中国工程院院士文集

柳百成院士文集

柳百成 著

机械工业出版社

《柳百成院士文集》收录了柳百成院士近年来的学术成果、国家制造业战略研究成果、代表性学术报告等各类学术类文章，以及个人专访文章、学生回忆类文章等。

全书共分6篇，第1篇为"铸造及凝固过程建模与仿真"代表性学术论文，第2篇为学术会议报告，第3篇为制造业发展及制造强国战略研究论文，第4篇为制造业发展及制造强国战略研究会议报告，第5篇为留学情结与学术人生相关的专访类文章，第6篇为祝贺与回忆类文章。

文集在展示柳百成院士近年来学术成果的同时，还展现了学术之外的内容，让读者可以更全面地认识柳百成院士。

图书在版编目(CIP)数据

柳百成院士文集/柳百成著.—北京：机械工业出版社，2022.6
ISBN 978-7-111-70493-5

Ⅰ.①柳⋯　Ⅱ.①柳⋯　Ⅲ.①柳百成-文集　Ⅳ.①K826.1-53

中国版本图书馆CIP数据核字(2022)第056057号

机械工业出版社(北京市百万庄大街22号　邮政编码100037)
策划编辑：孔　劲　　　责任编辑：孔　劲　李含杨
责任校对：陈　越　张　薇　封面设计：鞠　杨
责任印制：单爱军
北京虎彩文化传播有限公司印刷
2022年10月第1版第1次印刷
210mm×285mm·29印张·4插页·955千字
标准书号：ISBN 978-7-111-70493-5
定价：198.00元

电话服务　　　　　　　网络服务
客服电话：010-88361066　　机　工　官　网：www.cmpbook.com
　　　　　010-88379833　　机　工　官　博：weibo.com/cmp1952
　　　　　010-68326294　　金　书　网：www.golden-book.com
封底无防伪标均为盗版　机工教育服务网：www.cmpedu.com

自　　序

我 1933 年 2 月 11 日生于上海，籍贯为江苏常州。1945 年毕业于上海中西女中第二附属小学。1951 年毕业于上海圣芳济中学，曾任学生会副主席。1955 年毕业于清华大学机械工程系，获优秀毕业生金质奖章。1978—1981 年作为第一批赴美访问学者赴美国进修，并担任领队；在美国威斯康星大学及麻省理工学院材料科学与工程系从事科学研究。

我 1955 年毕业后留校在清华大学机械工程系工作，1984 年评为教授。2013 年至今，任清华大学机械工程学院及材料学院教授。1999 年当选为中国工程院院士。2015 年至今，兼任国家建设制造强国战略咨询委员会委员。曾任清华大学学术委员会委员、《清华大学学报》编委会主任、机械工程系学术委员会主任，及哈尔滨工业大学、上海交通大学、西安交通大学、西北工业大学等高等院校兼职教授。

我从事铸造及材料加工工程学科教育事业 60 余年。1981 年回国后，用英语讲授了多门新课，为国家培养了大批工程科技人才，已获博士学位的就有 50 余名，为培养铸造及材料加工学科工程科技人才做出贡献。获 1993 年北京市高校优秀教学成果一等奖。

在推动我国先进制造技术发展，应用电子计算机技术改造传统铸造行业以及铸铁结晶凝固基础研究与球墨铸铁生产技术应用研究等方面均做出了贡献。获奖成果近 20 项，其中省部级科技进步一等奖 4 项、省部级二等奖 9 项、国外奖励 2 项。完成国家发明专利 2 项。在主要学术刊物发表论文 400 余篇。

2002 年，获"光华工程科技奖"；2012 年及 2015 年，先后获中国机械工程学会"中国铸造杰出贡献奖"及"中国铸造终身成就奖"。

一、学术成就

1. 深入研究铸铁结晶凝固过程及石墨形态控制机理，为研究开发新型铸铁材料奠定科学基础

1978 年赴美国做访问学者，其间我努力学习并掌握扫描俄歇谱仪、电子显微探针等最新的材料分析仪器，因而在采用先进材料分析仪器探索铸铁结晶凝固机理领域，取得了一批创新成果。1981 年获美国铸造学会优秀论文奖。

回国后，在国内率先采用先进材料测试及实验手段，研究铸铁结晶凝固过程。1982 年获"机械工业部科技进步二等奖"。1984 年代表中国赴法国参加国际球墨铸铁标准会议。1988 年与沈阳铸造所等单位共同负责修订了国家标准《球墨铸铁件》。1988 年获"国家教育委员会科学技术进步奖"二等奖。负责并指导博士生共同完成在特殊条件下的铸铁结晶凝固过程研究，获 1995 年"国家教育委员会科学技术进步奖（基础类）"一等奖。

2. 在国内较早提出用计算机技术改造传统铸造行业，在多尺度建模与仿真领域取得创新成果

1979 年我在美国进修时，深深为计算机在科技及工程领域的广泛应用感到震惊，意识到计算机正在改变人类社会。回国后，立即带领博士生和硕士生开辟了铸造凝固过程宏观及微观模拟仿真研究的新领域。经过几十年的努力，我领导的研究团队在国际铸造学术界已占有一席之地，多次主持召开国际学术会议，或应邀在大会做特邀主题报告。

1992 年，研究开发完成商品化三维铸造工艺 CAD 及凝固过程模拟分析系统，1993 年被国家科委批准为"国家级科技成果重点推广计划"项目。研究成果在多个企业单位推广应用，达到优化铸造工艺、确保铸件质量、缩短试制周期及降低生产成本的目的，为工厂取得了显著的经济及社会效益。1996 年，获"国家教育委员会科学技术进步奖"二等奖。完成"铸件充型凝固过程的数值模拟研究"，获 1999 年"教育部科学技术进步奖（基础）"一等奖。完成国家科委 863/CIMS 关键技术攻关项目"并行工程"的子课题"并行工

程环境下铸造CAD/CAE"研究，总项目获1999年"教育部科学技术进步奖"二等奖。

1997—2001年，负责及领导研究团队完成国家攀登计划预选项目中有关铸造模拟领域的子课题。研究成果进一步在工程应用方面取得了显著效果。在德阳东方电机股份有限公司、上海沪东造船集团铸造厂、德阳东方汽轮机厂、中国第二重型机械集团有限公司（简称：中国二重）、马鞍山钢铁公司机械公司等国家重要工矿企业中应用，取得了显著的经济效益和社会效益。2002年，"砂型铸造过程数值模拟研究开发与工程应用"项目，获"北京市科学技术进步奖"二等奖。

研究开发完成的《铸造之星》软件，是国内第一个在Windows操作系统下运行的商品化软件，已先后在国内60余家单位应用。例如，与中国二重合作，负责长江三峡水轮机叶片铸造工艺方案的流场及温度场模拟仿真及优化分析。中国二重于2000年试制长江三峡水轮机叶片一次浇铸成功。由国务院三峡办、中国机械工业联合会共同主持召开的鉴定委员会认为"该叶片技术资料齐全，采用了计算机优化等先进技术，符合有关标准要求，达到国际同行业先进水平"。2002年马鞍山钢铁公司在没有生产特大型铸钢件设备和经验的情况下，采用《铸造之星》软件优化工艺，一次试制成功重达218t的大型轧钢机机架铸钢件。

近几年来，领导研究团队参加多项国家重点基础研究项目及国家自然科学重大基金项目，负责其中多项有关"精确成形过程多学科模拟仿真"的子课题等研究。研究团队涌现了一批年青学科带头人，在学科交叉、研究创新方面发挥了重要作用。2012及2014年，研究团队积极参与特大型铸件及钢锭的建模与仿真领域研究，先后获"教育部科学技术进步奖"二等奖2项；2018年，航空发动机高温合金叶片定向凝固多尺度建模与仿真技术及工程应用研究获"北京市科学技术进步奖"一等奖；2019年，铝、镁合金高致密压铸成形及建模仿真技术研究获"教育部科学技术进步奖"二等奖。

二、制造强国战略研究

"如何振兴我国制造业，发展先进制造技术"是我长期思考和关心的问题。1999年，当选中国工程院院士后，在中国工程院的直接领导下，积极参与振兴制造业、发展先进制造技术，为建设制造强国战略研究做出了贡献。

2002年，主持召开以"面向21世纪的材料成形加工技术与科学"为主题的第184次香山科学会议。

2003年，积极参与"国家中长期科技发展战略研究"第3课题"制造业发展科技问题"研究，多次代表课题组向国家科技领导小组汇报研究进展。

2004年陪同课题组组长中国工程院徐匡迪院长向国务院领导汇报研究成果，获得好评。

2005年，积极参与中国工程院大型咨询项目"装备制造业自主创新战略研究"，任副组长。主持编写综合报告，研究成果于2007年正式出版。

2013年，积极参与中国工程院大型咨询项目"制造强国战略研究"，任副组长。

2015年，国务院正式颁布实施《中国制造2025》，并受聘"国家制造强国建设战略咨询委员会"委员至今。先后多次在美国、韩国、德国、日本等国内外学术会议宣讲振兴中国制造业对策及加强研发关键核心技术，以及专门组团赴美国考察美国创新网络及制造业创新研究院，为我国制造业发展和振兴研究提供了有益经验和教训。

三、教书育人

我从事铸造及材料加工工程专业教育事业60余年，十分重视教书育人、以德为先；注意身体力行，严格要求学生既要勇于创新，又要学风严谨；既要重视基础科学理论，又要为国民经济发展做贡献。为国家培养了一大批铸造及材料加工工程学科的工程科技人才。"教授必须讲课"，1981年回国后，率先用英语讲授"多元相平衡图"及"现代材料加工工艺学"，为本科生讲授新课"材料加工工程概论"。已培养博士50余名，其中多数博士已在国内高校及研究院所等单位发挥了重要作用。

1987—1995年任全国高校铸造专业教学指导委员会主任，1996—2000年任全国高校材料加工专业教学指导委员会副主任兼铸造学科教学指导小组组长，为制订我国铸造学科工程科技人才的培养目标及规格、组织编写教材、指导教学改革等方面发挥了重要指导作用。因培养工程类型硕士研究生成绩卓著，获 1993 年 "北京市普通高等学校优秀教学成果奖"一等奖。

近年来，专门为全校博士研究生讲授"先进制造技术发展趋势"，多次参加为校内外研究生举办的"学术人生讲座"，以及在中国工程院为新疆、西藏等地优秀少先队员讲授"学术人生道路"。

四、国际学术交流

国际学术交流是学习国外先进科学技术的重要途径，也是展现我国科技水平的重要窗口。我作为"改革开放"后第一批赴美访问学者，并担任领队，亲身感受到我国改革开放政策的无比正确和远见卓识。出国访问，不仅学习了国际先进科学技术，也促进了国际民间友好往来；至今，我仍和威斯康星大学、麻省理工学院、通用和福特汽车研发中心等院校及机构的专家学者保持友好交往。

多年来我应邀出国访问近 100 次，先后赴美、英、德、法、韩、日等国近 30 所大学讲学、做学术报告；在国际学术会议宣读论文 30 余篇，并多次应邀在大会做主题报告；在国际铸造学术界享有盛誉。1992 年在美国讲学时，获美国密歇根州州长颁发的"特殊表彰"奖状。我积极参与并在国际学术组织及国际学术会议任职，为国家争得荣誉。1984—1996 年任国际铸造学会"稀土在铸造合金中应用"国际委员会学术秘书及主席，主持编写出版了《稀土在铸铁、铸钢及有色合金中应用综述报告》，获国际铸造学会高度评价。

我曾多次主持召开了国际学术会议。1995 年任第 61 届世界铸造会议组委会副主席兼学术委员会主席，主持大会学术论坛。1996 年在北京主持召开第 3 届环太平洋国际铸造及凝固模拟会议。2006 年在北京主持召开第 8 届国际铸铁科学与工艺会议。2011 年，受中国工程院委托，在清华大学主持召开"数字化设计与制造发展"国际高峰论坛。

他山之石，可以攻玉。我还多次组织国内制造企业、科研院所相关科研人员赴日本、韩国、美国考察先进制造技术及铸造与凝固过程建模仿真技术，促进了我国先进制造技术的发展。

五、体会

光阴如箭！我自 1951 年踏入清华园，已度过一个多甲子。一生从事高等工程教育及科学研究，深感要有所作为、有所贡献、有所成就，一是要有崇高的理想与奉献精神，二是要有创新思维、敢于站在学科前沿，三是要有顽强拼搏与求实的工作作风，四是要有健康的体魄，五是要全面发展、热爱生活。

1. 爱国奉献

我幼年是在日本帝国主义占领下的上海度过的，后来又处于国民党的反动腐败统治之下，深切盼望祖国强大、人民幸福。小学学到了文天祥正气歌中的名言"人生自古谁无死，留取丹心照汗青"，中学学到了范仲淹的"先天下之忧而忧，后天下之乐而乐"，那些世代传颂的经典诗篇，对我的一生都产生了难以磨灭的影响。新中国成立后来到清华大学，更增强了我的爱国意识。作为第一批访问学者赴美国进修时，我就下定决心，一定要尽量多地学习美国的先进科学技术，为祖国的建设服务。总之，一定要有远大理想，热爱祖国，热爱人民，努力用自己的智慧、知识和劳动，促进我国科教事业的发展，追赶世界先进水平。只有祖国强大了，才会有我们每个人的光辉前程。

2. 创新思维

作为传统的制造业及材料成形加工行业，如何适应一日千里的科学技术发展？只有勇于创新、学科交叉、跟踪前沿，利用世界上最先进的科学理论和信息技术来改造和促进传统制造业的技术进步，才能取得创新成果。1978 年赴美国做访问学者，看到了新的材料分析仪器，如扫描俄歇谱仪、电子显微探针等，我抓紧学习和掌握它们的操作技能。因此，在探索铸铁结晶凝固机理领域，取得了一批创新成果。

1978 年刚到美国时，我为计算机在工程领域的广泛应用感到震惊，敏锐地意识到计算机正在改变人类社会。在威斯康星大学，我学计算机语言，与美国大学生一起上课、上机、编程，节假日也和美国学生一样，提一包食物、一杯饮料埋头在学校计算机中心里。回国后，立即带领博士生和硕士生开辟铸造及凝固过程宏观及微观模拟仿真研究新领域。经过几十年来研究团队的共同努力，取得了一批理论创新成果，推进了我国铸造业的发展，领导的课题组在国际铸造学术界也占有一席之地。

3. 拼搏精神

在清华学习，在清华讲课，在国外做访问学者，回国后从事科学研究，顽强拼搏与实干精神始终是我的做事准则。在美国做访问学者期间，在材料分析实验室和计算机中心顽强奋战。学习计算机语言课程，每晚七八点钟就到学校计算机中心编程，直至凌晨三四点才回去睡觉。一分辛劳、一分收获，今天的这些成就是和早年乃至现在、仍然坚持的勤奋实干精神分不开的。只有靠脚踏实地、努力拼搏，才能够取得成绩，取得成功。

4. 健康体魄

我从小热爱体育运动。初中时就代表学校参加了全市篮球比赛，高中时参加了垒球队，并获全市中学生比赛冠军。大学时，南翔校长"为祖国健康工作五十年"的教诲一直鼓舞着我。足球、篮球、排球都有所涉足，更喜欢上了滑冰。毕业后，在清华冰场一直滑到七十岁高龄。20世纪六七十年代时，高校开门办学，有时要步行几十公里，到了目的地放下行李，还能立刻打一场全程篮球。

我既从事基础研究，又从事工程推广应用研究，经常带领研究生马不停蹄地奔赴各地进行考察、调研或试验。有时，晚上回到住地，我又通知和召集研究生讨论他们的论文进展情况。有的研究生早已累倒在床上，故经常感叹"身体还不如导师"。

5. 热爱生活

顽强拼搏不等于苦行僧似的枯燥生活。小学时学会的英文歌曲的歌词"Work while we work, and play while we play. That's the way to be happy and gay"，也经常鼓舞着自己，要热爱生活。

改革开放为我们知识分子带来了春天。在祖国及世界各地考察、参加会议的同时，也欣赏了祖国大好河山和世界美丽风光。我热爱摄影，1979年，刚到美国3个月，用节约省下的生活费用买了第1架相机，现在已拥有多台长变焦数码相机。先后在30多个国家、100多个地域奔波，及时运用各种"长枪短炮"，辛勤采集世界名胜古迹、自然奇特风采、民俗传统文化。2010—2014年，正式出版了《万里行踪》《五洲锦绣》《萍踪掠影》三本摄影集。由于风光宜人、山川迥异、人文情趣、异域奇观，加上经过特种处理，图片转为视频，更是异彩缤纷、独具风采，获得了不少中外专家、师生、亲友的称赞。摄影作品还多次在中国工程院、北京市、学校等摄影展展出并获奖。爱好摄影既提高了自己的审美情趣、文化修养，开阔了国际视野，也向学生和年轻教师展示了清华人热爱生活、全面发展的情操和志趣。

六、结束语

回顾80多年来的历程，我是随祖国的发展、强盛而成长的。新中国成立后我考进清华大学，受到祖国人民的培育、母校的教育、名师的指点、同学的爱护、团队的支持以及清华园"自强不息、厚德载物"校训潜移默化的熏陶，深感自己肩负的责任重大。几十年来，勤勤恳恳，丝毫不敢有松懈之心。虽然经历过各种曲折，却始终想以自己的绵薄之力报效我们伟大的祖国。改革开放为知识分子带来了春天，使我们这一代人重新焕发青春。我能为我国制造业和铸造行业的振兴及人才的培养贡献自己的微薄力量，能为祖国的强盛和人民的幸福而奋斗终生，感到由衷的高兴和莫大的喜悦。

"老骥伏枥，志在千里"。展望未来，面对祖国发展一日千里的大好时机，只有努力拼搏，为振兴中华继续奉献自己的一切。

柳百成

2021年7月

前　言

光阴如箭，日月如梭！

自 1951 年考进清华大学，1955 年毕业留校任教，至今生活在清华园已有 71 年。

2003 年，李言祥等教授为祝贺我 70 周岁生日，编辑出版《柳百成院士科研文选》。其中有我的自序，并收集了代表性论文 67 篇。

因此，此文集主要收集 2003 年以后的代表性论文 31 篇，主要是我指导博士生发表的论文，聚焦于多学科、多尺度铸造及凝固过程建模与仿真技术。

1999 年当选中国工程院院士后，在中国工程院的直接领导下，我积极参与《国家中长期科技发展规划战略研究》之三"制造业科技发展问题""装备制造业自主创新战略研究""制造强国战略研究"。2015 年，受聘为"国家制造强国建设战略咨询委员会"委员。文集专门收集了有关战略研究论文及会议报告。

1978 年，作为"改革开放"第一批赴美访问学者及总领队，进修 2 年。赴美留学成为我学术人生的重要里程碑，文集在"留学情结与学术人生"中收集了关于我的专访文章。文集最后，收录周昭喜等部分博士生的回忆文章。

老骥伏枥，志在千里。回顾我的学术人生道路，可以归纳为 20 个字、5 句话，即：爱国奉献、创新思维、顽强拼搏、健康体魄、热爱生活。

谨以此文集献给母校，感谢培育之恩。

柳百成

2021 年 7 月

出 版 说 明

为尊重文集中相关文献的内容，充分展现柳百成院士相关文献的原貌，特此就文集中相关文献的格式体例对广大读者进行说明：

1. 文集第 1 篇和第 3 篇收录了近年来柳百成院士在各类期刊中正式发表过的相关学术论文。其中，中文期刊中发表的学术论文，在保留原文格式的前提下，仅对文章中的个别词句、标点等进行适当调整，针对其中的外文图表添加了中文注解，包含参考文献在内的格式不做修改；外文期刊中发表的学术论文，在保留原文格式的前提下，仅对文章中的文献序号等进行格式调整，其余格式不做修改。

2. 文集第 2 篇和第 4 篇中收录了近年来柳百成院士的若干学术会议报告。其中，国内学术会议报告基本保留报告原貌，仅对内容中的个别段落做适当修改与调整；国际学术会议报告基本保留报告原貌，为便于读者查询，在目录及各报告正文的原英文标题后添加了中文标题，此外仅对个别内容做了适当修改与调整。

3. 文集第 5 篇收录了柳百成院士关于留学经历以及学术人生相关的文章，相关格式体例按出版规定进行了规范，并对部分文章进行了适当精简与调整。

4. 文集第 6 篇收录了柳百成院士所获两份奖项的颁奖词原文，以及早年毕业的部分博士生的回忆文章，相关格式体例按出版规定进行了规范，对部分内容进行了适当修改与调整。

目 录

自序
前言
出版说明

第1篇 "铸造及凝固过程建模与仿真"代表性学术论文

综述论文 ········ 2

1. 3D Modeling and Simulation of Dendritic Growth during Solidification ········ 3
2. 铸造过程的多尺度模拟研究进展 ········ 10
3. Phase-field simulation of solidification in multicomponent alloys coupled with thermodynamic and diffusion mobility databases ········ 22
4. Advances in Multi-scale Modeling of Solidification and Casting Processes ········ 28
5. 汽车工业镁合金压铸成形技术及模拟仿真 ········ 38
6. Simulation and experimental validation of three-dimensional dendrite growth ········ 50

航空及重燃叶片建模与仿真 ········ 57

7. MODELING OF DIRECTIONAL SOLIDIFICATION PROCESS OF SUPERALLOY TURBINE BLADE CASTINGS ········ 58
8. Numerical Simulation of Solidification Process on Single Crystal Ni-Based Superalloy Investment Castings ········ 65
9. Modeling of Grain Selection during Directional Solidification of Single Crystal Superalloy Turbine Blade Castings ········ 75
10. NUMERICAL SIMULATION OF TEMPERATURE FIELD IN DIRECTIONAL SOLIDIFICATION OF TURBINE BLADE BY LIQUID METAL COOLING METHOD ········ 81
11. Multiscale Modeling and Simulation of Directional Solidification Process of Turbine Blade Casting with MCA Method ········ 87
12. Numerical Simulation and Optimization of Directional Solidification Process of Single Crystal Superalloy Casting ········ 95
13. Deformation and recrystallization of single crystal nickel-based superalloys during investment casting ········ 106
14. Numerical simulation of dendrite growth in nickel-based superalloy and validated by in-situ observation using high temperature confocal laser scanning microscopy ········ 123
15. A model for simulation of recrystallization microstructure in single-crystal superalloy ········ 140

轻量化材料工艺建模与仿真 ········ 149

16. Preliminary Study on Simulation of Microporosity Evolution and Fatigue Life of Aluminum Alloy Casting ········ 150

17. Processing Technology and Mechanical Properties of Die-Cast Magnesium Alloy AZ91D ············ 156
18. Influences of Casting Pressure Conditions on the Quality and Properties of a Magnesium Cylinder Head Cover Die Casting ············ 161
19. Numerical Modeling of Microstructure Evolution and Dendrite Growth for Al-Si Alloy Casting during Low Pressure Die Casting ············ 168
20. Dendrite growth modelling of cast magnesium alloy ············ 174
21. Simulation of Magnesium Alloy AZ91D Microstructure Using Modified Cellular Automaton Method ············ 179
22. Cellular automaton simulation of three-dimensional dendrite growth in Al-7Si-Mg ternary aluminum alloys ············ 185
23. A phase field model for simulating the precipitation of multi-variant β-$Mg_{17}Al_{12}$ in Mg-Al-based alloys ············ 200

大型铸件及钢锭建模与仿真 ············ 206

24. Instability of Fluid Flow and Level Fluctuation in Continuous Thin Slab Casting Mould ············ 207
25. A Coupled Electrical-Thermal-Mechanical Modeling of Gleeble Tensile Tests for Ultra-High-Strength (UHS) Steel at a High Temperature ············ 214
26. Cellular Automaton Modeling of Austenite Nucleation and Growth in Hypoeutectoid Steel during Heating Process ············ 231
27. Deformation Prediction of a Heavy Hydro Turbine Blade During the Casting Process with Consideration of Martensitic Transformation ············ 242
28. Modeling of Species Transport and Macrosegregation in Heavy Steel Ingots ············ 255
29. Experimental Measurements for Numerical Simulation of Macrosegregation in a 36-Ton Steel Ingot ············ 264
30. Three-Dimensional Simulation of Macrosegregation in a 36-Ton Steel Ingot Using a Multicomponent Multiphase Model ············ 275
31. Analysis of internal crack in a six-ton P91 ingot ············ 286

第2篇 学术会议报告

国际会议 ············ 298

1. Experience on Modeling of Casting and Solidification Processes
（铸造及凝固过程建模研究经验）············ 299
2. Progress on Multi-scale Modeling of Solidification Process of Advanced Casting Technology
（先进铸造技术凝固过程的多尺度建模研究进展）············ 304
3. Numerical Simulation of Macrosegregation in Large Steel Ingot with Multicomponent and Multiphase Model（基于多成分和多相模型对大型钢锭中宏观偏析进行数值模拟研究）············ 314
4. Multiscale Modeling and Simulation of Directional Solidification Process of Ni-based Superalloy Turbine Blade Casting（镍基高温合金涡轮叶片铸件定向凝固过程的多尺度建模与仿真研究）············ 319

国内会议 ············ 324

5. 建模与仿真在装备制造中的作用与前景 ············ 325

 6. 高温合金定向凝固叶片铸件凝固过程建模与仿真进展 ········· 331

第3篇 制造业发展及制造强国战略研究论文

 1. 发展资源节约环境友好的先进制造技术 ········· 338
 2. 《中国制造2025》——建设制造强国之路 ········· 344
 3. 数字化设计与制造是智能制造关键共性技术 ········· 348
 4. 创新·强基·智能——建设制造强国 ········· 351

第4篇 战略研究会议报告

国际会议 ········· 360

 1. Trend of Advanced Manufacturing Technology（先进制造技术发展趋势） ········· 361
 2. Status and Forecast of China Manufacturing Industry（中国制造业的现状及展望） ········· 366
 3. CHINA MANUFACTURING 2025——An Action Program for Strong Manufacturing Industry
  （《中国制造2025》——建设制造强国行动纲领） ········· 371
 4. Developing Intelligent Manufacturing——For a Strong Manufacturing Industry
  （发展智能制造——建设制造强国） ········· 376
 5. Modeling and Simulation——Key Technology for Digital Transformation of
  Manufacturing Industry（建模与仿真——制造业数字化转型关键技术） ········· 379

国内会议 ········· 383

 6. 我国制造业科技发展战略 ········· 384
 7. 提高装备制造业自主创新能力 ········· 390
 8. 创新驱动 强化基础——建设制造强国 ········· 400
 9. 加强先进基础工艺创新能力 ········· 403

第5篇 留学情结与学术人生

 1. "中国留学生的四十年"之柳百成：新留学潮开启的见证者 ········· 408
 2. 改革开放四十年之亲历者记 柳百成：留学岁月照亮我的人生 ········· 413
 3. 西风千里话转折 水木数载铸人生——柳百成院士的学术人生 ········· 416
 4. 怀念南翔同志 学习南翔同志 ········· 426
 5. 顽强拼搏、报效祖国 ········· 428

第6篇 祝贺与回忆

 1. "中国铸造杰出贡献奖"颁奖词 ········· 434
 2. "中国铸造终身成就奖"颁奖词 ········· 435
 3. 桃李缘——贺导师柳百成院士清华任教60周年 ········· 周昭喜 436
 4. 跟着先生学知识学做人 ········· 郭景杰 437
 5. 久违的回忆 ········· 郝守卫 439

6. 科学严谨治学、厚德载物育人——写在柳百成先生从教60周年之际 ········· 程 军 **441**

7. 教书育人，勇攀科技高峰 ········· 李嘉荣 **443**

8. 贺柳老师执教六十年 ········· 康进武 **445**

9. 李文胜博士回忆 ········· **446**

附录 赴国外及中国港澳台地区参加重要学术交流活动表（1978—2019） ········· **448**

第1篇

"铸造及凝固过程建模与仿真"代表性学术论文

综述论文

1. 3D Modeling and Simulation of Dendritic Growth during Solidification

Zuojian LIANG, Qingyan XU and Baicheng LIU

Department of Mechanical Engineering, Tsinghua University, Beijing 100084, China

A mathematical model for the three-dimensional simulation of free dendritic growth and microstructure evolution was developed based on the growth mechanism of crystal grains and basic transfer equations such as heat, mass and momentum transfer equations. Many factors including constitutional undercooling, curvature undercooling and anisotropy, which had vital influences on the microstructure evolution, were considered in the model. Simulated results showed that final microstructural patterns and free dendritic growth could be predicted reasonably and calculated results were coincident with experimental. The simulated results of free dendritic growth indicated that the strength of anisotropy has significant effects on free dendritic growth, dendrite profile, micro solute and temperature distribution. The dendritic grain profiles with fully-grown parallel secondary arm tend to be formed at the intensive anisotropy, while near octahedral grain profiles with small protuberances of surface at low strength of anisotropy. The simulated results of free dendritic growth also indicated that there are small molten pools left in interdendritic areas. This is helpful to understand the fundamental of the formation of microstructure related defects such as microsegregation and microporosity.

Key words: Modeling and simulation. Dendritic grain growth, Microstructure evolution

1. Introduction

Solidification microstructure in cast alloys is one of most observed areas in the materials science and engineering. Mechanical properties of castings are influenced mostly by final microstructure patterns[1]. Dendritic growth is perhaps the most observed phenomenon in solidification of cast alloys. It is essential to make a fundamental understanding of dendritic growth and find the effective methods of microstructure control in order to obtain satisfied mechanical properties and service performance. In the last decades, to study the evolution of solidification microstructure most experimental techniques were developed by inspecting the nucleation and dendritic growth in transparent materials[2,3]. Nevertheless, The principle of free dendrite growth and microstructure evolution involves to different domains such as crystallography, thermodynamics, transport phenomena and micromechanics. Low efficiency and high cost of experiment prevents us from understanding the mechanism of microstructure evolution further. Numerical simulation, however, can extend our comprehension of microstructure formation and predict dendrite morphology, microstructure features, solid/liquid interface and microstructure related defects such as microsegregation and microporosity.

A few numerical models were developed for the simulation of dendrite growth in the last decades. They include deterministic techniques such as phase field method or spline mathematics approaches for simulation of dendrite morphology and microsegregation patterns, solidification kinetics deterministic models for calculating the evolution of solid and dendritic grain size, and probabilistic approaches such as Monte Carlo and Cellular Automaton techniques for simulating the evolution of dendritic morphologies[4-8].

The objective of the paper is to present a physical

and numerical model for three-dimensional simulation of microstructure and microsegregation based on the nucleation and growth of crystal grains and basic transfer equations such as heat transfer, mass transfer and momentum transfer. The model tries to consider more factors, which have vital influence on the evolution of microstructure and microsegregation, such as constitutional undercooling, curvature undercooling and anisotropy. Then simulation results of some cases were discussed in detail.

2. Mathematical Model

It is essential to establish a rational physical and mathematical model before computing and simulating the solidification microstructure and solute redistribution process. Although many mathematical models had been presented[9,10], most of them were only applicable to the two dimensional simulation. Recent work by the author has focused on the establishment of a three-dimensional mathe-matical model of microstructure evolution and free dendrite growth. The solidification process of binary alloys is governed by the evolution of the temperature field $T(x,y,z,t)$, concentration field $C(x,y,z,t)$, velocity field $u_x(x,y,z,t), u_y(x,y,z,t), u_z(x,y,z,t)$ and solid fraction $f_S(x,y,z,t)$. Most of governing equations have uniformed mathematical representation no matter where unit domain locates, in solid phase, or in liquid phase, or at the solid/liquid interface. The boundary conditions must be satisfied well at the moving solid/liquid interface and on the edge of cast domain. Besides the typical mass, heat and momentum transfer equations, equations that describe the physics of the solidification process are as follows.

Liquid species conservation equation:

$$\frac{\partial C_L}{\partial t} = D_L\left(\frac{\partial^2 C_L}{\partial x^2}+\frac{\partial^2 C_L}{\partial y^2}+\frac{\partial^2 C_L}{\partial z^2}\right) - \left(u_x\frac{\partial C_L}{\partial x}+u_y\frac{\partial C_L}{\partial y}+u_z\frac{\partial C_L}{\partial z}\right) \quad (1)$$

Solid species conservation equation:

$$\frac{\partial C_S}{\partial t} = D_S\left(\frac{\partial^2 C_S}{\partial x^2}+\frac{\partial^2 C_S}{\partial y^2}+\frac{\partial^2 C_S}{\partial z^2}\right) \quad (2)$$

Local equilibrium at the solid/liquid interface:

$$C_S^* = kC_L^* \quad (3)$$

Solute conservation at the solid/liquid interface:

$$V_n^* C_L^*(1-k) = D_L\left(\frac{\partial C_L}{\partial x}+\frac{\partial C_L}{\partial y}+\frac{\partial C_L}{\partial z}\right) - D_S\left(\frac{\partial C_S}{\partial x}+\frac{\partial C_S}{\partial y}+\frac{\partial C_S}{\partial z}\right) \quad (4)$$

The solidification process is governed by Eqs. (1) ~ (7). An explicit finite difference scheme is used for calculation of temperature and concentration field both in solid and liquid phases as well as velocity field in liquid phase. The difference scheme is stable when the following equation used to calculate the time step is satisfied:

$$\Delta t \leq \frac{1}{6}\min\left(\frac{\rho c(\min(\Delta x,\Delta y,\Delta z))^2}{\lambda}, \frac{(\min(\Delta x,\Delta y,\Delta z))^2}{\max(D_L,D_S)}, \min\left(\frac{\Delta x}{|u_x|},\frac{\Delta y}{|u_y|},\frac{\Delta z}{|u_z|}\right)\right) \quad (5)$$

The nucleation models of equiaxed grains, which are based on the heterogeneous nucleation theory, can be classified as two groups: the instantaneous nucleation model and the continuous nucleation model. The former assumes that all nuclei are generated at the nucleation temperature T_N. The latter, however, assumes a continuous dependency of N on temperature. Mathematical relationship is provided to correlate the nucleation velocity with undercooling, cooling rate and temperature. Another model, referred to as the dynamic nucleation, has been developed to consider the effect of melt convection on the breaking of dendritic arms and migration of nuclei. The continuous nucleation model used in the paper to calculate the nucleation velocity assumes that the grain density grows continuously with the increasing undercooling. The relationship between the nucleation velocity and the undercooling obeys Gaussian distribution and is given by

$$\frac{\partial N}{\partial(\Delta T)} = \frac{n_{max}}{\sqrt{2\pi}\Delta T_\sigma}\exp\left[-\frac{(\Delta T-\Delta T_N)^2}{2(\Delta T_\sigma)^2}\right] \quad (6)$$

where the maximum density of grains n_{max} that can form in the melt was set to $4.7\times10^{10}\mathrm{m}^{-3}$. The standard deviation of the distribution ΔT_σ ranges from 0.5K to 2.0K. The centre of the distribution ΔT_N is the mean nucleation undercooling. It was set to 2.5K for all cases.

The probability model of dendrite growth is based on the principle of minimum free energy. Capture probability of the neighboring liquid cells by a nucleus can be given by

$$P_G = \begin{cases} \exp(-\Delta G/k_B T) & \Delta G > 0 \\ 1 & \Delta G \leq 0 \end{cases} \quad (7)$$

where total free energy change ΔG is

$$\Delta G = \Delta G_V + \Delta G_J = -\frac{VL\Delta T}{T_L} + \sum (S_{SL}J_{SL} + S_{SS}J_{SS}) \quad (8)$$

the undercooling of liquid in Eq. (11) can be calculated by

$$\Delta T = \Delta T_c + \Delta T_t + \Delta T_k + \Delta T_r \quad (9)$$

only at very high solidification velocity the effect of kinetic undercooling ΔT_k is needed to calculate, so it is not taken into account in the model. In Eq. (12), other terms in the right hand side can be expressed respectively as

$$\Delta T_t = T_L - T \quad (10)$$
$$\Delta T_c = -(C_L^* - C_0)m_L \quad (11)$$
$$\Delta T_r = -\Gamma k f(\theta_i) \quad (12)$$

where $f(\theta_i)$ is the anisotropy function given by

$$f(\theta_i) = \prod_{i=x,y,z}(1 + \gamma_i \cos(\lambda_i \theta_i)) \quad (13)$$

where θ_i is the angle between the interfacial normal vector and the positive direction of x-, y- or z-axis. It is calculated by

$$\theta_i = \arccos \frac{|P_L - P_S|}{i_L - i_S} \quad (14)$$

3. Simulation Results and Discussion

The program code was written in C language. The medium and final values of T, C and f_S were stored to the same data file and shown in three-dimensional plots. Some parameters used in the simulation are listed in Table 1.

3.1 Nucleation rate

The relation between the nucleation rate and the undercooling is shown in Fig. 1. With the increase of undercooling, nucleation rate of grains obeys Gaussian distribution.

When the maximum density of grains n_{max} is set a

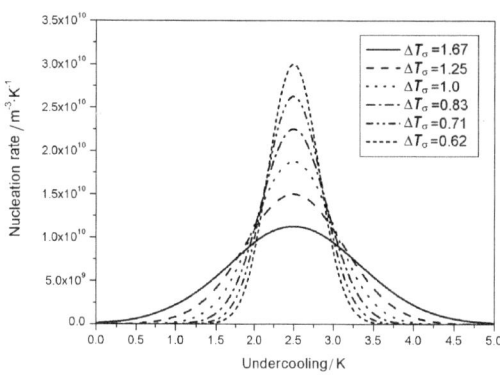

Fig. 1 Relations between undercooling and nucleation rate

constant, the undercooling starting to nucleate goes up and yet the undercooling finishing the nucleation goes down with the reduction of the standard deviation of the distribution ΔT_σ. Therefore, the undercooling range of nucleation becomes much narrower and the maximum nucleation rate rises gradually. As a result, most of nuclei are formed nearly at the same time, which contributes to the uniformity of grain size and refinement of grains. So it is an effective measure to control the final grain size by decreasing the standard deviation of the distribution during the solidification.

3.2 Columnar-to-equiaxed transition

To examine the CET process, simulation of the solidification microstructure of the cubic sample with the side length of 18mm was carried out. The simulated results in Fig. 2 were coincident with the experimental in Fig. 3 and both of them show that microstructure at the central cross section of the sample includes three zones: the chill zone of fine equiaxed grains in the surface layer, the zone of parallel columnar crystals normal to the inner wall of the mold and the zone of big equiaxed crystals at the center of the sample. The results at different pouring temperatures suggest that the microstructure profile with the wider columnar zone can be formed at the higher pouring temperature.

3.3 Free dendritic growth

It is assumed that the initial temperature of liquid is uniform in the calculated region. Some plots of free dendritic growth and concentration and temperature field from calculations are shown in Figs. 4 and 5 respectively. Photographs of typical dendrite pattern taken by glicksman are shown in Fig. 6. From three-dimensional dendrite profiles in Fig. 4 (a) and central cross sections of the dendrite in Figs. 4 (b), 4 (c) and 4 (d), it can be seen that secondary dendritic arms are parallel with each other and normal to primary dendritic stems, which was coincident with the experimental results in Fig. 6. Fig. 5 (a) and 5 (b) showed the concentration and temperature field during the evolution of free dendrite. For $k<1$ alloy system, the rejection of the solute from the solid/liquid interface to liquid phase can result in lower solid phase concentration and high liquid phase concentration. The primary stems, which are located at the junction of two secondary arms, correspond to the darkest area where the solute content is the lowest. Although the temperature at the center of dendrite is higher than that of liquid, as shown in Fig. 5 (b), it is lower than the temperature in other parts of the dendrite. Relatively high temperature at many locations is caused by the just released latent heat at the solid/liquid interface during solidification.

The variation of dendrite morphology with different strength of anisotropy γ_i was also simulated. The 3D and 2D dendrite profiles at different value of γ_i are shown in Figs. 7 and 8 respectively. With $\gamma_i = 0.04$, the dendrite tips tend to grow steadily along with the preferred growth direction and parallel secondary dendritic arm clusters may be formed. Finally tree-like profiles with fully-grown secondary branches can be obtained as shown in Fig. 7 (a). With the rise of γ_i, the structure of solid/liquid interface transits from irregular style to cellular and planar style. When γ_i is 0.02, the velocity of dendrite root is close to that of dendrite tip. The final dendrite profiles tend to have an appearance of near regular octahedron with lots of small protuberances of surface.

Table 1 Parameters used in the simulations

$c/\mathrm{J \cdot kg^{-1} \cdot K^{-1}}$	$C_0(\%)$	$D_S/\mathrm{m^2 \cdot s^{-1}}$	$D_L/\mathrm{m^2 \cdot s^{-1}}$	$n_{max}/\mathrm{m^{-3}}$	T_L/K	λ_i
569.43	0.4	1.0×10^{-10}	1.0×10^{-8}	4.7×10^{10}	1753	0.02~0.04
$\lambda/\mathrm{W \cdot m^{-1} \cdot K^{-1}}$	k	$L/\mathrm{J \cdot kg^{-1}}$	m_L/K	λ_i	$\rho/\mathrm{kg \cdot m^{-3}}$	$\Gamma/\mathrm{m \cdot K}$
50.66	0.28	2.72×10^5	-50.0	4	7.82×10^3	7.7×10^{-7}

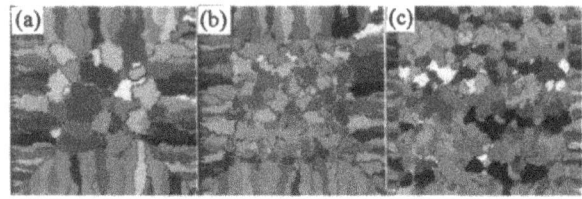

Fig. 2 Simulated results of columnar-to-equiaxed transition
(a) $T_p = 1823\mathrm{K}$, (b) $T_p = 1798\mathrm{K}$, (c) $T_p = 1773\mathrm{K}$

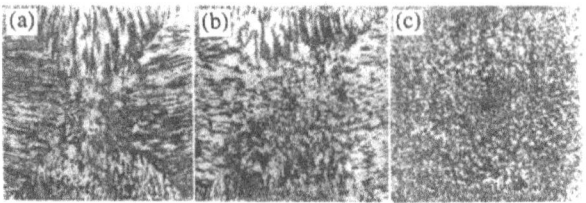

Fig. 3 Experimental results of columnar-to-equiaxed transition
(a) $T_p = 1823\mathrm{K}$, (b) $T_p = 1798\mathrm{K}$, (c) $T_p = 1773\mathrm{K}$

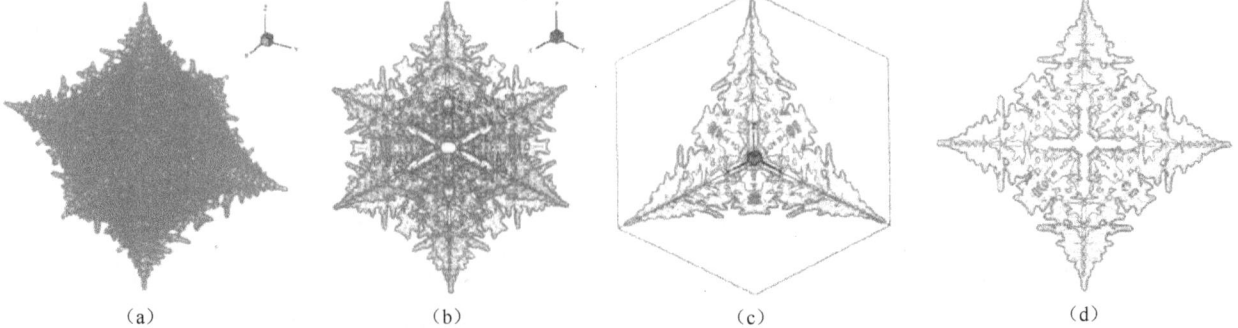

Fig. 4 Plots of 3D dendrite profiles and central cross sections from calculations
(a) 3D dendrite profiles, (b) central cross sections, (c) part of central cross sections, (d) single central cross section

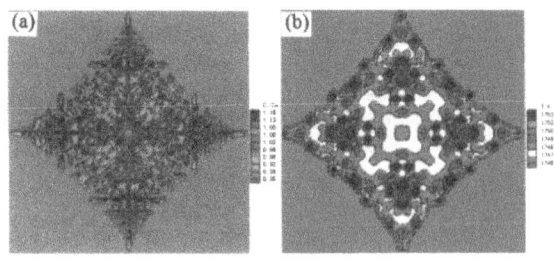

Fig. 5 Plots of the concentration and temperature field profiles at central cross section from calculations (a) concentration field, (b) temperature field

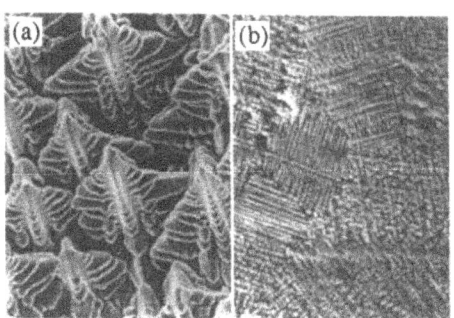

Fig. 6 Photographs of typical dendrite pattern taken by Glicksman (a) 3D dendrite growth, (b) dendrite pattern at a cross section

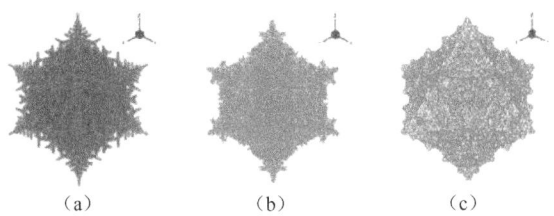

Fig. 7 Three-dimensional morphology of free dendrite with different γ_i (a) $\gamma_i=0.04$, (b) $\gamma_i=0.03$, (c) $\gamma_i=0.02$

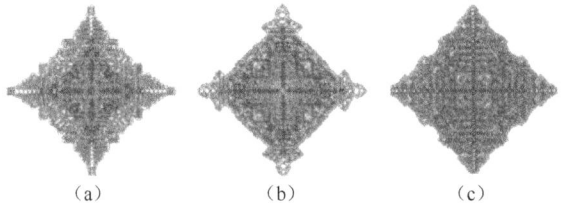

Fig. 8 Two-dimensional dendrite profiles at the central cross section with different γ_i (a) $\gamma_i=0.04$, (b) $\gamma_i=0.03$, (c) $\gamma_i=0.02$

The dendrite profiles shown in Fig. 4 also indicated that some small molten pools, in which the solute content is higher when $k<1$, exists in the interdendritic areas. Their existence is one of main reasons resulting in the formation of micro defects such as microsegregation and microporosity. So microstructure related defects could be predicted based on the calculated dendritic growth and final microstructure patterns and further the basic of their formation could be understood by numerical simulation.

4. Conclusions

A mathematical model for the three-dimensional simulation of free dendritic growth and microstructure evolution was developed based on the growth physics of crystal grains and basic transfer equations such as heat, mass and momentum transfer equations. Many factors including constitutional undercooling, curvature undercooling and anisotropy, which had vital influences on the microstructure evolution, were considered in the model. Simulated results show that final microstructural patterns and free dendritic growth could be predicted reasonably and calculated results were coincident with experimental results. The simulated results of free dendritic growth indicate that the strength of anisotropy has significant effects on free dendritic growth, dendrite profile, micro solute distribution and micro temperature distribution. The tree-like grain profiles with fully-grown parallel secondary dendritic arm clusters tend to be formed at the intensive anisotropy. Near octahedral grain profiles with small protuberances of surface tend to be obtained at low strength of anisotropy. The existence of small molten pools in the interdendritic areas could be predicted based on simulated results of free dendritic growth. This is helpful to understand the fundamental of the formation of microstructure related defects such as microsegregation and microporosity. Future work will involve: (1) a more thorough model validation through measurements of dendrite profile, temperature and solute distribution, (2) an investigation on influences of other parameters on dendrite profiles, (3) a complete consideration of segregation of multielements.

Acknowledgement

The work was sponsored by the Significant Project of National Natural Science Foundation of China (No. 59990470—3), the National Significant Fundamental Research Project of the Ministry of Science and Technology of China (No. G2000067208—3) and the Fundamental Research Project of Tsinghua University.

References

[1] M. C. Flemings and R. W. Cahn: *Acta Mater*, 2000, **48**, 371.
[2] M. E. Glicksman, E. Winsa, R. C. Hahn, et al: *Metall. Trans.*, 1987, **19A**, 1945.
[3] M. A. Chopra, M. E. Glicksman and N. B. Singh: *Metall. Trans.*, 1988, **19A**, 3087.
[4] L. Nastac: *Acta Mater.*, 1999, **47** (17) 4253.
[5] Baicheng LIU: *J. Mater. Sci. Technol.*, 1995, **11**, 313.
[6] Xu QY, Feng WM, Liu BC, et al: *Acta Metall. Sin.*, 2002, **38**, 799. (in Chinese)
[7] Q. Y. Xu and B. C. Liu: *Mater. Trans.*, 2001, **42**, 2316.
[8] Z. J. Liang, Q. Y. Xu, J. T. Li, et al: *Rare Metal. Mat. Eng.*, 2002, **31**, 353.
[9] W. Oldfield: *ASM Trans.*, 1966, **59**, 945.
[10] C. A. Gandin, C. Charbon and M. Rappaz: *ISIJ Inters.*, 1995, **35**, 651.

Nomenclature

c	Specific heat, $J \cdot kg^{-1} \cdot K^{-1}$	T_S	Solidus temperature, K
C	Species mass fraction, %	t	Time, s
C_L	Species mass fraction in liquid, %	u_x, u_y, u_z	Component of velocity, $m \cdot s^{-1}$
C_S	Species mass fraction in solid, %	V_n	Interface moving velocity, $m \cdot s^{-1}$
C_0	Initial species mass fraction, %	x, y, z	Coordinates, m
D_L	Species diffusion coefficient in liquid, $m^2 \cdot s^{-1}$	β_T	Thermal expansion coefficient, K^{-1}
D_S	Species diffusion coefficient in solid, $m^2 \cdot s^{-1}$	β_C	Solutal expansion coefficient
f_L	Mass fraction of liquid	γ_i	Strength of anisotropy
f_S	Mass fraction of solid	Γ	Gibbs-Thomson coefficient, $m \cdot K$
g_x, g_y, g_z	Component of gravity acceleration, $m \cdot s^{-2}$	ε	Emissivity
G	Grain size, m	θ_i	Angle between normal and i axis
i_L	Coordinate figure of interfacial liquid cell	κ	Curvature of interface, m^{-1}
i_S	Coordinate figure of interfacial solid cell	λ	Thermal conductivity, $W \cdot m^{-1} \cdot K^{-1}$
J	Interfacial tension, $J \cdot m^{-2}$	λ_i	Dimension of symmetry
K	Permeability, m^2	μ	Kinetic viscosity, $Pa \cdot s$
k	Equilibrium partition ratio	ρ	Density, kg/m^3
k_B	Boltzmann constant	ΔG	Total free energy change, J
L	Latent heat, $J \cdot kg^{-1}$	ΔG_V	Volume free energy change, J
m_L	Liquidus slope, K/%	ΔG_J	Interfacial free energy change, J
n_{max}	Maximum density of grain, m^{-3}	Δt	Time step, s
N	Density of grain, m^{-3}	ΔT	Undercooling, K
p	Pressure, Pa	ΔT_c	Constitutional undercooling, K
P_G	Capture probability	ΔT_k	Kinctic undercooling, K

P_L	Interfacial liquid cell	ΔT_N	Centre of distribution, K
P_S	Interfacial solid cell	ΔT_r	Curvature undercooling, K
S	Area, m^2	ΔT_t	Thermal undercooling, K
T	Temperature, K	ΔT_σ	Standard deviation of distribution, K
T_L	Liquidus temperature, K	$\Delta x, \Delta y, \Delta z$	Mesh size, m
T_P	Pouring temperature, K	Superscript *	Solid/liquid interface
T_R	Environmental temperature, K	Subscript *ref*	Reference

2. 铸造过程的多尺度模拟研究进展

柳百成　许庆彦　熊守美　康进武
(清华大学机械工程系　北京　100084)

摘　要：铸造行业对国民经济的发展具有重要作用，但我国与国外有很大差距，严重制约着经济的发展。铸造成形加工技术的发展趋势之一是用计算机模拟仿真技术来逐步代替传统的经验性研究方法。计算机模拟技术已成为改造传统铸造产业的必由之路，在生产中得到了越来越广泛的应用。随着铸造过程宏观模拟技术的成熟，研究者们把目光转向了微观过程模拟与多尺度模拟。主要针对目前的研究热点和发展趋势作了阐述，特别是对新一代精确铸造充型凝固过程模拟、铸造过程的应力应变分析、微观组织的形成与演变及并行工程环境下的多尺度模拟仿真等方面的国内外最新进展进行了分析，同时重点介绍了我国在这方面的研究成果。

关键词：精确铸造　模拟仿真　应力模拟　微观组织模拟　多尺度模拟
中图分类号：TG24

0　前言

铸造行业是制造业的重要组成部分，是汽车、电力、石化、造船、机械等支柱产业的基础制造技术。以液态铸造成形、固态塑性成形及连接成形等为代表的成形制造技术，不仅赋予零件以形状，而且决定了零件的最终组织、结构与性能。

我国有着悠久而灿烂的铸造历史。三千多年前我们祖先铸造的青铜器至今仍然令全世界惊叹不已。2001年我国铸件年产量已超过美国（1187万t），达到1488万t，是世界铸件生产第一大国。2002年中国第二重型机械集团有限公司成功地浇注了世界最大的轧钢机机架铸件，总共冶炼、浇注钢液730t。但是，我国的铸造行业与国外工业发达国家相比，仍有很大差距。例如，重大工程的关键铸件如长江三峡水轮机的第一个铸造拼焊结构的叶轮仍从加拿大进口，质量430t、价值为960万美元；航空工业发动机及其他重要的动力机械的关键铸件如燃气轮机叶片的核心铸造技术尚有待突破。因此，在振兴我国制造业的同时，要加强和重视铸造技术的发展。轻量化、精确化、高效化、数字化及绿色化将是未来铸造技术的重要发展方向。

随着计算机技术的发展，计算材料科学已成为一门新兴的交叉学科，是除试验和理论外解决材料科学中实际问题的第三个重要研究方法。它可以比理论和试验做得更深刻、更全面、更细致，可以进行一些理论和试验暂时还做不到的研究。因此，基于知识的以铸造为代表的材料成形工艺模拟仿真已成为材料科学与制造科学的前沿领域及研究热点。根据美国科学研究院工程技术委员会的测算，模拟仿真可提高产品质量5~15倍、增加材料出品率25%、降低工程技术成本13%~30%、降低人工成本5%~20%、增加投入设备利用率30%~60%、缩短产品设计和试制周期30%~60%等。

经过30多年的不断发展，铸造过程的宏观模拟在工程中应用已是一项十分成熟的技术，已有很多商业软件如MAGMA、PROCAST及中国的铸造之星（FT-STAR）等，并在生产中取得显著的经济及社会效益[1,2]。例如，在我国重型制造企业的共同努力下，长江三峡水轮机叶轮的不锈钢叶片（质量62t）已由德阳中国二重集团铸造厂于2001年首先试制成功，其铸造工艺方案采用了先进的计算机模拟仿真技术，经反复模拟得到了最优化的铸造工艺方案。由国务院三峡工程建设委员会办公室、中国机械工业联合会共同主持召开的鉴定委员会专家组认为：该叶片技术资料齐全，采用了计算机优化等先进技术，符合有关标准要求，达到国际同行业先进水平。

多学科、多尺度、多性能、高保真及高效率是模拟仿真技术的努力目标，而微观组织模拟（从毫

○ 本文刊登于《机械工程学报》，2003，39（10）：53-63。

米、微米到纳米尺度）则是近年来研究的新热点课题。通过计算机模拟，可深入研究材料的结构、组成及其在物理化学过程中宏观、微观变化机制，并由材料成分、结构及制备参数的最佳组合进行材料设计。

将就铸造过程建模与仿真的最新进展，主要是新一代精确铸造充型凝固过程，铸造过程的应力分析，微观组织演变及并行工程环境下的多尺度模拟仿真等方面的国内外最新进展进行讨论。

1 精确铸造成形过程的建模与仿真

砂型铸造充型及凝固过程的模拟已得到广泛的应用，研究重点已转向精确铸造成形工艺的建模与仿真。精确铸造成形方法主要有压力铸造、低压铸造、熔模铸造、消失模铸造和半固态铸造等。

1.1 压力铸造过程模拟仿真

压力铸造是目前广泛采用的精确铸造成形工艺，特别是铝及镁合金的压力铸造。在压铸成形条件下，型腔的填充模式是影响铸件质量的关键因素之一。因而，充型过程的流场控制是精确成形过程铸件质量控制的核心环节。同时，压铸过程是一个周期性循环生产的过程，在平衡状态下模具及铸件的温度场分布对铸件质量、模具使用寿命及生产效率有重要影响。因此，铸件充型及凝固过程数值模拟技术为压铸工艺设计、模具制造以及铸造工艺参数优化提供了快捷和有效的手段，可以缩短产品开发周期。

图 1 和图 2 是汽车镁合金压铸件的充型及凝固过程的模拟结果，其中充型模拟采用 ANYCASTING 软件，而凝固模拟则采用 FT-STAR 软件。

图 1 汽车气缸盖罩盖镁合金压铸件的充型过程

1.1.1 并行计算技术

因为对离散的流动控制方程的求解是一迭代过程，需要很长时间，因而提高计算效率仍是压铸模

图 2 汽车气缸盖罩盖镁合金压铸件的凝固过程

拟的研究重点。采用并行计算技术来加速流场的计算过程是重要的途径，作者利用基于机群的网络化并行计算环境，在对压铸充型过程的数学模型和计算模型进行分析的基础上，提出并建立了并行搜索计算模型。该模型以原有的 SOLA-VOF 串行算法为基础，通过效率参数的适当选择和调整，充分利用多节点的优势，最终实现并行计算优化串行过程的目的[3]。

采用微机并行计算系统 TH-NPSC2，对倒挡伺服器活塞零件的充型流动过程进行模拟。图 3 为充型流动过程的模拟结果。从充型过程可以看出，零件的圆筒形薄壁处是最后充填部位。由于气体集中于此，所以容易产生卷气、气孔等缺陷，影响零件质量。模拟结果为模具的设计、溢流槽的位置确定提供了有益的指导。

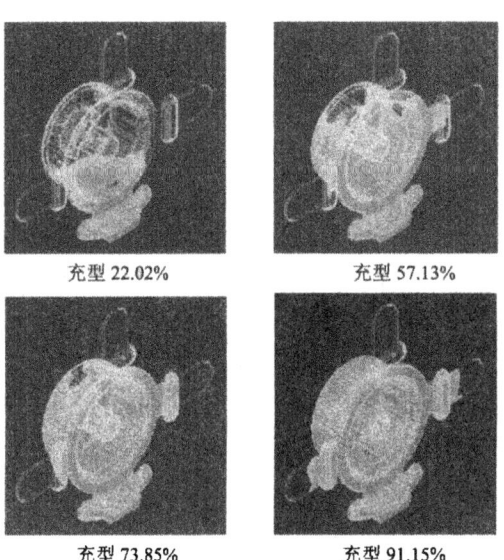

图 3 倒挡伺服器活塞充型模拟结果

1.1.2 分数步长法

采用分数步长法原理，对凝固过程中的热传导问题构造了相应的具有二阶精度的有限差分格式

如下

$$\begin{cases} \dfrac{T^{n+1/3}-T^n}{\tau}+\dfrac{1}{2}\Lambda_x^n(T^n+T^{n+1/3})=0 \\ \dfrac{T^{n+2/3}-T^{n+1/3}}{\tau}+\dfrac{1}{2}\Lambda_y^n(T^{n+1/3}+T^{n+2/3})=0 \\ \dfrac{T^{n+1}-T^{n+2/3}}{\tau}+\dfrac{1}{2}\Lambda_z^n(T^{n+2/3}+T^{n+1})=0 \end{cases}$$

式中 τ——分数步时间步长；

n——计算时间步，$n=0,1,2,\Lambda$；

Λ_x^n，Λ_y^n，Λ_z^n 分别为 $t_n \leq t \leq t_{n+1}$ 时对算子 $A_x = -\alpha\dfrac{\partial^2}{\partial x^2}$, $A_y = -\alpha\dfrac{\partial^2}{\partial y^2}$, $A_z = -\alpha\dfrac{\partial^2}{\partial z^2}$ 的近似。

由于该算法的无条件稳定性，所以时间步长可以在一定的范围内任意选择，因此可以极大地加快计算速度，提高计算效率[4]。

1.1.3 计算区域优化

根据 Barone 和 Caulk[5] 提出的"瞬态层"概念，及压铸过程的温度场变化特点和模具内温度分布特点，提出了对压铸件凝固模拟分析的分区计算方案。将整个模拟计算区域分为铸件区、瞬态区和稳态区。当采用分数步长法进行数值求解时，由于没有时间步长限制，可在模具"瞬态层"区域及铸件区域采用较小的空间步长和时间步长，而在模具"稳态区"则可采用较大的空间步长和时间步长。这样可大大提高整个系统的模拟计算效率。

对气缸盖罩盖镁合金压铸件及模具在压铸过程的温度场进行了模拟计算。在保证模拟计算精度的前提下，分别采用不同的方法进行了模拟计算效率的对比研究。下表给出了采用不同模拟方法进行实际压铸件凝固模拟计算效率比较结果。

从表 1 可以看出，采用分数步长法、分区域空间步长和分区域时间步长法等进行凝固模拟分析，可大大提高模拟计算效率，为快速有效地得到压铸工艺参数如浇注温度、模具预热温度等对铸件和模具温度场的影响的模拟结果，以及选取较优工艺参数提供科学的基础。

表 1 采用不同模拟计算方法进行实际压铸件凝固模拟计算效率比较

模拟方法	空间步长 l/mm	时间步长 t/s		网格划分数量		压铸每周期计算时间 T/min
		凝固阶段	其他阶段	网格总数	瞬态区网格数	
分数步长法	2	0.1	0.1	33019613		500
分阶段时间步长法	2	0.1	1	33019613		208
分区域空间步长法	不同空间步长	0.1	1	17119258		107
分区域时间步长法	不同空间步长	瞬态区 0.1 稳态区 0.2	瞬态区 1 稳态区 2	17119258	687661	51

图 4 显示了模具的温度场，图 5 是模拟计算中定镶块离铸件不同距离部位随时间变化的温度曲线。可以看出，模具内温度随着压铸周期的进行有周期性的上升和下降。在压铸第一阶段，压入金属液后，模具表面温度在极短的时间内上升至最高值，然后迅速下降，变化速度和幅度较大。而在第二、三、四段，模具温度的变化较平缓。随着到铸件距离的增大，温度上升的速度越慢，且变化幅度渐小，表明离铸件较远的模具温度受铸件温度的影响逐渐减小。

1.2 熔模铸造过程数值模拟

近年来，国内外熔模铸造技术发展迅速，熔模精铸件尤其是高温合金铸件在航空航天、国防军工等领域中的应用越来越广泛，如航空发动机压气机和燃气轮机的涡轮叶片等关键部件。由于熔模精铸件一般形状复杂、合金熔炼温度高和生产工序繁多

图 4 气缸盖罩盖镁合金压铸模具温度场

等原因，导致废品率和成本居高不下。利用计算机技术对熔模铸造过程进行数值模拟，有助于了解铸件凝固过程和预测铸造缺陷，从而改善铸造工艺，提高铸件质量。

清华大学与钢铁研究总院合作对钛铝增压涡轮进行了数学建模和模拟计算[6,7]。为考察铸件凝固规律和收缩缺陷，针对倒锥形浇注系统（方案 A）

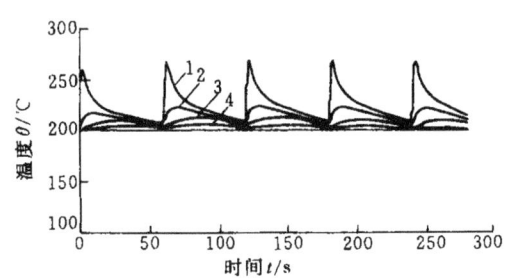

图 5 定镶块离铸件不同距离的温度变化曲线
1. 距铸件 1mm 处　2. 距铸件 5mm 处
3. 距铸件 9mm 处　4. 距铸件 13mm 处

和半球形浇注系统（方案 B）两种工艺分别进行了模拟，如图 6 所示。图 7a 和 b 所示分别为方案 A 和 B 的铸件凝固末期温度场。方案 B 的热节部位显著上移，有利于使收缩缺陷集中在浇注系统内部，减少铸件内部尤其是涡轮轴部位的缺陷。

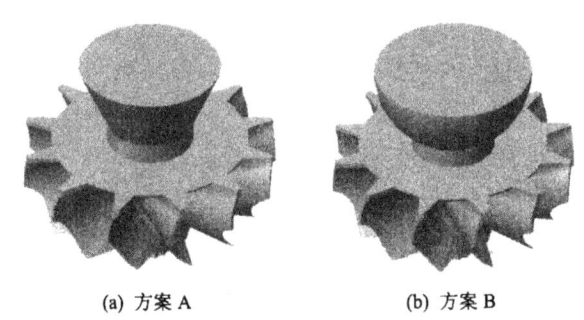

图 6 涡轮铸件三维实体形状

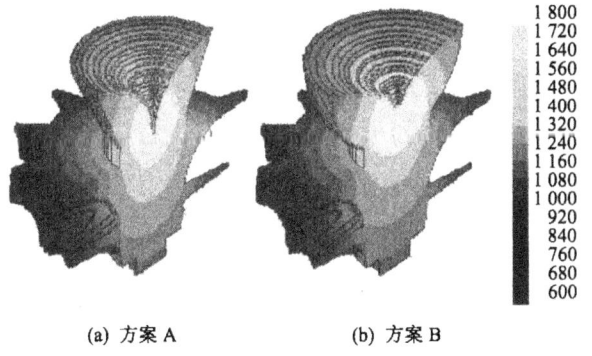

图 7 涡轮铸件凝固末期的温度场

2 铸造过程热应力建模与仿真

铸造过程热应力分析就是采用数值模拟的方法计算铸件/型芯在铸造过程中的热应力（将型芯的阻碍作用通过边界条件也纳入到热应力分析中）产生的变化，预测铸件热裂的产生、铸件的残余应力和残余变形，甚至型芯的变形和应力分布。通过对计算结果的分析进一步优化铸件结构或铸造工艺，从而消除热裂，最大限度地减小残余变形和残余应力。热应力分析的对象已从单一研究铸件的应力和变形，逐渐发展到研究铸件和型芯整个系统的热应力和变形分析[8]，因为不考虑型芯很难全面考虑铸件/型芯边界条件，并且在压铸生产中铸型的热应力模拟对预测压铸模具的使用寿命具有重要意义。另外，铸造过程热应力数值模拟研究逐渐从热力单向耦合向双向耦合发展。单向耦合即只考虑铸件传热对热应力的影响，而不考虑热应力对传热的影响。双向耦合为传热和应力发展相互影响。

2.1 力学模型

在铸件形成过程中，液态金属经过液态、固液两相共存区和固态三个阶段，而且同一时刻可能三个区域共存，因此凝固模拟涉及的应力应变本构关系非常复杂。铸件凝固过程热应力数值模拟也大致分为固液两相区的模拟和凝固以后阶段的模拟两部分。哈尔滨工业大学、清华大学和华北工学院等对一些铸造铝合金和铸钢进行了固液两相区的流变学性能的研究，得到了比较一致的流变学模型 [H]-[H|N]-[N|S][9]。同时，在半固态铸造方面对铝合金在半固态下的流变学性能进行了大量研究和测试，这也为固液两相区的应力分析奠定了基础。铸件凝固以后一般采用热弹塑性模型或热弹黏塑性模型[8,10]。目前凝固过程应力数值模拟的研究主要集中在凝固以后阶段，而在固液两相区的应力数值模拟方面的研究工作较少。另一方面砂型的力学模型也比较复杂，Bellet[8] 和 Samonds[10] 在铸件应力分析中将其处理为热弹塑性模型。

作者[11]开发了基于流变学模型 H-[H|N]-[N|S] 的铸件准固相区应力分析程序，对带热节的工字形试件在中间有无刚性约束条件进行了模拟，如图 8 所示。在流变学模型的基础上提出了热裂判据：当等效黏塑性应变大于临界黏塑性应变时产生热裂。

2.2 应用软件

铸造过程热应力模拟的分析手段经历了由简易专有程序、通用有限元应力分析软件到铸件凝固模拟专业软件三个阶段。早期的研究采用自行开发有限元应力分析程序，主要处理二维问题，如郑贤淑等[12]、邓康等[13]、金俊泽等[14]及张凤禄等[15]分别

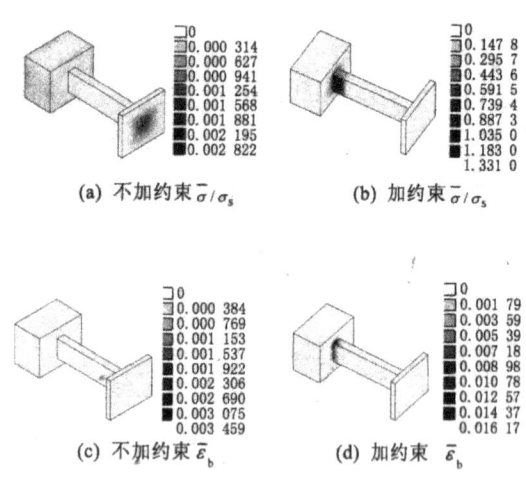

图 8 工字形试件在不同约束工艺下的结果比较

对应力框、大型汽轮机缸体、大型铸钢轧辊及水平连铸坯进行了热应力分析。近年来出现了一些大型的通用有限元分析软件如 ANSYS、ABAQUS、ADINA 及 I-DEAS 等，这些软件已经广泛应用，一般都提供热弹塑性模型等多种常用材料力学模型，并且具有强大的有限元前后处理功能。应用这些软件可以对铸件进行三维热应力分析。例如，林家骝等[16]和陈国权[17]分别采用 ABAQUS 和 ADINA & ADINAT 软件对带凹槽圆筒件和中空轴铸钢件进行了应力分析及热裂预测。但是，要完全适合铸造过程应力数值模拟，这些商业软件还需要进行二次开发。近几年来国内外开发了一些专业铸件凝固过程数值模拟软件，其中部分软件具有应力分析功能，如 MAGMA、PROCAST、CASTS、PHYSICA、THERCAST 及铸造之星等。

由于铸造过程应力分析实际上包括两部分，传热计算和应力计算。多数铸件凝固模拟软件采用有限差分法，而应力分析普遍采用有限元法。因此在该领域主要有两种方法：一种是温度场和应力场都采用相同的方法，主要是有限元法；另一种是采用不同的方法计算温度场和应力场，如用有限差分或有限体积法计算温度场，然后用有限元法计算应力。热分析和应力分析采用不同的方法是为了充分发挥各数值算法的优点，但是存在不同算法模型间的匹配问题以及由此带来的误差，如有限差分模型或有限体积模型和有限元模型的匹配。热分析和应力分析都采用相同的方法，温度场和应力场不需要进行匹配，并且能够实现应力场和温度场计算耦合，但计算复杂而且计算量大。

作者[18,19]采用有限差分法进行传热模拟，采用有限元法进行应力分析，建立了有限差分（FDM）/有限元（FEM）集成铸件热应力分析系统，如图 9 所示。系统实现了有限差分/有限元模型温度载荷的自动转换，采用流变学模型进行铸件准固相区热应力分析及热裂预测，在铸件凝固以后的应力分析可采用 ANSYS 或 I-DEAS 等商业软件中的热弹塑性模型。该系统已在铸造生产中得到应用，对多个实际铸件进行了热应力分析，并取得很好的结果，例如，不同落砂温度对于六缸发动机缸体残余应力的影响，压铸模具的应力及变形分布（图 10）及加强筋对大型鼓风机铸件局部残余应力的影响（图 11）。

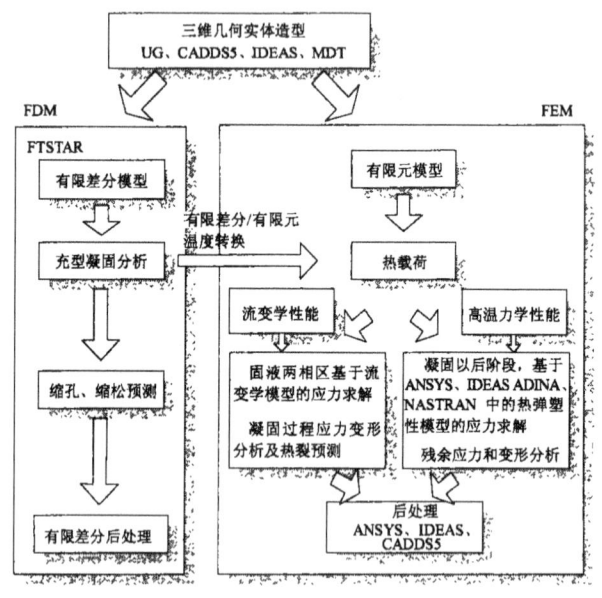

图 9 铸件凝固过程 FDM/FEM 集成热应力分析系统框图

Si Ho-Mum 等[20]也采用有限差分和有限元集成的方法进行铸件的热应力分析。Jinho Lee 等[21]则采用有限体积法和有限元法的集成对凝固金属进行热应力分析。J. H. Hattel 等[22]实现了基于控制体积有限差分法的热弹性应力分析，在采用有限差分法进行应力分析方面进行了探索。Frakeldey 等[20]将温度场/应力场以及微观组织模拟耦合起来，对铸件凝固过程中多物理现象进行了模拟，这也是将来铸件凝固模拟的一个发展方向。

3 凝固过程微观组织模拟仿真

凝固过程微观组织模拟已成为材料科学的研究热点之一，模拟方法一般可分为两大类：确定性模拟与随机性模拟。确定性模拟[23]以凝固动力学为基础，符合晶体生长的物理背景，但未考虑晶体生长

(a) 有限差分模型下的温度分布

(b) 转换到有限元模型下的温度载荷

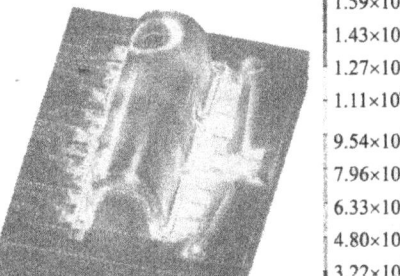

(c) 开模前模具中的等效应力分布

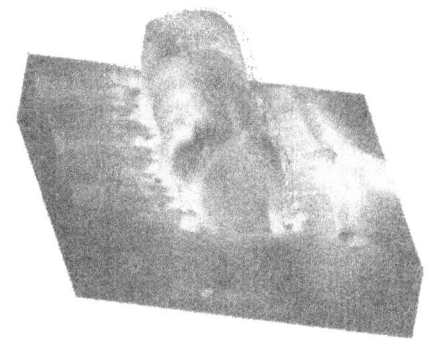

(d) 开模后模具的变形情况

图10 压铸模具中的等效应力分布及变形情况

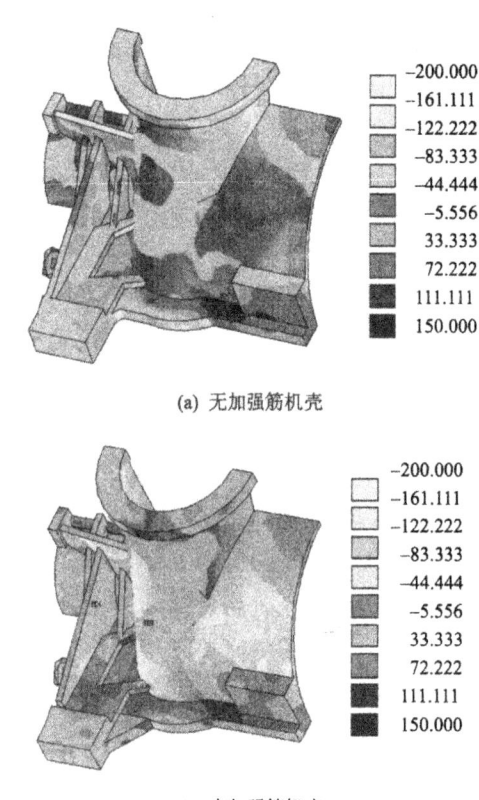

(a) 无加强筋机壳

(b) 有加强筋机壳

图11 大型鼓风机机壳铸铁件 x 方向残余应力（MPa）

过程中的一些随机现象。随机性方法中有代表性的是 Monte Carlo（MC）法[24] 与 Cellular automaton（CA）法[25,26]。在 MC 法中引入了概率论，对形核位置的分布与晶粒生长取向进行随机的处理，可得到与实际金相图片类似的图像，并体现出不同工艺参数的影响。CA 法以形核过程的物理机理和晶体生长动力学理论为基础，可得到晶粒的尺寸及分布，也可描述柱状晶的形成以及柱状晶向等轴晶的转变。最近相场方法[27]备受关注，在模拟晶粒三维生长方面有独特的优势。相场理论通过微分方程反映了扩散、有序化势及热力学驱动的综合作用，可以描述金属系统中固液界面的形态、曲率以及界面的移动。若与温度场、溶质场、速度场等外部场耦合，则可对金属液的凝固过程进行真实的模拟。但计算域较小，只能针对较大的过冷度，难以应用于实际的铸造过程。Steinbach 等提出了一种介观尺度的模拟方法[28]，采用整体数值模拟与局部解析解相结合的方法来描述多个等轴枝晶在过冷熔体中的非稳定长大，但能模拟的晶粒数目仍非常有限。

3.1 确定性方法（Deterministic model）

Thévoz 和 Rappaz 在等轴晶模拟中首先将溶质扩

散模型和枝晶生长动力学模型结合起来。他们可以求得平均晶粒尺寸分布及铸件的冷却曲线。但是他们只考虑了等轴晶组织，没有考虑对流传输和晶粒沉积效应。

Wang 和 Beckermann[29]将动量方程、能量方程和传质方程同时求解，考察了固相传输对等轴晶粒组织的影响，提出了多相溶质扩散模型。在枝晶组织中考虑了不同的长度尺度，认为控制体积中包含三种相：固相（等轴晶或柱状晶）、枝晶间液相及远端液相。枝晶的包络线被看作是固液界面，它的运动受枝晶尖端生长动力学所控制。该模型能体现枝晶的粗化过程，适用于柱状晶和等轴晶，但是忽略了热过冷熔体的对流的影响。

Brown 和 Hunt[30]使用界面追踪技术，通过设置标志粒子来研究枝晶前沿及等轴晶晶界的移动，并研究了 CET 转变。Gandin[31]采用二界面的前沿追踪技术，基于求解传热方程研究了定向凝固过程中共晶生长前沿和枝晶生长前沿的变化。Yang 和 Stefanescu[32]通过晶粒追踪模型可以精确模拟铝合金等轴晶粒的移动，并分析了晶粒移动对组织转变及最终组织的影响。

赵海东等[33,34]采用确定性模型对汽车球墨铸铁件进行了微观组织及性能预测模拟，铸件材质为 QT450-10。图 12 为实际球铁件的模拟预测结果，与生产实际结果吻合较好。

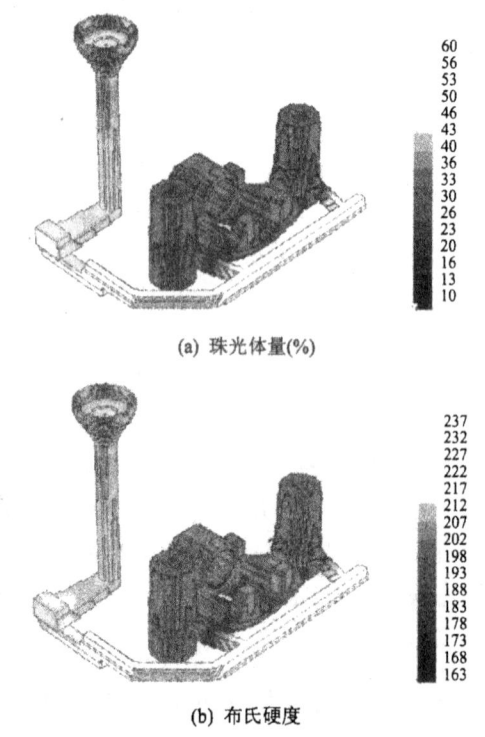

图 12　汽车球墨铸铁件微观组织及性能预测

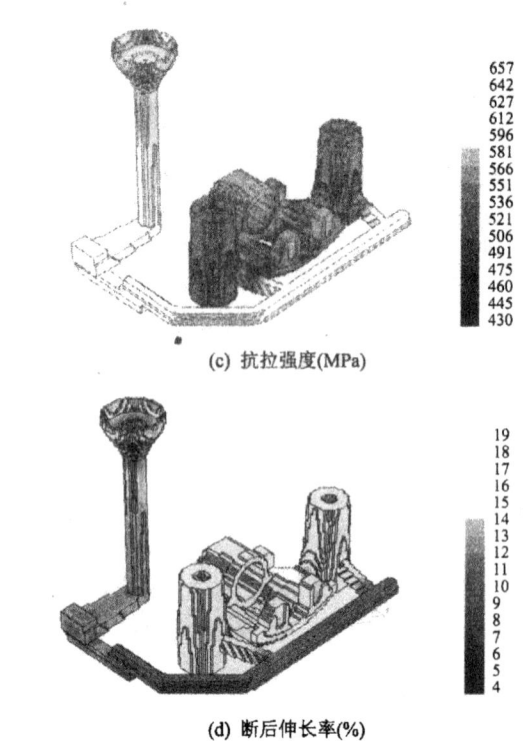

图 12　汽车球墨铸铁件微观组织及性能预测（续）

3.2　随机性方法（Stochastic model）

随机模型是指主要采用概率方法来研究晶粒的形核和长大，包括形核位置的随机分布和晶粒晶向的随机取向。主要包括有 MC 法和 CA 法。MC 法以概率统计理论为基础，以随机抽样为手段。它建立在界面能最小基础之上，不同属性的质点之间存在界面能（如固、液质点，或属于不同晶粒的质点）。Zhu 和 Smith[24]采用 MC 法对晶粒的形核与生长进行研究，基于固液相变时体自由能和界面自由能的变化计算了晶粒的生长，但没有考虑晶体生长过程中的择优取向。该方法忽略了宏观/微观传输过程的细节，缺乏物理背景。因此现在用这种方法模拟凝固组织已比较少见。

Rappaz 和 Gandin[35]提出了 CA 模型，考虑了非自发形核方法和生长过程的物理机制。在 FE-CA 的基础上，他们又发展了 3D CAFE 模型，并成功地模拟了铝硅棒晶粒组织的形成。作者等对 CA 法做了修正，采用简化的枝晶形状模拟了金属型和砂型试样的晶粒结构，并与试验进行了比较，如图 13 所示。

枝晶往往具有复杂的几何形状，如初生主干上会出现二次枝晶臂或高次分枝。传统的 CA 法没有考虑具体的枝晶形貌。Stefanescu 和 Pang 等[36]首先对枝晶形状的模拟做了尝试:在 10^{-6} m 尺度采用随机模型,而在 10^{-4} m 尺度下采用确定性模型,并将两者进行了耦合。同时还计算了枝晶臂粗化,主要是综合考虑了尖端生长速度和确定性的枝晶粗化模型。

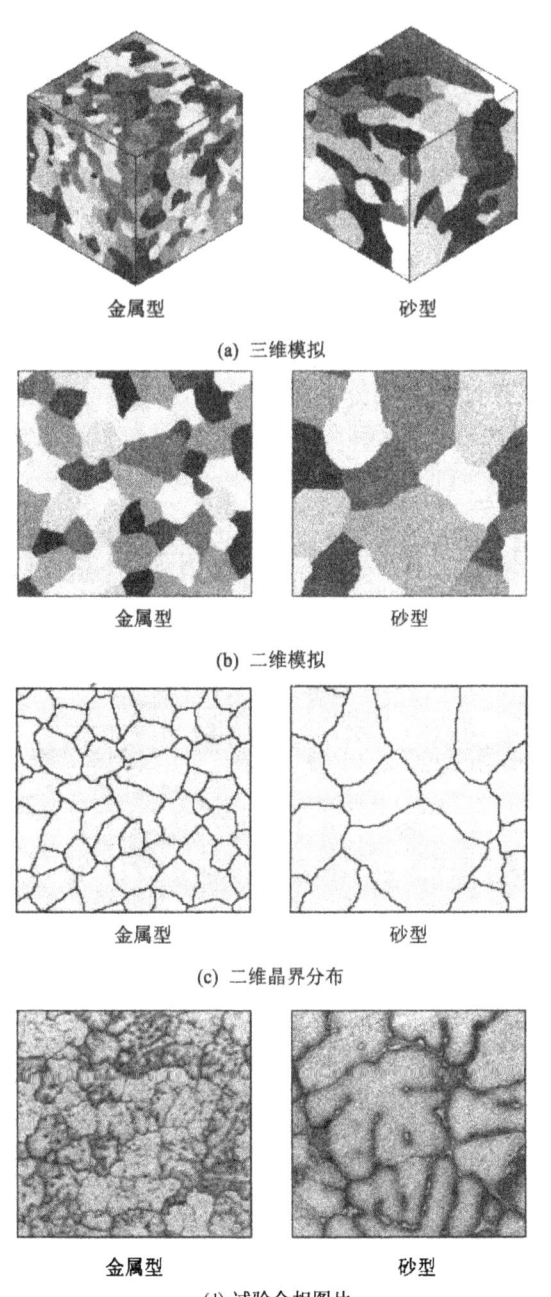

图 13 铝合金凝固组织模拟结果与金相组织的对比

Dilthey 等[37]利用改进的 CA 模型对枝晶形貌和晶粒长大进行了数值模拟,考虑了固液相中的溶质扩散和溶质再分配、溶质和曲面过冷对平衡界面温度的影响,定性再现了枝晶尖端的抛物线形态、二次和三次枝晶臂的发展、平界面的不稳定性、由曲率减小引起的粗化及在限制条件下枝晶的选择等。

Nastac[38]提出了一种更复杂的随机模型来模拟枝晶的形貌演变。这个模型包括与时间有关的温度分布计算、液相及固相中的溶质再分配、曲率和生长的各向异性。Zhu 和 Hong[39]也采用类似的方法模拟了枝晶形成。作者在这方面也做了一些工作,可模拟二维及三维枝晶的生长[38,39],对等轴枝晶的模拟结果如图 14 所示。

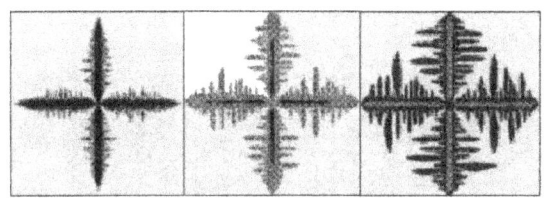
Nastac 的模拟结果(Al-7%Si)

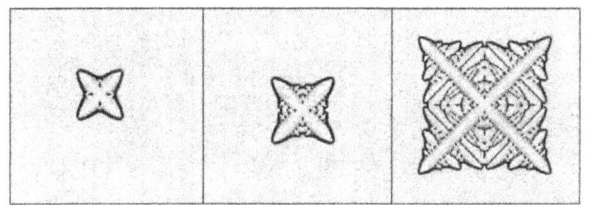
Zhu 和 Hong 的模拟结果(Al-2%Cu)

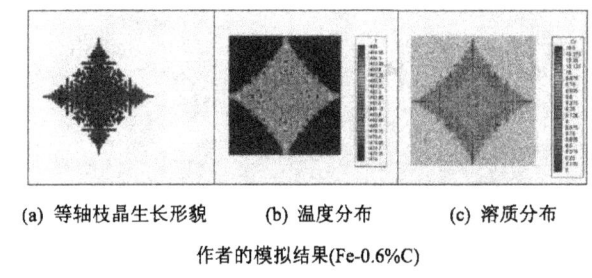
(a) 等轴枝晶生长形貌　(b) 温度分布　(c) 溶质分布
作者的模拟结果(Fe-0.6%C)

图 14 等轴枝晶生长的模拟

3.3 相场模型 (Phase field model)

相场方法引入相场变量 ϕ,ϕ 是一个有序参量,表示系统在空间/时间上每个位置的物理状态(液态或固态)。最近相场方法的研究成为微观组织模拟的热点。

相场方法的应用范围较广,从共晶到包晶、界面变化、枝晶生长,从二元到三元,从两相到多相,以及颗粒在界面上的迁移等问题。已有的工作包括:①多个晶粒生长时多元相场的耦合;②枝晶生长过程中相场与温度场或溶质场的耦合;③在包晶和共晶凝固中双相场与溶质场的耦合;④当存在强迫对流时相场与速度场的耦合。Nestler 等提出了一种新的多相场模型公式,考虑了表面能和界面动力学各向异性。Diepers 等[40]使用相场理论模拟了二元合金中对流引起的晶粒粗化,考虑熔体对流的影响,模拟了二维粗化问题。在纯扩散条件下,模拟结果与经典 LSW 理论稍有偏差。在强迫对流存在时,组织迅速粗化,曲率半径分布加宽,与 Ratke-Thieringer 理论一致。Tong 等[41]利用相场方法模拟了二维情况下的枝晶自由生长。当流体流动速度与尖端生长速度为同一个数量级时,流体的流动对枝晶的生长方向有重要影响。但是模拟中没有考虑干扰及高次枝晶的影响。

Grafe 等[42]采用多相场模型模拟了三元单晶 Ni-Al-Cr 在定向凝固时的组织变化及微观偏析。Nestler 等[43]提出了一个通用的二元多相合金系统的多相场模型,通过恰当地改变系统参数,可用来模拟共晶、包晶中的凝固现象,建立了多相场模型中自由能与特定相图之间的联系。Ode 等[44]利用相场方法研究了颗粒/界面问题,成功地再现了颗粒在界面前沿的推移和陷落现象。

张光跃等[45]采用相场方法对铝合金的生长过程进行了模拟。把 Karma 和 Rappel 的纯物质三维相场模拟扩展到了二元合金的三维相场模型[45]。图 15 对不同模型计算的三维枝晶形貌进行了对照。

(a) 纯物质尖锐界面相场模型　　(b) 二元合金弥散界面相场模型

图 15　相场法模拟的三维枝晶形貌

4　快速产品/工艺开发系统与多尺度模拟仿真

我国制造业的主要问题之一是缺乏创新产品的开发能力,因而缺乏国际市场竞争能力。随着全球化市场的激烈竞争,加快产品开发速度已成为竞争的重要手段之一。美国汽车工业希望汽车的研发周期缩短为 15~25 个月,而 20 世纪 90 年代汽车的研发周期为 5 年。并行工程、快速产品/工艺开发系统及网络化虚拟制造等就是在这样的背景下产生。

应该指出,产品设计及制造开发系统是以设计与制造过程的建模与仿真为核心内容,模拟仿真或称计算机辅助工程分析（CAE）已成为并行工程及产品虚拟开发的主要内容,如图 16 所示[46]。1992 年美国先进金属材料加工工程研究中心提出"合理的产品与工艺（成形加工）设计（Rational product and process design）",即在设计阶段进行成形工艺与产品设计（CAD）、铸造成形过程与性能分析、模具与产品的制造过程仿真（CAM）。它不仅提供产品零部件的可制造性评估,而且提供产品零部件的性能预测。最近,制造厂商又提出了"新产品一次研发成功"的理念,其核心仍然是从设计到制造全部过程的建模与仿真技术。快速产品/工艺开发系统与多尺度模拟仿真已在国外汽车及航空工业中得到应用,如图 17 所示。根据上述构思,针对铝合金铸件的性能和疲劳寿命预测,作者初步建立了铝合金铸件疲劳寿命模拟分析系统,如图 18 所示[47]。

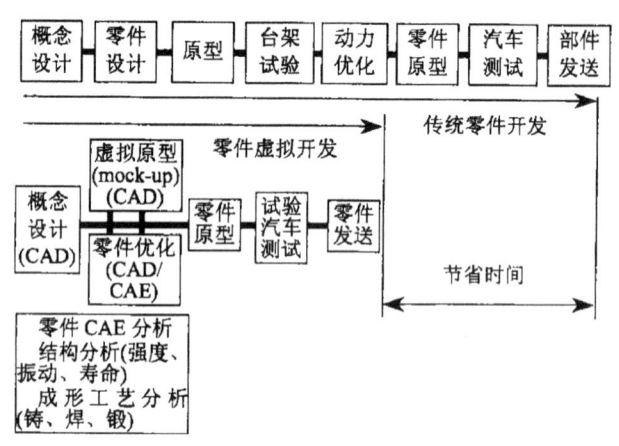

图 16　产品虚拟开发与传统方法比较

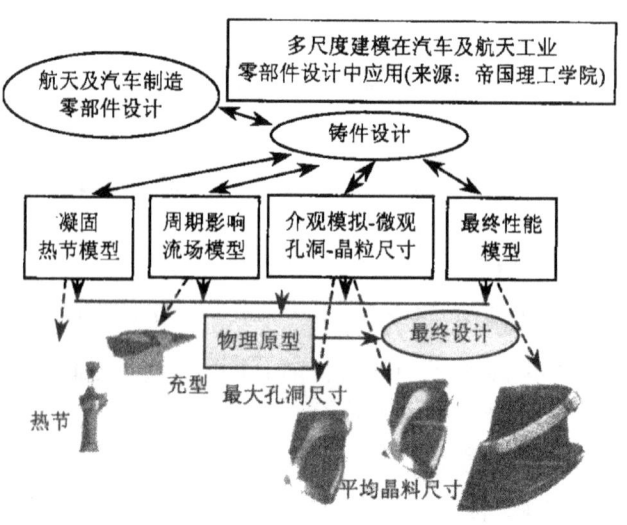

图 17　多尺度模拟仿真在国外汽车及航空工业中的应用

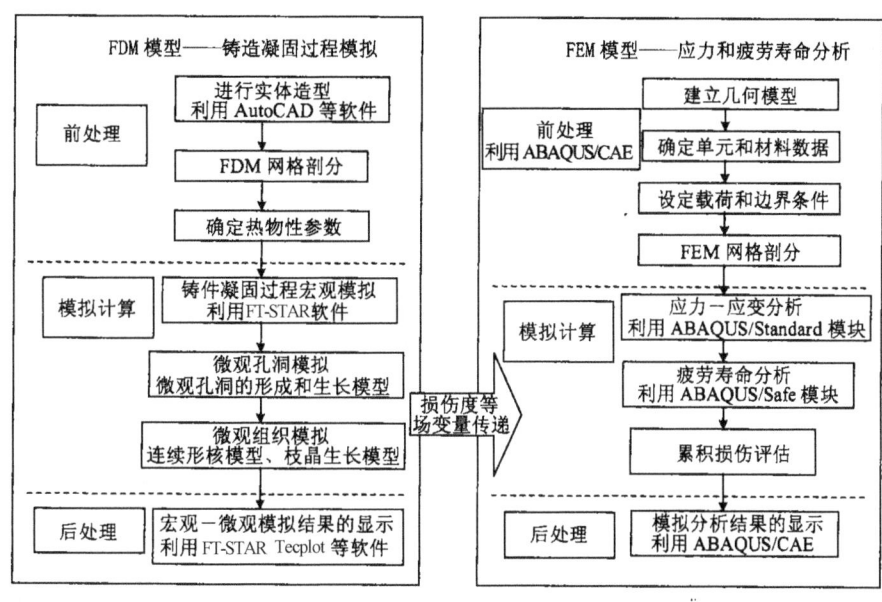

图18 铝合金铸件疲劳寿命模拟分析系统

5 结论

铸造行业是制造业的重要组成部分,在振兴我国制造业的同时,要加强和重视先进铸造技术的发展。基于知识的铸造成形过程模拟仿真是材料科学与制造科学的前沿领域及研究热点,铸造成形过程的宏观模拟已在生产中广泛应用。采用并行计算技术、分数步长法及分区域空间步长和分区域时间步长法可大大提高压力铸造充型及凝固过程数值模拟的计算效率。采用有限差分法进行传热模拟、采用有限元法进行应力分析的 FDM/FEM 集成铸件热应力分析系统已在生产中应用。系统实现了有限差分/有限元模型温度载荷的自动转换,采用流变学模型进行铸件准固相区热应力分析及热裂预测,采用热弹塑性模型进行铸件凝固后的应力。凝固过程微观组织模拟已成为计算材料科学的当前研究热点,在确定性方法、元胞自动机方法及相场方法等方面均取得可喜的进展。在网络化环境下、在快速产品/工艺研究开发系统中进行铸件的多尺度模拟仿真将是今后的发展趋势。

参考文献

[1] 柳百成,荆涛. 铸造工程的模拟仿真与质量控制. 北京:机械工业出版社,2001.

[2] 高志强,王春乐,邱伟,等. 考虑充型过程的铸钢件缩孔缩松预测研究. 机械工程学报,1997,33(6):46-52.

[3] Wang G, Xiong S M, Liu B C, et al. Parallel computation technique for mold filling simulation of die casting process by optimizing the computational parameters. Int, J. Cast. Metal. Res., 2002, 15(3): 143-147.

[4] Xiong S M, Lau F, Lee W B, et al. Numerical methods to improve the computational efficiency of thermal analysis for the die casting process. J. Mater Process Tech., 2003, 139(1~3): 457-461.

[5] Barone M R, Caulk D A. New method for thermal analysis of die casting. J. of Heat Transfer, 1993, 115(2): 284-293.

[6] 梁作俭,许庆彦,李俊涛,等. γ-TiAl 增压涡轮近净形铸造过程实验研究. 稀有金属材料与工程,2002(10): 353-357.

[7] 梁作俭,许庆彦,李俊涛,等. γ-TiAl 增压涡轮熔模铸造过程数值模拟研究. 稀有金属材料与工程,2003(3): 164-169.

[8] Bellet Michel, Aliaga Charles, Jaouen Olivier. Finite elements for a thermomechanical analysis of solidification processes. In: Sahm Peter R, Hansen Preben N, Coley James G, eds. Modeling of Casting, Welding and Advanced Solidification Processes IX. New York: The Minerals. Metals & Materials Society, 2000: 11-17.

[9] Li Q, Chen K, Liu Ch, et al. Rheological behavior in solid-liquid coexistence zone and simulation of stress-strain and cracking of Al-Cu alloy during solidification. AFS Trans, 1991, 99: 245-253.

[10] Samonds M, Zhu J Z. Coupled thermal-fluid-stress analysis of castings. In: Sahm Peter R, Hansen Preben N, Coley James G, eds. Modeling of Casting, Welding and Ad-

vanced Solidification Processes IX. New York: The Minerals, Metals & Materials Society, 2000: 81-87.
[11] Kang J, Liu B C, Xiong S M. Numerical simulation of thermal stress of shaped casting based on rheological model. J. Mater. Sci. Technol., 1999, 15 (3): 267-270.
[12] 郑贤淑, 金俊泽. 应力框动态应力的热弹塑性分析. 大连理工大学学报, 1983, 22 (3): 1-6.
[13] 邓康, 毛生根, 孙焕纯, 等. 大型汽轮机缸体铸件应力计算与热裂分析. 铸造技术, 1993 (2): 3-6.
[14] 金俊泽, 郑贤淑, 郭可忉. 大型铸钢轧辊铸造及热处理应力的数值模拟. 铸铁, 1988, 23 (10): 35-41.
[15] 张风禄, 博军隆. 水平连铸坯热应力的计算和分析. 北京科技大学学报, 1990, 12 (1): 25-31.
[16] 林家骝, 朱世根, 于震宗. 铸钢件凝固过程三维温度场热应力场的数值模拟与缩孔（缩松）的热裂的判定. 铸造, 1993, 42 (10): 1-9.
[17] 陈国权. 中空轴铸钢件凝固过程三维热应力场模拟及其热裂的研究: [博士学位论文]. 北京: 清华大学, 1994.
[18] Liu B C, Zhu R M. Residual stress computation and analysis of machine tool bed casting In: Proceedings of the Fifth International Symposium of the Plhysical Metallurgical of Cast Iron, France, 1994.
[19] Liu B C, Kang J W, Xiong S M. A study on the numerical simulation of thermal stress during the solidification of shaped casting. Science and Technology of Advanced Materials, 2001 (2): 157-164.
[20] Si Ho-Mun, Cho Chongdu, Kwahk Si-Young. A hybrid method for casting process simulation by combing FDM and FEM with an efficient data conversion algorithm. Journal of Materials Processing Technology, 2003, 133: 311-321.
[21] Lee Jinho. Hwang Ki-Young. A hybrid numerical analysis of heat transfer and thermal stress in a solidifying body using FVM and FEM. Int. J. Engng Sci, 1996, 34 (8): 901-922.
[22] Hattel J H, Hansen P N. A control volume based finite difference method for solving equilibrium equations in terms of displacement. Appl. Math Modeling. 1995 (19): 210-243.
[23] Zhao H D, Liu B C. Modeling of stable and metastable eutectic transformation of spheroidal graphite iron casting. ISIJ Inter., 2001, 41 (9): 986-991.
[24] Zhu P, Smith R W. Dynamic simulation of crystal growth by Monte Carlo method-I: model description and kinetics. Acta Metall. Mater, 1992, 40: 683-692.
[25] Xu Q Y, Liu B C. Modeling of As-cast microstructure of Al alloy with a modified cellular automaton method. Mater. Trans. 2001, 41 (7): 2316-2321.
[26] Feng W M, Xu Q Y, Liu B C. Microstructure simulation of aluminum alloy using parallel computing technique. ISIJ International, 2002, 42 (7): 702-707.
[27] Zhang G Y, Jing T, Liu B C. Microstructure simulation of aluminum alloy casting using phase field method. Int. J. Cast. Metal. Res., 2002, 15 (3): 237-240.
[28] Steinbach I, Beckermann C, Kauerauf B, et al. Three-dimensional modeling of equiaxed dendritic growth on a mesoscopic scale. Acta Mater, 1999, 47 (3): 971-982.
[29] Wang C Y, Beckermann C. Multi-scale/-phase modeling of dendritic alloy solidification. American Society of Mechanical Engineers, Heat Transfer Division, (Publication) HTD, Transport Phenomena in Solidification, 1994, 284: 75-95.
[30] Brown D J, Hunt J D. A model of columnar growth using a front-tracking technique. In: Modeling of Casting, Welding and Advanced Solidification Processes IX, Aachen, Germany. 2000: 437-444.
[31] Gandin Ch-A. From constrained to unconstrained growth during directional solidification of dendritic alloy. Acta Materialia, 2000, 48 (10): 2483-2501.
[32] Yang B J, Stefanscu D M. Solidification modeling with grain tracking, modeling of casting. In: Welding and Advanced Solidification Processes IX, Aachen, Germany. 2000: 582-589.
[33] 赵海东, 柳百成, 刘蔚羽, 等. 球墨铸铁件微观组织的数值模拟, 机械工程学报, 2000, 36 (2): 76-80.
[34] Zhao H D, Liu B C. Modeling of stable and metastable eutectic transformation of spheroidal graphite iron casting. ISIJ lntemational, 2001, 41 (9): 986-991.
[35] Gandin Ch-A, Rappaz M. Coupled finite clement-cellular automation model for the prediction of dendritic grain structures in solification processes. Acta Metall., 1994, 42: 2233-2246.
[36] Stefanescu D M, Pang H. Modeling of casting solidification: stochastic or deterministic. Canadian Metallurgical Quarterly, 1998, 37 (3, 4): 229-239.
[37] Dilthey U, Pavlik V. Numerical simulation of dendrite morphology and grain growth with modified cellular automata. In: Modeling of Casting. Welding and Advanced Solidification Processes VIII, 1998: 589-596.
[38] Nastac L. Numerical modeling of solidification morphologies and segregation patterns in cast dendritic alloys. Acta Mater., 1999, 47 (17): 4253-4262.
[39] Zhu M F, Hong C P. A modified cellular automaton model for the simulation of dendritic growth in solidification of alloys. ISIJ Intemational. 2001, 41 (5): 436-445.

[40] Diepers H-J, Beckermann C, Steinbach I. Simuiation of convection and ripening in a binary alloy mush using the phase-field method. Acta Materialia, 1999, 47 (13): 3663-3678.

[41] Tong X, Beckermann C, Karma A, et al. Phase-field simulations of dendritic crystal growth in a forced flow. Physical Review E, 2001, 63 (6): 1-16.

[42] Grafe U, Bottinger B, Tiaden J, et al. Coupling of multi-component thermodynamic databases to a phase field model: application to solidification and solid state transformations of superalloys. Scripta Materialia, 2000, 42 (12): 1179-1186.

[43] Nestler B, Wheeler A A. Multi-phase-field model of eutectic and peritectic alloys: numerical simulation of growth structures. Physica D: Nonlinear Phenomena, 2000, 138 (1): 114-133.

[44] Ode M, Kim S G, Suzuki T. Recent advances in the phase-field model for solidification. ISIJ International, 2001, 41 (10): 1076-1082.

[45] Zhang G Y, Jing T, Liu B C. Dendritic morphology simulation using the phase field method. Tsinghua Science and Technology, 2003, 8 (1): 117-120.

[46] Haldenwanger H G, Stich A. Casting simulation as an innovation in the motor vehicle development process. Modeling of Casting, Welding and Advanced Solidification Processes-IX. 2000: 44-51.

[47] Dong S Y, Zhuang Z, Xiong S M, et al. Modeling of micro-porosity evolution and fatigue life of aluminum alloy. In: Proceedings of the 10th International Modeling Conference on Casting, Welding and Advanced Solidification Processes, Florida, USA, 2003.

PROGRESS ON MULTI-SCALE MODELING OF CASTING PROCESS

Liu Baicheng   Xu Qingyan   Xiong Shoumei
Kang Jingwu
(*Tsinghua University*)

Abstract: Casting industry is critical to the national economy. However there exists big gap between the casting technologies at home and abroad. One of the important future trends is the application of *numerical simulation technique to substitute* the traditional empirical research methods. Numerical simulation has become the necessary way to up-grade the traditional casting industries and been paid with much more attention. With the mature of macro-modeling of casting process, micro-modeling and multi-scale modeling become one of the hottest research frontiers attracting many researchers and engineers. The current research hotspots and the development trends of modeling of casting processes are mainly introduced, especially on the mold filing and solidification processes of net shape casting, the stress and strain analyses, the prediction of the formation and evolution of microstructure and the multi-scale modeling under concurrent engineering environment. At the same time, the related achievements in our country are given with special emphasis.

Key words: Net shape casting   Modeling and simulation   Stress analysis   Microstructure simulation   Multi-scale modeling

作者简介：柳百成，男，1933年出生，中国工程院院士，清华大学教授，《机械工程学报》编委。长期从事铸铁结晶凝固过程和石墨形态控制的基础研究及提高铸铁性能和开发新型铸铁的应用研究，在国内较早提出用电子计算机技术改造传统铸造行业，在开拓多学科宏观及微观铸造过程模拟仿真研究新领域作出贡献。近年来，积极组织倡导开展轻量化、精密化、清洁化材料成形理论与技术研究。获部委科技进步一等奖2项、二等奖5项及三等奖4项，获国外奖励2项及国家发明专利2项。2002年获光华工程科技奖。发表论文300余篇，在国际学术会议宣读论文20余篇。

3. Phase-field simulation of solidification in multicomponent alloys coupled with thermodynamic and diffusion mobility databases

Ruijie Zhang[a], Tao Jing[a], Wanqi Jie[b], Baicheng Liu[a]

[a] Department of Mechanical Engineering, Tsinghua University, Beijing 100084, China
[b] College of Materials Science and Engineering, Northwestern Polytechnical University, Xi'an 710072, China Received 19 May 2005; received in revised form 10 January 2006; accepted 17 January 2006 Available online 24 March 2006

Abstract: To simulate quantitatively the microstructural evolution in the solidification process of multicomponent alloys, we extend the phasefield model for binary alloys to multicomponent alloys with consideration of the solute interactions between different species. These interactions have a great influence not only on the phase equilibria but also on the solute diffusion behaviors. In the model, the interface region is assumed to be a mixture of solid and liquid with the same chemical potential, but with different compositions. The simulation presented is coupled with thermodynamic and diffusion mobility databases, which can accurately predict the phase equilibria and the solute diffusion transportation in the whole system. The phase equilibria in the interface and other thermodynamic quantities are obtained using Thermo-Calc through the TQ interface. As an example, two-dimensional computations for the dendritic growth in Al-Cu-Mg ternary alloy are performed. The quantitative solute distributions and diffusion matrix are obtained in both solid and liquid phases.

© 2006 Acta Materialia Inc. Published by Elsevier Ltd. All rights reserved.

Key words: Phase-field models; Thermodynamics; Diffusion; Multicomponent solidification

1. Introduction

The phase-field model is becoming a powerful tool which can describe complex interface pattern evolution. The phase-field models were originally developed for solidification of pure materials[1-3] and then extended to binary alloys[4-6]. However, many general industrial alloys, such as iron, steel and aluminum alloys, are all multicomponent alloys. It can be said that the application of the phase-field model for solidification to practical technology is closely linked to our ability to model microstructural development in multicomponent alloys.

Most of the models[7-10] describing the solidification of multicomponent alloys are based on the assumption that the solute diffusion behaviors of the components are independent of each other. The diffusion fields in multicomponent alloys are then given by the same mathematical functions as in binary systems. There are several models that can describe the solute interactions in multicomponent alloy solidification[11-13]; however, they are limited to one-dimensional problems.

The aim of this work is to develop the phase-field model for dendritic solidification in multicomponent alloys with consideration of the solute interactions between different species. These interactions have a great influence not only on the phase equilibria but also on the solute diffusion behaviors. The simulation process presented is coupled with thermodynamic and diffusion mobility databases, which can accurately predict the phase equilibria and the solute diffusion transportation in the whole system. As an example, two-dimensional computations for the dendritic growth in Al-Cu-Mg ternary alloy are performed.

2. Phase-field model for multicomponent alloys

2.1 Governing equations

The total free energy of the system is defined as

$$F(\phi, C_1, C_2, \cdots, C_{n-1}) = \int_\Omega \left[f(\phi, C_1, C_2, \cdots, C_{n-1}) + \frac{1}{2}\varepsilon^2 |\nabla \phi|^2 \right] d\Omega \quad (1)$$

where F is the total free energy of the system, f is the free energy density, ε is the gradient energy coefficient and ϕ is the phase field ranging from zero in the liquid to one in the solid.

The governing equations for the phase field and the concentration field can then be expressed as[7]

$$\frac{\partial \phi}{\partial t} = -M \frac{\delta F}{\delta \phi} = M(\varepsilon^2 \nabla^2 \phi - f_\phi) \quad (2)$$

$$\frac{\partial C_k}{\partial t} = \nabla \sum_{i=1}^{n-1} M_{ki} \nabla f_{C_i}$$

$$= \nabla \sum_{j=1}^{n-1} \sum_{i=1}^{n-1} M_{ki} f_{C_i C_j} \nabla C_j + \nabla \sum_{i=1}^{n-1} M_{ki} f_{C_i \phi} \nabla \phi \quad (3)$$

where $f_\phi, f_C, f_{C\phi}$ and f_{CC} are $\partial f/\partial \phi$, $\partial f/\partial C_i$, $\partial^2 f/\partial C_i \partial \phi$ and $\partial^2 f/\partial C_i \partial C_j$, respectively. M_{ki} is determined from the diffusivity matrix:

$$D_{kj} = \sum_{i=1}^{n-1} M_{ki} f_{C_i C_j} \quad (4)$$

The diffusivity matrix in multicomponent alloys can be written as[14]

$$\mathbf{D} = \begin{pmatrix} D_{1,1} & D_{1,2} & \cdots & D_{1,n-1} \\ D_{2,1} & D_{2,2} & \cdots & D_{2,n-1} \\ \vdots & \vdots & & \vdots \\ D_{n-1,1} & D_{n-1,2} & \cdots & D_{n-1,n-1} \end{pmatrix} \quad (5)$$

If the off-diagonal terms are set to zero, i.e.,

$$D_{i,j} = 0, i \neq j \quad (6)$$

the solute diffusion transportation will be independent and can be determined by the same mathematical functions as in binary systems. In this paper, the diffusion matrix, both diagonal and off-diagonal terms, is accurately predicted by coupling with thermodynamic and diffusion mobility databases. This will be shown in Section 3.2.

When the diffusivity matrix, $\mathbf{D}$, is obtained, M_{ki} can be determined by solving Eq. (4).

In this work, the free energy density is defined as[15]

$$f(\phi, C_1, C_2, \cdots, C_{n-1}) = h(\phi) f^S(C_1^S, C_2^S, \cdots, C_{n-1}^S) + [1-h(\phi)] f^L(C_1^L, C_2^L, \cdots, C_{n-1}^L) + wg(\phi) \quad (7)$$

where

$$C_i = h(\phi) C_i^S + [1-h(\phi)] C_i^L \quad (8)$$

$$f_{C_i^S}^S(C_1^S, C_2^S, \cdots, C_{n-1}^S) = f_{C_i^L}^L(C_1^L, C_2^L, \cdots, C_{n-1}^L) \quad (9)$$

It is worth noting here that Eq. (9) is the equal chemical potential condition.

We choose:

$$h(\phi) = \phi^3(6\phi^2 - 15\phi + 10) \quad (10)$$

$$wg(\phi) = w\phi^2(1-\phi)^2 \quad (11)$$

2.2 Phase-field parameters

In the phase-field equation, there are three parameters: the mobility M, the gradient energy coefficient ε and the height of the parabolic potential w. the parameters w and ε can be obtained from the interface energy σ and the interface width 2λ. Using the one-dimension equilibrium solution

$$\phi_0(x) = \frac{1}{2}\left[1 - \tanh\left(\frac{\sqrt{2w}}{\varepsilon}x\right)\right] \quad (12)$$

we can obtain the following relationships:

$$\sigma = \frac{\varepsilon\sqrt{2w}}{3} \quad (13)$$

$$2\lambda = \alpha\sqrt{2}\frac{\varepsilon}{\sqrt{w}} \quad (14)$$

where α is a constant which is dependent on the definition of the interface thickness.

The phase-field mobility M is correlated with the interface kinetics and its equation is given as[6,7,15]

$$\Delta f_S = v_n \mu_k^{-1}$$

$$= v_n\left[\frac{\sigma}{M\varepsilon^2} - \frac{\varepsilon}{\sqrt{2w}} \xi(C_1^{L,e}, \cdots, C_{n-1}^{L,e}, C_1^{S,e}, \cdots, C_{n-1}^{S,e})\right] \quad (15)$$

$$\xi(C_1^{L,e}, \cdots, C_{n-1}^{L,e}, C_1^{S,e}, \cdots, C_{n-1}^{S,e})$$

$$= -\sum_{j=1}^{n-1}(C_j^{L,e} - C_j^{S,e})\sum_{k=1}^{n-1}(C_k^{L,e} - C_k^{S,e}) \times \int_1^0 \int_{\phi_0}^0 B_{jk}^e \frac{1-h(\phi)}{\phi(1-\phi)} h'(\phi_0) d\phi d\phi_0 \quad (16)$$

where B_{jk}^e is a component of the inverse matrix of $\tilde{M}$ at the equilibrium state. If we apply a vanishing kinetic coefficient[16], that is $\mu_k^{-1}=0$, the phase-field mobility can be expressed as

$$M^{-1} = \frac{\varepsilon^3}{\sigma\sqrt{2w}} \times \xi(C_1^{L,e},\cdots,C_{n-1}^{L,e},C_1^{S,e},\cdots,C_{n-1}^{S,e}) \quad (17)$$

The present interface kinetics analysis differs from the analysis of Karma[17], in which interface stretching and surface diffusion were considered.

3. Thermodynamics and diffusion mobility description in multicomponent alloys

3.1 Thermodynamics

In the case of multicomponent alloys, the integral Gibbs energy for each phase depends on the constitution, temperature and pressure, and this can be described by a thermodynamic model[18]

$$G = G^0 + G_{\text{mix}}^{\text{ideal}} + G_{\text{mix}}^{\text{xs}} \quad (18)$$

where G^0 is the contribution of the pure components of the phase to the Gibbs energy, $G_{\text{mix}}^{\text{ideal}}$ is the ideal mixing contribution and $G_{\text{mix}}^{\text{xs}}$ is the contribution due to non-ideal interaction between the components, also known as the Gibbs excess energy of mixing.

There are a large number of thermodynamic models for various substances in different states, such as the Redlich-Kister-Muggianu formalism[19] for face-centered cubic (fcc), body-centered cubic (bcc) and hexagonal closepacked (hcp) solid solution phases and the sublattice model[20] for the description of a phase with two or more sublattices. Such work has proved useful, since there are now several available software systems capable of estimating the phase equilibrium as a function of pressure, temperature and the composition of alloying elements, such as Thermo-Calc[21], PANDAT[22], MTDATA[23], etc.

3.2 Diffusion mobility

For the case that the elements are substitutional, the diffusion coefficient defined in the volume-fixed frame of reference, D_{ij}^V, can be expressed as[24]

$$D_{ij}^V = \sum_{k=1}^n (\delta_{ki} - x_i) x_k \Omega_k \frac{\partial \mu_k}{\partial x_j} \quad (19)$$

where x_i is the mole fraction of component i, μ_k is the chemical potential of component k and δ_{ki} is the Kronecker delta, i.e., $\delta_{ki}=1$ when $i=k$ and 0 otherwise. It can be noted that the quantity $\partial\mu_k/\partial x_j$ is a purely thermodynamic parameter and corresponds to the thermodynamic factor[25]. This quantity can thus be evaluated from the thermodynamic description of the system. The parameter Ω_k is the mobility of species k in a given phase and will be discussed later.

By eliminating the concentration element n, the chemical diffusion coefficients can be deduced as

$$D_{ij}^n = D_{ij}^V - D_n^V \quad (20)$$

where n is the solvent and D_{ij}^V are given as in Eq. (19). The diffusivity D_{ij}^n is the most convenient one for practical calculations. Determination the diffusion mobility parameter in Eq. (19) requires the use of experimental diffusion data. Tracer or self diffusivities, D_i^*, are generally determined from diffusion studies using isotopes and directly related to the mobility Ω_k by means of the Einstein relation:

$$D_i^* = RT\Omega_i \quad (21)$$

For the case that the elements are interstitial, the diffusion coefficient can be expressed as[24]

$$D_{ij}^n = D_{ij}^V \quad (22)$$

Using the diffusion coefficient expression in Eq. (20), the concentration of element n is eliminated and an $(n-1)\times(n-1)$ chemical diffusion matrix is obtained.

4. Application to Al-rich Al-Cu-Mg ternary alloys

4.1 Thermodynamics description

For fcc, bcc and hcp solid solution phases and liquid phase, the Gibbs energy G for ternary alloys can be written as[18]

$$G = \sum_{i=1}^n x_i G_i^0 + RT \sum_{i=1}^n x_i \ln x_i + G^{\text{ex}} \quad (23)$$

$$G^{\text{ex}} = \sum_{i=1}^2 \sum_{j=i+1}^3 x_i x_j \sum_{n=0}^m [L_{ij,n}(x_i - x_j)^n] + x_1 x_2 x_3 L^{\text{ter}} \quad (24)$$

The thermodynamic description of the Al-Cu-Mg system from Buhler et al.[26] can now be used. Using the parameters for the thermodynamic description of Al-rich ternary Al-Cu-Mg alloys, G^{ex} for liquid phase can be evaluated as

$$G^{ex}(\text{Liquid}) = x_{Al}x_{Cu}[(-66622+8.1T) + (46800-90.8T+10T\ln T)(x_{Al}-x_{Cu}) - 2812(x_{Al}-x_{Cu})^2] + x_{Al}x_{Mg}[(-12000+8.566T) + (1894-3T)(x_{Al}-x_{Mg}) + 2000(x_{Al}-x_{Mg})^2] + x_{Cu}x_{Mg}[(-36984+4.7561T) - 8191.29(x_{Cu}-x_{Mg})] \quad (25)$$

For fcc Al primary solution, G^{ex} is given by

$$G^{ex}(\text{fcc}) = x_{Al}x_{Cu}[(-53520+2T) + (38590-2T) \times (x_{Al}-x_{Cu}) + 1170(x_{Al}-x_{Cu})^2] + x_{Al}x_{Mg}[(4971-3.5T) + (900+0.423T)(x_{Al}-x_{Mg}) + 950(x_{Al}-x_{Mg})^2] + x_{Cu}x_{Mg}(-22279.28+5.868T) \quad (26)$$

4.2 Diffusion mobility data

Tracer diffusion is the diffusion of a tracer in the matrix of an alloy. Tracer diffusivities are generally functions of composition. Here, we assume that the tracer diffusivities have no composition dependence. Assuming x is the concentration of tracer A, the tracer diffusivity D_A^* is equivalent to self-diffusion for $x=1$ and impurity diffusion for $x \to 0$. The impurity or self-diffusivities, D_i^*, in the ternary Al-Cu-Mg are given in Table 1.

Table 1　Diffusion mobility data for Al-Cu-Mg alloy

Parameter	In liquid (m^2/s)	In fcc Al solution (m^2/s)
Impurity diffusion coefficient of Cu in Al[27]	$1.06 \times 10^{-7} \exp\left(\dfrac{-24000}{RT}\right)$	$4.44 \times 10^{-5} \exp\left(\dfrac{-133900}{RT}\right)$
Impurity diffusion coefficient of Mg in Al[27]	$9.9 \times 10^{-5} \exp\left(\dfrac{-71600}{RT}\right)$	$1.49 \times 10^{-5} \exp\left(\dfrac{-120500}{RT}\right)$
Self-diffusion coefficient of Al[28,29]	$1.16 \times 10^{-7} \exp\left(\dfrac{-21330}{RT}\right)$	$1.7 \times 10^{-4} \exp\left(\dfrac{-142000}{RT}\right)$

Thus the phase equilibria in the solid-liquid interface can be obtained by the equal chemical potential criterion, i.e., Eq. (9). And the diffusion matrix for Al-Cu-Mg multicomponent alloys can be determined from Eqs. (19) ~ (22). The other parameters for Al-Cu-Mg alloys used in the simulation process are given in Table 2.

Table 2　Parameters used in the simulation

Initial compositions, C^0	$C_{Cu}^0 = 2$ at.%, $C_{Mg}^0 = 3.5$ at.%
Interface energy, σ	0.093J/m^2
Molar volume, V_m	$1.06 \times 10^{-5} \text{m}^3/\text{mol}$
Grid size, Δx	$1.0 \times 10^{-8} \text{m}$

It is worth noting here that the phase equilibria and the thermodynamic factor in Eq. (19), $\partial \mu_k / \partial x_j$, are obtained using Thermo-Calc[21] through the TQ interface.

4.3 Simulation results

Taking advantage of the four-fold morphological symmetry, only a quarter of the entire dendrite is chosen as the computational cell, and a solid seed is placed at the bottom-left corner, that is, at the origin. Equiaxed dendrite shape and the solute concentration fields for Al-2 at.% Cu-3.5 at.% Mg alloy are shown in Fig. 1 at the evolution time of 6×10^{-5}s. It can be seen that primary stalk has a low concentration, but the regions between the secondary arms have the highest concentration. These features are commonly observed in real dendrites.

The diffusion matrix, both diagonal and off-diagonal items, is shown in Fig. 2. We can see that the diffusion coefficients are greatly concentration dependent. In the liquid phase, the absolute values of both diagonal and off-diagonal terms are larger at the interface than far from the interface, which correspond to the thick and dilute region, respectively. Some approximate analysis of the diffusion coefficients is given in Table 3. We can see that the ratio of off-diagonal to diagonal terms is approximately 10% for Cu and 15% for Mg.

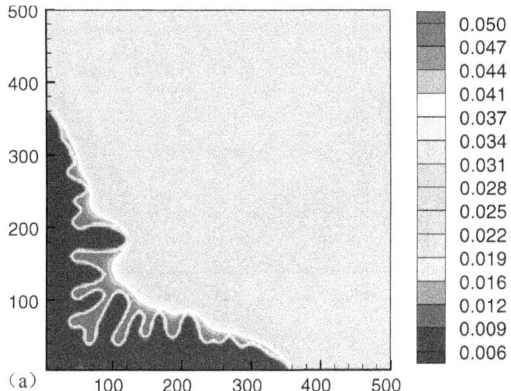

Fig. 1　Solute concentration profiles for the dendrite growth process of Al-2 at.% Cu-3.5 at.% Mg alloy at 900K ($t=6 \times 10^{-5}$s): (a) Cu, (b) Mg.

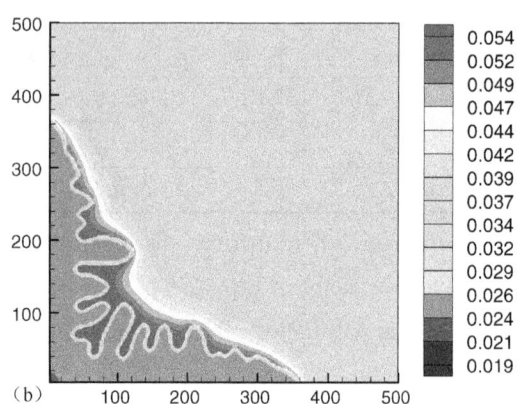

Fig. 1 Solute concentration profiles for the dendrite growth process of Al-2 at. % Cu-3. 5 at. % Mg alloy at 900K ($t=6\times10^{-5}$s): (a) Cu, (b) Mg. (Continued)

In Fig. 2 we can also see that the off-diagonal diffusion coefficients are negative, which means that the solutes have attractive diffusional interaction[14] in Al-Cu-Mg alloy. If the off-diagonal diffusion coefficients are positive, there will be repulsive diffusional interactions between solutes in the system.

Table 3 Some approximate analysis of the diffusion coefficients

	Liquid far from the interface	Liquid near the interface	Solid
$D_{CuCu}(m^2/s)$	4.4×10^{-9}	5.1×10^{-9}	6.5×10^{-13}
$D_{CuMg}(m^2/s)$	-3.9×10^{-10}	-6.9×10^{-10}	-4.2×10^{-14}
$|D_{CuMg}/D_{CuCu}|$ (%)	8.9	13.5	6.5
$D_{MgMg}(m^2/s)$	6.9×10^{-9}	7.2×10^{-9}	1.4×10^{-12}
$D_{MgCu}(m^2/s)$	-1.0×10^{-9}	-1.25×10^{-9}	-1.8×10^{-13}
$|D_{MgCu}/D_{MgMg}|$ (%)	14.4	17.4	12.9

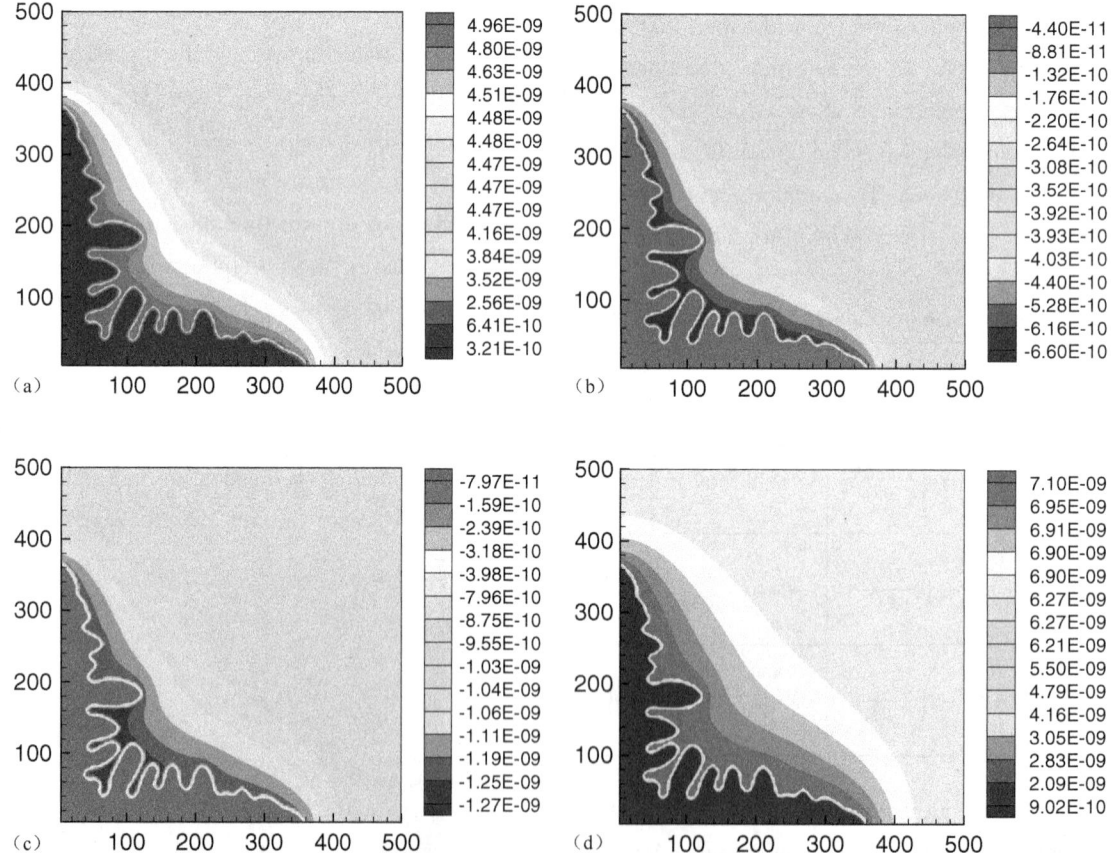

Fig. 2 Diffusion matrix profiles for the dendrite growth process of Al-2 at. % Cu-3. 5 at. % Mg alloy at 900K ($t=6\times10^{-5}$s): (a) D_{CuCu}, (b) D_{CuMg}, (c) D_{MgCu}, (d) D_{MgMg}.

5. Summary

A phase-field model for solidification of multicomponent alloys is presented coupled with thermodynamic and diffusion mobility databases. By making direct use of the assessed thermodynamic and mobility databases, the phase equilibria and the solute diffusion transportation can be accurately predicted in the whole system. As an example, the two-dimensional computations for the dendritic growth in Al-Cu-Mg ternary alloy have been performed. The quantitative solute distributions and diffusion matrix are obtained in both solid and liquid phase. It is found that the diffusion coefficients are greatly concentration dependent. It is also demonstrated that this simulation can quantitatively model the isothermal dendrite growth in solidification of multicomponent alloys.

Acknowledgement

The study was financially supported by the National Significant Fundamental Research Project of MOST (2005CB724105) and the State Key Fundamental Research Project (G2000067202-1).

References

[1] Kobayashi R. Physica D 1993; 63: 3410.
[2] McFadden GB, Wheeler AA, Braun RJ, Coriell SR, Sekerka RF. Phys Rev E 1993; 48: 2016.
[3] Karma A, Rappel WJ. Phys Rev E 1999; 60: 3614.
[4] Wheeler AA, Boettinger WJ, McFadden GB. Phys Rev A 1992; 45: 7424.
[5] Karma A. Phys Rev E 1994; 49: 2245.
[6] Kim SG, Kim WT, Suzuki T. Phys Rev E 1999; 60: 7186.
[7] Cha PR, Yeon DH, Yoon JK. Acta Mater 2001; 49: 3295.
[8] Qin RS, Wallach ER. Acta Mater 2003; 51: 6199.
[9] Kobayashi H, Ode M, Kim SG, Kim WT, Suzuki T. Scripta Mater 2003; 48: 689.
[10] Sakai K. J Cryst Growth 2002; 237-239: 144.
[11] Chen Q, Ma N, Wu KS, Wang YZ. Scripta Mater 2004; 50: 471.
[12] Zhu JZ, Wang T, Zhou SH, Liu ZK, Chen LQ. Acta Mater 2004; 52: 833.
[13] Borgenstam A, Engström A, Höglund L, Ågren J. J Phase Equilib 2000; 21: 269.
[14] Hunziker O. Acta Mater 2001; 49: 4191.
[15] Cha PR, Yeon DH, Yoon JK. J Cryst Growth 2005; 274: 281.
[16] Ode M, Lee JS, Kim SG, Kim WT, Suzuki T. ISIJ Int 2000; 40: 870.
[17] Karma A. Phys Rev Lett 2001; 87: 115701.
[18] Saunders N, Miodownik AP. Calphad: a comprehensive guide. Pergamon: Oxford; 1998. p. 91.
[19] Peng M, Qiao Z, Mikula A. Calphad 1998; 22: 459.
[20] Hillert M. J Alloys Compd 2001; 320: 161.
[21] Andersson JO, Helander T, Höglund L, Pingfang Shi, Sundman B. Calphad 2002; 26: 273.
[22] Chen SL, Daniel S, Zhang F, Chang YA, Yan XY, Xie FY, et al. Calphad 2002; 26: 175.
[23] Davies RH, Dinsdale AT, Gisby JA, Robinson JAJ, Martin SM. Calphad 2002; 26: 229.
[24] Andersson JO, Agren J. J Appl Phys 1992; 72: 1350.
[25] Lupis CHP. Chemical thermodynamics of materials. Oxford: North-Holland. p. 263.
[26] Buhler T, Fries SG, Spencer PJ, Lukas HL. J Phase Equilib 1998; 19: 317.
[27] Du Y, Chang YA, Huang BY, Gong WP, Jin ZP, Xu HH, et al. Mater Sci Eng A 2003; 363: 140.
[28] Cherne III FJ, Deymier PA. Scripta Mater 2001; 45: 985.
[29] Legzdina D, Parthasarathy TA. Metall Trans A 1987; 18: 1713.

4. Advances in Multi-scale Modeling of Solidification and Casting Processes

Baicheng Liu, Qingyan Xu, Tao Jing, Houfa Shen, and Zhiqiang Han

The development of the aviation, energy and automobile industries requires an advanced integrated product/process R&D systems which could optimize the product and the process design as well. Integrated computational materials engineering (ICME) is a promising approach to fulfill this requirement and make the product and process development efficient, econonic, and environmentally friendly. Advances in multi-scale modeling of solidification and casting processes, including mathematical models as well as engineering applications are presented in the paper. Dendrite morphology of magnesium and aluminum alloy of solidification process by using phase field and cellular automaton methods, mathematical models of segregation of large steel ingot, and microstructure models of unidirectionally solidified turbine blade casting are studied and discussed. In addition, some engineering case studies, including microstructure simulation of aluminum casting for automobile industry, segregation of large steel ingot for energy industry, and microstructure simulation of unidirectionally solidified turbine blade castings for aviation industry are discussed.

INTRODUCTION

Materials processing technologies play an important role for the manufacturing industry, for example, aluminum and magnesium alloy castings for the automobile industry, superalloy unidirectionally solidified turbine blade castings for the aviation industry, etc. On the other hand, modeling and simulation can play a significant role in guaranteeing the quality of these castings, to shorten the R&D time and to decrease the R&D cost. Recently, multi-scale modeling including macro-and micro-modeling has become a hot topic in computational materials engineering. Hence, macro- and micro-modeling of solidification and casting processes have been extensively studied in our research group, and some advances in macro- and micro-simulation of magnesium and aluminum alloy castings, macrosegregation of large steel ingots, and superalloy directionally solidified turbine blade casting are reported in the paper.

MODELING OF DENDRITE MORPHOLOGY OF CAST Mg ALLOY BY THE PHASE FIELD METHOD

Recently, numerical simulation for microstructural evolution by phase field method has become increasingly popular because of its advantages in morphology description—the dendritic morphology plays a key role in the final performance of cast Mg alloy components. The phase field method is based on Ginzburg-Landau theory, and reflects the influence of diffusion, ordering potential and thermodynamic driving force by using the differential equations. However, most previous research focused on metals with facecentered cubic (f.c.c.) structure, such as Al, Cu and Ni, while metals with hexagonal-close-packed (hcp) structure, such as Mg and Zn, were rarely referred to. Experimental results indicate that the dendritic morphology of metals with hcp structure is totally different from that with f.c.c. structure because of the different crystal lattice.[1-7]

Mathematical Models

Phase-Field Equations

The total free energy of the twophase system is described by a phenomenological Ginsburg-Landau model

> **How would you...**
>
> ...**describe the overall significance of this paper?**
>
> *Dendrite growth and microstructure during solidification process of super-alloy turbine blade casting, aluminum and magnesium alloy casting, and large steel ingot are extensively by experiments and Cellular Automaton Method.*
>
> ...**describe this work to a materials science and engineering professional with no experience in your technical specialty?**
>
> *This work is a general view of multi-scale modeling and simulation of solidification and casting processes, including single crystal turbine blade casting, aluminum and magnesium alloy castings, and large/heavy steel ingot.*
>
> ...**describe this work to a layperson?**
>
> *The work is to predict process-microstructure-property of important and critical castings, and hence to save R&D time and cost as well.*

as Equation 1, where F is the total free energy of the system, $f(\varphi, u, c)$ is the free energy density function, φ is the phase field variable parameter ranging from negative one in the liquid to positive one in the solid, u and c are the temperature and concentration, respectively, and $\gamma(n)$ and $\delta(n)$ are the gradient energy and concentration field coefficient, respectively. (All equations can be found in the table) The governing equations based on thermodynamic theory for the phase-field coupled with temperature field and solute field can then be expressed as Equation 2. In this equation, $\mu(n)$ is the kinetic coefficient, M_C is a concentration mobility parameter and is set as shown in Equation 2a. In this equation, $h(\varphi)$ is the solid fraction given by $\phi^2(3-2\phi)$, D_T is the thermal diffusion coefficient, L is the latent heat.

Thermodynamics Descriptions of Alloy System

The free energy density function of the system consists of the free energy of the bulk phases and an imposed parabolic potential which is given and can be written as Equation 3, where $g(\phi) - f^2(1-\phi)^2$, and W^A and W^B are the height of the parabolic potential which will be determined as Equation 4.

The Anisotropic Functions of Interface Energy and Mobility

An anisotropic function of interfacial free energy and mobility, which reflects underlying crystalline characteristics of the hexagonal close packed lattice, is proposed, as shown in Equations 5 and 6, where n_i is unit vector and is given as shown in Equation 5a and i represents x, y, z, respectively, g_0 and m_0 are, respectively, the mean values of interface free energy and kinetic, e_1, e_2, and x_1, x_2 are, respectively, the first-and second-order anisotropic parameters of crystal-melt interface free energy and mobility.

Numerical Simulation Results and Discussion

To yield well-developed threedimensional (3-D) dendritic morphologies, phase-field simulations of equiaxed dendritic solidification growth in undercooled melts were carried out. A nucleus was located in undercooled melts and an equiaxed solidification process, governed by both phase-field equation accompanied with associated temperature and solute field equations, was carried out.

Based upon two anisotropic parameters, phase-field calculations yield the entire dendritic solid-liquid interfacial morphologies as shown in Figure 1a, corresponding to the pattern of hexagonal dipyramid. X-ray tomography images based on synchrotron radiation of Figure 1b and the related two-dimensional (2-D) sectional pattern of Figure 1c also supply the proof of the possibility of three-dimensional results.

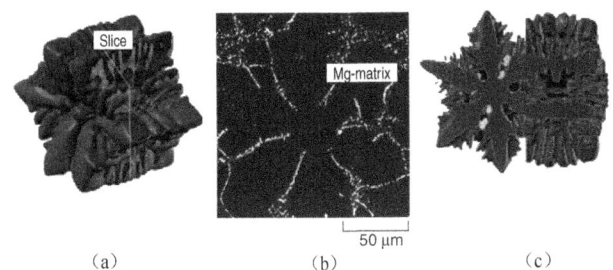

Fig. 1 Simulated result of dendrite morphology of magnesium alloy microstructures (Mg-9wt.% Al).
(a) Three-dimensional morphology; (b) synchrotron-radiation-based x-ray tomography slice extracted showing hcp phase patter;
(c) related sectional patter results from 3-D simulations.

MODELING OF DENDRITE MORPHOLOGY OF CAST Mg ALLOY BY CELLULAR AUTOMATON METHOD

Mathematical models based on the cellular automaton (CA) method are being used in micro-scale modeling of the dendrite growth, which can quantitatively reproduce most of the dendritic features with affordable computational costs. Böttger and Eiken et al.[8] simulated the dendrite morphology of Mg alloy using phase field (PF) method in two and three dimensions (2-D and 3-D). Huo et al.[9] simulated the 2-D and 3-D as-cast microstructure of AZ91D by using a modified cellular automaton (CA) method, where a prescribed dendrite profile was used instead of physics based simulation considering the solid-liquid interface anisotropy of Mg. Yin et al.[10] simulated the 2-D dendrite morphology of AZ91 Mg alloy using CA-finite element (FE) model under hexagonal mesh.

In this study 2-D and 3-D CA models have been developed to simulate the dendrite morphology evolution of cast Mg alloy and the experiments were caried out for validating the models.

Mathematical Models

The present CA model employs a scheme based on two sets of mesh. In the 2-D model, a hexagonal mesh is used to perform CA capture procedure to reflect the texture of Mg dendrites, and an orthogonal mesh is used to solve diffusion equations. In the 3-D model, the CA calculation is performed using a mesh defined by the hcp crystal lattice, and the diffusion is solved using a cubic mesh. The growth kinetics of solid-liquid interface is determined based on the difference between the local equilibrium liquid composition and the local actual composition obtained by solving the solute diffusion equation.[11] The solid-liquid interface curvature and growth anisotropy are also considered in the present model. Details of the model can be found in the literature.[12,13]

Simulation Results

The simulated morphology of equiaxed and columnar dendrites of AZ91D Mg alloy is shown in Figures 2 and 3. It can be seen that the present model reproduces the Mg dendrites pretty well and provides details about texture, solute segregation, and growth anisotropy and competition.

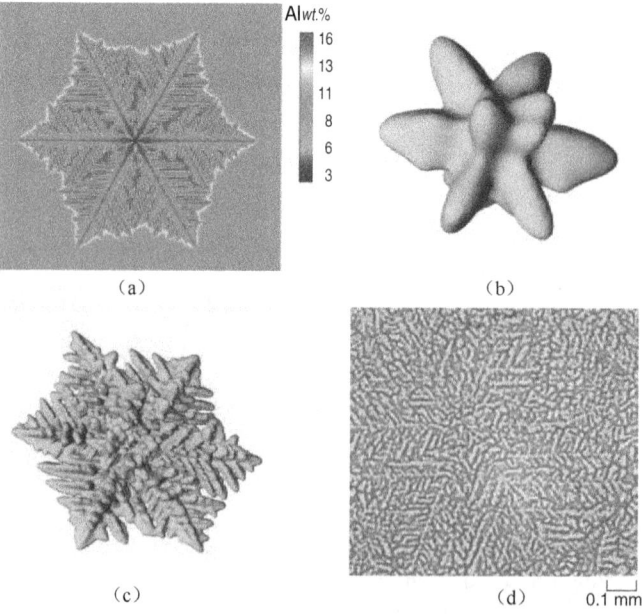

Fig. 2 (a,b,c) Simulated and (d) experimental results of Mg alloy dendrites.
(a) simulated 2-D equiaxed dendrite; (b) simulated 3-D equiaxed dendrite at early stage;
(c) fully developed 3-D equiaxed dendrite; (d) metallographic results showing texture of Mg alloy dendrites.

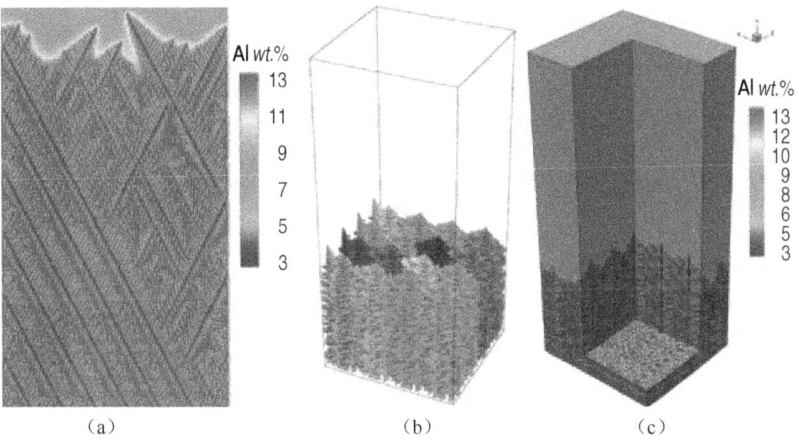

Fig. 3 Simulated columnar dendrite growth of Mg alloy in 2-D and 3-D.
(a) columnar dendrites in 2-D; (b) columnar dendrites in 3-D;
(c) section view showing the solute field at X-Y, Y-Z, and X-Z planes.

Equations

$$F = \int_V \left[f(\phi, u, c) - \frac{\gamma^2(n)}{2} |\nabla \phi|^2 - \frac{\delta^2(n)}{2} |\nabla C|^2 \right] dV \tag{1}$$

$$\mu(n)\frac{\partial \phi}{\partial t} = -\frac{\delta F}{\delta \phi}, \frac{\partial c}{\partial t} = \nabla \left[M_C c(1-c)\nabla\frac{\delta F}{\delta c} \right], \frac{\partial T}{\partial t} = D_T \nabla^2 T + L \frac{\partial h(\phi)}{\partial t} \tag{2}$$

$$\left[D_S + h(\phi)(D_L - D_S) \right] \frac{RT}{V_M} \tag{2a}$$

$$f(\phi, T, c) = h(\phi) f_{\text{sub-reg}}^{\text{hcp}}(T, c) + [1 - h(\phi)] f_{\text{sub-reg}}^L(T, c) + [(1-c)W^A + cW^B] g(\phi) \tag{3}$$

$$W^A = \frac{3\gamma^A}{\sqrt{2} T_{M_A} \delta_A}, W^B = \frac{3\gamma^B}{\sqrt{2} T_{M_B} \delta_B} \tag{4}$$

$$\gamma(n) = \gamma_0 \left[1 + \varepsilon_1 (n_x^6 - 15 n_x^4 n_y^2 + 15 n_x^2 n_y^4 - n_y^6) + \varepsilon_2 n_z^6 \right] \tag{5}$$

$$n_i = \frac{\partial \phi}{\partial i} / \sqrt{\left(\frac{\partial \phi}{\partial x}\right)^2 + \left(\frac{\partial \phi}{\partial y}\right)^2 + \left(\frac{\partial \phi}{\partial z}\right)^2} \tag{5a}$$

$$\mu(n) = \mu_0 \left[1 + \zeta_1 (n_x^6 - 15 n_x^4 n_y^2 + 15 n_x^2 n_y^4 - n_y^6) + \zeta_2 n_z^6 \right] \tag{6}$$

$$\rho c \frac{\partial T}{\partial t} = \lambda \left(\frac{\partial^2 T}{\partial x^2} + \frac{\partial^2 T}{\partial y^2} + \frac{\partial^2 T}{\partial z^2} \right) + \rho L \frac{\partial f_s}{\partial t} + Q_R \tag{7}$$

MICROSTRUCTURE MODELING OF ALUMINUM ALLOY CASTING BY THE MODIFIED CELLULAR AUTOMATON METHOD

Besides dendrite morphology, the microstructure evolution of Al 7wt.%Si alloy was also studied by MCA method.[14] A step-shaped sample casting to verify the model and then an engineering case study were carried out. The comparison between the simulated and experimental microstructure from specimens at different position s (20、40 and 60mm in thickness) of the step-shaped sample casting is shown in Figure 4. As shown in Figure 4, grain size and secondary dendrite arm space become smaller when the step thickness decreases.

For an engineering case study, a modified CA model coupled with finite difference method was used to simulate the microstructure evolution of an aircraft turbine wheel casting of Al-7wt.%Si alloy. The casting shape and the position of the specimens are schematically shown in Figure 5, and the thinnest part of the casting is only 2mm in thickness. Specimens were taken from the longitudinal cross-section of the wheel casting indexed as P1 to P7 in sequence. The comparison between the simulated and experimental microstructure of different specimen is shown in Figure 6.

Fig. 4 Comparison of simulated and experimental results of step-shaped casting (grain size).
(a) simulated results (b) experimental results.

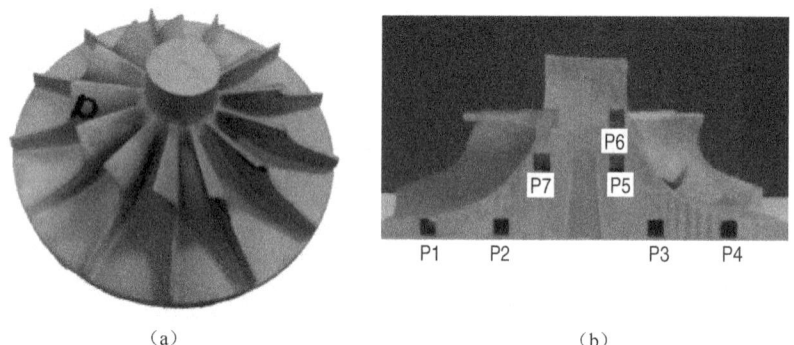

Fig. 5 Schematic of an aircraft turbine wheel casting.
(a) aircraft turbine wheel casting; (b) specimen positions.

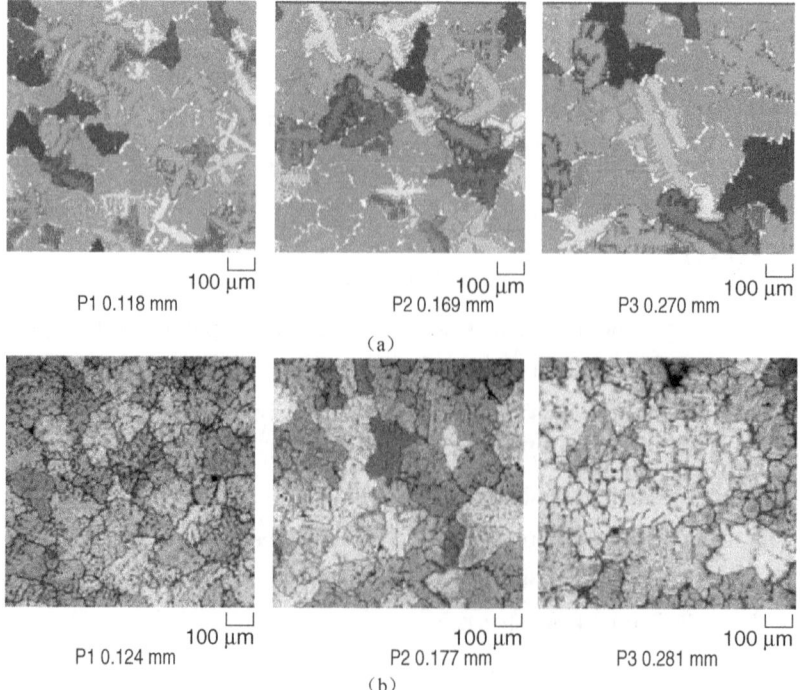

Fig. 6 (a) simulated and (b) experimental microstructure of an aircraft turbine wheel casting (grain size).

MICROSTRUCTURE MODELING OF SINGLE CRYSTAL TURBINE BLADE CASTING BY MCA

Unidirectionally solidified and single crystal Ni-based superalloy turbine blade castings produced by Bridgman directional solidification technology are currently used in both the aeronautic and energy industries as key parts of the gas turbine engines. The final microstructure of the blade casting directly determines the casting mechanical properties. As a powerful tool, numerical simulation technology could be used to study the directional solidification process and optimize the process parameters.

Physical and Mathematical Models

The schematic of the directional solidification process of turbine blade casting is shown in Figure 7. The metal pouring and solidification process take place in the directional solidification furnace under vacuum environment.

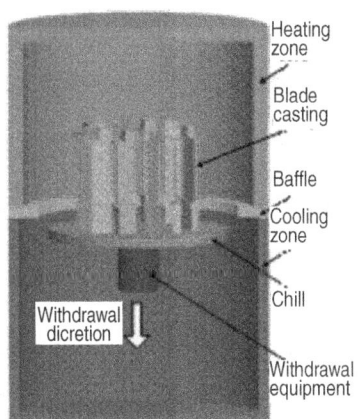

Fig. 7 Schematic of Bridgman directional solidification process.

Macro-heat Transfer

Complex heat transfer exists during the directional solidification process. The macro-temperature distribution within the casting and shell was calculated according to the transient nonlinear heat transport equation as shown in Equation (7), where T is the temperature, t is the time, ρ is the density, c is the specific heat, L is the latent heat, λ is the heat conductivity; x, y and z are the coordinates; f_s is the mass fraction of solid phase; Q_R is the heat radiation exchange between the shell surface and the furnace wall.

The huge number of memories required to calculate the view factors for each surface cell against others makes it extremely complicated and difficult for the heat radiation calculation in directional solidification. In this paper, a numerical method derived from the Monte Carlo method was proposed to compute the heat radiation in directional solidification, with much less memory required and a higher accuracy. The details can be seen in Reference [15].

The microstructure simulation was based on the modified CA method.[16] A continuous nucleation mode[17] was employed to calculate the nucleus number in the undercooled. The growth speed of the dendrite tip could be calculated based on the KGT model.[18]

Layer by Layer Calculation Method for Microstructure Simulation of Whole Turbine Blade

Considering the characteristic of directional solidification, a layer by layer method was proposed to calculate the microstructure formation of a single crystal turbine blade.[19] The mushy zone included several layers in longitudinal direction in macro-scale. We divided every layer into many cells further at microscale. At a macro-time step, the microstructure evolution in the micro-computational domain was calculated. Finally modeling results of all layers were combined together to form that of the whole turbine blade.

Each grain's orientation was randomly determined in this model. Therefore, the grains which were not well-aligned with respect to the maxi-mum gradient of the temperature field would grow at a much slower speed than those which were best aligned, which made them grow behind the growth front. This made it possible for those well-aligned grains to have their secondary and tertiary side arms grow out and occupy the space just in front of the less well-aligned grains. The above process can be used to describe the competitive grain growth in the starter block of grain selector.[20]

Simulation Results of Single Crystal Turbine Blade Castings

In order to investigate the influence of varying withdrawal rates on the casting microstructure, both experiments and simulation of two groups of Ni-based superalloy blade castings with different processing parameters (Group A and B) were carried out. The simulated microstructure evolution of blade casting at different time in group A, with a constant withdrawal rate of 7.0mm/min. is shown in Figure 8. It could be seen that stray grains existed at the edge of the platform of the blade. The simulated microstructure evolution of blade casting at different time in group B, with varying withdrawal rates is shown in Figure 9. It could be seen that no stray grains were found at the platform of the blade casting, and the produced casting was a whole single crystal super lloy blade.

The microstructures in different sections of the whole blade of group A by experiment with a constant withdrawal rate is shown in Figure 10. It could be seen both in the simulated and experimental results that stray grains appeared at the edge of the platform and grew up to the top of the blade. That explains why a high withdrawal rate would not be acceptable to get a complete single crystal blade casting.

The microstructures in different sections of the whole blade of group B by experiment with varying withdrawal rates is shown in Figure 11. No stray grains were found at the edge of the platform both in the simulated and experimental results.

Grain Competition and Evolution in the Grain Selector

The grain evolution process within the seed selector during solidification at different times is shown in Figure 12. The liquid is not displayed so that the solid-liquid interface could be clearly shown. It is indicated that a great number of tiny equiaxed grains emerged at the bottom surface of the starter block, and transferred into a much smaller number of columnar grains when growing upwards, which is well known as the grain competition process determined by the heat flux direction and the grain's fastest growth direction. The grain number decreased quickly in the starter block, leaving only less than ten columnar grains growing into the spiral. The grains in the spiral continued to decrease when growing upwards, and only one of them survived firom this grain selection, which finally grew into a whole single crystal casting. The measuring experiments from S1 to S7 sections were compared quantitatively with the simulation, which shows a reasonable correspondence.[20]

MODELING AND SIMULATION OF MACROSEGREGATION OF A LARGE STEEL INGOT

The production of large steel ingots with improved chemical homogeneity is of great concern for steelmakers

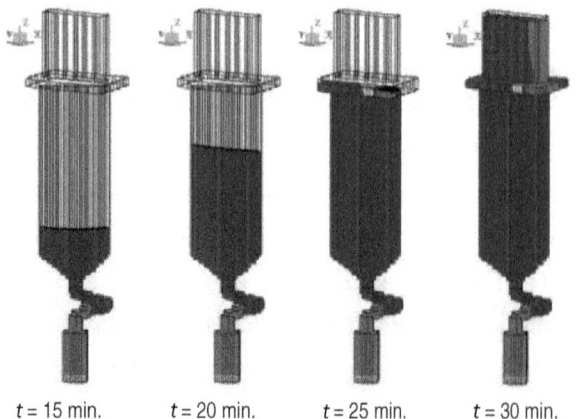

Fig. 8 Simulated microstructure evolution in group A at different time.

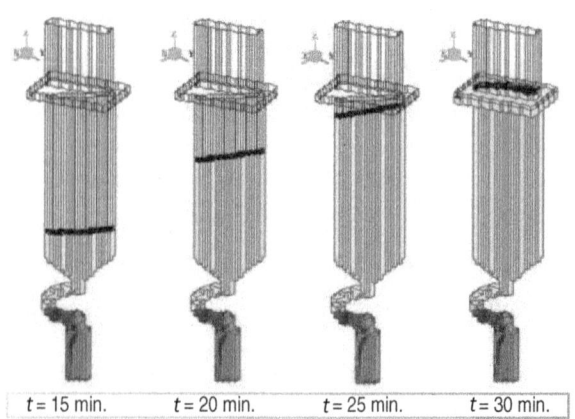

Fig. 9 Simulated microstructure evolution in group B at different time.

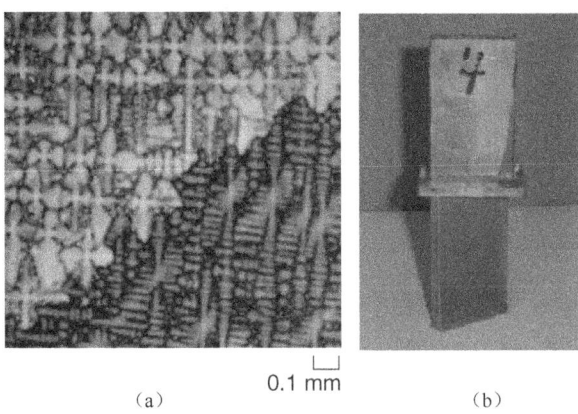

Fig. 10 Experimental microstructures of blade casting in group A with stray grains.

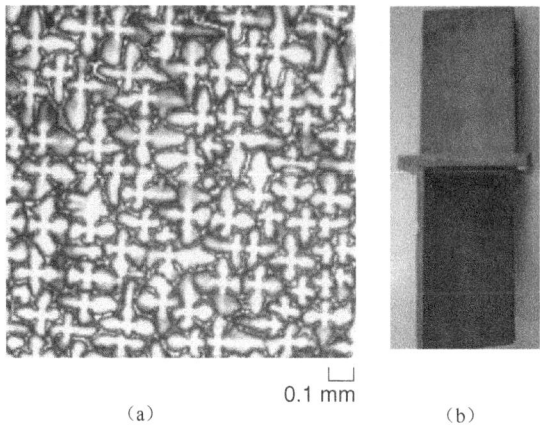

Fig. 11 Experimental microstructures of blade casting in group B without stray grains.

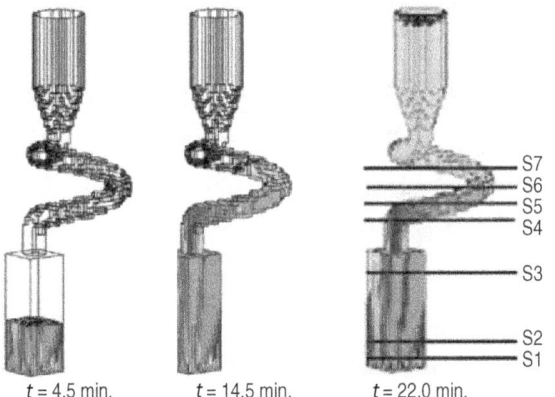

Fig. 12 Simulated grain evolution in the grain selector.

to meet stringent requirements for high quality and large integrated forgings typically used for pressure vessels of nuclear power plants. Macrosegregation, as one of the main defects in large steel ingot, refers to chemical inhomogeneity in cast metals at the scale of the product. It cannot be mitigated through the subsequent processing, and hence negatively impacts the properties of final products.[21,22] The multi-ladle pouring (MP) process, i.e., sequential pouring of liquid steel with different carbon contents,[23-26] has been widely used to suppress macrosegregation in large industrial steel ingots, especially several tons in weight. However, it is very difficult to completely avoid certain carbon segregation in a 360-t steel ingot, despite the MP process as well as other modern technologies of metallurgical production was used.[25]

This paper presents some simulated results based on recently developed macrosegregation model.[27] The model was first validated by using a benchmark test, and then used to simulate the macrosegregation in a 300-t MP steel ingot.

The model is based on the continuum theory, and it involves a fully coupled numerical solution of mass, momentum, energy, and species conservation equations in the liquid, solid, and mushy zones. The thermosolutal convection and the induced macrosegregation in large steel ingots can be numerically simulated by the model. It should be mentioned that multiphase solidification models are available in the literature that take into account melt convection and grain sedimentation (for example, References [28] and [29]). The application of these sophisticated models to large industrial ingots, however, is limited due to the large computational resources required to resolve the variety of the phenomena over the process scale.

The validation of the model was performed on the well-known Hebditch-Hunt (HH) benchmark experiment.[30] In this experiment, macrosegregation resulting from the solidification of a Pb-48wt.%Sn alloy in a rectangular cavity was measured. The thermophysical data and parameters used in the calculation were identical to the ones used in Reference[31] an existing benchmark simulation. Figure 13 shows the segregation ratio of tin in the solidifying cavity. It can be observed that the present predictions compare well with the corresponding results in Reference [31]. Furthermore, the predicted segregation maps at the end of solidification are generally in good agreement with the experimental results of HH (detailed comparison refers to Reference [27]).

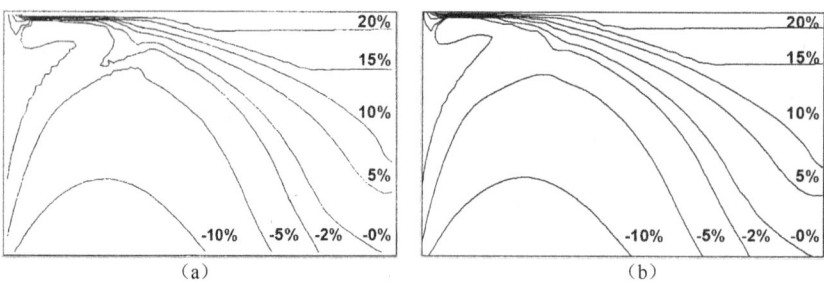

Fig. 13 Macrosegregation map in a solidifying cavity at t=400 s.
(a) Existing simulation; (b) present simulation.

Simulated Results and Discussion

The simulation was carried out for a large 300-t steel ingot (Fe-0.36wt.%C) 4.5 m in height and 3.4 m in mean width. Teeming was ignored, and no superheat was considered for the molten steel. The schematic of MP process is shown in the left side of Figure 14, showing that the first ladre contains 150-t molten steel, the second 90-t and the third 60-t, while the final macrosegregation pattern of carbon in the right side of Figure 14.

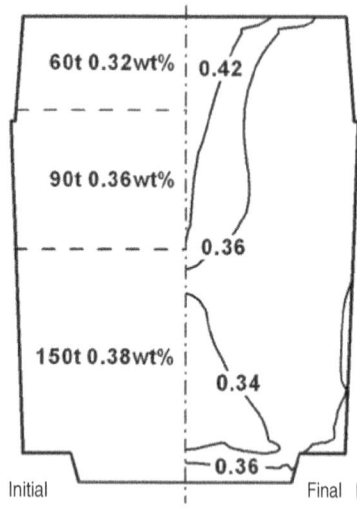

Fig. 14 Schematic of MP (left) and simulated results of final macrosegregation pattern (right) of a 300-t steel ingot.

The classical macrosegregation pattern in a large steel ingot is predicted, including an intense positive segregation in the hot top and a conically shaped negative segregation zone at the bottom of the ingot. It is indicated that certain carbon macrosegregation is not completely avoided in the simulated MP ingot. However, the MP process should have some positive effect on reducing macrosegregation from industrial experience and the simulation demonstrates the capability of the model to predict the macrosegregation for large steel ingot in industry. Nonetheless, the flow and mixture behavior of the molten steel from multiple ladles during the teeming process needs to be taken into account for further study.

CONCLUSIONS

Phase-field and cellular automaton models for simulating the dendrite morphology of cast Mg alloys have been developed, by incorporating the anisotropic formulae, which provide the insight into both the solid-liquid interfaces patterns and solidification morphologies evolution in hcp based metals or alloys. An MCA model was used to study the microstructure evolution of aluminum alloy casting for engineering application. A mathematical model for macrosegregation pattern of large steel ingot was also studied. Finally, a mathematical model based on CA-FD method was developed for the three dimensional simulation of grain evolution in unidirectional solidification process of superalloy turbine blade casting and the experimental results were studied and compared with the simulated results.

ACKNOWLEDGEMENTS

This work is financially supported by National Basic Research Program of China (Nos. 2005CB724105 and 2006CB605208), and National Important S & T Program No. 4 (2009 ZX04014).

References

[1] L. Gránásy, T. Pusztai, T. Börzsönyi, J. A. Warren, and J.

F. Douglas, *Nature Mater*, 3 (2004), pp. 645-650.
[2] S.-L. Wang, R. F. Sekerka, A. A. Wheeler, B. T. Murray, S. R. Coriell, R. J. Braun, and G. B. McFadden, *Physica D*, 69 (1993), pp. 189-200.
[3] G. Caginalp and W. Xie, *Phys, Rev. E*, 48 (1993), pp. 1897-1909.
[4] S. A. David ard T. DebRoy, *Science*, 257 (1992), pp. 497-500.
[5] A. Karma, "Prediction of Dendrite Growth Directions" (Presented at the TMS Annual Meeting, San Francisco, CA, 2005).
[6] K. Pattersen, O. Lohne, and N. Ryum, *Metall. Trans. A*, 21 (1990), pp. 221-230.
[7] F. Czerwinski, *Acta Mater.*, 50 (2002), pp. 3265-3281.
[8] J. Eiken, B. Böttger, and I. Steinbach, *Modeling of Casting, Welding and Advanced Solidification Processes-XI* (Warrendale, PA: TMS, 2006), pp. 489-496.
[9] Liang Huo et al., *Materials Science Forum*, 561-565 (2007), pp. 1797-1800.
[10] H. B. Yin and S. D. Felicelli, *Modeling and Simulation in Materials Science and Engineering*, 17 (7) (2009), 075011.
[11] M. F. Zhu and D. M. Stefanescu, *Acta Materialia*, 55 (2007), pp. 1741-1755.
[12] Liang Huo, Zhiqiang Han, and Baicheng Liu, "Twoand Three-dimensional Cellular Automaton Models for Simulating Dendrite Morphology Evolution of Cast Magnesium Alloys" (Presented at the 139th TMS Annual Meeting and Exhibition, Washington State Convention Center, Seattle, 14-18 February 2010).
[13] Liang Huo, Zhiqiang Han, ard Baicheng Liu, *Materials Science Forum*, 638-642 (2010), pp. 1562-1568.
[14] B. Li, Q. Y. Xu, and B. C. Liu, *Materials Science Forum*, 561-565 (2007), pp. 1787-1792.
[15] J. Yu et al., *J. Materials Science and Technology*, 23 (2007), p. 47.
[16] M. Rappaz and C. A. Gandin, *Acta Metallurgica et Materialia*, 41 (1993), p. 345.
[17] P. Thevoz, J. L. Desbiolles, and M. Rappaz, *Metall. Trans. A*, 20A (1989), p. 311.
[18] W. Kurz, B. Giovanola, and R. Trivedi, *Acta Metallurgica*, 34 (1986), p. 823.
[19] J. Yu et al., "Experimental Study and Numerical Simulation of Directionally Solidified Turbine Blade Casting" (Presented at the Asian Foundry Congress, Seoul, Korea, 2007).
[20] D. Pan et al, *JOM*, 62 (5) (2010), pp. 30-34.
[21] G. Lesoult, *Mater. Sci. and Eng. A*, 413-414 (2005), pp. 19-29.
[22] C. Beckermann, *Int. Mater. Rev.*, 47 (5) (2002), pp. 243-261.
[23] M. Tateno, *Transactions ISIJ* 25 (1985), pp. 97-108.
[24] H. Ushiyama, G. Yuasa, and T. Yajima, *Ironmaking and Steelmaking*, 5 (1978), pp. 121-134.
[25] V. I. Bogdanov, V. A. Durynin, and V. V. Tsukanov, *Russian Metallurgy (Metally)* (7) (2007), pp. 626-633.
[26] D. R. Liu et al., *Int. J. Cast Metals Research*, 23 (6) (2010), pp. 354-363.
[27] W. S. Li, H. F. Shen, and B. C. Liu, *Steel Research international*, 81 (11) (2010), pp. 994-1000.
[28] H. Combeau et al., *Metall. Mater. Trans. B*, 40 (2009), pp. 289-304.
[29] M. Wu and A. Ludwig. *Acta Materialia*, 57 (2009), pp. 5621-5631.
[30] D. J. Hebditch and J. D. Hunt, *Metall. Trans.*, 5 (1974), pp. 1557-1564.
[31] N. Ahmad et al., *Metall. Mater. Trans A*, 29 (1998), pp. 617-630.

Baicheng Liu, professor, Tao Jing, professor, Qingyan Xu, associate professor, Houfa Shen, professor, and Zhiqiang Han, associate professor, are with the Department of Mechanical Engineering, Tsinghua University, Beijing 100084, China. Prof. Liu can be reached at liubc@tsinghua.edu.cn.

5. 汽车工业镁合金压铸成形技术及模拟仿真

柳百成，熊守美

（清华大学 机械工程系，汽车安全与节能国家重点实验室，北京 100084）

摘 要：镁合金以其质量轻、比强度高、比刚度高、减振性好和易回收等优点被称为"21世纪的一种绿色工程材料"，广泛应用于航空、航天、汽车和电子等行业。在汽车工业，采用镁合金替代钢或铝合金是汽车轻量化的有效途径之一，可以降低汽车燃油消耗和减少气体排放。高压铸造是镁合金成形的主要成形工艺，通过模拟仿真及实验研究提高镁合金压铸件质量及开发高真空压铸等高性能成形工艺是镁合金发展的重要方向。本文介绍了作者在镁合金压铸工艺实验研究、镁合金真空压铸技术开发、镁合金压铸工艺过程数值模拟及优化等方面的研究进展。

关键词：汽车工业；镁合金；高压铸造；模拟仿真
中图分类号：TG 249.2，TG 292

High pressure die casting process of magnesium alloys and its modeling and simulation for automobile industry

LIU Baicheng XIONG Shoumei

(State Key Laboratory of Automobile Safety and Energy, Department of Mechanical Engineering, Tsinghua University, Beijing 100084, China)

Abstract: Magnesium alloy is widely used in aerospace, automobile, and electronic industries and is referred to as the most promising green engineering material for the 21 century due to its lightweight, high specific strength and stiffness, good dumping performance and recyclability. Using magnesium alloy instead of steel or aluminum alloy in automobile industry is one of the effective ways to realize light weighting of automobiles to reduce fuel consumption and exhaust gas emission. High-pressure die casting process is the dominant manufacturing process for magnesium structural applications. The experimental study and modeling and simulation on high-pressure die casting process of magnesium alloys as well as development of vacuum die casting technology are important research directions for magnesium alloys. This paper highlights the research progress in experimental study on magnesium die casting process, development of vacuum die casting technology for magnesium alloys, modeling and simulation technologies for high pressure die casting process and their applications for process optimization.

Key words: automobile industry; magnesium alloy; high-pressure die casting; modeling and simulation

镁合金作为实际应用中最轻的金属结构材料，具有密度小、比强度和比刚度高、减振性好以及屏蔽和导热性能优良等优点，已成为航天航空、国防建设、3C（通信、计算机、消费类电子）产业和现代汽车的备选材料，具有广泛的应用前景。由于节能、环境保护和轻量化的需求，镁合金在汽车上的应用越来越引起汽车工业的重视，并取得明显的轻量化效果。如通用汽车公司考维特Z06车型采用了的镁合金发动机支架（如图1所示），质量仅10.5kg，替代铝合金支架后减重35%[1]。福特汽车公司近期开发了一款镁合金汽车行李舱盖内衬板压铸件（如图2所示）替代了原来由6个零件组成的钢结构组装件，除减轻重量及减少零件装配时间外，还为外层盖板的设计提供了更多的自由度。同时，

⊖ 本文刊登于《汽车安全与节能学报》，2011，2（1）：1-11.

还使行李舱盖的开启高度增加了15mm[2]。

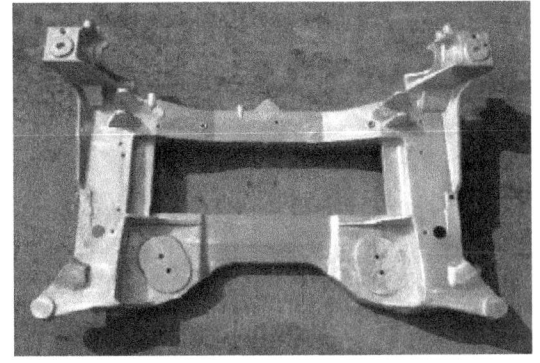

图1　通用汽车公司镁合金发动机支架[1]

图2　福特汽车公司镁合金行李舱盖内衬板[2]

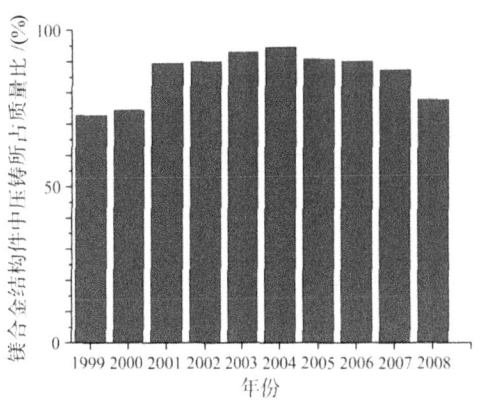

图3　美国1999年以来高压铸造在镁合金结构件成形方法中所占的比例

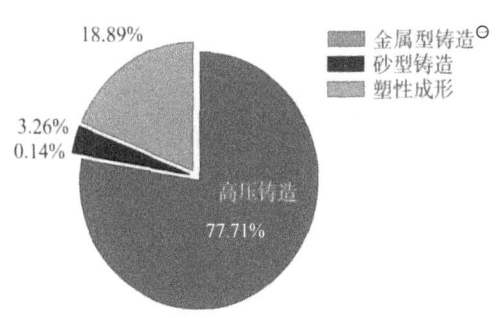

图4　2008年美国镁合金结构件成形主要方法及比例

但与铝合金相比，镁合金的研究和镁合金的应用也还很有限。限制镁合金广泛应用的主要问题是镁合金还存在着显著的缺点，如绝对强度仍然偏低，尤其是高温力学性能较差；室温塑性低、变形加工能力较差；化学活性高、易于氧化燃烧、使其熔炼加工困难；耐蚀性差，缺乏有效和积极的腐蚀防护途径。因此，发展高性能镁合金及其成形加工技术等是镁合金应用研究的重要课题[3]。

在现有的镁合金结构件的成形方法中，高压铸造是其主要成形方法，以美国原镁消耗结构中镁合金结构件的应用数据为例，高压铸造方法的占镁合金结构件应用的70%以上。图3和图4分别为美国近年来镁合金结构件成形方法中高压铸造所占的比例和2008年美国镁合金结构件主要成形方法[4]。

随着现代汽车工业的飞速发展，以及镁合金压铸生产设备的发展和压铸工艺的成熟，镁合金压铸件的需求及应用将更加广泛。然而，镁合金压铸过程中，液体金属在高速下充填型腔，容易产生气孔和夹杂缺陷，使其难以进行焊接或者用于气密性要求较高的零件。由于铸件中的气孔缺陷导致铸件不能进行热处理，其力学性能难以进一步提高，严重限制了镁合金在汽车上的进一步应用，尤其是镁合金复杂铸件的应用[5]。同时，由于压铸过程的工艺特征，铸件心部组织存在粗大的树枝晶，从表层到心部存在双缺陷带，压铸工艺对铸件组织、缺陷带的形成及力学性能具有显著影响。因此，开展镁合金压铸工艺及模拟仿真技术的研究以发展镁合金结构件的应用是镁合金研究切实可行的研究方向之一，具有重要的理论及实际意义。

○　图中金属型铸造比例为0.14%。——编者注

本文将重点讨论镁合金压铸过程工艺实验研究、镁合金真空压铸技术开发及镁合金压铸成形工艺过程模拟仿真技术的研究进展。

1 镁合金压铸工艺实验及组织性能研究

1.1 镁合金压铸工艺实验研究

镁合金压铸过程中，压铸工艺参数如低速速度、高速速度、低速-高速转换位置、压射压力、增压压力、增压时间等对压铸件组织及性能有着重要影响。采用阶梯试验件及扁平拉伸试样（如图 5 所示），系统研究了压铸工艺参数对镁合金压铸件组织及力学性能的影响。研究表明：随铸造压力增加，试样的力学性能有不同程度的提高；高速速度对试样的抗拉强度和延伸率影响较大。同时，高速速度对不同厚度的阶梯面影响规律不同；采用减速工艺可以明显提高压铸试样的力学性能[6]。

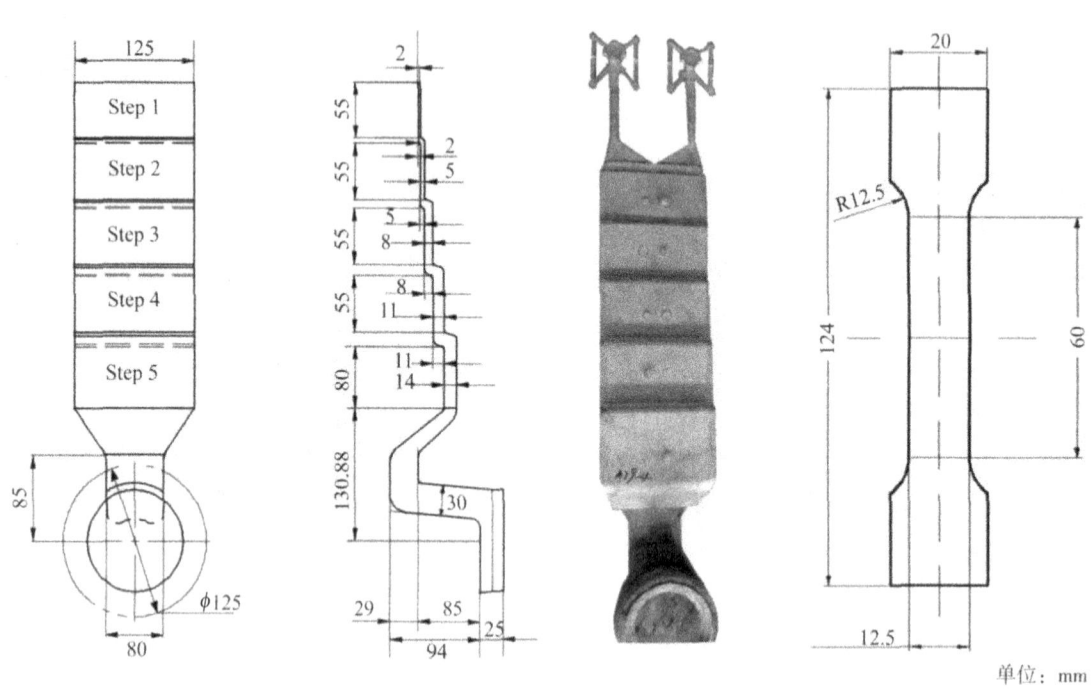

图 5 镁合金阶梯试验件及拉伸试样

图 6 为 AM50 合金试样的典型拉伸曲线。

图 7 为 AM50 合金压铸过程增压压力（p_c）、浇注温度（T_m）、模具温度（T_d）、高速速度（v_f）和增压时间等参数对试样抗拉强度的影响。

1.2 镁合金压铸件孔洞及组织对力学性能的影响

为研究镁合金压铸件的孔洞分布规律以及孔洞对拉伸过程的影响，采用超声显微扫描对压铸镁合金试样的孔洞分布进行了测量，实验研究了压铸镁合金微观组织，并采用显微拉伸动态观察了试样拉伸变形过程中孔洞及组织的变化，研究了孔洞及组织对拉伸性能的影响及断裂[7]。

图 8 显示了 AM50 合金压铸试样不同位置（表层到中心）试样的超声扫描的结果。从结果中可以看出，距表面一定深度的部分孔洞的含量最高。同

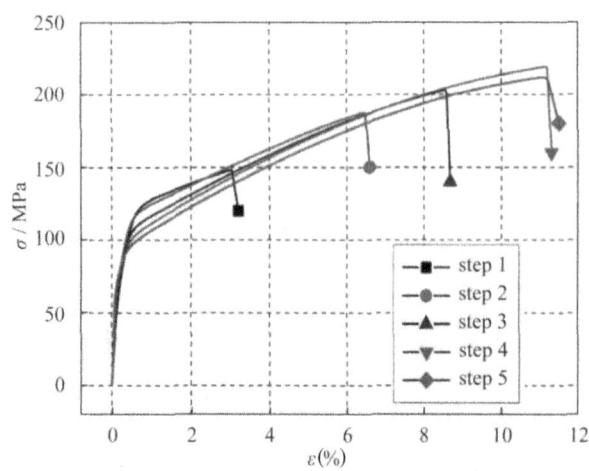

图 6 AM50 合金试样的典型拉伸曲线

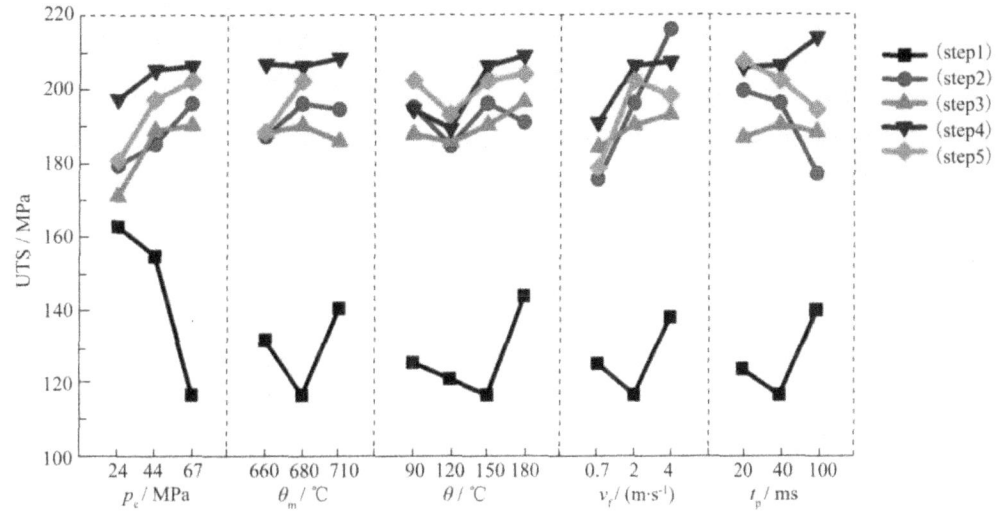

图 7 AM50 合金压铸工艺参数对试样抗拉强度的影响

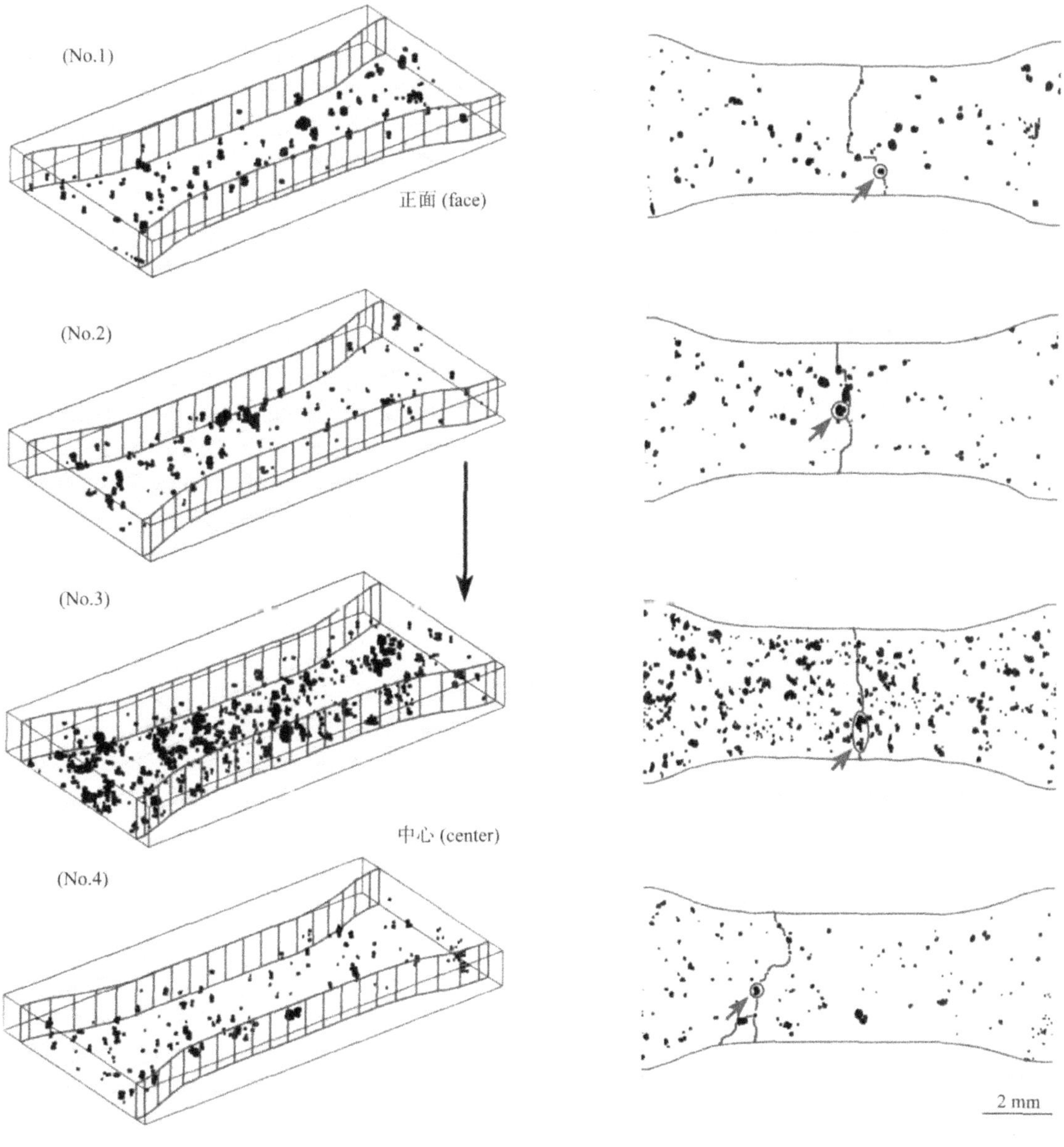

图 8 AM50 合金表层至心部原位拉伸试样显微超声扫描结果及试样断裂轨迹

时，根据试样孔洞的投影结果及试样拉伸过程中的断裂位置及断面可以看出断裂发生在较大的孔洞处。

原位显微拉伸结果表明抗拉强度和延伸率随着断裂处孔洞减小而降低，屈服强度与晶粒尺寸有关，而只有在断裂处孔洞的面积较大时，导致承载面积减小，才会对屈服强度产生影响。同时，铸件表层的性能与中心相比显著提高（见图9[8]）。

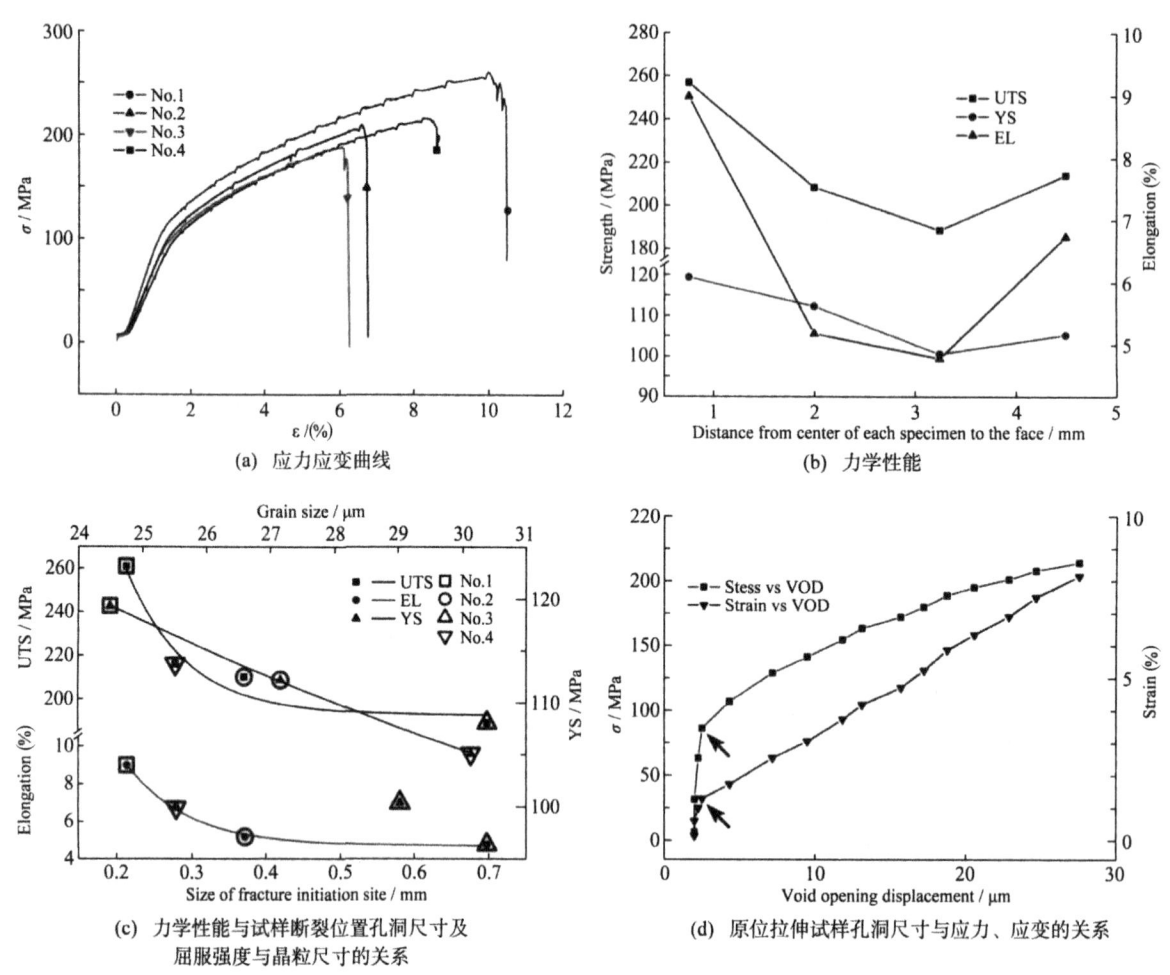

图9 AM50合金表层至心部原位拉伸试样的拉伸性能⊖

(a) 应力应变曲线
(b) 力学性能
(c) 力学性能与试样断裂位置孔洞尺寸及屈服强度与晶粒尺寸的关系
(d) 原位拉伸试样孔洞尺寸与应力、应变的关系

2 镁合金真空压铸工艺开发

真空压铸是利用真空技术在压铸过程中抽除型腔内空气，从而达到消除或减少铸件中的气孔缺陷，提高铸件性能的先进压铸工艺，其工作原理如图10所示。

针对真空压铸过程中模具密封、真空排气系统布置、真空排气阀及真空系统等关键技术问题，进行了系统的分析研究。研究及优化了高真空压铸的模具密封工艺及真空系统布置，建立了压铸真空系统排气过程的数理模型，优化了压铸真空系统设计，可以实现最低型腔真空压力不超过5kPa，真空时间1.5s的高真空压铸[9,10]。图11为采用改进的真空系统条件下，试验模具型腔及真空阀位置的真空压力曲线。由图11可以看出，真空时间约1s时，型腔及真空阀位置的真空度接近5kPa。

采用所开发的真空系统研究了镁合金真空压铸工艺参数对于铸件的铸造性能和力学性能（如密度、抗拉强度、屈服强度和伸长率）的影响规律，

⊖ 图中横纵坐标中英文对应关系如下，"Strength" 为 "强度"，"Elongation（EL）" 为 "延伸率"，"YS" 为 "屈服强度"，"Distance from center of each specimen to the face" 为 "试样中心至表面距离"，"Grain size" 为 "晶粒尺寸"，"Size of fracture initiation site" 为 "断裂位置孔洞尺寸"，"Strain" 为 "应变"，"Stess" 为 "应力"，"Void opening displacement（VOD）" 为 "孔洞尺寸"。——编者注

优化了镁合金真空压铸工艺规范。

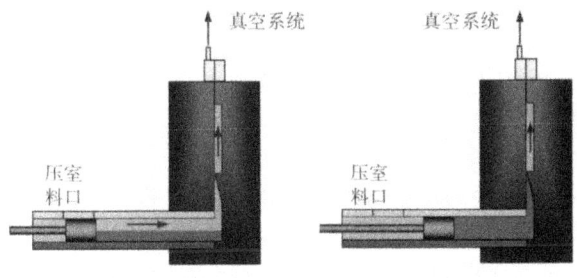

图 10 真空压铸工作原理

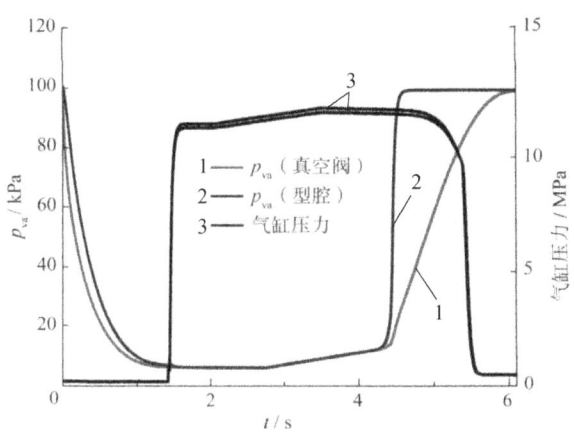

图 11 试验模具形腔及真空阀位置的真空压力曲线

图 12 显示了 AZ91D 合金真空压铸条件下真空度及铸造压力对压铸件抗拉强度的影响规律，随压铸真空度的提高（型腔真空压力降低），铸件抗拉强度明显提高。同时，研究了真空压铸镁合金压铸件的热处理工艺及性能，揭示了镁合金真空压铸件微观组织与力学性能关系。

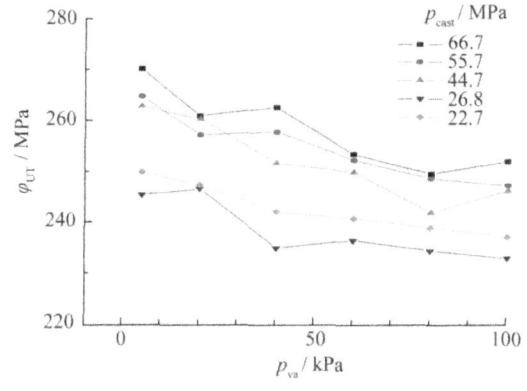

图 12 AZ91D 合金真空压铸抗拉强度与真空度、铸造压力的关系

图 13 显示了真空压铸在不同铸造压力下铸态及热处理态（T6 处理）AZ91D 合金的抗拉强度，从图中可以看出，通过热处理可以进一步提高 AZ91D 合金的力学性能[11]。

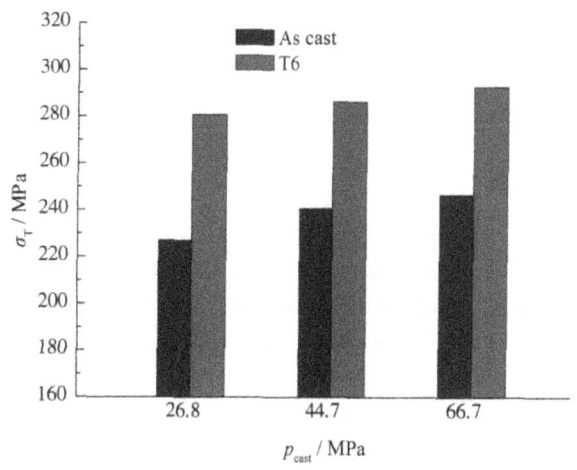

图 13 真空压铸 AZ91D 合金在不同的铸造压力下铸态及 T6 处理后的铸件抗拉强度

3 镁合金压铸过程模拟仿真及工艺优化

在冷室压铸机压铸生产过程中，液态或半固态的金属经过低速压射阶段后，在高速、高压下充型，并在高压下迅速凝固，容易产生气孔等铸造缺陷。由于镁合金压铸充型速度比铝合金更高，同时凝固速度更快，对镁合金压铸模具的流道系统及热平衡设计提出了更高的要求。数值模拟技术可以优化模具设计、加热冷却系统设计、预测压铸热平衡过程、模具寿命和铸件尺寸精度等，同时还可以优化压铸工艺，对实际压铸生产具有重要的指导意义。

3.1 低速压射工艺过程模拟及优化

压铸过程中液体金属的流动过程分为 3 个阶段：压室充填阶段、流道系统充填阶段和铸件充型阶段，其中压室充填阶段是由低速压射来完成的。低速阶段冲头的运动规律影响着压室中金属液和空气的流动状态，不恰当的低速参数选择会使金属液中卷入气体，形成气孔类缺陷，从而降低铸件的力学性能，并限制后续热处理或焊接工艺的实施。针对压室充填阶段，开发了考虑移动边界条件的压室液态金属流动的模拟分析系统[12-14]，对于压铸过程典型的两段压射工艺（如图 14 所示），分析了低速阶段的压射速度对压室液态金属流动形态及压室中气体卷入情况的影响,发现随压室充满度不同低速速度存在一个临界值,在该速度条件下,液体金属在压室中的流动将不会卷入气体,如图15所示。在此基础上,提出了优化的低速压射工艺,如图16所示。

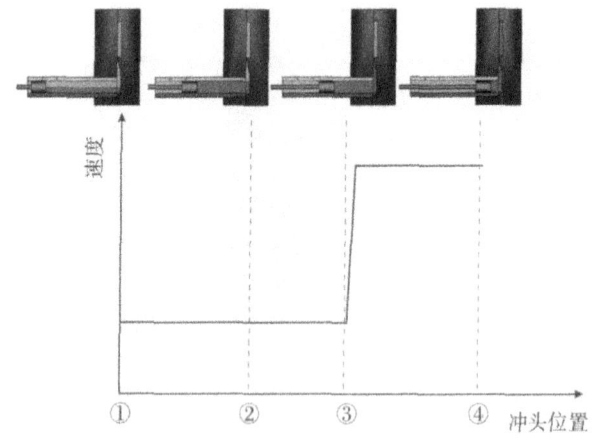

图14 压铸过程典型的两段压射工艺速度曲线

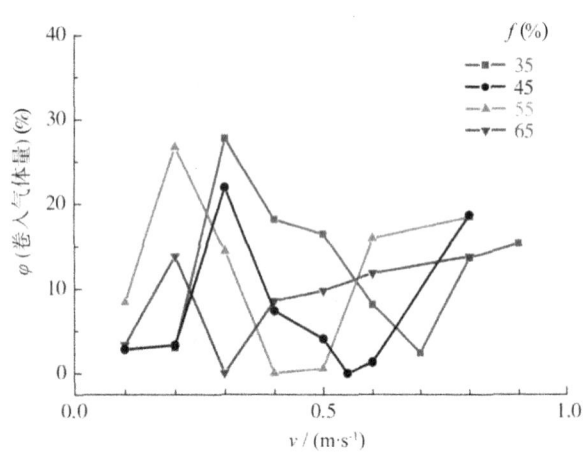

图15 不同压室充满度条件下低速对压室卷入气体量的影响

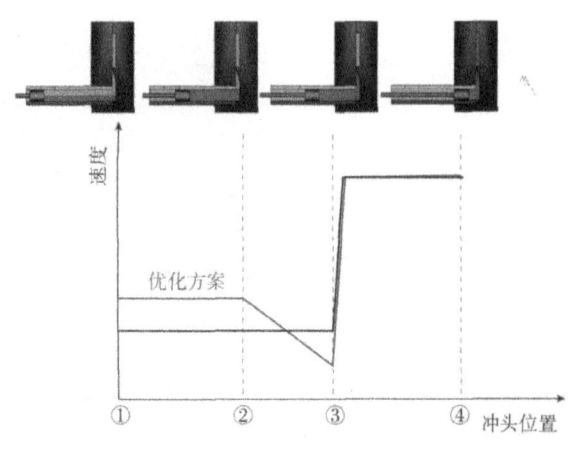

图16 低速压射工艺优化

3.2 压铸充型过程中卷入气体缺陷的数值模拟

在压铸过程中的铸件充型阶段,金属液在高速下填充型腔,在充型过程中会产生强烈的、不规则的紊态流动,致使型腔中部分空气来不及排出,被卷入金属液内部一起充填型腔,从而形成卷气现象。铸件中最终的卷气缺陷的大小及分布对铸件质量有着至关重要的影响,研究压铸充型过程中的卷气现象对于优化模具设计、改善工艺、提高铸件质量有着十分重要的意义。论文采用一种液-气两相耦合模型来模拟压铸充型过程中的卷气现象,建立了气泡的弥散化模型,采用气泡破碎判据和气体浓度输运方程,来跟踪和预测充型完毕后压铸件中最终的卷气缺陷分布,从而实现了对压铸工艺卷气缺陷从产生、发展至最终分布的全过程数值模拟[15,16]。

图17为压铸过程中金属液中的气泡卷入和演变过程。

图18为实际压铸件X射线检测结果与模拟预测的气体缺陷分布预测结果。

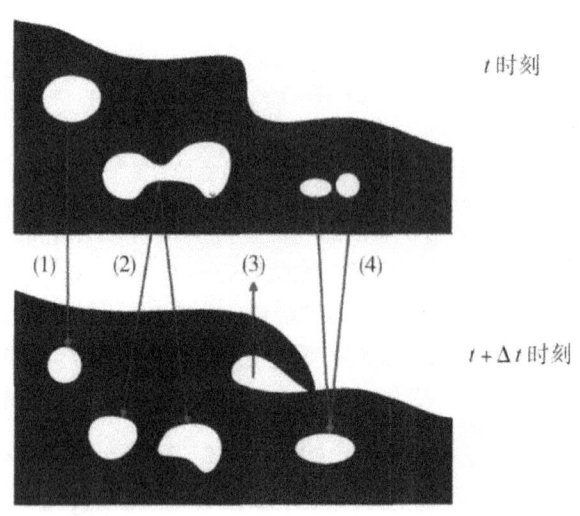

图17 液态金属充型过程中气泡演变的示意图

3.3 压铸过程中铸件/铸型界面传热及铸件凝固过程模拟

压铸过程是大规模连续生产过程,压铸过程中铸件/铸型界面换热条件及铸件的凝固过程对铸件质量及模具热平衡有着重要影响。论文基于热传导反算法,建立了求解压铸过程界面热流的反算模型,研究了计算参数及测温点位置对反算求解精度的影响,确定了最优反算计算参数及测温点位置的要求。

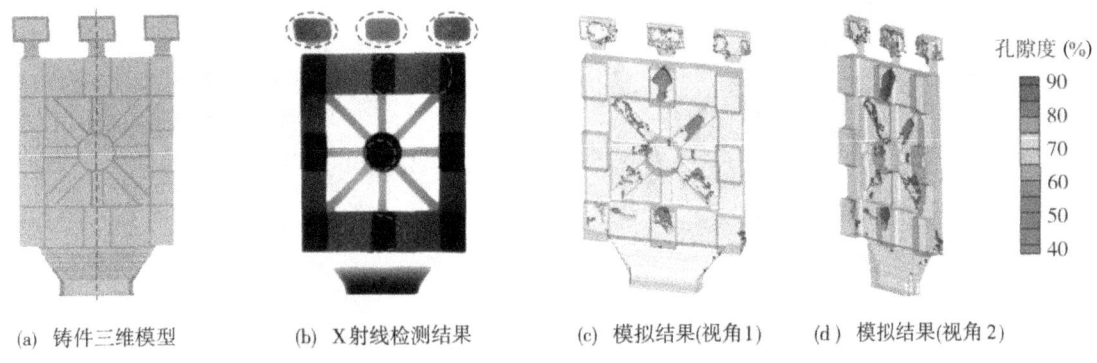

(a) 铸件三维模型　　(b) X射线检测结果　　(c) 模拟结果(视角1)　　(d) 模拟结果(视角2)

图 18　实际压铸件 X 射线检测结果与模拟预测的气体缺陷分布预测结果

采用图 5 所示的"阶梯"压铸件，系统地进行了压铸实验，准确地测量了不同合金及不同工艺条件下铸型内部的温度曲线。采用热传导反算模型，求解了不同合金及压铸工艺参数条件下的界面换热系数，图 19 为 AM50 合金典型测温曲线及热传导反算结果。图 19 中，A3、C3 分别为实测模具表面 1mm 和 6mm 处温度曲线。

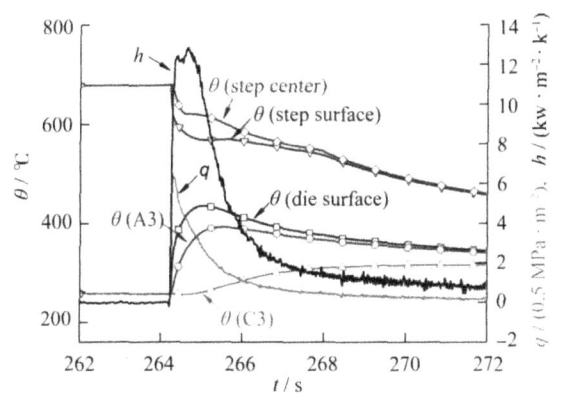

图 19　AM50 合金典型测温曲线及热传导反算结果

同时，系统研究了铸件壁厚、合金以及压铸工艺参数对换热系数的影响，建立了换热系数和铸件凝固分数，换热系数峰值和铸型初始表面温度的函数关系，在此基础上，将界面换热系数分为初始升高、峰值维持、快速下降以及低值保持 4 个阶段，建立了压铸过程铸件-铸型边界条件设定模型[17,18]，如图 20 所示。

采用所开发的边界条件处理模型及热平衡分析软件对汽车方向盘压铸件（AM50 合金）的实际压铸生产过程中铸件凝固模具热平衡进行了模拟，图 21 显示了铸件第 1 个循环周期中不同时间模具表面温度场变化。

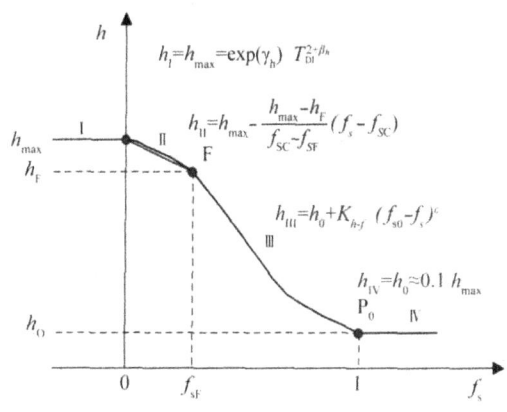

图 20　压铸过程界面换热系数边界条件设定模型

3.4　镁合金压铸过程微观组织模拟

镁合金压铸件的微观组织对最终使用性能有着重要的影响，研究压铸工艺对镁合金压铸件微观组织的影响规律，从而优化压铸工艺参数，有效地控制镁合金铸件在压铸过程中微观组织的形成过程，使铸件获得优良的使用性能，是镁合金压铸技术的重要发展方向。

由于镁合金具有密排六方的晶体结构特征，其枝晶形貌与具有面心立方（FCC）和体心立方（BCC）晶体结构金属的枝晶形貌有较大不同。针对镁合金枝晶形貌的特点，研究采用基于两套网格的"元胞自动机"（Cellular Automata，CA）方法，建立了模拟镁合金凝固过程枝晶形貌演化的二维模型。模型中，采用正六边形网格进行 CA 过程计算，采用四边形正交网格进行溶质场计算，图 22 为 CA 单元捕获规则的示意图。采用所开发的模型模拟计算了镁合金凝固过程中微观组织的演化。图 23 为二维条件下 AZ91D 镁合金单个等轴晶生长模拟和实验金相照片[19,20]。

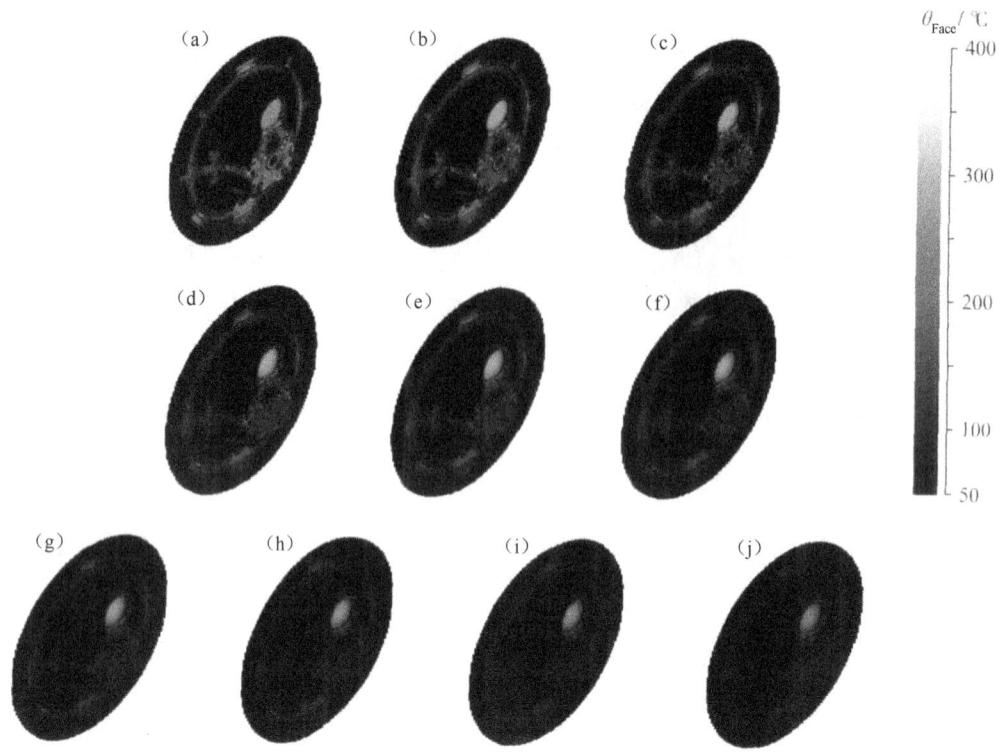

分图(a)~(j)的时间间隔为0.9 s

图 21 镁合金方向盘铸件凝固过程中模具（动模）表面温度场变化

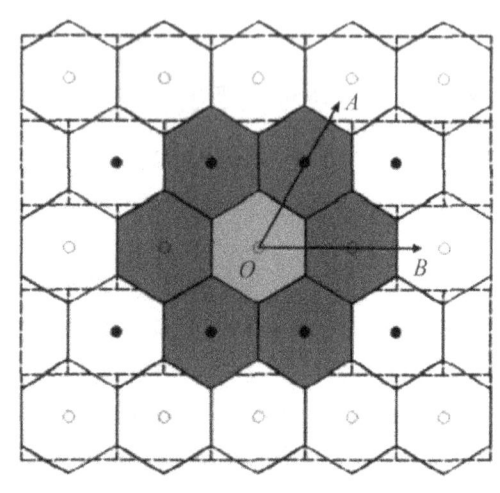

图 22 CA 单元的捕获规则示意图

以阶梯铸件热传导反算得到的压铸温度场为基础，分析了凝固过程冷却曲线，并根据实测得到的铸件晶粒尺寸，建立了以冷却速率与晶粒密度为对应关系的压铸形核模型。在压铸件表面附近及薄壁部位，冷却速率较高，产生激冷作用，形核密度与冷却速率近似满足线性关系；在压铸件厚壁靠近中心部位，冷却速率较低，形核密度与冷却速率近似满足指数函数关系。采用所建立的压铸形核模型及生长模型，模拟了不同浇注温度及模具温度下压铸镁合金 AM50 "阶梯" 压铸件的微观组织，得到的平均晶粒尺寸与金相实验结果相符[21]。

图 24 和图 25 分别为 AM50 合金压铸件表层和心部的形核模型。图 26 和图 27 分别为 AM50 合金阶梯铸件中心及表层组织模拟结果及实验观测结果。

4 结束语

高压铸造是镁合金成形的主要成形工艺，通过模拟仿真及实验研究提高镁合金压铸件质量及开发高真空压铸等高性能成形工艺是镁合金发展的重要方向。压铸工艺参数对铸件质量有重要影响，通过优化压铸工艺可以提高镁合金压铸件质量。研究了高真空压铸工艺的密封、真空系统及压铸工艺对镁合金真空压铸件质量的影响规律，采用高真空压铸工艺可以有效提高镁合金压铸件质量，可以进行铸件热处理以进一步提高铸件性能。开发了压铸过程低速压射过程、铸件充型过程、凝固过程及微观组织模拟仿真系统，可以优化铸造工艺及实现铸造缺陷预测，保证镁合金压铸件质量。

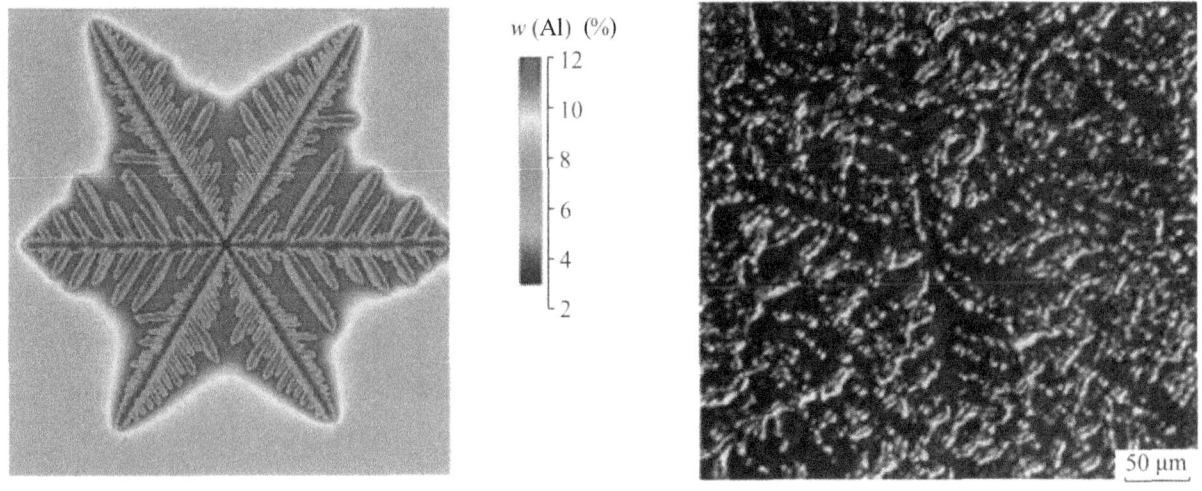

图 23　AZ91D 镁合金单个等轴晶生长模拟结果及实验结果

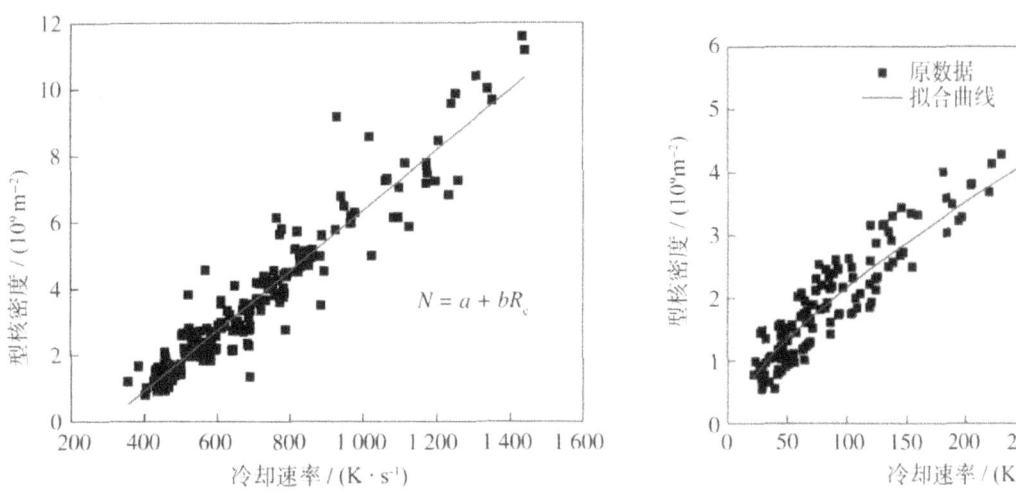

图 24　AM50 合金压铸件表层冷却速率与形核密度曲线　　图 25　AM50 合金压铸件心部冷却速率与形核密度曲线

图 26　AM50 合金 11mm 厚阶梯压铸试样中心微观组织模拟结果与金相实验结果

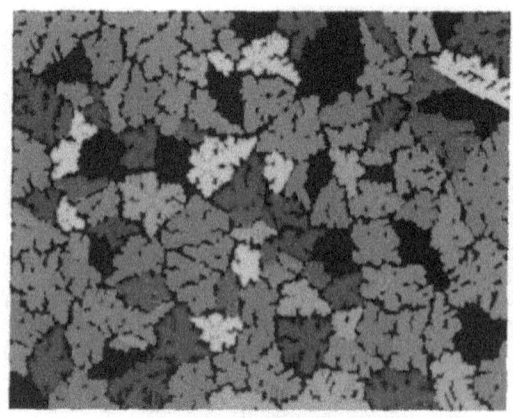 

图 27 AM50 合金 5mm 厚阶梯压铸试样表面微观组织模拟结果与金相实验结果

参考文献

[1] Alan A. Luo, Anil K. Sachdev and Bob R. Powell. Advanced casting technologies for lightweight automotive applications [J]. *China Foundry*, 2010, **7** (4): 63-469.

[2] NADCA. 2010 International Die Casting Competition Winners [J]. *Die Casting Engineer*, 2010 (7): 12-20.

[3] 丁文江, 吴玉娟, 彭立明, 等. 高性能镁合金及应用的新进展 [J]. 中国材料进展, 2010, **29** (8): 37-44.
DING Wenjiang, WU Yujuan, PENG Liming, et al. Research and application development of advanced magnesium alloys [J]. *Materials China*, 2010, **29** (8): 37-44. (in Chinese)

[4] Kramer D A. 2008 Minerals Yearbook-MagnesiumL: Advance Release [M]. US: U. S. Department of the Interior, U. S. Geological Survey, 2009.

[5] 熊守美. 镁合金压铸成形技术研究进展 [J]. 航空制造技术, 2006 (2): 32-35.
XIONG Shoumei. Research progress on high pressure die casting process of magnesium alloys [J]. *Aeronautical Manufacturing Technology*, 2006 (2): 32-35. (in Chinese)

[6] 宋杰. 压铸镁合金工艺、组织和性能关系的研究 [D]. 北京: 清华大学, 2009.
SONG Jie. Study on the processing-microstructure-mechanical property relationships of high pressure diecast magnesium alloys [D]. Beijing: Tsinghua University, 2009.

[7] SONG Jie, XIONG Shoumei, LI Mei, et al. In situ observation of tensile deformation of high-pressure diecast specimens of AM50 alloy [J]. *Materials Sci and Eng* A, 2009, **520** (1-2): 197-201.

[8] SONG Jie, XIONG Shoumei, LI Mei, et al. The correlation between microstructure and mechanical properties of high-pressure die-cast AM50 alloy [J]. *Journal of Alloys and Compounds*, 2009, **477** (1-2): 863-869.

[9] 胡泊、熊守美、村上正幸, 等. 真空压铸工艺参数对 AM50 镁合金力学性能的影响规律 [J]. 特种铸造及有色合金, 2009, **29** (12): 1156-1159.
HU Bo, XIONG Shoumei, MASAYUKI Murakami, et al. Influences of vacuum die casting process parameters on mechanical properties of AM50 magnesium alloy [J]. *Special Casting & Nonferrous Alloys*, 2009, **29** (12): 1156-1159. (in Chinese)

[10] 胡泊, 熊守美, 村上正幸, 等. AM50 镁合金真空压铸件孔洞分布与力学性能的关系 [J]. 铸造, 2009, **58** (11): 1115-1118, 1122.
HU Bo, XIONG Shoumei, MASAYUKI Murakami, et al. Relationship between porosity distribution and mechanical properties of vacuum die casting AM50 magnesium alloy [J]. *Foundry*, 2009, **58** (11): 1115-1118, 1122. (In Chinese)

[11] 胡泊, 熊守美, 村上正幸, 等. AZ91D 镁合金真空压铸力学性能研究 [J]. 铸造技术, 2007, **28** (12): 1579-1583.
Hu Bo, XIONG Shou-Mei, MASAYUKI Murakami, et al. Study on mechanical properties of vacuum die cast AZ91D alloy [J]. *Foundry Technology*, 2007, **28** (12): 1579-1583. (In Chinese)

[12] YUAN Lang, YANG Jie, XIONG Shoumei, et al. Water analogue validation of numerical model for fluid flow during slow shot phase in die casting process [J]. *Int J Cast Metals Res*, 2008, **21** (6): 401-407.

[13] YANG Jie, REN Yuxin, XIONG Shoumei. Numerical simulation of die-casting mold filling process by using fractional step method [J]. *Materials Sci Forum*, 2008, **575-578** (1): 104-108.

[14] 杨杰, 袁烺, 熊守美. 基于数值模拟的压铸过程低速工艺优化 [J]. 铸造, 2007, **56** (10): 1062-1065.

YANG Jie, YUAN Lang, XIONG Shoumei. Optimization of slow shot parameters in a die casting process by numerical simulation technique [J]. *Foundry*, 2007, **56** (10): 1062-1065. (in Chinese)

[15] 李帅君,熊守美,LI Mei,等. 压铸充型过程中卷气现象的数值模拟研究 [J]. 金属学报, 2010, **46** (5): 554-560.
LI Shuaijun, XIONG Shoumei, LI Mei, et al. Numerical simulation of air entrapment phenomenon during mold filling of high pressure die casting process [J]. *Acta Metallurgica Sinica*, 2010, **46** (5): 554-560. (in Chinese)

[16] 李帅君,熊守美,LI Mei,等. 应用两相流模型模拟压铸充型过程的卷气现象 [J]. 金属学报, 2009, **45** (10): 1153-1158.
LI Shuaijun, XIONG Shoumei, LI Mei, et al. A twophase flow model for simulating air entrapment during mold filling of high pressure die casting process [J]. *Acta Metallurgica Sinica*, 2009, **45** (10): 1153-1158. (in Chinese)

[17] GUO Zhipeng, XIONG Shoumei, LIU Baicheng, et al. Determination of the heat transfer coefficient at metal-die interface of high pressure die casting process of AM50 alloy [J]. *Int J Heat and Mass Transfer*, 2008, **51** (25-26): 6032-6038.

[18] GUO Zhipeng, XIONG Shoumei, LIU Baicheng, et al. Effect of process parameters, casting thickness, and alloys on the interfacial heat-transfer coefficient in the high-pressure die-casting process [J]. *Metallurgical and Materials Transactions A: Physical Metallurgy and Materials Science*, 2008, **39A** (12): 2896-2905.

[19] 刘志勇,许庆彦,柳百成. 铸造镁合金的枝晶生长模拟 [J]. 金属学报, 2007, **43** (4): 367-373.
LIU Zhiyong, XU Qingyan, LIU Baicheng. Modeling of dendritic growth for the cast magnesium alloy [J]. *Acta Metallurgica Sinica*, 2007, **43** (4): 367-373. (in Chinese)

[20] 霍亮,韩志强,柳百成. 基于两套网格的 CA 方法模拟铸造镁合金凝固过程枝晶形貌演化 [J]. 金属学报, 2009, **45** (12): 1414-1420.
HUO Liang, HAN Zhiqiang, LIU Baicheng. Modeling and simulation of microstructure evolution of cast magnesium alloys using CA method based on two sets of mech [J]. *Acta Metallurgica Sinica*, 2009, **45** (12): 1414-1420. (in Chinese)

[21] 吴孟武,熊守美. 基于改进 CA 方法的压铸镁合金微观组织模拟 [J]. 金属学报, 2010, **46** (12): 1534-1542.
WU Mengwu, XIONG Shoumei. Microstructure simulation of high pressure die cast magnesium alloys based on modified CA method [J]. *Acta Metallurgica Sinica*, 2010, **46** (12): 1534-1542. (in Chinese)

6. Simulation and experimental validation of three-dimensional dendrite growth

SHI Yu-feng, XU Qing-yan, LIU Bai-cheng

Key Laboratory for Advanced Materials Processing Technology, Ministry of Education,
Department of Mechanical Engineering, Tsinghua University, Beijing 100084,
China Received 19 October 2011; accepted 14 December 2011

Abstract: A three-dimensional (3-D) modified cellular automaton (MCA) method was developed for simulating the dendrite morphology of cubic system alloys. Two-dimensional (2-D) equations of growth velocities of the dendrite tip, interface curvature and anisotropy of the surface energy were extended to 3-D system in the model. Therefore, the model was able to describe the morphology evolution of 3-D dendrites. Then, the model was applied to simulate the mechanism of spacing adjustment for 3-D columnar dendrite growth, and the competitive growth of columnar dendrites with different preferred growth orientations under constant temperature gradient and pulling velocity. Directional solidification experiments of NH_4Cl-H_2O transparent alloy were performed. It was found that the simulated results compared well with the experimental results. Therefore, the model was reliable for simulating the 3-D dendrite growth of cubic system alloys.

Key words: modified cellular automaton; 3-D dendrite morphology; dendrite growth; directional solidification; NH_4Cl-H_2O transparent alloy

1 Introduction

The initial dendrite microstructure during solidification has significant influence on the properties of the castings. There are several approaches to investigate the mechanism of the dendrite evolution, such as experimental studies, theoretical approaches and numerical technique. The adjustment of primary dendrite arm spacing (λ_1) was observed by experimental research on transparent alloys[1-3]. Meanwhile, several theoretical models[4-6] were developed to describe the relationship between λ_1 and the solidification parameters (temperature gradient, G, and solidification rate, v). However, it is well known that the classical experimental and theoretical approaches are unable to describe the detailed microstructure phenomena including the branching and coarsening of secondary dendrite arms.

Recently, the phase field (PF) model and the cellular automaton (CA) approach have presented their considerable potential for quantitatively describing realistic phenomena associated with dendrite growth, including side arm branching and coarsening. KARMA and RAPPEL[7] studied the effect of surface anisotropy on the 3-D dendrite morphologies by a phase field model. NESTLER et al[8] developed a phase field model to simulate the crystal growth in a pure substance for different initial undercoolings. However, the algorithm of phase field model is complicated and the computational efficiency is lower. The CA model is more computationally efficient than the phase field model, because the computing grid can be coarser in CA model. Therefore, CA model is rapidly emerging as a choice for simulating the dendrite formation in solidification of commercial alloys[9-13]. YUAN and LEE[14] studied the effect of fluid motion on the 3-D dendrite morphology of Ni-4.85%Nb alloy by coupling CA model with basic flow equations, but the model ignored the anisotropy of interface energy.

PAN and ZHU[15] developed a 3-D CA model to simulate the effect of melt undercoolings and degrees of anisotropy of interface energy on the single dendrite morphologies of Fe-0.6% C alloy. CHEN and XIONG[16] developed a simple CA method to simulate columnar dendrite transformation to equiaxed dendrite (CET) of twin-roll continuous casting aluminum thin strip.

In the present study, a 3-D modified cellular automaton (MCA) model was developed to simulate the 3-D dendrite evolution in solidification of alloys based on the 2-D CA model. It proposed a simplified solution of the anisotropy of interface energy, which can affect the curvature undercooling and the dendrite morphology. Competitive growth of 3-D columnar dendrites in directional solidification was simulated by the model. In order to validate the model, the simulated results were compared with those derived by experiments.

2 Description of MCA model

2.1 Solute diffusion

In the 3-D MCA model, the domain is meshed by a set of uniform cubic cells, and the cell is characterized by the solid fraction (f_S): liquid ($f_S = 0$), solid ($f_S = 1$) or interface ($0 < f_S < 1$).

During the solidification process, for an alloy the solute diffusion is solved in the liquid and solid region, respectively, which is governed by

$$\frac{\partial C_L}{\partial t} = \nabla \cdot (D_L \nabla C_L) \quad (1)$$

$$\frac{\partial C_S}{\partial t} = \nabla \cdot (D_S \nabla C_S) \quad (2)$$

where C and D are the composition and solute diffusion coefficient, and the subscripts "L" and "S" means the liquid and solid, respectively, t is time, and k_0 is the solute partition coefficient.

2.2 Growth kinetics of dendrite tip

At the micro-scale level, the relationship between the equilibrium composition and the interface temperature is given by[17,18]

$$C_L^* = C_0 + [T^* - T_L + \Delta T_R]/m_L \quad (3)$$

$$C_S^* = k_0 C_L^* \quad (4)$$

where T^* is the interface temperature, T_L is the liquidus temperature, C_L^* and C_S^* are the equilibrium liquid and solid composition, respectively, C_0 is the initial composition, ΔT_R is the curvature undercooling, and m_L is the slope of the liquidus line.

The anisotropy of interfacial energy and the orientation dependence of the interfacial stiffness are incorporated into the equation of curvature undercooling, which can be expressed as follows[19,20]:

$$\Delta T_R = \frac{1}{\Delta S_F} \left[\left(\sigma(\theta,\psi) + \frac{\partial^2 \sigma(\theta,\psi)}{\partial^2 \theta} \right) K_1 + \left(\sigma(\theta,\psi) + \frac{\partial^2 \sigma(\theta,\psi)}{\partial^2 \psi} \right) K_2 \right] \quad (5)$$

where $\sigma(\theta,\psi)$ is the anisotropic interfacial free energy, θ and ψ are the two standard spherical angles of the normal to the solid-liquid interface. In a rectangular Cartesian coordinate system, θ is the angle between normal to the solid-liquid interface and z axis, and ψ is the normal projection in the x—y plane with respect to the x axis. K_1 and K_2 are the two principal interfacial curvatures. ΔS_F is the melting entropy of the alloys.

To simulate the growth of the typical cubic dendrites, a general form of the anisotropy function of interfacial energy with equal strength of anisotropy in the basal and in normal direction is given by[21,22]

$$\sigma(\theta,\psi) = \sigma_0 (1 - 3\varepsilon) \cdot \left[1 + \frac{4\varepsilon}{1-3\varepsilon} \left(\cos^4\theta + \sin^4\theta \left(1 - \frac{1}{2}\sin^2 2\psi\right) \right) \right] \quad (6)$$

$$\Gamma = \frac{\sigma_0}{\Delta S_F} \quad (7)$$

where σ_0 is the isotropic interfacial energy, Γ is the Gibbs-Thomson coefficient, and ε is the anisotropic coefficient.

In order to calculate θ and ψ, the unit vector normal to the interface $\boldsymbol{\eta}$ is simplified as follows:

$$\boldsymbol{\eta} = \nabla f_S / |\nabla f_S| = \eta_x \boldsymbol{i} + \eta_y \boldsymbol{j} + \eta_z \boldsymbol{k} \quad (8)$$

$$\begin{cases} \psi = \arccos\left(\frac{\partial f_S}{\partial x} \left[\left(\frac{\partial f_S}{\partial x}\right)^2 + \left(\frac{\partial f_S}{\partial y}\right)^2 \right]^{-1/2} \right) \\ \theta = \arccos\left(\frac{\partial f_S}{\partial z} \left[\left(\frac{\partial f_S}{\partial x}\right)^2 + \left(\frac{\partial f_S}{\partial y}\right)^2 + \left(\frac{\partial f_S}{\partial z}\right)^2 \right]^{-1/2} \right) \end{cases} \quad (9)$$

where η_x, η_y and η_z are the rectangular components of the vector $\boldsymbol{\eta}$.

The interface root mean square curvature of CA interface cell is calculated by a simplified computational method.

$$K = \left[1 - 2\left(f_S + \sum_{i=1}^{N} f_S^i\right)/(N+1)\right]/\Delta x \quad (10)$$

where Δx is the cell size, f_S^i is the solid fraction of the neighboring cells, and N is the total number of CA cells counted around the interface cell. In a 3-D system, N equals 26.

Solute conservation at the S/L interface is given by
$$v_n C_L^* (1-k_0) = -D_L \nabla C_L + D_S \nabla C_S \quad (11)$$
where v_n is the normal velocity of the interface. In three dimensional condition, $v_n = (v_x, v_y, v_z)$, which can be expressed as

$$v_x C_L^* (1 - k_0) = -D_L \frac{\partial C_L}{\partial x} + D_S \frac{\partial C_S}{\partial x} \quad (12)$$

$$v_y C_L^* (1 - k_0) = -D_L \frac{\partial C_L}{\partial y} + D_S \frac{\partial C_S}{\partial y} \quad (13)$$

$$v_z C_L^* (1 - k_0) = -D_L \frac{\partial C_L}{\partial z} + D_S \frac{\partial C_S}{\partial z} \quad (14)$$

After calculating the velocity components in x-, y- and z-directions, the increment of solid fraction at the interface is obtained by

$$\Delta f_S = [v_x \Delta t/\Delta x + v_y \Delta t/\Delta y + v_z \Delta t/\Delta z - v_x v_y \Delta t^2/(\Delta x \Delta y) - v_x v_z \Delta t^2/(\Delta x \Delta z) - v_y v_z \Delta t^2/(\Delta y \Delta z) + 2 v_x v_y v_z \Delta t^3/(\Delta x \Delta y \Delta z)] \quad (15)$$

$$f_S^{n+1} = f_S^n + \Delta f_S \quad (16)$$

where f_S^n and f_S^{n+1} are the solid fraction at the current time step and the next time step, respectively. When f_S equals 1, the interface cell becomes solid and captures the neighboring liquid cells, and the captured cells change its state to interface. Therefore, the dendrite can grow.

3 Simulation and experiment

3.1 Experimental setup

As shown in Fig. 1, NH_4Cl-H_2O transparent alloy was poured into a sample cell, and then subjected to directional solidification under constant pulling velocity (v_p) in a horizontal heating and cooling system, which can supply a constant temperature gradient (G). During the directional solidification process, the dendrite growth was observed by a microscope in real time.

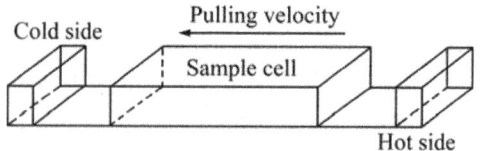

Fig. 1 Schematic illustration of experimental setup for directional solidification of NH_4Cl-H_2O transparent alloy

The thermal diffusion is several orders higher than the solute diffusion. Therefore, in the calculation domain, the temperature is controlled by G and v_p.

3.2 Simulation of selection of primary dendrite arm spacing

In order to validate the MCA model, the directional solidification of an NH_4Cl-74% H_2O (mass fraction) transparent alloy was simulated. The material properties were derived from Ref. [17].

At first, several seeds were set at the base x—y plane and the preferred growth direction of all the seeds aligned well with z-axis. The solidification parameters were used as follows: $G = 1 K/mm$, $v_p = 3 \mu m/s$, which were the same as experiments. The calculation domain was 1.8mm×0.12mm×2.4mm with cell size of 6μm.

From Fig. 2, it can be seen that two primary dendrite arms developed well. Some tertiary dendrites emanated from the secondary dendrite arms. However, they were blocked by the other secondary dendrites both from simulation (see Fig. 2(a)-(c)) and experimental result (see Fig. 2(d)). The two primary dendrites kept growing, the secondary arms began to coarsen, and the spacing remained constant (see Fig. 2 (e)-(h)). Above all, the simulated results agreed well with the experimental results.

Similar to the preliminary 3-D simulation of 2 seeds, the growth of 3 seeds at different time steps was simulated (see Figs. 3(a) and (e)) and observed by experiments (see Figs. 3(d) and (h)). At the beginning of simulation, 3 seeds were nucleated at the bottom with the <100> directions aligned well with z-axis, and the distance of the 2 seeds at the left side (see Figs. 3(c) and (d)) was closer than the right 2 seeds. Because of the dense packing of the left 2 seeds, the growth of one seed was suppressed after initial competition. It can be seen that, two dendrites with the same preferred growth

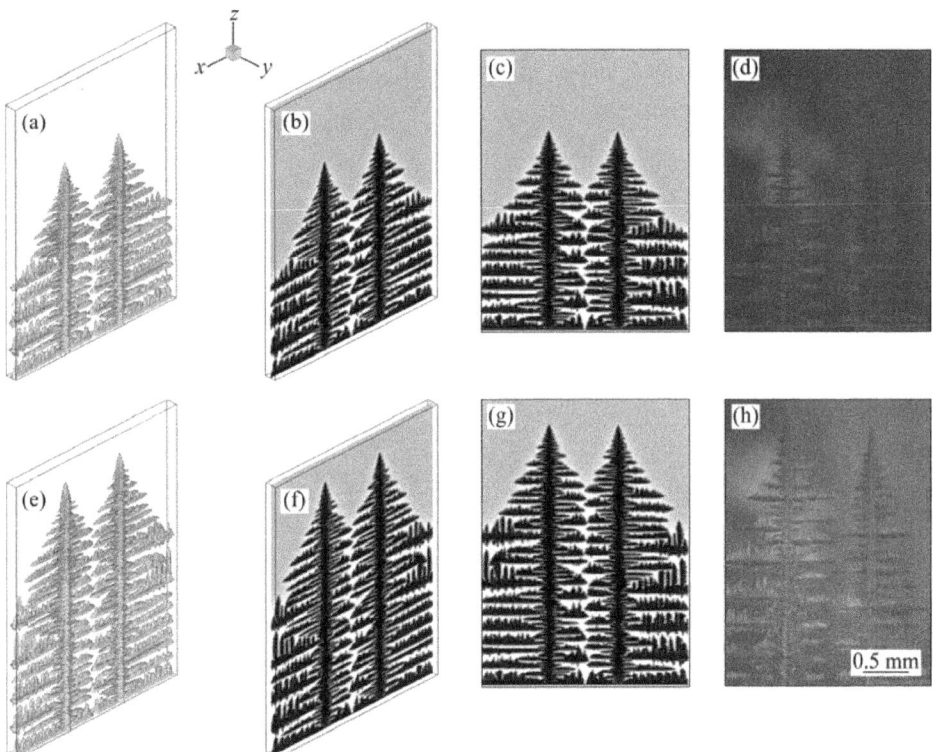

Fig. 2 Simulated and experimental results of 3-D columnar dendrite growth of NH_4Cl-74%H_2O transparent alloy with 2 seeds in directional solidification: (a) $t=430s$, 3-D morphology; (b,c) $t=430s$, x—z central slice of the solute field; (d) Experimental photograph; (e) $t=740s$, 3-D morphology; (f,g) $t=740s$, x—z central slice of the solute field; (h) Experimental photograph

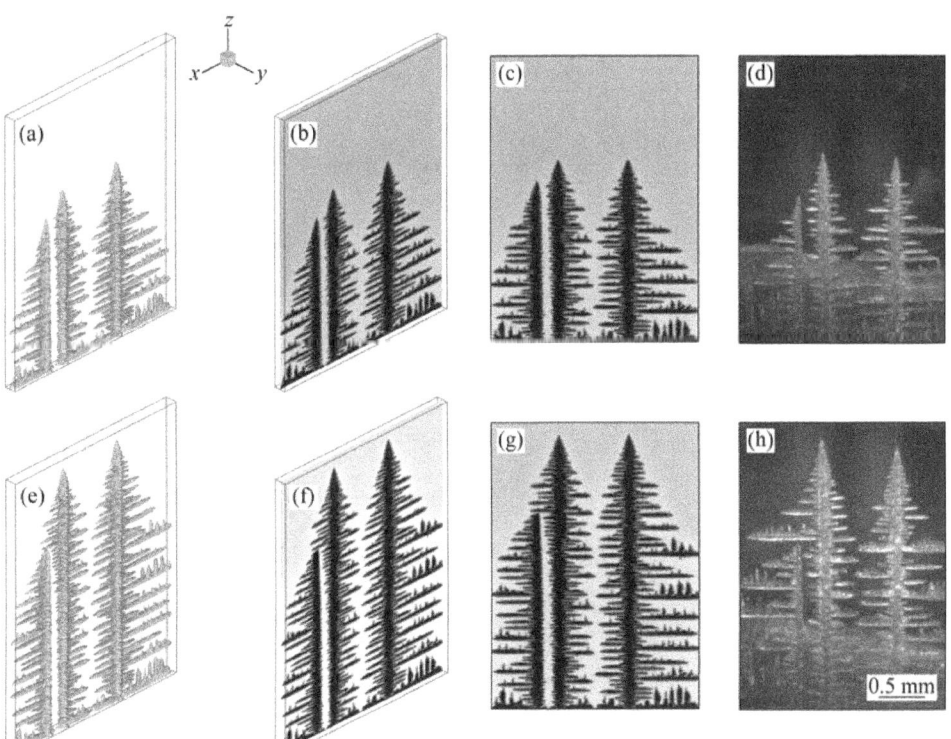

Fig. 3 Simulated and experimental results of 3-D columnar dendrite growth of NH_4Cl-74%H_2O transparent alloy with 3 seeds: (a) $t=420s$, 3-D morphology; (b,c) $t=420s$, x—z central slice; (d) Experimental photograph; (e) $t=750s$, 3-D morphology; (f,g) $t=750s$, x—z central slice; (h) Experimental photograph

direction overgrew the left one and kept growing steadily (see Figs. 3(a) and (e)). It was found that the experimental dendrites (see Figs. 3(d) and (h)) agreed well with that simulation (see Figs. 3(c) and (g)). Therefore, the MCA model can simulate the competitive growth of dendrites.

In classical models[4-6], the growth of dendrites with different numbers of seeds could result in the same final primary dendrite arm spacing (λ_1) when the solidification parameters were constant. λ_1 was determined as function of G and solidification rate v ($v \approx v_p$), $\lambda_1 \propto G^{-0.5} v^{-0.25}$. From Table 1, it can be seen that a smaller dendrite was overgrown by its neighbors when the initial spacing was too narrow, and the final primary dendrite arm spacing in the simulation compared well with the experimental results.

Table 1 Comparison of final primary dendrite arm spacing (λ_1) between initial and final state under constant G and v_p

State	Method	$\lambda_1/\mu m$	
		2 seeds	3 seeds
Initial state	Simulation	630	430
	Experiment	678	458
Final steady state	Simulation	630	620
	Experiment	678	664

3.3 Simulation of competitive growth of columnar dendrites

The simulation and experiment of competitive growth of columnar dendrites in a 3D block were performed with $G = 1 K/mm$, and $v_p = 10 \mu m/s$. In this 3-D simulation, temperature gradient stood perpendicularly to the x—y plane. The calculation domain consisted of $300 \times 20 \times 400$ CA cells and the cell size was $6 \mu m$. At the beginning, 4 seeds were set at the bottom plane with different preferred growth directions, and 2 seeds at the left wall were favorably oriented.

It can be seen that two dendrites aligned well with z-axis had the maximum growth rate (see Figs. 4(a) and 4(d)), and they were the leading dendrites, which grew faster than the dendrites with misaligned orientations (Figs. 4(e) and (h)). Finally, the development of secondary dendrite arms on the leading dendrites exceeded the tip of the lagging dendrite, and suppressed the growth of the lagging dendrites, which had the misaligned orientations. It was obvious that the predicted dendrite pattern was in good agreement with that obtained by experiments (see Fig. 4).

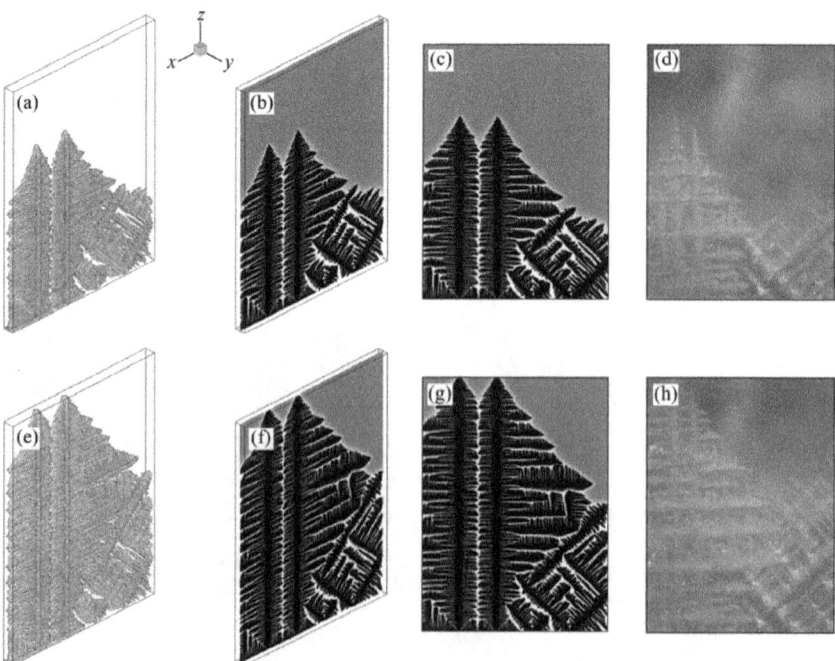

Fig. 4 Competitive growth of columnar dendrite of NH_4Cl-74%H_2O transparent alloy with different preferred growth orientations: (a) $t = 160s$; (b,c) $t = 160s$, x—z central slice; (d) Experimental result; (e) $t = 220s$; (f,g) $t = 220s$, x—z central slice; (h) Experimental result

4 Conclusions

A 3-D MCA model for the simulation of columnar dendrite growth in directional solidification process was developed. A simplified computational method of anisotropic interfacial energy was imported into the present model. The normal velocity of the interface was derived by solving the 3-D solute conservation equation subjected to the boundary conditions at the S/L interface. The MCA model was applied to simulate the selection and competition of columnar dendrites in directional solidification of NH_4Cl-H_2O transparent alloy. It was found that initial seed numbers had little effect on the primary dendrite arm spacing when the dendrite growth reached a stable state. It was also found that the crystal orientation parallel to heat flow direction can overgrow the misaligned one, which yield a relatively good quantitative agreement with experimental results. Above all, the present 3-D MCA model is possible to be a powerful tool to predict a number of interesting microstructure pattern formation issues of commercial alloys.

References

[1] SOMBOONSUK K, TRIVEDI R. Dynamical studies of dendritic growth [J]. Acta Metall, 1985, 33 (6): 1051-1060.

[2] SUKY M J, PARK Y M, KIM Y C. Dendrite spacing selection during directional solidification of pivalic acid-ethanol system [J]. J Mater Sci Technol, 2008, 24 (3): 340-342.

[3] WAN X, HAN Q, HUNT J D. Different growth regimes during directional dendritic growth [J]. Acta Mater, 1997, 45 (10): 3975-3979.

[4] LU S Z, HUNT J D. Numerical modeling of cellular/dendritic array growth: Spacing and structure predictions [J]. Metall Mater Trans A, 1996, 27: 611-623.

[5] KURZ W, FISHER D J. Dendritic growth and limit of stability tip radius and spacing [J]. Acta Metall, 1981, 29: 11-20.

[6] TRIVEDI R. Interdendritic spacing: part II. A comparison of theory and experiment [J]. Metall Mater Trans A, 1984, 15 (6): 977-982.

[7] KARMA A, RAPPEL W J. Quantitative phase-field modeling of dendritic growth in two and three dimensions [J]. Phys Rev E, 1998, 57 (4): 4324-4349.

[8] NESTLER B, DANILOV D, GALENKO P. Crystal growth of pure substances: Phase-field simulations in comparison with analytical and experimental results [J]. Journal of Computational Physics, 2005, 207: 221-239.

[9] NASTAC L. Numerical modeling of solidification morphologies and segregation patterns in cast dendritic alloys [J]. Acta Mater, 1999, 47: 4253-4262.

[10] BELTRAN-SANCHEZ L, STEFANESCU D M. Growth of solutal dendrites: A cellular automaton model and its quantitative capabilities [J]. Metall Mater Trans A, 2003, 34 (2): 367-382.

[11] WANG W, LEE P D, MCLEAN M. A model of solidification microstructures in nickel-based superalloys: Predicting primary dendrite spacing selection [J]. Acta Mater, 2003, 51: 2971-2987.

[12] LIU B C, XIONG S M, XU Q Y. Study on macro-and micromodeling of the solidification process of aluminum shape casting [J]. Metall Mater Trans B, 2007, 38: 525-532.

[13] LI B, XU Q Y, PAN D, LIU B C, XIONG Y C, ZHOU Y J, HONG R Z. Microstructure simulation of ZL114A alloy during low pressure die casting process [J]. Acta Metall Sin, 2008, 44 (2): 243-248. (in Chinese)

[14] YUAN L, LEE P D. Dendritic solidification under natural and forced convection in binary alloys: 2D versus 3D simulation [J]. Modelling Simul Mater Sci Eng, 2010, 18: 055008.

[15] PAN S Y, ZHU M F. A three-dimensional sharp interface model for the quantitative simulation of solutal dendritic growth [J]. Acta Mater, 2010, 58: 340-352.

[16] CHEN S D, XIONG S M. Simulation of microstructures in solidification of aluminum twin-roll casting [J]. Transactions of Nonferrous Metals Society of China, 2012, 22 (6): 1452-1456.

[17] SHI Y F, XU Q Y, GONG M, LIU B C. Simulation of NH_4Cl-H_2O dendritic growth in directional solidification [J]. Acta Metall Sin, 2011, 47 (5): 620-627. (in Chinese)

[18] WU M W, XIONG S M. Modeling of equiaxed and columnar dendritic growth of magnesium alloy [J]. Transactions of Nonferrous Metals Society of China, 2012, 22 (9): 2212-2219.

[19] NAPOLITANO R E, LIU S, TRIVEDI R. Experimental measurement of anisotropy in crystal-melt interfacial energy [J]. Interface Science, 2002, 10: 217-232.

[20] NAPOLITANO R E, LIU S. Three-dimensional crystal-melt Wulff-shape and interfacial stiffness in the Al-Sn binary system [J]. Phys Rev B, 2004, 70: 214103-1-11.

[21] JEONG J H, DANTZIG J A, GOLDENFELD N. Dendritic growth with fluid flow in pure materials [J]. Metall Mater Trans A, 2003, 34 (3): 459-466.

[22] ZHAO D P, JING T, LIU B C. Simulating the three-dimensional dendritic growth of Al alloy using the phase-field method [J]. Acta Phys Sin, 2003, 52: 1737-1742. (in Chinese)

航空及重燃叶片建模与仿真

7. MODELING OF DIRECTIONAL SOLIDIFICATION PROCESS OF SUPERALLOY TURBINE BLADE CASTINGS[⊖]

Jing Yu[1], Qingyan Xu[1], Kai Cui[1], Baicheng Liu[1]
Akihiko Kimatsuka[2], Yasunori Kuroki[2], Atsushi Hirata[2]

[1] Key Laboratory for Advanced Manufacturing by Materials Processing Technology, Department of Mechanical Engineering, Tsinghua University, Beijing 100084, China

[2] Ishikawajima-Harima Heavy Industries Co., Ltd., Isogo-Ku, Yokohama 235-8501, Japan

Key words: Directional solidification, Ni-based superlloy, Turbine blade, Numerical modeling.

Abstract: A mathematical model for three-dimensional simulation of directional solidification process of single crystal turbine blade of Ni-based superalloy investment castings was developed based on CA-FD method. Complex heat radiation among the multiple blade castings and the furnace wall were considered in the model. Temperature, grain growth interface and structure defects of single blade sample casting of single crystal and multiple turbine blade castings were investigated respectively. The experiments were carried out to validate the modeling results. It can be seen that the simulated results of microstructure evolution and structure defects were predicted reasonably and coincident with experimental. It is indicated that three-dimensional solidification simulation technique is a powerful tool for understanding the fundamental of directional solidification process and the formation of structure defects in directionally solidified and single crystal blade castings and finally for optimizing the product and process design as well.

Introduction

Ni-based superalloy turbine blade castings with columnar grain (DS) and single crystal (SX) produced by Bridgman directional solidification technology have been used in advanced gas turbine for aeronautic and energy industry as well. Since the last two decades of last century, great efforts have been done to study directional solidification technology. Original researches[1] were focused on one or two dimensional model without the consideration of radial temperature distribution to simulate the directional solidification process. K. O. Yu[2] studied the directional solidification process through commercial FEM software and developed the defects map which represented the correlation between the thermal gradient and casting defects. A two-dimensional model was developed by Saitou and Hirata[3] to analyze the shape of liquid-solid interface in Bridgman directional solidification. Compared with experimental results, Galantucci[4] investigated the directional solidification process of turbine blades through 2D FEM method. With the consideration of heat conduction and radiation, Wang and Overfelt[5] presented a new two-dimensional model which could solve the variational radiation view factor with the withdrawal process. J. R. Li[6] investigated the solidification process of single crystal investment castings by ProCast, a commercial software. From 1990s, microstructure simulation of castings became new research hot topics, many approaches have been presented for the computational modeling of microstructure evolution, such as deterministic, probabilistic models and phase field method, but few of them were used to study the single crystal solidification. Cellular automata (CA), dynamic systems in which space and time are discrete, was originally developed by Hesselbarth and Gobel[7] in recrystallization and applied first by Rappaz and Gandin[8] to the simulation of grain structure formation in solidification processes. Based on CA method, Xu[9] developed shape functions to describe the approximate contour of dendrite grain. Kermanpur and Rappaz[10] developed a CA-FE model and investigated the microstructure evolution of turbine blade produced by LMC method. On the assumption of given undercooling and nucleation parameters, Wang and Lee[11] analyzed the correlation of primary dendrite arm spacing and technical parameters of superalloy castings by CA-FE model without consideration of real turbine blade shape. Carter and Gandin[12] developed a process model for grain selection during the solidification of single crystal investment castings and study the geometrical factors influencing competitive growth and the efficacy of two designs of grain selector. Liang[13] investigated the directional solidification process and microstructure evolution of superalloy by CA-FD model.

In this paper, a stochastic modeling based on CA-FD method was studied for simulating the evolution of multiple superalloy turbine blades castings. Complex heat transfer between blades and furnace wall in the directional solidification of multiple turbine blades was considered in this model. The simulation results of solidification process, solidification interface and structure defects of turbine blade castings were compared with experimental results respectively.

Mathematical Model

Assumption

1. All the thermophysical properties are constant.
2. The temperature of heating and cooling zones is constant respectively.
3. Radiation exchanges in an enclosure composed of diffuse-gray surfaces.
4. The influence of melt convection is neglected.
5. The grain growth is controlled by thermal diffusion instead of solute diffusion.

Heat transfer model

The transient non-linear heat conduction equation is as follows:

$$\rho c \frac{\partial T}{\partial t} = \lambda \left(\frac{\partial^2 T}{\partial x^2} + \frac{\partial^2 T}{\partial y^2} + \frac{\partial^2 T}{\partial z^2} \right) + \rho L \frac{\partial f_s}{\partial t} + Q_{net} \quad (1)$$

Where T represents temperature; t is time; c is specific heat; L is latent heat; ρ is density; λ is heat conductivity; x, y and z are the coordinates, f_s is mass fraction of solid phase, Q_{net} is net energy exchange between body and external environment, Q_{net} is 0 for the interior of the body.

Since only radiative heat transfer occurs between shell mold and furnace wall, it is important to handle the heat radiation boundary condition. According to the law of gray body radiation, the net heat release of a diffuse-gray surface can be calculated as follows:

$$Q_{net,i} = (q_{out,i} - q_{in,i}) A_i \quad (2)$$

Where, $q_{out,i}$ is outgoing radiation energy flux of surface i, $q_{in,i}$ is radiation energy being received, A_i represents the surface area.

The incoming radiation energy is a combination of the outgoing radiant energy from all the surfaces being visible to surface i. The view factor φ_{i-j} is the ratio of radiant energy leaving from surface j to surface i to all the radiant energy leaving surface j. Thus:

$$q_{in,i} = \sum_{j=1}^{N} \varphi_{i-j} q_{out,j} \quad (3)$$

Where, N is the sum of the surfaces which are visible to surface i. Then the net heat release of surface i can be expressed:

$$Q_{net,i} = A_i \left(q_{out,i} - \sum_{j=1}^{N} \varphi_{i-j} q_{out,j} \right) \quad (4)$$

Although the theory of the net radiation energy can be derived easily, it is hard to deal with the view factor φ_{i-j}. For multiple blades heat radiation exists between shell and shell, between shell and furnace wall and also between the different blades. This will make the calculation of φ_{i-j} more complicated.

In this paper, a numerical method derived from Monte Carlo method[14] was adopted to deal with the heat radiation between every two discrete surfaces. Fig. 1 is a 2D schematics for the calculation of heat radiation between a cell and its visible shell cells or furnace wall. The radiation energy from a cell to the outside is divided averagely by a number of rays distributed uniformly in a semicircle (half sphere for 3D). The reaching end of each ray will be recorded, which maybe is the shell surface cell in the same or different blade, or the furnace wall. Then the temperature of the end of ray will be memorized to calculate the heat radiation along this ray.

$$Q_{net,i} = \sum_{j=1}^{N}(q_{out,i}/N - \varphi_{i-j}q_{out,j})A_i \quad (5)$$

$$Q_{net,i} = \sum_{j=1}^{n}A_i\sigma(T_i^4 - T_j^4)/((1-\varepsilon)/\varepsilon + n) \quad (6)$$

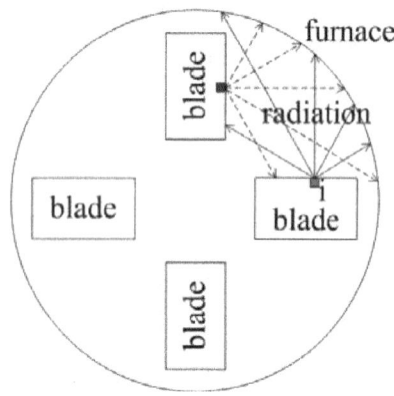

Fig. 1 Schematics for the calculation of heat radiation

where, σ is Stefan-Boltzman constant, ε is emissivity, n is the number of rays, T_i and T_j are temperature. Because the position of the shell surface relative to the furnace wall is changing in the withdrawal process, φ_{i-j} is not constant and changes in every time step. However, for the shell surface and its adjacent visible parts, φ_{i-j} is constant.

For a 3D finite difference surface cell I, there is 1 to 5 surface(s) involved into heat radiation, each of which can transfer heat by radiation with other visual surface cells. So the cell heat exchange by radiation can be expressed:

$$Q_{net,I} = \sum_{i} Q_{net,i} \quad (7)$$

Nucleation model

A continuous nucleation model was employed to calculate the nucleus density in the undercooled melts [8]:

$$n(\Delta T) = \int_0^{\Delta T}[1 - f_S(\Delta T')]\frac{dn}{d(\Delta T')}d(\Delta T') \quad (8)$$

$$\frac{dn}{d(\Delta T')} = \frac{N_{max}}{\sqrt{2\pi}\Delta T_\sigma}\exp\left[-\frac{1}{2}\left(\frac{\Delta T' - \Delta T_N}{\Delta T_\sigma}\right)^2\right] \quad (9)$$

where, N_{max} is the maximum nucleus density, ΔT_σ is the standard deviation of the distribution, ΔT_N is the average nucleation undercooling, $f_S(\Delta T')$ is the fraction of solid phase.

The growth model is based on the CA method. The detail of the CA method can be referred to references [9, 13].

Experimental

The Ni-based superalloy was used for experiments.

Single SX Blade Sample Casting

Before multiple blade castings experiment, single simplified SX blade sample casting was cast through Bridgman process in the laboratory at withdrawal rates of 270mm/h and 420mm/h respectively in order to validate the numerical model of microstructure evolution. The 3D sketch of single SX blade casting is shown in Fig. 2. Both temperature measurement and microstructure observation were carried out to validate the simulation results.

Multiple Turbine Blade Castings

The schematic of Bridgman process for multiple blade casting is shown in Fig. 3. Before casting, the ceramic shell mold with an open bottom of multiple DS/SX turbine blades was fixed on water-cooled copper chill and heated to a specified temperature. After pouring, the copper chill and the ceramic mold were withdrawn at a predetermined rate, v, from the heating zone to the cooling zone. The upper portion of mold above the baffle remained hot while the lower part of mold below it was cooled by water cooling unit and radiation.

Multiple DS and SX blades, placed on the chill plate with circular distribution, were cast at the rate of 200mm/h. There were 4 thermocouples placed on the surface of one of multiple blades for each case, as shown in Fig. 4, to record the temperatures. In DS blade, points 1 and 3 were at outboard side of blade with circular distribution, far from the center of the furnace, while points 2 and 4 were close to the center. In SX blade, points 3 was at outboard side and point 4 was at inboard side, points 1 and 2 were placed along the center line of the blade surface at different height.

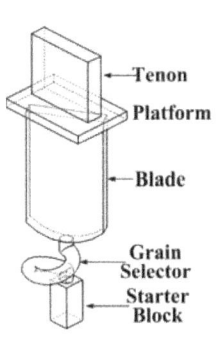 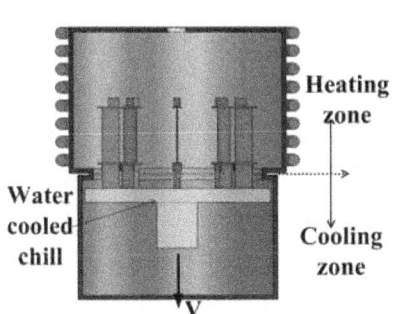 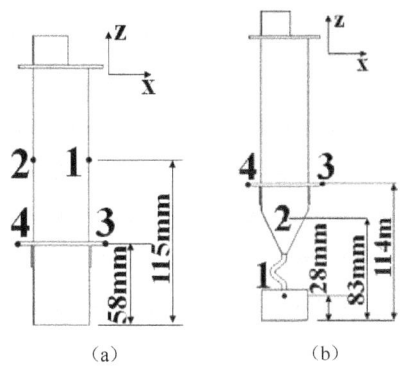

Fig. 2 3D sketch of single SX blade sample casting

Fig. 3 Directional solidification process of multiple turbine blade castings

Fig. 4 Sketch of thermocouple positions in the multiple blade castings
(a) DS model (b) SX model

Results

Single SX Blade Sample Casting

The simulated temperature distribution of single simplified SX blade sample casting was validated by the experimental results and agreed well. The crystal growth interface of single SX blade castings at different withdrawal rates is shown in Fig. 5. With the increase of withdrawal rate the curvature of solidification front increased gradually. When the withdrawal rate stepped from 270mm/h up to 420mm/h, remarkably concave growth interface appeared. When the whole solidification fraction went up to about 60%, the solidification front reached the bottom of the platform. Then, the nucleation of new grains occurred at the corners of platform of turbine blade casting at withdrawal rates of 420mm/h as shown in Fig. 5 (d). During the following stage of solidification, newly nucleated grains grew up and finally formed structure defects such as high angle boundaries (HAB). Experimental results of final microstructure in the platform are shown in Fig. 6. It can be seen that high angle boundaries were not found in turbine blade casting at the withdrawal rate of 270mm/h, as shown in Fig. 6 (a), while they existed in turbine blade casting at 420mm/h as shown in Fig. 6 (b).

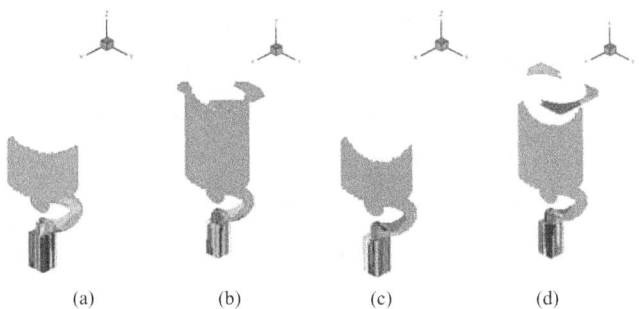 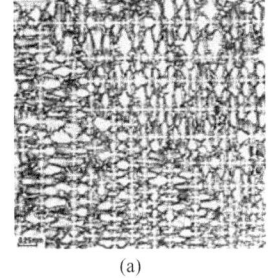 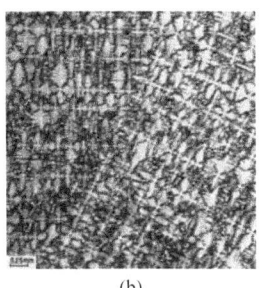

Fig. 5 Simulated microstructure evolution of single SX blade casting
(a) and (b) v=270mm/h, (c) and (d) v=420mm/h
(a) and (c) solidification fraction: 40%,
(b) and (d) solidification fraction: 60%

Fig. 6 Final microstructure in the platform of single SX blade casting at different withdrawal rates.
(a) v=270mm/h, no HAB
(b) v=420mm/h, HAB observed

Multiple Turbine Blade Castings

Cooling Curves. Fig. 7 shows the comparison between the experimental and calculated cooling curves of multiple DS blade castings at four positions. From Fig. 7, it can be seen that the calculated cooling curves agree well with the experimental ones. In the DS blade casting, the body of blade is symmetrical. Points 1 and 2 are at the same height and the points 3 and 4 as well. For the circular distribution of multiple blade castings, points 1 and 3 are close to the heater of the furnace and there exists great heat radiation between outside of the blade and the heater, while points 2 and 4 are in the inside of the circle and face other blades and the chill plate. As the blades were withdrawn with chill plate from heating zone to cooling zone, more radiation heat can loose from outside of the blades than the inside. As a result, the unsymmetrical heat boundary causes the great temperature difference between the different positions along the horizontal positions, as shown in Fig. 7 (b).

Fig. 8 shows the comparison between the experimental and calculated cooling curves of multiple SX blade castings at four positions. For SX blade point 3 is located at the outside, while point 4 inside. Great temperature difference occurs between point 3 and 4 because of the same reason as DS blade. From the cooling curves it can be seen that the simulated results are very close with the experimental ones.

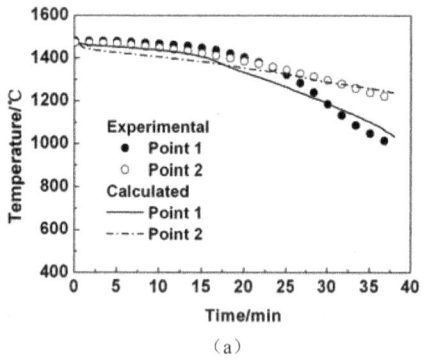 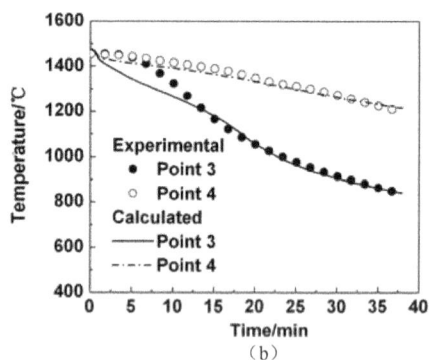

Fig. 7 Comparisons between calculated and measured cooling curves of multiple DS blade castings
(a) Points 1 and 2 (b) Points 3 and 4

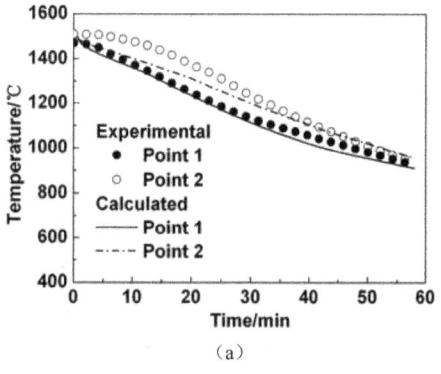 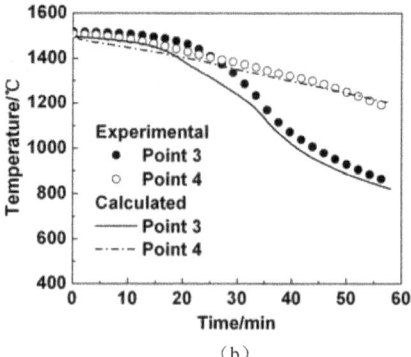

Fig. 8 Comparisons between calculated and measured cooling curves of multiple SX blade castings
(a) Points 1 and 2 (b) Points 3 and 4

Temperature Distribution. Fig. 9 shows the temperature distribution of multiple DS blade castings in the solidification at the withdrawal rate of 200mm/h. It can be seen that the isothermal lines are not horizontal. The temperature of the outside of the blade is lower than that of the inside due to the interaction among the multiple blades. On the solidification interface, the outboard temperature is still lower than that of the inboard side.

Fig. 10 shows the temperature distribution of multiple SX blade castings in solidification process at the withdrawal rate of 200mm/h. Similar with the DS model the solid/liquid interface is uneven. The outside of the interface is higher than the inside, and the outside temperature in front of the interface is lower than the inside, which agrees well with the experimental cooling curves.

Growth Interface. The simulated and experimental results of microstructure of the multiple DS blade castings are shown in Fig. 11. In the root of the blade, the grains grow upward directionally. Where there is abrupt change of blade section, the isothermal lines become uneven, which may lead to the new grains formation in the corner. During the growth process, the growth interface remains uneven. Fig. 11 (d) is the microstructure of a real DS blade casting from the experiment. It can be seen that the prediction result of microstructure is similar to that of the experimental result.

Fig. 12 shows the simulated results of grain growth of the multiple SX blade castings at the withdrawal rate 200mm/h. It can be seen that after only one grain grew upward out of the grain selector, new nucleation could form at the corner of the abrupt change of the blade section. Further experiments of microstructure evolution are in process.

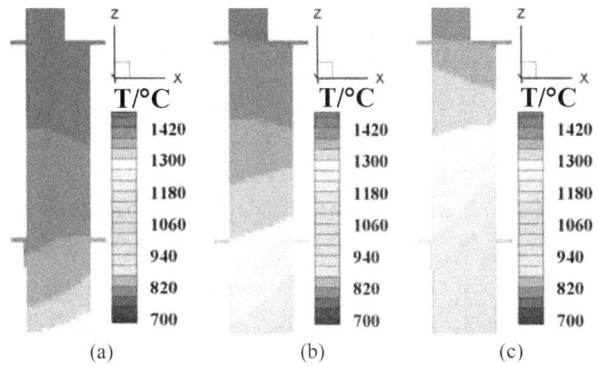

Fig. 9 Temperature distribution of multiple DS blade castings at different solidification time
(a) 10min (b) 20min (c) 30min

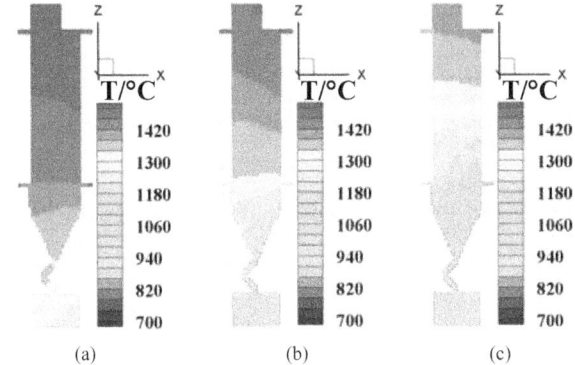

Fig. 10 Temperature distribution of multiple SX blades at different solidification time
(a) 15min (b) 30min (c) 45min

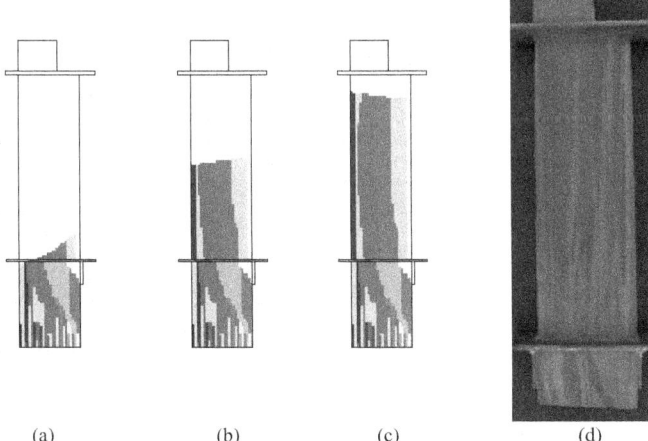

Fig. 11 Microstructure of multiple DS blade castings
(a), (b), (c) simulated results at different solidification time, (d) experimental result
(a) 10min (b) 20min (c) 30min

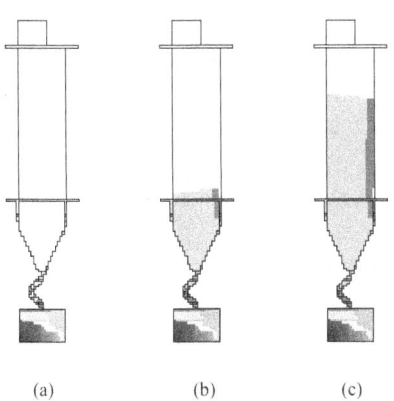

Fig. 12 Microstructure evolution of multiple SX blade castings at different solidification time
(a) 15min (b) 30min (c) 45min

Therefore, the simulated results of temperature distribution and microstructure evolution are helpful to optimize process parameters and to improve the turbine blade casting quality.

Conclusions

A mathematical model for 3D simulation of directional solidification and microstructure evolution of superalloy turbine blade castings was developed based on CA-FD method considering complex radiative heat transfer boundary condition. The numerical simulation has been carried out for the directional solidification process of single SX blade sample casting and multiple turbine blade castings respectively. The calculated cooling curves have been compared with the experimental ones and agreed well. The simulation results of microstructure evolution of single SX blade sample casting and multiple DS blade castings were validated by experimental results.

Acknowledgements

The research is financially supported by National Basic Research Program of China (No. 2005CB724105), NSF of China (No. 10477010) and IHI Research Funds.

References

[1] R. J. Naumann, "An Analytical Approach to Thermal Modeling of Bridgman-type Crystal Growth," *J. Cryst. Growth.*, 58 (1982), 554-568.

[2] K. O. Yu, "Solidification Modeling of Complex-Shaped Single Crystal Turbine Airfoils" (Paper presented at the Proceedings of the 7th International Symposium on Superalloys, Champion, PA, U.S.A., 20 September 1992), 135.

[3] Masatoshi Saitou, and Akira Hirata, "Numerical Calculation of Two-Dimensional Unsteady Solidification Problem," *J. Cryst. Growth.*, 113 (1991), 147-156.

[4] L. M. Galantucci, "A Computer-Aided Approach for the Simulation of the Directional-Solidification Process for Gas Turbine Blades," *J. Mater. Process. Tech.*, 77 (1998), 160-165.

[5] D. Wang et al., "Computer Heat Transfer Model for Directionally Solidified Castings" (Paper presented at the Proceedings of the Conference on Computational Modeling of Materials, Minerals and Metals Processing, San Diego, U.S.A., 23 September 2001), 461.

[6] Jiarong Li, and Shizhong Liu, "Solidification Simulation of Investment Castings Single Crystal Hollow Turbine Blade," *J. Mater. Sci. Technol.*, 19 (6) (2003), 532-534.

[7] H. W. Hesselbarth and I. R. Gobel, "Simulation of Recrystallization by Cellular Automata," *Acta Metall.*, 39 (1991), 2135-2143.

[8] M. Rappaz, "Probabilistic Modelling of Microstructure Formation in Solidification Processes," *Acta Metall. Mater.*, 41 (2) (1993), 345-360.

[9] Q. Y. Xu, W. M. Feng and B. C. Liu, "A Coupled Macro-Micro Simulation for Prediction of Microstructure of Al Alloy Castings" (Paper presented at the Proceedings of the 10th International Conference on Modeling of Casting, Welding and Advanced Solidification Processes, Destin, U.S.A., 25 May 2003), 149.

[10] Kermanpur. A, and Rappaz. M, "Thermal and Grain-Structure Simulation in a Land-Based Turbine Blade Directionally Solidified With the Liquid Metal Cooling Process," *Metal. Mater. Trans. B*, 31 (6) (2000), 1293-1304.

[11] P. D. Lee et al., "A Model of Solidification Microstructures in Nickel-Based Superalloys: Predicting Primary Dendrite Spacing Selection," *Acta Mater.*, 51 (2003), 2971-2987.

[12] P. Carter et al., "Process Modeling of Grain Selection During the Solidification of Single Crystal Superalloy Castings," *Mat. Sci. Eng.* A280 (2000), 233-246.

[13] Z. J. Liang, "Numerical Simulation of Solidification Process and Microstructure Formation of Investment Castings of Superalloy" (Ph. D. thesis, Tsinghua University, 2003).

[14] Robert Siegel, John R. Howell, *Thermal Radiation Heat Transfer*, 3rd Edition (U.S.A.: Braun-Brumfield, Inc. 1992).

8. Numerical Simulation of Solidification Process on Single Crystal Ni-Based Superalloy Investment Castings

Jing YU[1], *Qingyan XU*[1], *Kai CUI*[1], *Baicheng LIU*[1], *Akihiko KIMATSUKA*[2], *Yasunori KUROKI*[2] *and Atsushi HIRATA*[2]

[1] Key Laboratory for Advanced Materials Processing Technology, Ministry of Education, Department of Mechanical Engineering, Tsinghua University, Beijing 100084, China

[2] Ishikawajima-Harima Heavy Industries Co., Ltd., Isogo-Ku, Yokohama 235-8501, Japan [Manuscript received October 27, 2005, in revised form April 17, 2006]

Bridgman directional solidification of investment castings is a key technology for the production of reliable and highly efficient gas turbine blades. In this paper, a mathematical model for three-dimensional (3D) simulation of solidification process of single crystal investment castings was developed based on basic heat transfer equations. Complex heat radiation among the multiple blade castings and the furnace wall was considered in the model. Temperature distribution and temperature gradient in superalloy investment castings of single blade and multiple ones were investigated, respectively. The calculated cooling curves were compared with the experimental results and agreed well with the latter. It is indicated that the unsymmetrical temperature distribution and curved liquid-solid interface caused by the circle distribution of multiple turbine blades are probably main reasons why the stray grain and other casting defects occur in the turbine blade.

Key words: Directional solidification; Single crystal; Investment casting; Numerical simulation

1. Introduction

Single crystal (SX) Ni-based superalloy turbine blade castings have been widely used in advanced gas turbines for aeronautics and energy industries as well. It is necessary to control the processing conditions during directional solidification to avoid the formation of deleterious casting defects such as stray crystal, freckle, sliver and microporosity. Although the casting technology of advanced gas turbine blades was developed by trail and error in the past, numerical simulation is an effective and powerful tool to help us understand the fundamental of microstructure evolution during directional solidification process and the formation of deleterious casting defects.

Great efforts have been put into studying directional solidification process by numerical simulation in the last two decades. Original researches focused on one-dimensional (1D) model[1-4]. Yu et al.[5,6] studied the directional solidification process through commercial finite element method (FEM) software and developed the defects map which represented the correlation between the thermal gradient and casting defects. A two-dimensional (2D) model was developed by Saitou and Hirata[7] to analyze the shape of liquid-solid interface in Bridgman directional solidification. Galantucci and Tricarico[8] investigated the directional solidification process of turbine blades through 2D FEM with comparison of experimental results. In consideration of heat conduction and radiation, Wang and Overfelt[9] presented a new 2D model which considered the variational radiation view factor with the withdrawal process. Zhu et al.[10] focused on the boundary of heat radiation in directional solidification and developed the software package using regular and irregular mixed grids. Li et al.[11,12] investigated the solidification process of single crystal investment castings by ProCast, a commercial software. Liang et al.[13] simulated the directional solidification process of single turbine blade based on 3D finite difference method (FDM) model.

However, compared with the situation in single turbine blade casting, more complex heat transfer will occur between blades and furnace in the directional solidification of multiple turbine blades (that is the main technology for gas turbines to increase the productivity), and few of research work considered the multiple turbine blades interaction.

In this paper, 3D modeling on the basis of FDM method was performed to simulate the solidification of single crystal Ni-based superalloy investment castings. The simulation results of solidification process of single blade and multiple ones were compared with the experimental results, respectively. According to the simulation results, some suggestions were given to improve the directional process.

2. Physical Model

The schematics of the directional solidification process for single crystal turbine blade is shown in Fig. 1.

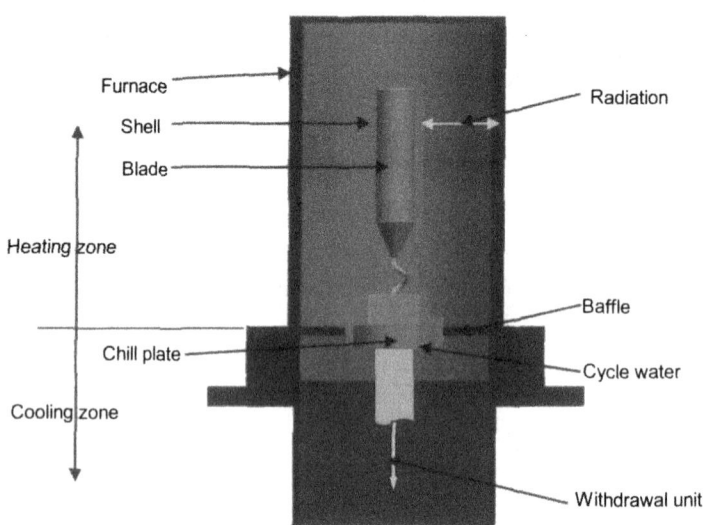

Fig. 1　Schematics of directional solidification process of superalloy turbine blade

The directional solidification process of superalloy investment castings can be described as follows: (1) The mold shell and the water-cooled copper chill plate are preheated to a given temperature. (2) Superalloy melt is poured from the top of the mold and then held for a certain time to keep the uniform temperature distribution. (3) Copper chill plate, mold shell and the high temperature superalloy melt are withdrawn from the heating zone to the cooling zone. During the withdrawal process, the heat transfers from the mold shell to the furnace wall by radiation and from melt to the shell and the chill plate by complex heat transfer. At the same time, the heat is conducted from the chill plate to the cycle-cooled water. (4) When all the parts enter into the cooling zone, the heat transfer continues and the blade completes the solidification process. (5) Due to the chill effect of the copper plate, the nucleation occurs in the melt near the plate and the grains grow continuously with the drop of the local temperature. When the grains grow into the grain selector, there is only one grain allowed to grow out of it. With the advancing of the withdrawal process, the final single crystal blade will be obtained.

In general, the heat transfer during the directional solidification process is determined by the heat conduction in the casting, mold shell and copper chill plate, heat convection between the casting and the mold shell and copper plate, heat radiation between the outside surface of the mold shell and furnace wall, etc.

3. Mathematical Models

The transient nonlinear heat conduction equation is as follows:

$$\rho c \frac{\partial T}{\partial t} = \lambda \left(\frac{\partial^2 T}{\partial x^2} + \frac{\partial^2 T}{\partial y^2} + \frac{\partial^2 T}{\partial z^2} \right) + \rho L \frac{\partial f_s}{\partial t} + Q_{net} \quad (1)$$

where T represents temperature, t is time, c is specific heat, L is latent heat, ρ is density, λ is heat conductivity, x, y and z are the coordinates, f_s is mass fraction of solid phase and Q_{net} is net energy exchange by radiation between body and external environment. Q_{net} is 0 for the interior of the body.

Since only radiative heat transfer occurs between shell mold and furnace, it is important to deal with the heat radiation boundary condition. According to the law of gray body radiation, the net heat radiation exchange between two gray bodies, Q_{net}, can be expressed by the following equation based on Stefan-Boltzman law[14]:

$$Q_{net} = A_1 \sigma (T_1^4 - T_2^4) / \left(\frac{1-\varepsilon_1}{\varepsilon_1} + \frac{1}{\varphi_{1,2}} + \frac{A_1}{A_2} \cdot \frac{1-\varepsilon_2}{\varepsilon_2} \right) \quad (2)$$

where ε_1 and ε_2 are emissivities of the gray bodies 1 and 2, respectively, $\varphi_{1,2}$ is view factor between two gray bodies, T_1 is the temperature of gray body 1, T_2 is temperature of gray body 2, A_1 and A_2 are areas of two visible surfaces of gray bodies, respectively, and σ is Stefan-Boltzman constant. $\varphi_{1,2}$ can be calculated as

$$\varphi_{1,2} = \frac{C_V}{A_1} \int_{A_2} \int_{A_1} \frac{\cos\theta_2 \cos\theta_1}{\pi R^2} dA_1 dA_2 \quad (3)$$

where θ_1 and θ_2 are the angle between the normal line of the surface of gray bodies and the line connecting the two bodies, respectively, R is distance between the two visible surface and C_V is visibility. C_V is 0 for non-visibility and 1 for visibility.

Although the analytical model of heat radiation is clear, it is hard to deal with the view factor of a real casting by numerical method. It needs large memory to store the view factors between every two surfaces of different cells and long CPU time to deal with various view factor every time step.

In this paper, a numerical method derived from Monte Carlo method[15] was adopted to deal with the heat radiation between every two discrete surfaces. For the discrete surface i, such as a surface of a finite difference element, the net heat exchange, $Q_{net,i}$, can be calculated as

$$Q_{net,i} = (q_{out,i} - q_{in,i}) A_i \quad (4)$$

where, $q_{out,i}$ is outgoing radiation energy flux of surface i, $q_{in,i}$ is radiation energy being received, A_i represents the surface area.

The incoming radiation energy is a combination of the outgoing radiant energy from all the surfaces being visible to surface i. The view factor φ_{i-j} is the ratio of radiant energy leaving from surface j to surface i to all the radiant energy leaving surface j. Thus:

$$q_{in,i} = \sum_{j=1}^{\infty} \varphi_{i-j} q_{out,j} \quad (5)$$

Then the net, heat release of surface i can be expressed as

$$Q_{net,i} = A_i \left(q_{out,i} - \sum_{j=1}^{\infty} \varphi_{i-j} q_{out,j} \right) \quad (6)$$

In Eq. (6), the second part is still hard to deal with numerically because of the large amount of visible surfaces j. The surfaces j may be scattered all around the surface i. So we divide the space enclosing the surface i regularly into limited domains where all surfaces j can locate. The number of domains is set with consideration of computation speed and efficiency. The surfaces located in the same domain could be considered as a single surface with average temperature T_{domain}. The net heat radiation exchange between surface i and a domain, $Q_{net,i\text{-}domain}$, can be derived from Eq. (2). The area of domain is larger than the discrete surface i. The view factors between the surface i and each domain are equal because we consider that outgoing energy from surface i to each domain is uniform. Based on Eq. (2), $Q_{net,i\text{-}domain}$ can be expressed as

$$Q_{net,i\text{-}domain} = A_i \sigma (T_i^4 - T_{domain}^4) / \left(\frac{1-\varepsilon_i}{\varepsilon_i} + \frac{1}{\varphi_{i,domain}} \right) \quad (7)$$

Then the $Q_{net,i}$ can be regarded as sum of net heat radiation exchange between surface i and each domain, seen in Eq. (8).

$$Q_{net,i} = \sum_{domain=1}^{n} Q_{net,i\text{-}domain} \quad (8)$$

where n domains are labeled by n rays from center of surface i to outer space. Figure 2 is a 2D schematics for the calculation of heat radiation between a cell and its visible cells or furnace wall. The rays are distributed uniformly in a semicircle (half sphere for 3D) space. The reaching end of each ray will be recorded, which may be the shell surface cell in the same or different blade, or the furnace wall. Then the temperature of the nearest end of ray will be memorized and regarded as the temperature of the domain.

A 3D FDM was adopted to solve the basic heat transfer equation. For a 3D finite difference cell I on the surface of shell, there may be 1 to 5 surface(s) involved into heat radiation, each of which can transfer heat by radiation with other visual surface cells. So the cell heat exchange by radiation can be expressed as:

$$Q_{net,I} = \sum_i Q_{net,i} \tag{9}$$

The simulation program was built with Visual C++ 6.0 by the author.

4. Experimental

Two experimental groups were carried out with Ni-based superalloy. One was for single turbine blade and the other for multiple blades. Figure 3 (a) and (b) show the 2D models of single blade and multiple ones, respectively. For the multiple blades, the normal line of the narrow plane was parallel to the radial direction of the furnace, shown in Fig. 3 (c). Both groups were withdrawn at the rate of 200mm/h. Thermocouples were placed on the surface of a blade in Fig. 3 (a) and (b) to record the temperatures. In Fig. 3 (a), thermocouples 1 and 2 were placed on the blade surface at different height. In Fig. 3 (b), thermocouple 3 was at outside, close to the furnace wall, and 4 was at inside, close to the center of the furnace; 1 and 2 were placed along the center line of the blade surface at different heights.

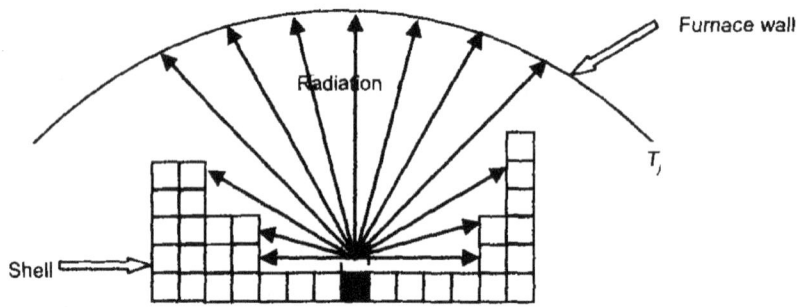

Fig. 2 Schematics for the calculation of heat radiation

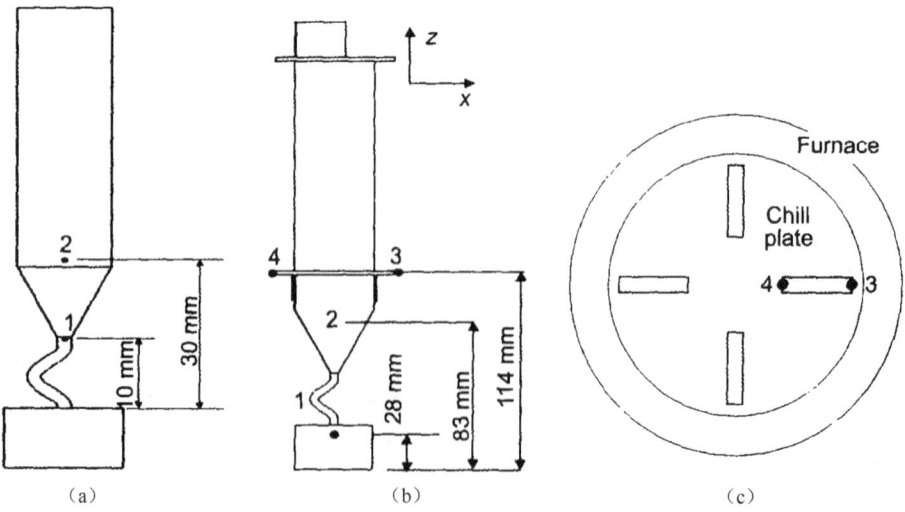

Fig. 3 Sketch of the thermocouple positions in the castings: (a) single blade, (b) multiple blades, (c) top view of multiple blades

5. Results and Discussion

5.1 Cooling curves

Figure 4 shows the comparison between the experimental and calculated cooling curves of single blade. Table 1 shows quantitative comparison between simulation and experimental results of single blade. From Fig. 4 and Table 1, it can be seen that the calculated cooling curves agreed well with the experimental ones and the maximum error between the experimental data and calculation is less than 5%.

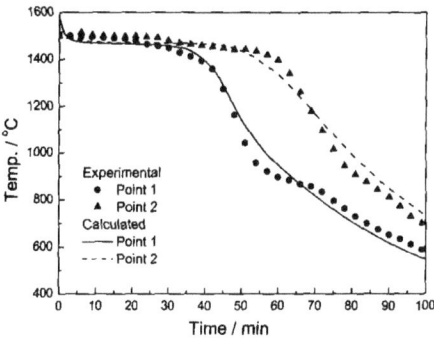

Fig. 4 Comparison between calculated and measured cooling curves of single blade at points 1 and 2

Figure 5 and Table 2 show the comparison between the experimental and calculated cooling curves of multiple blades at four positions. For the circle distribution of multiple blades, point 3 is close to the furnace and there is great heat radiation between outside of the blade and furnace both in heating zone and cooling zone, while point 4 is in the inside of the circle and faces other blades and the chill plate. As the blades are withdrawn with chill plate from heating zone into cooling zone, more radiation heat can dissipate from outside of the blades than the inside. Although the blade is geometrically symmetrical, the unsymmetrical heat boundary causes the great temperature difference between the different positions along the horizontal line. For multiple blades, points 1 and 2 are along the center line of the blade surface and different distance in vertical direction causes the temperature difference. The cooling curves demonstrate that the modeling results are very close to the experimental data, and the error between experimental data and calculation is less than 5%.

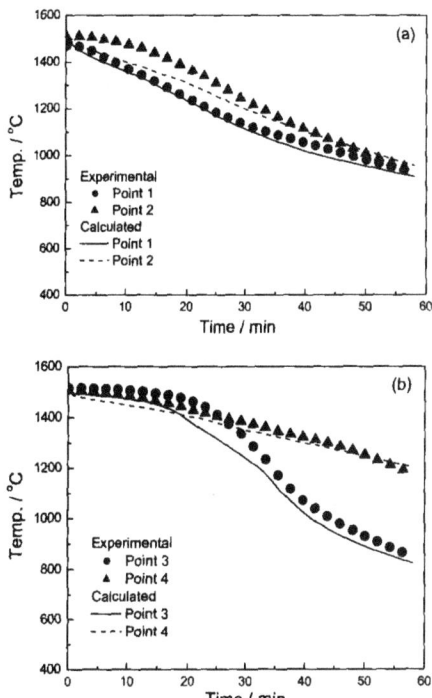

Fig. 5 Comparison between calculated and measured cooling curves of multiple blades: (a) points 1 and 2, (b) points 3 and 4

5.2 Temperature and temperature gradient distribution of single blade

Figure 6 shows the temperature distribution of single blade at different solidification time. At current withdrawal rate, the solidification front was very flat, the temperature isothermal line along transverse section was flat, and there was almost no temperature difference. This will help to avoid the formation of the stray crystal.

Table 1 Comparison of calculated and experimental results of single blade

Time/min	25			50			75			100		
	Exp.	Cal.	Err.	Exp.	Cal.	Err.	Exp.	Cal.	Err.	Exp.	Cal.	Err.
Point 1	1462	1462	0	1102	1143	3.7	796	759	-4.6	585	561	-4.1
Point 2	1495	1470	-1.7	1438	1436	-0.1	1035	1077	4.0	689	720	4.4

Notes: Exp.-experimental (℃), Cal.-calculated (℃), Err.-error (%)

Table 2 Comparison of calculated and experimental results of SX blade

Time/min	15			30			45			60		
	Exp.	Cal.	Err.	Exp.	Cal.	Err.	Exp.	Cal.	Err.	Exp.	Cal.	Err.
Point 1	1314	1299	−1.1	1132	1113	−1.7	1018	984	−3.3	922	910	−1.3
Point 2	1436	1367	−4.8	1235	1199	−2.9	1060	1060	0	935	956	2.2
Point 3	1494	1428	−4.8	1308	1249	−4.5	991	943	−4.8	851	822	−3.4
Point 4	1463	1449	−1.0	1381	1351	−2.2	1291	1273	−1.4	1176	1201	2.1

Figure 7 shows the variation of the longitudinal temperature gradient. From the modeling results we can see that the longitudinal temperature gradient in the mushy zone, which appears near the baffle, is larger than in the liquid metal. The temperature gradient is almost flat in the transverse section with the temperature distribution.

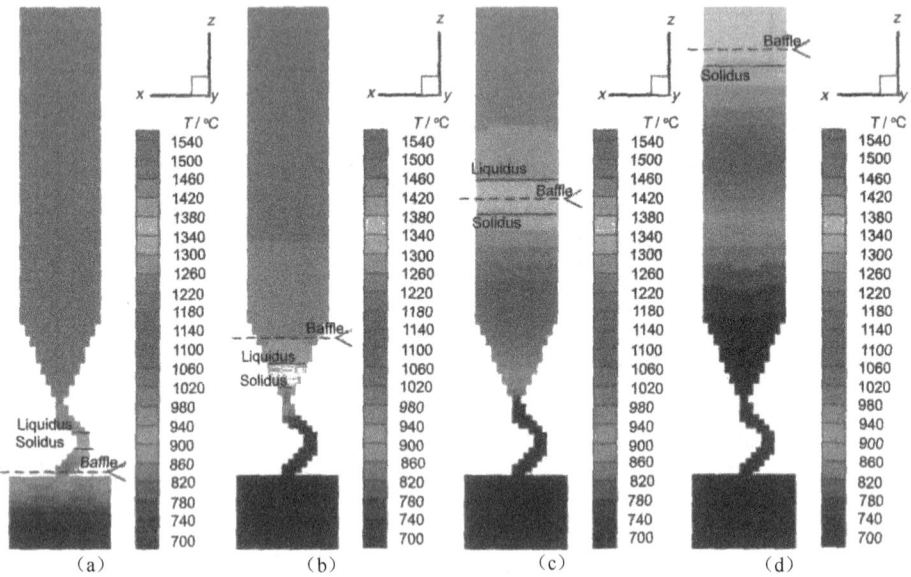

Fig. 6 Temperature distribution of single blade at different solidification time: (a) 25min, (b) 50min, (c) 75min, (d) 100min

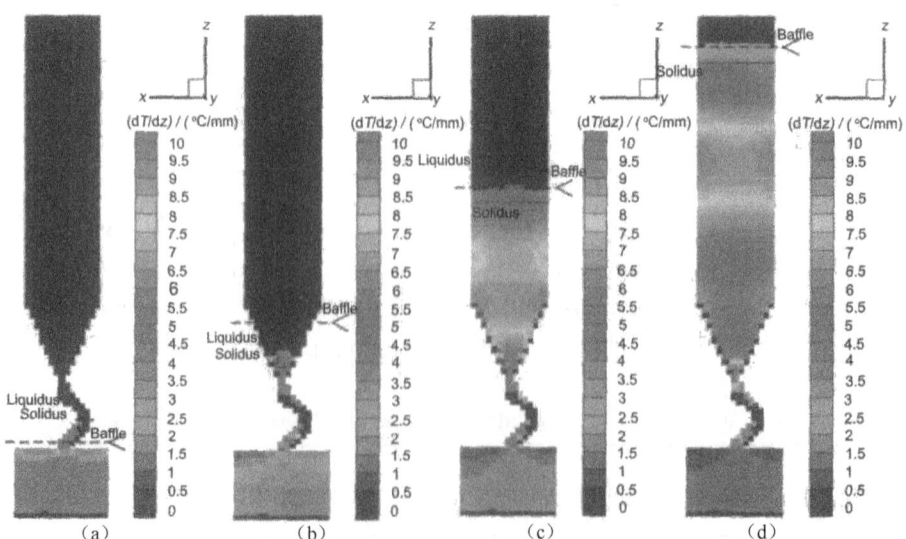

Fig. 7 Temperature gradient distribution of single blade at different solidification time:
(a) 25min, (b) 50min, (c) 75min, (d) 100min

5.3 Temperature and temperature gradient distribution of multiple blades

Figure 8 is the temperature distribution of multiple blades in solidification process at the withdrawal rate of 200mm/h. It can be seen that the isothermal lines are not horizontal compared with the single blade. The temperature of the right side of the blade below the baffle, which is close to furnace wall, is much lower than that of the left side which is close to the center of the furnace. This is due to the interaction among the multiple blades. In the cooling zone stronger radiation exists between the outside of the blade and furnace wall than that between the inside and the furnace wall because of the baffled action of other blades. But in the heating zone the outside is close to the heating unit of the furnace and could keep the high temperature. The inside of blade in the heating zone could hardly be heated directly by the furnace wall. On the other hand the inside of the blade in the heating zone is influenced by the shell mold covering the whole chill plate. The shell mold on the chill in the middle of the furnace has low temperature because of the heat conduction between the shell mold and the chill plate.

Figure 9 is the longitudinal temperature gradient distribution of the multiple blades during the solidification at the withdrawal rate of 200mm/h. It can be found that the maximum gradient is located at the right side of the blade, i.e. the maximum x value. Compared with the single blade case, the temperature gradient is not symmetrical.

5.4 Temperature field of starter block and grain selector of multiple blades

Figure 10 shows the temperature distribution of the starter block and grain selector of multiple blades. The model's screw part which links the body and starter is grain selector. For single crystal blade, lots of nucleus with different orientations formed after the melt was poured into the shell placed on the chill. The nucleus whose preferential growth direction is parallel to the maximum temperature gradient grows faster than others. After the competitive growth of grains in grain selector, only one grain can grow out from the top of selector and fill the body ideally in the end. When the only grain grows into the body, the temperature difference between the different positions along horizontal line can cause nucleation somewhere, as the undercooling of the liquid reaches a critical value. This may be the main reason why the stray crystal forms.

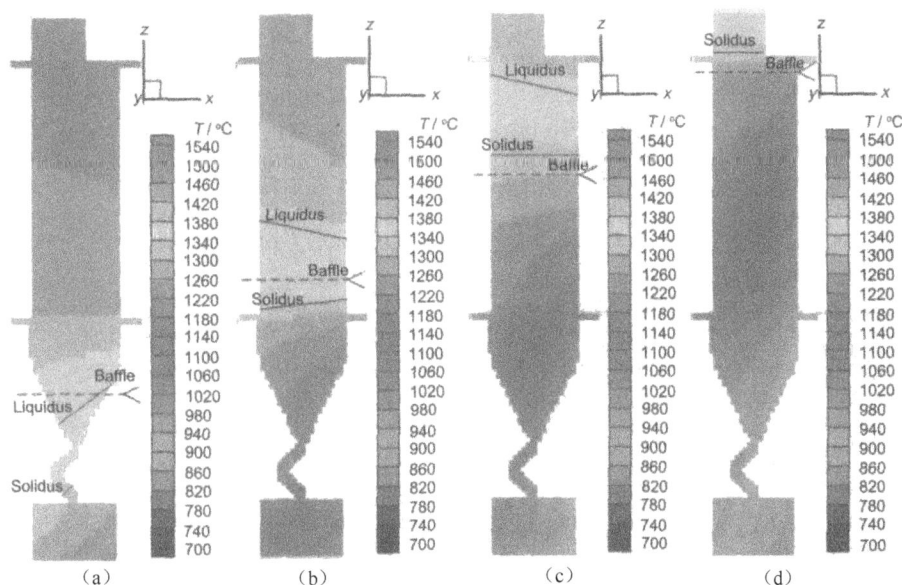

Fig. 8 Temperature distribution of SX multiple blades at different solidification time:
(a) 15min, (b) 30min, (c) 45min, (d) 60min

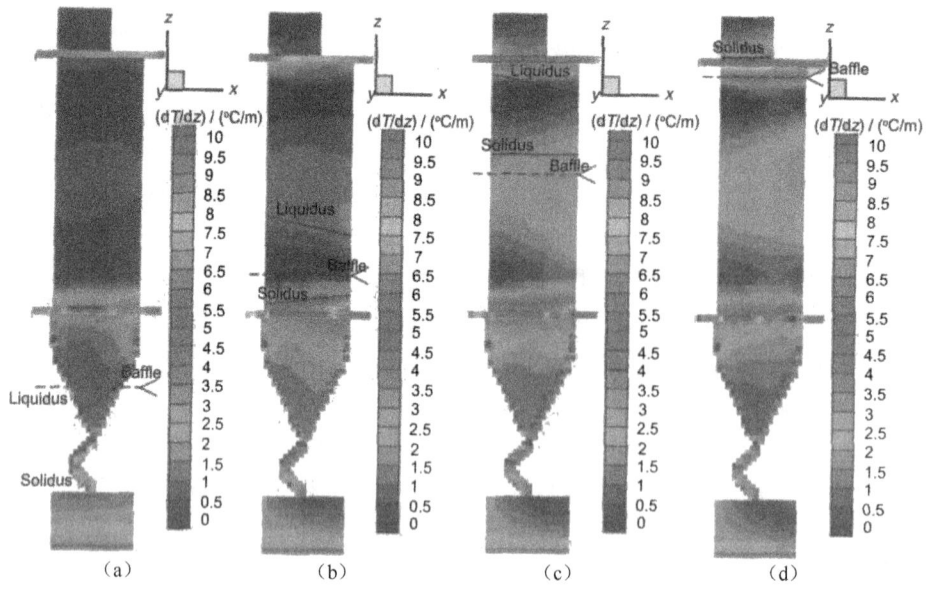

Fig. 9 Temperature gradient distribution of SX multiple blades at different solidification time:
(a) 15min, (b) 30min, (c) 45min, (d) 60min

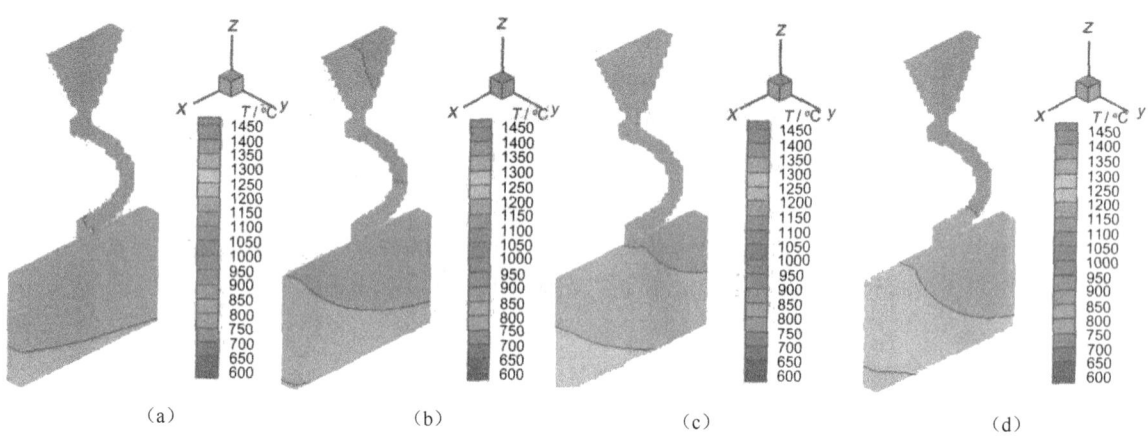

Fig. 10 Temperature distribution of start block of SX multiple blades at different solidification time:
(a) 5min, (b) 10min, (c) 15min, (d) 20min

To decrease and avoid the casting defects especially the stray grain, great efforts should be done to change and reduce the influence of unsymmetrical temperature distribution. We can take some measures as follows: (1) Reflector should be placed between every two blades to decrease the interaction; (2) To avoid the nucleation of new grain, the various withdrawal rate should be used. The blade casting can be withdrawn slowly when the transitional region passes the baffle; (3) For the blade with thin body, the normal line of the wide plane of the blade should be parallel to the radial direction of the furnace and towards the furnace instead of towards other blades. The suggested placement of multiple blades on chill plate was shown in Fig. 11. The temperature difference along the horizontal line could be decreased.

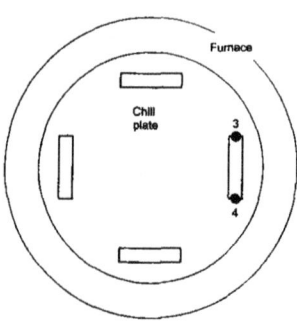

Fig. 11 Proposed placement of multiple blades on the chill plate

Figures 12 and 13 show the temperature and temperature gradient distribution of multiple blades with the proposed distribution of blades as shown in Fig. 11 on the chill plate. Compared with previous distribution the blades rotate 90° along z-axis. The normal line of the wide plane points to the center of the furnace. It can be seen that the temperature and temperature gradient distribution are similar to that of the single blade and the isothermal is almost horizontal. The maximal temperature gradient appears at the liquid-solid interface evenly. This temperature is suitable for the production of single crystal compared with the previous results of multiple blades. The simulation results show that changing the distribution of blades is an effective way for multiple blades investment castings.

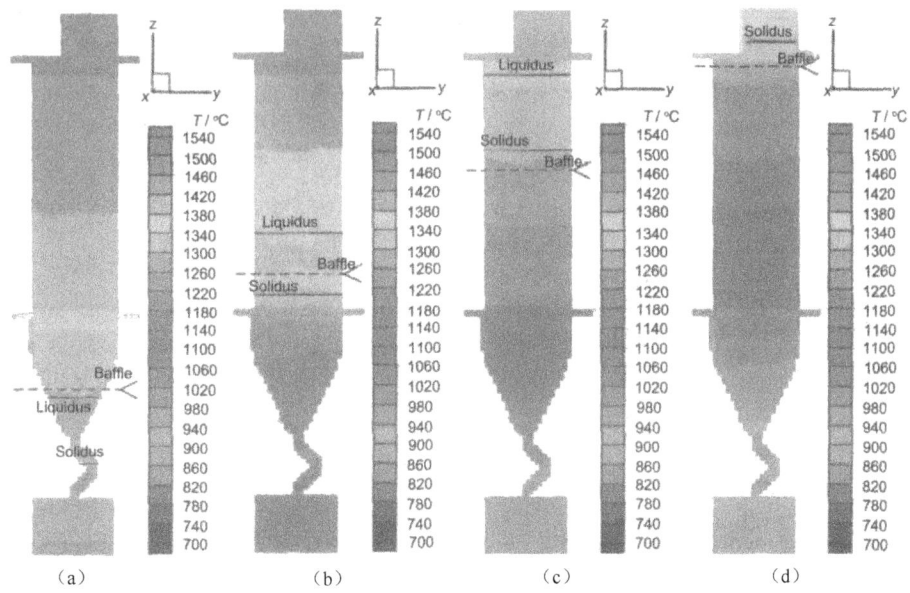

Fig. 12 Temperature distribution of multiple blades at different solidification time with modified blades distribution in Fig. 11: (a) 15min, (b) 30min, (c) 45min, (d) 60min

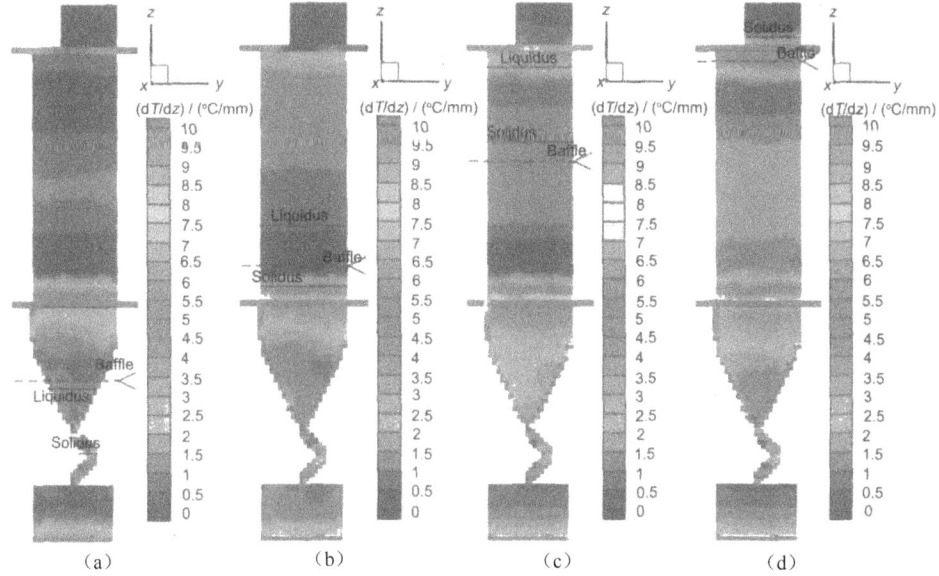

Fig. 13 Temperature gradient distribution of multiple blades at different solidification time with modified blades distribution in Fig. 11: (a) 15min, (b) 30min, (c) 45min, (d) 60min

6. Conclusions

(1) A mathematical model for 3D simulation of directional solidification of multiple turbine blades was developed based on basic heat transfer equations and consideration of radiative heat transfer.

(2) The numerical modeling has been carried out for the solidification process of single blade and multiple ones, respectively. The calculated cooling curves were compared with the experimental ones and agreed well with the latters.

(3) For the single blade, the isothermal lines and growth interface is almost horizontal and axis-symmetrical. For the multiple blades, however, the isothermal lines and solid/liquid interface are uneven to some extent. The blades with circular distribution on the copper plate have lower temperature and cool faster at the outside than inside.

Acknowledgements

This research was financially supported by the National Basic Research Program of China (No. 2005CB724105), the National Natural Science Foundation of China (No. 10477010) and Tsinghua-IHI Research Funds.

REFERENCES

[1] W. R. Wilcox: *J. Cryst. Growth*, 1980, **48**, 416.
[2] R. J. Naumann: *J. Cryst. Growth*, 1982, **58**, 554.
[3] T. Jasinski: *J. Cryst. Growth*, 1983, **61**, 339.
[4] T. Jasinski and R. J. Naumann: *J. Cryst. Growth*, 1984, **66**, 469.
[5] K. O. Yu, M. J. Beffel, M. Robinson, D. D. Goettsch, B. G. Thomas, D. Pinella and R. G. Carlson: *Trans. Am. Found. Soc.*, 1990, **53**, 417.
[6] K. O. Yu, J. A. Oti, M. Robinson and R. G. Carlson: in Proc. 7th Int. Symp. on *Superalloys*, eds. S. D. Antolovich, R. W. Stusrud, R. A. MacKay, D. L. Anton, T. Khan, R. D. Kissinger and D. L. Klarstrom, Champion, PA, USA, 1992, 135.
[7] M. Saitou and A. Hirata: *J. Cryst. Growth*, 1991, **113**, 147.
[8] L. M. Galantucci and L. Tricarico: *J. Mater. Process. Technol.*, 1998, **77**, 160.
[9] D. Wang and R. A. Overfelt: in Proc. Conf. *Compu. Model. Mater., Min. and Met. Process.*, eds. M. Cross and J. W. Evans, San Diego, Japan, 2001, 461.
[10] J. D. Zhu, I. Ohnaka, K. Kudo, S. Obara, A. Kimatsuka, T. M. Wang, F. Kinoshita and T. Murakami: in Proc. 10th Int. Symp. on *Model. Cast. Weld. Adv. Solidification Process.*, ed. D. M. Stefanescu, U. S. A., 2003, 447.
[11] J. R. Li, S. Z. Liu and Z. G. Zhong: *J. Mater. Sci. Technol.*, 2002, **18** (4), 315.
[12] J. R. Li, S. Z. Liu, H. L. Yuan and Z. G. Zhong: *J. Mater. Sci. Technol.*, 2003, **19** (6), 532.
[13] Z. J. Liang, J. R. Li, B. C. Liu, Q. Y. Xu, H. L. Yuan and S. Z. Liu: in *Multiph. Phenom. Model. Simul. Mater. Process.*, eds. TMS, Charlotte, 2004, 227.
[14] Weiheng JIANG: *Heat Transfer* 1st ed., Higher Education Press, Hebei, 1989, 172-190. (in Chinese)
[15] R. Siegel and J. R. Howell: *Thermal Radiation Heat Transfer*, 3rd ed., Braun-Brumfield, Inc., USA, 1992.

9. Modeling of Grain Selection during Directional Solidification of Single Crystal Superalloy Turbine Blade Castings

Dong Pan, Qingyan Xu, Baicheng Liu, Jiarong Li, Hailong Yuan, and Haipeng Jin

Single crystal superalloy turbine blades are currently widely used as key components in gas turbine engines. The single crystal turbine blade casting's properties are quite sensitive to the grain orientation determined directly by the grain selector geometry of the casting. A mathematical model was proposed for the grain selection during directional solidification of turbine blade casting. Based on heat transfer modeling of the directional withdrawing process, the competitive grain growth within the starter block and the spiral of the grain selector were simulated by using the cellular automaton method (CA). Validation experiments were carried out, and the measured results were compared quantitatively with the predicted results. The model could be used to predict the grain morphology and the competitive grain evolution during solidification, together with the distribution of grain orientation of primary <001> dendrite growth direction, with respect to the longitudinal axis of the turbine blade casting.

INTRODUCTION

Currently, single crystal Ni-based superalloy turbine blades produced by Bridgman directional solidification technology are widely used in both aeronautic and energy industries as key components of the gas turbine engines.[1,2] The single crystal turbine blade casting's properties are quite sensitive to the grain orientation determined directly by the grain selector geometry of the casting.[3,4] Numerical simulation technology is used to study the directional solidification process and predict the final microstructure.[5,6]

In this paper, a mathematical model is proposed for the three-dimensional simulation of the directional solidification process of single crystal castings. Based on heat

> **How would you...**
>
> **...describe the overall significance of this paper?**
> A single crystal superalloy turbine blade is one of the key parts of aero-engines, and its properties are quite sensitive to the grain orientation determined by the grain selector geometry. It is of great importance to understand the grain selection behavior and thus improve the blade's properties. Numerical simulation technology was used to reveal the grain selection mechanism within the grain selector and optimize geometry design.
>
> **...describe this work to a materials science and engineering professional with no experience in your technical specialty?**
> The properties of the single crystal superalloy turbine blades are quite sensitive to the grain orientation. The article proposes a mathematical model to predict grain morphology and distribution of grain's primary <001> dendrite growth direction during solidification. The simulated results are quantitatively compared with those of electron backscattered diffraction.
>
> **...describe this work to a layperson?**
> Single crystal superalloy turbine blades are widely being used in aero-engines. The blade's properties are greatly determined by the grain orientation. The grain selection during solidification is studied with a numerical simulation tool and quantitatively compared with experimental results. Modeling and simulation technology for quality control of single crystal superalloy turbine blades will become more significant over the coming years.

transfer modeling of the directional withdrawing process, the competitive grain growth within the starter block and the spiral of the grain selector (as shown in Figure 1) were simulated by using the cellular automaton method (CA). Validation experiments were carried out, and particular attention was paid to the grain morphology and grain orientation of primary <001> dendrite growth direction, with respect to the longitudinal axis of the turbine blade casting. The measured results were compared quantitatively with the predicted values.

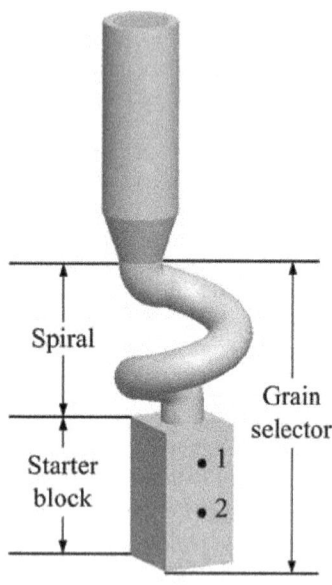

Fig. 1 Schematic of casting shape and thermocouple locations

PHYSICAL AND MATHEMATICAL MODELS

Macro Heat Transfer

As the foundation for the microstructure evolution simulation during directional solidification, the macro temperature distribution was calculated by the transient non-linear heat conduction equation as Equation (1), where T represents the temperature, t is the time, ρ is the density, c is the specific heat, L is the latent heat, λ is the heat conductivity, x, y and z are the coordinates; f_s is the mass fraction of solid phase, Q_R is the heat exchange between the casting surface and the ambient environment by radiation (Note that all equations are given in the table.)

It is difficult to calculate the heat radiation in directional solidification because of the memory required to store the view factors for each surface cell against others. In this paper, a numerical approach derived from Monte Carlo methods was adopted to deal with the radiation in directional solidification, with less memory required and higher accuracy. The details can be found in Reference [6].

Microstructure Nucleation and Growth

The microstructure simulation was based on the modified CA method.[7] A continuous nucleation model[8] was employed to calculate the nucleus number in the undercooled melts as given in Equations (2) and (3); where ΔT is the undercooling, $n(\Delta T)$ is the nucleus density, N_{max} is the maximum nucleus density, ΔT_σ is the standard deviation of the distribution, ΔT_N is the average nucleation undercooling, $f_s(\Delta T')$ is the fraction of solid phase.

Equations

$$\rho c \frac{\partial T}{\partial t} = \lambda \left(\frac{\partial^2 T}{\partial x^2} + \frac{\partial^2 T}{\partial y^2} + \frac{\partial^2 T}{\partial z^2} \right) + \rho L \frac{\partial f_s}{\partial t} + Q_R \quad (1)$$

$$n(\Delta T) = \int_0^{\Delta T} [1 - f_S(\Delta T')] \frac{dn}{d(\Delta T')} d(\Delta T') \quad (2)$$

$$\frac{dn}{d(\Delta T')} = \frac{N_{max}}{\sqrt{2\pi}\Delta T_\sigma} \exp\left[-\frac{1}{2} \left(\frac{\Delta T' - \Delta T_N}{\Delta T_\sigma} \right)^2 \right] \quad (3)$$

$$v(\Delta T) = \alpha_1 \cdot \Delta T^2 + \alpha_2 \cdot \Delta T^3 \quad (4)$$

The grain growth was calculated based on the KGT model[9] with a simplification.[10] The growth speed of the dendrite tip was calculated as Equation 4; where α_1 and α_2 are the coefficients.

Competitive Growth of Grains

In this model, each grain's orientation was randomly determined. Nevertheless, the growth velocity of the grain tip was equally calculated by the temperature gradient in front of the dendrite tip. Therefore, the grains which were not well-aligned with respect to the maximum gradient of the temperature field would grow at a much slower speed than those which were best aligned, which made them grow behind the growth front. This made it possible for those well-aligned grains to have their secondary and tertiary side arms grow out and occupy the space just in front of the less well-aligned grains, as shown in Figure 2. This is known as the grain's competitive growth.

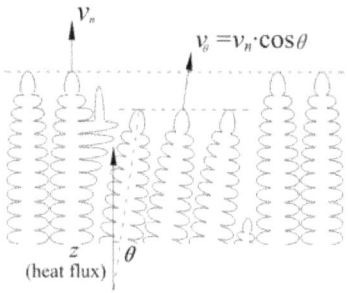

Fig. 2 Schematic of grain competitive growth.

EXPERIMENTAL PROCEDURE

Validation experiments of single crystal Ni-based superalloy casting were carried out. Cooling curves at different positions of the casting during directional solidification and the casting's final microstructures were measured and compared with the simulated results quantitatively. In the experiment, a group of three castings were produced together by the Bridgman directional solidification process, seen in Figure 3, for the schematic principle. The directional solidification furnace consists of a heating zone at the top, a cooling zone at the bottom, and a baffle in the middle to separate the heating and cooling zone, thus obtaining a steady high temperature gradient for the casting. At the beginning, the casting shell was placed on the top surface of the water-cooled chill plate, and heated by the heating zone for a certain time. After the melt metal was poured into the shell, the chill plate was withdrawn at a certain rate into the cooling zone. The withdrawal rate used in the experiment was 3.5mm/min. Thermocouples were placed on the surface of the casting for the temperature measurement. The casting shape and thermocouple locations are shown in Figure 1. The height of the casting is about 180mm.

The casting material used in the experiment was the DD6 Ni-based single crystal superalloy, nominal compositions[11] shown in Table 1.

Table 1 Nominal Compositions of DD6 Superalloy (wt.%)

Co	W	Ta	Al	Cr	Mo
9.0	8.0	7.5	5.6	4.3	2.0
Re	Nb	Hf	C	Ni	Ni
2.0	0.5	0.1	0.006	-The rest-	

RESULTS AND DISCUSSION

Cooling Curves and Grain Morphology

Figure 4 shows the simulated and experimental cooling curves at point 1 and 2. The temperatures at both points dropped sharply after approximately 7 minutes from the beginning, and the simulated cooling curves at both points agreed with the experimental well.

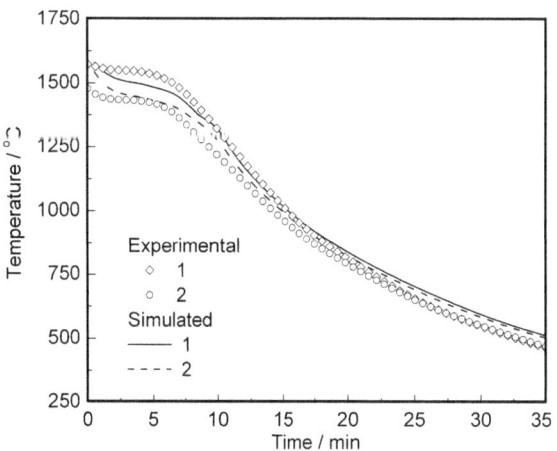

Fig. 4 simulated and experimental cooling curves.

Figure 5 shows the simulated and experimental microstructure of the starter block. The simulated microstructure had similar texture and grain sizes with the experimental microstructure.

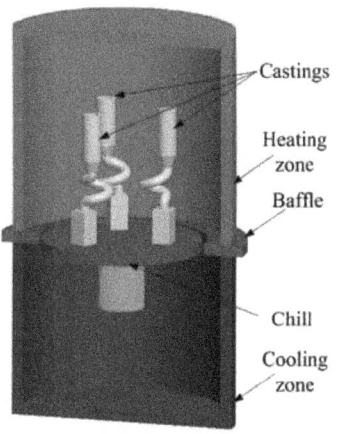

Fig. 3 Schematic of Bridgman directional solidification process.

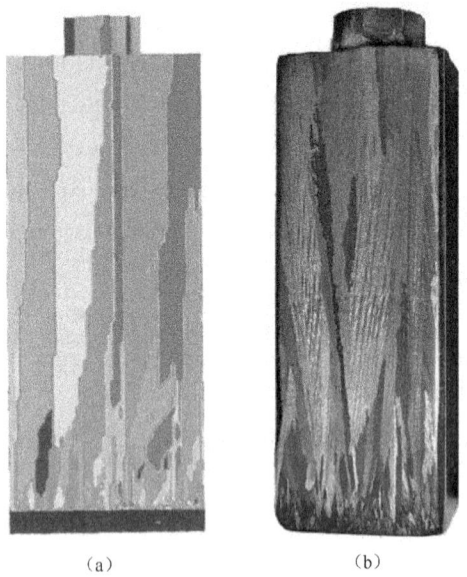

Fig. 5 (a) simulated and (b) experimental microstructure of the starter block.

Grain Competition and Evolution

Figure 6 shows the grain evolution process during solidification at different times. The liquid is not displayed so that the solid-liquid interface could be clearly shown. Figure 7 shows the simulated and measured grain number at different heights of the grain selector, in which the electron backscattered diffraction (EBSD) method was used for the experimental measurement of grain numbers at each transverse section. Good agreement was observed between the simulated and experimental results. It is indicated that a great number of tiny equiaxed grains emerged at the bottom surface of the starter block, and transferred into a much smaller number of columnar grains when growing upwards, which is well known as the grain competition process determined by the heat flux direction and the grain's fastest growth direction. The grain number decreased quickly in the starter block, leaving only less than 10 columnar grains growing into the spiral. The grains in the spiral continued to decrease when growing upwards, and only one of them survived from this grain selection, which finally grew into a whole single crystal casting.

Grain Orientation of Primary <001> Dendrite Growth Direction

Figure 8 shows the grain maps at different transverse sections of the grain selector, whose positions were previously indicated in Figure 6c. The results show that a great many small grains appeared at the bottom of the starter block and grew upwards. Only a few grains grew to the top of the starter block, which were allowed to grow into the spiral. In the spiral, the grains' growth was limited by the shape of the spiral, and only one of them survived in this selection. The simulated microstructure evolution results show that only one grain was left at the top of the casting, which initially nucleated at the bottom surface of the starter block and occupied the whole section in the middle circle of the spiral part.

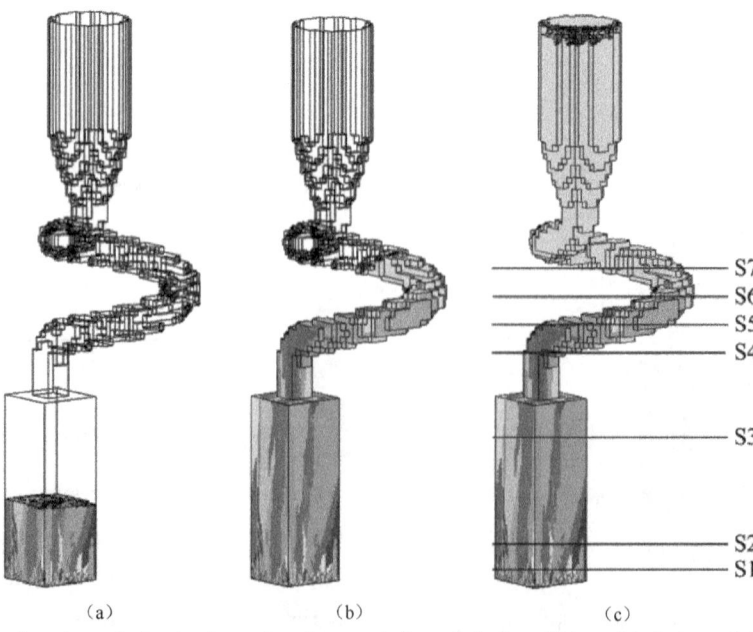

Fig. 6 Simulated grain evolution in the grain selector. (a) $t=4.5$min, (b) $t=14.5$min., (c) $t=22.0$min.

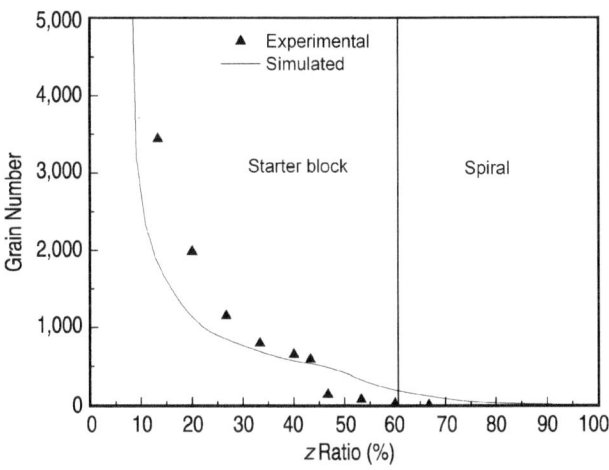

Fig. 7 Predicted and measured grain number at different positions of the grain selector.

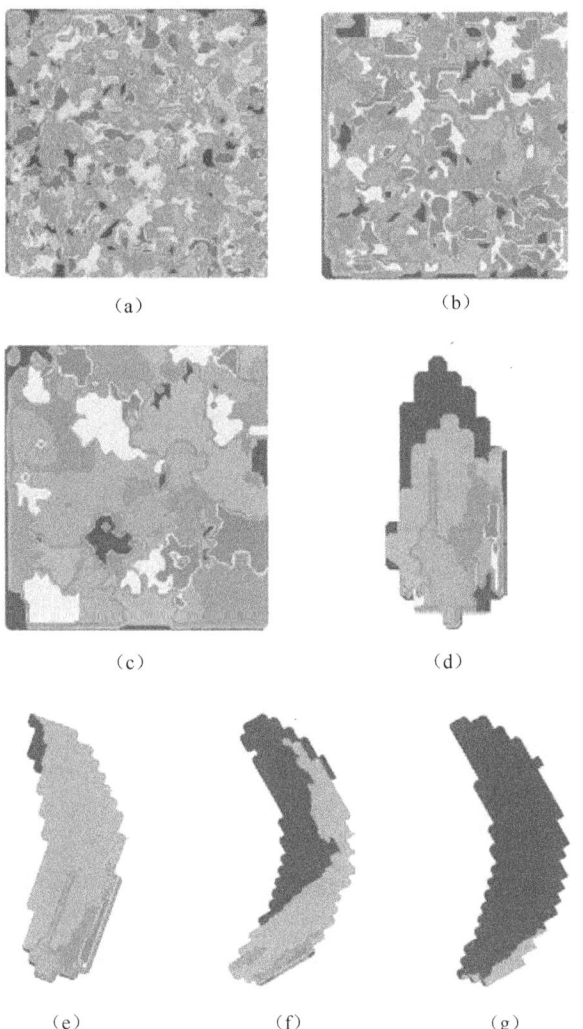

Fig. 8 Simulated grain maps of different transverse sections. (a) S1, (b) S2, (c) S3, (d) S4, (e) S5, (f) S6, (g) S7.

Figure 9 shows the comparison of predicted and measured variations of angle at several transverse sections in the starter block as indicated in Figure 6c, in which the angle is defined as the shortest angular rotation between the primary <001> direction of the grain and the normal of the chill surface. Both the simulated and experimental results show that the grain orientation near the bottom of the starter block was nearly random. Together with the decrease of the grain number caused

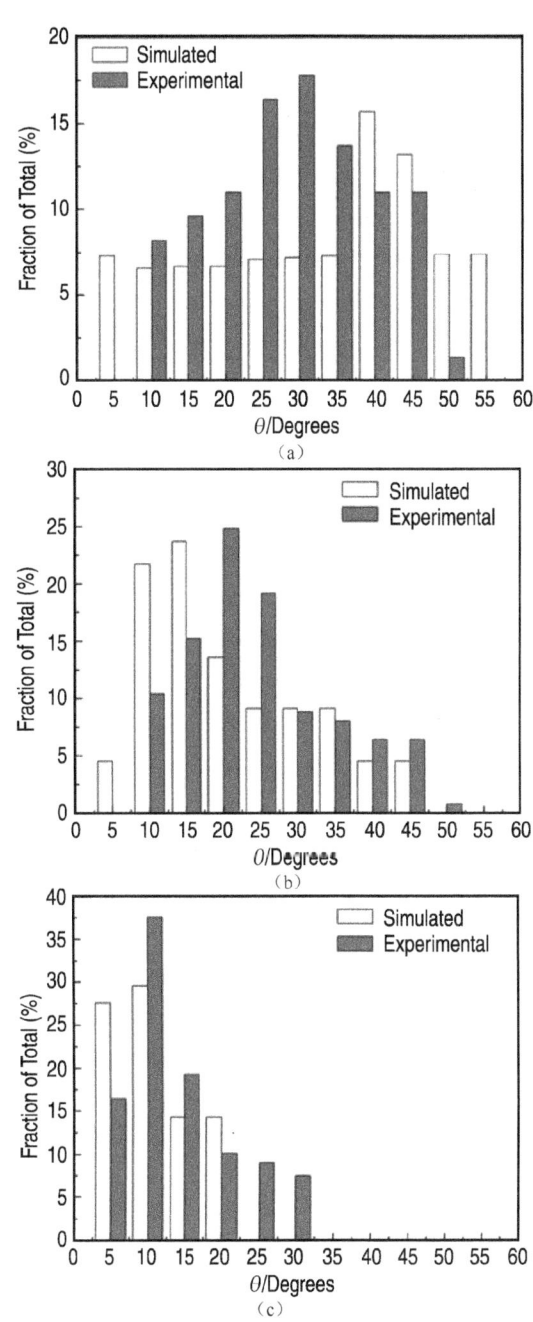

Fig. 9 Predicted and measured variations of grain orientation angle. (a) S1, (b) S2, (c) S3.

by the competitive growth in the starter block, the grain orientation clustered into a smaller range of angle. At the end of the starter block, the grain orientation clustered into a narrow 5°~15° range, showing the grain selection results caused by the competitive grain growth in the starter block. The predicted results show a reasonable correspondence to the measured results.

CONCLUSIONS

(1) A mathematical model was proposed for the three-dimensional simulation of grain selection during directional solidification of Ni-based single crystal superalloy turbine blade casting. Based on heat transfer modeling of the directional withdrawing process, the competitive grain growth within the starter block and the spiral were simulated by using cellular automaton method (CA).

(2) The simulated cooling curves and microstructures agree well with the experimental results. Only a few grains survived from the grain competition in the starter block and grew into the spiral, while just one of them was left at the middle height of the spiral and grew into a whole single crystal casting.

(3) The simulated grain orientation results of primary<001> dendrite with respect to the longitudinal axis of the turbine blade casting were compared quantitatively with the measured results, which shows a reasonable correspondence.

ACKNOWLEDGEMENTS

The work reported has been carried out under the financial support of National Basic Research Program of China (No. 2005CB724105), National Natural Science Foundation of China (No. 10477010), and National High Technology Research and Development Program of China (No. 2007AA04Z141).

References

[1] R. C. Reed, *The Superalloys Fundamentals and Applications* (New York: Cambridge University Press, 2006) pp. 18-29.

[2] R. E. Schafrik and Scott Walston "Challenges for High Temperature Materials in the New Millennium," *Proceedings of the 11th International Symposium on Superalloys*, ed. R. C. Reed et al. (Warrendale, PA: TMS, 2008), pp. 3-9.

[3] H. Esaka, K. Shinozuka, and M. Tamura, "Analysis of Single Crystal Casting Process Taking Into Account the Shape of Pigtail," *Materials Science and Engineering*, A413-414 (2005), pp. 151-155.

[4] Z. G. Zhong, "Making Method of Controlled Single Crystal Seed (in Chinese)," *Material Engineering*, 9 (1996), pp. 39-41.

[5] P. Carter et al., "Process Modelling of Grain Selection during the Solidification of Single Crystal Superalloy Castings," *Materials Science and Engineering*, A280 (2000), pp. 233-246.

[6] J. Yu et al., "Numerical Simulation of Solidification Process on Single Crystal Ni-based Superalloy investment Castings," *Journal of Materials Science and Technology*, (23) 2007, pp. 47-54.

[7] M. Rappaz and C. A. Gandin, "Probabilistic Modelling of Microstructure Formation in Solidification Processes," *Acta Metallurgica et Materialia*, 41 (1993), pp. 345-360.

[8] P. Thevoz, J. L. Desbiolles, and M. Rappaz, "Modeling of Eguiaxed Microstructure Formation in Casting," *Metallurgical Transactions A*, 20A (1989), pp. 311-322.

[9] W. Kurz, B. Giovanola, and R. Trivedi. "Theory of Microstructure Development during Rapid Solidification," *Acta Metallurgica*, 34 (1986), pp. 823-830.

[10] J. Lacaze, G. Lesoult. "Effects of Solidification-conditions on Austenitic Stainless-steel Solidification-mode," *Journal of Crystal Growth*, 89 (1988), pp. 531-544.

[11] J. R. Li et al., "Effects of Low Angle Boundaries on the Mechanical Properties of Single Crystal Superalloy DD6," *Proceedings of the 11th International Symposium on Superalloys*, ed. R. C. Reed et al. (Warrendale, PA: TMS, 2008), pp. 443-451.

Dong Pan, Ph. D. candidate, Qingyan Xu, associate professor, Baicheng Liu, professor, are with the Key Laboratory for Advanced Materials Processing Technology, Ministry of Education, Department of Mechanical Engineering, Tsinghua University, Beijing 100084, China; Jiarong Li, research fellow, Hailong Yuan and Haipeng Jin, engineers, are with the National Key Laboratory of Advanced High Temperature Structural Materials, Beijing Institute of Aeronautical Materials, Beijing 100095, China. Prof. Liu can be reached at liubc@ tsinghua. edu. cn.

10. NUMERICAL SIMULATION OF TEMPERATURE FIELD IN DIRECTIONAL SOLIDIFICATION OF TURBINE BLADE BY LIQUID METAL COOLING METHOD

TANG Ning, XU Qingyan, LIU Baicheng

Key Laboratory for Advanced Materials Processing Technology, Ministry Of Education,
Department of Mechanical Engineering, Tsinghua University, Beijing 100084 China

Key words: IGT blade; Directional solidification; parallel computing; numerical simulation

Abstract

Blades with excellent high temperature performance are required for industrial gas turbines (IGT). However, defects such as stray grains are almost inevitable, which sharply decrease the properties. Liquid metal cooling (LMC) is used as a new process in directional solidification of large blade castings in recent years, and it still needs to be improved. In order to optimize the casting process, the mathematical models of solidification during investment casting of IGT blade were developed. In this model, the convection between the shell and the cooling liquid metal as well as the influence of the height of liquid metal surface was taken into account. Due to large size of IGT blade, the massive data in the model consumes very much memory and CPU time. A modified FD method is established to reduce memory usage; parallel computing is developed to speed up the calculation. Based on simulation, the temperature and mushy zone evolution could be studied. Validation experiments were carried out. The cooling curves either from experiment or simulation corresponded well with each other.

Introduction

The properties of turbine increase with the temperature and pressure of the burning gas. The Hotter the Engine, the Better[1]. Thus, the mechanical property, such as fatigue life, creep resistance, etc, at high temperature of key parts, especially the blades, is very important. Directional solidified (DS) turbine blades are widely used in advanced gas turbines. A very strict process control is needed to prevent from defects occurring. However, defects easily occur during solidification.

In the past 10 years, Gas turbine blade casting is mainly manufactured by Bridgman directional solidification technology[2]. However, during Bridgman process, the mushy zone is sometimes very wide, and usually concave, which will easily result in stray grain. Some times Bridgman process cannot provide enough temperature gradient, especially for the blades with large transverse cross-section. A case in point is the heavy-duty gas turbine blade. In a word, Bridgman method is not appropriate to IGT blades.

In recent years, liquid metal cooling (LMC) is used as a new process in large blade casting[3], but it still needs to be improved. Fig. 1 is the schematic of a LMC furnace. In this process, low melting-point metal is used as cooling liquid metal. Instead of radiation, heat convection happens between the cooling liquid metal and the shell below the liquid surface. A new way is needed to find more optimized process by LMC without too many experiments.

With the development of solidification simulation technology, Numerical methods provide effective ways

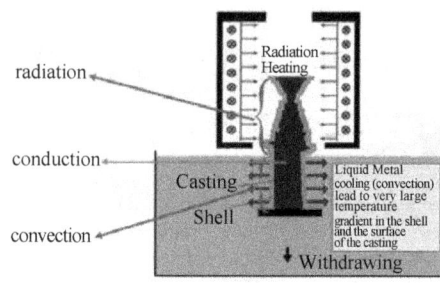

Fig. 1 Schematic of a LMC funace

to simulate the directional solidification process, and then to optimize the process[4]. studying the directional process and predicting the formation of casting defects are helpful to optimize technical parameters, avoid casting defects and reduce the development cycle and cost. Finite element (FE) and finite difference (FD) are most widely used discrimination methods in computer aided engineering. FE relatively reduces the memory cost. In the other side, FD can solve the microstructure coupled with temperature field, without the complex FE shape function. Computational efficiency is core problem of numerical simulation. With the popularity of computer aided engineering, the numerical models become larger and larger, consuming more and more memory and CPU time. Due to large size of IGT blade, the numerical model of temperature and grain growth of the casting is particularly huge; and it is difficult to be solved by ordinary serial program with tranditional FD method. Recently, with the constant advancement in computer manufacture and technology, computers are developing towards multi-core and multi-processor. Together with multi-core and multi-processor computers, parallel computation can greatly fasten the calculation.

Some experimental researches has been done by Giamei A F[3], Elliott A J[5], Liu C[6] and Zhang J[7], revealing that higher thermo gradient can be obtained by LMC, which get finer dendrite and precipitation as well as less defect. Haipeng J[8] and Dong H B[9] simulated the directional solidification of aero turbine blade by Bridgman process. They calculated temperature by FE and microstructure by FD. Their Microstructure calculation is limited in the start block and the grain selector because of too massive data, let alone the IGT blade has much larger volume than aero turbine blade. Simulation of temperature in LMC process is attempted only by Elliott A J[10], Kermanpur A[11]. Simulation of real IGT blade higher than 200mm is not reported.

In this paper, a model of casting, shell and furnace is established. The convection between the cooling liquid metal and the shell as well as the influence of the height of liquid metal surface is taken into account. To cope with the large model and to increase the computational efficiency, a quasi FE method is proposed and applied, as well as multithreading. The temperature evolution and solidification is calculated and the temperature result is validated by experiment.

Modeling

Mathematical model

Heat transferring equation: The non-linear conduction equation is described as follows:

$$\rho c \frac{\partial T}{\partial t} = \lambda \left(\frac{\partial^2 T}{\partial x^2} + \frac{\partial^2 T}{\partial y^2} + \frac{\partial^2 T}{\partial z^2} \right) + \rho L \frac{\partial f_s}{\partial t} + Q_R \quad (1)$$

Where T is the temperature, t is the time, ρ is the density, L is the latent heat, c is the specific heat, λ is the heat conductivity; x, y and z are the coordinates; f_s is the mass fraction of solid phase, Q_R is the heat radiaion exchange volume.

The type of heat transfer at the surface is determined by the value of z. Suppose the height of the cooling liquid metal surface is h, when $z > h$, the surface element radiates with the furnace wall, a Monte Carlo algorithm[12] is applied to calculate the view factor varying with withdrawal distance. When $z < h$, the following equation is used to calculate the heat transfer:

$$\rho c \frac{\partial T}{\partial t} = \alpha (T - T_l) \quad (2)$$

Where α is the convection coefficient, T_l is the temperature of liquid metal.

h is updated by:

$$\frac{dh}{dt} = \frac{dh_c}{dt} \frac{S_c}{S_c - S_p} \quad (3)$$

Where h_c is the withdrawal distance, S_c the area of the horizontal section of mould and casting at the liquid surface level, S_p is the area of the horizontal section of the liquid metal container.

Ouasi FE-modified FD method

FD method is applied to solve the temperature field. In traditional ordinary FD method, the 3D model is discretized into a 3D matrix whose size depends on the smallest circumscribed box of all the geometry. Fig. 2 schematically shows that the vacuum elements in white occupy memory as well, but they are never used in the solution.

Fig. 2 Geometry discretization in traditional FD

To reduce memory, the box method is abandoned. Similar to that of FE, only the solid elements are recorded, ignoring the vacuum elements. The topology relationship is stored in the variable of each element. This algorithm is not used only in temperature calculation; it will be even more helpful in microstructure calculation in further works.

Parallel computing

In spite of the reduced memory, the element number is still too large to calculate by single processor, it takes months to solve a casting, which delays the research period. Multi thread program with parallel algorism is constructed to save time (Fig. 3). Except for the temperature, microstructure calculation in future works will also be based upon parallel algorithm.

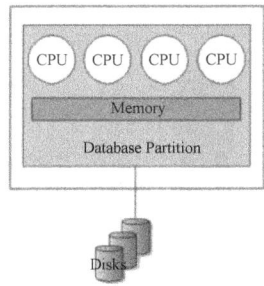

Fig. 3 Schematic of Parallel computation

The acceleration efficiency is defined as:

$$R_s = \frac{T_s}{T_m \cdot m}$$

Where T_s is the calculation time by single thread, T_m is the calculation time by multi thread, m is the thread number.

In parallel program with ideal efficiency, this ratio equals to 1, e.g. the speed is strictly in direct proportion to the number of cores. In practical parallel program, it will be less than 1 due to efficiency losses.

Experimental

Practical process is done in a LMC furnace (Fig. 4). W-Re thermocouples are installed in the casting, protected by quartz tube with 1mm thickness. Slurry is smeared on the thermocouple wires outside the thermocouple hole (Fig. 5). The geometry of the solidified slurry is also measured and meshed in the FD model. Four holes are prepared for thermocouples.

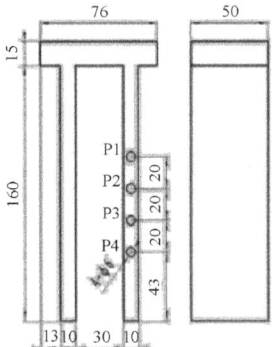

Fig. 4 Practical sample

Fig. 5 Shell ready to be filled in the experiment

Results and discussion

Modified FD sharply reduced the memory consumption (Table 1)

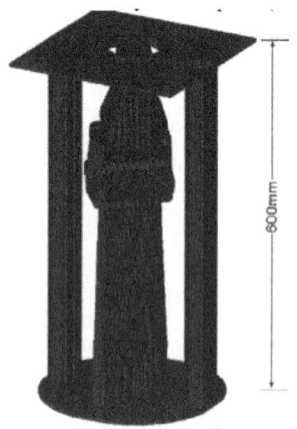

Fig. 6　Casting and shell used for memory test

Table 1　Memory consumption of two methods by the model in Fig. 6

Method	Solid elements/10^4	Elements stored/10^4	Memory used/Mb	Memory reducement
Traditional	393.25	3174	1289.48	76.5%
Modified	393.25	393.25	303.26	

By parallel computing, The speedup of a blade with 12.8×10^4 elements is show in Fig. 7 The calculating speed is defined as the iterative times per millisecond in calculation.

It is revealed that the acceleration efficiency is better with 8 or 4 threads except for single thread. 16 threads got the highest speed, but the acceleration efficiency is lowered by communication between threads.

The speedup of blades in different sizes is shown in Fig. 8. The heights of them vary from 200mm to 600mm. For comparison, the calculation time is normalized as time in hour divided by element number. The speed up ratio deceases sharply with the increase of element number. It has something to do with the Memory access optimization.

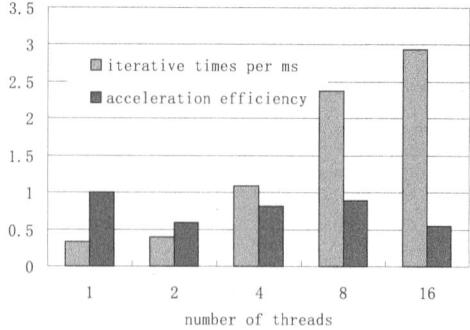

Fig. 7　Speedup of a blade

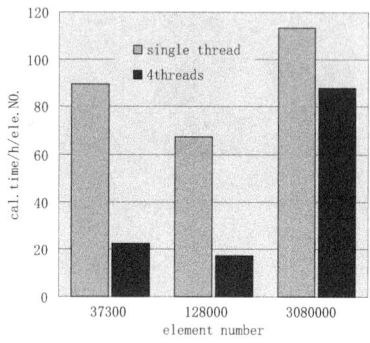

Fig. 8　Speedup of blades in different mesh sizes

As same as speedup, accuracy is also a core problem in calculation. Speedup often leads to Accuracy losses. The results by single and multi thread are compared, indicating the results are hearly identical (Fig. 9). That's to say, multi thread cause no more error than single thread.

A blade in real practical process is calculated (Fig. 10, Fig. 11). With the withdrawing mould, the mushy zone is convex at first. It becomes flat in the middle level, and get concave finally in the upper end.

The calculated temperature curves agree well with the experimental, shown in Fig. 12. The max error is approximately 6%.

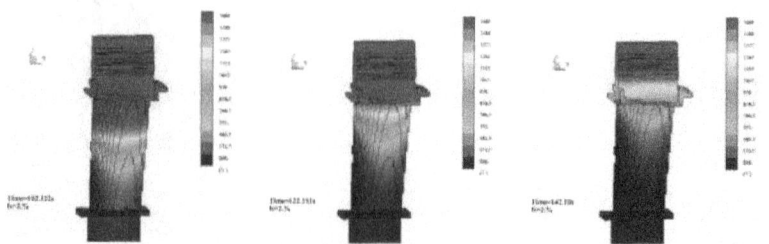

(a) solidify 102s, single thread　(b) solidify 122s, single thread　(c) solidify 142s, single thread

Fig. 9　Comparison of results by single and multi thread

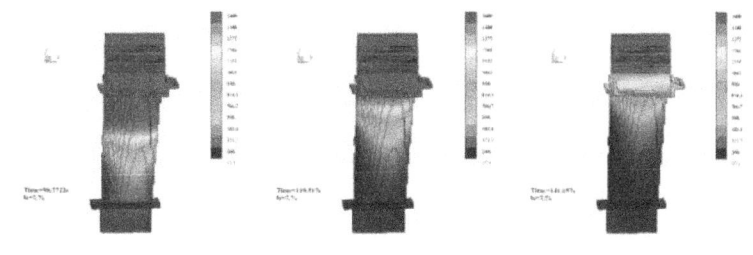

(d) solidify 98s,multithread (e) solidify 109s,multithread (f) solidify 141s,multithread

Fig. 9 Comparison of results by single and multi thread (Continued)

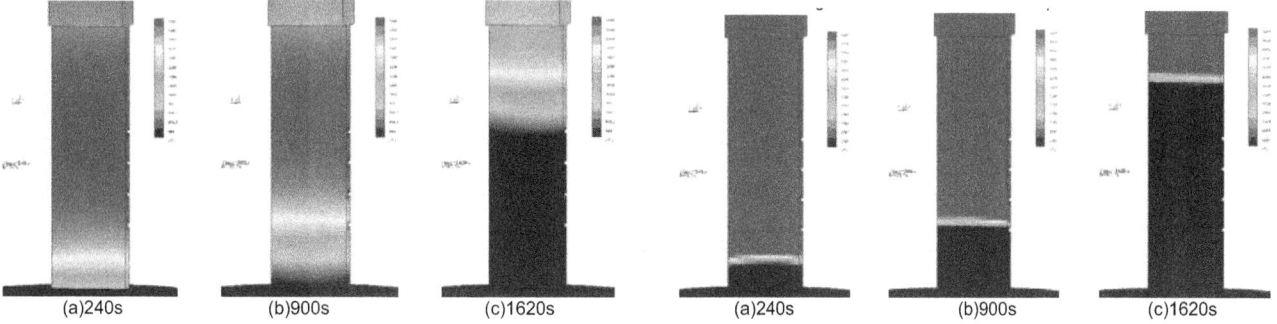

Fig. 10 Calculated result of temperature field

Fig. 11 Calculated result of mushy zone

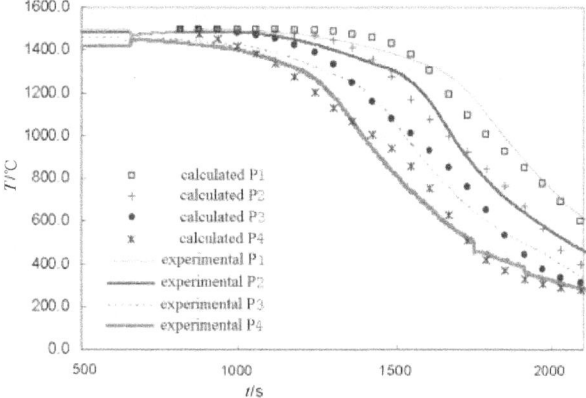

Fig. 12 Comparison of the calculated and experimental results

Conclusions

1) Numerical simulation can be used in directorial solidification of IGT by LMC to predict the temperature Field.

2) In FD modeling, data store and access by quasi FE method largely decreased the cost of computer memory and thus increased the utilization rate of memory.

3) Parallel computing is applied in this calculation; the solution speed is multiplied without significant loss of accuracy.

4) The calculated temperature curves agree well with the experimental. The simulation is demonstrated to be reliable.

Acknowledgements

The work is financially supported by National Basic Research Program of China (No. 2005CB724105, 2011CB706801), National Natural Science Foundation of China (No. 10477010), National High Technology Research and Development Program of China (No. 2007AA04Z141), and Important National Science &

Technology Specific Projects (2009ZX04006-041-04).

References

[1] Perepezko J H. The hotter the engine, the better [jet engines] [J]. Science, 2009, 326 (5956): 1068-1069.

[2] 潘冬, 许庆彦, 柳百成. 考虑炉壁温度变化的高温合金叶片定向凝固过程模拟 [J]. 金属学报, 2010 (3): 294-303.

[3] Giamei A F, Tschinkel J G. LIQUID METAL COOLING: A NEW SOLIDIFICATION TECHNIQUE [J]. Metallurgical Transactions A (Physical Metallurgy and Materials Science), 1976, 7A (9): 1427-1434.

[4] Stanford N, Djakovic A, Shollock B A, et al. Seeding of single crystal superalloys—role of seed melt-back on casting defects [J]. Scripta Materialia, 2004, 50 (1): 159-163.

[5] Elliott A J, Tin S, King W T, et al. Directional solidification of large superalloy castings with radiation and liquid-metal cooling A comparative assessment [J]. METALLURGICAL AND MATERIALS TRANSACTIONS, 2004, 35A: 3221-3231.

[6] Liu C, Shen J, Zhang J, et al. Effect of Withdrawal Rates on Microstructure and Creep Strength of a Single Crystal Superalloy Processed by LMC [J]. Journal of Materials Science & Technology, 2010, 26 (4): 306-310.

[7] Zhang J, Lou L. Directional solidification assisted by liquid metal cooling [J]. Journal of Materials Science and Technology, 2007, 23 (3): 289-300.

[8] Haipeng J, Jiarong L, Jing Y, et al. Study of Heat Transfer Coefficient Used in the Unidirectional Solidification Simulation Based on Orthogonal Design [J]. Rare Metal Materials and Engineering, 2010, 39 (5): 767-770.

[9] Dai H J, Dong H B, D'Souza N, et al. Grain Selection in Spiral Selectors During Investment Casting of Single-Crystal Components: Part II. Numerical Modeling [J]. 2011: 1-8.

[10] Elliott A J, Pollock T M. Thermal analysis of the bridgman and liquid-metal-cooled directional solidification investment casting processes [C]. 101 Philip Drive, Assinippi Park, Norwell, MA 02061, United States: Springer Boston, 2007.

[11] Kermanpur A, Varahram N, Davami P, et al. Thermal and grain-structure simulation in a land-based turbine blade directionally solidified with the liquid metal cooling process [J]. Metallurgical and Materials Transactions B: Process Metallurgy and Materials Processing Science, 2000, 31 (6): 1293-1304.

[12] Yu J, Xu Q, Cui K, Liu B, Kimatsuka A, Kuroki Y, Hirata A. Modeling of directional solidification process of superalloy turbine blade castings. vol. 2. Opio, France: Minerals, Metals and Materials Society, Warrendale, PA 15086, United States, 2006, p. 1011. [J].

11. Multiscale Modeling and Simulation of Directional Solidification Process of Turbine Blade Casting with MCA Method

QINGYAN XU, HANG ZHANG, XIANG QI, and BAICHENG LIU

Nickel-based superalloy turbine blade castings are widely used as a key part in aero engines. However, due to the complex manufacturing processes, the complicated internal structure, and the interaction between different parts of the turbine blade, casting defects, such as stray grains, often happen during the directional solidification of turbine blade castings, which causes low production yield and high production cost. To improve the quality of the directionally solidified turbine blade castings, modeling and simulation technique has been employed to study the microstructure evolution as well as to optimize the casting process. In this article, a modified cellular automaton (MCA) method was used to simulate the directional solidification of turbine blade casting. The MCA method was coupled with macro heat transfer and micro grain growth kinetics to simulate the microstructure evolution during the directional solidification. In addition, a ray tracing method was proposed to calculate the heat transfer, especially the heat radiation of multiple blade castings in a Bridgman furnace. A competitive mechanism was incorporated into the grain growth model to describe the grain selection behavior phenomena of multiple columnar grains in the grain selector. With the proposed models, the microstructure evolution and related defects could be simulated, while the processing parameters optimized and the blade casting quality guaranteed as well. Several experiments were carried out to validate the proposed models, and good agreement between the simulated and experimental results was achieved.

DOI: 10.1007/s11663-013-9909-6
© The Minerals, Metals & Materials Society and ASM International 2013

I. INTRODUCTION

A directionally solidified gas turbine blade has been widely used in aeronautical and energy industries, which is mainly manufactured by the Bridgman process. The processing parameters in directional solidification, such as the withdrawal rate, temperature gradient, pouring temperature, and so on, have great influence on the size and morphology of columnar grains as well as the performance of the final casting. The withdrawal rate, which affects temperature distribution and determines the formation of casting defects and the final quality, has been paid much more attention.[1-3] If the withdrawal rate is too high, it would cause an extremely concave solid-liquid (S/L) interface and lead to declining grains, transverse grains, or other defects. However, too low withdrawal rate would result in coarse grain, crack in the shell, or other defects and, thus, low productivity. Both experimental[4,5] and numerical methods[6-10] are extensively studied to learn more about the Bridgman process in the past few decades. Many kinds of numerical methods and models are proposed to simulate the directional solidification process and microstructure evolution in blade castings.

In this article, an integrated macro and micro multiscale model based on the modified cellular automaton (CA)-finite difference (FD) method was employed for the three-dimensional simulation of the microstructure evolution in the directional solidification process of super-alloy blade casting. The model was used to investigate the temperature distribution and grain evolution of the casting during solidification, and to predict the final grain morphology. Validation experiments were carried out. The simulated microstructure was compared with the experimental.

II. MATHEMATICAL MODELS

The metal pouring and solidification processes of the turbine blade castings take place in vacuum environment during the directional solidification process. The schematic of the directional solidification process is shown in Figure 1. In this model, the inner geometry of the furnace, the pattern of the blades on the chill plate, and the withdrawal rate are most important.

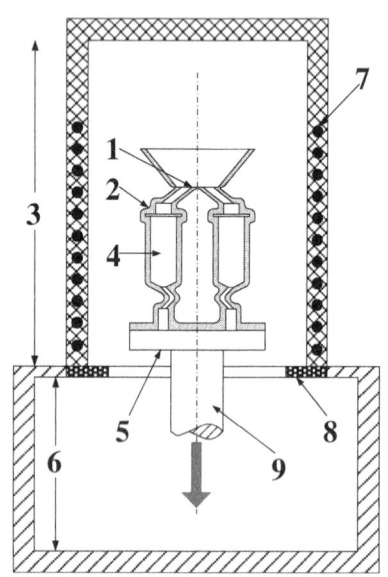

Fig. 1 Schematic of directional solidification
process of superalloy turbine blade:
1—gating system, 2—ceramic mold shell, 3—heating zone,
4—blade, 5—chilled copper plate, 6—cooling zone,
7—heating unit, 8—baffler, and 9—withdrawal unit.

Macro heat transfer during the directional solidification process can be calculated by the transient nonlinear heat conduction equation as follows:

$$\rho c \frac{\partial T}{\partial t} = \lambda \left(\frac{\partial^2 T}{\partial x^2} + \frac{\partial^2 T}{\partial y^2} + \frac{\partial^2 T}{\partial z^2} \right) + \rho L \frac{\partial f_S}{\partial t} + Q_R \quad (1)$$

where T represents the temperature; t is the time; ρ is the density; c is the specific heat; L is the latent heat; λ is the heat conductivity; x, y, and z are the coordinates; f_S is the mass fraction of solid phase; and Q_R is the heat exchange between the casting surface and the ambient environment by radiation.

Due to the huge number of memories required to store the variable view factors for each surface cell against others, it is difficult to calculate the heat radiation directly in directional solidification process. Here, a ray tracing method was adopted to solve the heat radiation in directional solidification: the details could be found in Reference 11.

Modified CA was used to calculate the microstructure formation and evolution during directional solidification.[12] A continuous nucleation model[13] was employed to get the nucleus number in the undercooled melts as follows:

$$n(\Delta T) = \int_0^{\Delta T} [1 - f_S(\Delta T')] \frac{dn}{d(\Delta T')} d(\Delta T') \quad (2)$$

$$\frac{dn}{d(\Delta T')} = \frac{N_{max}}{\sqrt{2\pi}\Delta T_\sigma} \exp\left[-\frac{1}{2}\left(\frac{\Delta T' - \Delta T_N}{\Delta T_\sigma}\right)^2\right] \quad (3)$$

where ΔT is the undercooling, $n(\Delta T)$ is the nucleus density, N_{max} is the maximum nucleus density, ΔT_σ is the standard deviation of the distribution, ΔT_N is the average nucleation undercooling, and $f_S(\Delta T')$ is the solid fraction.

The grain growth is calculated based on the KGT model[14] with a simplification, and the growth speed of the dendrite tip can be calculated as follows:

$$v(\Delta T) = \alpha_1 \cdot \Delta T^2 + \alpha_2 \cdot \Delta T^3 \quad (4)$$

where α_1 and α_2 are the coefficients.

Grain's competitive growth is shown in Figure 2. The grains that were not well aligned with respect to the heat flux direction would grow at a much slower speed than those best aligned. This made it possible for those wellaligned grains to have their secondary and tertiary side arms grow out and occupy the space just in front of the less well-aligned grains.

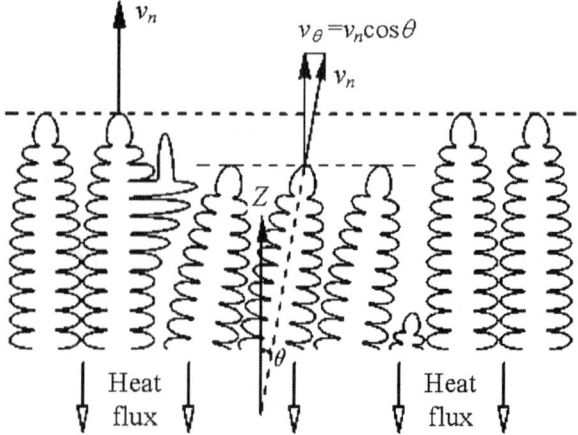

Fig. 2 Schematic of grain competitive growth.

III. NUMERICAL SIMULATION OF DIRECTIONALLY SOLIDIFIED (DS) TURBINE BLADE

The microstructure formation and evolution of DS blade was simulated. The temperature changing with time is shown in Figure 3 (where HZ, CZ, and Bf represent heating zone, cooling zone and baffler, respectively). When the withdrawal rate is low, the temperature of the blade above the baffler appears higher in the left side, which is close to the center of the furnace, but lower in the right side near the furnace wall. However, the temperature of the blade's part that below the baffler is almost even at a low withdrawal rate. As the withdrawal rate increases, the temperature distribution is similar to that of the low rate, but the slopes of the temperature isothermal lines become larger.

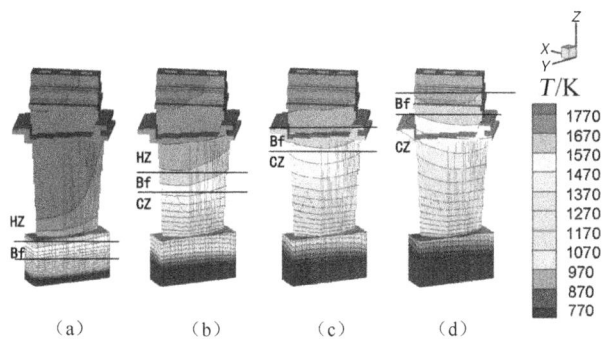

Fig. 3 Temperature distribution during solidification (back side): (a) $f_S = 40\%$, $t = 2$min, (b) $f_S = 50\%$, $t = 8$min, (c) $f_S = 60\%$, $t = 12$min, and (d) $f_S = 80\%$, $t = 16$min.

The mushy zone is defined as the zone where the temperature is below the liquidus and above the solidus, which is from 1568K to 1650K (1295℃ to 1375℃) for the alloy used in the experiments.[15] Figure 4 shows the mushy zone variation with the solid fraction increasing at certain withdrawal rates. The mushy zone has some characteristics. First, the length of this mushy zone is narrower and more horizontal compared with those at other withdrawal rates, and it becomes wider and wider with the solid fraction increasing gradually. When the withdrawal rate is low, there is enough time for heat transfer in the blade casting, so the temperature gradient near the baffler turns to be high and the length of the mushy zone becomes narrow and horizontal. As the withdrawal process is going, the main way by which the heat is dissipated changes from heat conduction through z coordinate to heat radiation toward the surrounded cooling zone. In ordinary directional solidification process, the efficiency of heat radiating is far lower than that of conducting; therefore, there is not enough time to dissipate heat as the heat transferring and the width of the mushy zone appears enlarged near the end of the solidification. Second, the location of the mushy zone is above the baffler's upper edge. This is because the growth rate of columnar grains is faster than the withdrawal rate. Then, the S/L interface develops faster than the movement of baffler. The location of baffler becomes lower than the S/L interface gradually.

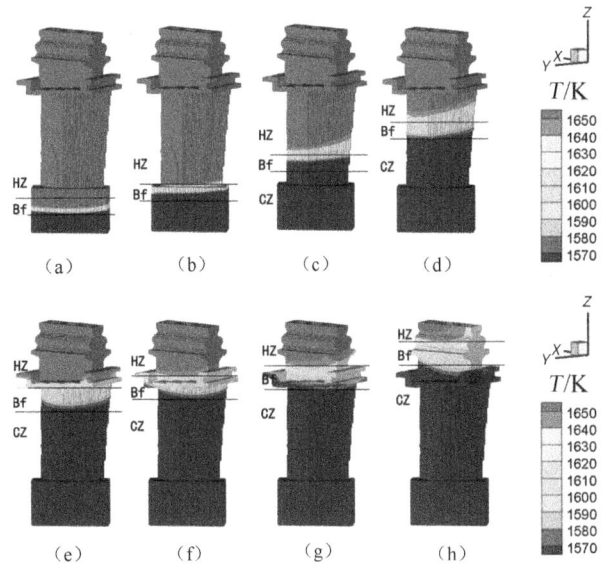

Fig. 4 Mushy zone distribution during the solidification (back side): (a) $f_S = 20\%$, $t = 1$min, (b) $f_S = 40\%$, $t = 2$min, (c) $f_S = 45\%$, $t = 5$min, (d) $f_S = 50\%$, $t = 8$min; (e) $f_S = 55\%$, $t = 11$min, (f) $f_S = 60\%$, $t = 12$min, (g) $f_S = 65\%$, $t = 13$min, and (h) $f_S = 80\%$, $t = 16$min.

Figure 5 is the grain growth in the turbine blade casting during solidification. Different colors represent different columnar grains, and the liquid metal is set as achromatic or transparent to present the morphology and location of the microstructure and solidifying front clearly. The columnar grains selected in the starter block grow steadily into the body of blade. Because two edges of the blade body cool faster, the grains in these places will incline. Some grains will transversely grow and become coarsen, so the width of the grains at the edge of the body is wider than that in the center.

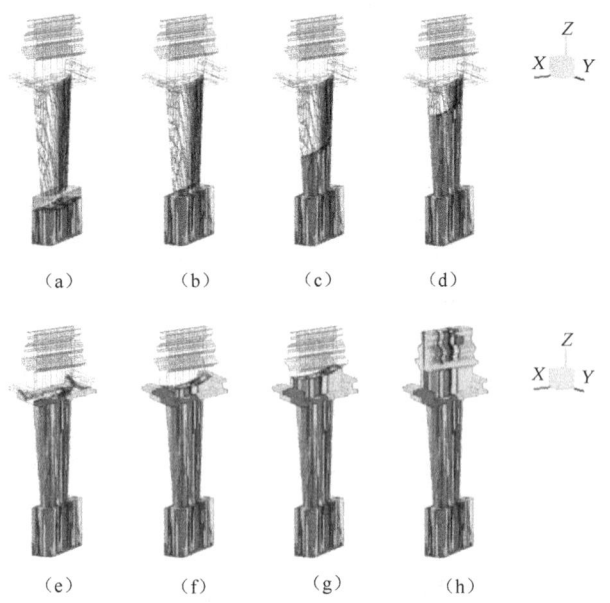

Fig. 5 The simulation result of microstructure size and morphology during the solidification: (a) $f_S = 20\%$, $t = 1$min, (b) $f_S = 40\%$, $t = 2$min, (c) $f_S = 45\%$, $t = 5$min, (d) $f_S = 50\%$, $t = 8$min; (e) $f_S = 55\%$, $t = 11$min, (f) $f_S = 60\%$, $t = 12$min, (g) $f_S = 65\%$, $t = 13$min, and (h) $f_S = 100\%$, $t = 19$min.

IV. MICROSTRUCUTRE SIMULATION OF SINGLE-CRYSTAL (SX) TURBINE BLADE

A. Grain Selection Behavior of Grain Selector

Grain selector is the key part of single-crystal blade casting. The grain selection behavior of real grain selector from the industry has been studied in a previous work.[16] In this article, some experimental results of newly designed grain selector with more parameters were further studied.

Figure 6 shows the grain evolution in the grain selector at different solidification times. Figure 7 shows the microstructure comparison in the starter block between the simulated and experimental results. Different colors represent different grains. The liquid is not displayed in the picture, so that the growth interface is clearly shown. The results show that a great many small grains appeared at the bottom of the starter block and grew upward, and only a few grains survived in the starter block and grew to a certain size. At the top of the starter block, several grains were allowed to grow into the pigtail. In the pigtail, the grains' growth was limited and interpreted by the shape of the pigtail, and just one of them survived in this selection in the middle height of the pigtail, which grew bigger and finally occupied the whole casting at the top, known as "single crystal." This result coincides with the experimental result, and grain selection behavior within the pigtail also agrees with published results by Zheng et al.[17] This indicates that the geometry of that grain selector is efficient to produce a single-crystal casting for the Ni-based DD6 superalloy.

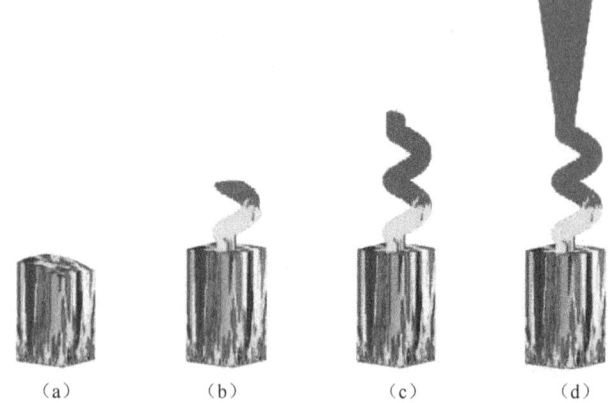

Fig. 6 Simulated grain evolution of Ni-based DD6 superalloy: (a) $t = 10.0$min, (b) $t = 17.0$min, (c) $t = 19$min, and (d) $t = 22.0$min.

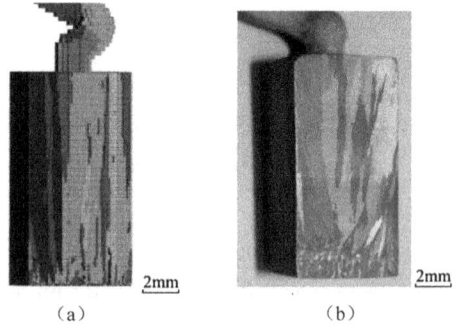

Fig. 7 Simulated and experimental microstructure of starter block.

Figure 8 shows the experimental grain structure observed by EBSD technique. It shows that the sizes of grain became bigger as the heights of the sections in the starter block increase. Some grains diminish or disappeared rapidly at the beginning. Figure 9 shows {001}

where the circles of 54.7 deg are full of points of <001> orientation. As the grains were growing on, the [001] orientations of these grains turned to be converging, and finally nearly all of the [001] orientations converged into the 10-deg circle, shown as Figures 9 (c) and (d) and Figures 10 (c) and (d). Both the simulated and experimental results show the competitive growth of grains in the starter block of the grain selector.

Figure 11 shows the grain maps at different transverse sections of the grain selector. The results show that a great many small grains appeared at the bottom of the starter block and grew upward. Only a few grains grew to the top of the starter block, which were allowed to grow into the spiral. In the spiral, the grains' growth was limited by the shape of the spiral, and only one of them survived in this selection. The simulated microstructure evolution results show that only one grain was left at the top the casting, which initially nucleated at the bottom surface of the starter block and occupied the whole section in the middle circle of the spiral part.

Figure 12 shows the comparison of predicted and measured grain structure at several transverse sections in the spiral part of the grain selector. The simulated

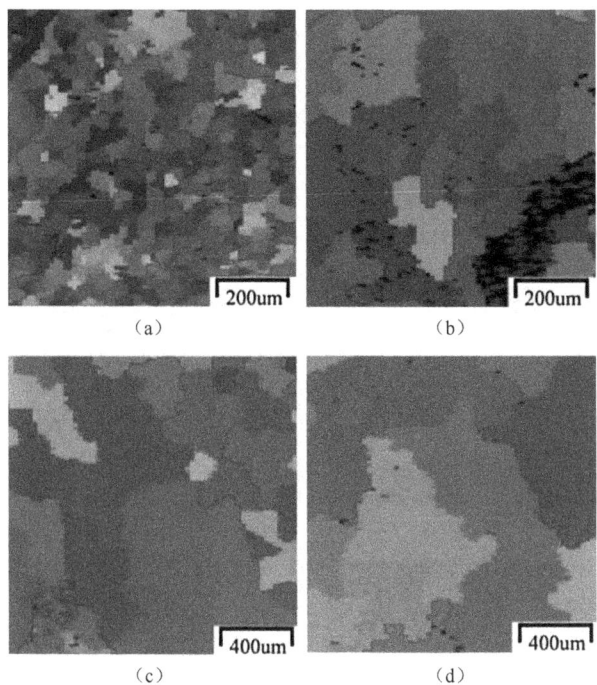

Fig. 8 EBSD results on the grain structure at different sections:
(a) 0.5mm, (b) 6mm, (c) 12mm, (d) 24mm.

pole figures of these sections by EBSD technique and Figure 10 are the simulated results. The orientations of grains were random, shown as Figures 9 (a) and 10 (a),

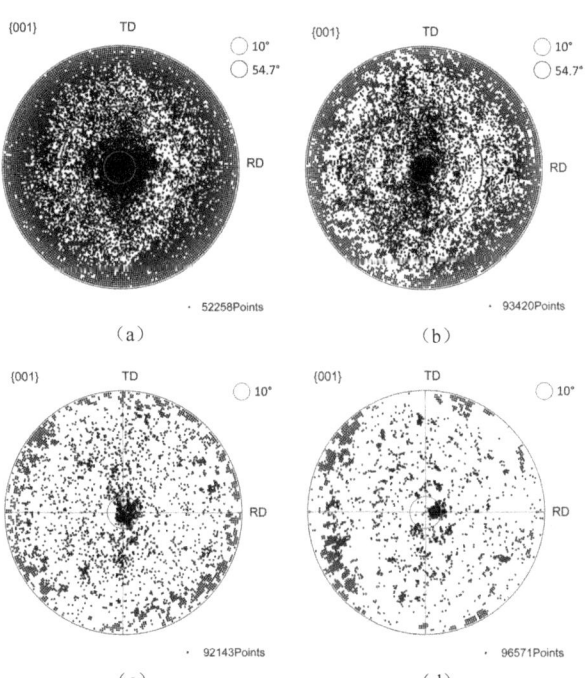

Fig. 9 Experimental {001} pole figures of different sections:
(a) 0.5mm, (b) 6mm, (c) 12mm, and (d) 24mm.

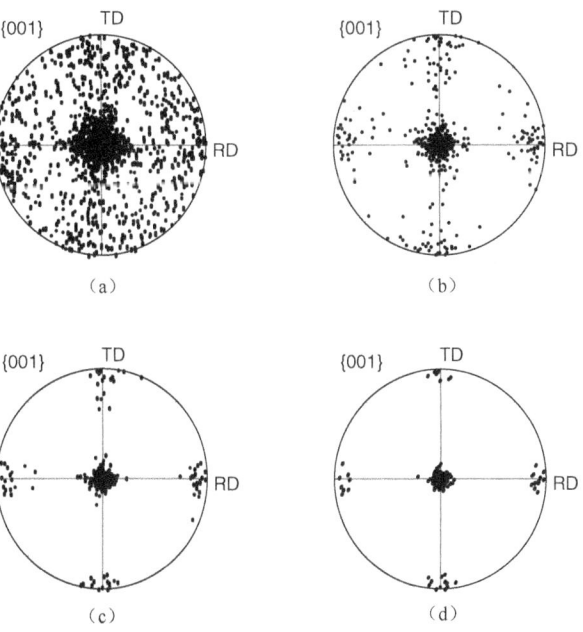

Fig. 10 Simulated {001} pole figures of different sections:
(a) 0.5mm, (b) 6mm, (c) 12mm, and (d) 24mm.

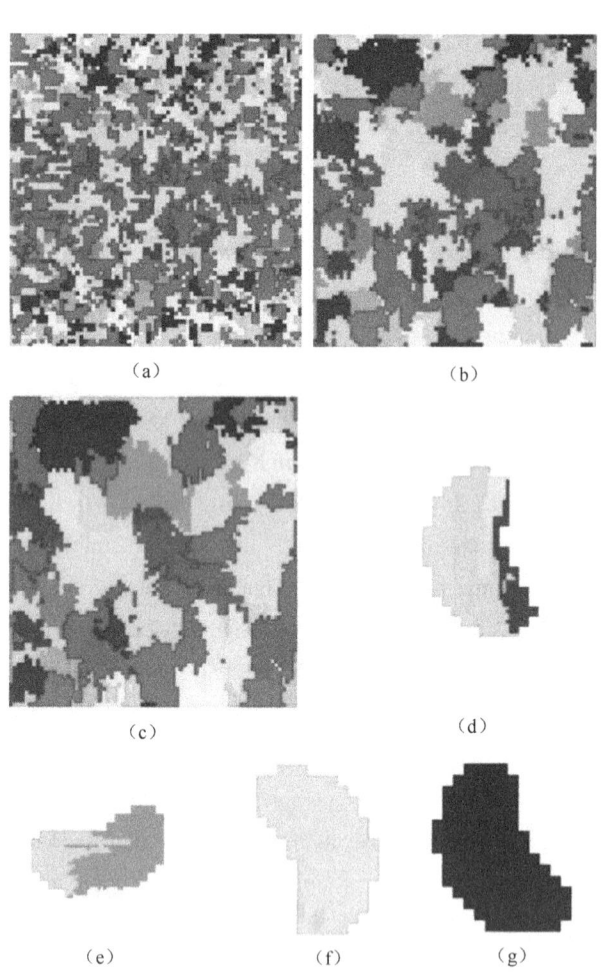

Fig. 11 Simulated grain maps of different transverse sections: (a) $S1=3$mm, (b) $S2=15$mm, (c) $S3=30$mm, (d) $S4=37.5$mm, (e) $S5=41$mm, (f) $S6=44.5$mm, and (g) $S7=51.5$mm.

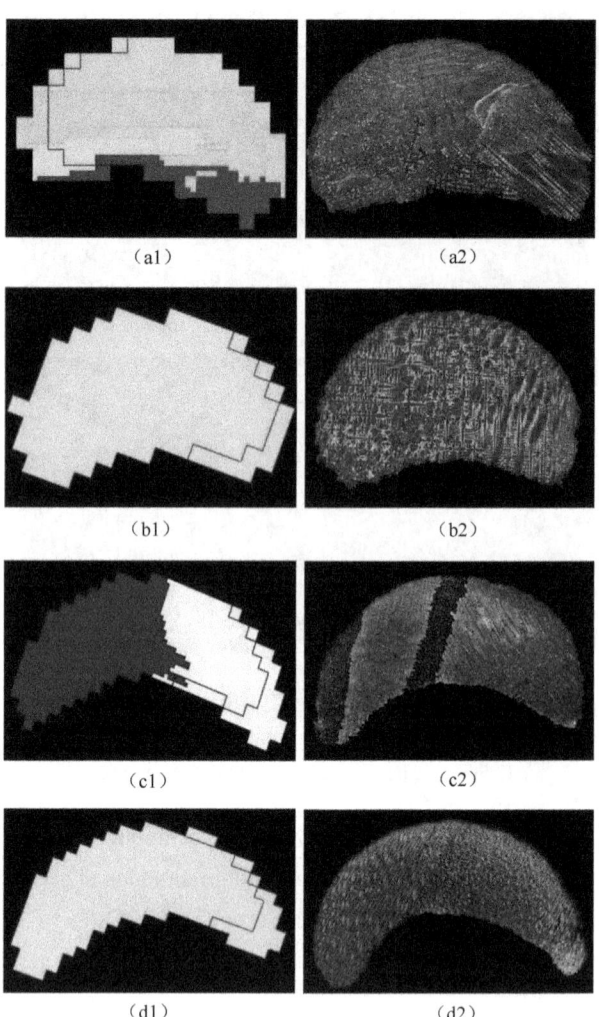

Fig. 12 Comparison of experiment results and simulated results of the spiral parts of the selector:
(a1), (a2), (b1), (b2): $R=8$mm group
(c1), (c2), (d1), (d2): $R=14$mm group.

results agreed well with the experimental. The grain number decreased quickly in the starter block, leaving only less than 10 columnar grains growing into the spiral. The grains in the spiral continued to decrease when growing upward, and only one of them survived from this grain selection, which finally grew into a whole single-crystal casting.

B. Microstructure Evolution of SX Turbine Blade

The modeling and simulation of the directional solidification process of single-crystal turbine blade casting have been studied in previous works.[18-20] Some further simulated and experimental results with a modified model and an improved computing technique are introduced in the article.

Based on all the above models, the microstructure evolution of the whole SX turbine blade can be calculated. To investigate the influence of varying withdrawal rates on the castings' microstructure, two groups of different processing parameters (groups A and B) were carried out for Ni-based superalloy. In group A, a constant withdrawal rate of 7.0mm/min was used during the withdrawal process, while varying withdrawal rates were used in groups B, with 7.0mm/min rate in the first 20min and then a 3.5mm/min rate until the end.

Figure 13 shows the simulated microstructure evolution of blade casting at different time in group A, with a constant withdrawal rate of 7.0mm/min. It could be seen that stray grains existed at the edge of the platform of the blade.

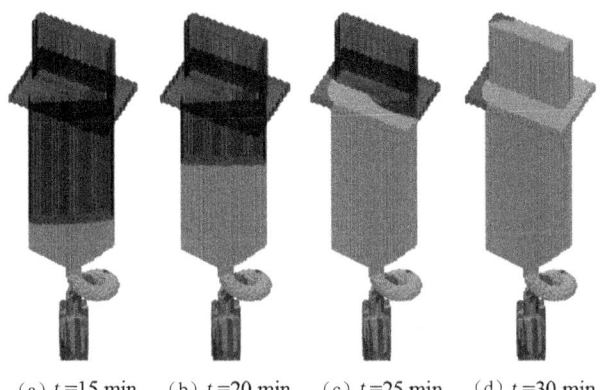

(a) $t=15$ min (b) $t=20$ min (c) $t=25$ min (d) $t=30$ min

Fig. 13 Simulated microstructure evolution in group A at different time.

Figure 14 shows the microstructures in different sections and the whole blade of group A by experiment with a constant withdrawal rate. It could be seen both in the simulated and experimental results that stray grains appeared at the edge of the platform and grew up to the top of the blade. That explains why a high withdrawal rate would not be acceptable to get a complete single-crystal blade casting.

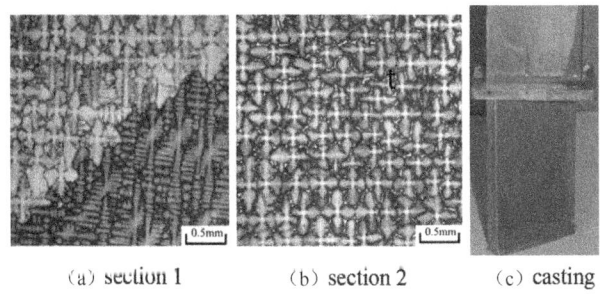

(a) section 1 (b) section 2 (c) casting

Fig. 14 Experimental microstructures of blade casting in group A.

Figure 15 shows the simulated microstructure evolution of blade casting at different time in group B, with varying withdrawal rates. It could be seen that no stray grains were found at the platform of the blade casting, and the produced casting was a whole single-crystal superalloy blade.

Figure 16 shows the microstructures in different sections and the whole blade of group B by experimenting with varying withdrawal rates. No stray grains were found at the edge of the platform both in the simulated and experimental results.

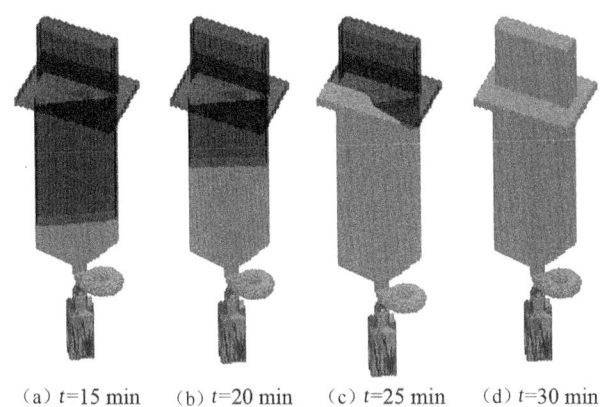

(a) $t=15$ min (b) $t=20$ min (c) $t=25$ min (d) $t=30$ min

Fig. 15 Simulated microstructure evolution in group B at different time.

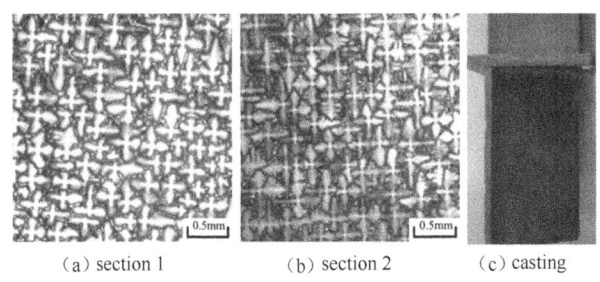

(a) section 1 (b) section 2 (c) casting

Fig. 16 Experimental microstructures of blade casting in group B.

V. CONCLUSIONS

1. Mathematical models were proposed for the three three-dimensional simulation of grain selection and microstructure evolution during the directional solidification of Ni-based superalloy turbine blade casting. Based on heat transfer modeling of the directional withdrawing process, the competitive grain growth within the starter block and the spiral were simulated by using CA method.

2. Only a few grains survived from the grain competition in the starter block and grew into the spiral, while just one of them was left at the middle height of the spiral and grew into a whole single-crystal casting.

3. The simulation results show that the withdrawal rate significantly influences the microstructure evolution of the DS turbine blade casting. A proper withdrawal rate can obtain a better microstructure and a higher yield rate.

4. Grain growth and microstructure evolution of the SX turbine blades were simulated to predict the casting defects and to investigate the influence of the processing parameters. To get high-quality blades, the directional solidification process must be optimized and improved.

ACKNOWLEDGMENTS

This research is funded by National Basic Research Program of China (Nos. 2011CB706801, 2005CB724105), National Natural Science Foundation of China (Nos. 51171089, 10477010), National Science & Technology Major Projects (Nos. 2012ZX04012-011, 2011ZX04014-052, and 2009ZX04006-041), and National High Technology Research and Development Program of China (No. 2007AA04Z141).

REFERENCES

[1] A. de Bussac and Ch.-A. Gandin: *Mater. Sci. Eng.*, 1997, vol. A237, pp. 35-42.
[2] L. Liu, T. W. Huang, J. Zhang, and H. Z. Fu: *Mater. Lett.*, 2007, vol. 61, pp. 227-30.
[3] A. Kermanpur and N. Varahraam: *Mater. Sci. Technol.*, 2000, vol. 16, pp. 579-86.
[4] A. Wagner, B. A. Shollock, and M. McLean: *Mater. Sci. Eng. A*, 2004, vol. A374, pp. 270-79.
[5] Z. Y. Liu, Y. Lei, and H. Z. Fu: *Acta Metall. Sin.*, 2000, vol. 36, pp. 1-6 (in Chinese).
[6] P. Carter, D. C. Cox, Ch. A. Gandin, and R. C. Reed: *Mater. Sci. Eng. A*, 2000, vol. A280, pp. 233-46.
[7] A. Kermanpur, N. Varahram, P. Davami, and M. Rappaz: *Metall. Mater. Trans. B*, 2000, vol. 31B, pp. 1293-1305.
[8] J. R. Li, S. Z. Liu, H. L. Yuan, and Z. G. Zhong: *J. Mater. Sci. Technol.*, 2003, vol. 19, pp. 532-34.
[9] W. Wang, P. D. Lee, and M. Mclean: *Acta Mater.*, 2003, vol. 51, pp. 2971-87.
[10] J. Yu, Q. Y. Xu, K. Cui, B. Liu, A. Kimatsuka, Y. Kuroki, and A. Hirata: *J. Mater. Sci. Technol.*, 2007, vol. 23, pp. 47-54.
[11] K. Cui, Q. Y. Xu, J. Yu, B. C. Liu, A. Kimatsuka, Y. Kuroki, and F. Yokoyama: *Acta Metall. Sin.*, 2007, vol. 43, pp. 465-71 (in Chinese).
[12] M. Rappaz and Ch.-A. Gandin: *Acta Metall. Mater.*, 1993, vol. 41, pp. 345-60.
[13] P. Thevoz, J. L. Desbiolles, and M. Rappaz: *Metall. Trans. A*, 1989, vol. A20, pp. 311-22.
[14] W. Kurz, B. Giovanola, and R. Trivedi: *Acta Metall.*, 1986, vol. 34, pp. 823-30.
[15] Editorial Committee: *Application Manual of Engineering Material*, China Standards Press, Beijing, China, 2002, pp. 771-73 (in Chinese).
[16] D. Pan, Q. Y. Xu, B. C. Liu, J. R. Li, H. L. Yuan, and H. P. Jin: *JOM*, 2010, vol. 62, pp. 30-34.
[17] Q. Zheng, G. C. Hou, and W. M. Tian: *Chin. J. Nonferrous Met.*, 2001, vol. 11, pp. 176-78 (in Chinese).
[18] Z. J. Liang: Ph. D. Thesis, Tsinghua University, Beijing, China, 2003, pp. 78-104 (in Chinese).
[19] J. Yu: Ph. D. Thesis, Tsinghua University, Beijing, China, 2007, pp. 50-74 (in Chinese).
[20] D. Pan: Ph. D. Thesis, Tsinghua University, Beijing, China, 2010, pp. 81-105 (in Chinese).

12. Numerical Simulation and Optimization of Directional Solidification Process of Single Crystal Superalloy Casting

*Hang Zhang, Qingyan Xu * and Baicheng Liu*

Key Laboratory for Advanced Materials Processing Technology, Ministry of Education, School of Materials Science and Engineering, Tsinghua University, Beijing 100084, China

Abstract: The rapid development of numerical modeling techniques has led to more accurate results in modeling metal solidification processes. In this study, the cellular automaton-finite difference (CA-FD) method was used to simulate the directional solidification (DS) process of single crystal (SX) superalloy blade samples. Experiments were carried out to validate the simulation results. Meanwhile, an intelligent model based on fuzzy control theory was built to optimize the complicate DS process. Several key parameters, such as mushy zone width and temperature difference at the cast-mold interface, were recognized as the input variables. The input variables were functioned with the multi-variable fuzzy rule to get the output adjustment of withdrawal rate (v) (a key technological parameter). The multivariable fuzzy rule was built, based on the structure feature of casting, such as the relationship between section area, and the delay time of the temperature change response by changing v, and the professional experience of the operator as well. Then, the fuzzy controlling model coupled with CA-FD method could be used to optimize v in real-time during the manufacturing process. The optimized process was proven to be more flexible and adaptive for a steady and straygrain free DS process.

Key words: numerical simulation; directional solidification; single crystal superalloy; fuzzy controlling strategy

1. Introduction

With the rapid development of computer and information technology, computer aided manufacturing technologies (computer-aided design (CAD), computer aided engineering (CAE), computer-aided manufacturing (CAM), etc.) are widely used in industrial production[1-10]. The numerical simulation method used in the directional solidification (DS) process of superalloys is receiving more attention in aviation and energy industries[11-18].

An important application of the numerical simulation is to predict casting defects, such as shrinkage cavity, hot cracking, and single crystal integrity during the directional solidification of the turbine blades[19-24]. The integrity of single crystal is a major index for the production of single crystal (SX) blades. Stray grain is a usual defect, which is a focal point of simulation studies[23-28].

The DS process, with many controlling parameters, is a complicated process. There are interactive effects among these parameters, which leads to a very narrow process window for the manufacturing of SX blades. Withdrawal rate is one of the important parameters influencing the DS process. A great deal of research has been done to study the relationship between withdrawal rate, microstructure, and properties[25,29-33]. A constant withdrawal rate is often used in industries because it is easy and convenient to control, however, it has less flexibility and leads to a low yield rate of SX blades. The experiment-based variable withdrawal rate for DS process develops quickly and is adopted more and more[34,35]. However, the main problem is that it needs many trials, increases cost, and enlarges time circles.

The numerical simulation used in DS process provides an effective way to lower the experimental circle and cost. In addition, some simple variable withdrawal rate processes were already proposed by simulation technology for an efficient and defect-free DS process[29,34,35]. However, these studies are still limited to modeling the experiment with a few times of rate changing. The process improvement lacked guidelines, which still meant a method of trial and error, and did not make full use of numerical simulation techniques. There are some studies[36,37] on the optimizing of DS processes, based on modeling and simulation, however, new models and algorithms need to be developed to deal with the system's variables, to instantly adjust the solidification parameters, and, finally, to improve the DS process.

The directional solidification is a complicate nonlinear system and hard to describe using a precise mathematical model. Fuzzy controlling method, based on fuzzy set theory[38], can deal with the fuzzy relation of semantic variables easily, according to certain fuzzy rules. It is an expert in nonlinear, close coupling, and uncertain systems[39-43]. In this work, the fuzzy controlling model was built to optimize the directional solidification process. The interface temperature gradient and average mushy zone width were studied in detail. Through optimizing the withdrawal rate instantly during the calculation of the directional solidification process, the fuzzy controlling model aims to get a higher temperature gradient and improve the stability of the directional solidification process.

2. Physical and Mathematical Models

2.1 Directional Solidification Process

There are different pieces of equipment used in DS processes, and the Bridgeman furnace is one of the most widely used. This furnace can be simplified and divided into five parts for modeling and simulation: heating zone, Baffler, Cooling zone, Chill, and Withdrawal unit, as shown in Figure 1. If the Cooling zone is equipped with water-cooled copper rings, the Bridgeman furnace is used for the high rapid solidification (HRS) technology, which is a main DS method to produce superalloy blade castings.

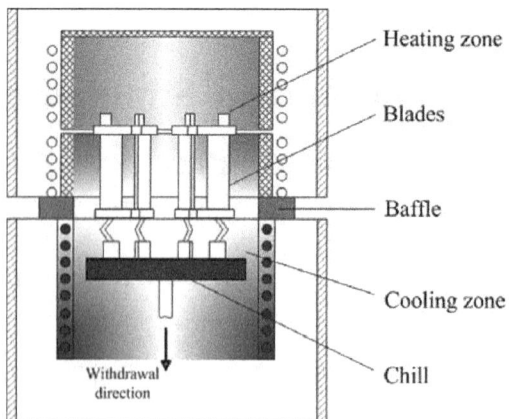

Fig. 1 Schematics of a Bridgman furnace.

In the HRS DS process, a group of mold shells are fixed on the chill. The liquid metal is poured into the mold and kept for minutes to make the temperature high enough. Then, the withdrawal unit starts, at certain speeds, of which the value is constant or variable. The baffler isolates the heating zone and cooling zone, then a unidirectional temperature gradient forms. When the liquid metal is drawn to pass the baffler, or entirely into the cooling zone, the mushy zone begins to freeze.

2.2 The Scheme of Optimizing DS Processes by Simulation Technology

Simulation technology was used to simulate DS processes for years. In this study, the fuzzy controlling model was built to optimize the withdrawal rate by simulation technology, as shown in Figures 2 and 3.

Firstly, the casting model was input and the withdrawal rate was pre-adjusted, based on the shape of the input model. Then, the DS process was simulated by the CA-FD method. The temperature field and microstructure growth were calculated step by step. Some key parameters, such as temperature gradient and mushy zone width, were analyzed by the fuzzy controlling model. The withdrawal rate was adjusted instantly. Then the optimized withdrawal rate was changed in the new simulation. During the simulating process, if there were stray grains appeared on the casting, the withdrawal rate would be post-adjusted and the simulating process would feed back to calculate again with a new withdrawal rate. Finally, when there is no defects predicted in the calculation, a withdrawal rate curve will be given out, which would be more effective and stable for the real DS process.

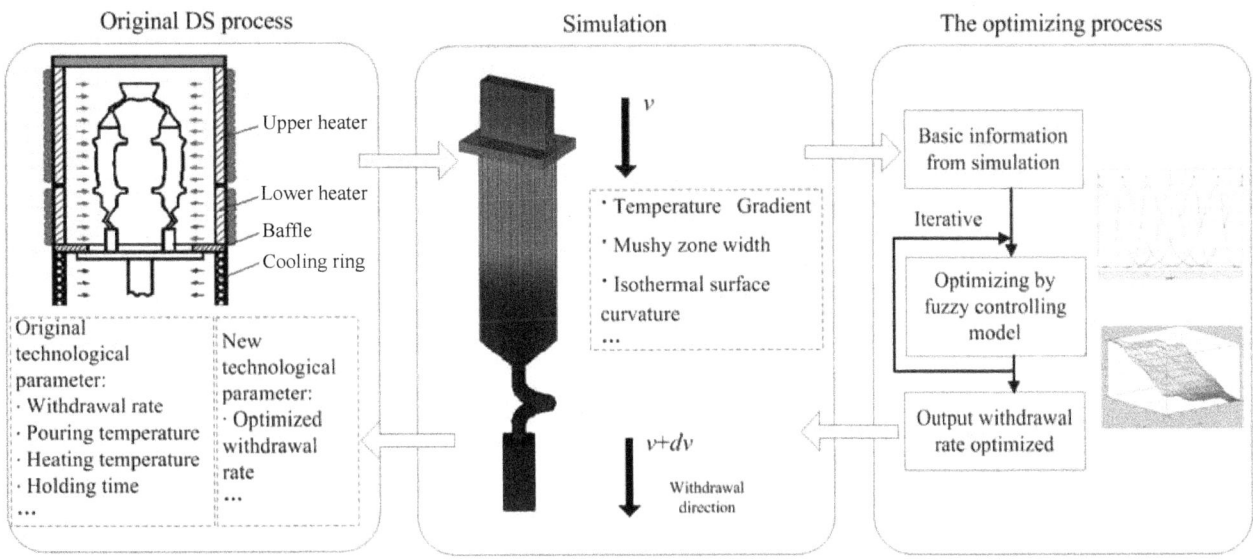

Fig. 2　The framework of DS processes, optimized by simulation.

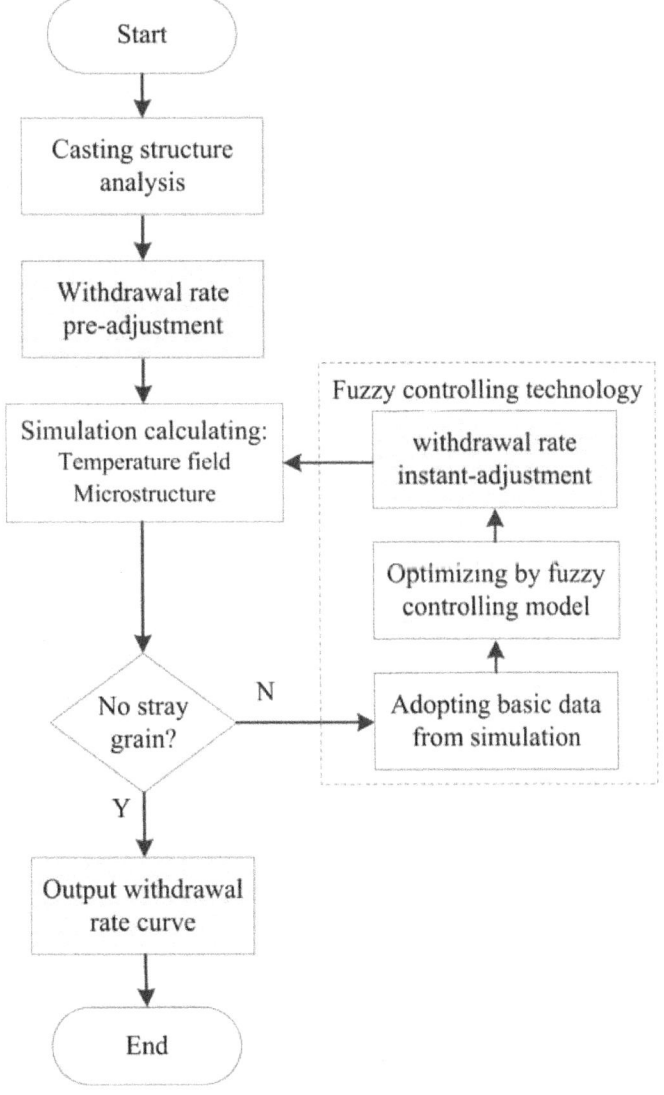

Fig. 3　The flow chart of withdrawal rate optimizing by simulation.

2.3 The Fuzzy Control Model for Optimizing DS Processes

A fuzzy control model was built to analyze the real time data derived from the simulation process, and some key variables were tracked to adjust the withdrawal rate.

2.3.1 The Fuzzy Controller

The mushy zone of DS process was studied by adopting a single output and three inputs model, as shown in Figure 4.

The three input variables are follows: ITE (the casting-mold interface temperature error) is the temperature difference between most inner cell's temperature in shell and the most outer cell's temperature in cast; ITEC is the change of ITE; WM is the average width of mushy zone. The output variable is SC (withdrawal speed change).

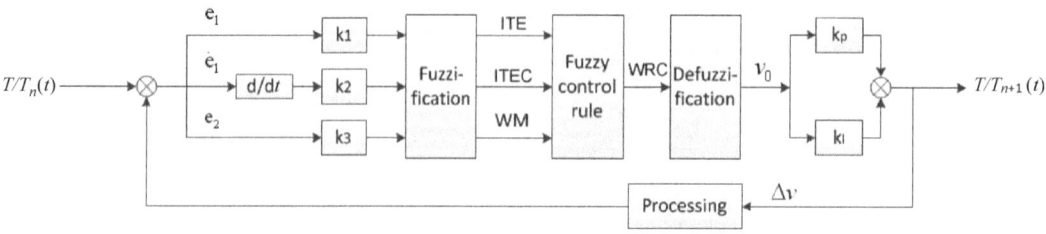

Fig. 4 The fuzzy controlling system.

2.3.2 The Domain of Discourse of Fuzzy Variables and Membership Functions

ITE was quantization into 13 grades, which are $\{-6, -5, -4, -3, -2, -1, +0, +1, +2, +3, +4, +5, +6\}$. The fuzzy subsets are $\{PB, PM, PS, O, NS, NM, NB\}$. e_1, $\dot{e}_1$ and e_2 are the accurate values of ITE, ITEC, and WM, respectively, and the corresponding quantification factors are k_{e_1}, $k_{\dot{e}_1}$, and k_{e_2}. The membership function of ITE is shown as Equation (1). The other fuzzy variables, such as ITEC, WM, and SC, are similarly treated with ITE. In the equation, a, b, and c are the parameters of the membership function.

$$f_{ITE}(x) = \begin{cases} \exp\left(-\dfrac{(x-a)^2}{2b^2}\right), & x \leqslant a \\ \exp\left(-\dfrac{(x-a)^2}{2c^2}\right), & x \geqslant a \end{cases} \quad (1)$$

2.3.3 Fuzzy Rules for Withdrawal Rate Adjustment

Fuzzy rules could be described as follows: if WM is WM_i and ITE is ITE_j, and ITEC is $ITEC_k$, SC is SC_{ijk}.

The fuzzy relation can be written as Equations (2) and (3):

$$\begin{aligned} R_{ijk} &= (WM_i \times SC_{ijk}) \wedge (ITE_j \times SC_{ijk}) \wedge (ITEC_k \times SC_{ijk}) \\ &= (WM_i \times ITE_j \times ITEC_k) \times SC_{ijk} \end{aligned} \quad (2)$$

$$R = R_{111} + R_{112} + \cdots + R_{ijk} + \cdots + R_{opq} = \bigcup_{i,j,k} R_{ijk}$$
$$i = 1, 2, \cdots, o \quad j = 1, 2, \cdots, p \quad k = 1, 2, \cdots, q \quad (3)$$

where WM_i, ITE_j, $ITEC_k$, and SC_{ijk} are the semantic input variables of WM, ITE, ITEC, and WRC, respectively.

During the simulation calculation of DS process, e_1, $\dot{e}_1$, and e_2 were received, as well as the semantic input variables, such as WM_i, ITE_j, and $ITEC_k$. The semantic output variable of fuzzy controller is calculated based on Equation (4):

$$\begin{aligned} SC^\delta &= (WM_r \times ITE_s \times ITEC_t) \circ R \\ &= (WM_r \times ITE_s \times ITEC_t) \circ \bigcup_{i,j,k} R_{ijk} \\ &= \bigcup_{i,j,k} (WM_r \times ITE_s \times ITEC_t) \circ \\ & \quad (WM_i \times ITE_j \times ITEC_k) \times SC_{ijk} \\ &= \bigcup_{i,j,k} \sup[(WM_r \times ITE_s \times ITEC_t) \wedge \\ & \quad (WM_i \times ITE_j \times ITEC_k)] \wedge SC_{ijk} \end{aligned} \quad (4)$$

$v(t)$ can be calculated based on the defuzzification of SC^δ, shown as Equation (5):

$$v(t) = \Delta v + v(t-1) = k_e \cdot \text{sgn}(SC^\delta) \cdot \text{Int}(SC^\delta + 0.5) + v(t-1) \quad (5)$$

k_e is the scale factor. $\text{sgn}(x)$ is sign function. $\text{Int}(x)$ is rounding function.

3. The Optimizing Process by Simulation

3.1 The Basic Simulation Condition

The SX sample blade designed has the main features of a real SX blade: the whole length is over 200mm; the platform has an abrupt change of section; the body of the blade rotates at a certain angle respective to the tenon. The experimental material was Ni-based superalloy DD6[44,45]. There were four schemes for simulation: group SG1 with the rate of 7.0mm/min, group SG2 with the rate of 4.5mm/min, group SG3 with the rate of 1.0mm/min and group SG4 with the rate optimized by fuzzy controlling model. Two groups were selected for experimental study: Group EG1 with the rate of 7.0mm/min and Group EG2 with the rate of 4.5mm/min. The parameters used in these simulating groups are shown as Table 1.

Table 1 The parameters used in the calculation (Superalloy DD6[44,45]).

Parameters	Unit	Value
Liquidus	℃	1370
Solidus	℃	1310
Density of alloy	g/cm³	8.78
Density of shell	g/cm³	2.50
Temperature of cooling water	℃	25

3.2 The Optimized Variable Withdrawal Rate Process

The optimized withdrawal rate of DS process was obtained in the group SG4. Figure 5 shows the curves of withdrawal rates of groups SG1—SG4. From the simulation results, it can be seen that the solidification time of SG4 was 75.5 min, which was half that of SG3, but longer than that of SG2.

The solidification processes of the four groups of DS were calculated. Then, the temperature distribution, mushy zones and temperature gradients of different processes could be analyzed by solidification times. Figure 6 is the temperature distributions of SG4 during the DS process. These temperature cloud charts show the unidirectional heat diffusion and temperature gradient distribution. The isothermal lines basically kept horizontal and some showed a slight slant, or concave or convex.

3.3 The Comparison of Constant and Optimized Withdrawal Rates Processes

Figure 7 is the microstructures of SG1-SG4 by simulation. SG1 with a constant rate of 7mm/min appeared some stray grains in the platform, contrast to other groups. These stray grains disqualified the casting, which had different orientations from the single grain grown from the blade body. In Figure 7, although there were no stray grains at the other blades, SG2 had a very narrow process window and would tend to form stray grains at small fluctuations of other process parameters, and SG3 was of too low efficiency and had too many defects to be applied in the industry production, which will be further explained below. Thus, SG4 could have a higher productivity and no stray grains.

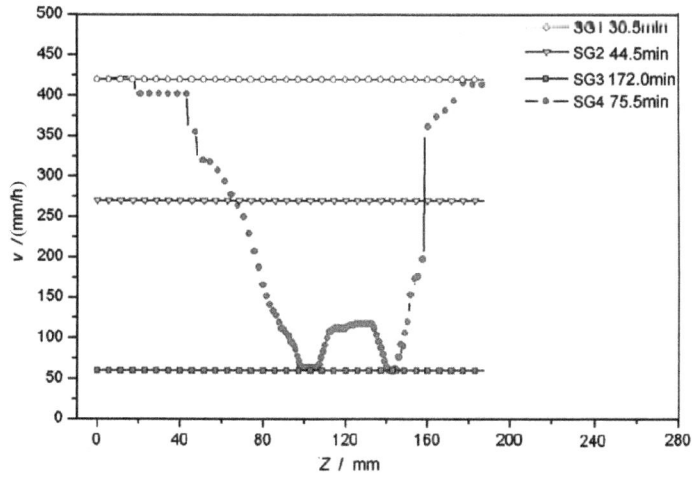

Fig. 5 Curves of withdrawal rates of SG1-SG4

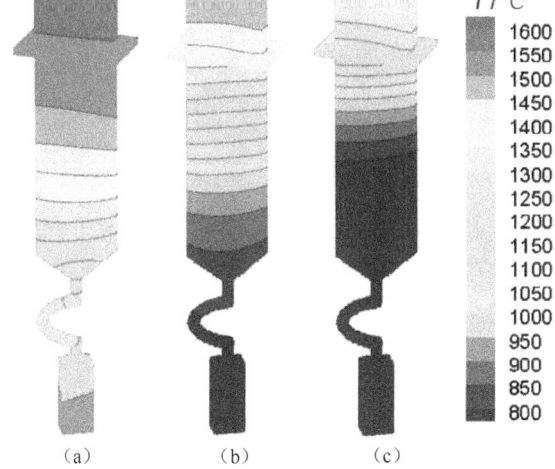

Fig. 6 Temperature distribution of SG4 at different time
(a) 19min; (b) 27.5min; (c) 36min.

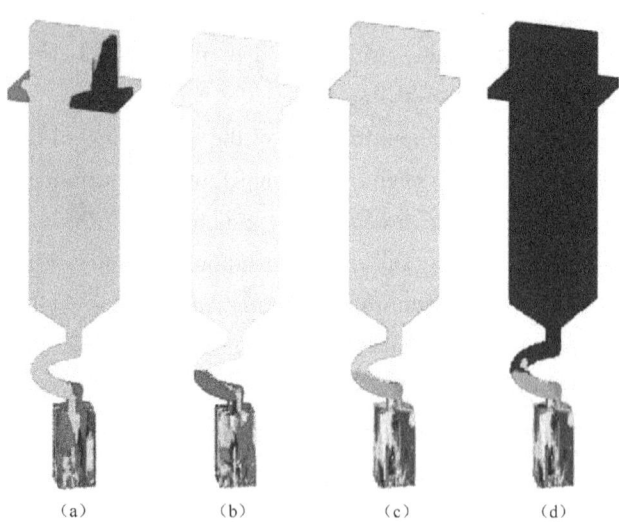

Fig. 7 Simulated Microstructures of the four groups
(a) SG1; (b) SG2; (c) SG3; (d) SG4.

Stray grain is one of most severe defects of SX blade. Figure 8 is the comparison of microstructure of EG1 and SG1. Both results of EG1 and SG1 showed that the stray grains mostly started and formed in the platform, where were far from the root of the tenon and at a deep overcooling, as shown in Figure 8a, c. From Figure 8b, the locations and boundaries of stray grains predicted by simulation were similarly with that by experiment. And it's proved that the simulating models for heat transfer and microstructure evolution were accurate to predict the DS process of SX blade well.

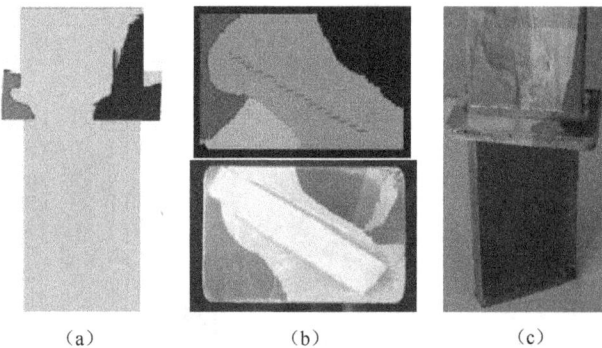

Fig. 8 The comparison of microstructure of SG1 with EG1
(a) The simualtion of microstructure of SX blade (partly);
(b) The comparison between simulation and experiment
(upward view, i.e., the bottom surface of the platform);
(c) The experimental result of EG1.

There are many reasons which caused stray grains, such as impurity of the melt, ceramic sunken surface, the surface of metal needles for fastening position, as well as the formation of deep undercooling zone. The deep undercooling will be the main factor leading to the stray grains in the real SX turbine blades.

In this study, SG1 and EG1 show obvious stray grains at the platform, as shown in Figure 9a, b. The undercooling zone was the main area that a stray grain nucleated and grew, which was caused by the non-uniform temperature distribution. As for SG1 and EG1, the stray grains formed at platforms. In Figure 9c, the special zones were marked in the simulated results, where the cells did not solidify but of which temperatures were lower than liquidus. These cells were named isolated undercooling zones (IUZs). IUZ provided the low temperature melt for stray grain nucleation and growth. IUZ was formed on certain condition of DS process, for example, a faster withdrawal rate.

According to the definition above, IUZ has some features: (a) Stray grains of SX blades are mainly formed in IUZs; (b) The location and range of an IUZ are influenced and divided based on the temperature distribution; (c) IUZ often appears at some tips of the casting where heat dissipation is faster; (d) The analysis of IUZ is a convenient way to predict areas of the stray grain formation.

Figure 10 shows the IUZs formed during the calculations of SG1—SG4. The IUZs of SG1 were larger in range and more in number, as shown in Figure 10a. IUZs of SG3 and SG4 were smaller than others, which was the main reason for no stray grains formed in these groups. In addition, IUZs of SG2 were inclined to formed stray grains, but at the critical status.

There are lots of factors influenced on the formation of IUZ, and withdrawal rate is an important one. The quick change of the cross-section area at the platform allowed more heat dissipation from the part below the platform, such as cooling zone or the water-cooled copper plate. Then at some edge or corner of the platform, the melt has a lower temperature than liquidus, but not turned to be solid, and the IUZs were formed.

Based on the analysis above, a smaller IUZ is expected by adjusting the withdrawal rate. A lower withdrawal rate is benefit for keeping the IUZs at the heating zone of the furnace as long as possible. Then, the heat radiation would warm up these IUZs and compress their regions. Then, stray grain has no time and space to nu-

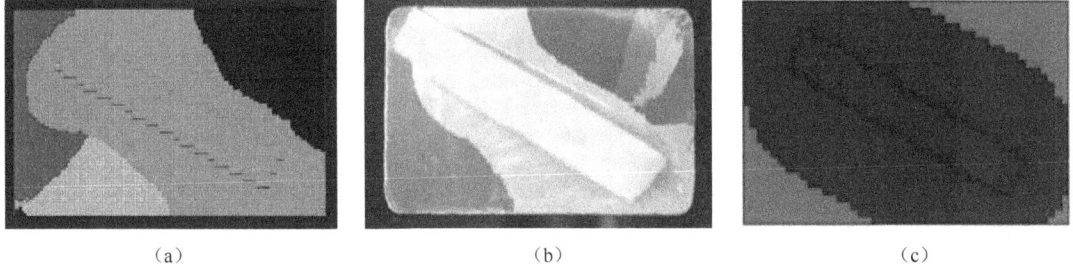

Fig. 9 The comparison beween the simulation and experiment to show stray grains formations (upward view, i.e., the bottom surface of the platform) (a) simulation result (SG1); (b) experiment result (EG1); (c) isolated undercooling zones (IUZ) of SG1.

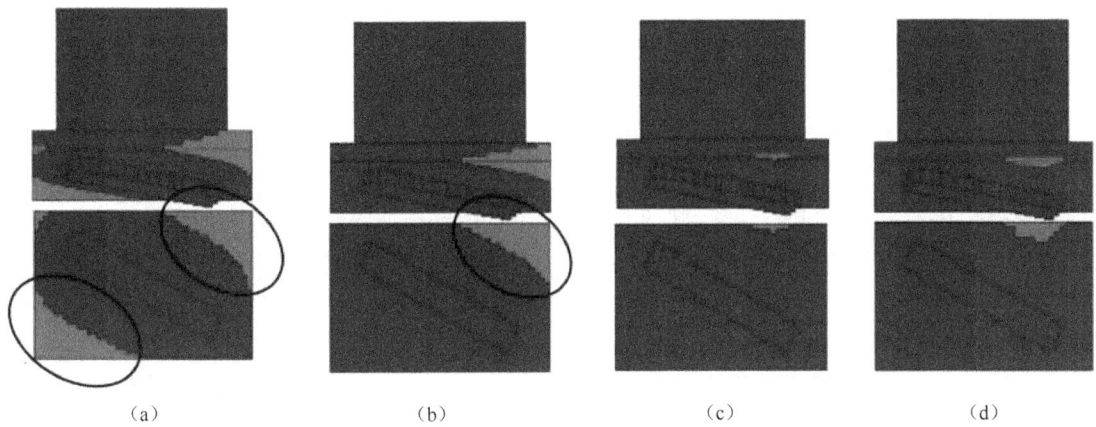

Fig. 10 The IUZ distributions of the four simulation groups (a) SG1; (b) SG2; (c) SG3; (d) SG4. The upper figures are side views in 3D, and the lower figures are the vertical views of the platform.

cleate and grow. It provides a method for the fuzzy controlling model to optimize withdrawal rate dynamically, as shown in Figure 10d.

4. Advantages of the Fuzzy Optimizing Model

4.1 To Get Higher Temperature Gradient

Temperature gradient of mushy zone is a major parameter of the DS process, which influences the grain growth and quality of final castings. In the study, temperature gradients in mushy zones during solidification process were sampled (interval: 0.5min), as shown in Figure 11. In all four groups, temperature gradients at bottom of starter block and at center of platform were higher than 6K/mm, which resulted from the fast heat transfer of water-cooled chill plate and the sudden change of section area at the platform, respectively.

Meanwhile, temperature gradients during the whole solidification process of SG3 and SG4 were higher than that of SG1 and SG2, which showed the advantages of these two processes.

In conclusion, SG4 had a short solidification time than SG3, as shown in Figure 5, but its temperature gradients were higher than others. That is to say, at a proper time span, the DS process with an optimized withdrawal rate is benefit for improving microstructure and properties, and increasing productivity and yield rate of SX blades.

4.2 To Enlarge the Process Window

DS process has many controlling parameters, which are complicate and coupled closely. Thus, the process is narrow for DS casting, which means a minor fluctuation may be amplified and lead to the formation of stray grains or other defects.

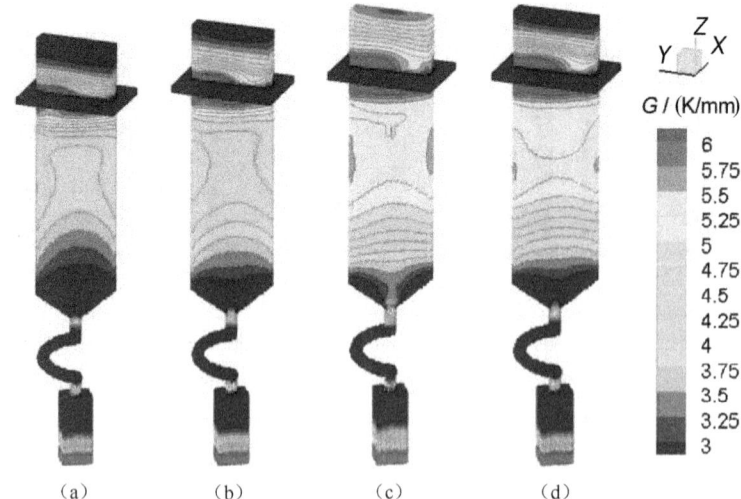

Fig. 11 Temperature gradients of mushy zones during DS process (a) SG1; (b) SG2; (c) SG3; (d) SG4.

In the work, the frequencies of ΔT (the physical value of ITE) and mushy zone width were studied during the whole solidification process, and the sampling interval is 30s. Figure 12 shows the frequencies of ΔT_s during the solidification process of the four groups. When the ΔT is zero, it means the transverse temperature gradient is eliminated, which is ideal for a DS process. In Figure 12d, most of ΔT_s were assembling around zero, which means the optimized process could keep a good unidirectional heat flux. Particularly noteworthy is that most frequencies of ΔT_s in Figure 12c were not good as those in Figure 12d. However, in Figure 12a, b, most frequencies of ΔT_s correspond to around 5℃ or more. The SG4 had a relative longer time when ΔT_s equaled to 0, which means a better DS condition than others.

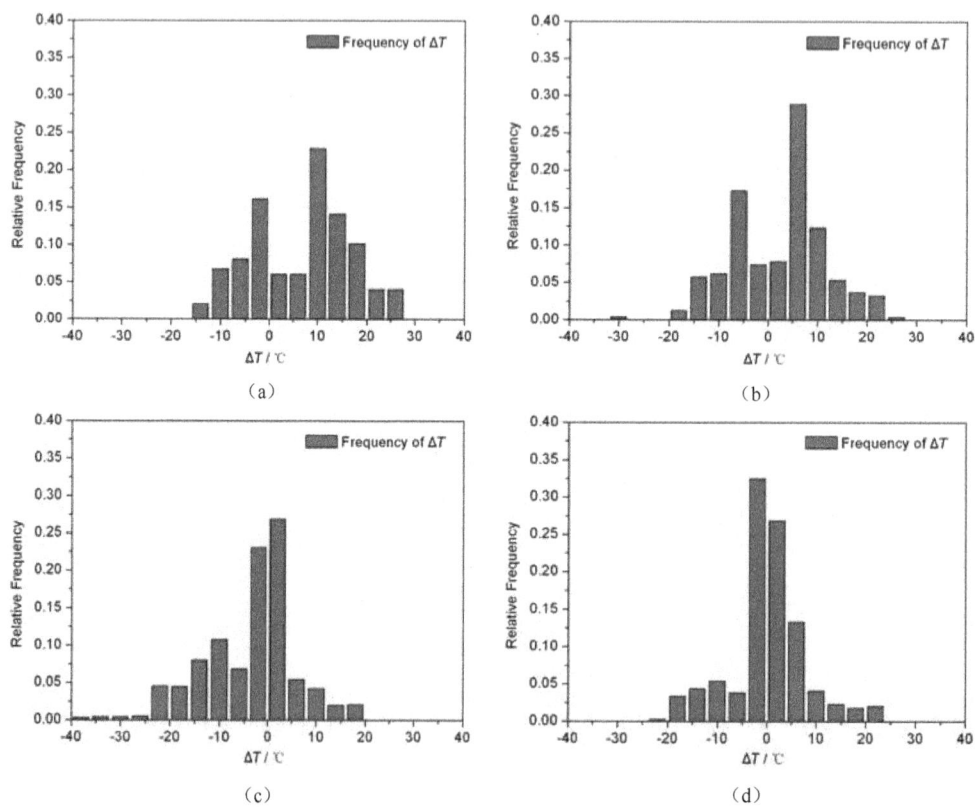

Fig. 12 The frequency distributions of ΔT during the solidification time
(a) SG1; (b) SG2; (c) SG3; (d) SG4.

Figure 13 shows the frequency distributions of WM of the four simulation groups. The frequency distributions of SG1 and SG2 were basically uniform and approximately distributed at the range of 7.5~20mm. Most frequencies of WMs of SG4 concentrated around 10mm and the frequency rate was above 0.25, better than that of SG3, as shown in Figure 13c. This concentration made sure the stabilities of WM and temperature gradient of mushy zone, which was benefit for a more stable DS process and allowed other solidification parameters to adjust in a lager range.

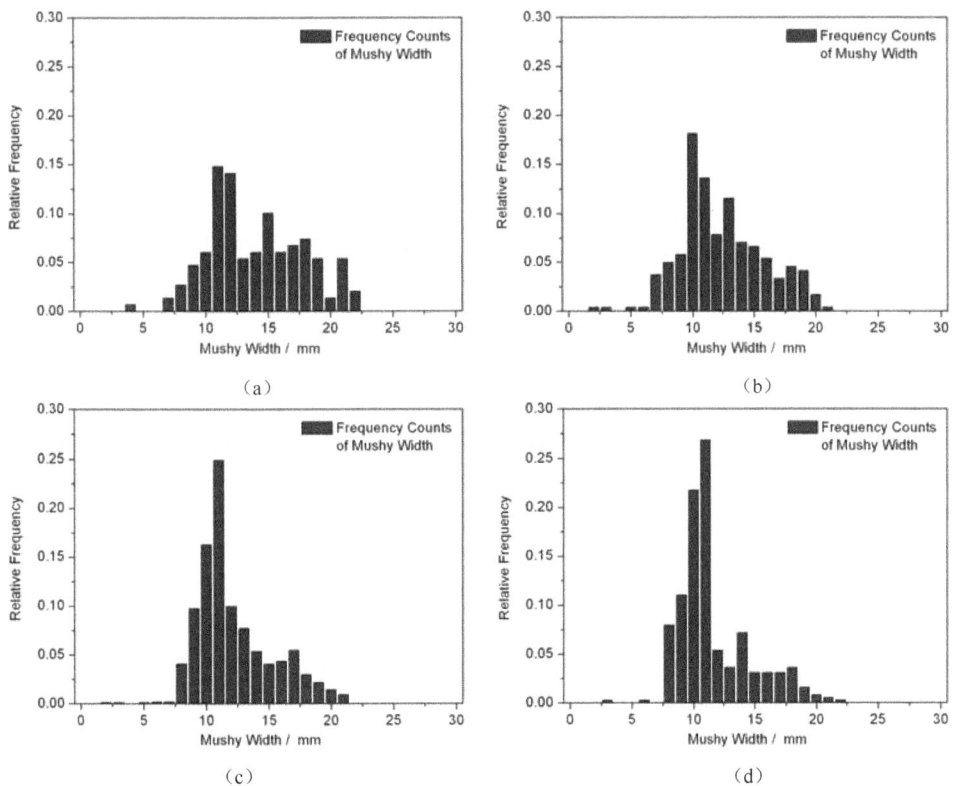

Fig. 13 The frequency distributions of mushy zone width of the four simulation groups
(a) SG1; (b) SG2; (c) SG3; (d) SG4.

5. Conclusions

The mathematical and physical models were built for the DS process. The SX blade was studied by numerical simulation and experimental methods. Stray grain formations were successfully predicted by simulation, and the IUZ was proposed to analyze the mechanism of stray grain formation at the platform.

A fuzzy controlling model for optimizing the DS withdrawal rate was built, and the withdrawal rate for SX blade casting was optimized. The optimized process could successfully get sound SX blade castings.

The advantages of optimized process were analyzed, based on the comparisons of temperature gradients, ITG, and WM. The proposed optimized technology in the paper that couples the intelligent controlling technology and the simulation technology is a useful way to optimize the DS process withdrawal rate and the model is useful to get a higher temperature gradient and enlarge the DS process window.

Acknowledgments

Thanks for the funds of National Basic Research Program of China (No. 2011CB706801), National Natural Science Foundation of China (Nos. 51171089 and 51374137), National Science and Technology Major Project (Nos. 2011ZX04014-052 and 2012ZX04012-011).

Conflicts of Interest

The authors declare no conflict of interest.

Author Contributions

In this research, Hang Zhang built the basic optimized model and finished the modeling and experiment. Qingyan Xu corrected the optimized model and Baicheng Liu reviewed this paper.

References

[1] Lee, A. Integrating computer aids [CAD/CAM]. *Engineer* **1982**, *6572*, 35.

[2] Shah, J. J.; Rogers, M. T. Functional requirements and conceptual design of the feature-based modelling system. *Comput. Aided Eng. J.* **1988**, *5*, 9-15.

[3] Roy, U.; Zhang, X. Establishment of a pair of concentric circles with the minimum radial separation for assessing roundness error. *Comput. Aided Design* **1992**, *24*, 161-168.

[4] De Martino, T.; Falcidieno, B.; Hassinger, S. Design and engineering process integration through a multiple view intermediate modeller in a distributed object-oriented system environment. *Comput. Aided Design* **1998**, *30*, 437-452.

[5] Liu, B. C. A new generation of precision casting forming process based on physical metallurgy and mathematical physics modeling. *China Mech. Eng.* **2000**, *1*, 67-69.

[6] Regli, W. C.; Cicirello, V. A. Managing digital libraries for computer-aided design. *Comput. Aided Design* **2000**, *32*, 119-132.

[7] Hoffman, C. M.; Lomonosov, A.; Sitharam, M. Decomposition plans for geometric constraint systems, part I: Performance measures for CAD. *J. Symb. Comput.* **2001**, *31*, 367-408.

[8] Sun, W.; Lin, F.; Hu, X. Computer-aided design and modeling of composite unit cells. *Compos. Sci. Technol.* **2001**, *61*, 289-299.

[9] Kim, K. Y.; Wang, Y.; Muogboh, O. S.; Nnajia, B. O. Design formalism for collaborative assembly design. *Comput. Aided Design* **2004**, *36*, 849-871.

[10] Sudarsan, R.; Fenves, S. J.; Sriram, R. D.; Wang, F. A product information modeling framework for product lifecycle management. *Comput. Aided Design* **2005**, *37*, 1399-1411.

[11] Gandin, C. A.; Rappaz, M.; Tintillier, R. 3-dimensional simulation of the grain formation in investment castings. *Metall. Mater. Trans. A* **1994**, *25*, 629-635.

[12] Yang, X. L.; Lee, P. D.; D'Souza, N. Stray grain formation in the seed region of single-crystal turbine blades. *JOM* **2005**, *57*, 40-44.

[13] Rappaz, M.; Gandin, C. A. Probabilistic modeling of microstructure formation in solidification processes. *Acta Metall. Mater.* **1993**, *41*, 345-360.

[14] Gandin, C. A.; Rappaz, M. A coupled finite-element cellular-automaton model for the prediction of dendritic grain structures in solidification processes. *Acta Metall. Mater.* **1994**, *42*, 2233-2246.

[15] Pan, D.; Xu, Q. Y.; Liu, B. C. Three-dimensional microstructure simulation of Ni-based superalloy investment castings. *Sci. China Phys. Mech. Astron.* **2011**, *54*, 851-855.

[16] Yu, J.; Xu, Q. Y.; Cui, K.; Liu, B. C.; Kimatsuka, A.; Kuroki, A.; Hirata, A. Numerical simulation of solidification process on single crystal Ni-based superalloy investment castings. *J. Mater. Sci. Technol.* **2007**, *23*, 47-54.

[17] Zhang, H.; Xu, Q. Y.; Tang, N.; Pan, D.; Liu, B. C. Numerical simulation of microstructure evolution during directional solidification process in directional solidified (DS) turbine blades. *Sci. China Technol. Sci.* **2011**, *54*, 3191-3202.

[18] Galantucci, L. M.; Tricarico, L. A computer-aided approach for the simulation of the directional-solidification process for gas turbine blades. *J. Mater. Process. Technol.* **1998**, *77*, 160-165.

[19] Yang, X. L.; Dong, H. B.; Wang, W.; Lee, P. D. Microscale simulation of stray grain formation in investment cast turbine blades. *Mater. Sci. Eng. A* **2004**, *386*, 129-139.

[20] Yang, X. L.; Ness, D.; Lee, P. D.; D'Souza, N. Simulation of stray grain formation during single crystal seed melt-back and initial withdrawal in the Ni-base superalloy CMSX4. *Mater. Sci. Eng. A* **2005**, *413-414*, 571-577.

[21] Zambaldi, C.; Roters, F.; Raabe, D.; Glatzel, U. Modeling and experiments on the indentation deformation and recrystallization of a single-crystal nickel-base superalloy. *Mater. Sci. Eng. A* **2007**, *454-455*, 433-440.

[22] He, Y. H.; Hou, X. Q.; Tao, C. H.; Han, F. K. Recrystallization and fatigue fracture of single crystal turbine blades. *Eng. Fail. Anal.* **2011**, *18*, 944-949.

[23] Fang, Y.; Li, Y.; He, W.; Lu, Y.; Li, P. Numerical simulation of residual stresses fields of DD6 blade during laser shock processing. *Mater. Design* **2013**, *43*, 170-176.

[24] Panwisawas, C.; Mathur, H.; Gebelin, J.; Putman, D.; Rae, C. M. F.; Reed, R. C. Prediction of recrystallization in investment cast single-crystal superalloys. *Acta Mater.* **2013**, *61*, 51-66.

[25] De Bussac, A.; Gandin, C. A. Prediction of a process window for the investment casting of dendritic single crystals. *Mater. Sci. Eng. A* 1997, *237*, 35-42.

[26] Yasuda, H.; Ohnaka, I.; Kawasaki, K.; Sugiyama, A.; Ohmichi, T.; Iwane, J.; Umetani, K. Direct observation of stray crystal formation in unidirectional solidification of Sn-Bi alloy by X-ray imaging. *J. Cryst. Growth* **2004**, *262*, 645-652.

[27] Zhou, Y. Formation of stray grains during directional solidification of a nickel-based superalloy. *Scr. Mater.* **2011**, *65*, 281-284.

[28] Zhao, X. B.; Liu, L.; Zhang, W. G.; Qu, M.; Zhang, J.; Fu, H. Z. Analysis of competitive growth mechanism of stray grains of single crystal superalloys during directional solidification process. *Rare Met. Mater. Eng.* **2011**, *40*, 9-13.

[29] Liu, S. Z.; Li, J. R.; Tang, D. Z.; Zhong, Z. G. Numerical simulation of directional solidification process of single crystal superalloys. *J. Mater. Eng.* 1999, 40-42.

[30] Liu, C. B.; Shen, J.; Zhang, J.; Lou, L. H. Effect of withdrawal rates on microstructure and creep strength of a single crystal superalloy processed by LMC. *J. Mater. Sci. Technol.* **2010**, *26*, 306-310.

[31] Liu, L.; Huang, T.; Qu, M.; Liu, G.; Zhang, J.; Fu, H. High thermal gradient directional solidification and its application in the processing of nickel-based superalloys. *J. Mater. Process. Technol.* **2010**, *210*, 159-165.

[32] Liu, G.; Liu, L.; Ai, C.; Ge, B.; Zhang, J.; Fu, H. Influence of withdrawal rate on the microstructure of Ni-base single-crystal superalloys containing Re and Ru. *J. Alloys Compd.* **2011**, *509*, 5866-5872.

[33] Jin, T.; Li, J. G.; Zhao, N. R.; Wang, Z.; Sun, X. F.; Guan, H. R.; Hu, Z. L. Effects of withdrawal rate on solidification parameters and microstructure of a nickel-based single crystal superalloy. *J. Mater. Eng.* **2002**, *3*, 36-39.

[34] Yu, J. Numerical Simulation of Directional Solidification Process and Microstructure Evolution of Superalloy Turbine Blade Castings. Master's Thesis, Tsinghua University, Beijing, China, April 2007.

[35] Pan, D. Numerical Simulation of Microstructure Formation and Evolution of Directional Solidified and Single Crystal Turbine Blade Casting. Master's Thesis, Tsinghua University, Beijing, China, April 2010.

[36] Monastyrskiy, V. Modeling and numerical optimization of withdrawal rate in directional solidification process. *IOP Conf. Ser. Mater. Sci. Eng.* **2012**, *33*, doi: 10.1088/1757-899X/33/1/012023.

[37] Hofmann, N.; Olive, S.; Laschet, G.; Hediger, F.; Wolf, J.; Sahm, P. R. Numerical optimization of process control variables for the Bridgman casting process. *Modell. Simul. Mater. Sci. Eng.* **1997**, *5*, doi: 10.1088/0965-0393/5/1/002.

[38] Takagi, T.; Sugeno, M. F. Fuzzy identification of systems and its applications to modeling and control. *IEEE Trans. Syst. Man Cybern.* **1985**, *SMC-15*, 116-132.

[39] Lee, C. C. Fuzzy-logic in control-systems-fuzzy-logic controller. 1. *IEEE Trans. Syst. Man Cybern.* **1990**, *20*, 404-418.

[40] Wang, H. O.; Tanaka, K.; Griffin, M. F. An approach to fuzzy control of nonlinear systems: Stability and design issues. *IEEE Trans. Fuzzy Syst.* **1996**, *4*, 14-23.

[41] Cao, S. G.; Rees, N. W.; Feng, G. Analysis and design for a class of complex control systems. Part I: Fuzzy modelling and identification. *Automatica* **1997**, *33*, 1017-1028.

[42] Hsu, Y.; Chen, G.; Tong, S.; Li, H. Integrated fuzzy modeling and adaptive control for nonlinear systems. *Inf. Sci.* **2003**, *153*, 217-236.

[43] Abonyi, J.; Nagy, L.; Szeifert, F. Adaptive fuzzy inference system and its application in modelling and model based control. *Chem. Eng. Res. Design* **1999**, *77*, 281-290.

[44] Li, J. R.; Zhong, Z. G.; Tang, D. Z.; Liu, S. Z.; Wei, P.; Wei, P. Y.; Wu, Z. T.; Huang, D. A low-cost second generation single crystal superalloy DD6. In Proceedings of the 10th International Symposium on Superalloys, Warrendale, PA, USA, 17 September 2000.

[45] Li, J. R.; Zhao, J. Q.; Liu, S. Z.; Han, M. Effects of low angle boundaries on the mechanical properties of single crystal superalloy DD6. In Proceedings of the 11th International Symposium on Superalloys, Champion, PA, USA, 14 September 2008.

13. Deformation and recrystallization of single crystal nickel-based superalloys during investment casting

Li Zhonglin[a], Xiong Jichun[b], Xu Qingyan[a], Li Jiarong[b], Liu Baicheng[a]

[a] School of Materials Science and Engineering, Key Laboratory for Advanced Materials Processing Technology, Ministry of Education, Tsinghua University, Beijing 100084, China

[b] National Key Laboratory of Advanced High Temperature Structural Materials, Beijing Institute of Aeronautical Materials, Beijing 100095, China

ARTICLE INFO

Article history: Received 28 August 2014 Received in revised form 21 October 2014 Accepted 23 October 2014 Available online 4 November 2014

Key words: Single crystal Superalloys Investment casting Plastic deformation Recrystallization

ABSTRACT: A semi-quantitative, macroscopic, phenomenon-based, thermo-elastic-plastic model was developed to predict the final plastic strains of single crystal nickel-based superalloys by considering their orthotropic mechanical properties. Various cases were considered and simulated to investigate the basic factors that influence the final plasticity. Thermo-mechanical numerical analysis was conducted to predict the recrystallization sites of simplified cored rods, with the results in good agreement with the experimental results. These hollowed rods with thin walls showed an increased propensity for recrystallization. The geometric features, especially stress concentration sites, are more significant to the induced plasticity than the material's orientation or shell/core materials. This paper also attempts to provide useful suggestions, such as introducing filets, to avoid causing plastic strains during the casting process that induce recrystallization.

© 2014 The Authors. Published by Elsevier B. V. This is an open access article under the CC BY license (http://creativecommons.org/licenses/by/3.0/).

1. Introduction

Turbine blades for gas turbine applications are fabricated by investment casting, often in single crystal form, which can allow higher inlet gas temperatures to be used and increase efficiency. However, the external and internal geometries of single crystal blades are becoming increasingly complicated, making them more difficult to cast as greater care is required to prevent defects, such as stray grains and freckles, being introduced during the manufacturing process. Recrystallization (RX) is one of the major difficulties and can be ascribed to plastic deformation, as demonstrated by Burgel et al. (2000). During the manufacture of new parts, plastic deformation can be caused by several possible sources: thermal contraction during solidification and subsequent cooling, removing the ceramic mold and core material mechanically, stamping identification marks, grinding the airfoil, etc. In practice, plastic deformation will induce RX during subsequent heat treatments or long-term service. For example, RX can introduce high-angle grain boundaries, which are obviously undesirable. As demonstrated by Meng et al. (2010) and Moverare et al. (2009), RX is potentially detrimental to creep and fatigue properties, respectively.

Work has been done to study the phenomenon of

RX in single crystal nickel-based superalloys. Some research has focused on the influence of microstructural features on RX, such as γ′-precipitates, carbides, and γ/γ′ eutectics. For example, Dahlen and Winberg (1980) have discussed the influence of γ′-precipitation on the RX of nickel-based superalloys. Wang et al. (2013) and Xiong et al. (2010) have investigated the effect of carbon content on the RX of single crystal (SX) nickel-based superalloys. In addition, Wang et al. (2009) studied the influence of eutectics on plastic deformation and the subsequent RX of the SX nickel-based superalloy CMSX-4. Meanwhile, some research has concentrated on the effect of different annealing conditions and crystallographic orientations on RX behavior. Wu et al. (2012) conducted surface RX of a Ni_3Al-based SX superalloy at different annealing temperatures and blasting pressures. Xie et al. (2012) studied the crystallographic orientation dependence of RX in a Ni-based SX superalloy. However, little attention has been paid to the effect of geometric features, ceramic shell and core material, and processing details. Certain critical questions need to be answered, such as at what temperature will RX occur? What is the critical plastic deformation required to induce RX?, and what is the influence of the geometric features, including holes and platforms? Answers to these questions will allow more efficient foundry processes, even process-friendly blade designs, to be developed. Modeling has been used to analyze the directional solidification of SX superalloys from thermal and microstructural perspectives. Pan et al. (2010) conducted multiscale modeling and simulations of the directional solidification process of turbine blade casting, which resulted in good predictions of temperature profiles and grain number. Dai et al. (2011) investigated grain selection in spiral selectors during investment casting of SX turbine blades through both experimental and numerical modeling techniques. One advantage simulation provides over experiments is that it can predict the plastic strains that cause RX.

The overarching goal of this study was to build a physics-based tool for predicting casting-induced plasticity and subsequent RX during the heat treatment of SX superalloys by considering the material's anisotropic mechanical properties. Panwisawas et al. (2013a, b) developed a mathematical model to predict plasticity and RX in investment-cast SX superalloys. However, this model considered SX superalloys as isotropic materials, which does not conform to the reality. Many mechanical models have been proposed to describe the mechanical properties of anisotropic materials. Ding et al. (2004) proposed a macroscopic phenomenon-based model built on a modified Hill plasticity model. Zambaldi et al. (2007) employed a microscopic crystal plasticity model, which was built on the physical deformation mechanisms of materials, to predict the distribution of crystallographic slip in SX nickel-based superalloys. The former gained great popularity for its concise equations, as well as its convenience and speed of calculations, though the latter model can give more accurate predictions of slips and grain size.

This paper proposed a mathematical thermo-mechanical model using the Hill's plasticity model as a basis, which considers the orthotropic mechanical properties of SX superalloys, and took into account both the scale effect and convenience. Numerical analysis using this model was performed to identify the major factors that cause the plasticity during investment casting and RX during the subsequent heat treatment. A series of simplified thermomechanical numerical analyses with the DD6 superalloy were conducted and compared with experimental results to test the validity of the model. This model could be employed to optimize processing conditions to reduce the likelihood of RX.

2. Mathematical model of SX superalloys

Plastic deformation during investment casting mainly occurs because of the different thermal expansion coefficients of the metals, and the ceramic shell and core. Assuming the plasticity is rate-independent, the thermal strain (ε_{th}), elastic strain (ε_{el}), and plastic strain (ε_{pl}) follow the relation below:

$$\varepsilon_{th} + \varepsilon_{el} + \varepsilon_{pl} = 0 \quad (1)$$

The thermal strain can be calculated as

$$\varepsilon_{th} = \alpha \Delta T = \alpha(T - T_{ref}) \quad (2)$$

Here, T_{ref} is the reference temperature, which is usually room temperature. The variable α denotes the thermal expansion coefficient, which is usually considered isotropic for SX materials (Green, 1998).

2.1 Orthotropic elastic properties

The elastic strain part of the model for SX superalloys considers the orthotropic characteristics. For materials with cubic structures (BCC or FCC), where the three principal orientations (denoted 1, 2, and 3) are identical, the elastic constitutive equation is determined with the generalized Hooke law, which can be expressed as follows:

$$\{\varepsilon\} = [S]\{\sigma\}$$
$$\{\sigma\} = [S]^{-1}\{\varepsilon\} = [C]\{\varepsilon\} \quad (3)$$
$$\{\varepsilon\} = [\varepsilon_{11} \varepsilon_{22} \varepsilon_{33} \gamma_{12} \gamma_{23} \gamma_{31}]^T$$
$$\{\sigma\} = [\sigma_{11} \sigma_{22} \sigma_{33} \tau_{12} \tau_{23} \tau_{31}]^T \quad (4)$$
$$[S] = [C]^{-1}$$

$$[S] = \begin{pmatrix} 1/E & -\mu/E & -\mu/E & 0 & 0 & 0 \\ -\mu/E & 1/E & -\mu/E & 0 & 0 & 0 \\ -\mu/E & -\mu/E & 1/E & 0 & 0 & 0 \\ 0 & 0 & 0 & 1/G & 0 & 0 \\ 0 & 0 & 0 & 0 & 1/G & 0 \\ 0 & 0 & 0 & 0 & 0 & 1/G \end{pmatrix} \quad (5)$$

where $\{\sigma\}$ and $\{\varepsilon\}$ are the stress and strain vectors, respectively. S_{ij} and C_{ij} denote the elastic compliance and stiffness constants, respectively, which measure the strain (or stress) necessary to maintain a given stress (or strain). E, μ, and G are the Young's modulus, Poisson's ratio, and shear modulus, respectively, in the three principal orientations: $\langle 0\,0\,1\rangle$, $\langle 0\,1\,0\rangle$, and $\langle 1\,0\,0\rangle$. The stiffness and compliance constants have the following relations:

$$S_{11} = \frac{C_{11}+C_{12}}{(C_{11}-C_{12})(C_{11}+2C_{12})} \quad (6)$$

$$S_{12} = \frac{C_{12}}{(C_{11}-C_{12})(C_{11}+2C_{12})} \quad (7)$$

$$S_{44} = \frac{1}{C_{44}} \quad (8)$$

The matrix phase, γ, and precipitate phase, γ', both exhibit FCC structures and have coherent interfaces. Therefore, the nickelbased SX superalloys can be considered approximately orthotropic materials with three identical principal orientations. There are only 3 independent constants in $[S]$.

By applying spatial geometry transformations, the Young's modulus, E', and shear modulus, G', in a given crystallographic orientation can be obtained as follows:

$$\frac{1}{E'} = S'_{11} = S_{11} - 2JS\left(\frac{S_{11}-S_{12}-S_{44}}{2}\right) \quad (9)$$

with the orientation parameters J and S given by:

$$J = l^2 m^2 + l^2 n^2 + m^2 n^2 \quad (10)$$
$$S = 2S_{11} - 2S_{12} - S_{44} \quad (11)$$

where l, m, and n represent the directional cosines relative to the axes 1, 2, and 3, respectively. Thus, the degree of anisotropy depends on the orientation parameter, which has a minimum value of zero along $\langle 0\,0\,1\rangle$, a maximum value of 1/3 along $\langle 1\,1\,1\rangle$, and a value of 1/4 along $\langle 0\,1\,1\rangle$. For a pure nickel SX at room temperature, typical values for the compliance constants are $S_{11} = 0.799 \times 10^{-5}$ MPa^{-1}, $S_{12} = -0.312 \times 10^{-5}$ MPa^{-1}, and $S_{44} = 0.844 \times 10^{-5}$ MPa^{-1}. It can be seen that the $\langle 1\,0\,0\rangle$ direction is the least stiff, while the $\langle 1\,1\,1\rangle$ direction is the stiffest, with $\langle 1\,1\,0\rangle$ between these two limits. The values of Young's modulus along these crystallographic orientations are $E_{\langle 0\,0\,1\rangle} = 125$ GPa, $E_{\langle 0\,1\,1\rangle} = 220$ GPa, and $E_{\langle 1\,1\,1\rangle} = 294$ GPa. SX superalloys display a similar degree of anisotropy. To determine the degree of elastic anisotropy in SX cubic materials, the anisotropic factor, A, is defined as:

$$A = \frac{2C_{44}}{C_{11}-C_{12}} = \frac{2(S_{11}-S_{12})}{S_{44}} \quad (12)$$

where $A = 1$ for isotropic materials. For example, the following cubic metals have A values of 2.44 (Ni), 3.19 (Cu), 2.97 (Ag), 2.90 (Au), 1.65 (Ge), and 1.22 (Al). Thus, Ni displays a fair degree of anisotropy, but it is not the most anisotropic cubic metal.

The Young's and shear moduli over a wide range of temperature can be obtained using many methods, with tensile testing and dynamic resonance techniques most widely used for their simple principles and high accuracy. The Poisson's ratio at low or high temperatures can be measured with Moire interferometry.

Fig. 1 shows the variation of the Young's and shear moduli for different SX nickel-based superalloys with crystallographic orientation and temperature. The moduli of DD6 were measured by tensile tests, with the values for all other alloys measured with dynamic resonance techniques. Bayerlein and Sockel (1992) provided data for MA760 and IN738LC, while the data for CMSX4, SRR99, and SX pure Ni are from Fahrmann et al. (1999), Hermann and Han (1996), and Reed (2006), respectively. It can be seen that the moduli between different SX superalloy systems are relatively close, and all decrease with increasing temperature, especially above 950℃.

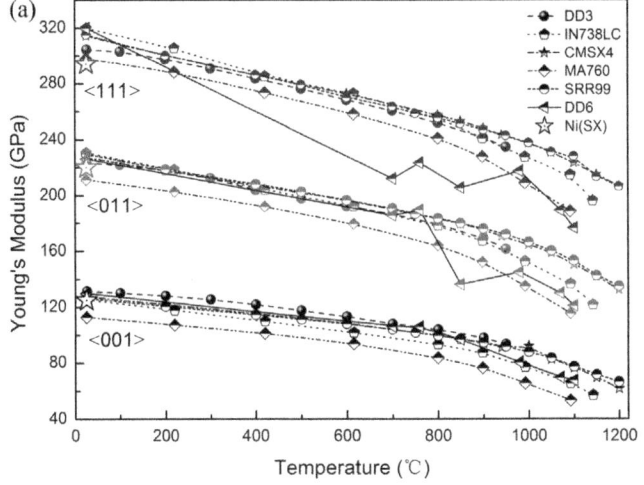 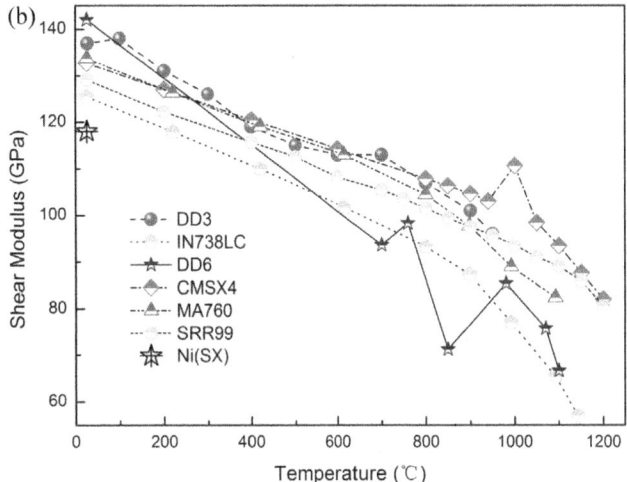

Fig. 1 Variation of the measured Young's and shear moduli of some SX Ni-based superalloys with crystallographic orientation and temperature (data of MA760, IN738LC, CMSX4 and SRR99 from literature, and data of DD3 and DD6 from the handbook).

2.2 Plastic behavior

For anisotropic materials, the Hill yield criterion, which is a simple extension of the von Mises criterion, is usually employed. Hill's potential function expressed in terms of rectangular Cartesian stress components has the following form:

$$f(\sigma) = \sqrt{F(\sigma_{22}-\sigma_{33})^2 + G(\sigma_{33}-\sigma_{11})^2 + H(\sigma_{11}-\sigma_{22})^2 + 2L\sigma_{23}^2 + 2M\sigma_{31}^2 + 2N\sigma_{12}^2} \qquad (13)$$

where F, G, H, L, M, and N are independent constants obtained from tensile or compression tests of the material in different orientations. If $f(\sigma) > \sigma_0$, the material will yield, where σ_0 is the user-defined reference yield stress specified for the metal plasticity definition, usually the yield strength in one principal orientation. In this article, $\sigma_0 = S_{\langle 001 \rangle}$, where $S_{\langle 001 \rangle}$ indicates the yield strength in one principal orientation. The mechanical properties are identical in the three principal orientations for FCC materials, and hence, $f(\sigma)$ can be expressed as:

$$f(\sigma) = \frac{1}{\sqrt{2}} \sqrt{(\sigma_{22}-\sigma_{33})^2 + (\sigma_{33}-\sigma_{11})^2 + (\sigma_{11}-\sigma_{22})^2 + 2K(\sigma_{23}^2 + \sigma_{31}^2 + \sigma_{12}^2)} \qquad (14)$$

where $K = L/F$ and denotes the anisotropic plastic parameter. This potential function will take the form of the von Mises criterion if $K = 3$, meaning that the material is isotropic. Theoretically, the yield stresses $S_{\langle 001 \rangle}$, $S_{\langle 011 \rangle}$, and $S_{\langle 111 \rangle}$ obtained through uniaxial tests have the following relations:

$$S_{\langle 111 \rangle} = \left(\frac{K}{3}\right)^{1/2} S_{\langle 001 \rangle} \qquad (15)$$

$$S_{\langle 011 \rangle} = \frac{1}{2}(1+K)^{1/2} S_{\langle 001 \rangle} \qquad (16)$$

Isotropic hardening criterion is employed for this model, with the flow rule used in this model as follows:

$$d\varepsilon^{pl} = d\lambda \frac{\partial f}{\partial \sigma} = \frac{d\lambda}{f} \boldsymbol{b} \qquad (17)$$

where λ denotes the plastic multiplier. From the above definition of $f(\sigma)$, $\boldsymbol{b}$ can be expressed as:

$$\boldsymbol{b} = \begin{bmatrix} \sigma_{11} - 0.5(\sigma_{22}+\sigma_{33}) \\ \sigma_{22} - 0.5(\sigma_{11}+\sigma_{33}) \\ \sigma_{33} - 0.5(\sigma_{11}+\sigma_{22}) \\ k\sigma_{12} \\ k\sigma_{31} \\ k\sigma_{23} \end{bmatrix} \qquad (18)$$

2.3 Validation of orthotropic mechanical properties

Validation of a mathematical model is very significant for modeling and simulation. This subsection will show the calculation of some critical mechanical parameters that were used in the simulations. Experimental data was used in the calculations to verify and validate the use of orthotropic mechanical properties.

Several methods have been developed to determine the elastic constants from measured moduli and Poisson's ratios. Hermann and Han (1996) developed the regression method, which is the simplest way to determine the elastic compliance constants. This method is based on Eqs. (9)-(11). The reciprocal values of the measured moduli, E^{-1}, for different orientations can be plotted against the orientation parameter, J. Plotting the reciprocal values of shear modulus will allow the elastic constant S_{44} to be determined. A linear regression with $J=0$ results in the calculation of elastic constant S_{11}, while S_{12} can be calculated with Eq. (11) from the slope of the regression lines. The slope of regression lines from plots of measured reciprocal elastic moduli against J is equal to $-2S$, as shown in Fig. 2. Therefore, the elastic compliance constants can be easily obtained with this method, as Young's and shear moduli in a given orientation can be measured experimentally. In addition, the more values obtained for moduli in various orientations, the more accurate the calculated compliance constants.

Sometimes Poisson's ratios are measured and reported instead of the shear modulus. In this case, the shear modulus can be calculated with another method, which will be illustrated next. By combining Eqs. (5) and (9) along $\langle 1\ 1\ 0 \rangle$ and $\langle 1\ 1\ 1 \rangle$, the following relations can be obtained:

$$\frac{1}{G} = \frac{3}{E_{111}} - \frac{1-2\mu}{E} \quad (19)$$

$$\frac{1}{G} = \frac{4}{E_{110}} - \frac{2-2\mu}{E} \quad (20)$$

Through Eqs. (14) and (15), the shear moduli G_1 and G_2 can be obtained, respectively. For the model, the shear modulus, G, is the average of G_1 and G_2:

$$G = \frac{G_1 + G_2}{2} \quad (21)$$

Figs. 3 and 4 show the compliance constants and anisotropic elastic factors of different SX superalloys obtained with the regression method. As the temperature increases, the stiffness of the materials decreases, especially above 950℃. Combining Eqs. (9) and (11), Young's moduli in all orientations can be determined, as shown in Fig. 5. Table 1 compares the calculated results from the regression plots and measured values of Young's moduli of the SX superalloy DD6. As shown by the similarity of the calculated and measured results, it is acceptable to use calculations based on orthotropic elastic properties in the model.

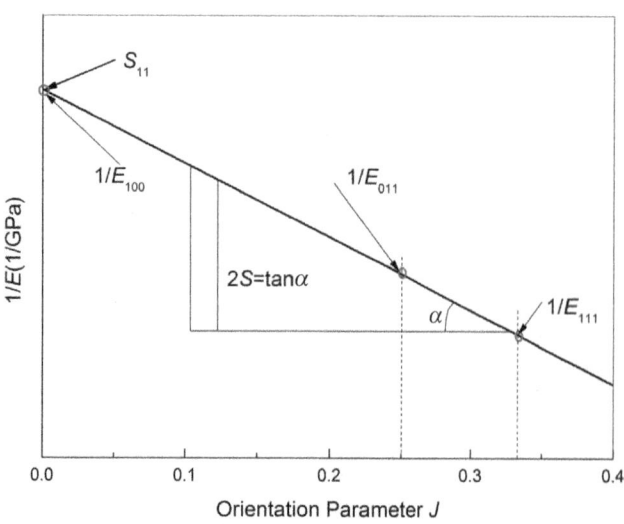

Fig. 2 Schematic of the regression method used to determine elastic compliance constants.

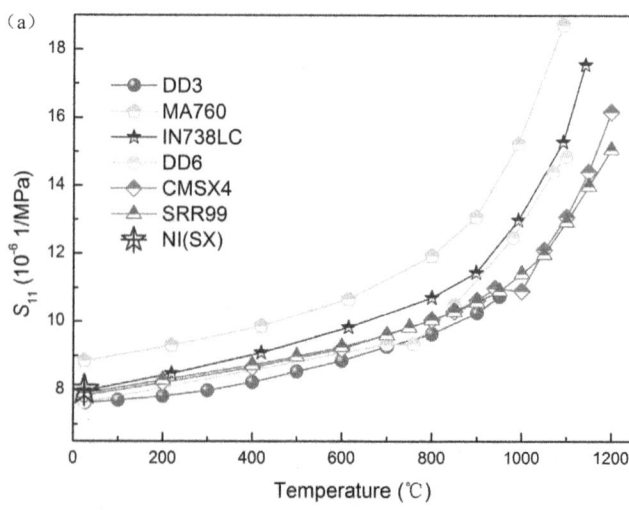

Fig. 3 Variation of elastic compliance constants for different SX Ni-based super-alloys with temperature.
The data was calculated with the regression method.

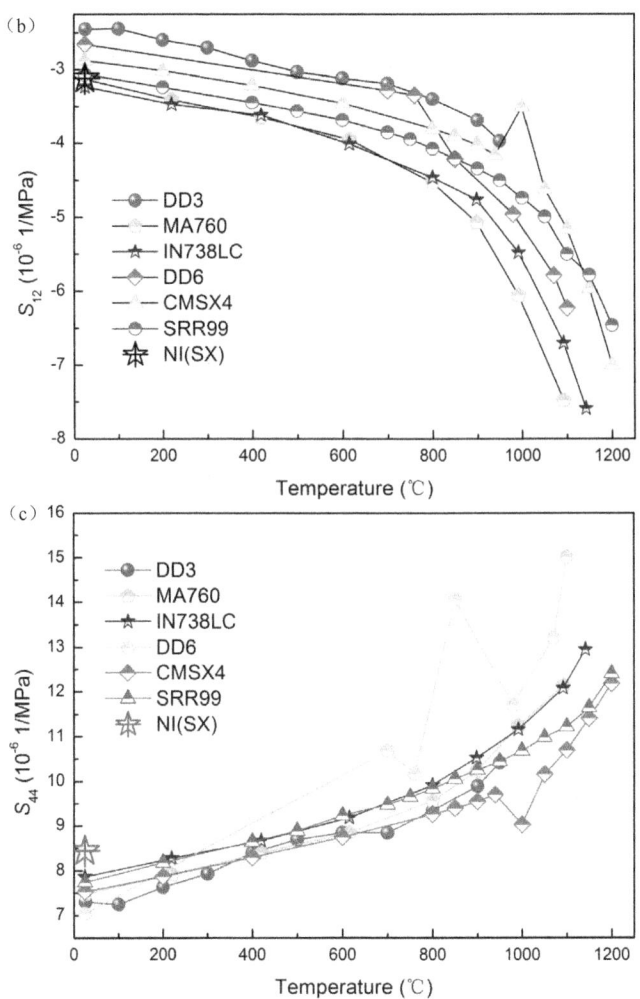

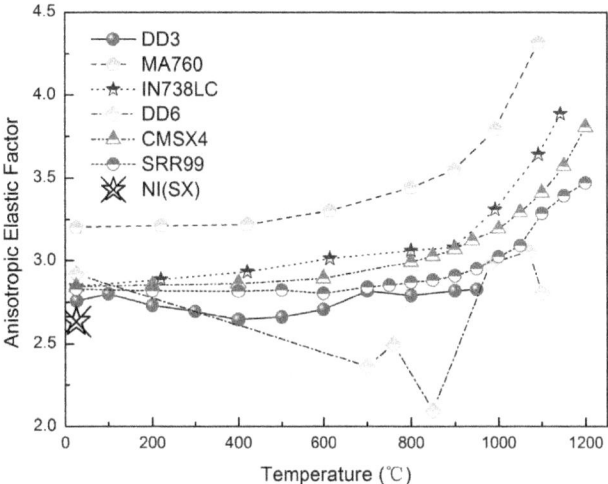

Fig. 4 Variation of anisotropic elastic factors for some SX Ni-based superalloys with temperature. The data was calculated using Eq. (12).

calculated anisotropic plastic parameter. For the SX superalloy DD6, the values of $S_{\langle 011\rangle}$ and ultimate tensile strength ($UTS_{\langle 011\rangle}$)

Fig. 3 Variation of elastic compliance constants for different SX Ni-based super-alloys with temperature. The data was calculated with the regression method. (Continued)

Using Eq. (15), the parameter K can be calculated using the yield strength and ultimate tensile strength, denoted K_p and K_b, respectively. For ease of calculation, the average of K_p and K_b is taken as the

predicted with the calculated K were compared with the experimental results, as shown in Table 2. It reveals that the calculated yield strength and ultimate tensile strength in the <0 1 1> direction are fairly accurate for temperatures of 850℃ and 980℃. The Hill's yield criterion is acceptable when modeling above 700℃, which is the temperature range this model is most concerned with.

It should be noted that the difference between the measured and calculated values for the elastic and plastic properties is not only from the measurement error, but also an inherent characteristic of engineered SX superalloys. Though the matrix and precipitate phases both exhibit FCC structures, all SX superalloys are not ideal

Table 1 Variation of calculation value and errors of Young's modulus in $\langle 0\ 0\ 1\rangle$, $\langle 0\ 1\ 1\rangle$ and $\langle 1\ 1\ 1\rangle$ with different temperatures.

Temperature (℃)	25	700	760	850	980	1070	1100
Calculation value of $E_{\langle 001\rangle}$ (GPa)	131.2	107.1	107	95.2	80.2	69.4	67.3
Calculation value of $E_{\langle 011\rangle}$ (GPa)	235.7	175.5	180.4	150.2	149.6	131.3	123.9
Calculation value of $E_{\langle 111\rangle}$ (GPa)	320.9	223	233.9	186	210.3	186.9	172.1
Error of $E_{\langle 001\rangle}$	-0.25%	0.82%	0.71%	-1.62%	-0.42%	-0.14%	-0.32%
Error of $E_{\langle 011\rangle}$	1.81%	-5.39%	-4.82%	10.21%	3.15%	10.26%	2.37%
Error of $E_{\langle 111\rangle}$	-1.85%	5.14%	4.69%	-9.48%	-3.33%	-1.10%	-2.47%

Table 2 Variation of the anisotropic parameter K and calculation error of $S_{\langle 011 \rangle}$ and $UTS_{\langle 011 \rangle}$ with different temperatures.

Temperature (℃)	25	700	760	850	980	1070	1100
Anisotropic plastic parameter K	6.2	3.47	3.44	2.46	1.87	2.15	2.36
Calculation error of $S_{\langle 011 \rangle}$	34.20%	—	—	—	-2.40%	-13.20%	-10.70%
Calculation error of $UTS_{\langle 011 \rangle}$	26.30%	11.10%	13.60%	-1.50%	-5.90%	-9.60%	5.30%

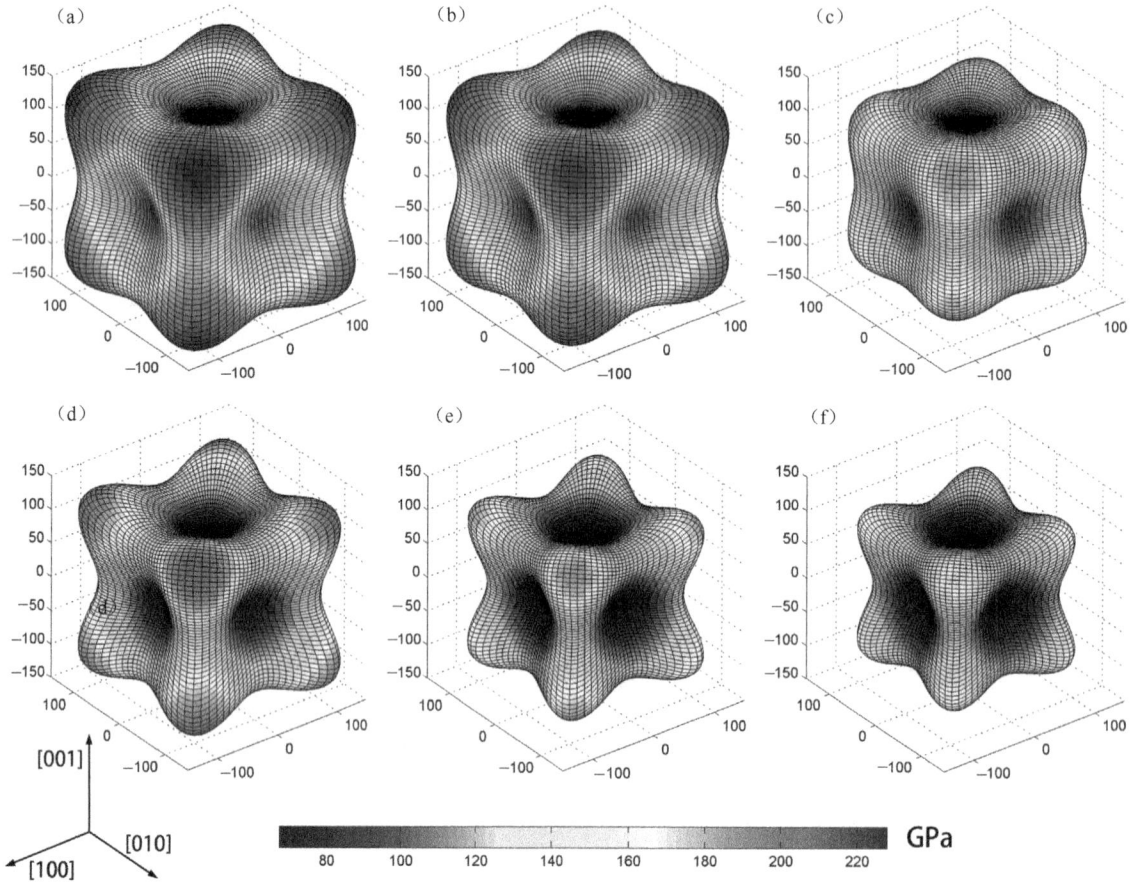

Fig. 5 Orientation and temperature dependence of Young's modulus of SX superalloy DD6:
(a) 700℃; (b) 760℃; (c) 850℃; (d) 980℃; (e) 1070℃; (f) 1100℃.

orthotropic materials in reality. Therefore, orthotropic elastic theory and Hill's yield criterion are unable to fully describe the elastic and plastic behavior of SX nickel-based superalloys. However, to some extent, they are valid for semi-quantitative analysis from an engineering perspective.

3. Experimental

3.1 Directional solidification

A simplified cored rod geometry was designed for investigating RX. Fig. 6 illustrates the geometric details of the test pieces, which are analogs of comparable size to a turbine blade aerofoil, with flanges to simulate the mechanical constraints provided by platforms and shrouds, as well as ceramic molds. Holes on both ends were created for core retaining. The gauge's length was 40mm, with a diameter of 10mm and a casting wall thickness of about 1.5mm. Filets with radii of 3mm were introduced where abrupt changes in section occurred. The nominal thickness of the shell was approximately 5mm. The second generation SX superalloy DD6 was used for the experiments. The composition of DD6 is given in Table 3. Thematerial exhibits a two-phase microstructure, with coherent and cuboidal γ'-precipitates that are surrounded by the γ-matrix. The cored rods were fabricated using an industrial-scale Bridgman facility in the Beijing Institute of Aeronautical Materials. Twelve rods were cast simultaneously with two rods per group, meaning that two rods shared one grain selector, as shown in Fig. 7. The SX alloy with ⟨0 0 1⟩ orientation was directionally solidified. A withdrawal rate of 5mm/min was used, and the molten metal was poured under vacuum conditions at 1550℃. The core was composed of silica-based material, while the shell consisted of alumina-silica-based material. The rods underwent standard heat treatment after casting, and a chemical etching process, with HCl/H_2O_2 as the etchant, was used to reveal whether RX had occurred.

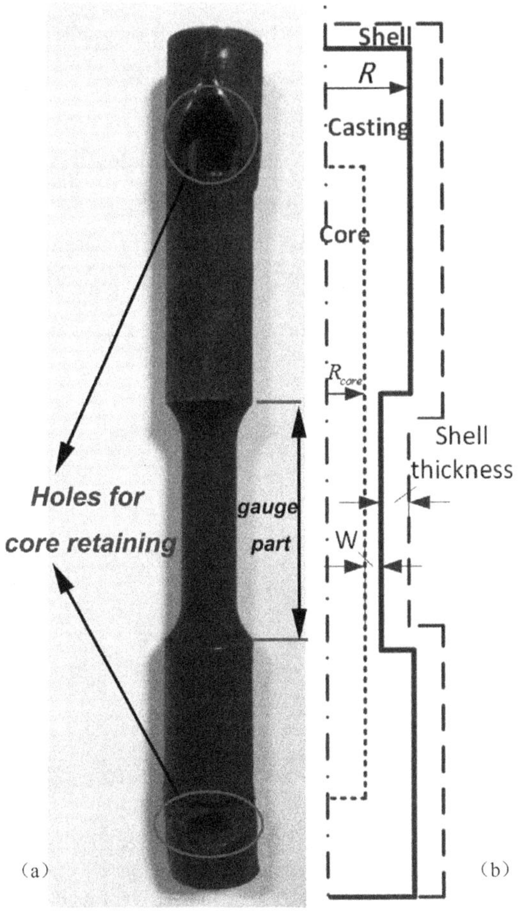

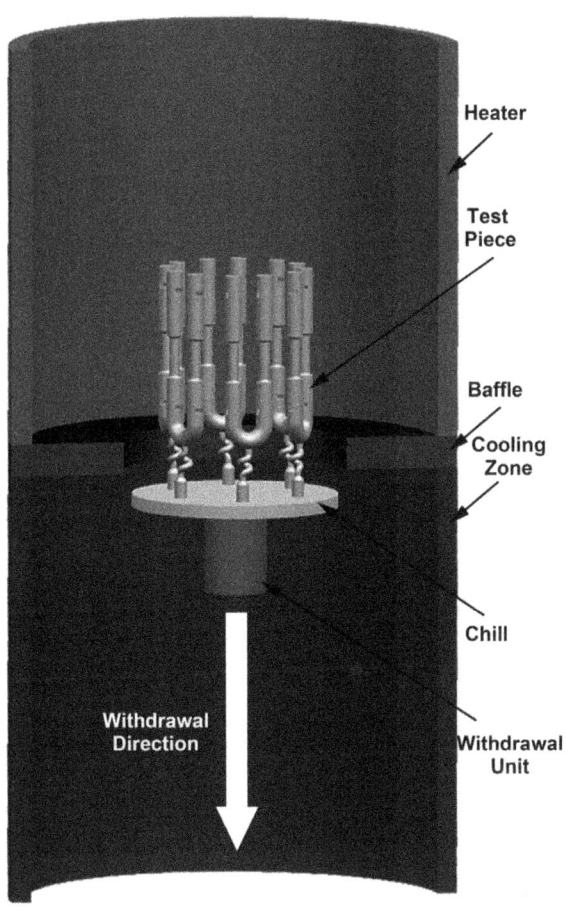

Fig. 6 Typical geometry of a test piece: (a) cored casting and (b) schematic of the geometry, where R_{core}, R, and W denote core radius, platform radius, and wall thickness, respectively.

Fig. 7 Schematic of the directional solidification process with the configuration of test pieces cast.

Table 3 Nominal composition of alloy DD6.

Element	Ni	Cr	Co	Mo	W	Ta	Re	Nb	AL	Hf
wt.%	Balance	4.3	9	2	8	7.5	2	0.5	5.6	0.1

3.2 Mechanical testing for yield strength

To improve the accuracy of the simulation, hot compression tests were conducted to obtain the yield strength of the as-cast SX superalloy DD6. Cylindrical pieces with a diameter of 6mm and a length of 10mm were cut using electrical discharge machining (EDM) from the as-cast test bars of SX DD6 with a diameter of 15mm and a length of 300mm. Compressive testing was carried out with a thermo-mechanical tester (Gleeble 3500) at different temperatures and a strain rate of $10^{-4} s^{-1}$. Great care was taken to ensure that only test pieces within 10° of the ⟨0 0 1⟩ axis were employed for the compressive testing. For tests below 1000℃, the pieces were heated at a rate of 15℃/s, and once the target tem-perature was reached, it was held for 1 min before compression. For tests above 1000℃, the heating rate was increased to 2℃/s above 1000℃. The holding time above 1000℃ was also 1 min. A vacuum was used to simulate the environment during investment casting. The yield strength data was extracted from the compression test results for modeling purposes. Typical stress-strain curves are shown in Fig. 8, and the variation of the flow stress with temperature for different SX superalloys is shown in Fig. 9. Panwisawas et al. (2013a, b) and Wang et al. (2009) provided the yield strength at different temperatures for the as-cast CMSX4 and as-heated SRR99, respectively. As can be seen, the flow stress of the as-cast DD6 is lower than that of the as-heated DD6.

pic mechanical properties of DD6 SX superalloy were considered using isotropic hardening criteria, including the elastic modulus, Poisson's ratio, yield stress, and ultimate yield strength. The stress, stored plastic energy, and strains, especially the plastic strains, were of primary interest. A 60° section of the whole model, with two test rods per group, was simulated because of its periodic symmetry. The interaction between the cores and shells was assumed to be free of friction during casting. It is supposed that cores and shells are connected. To model the shell and core, purely isotropic elastic properties were assumed. It should be noted that this hypothesis will lead to the prediction of larger stresses and strains because of the possible fracture of ceramic materials. This will be discussed later in this paper.

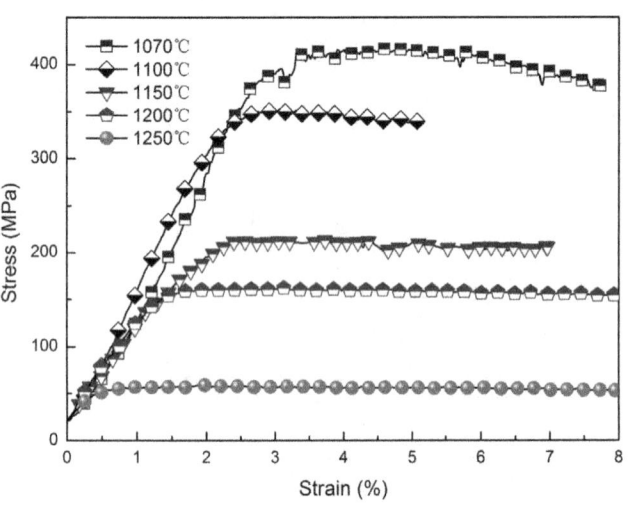

Fig. 8 Stress-strain curves at different temperatures for the as-cast DD6.

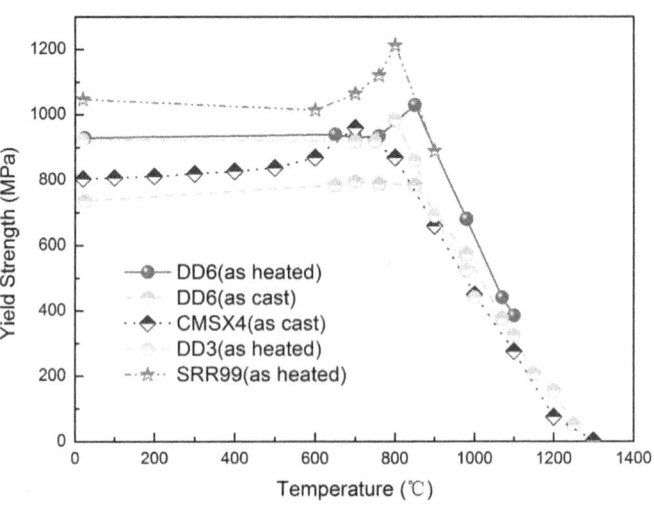

Fig. 9 Variation of yield strength of different SX Ni-based superalloys with temperature (as-cast DD6 from experiments; as-cast CMSX4, and as-heated SRR99, DD3 and DD6 from the literature).

4. Modeling approach

Commercially available finite element method software (Pro-CAST and ABAQUS) was used to model the temperature and strains. Thermo-elastic-plastic analysis was carried out, with the high temperature plasticity assumed to be rate-independent. Temperature-dependent material parameters for the DD6 superalloy were assumed. The following thermo-physical properties of DD6 and the ceramic molds were used as isotropic parameters: density, specific heat capacity, thermal conductivity, and thermal expansion coefficient. The orthotro-

Ignoring high temperature creep strain, static equilibrium was assumed during the calculation of the stress field, which also ignored the cooling rate. The following equations are employed to determine the equivalent effective plastic strain and plastic dissipation energy, denoted $\bar{\varepsilon}_{pl}$ and U_{pl}, respectively. They take the following forms:

$$\bar{\varepsilon}_{pl} \equiv \int_0^{\bar{\varepsilon}_{pl}} d\bar{\varepsilon}_{pl} = \int \frac{\sigma : d\varepsilon_{pl}}{f(\sigma)} \quad (22)$$

$$dU_{pl} = \int_0^{\varepsilon_{pl}} \sigma : d\varepsilon_{pl} \quad (23)$$

Thermal expansion coefficients are especially significant in this model, and therefore, temperature-dependent values were used, as illustrated in Fig. 10. Great care was taken to ensure that the mesh was sufficiently fine for the simulation results to be independent of element size. An explicit integration scheme was used, and the simulation results discussed below correspond to the integration points because of the high accuracy of these positions.

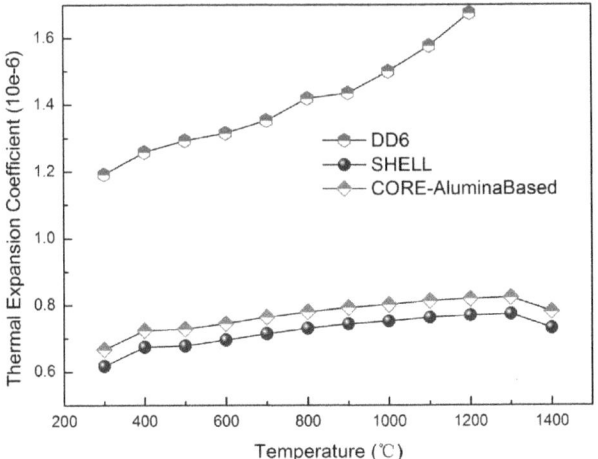

Fig. 10 Variation of thermal expansion coefficient of casting, shell and core with temperature (the reference temperature is 20℃).

5. Influence of geometric features

Before presenting the comparison of the simulated and experimental results for the test pieces, the influence of typical geometric features on the induced plasticity was investigated first, with the results discussed below. Though the preliminary research was based on simple assumptions, some of which are unachievable in reality, the results may be helpful for understanding what causes plastic deformation and the subsequent RX.

5.1 Cored rods with uniform walls

This case was investigated to evaluate the plasticity induced by the ceramic core, which is analogous to the strain induced on the inner surface of a turbine blade. The diameter of the rod was 20mm, and the rod axis was parallel to the casting crystallographic orientation ⟨0 0 1⟩ of the SX superalloy, as shown in Fig. 11 (a). It was assumed that the superalloy and core maintain the same temperature and interact without friction during the solidification and subsequent cooling from 1370℃ to 70℃. A quarter section of the cored rod model was simulated because of its four-fold crystallo-graphic symmetry.

The rod casting wall thickness of 5mm was chosen to investigate the evolution of stress and strain during solidification, and the modeled equivalent plastic strain contour results are illustrated in Fig. 11 (b). The final distribution of plastic strain on the circumference of the rod is non-uniform, with the maximum values in the primary ⟨0 1 1⟩ orientation. This finding can be explained by the maximum Young's and shear moduli of the (0 0 1) plane being found in the ⟨0 1 1⟩ direction. Fig. 12 shows the variation of simulated plastic, elastic, and thermal strain, as well as the plastic dissipation energy density, with temperature during the solidification of the cored rod. The SX Ni-based superalloy undergoes plastic deformation easily at high temperatures, especially above 1000℃, mainly because of the low yield strength. However, the plastic strain induced at this stage is usually smaller in scale compared with that below 800℃, as illustrated in Fig. 12. This can be explained by comparing the variation of the potential function and yield strength with the temperature, as shown in Fig. 13. The potential function was calculated from Eq. (14); a material will yield when the potential function is larger than the yield strength. The evolution of plastic strain may play a role in the characteristic yield strength of SX superalloy DD6. As seen in Fig. 13, the yield strength of DD6 increases significantly to its peak value around 800℃ during solidification, but below 800℃ the yield strength undergoes a small decline and remains relatively unchanged until room temperature is reached. On the other hand, the thermal strain and stress increase continuously, as shown in Fig. 12, with the majority of plastic strain occurring below 800℃. High equivalent plastic strain can be predicted without considering the fracture of the core. The plastic dissipation energy was also calculated, with only a small fraction needed to be stored in the material to act as the driving force for RX. According to classical theory, the driving force for RX in a deformed metal can be estimated with the following equation:

$$p = \frac{1}{2}\rho\mu b^2 \qquad (24)$$

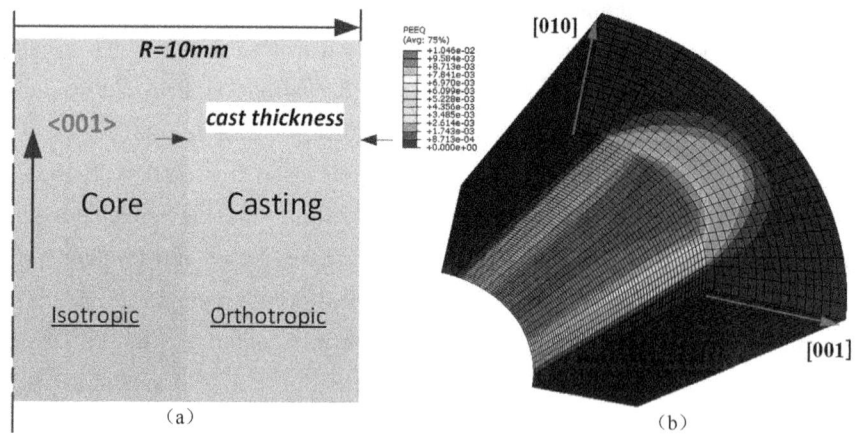

Fig. 11　Schematic of cored rod (a) and simulated equivalent effective plastic strain contour (b).

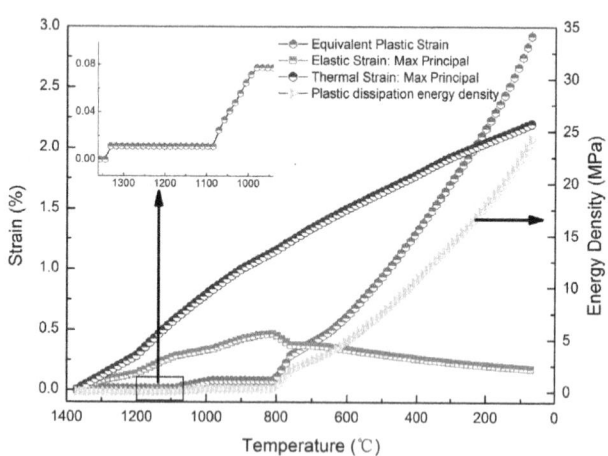

Fig 12　Variation of simulated equivalent plastic strain, elastic strain, thermal strain, and plastic dissipation energy density with temperature during solidification.

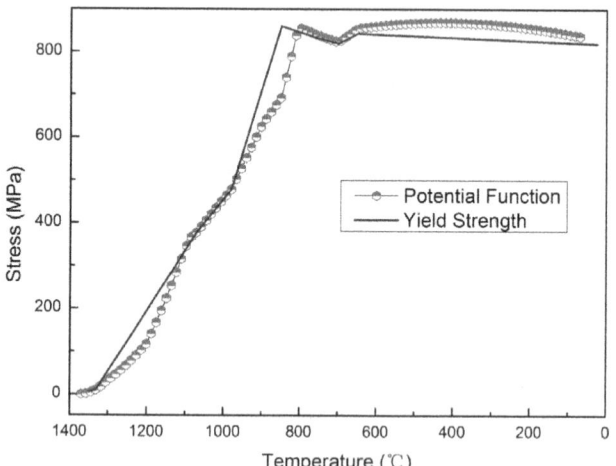

Fig 13　Comparison of simulated potential function and experimental yield strength during solidification, indicating when plasticity occurs.

with ρ, μ, and b representing dislocation density, shear modulus, and Burger's vector length, respectively. A rough estimate of the driving force can be made for the superalloy. Assuming ρ is 10^{15} m^{-2}, μ is about 50GPa, and b is 0.36nm, then the driving force p = 1.25MPa (1.8×10^6 J/m^3). This value is comparable to the calculated results, assuming about 2–5% plastic dissipation energy in the material.

The influence of different core/casting area ratios was investigated by changing the core's radius. As shown in Fig. 14, the thinner the casting wall, the larger the maximum equivalent plastic strain, meaning that RX is more likely to occur in thin-walled sections.

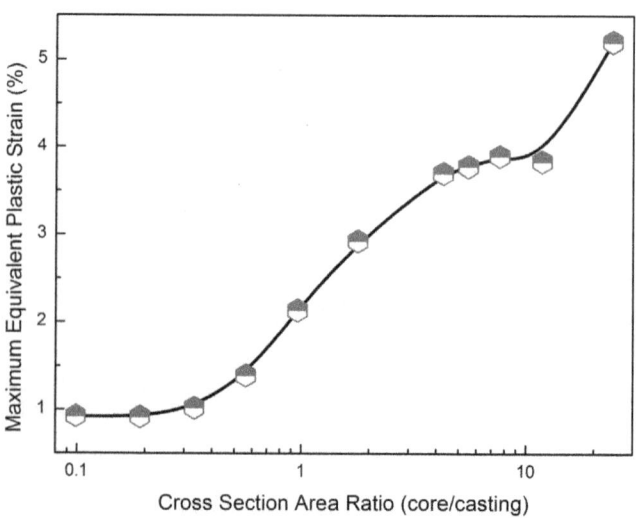

Fig. 14　Variation of maximum equivalent plastic strain with the area ratio (core/casting).

5.2 Decentralized-core rods

The wall thickness around the ceramic core is usually nonuniform for turbine blades. Therefore, decentralized-core rods were designed to simulate the influence of non-uniform wall thickness on the final plasticity. The diameters of rod and core were fixed at 20mm and 10mm, respectively, and the core deviated from the center at varied distances. The remaining simulation conditions were the same as those for the first case. Only half of the model was simulated because of the geometric symmetry. The correlation between maximum plastic strain and wall thickness was studied, with the parameter minimum wall thickness/core radius (MWTCR) used for convenience. The zone of maximum plasticity is influenced by the material's crystallographic orientation and MWTCR, as illustrated in Fig. 15. When MWTCR is large, meaning the wall thickness around the core is relatively uniform, plasticity is prone to occur in the zone approaching the $\langle 0\ 1\ 1 \rangle$ direction on the circumference. Otherwise, the area of maximum plasticity corresponds to the area with the thinnest wall. Fig. 16 confirms that the smaller MWTCR is, the larger the value of maximum equivalent plastic strain obtained. If the direction of the thinnest wall coincides with the $\langle 0\ 1\ 1 \rangle$ direction, the plasticity will reach its peak value. This may explain why the degree of irregularity of the wall thickness has a more significant influence on the final plasticity than elastic anisotropy. Concerning the solidification process, much higher plastic strains are found at temperatures of 1000℃ or above (Fig. 17), which means more damage occurs compared to the uniform simulation if the same plasticity is induced. This suggests that fabricating components with uniform wall thickness helps prevent RX.

5.3 Rods with changing cross-sections

This case was designed to simulate the mechanical constraints of flanges provided by platforms and shrouds in real turbine blades. Twelve castings were produced with the industrial Bridgman directional solidification method to make the process as close as possible to actual working conditions. The nominal withdrawal rate was 5mm/min. The rotational axes of the test rods were parallel to the $\langle 0\ 0\ 1 \rangle$ direction, like the first two cases. Fig. 18 (a) shows the geometric details of the test rods, excluding the runner system and grain selector. The top and bottom sections are cylinders 10mm in diameter and 20mm in length. The length of the middle part, the most pertinent part for this case, is 40mm, and the

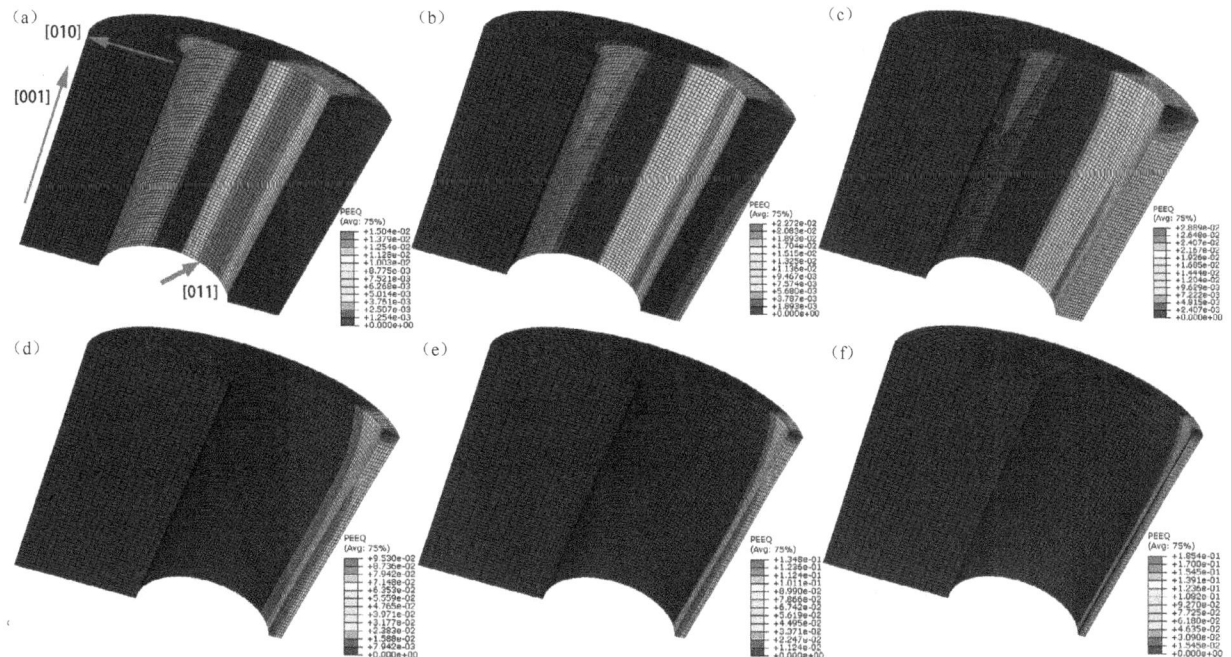

Fig. 15 Contour maps of the final plasticity of different cases with various offset distances:
(a) 1mm; (b) 2mm; (c) 3mm; (d) 4mm; (e) 4.2mm; (f) 4.4mm.

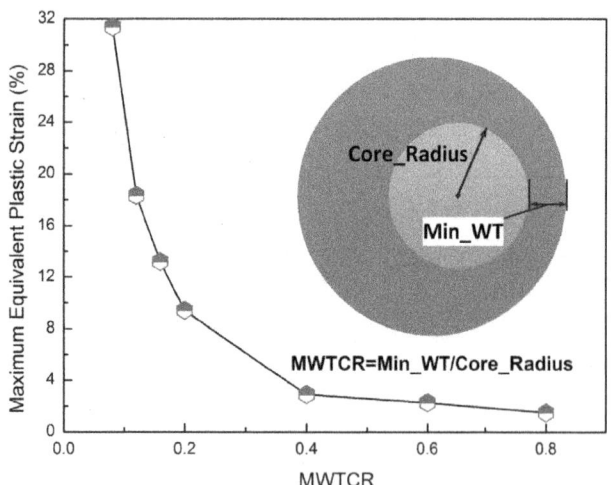

Fig. 16 Variation of maximum equivalent plastic strain with the parameter MWTCR.

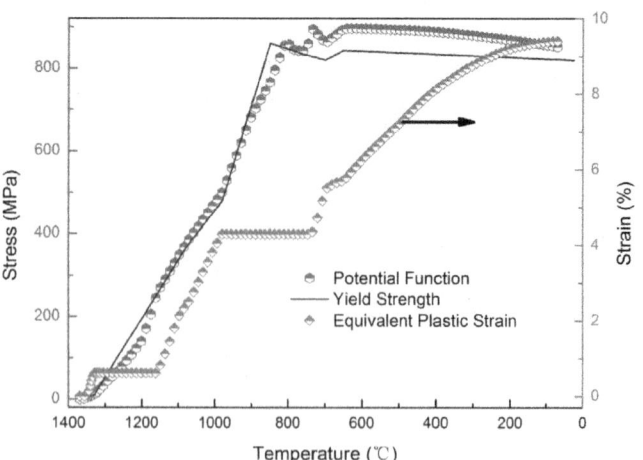

Fig. 17 Variation of simulated equivalent plastic strain, potential function, and yield strength with temperature during solidification (for the case of a 4mm-offset core).

diameter varies from 4mm to 18mm so that the effect of the cross-section ratio (small section/large section) could be investigated. The nominal shell thickness is 5mm. The reason for induced plastic strainsis illustrated in Fig. 18 (b). The middle part should bear tension stress because of the smaller thermal expansion coefficients of the ceramic-based shell compared to the cast. In addition, the temperature at the top of the middle part is relatively higher, resulting in lower yield strength. Therefore, plastic deformation will most likely occur in the region where the cross-section abruptly increases.

Rods without filets of different section ratios were simulated first. The simulation results confirm the above analysis, as shown in Fig. 19 (a). The maximum equivalent plastic strain is affected by the stress concentration at sharp corners and tensile stress of the part with the smaller section. The bottom part yields mainly because of the stress concentration. The former factor plays a more dominant role when the section ratio becomes larger, while the latter becomes more important if the section ratio is small. The minimum plastic strain is achieved when the section ratio lies between 0.2 and 0.5, giving a value of approximately 2%, as illustrated in Fig. 20. However, even this level of plasticity can give rise to RX during the subsequent heat treatment. Therefore, filets should be introduced to avoid large lev-

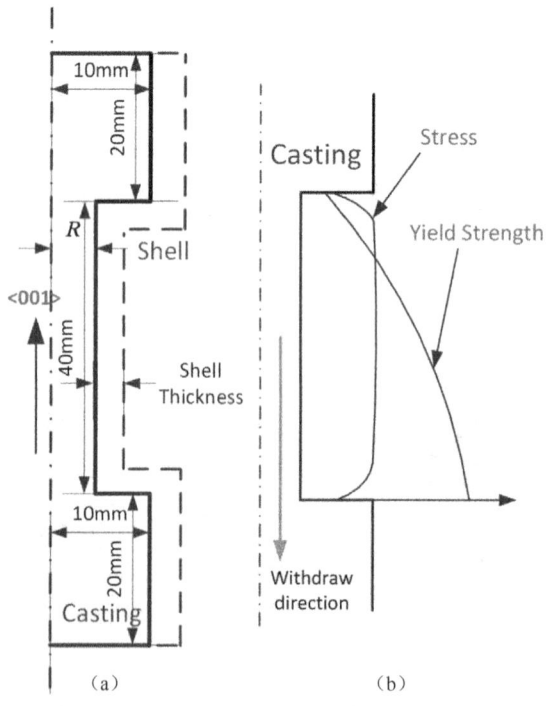

Fig. 18 Geometric details of a varying cross-section rod (a) and comparison between stress and yield strength of the middle part (b).

els of plasticity during solidification and the subsequent RX induced by section variation. The rod with a section ratio of 0.25 and filets was then simulated to verify this point. The result (Fig. 19(b)) shows that the maximum plastic strain (0.71%) is about only one-third compared to that of the rod of the same section ratio without filets (1.96%). Therefore, filets should be added to the sites with changing cross-sections in a turbine blade aerofoil to avoid RX. These kinds of sites include the joints between platform and blade, as well as leading (trailing) edges in a hollow blade. Combined with the second case modeled, another conclusion is that the geometric features are more significant than a material's orientation to the plasticity induced by the investment casting process.

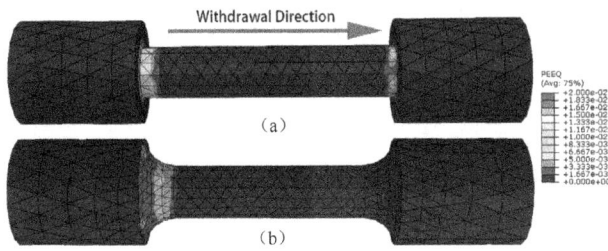

Fig. 19 Comparison of equivalent plastic strain contours between changing crosssection rods without filets (a) and with filets (b) (section ratio is 0.25).

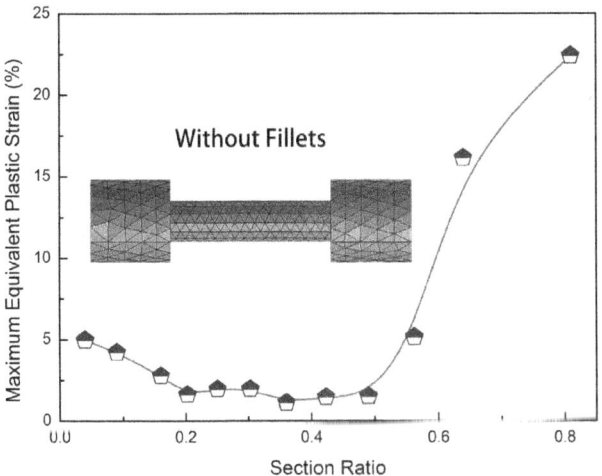

Fig. 20 Variation of maximum equivalent plastic strain with section ratio.

In addition, the effect of shell thickness, which was varied from 3mm to 9mm, was studied. The 0.25 section-ratio rods without filets were used in the simulation. Unexpectedly, the maximum plastic strain had no obvious correlation with shell thickness, and varied from 1.0% to 2.4%. By comparing these cases, a primary conclusion may be drawn: the influence of ceramic cores on plastic strain is more significant than that of the shell.

6. Comparison of models and experiments

Over 100 cored cross-section rods were fabricated with the Bridgman directional solidification method. It was found that the ceramic cores often buckled or broke during the preheating and casting processes, causing non-uniform wall thickness or the core to penetrate the wall (Fig. 21 (a) and (b)). RX occurred in most of the core-penetrated rods (Fig. 21 (c)), while little RX grains were found in the other rods, especially in normal cored rods. Interestingly, almost all of the RX grains appear below the holes as opposed to around the holes. To some extent, these findings were consistent with the simulation results (shown in Fig. 22). In the normal test bars, only a maximum of 6% effective plastic strain is predicted in the upper changing cross-section zone. For the test pieces with buckled cores, nearly 30% effective plastic strain is predicted in the zone below the hole, meaning that this zone will be more prone to RX during the subsequent heat treatment. This can be easily understood in the context of the case in Section 5.2. The zone below the hole is representative of a place with small MWTCR, which has the highest plastic strain. In this situation, the material orientation will also influence the final maximum plastic strain, which has been demonstrated by the previous simulations. It should be noted that most holes formed on the upper half of the middle part of the experimental samples because of their geometric characteristics. Thus, the area beneath the hole is thinner than the area above. Occasionally, the holes formed in the lower half of the middle part. In these cases, according to the models and the above analysis, RX grains should appear above the hole, which was confirmed by the experimental samples (the far right rod in Fig. 21 (c)). Thus, RX is likely to occur at the thin-walled sites below or above the hole instead of around the hole.

It should be pointed out that high plastic strains are predicted in zones A and B (see Fig. 22 (b)), where RX was not found. This can be explained by the following. First, the model is not a perfect replica of the real test pieces, giving rise to the differences found. These

Fig. 21 Test bars with buckled cores: (a) core does not penetrate the wall; (b) core penetrates the wall; (c) RX grains (marked with closed red lines) in test pieces with penetrating core. (For interpretation of the references to color in this figure caption, the reader is referred to the web version of this article.)

situations are difficult to completely describe in the model. Besides, higher plastic strains in some zones will be predicted because the fracturing of the core and shell was ignored.

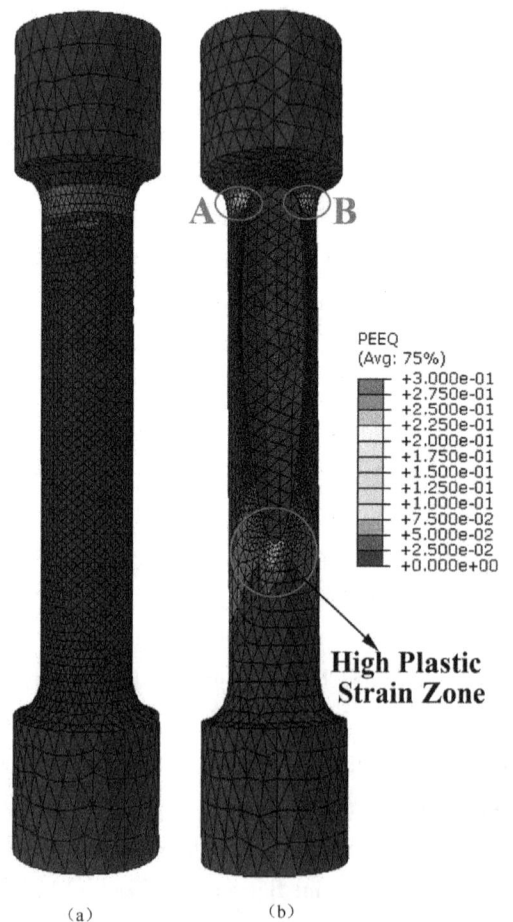

Fig. 22 Distribution of predicted effective plastic strains in normal (a) and core-buckled test pieces (b).

Most of the plastic strain occurs above 1000 ℃ for the normal test pieces (shown in Fig. 23), which is different from the case in Section 5.1. The zone with both changing cross-section and core is more prone to RX, and should be carefully treated during the manufacturing of SX components. The effect of core material on plasticity was also investigated with the model. Two distinct core systems were simulated: an alumina-based core (Core 1) and a silica-based core (Core 2). Though Core 1 was appreciably stiffer than Core 2, a little more plastic strain was induced within the metal cast around Core 2 than Core 1 because of the smaller thermal expansion coefficient of Core 2. Besides, the predicted plastic strains were very close between the two cores modeled, meaning that the effect of core material is less than that of geometric features when casting. In addition, the silica-based core can be leached out of the casting easily, leading to its employment in most situations.

Finally, it should be mentioned that the predicted plastic strains in this research may be larger than in reality. One of the reasons is that the shell and core were treated as ideal elastic materials, which ignores fracturing during the casting process. Evidence for this is that the core and shell usually underwent abnormally high stress during modeling. This can explain why RX was not found in certain areas of the normal cored rods fabricated, while the predicted plastic strain was as high as 6%. Therefore, the model presented in this research is only capable of predicting the sites of high plasticity, or in other words, it is only semi-quantitative.

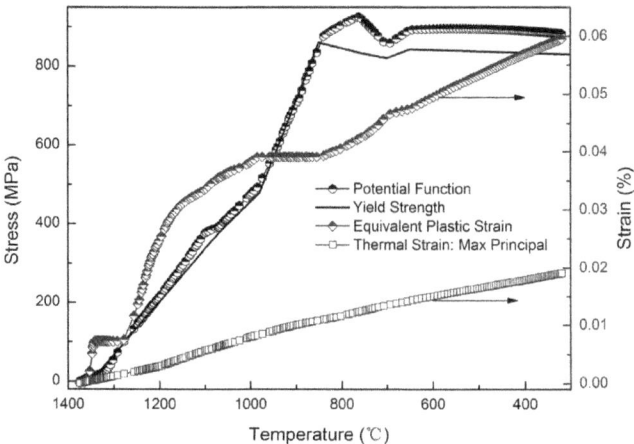

Fig. 23 Variation of potential function, equivalent plastic strain, and thermal strain with temperature (at the maximum integration point for normal test pieces with alumina cores and 1mm wall thickness).

7. Conclusions

A macroscopic, phenomenon-based, thermo-elastic-plastic model for the processing-induced plasticity during investment casting has been developed. Though only semi-quantitative, the model is capable of predicting the sites where localized plasticity can induce recrystallization during the heat treatment of single crystal superalloy castings. The following conclusions can be drawn.

(1) From an engineering perspective, orthotropic elastic properties and Hill's yield criterion can be employed in the thermomechanical modeling of single crystal nickel-based superalloys.

(2) The influence of ceramic cores on plastic strain is more significant than the shell. The thin-walled sections have an increased propensity for recrystallization.

(3) The geometric features are more significant than material orientation and material type. Filets should be introduced at the sites with abrupt changes of cross-section to avoid recrystallization.

(4) The thin-walled sites below or above the holes (along the withdrawal direction) have an increased propensity for recrystallization.

Acknowledgements

This research was funded by the National Basic Research Program of China (No. 2011CB706801) and National Natural Science Foundation of China (No. 51171089 and No. 51374137).

References

[1] Bayerlein, U., Sockel, H. G., 1992. Determination of single crystal elastic constants from DS-and DR-Ni-based superalloys by a new regression method between 20℃ and 1200℃. In: Antolovich, S. D., Stusrud, R. W., Mackay, R. A., Anton, D. L., Khan, T., Kissinger, R. D., Klarstrom, D. L. (Eds.), Superalloys. Warrendale, pp. 695-704.

[2] Burgel, R., Portella, P. D., Preuhs, J., 2000. Recrystallization in single crystals of nickel base superalloys. In: Pollock, T. M., Kissinger, R. D., Bowman, R. R., Green, K. A., Mclean, M., Olson, S., Schirra, J. J. (Eds.), Superalloys. Warrendale, pp. 229-238.

[3] Dahlen, M., Winberg, L., 1980. Influence of gamma'-precipitation on the recrystallization of a nickel-base superalloy. Acta Metall. 28 (1), 41-50.

[4] Dai, H. J., Dong, H. B., D'Souza, N., Gebelin, J. C., Reed, R. C., 2011. Grain selection in spiral selectors during investment casting of single-crystal components: Part Ⅱ. Numerical modeling. Metall. Mater. Trans. A 42A (11), 3439-3446.

[5] Ding, Z. P., Liu, Y. L., Yi, Z. Y., Yang, Z. G., Cheng, X. M., 2004. Elastic-plastic constitutive model of fcc single crystal materials. J. Cent. South Univ. Technol. 35 (3), 423-428.

[6] Fahrmann, M., Fahrmann, E., Pollock, T. M., 1999. Determination of matrix and precipitate elastic constants in (γ-γ') Ni-base model alloys, and their relevance to rafting. Mater. Sci. Eng. A 260 (1-2), 212-221.

[7] Green, D. J., 1998. An Introduction to the Mechanical Properties of Ceramics, first ed. Cambridge University Press, Cambridge, UK, pp. 13-69.

[8] Hermann, W., Han, J., 1996. Elastic properties and determination of elastic constants of nickel-base superalloys by a free-free beam technique. In: Kissinger, R. D., Deye, D. J., Anton, D. L., Cetel, A. D., Nathal, M. V., Pollock, T. M., Woodford, D. A. (Eds.), Superalloys. Warrendale, pp. 229-238.

[9] Meng, J., Jin, T., Sun, X. F., Hu, Z. Q., 2010.

Effect of surface recrystallization on the creep rupture properties of a nickel-base single crystal superalloy. Mater. Sci. Eng. A 527 (23), 6119-6122.

[10] Moverare, J. J., Johansson, S., Reed, R. C., 2009. Deformation and damage mechanisms during thermal-mechanical fatigue of a single-crystal superalloy. Acta Mater. 57 (7), 2266-2276.

[11] Pan, D., Xu, Q., Liu, B., Li, J., Yuan, H., Jin, H., 2010. Modeling of grain selection during directional solidification of single crystal superalloy turbine blade castings. J. Miner. Met. Mater. Soc. (JOM) 62 (5), 30-34.

[12] Panwisawas, C., Gebelin, J. C., Reed, R. C., 2013a. Analysis of the mechanical deformation arising from investment casting of directionally solidified nickel-based superalloys. Mater. Sci. Technol. 29 (7), 843-853.

[13] Panwisawas, C., Mathur, H., Gebelin, J., Putman, D., Rae, C. M. F., Reed, R. C., 2013b.

[14] Prediction of recrystallization in investment cast single-crystal superalloys. Acta Mater. 61 (1), 51-66.

[15] Reed, R. C., 2006. The Superalloys: Fundamentals and Applications, first ed. Cambridge University Press, New York, pp. 33-120.

[16] Wang, L., Xie, G., Lou, L. H., 2013. Effect of carbon content on the recrystallization of a single crystal nickel-based superalloy. Mater. Lett. 109, 154-157.

[17] Wang, L. N., Liu, Y., Yu, J. J., Xu, Y., Sun, X. F., Guan, H. R., Hu, Z. Q., 2009. Orientation and temperature dependence of yielding and deformation behavior of a nickel-base single crystal superalloy. Mater. Sci. Eng. A 505 (1-2), 144-150.

[18] Wu, Y. X., Yang, R. B., Li, S. S., Ma, Y., Gong, S. K., Han, Y. F., 2012. Surface recrystallization of a Ni_3Al based single crystal superalloy at different annealing temperature and blasting pressure. Rare Metals 31 (3), 209-214.

[19] Xie, G., Wang, L., Zhang, J., Lou, L. H., 2012. Orientational dependence of recrystallization in a Ni-base single-crystal superalloy. Scripta Mater. 66 (6), 378-381.

[20] Xiong, J. C., Li, J. R., Liu, S. Z., Zhao, J. Q., Han, M., 2010. Effects of carburization on recrystallization behavior of a single crystal superalloy. Mater. Charact. 61 (7), 749-755.

[21] Zambaldi, C., Roters, F., Raabe, D., Glatzel, U., 2007. Modeling and experiments on the indentation deformation and recrystallization of a single-crystal nickel-base superalloy. Mater. Sci. Eng. A 454, 433-440.

14. Numerical simulation of dendrite growth in nickel-based superalloy and validated by in-situ observation using high temperature confocal laser scanning microscopy

Xuewei Yan, Qingyan Xu, Baicheng Liu

Key Laboratory for Advanced Materials Processing Technology, Ministry of Education,
School of Materials Science and Engineering, Tsinghua University, Beijing 100084, China

ARTICLE INFO

Key words: Numerical simulation Dendrite growth In-situ observation HT-CLSM

ABSTRACT: Dendritic structures are the predominant microstructural constituents of nickel-based superalloys, an understanding of the dendrite growth is required in order to obtain the desirable microstructure and improve the performance of castings. For this reason, numerical simulation method and an in-situ observation technology by employing high temperature confocal laser scanning microscopy (HT-CLSM) were used to investigate dendrite growth during solidification process. A combined cellular automaton-finite difference (CA-FD) model allowing for the prediction of dendrite growth of binary alloys was developed. The algorithm of cells capture was modified, and a deterministic cellular automaton (DCA) model was proposed to describe neighborhood tracking. The dendrite and detail morphology, especially hundreds of dendrites distribution at a large scale and three-dimensional (3-D) polycrystalline growth, were successfully simulated based on this model. The dendritic morphologies of samples before and after HTCLSM were both observed by optical microscope (OM) and scanning electron microscope (SEM). The experimental observations presented a reasonable agreement with the simulation results. It was also found that primary or secondary dendrite arm spacing, and segregation pattern were significantly influenced by dendrite growth. Furthermore, the directional solidification (DS) dendritic evolution behavior and detail morphology were also simulated based on the proposed model, and the simulation results also agree well with experimental results.

1. Introduction

Nickel-based single crystal (SC) superalloys are widely used in modern advanced aero and power industry engines since they offer significantly improved high temperature fatigue resistance, creep strength, and corrosion resistance[1-3]. It is generally known that microstructures are the strategic link between materials process and performance[4]. Directional solidification (DS) process has revolutionized the development of SC superalloys over the past few decades[5-7]. However, the basic problem of understanding and controlling microstructures during DS process is still a challenge. Dendrites as the predominant microstructural constituents of solidified superalloys largely determines the final serving properties of turbine blades or other castings[8-11]. To improve the performance, numerous researchers and technologists have worked on the dendritic structure of castings to develop their solidification behaviors in the respects of theory and experiment. Kurz and Fisher[12] proposed a general framework which related to tip radius, interface undercooling and primary arm spacing in alloy dendrite growth. This simplified model permitted a semi-quantitative prediction of the relationship between growth conditions and primary arm spacing. Subsequently, Trivedi and Kurz[13] systematically summarized the important aspects and theoretical models of dendrite growth, including in the undercooled melt and DS process. Normally, the microstructural scales of dendrites is always characterized by means of optical microscope (OM) or scanning electron microscope (SEM) technologies[14]. However, only the dendrite morphology in solid state can be observed, while the nucleation and growth processes of dendrites cannot be captured by using these experimental methods. In-situ observation techniques are increasingly used and developed to study the microstructure evolution. Some in-situ observation techniques have been employed for the real-time observation of dendrite growth during melting and solidification[15,16]. Qian et al.[17] reported a growing crystalline dendrite in a DS experiment on succinonitrile containing 1% acetone, the dendrites grew rapidly into a side-branchlike feature according to the in-situ observation results. A columnar-to-equiaxed transition (CET) of an Al-15 wt% Cu alloy in DS process, presented by Dong and co-workers[18], was tracked and recorded by using synchrotron X-radiation imaging technique, the CET process and equiaxed dendrites growth were described from the viewpoint of dendrite detachment. However, extensive experimental studies of in-situ observations were always focused on succinonitrile or low melting point alloy, the dendrite growth of superalloys was rarely mentioned because of the high melting point and density. The high temperature confocal laser scanning microscopy (HT-CLSM) as a powerful tool can offer a great capability for real-time and continuous observation of phase transformation at high temperatures. Gu et al.[19] investigated the microstructure evolution of M2, 100Cr6 and C38LTT steel grades by using HT-CLSM and high energy X-ray microtomography, and discussed the observations in terms of microstructural development and liquid fraction during heating. Attallah et al.[20] studied the initiation of incipient melting of primary γ' in a Ni-base superalloy by using the HT-CLSM, and it was found that rapid heating prevented the dissolution of primary γ'. Although the HT-CLSM technique offers many advantages over classical experimental techniques, dendrite growth of in-situ observation in superalloy is still a challenge, due to the fact that it requires extremely high quality samples and complex operations.

In recent years, with the advancements of computer technology, numerical simulation as a powerful tool was used to investigate the dendrite growth during solidification[21-23]. Then, various simulation methods were emergence, and in particular phase field (PF) and cellular automaton (CA) approaches, which have permitted a validation of analytical theories as well as enabling predictions on dendrite growth and their evolution behavior. PF method is primarily rooted in continuum models of phase transitions that can precisely describe the dendrites interface and detailed morphology in two and even three dimensions[24,25]. However, large scale dendrites growth and 3-D polycrystalline solidification simulation using PF method are very difficult because of the need of enormous computational resources. CA method is another powerful computational approach that can reveal a wide range of micro/meso scale dendrite features, and has the advantage of a larger mesh size and much higher computational efficiency compared with PF method, and so it is extensively used in the investigation of dendrite growth[26-28]. In the last decade, important advances have been made in developing CA models and their algorithms of dendrite growth simulation. Initially, Rappaz and Gandin[29,30] proposed a CA coupled with finite element (FE) model in order to simulate the grain growth during solidification. Subsequently, there have been many studies on the simulation of DS dendrite growth and their evolution behavior using CA method. Wang et al.[31] developed a cellular automaton-finite difference (CA-FD) model to simulate solute diffusion controlled solidification of binary alloys, and found that perturbations significantly reduce the range of stable primary dendrite spacing. Pan et al.[32] built a 3-D sharp interface model for the quantitative simulation of dendrite growth, based on the local solutal equilibrium approach used to calculate the evolution of the S/L interface. Recently, Zhang et al.[33] presented a twotype directional dendrite growth model to realize the multi-scale simulation based on the CA-FD model considering macro DS parameters. However, most of studies mentioned above are 2-D or pseudo 3-D simulation for confining to calculation capability. Although some techniques such as the parallel computing and adaptive mesh refinement methods have been developed in order to enhance computational efficiency, large scale or 3-D dendrite growth simulation is still at the research stage.

The aim of this paper is to present a detailed study of dendrite growth in nickel-based superalloy using numerical simulation and in-situ observation technologies. A 3-D model are proposed to simulate dendrite growth, and the CA algorithm are also modified. Simulation parameters are calculated by dedicated software JMatPro, and the dendrite growth over a large scale in 2-D section and 3-D polycrystalline are simulated by the deterministic cellular automaton coupled with finite difference (DCA-FD) model. The instrumental device and the experimental procedure are described and the nucleation and growth during in-situ observation process are also analyzed. In addition, the samples are prepared a second time for dendritic morphology after HT-CLSM, and the simulation results are verified using these experimental results. Furthermore, the proposed model is also applied to the DS process to investigate the columnar dendrites growth.

2. Numerical modeling and experimental procedure

2.1 Solute diffusion coupling with temperature filed model

The dendrite growth is mainly controlled by solute redistribution and the temperature field during solidification. The solute distribution directly affects the dendrite morphology and dendrite arm spacing. Initially, the computational domain begins at a uniform composition, and the growing cells reject excess solute to its neighboring liquid cells with the solidification proceeding. Solute diffusion within the entire domain is then calculated coupled with the temperature field by Eq. (1) without considering nature and forced convection influence:

$$\frac{\partial C_i}{\partial t} = \nabla \cdot (D_i \nabla C_i) + C_i(1 - k_0)\frac{\partial f_s}{\partial t} \quad (1)$$

where C is the composition with its subscript i denoting solid or liquid, D is the solute diffusion coefficient and k_0 is the equilibrium partition coefficient. The last terms on the right hand denotes the amounts of solute rejected due to the increment of solid fraction at the S/L interface.

At the interface of the liquid and solid, the partitioning of solute in the growing cell is determined by Eq. (2).

$$C_S = k_0 C_L \quad (2)$$

where C_S and C_L are the average solute concentrations of the solid and liquid, respectively, in the solid at the liquid/solid interface, k_0 is the equilibrium partition coefficient.

The solute concentration, C_L, in the liquid within a growing cell, is given by Eq. (3).

$$C_L = C_L^* - \frac{1-f_S}{2}\Delta x G_C \quad (3)$$

where C_L^* is the concentration in the liquid at the S/L interface, Δx is the cell size, G_C is the concentration gradient in the S/L interface. C_L^* can be determined from a linearized equilibrium phase relation:

$$C_L^* = C_0 + \frac{1}{m_L}(T^* - T_L + \Gamma \kappa f(\theta_i)) \quad (4)$$

where C_0 is the original solute concentration in the liquid, m_L is the liquidus slope, T^* is the actual interface equilibrium temperature, T_L is the equilibrium liquidus temperature at initial solute composition, Γ is the Gibbs-Thomson coefficient, κ is curvature of S/L interface and $f(\theta_i)$ is a anisotropy function can be described by Eqs. (5) and (6).

$$\kappa = \frac{1}{a_m}\left\{1 - \frac{2}{N+1}\left[f_s + \sum_{i=1}^{N} f_s(i)\right]\right\} \quad (5)$$

$$f(\theta_i) = \prod_{i=l,m,n}[1 + \varepsilon \cos(\delta_i \theta_i)] \quad (6)$$

where N is the number of neighboring cells, a_m is the micro grid step length, f_s is the solid fraction, $f_s(i)$ is the solid fraction of i cell, ε is the anisotropy coefficient, δ_i is the anisotropic modulus, θ_i is the interface anisotropy angle, and l, m, n are the coordinates.

Assuming the local thermodynamic equilibrium exists at the scale of micro dendrite. Therefore, a simplified and well defined model was used to describe the temperature field in the calculation domain. For directional solidification process, adiabatic boundary was set up on both sides, as shown in Fig. 1. The cooling rate was R_c with a fixed temperature gradient G. It is assumed that the temperature was equivalent at the same micro grid, the temperature $T(t)$ in the macro cell (i,j) can be simply expressed as Eq. (7).

$$T(t) = T_{\text{liq}}(C_0) + G \cdot j \cdot \Delta x - R_C \cdot t \quad (7)$$

where the $T_{\text{liq}}(C_0)$ is the liquidus temperature at initial composition C_0, Δx is the cell size, t is the solidification time.

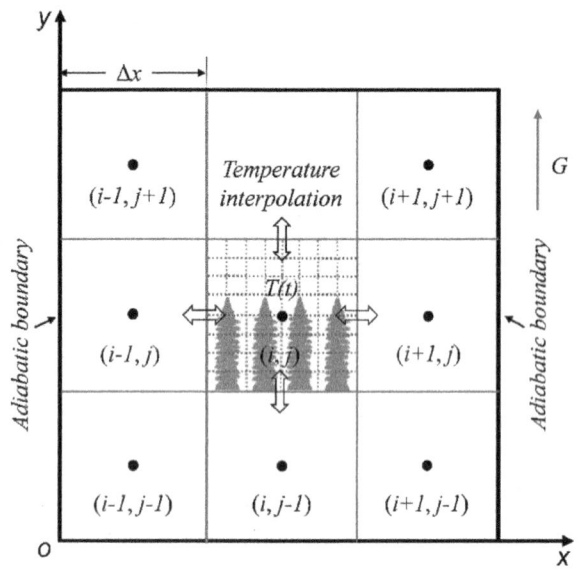

Fig. 1　Schematic illustration of coupling calculation of temperature field.

2.2　Algorithmic description of dendrite growth

According to Rappaz and Gandin[26,29,30], CA method should obey some rules. Firstly, the space was divided into many cells of equal size, usually squares or hexagons in two dimensions, arranged in a regular lattice. At the beginning of the simulation, each cell was given the same initial temperature above the liquidus of the alloy and a state index equal to zero which meaning it was liquid. Then, the time-stepping calculation was started. The temperature at each time-step was given by the cooling curve of the specimen, which was obtained either from a heat-flow computation or from a temperature measurement. Finally, when the temperature became lower than the liquidus point, the cells can become solid, as governed by the two mechanisms, of heterogeneous nucleation and growth. However, in this CA model, the locations of new nuclei were chosen at random among all of the remaining liquid cells and the crystallographic orientation of a new nucleus was also chosen randomly among equi-probabilistic orientation classes which will result in dendrites tending to grow brokenly and irregularly.

Fig. 2a shows a simple CA configuration in two dimensions, a grain with misorientation angle, θ, has nucleated at the central cell and is growing into a square shape. Subsequently, the liquid cells were captured in the two prior growth directions [01] and [10], that is to say, only the nearest-neighbor cells of a site location were considered. In this CA configuration, the growth direction was deterministic. In order to further develop this algorithm, a modified CA method was presented, which was named deterministic cellular automaton (DCA)

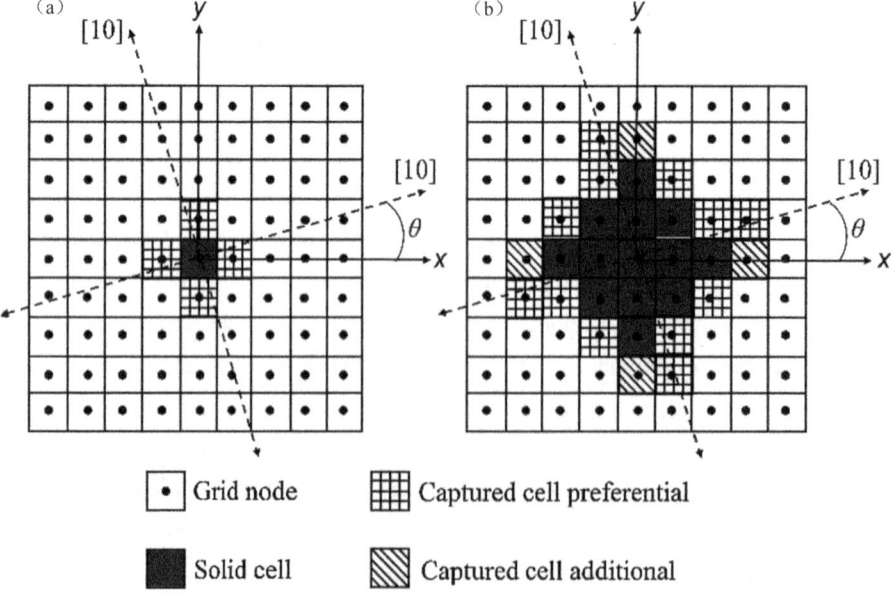

Fig. 2　Schematic illustration of CA algorithm in 2-D gridding:
(a) the simple CA configuration; (b) the deterministic cellular automaton (DCA) model.

model, as shown in Fig. 2b. In this DCA model, the liquid cells in the growth directions [01] and [10] were captured preferentially, and the cells in the direction which is vertical to the prior growth directions were also captured. These two capturing rules were the basic process of DCA model, which describe the dendrite growth and coarsening. Moreover, some special cells (additional cells in [01] and [10] directions shown in Fig. 2b) should be captured in this step to modify the grains directions and keep the [01] and [10] directions as the prior growth direction. This type of treatment to the discrete grids can release the reliance of different cells and enhance the computing efficiency.

The two dimensions DCA model is also extended into three dimensions, and the underlying approach is the same. A misoriented grain is considered to nucleate and grow within a regular array of cubic cells having an octahedral shape (Fig. 3). Assuming coordinate system of this grain is defined as (x, y, z), and the local coordinate system is (x_0, y_0, z_0). Therefore, the coordinate conversion from (x, y, z) to (x_0, y_0, z_0) can be uniquely determined using the rotation matrix which was defined as R_1, R_2 and R_3. The misorientation can be characterized by three Euler angles (α, β, γ). Accordingly, the rotation matrix within the volume is given by the following equations.

$$R_1 = \begin{pmatrix} 1 & 0 & 0 \\ 0 & \cos\alpha & -\sin\alpha \\ 0 & \sin\alpha & \cos\alpha \end{pmatrix}$$

$$R_2 = \begin{pmatrix} \cos\beta & 0 & \sin\beta \\ 0 & 1 & 0 \\ -\sin\beta & 0 & \cos\beta \end{pmatrix} \quad (8)$$

$$R_3 = \begin{pmatrix} \cos\gamma & -\sin\gamma & 0 \\ \sin\gamma & \cos\gamma & 0 \\ 0 & 0 & 1 \end{pmatrix}$$

$$\begin{pmatrix} x \\ y \\ z \end{pmatrix} = R_1 \cdot R_2 \cdot R_3 \begin{pmatrix} x_0 \\ y_0 \\ z_0 \end{pmatrix} \quad (9)$$

When the octahedron grows sufficiently large and its vertexes touch any of the neighboring liquid cells, the neighboring cell will then be changed so as to be in the interface state, meanwhile growth will continue from the vertex along <1 0 0> directions into the captured cells by generating a new octahedron. At each time step, the evolution of the distance $L(t)$ from the center to the vertex of the octahedron is related to the increment of the solid fraction Δf_s, and can be calculated based on the following equation:

$$L(t + \Delta t) = L(t) + \sqrt{2} \Delta x \cdot \Delta f_s \quad (10)$$

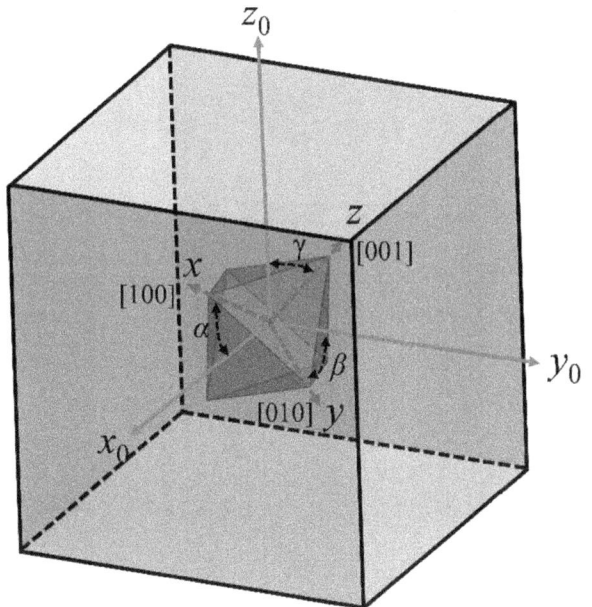

Fig. 3 Crystallographic orientations analysis of 3D individual dendrite in the regular cubic grid.

Once the value $L(t)$ has been calculated, the coordinates of the six vertexes of the octahedron in the local coordinate system are known, and their corresponding coordinates in the (x, y, z) coordinate system can be easily obtained through coordinate conversion.

2.3 Simulation parameters

In the present model, the approach for dendrite simulation of DD6 superalloy is used in conjunction with thermodynamic/kinetic/equilibrium phase diagram calculation databases in order to obtain the parameters required for the simulations. The solidification process of DD6 superalloy could be regarded as a single-phase (γ) solidification. For studying multicomponent alloys, this model is effective for using the equivalent binary alloy model to simplify the real alloy. Therefore, the equivalent binary Ni-X alloy was performed to simulate the solidification process variables on the development of the dendritic structure. Some equivalent parameters of Ni-X alloy were calculated using the professional metal performance calculation software JMatPro as shown in

Fig. 4. However, due to the fact that the limitation of the JMatPro software and issues with robustness, an optimized table-look-up technique is adopted to provide access to the data needed in the simulation. Some key thermophysical parameters of the Ni-X alloy are obtained from references which was shown in Table 1.

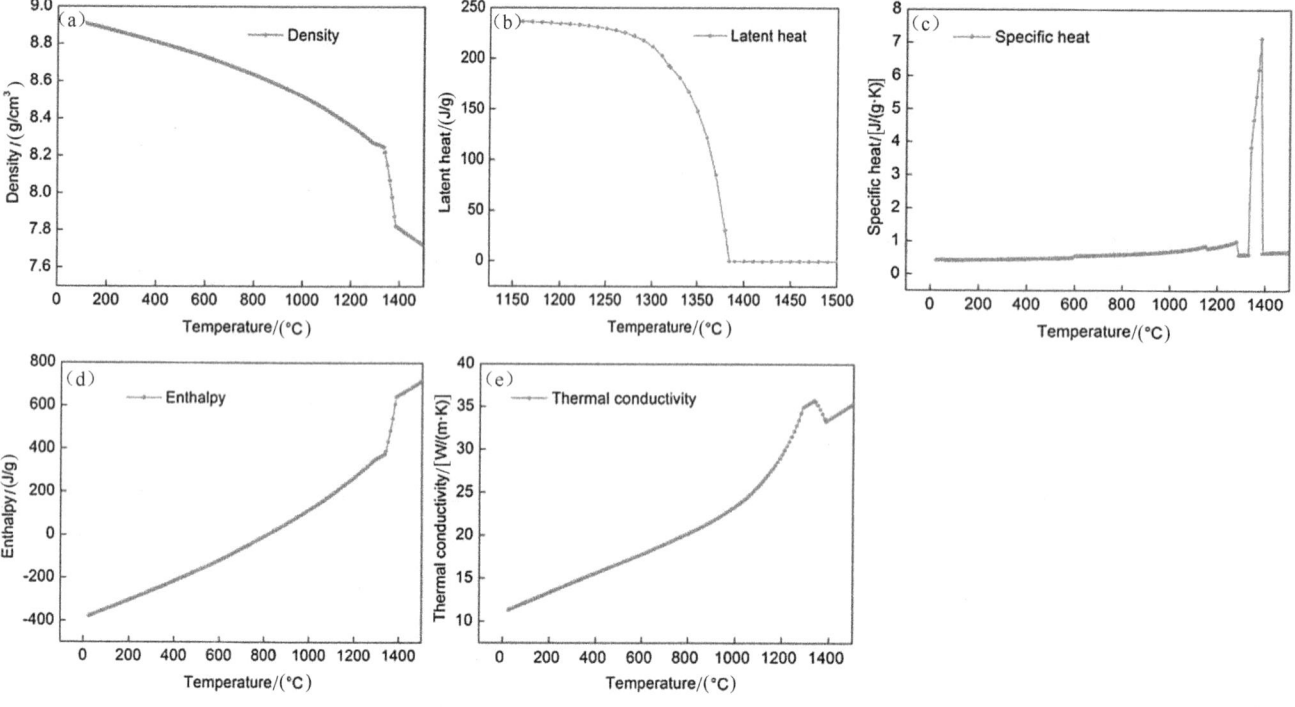

Fig. 4　Thermophysical properties of DD6 superalloy calculated by JMatPro software: (a) density; (b) latent heat; (c) specific heat; (d) enthalpy; (e) thermal conductivity.

Table 1　The thermophysical parameters of DD6 superalloy from Refs.[33,34].

Parameters	Values
Liquidus temperature (℃)	1399
Solidus temperature (℃)	1342
Liquidus slope	−3.95
Solute partition coefficient	0.788
Concentration (wt%)	39.006
Anisotropy coefficient ε	0.03
Gibbs-Thomson coefficient Γ (Km)	3.65×10^{-7}
Liquid diffusion coefficient D_L (m^{2}s^{-1})	3.6×10^{-9}
Solid diffusion coefficient D_s (m^{2}s^{-1})	1.0×10^{-12}

2.4　Experimental methods

A Lasertec™ VL2000.21W-SVF17SP.15FTC confocal laser scanning microscopy system (CLSM) was used to make some in-situ investigations of the dendrite growth directly during heating to the liquid state and during cooling to room temperature. It was combined with an imaging system (Fig. 5a) and a heating system (Fig. 5b). The imaging system uses a 1.5 mW He-Ne laser ($\lambda = 632.8$nm), with a 0.25μm diameter laser beam. The laser beam is reflected by the specimen and scanned at a rate of 15.7kHz by an acoustic optic detector in the horizontal direction, and by a dichroic mirror in the vertical direction at 60Hz. The obtained signal represents a quasi-topographical representation of the specimen surface through recording several captures at different depths, making it possible to distinguish the surface relief caused by any phase transformations. The heating system mounted at the focal point of an ellipsoidal gold-plated infrared image furnace, powered by a 1.5kW halogen lamp. This infrared heating system can reach temperature up to 1700℃ in a few minutes. The sample temperature is measured with a B-type thermocouple at the bottom of the Platinum sample holder.

In this study, the superalloy employed is DD6 (Ni-4.3Cr-5.6Al-2Mo-9Co-8W-2Re-7.5Ta-0.5Nb-0.1Hf, wt%), which is a typical second generation superalloy. Small samples 7mm in diameter and 2.5mm in height

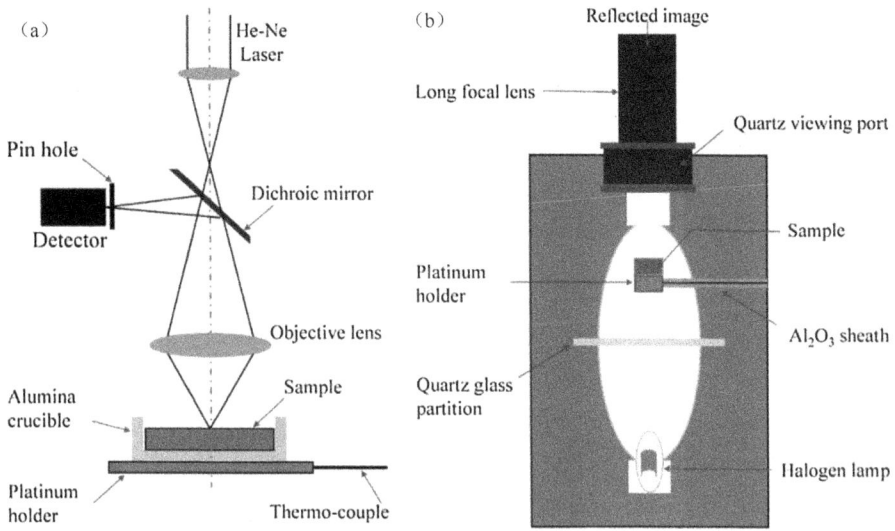

Fig. 5 Schematic illustration of HT-CLSM: (a) imaging system; (b) heating system.

were sectioned from a DD6 single crystal rod. The samples were then ground and mechanically polished down to 1μm. For the experiment, each sample was placed in an alumina crucible placed on the Pt holder in the HT-CLSM furnace below a quartz glass viewing window. Before heating stage, the HT-CLSM chamber is flushed three times with purified Argon before it is filled with Argon at atmospheric pressure in order to avoid the oxidation phenomenon. The sample was heated following the heating cycles shown in Fig. 6, the orange dotted line was the pre-set thermal cycle parameter and the blue line is the actual one by real-time measured. Initially, a low heating rate of 100℃ min^{-1} was performed to preheat the furnace which reached at ~100℃. Then, the sample was heated at a rapid heating rate of 500℃ min^{-1} to the predetermined temperature (~1400℃). Due to the nature of the temperature measuring and controlling system, it was not always possible to exactly achieve the exact target temperature during rapid heating or force a certain cooling schedule. Consequently, there is a difference in temperature between the preset and actual measured temperatures during the experiment. After 30s of isothermal holding at 1400℃, the sample was cooled down to 1100℃ at a control cooling rate 60℃ min^{-1}. Finally, a rapid cooling rate was set in order to make the sample temperature down to room temperature quickly. It is important to mention that thermal imaging calibration measurements showed that the temperature difference between the specimen surface and the recorded thermocouple temperature did not exceed ±15℃.

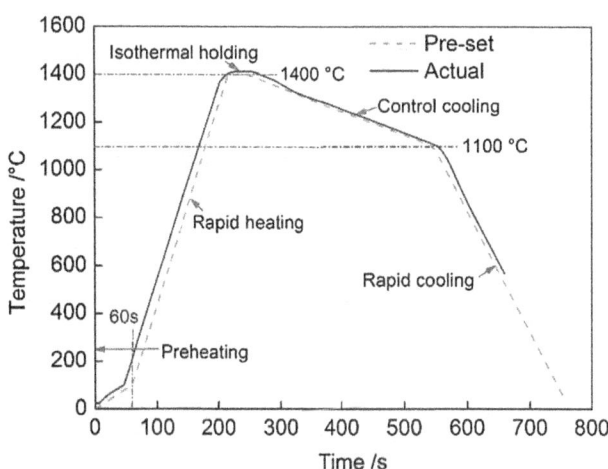

Fig. 6 The preset and actual thermal cycles performed in the HT-CLSM.

In order to investigate the evolution of dendrite morphology, samples before and after HT-CLSM were both prepared by mechanical polishing and chemical etching in mixed solution of 5mL HCl+2mL HF+2g CuSO$_4$ · 5H$_2$O + 23.5mL H$_2$O. And, the most remarkable, the sample after HT-CLSM experienced remelting and solidification, must be prepared a second time for dendrite morphology characterization at room temperature. Then, the samples were observed by using a LEICA DM6000M optical microscope (OM) and JSM-6301F field emission gun scanning electron microscope (FEG-SEM), equipped with a backscattered electrons (BSe) detector, operated at 5kV, and the distribution of different alloying elements was finally investigated using the equipped EDS system.

3. Results and discussion

3.1 Simulation of 2-D dendrite morphology

In order to investigate the feasible of the model, 2-D single dendrite morphology was simulated without considering nature and forced convection influence. A fixed nucleus was placed in the center of the calculation domain. The domain was a 100×100 cells square with the cell size of 5μm, which was large enough to eliminate the effects of boundary on the concentration field. The crystallographic orientations were aligned with the coordinate axes. No-flux conditions were imposed at the boundaries of the calculation domain. Initially, the temperature of the calculation domain was kept at the liquidus temperature, 1399℃, with a homogeneous composition C_0, and a constant cooling rate of 0.5K/s was applied to the calculation domain. The dendrite morphology, solute concentration are presented in Fig. 7. It can be seen that a fourfold symmetry of secondary dendrite arms formed a "cruciate flower". The initial tertiary dendrite arm with a random spacing grew perpendicular to the secondary arms which developed immediately behind the secondary dendrite tip (Fig. 7a). Since the solute diffusivity is much slower than the dendrite growth velocity, solute discharged from the newly solidified solid phase cannot sufficiently diffuse to the bulk liquid, especially in the regions between the secondary dendrite arms, as shown in Fig. 5b. As the solidification process continued, the solute in these regions may have become trapped between the solidified regions and resulted in microsegregation. As expected, this model can reveal the phenomenon of dendrite growth exactly, so more simulation cases will be performed based on this model.

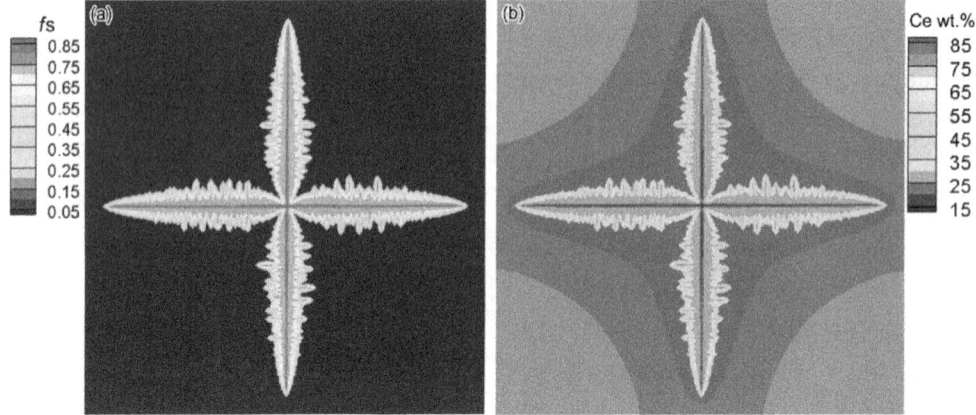

Fig. 7 Predicted dendritic growth morphology and concentration: (a) fraction solid; (b) solute concentration.

As mentioned above, dendrites are the substructure of grains, which are the strategic link between materials processing and materials behavior. Therefore, dendrites growth and distribution control is essential for any processing activity. However, the scale of the dendrite is very small and the growth stage is ordinary unobservable which will cause much hardship to study the dendrite. Although the simulation method can describe the process of the dendrite growth, over a large scale of simulation is still a challenge because of the computation bound. In this work, parallel algorithm and modified self-adaption mesh refinement method was used to simulate the dendrite growth at a large domain. A square calculation domain was selected and divided into 2000×2000 cells with the cell size of 5μm. Stochastic nucleation based on solute adjusted undercooling was used, with randomly assigned preferential growth directions. The simulation results are shown in Fig. 8, different dendrites with different Euler angles are presented in various colors. It can be observed that at the beginning of the solidification process, the fourfold symmetry dendrites developed steadily along the crystallographic orientations (Fig. 8a). As the solidification process, the primary trunk of dendrites became coarse accompanied

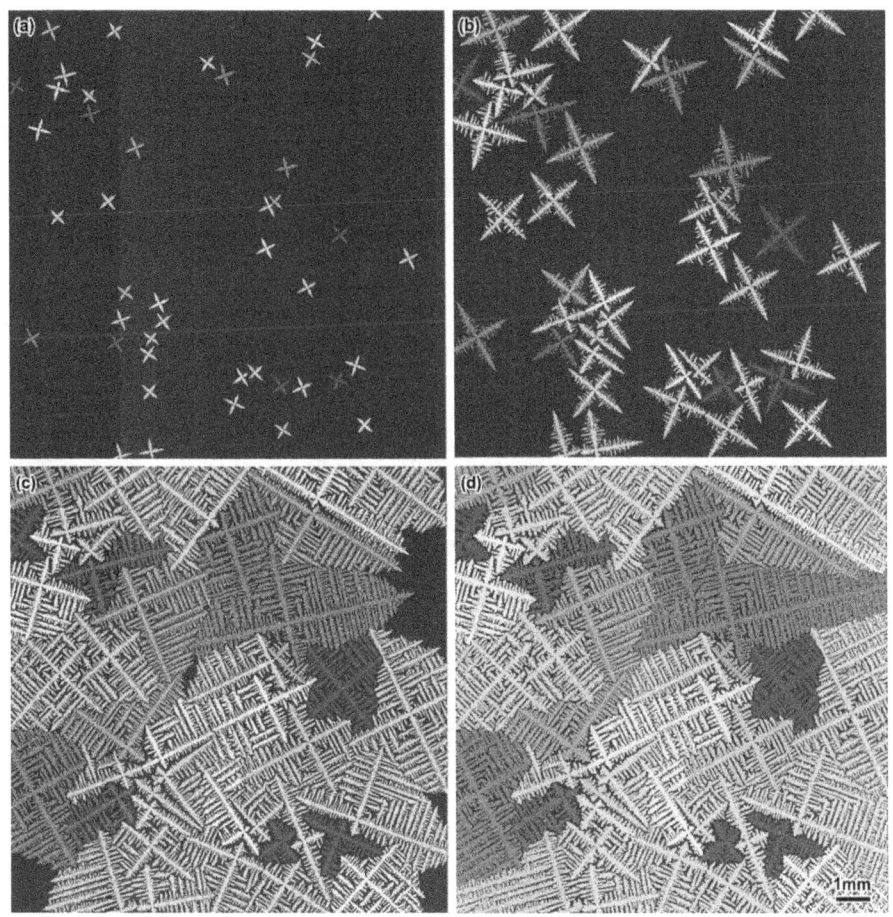

Fig. 8 Simulation of 2D dendritic distribution of a large domain:
(a) $t=3.5s$, $f_s=1.5\%$; (b) $t=6.9s$, $f_s=10.3\%$; (c) $t=10.4s$, $f_s=41.9\%$; (d) $t=17.4s$, $f_s=63.3\%$.

by side branching and the collision of dendrites, hindering the dendrite free growth (Fig. 8b and c). At the end of solidification, dendrite growth was significantly affected by the interaction between solute fields and the surrounding dendrites, forcing the dendrites to grow along the directions deviating from their initial crystallographic orientations, resulting in the complicated dendrite morphologies shown in Fig. 8d. In addition, it was also can be observed the simulation results can accurately predict the morphology and competitive growth of dendrites.

3.2 In-situ observation with HT-CLSM

To investigate the effect of element segregation to dendrite growth, EDS mapping measurements was used to observe the distribution of the alloying elements before in-situ observation, and the elemental maps are shown in Fig. 9. The location of surface scanning was in the junction of interdendritic and dendrite arm where the microsegregation was always presence. The elemental mapping indicated that the DD6 superalloy was rich in Ni, Al, Co, Cr, Mo, Re and W. The lighter pixels represent higher element content in the elemental maps, while the darker ones illustrate the element content was less. Moreover, the microsegregation behavior was observed, as that of other alloys, the microsegregation of DD6 superalloy is also divided into positive segregation and negative segregation. Due to the density of Aluminum is lower, positive segregation is likely to occur in the solidification process, while the larger density elements, such as W, Re, are often prone to negative segregation. However, as a result of the limitation of scope of observation, no microsegregation was observed in the Tungsten element map. Researches[14,19] have shown that element segregation behavior has an important influence on the microstructure of nickel-based superalloy.

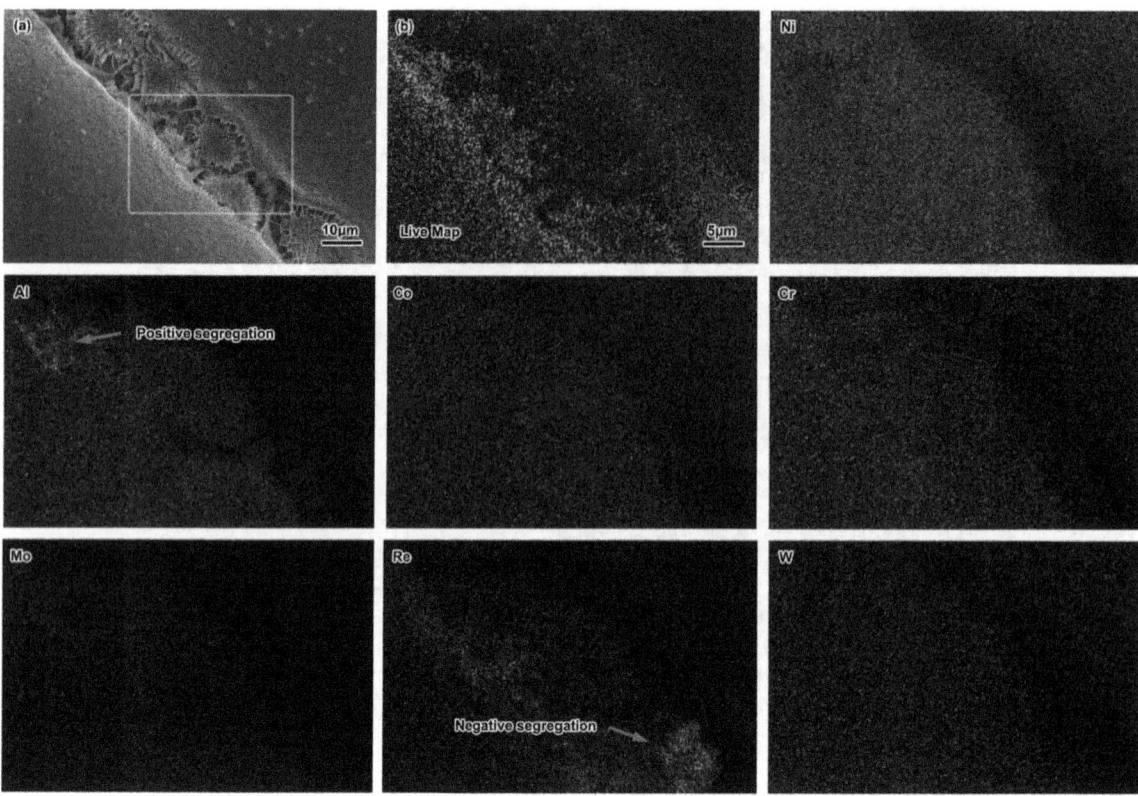

Fig. 9 SEM-EDS mapping of selected elements in as-received state DD6 superalloy: (a) SEM micrograph; (b) EDS live mapping.

The in-situ observation was performed according to the pro-set thermal cycles shown in Fig. 6, and the dendritic structure evolution and the liquid distribution were then investigated in particular, via partial remelting from the as-received state DD6 superalloy. Fig. 10 presents the snapshots taken at different temperature on DD6 superalloy during the heating and cooling processes. Due to the HT-CLSM is sensitive to the surface relief, so the electrochemical etching technology was used to process the sample before insitu observations, which leads to a rugged surface. During the heating, the sample surface remained unchanged until ~ 1194℃ as shown in Fig. 10a. With increasing temperature, the incipient melting occurred at ~ 1313℃, and the liquid appeared mainly in interdendritic regions; it was characterized by a topical change of the brightness of the image (Fig. 10b). Due to microsegregation of alloying elements during the solidification process, some elements, such as Al, Mo, Zr, can form low melting point intermetallic compounds with Ni in interdendritic regions which melted at temperature lower than that at which the bulk melts, which just to verify the result mentioned at Fig. 9. As the temperature further rises, the different elements began to diffuse in the semi-solid zone. The low melting point elements were transferred to other regions which resulting in solidification in the initial incipient melting regions (Fig. 10c). Given the temperature (below the liquidus), the liquid phase in Fig. 10c must also be the incipient melting. Some studies[35] indicate that incipient melting phenomenon has important influence on the formation of porosity and grain boundary cracking. When the liquidus temperature was reached, more liquid appeared along the interdendritic regions (Fig. 10d). Then, an interconnected liquid phase was formed with increasing temperature, and the liquid film finally recovered the whole surface of the sample, as shown in Fig. 10e. When comparing Fig. 10d and e, it was found that the content increased a lot during a very short time. Moreover, as the solubility of the liquid phase was higher, the alloying elements diffused into the liquid phase, so the surface of the sample was uniform. With decreasing temperature, liquid/solid phase transformation preferentially occurred under the liquid film because of the lower temperature relative to the surface. Initially, many nucleus were formed and began to grow in all directions, and some of them were observed on the surface (Fig. 10f). As the nucleus continues to grow, dendrites with "cruciate flower" appeared in the micro-filed, as shown in Fig. 10g, which just like the simulation result in Fig. 7. We can deduce from Fig. 10g that the zone marked with a blue circle in Fig. 10f must be a nucleation point. When temperature decreased below the solidus (~1342℃), some remaining liquid still existed in the interdendritic zone (Fig. 10h). It is believed that this phenomenon should be the alloying element segregation resulted in unusual composition undercooling. Finally, the liquid phase solidified completely, and the dendritic structure can be seen clearly in Fig. 10i. However, during the in-situ observation, many details were not captured because of the limitation of the magnification and the instantaneity of the solidification process. Therefore, after performing the thermal cycling which shown in Fig. 6, the sample would be further processed in order to observe the change of the microstructure.

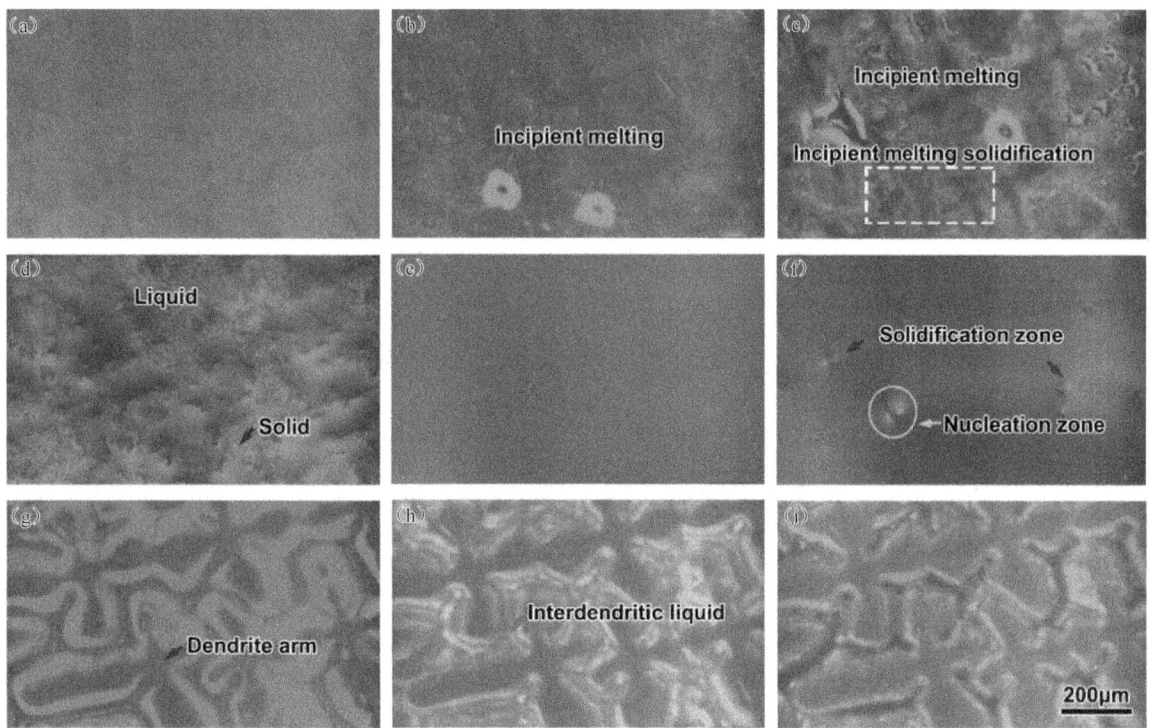

Fig. 10 HT CLSM snapshots for the sequence of partial remelting of DD6 superalloy during heating at 500℃·min^{-1} to a peak temperature of 1412℃ and the subsequent cooling: (a) $t=216$s, $T=1194$℃; (b) $t=233$s, $T=1313$℃; (c) $t=243$s, $T=1382$℃; (d) $t=258$s, $T=1410$℃; (e) $t=294$s, $T=1412$℃; (f) $t=312$s, $T=1353$℃; (g) $t=341$s, $T=1345$℃; (h) $t=352$s, $T=1332$℃; (i) $t=417$s, $T=1263$℃.

3.3 Comparison of simulation and experiment

During the cooling stage of HT-CLSM, the directions of heat flux were in all sides, so the equiaxed polycrystalline grew in random crystallographic orientations. However, the 2-D simulation results (Fig. 8) present a large deviation to the in-situ observations (Fig. 10), due to the heat transmission patterns in 2-D domain are oversimplified compared with the experimental conditions. Hence, this solidification process was also simulated by using the proposed 3-D dendrites growth model, and the simulation results are shown in Fig. 11. The calculation domain was a $400 \times 400 \times 400$ cells cube with the cell size of 5μm, and the cooling rate was 60℃·min^{-1} which same as the cooling stage of HTCLSM. The temperature was assumed to be uniform in the domain and was cooled down from the peak temperature (~1412℃), and the total nuclei number was equal to 20 in this simulation case, with randomly assigned location and preferential growth orientations. In this figure, the different colors represent different grains. Initially, the nucleated grains were randomly distributed in the domain and the dendrite arms started to develop along their preferential growth orientations which presented as having sixfold symmetry morphologies (Fig. 11a). As can be seen in the early stage of solidification, the size of the dendrites were relatively small, and the dendrites were far from each other with less interaction limitation. Although some tertiary dendrites were observed emanating from the secondary arms at the initial growth stage, they were blocked by the secondary dendrites growing from the primary dendrites. As the process of solidification, the solute rejected into the melt and the interaction effects of the solute field between the adjacent dendrites were intensified, so the tip growth of dendrites sufficiently slowed down, leading to the coarsening of the dendrite arms. In addition, impingement of dendritic tips also progressively hindered the growth of dendrite arms (Fig. 11b and c). It was noticed that further solidification will occur within the existing equiaxed dendrites, especially coarsening the secondary or tertiary dendrite arms, and causing the increase of solid fraction until they were completely solidified. The dendrites kept growing, the simulation was continued until 18.1s from the start of growth, and both branching and competitive growth phenomena were clearly observed in Fig. 11d. Comparing the 3-D simulation result with the experimental result (Fig. 10), it was found that multi-equiaxial dendrites growth was significantly influenced by solute diffusion and the adjacent dendrites, and the complex dendrite morphology was believed to be mainly attributed to their grain density, distribution, inherently preferred growth directions, and varying anisotropies.

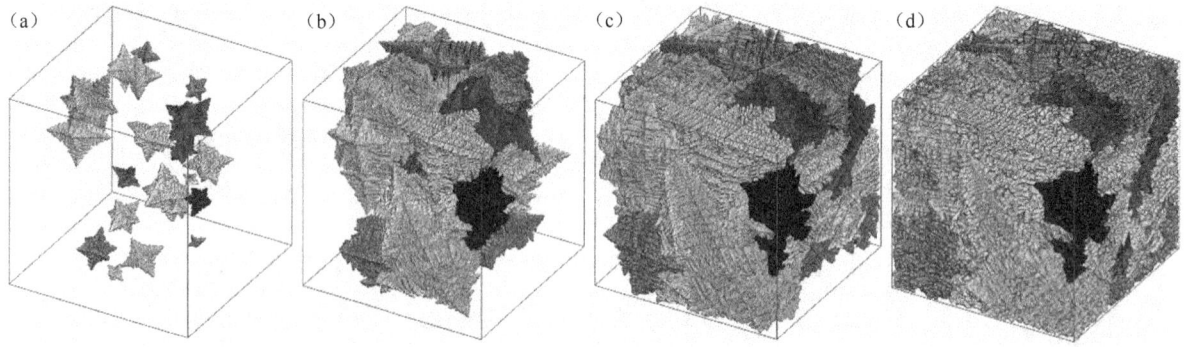

Fig. 11 Simulation results of multi-grain solidification of DD6 superalloy at the same cooling rate with HT-CLSM:
(a) $t=1.4s$, $f_s=3.3\%$; (b) $t=8.8s$, $f_s=51.7\%$; (c) $t=13.4s$, $f_s=69.5\%$; (d) $t=18.1s$, $f_s=82.8\%$.

After the in-situ observations, the sample was ground and observed to investigate the influence of the thermal cycle on the development of the final structure in the bulk. Fig. 12a presents the whole section dendrite morphology of the sample after HTCLSM. It can be seen in this figure, many equiaxial grains were developed during the remelting process, and each grain consists of dendrites with the same crystallographic orientation as the sub-structure. The boundary was formed between two different equiaxial grains which has traced by solid yellow line in the figure. The dendritic structure became refinedly and randomly, and the secondary and tertiary dendrite arms were more luxuriant because of the sufficient cooling efficiency. The competitive growth of dendrites was observed in zone I, and a larger image was shown in Fig. 12b. During solidification process, randomly oriented grain grew in the shape of dendrites along the direction of heat flow, and competitive growth took place between these dendrites where the collision occurred frequently. In this process, dendrite with [0 0 1] preferential crystallographic orientation that closely paralleled the heat flow direction would grow faster than the other one which exhibited different growth directions. The model of competitive growth has been presented by Walton and Chalmers[36], who found that the angle between the preferred growth direction and the heat flow direction was small, could keep growing by blocking unfavorably oriented dendrites. Based on this model, competitive growth of dendrites was simulated as shown in Fig. 12c. These two dendrites with different Euler angles encountered each other and formed a clear grain boundary. The left-hand side dendrite array had a [0 0 1] preferential growth direction close to the heat flow direction, which grew faster than the right one. It proved that the simulation result agree very well with the experimental result. Fig. 12d and e shows the dendrite morphology of zone II, obtained by experimental and simulation, respectively, and the view direction was [0 0 1]. It can be observed that the secondary dendrite arms were fragmentized and intermittent because of the fluctuations of heat transfer and solute diffusion during the solidification process. Researches[33,37] showed that the scale of dendrite subject to the cooling condition was measured by SDAS, which exerts a significant influence on the mechanical properties of castings. In addition, solidification defects, such as porosity, freckle, will be easily formed in the regions of broken dendrites.

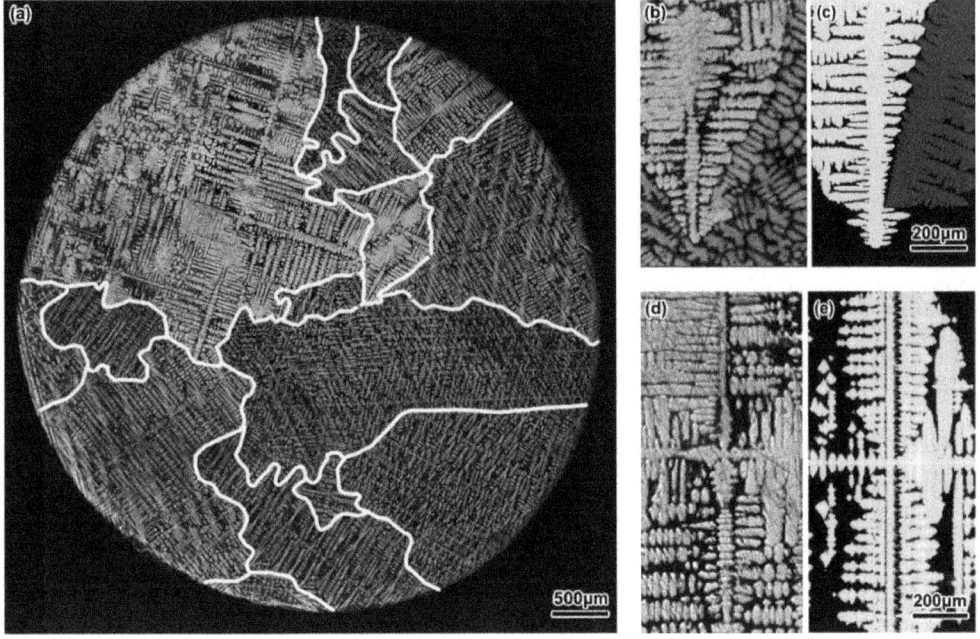

Fig. 12 Dendrite morphology in cross-section of the sample after IIT-CLSM: (a) optical micrograph of the whole section; (b) and (c) experimental and simulation results of dendrites competition growth at zone I; (d) and (e) experimental and simulation results of dendrites morphology in [0 0 1] view direction at zone II.

3.4 Simulation of 3D dendrite growth in DS process

Generally, high-performance turbine blades and other castings are usually produced by DS process, which can get access to columnar grains or single crystal structure. Therefore, the DS dendrites growth was also studied by the developed model. Fig. 13 shows the dendrite morphology of DD6 superalloy in as-received state, which prepared by DS process. The whole section dendrite morphology of sample was disposed by automatic puzzle technology (Fig. 11a), and the view direction is [0 0 1]. In this figure, the dendrites are distributed relatively equally in terms of the same crystallographic orientation. Four secondary arms of each individual dendrite emanate from the central primary dendrite, which presents a "cruciate flower" morphology, just like the simulation and in-situ observation results mentioned above. A higher magnification SEM micrograph of transverse section dendrite morphology is shown in Fig. 13b. It is observed that the primary dendrite arm spacing (PDAS) is close to 300μm. The approximate fourfold symmetry "cruciate flower" can be clearly distinguished, and the tertiary dendrite begin to develop on the secondary dendrite arm, which has not grown to a significant length. Fig. 13c shows the free-standing dendrites morphology which was obtained from the upper end of an as-grown single crystal (SC) cylindrical bar, where the solidifying material has run out of interdendritic melt material and free standing dendrites can be seen without further metallographic preparation. Although the tips of the dendrites are tiny and curving at the end of the solidification process, the growth direction of dendrites are always along with the [0 0 1], which suggests that the dendrites of DD6 superalloy during DS process will grow regularly following the specific crystallographic orientation.

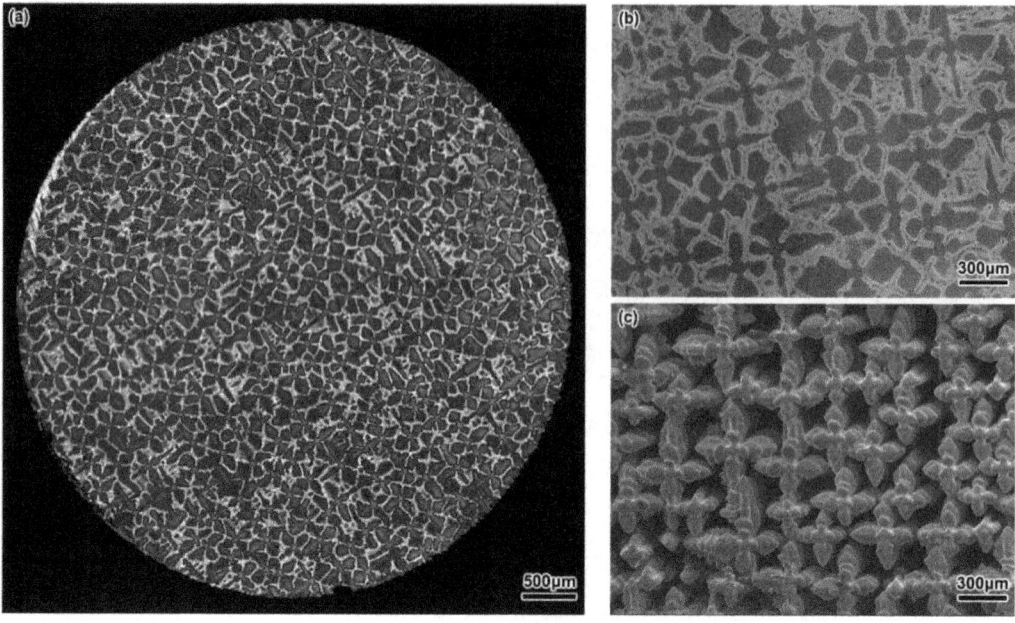

Fig. 13 Dendrite morphologies of DD6 superalloy in as-received state: (a) optical micrograph from the whole section of a small sample before HT-CLSM; (b) SEM micrograph with dendrites taken from a transverse section perpendicular to the growth direction; (c) SEM micrograph showing free-standing dendrites at the end of the cylindrical bar.

In order to investigate this specific dendrites growth pattern of DS process, simulation of columnar dendrites growth under DS process was performed on a domain of 400×400×800 cells with the cell size of 5μm, under conditions of a thermal gradient of 15K/mm and a constant withdrawal rate of 150μm/s. Without considering the influence of grain density on dendrite growth, 100 nuclei were planted at the bottom of the calculation domain, and they grew in the unidirectional temperature distribution (Fig. 14a). Initially, these grain seeds showed a severely competitive growth, and the dendrite arm spacing was adjusted accordingly (Fig. 14b). The uneven fluctuation of temperature and components led to grains with preferred orientation growing quickly, and other ones being blocked and eventually eliminated. The distribution of heat and solute then settled into a dynamic balance, which would lead to a stable growth of dendrites (Fig. 14c). Finally, the dendrites were stable growth and the dendrite arm spacing was equally distributed, as shown in Fig. 14d. In this figure, the dendrite tip had small radii of curvature, according to Langer and Müller-Krumbhaar[38], the tip morphology characteristics can be determined using the detailed numerical analysis of the wavelengths of instabilities along the sides of a dendrite which followed the predicted scaling law:

$$\lambda_2/R = 2.1 \pm 0.03 \quad (11)$$

where λ_2 is the secondary dendrite arm spacing, R is the steadystate dendrite tip radius.

Fig. 15 shows the simulation results of dendritic morphologies from the transverse section and top view respectively in DS process. It was observed that the dendritic morphology was not strictly symmetric. In some parts, the secondary arms were not developed, while in the other parts, they appeared to be tertiary or higher. Thus, this model was shown to describe the experimental results (Fig. 13b and c) very well, and the simulated dendrite "cruciate flower" morphology and arm spacing also agreed well with the experimental results.

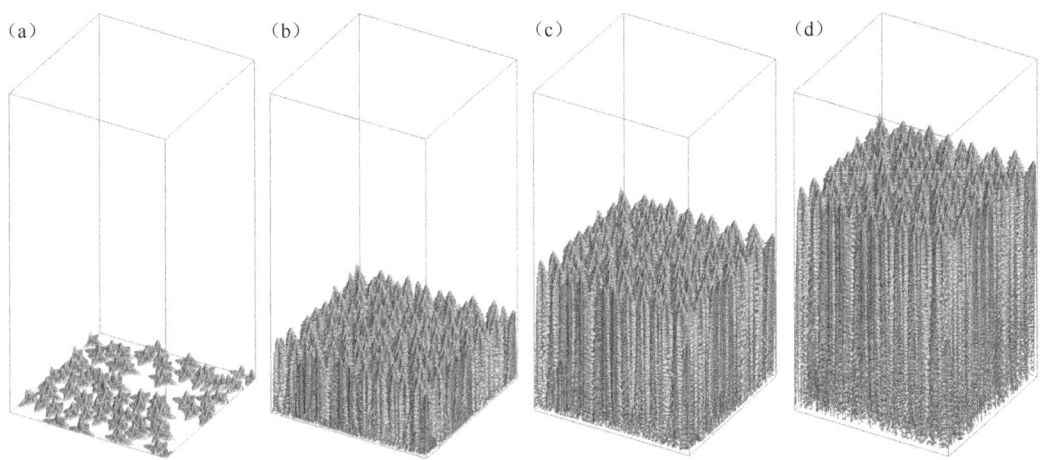

Fig. 14 3-D simulation results of directional solidification dendrite growth:
(a) $t=2.3s$, $f_s=0.79\%$; (b) $t=9.3s$, $f_s=7.5\%$; (c) $t=18.5s$, $f_s=22.7\%$; (d) $t=27.8s$, $f_s=42.5\%$.

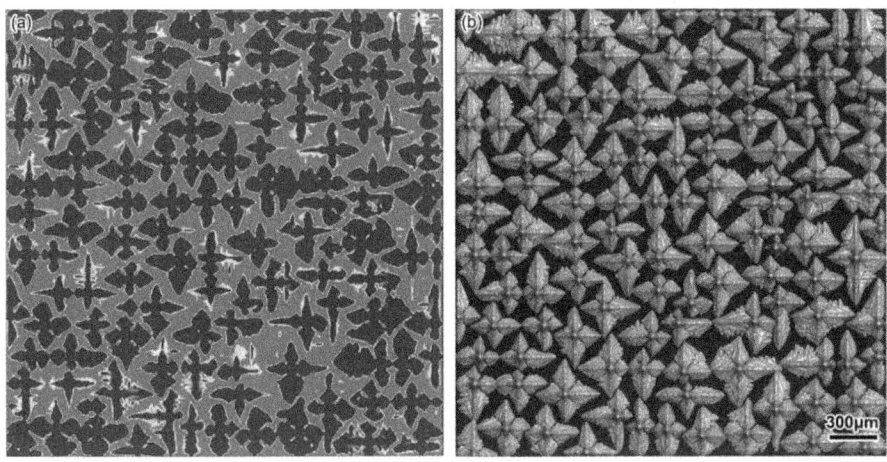

Fig. 15 Simulation results of dendritic morphologies: (a) transverse section; (b) top view.

4. Conclusion

In this work, numerical simulation and in-situ observation technologies have been used to investigate the dendrite growth of DD6 superalloy. A combined DCA-FD model was developed to simulate the dendrite growth partially in large scale in 2-D section, 3-D polycrystalline and DS columnar dendrites. The HT-CLSM as a powerful tool was used to observe the dendritic structure evolution during the heating and cooling thermal cycles. The main conclusions were as follows:

(1) The 3-D dendrite growth model was built, and the algorithm of cells capture was modified, a deterministic cellular automaton (DCA) model was proposed to describe neighborhood tracking. The dendritic morphologies, especially hundreds of 2-D dendrites distribution over a large scale and 3-D polycrystalline growth, were successfully simulated. The 3-D simulation results presented a reasonable agreement with the experimental observations under the same solidification conditions.

(2) According to the in-situ observation results, the single dendritic morphology in the final state presented a "cruciate flower" which just like the simulation result. The dendritic morphology of sample after HT-CLSM was observed by OM. It was found that many equiaxial grains consists of dendrites were developed, and the secondary dendrite arms of these dendrites were luxuriant and intermittent. The competitive growth of dendrites was also analyzed according to the experimental and simulation results, and they agreed well with each other.

(3) Finally, the developed model was applied to

the DS process, and the columnar dendrites evolution behavior and detail morphology were simulated based on the condition of a real DS process, and the corresponding experimental results observed by OM and SEM were used to verify the numerical model. The simulation and experimental results indicate that the proposed model is able to reproduce a wide range of DS process.

Acknowledgements

This work was supported by the National Basic Research Program of China [grant number 2011CB706801]; the National Natural Science Foundation of China [grant numbers 51374137, 51171089]; and the National Science and Technology Major Projects [grant numbers 2012ZX04012-011, 2011ZX04014-052].

References

[1] B. H. Kear, E. R. Thompson, Aircraft gas turbine materials and process, Science 208 (1980) 847-856.

[2] Q. Feng, T. K. Nandy, S. Tin, et al., Solidification of high-refractory rutheniumcontaining superalloys, Acta Mater. 51 (2003) 269-284.

[3] M. Montakhab, M. Bacak, E. Balikci, Low melt height solidification of superalloys, Metall. Mater. Trans. A 47A (2016) 3031-3039.

[4] M. Asta, C. Beckermann, A. Karma, et al., Solidification microstructures and solid-state parallels: recent developments, future directions, Acta Mater. 57 (2009) 941-971.

[5] Y. Z. Zhou, Formation of stray grains during directional solidification of a nickel-based superalloy, Scripta Mater. 65 (2011) 281-284.

[6] Q. Y. Xu, H. Zhang, B. C. Liu, Multiscale modelling and simulation of single crystal superalloy turbine blade casting during directional solidification process, China Foundry 11 (2014) 268-276.

[7] J. D. Miller, T. M. Pollock, Stability of dendrite growth during directional solidification in the presence of a non-axial thermal field, Acta Mater. 78 (2014) 23-36.

[8] M. Rappaz, Modeling and characterization of grain structures and defects in solidification, Curr. Opin. Solid Mater. Sci. 20 (2016) 37-45.

[9] I. M. McKenna, S. O. Poulsen, E. M. Lauridsen, et al., Grain growth in four dimensions: a comparison between simulation and experiment, Acta Mater. 78 (2014) 125-134.

[10] R. Trivedi, H. Miyahara, P. Mazumder, et al., Directional solidification microstructures in diffusive and convective regimes, J. Cryst. Growth 222 (2001) 365-379.

[11] Y. Y. Lian, D. C. Li, K. Zhang, A method for flattening the solidification front in directional solidification technology, J. Cryst. Growth 426 (2015) 186-197.

[12] W. Kurz, D. J. Fisher, Dendrite growth at the limit of stability: tip radius and spacing, Acta Metall. 29 (1980) 11-20.

[13] R. Trivedi, W. Kurz, Dendritic growth, Int. Mater. Rev. 39 (1994) 49-74.

[14] C. Sun, M. Kirk, M. Li, et al., Microstructure, chemistry and mechanical properties of Ni-based superalloy Rene N4 under irradiation at room temperature, Acta Mater. 95 (2015) 357-365.

[15] D. X. Ma, Development of dendrite array growth during alternately changing solidification condition, J. Cryst. Growth. 260 (2004) 580-589.

[16] S. Karagadde, L. Yuan, N. Shevchenko, et al., 3-D microstructural model of freckle formation validated using in situ experiments, Acta Mater. 79 (2014) 168-180.

[17] X. W. Qian, H. Z. Cummins, Dendritic sidebranching initiation by a localized heat pulse, Phys. Rev. Lett. 64 (1990) 3038-3041.

[18] Q. Dong, J. Zhang, J. F. Dong, et al., In situ observation of columnar-to-equiaxed transition in directional solidification using synchrotron X-radiation imaging technique, Mater. Sci. Eng. A 530 (2011) 271-276.

[19] G. C. Gu, R. Pesci, L. Langlois, et al., Microstructure observation and quantification of the liquid fraction of M2 steel grade in the semi-solid state, combining confocal laser scanning microscopy and X-ray microtomography, Acta Mater. 66 (2014) 118-131.

[20] M. M. Attallah, H. Terasaki, R. J. Moat, et al., In-Situ observation of primary γ' melting in Ni-base superalloy using confocal laser scanning microscopy, Mater. Charact. 62 (2011) 760-767.

[21] H. Zhang, Q. Y. Xu, B. C. Liu, Numerical simulation and optimization of directional solidification process of single crystal superalloy casting, Materials 7 (2014) 1625-1639.

[22] H. Yin, S. D. Felicelli, L. Wang, Simulation of a dendritic microstructure with the lattice Boltzmann and cellular automaton methods, Acta Mater. 59 (2011) 3124-3136.

[23] J. D. Miller, L. Yuan, P. D. Lee, et al., Simulation of diffusion-limited lateral growth of dendrites during solidification via liquid metal cooling, Acta Mater. 69 (2014) 47-59.

[24] T. Takaki, M. Ohno, Y. Shibuta, et al., Two-dimension-

al phase-field study of competitive grain growth during directional solidification of polycrystalline binary alloy, J. Cryst. Growth. 442 (2016) 14-24.

[25] D. Tourret, A. Karma, Growth competition of columnar dendritic grains: a phase-field study, Acta Mater. 82 (2015) 64-83.

[26] C. A. Gandin, M. Rappaz, A 3D cellular automaton algorithm for the prediction of dendritic grain growth, Acta Mater. 45 (1997) 2187-2195.

[27] M. F. Zhu, S. Y. Lee, C. P. Hong, Modified cellular automaton model for the prediction of dendritic growth with melt convection, Phys. Rev. E 69 (061610) (2004) 1-12.

[28] J. Yu, Q. Y. Xu, K. Cui, et al., Numerical simulation of microstructure evolution based on a modified CA method, Acta Metall. Sin. 43 (2007) 731-738.

[29] M. Rappaz, C. A. Gandin, Probabilistic modelling of microstructure formation in solidification process, Acta Metall. Mater. 41 (1993) 345-360.

[30] C. A. Gandin, M. Rappaz, A coupled finite element-cellular automaton model for the prediction of dendritic grain structures in solidification processes, Acta Metall. Mater. 42 (1994) 2233-2246.

[31] W. Wang, P. D. Lee, M. McLean, A model of solidification microstructures in nickel-based superalloys: predicting primary dendrite spacing selection, Acta Mater. 51 (2003) 2971-2987.

[32] S. Y. Pan, M. F. Zhu, A three-dimensional sharp interface model for the quantitative simulation of solutal dendritic growth, Acta Mater. 58 (2010) 340-352.

[33] H. Zhang, Q. Y. Xu, Multi-scale simulation of directional dendrites growth in superalloys, J. Mater. Process. Technol. 238 (2016) 132-141.

[34] R. Chen, Q. Y. Xu, B. C. Liu, Cellular automaton simulation of three-dimensional dendrite growth in Al-7Si-Mg ternary aluminum alloys, Comput. Mater. Sci. 105 (2015) 90-100.

[35] H. X. Li, T. K. Chaki, Incipient melting of grain boundaries in Ni_3Al alloys containing zirconium, Mater. Sci. Eng. A 192 (193) (1995) 570-576.

[36] D. Walton, B. Chalmers, The origin of the preferred orientation in the columnar zone of ingots, Trans. Metall. Soc. AIME 215 (1959) 447-457.

[37] M. Rappaz, Modelling of microstructure formation in solidification processes, Int. Mater. Rev. 34 (1989) 93-123.

[38] J. S. Langer, H. Müller-Krumbhaar, Theory of dendritic growth-I. Elements of a stability analysis, Acta Metall. 26 (1978) 1681-1687.

15. A model for simulation of recrystallization microstructure in single-crystal superalloy

Run-Nan Wang, Qing-Yan Xu, Bai-Cheng Liu

Abstract: In the present investigation, a coupled crystal plasticity finite-element (CPFE) and cellular automaton (CA) model was developed to predict the microstructure of recrystallization in single-crystal (SX) Ni-based superalloy. The quasi-static compressive tests of [001] orientated SX DD6 superalloy were conducted on Gleeble3500 tester to calibrate the CPFE model based on crystal slip kinematics. The simulated stress-strain curve agrees well with the experimental results. Quantitative deformation amount was introduced in the deformed samples of simulation and experiment, and these samples were subsequently subjected to the standard solution heat treatment (SSHT). Results of CA simulation show that the recrystallization (RX) nucleation tends to occur at the third stage of SSHT process due to the high critical temperature of RX nucleation for the samples deformed at room temperature. The inhomogeneous RX grains gradually coarsen and compete to reach more stable status by reducing the system energy. Simulated RX grain density decreases from 7.500 to 1.875 mm^{-1}, agreeing well with the value of 1.920 mm^{-1} from electron backscattered diffraction (EBSD) detection of the experimental sample.

Key words: Recrystallization; Single crystal; Crystal plasticity; Cellular automaton; Microstructure

1 Introduction

Single-crystal (SX) Ni-based superalloy has been widely used in the extreme conditions due to its superior mechanical properties and resistance to corrosion[1,2]. However, the defects induced during directional solidification (DS) and heat treatment process, for example, the stray grains[3,4], sliver[5] and recrystallization (RX)[6], seriously restrict the cost and application of SX castings. The high-angle boundaries induced by RX defects can degrade the creep and fatigue properties significantly.

In the past decades, the investigations of RX in SX superalloy mainly focused on the mechanical properties[6-10], microstructure[11-14], annealing conditions[15] and RX nucleation[16,17]. Mathur et al.[16] found that the formation of RX in SX superalloy was induced by the dislocations and micro γ′ in the surface eutectic particles formed during the DS process. The evolution of temperature field and the microstructure of castings during DS process have been studied by experiments and simulations, and corresponding works were reported in Refs.[18-22]. Lots of researches have been performed to simulate the recrystallization behavior for enhancing the material properties such as in steel and nonferrous alloy[23-25], while the microstructure simulation of RX defect in SX Nibased superalloy has rarely been reported. Li et al.[26] and Zambaldi et al.[27] have done the related work, but neither phenomenon-based model nor indentation test can give the accurately quantitative deformation amount in experiment and simulation at the same time.

In this study, the quasi-static compressive tests were conducted for SX DD6 superalloy by experiment and simulation based on crystal plasticity finite-element method (CPFEM). A cellular automaton (CA) model for microstructure simulation of RX was developed based on the calculated deformation. The samples deformed to 5% plasticity were subjected to the standard solution heat treatment. The evolution of RX microstructure was simulated to make comparison with the final grain morphology and density from electron backscattered diffraction (EBSD) detection.

2 Coupled CPFEM and CA model

The crystal plasticity theory developed by Taylor[28], Hill[29] and Hill and Rice[30] has gained a lot of popularity in describing the flow behavior of metals for a long time. It was coupled with finite-element method (FEM) to analyze the single-crystal deformation[31-33]. The driving force for RX nucleation and growth is the plastic deformation induced prior to the heat treatment, so an accurate calculation of plastic strain field during deformation is of crucial importance to the simulation of RX microstructure. In this study, the crystal plasticity theory was coded into a UMAT file (user-defined material), which acts as an interface between user and ABAQUS to be called during simulation. Simulated accumulated slip was imported to the CA model as the driving force for RX.

2.1 Crystal plasticity model

2.1.1 Kinematics and constitutive laws

The plastic deformation is assumed to arise from the crystallographic dislocation slip. The Schmid stress, or resolved shear stress on a slip system, is assumed here to be the driving force for slip. The total deformation gradient ($\mathbf{F}$) can be expressed as:

$$\mathbf{F} = \mathbf{F}^e \mathbf{F}^p, \quad (1)$$

where $\mathbf{F}^p$ and $\mathbf{F}^e$ represent the plastic shear and stretching and rotation of the lattice, respectively. The rate of change of $\mathbf{F}^p$ is related to the slipping rate ($\dot{\gamma}^\alpha$) of the α slip system by:

$$\dot{\mathbf{F}}^p (\mathbf{F}^p)^{-1} = \sum_\alpha \dot{\gamma}^\alpha \mathbf{s}^\alpha \otimes \mathbf{m}^\alpha, \quad (2)$$

where the sum ranges over all activated slip systems, unit vectors $\mathbf{s}^\alpha$ and $\mathbf{m}^\alpha$ are the slip direction and normal to slip plane in the reference configuration, respectively. $\mathbf{s}^{e(\alpha)} = \mathbf{F}^e \mathbf{s}^\alpha$ is the vector lying along the slip direction of system α in the deformed configuration. A normal to the slip plane which is the reciprocal base vector to all such vectors in the slip plane follows:

$$\mathbf{m}^{e(\alpha)} = \mathbf{m}^\alpha (\mathbf{F}^e)^{-1} \quad (3)$$

The velocity gradient ($\mathbf{L}$) in the current state is:

$$\mathbf{L} = \dot{\mathbf{F}} \mathbf{F}^{-1} = \mathbf{D} + \mathbf{\Omega}, \quad (4)$$

where $\dot{\mathbf{F}}$ is the time derivative of $\mathbf{F}$, and the symmetric rate of stretching ($\mathbf{D}$) and the antisymmetric spin tensor ($\mathbf{\Omega}$) can be decomposed into lattice parts ($\mathbf{D}^e$ and $\mathbf{\Omega}^e$) and plastic parts ($\mathbf{D}^p$ and $\mathbf{\Omega}^p$) as: $\mathbf{D} = \mathbf{D}^e + \mathbf{D}^p$, $\mathbf{\Omega} = \mathbf{\Omega}^e + \mathbf{\Omega}^p$, $\mathbf{D}^e + \mathbf{\Omega}^e = \dot{\mathbf{F}}^e (\mathbf{F}^e)^{-1}$ and $\mathbf{D}^p + \mathbf{\Omega}^p = \sum_\alpha \dot{\gamma}^\alpha \mathbf{s}^{e(\alpha)} \mathbf{m}^{e(\alpha)}$.

The relationship between Jaumann rate ($\overset{\nabla^e}{\boldsymbol{\sigma}}$) and Cauchy stress ($\boldsymbol{\sigma}$) follows:

$$\overset{\nabla^e}{\boldsymbol{\sigma}} + \boldsymbol{\sigma}(\mathbf{I} : \mathbf{D}) = \mathbf{L} : \mathbf{D}^e, \quad (5)$$

$$\overset{\nabla^e}{\boldsymbol{\sigma}} = \overset{\nabla}{\boldsymbol{\sigma}} + (\mathbf{\Omega} - \mathbf{\Omega}^e) \cdot \boldsymbol{\sigma} - \boldsymbol{\sigma} \cdot (\mathbf{\Omega} - \mathbf{\Omega}^e), \quad (6)$$

$$\overset{\nabla}{\boldsymbol{\sigma}} = \dot{\boldsymbol{\sigma}} - \mathbf{\Omega} \cdot \boldsymbol{\sigma} + \boldsymbol{\sigma} \cdot \mathbf{\Omega}, \quad (7)$$

where $\mathbf{I}$ is the second-order unit tensor, $\dot{\boldsymbol{\sigma}}$ the material derivative of $\boldsymbol{\sigma}$ and $\overset{\nabla}{\boldsymbol{\sigma}}$ is the corotational stress rate on axes spinning with the material. The crystalline slip depends on the current stress ($\boldsymbol{\sigma}$) through the Schmid stress, $\tau^\alpha = \mathbf{m}^{e(\alpha)} \cdot \frac{\rho_0}{\rho} \boldsymbol{\sigma} \cdot \mathbf{s}^{e(\alpha)}$, where ρ_0 and ρ are the reference and current mass density. Rate of change of Schmid stress ($\dot{\tau}^\alpha$) follows:

$$\dot{\tau}^\alpha = \mathbf{m}^{e(\alpha)} \cdot [\overset{\nabla}{\boldsymbol{\sigma}} + \boldsymbol{\sigma}(\mathbf{I} : \mathbf{D}^e) - \mathbf{D}^e \cdot \boldsymbol{\sigma} + \boldsymbol{\sigma} \cdot \mathbf{D}^e] \cdot \mathbf{s}^{e(\alpha)} \quad (8)$$

2.1.2 Hardening of rate-dependent crystalline materials

According to the rate-dependent model, the shearing rate follows: $\dot{\gamma}^\alpha = \dot{\gamma}_0 \mathrm{sgn}(\tau^\alpha) \left| \frac{\tau^\alpha}{g^\alpha} \right|^m$, $\dot{g}^\alpha = \sum_\beta h_{\alpha\beta} \dot{\gamma}^\beta$, where $\dot{\gamma}_0$, τ^α and g^α are reference shearing rate, resolved shear stress and slip resistance of the α slip system. $\dot{\gamma}^\beta$ is the shearing rate of the β slip system. $h_{\alpha\beta}$ is the matrix of hardening modulus.

Self-hardening:

$$h_{\alpha\beta} = h(\gamma) = h_0 \mathrm{sech}^2 \left| \frac{h_0 \gamma}{\tau_s - \tau_0} \right|, \quad \gamma = \sum_\alpha \int_0^t |\dot{\gamma}^\alpha| \mathrm{d}t \quad (9)$$

Latent hardening:

$$h_{\alpha\beta} = q h(\gamma), \quad (10)$$

where h_0 is the initial hardening modulus, τ_0 is the yield stress, and τ_s is the saturated stress and q the constant. Verification of model was performed by the uniaxial compression of [001] oriented SX CMSX-4 superalloy. The parameters used in the CPFEM simulation are presented in Table 1, where RT, AHT and AC are short for room temperature, as-heat treated and as-cast conditions, respectively. Figure 1 shows stress-strain curve for the quasi-static compressive test of [001] oriented SX CMSX-4 superalloy. The experimental data are from Ref.[27].

Table 1 Parameters used in CPFEM simulations (RT)

Parameters	Symbol	CMSX-4 (AHT)	DD6 (AC)
Elastic moduli/GPa	C_{11}	252	25.6
	C_{12}	161	12.1
	C_{44}	131	14.9
Reference strain rate/s^{-1}	$\dot{\gamma}_0$	0.001	0.001
Initial slip resistance/MPa	τ_0	245	145
Saturation slip resistance/MPa	τ_s	775	580
Power law exponent	m	20	20
Initial hardening modulus/MPa	h_0	350	320
Hardening ratio	q	1	1

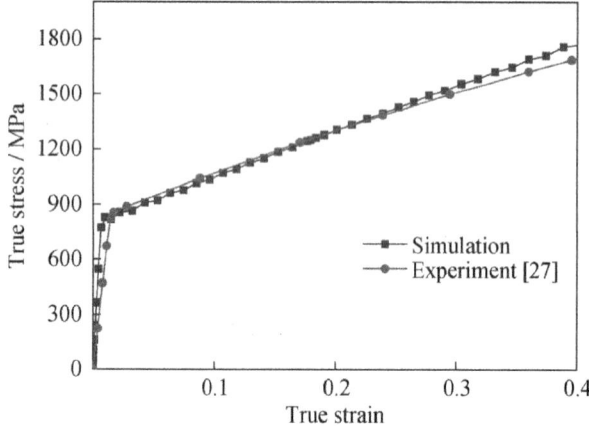

Fig. 1 Stress-strain curve for quasi-static compressive test of [001] oriented SX CMSX-4 superalloy

2.2 CA model for recrystallization simulation

The driving force of RX is plastic deformation which is essentially the dislocation slip produced prior to heat treatment. The stored deformation energy for CA modeling is expressed in terms of a reference dislocation density, which is related to the amount of accumulated shear. The effect of as-cast dendritic morphology on RX behavior was taken into consideration through different activation energy in dendritic arms (DAs) and interdendritic regions (IDRs).

2.2.1 Model of RX nucleation

The RX nucleus usually occurred in the region with large deformation, so the continuous nucleation model is suitable for describing this process. Considering the temperature of heat treatment and the heterogeneity of as-cast sample, the nucleation rate (N) follows:

$$N = C_0(P - P^c)\exp\left(-\frac{Q_a}{RT}\right), \quad (11)$$

where C_0 is constant coefficient ($1.0 \times 10^9 \text{s}^{-1} \cdot \text{J}^{-1}$); R, T and P denote universal gas constant, degree kelvin and driving force for RX, respectively; P is related to the reference dislocation density of $2 \times 10^5 \text{J} \cdot \text{m}^{-2}$, which was multiplied by the local amount of accumulated shear (γ); and Q_a and P^c are activation energy and critical stored energy of RX nucleation, respectively.

$$P^c = \frac{10^7 \gamma_c}{2.2\gamma_c + 1.1} E_{\text{lagb}} \quad (12)$$

where γ_c is critical shear set 2% in this study, and E_{lagb} is the low-angle grain boundary energy set $0.6 \text{J} \cdot \text{m}^{-2}$. According to our previous research, the onset temperature of RX formation varies with temperature at which the samples are deformed[34]. For the samples with 5% plastic strain deformed at RT, RX grains only form at the annealing temperature above 1310℃. Hence, the critical temperature of RX nucleation is set 1311℃.

2.2.2 Model of RX coarsening and growing

The velocity of interface migration (v) depends on the grain boundary mobility for the static recrystallization (M) and driving pressure for the grain boundary movement (P), as shown in Eq. (13). M can be described by the Arrhenius formula:

$$V = MP \quad (13)$$

$$M = M_0 \exp\left(-\frac{Q_b}{RT}\right) = \frac{D_0 b^2}{kT}\exp\left(-\frac{Q_b}{RT}\right) \quad (14)$$

where M_0 is grain boundary mobility, Q_b is the activation energy for grain boundary motion, D_0 is the diffusion constant, k is the Boltzmann constant and b is the Burger's vector.

When RX process is completed, the grains will still coarsen under the control of grain boundary energy (E) in Eq. (15) and curvature (k) in Eq. (16). The misorientation angle (θ) is calculated from Euler angle (ϕ_1, Φ, ϕ_2) of adjacent grains, and the corresponding algorithm can be found from Ref. [26].

$$P = E\kappa \quad (15)$$

$$E = E_m \left(\frac{\theta}{\theta_m}\right)\left(1 - \ln\left(\frac{\theta}{\theta_m}\right)\right) \quad (16)$$

$$\kappa = \frac{\alpha}{c_s} \frac{\text{Kink} - c_i}{N'} \quad (17)$$

where E_m is the large grain boundary energy, θ_m is the critical misorientation of large grain boundary, α is the constant, c_s is the CA element size, c_i is the number of elements which have the same state of central element, $N' = 25$ and Kink = 15 for 2D simulation. In view of the inconformity of meshes used in CA and FEM, the simulated results of FEM calculation (M_n^{FEM}) must be mapped to CA meshes by a conversion algorithm, and the mapped result in CA cell (f_{CA}) follows:

$$f_{\text{CA}}(i,j,k) = \sum_{n=0}^{l} d_n^{-1} \cdot M_n^{\text{FEM}} (d_n < R) \quad (18)$$

where l is the number of FEM nodes within R distance from the CA cell (i,j,k), and d_n is the real distance between the CA cell and FEM node. The key parameters used in the simulation are listed in Table 2. Different symbol values were used to distinguish the cells of DAs and IDRs in the computational domain.

Table 2 Key parameters used in CA simulation

Parameters	Value
Activation energy for nucleation in DAs, $Q_{a1}/(\text{kJ} \cdot \text{mol}^{-1})$	280~290
Activation energy for nucleation in IDRs, $Q_{a2}/(\text{kJ} \cdot \text{mol}^{-1})$	260~270
Activation energy for recrystallization in DAs, $Q_{m1}/(\text{kJ} \cdot \text{mol}^{-1})$	250~265
Activation energy for recrystallization in IDRs, $Q_{m2}/(\text{kJ} \cdot \text{mol}^{-1})$	330~340
Time step/s	0.01
Burgers vector, b/nm	0.36
Cell size/mm	0.005

3 Experimental

The second-generation SX superalloy DD6, whose nominal chemical composition is presented in Table 3[35], was used in this study. DD6 superalloy ingot was melted, and directional solidification (DS) was performed in an industrial vacuum Bridgman furnace to obtain the SX cylinder bars which are 180mm in length and 15mm in diameter. The small cylinder specimens, whose diameter is 6mm and the length is 10mm, were cut from as-cast cylinder bars using electrical discharge machining. Only the samples within 10° misorientation angle from [001] direction were employed. The compression flow curves were used to calibrate the crystal plasticity model. Compressive test was performed on Gleeble3500 tester at room temperature at a low strain rate of $1 \times 10^{-3} \text{s}^{-1}$ to simulate the quasi-static compressive process. For the samples of quasi-static compressive test, the relationship between true and engineering strain (ε_t, ε_e)/stress (σ_t, σ_e) follows: $\varepsilon_t = -\ln(1 - \varepsilon_e)$ and $\sigma_t = \sigma_e \cdot (1 - \varepsilon_e)$, respectively.

Table 3 Nominal chemical composition of DD6 superalloy (wt%)

Cr	Co	Mo	W	Ta	Re	Nb	Al	Hf	Ni
4.3	9.0	2.0	8.0	7.5	2.0	0.5	5.6	0.1	Bal.

The as-cast samples with a quantitative deformation of 5% were chosen to undergo the standard solution heat treatment (SSHT 1290℃, 1h + 1300℃, 2h + 1315℃, 4h, air cooling). The annealed sample was cut from the middle cross section of cylinder to perform polishing. The as-polished samples were etched using the Marble's reagent and then observed by optical microscope (OM, Zeiss AM10 OM). The samples for electron backscattered diffraction (EBSD) detection were electrochemical polished using $HClO_4$ (10%) and C_2H_5OH (90%). The data were collected from a MIRA3 LMH FSEM equipped with an Oxford EBSD detector at an accelerating voltage of 20kV and step size of 2-10μm range. High-angle grain boundaries (>15°) were shown by black lines in inverse pole figure (IPF). The critical value of area to define a true grain was set to be 20μm² because of the existence of EBSD calibration error. The density of RX grains in the viewing zone can be calculated by: N/A, where N and A are the number of RX grains and the area of viewing zone, respectively. For the RX grains located at the side and corner of the viewing zone, the number should be multiplied by 1/2 and 1/4, respectively.

4 Results and discussion

4.1 Simulated and experimental quasi-static compression

The compression flow curves were used to calibrate the crystal plasticity model. Two cylinder samples were compressed, and the true stress-strain curves for quasi-static compressive test of [001] oriented as-cast DD6 superalloy are shown in Fig. 2. The material parameters for CPFEM simulation are demonstrated in Table 1. The simulated curve of the same process is shown as the red line in Fig. 2. It conforms well to the experimental results, revealing that the simulation results based on crystal plasticity can accurately describe the deformation scale and status in SX samples. By employing the deformation of 5% plasticity, the total cumulative shear strain γ on the middle section of sample is shown in Fig. 3. Accumulated shear strain gradually decreases from the center of the circle to the periphery.

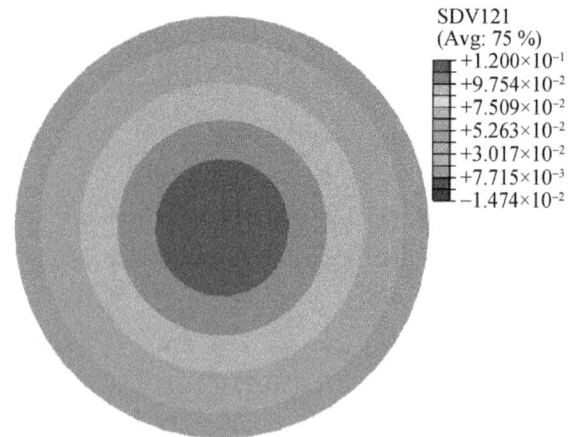

Fig. 3 Total cumulative shear strain γ on middle section of sample with 5% plastic strain

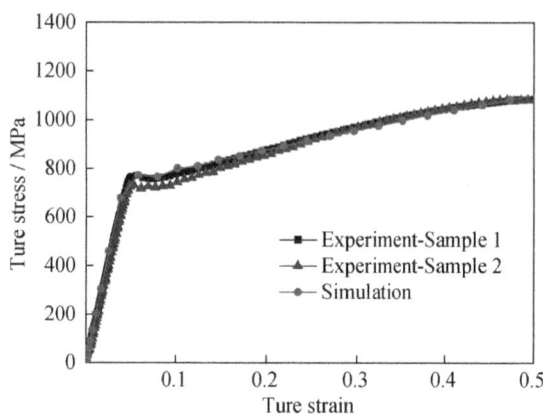

Fig. 2 Stress-strain curves for quasi-static compressive test of [001] oriented as-cast DD6 superalloy

In addition, during compression process, the inhomogeneous strain distribution can be induced by the anisotropy of SX material with fcc structure as well as the friction between the head face of sample and the pressure head of Gleeble tester. For the Ni-based superalloy deformed at RT, the slip face and direction are {111} and <110>, respectively. Three end-fixed samples, whose axial direction is along [001], [110] and [111], were simulated to test the anisotropy. The black dashed lines in Fig. 4a, c, e represent that the axial directions of the cylinder samples coincide with [001], [110] and [111] orientation of fcc lattice, respectively. The shear strain on the head faces of deformed samples expresses fourfold, threefold and double symmetric distributions (Fig. 4b, d, f), which conform to the periodicity and symmetry of {111} <110> slip system for fcc structure. Owing to the long distance between the head face and the middle cross section, the anisotropy does not influence the distribution of shear strain on the middle cross section (Fig. 3).

4.2 Evolution of RX microstructure during heat treatment

The evolution of the optical metallographic microstructure during SSHT process is shown in Fig. 5. For the samples in as-cast deformed condition (Fig. 5a) and first stage of SSHT (1290℃, 0.5h Fig. 5b), the DA and IDRs can be clearly distinguished. RX grain has not nucleated at this stage. The degree of element segregation gradually decreases with the SSHT proceeding. Consequently, the DA and IDRs become almost uniform at the max SSHT temperature (1315℃), but slight IDRs and eutectic particles can still be identified in Fig. 5c (1290℃, 1h + 1300℃, 2h + 1315℃, 0.5h). Figure 5d shows the final microstructure of samples subjected to complete SSHT process. As shown in Fig. 5c, d, RX grains can be clearly observed when the annealing temperature reaches 1315℃. The morphologies of RX grains in Fig. 5d are more homogeneous than those in Fig. 5c, and the sizes of grains are bigger.

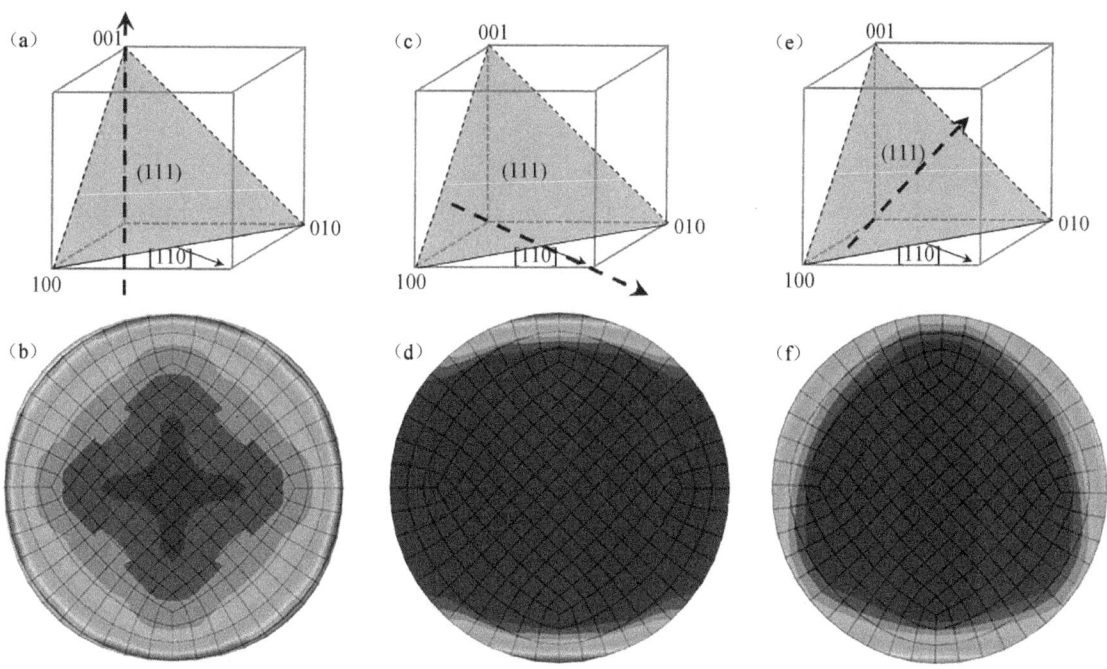

Fig. 4 Anisotropy of shear strain distribution on head face of deformed samples with axial directions of samples lying along different orientations of fcc lattice: (a) (b) [001], (c) (d) [110] and (e) (f) [111]

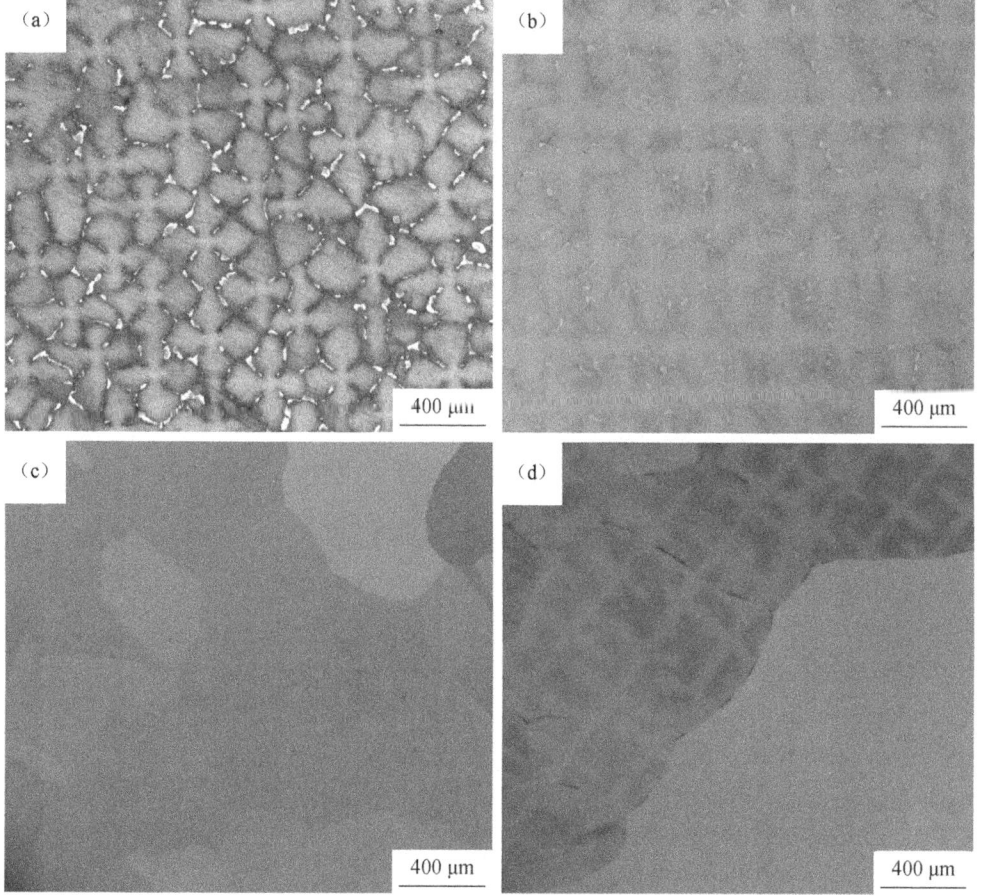

Fig. 5 OM images for microstructural evolution of deformed samples during SSHT: (a) as-cast deformed; (b) 1290℃, 0.5h; (c) 1290℃, 1h+1300℃, 2h+1315℃, 0.5h; (d) 1290℃, 1h+1300℃, 2h+1315℃, 4h

The simulated evolution of RX microstructure during SSHT is shown in Fig. 6a-d, as well as the experimental results of EBSD measurement (Fig. 6e, f). Before heat treatment of 1315℃, no RX grain appears in the deformed region. At the beginning of solvus heat treatment (3.05h), many misoriented RX grains begin to nucleate, and RX grains of different sizes inhomogeneously coexist in the simulated area. Subsequently, these grains gradually coarsen and compete to reach more stable status by reducing the system energy. Finally, the number of RX grains becomes less and less, and the large grains get the dominant position, as shown in the simulated (Fig. 6d) and experimental (Fig. 6f) results.

Fig. 6 Simulated (a-d) and EBSD detected (e, f) RX microstructures of samples subjected to SSHT: (a) 0h (inset showing dendritic morphology of as-cast sample for simulation), (b) 3.05h, (c) 4.00h, (d) 7.00h, (e) 3.50h and (f) 7.00h (misoriented grains with different Euler angles marked by different colors)

The variation of simulated and experimentally measured grain density during the SSHT process is presented in Fig. 7. RX grains begin to nucleate at the third stage of SSHT, and the density of RX grains rapidly increases to 7.500mm^{-1}. With the increase of annealing time, the value gradually decreases. The simulated grain density decreases to 5.5mm^{-1} at 3.50h and finally to 1.875mm^{-1}. From the EBSD observation, the grain densities on the middle sections of samples at 3.50 and 7.00h are 4.950 and 1.920mm^{-1}, respectively. The grain size and density usually depend on the activation energy for boundary migration. The velocity of interface migration under the solvus condition is faster than that under subsolvus condition. Hence, this leads to big grain size and small density.

It is well known that many small RX nuclei tend to

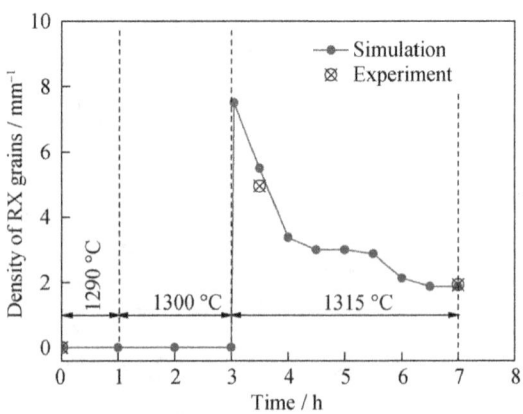

Fig. 7 Density of RX grains varying with annealing time and solution temperature

appear in the dendritic arms from the onset of heat treatment[26,36]. Subsequently, by undergoing long-time SSHT at high temperature (solvus and sub-solvus), the small grains will overgrow the dendritic arms and enter the interdendritic regions. RX behavior of deformed matrix at this stage is caused by the release of deformation stored energy. However, the behavior of RX nucleation strongly depends on the deformation temperature of samples. According to previous researches[34,37], critical temperature of RX nucleation reaches as high as 1310℃ for the samples with 5% plastic strain induced at room temperature. Hence, there is no RX nucleation until the solution temperature comes to the solvus 1315℃. At this time, the interdendritic regions and dendritic arms have become homogenized, and then the RX nucleation can rapidly grow and coarsen to decrease the interfacial energy (IFE). The process of RX grains growing and coarsening is controlled by the difference of IFE between small and large RX grains. The amount of grain boundaries and the scale of IFE can be reduced during this process spontaneously. Thus, large RX grains get the dominant position instead of fine grains after SSHT process.

5 Conclusion

A coupled CPFEM and CA model was developed to simulate the RX microstructure of SX Ni-based superalloy. Quasi-static compressive tests were conducted to calibrate the CPFEM model. The simulated stress-strain curves for as-heat-treated CMSX-4 and as-cast DD6 SX superalloy agree well with the experimental results. As the driving force for RX, the plasticity which is represented by local dislocation density was quantitatively introduced in simulation and experiment. Then, the samples with 5% plastic strain were subjected to SSHT process. Simulated results show that high critical temperature of RX nucleation for the samples deformed at room temperature results in different RX behaviors in three stages of SSHT. RX nucleation tends to occur at the third stage (solvus) of SSHT process, and the inhomogeneous RX grains gradually coarsen and compete to reach stabilization by reducing the system energy. Finally, the large grains get the dominant position. Simulated RX grain density decreases from 7.500 to 1.875mm^{-1}, which agrees well with the value of 1.920mm^{-1} from experimental sample by EBSD detection.

Acknowledgements This study was financially supported by the National Key R&D Program of China (No. 2017YFB0701503) and the National Basic Research Program of China (No. 2011CB706801).

References

[1] Reed RC. The superalloys fundamentals and applications. New York: Cambridge University Press; 2006.1.

[2] Perepezko JH. The hotter the engine, the better. Science. 2009; 326 (5956): 1068.

[3] Meng XB, Li JG, Chen ZQ, Wang YH, Zhu SZ, Bai XF, Wang F, Zhang J, Jin T, Sun XF, Hu ZQ. Effect of platform dimension on the dendrite growth and stray grain formation in a Ni-base single-crystal superalloy. Metall Mater Trans A. 2012; 44 (4): 1955.

[4] Meng XB, Li JG, Zhu SZ, Du HQ, Yuan ZH, Wang J, Jin T, Sun XF, Hu ZQ. Method of stray grain inhibition in the platforms with different dimensions during directional solidification of a Ni-base superalloy. Metall Mater Trans A. 2013; 45 (3): 1230.

[5] Aveson JW, Tennant PA, Foss BJ, Shollock BA, Stone HJ, Souza ND. On the origin of sliver defects in single crystal investment castings. Acta Mater. 2013; 61 (14): 5162.

[6] Meng J, Jin T, Sun X, Hu Z. Effect of surface recrystallization on the creep rupture properties of a nickel-base single crystal superalloy. Mater Sci Eng A. 2010; 527 (23): 6119.

[7] Zhang B, Lu X, Liu D, Tao C. Influence of recrystallization on high-temperature stress rupture property and fracture behavior of single crystal superalloy. Mater Sci Eng A. 2012; 551: 149.

[8] He YH, Hou XQ, Tao CH, Han FK. Recrystallization and fatigue fracture of single crystal turbine blades. Eng Fail Anal. 2011; 18 (3): 944.

[9] Wang DL, Jin T, Yang SQ, Wei Z, Li JB, Hu ZQ. Surface recrystallization and its effect on rupture life of SRR99 single crystal superalloy. Mater Sci Forum. 2007; 546-549: 1229.

[10] Zhang B, Liu C, Lu X, Tao C, Jiang T. Effect of surface recrystallization on the creep rupture property of a single-crystal superalloy. Rare Met. 2010; 29 (4): 413.

[11] Zhuo L, Liang S, Wang F, Xu T, Wang Y, Yuan Z, Xiong J, Li J, Zhu J. Kinetics and microstructural evolution during recrystallization of a single crystal superalloy. Mater Charact. 2015; 108: 16.

[12] Wang L, Xie G, Zhang J, Lou LH. On the role of carbides during the recrystallization of a directionally solidified nickel-base superalloy. Scr Mater. 2006; 55 (5): 457.

[13] Wang L, Pyczak F, Zhang J, Lou LH, Singer RF. Effect of eutectics on plastic deformation and subsequent recrystallization in the single crystal nickel base superalloy CMSX-4. Mater Sci Eng A. 2012; 532: 487.

[14] Wu Y, Yang R, Li S, Ma Y, Gong S, Han Y. Surface recrystallization of a Ni_3Al based single crystal superalloy at different annealing temperature and blasting pressure. Rare Met. 2012; 31 (3): 209.

[15] Cox DC, Roebuck B, Rae C, Reed RC. Recrystallisation of single crystal superalloy CMSX-4. Mater Sci Technol. 2003; 19 (4): 440.

[16] Mathur HN, Panwisawas C, Jones CN, Reed RC, Rae CMF. Nucleation of recrystallisation in castings of single crystal Ni-based superalloys. Acta Mater. 2017; 129: 112.

[17] Zhuo L, Xu T, Wang F, Xiong J, Zhu J. Microstructural evolution on the initiation of sub-solvus recrystallization of a grit-blasted single-crystal superalloy. Mater Lett. 2015; 148: 159.

[18] Zhang H, Xu Q. Multi-scale simulation of directional dendrites growth in superalloys. J Mater Process Technol. 2016; 238: 132.

[19] Tang N, Wang YL, Xu QY, Zhao XH, Liu BC. Numerical simulation of directional solidified microstructure of wide-chord aero blade by Bridgeman process. Acta Metal Sin. 2015; 51 (4): 499.

[20] Wang R, Yan X, Li Z, Xu Q, Liu B. Effect of construction manner of mould cluster on stray grain formation in dummy blade of DD6 superalloy. High Temp Mater Process. 2017; 36 (4): 399.

[21] Zhang W, Liu L. Solidification microstructure of directionally solidified superalloy under high temperature gradient. Rare Met. 2012; 31 (6): 541.

[22] Liu G, Liu L, Han Z, Zhang G, Zhang J. Solidification behavior of Re-and Ru-containing Ni-based single-crystal superalloys with thermal and metallographic analysis. Rare Met. 2017; 36 (10): 792.

[23] Chun YB, Hwang SK. Monte carlo modeling of microstructure evolution during the static recrystallization of cold-rolled, commercial-purity titanium. Acta Mater. 2006; 54 (14): 3673.

[24] Crumbach M, Gottstein G. Modelling of recrystallisation textures in aluminium alloys: i. Model set-up and integration. Acta Mater. 2006; 54 (12): 3275.

[25] Crumbach M, Gottstein G. Modelling of recrystallisation textures in aluminium alloys: ii. Model performance and experimental validation. Acta Mater. 2006; 54 (12): 3291.

[26] Li Z, Xu Q, Liu B. Microstructure simulation on recrystallization of an as-cast nickel based single crystal superalloy. Comput Mater Sci. 2015; 107: 122.

[27] Zambaldi C, Roters F, Raabe D, Glatzel U. Modeling and experiments on the indentation deformation and recrystallization of a single-crystal nickel-base superalloy. Mater Sci Eng A. 2007; 454: 433.

[28] Taylor GI. Plastic strain in metals. J Inst Met. 1938; 62: 307.

[29] Hill R. A self-consistent mechanics of composite materials. J Mech Phys Solids. 1965; 13: 213.

[30] Hill R, Rice JR. Constitutive analysis of elastic-plastic crystals at arbitrary strain. J Mech Phys Solids. 1972; 20: 401.

[31] Peirce D, Asaro RJ, Needleman A. Material rate dependence and localized deformation in crystalline solids. Acta Metall. 1983; 31: 1951.

[32] Zambaldi C, Zehnder C, Raabe D. Orientation dependent deformation by slip and twinning in magnesium during single crystal indentation. Acta Metall. 2015; 91: 267.

[33] Eidel B. Crystal plasticity finite-element analysis versus experimental results of pyramidal indentation into (001) fcc single crystal. Acta Metall. 2011; 59 (4): 1761.

[34] Li Z, Xu Q, Liu B. Experimental investigation on recrystallization mechanism of a Ni-base single crystal superalloy. J Alloys Compd. 2016; 672: 457.

[35] Editorial committee. Engineering Materials Handbook. Beijing: Standards Press of China; 2001. 812.

[36] Porter AJ, Ralph B. Ralph, Recrystallization of a nickel-base superalloy: kinetics and microstructural development. Mater Sci Eng. 1983; 59 (1): 69.

[37] Li Z, Fan X, Xu Q, Liu B. Influence of deformation temperature on recrystallization in a Ni-based single crystal superalloy. Mater Lett. 2015; 160: 318.

轻量化材料工艺建模与仿真

16. Preliminary Study on Simulation of Microporosity Evolution and Fatigue Life of Aluminum Alloy Casting

S. Y. Dong[1], Z. Zhuang[2], Q. Y. Xu[1], S. M. Xiong[1], B. C. Liu[1]

[1] Department of Mechanical Engineering, Tsinghua University, Beijing 100084, China
[2] Department of Engineering Mechanics, Tsinghua University, Beijing 100084, China

A mathematical model to simulate the microporosity evolution and to predict the fatigue life of aluminum alloy casting was presented. The failure probability caused by the microporosity was determined by fatigue life analysis. Firstly, a two dimensional mathematical model to calculate the size and distribution of the microporosity was studied and coupled with a probabilistic microstructure evolution model. The nucleation and growth of grains were modeled with a probabilistic method that uses the results from a macro scale heat transfer model to determine the rules of transition for grain evolution. By using the calculated size and distribution of porosity, the fatigue life of the casting was then predicted by using ABAQUS software. Finally, preliminary experiments were made to validate the proposed model and the calculated results for the aluminum alloy castings matched the experimental results.

Key words: casting, numerical simulation, microporosity prediction, fatigue life

Introduction

The application of aluminum alloys in the automotive and aerospace industries has increased dramatically in recent years because of their favorable performance and manufacturability. However, in many applications, defects in the cast microstructure undermine the performance characteristics of the components. One of the most serious defects is microporosity, which decreases the tensile strength, the elongation and the fatigue properties as well. Porosity in castings has been classified into macroporosity and microporosity according to the size of the pores. Macroporosity can be predicted accurately using existing continuum heat transfer models.[1] Therefore, many studies now focus on the simulation of the microporosity evolution. Both shrinkage and gas driving forces contribute to this porosity and hence the resultant pore structure is simply termed microporosity. Quantitative information on the development of microporosity as a function of alloy variables and casting process conditions is particularly important for designers of safety critical components.

In this paper, a two dimensional mathematical model to predict the size and distribution of microporosity coupled with a probabilistic microstructure evolution model was studied. Combined with the calculated distribution of the porosity, the fatigue life of the subject castings was then predicted with the porous elastic model.

Computational Model

Grain Structure Evolution Modeling

The probabilistic model to simulate the dendrite structure evolution was based on a two-dimensional CA (cellular automata) method. In this study, a continuous nucleation model with Gaussian distributions was used to describe the heterogeneous nucleation.[2] The expression of Gaussian function is as follows:

$$\frac{dn}{d(\Delta T)} = \frac{n_{max}}{\sqrt{2\pi}\Delta T_\sigma} \exp\left[-\frac{1}{2}\left(\frac{\Delta T - \Delta T_N}{\Delta T_\sigma}\right)^2\right] \quad (1)$$

Where ΔT_N, ΔT_σ and n_{max} are the mean undercooling, the standard deviation and the maximum density of grains respectively. Therefore, the total density of grains is given by the integral of this distribution.

According to the KGT (Kurz-Giovanola-Trivedi) model,[3] the relationship between the growth velocity of the dendrite tip, $v(\Delta T)$, and local undercooling, ΔT, can be simplified as:

$$v(\Delta T) = a\Delta T^2 + b\Delta T^3 \qquad (2)$$

Where a and b are the coefficients and based on experiments.

Pore Evolution Modeling

The governing equations of microporosity evolution include the motion equation and the continuity equation of metals and the hydrogen mass balance equation.[4,5]

From a mass balance for a volume element, the continuity equation of metals is shown in equation (3) as follows:

$$\frac{\partial \rho}{\partial t} + \nabla \cdot (\rho \bar{u}) = 0 \qquad (3)$$

Where ρ is the density, t is the time and $\bar{u}$ is the interdendritic flow velocity vector.

The motion equation describing the interdendritic flow follows the Darcy's law as follows:

$$\bar{u} = -\frac{K}{\mu f_l}(\nabla P_s + \rho_l g) \qquad (4)$$

Where K is the permeability of the medium, μ is kinetic viscosity, f_l is the volume fraction of the liquid metal, P_s is the shrinkage pressure, ρ_l is the density of liquid metal and g is the acceleration due to the gravity.

Hydrogen alone can dissolve in an aluminum alloy. Since the diffusion distance of the hydrogen and the dendrite arm spacing of an aluminum alloy are of the same order, the hydrogen atoms can be assumed to have enough time to diffuse from the solid to the liquid in permanent mold Al alloy castings.[4] Under a complete equilibrium state assumption, the hydrogen mass balance equation can be expressed as:

$$[H_0]\rho_l = [H_s]\rho_s f_s + [H_l]\rho_l(1-f_s-f_g) \qquad (5)$$

Where $[H_0]$ is the initial hydrogen content in the melt, $[H_s]$ and $[H_l]$ are the hydrogen content in the solid and liquid respectively. ρ_s is the density of the solid metal. f_s and f_g are the volume fraction of the solid and the porosity respectively. α is the gas conversion factor, P_g is the gas pressure, and T is the local temperature.

Pore evolution is a complex phenomenon as shown in Fig. 1. The conditions for a gas pore to form and grow in the solidifying melt is that the gas pressure has to be equal or greater than the total local external pressure, $P_{\exp}$:

$$P_g \geqslant P_{\exp} = P_a + P_h + P_s + P_\sigma \qquad (6)$$

Where P_a, P_h and P_σ are the ambient pressure, the metallostatic pressure and the surface tension between the gas and the liquid respectively.

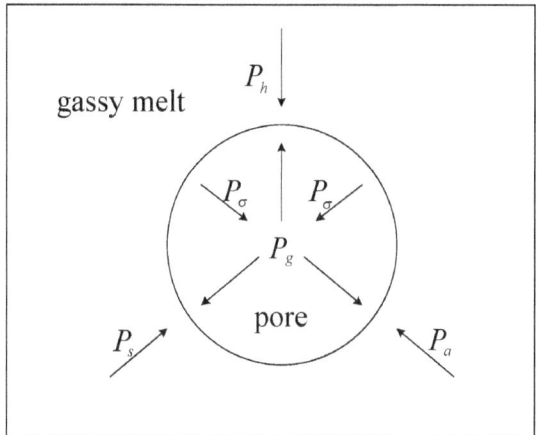

Fig. 1 The scheme of the criteria of pore formation and growth

Fatigue Life Analysis

The aluminum castings with microporosity can be regard as a kind of porous materials. Usually, the elastic part of the volumetric behavior of porous materials is modeled accurately by assuming that the elastic part of the change in volume of the material is proportional to the logarithm of the pressure stress:[6]

$$\frac{\kappa}{1+e_0}\ln\left(\frac{p+p_t^{el}}{p_0+p_t^{el}}\right) = 1 + J^{el} \qquad (7)$$

Where e_0 is the void ratio; p is the equivalent pressure stress; p_0 is the initial value of the equivalent pressure stress; κ is the logarithmic bulk modulus; J^{el} is the elastic part of the volume ratio between the current and reference configurations; and p_t^{el} is the elastic tensile strength of the material. To model metal material with a dilute concentration of voids, the results of this model compare well with those of the effective model considered void fraction.

Calculation Procedure

In order to simulate the microporosity evolution, the micro modeling for the porosity and grain structure evolution needs to couple with the macro modeling of solidification process of castings. Macroscopic heat transfer models are used to simulate the temperature and solid fraction distributions, and local solidification time during solidification process. In the micro model, the microporosity modeling follows the grain structure modeling and predicts the size and distribution of the pores. The computation process is looped until every element solidifies. By using the results of casting process simulation and the porous elastic model, the mechanical behavior and the fatigue life of the aluminum casting were modeled accurately by using ABAQUS. The flow chart for the subject model is shown in Fig. 2.

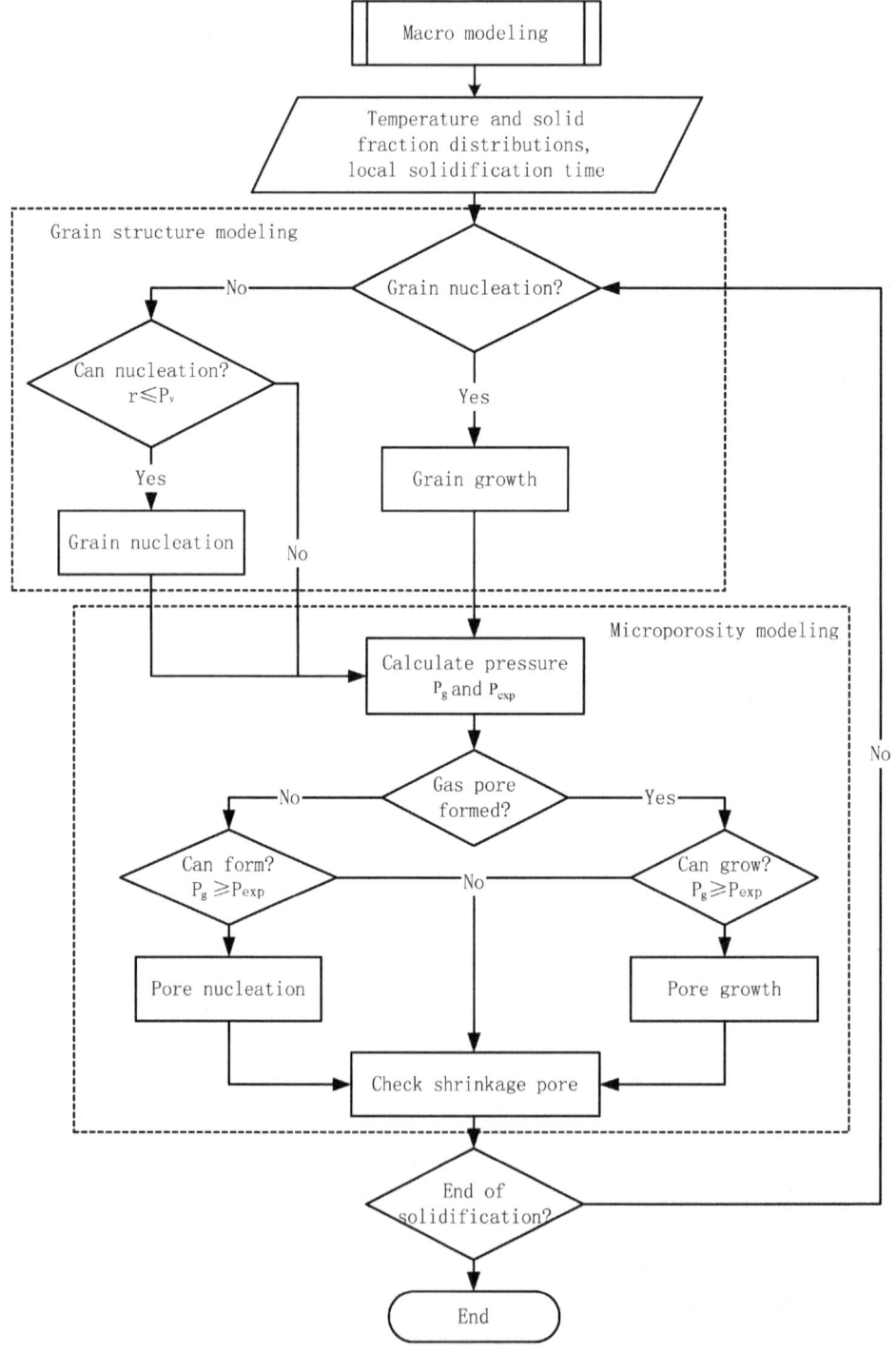

Fig. 2　Flow chart for the subject model

Experimental Procedure

In order to verify the mathematical models described above, two groups of experiments were performed. Several step-shape castings as shown in Fig. 3 were made with permanent metallic mold. The step-shape castings were 50mm in width, 290mm in length and with 10, 20, 30, 40 and 50mm in thickness respectively. The riser was 40mm in diameter and 100mm in height.

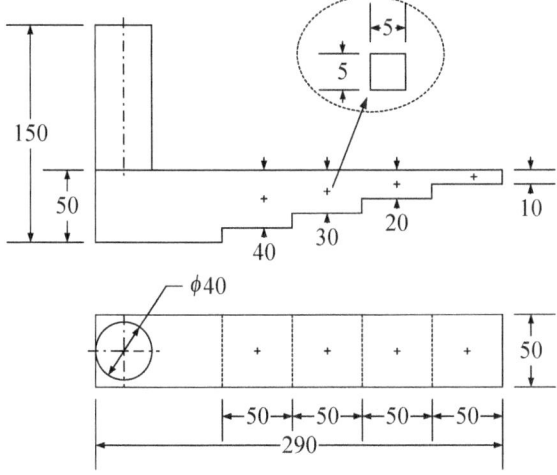

Fig. 3 Geometry of the step-shape sample casting and locations of specimen for optical image analysis. (unit in mm)

The experiments were divided into two groups. For Group I, the melt was not modified or refined, while for Group II, the strontium level in the melt was maintained at 0.022 wt.%, and the titanium level at 0.068 wt.%. The holding furnace was maintained at around 750℃. The initial hydrogen content of the melt was monitored using a commercial HYSCAN II hydrogen analyzer. A small amount of melt was taken for chemical composition analysis. For optical image analysis, specimens were excised from the each step center of the castings. The geometry and location of the specimen were shown in Fig. 3. The microphotographs were scanned and analyzed with an image analysis software to evaluate the pore fraction.

Results And Discussion

The experiment results showed that with the increase of cooling rate in the casting the fraction and the average diameter of pores decreased obviously, while the distribution became more uniform. For a given hydrogen content, $[H_0] = 0.14 cm^3/100g$, the effect of cooling rate, R, on fraction of pores, f_g, and average diameter of pores, d_{ave} was shown in Fig. 4. The experimental results also illustrated that when Sr modifier and TiB_2 grain refiner were used, the amount and size of pores became smaller and the distribution of pores became uniform.

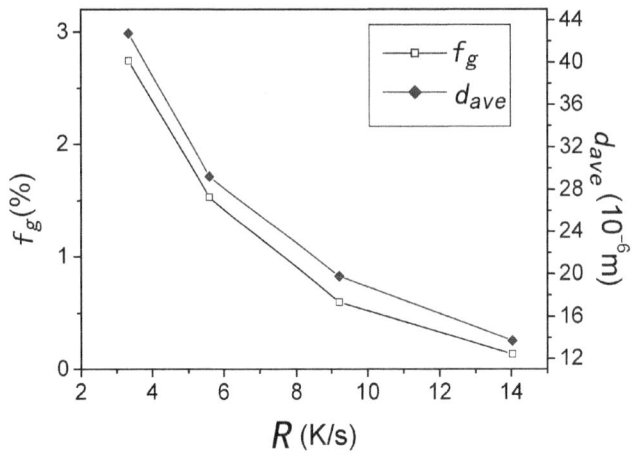

Fig. 4 The effect of cooling rate on fraction and average diameter of pores

After the macroscopic heat transfer simulation was done, one section of the specimen was selected for the microporosity calculation. To model the effect of Sr modification, different values of the surface tension of the liquid and the volume shrinkage were used in calculation. To model the effect of grain refiner, Ti-B, higher grain density value was used. Fig. 5 and Fig. 6 showed the optical and computed microstructure for two separate castings. The castings were taken from the two groups of experiments. The casting (Group I) in Fig. 5 had medium level of hydrogen content in the melt and was not refined or modified. The casting (Group II) in Fig. 6 had close level of hydrogen content in the melt and was modified and grain refined with 0.022 wt.% Sr and 0.068 wt.% Ti. The black spots in both experimental and computed images represented pores. Comparison of the experimental and calculated fraction of porosity was shown in Table 1. Both simulation results (Fig. 5a and Fig. 6a) showed good agreement with the corresponding microphotographs (Fig. 5b and Fig. 6b).

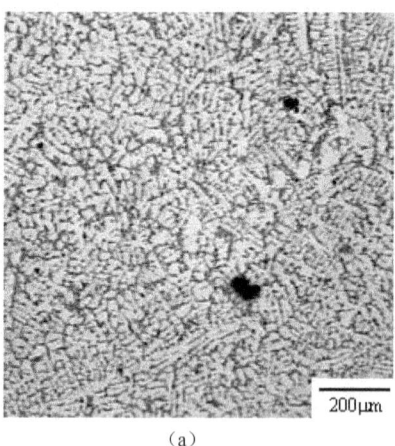 

(a)   (b)

Fig. 5 Comparison of experimental (a) and computed (b) microstructure of the step casting without modification or grain refinement ($[H_0] = 0.14 \text{cm}^3/100\text{g}$).

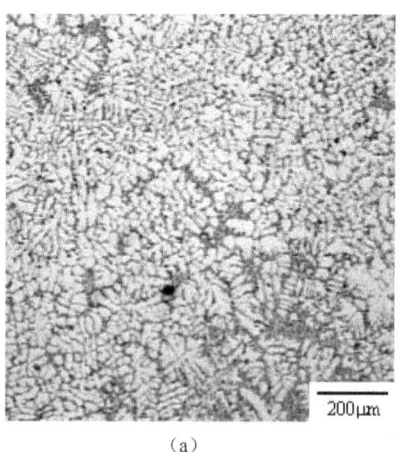 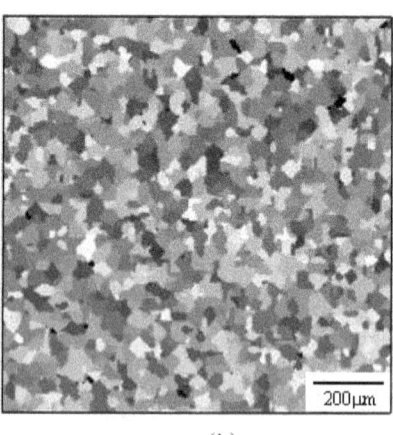

(a)   (b)

Fig. 6 Comparison of experimental (a) and computed (a) microstructure of the step casting with modification and grain refinement ($[H_0] = 0.11 \text{cm}^3/100\text{g}$).

Table 1 Comparison of calculated and experimental fraction of porosity.

Group	$[H_0]$ (cm^3/100g)	f_v(%) (image analysis)	f_v(%) (calculated)
I	0.14	1.32	1.41
II	0.11	0.53	0.42

By using the calculated distribution of voids (microporosity), the fatigue life of one section for plane-strain problem was modeled with porous elastic model. The section was 50mm length, 20mm in width. It was assumed that the left end is fixed in the x and y directions, the right end was loaded with a concentrate force, and the load ratio used in the fatigue analysis was $r = -1$. Fig. 7 and Fig. 8 showed the contour plot of the maximum principal stress and fatigue life. The amplitude of the stress at upper part was much higher than that at the lower part, as shown in Fig. 7. Since the fatigue load was alternatively applied, the stress distribution is also alternative in variation. For the estimation of duration, only the maximum stress was considered and the corresponding fatigue life was shown in Fig. 8. Since the fatigue stress was alternative in variation, the fatigue life was symmetric in distribution.

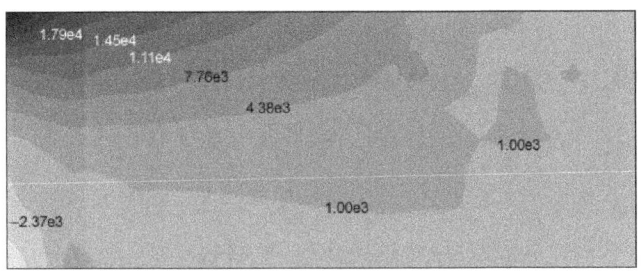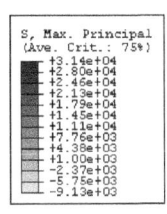

Fig. 7 Contour plot of maximum principal stress

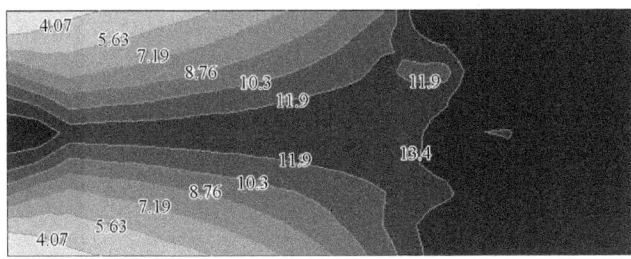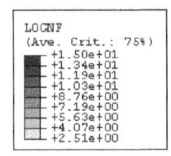

Fig. 8 Contour plot of fatigue life

Conclusions

1. A two dimensional mathematical model to predict the size and distribution of microporosity coupled with a probabilistic microstructure evolution model was studied. The micro modeling of porosity and grain structure was also coupled with the macro modeling of solidification process of castings.

2. A step-shape casting was designed and two groups of experiments were conducted to validate the proposed models. The experiment results for A356 alloy showed that the amount and size of pores are affected by the cooling rate and the use of grain refiner and modifier. The calculated results agreed with the experimental results reasonably.

3. With the results of microporosity simulation of castings, the modeling of the mechanical behavior and the fatigue life of aluminum castings was studied by considering castings with microporosity as a porous material and implemented by using ABAQUS software.

Acknowledgements

The paper was financially supported by the Key Project of NSFC (59990470-3), and State Significant Fundamental Research Program of MOST (G2000067208-3).

References

[1] S. M. Xiong, B. C. Liu, "Study on numerical simulation of mold-filling and solidification processes of shaped casting". Chinese J. Mechanical Engineering, 1999, 12 (1), 4-10

[2] M Rappaz, A. Gandin, "Probabilistic modelling of microstructure formation in solidification process". Acta Metall., v41, 1993, 345-360.

[3] W. Kurz, B. Giovanola, and R. Trivedi, "Theory of Microstructural Development During Rapid Solidification", Acta Metall., 1986, 34, 823-830.

[4] K. Kubo, R. Phelke, "Mathematical modeling of porosity formation in solidification", Metall. Trans., 16B, June 1985, 359-366.

[5] J. Huang, T. Mori and J. G. Conley, "Simulation of microporosity formation in modified and unmodified A356 alloy castings", Met. and Mat. Trans., 29B, 1998, 1249-1260.

[6] ABAQUS/Standard User's Manual, V. 6.2, HKS Inc., 2001.

17. Processing Technology and Mechanical Properties of Die-Cast Magnesium Alloy AZ91D

LIU Yan'gai (刘艳改), *LIU Wenhui* (刘文辉), *XIONG Shoumei* (熊守美),
LIU Baicheng (柳百成), *Wang Gang* (王罡), *MATSUMOTO Yoshihide*, *MURAKAMI Masayuki*

Department of Mechanical Engineering, Tsinghua University, Beijing 100084, China;
Toyo Machinery and Metal Co., Ltd., Hyogo 674-0091, Japan

Abstract: The mechanical properties of magnesium die-casting components can be improved with improved die-casting processing technology. An orthogonal experiment with four factors and three levels ($L_q, 3^4$) was used to evaluate the effect of various die-casting processing parameters on the quality and mechanical properties of an AZ91D magnesium alloy cylinder head cover component. The results show that the injection speed and casting and die temperatures all influence the component quality, with the influence of the casting pressure being the smallest. The injection speed and casting pressure are the two most important factors influencing the tensile strength. The best die-casting parameters for the magnesium alloy cylinder head cover component were determined to be a casting temperature of 660℃, a die temperature of 200℃, an injection speed of 70mgs^{-1}, and a casting pressure of 65MPa. The porosity is one of the most important parameters influencing the casting strength.

Key words: AZ91D; die casting; magnesium; process parameters; mechanical properties

Introduction

Lightweight design and the demand for recyclable materials that could help ameliorate environmental problems have led to an overwhelming increase in the research and development of magnesium alloys for practical industrial applications, particularly in the automobile sector[1-7]. The low density of magnesium (2/3 aluminum, 1/4 steel) gives it a remarkable ability to produce lightweight components and has driven 20% annual growth over the past 10 years, from 1.2 kg/vehicle in 1992 to over 4 kg/vehicle in 2002[8]. The magnesium alloy AZ91D (Mg-9 wt.% Al-1 wt.% Zn) is most widely used due to its good castability, corrosion resistance, and mechanical properties. There have been a few reports on the influence of various diecasting parameters on the mechanical properties of magnesium alloy specimens[9-12], but the available data is still rather fragmentary. Also, the influence of these parameters on the external quality of practical components is still uncertain. Moreover, the dependence of the mechanical properties of the magnesium alloys on the die-casting parameters is greatly influenced by the shape of components. Therefore, differences exist between practical components and experimental specimens. Cylinder head cover components were among the first to employ magnesium alloys in large quantities in the Chinese automobile industry with the first Mg alloy die castings by the Chinese First Automobile Works (FAW). The present paper investigates the processing technology and mechanical properties of AZ91D magnesium alloy die-casting cylinder head covers with the purpose of developing a data base and mathematical model describing the dependence of the mechanical properties on the processing parameters.

1 Experimental Procedure

1.1 Experimental design

The magnesium alloy cylinder head covers were produced on a die-casting machine 650T (BD-650V4-N). Seven castings were made for each experiment with 5 used to evaluate the external quality and the mechanical properties of the components. The sample densities were determined by flotation. An optical microscope was used to examine the porosity (shrinkage and gas and/or air) in the castings. The tensile tests used 8mm × 1.5mm specimens taken from the castings. The tensile strength was measured on an Electronic Universal Material Testing Machine Instron-1186. The specimen fracture surfaces were investigated using the scanning electron microscopy (SEM).

An orthogonal experiment with four factors and three levels ($L_q, 3^4$) given in Table 1 was used to study the influence of processing parameters on the external quality and mechanical properties of die-casting components, where t_c is the casting temperature, t_d is the die temperatures, V_i is the injection speed, and P_c is the casting pressure. The density (ρ), tensile strength (σ), and defect index (Q) of the die castings were evaluated in the tests.

Table 1 Die-casting parameters for orthogonal experiments

Level	t_c/℃	t_d/℃	V_i/(m·s^{-1})	P_c/MPa
1	640	150	40	25
2	660	200	70	45
3	680	250	100	65

1.2 Casting structure and die design

The casting structure of the cylinder head cover is shown in Fig. 1 with the die runner system, in which points P_1 and P_2 are the sample locations used to test the density and tensile strength of the casting. The castings had a mass of 1099g, a projected area of 73780mm^2, a thinnest wall thickness of 2.3mm, the proportion of the thinnest part of the casting to the whole casting was 85%, the thickest wall thickness was 10mm, the proportion of the thickest part of the casting to the whole casting was 6%, and the space diagonal length was 462mm.

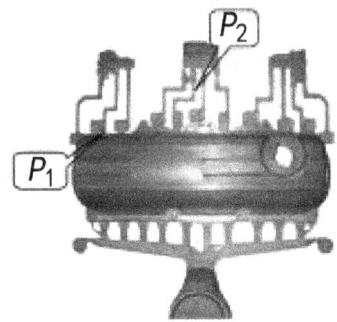

Fig. 1 Casting structure and runner system for the cylinder head cover

The die casting had a shoot sleeve area of 7850mm^2, a gate area of 326mm^2, an inner gate thickness of 1.3mm, and a shoot sleeve length of 315mm.

2 Determination of External Casting Quality

The external defects of cast parts, such as cold laps, misruns, surface folds, flow marks, cracks, and sink marks, were examined by direct observation and evaluated by calculating a defect index Q:

$$Q = \sum_{j=1}^{m} \sum_{i=1}^{n} \eta_i \mathrm{g} \omega_j \mathrm{g} \overline{P}_{ij} \qquad (1)$$

where m is the number of zones in the casting used to evaluate the influence of defects on the casting performance, n is the number of external defects considered, η_i is the weight factor of defect i indicating the influence of a defect on the casting performance according to the technical specifications and performance requirements of the casting, ω_j is the weight factor of zone j which is determined according to the quality requirement of the zone, and $\overline{P}_{ij}$ is the average defect index contributed by defect i in zone j which is given by averaging all the defect indices of defect i in the same zone j for all the castings considered.

According to the casting specifications and performance requirements, defect indices less than 50 are regarded as sound castings, while those higher than 50 will be rejected.

3 Results and Discussion

3.1 Orthogonal experiment

The orthogonal experiment results given in Tables 2 and 3 show that the influences of the processing parameters on the density and tensile strength of points P_1 and P_2 of the die casting are inconsistent. The greatest factor influencing the density of point P_1 is P_c, followed by t_c, V_i, and t_d. For point P_2, the factors influencing the density from the greatest to the smallest are t_c, P_c, V_i, and t_d. Of the factors influencing the strength of point P_1, V_i is the greatest, followed by P_c, t_c, and t_d. But for the strength of point P_2, t_c, P_c, and V_i were almost equally important with the influence of t_d as the smallest. For the defect indices, V_i, t_c, and t_d were all important factors with the influence of P_c being the smallest.

Table 2 Orthogonal experiment results

Set	t_c	t_d	V_i	P_c	$\rho/(\mathrm{kg \cdot m^{-3}})$		Q	σ_b/MPa	
					P_1	P_2		P_1	P_2
1	1	1	1	1	1785.76	1783.36	113.39	177.59	132.26
2	1	2	2	2	1805.34	1787.25	77.07	247.95	186.45
3	1	3	3	3	1814.45	1788.90	46.00	269.20	195.64
4	2	1	2	3	1810.62	1792.06	65.70	276.60	188.92
5	2	2	3	1	1780.75	1757.57	39.03	262.51	187.25
6	2	3	1	2	1768.91	1749.83	52.33	212.71	205.17
7	3	1	3	2	1801.67	1781.68	50.36	271.25	236.05
8	3	2	1	3	1813.94	1792.61	54.47	250.34	175.25
9	3	3	2	1	1796.24	1783.18	47.30	232.73	207.49

Table 3 Extreme difference of the four factors in orthogonal experiment

$\Delta \bar{k}_{ij}$	t_c	t_d	V_i	P_c
ρ_{P_1}	17.19	6.81	14.53	25.42
ρ_{P_2}	20.02	11.73	12.23	18.27
Q	28.11	27.94	28.27	11.18
σ_{b,P_1}	19.86	15.39	54.11	41.10
σ_{b,P_2}	34.81	19.78	35.42	33.56

Δk_{ij} is the extreme difference which indicates the influencing degree of the factor on the experimental results.

Location P_1 was nearer the runner gate than P_2, so P_1 was closer to the piston and the liquid metal near position P_1 is near to sequential solidification. Thus, P_c more directly affects the porosity (shrinkage and gas and/or air) at this position in the casting which, therefore, affects the density at P_1. As t_c increases, the time until the liquid meal solidifiation increases which affects not only the sequential solidification time but also the effective acting time for P_c, which reduces the porosity in the casting and increases the density. Therefore, t_c also greatly influences the casting density. t_d has little effect on the solidification, so it has little influence on the casting density. The solidification rate at P_2 is different from that of P_1 for several reasons. Since the casting at P_2 is thicker than at most locations before the liquid metal reaches P_2, the pressure channel may be solidified before P_2 solidifies completely. Since the pressure channel solidification depends greatly on t_c, t_c greatly influences the density at P_2. P_c is one of the important factors influencing the density at P_2 before the pressure channel closes. V_i is related to the gas entrapped in the casting. Since the amount of entrapped gas was almost the same for locations P_1 and P_2, the influence of V_i on the density of points P_1 and P_2 was almost the same.

External defects on the cast parts were mostly cold laps, flow marks, and misruns. There were also a few cracks and sink marks. The temperature gradient in the casting during the die casting, which is influenced by the solidification time, the mold filling time, and the casting structure, is the main factor causing external defects, such as cold laps, flow marks, misruns, and cracks. Since the solidification time and mold filling time strongly depend on t_c, t_d, and V_i, these three factors all affect the external casting quality.

The results in Table 2 show that higher casting densities are related to higher tensile strengths, i.e., the die-casting strength strongly depends on the porosity. V_i directly influences the entrapped gas as well as the porosity size and distribution in the casting. At P_1 with sequential solidification, an increased P_c will lead to a reduced casting porosity and an increased casting strength. At P_2 location with non-sequential solidification, P_c directly influences the casting porosity before the pressure channel closes. Therefore, V_i and P_c both greatly influence the casting strength at both P_1 and P_2. In addition, increasing t_c can extend the time for closing the feeding channel to P_2, which also greatly influences the porosity size and distribution at P_2. Therefore, the strength at location P_2 also depends on t_c.

The experimental results show that the best diecasting parameters for the magnesium alloy cylinderhead cover are: $t_c = 660\,^\circ\!C$, $t_d = 200\,^\circ\!C$, $V_i = 70\,\text{mgs}^{-1}$, and $P_c = 65\,\text{MPa}$.

3.2 Influence of process parameters on casting porosity

Some optical micrographs of the porosity distribution in samples taken from point P_1 in the castings from the 4 tests are shown in Fig. 2. The statistical results for the porosity area percentage for the 9 samples are listed in Table 4. The porosities in castings 3, 4, 5, and 7 were relatively lower. Accordingly, the strengths of these specimens were found to be higher.

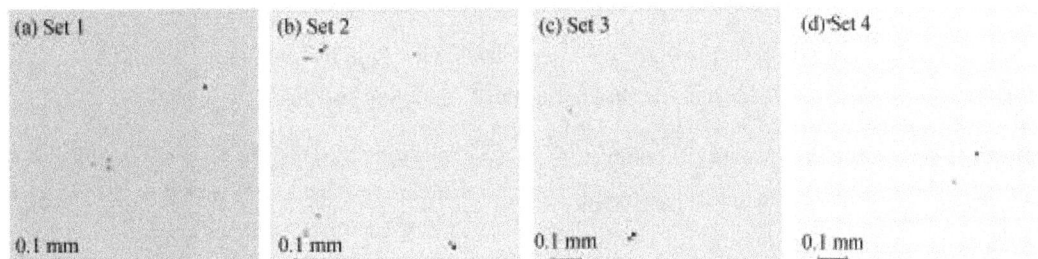

Fig. 2 Porosity distribution at P_1 in the castings for sets 1-4 of die-casting parameters in Table 2

Table 4 Statistics of porosity area percentage at location P_1 in the castings for the 9 different sets of die-casting parameters listed in Table 2

Specimen(No.)	1	2	3	4	5	6	7	8	9
Porosity area (%)	0.25	0.42	0.14	0.24	0.21	0.34	0.21	0.29	0.20

3.3 Casting fractographs

Some SEM fractographs of the tensile samples taken from point P_1 for the 9 test samples are shown in Fig. 3. Much more porosity was observed in the SEM fractographs of samples 1, 2, 6, and 9 than in samples 3, 4, 5, and 7. Since the samples with higher porositiys all had lower strength, the fractograph observations suggest that the casting porosity is one of the important factors influencing casting strength, which corresponds to the results of the orthogonal experiment.

4 Conclusions

1) The orthogonal experimental results show that the injection speed, the casting temperature, and the die temperature were all important factors influencing the external quality of the AZ91D magnesium die-casting components with the casting pressure having the smallest effect. The injection speed and casting pressure have the greatest influence on the tensile strength while the die temperature had the smallest effect.

2) The best die-casting processing parameters for the magnesium alloy cylinder head cover were a casting temperature of $660\,^\circ\!C$, a die temperature of $200\,^\circ\!C$, an injection speed of $70\,\text{mgs}^{-1}$, and a casting pressure of $65\,\text{MPa}$.

3) Lower porosities and, hence, higher densities resulted in higher tensile strength in the castings. The

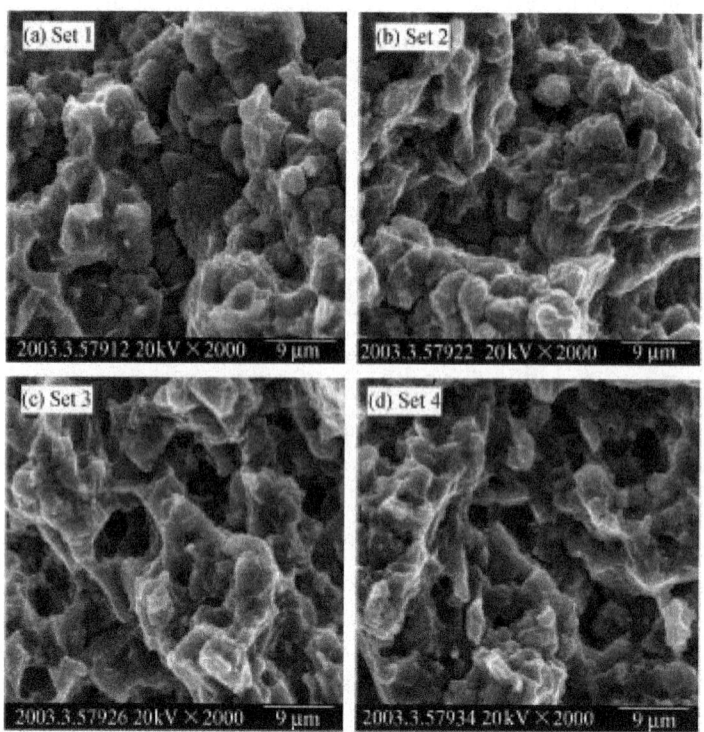

Fig. 3 Fractographs of tensile samples taken from location P_1 in the castings for Sets 1-4 of die-casting parameters listed in Table 2 for Figs. 3a-3d

fractograph observation suggests that porosity is one of the most important factors influencing the casting strength. This corresponds to the orthogonal experimental results.

Acknowledgements

Special thanks are due to the Institute of Foundry Technology of the First Automobile Works for their support in providing the die-casting die for the experiments.

References

[1] Kojima, Y, Aizawa T, Kamado S, Higashi K. Progressive steps in the platform science and technology for advanced magnesium alloys. *Materials Science Forum Vols.*, 2003, **419-422**: 3-20.

[2] Kamado S, Koike J, Kondoh K, Kawamura Y. Magnesium research trend in Japan. *Materials Science Forum Vols.*, 2003, **419-422**: 21-34.

[3] Mordike B L, Ebert T. Magnesium properties-apllications-potential. *Mater. Sci. Eng.*, 2001, **A302**: 37-45.

[4] Ambat R, Aung N N, Zhou W. Evaluation of microstructural effects on corrosion behaviour of AZ91D magnesium alloy. *Corrosion Sci.*, 2000, **42**: 1433-1455.

[5] Schumann S, Friedrich H. Current and future use of magnesium in the automobile industry. *Materials Science Forum Vols.*, 2003, **419-422**: 51-56.

[6] Luo A A. Recent magnesium alloy development for automotive powertrain applications. *Materials Science Forum Vols.*, 2003, **419-422**: 57-66.

[7] Kaneko T, Suzuki M. Automotive applications of magnesium alloys. *Materials Science Forum Vols.*, 2003, **419-422**: 67-72.

[8] Cole G S. Issues that influence magnesium's use in automotive industry. *Materials Science Forum Vols.*, 2003, **419-422**: 43-50.

[9] Emlry E F. Principles of Magnesium Technology. Oxford: Pergamon, 1996: 193, 431.

[10] Gutman E M, Unigovski Y, Levkovich M, Koren Z, Aghion E, Dangur M. Influence of technological parameters of permanent mold casting and die casting on creep and strength of Mg alloy AZ91D. *Mater. Sci. Eng.*, 1997, **A234-236**: 880-883.

[11] El-Mahallawy N A, Taha M A, Pokora E, Klein F. On the influence of process variables on the thermal conditions and properties of high-pressure die-cast magnesium alloys. *J. Mater. Proc. Tech.*, 1998, **1-3**: 125-138.

[12] Gutman E M, Unigovski Y B, Eliezer A, Abramov E, Aghion E. Processing effect on mechanical properties of die cast magnesium alloys. *Mater. Tech.*, 2001, **2**: 126-132.

18. Influences of Casting Pressure Conditions on the Quality and Properties of a Magnesium Cylinder Head Cover Die Casting

Wenhui LIU[1], *Yangai LIU*[1], *Shoumei XIONG*[1], *Baicheng LIU*[1], *Y. Matsumoto*[2] *and M. Murakami*[2]

[1] Department of Mechanical Engineering, Tsinghua University, Beijing 100084, China
[2] Toyo Machinery & Metal Co., Ltd., Japan

[Manuscript received September 26, 2003, in revised form December 20, 2003]

Casting pressure conditions have great influences on the casting defects, such as gas porosity, shrinkage porosity and gas holes. A Mg cylinder head cover die casting was used to experimentally study the influences of casting pressure, the loading time and the piston position of pressure intensification on the variation of pressure and the quality of casting. The results show that casting pressure, the loading time and the piston position of pressure intensification have great influences on the pressure variations in the mold, the quality and performance of casting. The external quality, the density and the tensile strength of casting were improved with the increase of casting pressure and the piston position of pressure intensification and the decrease of the loading time of pressure intensification.

Key words: Magnesium alloy; Pressure; Die casting; Quality; Properties

1. Introduction

High pressure die casting is an important method in making Mg alloys for both auto parts and 3C products[1,2]. It is estimated that the amount of Mg alloy die castings is more than 90% of structural components of Mg alloy. Because of the characteristics of low latent heat of phase change and low density[3,4], Mg alloy has obvious characteristics during high pressure die casting compared to Al alloy. In order to improve the quality of Mg castings, it is necessary to study the die casting process of Mg alloy systematically[5~8]. This is also helpful to promote the wide use of Mg. The pressure conditions are the most important factors of die casting and have direct effects on the process as well as the quality of castings. In this paper, a Mg cylinder head cover die casting was produced to experimentally study the influences of die casting pressure conditions on the quality and properties of the castings. The results are assistant to accumulate experimental data and theoretical base for the process design of Mg die casting.

2. Experimental

2.1 Experimental design

A Mg cylinder head cover was used to experimentally study the influences of casting pressure (p_c), the loading time of pressure intensification (t_{PI}) and piston position of pressure intensification (L_{PI}) on the pressure variations in the mold during mold filling and the quality of the castings. The employed alloy is AZ91D and the experimental process parameters are shown in Tables 1 and 2. During the experiments, cavity pressure sensors were placed in the die for the measurement of the pressure variations.

The experiments were conducted on a 650T (BD-650V4-N) die casting machine. 5 castings were made for each experiment to determine and estimate the external quality, density and mechanical properties of the casting with averaging results. The density of the samples was determined by Archimedes method. The gas porosity of the test samples was observed by optical microscope.

X-ray inspection technique was used to examine the gas holes and shrinkage porosity in the castings. For the tensile test, the samples were cut into specimens with a section dimension of 8mm×1.5mm. The tensile strength was evaluated by Instron-1186 model electronic universal material testing machine.

Table 1 Experimental parameters

Die temperature, T_D/℃	200
Pouring temperature, T_P/℃	660
Shot sleeve temperature, T_{SS}/℃	230
Biscuit thickness, W_B/mm	20
Start position of high speed injection stage, L_{HSI}/mm	210
Velocity of the high speed injection stage, v_{HSI}/(m/s)	70
Velocity of the low speed injection stage, v_{LSI}/(m/s)	0.4

Table 2 Experimental schemes of the die casting process

		t_{PI}/ms	p_C/MPa	L_{PI}/mm
p_C/MPa	26.9	30	26.9	265
	38	30	38	265
	63	30	63	265
t_{PI}/ms	20	20	63	265
	30	30	63	265
	70	70	63	265
L_{PI}/mm	245	30	63	245
	265	30	63	265
	290	30	63	290

2.2 Casting structure and die design

The casting structure with the runner system of the cylinder head cover component is shown in Fig.1, in which positions P1 and P2 are locations for the pressure measurement in die cavity and the quality test of samples.

3. Determination of External Quality of the Casting

External defects of cast parts, such as cold laps, misrun, surface folds, flow marks, cracks, sink marks, *etc.*, were examined by direct observation after polishing the casting surface and evaluated by calculating a defect index Q according to Eq. (1):

$$Q = \sum_{j=1}^{m} \sum_{i=1}^{n} \eta_i \cdot \omega_j \cdot \overline{P}_{ij} \quad (1)$$

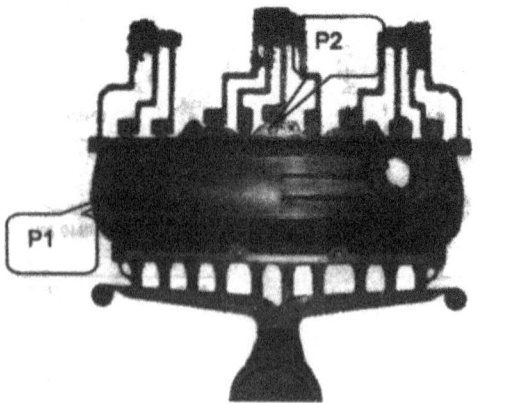

Fig. 1 Casting structure and runner system of the cylinder head cover component

where Q is the defect index of a casting, m is the number of zones of a casting divided for evaluating the influence of different zones with defects on the performance of a casting, n is the number of external defects considered, η_i is the weight factor of defect i, indicating the influence of the defect on the performance of the casting according to the technical specification and performance requirement of a casting, ω_j is the weight factor of zone j, $\overline{P}_{ij}$ is the average defect index contributed by defect i in zone j, which is given by averaging all the defect indexes of defect i in the same zone j for all the castings considered.

According to the specifications and the performance requirements of the casting, the critical defect index Q of the casting is 50, castings under the defect index are regarded as sound castings, and those with higher defect indexes will be rejected.

4. Results and Discussion

4.1 Influence of pressure conditions on the pressure variations in the mold during mold filling and solidification stages

The pressure variations in the mold during mold filling and solidification stages were determined by measuring the pressures at positions P1 and P2. Figure 2 gives the curves of the pressure at positions P1 and P2 as function of time under different casting pressure conditions. Filling pressure (p_F), the pressure during pressure intensification stage (p_{PI}) and t_{PI} have great influences on the quality of the castings during die casting. Of the three factors, p_F reflects the kinetic energy of the liquid metal during mold filling. Therefore, it has great influence on the quality and the performance of the castings. The defects like cold laps, misrun, surface folds and flow marks will decrease with the increase of p_F. t_{PI} represents the rate of pressure intensification after the mold is filled completely. The shorter the t_{PI}, the faster the pressure established during the pressure intensification stage. As a result, some defects produced during mold filling can be eliminated to some extent. Therefore, shorter t_{PI} is helpful to produce castings with high quality. p_{PI} is the highest pressure that the system can act on the liquid metal during the pressure intensification stage. If p_{PI} increases, the liquid metal will produce solidification at higher pressure, resulting in the improvement of the feeding conditions of the castings. Accordingly, the external sink marks as well as internal gas porosity and shrinkage porosity tend to decrease. The size of porosities also decreases.

It can be seen from Fig. 2 that p_{PI} increases greatly with the increase of p_C and that p_F changes a little under different casting pressures. Experimental results also show that p_F takes no evident changes with the decrease of t_{PI}. But the time for establishing pressure in the mold is shortened and p_{PI} is enhanced rapidly. In addition, the decrease of L_{PI} results in the decrease of p_F and a little decrease of p_{PI}, but no evident changes are observed for t_{PI}.

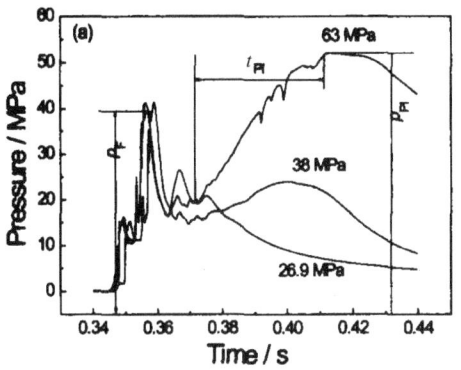 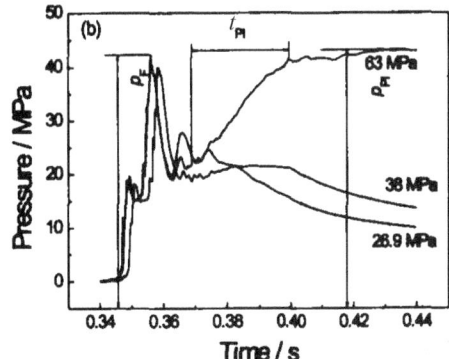

Fig. 2 Pressure variations in the mold during mold filling and solidification stages under different casting pressure conditions: (a) position P1 and (b) position P2

4.2 Influence of pressure conditions on the external quality of the casting

By examining external defects of the cast parts under different pressure conditions, the defect indexes were calculated and the results are shown in Fig. 3. It can be found that the surface quality of the castings improves with the increase of p_C. This is mainly due to the increase of feeding pressure during the solidification process of the casting caused by the increase of p_C. As a result, the sink mark reduces. At the same time, the defects like cold laps and misrun produced during mold filling can be fed further under pressure conditions with the increase of p_C.

The decrease of t_{PI} also leads to the improvement of the surface quality of the cast parts. Based on the measurement of pressure variations, p_{PI} in the mold can be enhanced a little with the decrease of t_{PI}. This is helpful to reduce the sink marks of the castings. At the same time, faster establishment of the pressure in the mold and the increased p_{PI} are also contributed to the modification of the defects that has formed in the castings before.

The surface defects of the castings decrease as L_{PI} increases in a certain range. The increase of L_{PI} leads to the increase of p_{PI} in the mold. This is contributed to the decrease of the sink marks of the castings. It has been known from the pressure variations in the mold that p_F decreases greatly when L_{PI} is too small. This will result in the increase of the surface defects of the castings.

Therefore, in order to improve the surface quality of the castings, pressure intensification should not start up too early.

4.3 Influence of pressure conditions on gas holes of the casting

X-ray inspection shows that gas holes were found at a thicker part (8mm in thickness) far from the gate area as shown in Fig. 4. Statistical data of the size and total area of gas holes at this location of the castings under different conditions are shown in Fig. 5. It is found that the average diameter and total area of gas holes decrease as p_C increases, increase as t_{PI} increases and decrease as L_{PI} increases. The increase of p_C and L_{PI} and decrease of t_{PI} all contribute to the increase of p_{PI}. Therefore, the feeding pressure during solidification process of the casting will increase, leading to the decrease of gas holes in the casting. At the same time, the entrapped gas will be compressed into smaller gas porosity when the liquid metal solidifies under higher pressure. Therefore, the gas holes in the cast parts will be small in size.

Samples taken from positions P1 and P2 of the castings were examined by optical microscope in order to observe the shape of porosities. The results are shown in Figs. 6 and 7, respectively. It can be found that the size of porosities at position P1 is smaller than that at position P2. Besides, larger porosities appear at position P2. To the reason is that position P2 is at the end of the casting and far from the inner gate. The front liquid metal with more gas entrapped during mold filling will stay here, resulting in the formation of more pores. In addition, the wall at position P2 is thicker than that at position P1. The pressure channel for the feeding of position P2 will be closed earlier during the solidification process since the wall before point P2 is thinner. As a result, the pressure remained at the end of solidification process of position P2 is not efficient enough for feeding, leading to the formation of shrinkage porosities. In addition, the size of the porosities will increase because of the decrease of p_{PI} in the mold. It also can be seen from Figs. 6 and 7 that both the size and the number of the pores decrease with the increase of p_C. This is mainly due to the increase of p_{PI} in the mold with the increase of p_C.

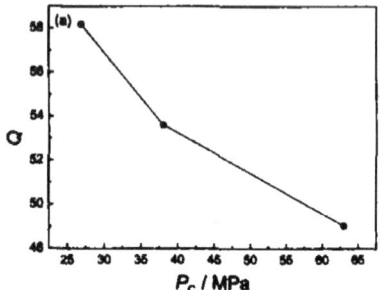
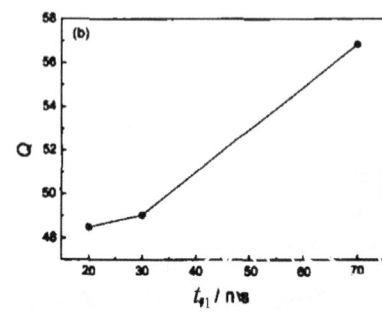
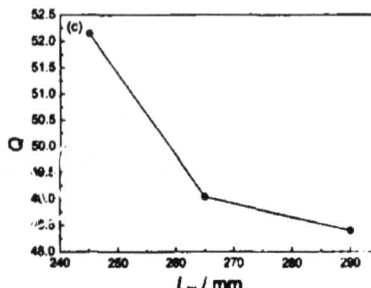

Fig. 3 Defect indexes of castings as function of p_C (a), t_{PI} (b) and L_{PI} (c)

Fig. 4 Location of gas holes (a) and one of the X-ray inspection results (b)

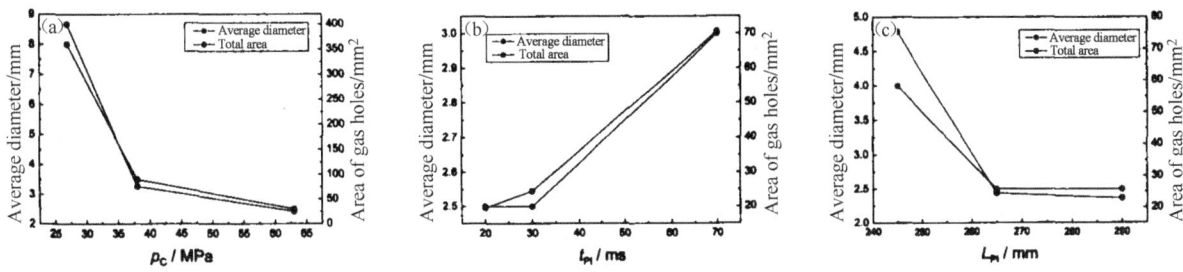

Fig. 5 Average diameter and total area of gas holes of the castings as function of p_C (a), t_{PI} (b) and L_{PI} (c)

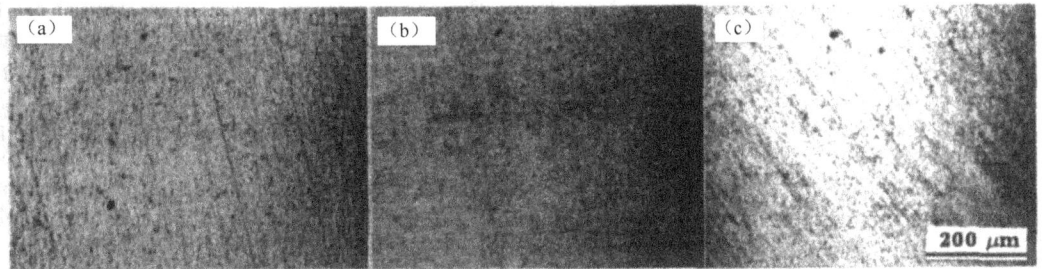

Fig. 6 Porosity distribution at position P1 in the casting under difference casting pressures:
(a) 26.9MPa, (b) 38MPa and (c) 63MPa

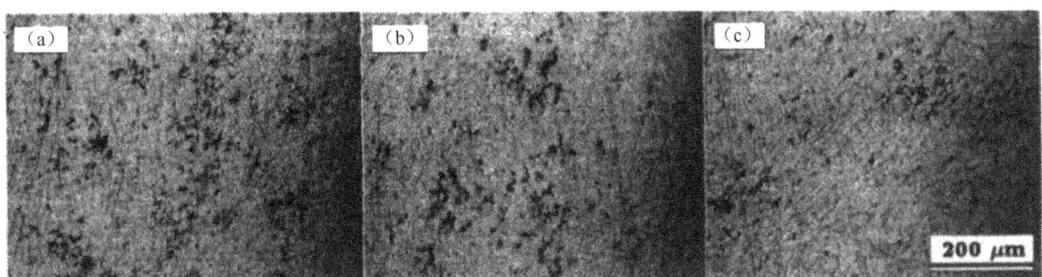

Fig. 7 Porosity distribution at position P2 in the casting under different casting pressures:
(a) 26.9MPa, (b) 38MPa and (c) 63MPa

The experimental results also show that both the decrease of t_{PI} and the increase of L_{PI} lead to the decrease of the size and the number of porosities in the casting. Based on the analysis of pressure variations, p_{PI} will be enhanced with the decrease of t_{PI} and the increase of L_{PI}, which is helpful to the decrease of the number and the size of shrinkage porosities in the casting.

4.4 Influence of pressure conditions on the density and the tensile strength of the casting

The density and the tensile strength of the samples taken from positions P1 and P2 of the castings were examined. The results are shown in Figs. 8, 9 and 10, respectively. The results show that the density and the strength of the samples from position P1 are much higher than those from position P2. This is related to the fact that there are more porosities formed at position P2.

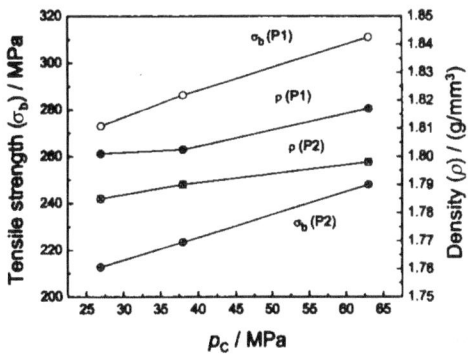

Fig. 8 Tensile strength and the density of the samples as function of p_C

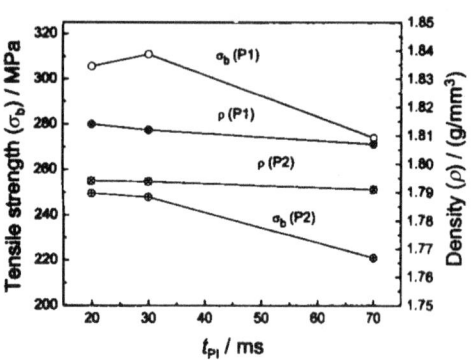

Fig. 9 Tensile strength and the density of the samples as function of t_{PI}

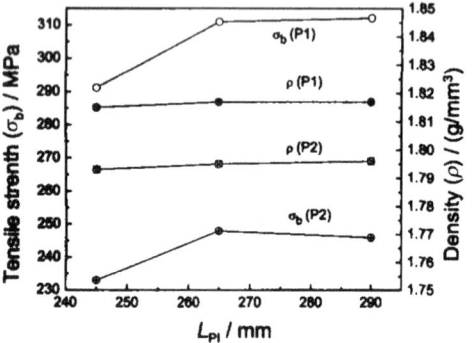

Fig. 10 Tensile strength and the density of the samples as function of L_{PI}

It can be seen from Fig. 8 that both the tensile strength and the density of the castings increase with the increase of p_C. The increase of p_C causes a great increase of p_{PI} in the mold. This will contribute to the enhancement of the cooling rate of the casting during solidification process, resulting in the refining of the microstructure. In addition, when the casting solidifies under higher pressure, the number of gas holes and shrinkage porosities tends to decrease and the size of porosities also decreases. Accordingly, the density of the casting increases. At the same time, the tensile strength of the casting improves.

The decrease of t_{PI} leads to the increase of both the strength and the density of the casting, as can be seen from Fig. 9. p_{PI} in the mold will increase with the decrease of t_{PI}, resulting in the increase of the pressure during solidification process of the casting. Therefore, the strength and the density of the casting improve.

It can be seen from Fig. 10 that, both the strength and the density of the casting improve with the increase of L_{PI}. Moreover, the strength increases greatly when L_{PI} is less than 265mm. When L_{PI} is too small, more gas will be entrapped since the shot sleeve is not well filled. Additionally, p_{PI} becomes lower. These factors all lead to the decrease of the strength and the density of the casting. Based on the analysis of pressure variations in the mold, when L_{PI} starts at 245mm, p_{PI} is much less than that when L_{PI} starts at 265mm. But there is small difference for p_{PI} when L_{PI} increases from 265mm to 290mm. Accordingly, the strength and the density take small changes when L_{PI} is more than 265mm.

5. Conclusions

(1) The increase of casting pressure leads to a great increase of the pressure during intensification of pressure stage and a minor variation of filling pressure. The pressure during pressure intensification stage increases with the increase of the piston position of pressure intensification and the decrease of the loading time of pressure intensification. Filling pressure is enhanced as the piston position of pressure intensification increases.

(2) The external quality, the density and the tensile strength of the castings are all improved with the increase of casting pressure and the piston position of pressure intensification and the decrease of the loading time of pressure intensification. At the same time, the number and the size of shrinkage porosities and gas holes decrease.

Acknowledgements

The research is a part of the research project of Tsinghua-Toyo R&D center of Mg and Al alloys processing technology funded by Toyo Machinery & Metal Co., Ltd. Additionally, the study was also financially supported by the National Natural Science Foundation of China under grant number 50275081, the internal research fund from Tsinghua University and the Post-Doctoral Foundation from the Ministry of Education of China. Special thanks are due to the Institute of Foundry Technology of FAW for the support in providing the die-casting die of the experiments.

REFERENCES

[1] Peter Wong: *Papers of Sinomag Magnesium Seminar*, Yanxiang Hotel, Beijing, 2002, 177.

[2] B. L. Mordike and T. Ebert: *Mater. Sci. Eng.*, 2002, **A302**, 37.

[3] Zheng LIU, Zhongguang WANG, Yue WANG, Feng LI and Huijie ZHAO: *Chin. J. Mater. Res.*, 1999, **13**, 641. (in Chinese)

[4] B. H. Hu, K. K. Tong, X. P. Niu and I. Pinwill: *J. Mater. Proc. Technol.*, 2000, **105**, 128.

[5] W. P. Sequeira, M. T. Murray, G. L. Dunlop and D. H. StJohn: Proc. of the 1997 TMS Annual Meeting, *Automotive Alloys*, Orlando, FL, USA, 1997, 169.

[6] Weiss Konrad and Honsel Christoph: Proc. of the 2003 TMS Annual Meeting, *Magnesium Technology*, San Diego, CA, United States, 2003, 109.

[7] E. M. Gutman, Y. B. Unigovski, A. Eliezer, E. Abramov and E. Aghion: *Mater. Technol.*, 2001, **16**(**2**), 126.

[8] Y. J. Huang, B. H. Hu, I. Pinwill, W. Zhou and D. M. R. Taplin: *Mater. Manufact. Proc.*, 2000, **15**(1), 97.

19. Numerical Modeling of Microstructure Evolution and Dendrite Growth for Al-Si Alloy Casting during Low Pressure Die Casting

B. Li[1,a], Q. Y. Xu[1,b], B. C. Liu[1,c]

[1]Key Laboratory for Advanced Materials Processing Technology (MOE), Department of Mechanical Engineering, Tsinghua University, Beijing 100084, China

[a]libin03@mails.tsinghua.edu.cn, [b]scjxqy@tsinghua.edu.cn, [c]liubc@tsinghua.edu.cn

Key words: Microstructure simulation, Aluminum alloy, Low pressure die casting

Abstract: A modified Cellular Automaton model was presented to simulate the evolution of dendritic microstructure in low pressure die casting of Al-Si Alloy, which accounted for the heterogeneous nucleation, the solute redistribution both in liquid and solid, the interface curvature and the growth anisotropy during solidification. The free growth of single equiaxed dendrite and the evolution of multi dendrites with various crystallographic orientations were predicted. The variation of the dendrite tip velocity and local solute concentration at the solid/liquid interface were analyzed. The grain morphology of aircraft turbine wheel casting at different specimen points were predicted and compared with experimental results.

Introduction

Solidification microstructure can affect the performances of the final castings to a great extent. So it is very important to better understand and control the formation of solidification microstructure. Besides physical experiments and analytical techniques, numerical simulation is a very powerful tool to study microstructure evolution because of its high efficiency and low cost.

In recent decades, microstructure simulation of aluminum alloys during solidification has been studied extensively by many groups in the world from meso-scale to micro-scale. Cellular Automaton models[1-7] and Phase Field models[8,9] are two kinds of ones which are applied most popularly till now. Phase field (PF) models can simulate the kinetics of dendrite growth and realistic dendritic morphology using entropy or free energy formulation. However, PF models demands a large number of computer resources, so it can only simulate a few dendrites in a smaller domain. CA models are closer to practical application because it is simpler to program and solve in a PC and the simulated domain is larger.

In this paper, the solidification of Al-7wt% Si-0.5wt% Mg alloy during low pressure die casting was analyzed, and nucleation model of the alloy was established based on a number of experimental data. A modified CA method coupled with finite difference method was used to simulate the evolution of the alloy microstructure. The preferential growth orientation, the solute redistribution in both liquid and solid, the solid/liquid interface curvature and the growth anisotropy were all taken into account in the model, reproducing the growth of multi dendritic grains with different crystallographic orientation. The grain size at different position of the aircraft turbine wheel casting were predicted and compared with experimental results.

Model description

Alloy Solidification Process Analysis. The equilibrium structure of Al-7wt%Si-0.5wt%Mg is primary α Al, Al-Si eutectic and Mg_2Si reinforced phase. The content of Mg_2Si is usually less and it is distributed dispersedly so that it is hard to identify[10]. On the other hand, based on the calculated results of THERMO-CALC software, at the end of binary eutectic transformation L→Al+Si, solid fraction of primary and eutectic microstructure is already above 95 percent. Then ternary eutectic transformation begins and complex phases can appear. So the solidification process of Al-7wt% Si-0.5wt%Mg alloy can be simplified into that of Al-7wt% Si alloy, which can still represent the main characteristic of microstructure evolution. The pressure under which the alloy solidifies is below 0.1MPa for low pressure die casting, so the influence of the pressure on solidification process and final microstructure can be neglected.

Nucleation Model. The continuous nucleation model based on Gaussian distribution was used popularly for Aluminum alloy solidification[11,12]. Grain density $n(\Delta T)$ at one certain undercooling is calculated as follows:

$$n(\Delta T) = \int_0^{\Delta T} [1 - f_s(\Delta T)] \frac{dn}{d(\Delta T)} d(\Delta T) \quad (1)$$

$$\frac{dn}{d(\Delta T)} = \frac{n_{max}}{\sqrt{2\pi}\Delta T_\sigma} \exp\left[-\frac{1}{2}\left(\frac{\Delta T - \Delta T_N}{\Delta T_\sigma}\right)^2\right] \quad (2)$$

Where ΔT is the actual undercooling, n_{max} is the maximum density of nucleation sites, ΔT_N is the mean nucleation undercooling, ΔT_σ is the standard deviation of the distribution.

However, for the solidification process under practical processing condition, it is not exact to reflect the characteristic of nucleation process if following the previous model parameters completely. So it is necessary to carry through numerical statement and analysis based on a number of experimental data, and then the related experimental nucleation parameters can be concluded. Twelve sets of experiments for plate-shaped and step-shaped castings were designed in the present study, and cooling rate and grain size at every specimen position were measured. The final calculated results based on statistics and analyses for acquired experiment data are as follows: $n_{max} = 7.0 \times 10^9$; $\Delta T_N = 20K$; $\Delta T_\sigma = 0.1K$.

Dendrite Growth Model. After the primary α Al begins to nucleate, it grows with dendritic shape for alloy equiaxed solidification condition. As the dendrite grows, latent heat and solute are released into the solid/liquid interface. Besides, the dendrite shape also changes the interface curvature. The changing thermal/solute field and interface curvature all influence the equilibrium interface undercooling/movement. So the heat and mass transport will continue through the whole solidification process. Solid/liquid interface equilibrium composition during alloy solidification process was calculated in this paper based on thermal and solutal conservation. Constitutional undercooling, curvature undercooling and anisotropy factor at solid/liquid interface were considered to establish interface kinetics model. Microstructure evolution was simulated through solving governing variables such as temperature, concentration, solid fraction and interface velocity. Modified CA method can describe not only grain profile, but also dendrite morphology with different crystallographic orientations. The related governing equations are as follows.

(1) Equilibrium composition and solute conservation at solid/liquid interface

The local interface equilibrium composition and solute conservation are calculated by the following equations:

$$C_L^* = C_0 + (T^* - T_L + \Gamma \bar{k} f(\varphi, \theta))/m_L \quad (3)$$

$$C_S^* = k_0 C_L^* \quad (4)$$

$$v_n^* C_L^* (1-k) = D_L\left(\frac{\partial C_L}{\partial x} + \frac{\partial C_L}{\partial y}\right) - D_S\left(\frac{\partial C_S}{\partial x} + \frac{\partial C_S}{\partial y}\right) \quad (5)$$

Where C_S^* is the solid equilibrium composition at the solid/liquid interface, k_0 is the equilibrium partition ratio, v_n^* is the normal velocity of the solid/liquid interface.

(2) Interface curvature and anisotropy factor at solid/liquid interface

The variation of the interface curvature can directly reflect dendrite morphology. Besides, it can result in the change of the temperature at solid/liquid interface (curvature undercooling), which affects the growth of dendrite front. For the CA cell at the solid/liquid interface, its curvature is determined by the solid fraction of itself and its neighborhood cells. The growing dendrites in the simulated domain have different preferential growth direction (crystallographic orientation) which is determined by crystal anisotropy including the influence of interface energy and growth kinetics[2,5,13]. The interface curvature and anisotropy factor are calculated by the following equations.

$$\bar{k} = \frac{1}{l}\left(1 - 2\frac{f_S + \sum_{k=1}^{N} f_S(k)}{N+1}\right) \quad (6)$$

$$f(\varphi,\theta) = 1 + \gamma\cos[4(\varphi-\theta)] \quad (7)$$

$$\varphi = \arccos\left(\frac{\partial f_s/\partial x}{[(\partial f_s/\partial x)^2 + (\partial f_s/\partial y)^2]^{1/2}}\right) \quad (8)$$

Where N is the number of neighbors of the interface cell. 24 cells can be counted if two-layer cells around the interface cell are considered in 2D, which means $N=24$. γ is the anisotropy factor and here equals to 0.04, $f(\varphi,\theta)$ is a function describing the anisotropy of the surface tension, φ is the angle of the normal to the interface with respect to the reference axis, θ is the angel of the preferential growth direction (crystallographic orientation) with respect to the reference axis.

In this paper, the grids rotating and coordinate transformation method was used to overcome the anisotropy introduced by the mesh of square cells. The details are described in the reference [7].

Results and discussions

Single dendrite growth. The simulation of single dendrite growth for Al-7wt%Si alloy were performed in a domain consisting of 500×500 square meshes with mesh length of 2μm. One crystal nucleus was set at the center of the domain and grew at a constant cooling rate 70k/s. Fig. 1 shows the simulated dendrite morphology when the growth time was about 2.96s. Fig. 1 (a), (b), (c) is solute concentration field, dendrite tip growth velocity field and Si concentration distribution along the horizontal center line of the domain, respectively. As shown in Fig. 1, the solute concentration decreases with bigger gradient in liquid, while smaller in solid. The solute accumulates most at the solid/liquid interface because large amounts of solute are released into the adjacent liquid when interface cells solidify and the solute diffuses slowly in liquid. The concentration in liquid decreases quickly. The diffusion is slower in solid, so the concentration changes slowly in solid. Due to solute pileup between the dendrites, the velocity at the tip of dendrites is higher than that between the dendrites.

Fig. 2 shows the variation of dendrite tip growth and solute concentration in liquid and solid with time. As shown in Fig. 2, at the beginning of the solidification, the tip velocity is close to zero because the undercooling is very small. As the solidification proceeds, the undercooling increases gradually and the tip velocity increases correspondingly. At the same time, dendrite tip liquid composition also increases. When the growth time was around 2.96s, the growing dendrite tip is close to the boundary of the simulated domain and the tip velocity becomes the biggest, and after this, decreases rapidly due to too much solute pileup as well as boundary obstruction.

Multi-dendrites growth. The simulation were performed in a domain consisting of 500×500 square meshes with mesh length 2μm. The temperature in the entire domain was assumed to be homogeneous and cooled down with a constant rate 70K/s. Fig. 3 shows the growth evolution of multi-dendrites with different crystallographic orientations. As shown in Fig. 3, at the initial stage of solidification, equiaxed crystal nuclei begin to

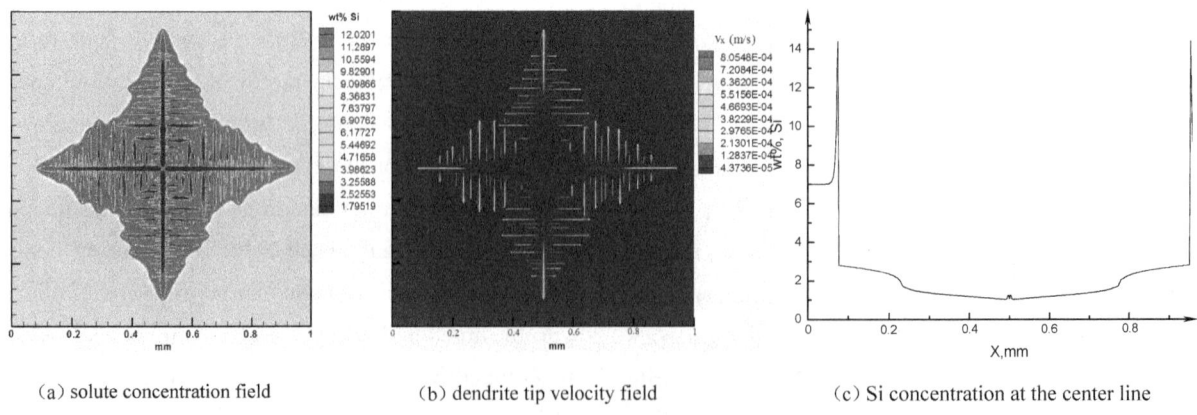

(a) solute concentration field (b) dendrite tip velocity field (c) Si concentration at the center line

Fig. 1 Simulated dendrite morphology of Al-7wt%Si alloy

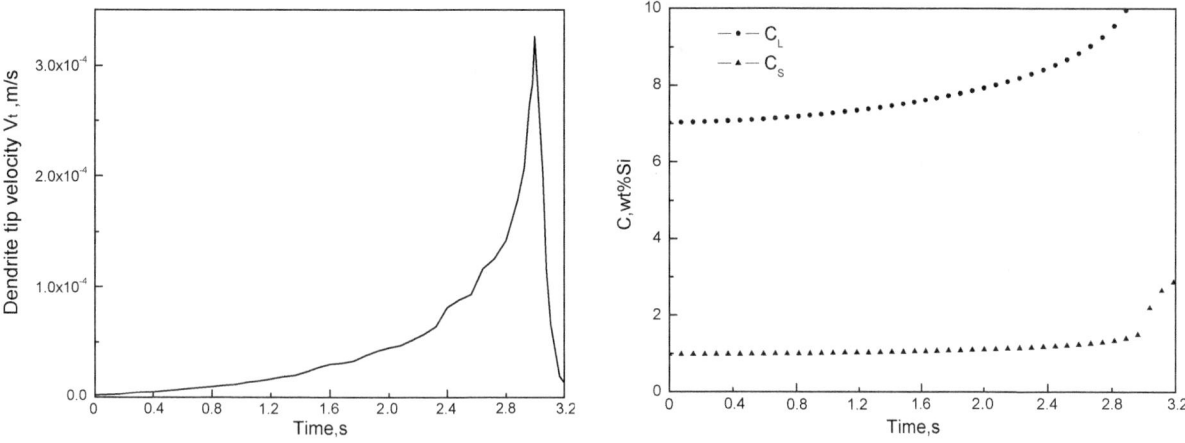

Fig. 2 Variation of dendrite tip velocity (left) and dendrite tip liquid and solid composition (right) with time

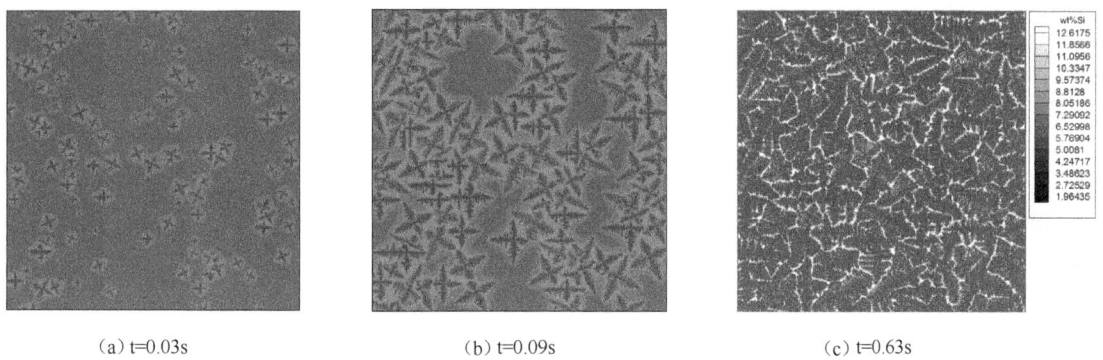

(a) t=0.03s   (b) t=0.09s   (c) t=0.63s

Fig. 3 Multi-dendrites growth of Al-7wt%Si alloy

appear randomly in the undercooled liquid with different crystallographic orientations, and then grow with dendritic shape. Secondary dendrite arms grow on the primary dendritic arms and even ternary arms appear. As the solidification proceeds, the solutes are rejected from the solid/liquid interface into the remaining liquid gradually. The solute concentration between the dendrites is higher and higher. When the concentration is up to 12.6%, the dendrites stop growing. The eutectic structures finally form at grains boundaries and the interdendrite regions.

Microstructure simulation application in aircraft turbine wheel. To validate the model presented in this paper, an aircraft turbine wheel casting made of Al-7wt%Si-0.5wt%Mg alloy was selected to compare simulation results of solidification microstructure with those in experiment. The pouring temperature is 710℃; the supercharged pressure is 0.05MPa. The size of the casting is 30mm(height)×135mm (diameter) and the thickness of the thinnest position is only 2mm. The number of the casting cells and the chill cells is 157,558 and 133,560, respectively and the total number of macro cells including sand mould cells is 2,073,600. Seven 5mm×5mm specimens were taken from the longitudinal section at the center of the wheel and indexed as P1~P7 in order. The casting shape and the positions of the specimens are schematically shown in Fig. 4.

Modified CA model coupled with finite difference method was used to simulate the evolution of the microstructure of the above casting. The macro cell size for heat transfer calculation is 1mm×1mm×1mm and the 2D micro cell size for microstructure calculation is 2μm×2μm. Fig. 5 is the comparison between the simulated and experimental microstructure at different specimen point of the aircraft turbine wheel casting. The order of cooling rate of specimen positions from fast to slow is: P1>P3>P6>P5. As shown in Fig. 5, grain size is smaller and secondary dendrite arm space is also smaller as the cooling rate increases. These can be understood due to the fact that the increase of the cooling rate will lead to the increase of the undercooling and the number of nuclei in one certain domain, which causes the grains refining.

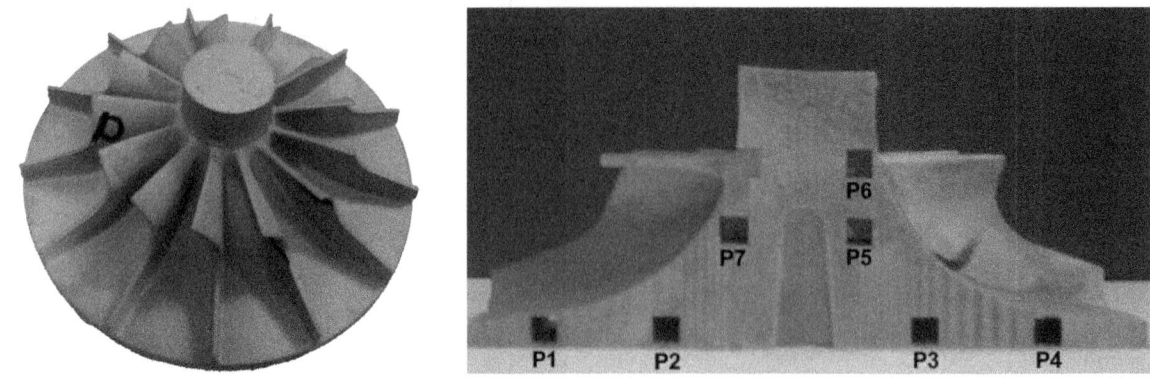

Fig. 4　Schematics of aircraft turbine wheel casting (left) and specimen positions (right)

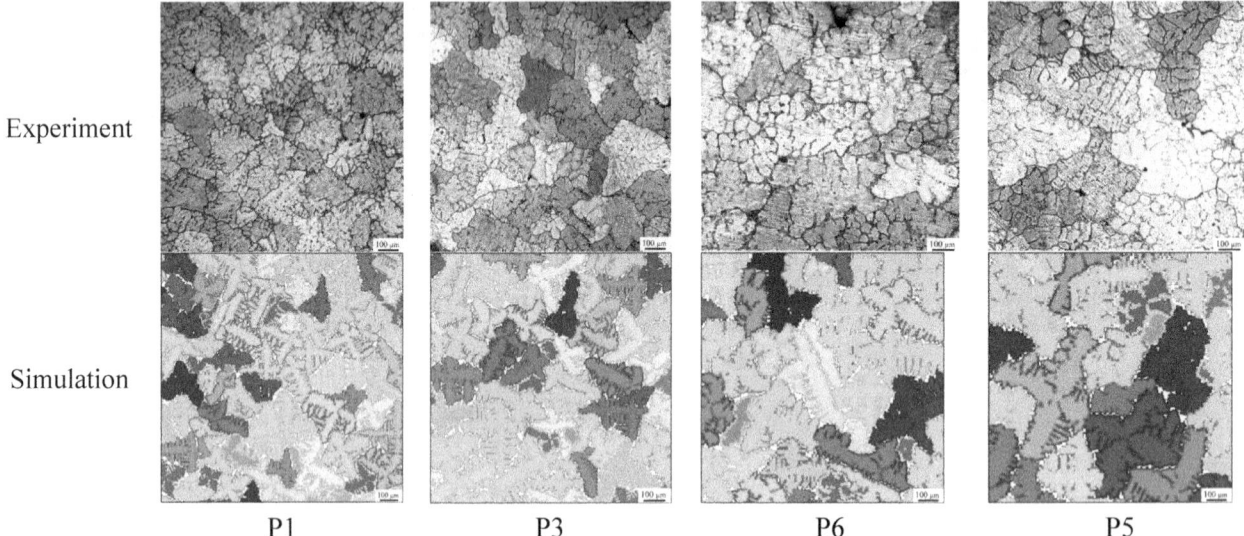

Fig. 5　Comparison of simulated and experimental microstructure for turbine wheel casting

Conclusions

(1) The dendrite growth model was established considering the solute redistribution in both liquid and solid, the solid/liquid interface curvature, the growth anisotropy, reproducing the growth of multi dendrites with different crystallographic orientation. The variation of the dendrite tip velocity and local solute concentration at the solid/liquid interface were analyzed.

(2) A modified CA method coupled with finite difference method was presented to simulate the evolution of Al-7wt%Si alloy microstructure. The grain morphology at different position of the aircraft turbine wheel casting were predicted and compared with experimental results and they agreed with each other well.

References

[1] Gandin Ch-A, Rappaz M. Acta Mater. Vol. 45, (1997), p. 2187.

[2] L. Nastac, Acta Mater. Vol. 47, (1999), p. 4253.

[3] M. F. Zhu, and C. P. Hong. ISIJ Int. Vol. 41, (2001), p. 992.

[4] M. F. Zhu, and C. P. Hong. ISIJ Int. Vol. 42, (2002), p. 520.

[5] L. Beltran-Sanchez, and D. M. Stefanescu. Metall Mater Trans A. Vol. 34, (2003), p. 367.

[6] H. B. Dong, and P. D. Lee. Acta Mater. Vol. 53, (2005), p. 659.

[7] Y. Liu, Q. Y. Xu, and B. C. Liu. Tsinghua Science and Technology. Vol. 11, (2006), p. 495.

[8] C. Beckermann, Q. Li, X. Tong. Science and Technology of Advanced Materials. Vol. 2, (2001), p. 117.

[9] I. Steinbach, C. Beckermann, B. Kauerauf, Q. Li, J. Guo. Acta Mater. Vol. 47, (1999), p. 971.

[10] B Closset, J E Gruzleski. AFS Transaction. Vol. 90, (1982), p. 453.

[11] P. Thévoz, J. L. Desbiolles, and M. Rappaz. Metall Mater Trans A. Vol. 20, (1989), p. 311.

[12] C. A. Gandin, C. Charbon, and M. Rappaz. ISIJ Int. Vol. 35, (1995), p. 651.

[13] L. Beltran-Sanchez, and D. M. Stefanescu. Metall Mater Trans A. Vol. 35, (2004), p. 2471.

20. Dendrite growth modelling of cast magnesium alloy

Z. Y. Liu, Q. Y. Xu and B. C. Liu

Cast magnesium alloy are commonly used in 3C electronic and auto industry. Therefore, microstructure simulation of Mg alloy during solidification process not only has important academic values, but also has strong background in industrial application. Based on the crystallographic feature of magnesium alloy with hexagonal close packed structure, twodimensional growth model of dendrite was established, which employed dendrite shape functions to describe the growing contours of dendrite arms and considered the kinetics of dendrite growth and the coarsening of the secondary dendrite arms. Then a new stochastic simulation method named virtual growth centre calculation model was proposed. Finally, a step shaped sample casting of magnesium alloy was cast to validate the proposed models.

Key words: Modelling, Dendrite growth, Magnesium alloy, Microstructure

Introduction

The performance of cast Mg alloy largely depends on the structure and defects formed in the solidification. It is very important to quantitatively study the influence of different alloy compositions and temperature conditions on grain size and morphology. In addition to experiment, microstructure simulation is also an important and effective research instrument.

Mg alloy has hexagonal close packed (HCP) crystal structure. However, previous simulation mainly focused on the alloys with cube crystal structure, which is unable to reveal the anisotropy of HCP crystal structure and hence can not accurately represent the morphology of grain structure of Mg alloy. Due to the complexity of modelling and experimental validation, the research on the HCP crystal structure is still underway so far. For pure zinc, whose crystal structure is similar to magnesium, the equilibrium shape of the solid in its melt was measured,[1] showing a lens shaped structure. This indicates that instabilities in the basal plane might be also favoured in the growth structure. In the context of phase field modelling of dendritic solidification with non-cubic symmetry, Semoroz et al.[2] deals with the growth of zinc dendrites in coatings of steel. Recently, Eiken adopted a multiphase field model to simulate microstructure evolution of magnesium based alloys and introduced hexagonal anisotropy functions to describe the growth of the HCP magnesium phase.[3] Therefore, for meeting the increasing demand of the research of Mg alloy theory and application, it is necessary to develop a new model to simulate the dendrite growth of cast Mg alloy.

In this paper, the physical model of dendrite growth of Mg alloy was founded. Considering the dendrite growth kinetics and secondary dendrite arm coarsening, a new calculation method was proposed. Finally, the simulated results were compared with the experimental ones.

Mathematical and physical description of models

Physical model of cast Mg alloy

A specific feature of Mg alloys is the hexagonal structure of the crystal lattice. There is a sixfold symmetry in the basal plane and a twofold symmetry in the normal direction to this plane. Apparent anisotropy of grain growth is represented in the crystal growth and the preferential growth direction is <10$\bar{1}$0>. From experimental observations, the sixfold growth in the basal plane seems to dominate the dendritic structure.[3,4] Considering the complex dendritic morphology of actual dendrite grains of Mg alloy, mathematical construction method was used to simply describe the two-dimensional (2D) dendrite profile. The 2D contour of grain is supposed as shown in Fig. 1a, without considering tertiary and above arm branching. The following conic equations were used to represent the contours of primary dendrite arms, as shown in Fig. 1b

$$\begin{cases} x^2 = L_{1a}^2 - \Phi_{1a}^2 y^2 \\ x^2 = L_{1b}^2 - \Phi_{1b}^2 y^2 \\ \left(x\cos\frac{\pi}{3} + y\sin\frac{\pi}{3}\right)^2 = L_{1c}^2 - \Phi_{1c}^2 \left(-x\sin\frac{\pi}{3} + y\cos\frac{\pi}{3}\right)^2 \\ \left(x\cos\frac{\pi}{3} + y\sin\frac{\pi}{3}\right)^2 = L_{1d}^2 - \Phi_{1d}^2 \left(-x\sin\frac{\pi}{3} + y\cos\frac{\pi}{3}\right)^2 \\ \left(x\cos\frac{2\pi}{3} + y\sin\frac{2\pi}{3}\right)^2 = L_{1e}^2 - \Phi_{1e}^2 \left(-x\sin\frac{2\pi}{3} + y\cos\frac{2\pi}{3}\right)^2 \\ \left(x\cos\frac{2\pi}{3} + y\sin\frac{2\pi}{3}\right)^2 = L_{1f}^2 - \Phi_{1f}^2 \left(-x\sin\frac{2\pi}{3} + y\cos\frac{2\pi}{3}\right)^2 \end{cases} \quad (1)$$

L_{1a}, L_{1b}, L_{1c}, L_{1d}, L_{1e} and L_{1f} are the primary dendrite radius along six directions respectively, which are related to the growth velocity of dendrite tip and solved by KGT model.[5,6] Φ_{1a}, Φ_{1b}, Φ_{1c}, Φ_{1d}, Φ_{1e} and Φ_{1f} are the shape factors related to the solid fraction of grain.[7,8] θ is the inclination of primary dendrite arm relative to x axis. The similar equations were used to represent the contours of secondary dendrite arms, as shown in Fig. 1c.

Secondary dendrite spacing model

Kattamis et al.[9] had made quantitative analysis on the radial melting model. The time t_c that melting the thinner arms takes can be presented as follows

$$t_c = \frac{\Delta T_s}{\dot{T}} = \frac{1}{16} \frac{\rho \Delta H m_L C_L (1-k)}{\sigma T_L D_L} \lambda_2^3 \quad (2)$$

where λ_2 is the secondary dendrite arm spacing (SDAS), σ is the surface energy, C_L is the liquid concentration among the secondary dendrite arms, D_L is the solute diffusion coefficient, m_L is the liquidus slope, k is the solute partition coefficient, ΔH is the melting latent heat, T_L is the liquidus temperature, ρ is the density of the alloy, ΔT_s is the temperature span of non-equilibrium solidification, $\dot{T}$ is the cooling rate. Thus, the formula about λ_2 can be deduced as follows

$$\lambda_2 = \left[\frac{16\sigma T_L D_L \Delta T_s}{\rho \Delta H m_L C_L (1-k) \dot{T}}\right]^{1/3} \quad (3)$$

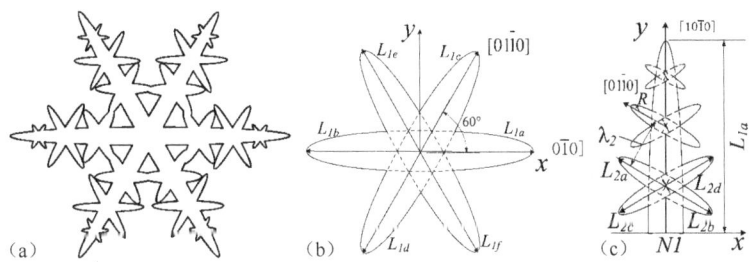

(a) profile of dendrite; (b) primary dendrite arms; (c) secondary dendrite arms

Fig. 1 Profile of dendrite grain and growth radius of dendrite arms

Calculation model and algorithm

To simulate the dendrite growth of HCP crystal, virtual growth centre calculation model was proposed. Virtual growth centre is not actual nucleus, but supposed growth centre of primary or secondary dendrite arm in different preferential growth directions in numerical calculation. Figure 2 shows the schematic of virtual growth centre model.

As can be seen in Fig. 2, circle signed N denotes the original nucleus, hollow white circle denotes the node of cell and solid black circle denotes the virtual growth centre in certain preferential growth direction of original nucleus. The phase state of every cell is liquid at the very beginning of the simulation with the phase state sign $P_i = 0$. At certain time t_0, suppose that a grain of primary phase nucleates at N, whose inclination of [10$\bar{1}$0] crystallography orientation relative to x axis is θ. Herein, this cell is assigned as original nucleus cell, whose phase state sign is changed to $P_N = 1$ and inclination is θ. Taking into account of anisotropy growth, six virtual growth centres N1-N6 with different growth directions are derived from the original nucleus cell N.

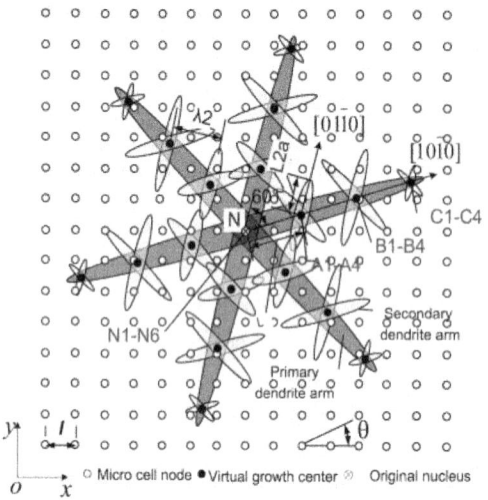

Fig. 2 Schematic of virtual growth centre model of dendrites

Taking the growth centre N1 of primary dendrite arm in $[10\overline{1}0]$ direction as example. At the time t_1, the growth length $L_{1a}^{t_1}$ of primary dendrite is given as

$$L_{1a}^{t_1} = \int_{t_0}^{t_1} v_{1a}[\Delta T_{1a}(\tau)]d\tau \quad (4)$$

v_{1a} is the growth velocity of primary dendrite tip along $[10\overline{1}0]$ direction, which is a function of local undercooling ΔT_{1a}. The relationship between v_{1a} and ΔT_{1a} is given by growth kinetics model. After time Δt, the growth tip will capture the ahead cell and ΔT_{1a} ($t_1+\Delta t$) will be calculated by the temperature of new captured cell.

After several time step, assuming at the time t_n, the growth length of primary dendrite arm from N1 reaches the SDAS λ_2 which is related to cooling rate. Here, four new virtual growth centres will generate on this primary dendrite arm, which are denoted by A(1-4), as shown in Fig. 2. Each of them represents the virtual growth centre of secondary dendrite arm in one of the four preferential growth directions. Taking the neighbour cell nearest to virtual growth centre as growth centre cell, the phase state sign becomes $P_A = 1$ and the inclination of crystallographic orientation can be calculated by that of original nucleus. Taking A1 in $[01\overline{1}0]$ orientation for example, the inclination of $[01\overline{1}0]$ relative to x axis can be presented as $\theta[01\overline{1}0] = \theta + \pi/3$. The nearest cell is selected as growth centre cell and the growth length $L_{2a}^{t_2}$ of secondary dendrite arm at time t_2 is evaluated by

$$L_{2a}^{t_2} = \int_{t_n}^{t_2} v_{2a}[\Delta T_{2a}(\tau)]d\tau \quad (5)$$

v_{2a} is the growth velocity of secondary dendrite tip along $[01\overline{1}0]$ direction, which is a function of local undercooling ΔT_{2a} at the tip of secondary dendrite arm. Following the same capture rule, the growth process of the primary and secondary dendrite arms along other directions can also be calculated, and finally the whole dendrite grain of primary phase will be formed.

Simulation results and experiment validation

Experiment method

In this experiment, step shaped sand casting of magnesium alloy is used to study the influence of different cooling rates on the final microstructure. The profile of the step shaped casting and positions where the samples were taken from is shown in Fig. 3. AZ91D alloy is adopted, pouring temperature is 1023K, room temperature is 298K, and pouring time is 5s. Figure 4 shows the actual step shaped casting including the runner system. The thickness of the four steps is 5, 10, 15 and 20mm respectively. The four samples were cut from different steps of the casting and the positions 1-4 are shown in Figs. 3 and 4.

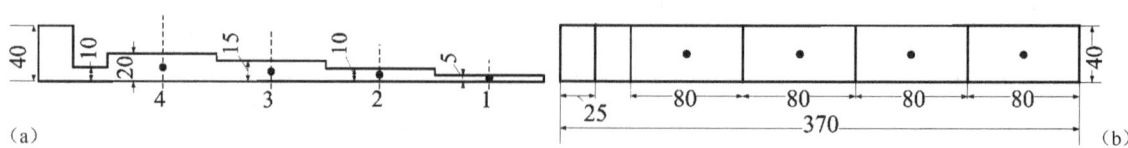

(a) front elevation; (b) planform

Fig. 3 Sample positions on step shaped casting (mm)

Fig. 4 Actual step shaped casting and sample positions

Simulation parameters

With the same experimental parameters, the simulation of 2D dendrite growth was carried on with proposed models. Partial simulation parameters are as follows: macromesh size is 3.5×3.5mm, microcell size is 7×7μm, thermal conductivity factor is 80W · m^{-1} · K^{-1}, specific heat capacity is 1320J · kg^{-1} · K^{-1}, latent heat is 6.7513×10^8 J · m^{-3}.

Comparison of simulation and experimental results

Figure 5a-d shows the comparison of experimental micrographs of different positions, and the corresponding simulation results are shown in Fig. 5e-h. As shown in Fig. 5, the simulated dendritic morphology is similar to that of experimental micrographs. With increasing thickness of the steps from 1 to 4, the grain size of the corresponding sample varies from small to big and the secondary dendritic arms varies from thin to thick. The reason is the different cooling rates in the casting due to the different thickness and location of the steps.

Table 1 shows a comparison of experimental results of λ_1 and λ_2 and those simulated. From sample 1 to sample 4, λ_1 increases with decreasing cooling rate as well as λ_2. In Table 1, the comparison shows that the experimental results of average grain diameter and SDAS are in good agreement with those of simulation.

Full developed dendrite morphology appears in the sand casting, especially for the sample 4 with the lowest cooling rate. Typical dendrite morphology at two positions of sample 4 is shown in Fig. 6, which represents obvious sixfold symmetry of the dendrite grain.

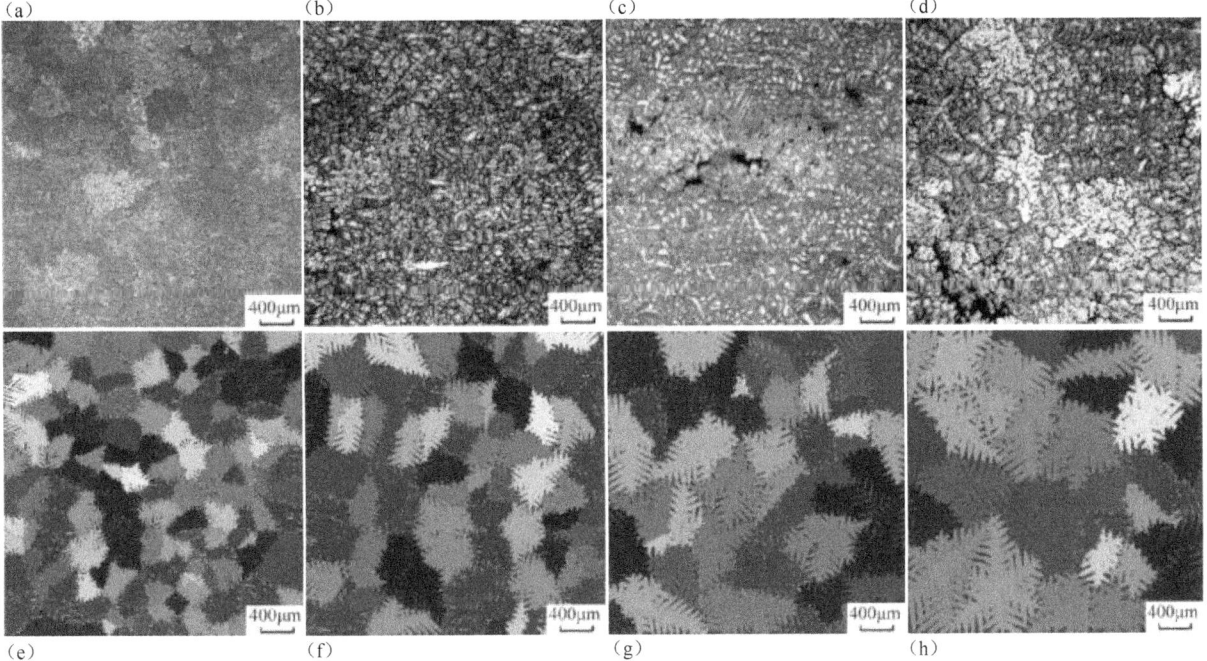

(a) micrograph 1; (b) micrograph 2; (c) micrograph 3; (d) micrograph 4; (e) simulated result 1; (f) simulated result 2; (g) simulated result 3; (h) simulated result 4

Fig. 5 Comparison of experimental micrographs and modelling results for positions 1-4 on step shaped casting

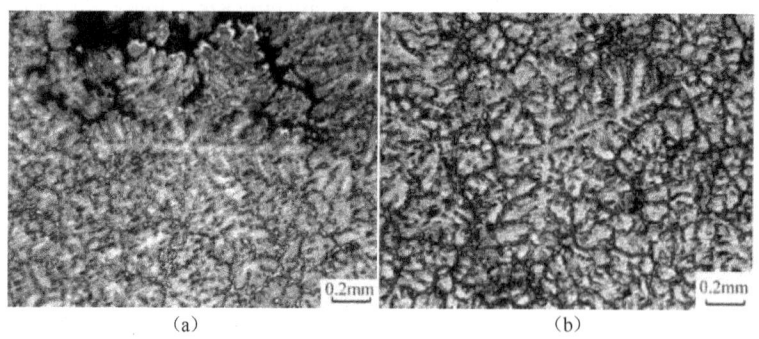

(a) position 1; (b) position 2

Fig. 6 Typical dendrite morphology in sample 4

Table 1 Average grain diameter λ_1 and SDAS λ_2

Sample	λ_1, mm		λ_2, mm	
	Experiment	Simulation	Experiment	Simulation
1	0.307	0.322	0.038	0.042
2	0.398	0.385	0.061	0.058
3	0.494	0.502	0.072	0.067
4	0.582	0.569	0.084	0.089

Conclusions

1. A new stochastic simulation method named virtual growth centre calculation model was proposed to deal with the anisotropic growth of HCP crystal.

2. A step shaped sample casting of magnesium alloy was cast to validate the proposed models. The experimental results verified the sixfold symmetric dendritic morphology of Mg alloy and the simulated results predicted the different microstructures at four steps successfully.

Currently, the experience and information of the growth morphology with HCP structure are very deficient, as well as the integrated theory system. Therefore, the further modification and development of the models established in this paper are continuing.

Acknowledgements

The research was sponsored by National Basic Research Program of China (2005CB724105) and National Natural Science Foundation of China (10477010). Based on a presentation at SP07, the 5th Decennial Conference on Solidification Processing, organised by the University of Sheffield, UK on 23-25 July 2007.

References

[1] A. Passerone and N. Eustathopoulos: *Acta Mater.*, 1982, **30**, 1349-1356.

[2] A. Semoroz, S. Henry and M. Rappaz: *Mater. Trans. A*, 2000, **30A**, 487-495.

[3] J. Eiken, B. Bottger and I. Steinbach: in 'Modeling of casting, welding and advanced solidification processes XI', (ed. C.-A. Gandin and M. Bellet), 489-496; 2006, Warrendale, PA, TMS.

[4] A. K. Dahle, Y. C. Lee, M. D. Nave, P. L. Schaffer and D. H. St. John: *J. Light Met.*, 2001, (1), 61-72.

[5] W. Kurz, B. Giovanola and R. Trivedi: *Acta Metall.*, 1986, **34**, (5), 823-830.

[6] M. Rappaz and P. Thévoz: *Acta Metall.*, 1987, **35**, (7), 1487-1497.

[7] I. Steinbach, C. Beckermann, B. Kauerauf, J. Guo and Q. Li: *Acta Mater.*, 1999, **47**, (3), 971-982.

[8] Q. Y. Xu, W. M. Feng and B. C. Liu: *J. Mater. Sci. Technol.*, 2003, **19**, (5), 391-394.

[9] T. Z. Kattamis, J. C. Coughlin and M. C. Flemings: *Trans. Met. Soc. AIME*, 1967, **239**, 1504.

21. Simulation of Magnesium Alloy AZ91D Microstructure Using Modified Cellular Automaton Method

HUO Liang (霍亮), *LI Bin* (李斌), *SHI Yufeng* (石玉峰), *XU Qingyan* (许庆彦),
HAN Zhiqiang (韩志强), *LIU Baicheng* (柳百成)

Key Laboratory for Advanced Materials Processing Technology of the Ministry of Education,
Department of Mechanical Engineering, Tsinghua University, Beijing 100084, China

Abstract: A two-dimensional modified cellular automaton model was developed to simulate the solidification process of magnesium alloy. The stochastic nucleation, solute redistribution, and growth anisotropy effects were taken into account in the present model. The model was used to simulate the grain size of magnesium alloy AZ91D for various cooling rates during the solidification process. To quantitatively validate the current model, metallographic experiments were carried out on specimens obtained from sand mold AZ91D step castings. The metallographic results agree well with the prediction results. The current model can be used to accurately predict the grain sizes of cast AZ91D magnesium alloy.

Key words: magnesium alloy; AZ91D; microstructure; numerical simulation; cellular automaton method

Introduction

Magnesium alloys are widely used in various industrial fields, such as transportation, aviation and aerospace, and mobile electric devices, due to their superior properties such as high specific strength and stiffness[1,2]. However, the performance of cast magnesium parts is strongly influenced by the as-cast microstructure formed during solidification, for example, the grainsize, secondary arm spacing, and micro-segregation. Thus, precise control of the solidification process is necessary to get the intended properties. Numerical simulations are an effective, cost-effective method to predict the final microstructure and solute field during solidification to optimize the processing parameters and to predict the magnesium casting performance.

The cellular automaton (CA) method has been widely used to simulate solidification microstructures[3,4]; however, it has not been widely applied to magnesium alloy systems. Liu et al.[5] used a geometric shapebased CA method to represent the two- and three- dimensional dendritic morphology of magnesium alloy. Fu et al.[6] represented the six-fold symmetry of magnesium AM50, AZ91D, and AZ31 using a special neighborhood configuration in CA cells.

In the present work, a modified CA model is used to simulate the microstructure evolution of the AZ91D magnesium alloy during solidification. The stochastic nucleation, competitive growth of many grains with different orientations, solute redistribution and diffusion during dendrite solidification, and growth anisotropy effects are taken into account in the model. The grain sizes for different cooling rates are predicted by the current model. Specimens obtained from sand mold step castings of AZ91D magnesium alloy are used to validate the model.

1 Model Description

Since the content of Zn, Mn, and other elements in the AZ91D magnesium alloy are less than 1%, the alloy system is assumed to be a Mg-Al binary system. During solidification, the primary α phase dendrites first stretch freely in the undercooled melt until the den-

---

本文刊登于《TSINGHUA SCIENCE AND TECHNOLOGY》, 2009, 14 (3): 307-312.

drite arms collide. According to the equilibrium phase diagram, the AZ91D alloy composition does not cross the eutectic line (the maximum solubility of Al in Mg is 12.7%). However, in real castings the eutectic β phase exists at the grain boundaries[7], which indicates that the solidification process of Mg castings is a nonequilibrium process. As the solidification proceeds, solute concentration continues to increase. When the temperature falls below the eutectic point, the rest of the liquid transforms into the eutectic phase. The solidification process of AZ91D is illustrated in Fig. 1.

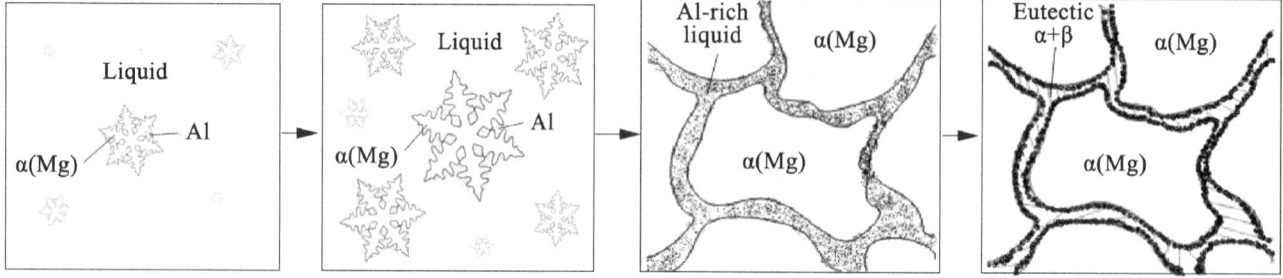

Fig. 1 AZ91D magnesium alloy solidification process

1.1 Energy equation

The temperature field in the calculation domain was obtained by solving the macro-scale transient energy equation by the finite difference method (FDM)[8]:

$$\rho c \frac{\partial T}{\partial t} = \lambda \left(\frac{\partial T^2}{\partial x^2} + \frac{\partial T^2}{\partial y^2} + \frac{\partial T^2}{\partial z^2} \right) + \rho L \frac{\partial f_S}{\partial t} \quad (1)$$

where ρ is the density, c is the specific heat, T is the temperature, λ is the thermal conductivity, L is the latent heat, f_S is the solid fraction, and t is the time.

1.2 Nucleation model

Gaussian-distribution-based continuous nucleation model was used to model the real heterogeneous nucleation process during solidfication[9]. The distribution of the nucleation density as a function of the undercooling was decided by

$$\frac{\partial N}{\partial (\Delta T')} = \frac{N_s}{\sqrt{2\pi} \Delta T_\sigma} \exp\left[-\frac{(\Delta T' - \Delta T_N)^2}{2(\Delta T_\sigma)^2} \right] \quad (2)$$

where $\Delta T'$ is the undercooling of liquid, ΔT_N is the average undercooling, ΔT_σ is the standard curvature undercooling, N_s is the number of heterogeneous nucleation sites, and N is the total number of nuclei.

The total number of nuclei was calculated by

$$N(\Delta T) = \int_0^{\Delta T} [1 - f_S(\Delta T')] \frac{\partial N}{\partial (\Delta T')} \mathrm{d}(\Delta T') \quad (3)$$

1.3 Solute redistribution and diffusion

Since the solute diffusion in magnesium alloy lags far behind the thermal diffusion (always several orders of magnitude), the solute diffusion can be assumed to occur only within the macro-scale lattice (i.e., the calculation domain is an isolated system for the solute diffusion). Therefore, the solute diffusion fields in the liquid and solid are governed by

$$\frac{\partial C_L}{\partial t} = D_L \left(\frac{\partial^2 C_L}{\partial x^2} + \frac{\partial^2 C_L}{\partial y^2} \right) \quad (4)$$

$$\frac{\partial C_S}{\partial t} = D_S \left(\frac{\partial^2 C_S}{\partial x^2} + \frac{\partial^2 C_S}{\partial y^2} \right) \quad (5)$$

where C_L and C_S are the liquid and solid solute concentrations and D_L and D_S are the liquid and solid solute diffusion coefficients.

In the alloy system, the solute concentration field determines the dendrite morphology rather than the temperature field. The present model includes the curvature and anisotropy effects in the solute redistribution model with the concentrations at the solid-liquid interface represented by

$$C_L^* = C_0 + (T^* - T_L + \Gamma \bar{k} f(\varphi, \theta))/m_L \quad (6)$$

$$C_S^* = k_0 C_L^* \quad (7)$$

where T^* is the equilibrium temperature and C_L^* and C_S^* are the equilibrium liquid and solid concentrations at the interface, T_L is the equilibrium liquidus temperature,

Γ is the Gibbs-Thomson coefficient, m_L is the slope of the liquidus, $\bar{k}$ is the interface curvature, $f(\varphi, \theta)$ is the anisotropy function, and k_0 is the solute redistribution coefficient.

1.4 Growth model

The interface velocity in a cell obtained by solving the solute conservation equation is given by

$$v_n^* C_L^* (1-k) = D_L \left(\frac{\partial C_L}{\partial x} + \frac{\partial C_L}{\partial y} \right) - D_S \left(\frac{\partial C_S}{\partial x} + \frac{\partial C_S}{\partial y} \right) \quad (8)$$

where v_n^* represents the normal velocity of the interface.

2 Simulation Algorithm

2.1 Stochastic nucleation

At the beginning of the simulation, all the CA cells were assumed to be liquid and their state indexes were assigned to zero. As the nucleation proceeds, some cells experienced nucleation with their indexes changed to an integer larger than zero, n, which also reflects the preferential growth direction.

The location of the nucleated cells was randomly assigned by producing random numbers in the calculation domain to represent the stochastic heterogeneous nucleation process in real castings.

2.2 Growth algorithm and interface determination

The interface velocity was obtained by solving Eq (8) using the finite difference method. As shown in Fig. 2, the interface velocity in the x direction v_x, was calculated by Eq. (9). The velocity determination in the y direction was similar.

$$v_x^{(i,j)} = \frac{D_L}{\Delta h(1-k)} \cdot$$
$$\left[\left(1 - \frac{C_L^{(i-1,j)}}{C_L^{*(i,j)}} \right) f_L^{(i-1,j)} + \left(1 - \frac{C_L^{(i+1,j)}}{C_L^{*(i,j)}} \right) f_L^{(i+1,j)} \right] +$$
$$\frac{kD_S}{\Delta h(1-k)} \left[\left(1 - \frac{C_S^{(i-1,j)}}{kC_L^{*(i,j)}} \right) f_S^{(i-1,j)} + \left(1 - \frac{C_S^{(i+1,j)}}{kC_L^{*(i,j)}} \right) f_S^{(i+1,j)} \right]$$
$$(9)$$

In the traditional CA method, when a cell is captured, its state immediately turns from liquid to solid.

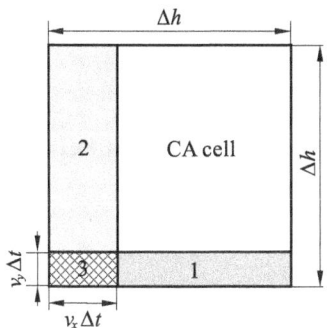

Fig. 2 Relationship between interface velocity and solid fraction in one CA cell

Even though the cell is quite small, commonly dozens of micro-meters, it has a specific volume, so the actual physical procedure is that the cell turns from solid to semi-solid, then to fully solid after some time. To represent this physical procedure, a solid fraction factor is assigned to each cell to indicate how much of the cell is solidified[10]. This solid fraction is calculated as

$$\delta f_S = \frac{\delta t}{\Delta h} \left(v_x + v_y - v_x v_y \frac{\delta t}{\Delta h} \right) \quad (10)$$

$$f_S^{t+\delta t} = f_S^t + \delta f_S \quad (11)$$

where v_x and v_y are the growth velocities along the x and y axes and Δh is the length of the CA cell.

Thus, the present modified CA model calculates the solid fraction in each CA cell rather than the explicit interface position which can be related to v_x, v_y, and f_S in each interface cell.

2.3 Calculation of interface curvature and anisotropy

The solidification front curvature causes capillary effects which alter the liquidus temperature and cause curvature undercooling. In addition, the interface curvature also affects the shape of the dendrite tip.

The interface curvature was calculated by[11,12]

$$\bar{k} = \frac{1}{\Delta h} \left[1 - 2 \frac{f_S + \sum_{k=1}^{N} f_S(k)}{N+1} \right] \quad (12)$$

where N is the total number of neighboring cells.

The surface tension anisotropy was obtained from[4,13]

$$f(\varphi, \theta) = 1 + \gamma \cdot \cos[4(\varphi - \theta)] \quad (13)$$

$$\varphi = \cos^{-1} \left(\frac{\partial f_S / \partial x}{\sqrt{(\partial f_S / \partial x)^2 + (\partial f_S / \partial y)^2}} \right) \quad (14)$$

where θ is the preferential crystallographic orientation angle, φ is the growth angle, and γ is the anisotropy coefficient.

3 Simulation Results and Experimental Validation

3.1 Experimental methods

AZ91D step-shaped sand-mold castings were poured to study the influence of different cooling rates on the final microstructure.

The profile of the step-shaped casting and the positions where the samples were taken are shown in Fig. 3. The thicknesses of the four steps were 5, 10, 15, and 20mm. Four samples with cross sections of 8mm×8mm were cut from the center of each step. The experimental conditions are listed in Table 1.

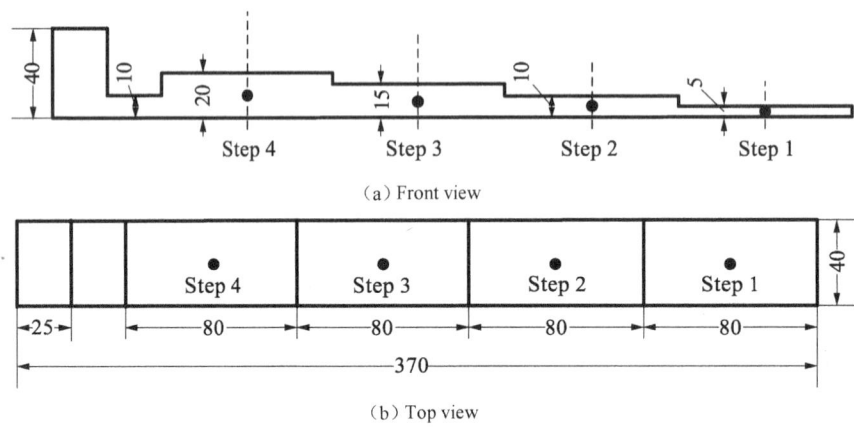

Fig. 3 Sample positions on the step-shaped casting (mm)

Table 1 Experimental conditions

Material	Pouring temperature (K)	Environmental temperature (K)	Pouring time(s)
AZ91D	1023	298	5

3.2 Simulation parameters

Some of the simulation parameters for the simulation are shown in Table 2.

Table 2 Simulation parameters

Macro mesh size (mm^2)	1×1
Micro cell size (μm^2)	2×2
Liquidus temperature (K)	868
Solidus temperature (K)	743
Eutectic temperature (K)	710
Thermal conductivity (W·m^{-1}·K^{-1})	80
Specific heat capacity (kJ·kg^{-1}·K^{-1})	1.32
Mass density (kg·m^{-3})	1810
Latent heat (kJ·kg)	373

3.3 Comparison and validation

Figure 4 compares the experimental micrographs and simulation results for the four steps.

The grain sizes of the samples in the different steps vary due to the different cooling rates, as can be seen in both the experimental micrographs and the simulation results. The thinnest step has the fastest cooling rate, which results in the finest grains. As the cooling rate decreases, the nuclei density and interface velocity decrease, which results in coarser grains.

The simulated and experimental grain sizes are compared in Table 3 which shows that the simulation results agree well with the experimental data.

Table 3 Comparison of experimental and simulated grain sizes

Position	Simulated grain size (μm)	Experimental grain size (μm)
Step 1	298	307
Step 2	384	398
Step 3	511	494
Step 4	602	582

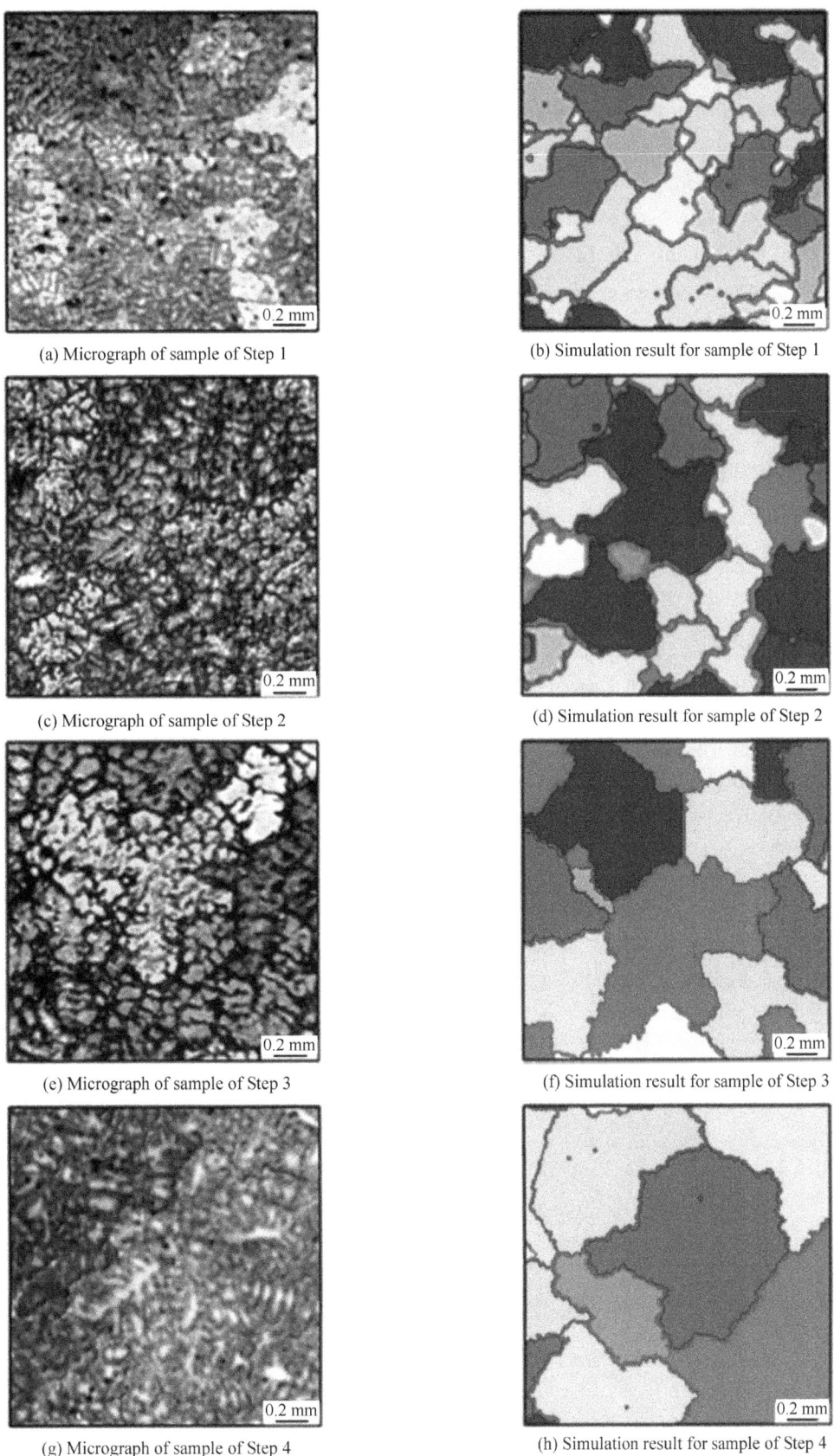

Fig. 4 Comparison of experimental and simulation results

4 Conclusions

(1) A microstructure evolution model for cast AZ91D magnesium alloys was developed using a modified cellular automaton method.

(2) The model includes stochastic nucleation, competitive growth of many grains with different orientations, solute redistribution, interface curvature, and anisotropic growth.

(3) The predicted grain sizes for the AZ91D magnesium alloy step castings agree well with experimental results.

(4) The modified CA-based model can be used to predict the grain sizes of the AZ91D magnesium alloy.

References

[1] Michael M A, Hugh B. Magnesium and Magnesium Alloys (ASM Handbook). New York: ASM International, 1999: 3-6.

[2] Mordike B L, Eert T. Magnesium properties—Applications & potential. *Mater. Sci. Eng.*, 2001, **A302**: 37-45.

[3] Li B, Xu Q Y, Xiong Y C, et al. Experiment and numerical simulation of microstructure of ZL114A alloy in low pressure casting. *Special Casting & Nonferrous Alloy*, 2007, **10** (27): 759-762. (in Chinese)

[4] Li B, Xu Q Y, Liu B C. Establishment of nucleation model and microstructure simulation of Al-Si alloy for low pressure die casting. In: Mater. Sci. & Tec. Detroit: Grayden Press, 2007: 367-376.

[5] Liu Z Y, Xu Q Y, Liu B C. Microstructure simulation of die casting AZ91D alloy. In: Materials Science Forum, Beijing International Materials Week. Beijing, China, 2006: 109-112.

[6] Fu Z N, Xu Q Y, Xiong S M. Numerical simulation on dendrite growth process of Mg alloy using cellular automaton methods based on probability capturing model. *The Chinese Journal of Nonferrous Metals*, 2007, **17** (10): 1567-1573. (in Chinese)

[7] Song G, Atrens A. Corrosion mechanisms of magnesium alloys. *Adv. Eng. Mater.*, 1999, **1** (1): 11-33.

[8] Xiong S M, Xu Q Y, Kang J W. Modeling and Simulation Technology in Casting Process. Beijing: China Machine Press, 2004: 133-170. (in Chinese)

[9] Thévoz Ph, Desbiolles J L, Rappaz M. Modeling of equiaxed microstructures formation in casting. *Metall. Trans. A*, 1989, (20): 311-322.

[10] Dilthey U, Pavlik V. Numerical simulation of dendritic morphology and grain growth with modified cellular automata. In: Thomas B G, Beckermann C, eds. Proc. of the Modeling of Casting: Welding and Advance Solidification Processes (Ⅷ). TMS, Warrendale, PA, 1998: 589-596.

[11] Sasikumar R, Sreenivisan R. Two dimensional simulation of dendrite morphology. *Acta Mater.*, 1994, **42** (7): 2381-2386.

[12] Nastac L. Numerical modeling of solidification morphologies and segregation patterns in cast dendritic alloys. *Acta Mater.*, 1999, **47** (17): 4253-4262.

[13] Beltran-Sanchez L, Stefanescu D M. Growth of solutal dendrites: A cellular automaton model and its quantitative capabilities. *Metall. Mater. Trans.*, 2003, (34A): 367-382.

22. Cellular automaton simulation of three-dimensional dendrite growth in Al-7Si-Mg ternary aluminum alloys

Rui Chen, Qingyan Xu, Baicheng Liu

Key Laboratory for Advanced Materials Processing Technology, Ministry of Education,
School of Materials Science and Engineering, Tsinghua University, Beijing 100084, China

ARTICLE INFO

Key words: Al-7Si-Mg alloy Cellular automaton Three dimensions Crystallographic orientation Dendrite growth

Abstract: Due to the extensive applications in the automotive and aerospace industries of Al-7Si-Mg casting alloys, an understanding of their dendrite microstructural formation in three dimensions is of great importance in order to control the desirable microstructure, so as to modify the performance of castings. For this reason, a three-dimensional cellular automaton model (3-D CA) allowing for the prediction of dendrite growth of ternary alloys is presented. The growth kinetics of the solid/liquid (S/L) interface is calculated based on the solutal equilibrium approach. This proposed model introduces a modified decentered octahedron algorithm for neighborhood tracking, in order to eliminate the effects of mesh dependency on dendrite growth. The thermodynamic and kinetic data needed in the simulations are obtained through coupling with the Pandat software package in combination with thermodynamic/kinetic/equilibrium phase diagram calculation databases. The solute interactions between alloying elements are considered in the model. The model was first used to simulate the Al-7Si dendrite, followed by a validation using theoretical predictions. The influence of Mg content on the dendrite growth dynamics and dendrite morphologies was investigated. Also, the model was applied to Al-7Si-0.5Mg dendrite simulation both with and without a consideration of solute interactions between the Si and Mg alloying elements and the effects on dendrite growth process was analyzed using the simulation results. This model was finally used in order to simulate the dendrite growth in different crystallographic orientations in an Al-7Si-0.36Mg ternary alloy during polycrystalline solidification, resulting in a predicted secondary dendrite arm spacing (SDAS) and dendrite volume fraction data that show a reasonable agreement with experimental results. The single dendrite and polycrystalline growth simulations effectively demonstrate the capability of this model in predicting the three-dimensional dendrite microstructure of ternary alloys.

1. Introduction

Due to an excellent combination of castability, high corrosion resistance, and comprehensive mechanical properties, Al-Si casting alloys play an important role in the automotive and aerospace industries as structural components[1-3]. The addition of small amounts of the alloying element Mg into Al-Si alloys can alter their solidification behavior, and can induce significant age-hardening behavior through Mg_2Si precipitates, and provides a good engineering alloy[4]. The most widely used Al-Si alloys are the A356 and A357 alloys containing 0.3-0.7 wt% Mg and an as-cast microstructure mainly comprised primary α-Al dendrite and eutectic phase. It is generally accepted that the primary α-Al dendrite microstructure features, such as morphology, size and composition distribution are of great importance in determining the quality of the final casting. Although extensive experimental studies have been carried out on these features, most of the results obtained have been limited to two-dimensions, as an investigation of complex dendrite microstructure in three dimensions using experimental approaches such as X-ray tomography is still a challenge, due to the fact that they require extremely high quality equipment and samples.

Advancements in computer technology in recent decades have allowed the use of numerical modeling and simulation as powerful tools for developing our understanding of dendrite formation during solidification[5-9]. Many efforts have been made to develop numerical models for 3-D dendrite simulation; among these, 3-D phase-field (PF) models and 3-D cellular automaton (CA) models are the most promising methods for describing 3-D dendrite features comparable to those observed in experiment. Recently, several studies have carried out for the comparisons for simulations of dendrite growth between PF and CA models[10-12]. Phase field modeling is a powerful method that can precisely reproduce the dendrite interface, as it describes the solid/liquid (S/L) interface through the introduction of a smooth transition variation in an order parameter φ, avoiding explicit tracking of the S/L interface[13,14]. PF models have been successfully applied in order to quantitatively simulate three-dimensional dendrite growth, and the dendrite morphologies and tip growth behavior were investigated and showed a good agreement with theoretical predictions[15,16]. Although some techniques such as the parallel computing and adaptive mesh refinement methods have been developed in order to enhance computational efficiency, 3-D dendrite growth simulation using PF method is still a challenge, as it requires significant computational resources, especially when examining the case of 3-D polycrystalline solidification processes. The cellular automaton method is another computational approach that can reveal a wide range of micro/meso-scale dendrite features, and has the advantage of a larger mesh size and much higher computational efficiency compared with PF models, and so it is extensively used in the investigation of dendrite growth[5]. In the last decade, there have been attempts to develop 3-D CA models and algorithms for use in dendrite growth simulation. A three-dimensional CA model coupled with finite element (FE) in order to obtain the non-uniform temperature field, originally proposed by Rappaz and Gandin[17], was developed to simulate grain growth during solidification.

Lee and co-workers[6] developed a 3-D CA model in order to simulate the dendrite growth of binary alloys based on solute diffusion-controlled conditions, while neglecting the influence of the anisotropy of interfacial energy. The effects of grid anisotropy were eliminated using a decentered octahedron growth technique, allowing the model to simulate dendrite growth in different crystallographic orientations. This model was later extended in order to study fluid motion effects on 3-D dendrite morphology[18]. Yu and Xu[19] presented a mathematical model for 3-D dendrite simulation, in which the different crystallographic orientations were generated through a continuous artificial correction of capturing directions. Pan and Zhu[20] developed a 3-D sharp interface model to simulate the dendrite growth of binary alloys, based on the local solutal equilibrium approach used to calculate the evolution of the S/L interface. In order to describe the specific crystallographic orientation of dendrite growth in three dimensions, the weight mean curvature (wmc) together with the effect of the anisotropic surface energy was presented. Eshraghi et al.[21] introduced a solute-driven 3-D dendrite growth CA model using the lattice Boltzmann (LB) technique in order to calculate the transport phenomena. Using this model, the effect of the anisotropic surface energy on the dendrite growth kinetics and morphologies was studied. In order to reduce the mesh induced anisotropy caused by CA capture rules, a 3-D CA model coupled with a limited neighbor solid fraction, referred to as the LNSE method, was developed by Wei et al.[22], as this model was suitable for use in describing the solidification of a pure substance. In this model, two interface free energy anisotropy parameters were employed in order to simulate the dendrite orientation selection. Zhao et al.[23] developed a new tracking neighborhood rule forsimulating 3-D dendrite growth in different crystallographic orientations, while the migration of the S/L interface is determined using the phase transition driving force obtained from a thermodynamic database. Zhang et al.[24] recently developed a cellular automaton model for describing dendrite growth in multi-component alloys in which the interactions between alloying elements were considered through a coupling of kinetic and thermodynamic calculations.

Most of 3-D CA models mentioned above are confined to describing the single dendrite of binary alloys with well-defined crystallographic axes. In practice however, most commercial alloys are multicomponent, containing three or more elements, and their solidification process involves complex polycrystalline growth in different crystallographic orientations. Hence, the existing work on three-dimensional dendrite simulation of multicomponent alloys is still far from satisfactory and further efforts are still required. The objective of the present study is to investigate the dendrite growth process of Al-7Si-Mg alloys by establishing a 3-D CA model for ternary alloys. The thermodynamic and kinetic data needed to describe the dendrite growth are obtained using the Pandat software package in combination with thermodynamic/kinetic/equilibrium phase diagram calculation databases[25]. The evolution of the S/L interface is calculated based on the local solutal equilibrium approach. In order to describe 3-D dendrite growth in different crystallographic orientations, this model adopts the modified decentered octahedron algorithm for neighborhood tracking. The model was first used to simulate binary dendrite, and then it was validated by comparing the simulation results with theoretical predictions, after which the model was then used to simulate single dendrite and the polycrystalline growth of Al-7Si-Mg alloys in three dimensions.

2. Model description and numerical algorithm

The first solid phase of Al-7Si-Mg alloys precipitated from the melt is that of α-Al dendrite, followed by (α-Al+Si) eutectic and (α-Al+Si+Mg$_2$Si). The dendrite microstructure evolutions of Al-7Si-Mg alloys are simulated by the 3-D CA model. In order to simulate 3-D dendrite growth, a cubic calculation domain is uniformly divided into an orthogonal arrangement of cubic cells, in which each cell is characterized using variables such as temperature, solute composition, solid fraction, and crystallographic orientation. The calculation starts with all the cells in the liquid state, and the solid seeds with randomly determined preferential growth orientations are assigned in the domain. Since the local interface equilibrium composition of an interfacial cell is larger than its actual local liquid composition, in order to strive for equilibrium, part of the liquid in the cell solidifies to reject the redundant solute. For the sake of simplicity, the temperature of the calculation domain was assumed to be uniform.

2.1 Solute distribution calculation including solute interaction

In order to describe mass transfer of Al-7Si-Mg ternary system, the solute fields of Si and Mg need to be calculated separately. Without considering natural and forced convection, solute diffusion within the entire domain is calculated based on the following equation

$$\frac{\partial w_i^\phi}{\partial t} + \nabla \cdot J_i = w_i^\phi (1-k_i) \frac{\partial f_S}{\partial t} \qquad (1)$$

where w is the composition with a superscript ϕ, denoting the liquid or solid phase, and a subscript i, denoting the alloying element Si or Mg. k_i is the composition and temperature dependent equilibrium partition coefficient which is obtained through coupling with the data from equilibrium phase diagram calculation databases. f_S is the solid fraction. J_i is the diffusion flux of element i, given by the Fick-Onsager law as:

$$J_i = -\sum_{j=\text{Si,Mg}} D_{ij}^\phi \nabla w_j^\phi \qquad (2)$$

where D_{ij}^ϕ is the solute diffusivity matrix for the phase ϕ. Due to the fact that Si and Mg atoms are substitutional, D_{ij}^ϕ can be expressed as[26]:

$$D_{ij}^\phi = \sum_{v=\text{Al,Si,Mg}} (\delta_{vi} - x_i^\phi) x_v^\phi M_v^\phi \left(\frac{\partial \mu_v^\phi}{\partial x_j^\phi} - \frac{\partial \mu_v^\phi}{\partial x_{\text{Al}}^\phi} \right) \qquad (3)$$

where x_v^ϕ is the mole fraction of component v, and the parameter M_v^ϕ is the atomic diffusion mobility of element v in the given phase ϕ. M_v^ϕ can be determined from the experimental data by means of the Einstein relation, $D_v^* = \text{RTM}$ (D_v^* is the tracer diffusivity of element v), or can also be obtained using the kinetics database. δ_{ji} is the Kronecker delta, equal to 1 when $j = i$, otherwise $\delta_{ji} = 0$. The term $\partial \mu_v^\phi / \partial x_j^\phi$ corresponds to the thermodynamic factor and can be obtained from the thermodynamic database.

By coupling the kinetic and thermodynamic calculations in the Pandat databases, the diffusion matrix D_{ij}^ϕ in Eq. (2) is obtained. In order to overcome the problem of composition discontinuity at the S/L interface that occurs when using Eq. (1), the solution proposed in Ref. [8] is adopted.

2.2 Growth kinetics and solid fraction calculation

It is assumed that local thermodynamic equilibrium exists at the interface, caused by the influence of constitutional undercooling and curvature undercooling, and so the interface equilibrium temperature is characterized by the following equation neglecting the kinetic undercooling

$$T(t) = T_L^{liq}(w_{Si}^L, w_{Mg}^L) - \Delta T_C - \Delta T_R \quad (4)$$

where $T_L^{liq}(w_{Si}^L; w_{Mg}^L)$ is the liquidus temperature, obtained from the multicomponent phase diagram at a given set of concentrations $(w_{Si}^L; w_{Mg}^L)$. ΔT_C and ΔT_R are the constitutional and curvature undercooling, respectively. In order to consider the influence of different alloying elements on constitutional undercooling, a commonly used method is to superpose the effects of each alloying element. Therefore, the constitutional undercooling can be expressed as the following:

$$\begin{aligned}\Delta T_C &= T_L^{liq}(w_{Si}^L, w_{Mg}^L) - T_L^{liq}(w_{Si}^{L*}, w_{Mg}^{L*})\\ &\approx \frac{\partial T_L^{liq}(w_{Si}^L, w_{Mg}^L)}{\partial w_{Si}^L}(w_{Si}^L - w_{Si}^{L*})\\ &+ \frac{\partial T_L^{liq}(w_{Si}^L, w_{Mg}^L)}{\partial w_{Mg}^L}(w_{Mg}^L - w_{Mg}^{L*})\end{aligned} \quad (5)$$

where the term $\partial T_L^{liq}(w_{Si}^L, w_{Mg}^L)/\partial w_i^L$ (i refers to either Si or Mg) is the slope of the liquidus surface with respect to the solute element i (i.e., m_i^L) at the composition $(w_{Si}^L; w_{Mg}^L)$. w_i^{L*} is the local equilibrium composition at the interface, obtained through a calculation described later in this work.

It is well known that in the case of three-dimensional dendrite growth, the curvature undercooling ΔT_R can be related to the weighted mean curvature (wmc), which is expressed as the following[27]:

$$\Delta T_R = \frac{1}{\Delta S_F} \sum_{i=1}^{2} \left(\gamma(\mathbf{n}) + \frac{\partial^2 \gamma(\mathbf{n})}{\partial \theta_i^2} \right) \cdot \kappa_i \quad (6)$$

where ΔS_F is the melting entropy and κ_1, κ_2 are the two local principal curvatures of the S/L surface. θ_1, θ_2 are the two standard spherical angles of the interface normal, $\mathbf{n}$, and $\gamma(\mathbf{n})$ is the anisotropic surface energy function. It is complicated to quantify these two principal curvatures and accurately determine their directions. In order to simplify this expression and allow numerical computation, it is assumed that these two principal curvatures are equal[24]. The curvature undercooling can therefore be approximately expressed as the following:

$$\Delta T_R = \frac{1}{\Delta S_F} \cdot \kappa \sum_{i=1}^{2} \left(\gamma(\mathbf{n}) + \frac{\partial^2 \gamma(\mathbf{n})}{\partial \theta_i^2} \right) \quad (7)$$

The function describing the dependence of the surface energy on the normal direction, $\mathbf{n}$, in the case of cubic symmetry is given by[28]:

$$\begin{aligned}\gamma(\mathbf{n}) &= \gamma_0(1-3\varepsilon)\left[1 + \frac{4\varepsilon}{1-3\varepsilon}(n_x^4 + n_y^4 + n_z^4)\right]\\ &= \gamma_0(1-3\varepsilon)\left\{1 + \frac{4\varepsilon}{1-3\varepsilon}\left[\cos^4\theta_1 + \sin^4\theta_1(1-2\sin^2\theta_2\cos^2\theta_2)\right]\right\}\end{aligned} \quad (8)$$

where γ_0 is the isotropic interfacial energy with an average Gibbs-Thomson coefficient given by $\Gamma = \gamma_0/\Delta S_F$, ε is the strength of the fourfold anisotropy, and n_x, n_y, n_z are the components of the normal unit vector $\mathbf{n}$ in Cartesian coordinates (i.e., $\mathbf{n} = n_x \vec{i} + n_y \vec{j} + n_z \vec{k}$). $n_i = \frac{\partial f_S}{\partial i} / \sqrt{\left(\frac{\partial f_S}{\partial x}\right)^2 + \left(\frac{\partial f_S}{\partial y}\right)^2 + \left(\frac{\partial f_S}{\partial z}\right)^2}$, while i denotes the x, y and z directions. $\theta_1 = \arccos\left(\frac{\partial f_S}{\partial x} / \sqrt{\left(\frac{\partial f_S}{\partial x}\right)^2 + \left(\frac{\partial f_S}{\partial y}\right)^2}\right)$, $\theta_2 = \arccos\left(\frac{\partial f_S}{\partial z} / \sqrt{\left(\frac{\partial f_S}{\partial x}\right)^2 + \left(\frac{\partial f_S}{\partial y}\right)^2 + \left(\frac{\partial f_S}{\partial z}\right)^2}\right)$. The interface curvature of a cell with a solid fraction, f_S (where $0 < f_S < 1$), is approximated using the counting method in an expression given by the following[29]:

$$\kappa = \frac{1}{\Delta x}\left[1 - 2\left(f_S + \sum_{i=1}^{N} f_S^i\right)/(N+1)\right] \quad (9)$$

where Δx is the cell size, f_S^i is the solid fraction of the neighboring cells, and N is the total number of the first layer neighboring cells, which is equal to 26.

Assuming that on the length scale of an interfacial cell, the concentrations are uniform, and the solid and liquid are well mixed with a local equilibrium[21], the lever rule can be adopted to calculate the increment of the solid fraction. The solute conservation of each solute element during each time step for the interfacial cells yields the following defining equation for solid fraction variation

$$\Delta f_\mathrm{S} = \frac{w_\mathrm{Si}^{\mathrm{L}*} - w_\mathrm{Si}^\mathrm{L}}{w_\mathrm{Si}^{\mathrm{L}*}(1-k_\mathrm{Si})} = \frac{w_\mathrm{Mg}^{\mathrm{L}*} - w_\mathrm{Mg}^\mathrm{L}}{w_\mathrm{Mg}^{\mathrm{L}*}(1-k_\mathrm{Mg})} \quad (10)$$

Expressions for the analytical solutions of the interfacial equilibrium concentrations ($w_\mathrm{Si}^{\mathrm{L}*}$, $w_\mathrm{Mg}^{\mathrm{L}*}$) and Δf_S can be directly obtained through a combination of Eqs. (4) and (10). In order to produce small perturbations in the solid fraction evolution, Δf_S, calculated using Eq. (10), the term $(1+0.1\times(1-\zeta))$ is introduced where ζ is a random number between 0 and 2.

2.3 Algorithmic description of 3-D polycrystals with different crystallographic orientations

In CA models, due to the influence of mesh-induced anisotropy, the traditional capture process will result in dendrites tending to grow along the mesh axis, independent of the original crystallographic orientation. In practice however, the growth orientations of the dendrites in an undercooled melt vary from one to the other, as shown in Fig. 1 (a). In the present paper, in order to address the issue of different crystallographic orientations for polycrystalline growth in three dimensions, a space coordinate conversion algorithm is adopted. As demonstrated in Fig. 1 (a), every individual dendrite is assigned to a local coordinate system (i.e., the x_0, y_0, z_0 axes in Fig. 1), which are chosen to be parallel to the [100] directions of the dendrite arm. Therefore, the relative coordinate conversion from (x_0, y_0, z_0) to (x, y, z) can be uniquely determined using a rotation matrix (defined as Rotate_1, Rotate_2, Rotate_3) which is expressed in the terms of three Euler angles (α, β, γ) as described in Eqs. (11) and (12) and Fig. 1 (b).

$$\mathrm{Rotate}_1 = \begin{pmatrix} \cos\gamma & -\sin\gamma & 0 \\ \sin\gamma & \cos\gamma & 0 \\ 0 & 0 & 1 \end{pmatrix}$$

$$\mathrm{Rotate}_2 = \begin{pmatrix} \cos\beta & 0 & \sin\beta \\ 0 & 1 & 0 \\ -\sin\beta & 0 & \cos\beta \end{pmatrix} \quad (11)$$

$$\mathrm{Rotate}_3 = \begin{pmatrix} 1 & 0 & 0 \\ 0 & \cos\alpha & -\sin\alpha \\ 0 & \sin\alpha & \cos\alpha \end{pmatrix}$$

$$\begin{pmatrix} x \\ y \\ z \end{pmatrix} = \mathrm{Rotate}_1 \cdot \mathrm{Rotate}_2 \cdot \mathrm{Rotate}_3 \begin{pmatrix} x_0 \\ y_0 \\ z_0 \end{pmatrix} \quad (12)$$

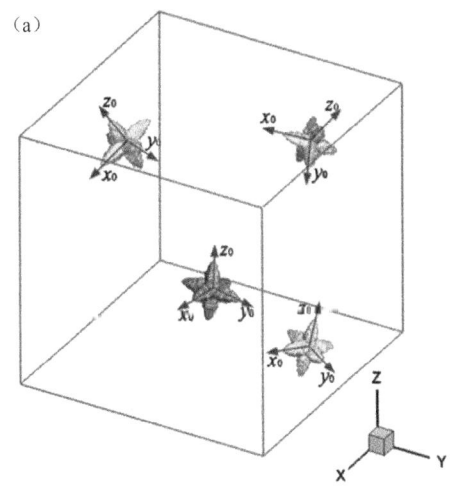 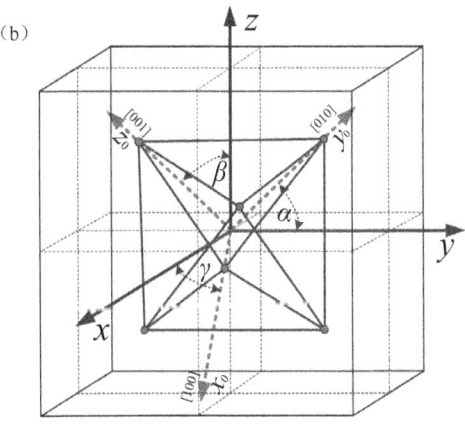

Fig. 1 (a) Schematic diagram of the different growth orientations of various grains, and (b) the definition of new centers in neighboring cells using a rotation matrix for the local coordinate system.

The underlying capture approach here is similar to the 3-D decentered octahedron growth technique. A misoriented grain with the preferential angle (α, β, γ) nucleates at the center and the cell turns into interface and begins to grow into an octahedron shape. At each time step, the evolution of the distance $L(t)$ from the center to the vertex of the octahedron is related to the increment of the solid fraction Δf_S, and can be calculated based on the following equation

$$L(t+\Delta t) = L(t) + \sqrt{2}\Delta x \cdot \Delta f_\mathrm{S} \quad (13)$$

Once the value $L(t)$ has been calculated, the coordinates of the six vertexes of the octahedron in the local coordinate system are known, and their corresponding coordinates in the (x,y,z) coordinate system can be easily obtained through coordinate conversion. Once the octahedron grows sufficiently large and its vertexes touch any of the neighboring liquid cells, the neighboring cell will then be changed so as to be in the interface state, meanwhile it is assigned to the same preferential orientation as that of the nuclei'. A new octahedron is then generated for the new interfacial cell and it can continue to growing along the same direction as that of the nuclei'.

2.4 Coupling with the Pandat software package

In the present model, the approach for microstructural simulation of Al-7Si-Mg ternary alloys is used in conjunction with thermodynamic/kinetic/equilibrium phase diagram calculation databases in order to obtain the data required for the simulations[25]. Due to the fact that the direct coupling approach exhibits very low computational efficiency and issues with robustness, an optimized table-look-up technique is adopted to provide access to the data needed in the simulations. The atomic diffusion mobility and thermodynamic factors needed for the calculation diffusion matrix are obtained using thermodynamic and kinetic databases, respectively, while the equilibrium phase diagram data, including the liquidus temperature $T_L^{liq}(w_{Si}^L, w_{Mg}^L)$, the partition coefficients (k_{Si}, k_{Mg}) and the slope of the liquidus surface (m_{Si}^L, m_{Mg}^L) as a function of liquid concentrations (w_{Si}^L, w_{Mg}^L) are generated using PanEngine, and the relevant liquid concentrations (w_{Si}^L, w_{Mg}^L) are stored with an uniform composition range of 0.01 wt%. For each interfacial cell with given concentrations and temperature, the corresponding parameters can always be obtained.

3. Results and discussion

3.1 Single dendrite morphologies of Al-7Si

Simulations were carried out in order to investigate the influence of undercooling on dendrite morphologies and tip growth velocity. The thermophysical parameters of the Al-7Si (wt%) alloy used are presented in Table 1. The computational domain was 150×150×150 cells with a cell size of 2μm, and a single solid seed with an initial composition of $k_{Si} w_{Si}^0$ and a preferential crystallographic orientation (0°,0°,0°) parallel to the axis of the (x,y,z) coordinate system was placed at the center of the domain. No-flux conditions were imposed at the boundaries of the calculation domain, which was described by $\partial w_i^\phi / \partial \mathbf{n} = 0$. Various constant undercooling values, ΔT (defined as $T_L^{liq}(w_{Si}^0) - T^*$ in which T^* is the constant temperature imposed on the calculation domain), in the range between 2K and 8K were used to simulate the dendrite growth. Fig. 2 shows the simulated dendrite morphologies at different solidification times, obtained using an undercooling of 2K and 6K. It can be seen that at the initial solidification stage, the dendrites subject to both undercooling conditions steadily grew along the crystallographic orientation without secondary dendrite arm formation. As solidification proceeded, the dendrite subject to an undercooling of 6K (Fig. 2(b1)-(b4)) exhibited well-developed side branching. The secondary dendrite arms grew perpendicular to the primary arms, and the initial secondary dendrite arm spacing, λ_2, that developed immediately behind the primary dendrite tip had a random spacing, whereas spacing increased with distance from the dendrite tip as a result of the coarsening process. The dendrite tip morphology characteristics, determined using the detailed numerical analysis of the wavelengths of instabilities along the sides of a dendrite by Langer and Müller-Krumbhaar[30], followed the predicted scaling law:

$$\lambda_2 / R = 2.1 \pm 0.03 \qquad (14)$$

Table 1 Properties of the Al-7Si (wt%) binary alloys used in the following simulations.

Definition and symbols	Values
Initial compositions w_{Si}^0(wt%)	7.0
Liquidus temperature $T_L^{liq}(w_{Si}^0)$ (K)	889.8
Liquidus slope m_{Si}^L(K wt%$^{-1}$)	-6.83
Partition coefficient k_{Si}	0.113
Gibbs-Thomson coefficient Γ(Km)	2.4×10^{-7}
Anisotropy coefficient ε	0.03
Liquid diffusion coefficient D_{Si}^L(m$^2 \cdot$s^{-1})	2.4×10^{-9}
Solid diffusion coefficient D_{Si}^S(m$^2 \cdot$s^{-1})	1.5×10^{-12}
Time step δt(s)	$\Delta x^2 / 6D_{Si}^L$

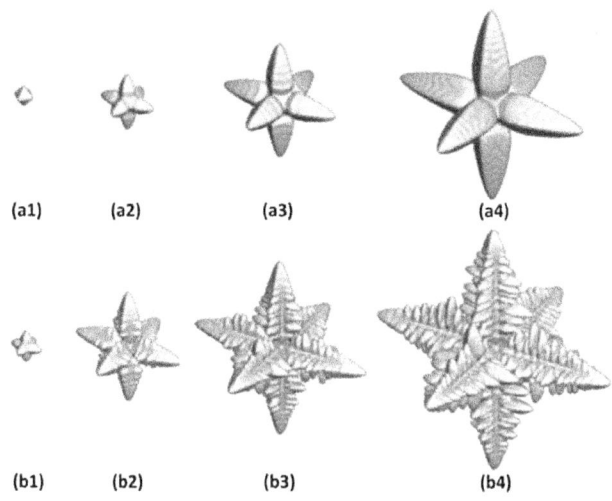

Fig. 2 The evolution of dendrite morphologies subject to different undercooling conditions, (a1-a4) $\Delta T = 2K$, from left to right, after 0.22s, 0.89s, 2.22s, 4.17s and (b1-b4) $\Delta T = 6K$, from left to right, after 0.09s, 0.40s, 0.67s, 0.98s.

where R is the steady-state dendrite tip radius. In order to measure the tip radius of the simulated dendrite, the parabola fitting approaches have been used[5], and the 3-D isosurface plot is depicted for $f_S = 0.5$. For $\Delta T = 6K$, the parabolic line is determined to be $y = 0.1434 x^2 + 0.032 x + 5.973$ as shown in Fig. 3, and the tip radius is determined to be $R = 3.49 \mu m$. The secondary dendrite arm spacing, λ_2, near the dendrite tip was found to be approximately $8.0 \mu m$. Therefore, the value of λ_2/R is equal to 2.29, which is close to the theoretical value obtained using Eq. (14). From Fig. 2, it can also be observed that the dendrite subject to $\Delta T = 2K$ (Fig. 2 (a1)-(a4)) exhibits a branchless needle shape during the whole solidification process, and so is consistent with the fact that a higher undercooling tends to lead to the appearance of side branching.

In order to draw comparison with the predictions of the Lipton-Glicksman-Kurz (LGK) analytical model, the steady-state tip growth velocity under different undercooling has been measured. The concepts to determine the steady growth velocities can be found in Ref. [8]. Since the selection parameter σ^* varies with the anisotropy parameter ε predicted by microsolvability theory, according to the 3-D linearized solvability theory, the value of σ^* for the 3-D dendrite is 0.085, corresponding to the value of $\varepsilon = 0.03$ used in the simulations. A comparison of the simulated dendrite tip velocities with the values calculated using the LGK model as a function of undercooling are shown in Fig. 4. Both sets of model predictions followed the same trends and their values appeared to give a reasonable agreement. As could be expected, the tip velocity increased with increased undercooling.

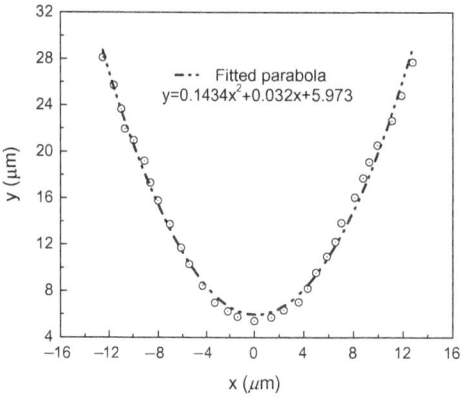

Fig. 3 The fitted parabola for the 3-D dendrite tip in Fig. 2 (b4). The circles indicate the S/L interface position near the dendrite tip, and the dashed line gives the fitted parabola.

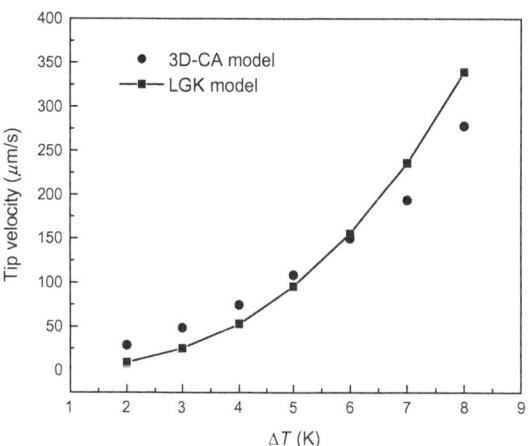

Fig. 4 The steady-state dendrite tip velocity calculated using the present model and the theoretical LGK model, as a function of undercooling.

3.2 Isothermal dendrite morphologies and solute distribution of Al-7Si-xMg

Adding Mg to the Al-7Si casting alloy can significantly improve its mechanical properties, and it has been reported that Mg content can affect the dendrite morphologies and eutectic structure, as well as their volume fractions[31]. Therefore, in order to investigate the effect of different levels of Mg concentration on dendrite growth, simulations were performed on a domain containing 150×150×150 cells with a cell size of 2μm, and isothermal solidification was adopted at a constant temperature, $T^* = 881K$. In this section, the effect of interactions between alloying elements was not taken into account and the diffusion coefficients of Si and Mg in the liquid were taken to be constants with the values $D_{Si}^L = 2.4×10^{-9} m^2/s$ and, $D_{Mg}^L = 4.9×10^{-9} m^2/s$, respectively. Fig. 5 depicts the simulated dendrite morphologies and the distribution of the Si solute in a 2-D slice for Al-7Si-Mg alloys of a varying Mg content. The dendrite clearly exhibited well-developed side branching when Mg concentration was 0.5 wt% (Fig.5(a)), and as the Mg concentration increased to 1.0 wt%, the growth of secondary dendrite arms was constrained (Fig. 5 (b)). When the Mg content further increased to 1.5 wt%, the dendrite tended to a branchless needle shape (Fig.5(c)). A similar result for dendrite morphology evolution was observed in the phase field simulations presented in Ref.[32]. This phenomenon can be explained as follows: according to the phase-diagram, an increase in Mg content causes a significant decrease in the equilibrium liquidus temperature T^{eq}, and reduces the degree of the undercooling in front of the dendrite, defined as $T^{eq} - T^*$. The decreased undercooling slows down the dendrite growth rate, as shown in Table 2, and causes an enhancement in the interface stability, thus reducing the tendency for side branching.

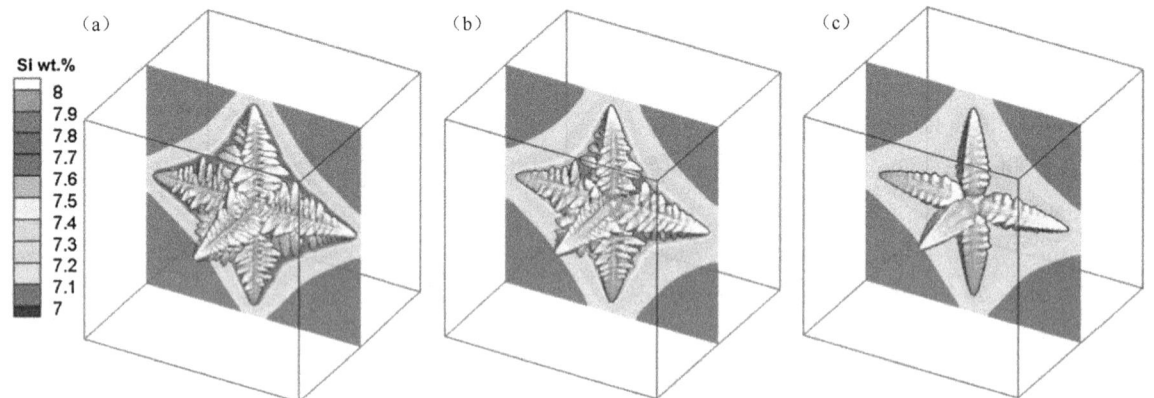

Fig. 5　Simulated dendrite morphologies and the distribution of the Si solute in Al-7Si-xMg alloys containing varying Mg contents, at a constant temperature $T^* = 881K$. (a) Al-7Si-0.5Mg, (b) Al-7Si-1.0Mg, (c) Al-7Si-1.5Mg.

Table 2　The steady-state dendrite tip velocity of Al-7Si-xMg alloys containing varying Mg contents, at a temperature $T^* = 881K$.

Concentration of Mg (wt%)	Tip velocity (μm/s)
Al-7Si-0.5Mg	189
Al-7Si-1.0Mg	103
Al-7Si-1.5Mg	59

Since the diffusivity of solute is much smaller than the dendrite growth velocity, the solute discharged from the newly solidified solid phase can not sufficiently diffuse to the bulk liquid. It can be clearly seen from Fig. 5 that the Si were piled up just ahead of the dendrite interface as a result of solute redistribution, especially in the regions between the secondary dendrite arms. As the solidification process continued, the solute in these regions may have become trapped between the solidified regions and resulted in microsegregation. It can be noted from Fig. 5 that the Si concentration field is clearly influenced by the amount of additional Mg. The quantitative data on Si concentration, measured along the horizontal dendrite arms from the center of the dendrite are given in Fig. 6. It can be observed that the liquid concentration of Si at the interface decreases as the Mg concentration increases, which can be explained by the fact that an increase in Mg concentration causes a decreases in the liquidus temperature, slowing down the dendrite growth rate, and so more time is available for the diffusion of the accumulated solute, leading to the lower tip concentration shown in Fig. 6.

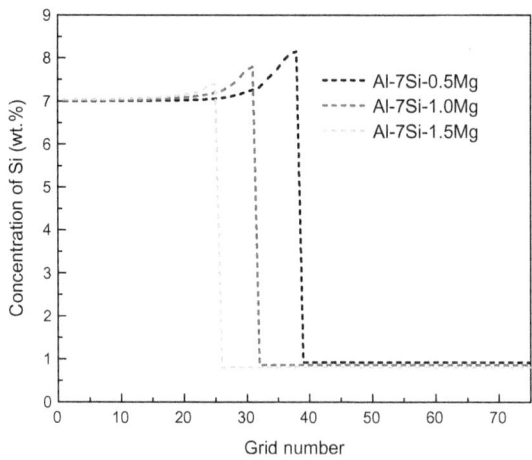

Fig. 6 Si solute concentration profiles along the dendrite arm direction for Al-7Si-xMg alloys containing varying Mg content, at a temperature $T^* = 881$K.

3.3 Effect of interactions between alloying elements

In order to study the influence of solute interactions on dendrite growth, a single equiaxed dendrite of the Al-7Si-0.5Mg alloy, solidified in an undercooled melt with a constant temperature of $T^* = 881$K has been simulated. The calculation domain was $200 \times 200 \times 200$ cells with a cell size of $2\mu m$ and the diffusion coefficient D_{ij} was obtained through coupling with the Pandat databases. Fig. 7 shows the diffusion matrix in a 2-D slice, both for the diagonal (D_{SiSi} and D_{MgMg}) and off-diagonal terms (D_{SiMg} and D_{MgSi}). It has been found that in the liquid region, the diffusion coefficients are concentration dependent, and the off-diagonal terms are negative, which implies an attractive interaction between the alloying solutes. It can be seen that the values of the off-diagonal terms (D_{SiMg} and D_{MgSi}) and diagonal term (D_{MgMg}) at the interface are smaller than those far from the interface, while the diagonal term (D_{SiSi}) at the interface is larger than that was found at other positions. Fig. 8 represents the diagonal diffusion coefficients of the Al-7Si-0.5Mg alloy, with varying concentrations of Si and Mg, at the isothermal temperature of 881K. It can be observed that the diffusion coefficient D_{MgMg} decreases with increasing of Si and Mg. In the case of the diffusion coefficient D_{SiSi}, there is an increase from approximately 2.385×10^{-9} m^2/s to 2.405×10^{-9} m^2/s as the amount of Si varies from 7 wt% to 8 wt%, while there is a decrease from 2.385×10^{-9} m^2/s to 2.380×10^{-9} m^2/s with the increase in Mg from 0.5 wt% to 0.8 wt%. It can therefore be observed that the evolution of diffusion coefficient D_{SiSi} is more sensitive to the changes in Si concentration and that explains the reason why the value of D_{SiSi} near the dendrite interface is larger than at position far from the interface, as shown in Fig. 7 (a).

In Fig. 7, the off-diagonal diffusion coefficients are smaller than those of the diagonal term by approximately one order of magnitude. In order to illustrate the influence of solute interaction on dendrite growth, Fig. 9 shows a comparison of the solute concentrations at the dendrite tip in the liquid phase as a function of dendrite growth time, both by considering and ignoring solute interaction. It is interesting to note that the concentration of Si is found to be slightly lower for the case that consider solute interaction than those that ignore it, while in the case of Mg content, the concentration at the dendrite tip is higher when considering of solute interaction compared with the case without solute interaction. A brief analysis of this phenomenon can be described as follows: attractive interactions tend to drive both of the Si and Mg elements toward the solid-liquid interface by the concentration gradient of the other solute, slowing down the diffusion behavior from the interface to the bulk liquid, which tends to make solute concentration at the dendrite tip higher when considering solute interaction. The higher solute concentration at the dendrite tip when considering solute interaction leads to a decrease in the undercooling and a further decrease in the tip growth velocity. Through measuring the average growth velocity during a solidification time from 0.2 to 0.7s, the value when considering solute interaction is found to be $183\mu m/s$, whereas solute interaction is ignored, it is $191\mu m/s$. The lower growth velocity occurring when the effect of solute interaction is taken into consideration allows more time for the solute in front of the dendrite to diffuse. As the Si content is much higher than Mg in the Al-7Si-0.5Mg alloy, the contribution of the cross diffusion term (D_{SiMg}) to the Si solute distribution is much smaller compared to the contribution of D_{MgSi} to the distribution of the Mg solute. Both of the reasons result in the difference in the solute distribution behavior between Si and Mg observed in Fig. 9.

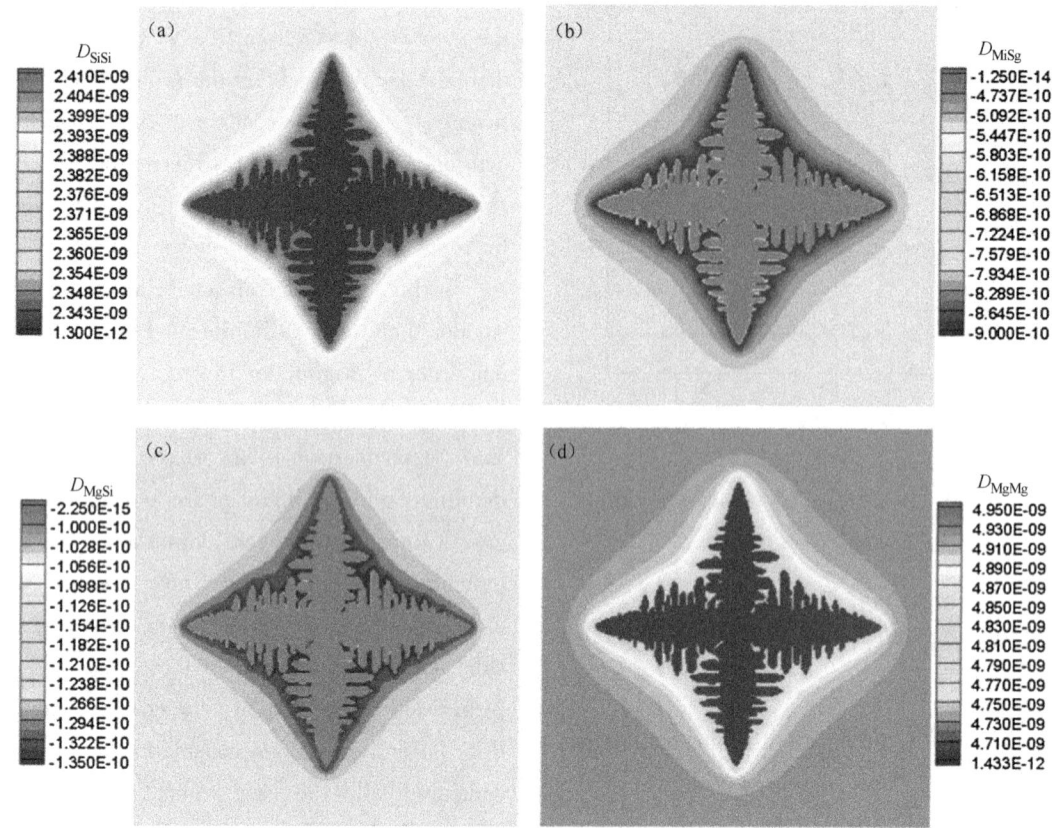

Fig. 7 Concentration dependent diffusion matrix profiles for the Al-7Si-0.5Mg alloy, solidified at a constant temperature of 881K. (a) D_{SiSi}, (b) D_{SiMg}, (c) D_{MgSi}, (d) D_{MgMg}.

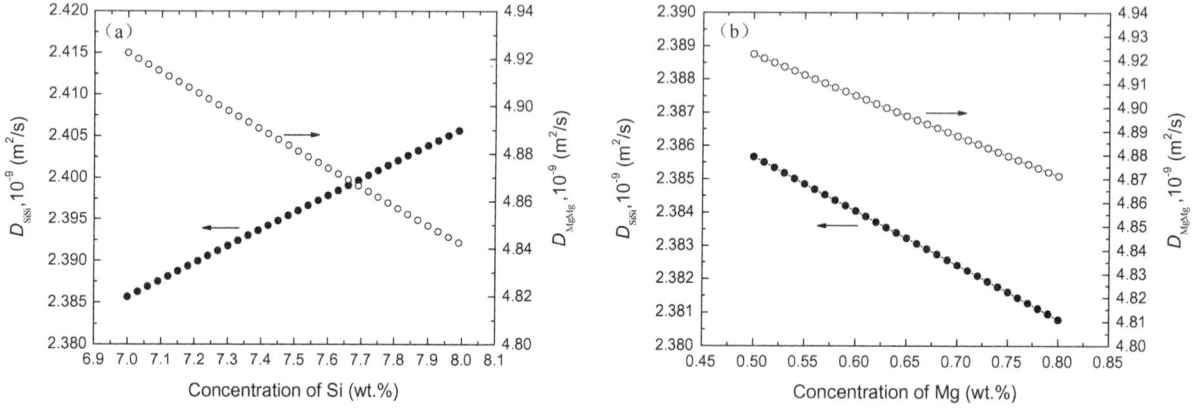

Fig. 8 Variation in the diagonal diffusion coefficients D_{SiSi} and D_{MgMg} in the liquid as a function of concentration of Si and Mg at the isothermal temperature of 881K. (a) Si content varies from 7 wt% to 8 wt% while the Mg content is equal to 0.5 wt%. (b) Mg content varies from 0.5 wt% to 0.8 wt% while Si content is equal to 7 wt%.

3.4 Application to polycrystalline growth

Since most practical industrial casting processes of Al-7Si-Mg casting alloys involve equiaxed polycrystalline growth in random crystallographic orientations, and the majority of cooling rates are at no more than 20K/s, this case was also simulated using the present model for Al-7Si-0.36Mg (wt%) alloy. Simulations were performed on a domain with a size of $1\times1\times1\text{mm}^3$, and various constant cooling rates between 0.5K/s and 10K/s were applied. The temperature was assumed to be uni-

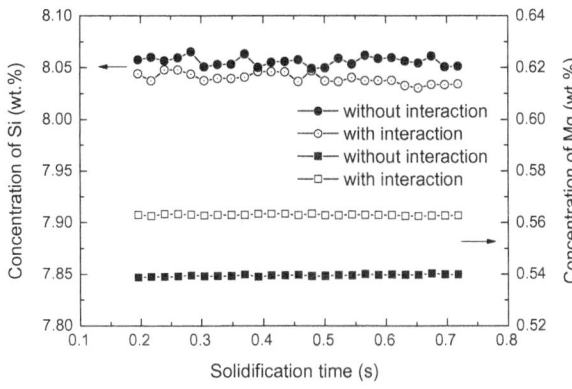

Fig. 9 Steady state concentrations of Si and Mg in front of the dendrite tip, varying with the solidification time both with and without consideration of off-diagonal terms in the diffusion matrix.

form in the domain and was cooled down from the liquid temperature (i.e., $T_{liq} = 887.7K$), and as soon as the eutectic temperature (i.e., $T_e = 847.4K$ obtained from Pandat software) was reached during solidification, simulation was terminated. Without considering the influence of grain density on dendrite growth, it was assumed that the total nuclei number was equal to 60 in all simulation cases, with randomly assigned preferential growth orientations. Fig. 10 represents the simulated evolution of polycrystalline growth of the ternary Al-7Si-0.36Mg alloy at the cooling rates of 2K/s and 5K/s, respectively. It can be observed that at the beginning of the solidification process, primary dendrite arms steadily develop along the crystallographic orientations and the dendrite morphology is presented as having sixfold symmetry (Fig. 10(a1) and (b1)). As the solidification process, with the growth and coarsening of primary trunks, it is accompanied by side branching and the collision of dendrites, hindering the dendrite free growth

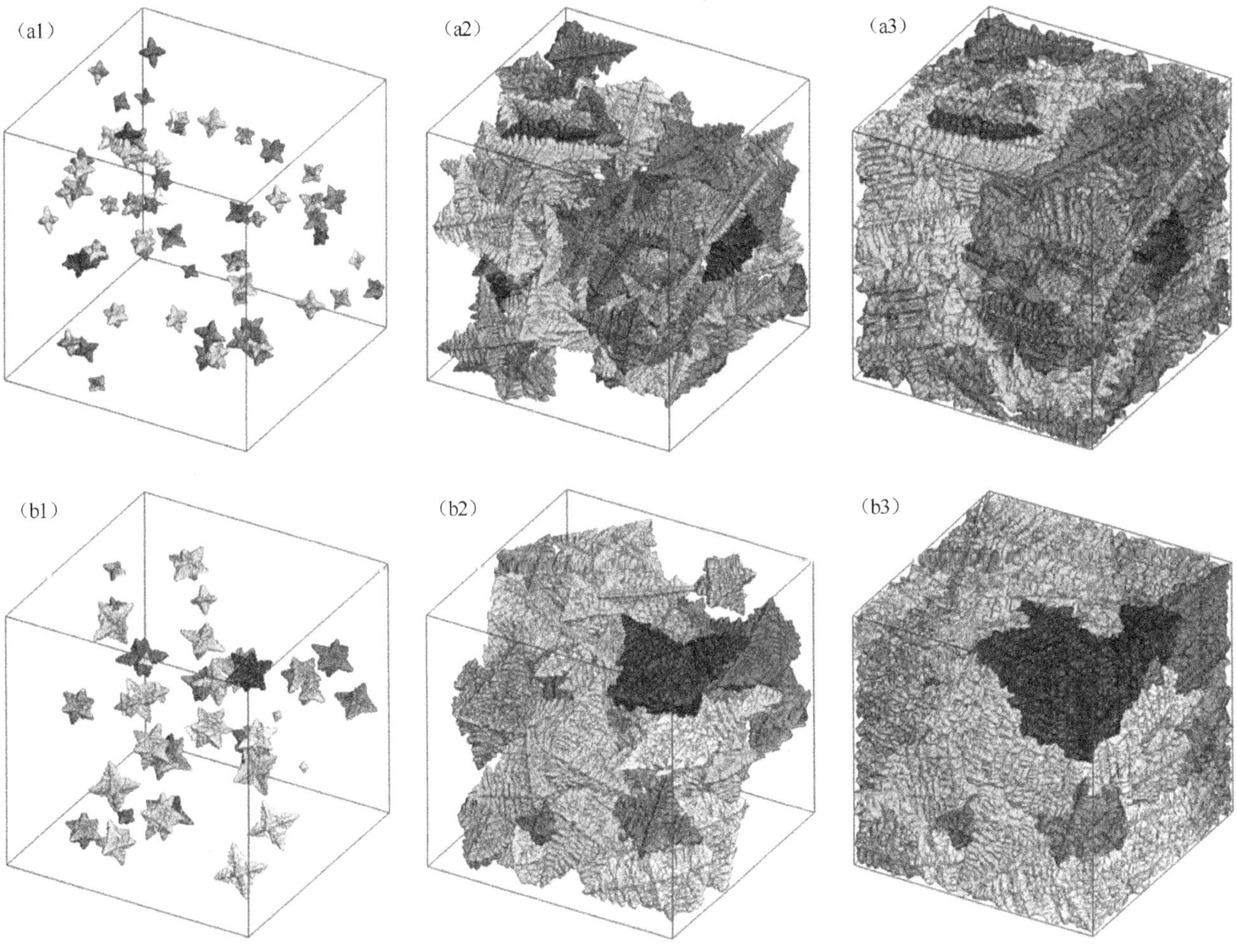

Fig. 10 Simulated multigrain solidification of an Al-7Si-0.36Mg alloy at a constant cooling rate of 2K/s for (a1-a3) and 5K/s for (b1-b3). The different colors represent different grains. (a1) $f_s = 2\%$, $t = 1.98s$, (a2) $f_s = 21\%$, $t = 3.47s$, (a3) $f_s = 44\%$, $t = 9.42s$. (b1) $f_s = 3\%$, $t = 1.49s$, (b2) $f_s = 24\%$, $t = 2.48s$, (b3) $f_s = 52\%$, $t = 6.44s$.
(For interpretation of the references to colour in this figure legend, the reader is referred to the web version of this article.)

(Fig. 10(a2) and (b2)). At the end of solidification, dendrite growth is significantly affected by the interaction between solute fields and the surrounding dendrites, forcing the dendrites to grow along the directions deviating from their initial crystallographic orientations, resulting in the complicated dendrite morphologies shown in Fig. 10 (a3) and (b3). This appearance of the single dendrite morphology obtained from polycrystalline simulations is similar to that of the experimental results, as shown in Fig. 11, in terms of the complexity of the dendrite morphologies. According to the analysis of Wang et al.[33], based on phase field simulation and 3-D X-ray tomography experimental observations of α-Mg dendrites subject to polycrystalline solidification, the complex dendrite structure of polycrystalline solidification is believed to be mainly attributed to its grain density, distribution, inherently preferred growth directions, and its complex and varying anisotropies, as well as interactions with adjacent dendrites.

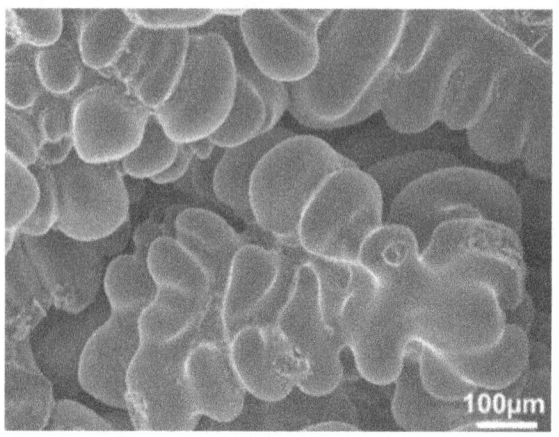

Fig. 11 SEM image showing the complicated dendrite structure observed in experiments of Al-7Si-0.36Mg casting alloy.

Fig. 12 describes the two dimensional transverse section dendrite morphologies across the center of the calculation domain at cooling rates of 2K/s and 5K/s, together with the experimentally obtained metallographic microstructures at cooling rates of 1.75K/s and 6.25K/s. It can be observed that the microstructure was refined as the cooling rate increased. The scale of the microstructures subject to different cooling conditions were analyzed by measuring the secondary dendrite arm spacing (SDAS), which exerts a marked influence on the mechanical properties of castings. From Fig. 13, which de-

scribes the SDAS as a function of cooling rate, it can be observed that SDAS decreases as the cooling rate increases, and that the formula fitted according to the simulated results, i.e., SDAS = $40.5R_c^{-0.31}$, is in agreement with the results reported in Ref.[34]. Those findings indicated that the SDAS in A356/A357 alloys fitted well with the empirical equation, i.e., SDAS = $39.4R_c^{-0.317}$, thus proving the reliability of the present model in predicting SDAS. In addition to the SDAS, a variation in the cooling rate also affects the volume fraction of α-Al dendrite. Fig. 14 shows the simulated variation of dendrite volume fraction as a function of cooling rate. It should be noted that the eutectic point shifting, i.e., the eutectic undercooling, was not considered in the model. For this reason, we can conclude that the predicted value shown in Fig. 14 is a slight undervaluation. According to the evolution of the predicted amounts of α-Al dendrite shown in Fig. 12, one can observe that increasing the cooling rate significantly decreases the amount of α-Al dendrite present in the range of slow cooling, while in the range between 2K/s and 10K/s, the volume fraction increases slightly. This phenomenon was also found in recent experimental observations on Al-Cu alloys[35]. It is commonly accepted that higher cooling rates allow less time for diffusion and the creation of finer microstructure, i.e., a larger area of solid/liquid interface per unit volume, which is beneficial for reducing the extent of microsegregation by means of back diffusion. Both of these would affect the degree of back diffusion, thus influencing microsegregation and the α-Al dendrite volume fraction[35]. This implies that if the microstructure is sufficiently fine and the corresponding solute gradients are increased by the higher cooling rates, back diffusion is so efficient that it can decrease the degree of microsegregation, thus increasing the volume fraction of primary dendrites. Further supporting evidence of the effect of finer microstructure in increasing dendrite volume fraction is the severe coarsening theory in the faster cooling case. According to the investigation of Du et al.[36], a higher cooling rate produces a much more obvious side branching and with the impinging, ripening and coalescence between branches, leading to the presence of more core regions, indicated by the circles in Fig. 12, in which solute enrichment might be higher than in other liquid regions. The solute enrichment in the core regions might result in a higher amount volume fraction of α-Al dendrite. In the case of slow cooling conditions, i.e., $R_c <$ 2K/s given in Fig. 14, the degree of microsegregation is lower, due to a longer solidification time and more time is available for the solute diffusion, resulting in a higher volume fraction of the primary phase.

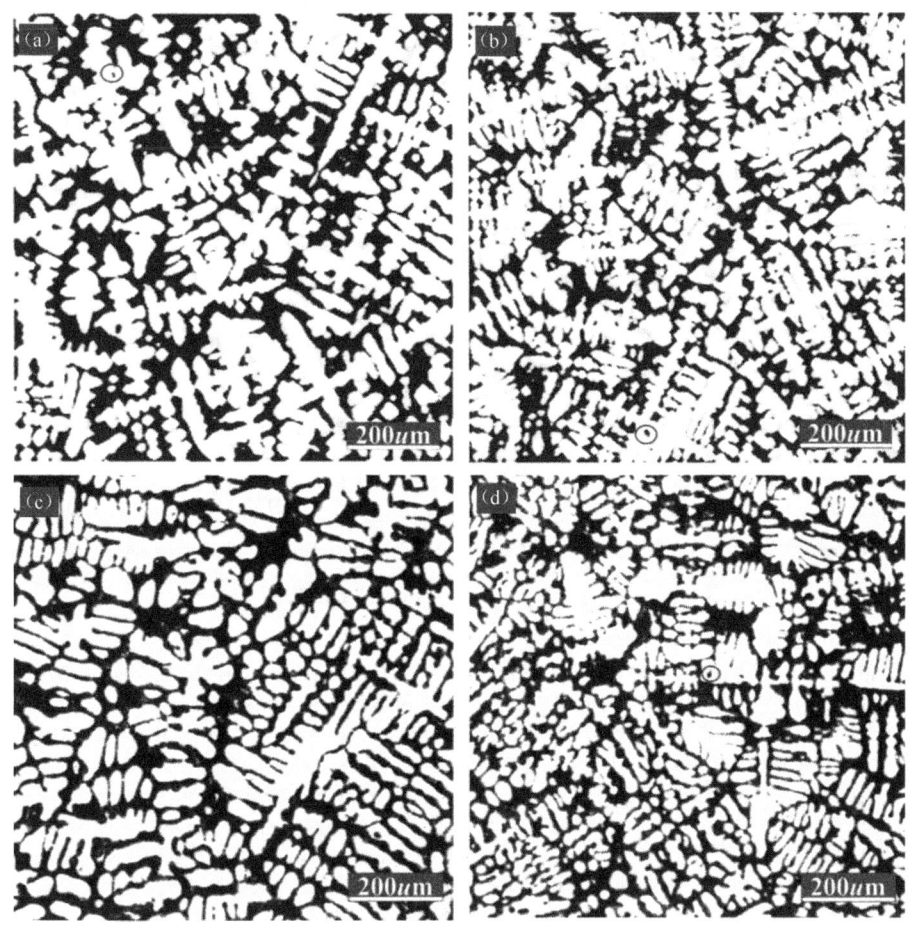

Fig. 12 Simulated and experimentally obtained metallographical microstructures at different cooling rates: (a) simulated, $R_c = 2$K/s, (b) simulated, $R_c = 5$K/s, (c) experimental, $R_c = 1.75$K/s, (d) experimental, $R_c = 6.25$K/s. (R_c: average cooling rate).

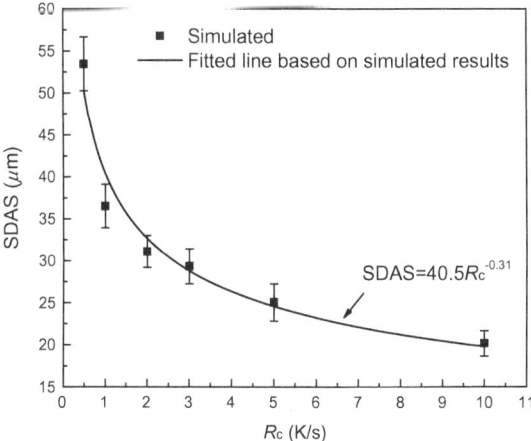

Fig. 13 Calculated secondary dendrite arm spacing for an Al-7Si-0.36Mg alloy solidified at different cooling rates.

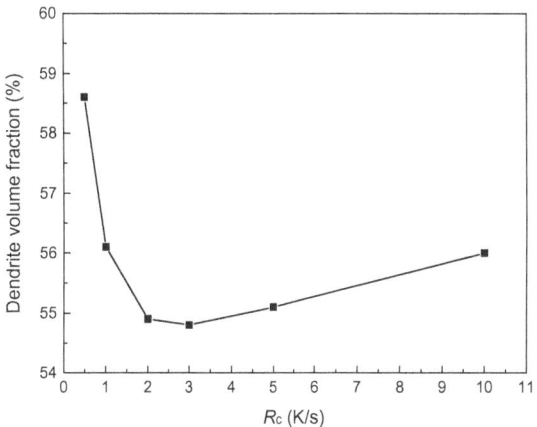

Fig. 14 Simulated dendrite volume fraction as a function of cooling rate for an Al-7Si-0.36Mg alloy.

4. Conclusion

In this paper, a three-dimensional cellular automaton model for the prediction of ternary dendrite growth during solidification processes has been developed. The growth kinetics of the S/L interfacial cells are determined from the difference between the local interface equilibrium composition (w_i^{L*}) and the local actual liquid composition (w_i^L) using an efficient calculation method. The solute interactions between various alloying elements are considered in the model. In the case of polycrystalline solidification in various crystallographic orientations, the modified decentered octahedron algorithm for neighborhood tracking has been applied in order to eliminate the influence of mesh-induced anisotropy on dendrite growth. The model is coupled with thermodynamic/kinetic/equilibrium phase diagram calculation databases incorporated in the Pandat software package using an optimized table-look-up strategy.

The proposed model was applied to simulate the dendrite growth of Al-Si binary and Al-7Si-Mg ternary alloys. Detailed model validations were performed, with the simulated steady-state tip parameters being in good agreement with the LGK predictions and the wavelength of instabilities theory. The dynamics and dendrite morphologies of Al-7Si-xMg ternary alloys containing different amounts of Mg under isothermal solidification were investigated. It was found that an increase in Mg content can weaken the ability of the dendrite to exhibit side branching, due to a significant decrease of the equilibrium liquidus temperature, reducing the degree of undercooling and slowing down the growth velocity. The proposed model was also applied to Al-7Si-0.5Mg dendrite simulation, both with and without consideration of solute interaction between Si and Mg alloying elements, and the effects on dendrite growth process have been analyzed.

Finally, the developed model was applied to simulation of polycrystalline growth in different crystallographic orientations for an Al-7Si-0.36Mg ternary alloy, with the simulated SDAS data obtained from arbitrarily cross sections showing a reasonable agreement with empirical calculations. The dendrite volume fraction was also predicted and the effect of the cooling rate on dendrite volume fraction was analyzed using the back diffusion and coarsening theory. The simulation results indicate that the proposed model is able to reproduce a wide range of complex dendrite growth phenomena such as side branching in dendrite morphologies, coarsening of dendrite arms, as well as interactions among neighboring dendrites.

Acknowledgments

The authors gratefully acknowledge the financial support of the National Basic Research Program of China (Grant No. 2011CB706801), the National Natural Science Foundation of China (Grant Nos. 51374137, 51171089), and the National Science and Technology Major Projects (Grant Nos. 2012ZX04012-011, 2011ZX04014-052).

References

[1] P. T. Li, S. D. Liu, L. L. Zhang, X. F. Liu, Mater. Des. 47 (2013) 522-528.
[2] M. Zhu, Z. Y. Jian, G. C. Yang, Y. H. Zhou, Mater. Des. 36 (2012) 243-249.
[3] M. O. Shabani, A. Mazahery, JOM 63 (2011) 132-316.
[4] M. Yildirim, D. Özyürek, Mater. Des. 51 (2013) 767-774.
[5] L. Beltran-Sanchez, D. M. Stefanescu, Metall. Mater. Trans. A 35 (2004) 2471-2485.
[6] W. Wang, P. D. Lee, M. McLean, Acta Mater. 51 (2003) 2971-2987.
[7] M. Plapp, J. Cryst. Growth 303 (2007) 49-57.
[8] M. F. Zhu, D. M. Stefanescu, Acta Mater. 55 (2007) 1741-1755.
[9] J. J. Li, Z. J. Wang, Y. Q. Wang, J. C. Wang, Acta Mater. 60 (2012) 1478-1493.
[10] M. A. Zaeem, H. Yin, S. D. Felicelli, Appl. Math. Model. 37 (2012) 137-146.
[11] M. A. Zaeem, H. Yin, S. D. Felicelli, J. Mater. Sci. Technol. 28 (2013) 3495-3503.
[12] A. Choudhury, K. Reuther, E. Wesner, A. August, B. Nestler, M. Rettenmayr, Comput. Mater. Sci. 55 (2012) 263-268.
[13] W. D. Tan, N. S. Bailey, Y. C. Shin, Comput. Mater. Sci. 50 (2011) 2573-2585.
[14] S. C. Michelic, J. M. Thuswaldner, C. Bernhard, Acta Mater. 58 (2010) 2738-2751.

[15] A. Karma, W. Rappel, Phys. Rev. E 57 (1998) 4323-4349.
[16] A. Karma, Y. H. Lee, M. Plapp, Phys. Rev. E 61 (2000) 3996-4006.
[17] Ch.-A. Gandin, M. Rappaz, Acta Mater. 45 (1997) 2187-2195.
[18] L. Yuan, P. D. Lee, Model. Simul. Mater. Sci. Eng. 18 (2010) 055008.
[19] J. Yu, Q. Y. Xu, K. Cai, B. C. Liu, Acta Metall. Sin. 43 (2007) 731-738.
[20] S. Y. Pan, M. F. Zhu, Acta Mater. 58 (2010) 340-352.
[21] M. Eshraghi, S. D. Felicelli, B. Jelinek, J. Cryst. Growth 354 (2012) 129-134.
[22] L. Wei, X. Lin, M. Wang, W. D. Huang, Physica B 407 (2012) 2471-2475.
[23] Y. Zhao, D. F. Chen, M. J. Long, T. T. Arif, R. Qin, Metall. Mater. Trans. B 45 (2014) 719-725.
[24] X. F. Zhang, J. Z. Zhao, H. X. Jiang, M. F. Zhu, Acta Mater. 60 (2012) 2249-2257.
[25] W. Cao, S.-L. Chen, F. Zhang, K. Wu, Y. Yang, Y. A. Chang, R. Schmid-Fetzer, W. A. Oates, Calphad 33 (2009) 328-342.
[26] R. J. Zhang, Z. He, X. Y. Wang, W. Q. Jie, Mater. Lett. 59 (2005) 2765-2768.
[27] J. E. Taylor, J. W. Cahn, C. A. Handwerker, Acta Metall. Mater. 40 (1992) 1443-1474.
[28] S. Gurevich, A. Karma, M. Plapp, R. Trivedi, Phys. Rev. E 81 (2010) 11603.
[29] L. Nastac, Acta Mater. 47 (1999) 4253-4262.
[30] J. S. Langer, H. Müller-Krumbhaar, Acta Metall. 26 (1978) 1681-1687.
[31] Q. G. Wang, C. J. Davidson, J. Mater. Sci. 36 (2001) 739-750.
[32] W. Y. Long, Q. Z. Cai, B. K. Wei, L. L. Chen, Acta Phys. Sin. 55 (2006) 1341-1345.
[33] M. Y. Wang, Y. J. Xu, Q. W. Zheng, S. J. Wu, T. Jing, N. Chawla, Metall. Mater. Trans. A 45 (2014) 2562-2574.
[34] Q. G. Wang, C. H. Cáceres, Mater. Sci. Forum 242 (1996) 159-164.
[35] D. G. Eskin, Q. Du, D. Ruvalcaba, L. Katgerman, Mater. Sci. Eng., A 405 (2005) 1-10.
[36] Q. Du, D. G. Eskin, A. Jacot, L. Katgerman, Acta Mater. 55 (2007) 1523-1532.

23. A phase field model for simulating the precipitation of multi-variant β-$Mg_{17}Al_{12}$ in Mg-Al-based alloys

Guomin Han,[a] Zhiqiang Han,[a] Alan A. Luo,[b] Anil K. Sachdev[b] and Baicheng Liu[a,c]

[a] Key Laboratory for Advanced Materials Processing Technology, Ministry of Education, Department of Mechanical Engineering, Tsinghua University, Beijing 100084, China

[b] Chemical and Materials Systems Laboratory, General Motors Global Research and Development Center, Warren, MI 48090-9055, USA

[c] State Key Laboratory of Automotive Safety and Energy, Department of Automotive Engineering, Tsinghua University, Beijing 100084, China

A phase field model for simulating the precipitation of multi-variant β-$Mg_{17}Al_{12}$ phase during the aging process of Mg-Al-based alloys was developed in which the interface anisotropy and the elastic strain energy were taken into account. A special numerical technique based on a hexagonal and an orthogonal mesh was employed to deal with the precipitate orientation and calculate the elastic strain energy. The model reveals the contribution of the interface anisotropy and the elastic strain energy in the evolution of the precipitates.

Key words: Mg-Al-based alloys; Multi-variant precipitation; Phase-field model; Elastic strain energy; Interface anisotropy

Mg-Al-based alloys are important lightweight materials that are widely used in the automobile and aerospace industries[1]. The alloys can be strengthened through heat treatment due to the precipitation of intermetallic phase, β-$Mg_{17}Al_{12}$, during the aging process. The morphology, size and distribution of the precipitating phase have significant effects on the mechanical properties of the alloys. Thus it is vital to understand the evolution mechanism of the morphology as well as the growth kinetics of the β-$Mg_{17}Al_{12}$ phase.

Extensive experimental investigations have reported β-$Mg_{17}Al_{12}$ phase precipitation[2-5]. Studies involving the morphology or crystallography of the precipitates have mainly been carried out using transmission electron microscopy (TEM). However, the mechanisms of the evolution of the precipitate morphology cannot be revealed by only observing the final forms of the precipitates. A phase field method based on thermodynamic driving force and ordering potential is an effective approach to model the evolution of precipitates, whereby the governing variables of the precipitation can be studied quantitatively. Wang et al.[6] adopted a phase field method to study the precipitation of a prototype alloy, whereby the transformation-induced elastic strain was considered. Zhu et al.[7] investigated the coarsening process of γ' precipitates of an Ni-Al system using a phase field model that considered the effect of elastic strain energy. Vaithyanathan et al.[8] simulated the precipitation of θ' phase in an Al-Cu alloy using a phase field method. In their model, not only was the elastic strain energy considered, but the interface anisotropy was also taken into account. Li et al.[9] made an early attempt to simulate the precipitates in AZ91 (Mg-9Al-1Zn; all compositions are in wt.% unless otherwise stated) alloy. Later Gao et al.[10] simulated the precipitation of β_1 phase in Mg-Y-Nd alloy using a phase field model and discussed the effect of elastic strain energy on the precipitation. Han et al.[11] simulated the precipitation of β-$Mg_{17}Al_{12}$

using a phase field model that considered interfacial anisotropy, and discussed the effects of the two types of solution approximation on the morphology evolution of the precipitate. The evolution of precipitates from a saturated matrix is a solid-state transformation that is significantly affected by the crystal structure and orientation of both the new phase and the matrix. For a particular alloy system, the crystal structure and orientation of the precipitate and the matrix are unique, thus special attention needs to be paid to deal with the interfacial anisotropy and elastic strain energy. Mg-Al-based alloys have a matrix with a hexagonal close-packed (hcp) crystal structure and a precipitate with a body-centered cubic (bcc) crystal structure. However, a thorough understanding of the effects of the interfacial anisotropy and elastic strain energy on the evolution of β-$Mg_{17}Al_{12}$ phase in the Mg-Al system is still lacking. Furthermore, precipitates usually have a series of variants with different orientations[12]; thus, the modeling of multi-variant precipitation is of significance in the simulation of the actual distribution, morphology and size of the precipitates. However, it is still a great challenge to model the variants in the Mg-Al system and, to the authors' knowledge, no phase field model describing the multi-variance of the precipitates in Mg-Al alloy has yet been reported.

In this paper, a two-dimensional phase field model was developed to simulate the multi-variant precipitation in Mg-Al alloy in which the interfacial anisotropy and elastic strain energy were taken into account. A special numerical technique based on two sets of mesh was employed to combine the advantages of hexagonal mesh in dealing with the precipitate orientation and those of orthogonal mesh in computing the elastic strain energy. The chemical free energy of the precipitate and the matrix was calculated by real-time coupling with a commercial thermodynamic database. The effects of the interfacial anisotropy and elastic strain energy on the precipitation are revealed.

The predominant precipitation of β-$Mg_{17}Al_{12}$ in Mg-Al system has the crystallographic characteristics of hcp→bcc phase transformation, with the following orientation relationship between the β-phase and the matrix[5]:

$$(0001)_\alpha \parallel (110)_\beta, [1\bar{2}10]_\alpha \parallel [1\bar{1}1]_\beta$$

Where α and β denote the matrix and precipitate, respectively. TEM observation[3,5] showed that the β-phase has 12 variants. Due to the symmetrical distribution of the variants in the basal plane, it is adequate to investigate the evolution of three typical precipitate variants (variant-1, variant-2 and variant-3) with an interval of 60° in the simulation. Thus three non-conserved quantities (the structural order parameter η_p, $p = 1-3$) and one conserved quantity (molar fraction of the solute Al atom, c) are introduced, and a phase field model for multi-variant precipitation can be constructed based on the Kim-Kim-Suzuki model[13],

$$\frac{\partial \eta_p}{\partial t} = -M \frac{\delta F}{\delta \eta_p}, \quad p = 1-3 \quad (1)$$

$$\frac{\partial c}{\partial t} = \nabla \cdot \left(\frac{D(T)}{f_{cc}} \nabla(f_c) \right) \quad (2)$$

Eq. (1) is a governing equation of the non-conserved field, i.e. the structural order parameter η_p is defined as 1 in the precipitate phase and 0 in the matrix. M is the interface mobility coefficient. F is the total energy of the system, including chemical free energy, gradient energy and elastic strain energy. Eq. (2) is a governing equation of the conserved field, i.e. the molar fraction of solute, c. $D(T)$ is the solute diffusivity. f_c and f_{cc} are the first- and second-order derivatives of the total energy density f with respect to concentration, respectively.

The total energy F can be expressed as follows:

$$F(c, \{\eta_p\}, T) = \int_v \left[f(c, \{\eta_p\}, T) + \sum_{p=1}^{3} \frac{\varepsilon^2(\varphi_p)}{2} (\nabla \eta_p)^2 \right] dv + E^{ela} \quad (3)$$

where the first integral term denotes the free energy, including the contribution of the chemical free energy and the gradient energy. $\varepsilon(\varphi_p)$ is the gradient energy coefficient related to interface anisotropy and φ_p is the interface anisotropy angle of variant-p, defined as the angle between the interface normal direction and the x axis. The second term on the right, E^{ela}, denotes the elastic strain energy.

The chemical free energy density f can be expressed by the following equation[13]:

$$f(c, \{\eta_p\}, T) = h(\{\eta_p\}) f^\beta(c_\beta, T) + (1 - h(\{\eta_p\})) f^\alpha(c_\alpha, T) + wg(\{\eta_p\}) \quad (4)$$

where c_α and c_β are the molar fractions of atomic Al in the matrix and in the β-$Mg_{17}Al_{12}$ precipitate, respectively. $h(\{\eta_p\})$ is a monotonic function varying from 0 to 1, $g(\{\eta_p\})$ is a double-well potential and w is the double-well potential's height. $f^\alpha(c_\alpha, T)$ and $f^\beta(c_\beta, T)$ denote the chemical free energy density of the matrix and of the precipitate, respectively, which can be calculated through the chemical free energy divided by the molar volume of the system.

In the simulation, for each time step, an iterative algorithm was employed to calculate c_α and c_β, as well as the corresponding chemical free energy and chemical potential of the precipitate and matrix, in which the constraints of Eqs. (5) and (6) were applied and the commercial thermodynamic database Thermo-Calc was coupled. The calculated chemical free energy and chemical potential were used as input parameters for the governing equations to calculate the order parameter and the molar fraction of the solute for next step of the simulation.

$$c = (1 - h(\{\eta_p\}))c_\alpha + h(\{\eta_p\})c_\beta \quad (5)$$

$$\frac{\partial f^\alpha(c_\alpha, T)}{\partial c_\alpha} = \frac{\partial f^\beta(c_\beta, T)}{\partial c_\beta} \quad (6)$$

The elastic strain energy E^{ela} can be calculated as follows using Khachaturyan's elastic strain theory [12],

$$E^{ela} = \frac{1}{2} \sum_{p,q=1}^{3} \int \frac{d^3 \vec{g}}{(2\pi)^3} B_{p,q}(\vec{n}) \{\eta_p^2\}_{\vec{g}} \{\eta_q^2\}_{\vec{g}}^* \quad (7)$$

$$B_{p,q}(\vec{n}) = [C_{ijkl}\varepsilon_{ij}^0(p)\varepsilon_{kl}^0(q) - n_i\sigma_{ij}^0(p)\Omega_{jk}(\vec{n})\sigma_{kl}^0(q)n_l] \quad (8)$$

$$\varepsilon_{ij}^0(r) = \sum_{p=1}^{3} \varepsilon_{ij}^0(p)\eta_p^2 \quad (9)$$

where $B_{p,q}(\vec{n})$ is the elastic interaction energy in Fourier space. $\vec{g}$ is a vector of the Fourier space and $\vec{n} = \frac{\vec{g}}{|\vec{g}|}$. $\{\eta_p^2\}_{\vec{n}}$ denotes Fourier transform of η_p^2, and $\{\eta_q^2\}_{\vec{g}}^*$ denotes the complex conjugate of $\{\eta_q^2\}_{\vec{g}}$. $\Omega_{ik}^{-1}(\vec{g}) = C_{ijkl}n_jn_l$, $\sigma_{ij}^0(p) = C_{ijkl}\varepsilon_{kl}^0(p)$. C_{ijkl} is the elastic modulus tensor. For the sake of numerical computation, an assumption that the modulus of the precipitate is the same as that of the matrix was made. The components of the elastic modulus tensor are $C_{11} = 58$ GPa, $C_{12} = 25$ GPa, $C_{13} = 20.8$ GPa, $C_{33} = 61.2$ GPa and $C_{44} = 16.6$ GPa [9]. $\varepsilon_{ij}^0(r)$ is the stress-free strain tensor. $\varepsilon_{ij}^0(p)$ is the eigen strain tensor of precipitation transformation of variant-p, and its matrix form for variant-1 [14] is expressed as:

$$\varepsilon_{ij}^0(1) = (R5.26°)^T \begin{pmatrix} \frac{\alpha_\beta\sqrt{3} - 6a_\alpha}{6a_\alpha} & 0 & 0 \\ 0 & \frac{\alpha_\beta\sqrt{11} - 6\sqrt{3}a_\alpha}{6\sqrt{3}a_\alpha} & 0 \\ 0 & 0 & \frac{\alpha_\beta\sqrt{2} - 3\sqrt{c_\alpha}}{3c_\alpha} \end{pmatrix} (R5.26°) \quad (10)$$

where a_α and c_α are lattice parameters of the matrix with hcp structure. α_β is the lattice parameter of the precipitate phase with bcc structure. $(R5.26°)$ is the matrix of rigid-body rotation transformation, and is defined as:

$$(R5.26°) = \begin{pmatrix} \cos 5.26° & \sin 5.26° & 0 \\ -\sin 5.26° & \cos 5.26° & 0 \\ 0 & 0 & 1 \end{pmatrix} \quad (11)$$

$(R5.26°)^T$ is the transpose of $(R5.26°)$. The eigen-strain tensor of the other two variants can be obtained via coordinate rotation transformation as follows:

$$\varepsilon_{ij}^0(2) = (R60°)^T \varepsilon_{ij}^0(1)(R60°) \quad (12)$$

$$\varepsilon_{ij}^0(3) = (R120°)^T \varepsilon_{ij}^0(1)(R120°) \quad (13)$$

where $(R60°)$ and $(R120°)$ are rotation transformation matrices that are similar to $(R5.26°)$.

The interface between the precipitate and the matrix was assumed to be composed of semi-coherent and non-coherent interfaces. The interfacial energy anisotropy is defined as:

$$\sigma(\varphi_p) = \sigma_{semi-coherent} + (\sigma_{non-coherent} - \sigma_{semi-coherent})f(\varphi_p) \quad (14)$$

where $\sigma_{non-coherent}$ and $\sigma_{semi-coherent}$ are the interfacial energies of the non-coherent and the semi-coherent interfaces, taking values of 300 and 60 mJm^{-2} from first principles, respectively. $f(\varphi_p)$ is the interface anisotropy coefficient. Figure 1 shows the interface anisotropy coefficient $f(\varphi_p)$ for the three variants in polar coordinate system.

Mesh-induced anisotropy is a common issue in phase field simulation, and is more serious when interfacial anisotropy has to be dealt with in the simulation [15]. In order to reduce the mesh-induced anisotropy, a special numerical technique based on two sets of mesh, a hexagonal one and an orthogonal one, was employed to simulate the multi-variant precipitation. The

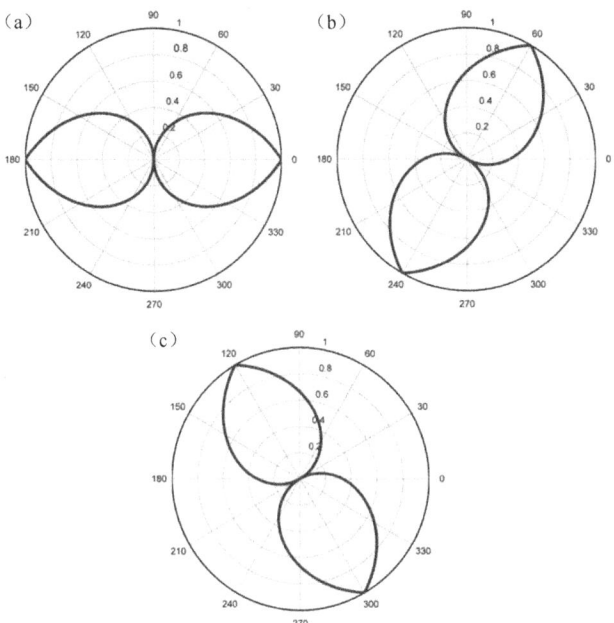

Fig. 1 The interface anisotropy coefficient in the polar coordinate system: (a) variant-1, (b) variant-2 and (c) variant-3.

hexagonal mesh was used to solve the equations governing the phase field, and the orthogonal mesh was adopted to compute the elastic strain energy. The three typical precipitate variants are distributed in the basal plane with intervals of 60°, thus the evolution of the variants in the directions of 60° and 120° would be strongly interfered with by the mesh-induced anisotropy if only the orthogonal mesh was employed in the simulation. Additionally, the calculation of the elastic energy involves a necessary transformation between the Fourier space and real space, and it would be difficult to conduct this transformation if only the hexagonal mesh was used in the simulation. The numerical technique based on the two sets of mesh combines the advantages of the hexagonal mesh in dealing with the precipitate orientation and those of the orthogonal mesh in computing the elastic strain energy. Figure 2 shows the layout of the two meshes (the hexagonal mesh is in red and the orthogonal is in blue), and the two sets of mesh were coupled via data interpolation.

The morphology and distribution of the precipitate variants were simulated using the model and numerical technique developed in this study. In the simulation, round seeds were placed as precipitate nuclei in the simulation domain. The initial composition of the precipitates and the matrix are 0.414 (molar fraction) and 0.0827, respectively. The molar volume of the alloy system is $V_M = 1.3397 \times 10^{-5} m^3 mol^{-1}$. The temperature of domain was assigned to be 441K.

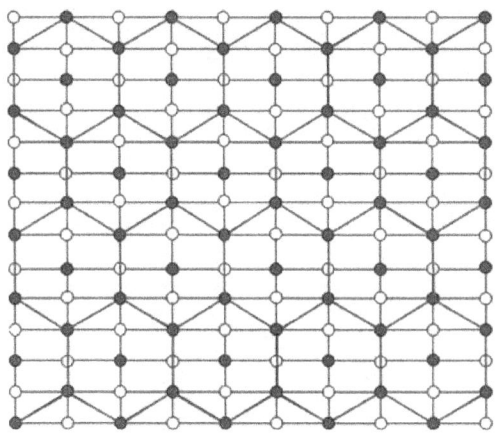

Fig. 2 A schematic of the hexagonal and orthogonal meshes employed in the simulation.

Figure 3 (a) shows the simulation results of the multivariant precipitates at 1600s, with both the interface anisotropy and the elastic strain energy being taken into account. The blue areas in Figure 3 are the matrix, and the red areas represent the precipitate phase. It can be seen that the precipitate phase has a lath shape with lozengeshaped ends, and the three variants are distribute in directions with intervals of 60°. Figure 3 (b) is the TEM brightfield image obtained from AZ91 aged at 441K for 16h, where three typical precipitate variants, with lath shapes and lozenge-shaped ends, can be seen in the basal plane. The angle between variant-1 and variant-2 is about 80°, and that between variant-1 and variant-3 is about 120°. Due to twinning symmetry, the variants have an angular deviation of 2-32° as compared with the reference orientations[3]. The simulation results of the morphology and distribution of the precipitate variants show good agreement with the experimental observations. The growth kinetics of the precipitates between the simulation and experiments are also comparable.

In addition, case studies were conducted in order to understand the effects of the interface anisotropy and elastic strain energy on the morphology and distribution of the precipitates. Figure 3 (c) presents the simulation results without considering the interface anisotropy or elastic strain energy, and shows round shapes in the

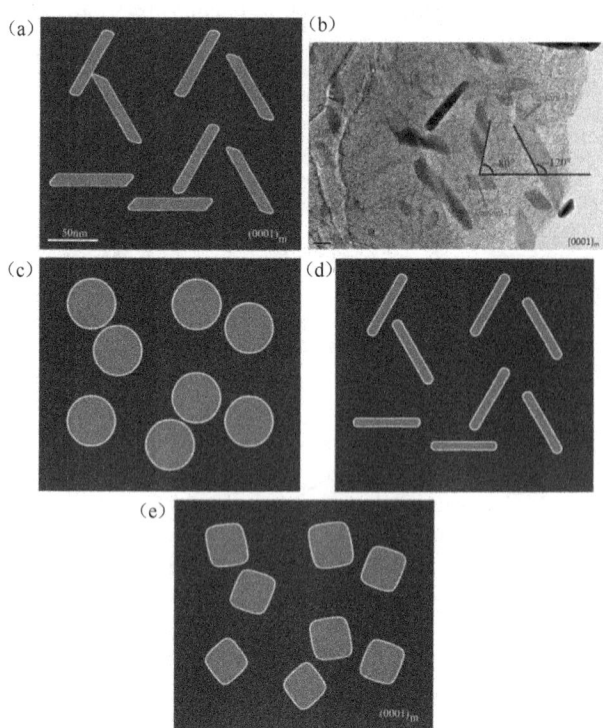

Fig. 3 Simulation and TEM observation of multi-variant precipitation, (a) considering the interface anisotropy and the elastic strain energy, (b) TEM bright-field image of the precipitates for AZ91 aged at 441K for 16h, (c) without considering the interface anisotropy and the elastic strain energy, (d) considering only the interface anisotropy and, (e) considering only the elastic strain energy.

morphology of the precipitates. When the effect of the interface anisotropy is added, all the precipitates show a lath shape with two round ends, and are distributed in directions with an angular interval of 60° (Fig. 3(d)). This implies that the lath morphology arises from the interface anisotropy. However, the morphology of the ends of the precipitates is still different from the experimental observations. Figure 3 (e) presents the simulation results when only the elastic strain energy is considered, and shows that the precipitates are in a diamond shape. The difference in morphology of the ends in Figure 3 (a) and (d) is attributed to the effect of elastic strain energy. It is clear that the morphology and distribution of the precipitates are governed by both the interface anisotropy and the elastic energy, and when both of them were considered, the phase field simulation agrees well with the experimental results.

A two-dimensional phase field model has been developed to simulate the multi-variant β-$Mg_{17}Al_{12}$ phase precipitation in Mg-Al alloy that considers the interface anisotropy and elastic strain energy. A special numerical technique based on two sets of mesh was employed to combine the advantages of hexagonal mesh in dealing with the precipitate orientation and those of orthogonal mesh in computing the elastic strain energy. The model shows that the morphology and distribution of the precipitates are affected by the interface anisotropy and the elastic strain energy. When they are both considered in simulation, the simulated precipitates have a lath shape with lozenge-shaped ends, and the precipitate variants are distributed in directions with an angular interval of 60°, which is in good agreement with experimental observations. The numerical simulation indicated that the lath morphology arises from the interface anisotropy and the morphology of the lozenge-shaped ends is attributed to the effect of the elastic strain energy.

This work is funded by the National Natural Science Foundation of China (Grant No. 51175291), the General Motors Global Research and Development Center, Tsinghua University Initiative Scientific Research Program (Grant No. 2011Z02160) and the MoST (Ministry of Science and Technology) of China under the Contract Nos. 2010DFA72760 and 2011DFA50909.

[1] B. L. Mordike, T. Ebert, Mater. Sci. Eng. A 302 (2001) 37.
[2] J. B. Clark, Acta Metall. 16 (1968) 141.
[3] S. Celotto, Acta Mater. 48 (2000) 1775.
[4] D. Duly, J. P. Simon, Y. Brecher, Acta Metall. Mater. 43 (1995) 101.
[5] C. R. Hutchinson, J. F. Nie, S. Gorsse, Metall. Mater. Trans. A 36 (2005) 2093.
[6] Y. Z. Wang, L. Q. Chen, A. G. Khachaturyan, Acta Metall. Mater. 41 (1993) 279.
[7] J. Z. Zhu, Z. K. Liu, V. Vaithyanathan, L. Q. Chen, Scripta Mater. 46 (2002) 401.
[8] V. Vaithyanathan, C. Wolverton, L. Q. Chen, Acta Mater. 52 (2004) 2973.
[9] M. Li, R. J. Zhang, J. Allison, in: S. Agnew, N. R. Neelameggham, E. A. Nyberg, W. Sillekens (Eds.), Magnesium Technology, TMS, Seattle, 2010, pp. 623-627.
[10] Y. P. Gao, H. Liu, R. Shi, N. Zhou, Z. Xu, Y. M. Zhu, J. F. Nie, Y. Z. Wang, Acta Mater. 60 (2012) 4819.

[11] G. M. Han, Z. Q. Han, A. A. Luo, S. K. Sachdev, B. C. Liu, Mater. Sci. Eng. 33 (2012) 012110.

[12] A. G. Khachaturyan, Theory of Structural Transformation in Solids, Wiley-Interscience, New York, 1983.

[13] S. G. Kim, W. T. Kim, T. Suzuki, Phys. Rev. E: Stat. Phys. 60 (1999) 7186.

[14] N. Katarzyna, M. Braszczynska, in: F. Czerwinski (Ed.), Magnesium Alloys-Design, Processing and Properties, In-Tech Press, Croatia, 2011, pp. 95-112.

[15] A. M. Mullis, Comput. Mater. Sci. 36 (2006) 345.

大型铸件及钢锭建模与仿真

24. Instability of Fluid Flow and Level Fluctuation in Continuous Thin Slab Casting Mould

Bingzhen SHEN, Houfa SHEN and Baicheng LIU
Key Laboratory for Advanced Materials Processing Technology, Department of
Mechanical Engineering, Tsinghua University, Beijing, 100084 China.
E-mail: shenbz00@tsinghua.edu.cn, shen@tsinghua.edu.cn, liubc@tsinghua.edu.cn

A full scale water modeling experiment has been conducted to address the relationship between the instability of fluid flow and level fluctuation in the continuous thin slab casting mould with the particle image visualization. The results show that the internal fluid flow and level fluctuation are unsteady and periodical. The probabilities of fluctuated meniscus and moving circumfluence center position seem Possion distributions with the highest frequency near the average position. The circumfluence and meniscus profile are asymmetrical, and the phase difference of wave height and circumfluence center in the two sides of mould centerline is half period. The average meniscus profile, the highest and lowest meniscus positions are generally symmetry about the mould centerline, and the circumfluence center swings with a similar trace. The wave height mainly depends on the circumfluence center position along the mould height. The wave height has an inverse relation with the circumfluence center depth, and the wave height decreases with descending circumfluence.

Key words: continuous thin slab casting; mould; water modeling; fluid flow; level fluctuation.

1. Introduction

With the growth of continuous casting, both experimental and numerical work has been carried out to study the fluid flow in the mould. During the continuous casting of steel, transient flow is very important to the strand quality, and the level fluctuation is believed to have significant contribution to mould powder entrapment. So, control of fluid flow and level fluctuation plays an important role in attaining a better product quality.

For the study of internal flow instability in the mould, Robertson et al.[1] found that the flow asymmetry in a slab mould was either fluctuating or persistent. Gupta et al.[2-4] carried out a water model and found that the flow pattern in the mould was oscillating and asymmetric about the central plane with a random period. Gupta also found the non-uniform flow at the mould exit and pointed out that these nonuniform discharge characteristics were directly related to the asymmetric recirculation pattern. Honeyands et al.[5] constructed a 1 : 6 scale model of the thin slab caster water model to investigate the time dependent flow phenomena and observed that the fluid condition were neither steady nor symmetrical, and instead oscillated periodically. Honeyands pointed out that the interaction between the confined jets and the recirculating fluid eddies could be a critical factor responsible for the oscillation in the thin slab flow system. Ramos-Banderas et al.[6] studied the fluid flow of water in the slab mould using Digital Particle Image Velocimetry (DPIV) and found that the asymmetry of fluid flows and the flow pattern changed with time as a consequence of the vertical oscillation of the jet core. The jet angle and its impinging position on the mould narrow face varied with time corroborating the oscillatory motion of the entry jet. Vanka and Thomas et al.[7,8] studied the fluid flow in a 0.4-scale water mould using

Particle Image Velocimetry (PIV) and the Large Eddy Simulation (LES) methods and found that the flow in the upper region was oscillating between a large single vortex and multiple vortices of various smaller sizes. Davidson et al.[9,10] observed the jet oscillation in thin slab continuous casting using a two-dimensional transient numerical model and found that the oscillation relied on the exchange of fluid between recirculation cells on each side of the jet via a cross-flow through the gap between the nozzle shaft and the broad face of the mould. Davidson et al.[11] also used Laser Doppler Anemometry (LDA) measurements in a 1 : 3 scale water model of the thin slab casting mould with two lateral jets through a bifurcated nozzle and found that the time averaged flow pattern was almost symmetric across the broad face of the mould.

For the study of level fluctuation in the mould, Matsushita et al.[12] measured the meniscus of the molten steel directly through a quartz glass window mounted on the mould wall and found that the meniscus was not stationary but fluctuated at the same period and phase as those of mould oscillation. Gupta et al.[13] found that the meniscus profile kept on fluctuating and was not always symmetric on either side of the nozzle, but the time-average value showed a symmetric pattern. Miranda et al.[14] studied the free surface fluctuations using a 1 : 3 scale cold water model and found that the free surface level fluctuation showed an erratic behavior. Ramírez-López et al.[15] studied the structure of the turbulent flow in a slab mould using a water model and mathematical simulation and found that the meniscus stability depended on the turbulence structure of the flow in the mould.

It is known that the fluid flow is much turbulent in the continuous thin slab casting and the flow instability may be much complicated in the specified mould. A quantitative description of the instability of the fluid flow and level fluctuation in the mould can be relied on design of the SEN structure and the process parameters. The present work aims to investigate the relationship among the flow instability characters such as circumfluence position, level fluctuation and wave height by using a full scale funnel type continuous thin slab casting mould.

2. Experimental

Direct observation of fluid flow in the real mould during continuous casting is very difficult, or even impossible. For this reason, the present study was performed using a full scale water model with the dimension of a practical mould and a two-port down-through submerged entry nozzle (SEN). The full scale water model satisfies Reynolds-Froude similarity requirements, which means that what is observed in the water model reasonably represents the phenomena occurring in the prototype. **Figure 1** shows the water modeling experimental setup of continuous thin slab casting consisting a mould, a tundish and a water reservoir. A stopper with height adjustment was used for flow rate control. The flow circuit of water model led fluid from the reservoir to the tundish, then the fluid was discharged into the mould via the two-port down-through SEN and finally returned back into the reservoir. The flow circuit was maintained by a centrifugal pump. The water level in the tundish was kept stable using two baffles and an overflow pipe. To monitor the flow rate through the water modeling system, an electromagnetic flow meter was installed between the mould and the reservoir. The mould was made in Plexiglas with width of 1600mm and thickness at the mould outlet of 70mm. In order to find detail flow information near the mould outlet, the height of experimental mould was extended to 2000mm. SEN immersion depth i.e., the distance from the meniscus to the SEN bottom was 255mm. The experiment was carried out with the casting speed of 6.0m/min. To ensure an even outflow from the bottom of the mould, some holes were spaced uniformly on mould bottom. The SEN was fixed strictly at the mould center and the geometrical construction of the mould was symmetrical. Flow visualization was realized by using particle tracing method and the tracing particles with density close to water were added when the system was time averaged stable in global. The transient flow in the mould with constant process parameters was recorded using a digital camera and video. The wave fluctuation and meniscus profile were recorded by a wave gauge and 12 wave height sensors with the mark of L1~L6 and R6~R1 in the left and right sides of the mould centerline, and the recording time interval was 0.25s with whole time of 512s. The wave height sensors were located at the meniscus with the same spacing along the mould width direction.

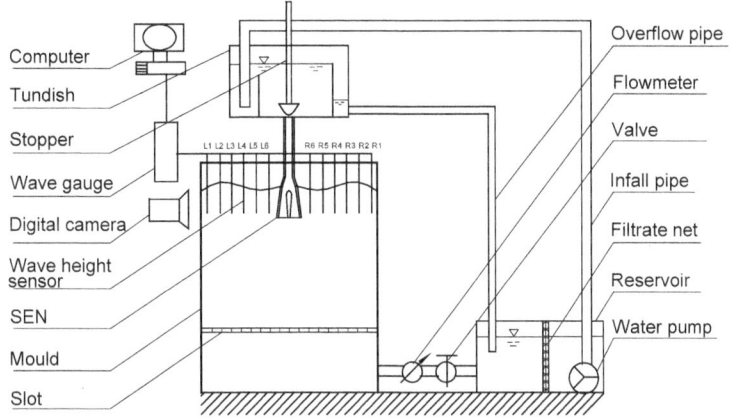

Fig. 1 Schematic of water modeling experimental setup for the fluid flow in continuous thin slab casting mould.

Figure 2 shows a photo of the fluid flow along the mould broad face using the particle image visualization method. In order to quantitatively analyze the circumfluence region and the circumfluence center position with time, the grids in size of 50mm×50mm were marked on the mould broad face. According to the fluid flow characteristic with the present experimental condition, a definition about the wave heights (W_L, W_R) and circumfluence center positions (X_L, Y_L and X_R, Y_R) in the left and the right sides of mould centerline are indicated in **Fig. 3**. In this paper, the wave height is defined as the distance between the wave crest and valley of the meniscus profile. The origin of coordinate is at the intersection of the liquid level and mould centerline.

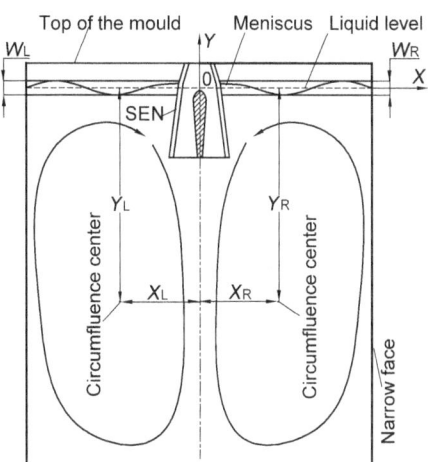

Fig. 3 Definition of circumfluence center position (X, Y) and wave height (W).

3. Results and Discussion

3.1 Instability of Level Fluctuation

From the experiment, it is found that the meniscus is unstable and the liquid level fluctuates with time in the mould. The average meniscus wave profile during the monitoring time of 512s is shown with a dense line in **Fig. 4**. The typical meniscus profile in the mould looks like a saddle with two crests near the mould narrow faces and two valleys near the mould centerline where the SEN locates. In order to describe the instability of meniscus, the highest and the lowest positions of the meniscus are ranged around the averaged meniscus profile and the

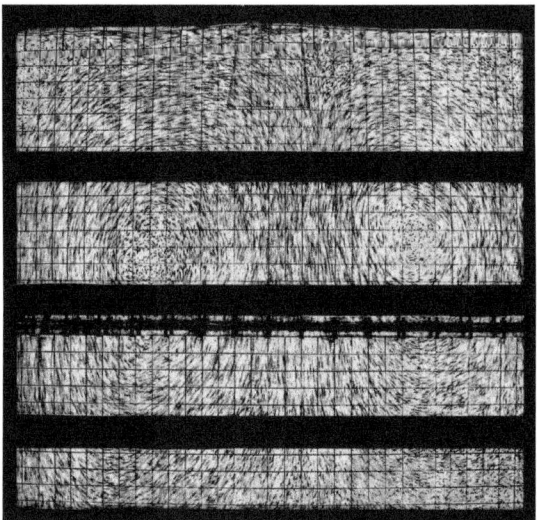

Fig. 2 Flow pattern along the continuous thin slab casting mould broad face with the mesh size of 50×50mm.

probability of the fluctuated wave position between the highest and the lowest positions of the meniscus are also illustrated in Fig. 4. The dash line in Fig. 4 indicates the average liquid level along the mould width. The average wave profile, the highest and the lowest positions of the meniscus as well as the probability of the fluctuated wave position in Fig. 4 are generally symmetrical about the mould centerline. The average wave height of the meniscus i.e., the average of the left and the right wave heights is 6.7mm. The range of the fluctuated meniscus between the highest and lowest positions is about 25.4mm. The probabilities of the fluctuated wave at 12 wave height sensor positions look like Possion distributions with the maximum frequency near the average wave height and the minimum frequency near the highest and the lowest positions of the meniscus. It is known that the steel slag interfacial disturbances should be kept a minimum to avoid any entrainment of impurities into steel. So, these characteristic values can be recommended as guidance to quantitatively analyze the flow conditions at the meniscus of continuous casting.

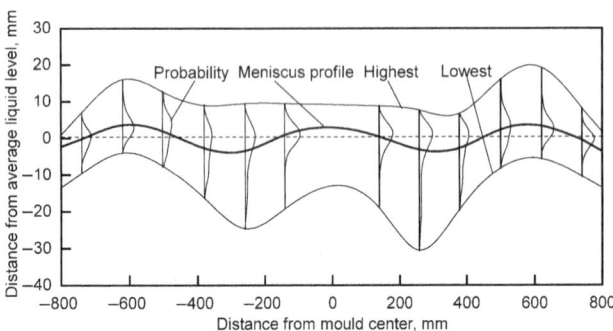

Fig. 4 Meniscus profile and probabilities of the fluctuated wave positions along the mould broad face.

3.2 Instability of Fluid Flow in Mould

For the two-port SEN with the outlet angle directly downward, the jets from each port of SEN are discharged to the mould bottom and the part of fluid flows back to the meniscus as shown in Fig. 2. In this case, it is hard to found the impinging area at the mould narrow face, so only two dominant circumfluences occupy in the left and the right sides of mould centerline with rotation directions in clockwise and anticlockwise respectively. According to the movie of particle image visualization, it is found that the circumfluence area and the circumfluence center swings with time. **Figure 5** shows the positions of the two circumfluence centers with scattered dot and the probabilities of the circumfluence center position along the mould width and height. The moving range of two circumfluence centers is about 200mm in mould width and 500mm in mould height direction. The average position of the left circumfluence center is at (−379,−653) and the right one is at (378,−651). The probability of the moving circumfluence center is like a Possion distribution with the maximum value of about 0.2 near the average circumfluence center. Both the occurring position and its probability of circumfluence center are generally symmetrical about mould centerline.

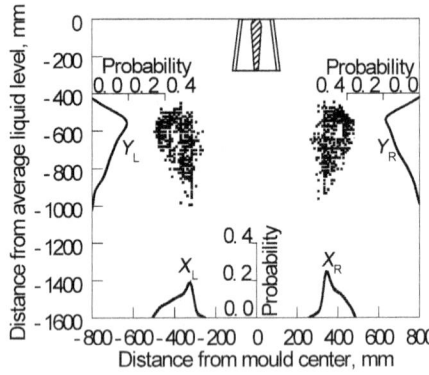

Fig. 5 Position and probability of circumfluence center along the mould broad face.

Figure 6 shows the trajectories of two swing circumfluence centers. It is found that the left circumfluence center moves in counter-clockwise while the right circumfluence center moves in clockwise, and they all move around their average circumfluence center position with a certain period (T) and a similar trace.

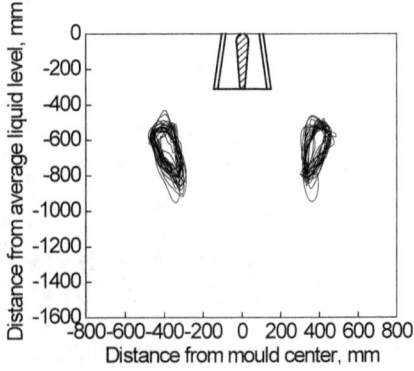

Fig. 6 Contrail of two swing circumfluence centers along the mould broad face.

3.3 Relation of Level Fluctuation and Fluid Flow

In order to explore the influence of swing circumfluence on the fluctuated meniscus, two characteristic points near the meniscus valley were selected with the wave sensor marked numbers of L4 and R4 as indicated in Fig. 1. **Figure 7** shows the variation of circumfluence center positions (X_L, Y_L and X_R, Y_R), level fluctuation at characteristic points (F_{L4}, F_{R4}) and wave heights (W_L, W_R) in two sides of mould centerline. It is found that the circumfluence center, level fluctuation and wave height vary with a similar period of about 23.3s during the monitoring time of 512s. The wave height (W_L, W_R) is coherently related to the fluctuation near the meniscus valley (F_{L4}, F_{R4}) with the opposite variation, i.e., the wave height increases with decreasing fluctuation near the meniscus valley. The wave height variation has a same phase with the circumfluence center position along the mould height (Y_L and Y_R), and there is a phase difference about a quarter of period between the circumfluence center position along the mould width (X_L and X_R) and that along the mould height (Y_L and Y_R). The wave height increases with rising circumfluence while circumfluence center departs from the SEN, and the wave height decreases with descending circumfluence while the circumfluence center approaches to the SEN. Therefore, the movement of meniscus is mainly depends on swing of circumfluence. Comparing Figs. 7(a) and 7(b), it can be found that the phase difference of both the wave height and circumfluence position in the left and the right sides of mould is about half period. According to the parameters variation in Fig. 7, the phase differences of wave height, characteristic level fluctuation and circumfluence position are indicated in **Table 1** with the reference phase of wave height in the mould left side as 0.

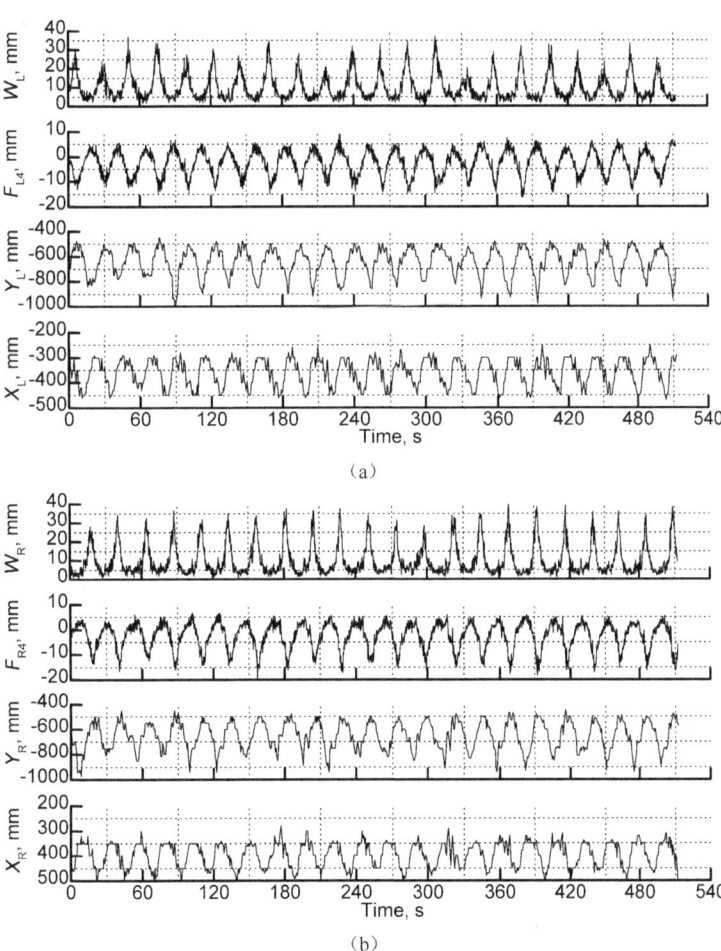

Fig. 7 Variation of wave height (W), characteristic level fluctuation (F) and circumfluence position (X, Y).
(a) In the left side of mould centerline; (b) in the right side of mould centerline.

Table 1 Phase differences of wave height, characteristic level fluctuation and circumfluence position.

	wave height	flucuation at meniscus valley	circumfluence center position in mould height	circumfluence center position in mould width
In mould left side	0	T/2	T/4	T/2
In mould right side	T/2	T	3T/4	T

The relation of circumfluence center position and level fluctuation can be described more clearly in **Fig. 8**, which indicates the variation of circumfluence center position and meniscus profile in an arbitrarily period from the monitoring time of 50.75 – 74.00s in Fig. 7. In order to investigate the evolution of meniscus profile and circumfluence center position, eight intervals is equally divided in the period. For a moment, the circumfluence center position and wave profile is not symmetrical about the mould centerline. For example, at the 1/8 period the meniscus valley in the mould left side is at the lowest position and the circumfluence center position in the mould left side is at the highest, while the meniscus valley in the mould right side is at the highest position and the circumfluence center position in the mould right side is at the lowest (as indicated with number 1 in Fig. 8). After half period, this asymmetry of both circumfluence and meniscus reverses in mirror about the mould centerline. According to the characteristic of meniscus profiles with the same time interval, it is found that the meniscus fluctuates more quickly when the meniscus valley is near to the lowest position.

Figure 9 shows quantitative relation of the wave height (W_L, W_R) with the circumfluence position along the mould height (Y_L, Y_R) in the left and the right sides of the mould centerline. It can be seen that they have inverse relation. However, it is sure that there is a relation of the wave height W with the circumfluence position along the mould width X because there is a phase difference between the circumfluence center position along the mould width and height.

According to the foregoing results, it can be found that the level fluctuation is decided by the instabilities of fluid flow, which is characterized by the period and the swing aptitude of the circumfluence in the continuous casting mould. It is estimated that these characteristic values would be affected by the SEN structure and the process parameters. Therefore, a further investigation on the optimization of the SEN structure and the process parameters with certain instabilities criteria for the practice will be helpful for the control of level fluctuation and fluid flow in the continuous thin slab casting.

4. Conclusions

The instability of level fluctuation and fluid flow in continuous thin slab casting mould with a two-port downthrough submerged entry nozzle has been investigated by wave measurement and particle image visualization in a full scale water modeling system. Conclusions are summarized as following:

(1) The circumfluence center swings and the meniscus profile fluctuates with time. The probabilities of fluctuated meniscus and swing circumfluence center position seem Possion distributions with the highest frequency near the average position.

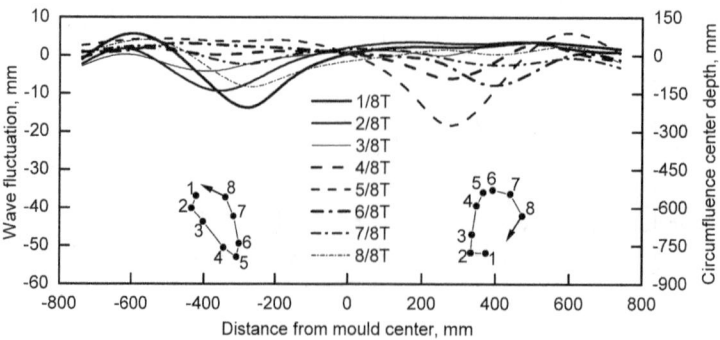

Fig. 8 Variation of circumfluence center position and meniscus profile in one period.

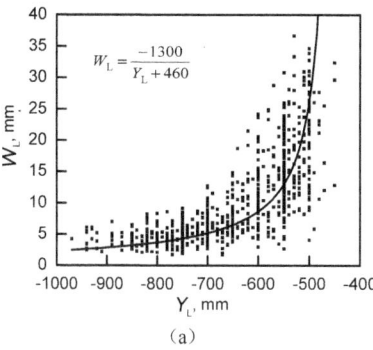
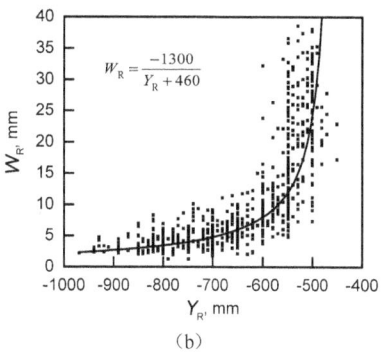

Fig. 9 Quantitative relation of wave height (W) with circumfluence position in mould height Y.
(a) In the left side of mould centerline; (b) in the right side of mould centerline.

(2) The level fluctuation and circumfluence movement is periodical with a similar period. The circumfluence and meniscus profile may be asymmetrical for a moment, and the phase difference of wave height and circumfluence center in the two sides of mould centerline is half period. However, the average circumfluence center position, the average meniscus wave profile, the highest and lowest meniscus positions are generally symmetry about the mould centerline, and circumfluence center swings with a similar trace.

(3) The wave height mainly depends on the circumfluence position with constant process parameters. The wave height has an inverse relation with the circumfluence center position in mould height, and the wave height decreases with descending circumfluence.

Acknowledgement

The work is financially supported by the Iron and Steel Research Joint Fund of NSFC and Baoshan Steel Complex of Shanghai in China (50474088).

REFERENCES

[1] T. Robertson, P. Moore and R. J. Hawkins: *Ironmaking Steelmaking*, **13** (1986), 195.

[2] D. Gupta and A. K. Lahiri: *Metall. Mater. Trans. B*, **27B** (1996), 757.

[3] D. Gupta, S. Chakraborty and A. K. Lahiri: *ISIJ Int.*, **37** (1997), 654.

[4] D. Gupta, S. Subramaniam and A. K. Lahiri: *Process. Metall.*, **62** (1991), 496.

[5] T. Honeyands and J. Herbertson: *Process. Metall.*, **66** (1995), 287.

[6] A. Ramos-Banderas, R. Sánchez-Peréz, R. D. Morales, J. PalafoxRamos, L. Demedices-García and M. Díaz-Cruz: *Metall. Mater. Trans. B*, **35B** (2004), 449.

[7] Q. Yuan, S. Sivaramakrishnan, S. P. Vanka and B. G. Thomas: *Metall. Mater. Trans. B*, **35B** (2004), 967.

[8] B. G. Thomas, H. Bai, S. Sivaramakrishnan and S. P. Vanka: Int. Symp. on Cutting Edge of Computer Simulation of Solidification and Processes, ISIJ, Tokyo, (1999), 113.

[9] B. M. Gebert, M. R. Davidson and M. J. Rudman: *Appl. Math. Model.*, **22** (1998), 843.

[10] M. R. Davidson and N. J. Lawson: Second Int. Conf. on CFD in the Minerals and Process Industries, CSIRO, Melbourne, (1999), 6.

[11] N. J. Lawson and M. R. Davidson: *Trans. ASME J. Fluid Eng.*, **124** (2002), 535.

[12] A. Matsushita, K. Isogami, M. Temma, M. Temma, T. Ninomiya and K. Tsutsumi: *Trans. Iron Steel Inst. Jpn.*, **28** (1988), 531.

[13] D. Gupta and A. K. Lahiri: *Metall. Mater. Trans. B*, **25B** (1994), 227.

[14] R. Miranda, M. A. Barron, J. Barreto, L. Hoyos and J. Gonzalez: *ISIJ Int.*, **45** (2005), 1626.

[15] P. Ramírez-López, R. D. Morales, R. Sánchez-Pérez, L. G. Demedices and O. Dávila: *Metall. Mater. Trans. B*, **36B** (2005), 787.

25. A Coupled Electrical-Thermal-Mechanical Modeling of Gleeble Tensile Tests for Ultra-High-Strength (UHS) Steel at a High Temperature

CHANGLI ZHANG, MICHEL BELLET, MANUEL BOBADILLA, HOUFA SHEN, and BAICHENG LIU

A coupled electrical-thermal-mechanical model is proposed aimed at the numerical modeling of Gleeble tension tests at a high temperature. A multidomain, multifield coupling resolution strategy is used for the solution of electrical, energy, and momentum conservation equations by means of the finite element method. Its application to ultra-high-strength steel is considered. After calibration with instrumented experiments, numerical results reveal that significant thermal gradients prevail in Gleeble tensile steel specimen in both axial and radial directions. Such gradients lead to the heterogeneous deformation of the specimen, which is a major difficulty for simple identification techniques of constitutive parameters, based on direct estimations of strain, strain rate, and stress. The proposed direct finite element coupled model can be viewed as an important achievement for subsequent inverse identification methods, which should be used to identify constitutive parameters for steel at a high temperature in the solid state and in the mushy state.

DOI: 10.1007/s11661-010-0310-7

© The Minerals, Metals & Materials Society and ASM International 2010

I. INTRODUCTION

VARIOUS defects on as-cast products often are encountered in shape or continuous casting production. Hot tears formed at the end of solidification or cracks formed at a lower temperature in the solid state are frequent defects in industrial practice. They can be found at or near the surface or in the core of products. Such defects cannot be eliminated by postthermomechanical treatments. From many studies, it is known that hot tears, which are also called solidification cracks, initiate just above solidus temperature in the mushy zone when it is subjected to a tensile state.[1] To predict the initiation of such cracks, many hot tearing "macroscopic" criteria have been proposed that mostly involve critical stress,[2] critical strain,[3-5] or critical strain rate.[6] Therefore, the mathematical modeling of the formation of such cracks in cast products is a complex task, which should be based on a reliable prediction of the local thermomechanical state in castings, which requires, in turn, reliable and accurate constitutive relations for the considered materials, especially at high temperature.

Experimental studies of the rheological behavior of metals have been reported extensively in literature for many years. However, several articles deal with the characterization of steels at a very high temperature, namely higher than 1473K (1200°C), and up to the mushy state. The difficulties mainly are caused by the very high level of steel melting points in comparison with nonferrous metals like aluminum alloys, which demand strict requirements for the experimental devices. Gleeble thermosimulator systems are efficient tools for this subject, as they provide means for characterizing metals at a high temperature, under vacuum, and along complex thermal-mechanical paths.[7,8] However, it should be noted that, as reported in literature,[7-9] thermal gradients always exist at a high temperature in Gleeble-type tension or compression specimens. Because the mechanical properties of steel are temperature dependent, such thermal gradients become the source of deformation heterogeneities in specimens. As a consequence, an accurate analysis of Gleeble tension or compression tests, in view of identifying parameters of constitutive equations, cannot be carried out based on the usual assumption of uniform stress, strain rate, and strain in the working zone of the specimen. The identification task then must be based on the inverse methods involving an accurate direct numerical modeling of such tests.

The current article focuses on the direct modeling of Gleeble tensile tests for steel at a high temperature, with the intention of providing a reliable direct numerical simulation of tests for subsequent inverse identification. During Gleeble tension tests, complex phenomena occur concurrently, such as electrical, thermal, and mechanical phenomena, which are seldom taken into account. Most articles that deal with numerical modeling of Gleeble tests only consider the electrical-thermal problem, like Brown et al.,[10] Norris and Wilson,[11] and Solek et al.,[12] for instance, which are already of great help in the design of Gleeble specimens. In the present study, a coupled electrical-thermal-mechanical model, which is the subject of this work, is described and applied to the direct modeling of Gleeble tensile tests on steel specimens at a high temperature, which provides the basis for the automatic inverse identification of constitutive parameters for steels at a very high temperature.

II. EXPERIMENTAL PROCEDURE

An ultra-high-strength (UHS) steel is considered in the current study; the main chemical composition of which is 0.16 wt pct C, 0.23 wt pct Si, and 1.89 wt pct Mn. Cylindrical tensile specimens with 10-mm diameter and 120-mm length (Figure 1(a)) have been tested using a Gleeble machine (model 1500D, Dynamic Systems Inc., Poestenkill, NY), which is shown schematically in Figure 1(b). The specimen is heated by an alternate current (AC), which is introduced through the copper grips. The vacuum atmosphere in the chamber is maintained at 5×10^{-4} torr (about 0.067Pa) to prevent oxidation of the specimen and also to minimize heat losses by convection. A transparent quartz tube is used to cover the working zone of the specimen to retain the possible melt.

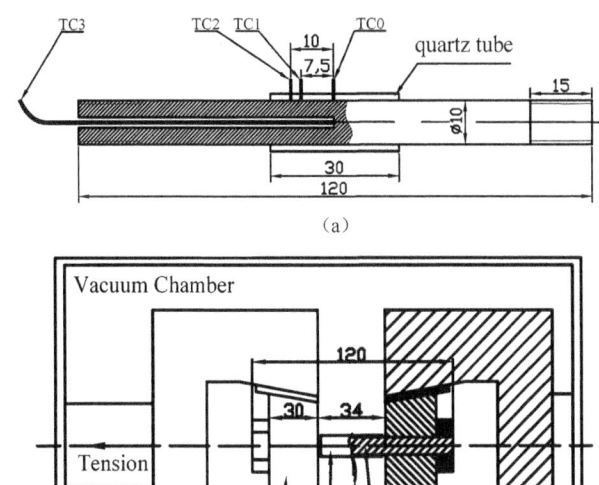

Fig. 1 Schematics of Gleeble 1500D tensile testing system. (a) Temperature measurements of the cylindrical specimen in specially dedicated tests. (b) Section view of the tensile specimen installed in the machine.

In the first step, as shown in Figure 2, the specimen is heated rapidly to 1323K (1050℃) with a heating rate of 15K/s (15℃/s) and held for 1 minute for homogenization. In the second step, it is heated to the testing temperature (at 2K/s (2℃/s)) and is maintained there for 1 minute before mechanical loading. During the entire testing period, including heating and mechanical loading, the electrical input is monitored according to the temperature measured by the thermocouple welded on the surface of the specimen at midlength (TC0 in Figure 1(b)). In the subsequent sections of the article, in the absence of complementary information, the temperatures that are mentioned are those measured or predicted at this location TC0.

To obtain data for the temperature distribution in the specimen, temperatures were measured continuously at the following locations in specifically dedicated tests (see Figure 1(a)):

(a) At the following locations along the surface of the specimen: midlength (TC0), 7.5mm, and 10mm from the center (TC1 and TC2, respectively). This measurement provides information on the axial temperature gradient. In addition, the temperature measurement in position TC0 is used all along the test for the monitoring of the electrical input.

(b) In the core center on the symmetry axis, which is in the midtransverse section of the specimen (TC3). By comparing these data with TC0 it provides access to the radial temperature gradient.

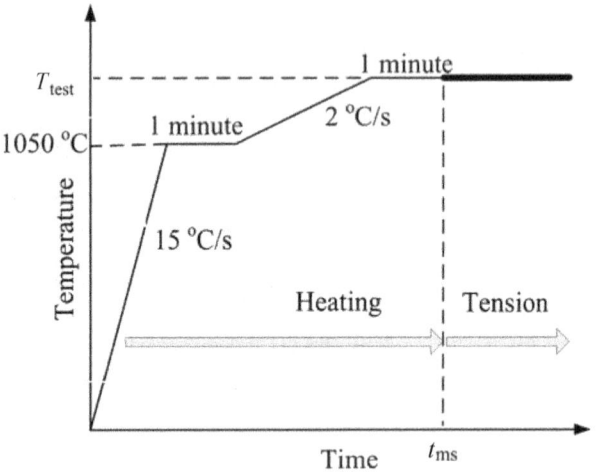

Fig. 2 Schematic diagram of the thermal-mechanical history for tensile tests.

III. NUMERICAL MODELING OF GLEEBLE TENSION TESTS

A. Geometrical Model

In the numerical simulation of Gleeble tension tests, both the specimen and the copper grips are taken into account and assumed as axisymmetric, without considering the nuts at both ends of the specimen, as shown in Figure 3. The free surfaces and contact interfaces mentioned in the following paragraphs also are indicated. The boundaries $\partial\Omega_{gf1}$ and $\partial\Omega_{gf2}$ are the two lateral surfaces of the grips in contact with the Gleeble framework. $\partial\Omega_{sg}$ is the contact interface between the grips and the specimen. The boundary $\partial\Omega_s$ is the surface of the specimen between the two grips. Finally, the boundaries $\partial\Omega_{g\_es}$ and $\partial\Omega_{g\_is}$ are the outer-and innerside surfaces of the grips, respectively.

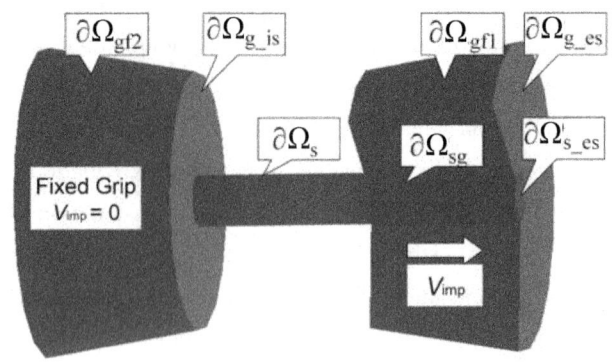

Fig. 3 Schematic geometric model used for the modeling of Gleeble tensile tests.

B. Electrical Solution

The electrical potential field in a conductor is governed by Maxwell's equation of conservation of electrical charge. When assuming a steady-state direct current (DC), the equations can be written as follows[13]:

$$\mathbf{J} = -\sigma_{elec}\nabla\phi \quad (1)$$

$$\nabla \cdot \mathbf{J} = 0 \quad (2)$$

where ϕ is the electrical potential, σ_{elec} is the electrical conductivity, and $\mathbf{J}$ is the electrical current density vector. The solution of the electrical problem consists of solving the following Poisson type equation for the following electrical potential:

$$\nabla \cdot (\sigma_{elec}\nabla\phi) = 0 \quad (3)$$

The following three types of boundary conditions may be used:

$$\phi = \phi_{imp} \quad (4a)$$

$$-\mathbf{J} \cdot \mathbf{n} = J_{imp} \quad (4b)$$

$$\mathbf{J} \cdot \mathbf{n} = h_{elec}(\phi - \phi_{contact}) \quad (4c)$$

Equation (4a) represents a prescribed electrical potential ϕ_{imp} at the boundary. This boundary condition is used on the surface $\partial\Omega_{gf2}$ of the fixed grip with $\phi_{imp}=0$.

Equation (4b) corresponds to the imposition of an electrical current density J_{imp}, with $\mathbf{n}$ denoting the local outward unit normal vector. This boundary condition is used on the surface $\partial\Omega_{gf1}$ of the mobile grip, the value of J_{imp} being possibly automatically calculated and dynamically updated to control the specimen temperature, as explained further.

Equation (4c) expresses a nonperfect electrical contact; the input electrical current density then is related to the local difference of electrical potential. ϕ_{contact} is the local electrical potential at the surface of the neighbor domain, and h_{elec} is an effective electrical transfer coefficient. This condition is used along the interface $\partial\Omega_{\text{sg}}$ between the specimen and the grips. For a quasiperfect electrical contact, an arbitrary large value for h_{elec} is used, resulting in a very small difference between the electrical potentials, which expresses the quasicontinuity of ϕ through the interface.

Using Green's (divergence) theorem, the weak or global form of Eq. (3) is as follows:

$$\forall \phi^*, \quad \int_{\Omega} \sigma_{\text{elec}} \nabla\phi \cdot \nabla\phi^* \, d\Omega + \int_{\partial\Omega} \phi^* \mathbf{J} \cdot \mathbf{n} d\Gamma = 0 \quad (5)$$

where ϕ^* denotes scalar test functions and $\partial\Omega$ denotes the surface of the specimen, which can be decomposed as indicated in Figure 3 with boundary conditions specified in Eq. (4). A classic Galerkin finite element formulation is used to discretize this equation, leading to a set of linear equations to be solved for the nodal values of the electrical potential. A multidomain resolution strategy is used to solve the electrical potential in the grips and the specimen with details expanded in Section III-E.

C. Energy Equation Resolution

Considering the Joule heat input but neglecting the heat source associated with deformation power (as only very low strain rates are envisaged here), the energy conservation is as follows[13]:

$$\rho \frac{dh}{dt} - \nabla \cdot (\lambda \nabla T) - P_v^{\text{elec}} \quad (6)$$

where ρ denotes the density, h is the specific enthalpy, λ is the heat conductivity, and T is the temperature. The specific enthalpy h is defined as follows:

$$h = \int_{T_{\text{ref}}}^{T} c_p(\tau) d\tau + f_l L \quad (7)$$

with T_{ref} as an arbitrary reference temperature, c_p is the specific heat, f_l is the mass fraction of liquid, and L is the specific latent heat of fusion. In the current study, mass and volume fractions are assumed identical and are given as a function of temperature. Therefore, the value of the specific enthalpy can be calculated for any value of the temperature.

In Eq. (6), P_v^{elec} is the volume heat source associated with resistance heating, which is given by the following Joule's law[13]:

$$P_v^{\text{elec}} = \sigma_{\text{elec}}^{-1} \mathbf{J} \cdot \mathbf{J} = \sigma_{\text{elec}} \nabla\phi \cdot \nabla\phi \quad (8)$$

The following three types of thermal boundary conditions may be used:

$$-\lambda \nabla T \cdot \mathbf{n} = q_{\text{imp}} \quad (9a)$$

$$-\lambda \nabla T \cdot \mathbf{n} = h_c (T - T_{\text{contact}}) + \frac{b}{b + b_{\text{contact}}} P_{\text{interface}}^{\text{elec}} \quad (9b)$$

$$-\lambda \nabla T \cdot \mathbf{n} = h_{\text{th\_eff}} (T - T_{\text{env}}) \quad (9c)$$

where

$$b = \sqrt{\lambda \rho c_p} \quad \text{and} \quad P_{\text{interface}}^{\text{elec}} = h_{\text{elece}} (\phi - \phi_{\text{contact}})^2$$

Equation (9a) means a prescribed heat flux. Such a condition is applied to the inner and outer side surfaces of grips $\partial\Omega_{\text{g\_es}}$ and $\partial\Omega_{\text{g\_is}}$ and to the end surface of the specimen $\partial\Omega_{\text{s\_es}}$, with $q_{\text{imp}} = 0$ for both cases, expressing assumed adiabatic boundary conditions.

Equation (9b) represents the nonperfect thermal contact condition at the interface between specimen and grips $\partial\Omega_{\text{sg}}$. T_{contact} is the local temperature at the surface of the neighbor domain, and h_c is an effective heat transfer coefficient defined at the interface between specimen and grips. The Joule heat power is distributed between the two domains in contact according to their respective thermal effusivities b.

Because of the complex heat-transfer conditions among the specimen, the transparent quartz tube, and the environment, an equivalent heat transfer model (Eq.(9c)) between the specimen and the environment is assumed by defining an effective heat transfer coefficient $h_{\text{th\_eff}}$, which is determined by an inverse numerical calculation based on the experimental temperature measurements. This point is discussed later on, in Section IV-B.

Multidomain resolution strategy is used, which is detailed in Section III-E. It should be noted that when computing the solution in one of the grips, the heat transfer model of Eq. (9c) also is used at the surface ($\partial\Omega_{\text{gf1}}$ or $\partial\Omega_{\text{gf2}}$) in contact with the framework.

The weak form of Eq. (6) is as follows:

$$\forall \varphi^*, \quad \int_{\Omega} \rho \frac{dh}{dt} \varphi^* d\Omega + \int_{\Omega} \lambda \nabla T \cdot \nabla \varphi^* d\Omega + \int_{\partial\Omega} -\lambda \nabla T \cdot \mathbf{n} \varphi^* d\Gamma - \int_{\Omega} P_v^{\text{elec}} \varphi^* d\Omega = 0 \quad (10)$$

where φ^* are scalar test functions. Like for the electrical solution, a classic Galerkin finite element formulation is used to discretize this equation. This leads to a set of nonlinear equations to be solved for the nodal values of specific enthalpy. This set is linearized by an implicit formulation and a Newton-Raphson method, for which the tangent stiffness matrix involves the nodal values of $\partial T/\partial h$. When the energy equation is solved in grips, temperature T is chosen as the primary unknown, and the weak form of Eq. (10) can be reduced to the following:

$$\forall \varphi^*, \quad \int_\Omega \rho c_p \frac{dT}{dt} \varphi^* d\Omega + \int_\Omega \lambda \nabla T \cdot \nabla \varphi^* d\Omega + \int_{\partial\Omega} -\lambda \nabla T \cdot \mathbf{n}\varphi^* d\Gamma - \int_\Omega P_v^{elec} \varphi^* d\Omega = 0 \quad (11)$$

In this case, taking the values of ρ, λ, and c_p, which generally depend on T, at the beginning of the time step, we get a set of linear equations to be solved for the nodal temperatures.

D. Mechanical Momentum Equation Resolution

The constitutive models considered in the present study should cover the solid state and the mushy state, which can be present at the same time in a tensile specimen, which is why we use the hybrid approach developed by Bellet et al. for the modeling of solidification processes.[14,15] This approach is summarized briefly.

In the mushy state, a pure thermo-viscoplastic (THVP) law is used above the solidus temperature and is described by the following equations:

$$\dot{\boldsymbol{\varepsilon}} = \dot{\boldsymbol{\varepsilon}}^{vp} + \dot{\boldsymbol{\varepsilon}}^{th} \quad (12a)$$

$$\dot{\boldsymbol{\varepsilon}}^{vp} = \frac{3}{2K_{vp}} \dot{\bar{\varepsilon}}^{1-m} \mathbf{s} \quad (12b)$$

$$\dot{\boldsymbol{\varepsilon}}^{th} = -\frac{1}{3\rho} \frac{d\rho}{dt} \mathbf{I} \quad (12c)$$

The strain-rate tensor is decomposed into a viscoplastic and a thermal part, as indicated by Eq. (12a); no elasticity is considered. In Eq. (12c), the change of the material density ρ expresses the shrinkage term associated with the liquid-solid phase change. $\mathbf{I}$ denotes the identity tensor. Eq. (12b) is the classic constitutive equation of a generalized non-Newtonian fluid. K_{vp} is the so-called viscoplastic consistency of the material, m is the strain-rate sensitivity coefficient, and $\mathbf{s}$ is the deviatoric stress tensor as deduced from the Cauchy stress tensor $\boldsymbol{\sigma}$ as follows:

$$\mathbf{s} = \boldsymbol{\sigma} - \frac{1}{3} tr(\boldsymbol{\sigma}) \mathbf{I} \quad (13)$$

Denoting $\dot{\bar{\varepsilon}}$ and $\bar{\sigma}$, the von Mises equivalent strain rate and the equivalent stress, respectively, and are defined as follows:

$$\dot{\bar{\varepsilon}} = \sqrt{\frac{2}{3} \dot{\varepsilon}_{ij}^{vp} \dot{\varepsilon}_{ij}^{vp}}, \quad \bar{\sigma} = \sqrt{\frac{3}{2} s_{ij} s_{ij}} \quad (14)$$

From Eqs. (12b) and (14), the one-dimensional power-law-type relationship between stress and strain-rate invariants can be achieved as follows:

$$\bar{\sigma} = K_{vp} \dot{\bar{\varepsilon}}^m \quad (15)$$

Below the solidus temperature, the alloy is modeled by a thermo-elastic-viscoplastic (THEVP) constitutive law, which is more representative of solid-like behavior. The solid-like constitutive equations are described by the following equations in which small deformations and rotations are assumed, which is consistent with our application field:

$$\dot{\boldsymbol{\varepsilon}} = \dot{\boldsymbol{\varepsilon}}^{el} + \dot{\boldsymbol{\varepsilon}}^{vp} + \dot{\boldsymbol{\varepsilon}}^{th} \quad (16a)$$

$$\dot{\boldsymbol{\varepsilon}}^{el} = \frac{1+v}{E} \dot{\boldsymbol{\sigma}} - \frac{v}{E} tr(\boldsymbol{\sigma}) \mathbf{I} \quad (16b)$$

$$\dot{\boldsymbol{\varepsilon}}^{vp} = \frac{3}{2\bar{\sigma}} \dot{\bar{\varepsilon}} \mathbf{s} \quad (16c)$$

The strain-rate tensor $\dot{\boldsymbol{\varepsilon}}$ is split into an elastic component, an inelastic (nonreversible) component, and a thermal component. Here, E and v are the notations for Young's modulus and Poisson's ratio, respectively.

Different constitutive equations can be introduced to describe the relation between the von Mises equivalent strain rate and stress. In the present work, the following constitutive equation is chosen in which strain hardening and strain-rate sensitivity effects are taken into account by an additive formulation[16]:

$$\bar{\sigma} = \sigma_y + H_{evp} \bar{\varepsilon}^n + K_{evp} \dot{\bar{\varepsilon}}^m \quad (17)$$

In this expression, σ_y denotes the initial yield stress. The current yield stress is assumed to depend on the cumulated plastic strain, with its value being $\sigma_y + H_{evp} \bar{\varepsilon}^n$ as a result of strain hardening. Strain-rate sensitivity is taken into account through a power law of coefficients K_{evp} and m. In this case, Eq. [16c] takes the following form:

$$\dot{\boldsymbol{\varepsilon}}^{\mathrm{vp}} = \frac{3}{2\bar{\sigma}}\left[\frac{\bar{\sigma}-(\sigma_{\mathrm{y}}+H_{\mathrm{evp}}\bar{\varepsilon}^{n})}{K_{\mathrm{evp}}}\right]^{1/m}\mathbf{s} \quad (18)$$

The expression between Macauley brackets [·] is reduced to zero when negative, expressing plastic yield.

The local mechanical equilibrium is governed by the momentum conservation equation in which, regarding the low velocities in such Gleeble tests, inertia effects are ignored as follows[13]:

$$\nabla \cdot \boldsymbol{\sigma} + \rho \mathbf{g} = 0 \quad (19)$$

In regard to mechanical boundary conditions, the grips are assumed nondeformable. One grip is fixed, whereas the mobile grip has a prescribed time-dependent velocity $V_{\mathrm{imp}}(t)$. The specimen undergoes mechanical boundary conditions at the interface with grips $\partial\Omega_{\mathrm{sg}}$ only. In the present study, as will be discussed later (Section IV-C), two kinds of contact conditions are addressed at this interface—bilateral sticking contact and bilateral sliding contact without friction. Denoting $\mathbf{v}$ and $\mathbf{v}_{\mathrm{g}}$ as the velocity fields in the specimen and in the grips, respectively, the bilateral sticking condition can be expressed by the following:

$$\mathbf{v} - \mathbf{v}_{\mathrm{g}} = 0 \quad (20)$$

$$\mathbf{T} = \boldsymbol{\sigma}\mathbf{n} = -\chi_{\mathrm{p}}(\mathbf{v} - \mathbf{v}_{\mathrm{g}}) \quad (21)$$

The fulfillment of Eq. (20) is obtained by means of a penalty method, which consists of applying a stress vector $\mathbf{T}$ (Eq. (21)) to the surface of the specimen, with χ_{p} denoting the penalty coefficient (a large positive number).

The bilateral frictionless sliding condition can be expressed as follows:

$$(\mathbf{v} - \mathbf{v}_{\mathrm{g}}) \cdot \mathbf{n} = 0 \quad (22\mathrm{a})$$

$$\mathbf{T} = \boldsymbol{\sigma}\mathbf{n} = -\chi_{\mathrm{p}}((\mathbf{v} - \mathbf{v}_{\mathrm{g}}) \cdot \mathbf{n})\mathbf{n} \quad (22\mathrm{b})$$

The mechanical problem is solved using a mixed formulation with velocity and pressure as primitive variables. The problem to be solved then consists of two equations. The first one is the weak form of the momentum equation, also known as the principle of virtual power. Because p is kept as a primitive variable, only the deviatoric part of constitutive equations is accounted for and has to be solved locally to determine the deviatoric stress tensor $\mathbf{s}$. Therefore, the second equation consists of the weak form of the volumetric part of the constitutive equations. It expresses the incompressibility of the plastic deformation. This leads to the following[17,18]:

$$\begin{cases} \forall \mathbf{v}^{*} \quad \int_{\Omega}\mathbf{s}:\dot{\boldsymbol{\varepsilon}}^{*}\mathrm{d}\Omega - \int_{\Omega}p\nabla\cdot\mathbf{v}^{*}\mathrm{d}\Omega - \int_{\partial\Omega}\mathbf{T}\cdot\mathbf{v}^{*}\mathrm{d}\Gamma \\ \qquad - \int_{\Omega}\rho\mathbf{g}\cdot\mathbf{v}^{*}\mathrm{d}\Omega = 0 \\ \forall p^{*} \quad \int_{\Omega}p^{*}\,\mathrm{tr}\,\dot{\boldsymbol{\varepsilon}}^{\mathrm{vp}}\mathrm{d}\Omega = 0 \end{cases} \quad (23)$$

where v^{*} and p^{*}, respectively, are a vector and a scalar test functions that can be seen as virtual velocity and pressure fields.

The form of the term integrated in the second equation varies according to the local state of steel (i.e., solid or mushy). For a solid-like constitutive equation (solid state, elastic-viscoplastic behavior), it is as follows:

$$\mathrm{tr}\dot{\boldsymbol{\varepsilon}}^{\mathrm{vp}} = \mathrm{tr}\dot{\boldsymbol{\varepsilon}} - \mathrm{tr}\dot{\boldsymbol{\varepsilon}}^{\mathrm{el}} - \mathrm{tr}\dot{\boldsymbol{\varepsilon}}^{\mathrm{th}} = \nabla\cdot\mathbf{v} + \frac{3(1-2v)}{E}\dot{p} - \frac{1}{\rho}\frac{\mathrm{d}\rho}{\mathrm{d}t} = 0 \quad (24)$$

For a liquid-like constitutive equation (mushy state, pure viscoplastic behavior), it is as follows:

$$\mathrm{tr}\dot{\boldsymbol{\varepsilon}}^{\mathrm{vp}} = \mathrm{tr}\dot{\boldsymbol{\varepsilon}} - \mathrm{tr}\dot{\boldsymbol{\varepsilon}}^{\mathrm{th}} = \nabla\cdot\mathbf{v} - \frac{1}{\rho}\frac{\mathrm{d}\rho}{\mathrm{d}t} = 0 \quad (25)$$

Accordingly, the stress deviator $\mathbf{s}$ is deduced either from a viscoplastic law or from an elastic-viscoplastic constitutive equation. In the first case, s can be deduced easily from Eq. (12), from which we get the following:

$$\mathbf{s} = \frac{2}{3}K_{\mathrm{vp}}\dot{\bar{\varepsilon}}^{m-1}\mathrm{dev}(\dot{\boldsymbol{\varepsilon}}) \quad (26)$$

In the second case (elastic-viscoplastic behavior), the resolution of Eq. (26) consists of solving a nonlinear scalar equation. This can be achieved with a Newton method.[19]

After spatial discretization with the triangular minielement (P1+/P1), for that details can be found in literature,[20] Eq. (23) can be cast in a set of nonlinear equations; the unknowns of which are the nodal velocities and pressure. This system is solved by a Newton-Raphson method.

E. Finite Element Discretization and Multidomain Multifield Coupling Resolution Strategy

The specimen and two grips are discretized spatially on linear triangle elements, which are shown in Figure 4.

To capture the thermal and mechanical gradients in the working zone of the specimen, a fine mesh is generated in this region with mesh size about 0.2mm.

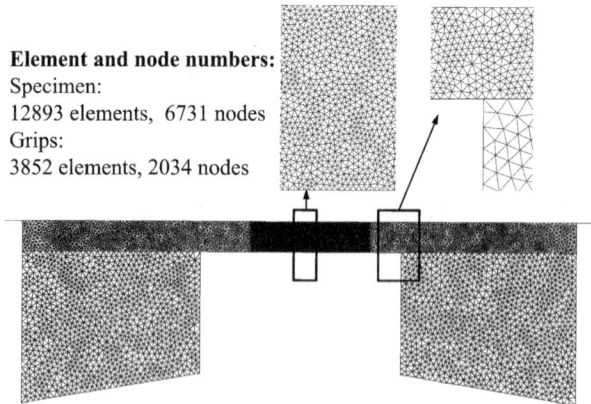

Fig. 4 Finite element meshes of the specimen and Gleeble grips (linear triangular elements).

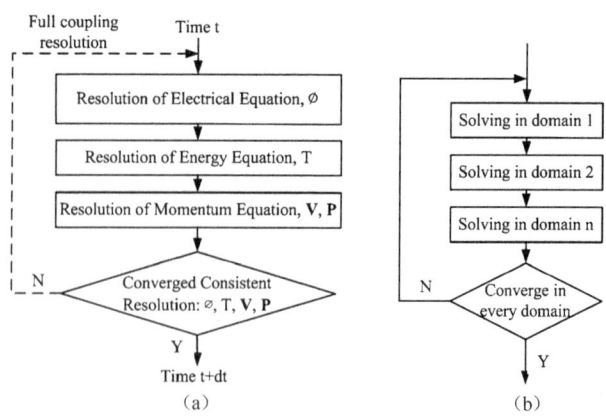

Fig. 5 Multidomain resolution strategy. (a) Electrical, thermal and mechanical coupling resolution strategy; (b) multidomain electrical or thermal resolution.

The electrical, thermal, and mechanical equations (Eqs. (5), (10), and (23)) are solved by the two-dimensional axisymmetric finite element code R2SOL-CA developed at Centre de Mise en Forme des Matériaux. Within each time increment, the converged consistent resolutions of electrical, energy, and momentum conservation equations can be achieved through multifield coupling iterations, as is shown in Figure 5(a). At each coupled iteration, the electrical and the energy equations must be solved in all domains, which are the specimen and the two grips in the present context. Local converged resolutions of each physical field are achieved by inner iterations between domains, as is shown in Figure 5(b). In the present study, because there is no severe coupling relationship between electrical, thermal, and mechanical variables, a weak coupling resolution strategy can be used in practice rather than the full coupling resolution method indicated in Figure 5(a). This saves computational time and does not affect the accuracy of the solution.

IV. RESULTS AND DISCUSSION

The electrical, thermal, and mechanical properties of the considered UHS steel, which are used in the present numerical modeling of Gleeble tests, are listed in the Appendix.

A. Electrical Simulation Analysis

As shown in Figure 2, the specimen is heated by the electrical current, according to the prescribed heating history. In regard to boundary conditions, the electrical transfer coefficient along the interface with grips helec is unknown. This coefficient may affect the potential distribution. It also may affect the temperature distribution, especially the axial profile, together with the heat transfer coefficient along the same interface h_c. Therefore, both coefficients should be identified. Moreover, because of the smooth and tight contact conditions between the grips and the specimen, it can be thought that the two transfer coefficients take high values, leading to quasicontinuous profiles of electrical potential and temperature through the interface. To simplify the numerical determination procedure, an arbitrary high value is chosen for the electrical transfer coefficient $h_{elec} = 3 \times 10^8 \Omega^{-1} m^2$. Thus, only the heat-transfer coefficient h_c has to be determined by a numerical inverse determination procedure based on temperature measurements. It is shown in Section IV-B that this strategy leads to a good agreement between measured and calculated temperatures.

Zero potential is imposed on the surface $\partial\Omega_{gf2}$, and the electrical current density J_{imp} is imposed on $\partial\Omega_{gf1}$. The value of J_{imp} is regulated by a simple proportional-integral-derivative (PID) algorithm to control the heating rate of the specimen according to the prescribed heating history. At each time increment, the incremental correction for J_{imp} is calculated as a function of the errors between the calculated and prescribed temperatures as follows[21]:

$$\Delta J_{imp} = k_p e^t + k_i \sum_{t=0}^{t} e^t + k_d(e^t - e^{t-1}) \quad (27)$$

where k_p, k_i, and k_d are proportional, integral, and derivative constants, respectively. t represents the time indicator, and e^t is expressed as follows:

$$e^t = T_{obj}^t - T_{cal}^t \quad (28)$$

The imposed J_{imp} is then updated with the following:

$$J_{imp}^t = J_{imp}^{t-1} + \Delta J_{imp} \quad (29)$$

The electrical potential distribution and the electrical current density distribution are shown in Figure 6. Basically, the electrical potential gradient reaches its maximum value in the middle part of the specimen. Consequently, the electrical current density reaches its maximal value at the same location. It is shown in Figure 6(b) that the current density is found almost uniform in the middle part of the specimen on a length of approximately 28mm and decreases to zero at both ends of the specimen. This characteristic distribution of electrical current explains the rapid and effective heating of most of the working zone (34mm between grips) of the specimen as well as the axial temperature gradients prevailing in this zone. This is discussed in the next section.

B. Thermal Simulation Analysis

The nonsteady-state heat transfer is modeled in the whole set up, including grips. Before discussing the boundary conditions, the transient temperature control of the specimen is presented first. As explained, a PID numerical algorithm is used to regulate the prescribed electrical current to minimize the difference between the calculated and the aimed nominal temperature at the location of the thermocouple TC0 in Figure 1(b). As shown by the temperature curves in Figure 7 and as expected, the history of the calculated temperature at this position reproduces exactly the desired heating path. A similar control is obtained experimentally through the monitoring procedure of the Gleeble machine. Both monitoring procedures (experimental and numerical) then are satisfying and consistent, allowing the operator and the code user to get the prescribed temperature-evolution curve.

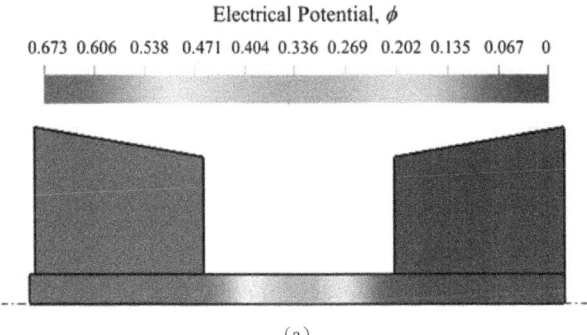

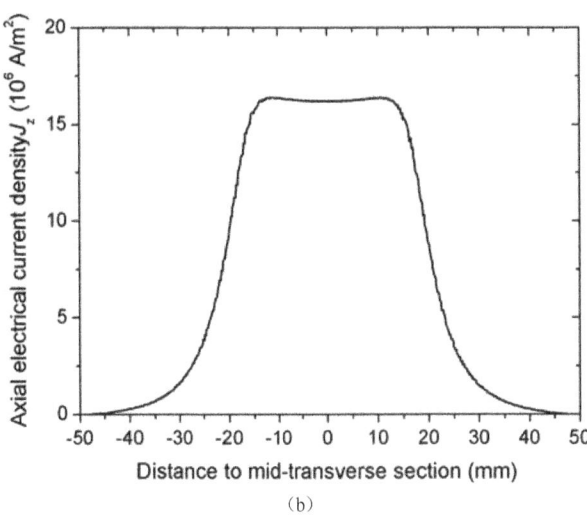

Fig. 6 (a) Electrical potential distribution in a longitudinal section of the tensile set up. (b) Electrical current density axial profile in the specimen.

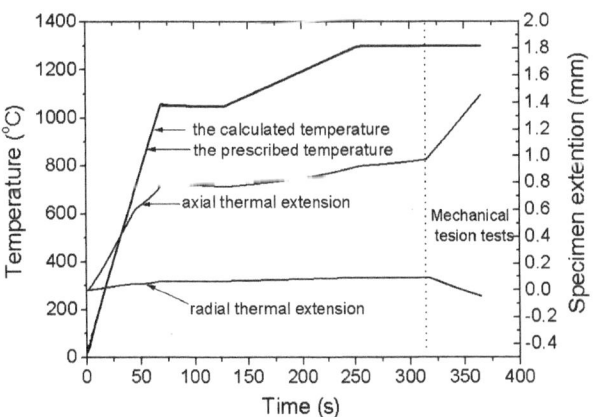

Fig. 7 Calculated and prescribed heating history together with the evolution of the calculated axial and radial thermal expansions.

The framework of the Gleeble machine is water-cooled. In regard to the grips, the strong heat transfer between the copper grips and the steel framework is taken into account by setting the local heat-transfer coefficient $h_{th\_eff} = 2000 \text{Wm}^{-2}\text{K}^{-1}$ (Eq. (9c)) along interfaces $\partial \Omega_{gf1}$ and $\partial \Omega_{gf2}$. The heat-transfer coefficient h_c along the interfaces between the grip and the specimen are determined inversely based on the surface temperature measurements along the axis, which is detailed in the following paragraphs.

In regard to the specimen, the temperature difference between the surface and the core (i.e., the radial gradient) mainly is affected by h_{th_eff} (Eq. (9c)). This heat-transfer coefficient is determined after the temperature of the specimen has been stabilized (between 70 seconds and 130 seconds, see Figure 7). A numerical inverse method is used to decrease the error between the calculated and measured surface temperature (T_s, measured at position TC0) and the core temperature (T_c, measured at position TC3). Figure 8 shows the temperature difference ($T_c - T_s$) between the core (T_c) and the surface temperature (T_s) vs the surface temperature. It is shown, as expected, that the radial temperature gradient increases significantly with the surface temperature of the specimen. For temperatures as high as the solidus temperature of the UHS steel (1710K (1437℃)), it can be anticipated by extrapolation of these results that the temperature difference between the core and the surface should reach 70K (70℃) to 80K (80℃).

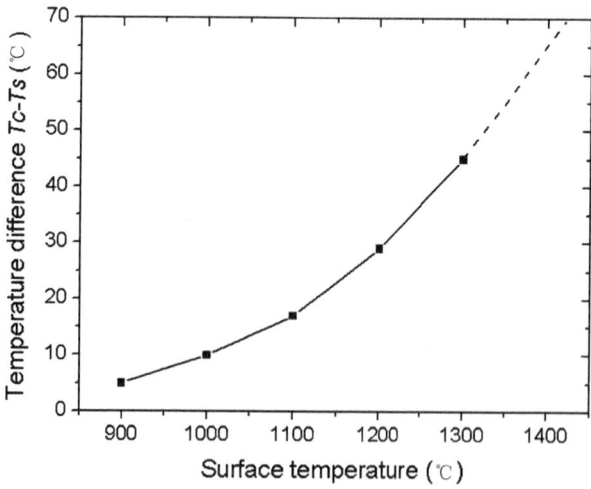

Fig. 8 Measured radial temperature difference (core with respect to surface) in the medium transverse section of the specimen as a function of surface temperature.

Let us now consider the axial thermal gradient taking place in the specimen. The quasiuniform profile of electrical current density in most of the working zone (Figure 6(b)) ensures that the Joule heat-source term is distributed uniformly in this region. However, thermal axial diffusion toward the cooler grips gives birth to an axial temperature gradient in the working zone. The heat-transfer coefficient along the grip-specimen interfaces h_c is determined by decreasing the difference between the calculated and the measured temperature profiles along the surface of the specimen during the homogenization period (from 70 seconds to 130 seconds). Figure 9(a) shows a comparison between calculated and measured longitudinal temperature profiles along the surface of the specimen in its central region (up to 12mm from the midlength transverse section in the region of the three thermocouples TC0, TC1, and TC2). This comparison is given for three controlled temperatures for the central thermocouple TC0—1473K (1200℃), 1573K (1300), JC, and 1673K (1400℃). Thanks to the numerical PID monitoring of the calculated temperature in the numerical simulation (as well as for the TC0 temperature in the experiment), there is a perfect agreement between the simulation and the experiment for this position. Figure 9(a) also shows a good agreement at the TC1 and TC2 locations.

Although the vacuum chamber and the quartz tube are used in the tests, surface heat losses exist from the free surface of the specimen between grips. The radial thermal gradients are increased with the increasing surface temperature (TC0 location), which can be observed clearly in the simulation results in Figure 9(b). In this figure, it also is shown that the identification of coefficient h_{th_eff} yields core temperatures in excellent agreement with the measurements already reported in Figure 8.

The previous results are interesting because they show that despite the rather extended (30mm) central zone with a homogeneous electrical current density (Figure 6(b)), there is actually no real homogeneity of temperature in the working zone, neither is there homogeneity in the axial or radial directions. It also should be noted that the different distributions also depend on the material parameters themselves, especially the temperature dependence of the electrical conductivity.

Because of the existence of these thermal gradients, the fusion of steel and then a mushy zone first will ap-

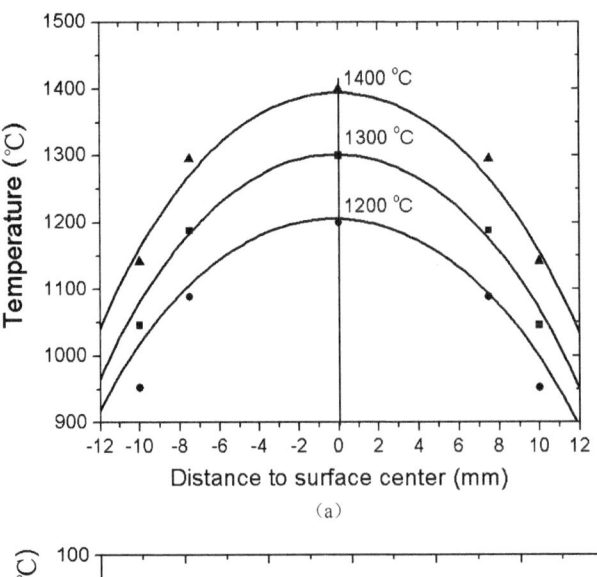

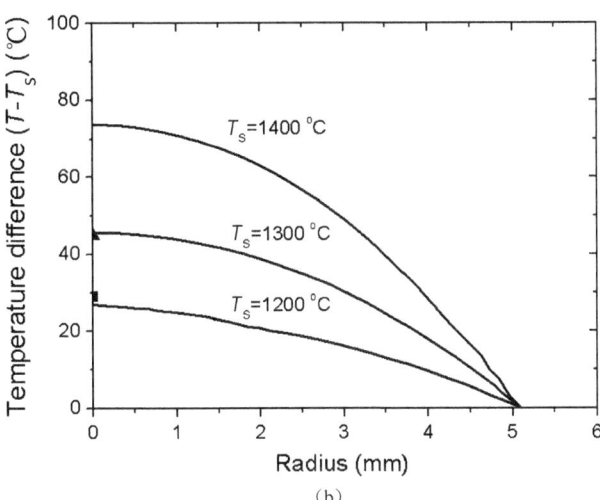

Fig. 9 Temperature distribution for three different nominal temperatures. (a) Calculated surface temperature profile in the axial direction together with experimental measurements. (b) Calculated radial temperature distribution in the midtransverse section. Superimposed are two measurements at position TC3 (center of specimen).

pear in the central core zone of the specimen when the nominal surface temperature increases and exceeds a certain value. Figure 10(a) shows the calculated temperature distribution with surface temperature 1673K (1400℃). The axial and radial temperature gradients result in a central ellipsoidal mushy zone; the surface of which is determined by the isotemperature surface $T = 1710K$ (1437℃) (solidus temperature of the UHS steel). The axial extension of the calculated mushy zone is about 11mm, whereas its radial extension is about 7.5mm. Inside the mushy zone, thermal gradients are associated with liquid fraction gradients, as is shown in Figure 10(b) (the maximum liquid fraction in this case is 0.22).

C. *Mechanical Simulation Analysis*

During the heating stage for real specimens, if the grips are kept fixed, then dilatation effects (Eq. (12c)) lead to substantial compressive stresses in the material, which may cause damage. This is why in real Gleeble tests, a so-called "zero force" technique is used for grip adjustment to reduce thermal stresses, which means that the movable grip can move freely to reduce the detected force under a small tolerance force (near zero). During the present numerical simulation, to model this "zero force" control, a boundary condition switch technique has been developed, using bilateral frictionless sliding before starting mechanical tension and then using bilateral sticking during mechanical tension. As shown in Figure 7, after heating and temperature homogenization at time 320 seconds, just before loading, the numerical simulation shows that the specimen has extended by 0.9mm axially (0.75 pct of total length) and 0.09mm radially (1.8 pct of the radius in the working zone). Although the moving grip is left free during the heating stage, the numerical simulation reveals that there is a substantial thermal stress from the radial constraint exerted by grips in the grip-holding region, as shown in Figure 11 for a nominal temperature of 1573K(1300℃). However, it should be noticed that such a stress state probably is overestimated because the grips are being assumed rigid in the simulation, and dilatation effects are not taken into account in the grips themselves. Despite this rough approximation, it can be noted that actually small thermal stress is observed in the central part of the specimen (<1MPa).

As expected, the nonuniform temperature distribution in the specimen gives birth to strong deformation heterogeneity. This is evidenced by Figure 12(a); the calculated strain rate in the specimen is actually far from being uniform. Because of axial and radial temperature gradients, there is a strain concentration in the vicinity of the core center of the specimen where the equivalent strain rate $\dot{\bar{\varepsilon}}$ reaches a maximum of $1.2 \times 10^{-3} s^{-1}$ for a nominal temperature of 1473K (1200℃) and a constant velocity $V_{imp} = 0.01$ mm/s of the moving grip. The effective working zone (in which material deforms) is about 20mm long in the central part. It can be noted that, during tension, this effective working zone is enlarged to 25mm (see Figure 12(a)), yielding a lower maximum strain rate of $0.8 \times 10^{-3} \, s^{-1}$. Besides, the radial heterogeneity of the deformation is shown clearly in Figure 12(b).

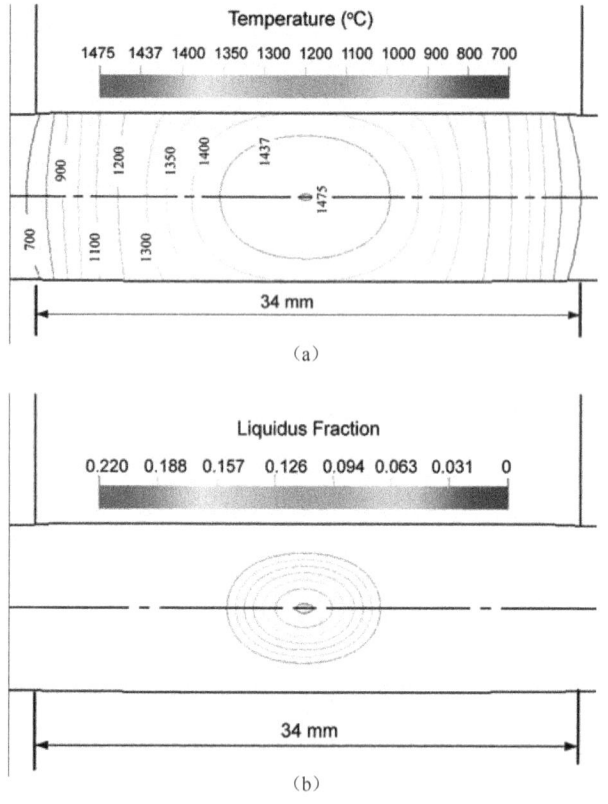

Fig. 10 (a) Temperature and (b) liquid fraction distributions in a longitudinal section of the working zone of the specimen for a nominal surface temperature 1673K (1400℃).

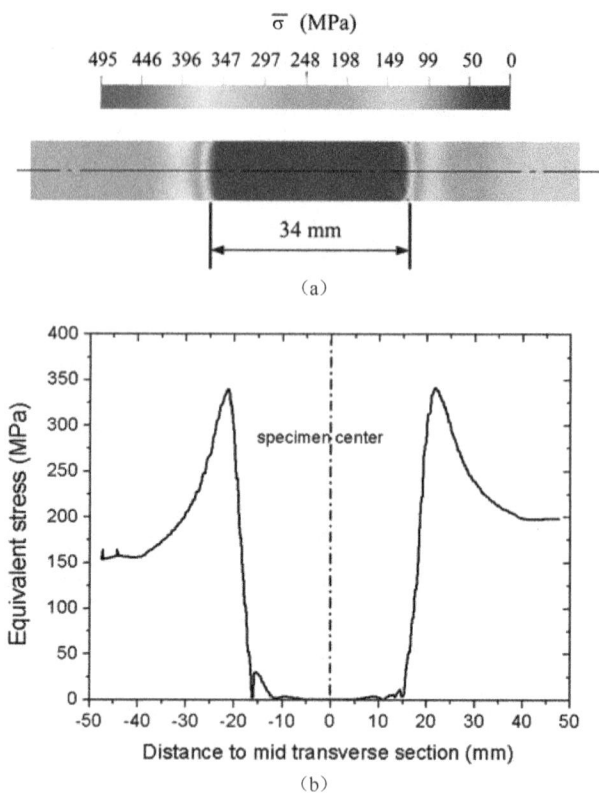

Fig. 11 Distribution of the von Mises equivalent stress caused by thermal dilatation before mechanical tension.
(a) Equivalent stress distribution in the longitudinal section of the specimen. (b) Equivalent stress profile along symmetry axis.

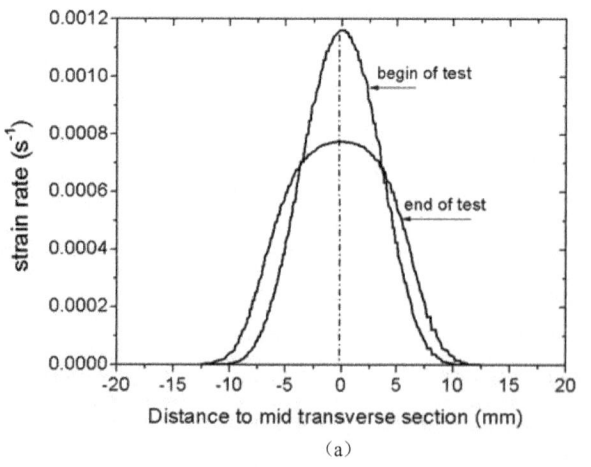

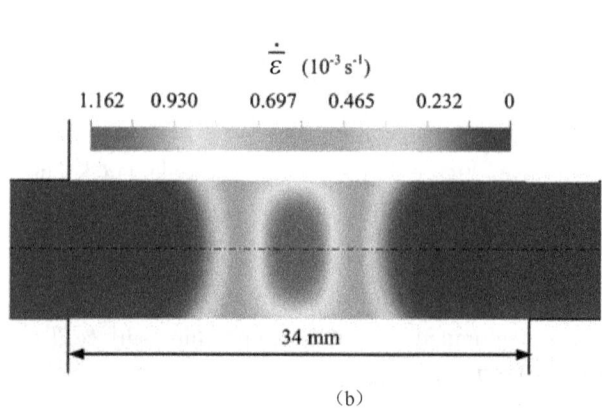

Fig. 12 Calculated distribution of the equivalent strain rate $\dot{\bar{\varepsilon}}$ in the specimen at nominal testing temperature 1473K (1200℃) and for a constant velocity of the moving grip $V_{imp} = 0.01$mm/s. (a) Axial profiles of $\dot{\bar{\varepsilon}}$ at the core at the beginning and end (50s) of the test; (b) distribution map of $\dot{\bar{\varepsilon}}$ at the beginning of the mechanical test (maximum = $1.16 \times 10^{-3} s^{-1}$).

1. Influence of the Constitutive Equation

It is interesting to realize that such deformation heterogeneities are highly dependent on the constitutive model chosen for the alloy. To demonstrate, let us consider an alternative equation to Eq. (17) provided by Han et al.[22] as follows:

$$\overline{\sigma} = \frac{\overline{\varepsilon}^n}{\alpha}\mathrm{arsinh}\left[\left(\frac{1}{A}\exp\left(\frac{Q}{RT}\right)\right)^m \dot{\overline{\varepsilon}}^m\right] \quad (30)$$

The corresponding material parameters for the considered UHS steel are taken from Seol et al.[8] and can be found in the Appendix (Table AII).

Using this model, the strain-rate distribution is quite different, as shown in Figure 13. It is shown that in contrast to the previous model, the strain-rate concentration is lower; the maximum strain rate in the beginning of the test is limited to $0.85 \times 10^{-3} \mathrm{s}^{-1}$ instead of $1.16 \times 10^{-3} \mathrm{s}^{-1}$. The effective working zone is slightly larger in the beginning of the test, and it does not vary during the test, contrary to the previous case. In addition, during the test, a slight increase of the maximum strain rate now is observed instead of a larger decrease using the additive model. These different evolutions are illustrated in Figure 14.

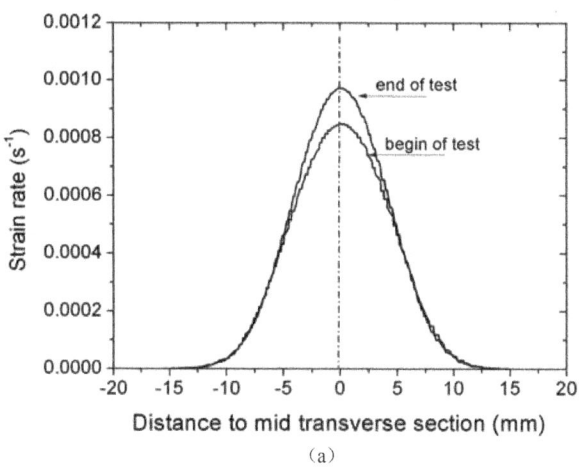

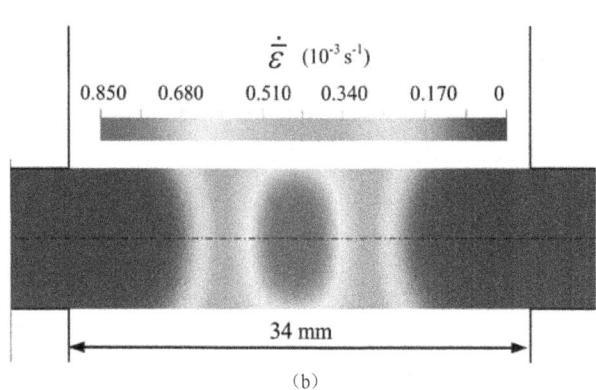

Fig. 13 Strain rate and strain axial distributions calculated by Eq. (30) in the specimen at nominal testing temperature 1473K (1200℃) and for a constant velocity of the moving grip: $V_{\mathrm{imp}} = 0.01$ mm/s. (a) Strain rate axial profiles at the core at the beginning and end (50s) of mechanical tests. (b) Strain rate distribution map at the beginning of mechanical tests (maximum = $0.85 \times 10^{-3} \mathrm{s}^{-1}$).

As classified by Lemaître and Chaboche,[16] the effects of strain hardening and strain-rate hardening can be combined in the following two ways in viscoplastic constitutive models: additive and multiplicative, which can be written simply into the following two equation types:

Additive: $\overline{\sigma} = H_{\mathrm{evp}}\overline{\varepsilon}^n + K_{\mathrm{evp}}\dot{\overline{\varepsilon}}^m$ or

$$\dot{\overline{\varepsilon}} = ((\overline{\sigma} - H_{\mathrm{evp}}\overline{\varepsilon}^n)/K_{\mathrm{evp}})^{1/m} \quad (31)$$

Multiplicative: $\overline{\sigma} = K_{\mathrm{evp}}\overline{\varepsilon}^n \dot{\overline{\varepsilon}}^m$ or

$$\dot{\overline{\varepsilon}} = (\overline{\sigma}/(K_{\mathrm{evp}}\overline{\varepsilon}^n))^{1/m} \quad (32)$$

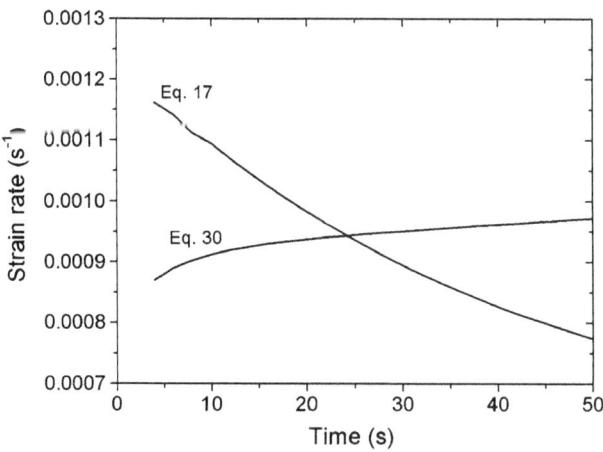

Fig. 14 Evolution of the maximum strain-rate (found at the center of the specimen) during the tensile test for the additive model (Eq. (17)) and the hyperbolic sine model (Eq. (30)).

It can be thought that the second form, in which the term $\overline{\varepsilon}^n$ is found in the numerator, promotes the influence of the strain-hardening effect, leading to lower strain-rate concentrations. This seems to be consistent with Figures 12 and 13.

2. *About Forthcoming Parameters Identification*

From the different thermal and mechanical results shown previously, it can be anticipated that the identification of material behavior at a high temperature in the solid state and a fortiori in the mushy state is really challenging. The only way through it probably consists of inverse numerical modeling based on the measurement of traction force and displacement. Success in this matter will rely on three essential requirements (1) reliable direct numerical simulation and inverse optimization module, (2) accurate temperature measurements, and (3) good knowledge of thermophysical properties of the material.

Inverse identification would consist of finding the set of material parameters minimizing the difference between measured and calculated force-elongation curves for a set of tensile tests performed in different conditions (traction velocity and temperature). As mentioned previously, in the current numerical model, traction velocity is prescribed directly, and the nominal temperature is well controlled like in real tests. In regard to elongation, it is obtained directly in the simulation by the following integration:

$$\Delta l(t) = \int_{t_{ms}}^{t} V_{imp}(\tau) \, d\tau \qquad (33)$$

where t_{ms} denotes the time at which tension is started and V_{imp} is the velocity that is imposed on the movable grip. As for the tensile force, its calculation is more delicate. In our finite element approach, it is calculated by two methods. The first one consists of summing all contact nodal forces associated with the penalty treatment of sticking contact as follows:

$$F(t) = \sum_{\text{contact nodes } n} \mathbf{T}_n(t) \cdot \mathbf{e}_z 2\pi r_n l_n \qquad (34)$$

where the nodal stress vector (surface force) is calculated by Eq. [21], $\mathbf{e}_z$ denotes the unit vector along the axial direction, r_n and l_n are the radial coordinate and the control length associated with any boundary node n, respectively. In the second method, the force is deduced from the distribution of axial stress components along the central transverse section of the specimen as follows:

$$F(t) = \sum_{e} \sigma_{zz}(e) 2\pi r_e \Delta r_e \qquad (35)$$

where the summation is applied to the triangular elements e crossed by the central transverse section, $\sigma_{zz}(e)$ is the axial stress component calculated at the center of element e, r_e is the radial coordinate of the center of element e, and Δr_e is the dimension of element e along the radial direction. It has been checked that the two methods lead to extremely close values of F.

Figure 15 shows the calculated curves—traction force *vs* elongation—for three different temperatures and a constant grip velocity 0.01mm/s, using the additive constitutive model. Temperature and strain-hardening effects are clearly evidenced. The large differences are recorded between measured and calculated curves, illustrating the need of a complementary identification of constitutive parameters through a procedure based on inverse finite element analysis.

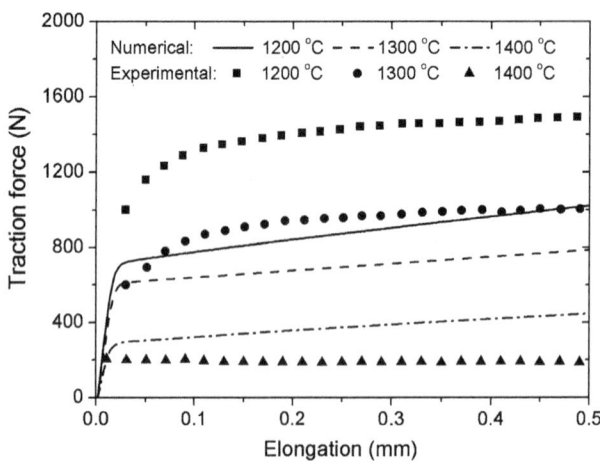

Fig. 15 Comparison between the experimentally measured and the calculated traction force *vs* the elongation curves during Gleeble tension tests with imposed grip velocity 0.01mm/s and three nominal temperatures. Calculations are done with the additive constitutive model.

V. CONCLUSION

Through this study, a coupled electrical-thermal-mechanical model has been proposed and discussed for the direct numerical modeling of Gleeble tests at a high temperature and in the mushy state. The direct modeling of Gleeble tension tests for a UHS steel has revealed that thermal gradients resulting from a coupled electricalthermal problem significantly affect the material and result in a heterogeneous deformation of the specimen. This point constitutes a major difficulty for the simple identification of constitutive parameters, using direct estimations of strain, strain rate, and stress. Given such marked heterogeneities, the only safe procedure seems to be inverse numerical modeling based on direct coupled finite element models, such as the one presented here. Identification then should be performed with an optimization module aimed at the minimization of the difference between force-displacement curves (or the possible specimen shape difference between the calculations and the measurements) for a set of tests achieved under different conditions (temperature and imposed velocity). Success in this matter will require the following:

1. A reliable direct coupled numerical simulation
2. A robust and efficient optimization module
3. Accurate temperature measurements during real tests
4. A good knowledge of thermophysical properties of the material

ACKNOWLEDGMENTS

This study has been financially supported by the company ArcelorMittal, which supported a two-year period passed by Changli Zhang in CEMEF laboratory.

APPENDIX: MATERIAL PROPERTIES OF THE UHS STEEL

To calculate the solidification path of the considered UHS steel, the microsegregation model presented by Won et al.[23] is used here, which takes into account the steel composition and cooling rate. The model is listed briefly as follows:

$$f_s = \left(\frac{1}{1-2\beta k}\right)\left[1-\left(\frac{T_f-T}{T_f-T_L}\right)^{(1-2\beta k)/(k-1)}\right]$$

$$\beta = a\left[1-\exp\left(\frac{-1}{a}\right)\right] - \frac{1}{2}\exp\left[\frac{-1}{2a}\right]$$

$$a = 33.7\,\dot{T}^{-0.244}$$

where k is the equilibrium partition coefficient of carbon (taken as 0.265) and T_f is the melting temperature of pure Fe (taken as 1808K (1535℃)). The liquidus temperature can be determined by the following:

$T_L = 1808 - 78(\text{pct C}) - 7.6(\text{pct Si})$
$\quad -4.9(\text{pct Mn}) - 34.4(\text{pct P}) - 38(\text{pct S})$

where temperature is K. The cooling rate $\dot{T}$ is taken as 0.17K/s. The calculated relation between temperature and solid fraction is shown in Figure 16. The latent heat L is 272kJ/kg. Thermophysical and electrical properties are given in Table 1.

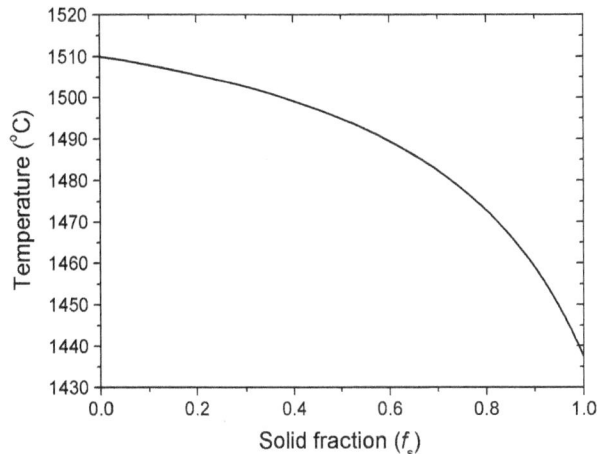

Fig. 16 The calculated relation between solid fraction and temperature for the steel.

Table 1 Thermal and Electrical Properties of the Considered UHS Steel

$T[\text{K}(℃)]$	λ [Wm⁻¹ K⁻¹]	c_p [Jkg⁻¹ K⁻¹]	ρ [kg⁻¹ m⁻³]	σ_{elec} [Ω⁻¹ m⁻¹]
298(25)	38.9	447.0	7780.0	6.65×10⁶
373(100)	40.5	479.0	7757.1	5.23×10⁶
473(200)	41.0	526.0	7722.5	3.92×10⁶
573(300)	41.6	582.0	7687.5	3.03×10⁶
673(400)	40.6	640.0	7649.7	2.40×10⁶
773(500)	39.5	710.0	7613.7	1.93×10⁶
873(600)	37.5	810.0	7579.9	1.61×10⁶
973(700)	33.9	1018.0	7556.0	1.30×10⁶
1073(800)	35.8	1051.0	7561.8	1.03×10⁶
1173(900)	24.8	610.0	7539.1	0.98×10⁶
1273(1000)	27.2	625.0	7494.1	0.95×10⁶
1373(1100)	29.1	641.0	7448.7	0.92×10⁶
1473(1200)	29.7	656.0	7408.0	0.89×10⁶
1573(1300)	30.7	672.0	7365.4	0.86×10⁶
1673(1400)	32.3	688.0	7325.7	0.83×10⁶
1710(1437)	33.6	710.0	7290.0	0.82×10⁶
1783(1510)	40.0	814.0	7030.9	0.76×10⁶

In regard to the mechanical behavior, the UHS steel is supposed to behave as an elastic-viscoplastic material, obeying the classical J_2 theory with isotropic linear hardening. The Young's modulus is taken from Mizukami et al.[24] and is as follows:

$$E[\text{GPa}] = 968 - 2.33(T-273) + 1.90 \times 10^{-3}(T-273)^2 - 5.18 \times 10^{-7}(T-273)^3$$

Poisson's ratio is arbitrarily taken as 0.3. Two different constitutive viscoplastic models have been considered in the present study.

The additive model from Kozlowski et al. (model III)[25] corresponds to Eq. (17) and is as follows:

$$\bar{\sigma} = \sigma_y + H_{evp}\bar{\varepsilon}^n + K_{evp}\dot{\bar{\varepsilon}}^m$$

The material exhibits a plastic yield stress under which its behavior is purely elastic. This plastic yield stress is the sum of the initial yield stress σ_y and the strainhardening contribution $H_{evp}\bar{\varepsilon}^n$. The following constitutive parameters used here are taken from Reference [25], and they are supposed to cover a wide range of austenitic plain carbon steels:

$$\sigma_y = 0$$
$$m = 1/(8.132 - 1.540 \times 10^{-3} T)$$
$$n = -0.6289 + 1.114 \times 10^{-3} T$$
$$H_{evp} = 130.5 - 5.128 \times 10^{-3} T$$
$$K_{evp} = \left(\frac{1}{C}\exp\left(\frac{Q}{RT}\right)\right)^m$$

where $C = 46550 + 71400c + 12000c^2$, $Q = 371.2$ kJ/mol. The carbon content c is in wt pct, and the stress H_{evp} and K_{evp} is in MPa.

The model proposed by Han et al.[22] corresponds to Eq. (30) and is as follows:

$$\bar{\sigma} = \frac{\bar{\varepsilon}^n}{\alpha}\text{arsinh}\left[\left(\frac{1}{A}\exp\left(\frac{Q}{RT}\right)\right)^m \dot{\bar{\varepsilon}}^m\right]$$

The corresponding material parameters used here are taken from Seol et al.,[8] who characterized a steel grade with a composition approaching the composition of the grade considered here—0.14 wt pct C, 0.40 wt pct Si, and 1.28 wt pct Mn. Their parameters are listed in Table 2.

To illustrate the differences between these two constitutive models, stress-strain curves have been plotted for a constant strain rate 0.001 s^{-1} and three different temperatures (Figure 17). Significant differences are observed between the calculated curves.

Table 2 Parameters Value of Eq. (30), Taken from Seol et al.[8]

$A(\text{s}^{-1})$	$Q(\text{kJ} \cdot \text{mol}^{-1})$	$\alpha(\text{MPa}^{-1})$	m	n
1.192×10^{10}	422.9	0.0715	0.2038	0.1544

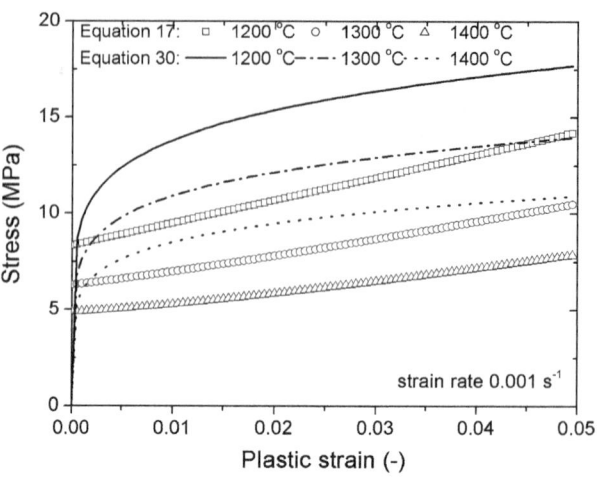

Fig. 17 Plotted stress-strain curves of Eq. (17) with parameters taken from Ref. 25 and of Eq. (30) with parameters taken from Ref. 8.

NOMENCLATURE

A	Material constant, s^{-1}
C	Material constant, N$^{-1/m}$ m$^{2/m}$ or Pa$^{-1/m}$
E	Elastic Young's modulus, Nm^{-2} or Pa
F	Traction force, N
H_{evp}	Temperature dependant constant, Nm^{-2} or Pa
I	The identity tensor
J_{imp}	Imposed electrical current density, Am^{-2}
J	Electrical current density vector, Am^{-2}
K_{vp}	The so-called viscoplastic consistency in TH-VP law, Nm^{-2} or Pa
K_{evp}	The so-called viscoplastic consistency in THEVP law, Nm^{-2}, or Pa
L	Specific latent heat, Jkg^{-1}
P_v^{elec}	Volume heat source caused by Joule effect (resistance heating), Wm^{-3}
$P_{interface}^{elec}$	Interface heat source caused by Joule effect (resistance heating), Wm^{-2}
Q	Apparent activation energy, Jmol^{-1}
R	Gas constant
T	Temperature, K

$T_{contact}$	Local temperature at the contact surface of the neighbor domain, K	$\dot{\bar{\varepsilon}}$	von Mises equivalent strain rate, s^{-1}
T_{env}	Environment temperature, K	λ	Heat conductivity, Wm^{-1} K^{-1}
T	Stress vector, Nm^{-2} or Pa	ρ	Density, kgm^{-3}
V_{imp}	Imposed grip velocity, ms^{-1}	ϕ	Electrical potential, V
a	Parameter in microsegregation model	ϕ_{imp}	Imposed electrical potential, V
b	Thermal effusivity, Jm^{-2}K^{-1}s$^{-1/2}$	$\phi_{contact}$	Local electrical potential at the contact surface of the neighbor domain, V
$b_{contact}$	Thermal effusivity at the contact surface of the neighbor domain, Jm^{-2}K^{-1}s$^{-1/2}$	σ_{elec}	Electrical conductivity, AV^{-1} m^{-1} or Ω^{-1} m^{-1}
c	Carbon content, wt pct	σ	Cauchy stress tensor, N m^{-2} or Pa
c_p	Specific heat, Jkg^{-1} K^{-1}	$\bar{\sigma}$	von Mises equivalent stress, N m^{-2} or Pa
e	Estimated error in PID method, K	σ_y	Initial yield stress, N m^{-2} or Pa
e$_z$	Unit vector along axial direction	σ_{zz}	Axial stress component, N m^{-2} or Pa
f_l	Liquid mass fraction	v	Poisson's ratio
g	Gravity vector, m s^{-2}	χ_p	Penalty coefficient
h	Specific enthalpy, J kg^{-1}		
h_c	Heat-transfer coefficient at interface between specimen and grips, Wm^{-2} K^{-1}		
h_{elec}	Effective electrical transfer coefficient, Am^{-2} V^{-1} or Ωm^{-2}		
h_{th_eff}	Effective heat transfer coefficient, Wm^{-2} K^{-1}		
k_p, k_i, k_d	Proportional, integral and derivative constants in PID method, K^{-1} or °C^{-1}		
l_n	The control length associated with boundary node n		
m	Strain-rate sensitivity coefficient		
n	Outward unit normal vector		
p	Pressure, Nm^{-2} or Pa		
q_{imp}	Imposed heat flux density, Wm^{-2}		
r_e	Radial coordinate of the center of element e, m		
r_n	Radial coordinate of node n, m		
s	Deviatoric stress tensor, Nm^{-2} or Pa		
t	Time, s		
v	Velocity vector, ms^{-1}		
v$_g$	Grip traction velocity vector, ms^{-1}		
Δl	Elongation of specimen, m		
Δr_e	Element dimension along radial direction, m		
α	Material constant, N^{-1} m^2 or Pa^{-1}		
β	Parameter in microsegregation model		
$\dot{\varepsilon}$	Total strain rate tensor, s^{-1}		
$\dot{\varepsilon}^{el}$	Elastic strain rate tensor, s^{-1}		
$\dot{\varepsilon}^{th}$	Thermal strain rate tensor, s^{-1}		
$\dot{\varepsilon}^{vp}$	Irreversible (viscoplastic) strain rate tensor, s^{-1}		

REFERENCES

[1] D. G. Eskin and L. Katgerman: *Metall. Mater. Trans. A*, 2007, vol. 38A, pp. 1511-19.

[2] D. J. Lahaie and M. Bouchard: *Metall. Mater. Trans. B*, 2001, vol. 32B, pp. 697-705.

[3] S. Nagata, T. Matsumiya, K. Ozawa, and T. Ohashi: *Tetsu to Hagané*, 1990, vol. 76, pp. 214-21.

[4] Y. M. Won, T. J. Yeo, D. J. Seol, and K. H. Oh: *Metall. Mater. Trans. B*, 2000, vol. 31B, pp. 779-94.

[5] M. Bellet, O. Cerri, M. Bobadilla, and Y. Chastel: *Metall. Mater. Trans. A*, 2009, vol. 40A, pp. 2705-17.

[6] M. Rappaz, J. M. Drezet, and M. Gremaud: *Metall. Mater. Trans. A*, 1999, vol. 30A, pp. 449-55.

[7] K. Kim, K. H. Oh, and D. N. Lee: *Scripta Mater.*, 1996, vol. 34, pp. 301-07

[8] D. J. Seol, Y. M. Won, T. J. Yeo, K. H. Oh, J. K. Park, and C. H. Yim: *ISIJ Int.*, 1999, vol. 39, pp. 91-98.

[9] M. Hojny and M. Glowacki: *Steel Res. Int.*, 2008, vol. 79, pp. 868-74.

[10] S. G. R. Brown, J. D. James, and J. A. Spittle: *Model. Simul. Mater. Sci. Eng.*, 1997, vol. 5, pp. 539-48.

[11] S. D. Norris and I. Wilson: *Model. Simul. Mater. Sci. Eng.*, 1999, vol. 7, pp. 297-309.

[12] K. Solek, Z. Mitura, and R. Kuziak: *Proc. 3rd MIT Conf. Computational Fluid and Solid Mechanics*, K. J. Bathe, ed., MIT, Boston, MA, 2005, pp. 1001-03.

[13] M. Rappaz, M. Bellet, and M. Deville: *Numerical Modeling in Materials Science and Engineering*, Springer-Verlag, New York, NY, 2003.

[14] M. Bellet and V. D. Fachinotti: *Comput. Meth. Appl. Mech.*

Eng., 2004, vol. 193, pp. 4355-81.

[15] B. G. Thomas and M. Bellet: *ASM Handbook* vol. 15, *Casting Division 4: Modelling and Analysis of Casting Processes*, AMS, Materials Park, OH, 2008, pp. 449-61.

[16] J. Lemaître and J. -L. Chaboche: *Mechanics of Solid Materials*, Cambridge University Press, Cambridge, UK, 1990.

[17] O. Jaouen: Ph. D. Dissertation, Mines-ParisTech, Paris, France, 1998.

[18] M. Bellet, O. Jaouen, and I. Poitrault: *Int. J. Numer. Meth. Heat. Fluid Flow*, 2005, vol. 15, pp. 120-42.

[19] M. Bellet, F. Decultieux, M. Menai, F. Bay, C. Levaillant, J. L. Chenot, P. Schmidt, and I. L. Svensson: *Metall. Mater. Trans. B*, 1996, vol. 27B, pp. 81-99.

[20] M. Bellet and A. Heinrich: *ISIJ Int.*, 2004, vol. 44, pp. 1686-95.

[21] G. A. Perdikaris: *Computer Controlled Systems: Theory and Applications*, Kluwer Academic Publishers, Dordrecht, The Netherlands, 1991.

[22] H. N. Han, Y. G. Lee, K. H. Oh, and D. N. Lee: *Mater. Sci. Eng. A*, 1996, vol. 206, pp. 81-89.

[23] Y. M. Won, K. H. Kim, T. J. Yeo, and K. H. Oh: *ISIJ Int.*, 1998, vol. 38, pp. 1093-99.

[24] H. Mizukami, K. Murakami, and Y. Miyashita: *Tetsu to Hagané*, 1977, vol. 63, p. 562.

[25] P. F. Kozlowski, B. G. Thomas, J. A. Azzi, and H. Wang: *Metall. Trans. A*, 1992, vol. 23A, pp. 903-18.

26. Cellular Automaton Modeling of Austenite Nucleation and Growth in Hypoeutectoid Steel during Heating Process

Bin SU, Zhiqiang HAN and Baicheng LIU

Key Laboratory for Advanced Materials Processing Technology (Ministry of Education), Department of Mechanical Engineering, Tsinghua University, Beijing, 100084 China.

A cellular automaton model has been developed to simulate the austenite nucleation and growth of hypoeutectoid steel during heating process. In the model, the dissolution of pearlite, the transformation of ferrite into austenite and austenite grain coarsening were simulated. To validate the model, dilatometric and quenching experiments were carried out. The dilatometric experiment was conducted using a DIL805A dilatometer, and experimental data was employed to study phase transformation kinetics and validate the model. While the quenching experiment was conducted using a chamber electric furnace, and metallographic examination was carried out. The simulated results were compared with the experimental results and the capability of the model for quantitatively predicting the microstructure evolution of the steel in heating process was assessed.

Key words: austenite nucleation and growth; heating process; cellular automaton; numerical simulation.

1. Introduction

Austenitization is a very important process in heat treatment of steels, because the steels are frequently processed in the austenitic state in some industrial production.[1-3] Till now, less attention has been paid to the study of austenitization compared with the vast amount of research on austenite decomposition. This is because the properties of steel depend basically on the transformation during the cooling process following austenitization. However, austenitization usually affects the austenite grain size and the concentration homogeneity of the materials, which have a great impact on the kinetics of phase transformation in the subsequent cooling process and the mechanical properties of steel. Therefore, it is of great significance to study the kinetics and microstructure evolution during the austenitization process of steels.[4]

The typical microstructure of a medium-carbon steel consists of pearlite and ferrite. Austenitization in hypoeutectoid steels occurs in two steps: (a) P→γ, and (b) α→γ, where P is pearlite, γ is austenite, and α is ferrite. Nucleation of austenite grains in pearlite region takes place just above the eutectoid temperature and the transformation of pearlite into austenite is very fast since the diffusion distance for solute atoms are relatively small. The transformation of ferrite into austenite occurs at a higher temperature and is completed above the (γ+α)/γ line in the phase diagram.[4] After the full austenite microstructure is formed, austenite grain coarsening occurs and it becomes more visible with increasing temperature. The mechanism and the kinetics of the austenitization process mentioned above have been widely discussed in literatures.[1-6]

Numerical simulation has become a powerful tool for simulating the microstructure evolution. In recent years, some computer models have been developed to simulate the microstructure evolution during austenitization process. Caballero et al.[3,6,7] used the Avrami equation to quantitatively model transformations during continuous heating in eutectoid and hypoeutectoid steels. It is a type of analytical model by which the variation of phase fractions can be predicted. While in many cases not only the phase fraction but the phase morphology is also necessarily to be predicted. Jacot and Rappaz[5] simulated the nucleation and growth process of austenite grain in a hypoeutectoid steel using Monte Carlo model, and Yang et al.[2] used a cellular automaton (CA) model to simulate the austenitization of hypoeutectoid steel. In their models, the dissolution of pearlite and the transformation of ferrite into austenite were simulated. While the influence of the pearlite morphology on the nucleation and growth of austenite grains was ignored. A variety of grain growth models were developed during past decades to study the grain size and the distribution of grain size during grain coarsening.[8-13] However, initial state of microstructure was set by using experimental data or sometimes invoking assumptions. Moreover, in most of the reported models, the transformation of ferrite into austenite was only assumed to be governed by the diffusion of carbon. In fact, many alloying elements have a great influence on the austenitization, especially the transformation of ferrite into austenite.[14-18] To date, there was little report about a model which is able to simulate the dissolution of pearlite, the transformation of ferrite into austenite, and austenite grain coarsening, and simultaneously to consider the diffusion of multicomponent and the effect of the initial as-cast microstructure on austenitization. Further, it is necessary to make more efforts to validate the microstructure simulation models.

In this paper, a CA model has been developed to simulate the microstructure evolution of hypoeutectoid steel during heating process. This model will be integrated with a model developed to predict the as-cast microstructure, including the grain size and area fraction of α phase as well as the mean interlamellar spacing of pearlite.[18] In the present model, the thermodynamics and solute diffusion of the multicomponent system were taken into account by using Thermo-Calc[19] and Dictra[20] software. The dissolution of pearlite, the transformation of ferrite into austenite and the austenite grain coarsening were simulated by using the developed model. To validate the model, dilatometric and quenching experiments were carried out. The simulated results were compared with the experimental results and the capability of the model for quantitatively predicting the microstructure evolution of the steel in heating process was assessed.

2. Mathematical Model

2.1 Nucleation

A continuous nucleation model[3,4,6,7] was employed to calculate the nucleus density of austenite grain in the pearlite region:

$$n_\gamma(\Delta T) = f_N \exp\left(\frac{-Q_N}{k\Delta T}\right) \quad (1)$$

where ΔT is the value of overheating, $n_\gamma(\Delta T)$ is the nucleus density, f_N is the factor representing the influence of pearlite structure on the nucleation, Q_N is the activation energy of nucleation, and k is Boltzmann's constant.

2.2 Growth Model

The dissolution of pearlite and the transformation of ferrite into austenite were considered here. Austenite grains grow into the pearlite region at a velocity $v^{\gamma/P}$:[3,4,6,7]

$$v^{\gamma/P}(\Delta T) = f_G \exp\left(\frac{-Q_G}{k\Delta T}\right) \quad (2)$$

where f_G is the factor representing the influence of pearlite structure on the growth rate, and Q_G is the activation energy of growth.

A mixed-mode model[4,17,18,21] was employed to calculate the growth velocity of the γ/α interface, where both the finite interface mobility and the finite diffusivity of the alloying elements are taken into account:

$$v^{\gamma/\alpha} = M^{\gamma/\alpha} \Delta G_{\alpha \to \gamma} \quad (3)$$

where $v^{\gamma/\alpha}$ is the interface growth velocity, $M^{\gamma/\alpha}$ is the interface mobility, and $\Delta G_{\alpha \to \gamma}$ is the chemical driving force and can be calculated by:

$$\Delta G_{\alpha \to \gamma} = \sum_{i=1}^{N} c_i^\gamma \bigg|_{\gamma/\alpha} (\mu_i^\alpha - \mu_i^\gamma) \quad (4)$$

where N is the number of chemical components in the system, $c_i^\gamma \big|_{\gamma/\alpha}$ is the mole fraction of component i in γ at the interface, and μ_i^α and μ_i^γ are the chemical potentials per mole of component i in α and γ at the interface, respectively.

The chemical potential depends on the chemical composition and can be calculated by using Thermo-Calc thermodynamic database. The interface mobility can be described by:

$$M^{\gamma/\alpha} = M_0^{\gamma/\alpha} \exp\left(-\frac{E^{\gamma/\alpha}}{RT}\right) \quad (5)$$

where $M_0^{\gamma/\alpha}$ is the pre-exponential factor, $E^{\gamma/\alpha}$ is the activation energy for atom motion at the interface, and R is the gas constant.

Austenite and ferrite have different crystal structure and contain different mole fractions of the solute. With γ/α interface moving, solute atom continuously transfers into ferrite from austenite. The governing equation for the atom diffusion in ferrite or austenite phase interior is given by:

$$\frac{\partial c_i^u}{\partial t} = D_i^u \nabla^2 c_i^u \quad (6)$$

where c_i^u is concentration of component i in phase u (γ or α), and D_i^u is diffusion coefficient of component i in phase u and can be calculated by Dictra software.

2.3 Grain Coarsening

Grain coarsening is resulted from the competitive growth of grains with the same phase. Boundary morphology is determined by how grain boundaries join together. According to Burke and Turnbull's theory, the velocity of a grain boundary segment can be expressed by:[4,8,22-24]

$$v^{\gamma/\gamma} = M^{\gamma/\gamma} P \quad (7)$$

where $M^{\gamma/\gamma}$ is the boundary mobility between austenite grains and can be expressed by:

$$M^{\gamma/\gamma} = M_0^{\gamma/\gamma} \exp\left(-\frac{E^{\gamma/\gamma}}{RT}\right) \quad (8)$$

where $M_0^{\gamma/\gamma}$ is the pre-exponential factor, and $E^{\gamma/\gamma}$ is the activation energy for grain boundary migration.

The driving force for grain boundary migration, P, can be calculated by:

$$P = E\kappa \quad (9)$$

where E is the austenite grain boundary energy and can be calculated by the Read-Shockley equation:[4,8,23]

$$E = E_m \left(\frac{\theta}{\theta_m}\right) \left[1 - \ln\left(\frac{\theta}{\theta_m}\right)\right] \quad (10)$$

where $E_m = 0.79 \text{J} \cdot \text{m}^{-2}$ and $\theta_m = 15°$. θ is the grain boundary misorientation and can be formulated as:

$$\theta = 2\pi \frac{|S_j - S_i|}{Q} \quad (11)$$

where S is crystallographic orientation number, Q is the maximum of the crystallographic orientation number, $1 \leq S \leq Q$, and S_j and S_i are the crystallographic orientation numbers of grains j and i, respectively. When the grain boundary becomes a high angle boundary, $\theta > 15°$, E remains independent on the misorientation angle and $E = E_m$.

κ is the austenite grain boundary curvature and can be calculated by using the model described in reference:[8,23]

$$\kappa = \frac{A}{\Delta h} \frac{Kink - N_i}{N+1} \quad (12)$$

where $A = 1.28$ is a coefficient, Δh is the size of a square CA cell, N is the number of the first and second nearest neighbors for the cell, N_i is the number of cells within the neighborhood belonging to grain i, and $Kink$ is the number of cells within the neighborhood belonging to grain i for a flat interface.

3. Cellular Automaton Algorithm

Cellular automaton method was used in the simulation.[4] A two-dimensional computational domain was discretized into square cells. Each cell has the following variables, (1) grain identifying variable, (2) cell status, which is one of P, α, γ, and γ/α interface, (3) concentration, and (4) interface migration distance. In the simulation, the effect of carbon and manganese were considered and their concentrations were obtained by solving diffusion equations. The interface migration distance was calculated based on the growth kinetics and was used in cell capturing in the CA model.

In our previous work,[4,18] the microstructure evolution of ASTM A216 WCA cast steel during solidification and consequent cooling process was simulated using a CA model. In the simulation, the peritectic solidification, α phase precipitation, and eutectoid transformation were simulated, and the grain size and area fraction of α phase as well as the mean interlamellar spacing of pearlite were obtained. To validate the model, a sand mold step-shaped casting was produced and metallographic examination was carried out. It was shown that the simulated results were in good agreement with the experimental results. Therefore, the simulated as-cast microstructure was used as the initial conditions for simulation of the austenitization.

At the beginning of the simulation, each cell is set as P or α with the same initial temperature T_{ini} and the equilibrium concentration at eutectoid temperature. When $T>A_1$, the nucleus density in pearlite zone can be calculated by Eq. (1), and the total number of austenite grains in the calculation domain can be obtained:

$$N_\gamma(\Delta T) = \sum_{(i,j) \in P} n_\gamma(i,j) S_{cell} \quad (13)$$

where cell (i,j) represents the pearlite cell, and S_{cell} is the area of a cell. It was assumed that the nucleation probability was the same for every cell in the pearlite region, and the nucleation sites are obtained by randomly choosing cells. The orientation of each nucleated austenite cell is given a random integer in the range of 1 to Q. Austenite grains grow into the pearlite region at a uniform velocity, which is calculated by Eq. (2). The radius of the grains at time t, R_t can be obtained:

$$R_t = R_{t-\Delta t} + v^{\gamma/P} \Delta t \quad (14)$$

where Δt is the time step, and $R_{t-\Delta t}$ is the radius at the previous step.

Another process is the transformation of ferrite to austenite (as seen in **Fig. 1**). At time t_0, the mole fraction of component i in γ and α in the γ/α interface cell (k,l) are $c_i^\gamma |_{\gamma/\alpha}^{t_0}$ and $c_i^\alpha |_{\gamma/\alpha}^{t_0}$, and the growth length in the interface cell is $l_{t_0}^{\gamma/\alpha}$. The interface velocity in this cell can be calculated by Eq. (3). The growth length in one time step, $\Delta l^{\gamma/\alpha}$, can be calculated:

$$\Delta l^{\gamma/\alpha} = \int_{t_0}^{t_0+\Delta t} v^{\gamma/\alpha} dt \quad (15)$$

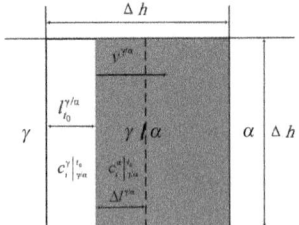

Fig. 1 The relationship between interface velocity and transformation in a CA cell.

At time $t_0+\Delta t$, the growth length in the interface cell is $l_{t_0+\Delta t}^{\gamma/\alpha}$:

$$l_{t_0+\Delta t}^{\gamma/\alpha} = l_{t_0}^{\gamma/\alpha} + \Delta l^{\gamma/\alpha} \quad (16)$$

if $l_{t_0+\Delta t}^{\gamma/\alpha} \geq \Delta h$, the γ/α interface cell (k,l) will change to a γ phase cell, where Δh is the size of a square CA cell.

4. Materials and Experimental Procedures

To validate the model, dilatometric and quenching experiments were carried out to study the microstructure evolution during heating process. The variation of fractions of different phases results in volumetric change of the samples, so the dilatometry results can be used to validate the model and phase transformation kinetics. In the quenching process, the austenite transforms to martensite. The fraction of the austenite can be derived by measuring the fraction of the martensite in the quenched samples. Meanwhile, the microstructure of the samples was examined to determine average austenite grain size and the distribution of austenite grain size.

The steel studied was ASTM A216 WCA steel with the chemical composition listed in **Table 1**. The dilatometric experiment was conducted using a DIL805A dilatometer with cylindrical samples (4mm diameter and 10mm long). The temperature of the sample was measured using thermocouples welded on the sample surface. The dilatometric curve for the heating rate of 80℃/h to 900℃ is illustrated in **Fig. 2**. It can be seen that the heating process represented by the dilatometric curve of length change, $\dfrac{\Delta L}{L_0}$, can be divided in three stages. In the first stage, the dilatometric curve exhibits a linear expansion with temperature change. This is a pure thermal expansion of the steel sample without phase change. In the second stage, the slope of the dilatometric curve reduced due to the volume change caused by the dissolution of pearlite and the transformation of ferrite into austenite. This was a result of the competition between the thermal expansion and the volume change induced by austenitization. In the third stage, the sample was fully austenitized, and the curve exhibits again a linear expansion feature reflecting the thermal expansion of the austenite.

Table 1 The chemical composition of the steel (wt.%)

C	Si	Mn	S	P	Ni	Cr	Cu	Mo
0.28	0.36	0.90	0.025	0.025	0.20	0.25	0.25	0.15

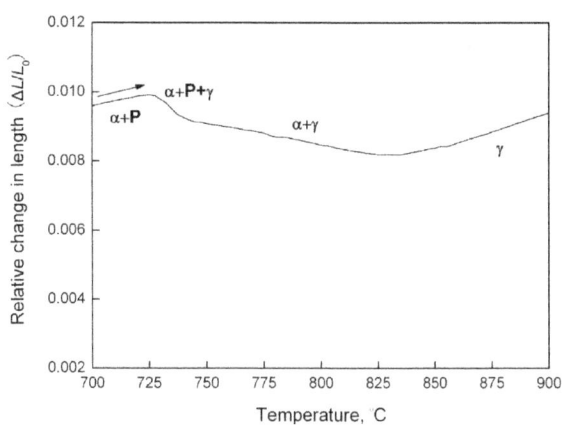

Fig. 2 Dilatometric curve of length change as a function of temperature for the heating rate of 80°C/h.

In the quenching experiments, steel samples were heated at a rate of 80°C/h to different temperatures (680, 730, 750, 810, 860 and 900°C) and soaked for different time (0, 1, 2, 5, 10 and 20h) at 900°C using a chamber electric furnace, then they were dropped into a water tank immediately. The microstructure of the samples was examined to determine the fraction of different phases, average austenite grain size and the distribution of austenite grain size. The microstructure was characterized by using optical microscopy and different etchants. LePera's etchant was employed to identify the martensite transformed from pearlite, and 4% nital was used to distinct ferrite and martensite, and saturated aqueous picric acid was adopted to exhibit the grain boundaries of the prior austenite. The austenite grains were observed by using a Zeiss Axio Imager A1 microscope, and more than 6 visual fields were selected in every sample. The grain size of austenite was measured by using the linear intercept method (ASTM E112), and more than 300 grains were counted in every sample to ensure the measurement accuracy.

5. Simulation Results and Discussion

The initial microstructure of the samples consists of pearlite (mean interlamellar spacing is 0.63μm) and ferrite (area fraction is 0.592 and mean grain size is 141μm). The computational domain was divided into 150×100 rectangular cells. The cell size is 5×5μm. For simulation the boundary was adiabatic so heat flux and atom flux are zero on the boundary. The temperature is uniform throughout the domain with initial temperature $T_{ini} = 650$°C. The parameters used in the simulation are shown in **Table 2**.

Table 2 The parameters used in the simulation.

Parameter	Value	Unit	Source
Eutectoid temperature (A_1)	707	°C	Thermo-Calc database
Nucleation factor (f_N)	$8.0×10^7$	$m^{-2} \cdot s^{-1}$	—
Activation energy of nucleation (Q_N)	$3.5×10^{-23}$	$J \cdot mol^{-1}$	Ref.[3,6,7]
Growth factor (f_G)	$1.0×10^{-4}$	$m \cdot s^{-1}$	—
Activation energy of growth (Q_G)	$4.1×10^{-23}$	$J \cdot mol^{-1}$	Ref.[3,6,7]
Activation energy for atom motion at the γ/α interface ($E^{\gamma/\alpha}$)	147	$kJ \cdot mol^{-1}$	Ref.[2]
Pre-exponential factor ($M_0^{\gamma/\alpha}$)	$1.0×10^{-4}$	$mol \cdot m \cdot J^{-1} \cdot s^{-1}$	—
Activation energy for grain boundary migration ($E^{\gamma/\gamma}$)	147	$kJ \cdot mol^{-1}$	—
Pre-exponential factor ($M_0^{\gamma/\gamma}$)	$1.0×10^{-3}$	$m^4 \cdot J^{-1} \cdot s^{-1}$	—
Maximum of the crystallographic orientation number (Q)	256	—	—

The simulated microstructure evolution during heating process at the rate of 80°C/h is shown in **Figs. 3** (a)-3(e). Figures 3(a)-3(c) show the transformation of pearlite into austenite, where the black area represents pearlite and the red area represents ferrite. The other color areas represent γ phase, and different colors represent γ grains with different crystallographic orientations. Figures 3(d) and 3(e) show the transformation of ferrite into austenite. The corresponding carbon and manganese concentration distribution during the transfor-

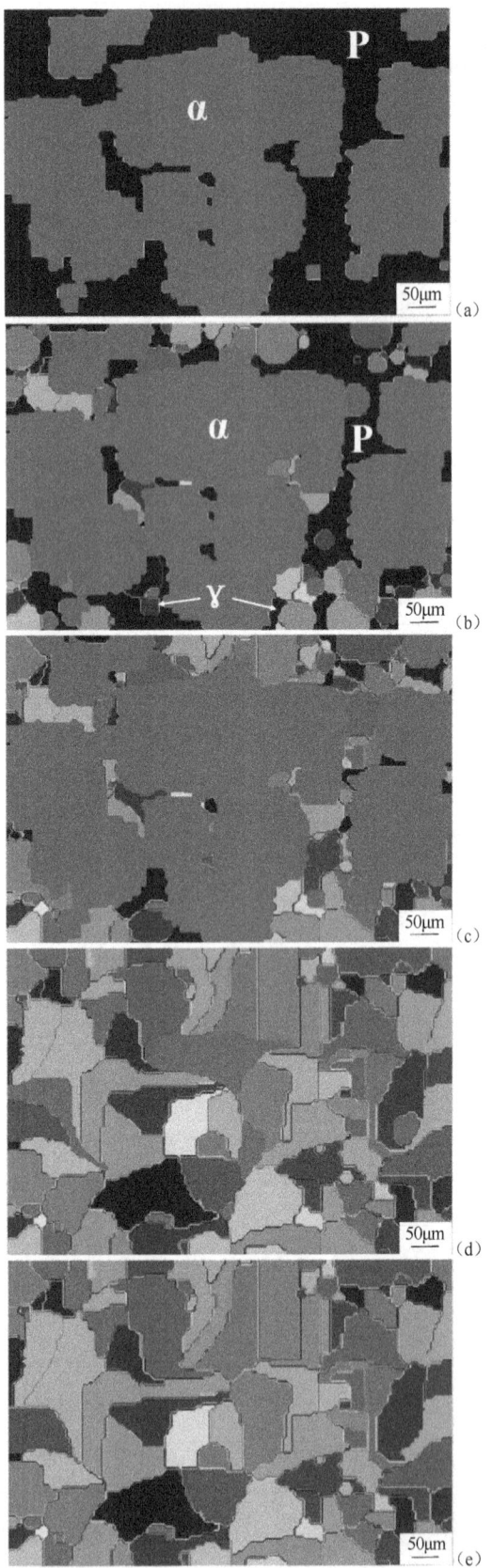

mation from ferrite to austenite is shown in **Figs. 4** and **5**, respectively. It can be seen that the carbon and manganese concentration in austenite formed in earlier stage is at a high level. However, the carbon and manganese concentration of newly formed austenite in original ferrite region is still at a relatively low level, so a remarkable solute concentration gradient in austenite develops, which results in the diffusion of carbon and manganese from austenite phase interior to the γ/α interface. In the model, the driving force changes with the change of carbon and manganese concentration in austenite at the interface, and the migration velocity of γ/α interface will change according to Eq. (3). Therefore the interaction between interface mobility and solute diffusion determines the solute concentration in austenite at the interface and controls the migration of γ/α interface.

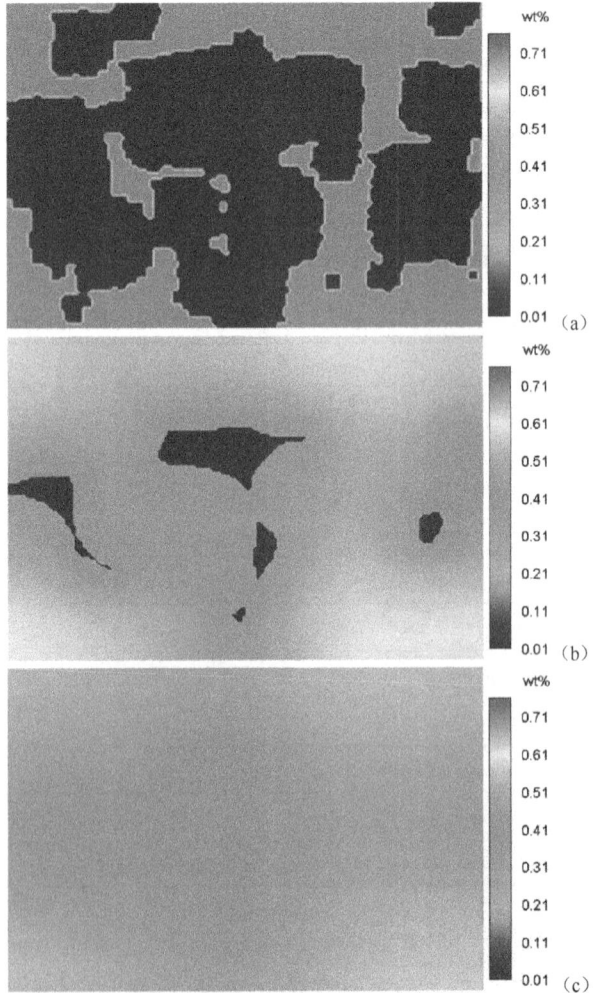

Fig. 3 The simulated microstructure at different temperatures during the heating process. (a) 680℃, (b) 730℃, (c) 750℃, (d) 810℃, (e) 860℃, where P is pearlite, γ is austenite and α is ferrite.

Fig. 4 The distribution of carbon concentration field during the transformation from ferrite to austenite. (a) 750℃, (b) 810℃, (c) 860℃.

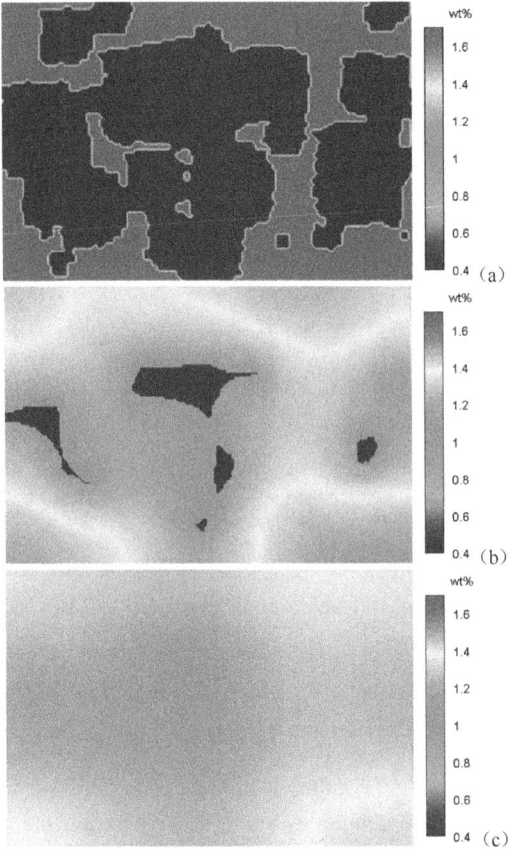

Fig. 5 The distribution of manganese concentration field during the transformation from ferrite to austenite. (a) 750℃, (b) 810℃, (c) 860℃.

Figures 6(a)-6(e) show the metallographic photos of the sample quenched at 680℃, 730℃, 750℃, 810℃, and 860℃, respectively. The microstructure in Fig. 6 (a) consists of ferrite and pearlite. The microstructure in Fig. 6 (b) consists of ferrite, residual pearlite, and martensite. The microstructure in Figs. 6 (c) and 6 (d) consist of residual ferrite and martensite. The microstructure in Fig. 6 (e) is martensite. All the martensite was austenite before quenching. Figure 6 (e) exhibits the grain boundaries of the prior austenite.

Comparison between the calculated fractions of different phases during heating with experimental data is shown in **Fig. 7.** As might be expected, formation of austenite from the pearlite occurs at a higher rate than the formation of austenite from ferrite. The pearlite dissolution is very fast and the transformation of ferrite into austenite is slower and is almost completed at 850℃. It can be seen that the simulated results are in good agreement with the experimental data.

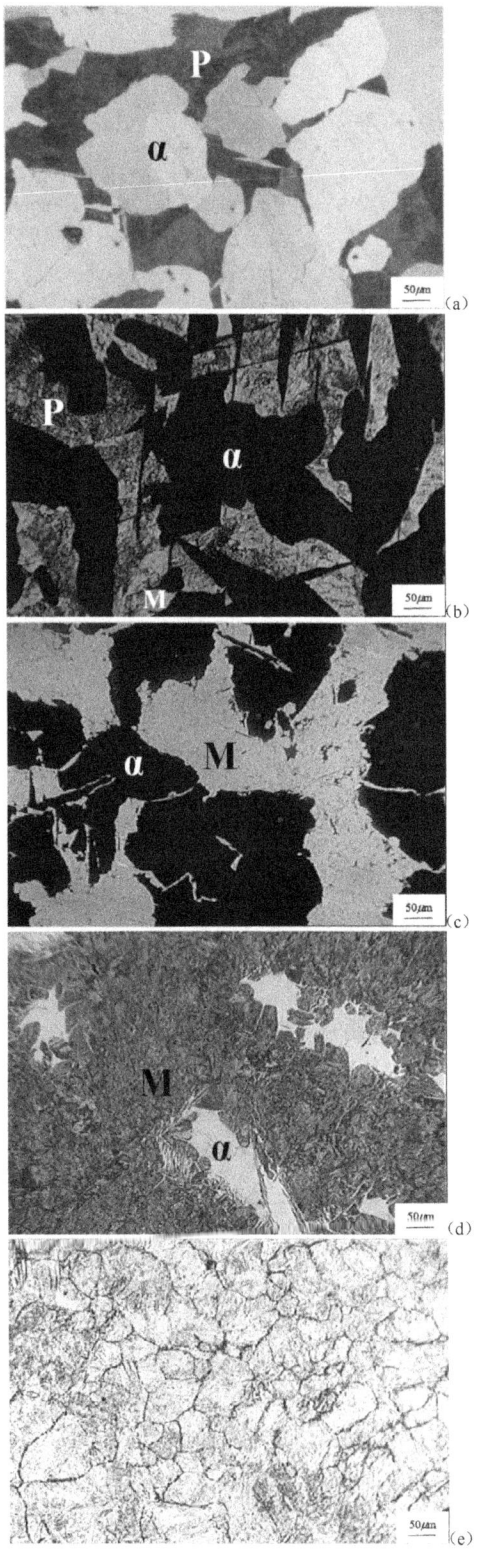

Fig. 6 The metallographic photos of the samples. The microstructure of the sample quenched at (a) 680℃ (4% nital), (b) 730℃ (LePera's etchant), (c) 750℃ (LePera's etchant), (d) 810℃ (4% nital), and (e) quenched at 860℃ (saturated aqueous picric acid), where M is martensite, P is pearlite, and α is ferrite.

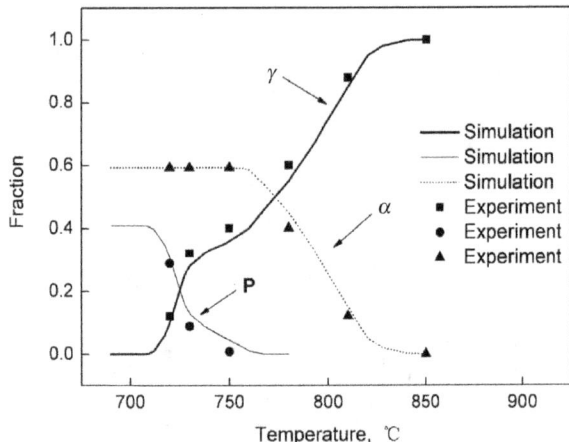

Fig. 7 Fractions of different phases as function of temperature for the heating rate 80℃/h.

Assuming that the sample expands isotropically, for small volume changes, the change of the sample length ΔL referred to the initial length L_0 at room temperature is related to the volume change ΔV and the initial volume V_0 at room temperature for small changes as follows:[3,6,7]

$$\frac{\Delta L}{L_0} = \frac{L-L_0}{L_0} = \frac{V-V_0}{3V_0} \quad (17)$$

Therefore, $\frac{\Delta L}{L_0}$ can be calculated from the fractions of the different phases in the microstructure during continuous heating:[3,6,7]

$$\frac{\Delta L}{L_0} = \frac{1}{3}\left[\frac{\left(2V_\alpha a_\alpha^3 + \frac{1}{3}V_\theta a_\theta b_\theta c_\theta + V_\gamma a_\gamma^3\right) - \left(2V_{\alpha_0} a_{\alpha_0}^3 + \frac{1}{3}V_{\theta_0} a_{\theta_0} b_{\theta_0} c_{\theta_0}\right)}{\left(2V_{\alpha_0} a_{\alpha_0}^3 + \frac{1}{3}V_{\theta_0} a_{\theta_0} b_{\theta_0} c_{\theta_0}\right)}\right] \quad (18)$$

where V_{α_0} and V_{θ_0} are the initial fractions of ferrite and cementite at room temperature, respectively. V_α, V_θ and V_γ are the fractions of ferrite, cementite and austenite at any transformation temperature, which were calculated using the model described above. Fractions of ferrite and of cementite in pearlite are considered to be 0.88 and 0.12, respectively. a_{α_0} is the lattice parameter of ferrite at room temperature, given by 2.866Å. a_{θ_0}, b_{θ_0} and c_{θ_0} are the lattice parameters of cementite at room temperature, given by 4.5246, 5.0885 and 6.7423Å, respectively. a_{γ_0} is the lattice parameter of austenite at room temperature:

$$a_{\gamma_0} = 3.573 + 0.033C + 0.00095Mn - 0.0002Ni + 0.0006Cr + 0.0031Mo + 0.0018V \quad (19)$$

where the chemical composition is measured in wt% and a_{γ_0} is in Å. a_α, a_θ, b_θ, c_θ and a_γ are the lattice parameters of ferrite, cementite and austenite at any transformation temperature, which can be calculated as follows:

$$a_\alpha = a_{\alpha_0}[1+\beta_\alpha(T-300)] \quad (20a)$$
$$a_\gamma = a_{\gamma_0}[1+\beta_\gamma(T-300)] \quad (20b)$$
$$a_\theta = a_{\theta_0}[1+\beta_\theta(T-300)] \quad (20c)$$
$$b_\theta = b_{\theta_0}[1+\beta_\theta(T-300)] \quad (20d)$$
$$c_\theta = c_{\theta_0}[1+\beta_\theta(T-300)] \quad (20e)$$

where β_α and β_γ are the linear thermal expansion coefficients of ferrite and austenite, given by $1.244\times10^{-5}K^{-1}$ and $2.065\times10^{-5}K^{-1}$. β_θ is the linear thermal expansion coefficient of cementite, which can be calculated by:

$$\beta_\theta = 6.0\times10^{-6} + 3.0\times10^{-9}(T-273) + 1.0\times10^{-11}(T-273)^2 \quad (21)$$

where T is the temperature in K. The parameters used mentioned above can be obtained from reported literatures.[3,6,7]

The dilatometric curve calculated for samples together with the corresponding experimental curve are shown in **Fig. 8**. In general, the simulated relative change in length is consistent with the experimental result. It also can be used to validate the microstructure simulation models.

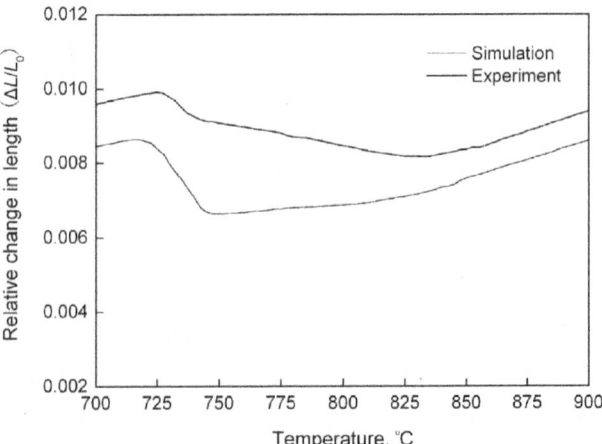

Fig. 8 Calculated and experimental dilatometric curves of the studied steel for the heating rate 80℃/h.

After the full austenite microstructure is formed, grain coarsening is evident. **Figure 9** displays simulated and experimental microstructural evolution during the grain growth. From Fig. 9, it can be seen that grains grow gradually with the increase of soaking time. **Figure 10** indicates the distribution of austenite grain size at the temperature of 900℃ with different soaking time. As seen from Fig. 10, the distribution of austenite grain size is close to lognormal distribution. The austenite grain size shown in Fig. 10 (a) is mostly in the range of 20-70μm at a soaking time of 0h. And the austenite grain size shown in Fig. 10 (c) is mostly in the range of 40-100μm at a soaking time of 20h. The changing of average austenite grain size with the soaking time is shown in **Fig. 11.** As seen from Fig. 11, austenite grain growth rate is initially high and then decreases later.

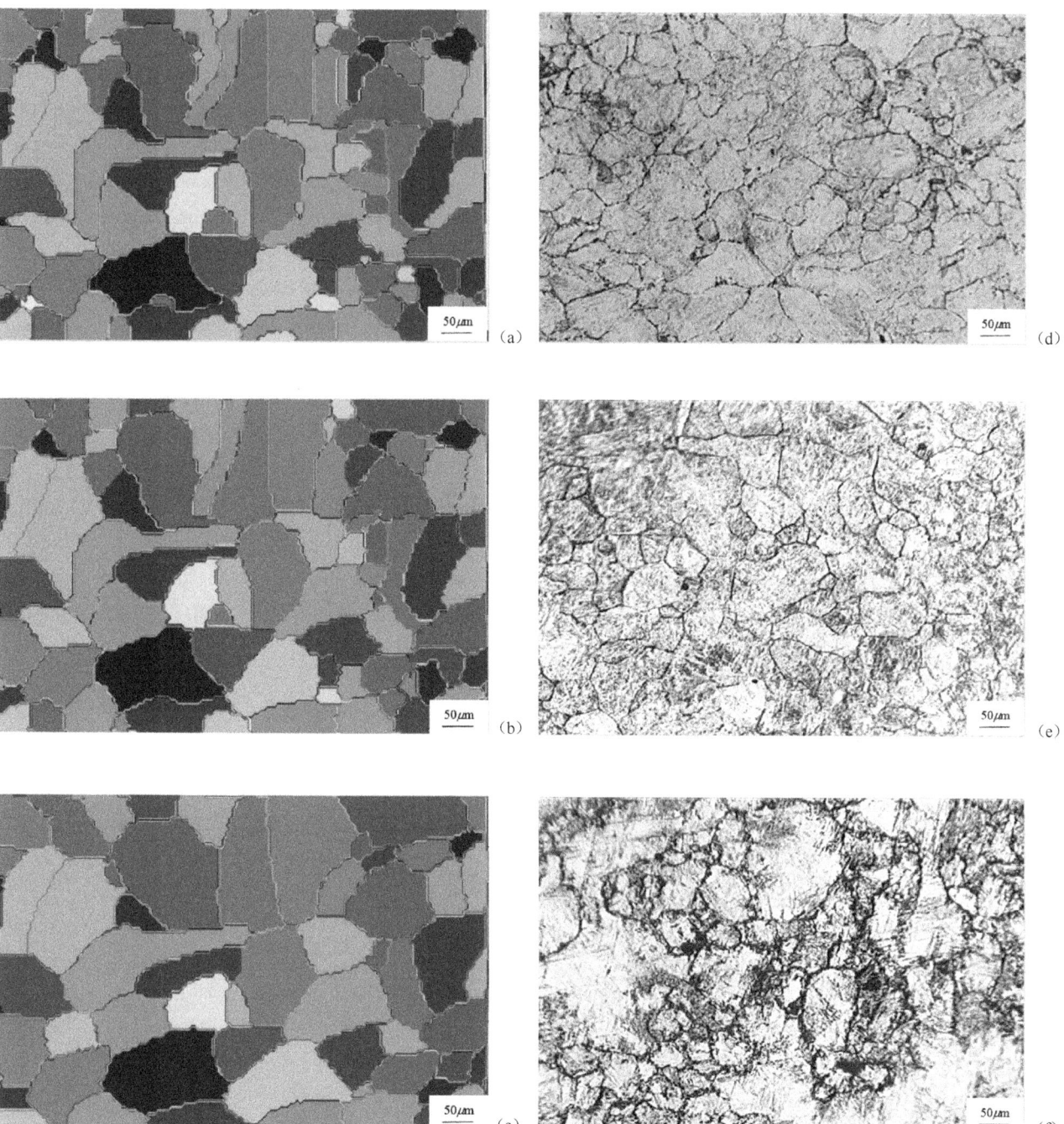

Fig. 9 Simulation results (a-c) and optical micrographs (d-f) representing grain size for different soaking time. (a, d) 0h, (b, e) 5h, (c, f) 20h.

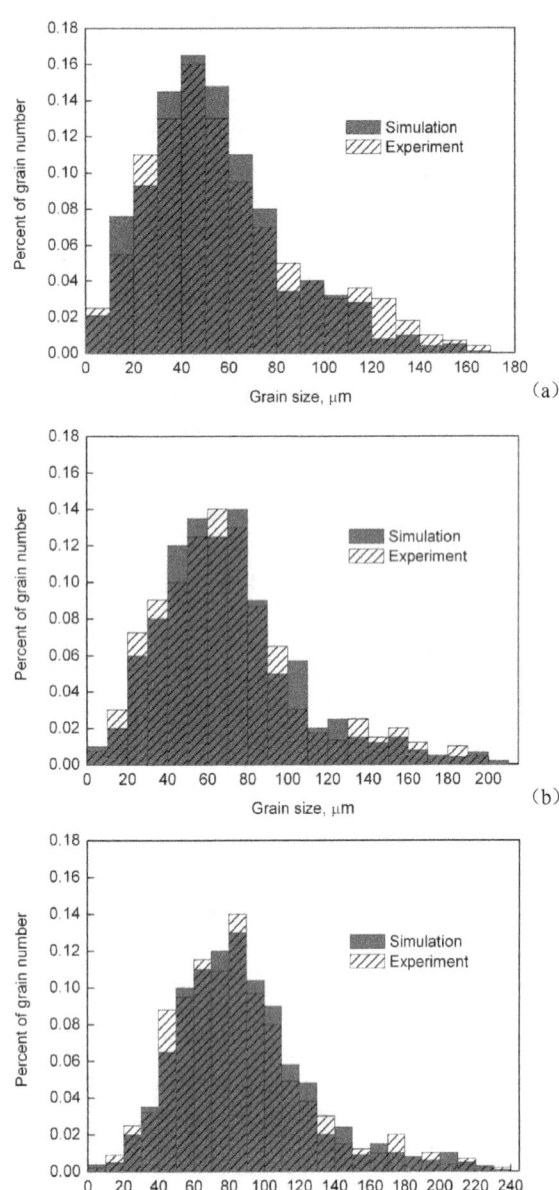

Fig. 10 The distribution of austenite grain size at heating temperature of 900℃ with different soaking time. (a) 0h, (b) 5h, (c) 20h.

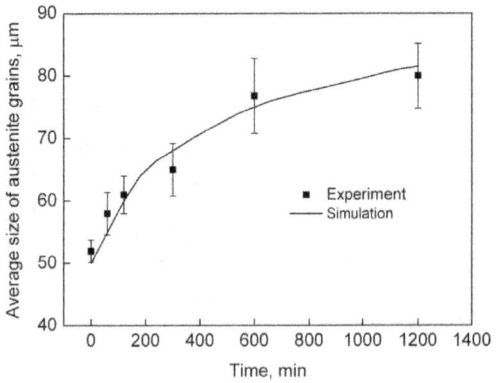

Fig. 11 Effect of soaking time on average grain size.

6. Conclusion

A cellular automaton model has been developed to simulate the austenitization process of ASTM A216 WCA steel during heating process. The dissolution of pearlite was described by continuous nucleation and growth of austenite grains. A mixed-mode model for multicomponent system was employed to calculate the growth velocity of the γ/α interface. The austenite grain coarsening induced by γ/γ grain boundary migration was considered and the migration velocity of the grain boundaries was calculated based on Burke and Turnbull's theory. To validate the model, dilatometric and quenching experiments were carried out, and the microstructure of the quenched samples was examined and compared with the simulation results. It was shown that the simulated results, including the fraction of the austenite, average austenite grain size and the distribution of austenite grain size, are in good agreement with the experimental results.

Acknowledgement

This work is funded by the National Science and Technology Major Project of China (2011ZX04014-052 and 2012ZX04012011).

REFERENCES

[1] F. L. G. Oliveira, M. S. Andrade and A. B. Cota: *Mater. Charact.*, **58** (2007), 256.

[2] B. J. Yang, L. Chuzhoy and M. L. Johnson: *Comput. Mater. Sci.*, **41** (2007), 186.

[3] F. G. Caballero, C. Capdevila and C. Garía de Andrés: *ISIJ Int.*, **41** (2001), 1093.

[4] B. Su, Z. Q. Han, B. C. Liu, Y. R. Zhao, B. Z. Shen and L. Z. Zhang: *IOP Conf. Ser.: Mater. Sci. Eng.*, **33** (2012), 012080.

[5] A. Jacot and M. Rappaz: *Acta Mater.*, **47** (1999), 1645.

[6] F. G. Caballero, C. Capdevila and C. Garía de Andrés: *J. Mater. Sci.*, **37** (2002), 3533.

[7] F. G. Caballero, C. Capdevila and C. Garía de Andrés: *Scr. Mater.*, **42** (2000), 1159.

[8] Y. J. Lan, D. Z. Li and Y. Y. Li: *Metall. Mater. Trans. B*, **37B** (2006), 119.

[9] J. Geiger, A. Roósz and P. Barkóczy: *Acta Mater.*, **49** (2001), 623.

[10] S.-J. Lee and Y.-K. Lee: *Mater. Des.*, **29** (2008), 1840.

[11] K. H. Jung, H. W. Lee and Y. T. Im: *Int. J. Mech. Sci.*, **52** (2010), 1136.

[12] F. A. Hua, Y. S. Yang, D. Y. Guo, W. H. Tong and Z. L. Hu: *Acta Metall. Sin.*, **40** (2004), 1210.

[13] Q. Yu and S. K. Esche: *Mater. Lett.*, **56** (2002), 47.

[14] J. Odqvist, M. Hillert and J. Ågren: *Acta Mater.*, **50** (2002), 3211.

[15] O. Thuillier, F. Danoix, M. Gouné and D. Blavette: *Scr. Mater.*, **55** (2006), 1071.

[16] F. Fazeli and M. Militzer: *Metall. Mater. Trans. A*, **36A** (2005), 1395.

[17] C. Bos and J. Sietsma: *Acta Mater.*, **57** (2009), 136.

[18] B. Su, Z. Q. Han, Y. R. Zhao, B. Z. Shen, L. Z. Zhang and B. C. Liu: *Acta Metall. Sin.*, **47** (2011), 1388.

[19] J. Andersson, T. Helander, L. Höglund, P. F. Shi and B. Sundman: *Calphad*, **26** (2002), 273.

[20] A. Borgenstam, A. Engstrom, L. Hoghund and J. Agren: *J. Phase Equilib.*, **21** (2000), 269.

[21] M. Hillert: *Acta Mater.*, **47** (1999), 4481.

[22] J. E. Burke and D. Turnbull: *Prog. Metal Phys.*, **3** (1952), 220.

[23] D. Z. Li, N. M. Xiao, Y. J. Lan, C. W. Zheng and Y. Y. Li: *Acta Mater.*, **55** (2007), 6234.

[24] J. Geiger, A. Roósz and P. Barkóczy: *Acta Mater.*, **49** (2001), 623.

27. Deformation Prediction of a Heavy Hydro Turbine Blade During the Casting Process with Consideration of Martensitic Transformation

JINWU KANG, TIANJIAO WANG, TIANYOU HUANG, and BAICHENG LIU

Heavy hydro turbine castings are made of martensitic stainless steel, which undergoes martensitic transformation during the casting process. Therefore, both residual stress and deformation are affected not only by uneven cooling but also by martensitic transformation. In this paper, a coupled thermo-martensitic phase transformation-stress model was established and it was implemented by further development with ABAQUS, which also incorporated the thermal and mechanical boundaries, and the contact pair between the casting and mold. The system was applied to the analysis of a heavy hydro blade casting. Results of stress, displacement, and martensite phase fraction were obtained. It is found that martensitic transformation has a significant effect on the stress and deformation results. The displacement in the normal direction of local areas was calculated to represent deformation in the x, y, and z directions. The deformation of the blade casting occurred mainly at the two thin corners with 18 and 22mm in opposite tendency. The simulated results were compared with the measured machining allowance, and they are basically in agreement.

DOI: 10.1007/s11661-013-1856-y

© The Minerals, Metals & Materials Society and ASM International 2013

I. INTRODUCTION

DEFORMATION is a common defect in casting production, which mainly results from uneven cooling. Modeling and numerical simulation can be used to predict stress and deformation in which thermomechanical modeling, thermal and mechanical boundary conditions between casting and mold, and the analysis of deformation are the main concerns. Thermo-elastic and thermo-elasto-plastic models are commonly used in stress analysis. Because both the liquid and solid phases and their mixture are involved in the casting process, thermo-elasto-visco-plastic or rheological models are also applied, especially for the prediction of hot tearing.[1-3] The effect of the mold on stress and strain results is very complicated, and it used to be considered as rigid or elastic. In a contact problem between the casting and mold, sometimes a gap forms and sometimes forced contact occurs. Liu et al.[4] considered the effect of sand mold on casting using the contact element method. These results showed that the mold had an obvious effect on the stress and deformation of heavy runner band castings. On the other hand, the casting/mold interface heat transfer is affected by the formation of the air gap resulting from deformation of both the casting and mold. Xu et al.[5] coupled the thermal and mechanical boundaries between the casting and mold, using the contact element method for the mechanical action between the casting and mold, and the air gap resulting from deformation is fed back to the thermal contact condition by modifying the interfacial heat transfer coefficient. Kron et al.[6] systemically investigated the effect of the thermo-mechanical boundary on the thermal histories and displacements of the casting and mold. These results showed that heat transfer between the casting and mold is affected by air gap formation. Shake-out of casting alters the mechanical boundary condition, which was studied by Lee and Lee[7] with the effect of shake-out on the deformation of a large marine propeller casting during solidification and the subsequent cooling. It is found that the later shake-out of the casting, the smaller its deformation. In order to control the deformation of the propeller casting, slow shake-out was much better than sudden shake-out. The aim of deformation prediction is to control deformation finally. So, Chen et al.[8] carried out the stress analysis of an impeller casting, and the displacement was annulled by modifying the casting geometry in the subsequent simulations. Iterations were performed until uniform machining allowances were achieved.

Usually, displacement, a kind of direct result of stress analysis, is used to represent deformation. However, contraction occurs during the casting process which contributes to the displacement as well. The total displacement is a combination of contraction and deformation. The authors[9] proposed three methods to predict net deformation; one method is to separate deformation from displacement by subtracting the contraction component. Another method is to use the machining allowance to describe deformation. The third method employs the variation of the normal direction of the local surface area. The authors carried out numerical simulation of the Three Gorges Project hydro turbine blade casting where the machining allowance distribution is used to determine the desired deformation, and an algorithm was proposed to determine the inverse deformation for the compensation of the deformation.[10]

Heavy hydro turbine blade castings, usually made of martensitic stainless steel, undergo martensitic transformation during the casting process. For these castings, it is necessary to take martensitic transformation into account. However, in the modeling and simulation of the casting process, solid phase transformation is always neglected. In the heat treatment aspect, the Koistinen-Marburger equation is used to describe martensitic transformation.[11] During martensitic transformation, plastic strain occurs under stress less than yield stress or even without stress, which is called transformation-induced plasticity (TRIP). Different from classical plastic strain, this strain complies with the Greenwood-Johnson mechanism.[12,13] The TRIP steel refers to that utilizing the TRIP phenomena. For this type of steel, the retained austenite undergoes martensitic transformation under load during service, which can improve its strength and plasticity.[14,15] The coupling of phase transformation and stress for parts during the heat treatment process was studied by Inoue and Wang,[16] Denis et al.,[17] Liu et al.,[18] and Sun et al.[19] The phase transformation plasticity was taken into account in their study. Sun et al.[19] and Dai et al.[20] determined the transformation kinetics coefficient of the transformation plasticity based on dilatometry measurements under different loads. The authors[21] also carried out the thermo-mechanical coupled stress analysis for heavy hydro turbine blades during the normalizing process by DEFORM. Both the plasticity and strain caused by the phase transformation from austenite to martensite were considered along with the elastic, plastic, and thermal strains. The results show that martensitic phase transformation has a great effect on the deformation of these blades. However, this model has not been applied to the casting process because thermal and mechanical boundaries between the casting and mold were not included in DEFORM.

In this paper, a coupled thermo-martensitic phase transformation-mechanical model is developed for the numerical simulation of the casting process of martensitic stainless steels. The contact boundary condition between casting and mold is integrated. The deformation of a heavy hydro blade casting will be studied and the effect of martensitic transformation will be considered.

II. MODEL DESCRIPTION

During the casting process of martensitic stainless steels, the cooling process is accompanied by solidification, martensitic transformation, and stress evolution. These three phenomena are closely linked, as illustrated in Figure 1. Cooling determines phase transformation, and the latent heat released during solidification contributes to temperature fields. Because of uneven cooling and phase transformation, stress evolves. The deformation resulting from stress fields has an effect on the contact condition between the casting and mold which may alter the interfacial heat transfer coefficient. However, it is neglected here. The heat resulting from deformation is usually neglected as well. For martensitic stainless steels, austenite transforms into martensite during the casting process. Expansion and the plasticity induced by martensitic transformation contribute to stress fields.

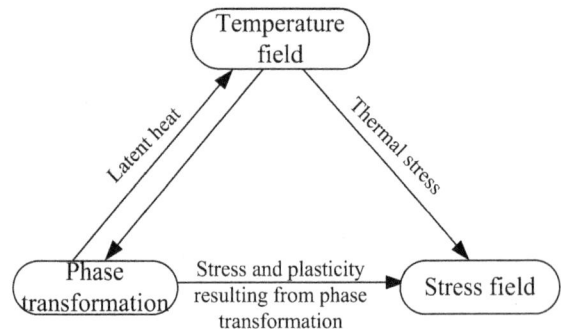

Fig. 1 Schematic diagram of temperature, phase transformation, and stress analysis during the casting process.

A. Martensitic Phase Transformation

The phase transformation from austenite to martensite is not controlled by diffusion. Instead, the fraction of martensite is described by the Koistinen-Marburger equation

$$\xi_M = 1 - e^{c(T-M_s)} \quad (1)$$

where ξ_M is the fraction of martensite, T is temperature, M_s is the start temperature of martensitic transformation, c is the kinetic coefficient, and $c = 0.014$, as determined by experiment.[21]

The variation of density of new and old phases during martensitic phase transformation leads to strain. This strain increment is

$$d\{\varepsilon_{tr}\} = \beta_M d\xi_M \quad (2)$$

where β_M is the temperature-dependent expansion coefficient of phase transformation.

During martensitic phase transformation, there is plasticity induced by phase transformation even though no yielding occurs. This plastic strain increment is determined by the Greenwood-Johnson model

$$d\{\varepsilon_{tp}\} = 3K\{s\}(1-\xi_M)d\xi_M \quad (3)$$

where K is the coefficient of phase transformation, $K = 8.74 \times 10^{-5}$ MPa^{-1}, as determined by experiment,[21] and $\{s\}$ is the stress deviation.

B. Thermo-Martensitic Transformation-Mechanical Model

The total strain increment is composed of elastic, plastic, thermal, and phase transformation-related terms as follows:

$$d\{\varepsilon\} = d\{\varepsilon_e\} + d\{\varepsilon_p\} + d\{\varepsilon_{th}\} + d\{\varepsilon_{tr}\} + d\{\varepsilon_{tp}\} \quad (4)$$

where $d\{\varepsilon\}$ is total strain increment tensor and $d\{\varepsilon_e\}$, $d\{\varepsilon_p\}$, and $d\{\varepsilon_{th}\}$ are elastic, plastic, and thermal strains, respectively.

The elastic strain is determined by Hooke's law as follows:

$$d\{\varepsilon_e\} = [\overline{D}_e]^{-1}d\{\sigma\} \quad (5)$$

where $[\overline{D}_e]$ is the modulus matrix, which is a function of temperature and the martensite volume fraction.

The plastic strain is governed by the Prandtl-Reuss principle

$$d\{\varepsilon_p\} = d\overline{\varepsilon}_p \frac{\partial \overline{\sigma}}{\partial \{\sigma\}} \quad (6)$$

where $\overline{\sigma}$ is the equivalent stress.

The thermal strain is

$$d\{\varepsilon_{th}\} = \overline{\alpha}dT \quad (7)$$

where $\overline{\alpha}$ is the equivalent thermal expansion coefficient, which is a function of temperature and microstructure.

Substituting Eqs. (2), (3), (5), (6), and (7) into Eq. (4), the total stress increment is obtained

$$d\{\sigma\} = [\overline{D}_e]\left[d\{\varepsilon\} - \overline{\alpha}dT - (\beta_M + 3K\{s\}(1-\xi_M))d\xi_M - \frac{\partial \overline{\sigma}}{\partial \{\sigma\}}d\overline{\varepsilon}_p\right]. \quad (8)$$

Assuming isotropic hardening, the Mises yield principle is

$$f(\overline{\sigma}, \overline{\varepsilon}_p) = \overline{\sigma} - H\left(\int d\overline{\varepsilon}_p\right) = 0 \quad (9)$$

where H is a hardening function.

During plastic loading, stress is located on the yielding plane, $df(\overline{\sigma}, \overline{\varepsilon}_p) = 0$, so

$$\left\{\frac{\partial \overline{\sigma}}{\partial \{\sigma\}}\right\}^T d\{\sigma\} - H'd\overline{\varepsilon}_p = 0 \quad (10)$$

where H' is the hardening modulus.

Substituting Eq. (8) into Eq. (10), the relationship between the equivalent plasticity increment and the total strain increment is as follows:

$$d\overline{\varepsilon}_p = \frac{\left\{\frac{\partial \overline{\sigma}}{\partial \{\sigma\}}\right\}^T [\overline{D}_e]}{H' + \left\{\frac{\partial \overline{\sigma}}{\partial \{\sigma\}}\right\}^T [\overline{D}_e]\frac{\partial \overline{\sigma}}{\partial \{\sigma\}}}[d\{\varepsilon\} - \overline{\alpha}dT - (\beta_M + 3K\{s\}(1-\xi_M))d\xi_M]. \quad (11)$$

Substituting Eq. (11) into Eq. (8),

$$d\sigma = \left[[\overline{D}_e] - \frac{[\overline{D}_e]\frac{\partial\overline{\sigma}}{\partial\{\sigma\}}\left\{\frac{\partial\overline{\sigma}}{\partial\{\sigma\}}\right\}^T[\overline{D}_e]}{H' + \left\{\frac{\partial\overline{\sigma}}{\partial\{\sigma\}}\right\}^T[\overline{D}_e]\frac{\partial\overline{\sigma}}{\partial\{\sigma\}}}\right][d\{\varepsilon\} - \overline{\alpha}dT$$
$$-(\beta_M + 3K\{s\}(1-\xi_M))d\xi_M]. \quad (12)$$

Then, the coefficient term can be simplified as

$$[\overline{D}_{ep}] = \left[[\overline{D}_e] - \frac{[\overline{D}_e]\frac{\partial\overline{\sigma}}{\partial\{\sigma\}}\left\{\frac{\partial\overline{\sigma}}{\partial\{\sigma\}}\right\}^T[\overline{D}_e]}{H' + \left\{\frac{\partial\overline{\sigma}}{\partial\{\sigma\}}\right\}^T[\overline{D}_e]\frac{\partial\overline{\sigma}}{\partial\{\sigma\}}}\right] \quad (13)$$

where $[\overline{D}_{ep}]$ is the equivalent elasto-plastic matrix.

Then, Eq. (12) can be simplified to

$$d\{\sigma\} = [\overline{D}_{ep}][d(\varepsilon) - \overline{\alpha}dT - (\beta_M + 3K\{s\}(1-\xi_M))d\xi_M] \quad (14)$$

Equation (14) is the stress-strain relationship considering martensitic phase transformation.

The effect of stress-induced phase transformation is neglected here because no external load is exerted during the casting process.

III. MODEL IMPLEMENTATION

Based on the thermo-phase transformation-mechanical model described above, a platform was established for the stress analysis of the casting process by applying ABAQUS, the commercial software package for simulation of heat transfer and stress analysis. User-defined material mechanical behavior (UMAT subroutine) provided by ABAQUS was used to define the thermomartensitic transformation-mechanical model. The flowchart of the implementation of the coupled model is shown in Figure 2. FT-STAR, a self-developed software for the numerical simulation of casting processes, is used for thermal analysis. The simulated temperature fields are converted to thermal inputs in ABAQUS load step for stress analysis. The casting/mold surface to surface contact boundary condition[4] is set in ABAQUS. For each iteration, in each increment of each step, UMAT is called, in which the martensitic phase transformation kinetics, phase transformation strain, and phase transformation-induced plasticity are calculated, as shown in Figure 3. In the UMAT routine, the martensitic phase transformation is calculated according to the temperature development. Then, the thermal mechanical properties are updated according to the fraction of martensite and temperature. The elastoplastic matrix and yield stress are updated. Based on Eq. (14), stress, strain, and Jacobian matrix are updated as well.

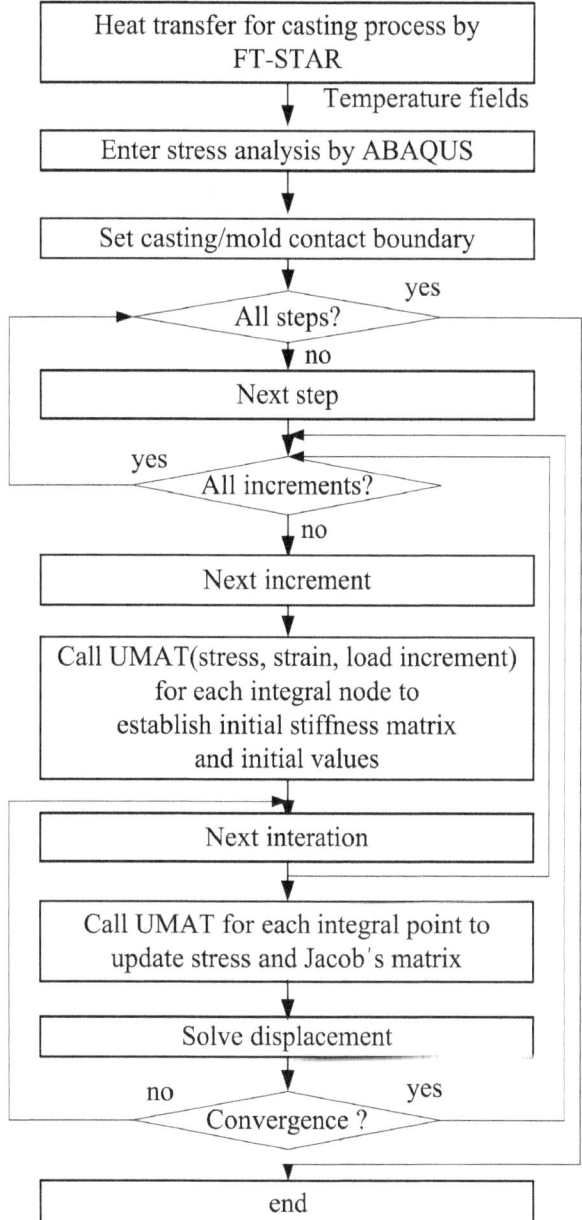

Fig. 2 Solution flowchart of thermo-phase transformation-stress model in ABAQUS.

IV. VALIDATION

To validate the thermo-phase transformation-mechanical model, the simulated results by the developed platform of a quenched tube were compared to the experimental results cited from Reference [22]. The geometry

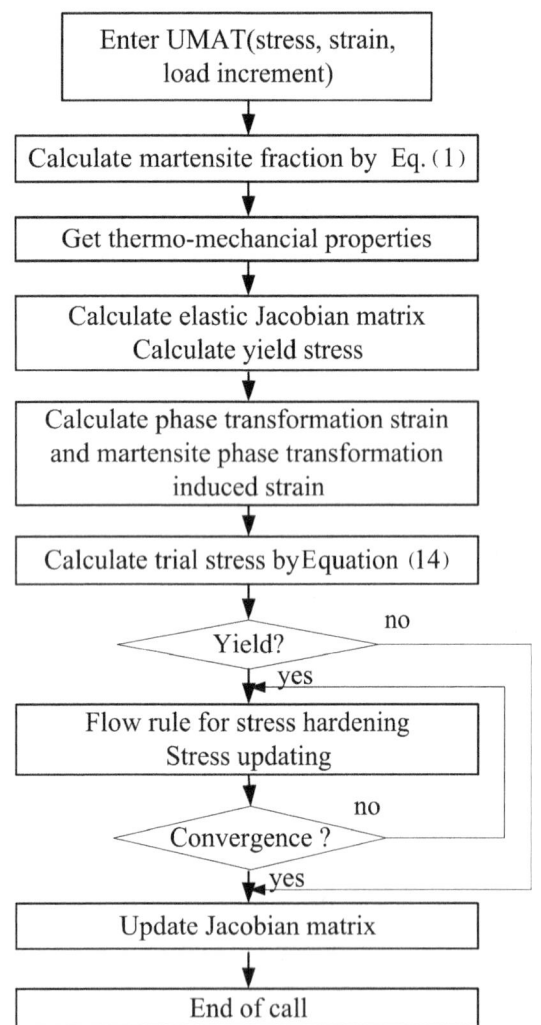

Fig. 3 The flowchart of the UMAT routine for material model.

1093K (820℃) in a furnace. After holding for 2 hours, it was quenched; martensitic phase transformation occurred during quenching. In the reference, residual stress of the tube was measured by the ring-core method. In this method, a circular trough is cut with strain gages attached at the core surface. During the sectioning operation, the residual strains in the part are relieved. The changes in strains are monitored by an on-line computer as a function of cut depth. The principal residual stresses are determined using the derivative of the strain vs depth data. Before the measurement, calibration was performed, and temperature compensation was considered during the measurement. The simulated temperature of point P, axial stress, and circumferential stress along line l was compared with the measured results, as shown in Figure 5. It can be seen they are in good agreement.

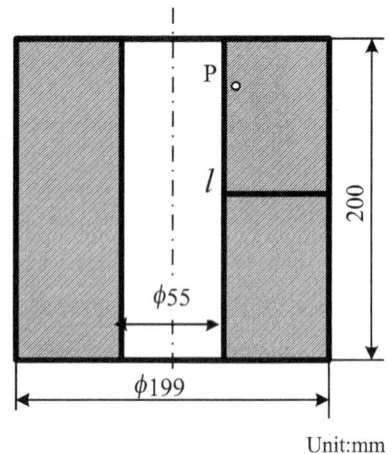

Fig. 4 Geometry of the validation specimen—a tube.

of the tube is shown in Figure 4. It is made of 26Cr2Ni4MoV (C: 0.26 pct, Cr: 2 pct, Ni: 4 pct). The tube is heated at rate of 200K/h (200℃/h) from room temperature to

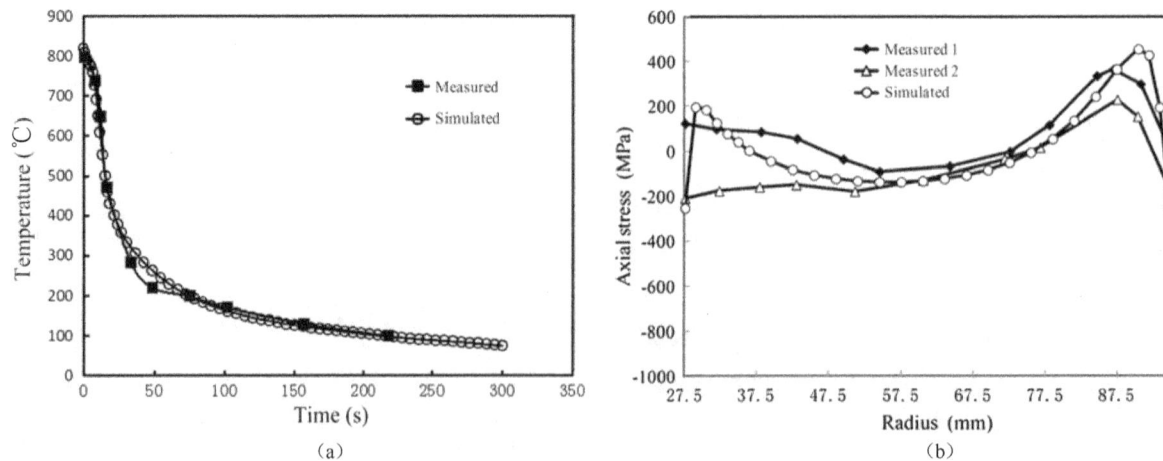

Fig. 5 Comparison of simulated (a) temperature of point P, (b) axial stress, and (c) circumferential stress and the measured results along line l.

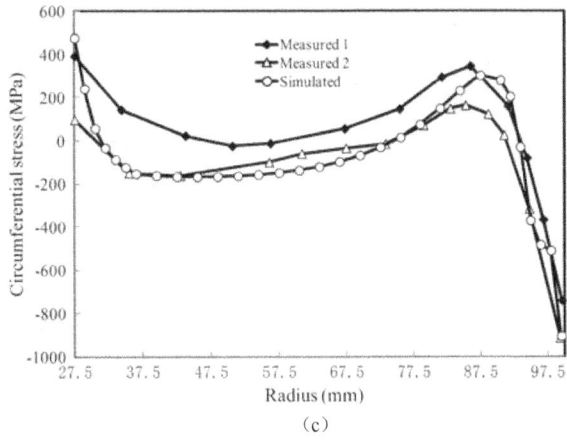

Fig. 5 Comparison of simulated (a) temperature of point P, (b) axial stress, and (c) circumferential stress and the measured results along line *l*. (Continued)

V. NUMERICAL SIMULATION

The hydro turbine blade casting for the Three Gorges Project in China is made of martensitic stainless steel ZG0Cr13Ni4Mo (Chinese standard, as listed in Table 1) with as-cast martensite microstructure. It is of a curved shape, having dimensions 4687 × 4268 × 1753mm³, and is 80 to 350mm thick varying from the outlet edge to the inlet edge, as shown in Figures 6 and 7 (a). Its gross weight is 16.5 t. It is prone to deformation during the casting process.

Fig. 6 Three Gorges Project hydro turbine blade casting.

The heat transfer of the casting and mold was calculated by FT-STAR. The simulated temperature fields at different times were mapped to the finite element models of the casting and mold for the further phase transformation and stress analysis by ABAQUS. In the thermal analysis, variation of heat transfer coefficient between the casting and mold was neglected. The cooling process after solidification, instead of solidification itself, mainly contributes to stress and deformation. And martensitic phase transformation occurs below 573K (300℃). Therefore, the heat transfer coefficient between the casting and mold was assumed to be constant, 400W/m² K. The finite element models of the casting and mold are illustrated in Figure 7. During the stress analysis, the contact element model provided by ABAQUS was used at the contact surface between the casting and mold. Thermo-mechanical properties of the blade are dependent on temperature and microstructure, as shown in Figure 8.[22] Above 1273K (1000℃), the microstructure is fully austenite, and its thermo-mechanical properties are listed in Table 2.

Table 1 Chemical Composition of the Martensitic Stainless Steel ZG0Cr13Ni4Mo (Percentage)

C	Si	Mn	P	S	Ni	Cr	Mo	Cu
0.03	0.46	0.52 to 0.55	0.011	0.012 to 0.025	4.25	13.46 to 13.61	0.60 to 0.65	0.08 to 0.09

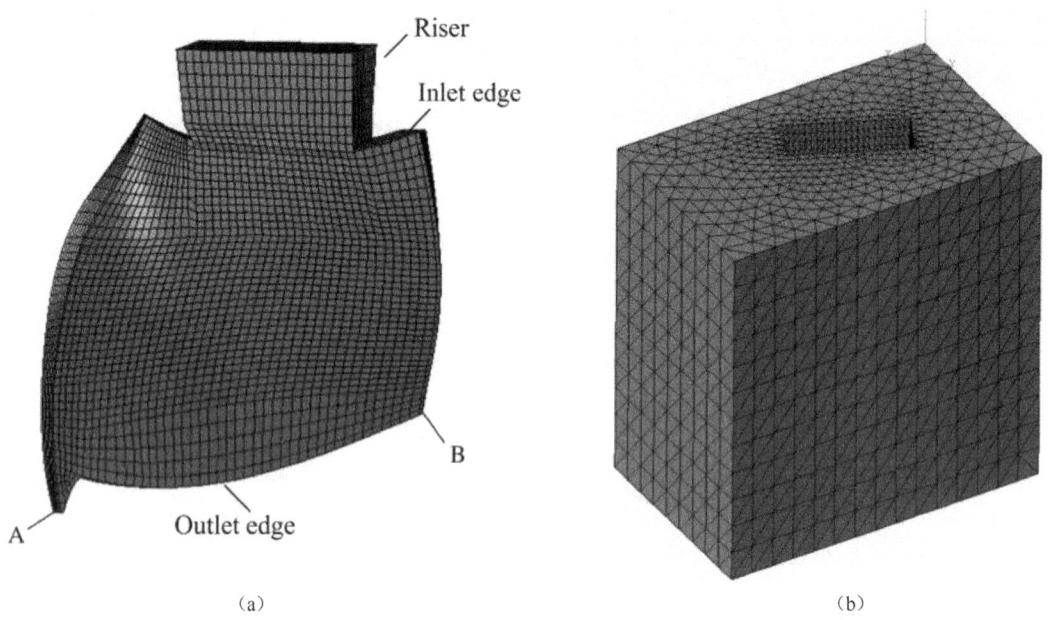

Fig. 7 Finite element model of the hydro turbine blade and sand mold: (a) casting and (b) sand mold.

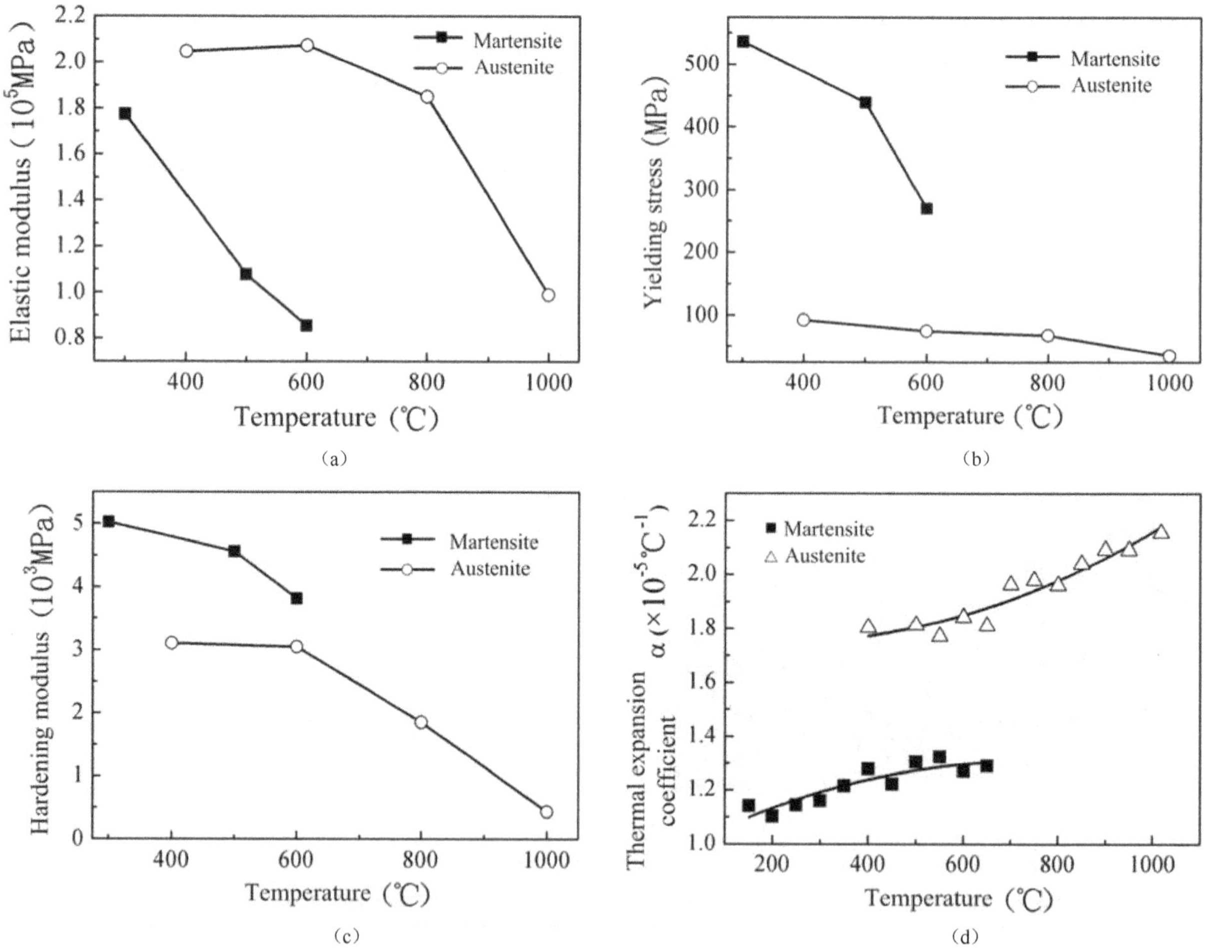

Fig. 8 Thermo-mechanical properties of the austenite and martensite of ZG0Cr13Ni4Mo steel below 1273K (1000℃). (a) Elastic modulus, (b) yield stress, (c) hardening coefficient, and (d) thermal expansion coefficient.

Table 2 Thermo-Mechanical Properties of the Martensitic Stainless Steel Above 1273K (1000℃)[23]

Temperature [K (℃)]	Elastic Modulus (MPa)	Hardening Modulus (MPa)	Yield Stress (MPa)
1473 (1200)	3090	24	25
1573 (1300)	2200	13	22.5
1623 (1350)	1100	0	20
1673 (1400)	1083	0	12.5

VI. RESULTS AND DISCUSSION

A. Temperature Fields

The temperature distributions at two times from pouring are shown in Figure 9. After 50 hours of cooling, the (outlet) bottom edge, which is of the thinnest section, cools below the start point of martensitic phase transformation 549K (276℃).[21] Note that after 150 hours of cooling, almost 70 pct of the blade has been cooled into the phase transformation zone.

B. Phase Transformation

The martensite percentage during the casting process is shown in Figure 10. After 150 hours of cooling, the martensitic phase transformation occurs over almost the entire blade, but only the bottom edge is close to finishing. At the end, the entire blade transforms to martensite, as shown in Figure 10 (b).

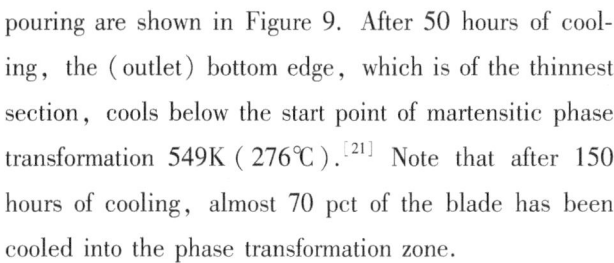

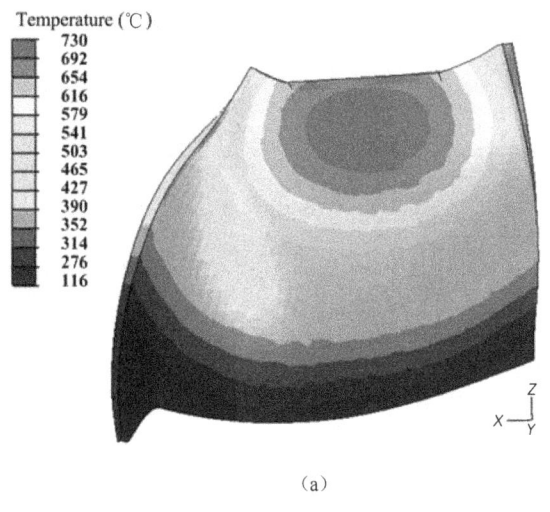
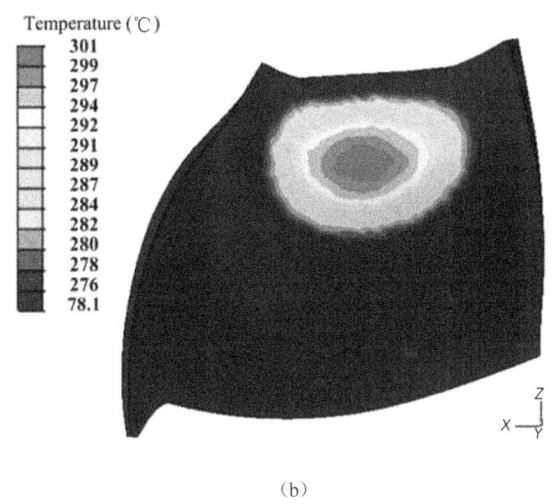

Fig. 9 Temperature distribution during the casting process: (a) 50h, phase transformation occurs at the bottom edge and (b) 150h, most area is under phase transformation.

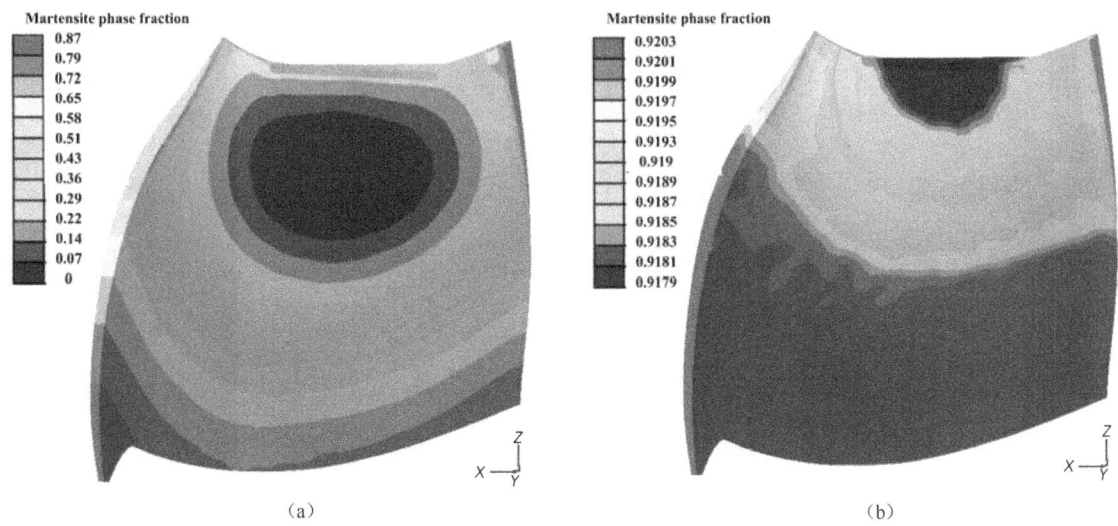

Fig. 10 Martensitic phase transformation during the casting process: (a) 150h and (b) final.

C. Stress

The equivalent stress (Von Mises) distributions of the blade after 150 hours from pouring and at the end of cooling to room temperature are shown in Figure 11. It can be seen that the final residual stress is lower than the stress after 150 hours of cooling. The maximum residual equivalent stress is 350MPa and the average stress is 60MPa.

D. Displacement

The displacement results of the blade are shown in Figure 12 where the blade is parallel to xz plane, with the colored contour showing the y-displacement (in the y-direction). The wireframe shows the original shape and the colored contour shape is the deformed shape. The maximum deformation occurs at the two corners A and B (as shown in Figure 7(a)) which have the largest curvature. The directions of displacements are opposite because of their initial opposite bending direction. The final y-direction deformation of corner A is −38.5mm, while, corner B is +65.3mm. The signs of the values mean the direction, "−" the negative y-direction, and "+" the positive y-direction. The final displacement tends to flatten the blade.

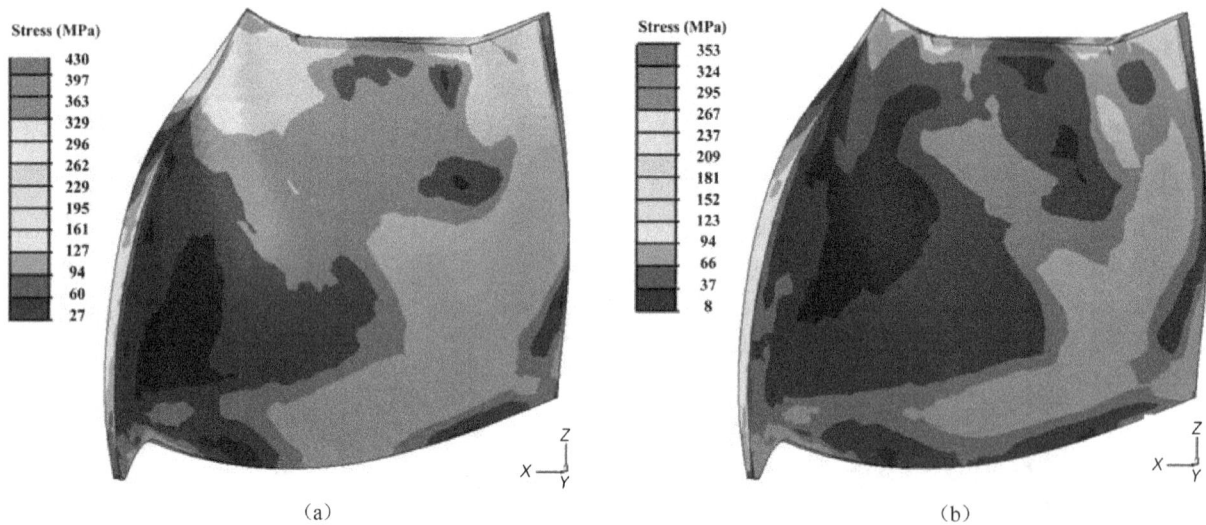

Fig. 11 Stress distribution of the blade at (a) 150h and (b) final at room temperature.

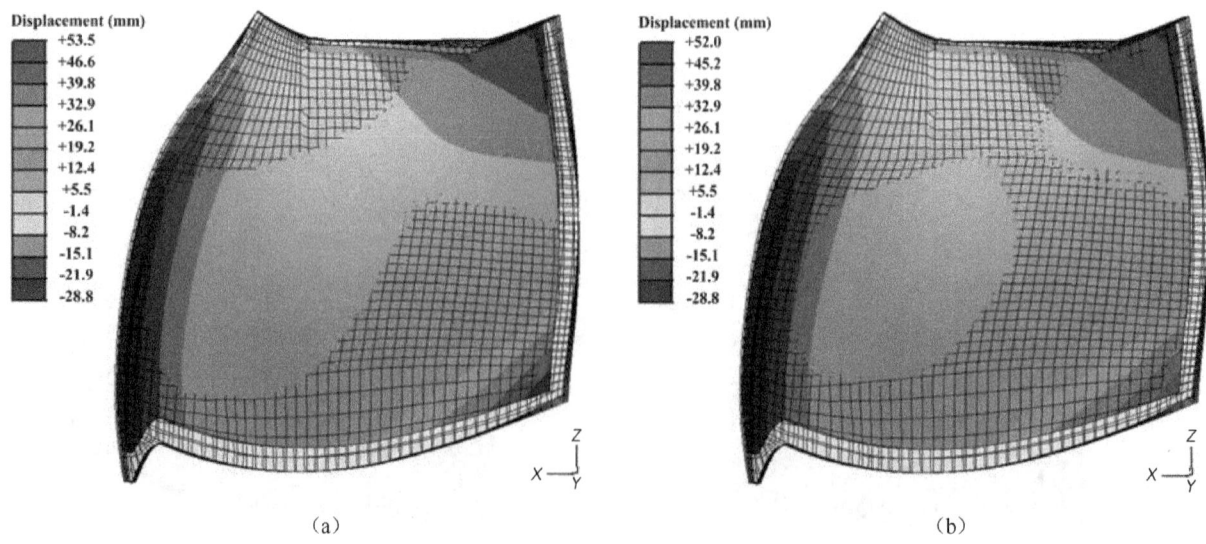

Fig. 12 Displacement in y-direction of the blade during the casting process: (a) 150h and (b) final.

E. Effect of Phase Transformation on Stress and Displacement

To elucidate the effect of martensitic phase transformation, results obtained by the thermo-phase transformation-mechanical and thermo-mechanical models are compared. This comparison for the equivalent stress evolution with time is shown in Figure 13. There is a big difference in stress evolution; the mean equivalent stress is 60MPa with the consideration of phase transformation, while it is 160MPa without it. There is no difference before 50 hours. However, after 150 hours, the equivalent stress decreases as phase transformation proceeds over the entire casting because of phase transformation-induced plasticity.

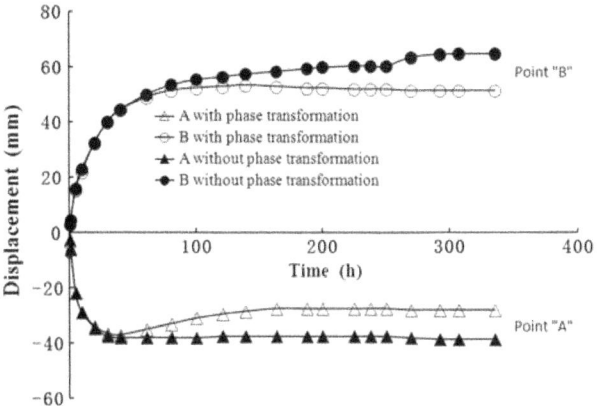

Fig. 14 Effect of martensitic phase transformation on the displacement evolution of corners A and B in the y-direction during the casting process.

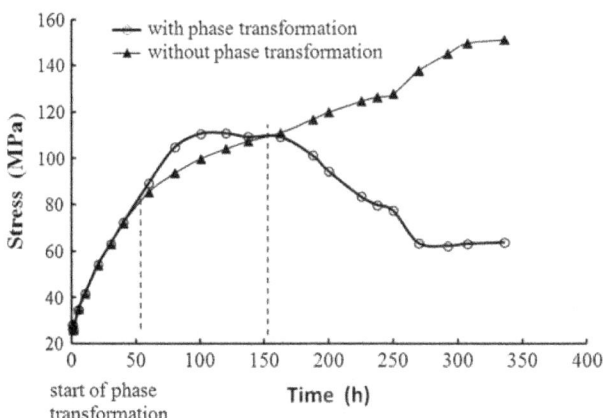

Fig. 13 Effect of martensitic phase transformation on the mean equivalent stress variation during the casting process.

A comparison of the displacements in the y-direction of the corners A and B with and without phase transformation is shown in Figure 14. Note there is also a big difference between these results. Without consideration of the phase transformation, the displacement increases continuously over time. However, as phase transformation is considered, both of the displacements of corners A and B differ from those without consideration of phase transformation when phase transformation starts, and their final displacements come to be smaller. Martensitic transformation results in the displacement of corner A recovering and that of B maintaining at a certain level. The reason for this is that the casting expands during phase transformation, which annuls the contraction resulting from the cooling. Both the uneven cooling and phase transformation cause stress and deformation.

From the above comparisons of these stress and displacement results, it can be concluded that uneven cooling is responsible for the stress and deformation of the blade before martensitic transformation; during the transformation, both uneven cooling and martensitic transformation determine the stress and displacement evolution of the blade. Clearly, martensitic transformation cannot be neglected in the numerical simulation of the casting process of the blade.

F. Displacement in Local Normal Direction

Generally speaking, castings are required to be machined into parts for assembly. Therefore, their deformation directly influences the actual machining allowance which is perpendicular to the local surface area. Therefore, it is useful to evaluate deformation by the displacement in normal direction of the local area which determines the actual machining allowance. If the actual machining allowance is in agreement with the designed value, the casting is free of deformation; otherwise, there is excess machining allowance somewhere and insufficient machining allowance somewhere else. In both the casting and machining workshops, the actual machining allowance distribution of the entire blade is usually used as a criterion for deformation.

Take the displacement vector $\vec{\delta}$ of node Q (in Figure 15), for example,

$$\vec{\delta} = (\delta_x, \delta_y, \delta_z)^T \qquad (15)$$

where δ_x, δ_y, δ_z are the displacement components of node Q.

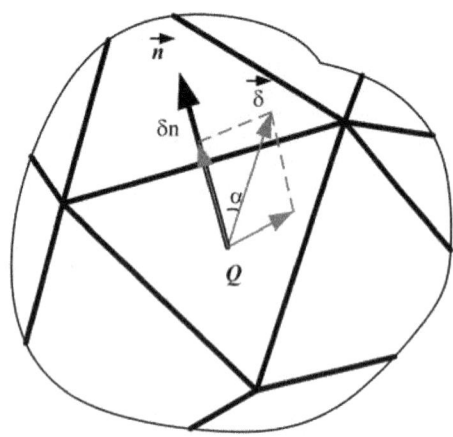

Fig. 15 Illustrative diagram of displacement in the normal direction calculation.

Because the displacement components do not exactly comply with the local area orientation, the displacement $\vec{\delta}$ is projected to the normal direction of the surface area around node Q; the local area is denoted by a triangle, as shown in Figure 15. It is calculated as follows:

$$\delta_n = \vec{\delta} \cdot \vec{n} \qquad (16)$$

where $\vec{n}$ is the unit normal direction of surface area of the node Q and δ_n is the length of the displacement projected in the normal direction, which is related to the machining allowance of node Q.

The displacements of corners A and B in the direction perpendicular to their local surface area are shown in Figure 16. It can be seen that they increase mainly during the beginning period, then grow gradually, and finally reach 18 and 22mm, respectively. Their displacements in the normal direction are smaller than the y-displacement values, which means the normal direction of the local surface area is not exactly the y-direction. The displacement in the normal direction is useful to the pattern makers. To compensate for deformation, the pattern will be bent in the opposite direction. During the casting process, the casting will deform to the normal shape, so the final shape will be free of deformation. This deformation given to the pattern is called in-verse deformation here, which is a typical measure taken in the casting production. In the production of the first hydro turbine blade casting for the Three Gorges Project, inverse deformation is given to the two corners A and B to compensate for deformation based on practice, which is 45mm in positive y-direction and 30mm in negative y-direction, respectively. These inverse deformations of corner A and B are in the opposite directions with respect to the simulated displacements, which proves that the simulated results are correct in direction.

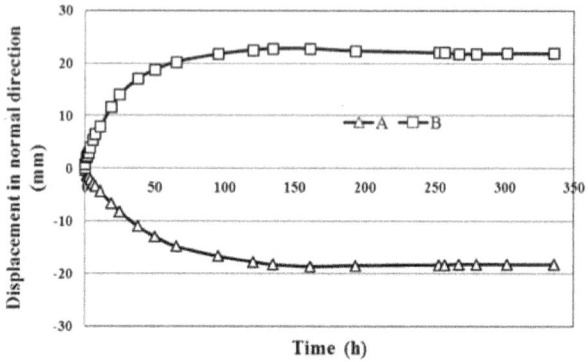

Fig. 16 Displacement in the normal direction of points A and B.

As the blade deforms during the casting process, there will be insufficient machining allowance of corner A on the front side (positive y-direction) and corner B on the back side (negative y-direction). The blade contour was measured with a photoelectric theodolite on-site by the manufacturer. The spatial coordinates of the evenly distributed points on the blade surface were acquired. Then, these points were fit into spatial curved surface. Comparing this surface with the original casting design, the machining allowance of each point on this surface was obtained, as shown in Figure 17. As the inverse deformation was given at corners A and B, the machining allowance of corner A on the front side is 55mm, about 20mm greater than the set value 35mm. That is roughly proved by the simulated normal displacement 22mm, which means the inverse deformation should be 22mm. As 45mm is given, there is excess machining allowance of 23mm on this side which is close to the measured value 20mm. As the bending of corner B is in the negative y-direction, the machining allowance of the back side should be compared. The machining allowance of corner B at the front surface is between 10 and 18mm, around 20mm less than the set value, i. e., the machining allowance of the back side is 20mm more than the set value. The simulated normal displacement toward the back side is 18mm, while the set inverse deformation is 30mm, so that will result in excess machining allowance of 12mm on the back side which is approximately the same as the measured value 20mm. Thus, the simulated results are basically in agreement with the measured ones.

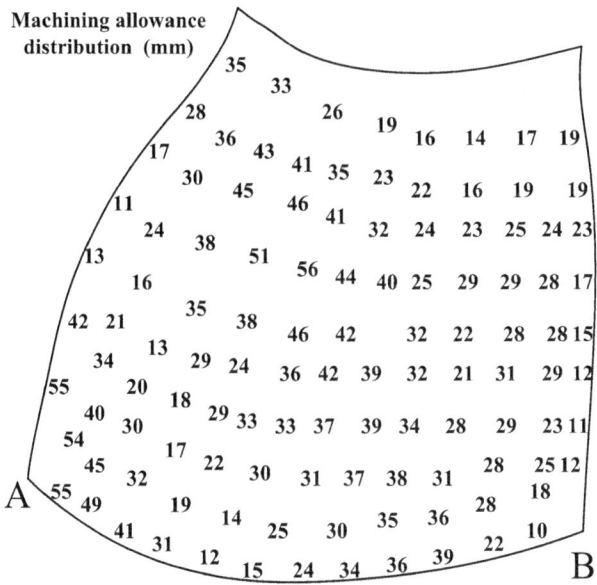

Fig. 17 Measured machining allowance distribution of the blade after casting. The lines are the illustrative surface of the blade casting, and the values are the machining allowance of the measured points.

The temperature difference between the two sides of the blade drives the deformation. The temperature difference at corner A is calculated, as shown in Figure 18, together with temperature and displacement. It can be seen that the temperature difference at the beginning is significant and varies from 307K (34℃) initially to 274K (1℃) after cooling for 65 hours. The displacement mainly occurs during this period. The cooling of the area around A mainly happens during this period and it reaches 382K (109℃). Therefore, the temperature difference of the two sides during the casting process causes deformation. By controlling the temperature difference, the deformation can be reduced or eliminated due to even cooling of the two sides of the blade.

VII. CONCLUSIONS

A thermo-phase transformation-mechanical model is presented for martensitic stainless steel with consideration of the phase transformation-induced strain and the phase transformation-induced plasticity. A numerical simulation method is established by applying ABAQUS.

Numerical simulation of the casting process of the Three Gorges Project hydro turbine blade casting was performed. At the beginning of the casting process, the uneven cooling results in stress and deformation of the blade. Then, as martensitic transformation occurs, both uneven cooling and phase transformation determine the residual stress and deformation. There is significant deformation during the casting process with large deformation occurring at the corners A and B. The displacement in the normal direction of the local area is used as a measure of deformation with respect to machining allowance. The normal displacement of corners A and B is 18 and 22mm, respectively. The simulated results were compared with the measured machining allowance and they are basically in agreement. It is also shown that the phase transformation cannot be neglected during the numerical simulation of the casting process. When phase transformation is considered, the deformation recovers partially or is restricted to a certain level and the residual stress level is lowered. The temperature difference between the two sides of the blade is calculated and it drives the displacement evolution. Therefore, it is shown that the temperature difference resulting from uneven cooling of the two sides of the blade causes the deformation of the blade. The simulated results can assist both casting and pattern design. Controlling the tempera-

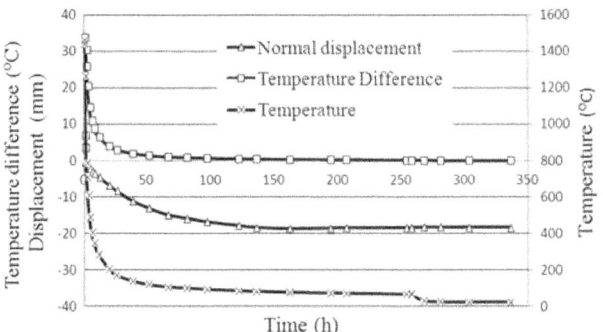

Fig. 18 Temperature, temperature difference, and displacement in the normal direction of points A during the casting process.

ture difference of the two sides of the blade by even cooling can reduce or eliminate its deformation.

ACKNOWLEDGMENTS

The project was funded by the Major National SciTech Project of China No. 2011ZX04014-052.

REFERENCES

[1] T. Inoue and D. Y. Ju: *J. Therm. Stresses*, 1992, vol. 15, pp. 109-28.

[2] J. W. Kang, B. C. Liu, and S. M. Xiong: *J. Mater. Sci. Technol.*, 1999, vol. 15, pp. 267-70.

[3] P. M. M. Vila Real, C. A. M. Oliveira, and J. T. Barbosa: *Int. J. Mech. Sci.*, 2004, vol. 46, pp. 245-61.

[4] X. G. Liu, J. W. Kang, T. Y. Huang, and B. C. Liu: *TMS Annual Meeting*, 2007, pp. 11-18.

[5] Y. Xu, J. W. Kang, T. Y. Huang, and Y. Y. Hu: *Tsinghua Sci. Technol.*, 2008, vol. 13, pp. 132-36.

[6] J. Kron, M. Bellet, A. Ludwig, B. Pustal, J. Wendt, and H. Fredriksson: *Int. J. Cast Met. Res.*, 2004, vol. 17, pp. 295-310.

[7] S. M. Lee and W. J. Lee: *J. Mater. Eng. Perform.*, 2005, vol. 14, pp. 388-94.

[8] L. Q. Chen, Y. Ling, X. H. Kang, L. J. Xia, and D. Z. Li: *J. Mater. Sci. Technol.*, 2008, vol. 24, pp. 364-68.

[9] J. W. Kang, H. M. Long, T. J. Wang, T. Y. Huang, and B. C. Liu: *Int. J. Cast Met. Res.*, 2011, vol. 24, pp. 228-32.

[10] J. F. Zhang, J. W. Kang, B. C. Liu, Y. Wu, J. S. Zhang, Z. C. Rong, and C. C. Zhang: *Int. J. Cast Met. Res.*, 2008, vol. 21, pp. 304-07.

[11] D. P. Koistinen and R. E. Marburger: *Acta Metall.*, 1959, vol. 7, pp. 59-60.

[12] G. W. Greenwood and R. H. Johnson: *Proc. R. Soc.*, 1965, vol. 238, pp. 403-22.

[13] R. H. Johnson and G. W. Greenwood: *Nature*, 1962, vol. 195, pp. 138-39.

[14] I. Tamura: *Met. Sci.*, 1982, vol. 16, pp. 245-53.

[15] F. D. Fischer, G. Reisner, E. Werner, K. Tanaka, G. Cailletaud, and T. Antretter: *Int. J. Plast.*, 2000, vol. 16, pp. 723-48.

[16] T. Inoue and Z. G. Wang: *Mater. Sci. Technol.*, 1984, vol. 1, pp. 845-50.

[17] S. Denis, S. Sjostrom, and A. Simon: *Metall. Trans. A*, 1987, vol. 18A, pp. 1203-12.

[18] C. C. Liu, K. F. Yao, and Z. Liu: *J. Comput. Aided Mater. Des.*, 2000, vol. 7, pp. 63-69.

[19] C. Y. Sun, G. Fang, L. P. Lei, and P. Zeng: *Trans. Mater. Heat Treat.*, 2008, vol. 29, pp. 161-66.

[20] H. Dai, R. Moat, A. F. Mark, and P. J. Withers: *American Society of Mechanical Engineers, Pressure Vessels and Piping Division (Publication) PVP*, 2010, vol. 6, pp. 1325-32.

[21] J. W. Kang, R. Zhang, T. Y. Huang, and B. C. Liu: *TMS Annual Meeting*, 2010, pp. 553-61.

[22] Z. H. Liu, Z. J. Wu, and J. Z. Wu: *Numerical Simulation of Heat Treating Process*, Science Press, Beijing, 1996, pp. 195-96.

[23] J. W. Kang: Ph. D. Thesis, Department of Mechanical Engineering, Tsinghua University, Beijing, China, 1998.

28. Modeling of Species Transport and Macrosegregation in Heavy Steel Ingots

WENSHENG LI, HOUFA SHEN, XIONG ZHANG, and BAICHENG LIU

In the current study, two significant phenomena involved in heavy steel ingot casting, *i.e.*, species transport and macrosegregation, were numerically simulated. First, a ladle-tundish-mold species transport model describing the entire multiple pouring process of heavy steel ingots was proposed. Carbon distribution and variation in both the tundish and the mold of a 292-ton steel ingot were predicted. Results indicate high carbon concentration in the bottom of the mold while low concentration carbon at the top of mold after the pouring process. Such concentration distribution helps in reducing both negative segregation in the bottom of the solidified ingot and positive segregation at the top. Second, a two-phase multiscale macrosegregation model was used to simulate the solidification process of industrial steel ingots. This model takes into account heat transfer, fluid flow, solute transport, and equiaxed grain motion on a system scale, as well as grain nucleation and growth on a microscopic scale. The model was first used to analyze a three-dimensional industry-scale steel ingot as a benchmark. Then, it was applied to study macrosegregation formation in a 53-ton steel ingot. Macrosegregation predicted by the numerical model was presented and compared with experimental measurements. Typical macrosegregation patterns in heavy steel ingots are found to be well reproduced with the two-phase model.

DOI: 10.1007/s11663-013-9862-4

I. INTRODUCTION

HEAVY steel ingots are typically used to manufacture mill rolls, pressure vessels, and turbine rotor shafts in metallurgy, petrochemistry, energy, and other heavy industries. Macrosegregation is a major defect in these large ingots. It seriously deteriorates material homogeneity and thus affects the final properties and the performance of the key forging components manufactured.

Multiple pouring (MP) process[1,2] is widely used to minimize macrosegregation in large ingots (*e.g.*, 100 to 670 tons). It sequentially pours molten steel using different ladle compositions. It has been recognized that carbon concentration distribution in the ingot at the end of the MP process is crucial for the macrosegregation formation in the subsequent solidification process. However, few numerical or experimental studies of species transport during the MP process of large ingots have been reported in the literature.

On the other hand, modeling of macrosegregation formation during industrial steel ingot solidification is still challenging.[3-5] In the last two decades, multiphase solidification models have been developed to predict macrosegregation. Beckermann and co-workers[4,6,7] first proposed a multiphase model that accounts for melt convection and grain motion. Ludwig and co-workers[8-11] developed a series of sophisticated multiphase models. A pioneering application of these multiphase models to industry-scale steel ingots has been performed recently by Combeau and co-workers.[12-15] Macrosegregations in ingots of 3.3 and 6.2 ton were experimentally measured and numerically simulated in their study. Most recently, Combeau and co-workers[16] applied a multiphase model to a 65-ton steel ingot. Simulation results of macrosegregation in the ingot were compared with experiments. The authors pointed out: "These results are encouraging and show that the model is on the good way for being fully predictive." They also claimed that the model needed to be further improved.

Recent progress made by the authors of the current study on numerical modeling of species transport and macrosegregation in heavy steel ingots is reported in this article. A ladle-tundish-mold species transport model for the MP process is first applied to a 292-ton steel ingot. Simulation results of macrosegregation formation during the solidification process of a 53-ton steel ingot using a two-phase model are then presented.

II. NUMERICAL SIMUALTION OF MP PROCESS

A. Description of MP Process

The ingot simulated in the current study was produced by CITIC Heavy Industries Co., Ltd. It was a large 292-ton steel ingot of 4.5m in height and 3.4m in mean width. The MP process of this ingot is illustrated in Figure 1. Three ladles with different carbon concentrations were used in the MP process. The first ladle contained 150 tons of molten steel (0.38 wt pct C), the second 90 tons (0.36 wt pct C), and the third 60 tons (0.32 wt pct C). Consequently, the nominal carbon content of the ingot was 0.362 wt pct. An 80-ton tundish of 3.0m in height and 2.4m in diameter was also used.

When the casting process starts, the tundish inlet is opened first. Refined molten steel is then poured from the first ladle into the tundish. After the melt reaches a certain bath height, the tundish inlet is closed, and molten steel stabilizes in the tundish for a set period. This stage is called the filling process. In the second step called the holding process, the inlet and the outlet of the tundish are opened simultaneously. Molten steel in the tundish begins to flow into the mold. During this process, tundish inlet and outlet flow rates are carefully controlled so that the bath level is maintained at almost the same height. In the final step, namely the draining process, after the molten steel in all ladles has been completely poured into the tundish, the bath level begins to drop. When the bath level reaches a certain critical height, the outlet of the tundish is closed and the whole pouring process is completed.

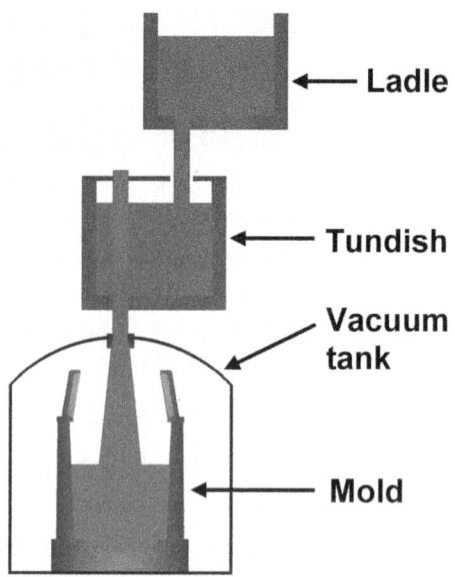

Fig. 1 Schematic of multiple pouring process for 292-ton steel ingot.

It should be noted that at time zero ($t = 0$ seconds), the molten steel starts to pour from the first ladle into the tundish. The draining process ends at $t = 3030$ seconds.

B. Model

The ladle-tundish-mold species transport model for the entire MP process was proposed in a previous study.[17] Important phenomena, including turbulent flow of molten steel in the tundish and the mold cavity, multiphase flow, heat transfer, and solute elements transport, were modeled using the combined Realizable k-ε and volume of fluid multiphase model. Threedimensional simulations were performed because of the complex geometry of the tundish and mold system. The governing equation describing species transport in the molten steel is expressed as follows:

$$\frac{\partial}{\partial t}(\rho C) + \nabla \cdot (\rho \mathbf{u} C) = \nabla \cdot (\rho D \nabla C) \quad (1)$$

where ρ is the density of molten steel, C the concentration, t the time, $\mathbf{u}$ the velocity vector, and D the mass diffusivity. More details on the model can be found in Reference 17.

C. Results and Discussion

Figure 2 shows the predicted carbon mixing in the tundish during the holding process. Representative times are selected to illustrate the mixing process, with Figures 2 (a) through (c) showing melt pouring from the second ladle and Figures 2 (d) through (f) from the third ladle. At the beginning (before 890 seconds), all melt comes from the first ladle. Carbon concentration in the tundish is homogenous (i.e., 0.38 wt pct). At 890 and 1800 seconds, molten steel from the second and the third ladles, with carbon concentration of 0.36 and 0.32 wt pct, respectively, starts to flow into the tundish.

With the addition of such fresh molten steel, high carbon concentration regions begin to form in the middle of the tundish and at several circumfluence spots. Gradually, carbon concentration in the tundish is diluted and homogenized by mixing effect from convection and diffusion, as shown in Figures 2 (b) through (f). Carbon mixing first occurs in spots where plunging jet directly flows through, then spreads throughout the tundish, which shows mixing is mainly driven by convection. It can also be noted that carbon concentration at the tundish outlet comes from a mixture of the high carbon content flow from the middle of the tundish and the low content flow from the jet.

Figure 3 shows the carbon mixing process in the tundish during the draining process. The bath level in the tundish decreases with time as fluid flows out. The resulting transient turbulent flow enhances mixing and facilitates solute transport. At the last stage of draining (Figure 3(c)), carbon concentration is almost homogeneous in the tundish, higher than that in the third ladle because of the remaining fluid from the first and the second ladles.

Figure 4 shows the simulated carbon concentration at the tundish outlet during the MP process. This concentration is averaged across the outlet cross section. Cleary shown in the figure, concentration level decreases as fresh molten steel with lower carbon content is being added from the second and third ladles. The concentration reduction rate is determined by the concentration difference between the ladles. However, the reduction

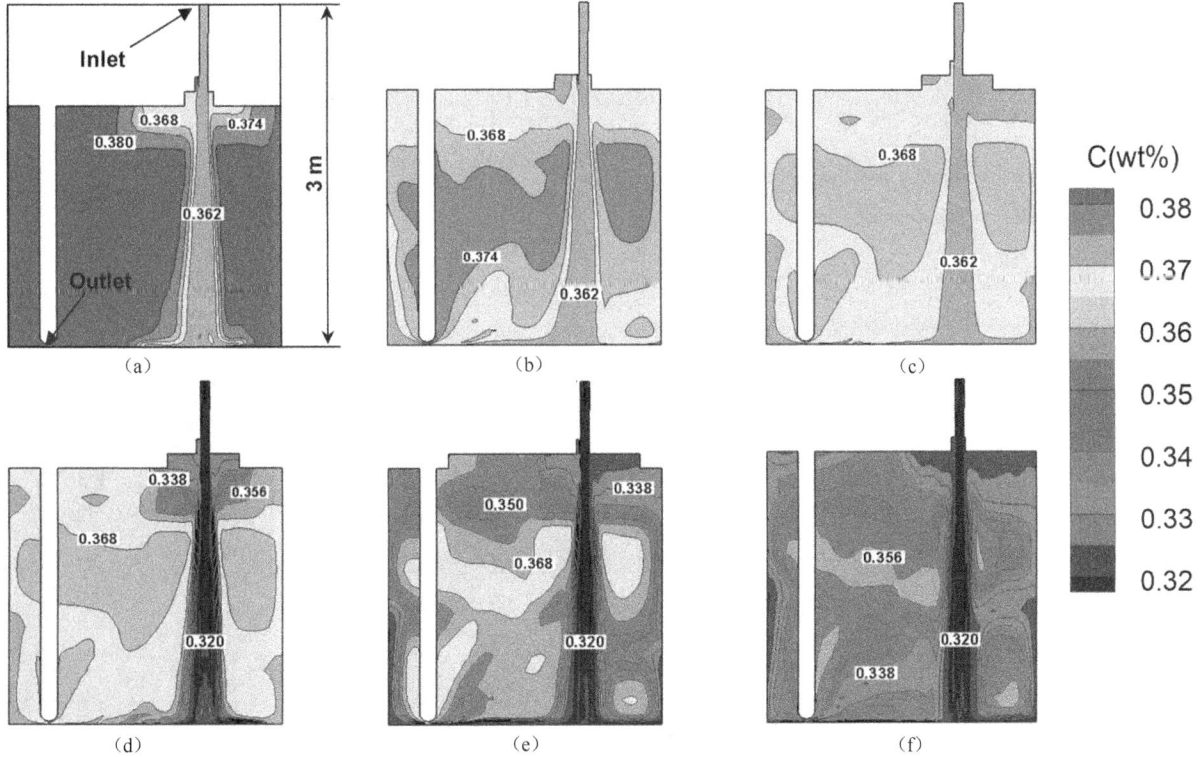

Fig. 2 Distribution of carbon concentration in tundish at different times during holding process.
(a) 910s, (b) 1360s, (c) 1750s, (d) 1800s, (e) 2060s, and (f) 2290s. Note that times
(a) through (c) correspond to the second ladle, while (d) through (f) the third ladle.

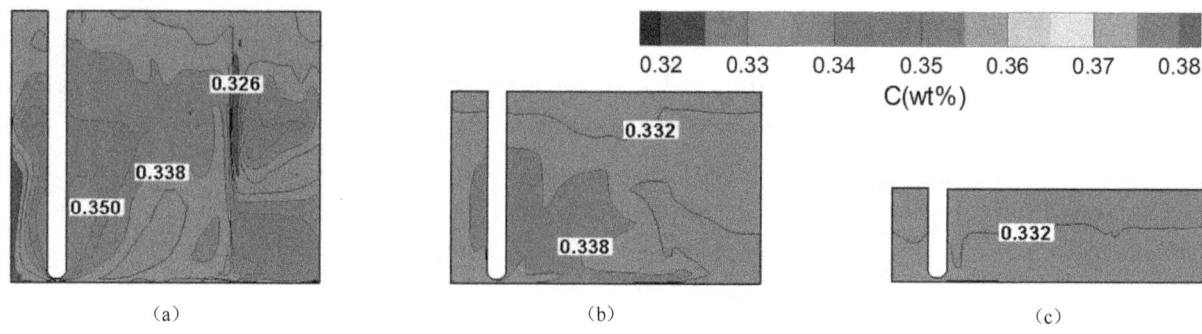

Fig. 3 Distribution of carbon concentration in tundish during draining process. (a) 2300s, (b) 2600s, and (c) 3000s.

rate fluctuates because of the competition of the direct flow and circumfluence in the tundish. Concentration at the outlet increases slightly when circumfluence flow dominates, and vice versa.

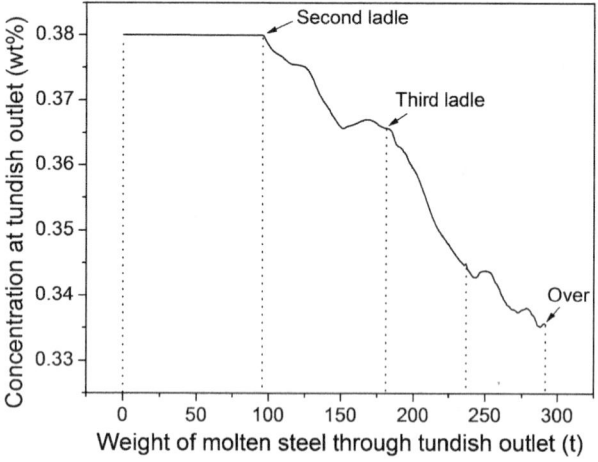

Fig. 4 Carbon concentration variation at tundish outlet during multiple pouring process.

Figures 5 (a) through (d) present the carbon distribution in the mold during the pouring process. In Figure 5 (a), molten steel with varying concentration from the tundish outlet flows into the mold and spreads gradually. The mixing region is mainly determined by the impact action of the inlet flow into the mold. Since the impact intensity of flow near the mold axis is stronger than that in edge, the impact depth reaches to about 1 m and the mixing region takes on a V-shape in the upper region of the mold. In Figures 5 (b) through (d), as the bath level increasing, an additional/secondary V-shape mixing region forms above the first V-shape region by the impact action.

The final carbon concentration distribution in the mold at the end of the MP process is shown in Figure 5 (d). A high concentration zone exists at the bottom of the mold and a low concentration zone at the hot top. Generally, negative segregation in the bottom part of the ingot and positive at the top develop during steel ingot solidification. Thus, it is believed that this reversed concentration distribution produced by the MP process is favorable to suppress the final macrosegregation in the fully solidified 292-ton ingot.

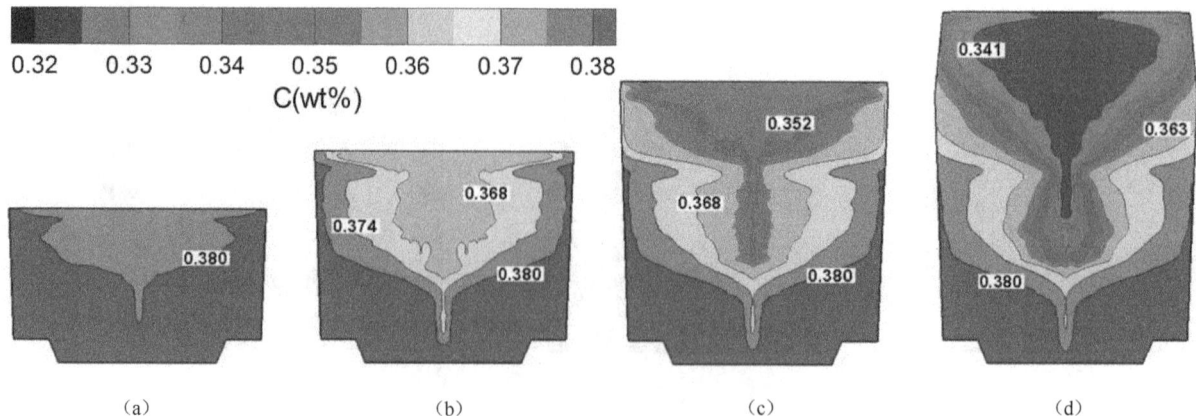

Fig. 5 Distribution of carbon concentration in mold at different times. (a) 1074s, (b) 1770s, (c) 2410s, and (d) 3030s.

III. MACROSEGREGATION MODELING

A. Model Description

A two-phase multiscale solidification model[18-20] was recently developed to predict macrosegregation in industrial steel ingots. The model takes into account heat and solute transfer, melt convection, and equiaxed grains motion on a system scale. On the microscopic scale the model accounts for nucleation, constitutional undercooling, and grain growth. A brief summary of the model is provided below.

The model considers two phases: solid and liquid. The species conservation of the two phases can be written as follows:

$$\frac{\partial}{\partial t}(g_s \rho_s C_s) + \nabla \cdot (g_s \rho_s \mathbf{u}_s C_s) = \frac{S_V \rho D_s}{\delta_s}(C_s^* - C_s) + C_s^* M_{ls} \quad (2)$$

$$\frac{\partial}{\partial t}(g_l \rho_l C_l) + \nabla \cdot (g_l \rho_l \mathbf{u}_l C_l) = \frac{S_V \rho D_l}{\delta_l}(C_l^* - C_l) - C_l^* M_{ls} \quad (3)$$

where g is the volume fraction, S_V the interfacial area concentration, δ the solute diffusion length, and M_{ls} the interfacial phase change rate. Subscripts "s" and "l" stands for solid and liquid, respectively. Superscript "*" denotes equilibrium at the solid-liquid interface.

Solute transport at the solid-liquid interface controlling phase change is described by the solute balance equation:

$$\frac{S_V \rho D_s}{\delta_s}(C_s^* - C_s) + C_s^* M_{ls} + \frac{S_V \rho D_l}{\delta_l}(C_l^* - C_l) - C_l^* M_{ls} = 0. \quad (4)$$

Average solute concentration is calculated as follows:

$$C = g_s C_s + g_l C_l. \quad (5)$$

The conservation equations are discretized using a finite volume method with an orthogonal mesh. The resolution of the velocity-pressure coupling for the specific two-phase system is carried out by a variant of IPSA (inter-phase slip algorithm). This algorithm is an extension of the single-phase solution algorithm semiimplicit method for pressure-linked equations-consistent for multiphase flows. The sparse linear systems of the discretized equations are solved by conjugate gradienttype methods.

B. Benchmark Case

The solidification of a benchmark 3.3-ton steel ingot, about 2m in height and 0.6m in average diameter, was numerically simulated in three dimensions. The solid phase was assumed to be fixed in this simulation. Shrinkage cavity formation at the top of the ingot was calculated as well. Owing to symmetry, a quarter of the system was simulated. A three dimensional 10 × 10 × 15mm mesh was used, resulting in 277,196 elements, in which 84,267 elements were contributed to the steel ingot. The time step was chosen as 0.5 seconds. The steel was simplified as a binary iron-carbon alloy with a nominal composition of $C_0 = 0.36$ wt pct C. Values of the thermophysical properties, boundary conditions, and numerical parameters used in the current study are summarized in References 18 and 21.

Figure 6 illustrates the model results of both solidification and macrosegregation in the ingot (at 1600 seconds), with the left panel showing the velocity vectors and the solid volume fraction (g_s), and the right panel presenting the segregation ratio. The flow ascends along the mold side wall and descends in the ingot center, because solutal buoyancy dominates over thermal buoyancy under simulated thermophysical conditions. It should be noted that the melt velocity has a maximum magnitude of approximately 3.2mm/s. The upward, solute-rich melt flow along the mold wall side leads to a continual enrichment of the remaining melt at the top part of the ingot. Thus, a vertical concentration gradient is created in the core, and the hot top is positively segregated, while a conically shaped negative segregation zone forms at the bottom part of the ingot. Predictions of final macrosegregation in the ingot agree well with the literature experiment results.[12]

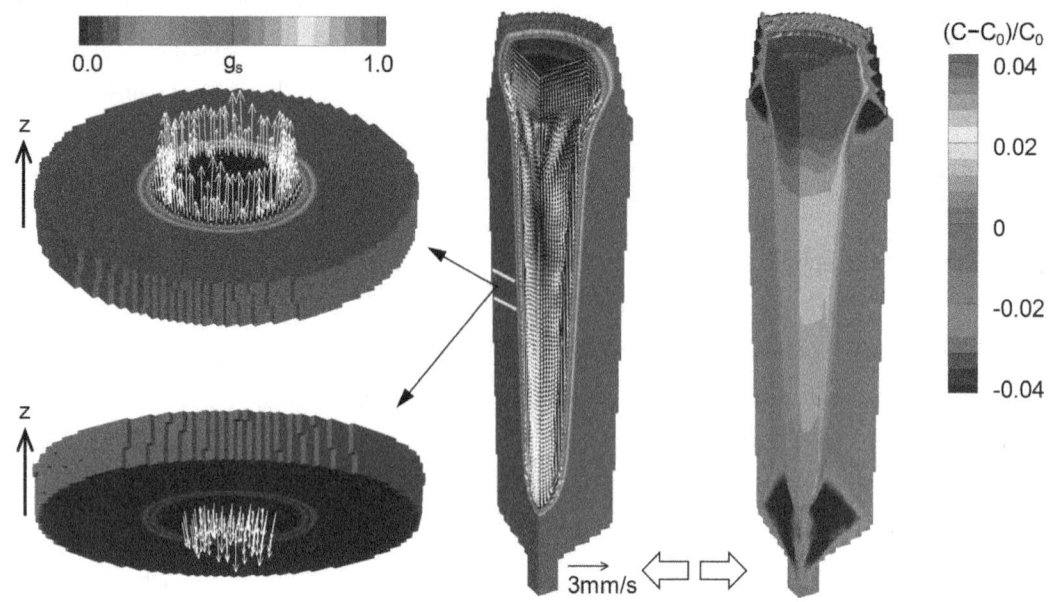

Fig. 6 Model results for a 3.3-ton steel ingot (at solidification time of 1600s).
Left velocity vectors and solid volume fraction. *Right* macrosegregation.

C. *Industrial Application*

The two-phase model with its full capacity was applied to analyze a 53-ton steel ingot cast by the steel plant of CITIC Heavy Industries Co., Ltd. The dimensions of the ingot system are illustrated in Figure 7. The molten metal was top poured at a temperature of 1823.15K (1550℃) in a cast-iron mold with a refractory insulation sleeve. After teeming, a layer of exothermic powder was overlaid. The complete solidification time for this ingot was ~15 hours. Carbon concentration was measured in the longitudinal section of the hot top.

Symmetry along the centerline axis was assumed in the analysis. A grid system consisting of 15376 elements was used with a mesh size of 20mm. At the beginning of solidification, the time step was in the order of 0.01 seconds. As solidification proceeds, the time step was increased gradually to 0.5 seconds. The steel was simplified as a binary Fe-C system with a nominal concentration of 0.41 wt pct, neglecting the other alloying elements. Thermophysical properties, boundary conditions, and other major parameters of the model are reported in Reference 19.

The predicted solidification sequences are shown in Figure 8. Nearer the mold wall, the melt is the coolest, and heterogeneous nucleation initially takes place. The

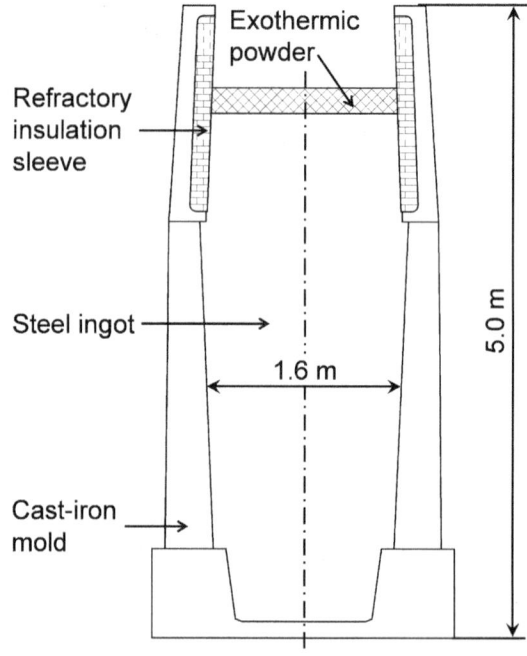

Fig. 7 Schematic of 53-ton steel ingot used in simulation.

equiaxed grains produced by nucleation descend along the columnar layer at the surface and entrain the surrounding liquid with them, inducing a downward melt flow at the mold side. The solute-depleted grains are concentrated at the ingot bottom, leading to a negative segregation. The equiaxed grain motion progressively slows down as solidification proceeds. At a later stage of solidification (*e.g.*, at 5.0 hours), the thermosolutal

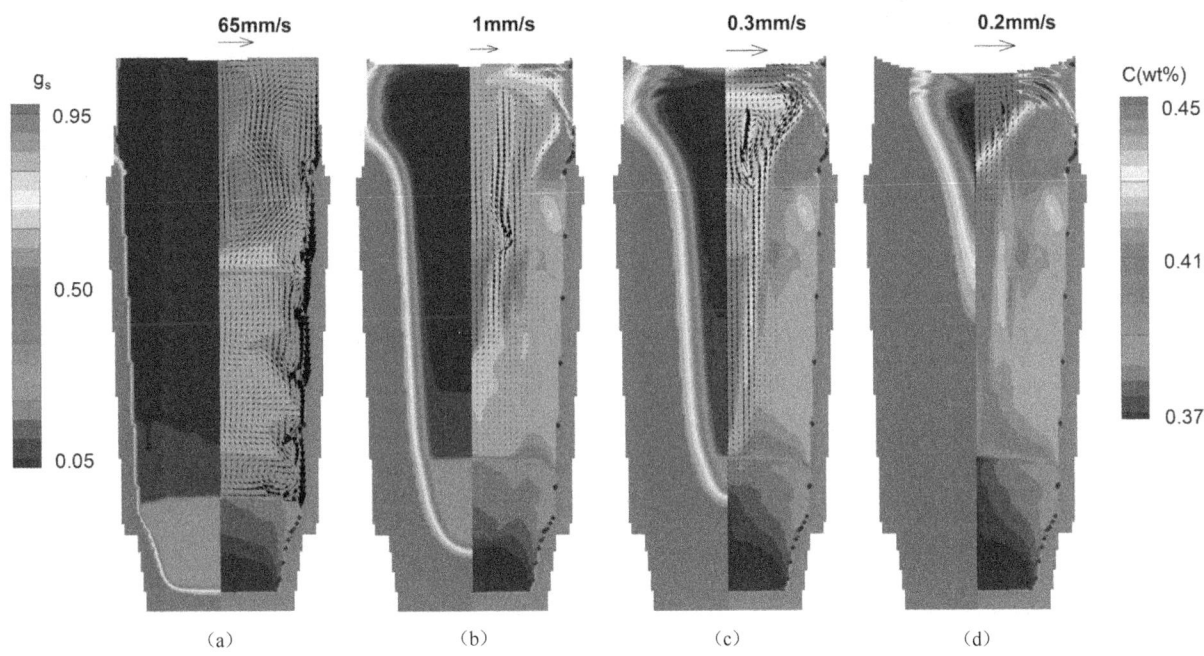

Fig. 8 Predicted solidification sequence of 53-ton ingot. *Left* solid volume fraction. *Right* macrosegregation and liquid velocity. (a) 0.5h, (b) 2.5h, (c) 5.0h, and (d) 10h.

convection dominates and thus induces a counter-clockwise flow, descending at the center and ascending at the surface of the ingot. The highest liquid velocities shown in Figures 8 (a) through (d) are 7.78×10^{-2}, 6.36×10^{-4}, 2.12×10^{-4}, and 5.75×10^{-5} m/s, respectively. A-segregates develop in the hot top as a result of instabilities in the mushy zone growth that perturb the fluid flow at the scale of a few centimeters.[12] The formation mechanism of the banded channel segregation was systematically analyzed in detail in the recent studies of the authors of the current study,[19] Combeau and co-workers,[22] and Luwdig and co-workers.[23] It is interesting to note that local recirculation loops are present in Figure 8 (a) and the corresponding low carbon spots near the rim of the ingot are shown in Figures 8 (b) through (d). This could be because the orthogonal computational mesh used was not able to capture precisely the mold inclination along the ingot-mold interface.

Figure 9 illustrates the predicted final carbon macrosegregation pattern in the fully solidified ingot. A negative segregation zone with a characteristic conic shape is present in the ingot bottom, and a strong positive segregation is found at the hot top. Furthermore, a striking feature is observed: the A-segregates, appearing as strong, banded channel segregations, are predicted in the hot top. This demonstrates that the typical macrosegregation patterns found in a heavy steel ingot are reproduced with the present model.

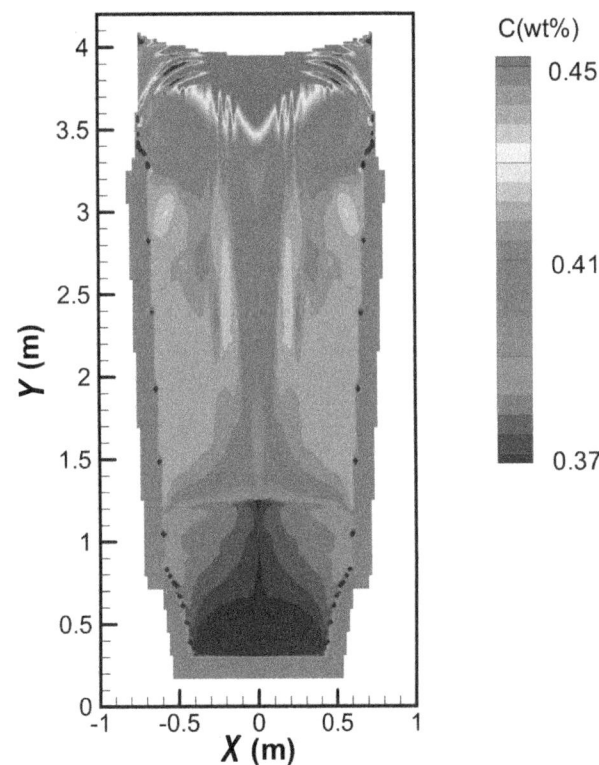

Fig. 9 Predicted final macrosegregation in fully solidified 53-toningot.

Figure 10 shows comparison of the predicted and measured carbon macrosegregation along transverse sections of the hot top in the ingot. From the center to the ingot surface, the measured segregation exhibits a positive-to-negative transition. The simulation results are generally in good agreement with measured tendencies. However, both the positive segregation near the center and the negative segregation near the ingot surface are underestimated in the simulation compared with measurements. The discrepancy could be attributed to the two-dimensional simplification of the geometry, the uncertainties in model parameters, and the preliminary nature of the model. Future experiments should be designed and performed considering more details to provide a sound basis for assessing model predictions, such as (1) sufficient measurement points to construct a high-resolution segregation map for a whole ingot section, and (2) a longitudinal macro-etch at the hot top part to validate the simulated shape and depth of the shrinkage cavity.

Despite the difficulties confronted, a study using the two-phase model accounting for equiaxed grain motion in a 292-ton steel ingot is in progress. Thus, a synthetic analysis of both the ladle-tundish-mold species transport model and the two-phase solidification model to such a heavy steel ingot remains the scope of a future study.

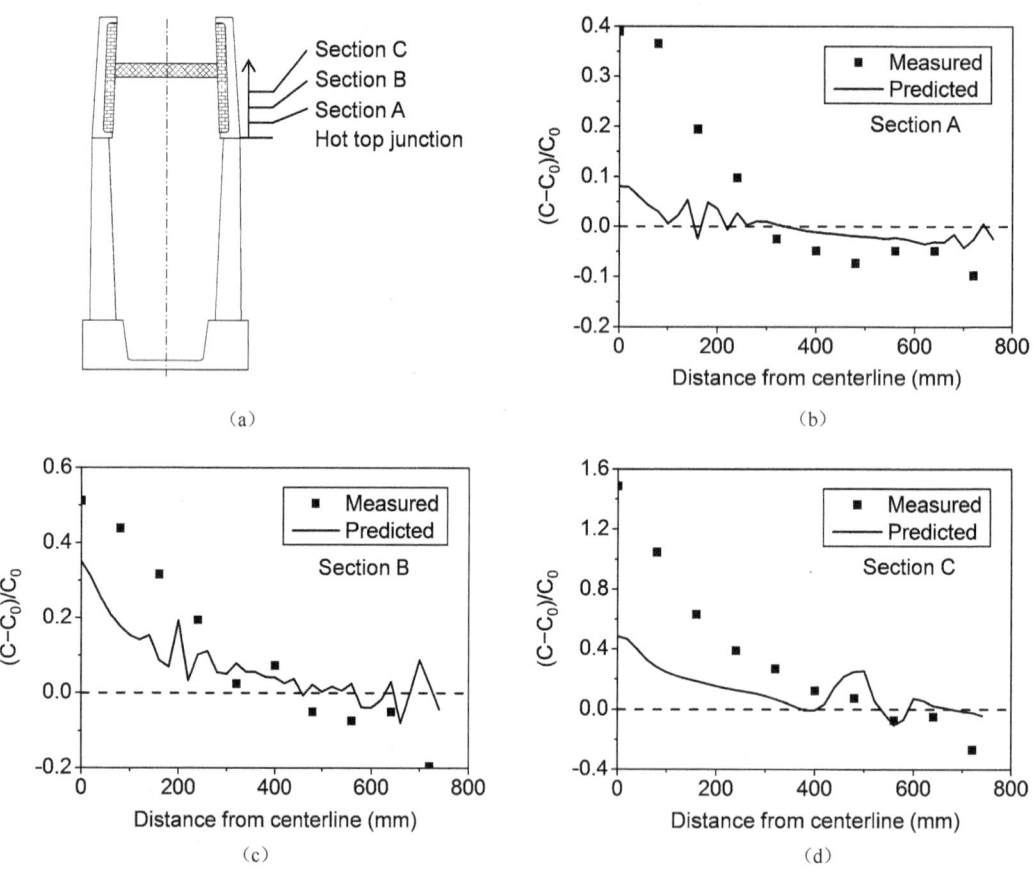

Fig. 10 (a) Schematic showing different transverse sections in hot top of 53-ton ingot. Comparison between measured and predicted segregations of (b) section A, (c) section B, and (d) section C.

IV. CONCLUSIONS

Carbon distributions in both the tundish and the mold of a steel ingot casting system were simulated using a ladle-tundish-mold species transport model throughout the MP process. Carbon concentration at the tundish outlet declines along the casting process, with fluctuations caused by the competition between the low concentration flow from the plunging steel jet and the high concentration flow in the middle of the tundish. The predicted carbon distribution in the mold at the end of the pouring process shows a low concentration zone in the upper region and a high concentration zone in the bottom. This specific concentration distribution is believed to be favorable for preventing the formation of macrosegregation during ingot solidification.

Furthermore, a two-phase solidification model tackling the motion of equiaxed grains was applied to investigate macrosegregation formation in a steel ingot that was characterized experimentally. A conically shaped negative segregation zone was predicted in the bottom of the ingot, while positive segregation was predicted at the hot top. Such results show that this model is capable of predicting major macrosegregation patterns in steel ingots. Further research, both experimental and numerical, is required to achieve a better quantitative agreement between macrosegregation measurements and predictions. The limitation of current computational resources will probably be the big obstacle to accurately simulate the coupled micro and macroscopic phenomena involved in the solidification process of heavy steel ingots.

ACKNOWLEDGMENTS

This study was financially supported by the National Basic Research Program of China under Grant No. 2011CB012900 and the National Science and Technology Major Project of the Ministry of Science and Technology of China under Grant No. 2012ZX04012011. The cooperation and the assistance of personnel, especially by Dr. Bingzhen Shen of CITIC Heavy Industries Co., Ltd., Luoyang, P. R. China during the plant trials, are gratefully acknowledged.

REFERENCES

[1] B. C. Liu, Q. Y. Xu, T. Jing, H. F. Shen, and Z. Q. Han: *JOM*, 2011, vol. 63, pp. 19-25.
[2] Y. Tanaka and I. Sato: *J. Nucl. Mater.*, 2011, vol. 417, pp. 854-59.
[3] M. C. Flemings: *ISIJ Int.*, 2000, vol. 40, pp. 833-41.
[4] C. Beckermann: *Int. Mater. Rev.*, 2002, vol. 47, pp. 243-61.
[5] G. Lesoult: *Mater. Sci. Eng. A*, 2005, vols. 413-414A, pp. 19-29.
[6] J. Ni and C. Beckermann: *Metall. Trans. B*, 1991, vol. 22B, pp. 349-61.
[7] C. Y. Wang and C. Beckermann: *Metall. Mater. Trans. A*, 1996, vol. 27A, pp. 2754-64.
[8] M. Wu and A. Ludwig: *Metall. Mater. Trans. A*, 2006, vol. 37A, pp. 1613-31.
[9] M. Wu and A. Ludwig: *Metall. Mater. Trans. A*, 2007, vol. 38A, pp. 1465-75.
[10] M. Wu and A. Ludwig: *Acta Mater.*, 2009, vol. 57, pp. 5621-31.
[11] M. Wu, A. Fjeld, and A. Ludwig: *Comput. Mater. Sci.*, 2010, vol. 50, pp. 32-42.
[12] H. Combeau, M. Zaloznik, S. Hans, and P. E. Richy: *Metall. Mater. Trans. B*, 2009, vol. 40B, pp. 289-304.
[13] M. Zaloznik and H. Combeau: in *Modeling of Casting, Welding and Advanced Solidification Processes—XII*, S. L. Cockroft and D. M. Maijer, eds., TMS, Warrendale, PA, 2009, pp. 165-72.
[14] H. Combeau, A. Kumar, and M. Zaloznik: *Trans. Indian Inst. Met.*, 2009, vol. 62, pp. 285-90.
[15] A. Kumar, M. Zaloznik, and H. Combeau: *Int. J. Adv. Eng. Sci. Appl. Math.*, 2010, vol. 2, pp. 140-48.
[16] H. Combeau, A. Kumar, M. Zaloznik, I. Poitrault, G. Lacagne, A. Gingell, T. Mazet, and G. Lesoult: in *1st International Conference on Ingot Casting, Rolling and Forging*, Aachen, Germany, 2012.
[17] X. Zhang: Master's Thesis, Tsinghua University, Beijing, P. R. China, 2012.
[18] W. S. Li, H. F. Shen, and B. C. Liu: *Int. J. Miner. Metall. Mater.*, 2012, vol. 19, pp. 787-94.
[19] W. S. Li: Ph. D. Thesis, Tsinghua University, Beijing, P. R. China, 2012.
[20] W. S. Li, B. Z. Shen, H. F. Shen, and B. C. Liu: *IOP Conf. Ser.: Mater. Sci. Eng.*, 2012, vol. 33, p. 012090.
[21] W. S. Li, H. F. Shen, and B. C. Liu: *Steel Res. Int.*, 2010, vol. 81, pp. 994-1000.
[22] M. Zaloznik and H. Combeau: *Int. J. Therm. Sci.*, 2010, vol. 49, pp. 1500-09.
[23] J. Li, M. Wu, J. Hao, A. Kharicha, and A. Ludwig: *Comput. Mater. Sci.*, 2012, vol. 55, pp. 419-29.

29. Experimental Measurements for Numerical Simulation of Macrosegregation in a 36-Ton Steel Ingot

ZHENHU DUAN, WUTAO TU, BINGZHEN SHEN, HOUFA SHEN, and BAICHENG LIU

In order to cognize the macrosegregation formation with solidification conditions, a 36-ton steel ingot has been experimentally investigated. Temperature variations of fourteen specified positions, for both the mold and ingot, were monitored to acquire the thermal conditions during solidification. Calibrated heat transfer coefficients between the ingot and mold were determined based on the temperature measurements and the empirical formula. Besides, concentration distributions of both carbon and sulfur in the ingot longitudinal section were mapped by 1800 drilled samples. Macrosegregation patterns were obtained, and notable negative segregations along the side walls of hot-top as well as typical segregation characteristics were presented in the maps. Segregation extent of sulfur was greater than that of carbon, and the segregated sulfur was relevant to the segregated carbon in a certain extent on statistical analysis with a standard correlation coefficient $r = 0.68872$. Finally, a two-phase multiscale multicomponent solidification model was preliminarily utilized to predict the species segregation. General good agreements are exhibited for the comparisons between the prediction and measurement of concentration profiles of carbon and sulfur in ingot.

DOI: 10.1007/s11661-016-3531-6

I. INTRODUCTION

STEEL ingots are necessary for mono-block forgings, such as the pressure vessels for nuclear reactor and the shaft rotors for steam turbine. Macrosegregation, as a compositional heterogeneity, is a common solidification defect in steel ingots. It deteriorates the mechanical properties of products and haunts the manufacturers over decades. Numerous efforts have been devoted to study the macrosegregation in steel ingots. The thermo-solutal convection, shrinkage-induced flow, equiaxed grains movements, and solid skeleton deformation are believed to be the main reasons responsible for macrosegregation formation.[1-3] Nowadays, mathematical modeling acts as an indispensable tool for the research of macrosegregation, and it facilitates the design and the optimization of ingot process. Since the pioneering local solute redistribution equation derived by Flemings *et al.*[4] in 1960s, various models[5-9] have been proposed to predict macrosegregation. Among the models, the continuum model[5] and volume averaged model[6] treated the solidification system as a continuum mixture. The two-phase model[7] divided the system into solid and liquid phase focused on the interface transport behavior, and it was further developed into multi-phase models[8,9] considering the different characteristics of sub-phases in solid or liquid. However, the utilizable perspective of mathematical models is still limited due to the contradiction between their accuracies and efficiencies, and the model validation still needs more benchmarks. For the purpose of verification and validation of mathematical models, a call for benchmark contributions has been co-launched by many researchers in 2009.[10]

Direct dissection methods have been adopted to investigate macrosegregation in steel ingots. Sulfur prints and local concentration sampling are usually used to acquire the basic knowledge of macrosegregation maps. Sulfur prints give qualitative macrosegregation maps of sulfur solute and exhibit the possible macrosegregation channels.[11] Local sampling helps to construct the quantitative macrosegregation maps, and the map resolution

---

本文刊登于《Metallurgical and Materials Transactions A》, 2016, 47A (7): 3597-3606.

relies on the sampling densities. With the increase of sampling points, more details of macrosegregation can be illustrated on the maps. Figure 1 exhibits the typical carbon macrosegregation maps of steel ingots from literatures.[11-15] Figure 1 (a) is a carbon concentration contour map of a 2.45-ton steel ingot with 1.682m in height and 0.482m in mean diameter.[12] The macrosegregation map was reconstructed from 54 drilling samples as labeled by the solid circles in Figure 1 (a). Figures 1 (b) through (d) show the carbon segregation maps in the longitudinal section of 3.3 tons steel ingots with 2m in height and 0.6 m in mean width.[13-15] Hans et al. built the carbon macrosegregation map under concentration measurements of about 26 points[13] as shown in Figure 1 (b). Another two similar carbon segregation maps for 3.3 tons ingot were constructed by Combeau et al.[14,15] in Figures 1 (c) and (d). The two maps were reconstructed by 114 chemical analysis results as shown in Figure 1 (d). Interpolation methods improved the resolution of maps. Synthetical illustration of macrosegregation and macrostructure of a 65-ton steel ingot[11] is shown in Figure 1 (e). It was an ingot with a height of 3.8m and an average diameter of 1.8m. Unlike the former macrosegregation maps with legends, the right half of this map was schematically drawn with colors according to measurements. All the above macrosegregation maps have further demonstrated the typical macrosegregation patterns, including a negative segregation zone in the lower region and a positive segregation zone in the upper region, and have deepened the popular understanding of macrosegregation in steel ingots. It should be noted that the above macrosegregation maps were constructed with sample points by interpolation methods. Since the sample points were generally limited, the macrosegregation maps included regions covered by no measurements and the maps should be used with caution.[15,16] A 12-ton steel ingot was chemically analyzed by X-ray fluorescence spectroscopy (XRF) and concentration maps of over 71000 points were rebuilt on the longitudinal section.[16]

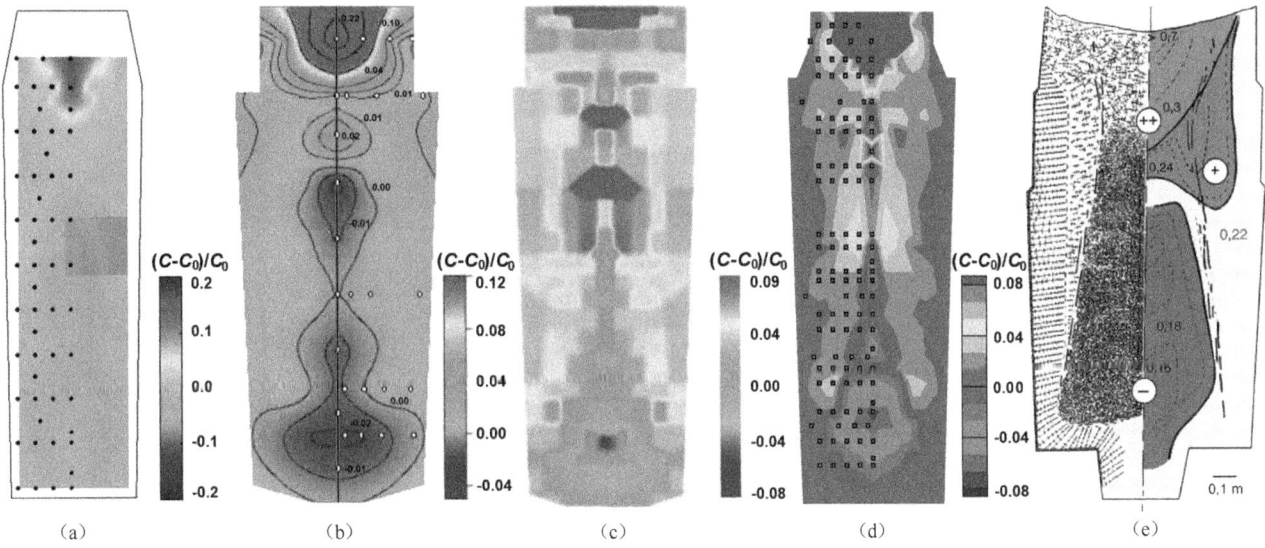

Fig. 1 Typical reconstructed macrosegregation maps according to the concentration measurements in literatures. (a) 2.45 tons ingot,[12] (b) through (d) 3.3 tons ingots,[13-15] (e) 65 tons ingot.

Besides the above reconstructed macrosegregation maps with the grid sampling in ingot section, segregation profiles along certain directions were also reported to indicate the carbon variations. Centerlines, as a typical position for the long-range variations covered the whole solidification process of ingot, were often selected for model validations. Concentrations investigated along the centerline in steel ingots varied from 2.45 to 650 tons.[11,12,14-18] Transverse section lines (or radius) lying in the ingot bottom or the hot-top were other common selected lines for quantitative comparisons. The representatives of these zones in ingot, bottom for the negative segregation and hot-top for the positive, were the primary considerations.[19-21] Considering the spatial locality of the results along certain lines, one should keep in mind that these results can only be served as necessary but not necessarily sufficient conditions for the validation.

In current research, 1800 sample points were chemically measured to construct the macrosegregation maps of both carbon and sulfur in a 36-ton steel ingot. Temperature variations of both the mold and ingot after filling were recorded to define the solidification condition. As an attempt for modeling macrosegregation of ingot with validation, a two-phase multiscale multicomponent solidification model was applied.

II. EXPERIMENTAL PROCESS

A 36-ton steel ingot was cast in CITIC Heavy Industries Co., Ltd., People's Republic of China. The configuration of the ingot/mold system is shown in Figure 2 (a) and the steel melt composition is listed in Table 1. The ingot is 3200mm in height and 1500mm in mean diameter. Molten steel was poured from the mold bottom at 1833K (1560℃) and a layer of exothermic power was overlaid on the melt top. Fourteen thermocouples were arranged to monitor the temperature variations at specific positions as shown in Figure 2 (a). Twelve thermocouples with each group of three (TA, TB, and TC) were horizontally located at four different heights (0.8, 1.6, 3.0, and 3.4m over the bottom face of mold). Four S-type thermocouples (TAs: TA1~TA4) were immersed into the ingot (i.e., mold cavity before pouring) at 30mm depth along radius, other four S-type thermocouples (TBs: TB1~TB4) were at the very inner face of the mold, and four K-type thermocouples (TCs: TC1~TC4) were located within the mold at 30mm away from the inner face. The last two S-type thermocouples (TA5 and TA6) were inserted into the ingot vertically from the very top with the depth of 200mm. TA5 was in the ingot centerline, and TA6 was 400mm away the centerline. All the thermocouples had been carefully calibrated before the experiment and the temperature data were recorded by an acquisition system at a frequency of 1 Hz.

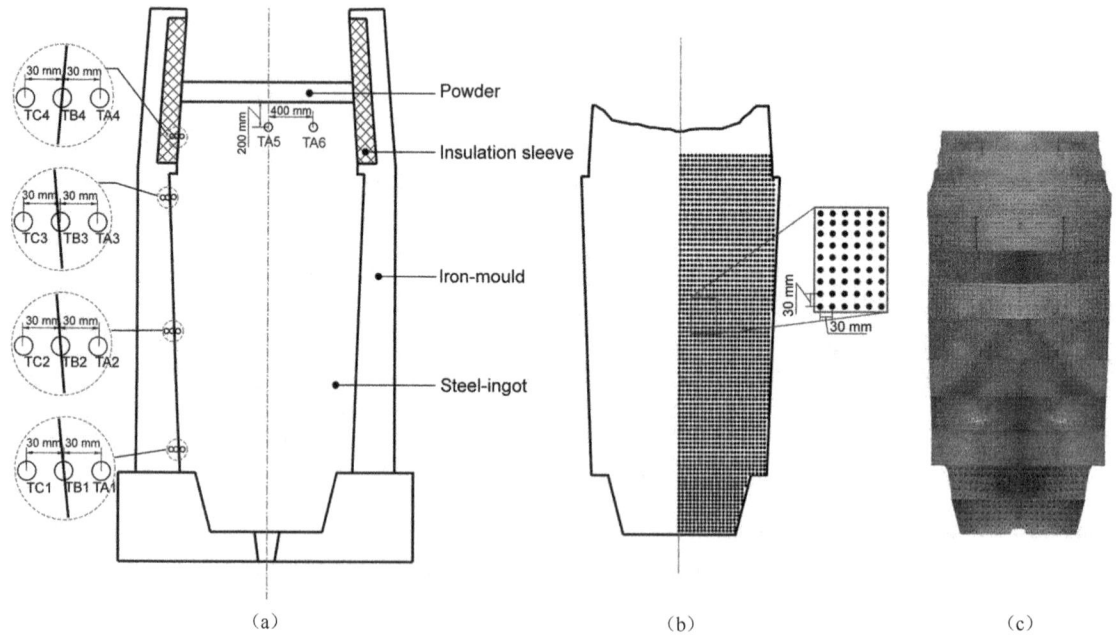

Fig. 2 (a) Schematic of 36-ton ingot/mold system with 14 temperature measurement positions, (b) schematic of concentration measurement positions in the longitudinal section, and (c) view of sampling positions in ingot.

Table 1 Composition of Steel Ingot

Elements	C	Si	Mn	S	P	Ni
(Wt Pct)	0.51	0.23	0.60	0.006	0.009	0.13

After stripping out, the ingot was cut along the axial plane by flame gas in as-cast condition. A plate of 500mm thickness was sliced by milling machine. Residual stresses were released by regular stress relief annealing. Considering the symmetry, the plate was cut along the centerline into two halves. One half was etched to obtain the as-cast macrostructure, while the other was for chemical analysis using infrared carbon-sulfur analyzer. For the chemical analysis, 1800 sample points were drilled in the positions of ingot as shown in Figures 2 (b) and (c). To avoid the possible errors by interpolations for areas covered by no measurements, current measurement point assembly has covered the half plate completely. The resolution of the measurement grids is $30 \times 30 \text{mm}^2$.

III. EXPERIMENTAL RESULTS

A. Temperature Variations

Figure 3 shows the temperature variations at the 14 characteristic positions in 36-ton steel ingot/mold system, which are indicated in Figure 2 (a). In Figure 3 (a), all the four temperature curves (i.e., TA1~4 in the ingot) increase sharply to a maximum value and then decrease with time. The increase corresponds to the contact of molten steel during filling while the decrease represents the cooling during solidification. As a consequence of the different heights for TA1~4, different temperature maximum values have been reached. Recalescences are recorded for TA1~3, and the recalescences take place due to the fact that the heat extraction is overwhelmed by the release of latent heat. A failure of recording is noticed for TA3 after 2 hours, which may be explained by the accident broken of thermocouples attributed to the large deformation of mold and ingot. Owing to the existence of insulating sleeve in the riser, a much slower decreasing is recorded for TA4 compared with the others and no recalescence is recorded. The four temperature curves TB1~4 at the mold/ingot interface in Figure 3 (b) show similar trends, including the increases at the initial, the possible recalescences and the later decrease at the end, compared with the curves in Figure 3 (a). As the thermocouples are not immersed into the melt but only kept aligned with the inner face of mold or sleeve, the temperatures of TB1~4 are lower compared with the ones in Figure 3 (a). As illustrated in Figure 3 (c), temperatures for TC1~4 in the mold are in general increasing trends corresponding to the heating of mold or sleeve during ingot solidification. Due to the different heat transfer capabilities, the temperature of TC4 for the sleeve increases faster to a higher maximum compared with the ones of TC1~3. As for temperature variations of TA5 and TA6 in the hot-top of ingot, almost the same curves are recorded as shown in Figure 3 (d). As the final solidified region in the ingot, the hot-top has experienced the whole solidification stage.

B. Concentration Distributions

The macrosegregation maps of carbon and sulfur constructed by 1800 concentration measurements are shown in Figures 4 (a) and (b), respectively. Typical macrosegregation patterns are reproduced in both maps: the positive segregations in the center upper region, and the negative ones near the bottom of ingot. Moreover, another negative segregation is indicated along the side wall of the hot-top, which is rarely noticed in literatures. Besides the main segregation patterns, some concentration islands exist in the segregation maps, which can be associated with the existence of possible segregation channels and the insufficient sampling points.

For further quantitative comparison of segregation extent between the carbon and sulfur, the frequency distributions of segregation ratio for both carbon and sulfur are illustrated in Figure 5. The segregation ratio R_i for solute element i (carbon or sulfur) is defined as

$$R_i = (C_i - C_{0,i})/C_{0,i}, \quad (1)$$

where C_i is the local concentration value and $C_{0,i}$ is the nominal concentration value. As shown in the frequency histogram, sulfur segregation extent is greater than carbon solute (i.e., large segregation ratio with high frequency). For a low segregation range ($|R_i| < 0.06$), the frequency of carbon is 65 pct while the one for sulfur is 33.5 pct. On the contrary, the frequency of sulfur for a high segregation range ($|R_i| > 0.1$) is 49 pct while the one for carbon is 17.18 pct. Another index, the global segregation index S_i, is adopted to compare the segregation extent of carbon and sulfur globally. Here, the S_i is defined as[22]

$$S_i = \frac{1}{C_{0,i}} \left[\frac{1}{V_{\text{ingot}}} \int_V (C_i - C_{0,i})^2 dV \right]^{1/2} \quad (2)$$

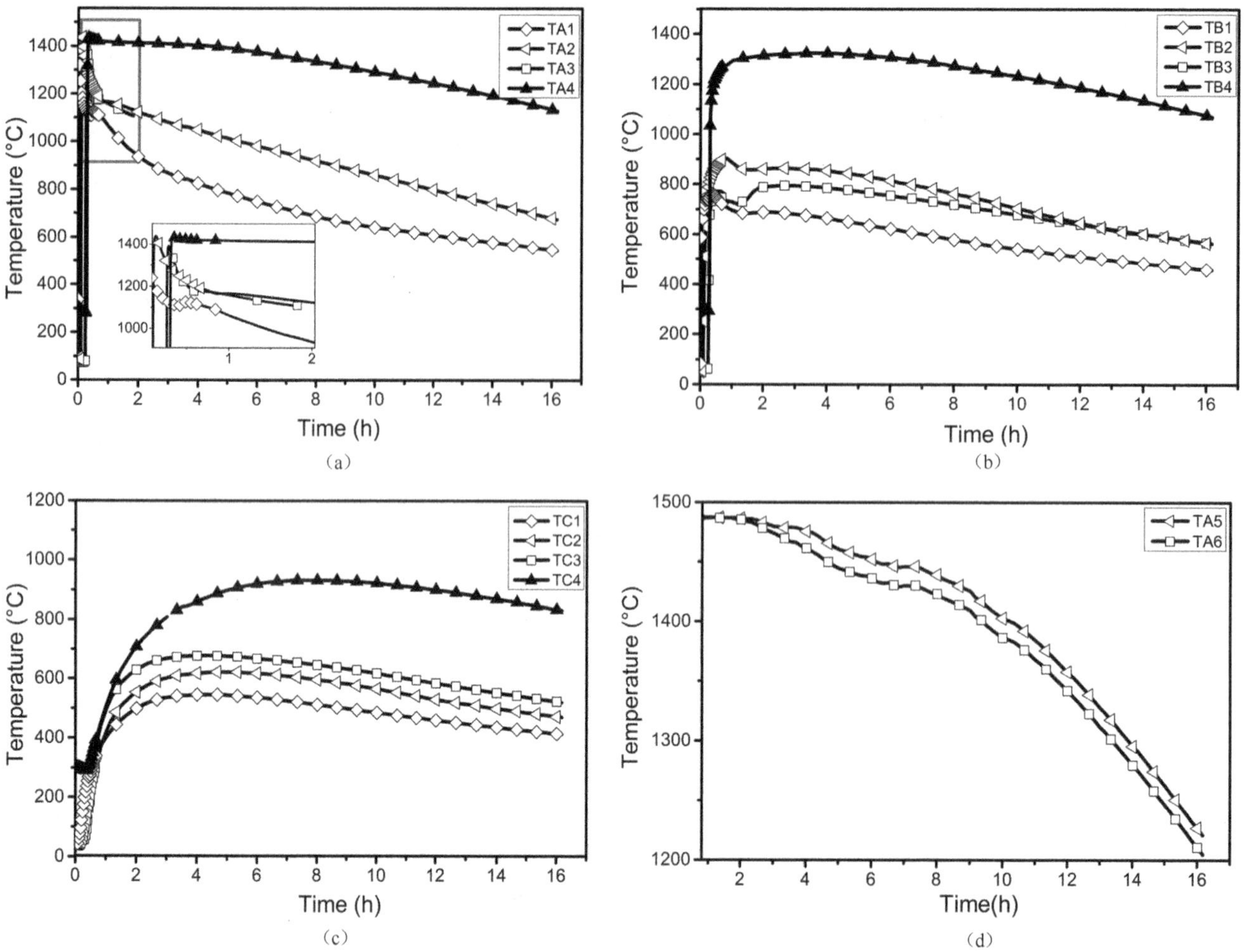

Fig. 3 Temperature variations at different positions after pouring. (a) TA1~4 in ingot, (b) TB1~4 at the ingot/mold interface, (c) TC1~4 in mold, (d) TA5~6 in ingot.

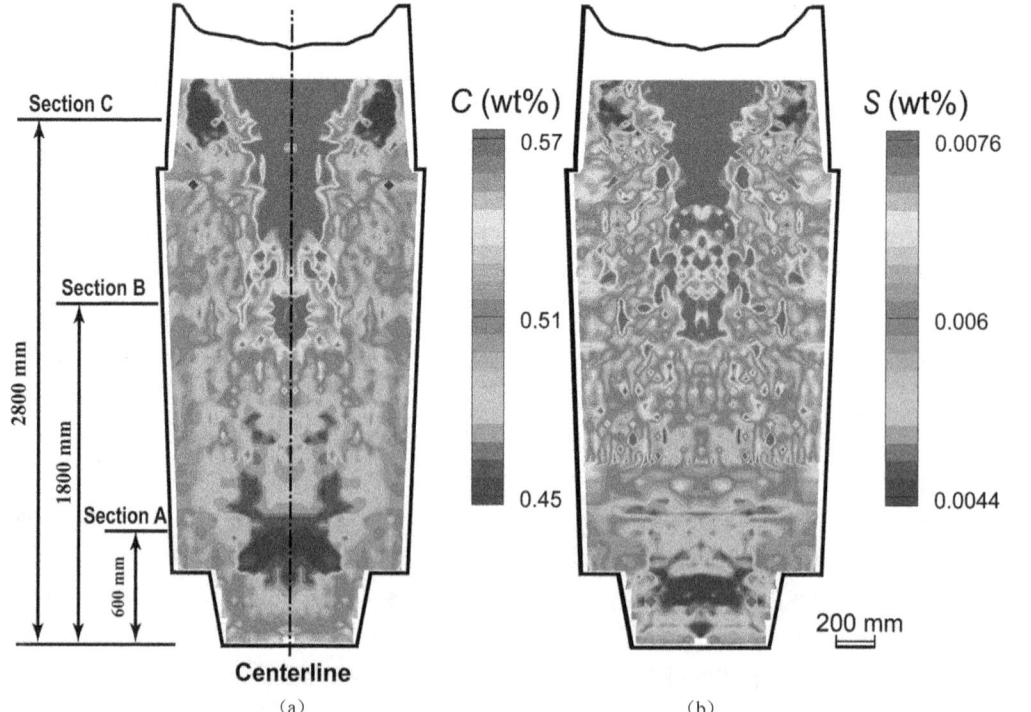

Fig. 4 Reconstructed macrosegregation maps in 36-ton ingot. (a) Carbon, (b) Sulfur.

where V_{ingot} is the volume of the ingot. Since the integration over the whole volume, S_i can be interpreted as a measure of segregation ratio for solute throughout the ingot. Assumed that the volume of each measurement grid is equal, then S_i is simplified as

$$S_i = \frac{1}{C_{0,i}} \cdot \left[\frac{\sum (C_i - C_{0,i})^2}{N} \right]^{1/2} \quad (3)$$

where N is the number of the measured grids. In current measurements, the global segregation index S_i for carbon and sulfur solute is 0.129 and 0.310, which can also be concluded that the segregation extent of sulfur is greater than the segregation extent of carbon in the 36-ton ingot.

Then the relevancy between the carbon segregation and sulfur segregation has been investigated in Figure 6. Here, the natural logarithm of segregation degree index D_i is adopted to indicate the solute segregation extent.

$$D_i = C_i / C_{0,i} (= R_i + 1) \quad (4)$$

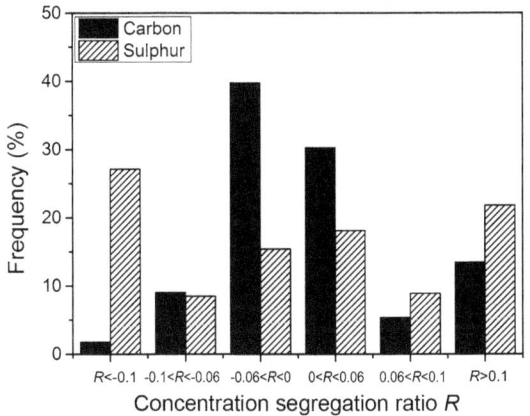

Fig. 5 Frequency distributions of concentration segregation ratios.

The scatters (lnD_c, lnD_s) for all sampling measurements along with the best fit line are drawn in Figure 6. To linearly fit the measurement data, the least-squares method is applied. The standard correlation coefficient r is used to quantitatively describe the quality of the linear fitting for the measurement data. Here r is calculated as

$$r = \frac{\sum_i (D_c - \overline{D}_c)(D_s - \overline{D}_s)}{\left[\sum_i (D_c - \overline{D}_c)^2 \cdot \sum_i (D_s - \overline{D}_s)^2 \right]^{1/2}} \in [-1, 1] \quad (5)$$

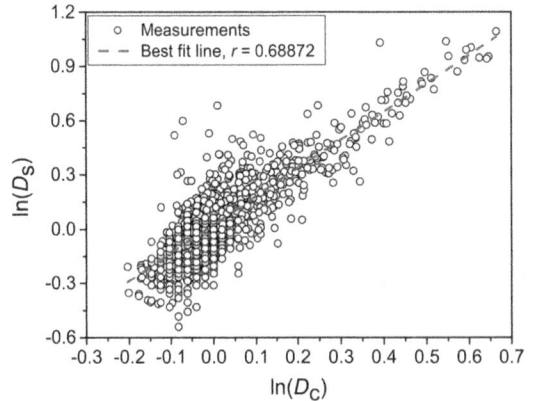

Fig. 6 The relevancy of carbon and sulfur segregation degree of all samples in ingot.

If $|r| = 1$, it means all the measurement data do locate in the best fit line. As shown in Figure 6, a general good correlation of the linear fitting to all the measurements is exhibited with $r = 0.68872$.

IV. NUMERICAL SIMULATION

A two-phase multiscale model is applied to predict macrosegregation in this 36-ton ingot. Heat transfer coefficients (HTCs) between the ingot and mold, as the necessary boundary conditions in macrosegregation simulation, are determined by verifying the measured temperatures in the ingot/mold system (Figure 3). Four concentration profiles along selected positions, including the centerline and three transverse lines as shown in Figure 4 (a), are quantitatively compared between predictions and measurements. The main parameters in current simulations are summarized in Table 2.

Table 2 Main Parameters Used in the Simulation

Initial concentration	Fe—0.51 wt pct C—0.006 wt pct S
Liquidus	1532−7175.17 C−3271.05 S ℃
Partition coefficient of carbon solute	0.324
Partition coefficient of sulfur solute	0.014

	(Continued)
Thermal expansion coefficient	$1.07 \times 10^{-4} \text{K}^{-1}$
Carbon solutal expansion coefficient	1.4164
Sulfur solutal expansion coefficient	1.27
Viscosity	$0.0042 \text{kgm}^{-1}\text{s}^{-1}$
Density	6990kgm^{-3}
Specific heat	$500 \text{Jkg}^{-1}\text{K}^{-1}$
Thermal conductivity	$39.3 \text{Wm}^{-1}\text{K}^{-1}$
Latent heat	271000Jkg^{-1}

A. Determination of HTC

Due to the contraction of steel ingot during solidification, an air gap will form and develop at the interface between ingot and mold. The heat transfer at the interface is complex with convection, radiation, and gas conduction. The formation of the air gap between the ingot and mold is simulated with thermo-elastic-viscoplastic and thermo-elastic models considering both the expansion of mold and contraction of the ingot. The related equations are listed as follows:[23]

The total strain rate is

$$\varepsilon = \varepsilon^{el} + \varepsilon^{vp} + \varepsilon^{th} \quad (6)$$

where ε^{el}, ε^{vp}, and ε^{th} are the elastic, viscoplastic, and thermal strain rate tensors, respectively.

$$\varepsilon^{vp} = \lambda m \quad (7)$$

where λ is a non-negative parameter, specifying the magnitude of viscoplastic strain rate and m determines the direction of the viscoplastic strain rate.

$$\varepsilon^{th} = \int_{T_0}^{T} \alpha(T) \, dT_\delta \quad (8)$$

where α is thermal expansion coefficient, T_0 is the reference temperature, and δ is the Kronecker's delta.

The stress rate equation is

$$\sigma = \underline{\underline{D}}^{el} : \varepsilon^{el} \quad (9)$$

where $\underline{\underline{D}}^{el}$ is the fourth-order isotropic elastic stiffness modulus tensor.

During the thermal-stress simulation, the HTC at the interface is continuous adjusted to minimize the sum residual between the temperature predictions and measurements at the 14 positions labeled in Figure 2 (a). Then, the HTC is transferred into an equivalent form calculated by an empirical equation,[24,25] and is applied as the boundary conditions of macrosegregation modeling below. The equivalent HTC is calculated with a gage time t_{gap} of air gap's initialization. The time evolutions of air gap widths in three different heights (H1 = 800mm, H2 = 1600mm, and H3 = 3000mm) at the ingot/mold interface are shown in Figure 7. The positions of H1, H2, and H3 are identical to the ones of thermocouples TB1, TB2, and TB3 as shown in Figure 2 (a). The t_{gap} is gauged to be 2800, 1600, and 2700 seconds at H1, H2, and H3 with the width of 1mm, respectively. The equivalent HTCs at the ingot/mold interface are shown in Figure 8. All the equivalent HTCs initialize at a maximum value ($\sim 3000 \text{Wm}^{-2}\text{K}^{-1}$) which results from the best contact of liquid metal with the mold. Then HTCs decrease with time sharply to a critical value (100 to $200 \text{Wm}^{-2}\text{K}^{-1}$) for the broken of good contact between the ingot and mold.

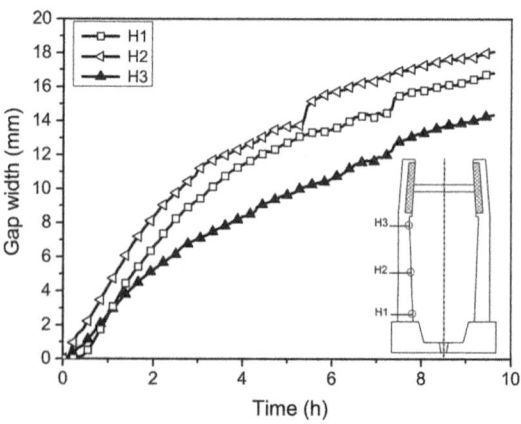

Fig. 7 Simulated air gap widths at the ingot/mold interface.

B. Macrosegregation Modeling

Adopting the equivalent HTCs calculated above, a previous two-phase multiscale solidification model[19,20]

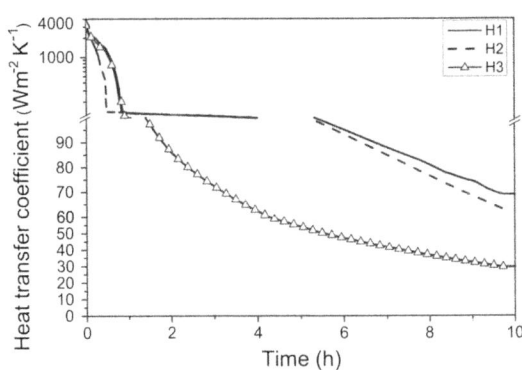

Fig. 8 Calculated equivalent HTCs at the ingot/mold interface (H1, H2, and H3 are the same as those in Fig. 7).

for binary alloy is improved to predict macrosegregation in this 36-ton ingot. Two sets of conservation equations are developed in the two-phase model for the considerations of the different transport behaviors of solid and liquid phase during solidification. The mass, momentum, heat, and species transport on macroscopic scale is coupled with the microscopic descriptions of solid grains' nucleation and growth. The solid grains are assumed to be ideal spheres. Full details of the mathematic model are available in References 19 and 20.

In current simulation, the previous developed twophase model is extended to ternary system. The buoyancy term in the momentum conservation is revised to include the second solute according to the Boussinesq approximation:

$$\rho_1^b = \rho_0 [1 - \beta_T (T - T_{ref}) - \beta_1 (C_{1,1} - C_{ref,1}) - \beta_2 (C_{1,2} - C_{ref,2})] \quad (10)$$

where ρ_0 is the reference density value, β_T is the thermal expansion coefficient, β_1 and β_2 are the solutal expansion coefficients for the first and second solute element, T_{ref} is the reference temperature value, $C_{ref,1}$ and $C_{ref,2}$ are the reference values for the solute concentration, T is the temperature, $C_{1,1}$ and $C_{1,2}$ are the liquid solute concentrations.

The second solute transport equation is added:

$$\frac{\partial}{\partial t}(g_k \rho_k C_{k,2}) + \nabla \cdot (g_k \rho_k \boldsymbol{u}_k C_{k,2})$$
$$= \frac{S_V \rho_k D_k}{\delta_k}(C_{k,2}^* - C_{k,2}) + C_{k,2}^* \Gamma_k \quad (11)$$

where g is the mass fraction, $\boldsymbol{u}$ is the velocity, C is the concentration, S_V is the interfacial area concentration, D is the concentration diffusion coefficient, δ is the interfacial solute diffusion length, and Γ is the interfacial phase change rate. The subscript k refers to the general k phase (liquid or solid), and the superscript * stands for the solid-liquid interface. Besides, extended interfacial balance, added in the Appendix, is adopted to build the constraint between the interface solute element evolutions:

$$\frac{D_{1,1}}{\delta_{1,1}} \cdot \frac{(C_{1,1}^* - C_{1,1})}{C_{1,1}^*(1-k_1)} = \frac{D_{1,2}}{\delta_{1,2}} \cdot \frac{(C_{1,2}^* - C_{1,2})}{C_{1,2}^*(1-k_2)} \quad (12)$$

where k_1 and k_2 are the solute partition coefficients for the first and second solute, respectively.

Due to the limitation of present models and the other uncertainty of process parameters, it is still hard to simulate whole macrosegregation maps with similar elements segregation degree and area as shown in Figure 4. Therefore, focus has now been made on concentration profiles along certain positions of ingot as discussed below.

The carbon and sulfur concentration profiles along the ingot centerline are compared between the predictions and measurements as shown in Figure 9 (a). Generally, the predictions are in good agreements with measurements. However, the concentrations of both carbon and sulfur in predictions are underestimated for the positive segregation zone (the distance to the bottom higher than 2.5m). The reason for the underestimation may lie in the neglect of the alloying elements which increase the thermal-solutal convection during solidification.

Three typical transverse sections in ingot as shown in Figure 4 (a), are selected to further investigate the capability of current model. Section A is located at the bottom representing the negative segregation zone due to the sedimentation of solute-lean solid grains, and section B is in the concerned ingot body zone for practical use, while section C is located at the hot-top standing for the positive segregation zone formed by the solidification of solute-rich melt at late stages. Section A, section B, and section C are at the heights of 600, 1800, and 2800mm over the ingot bottom, respectively. Figures 9 (b) through (d) exhibit the comparisons of carbon and sulfur concentrations along the three sections between predictions and measurements. For section A, slight un-

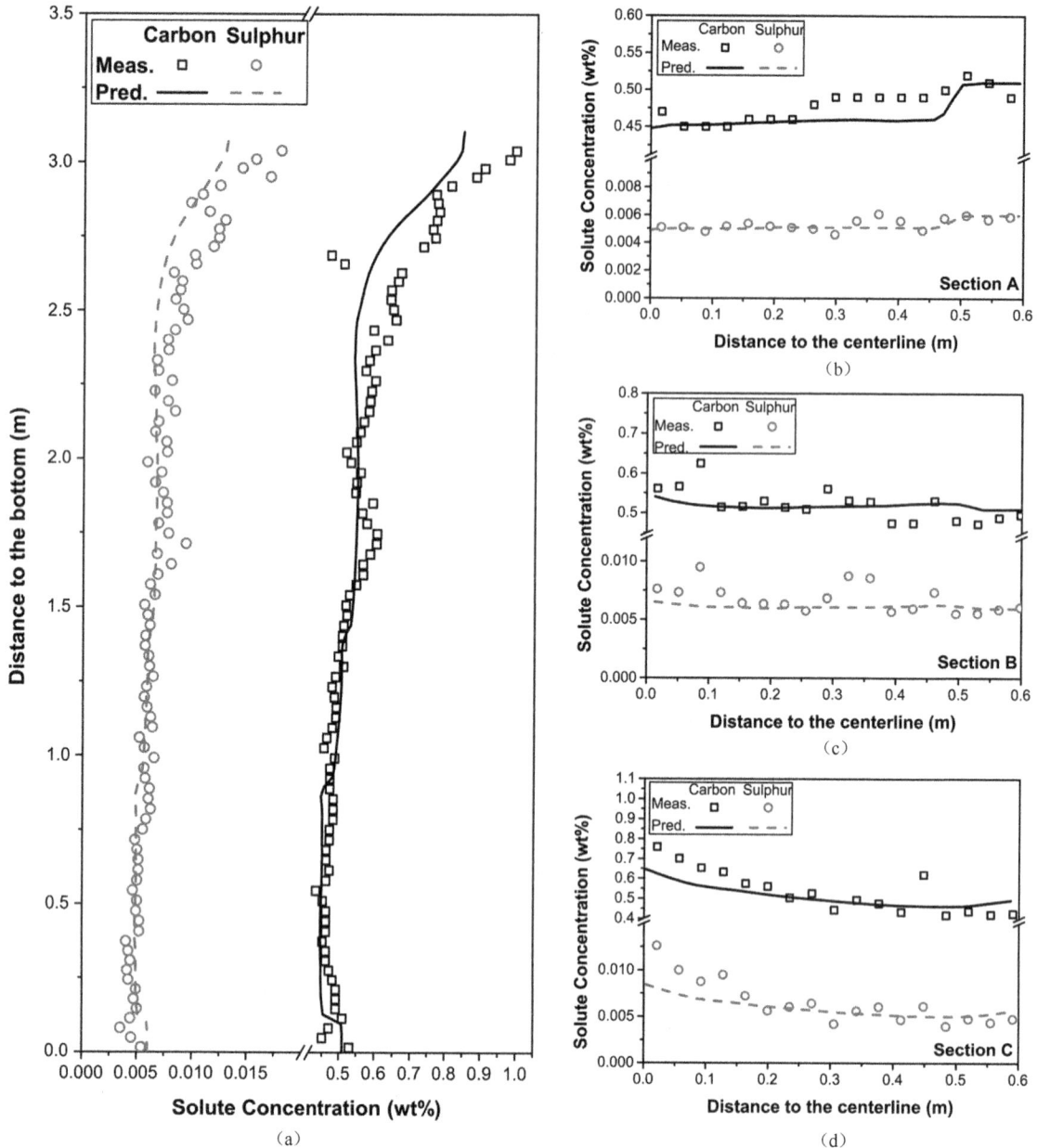

Fig. 9 Solute concentration profiles along (a) the ingot centerline, (b) section A, (c) section B, and (d) section C (positions as shown in Fig. 4a).

derestimations are observed for the predictions compared with measurements as shown in Figure 9 (b). As analyzed by Combeau et al.,[14] the simplification of solid grain morphology should be responsible for this underestimation. The ideal spherical grains are of greater sedimentation speed due to the larger ratio of volume to surface (thus, the ratio of sedimentation to buoyancy) compared with the probable dendritic solid grains in practice. For section B, relative flat prediction curves follow measurements with fluctuations as shown in Figure 9 (c). As for section C, both the predictions and measurements are in a general decreasing trend as shown in Figure 9 (d). However, the concentrations are also underestimated in predictions compared with measurements. This underestimation could be attributed to the neglect of alloying elements as stated above.

Anyway, experimental analysis concerned the determination of uncertain parameters for grain nucleation and growth, and numerical considerations of complex solid grain morphology, etc., in multicomponent alloy solidification should be included in future research.

V. CONCLUSIONS

Experimental measurements and numerical simulations have been conducted to investigate the macrosegregation in a 36-ton steel ingot. It is hoped that the experimental results can be served as basic data for the validation of numerical codes. Temperature evolutions at specified positions in the ingot/mold system were measured, and carbon as well as sulfur macrosegregation maps were reconstructed with chemical analysis of 1800 grid samples in ingot. Preliminary simulations were made for a basic validation of numerical codes with measurements.

1. Fourteen temperature variations in the mold, in the ingot, and at the ingot/mold interface were obtained, which provided the necessary solidification conditions of ingot.
2. Macrosegregation maps were reconstructed by chemical analysis of both the carbon and sulfur on the ingot longitudinal section. Typical macrosegregation patterns, including the positive segregation in the hot-top and negative segregation in the bottom, were reproduced. Notable negative segregations appeared along the side walls of hot-top. Segregation extent of sulfur was greater than that of carbon.
3. Relevancy between the carbon segregation and sulfur segregation in ingot were obtained and a general relevancy was illustrated for all the measurement data with a standard correlation coefficient $r=0.68872$.
4. The equivalent heat transfer coefficient (HTC) between the ingot and mold was calibrated with the temperature measurements. HTCs initialized at a maximum value ($\sim 3000 \mathrm{Wm}^{-2}\mathrm{K}^{-1}$) and then decreased sharply to critical points (100 to $200 \mathrm{Wm}^{-2}\mathrm{K}^{-1}$) for the broken of good contact between the ingot and mold.
5. A two-phase multiscale multicomponent solidification model was improved to predict the macrosegregation in the 36-ton steel ingot. Comparisons were made between the predicted and measured segregation profiles of both carbon and sulfur, and the general good agreements were obtained. Further developments should be done for considerations of the complex solid grain morphology for multicomponent alloy.

ACKNOWLEDGMENTS

This work was financially supported by the National Basic Research Program of China (No. 2011CB012900) and the National Science and Technology Major Project the Ministry of Science and Technology of China (No. 2012ZX04012011).

APPENDIX

The concentration solute transport equations[19,20] for the liquid and solid phase is improved as follows:

$$\frac{\partial}{\partial t}(g_s \rho_s C_{s,1}) + \nabla \cdot (g_s \rho_s \boldsymbol{u}_s C_{s,1})$$
$$= \frac{S_V \rho_s D_{s,1}}{\delta_s}(C_{s,1}^* - C_{s,1}) + C_{s,1}^* \Gamma_s \quad (A1)$$

$$\frac{\partial}{\partial t}(g_1 \rho_1 C_{1,1}) + \nabla \cdot (g_1 \rho_1 \boldsymbol{u}_1 C_{1,1})$$
$$= \frac{S_V \rho_1 D_{1,1}}{\delta_1}(C_{1,1}^* - C_{1,1}) - C_{1,1}^* \Gamma_s. \quad (A2)$$

According to the interface solute balance, it can be derived as

$$\frac{S_V \rho_s D_{s,1}}{\delta_{s,1}}(C_{s,1}^* - C_{s,1}) + C_{s,1}^* \Gamma_s + \frac{S_V \rho_1 D_{1,1}}{\delta_{1,1}}(C_{1,1}^* - C_{1,1})$$
$$- C_{1,1}^* \Gamma_s = 0. \quad (A3)$$

Considering the fact that diffusion in solid is negligible compared with the diffusion in liquid ($D_{s,1} \ll D_{1,1}$), it can be simplified as

$$C_{s,1}^* \Gamma_s + \frac{S_V \rho_1 D_{1,1}}{\delta_{1,1}}(C_{1,1}^* - C_{1,1}) - C_{1,1}^* \Gamma_s = 0 \quad (A4)$$
$$\Rightarrow \Gamma_s = \frac{S_V \rho_1 D_{1,1}}{\delta_{1,1}} \cdot \frac{(C_{1,1}^* - C_{1,1})}{C_{1,1}^*(1-k_1)}$$

Similarly, the interfacial phase change rate can also be expressed as

$$\Gamma_s = \frac{S_V \rho_1 D_{1,2}}{\delta_{1,2}} \cdot \frac{(C_{1,2}^* - C_{1,2})}{C_{1,2}^*(1-k_2)}. \quad (A5)$$

Combining Eqs. [A4] and [A5], the constraint between the interface solute element evolutions is

$$\frac{D_{1,1}}{\delta_{1,1}} \cdot \frac{(C_{1,1}^* - C_{1,1})}{C_{1,1}^*(1-k_1)} = \frac{D_{1,2}}{\delta_{1,2}} \cdot \frac{(C_{1,2}^* - C_{1,2})}{C_{1,2}^*(1-k_2)} \quad (A6)$$

REFERENCES

[1] C. Beckermann: *Int. Mater. Rev.*, 2002, vol. 47, pp. 243-61.

[2] E. J. Pickering: *ISIJ Int.*, 2013, vol. 53, pp. 935-49.

[3] D. Z. Li, X. Q. Chen, P. X. Fu, X. P. Ma, H. W. Liu, Y. Chen, Y. F. Cao, Y. K. Luan, and Y. Y. Li: *Nat. Commun.*, 2014, vol. 5, p. 5572, DOI: 10.1038/ncomms6572.

[4] M. C. Flemings and G. E. Nereo: *Trans. Metall. Soc. AIME*, 1967, vol. 239, pp. 1449-61.

[5] W. D. Bennon and F. P. Incropera: *Int. J. Heat Mass Transfer*, 1987, vol. 30, pp. 2161-70.

[6] C. Beckermann and R. Viskanta: *Physicochem. Hydrodyn.*, 1995, vol. 10, pp. 195-213.

[7] J. Ni and C. Beckermann: *Metall. Trans. B*, 1991, vol. 22B, pp. 349-61.

[8] C. Y. Wang and C. Beckermann: *Metall. Mater. Trans. A*, 1996, vol. 27A, pp. 2754-64.

[9] M. Wu and A. Ludwig: *Metall. Mater. Trans. A*, 2006, vol. 37A, pp. 1613-31.

[10] M. Bellet, H. Combeau, Y. Fautrelle, D. Gobin, M. Rady, E. Arquis, O. Budenkova, B. Dussoubs, Y. Duterrail, A. Kumar, C. A. Gandin, B. Goyeau, S. Mosbah, and M. Založnik: *Int. J. Therm. Sci.*, 2009, vol. 48, pp. 2013-16.

[11] G. Lesoult: *Mater. Sci. Eng. A*, 2005, vols. 413-414A, pp. 19-29.

[12] J. Li, M. Wu, A. Ludwig, and A. Kharicha: *Int. J. Heat Mass Transfer*, 2014, vol. 72, pp. 668-79.

[13] S. Hans, P. E. Richy, B. Lusson, and A. Grellier: in *1st Multidisciplinary Congress on Materials*, Tours, France, 2002, AF16005.

[14] H. Combeau, B. Rabia, S. Charmond, S. Hans, and P. E. Richy: in *2nd Multidisciplinary Conference on Materials*, Dijon, France, 2006.

[15] H. Combeau, M. Založnik, S. Hans, and P. E. Richy: *Metall. Mater. Trans. B*, 2009, vol. 40B, pp. 289-304.

[16] J. Pickering, C. Chhesman, S. Al-Bermani, M. Holland, P. Davies, and J. Talamantes-silva: *Metall. Mater. Trans. B*, 2015, vol. 46B, pp. 1860-74.

[17] P. Machovcak, A. Opler, Z. Carbol, A. Trefil, K. Merta, J. Zaoral, M. Tkadleckova, and K. Michalek: *Arch. Mater. Sci. Eng.*, 2012, vol. 58, pp. 22-27.

[18] K. Kajikawa, S. Suzuki, F. Takahashi, S. Yamamoto, T. Suzuki, S. Ueda, T. Shibata, and H. Yoshida: in *1st International Conference on Ingot Casting, Rolling and Forging*, Aachen, Germany, 2012.

[19] W. S. Li, H. F. Shen, X. Zhang, and B. C. Liu: *Metal. Mater. Trans. B*, 2014, vol. 45B, pp. 464-71.

[20] W. Tu, H. Shen, and B. Liu: *ISIJ Int.*, 2014, vol. 54, pp. 351-55.

[21] Z. Duan, H. Shen, and B. Liu: in *The 14th Modelling of Casting, Welding and Advanced Solidification Process*, Hyogo, Japan, 2015, p. 012048.

[22] M. C. Schneider and C. Beckermann: *Metal. Mater. Trans. A*, 1995, vol. 9A, pp. 2373-88.

[23] ProCAST software, version 2011, https://www.esi-group.com/software-services/virtual-manufacturing/casting/procast-quikcast.

[24] W. S. Li, B. Z. Shen, H. F. Shen, and B. C. Liu: in *The 69th World Foundry Congress*, Hangzhou, P. R. China, 2010, pp. 0537-40.

[25] Z. Liu, Y. Zhao, Y. Zhang, H. L. Zhao, and Y. T. Yang: *J. Iron. Steel. Res*, 1993, vol. 5, pp. 23-32.

30. Three-Dimensional Simulation of Macrosegregation in a 36-Ton Steel Ingot Using a Multicomponent Multiphase Model

WUTAO TU,[1,2] ZHENHU DUAN,[1,3] BINGZHEN SHEN,[4] HOUFA SHEN,[1,5] and BAICHENG LIU[1]

1.—School of Materials Science and Engineering, Tsinghua University, Beijing 100084, People's Republic of China. 2.—SMIC Advanced Technology Research & Development (Shanghai) Corporation, Shanghai 201203, People's Republic of China. 3.—Engineering School, Lishui University, Lishui 323000, Zhejiang, People's Republic of China. 4.—China North Industries Group Corporation, Beijing 100089, People's Republic of China. 5.—e-mail: shen@tsinghua.edu.cn

A multicomponent multiphase solidification model has been developed to predict macrosegregation of steel ingots in three dimensions. The interpenetrating continua of liquid melt and solid grains is coupled with air for the mass, momentum, concentration, and heat transfer. Interfacial solute constraint relationships are derived to close the model by solving the solidification paths of multicomponent alloy. The upward unidirectional solidification case of a ternary Al-6.0 wt.%Cu-1.0 wt.%Si alloy is taken as a basic validation. Predictions have well captured the inverse segregation profiles induced by shrinkage during solidification. Then, the model is applied to a 36-ton steel ingot, which was experimentally investigated by temperature recording and concentration analysis. Predictions have reproduced the macrosegregation patterns in the measurements. Confidence levels of current predictions compared to the concentration measurements have been presented. General good agreements are exhibited in quantitative comparisons between measurements and predictions of carbon and sulfur variations along selected positions.

INTRODUCTION

Macrosegregation, namely compositional heterogeneity, is a common defect occurring in large steel ingots. It has arisen from the solute partition during solidification, and the relative motion between the liquid and solid phase translates the solute microscopic inhomogeneity into the difference of chemical composition on a macroscopic scale. The origin of the relative motion is multifold, and it mainly develops in the form of thermosolutal buoyancy, solid grains sedimentation and shrinkage-induced flow.[1,2] Macrosegregation, which may lead to non-uniform distribution of the microstructure and possible deleterious effects on mechanical properties, has haunted steelmakers for decades. Macrosegregation cannot be alleviated by downstream hot-working process, thus it is important to control the formation of macrosegregation during solidification. Considering the size of large steel ingots, it is high-cost and time-consuming using pure experiment tests. Thus, numerical simulation has become an indispensable tool for the investigation of macrosegregation in steel ingots.

Since the pioneering work of Flemings and Nereo in the 1960s,[3] numerous efforts have been devoted to studying the macrosegregation in steel ingots. Among them, most of the research work has focused on the Fe-C binary systems due to the fact that carbon has the strongest effect on the solutal buoyancy forces. Combeau et al.[4] adopted a volume-averaged model to investigate macrosegregation in a 65-ton Fe-0.22 wt.%C steel ingot. Comparisons were made between predictions and measurements of composition with 35 points on the ingot longitudinal section. Due to the limitation of the volume-averaged model, the prediction cannot capture the negative segregation caused by the equiaxed grain sedimentation at the ingot bottom. Inspired by the two-phase model proposed by Ni and Beckermann,[5] Combeau et al. applied a two-phase equiaxed model to a 3.3-ton steel ingot[6] measured by 114 points of composition. The steel was simplified as Fe-0.36 wt.%C and the effects of solid grainmorphology were examined. A similar two-phase model was applied to a 53-ton steel ingot by Li et al.[7] and the effects of thermo-solutal buoyancy, solid grains sedimentation, and primary shrinkage pipe were investigated. Comparisons of carbon variations were made between the measurements and predictions on three transverse sections in the ingot hottop. In addition, Ludwig et al. utilized a three-phasecolumn-equiaxed model to study the macrosegregation in a 2.45-ton ingot.[8] The column-equiaxed transition (CET) was taken into account and carbon solute along the ingot centerline was compared with measurements. All the above binary Fe-C alloy applications have enjoyed a measure of success in predicting the general solidification behaviors of steel ingots. However, other solute elements in real steel may also have significant effects on thermosolutal motion especially at the late solidification stage when solutes have been aggregated for a long time. In addition, the phases in the binary alloy are limited and solidification paths are relatively simplified, while various phases may coexist and complicated solidification paths will occur during solidification of the practical steel ingot.

The first numeric attempt of macrosegregation in multicomponent steel alloys was made by Fujii et al.[9] with an analytical mushy zone model. The local solute redistribution equation by Flemings and Nereo[3] was extended to multicomponent alloy systems to analyze the occurrence of channel-type segregations, and the effects of alloying elements were investigated. Subsequently, Schneider and Beckermann[10] extended a binary continuum model to multicomponent alloy systems for the investigation of various solute macrosegregation in steel ingots. The importance of accurate thermo-dynamic data of phase diagram had been addressed. Gu and Beckermann[11] applied the model to predict the macrosegregation in a 43-ton ingot. Good agreements were obtained in comparisons of carbon and sulfur variations along the ingot centerline, except that the negative segregation in the bottom was absent in predictions due to the limitation of the continuum model.

In current research, a multicomponent multiphase model has been developed to predict the macrosegregation of steel ingots in three dimensions. The interpenetrating continua of liquid melt and solid grains is coupled with air for the mass, momentum, concentration and heat transfer. Full coupling of temperature and interface concentrations, through thermodynamic equilibrium at the liquid-solid interface with the interfacial solute constraint relationships, is derived to close the model. An upward unidirectional solidification case of a ternary Al-6.0 wt.%Cu-1.0 wt.%Si alloy is taken as a basic validation of the model. Then, the model was applied to a 36-ton steel ingot of which the macrosegregation maps have been rebuilt with 1800 sampling points. Confidence levels of current predictions to measurements have been presented. Solute variations along four selected lines in the ingot are compared between measurements and predictions.

MATHEMATIC MODEL

The multicomponent multiphase model is an extension of the previous binary two-phase model by Li et al.[7,12] The air phase is added for the consideration of solidification shrinkage of the ingot. In addition, additional solute conservations are included, and the interface solute balance constraint relationships coupled with thermo-dynamic data of the multicomponent alloy phase diagram are derived to close the model. The model is numerically solved by a self-developed program based on the SIMPLE algorithm.

Basic assumptions in the model are summarized as follows:

(1) Three phases, the liquid phase (l), the solid phase (s), and air phase (a), are incorporated in the system. The mass of air is negligible compared with the liquid and solid, and the concentration of air is zero. Full interaction for the mass, momentum, heat and solute transfer is constructed between the liquid and the solid phase, while only the heat and the momentum interaction is modeled

between the air and the others.

(2) The drag force between the liquid and solid is modeled by the Gidaspow model.[13] A constant value is chosen as the critical solid fraction (g_{sc}). When the solid fraction is smaller than the critical value ($g_s < g_{sc}$), the flow between the liquid and solid is tackled as the slurry flow where the equiaxed grains can freely move in the surrounding liquid. Otherwise, a porous regime is used where the solid is assumed to be a rigid skeleton through which the liquid flow travels.

(3) A three-parameter heterogeneous nucleation law[14] is adopted to calculate the nucleation of the solid grains, and a diffusion-controlled growth mechanism is used to calculate the growth of the grains. The morphologies of the grains are simplified as ideal spheres.

Mass Conservation

$$\frac{\partial}{\partial t}(g_s \rho_s) + \nabla \cdot (g_s \rho_s \mathbf{v}_s) = \Gamma_s \tag{1}$$

$$\frac{\partial}{\partial t}(g_l \rho_l) + \nabla \cdot (g_l \rho_l \mathbf{v}_l) = -\Gamma_s \tag{2}$$

where t is the time, g is the mass fraction, ρ is the density, $\mathbf{v}$ is the velocity, and Γ_s is the interfacial solid phase change rate. The subscripts "s" and "l" refer to the solid phase and liquid phase, respectively. It should be noted that the densities are not equal, $\rho_s > \rho_l$ for most alloys, then the overall density $\rho = g_s \rho_s + g_l \rho_l$ will be varied with time which is the origin for the shrinkage-induced flow.[15]

Volume Conservation

$$\Delta V = \left(\frac{\rho_s}{\rho_l} - 1\right) \sum (V_{cell} \cdot \Delta g_s) \tag{3}$$

where ΔV is volume change of the liquid-solid solidification system during a computation time step, and V_{cell} is the volume computation cell. The integration of ΔV forms the shrinkage cavity filled with the air phase compensating the solidification shrinkage. A vertical velocity of the air phase is imposed at the top of the computation domain according to the method by Zhang et al.[16]

$$v_a = \frac{\left(\frac{\rho_s}{\rho_l} - 1\right) \sum (V_{cell} \cdot \Delta g_s)}{A \cdot \Delta t} \tag{4}$$

where A is the top area of calculation domain, and Δt is the time step.

Momentum Conservation

$$\frac{\partial}{\partial t}(g_l \rho_l \mathbf{v}_l) + \nabla \cdot (g_l \rho_l \mathbf{v}_l \mathbf{v}_l) \tag{5}$$
$$= -g_l \nabla p + \nabla \cdot (g_l \mu_l \nabla \mathbf{v}_l) - K_{ls}(\mathbf{v}_l - \mathbf{v}_s) + g_l \rho_l^b \mathbf{g}$$

$$\frac{\partial}{\partial t}(g_s \rho_s \mathbf{v}_s) + \nabla \cdot (g_s \rho_s \mathbf{v}_s \mathbf{v}_s) \tag{6}$$
$$= -g_s \nabla p + \nabla \cdot (g_s \mu_s \nabla \mathbf{v}_s) + K_{ls}(\mathbf{v}_l - \mathbf{v}_s) + g_s \rho_s \mathbf{g}$$

where μ is the viscosity, K_{ls} is the drag coefficient between the solid and liquid phases, and $\mathbf{g}$ is the gravity force. The superscript b denotes the buoyancy. The drag coefficient is modeled according to the Gidaspow model,[13] and the details can be referenced to Ref. 12. Due to the fact that the solid density ρ_s is greater than the liquid density ρ_l, the unpacked solid grains will sedimentate downwards, which is called the grain sedimentation.

The liquid buoyancy density is calculated as

$$\rho_l^b = \rho_l [1 - \beta_T(T - T_0) - \sum (\beta_{C,i}(C_{l,i} - C_0))] \tag{7}$$

where β_T is the thermal buoyancy coefficient, T is the temperature, T_0 is the reference temperature, $\beta_{C,i}$ is the solutal buoyancy coefficient of solute i, C_l, i is the liquid concentration, and C_0 is the reference concentration. It should be noticed that all the solute elements should be taken into account for the liquid buoyancy density, and that the thermo-solutal buoyancy flow is driven by the variation of the liquid buoyancy term.

Concentration Conservation

$$\frac{\partial}{\partial t}(g_s \rho_s C_{s,i}) + \nabla \cdot (g_s \rho_s \mathbf{v}_s C_{s,i})$$
$$= \nabla \cdot (g_s \rho_s D_{s,i} \nabla C_{s,i}) + \frac{S_V \rho_s D_{s,i}}{\delta_s}(C_{s,i}^* - C_{s,i}) + C_{s,i}^* \Gamma_s \tag{8}$$

$$\frac{\partial}{\partial t}(g_l \rho_l C_{l,i}) + \nabla \cdot (g_l \rho_l \mathbf{v}_l C_{l,i})$$
$$= \nabla \cdot (g_l \rho_l D_{l,i} \nabla C_{l,i}) + \frac{S_V \rho_l D_{l,i}}{\delta_l}(C_{l,i}^* - C_{l,i}) - C_{l,i}^* \Gamma_s \tag{9}$$

where D is the concentration diffusion coefficient, S_v is the interfacial area concentration, and δ_l is the interfacial concentration diffusion layer length. The subscript i denotes the solute i and the superscript $*$ stands for the liquid-solid interface.

The second and the third terms on the right hand of Eqs. (8) and (9) are the interfacial concentration diffusion by concentration gradient and the interfacial concentration transfer due to phase change, respectively. Here, the interfacial concentration balance is derived as,

$$\frac{S_V \rho_s D_{s,i}}{\delta_{s,i}}(C^*_{s,i}-C_{s,i})+C^*_{s,i}\Gamma_s+\frac{S_V \rho_l D_{l,i}}{\delta_{l,i}} \\ (C^*_{l,i}-C_{l,i})-C^*_{l,i}\Gamma_s=0 \quad (10)$$

Given the fact that diffusion in the solid is negligible compared with the diffusion in the liquid ($D_{s,i} \ll D_{l,i}$), Eq. (10) can be simplified as:

$$C^*_{s,i}\Gamma_s+\frac{S_V \rho_l D_{l,i}}{\delta_{l,i}}(C^*_{l,i}-C_{l,i})-C^*_{l,i}\Gamma_s=0 \\ \Rightarrow \Gamma_s = \frac{S_V \rho_l D_{l,i}}{\delta_{l,i}} \cdot \frac{(C^*_{l,i}-C_{l,i})}{C^*_{l,i}-C^*_{s,i}} \quad (11)$$

Similarly, the interfacial solid phase change rate Γ_s can be expressed as:

$$\Gamma_s = \frac{S_V \rho_l D_{l,1}}{\delta_{l,1}} \cdot \frac{(C^*_{l,1}-C_{l,1})}{C^*_{l,1}-C^*_{s,1}} = \frac{S_V \rho_l D_{l,2}}{\delta_{l,2}} \cdot \frac{(C^*_{l,2}-C_{l,2})}{C^*_{l,2}-C^*_{s,2}} \\ = \cdots = \frac{S_V \rho_l D_{l,n-1}}{\delta_{l,n-1}} \cdot \frac{(C^*_{l,n-1}-C_{l,n-1})}{C^*_{l,n-1}-C^*_{s,n-1}} \quad (12)$$

Equation (12) is termed the interfacial concentration constraint relationsships for the multicomponent alloy system. Coupled with the thermodynamic data of the multicomponent phase diagram, the solidification paths are calculated to close the model by applying the interfacial concentration copyconstraint relationships. The application of interfacial concentration constraint relationships to a typical eutectic ternary alloy system for closing the model is illustrated in detail in the supplementary file.

Energy Conservation

$$\frac{\partial}{\partial t}[(g_s \rho_s c_{ps}+g_l \rho_l c_{pl})T_{s(l)}] \\ +\nabla \cdot [(g_s \rho_s c_{ps} \mathbf{v}_s+g_l \rho_l c_{pl} \mathbf{v}_l)T_{s(l)}] \\ = \nabla \cdot [(g_s \lambda_s+g_l \lambda_l)\nabla T_{s(l)}]+\Gamma_s L \quad (13)$$

where c_p is the heat capacity, k is the thermal conductivity and L is the latent heat. Here, only the temperatures of the liquid phase and solid phase are considered while the temperature of the air is constant. The influence of the air on the temperature is introduced by setting a heat transfer coefficient at the air interface.

The supplementation relationships on the microscale, including the descriptions of the interfacial area concentration, the interfacial concentration diffusion layer length, etc., can be found in Ref. [12].

MODEL VALIDATION

The upward unidirectional solidification case of a ternary Al-6.0 wt.%Cu-1.0 wt.%Si alloy proposed by Ferreira et al.[17] is taken as a basic validation. This ternary alloy was solidified in a cylindrical mold with a diameter of 50mm. The mold was chilled from the bottom while the other surfaces were kept adiabatic. The schematic of the experiment is shown in Fig. 1a.

The Thermo-Calc software[18] has been used to calculate the three-dimensional ternary Al-Cu-Si phase diagram by the TQ interface routine with the TTAL5 aluminium-based alloy database. The calculated Al-rich corner of the phase diagram is shown in Fig. 1b with Cu varied from 0 wt.% to 35 wt.% and Si varied from 0 wt.% to 12 wt.%. Coupled with the Al-Cu-Si ternary phase diagram data, the interfacial concentration constraint relationships are used to calculate the solidification paths to close the model. The solidification paths of the concentration point (0.06, 0.01) predicted by the constraint relationship, labeled by the line with open circles in Fig. 1c, have overlapped with the calculations by the Thermo-Calc POLY3 module.

The parameters used in the current simulation are summarized in Table 1. According to the experiment results, the solidification macrostructure is columnar. Therefore, the solids in the current simulations are viewed as fixed.

The predicted concentration distribution of Cu at t = 120s is shown in Fig. 2a, on which the liquid flow vectors along with the solid fraction isolines are superimposed. As shown in Fig. 2a, the concentrations near the chilling bottom exhibit positive segregation patterns which

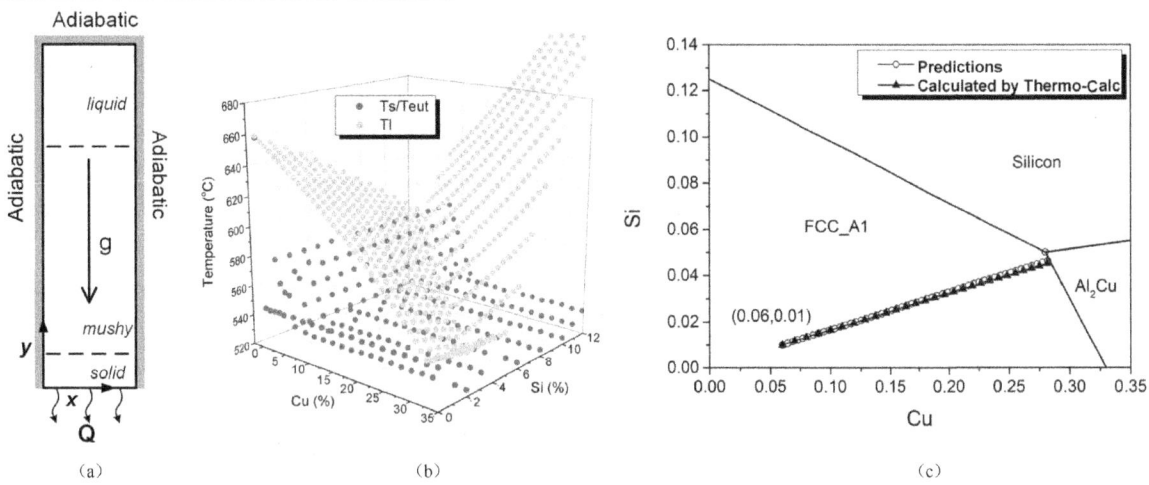

Fig. 1 (a) Schematic of the Al-6.0 wt.%Cu-1.0 wt.%Si unidirectional solidification experiment, and (b) calculated Al-Cu-Si phase diagram, (c) solidification paths for the concentration point of Al-6.0 wt.%Cu-1.0 wt.%Si.

are termed inverse segregation. As shown by the magnified section in Fig. 2a, a negative segregation makes its appearance at the zone in the solid fraction of (0.2, 0.8) with the liquid flow vectors vertical. The species accumulated at the bottom are dragged downwards from the mushy zone in the middle by the vertical liquid flow. As analyzed by Ferreira et al.,[17] the main driving force for the vertical liquid flow is the solidification shrinkage.

The final concentration distributions of Cu and Si near the bottom along the vertical section centerline after solidification are shown in Fig. 2b. Predictions with and without shrinkage are compared with the experiments. The inverse segregations of both Cu and Si are exhibited in the experiments and predictions with shrinkage, while slight negative segregations are predicted in simulations without shrinkage. As analyzed above, the shrinkage-induced flow drives the formation of inverse segregations. Good agreements are obtained by quantitative comparisons of current predictions with the measurements.

Table 1 Simulation parameters

Properties	Values	Units
Mesh size	0.05	mm
Initial concentration Cu/Si	0.06/0.01	
Initial temperature	650	℃
Chilling bottom base temperature	25	℃
Liquid/solid density	2713.4/2529.5	$kg \cdot m^{-3}$
Liquid/solid heat capacity	1063/1125	$J \cdot kg^{-1} \cdot K^{-1}$
Liquid/solid thermal conductivity	87.9/180	$W \cdot m^{-1} \cdot K^{-1}$
Latent heat	380554	$J \cdot kg^{-1}$
Liquid viscosity	3×10^{-3}	$kg \cdot m^{-1} \cdot s^{-1}$
Solutal expansion coefficient	0.72	
Thermal expansion coefficient	4.95×10^{-5}	K^{-1}
Concentration diffusion coefficient for Cu/Si	$3.0 \times 10^{-9}/1.0 \times 10^{-9}$	$m^2 \cdot s^{-1}$
Heat transfer coefficient between the chilling bottom and the melt	$14,000 \times t^{-0.08}$	$W \cdot m^{-2} \cdot K^{-1}$

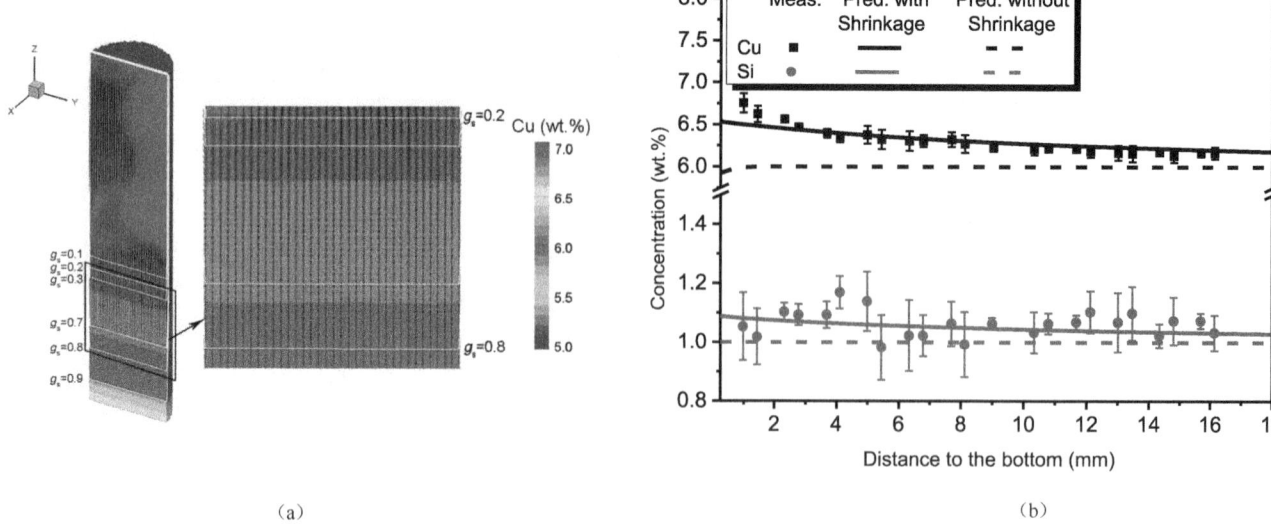

Fig. 2 (a) Predicted concentration of Cu at $t=120$ s in the Al-Cu-Si unidirectional solidification, and (b) concentration profiles near the chilling bottom after Al-Cu-Si unidirectional solidification.

RESULTS AND DISCUSSION

After the basic validation, the model has been applied to a 36-ton steel ingot. The ingot was cast in the steel plant of CITIC Heavy Industries. The ingot was 3.2m in height and 1.5m in mean diameter. A plain carbon steel was chosen with the composition as shown in Table 2. The ingot was bottom-poured at 1560℃ and temperature variations at specific positions, as shown with the open circles in Fig. 3a, were recorded to acquire the necessary heat transfer conditions between the ingot and mold. After being stripped out of the mold, the ingot was dissected into slices along the center plane, and samples in a matrix of 1800 points were taken to analyze the concentration distribution. A resolution of 30mm×30mm was chosen for the measurement sampling points (Fig. 3b). The reconstructed concentration distributions of carbon and sulfur from measurements are shown in Fig. 3c and d.

Table 2 Steel grade (wt.%)

C	Si	Mn	S	P	Ni
0.51	0.23	0.60	0.006	0.009	0.13

In current simulations, symmetry along the centerline axis has been assumed and only a quarter of the ingot system is simulated. A grid system of 184,823 cells was used with a mesh size of 30mm×30mm×30mm. A variable timestep from 0.02s to 0.5s was used. The initial concentration has been simplified as Fe-0.51 wt.% C-0.006 wt.% S. Necessary simulation parameters are listed in Table III. It should be noticed that the liquidus temperature and the solute partition coefficients for the ternary Fe-C-S alloy system are calculated by Thermo-Calc with the TCFE4 Fe alloy database for the Fe-rich corner in the solute range of C ∈ [0 wt.%, 1.5 wt.%] and S ∈ [0 wt.%, 0.02 wt.%]. Here, the focus has been put on the effects of multicomponent elements on the liquidus surface and solute partition coefficients due to the interaction among the solute elements, and only the primary solidification, i.e. the austenite phase solidified from liquid ($L \rightarrow \gamma$), is considered. A calculation interval of 0.005 wt.%C and 0.001 wt.%S is chosen. The linear regression method is used to fit the calculated phase-diagram scatters (~6000 points) for the liquidus temperature and solute partition coefficients as shown in Table 3. Other parameters, including the basic thermophysical property parameters of the ingot system and necessary initial and boundary conditions, are identical to the ones in Ref. [19].

The predicted concentration distributions are shown in Fig. 4a and b. Both carbon and sulfur concentrations exhibit similar patterns including the upper positive segregations and lower negative segregations. In addition, negative segregations along the side wall of the hot-top have been predicted while similar segregation patterns have

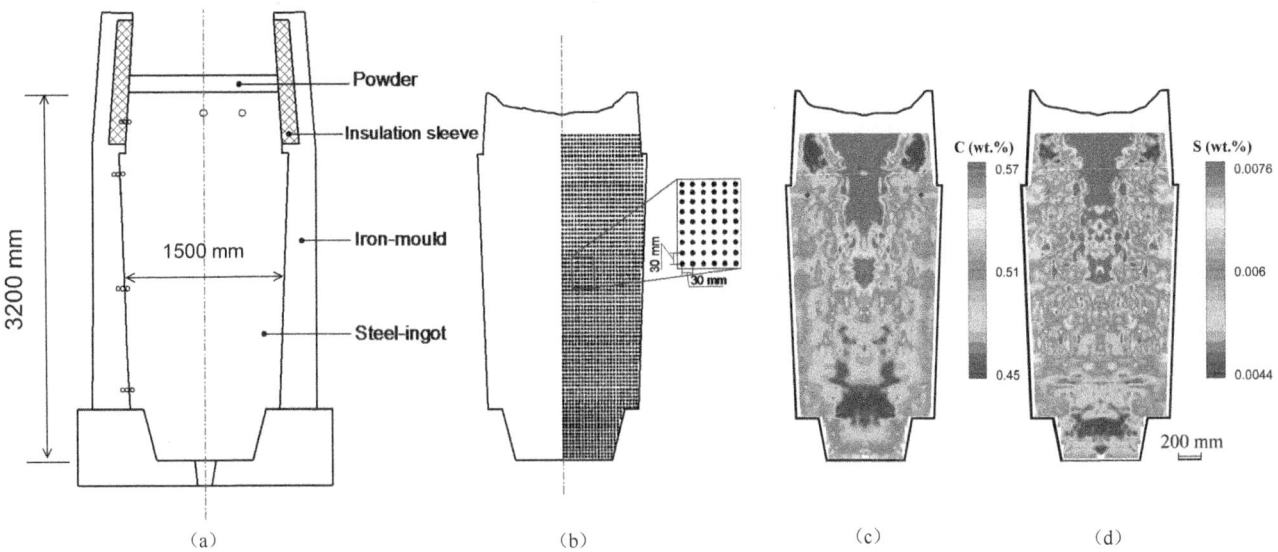

Fig. 3 (a) Schematic of ingot system, (b) schematic of concentration sampling positions, (c) re-constructed concentration map of carbon, and (d) re-constructed concentration map of sulfur.

Table 3 Simulation parameters for the Fe-C-S alloy system

Property	Value	Unit
Melting temperature of pure iron	1532	℃
Liquid density	6990	kg·m^{-3}
Solid density	7300	kg·m^{-3}
Liquidus temperature	$1532-7175.17033 \cdot C-3271.05413 \cdot S$	℃
Specific heat capacity	500	J·kg^{-1}·K^{-1}
Thermal conductivity	39.3	W·m^{-1}·K^{-1}
Latent heat	2.71×10^5	J·kg^{-1}
Carbon solute partition coefficient	$0.30075+4.77466 \cdot C-2.07705 \cdot S$	1
Sulfur solute partition coefficient	$0.01525-0.22988 \cdot C+0.39878 \cdot S$	1
Carbon solute expansion coefficient	1.4164×10^{-2}	wt.%$^{-1}$
Sulfur solute expansion coefficient	1.27×10^{-2}	wt.%$^{-1}$
Thermal expansion coefficient	1.07×10^{-4}	K^{-1}
Carbon solute diffusion coefficient in liquid	2×10^{-8}	m^2·s^{-1}
Sulfur solute diffusion coefficient in liquid	2×10^{-8}	m^2·s^{-1}
Carbon solute diffusion coefficient in solid	5.6×10^{-10}	m^2·s^{-1}
Sulfur solute diffusion coefficient in solid	3.3×10^{-11}	m^2·s^{-1}
Maximum grain density	5×10^{16}	m^{-3}
Undercooling for maximum production rate	5	K
Gaussian distribution width of the nucleation law	1	K

been observed in the measurements (Fig. 3c and d). As analyzed by Combeau et al.,[6] the melt in the opposite direction of the temperature gradient drags the concentration from the mushy zone to the liquid melt, and the negative segregations have been formed. For further illustrations of segregation pattern, the characteristic segregations ($C>0.54$ wt.% or $C<0.48$ wt.%) are extracted in Fig. 4c from the carbon predictions (Fig. 4a). As shown in Fig. 4c, a conically shaped negative segregation zone locates at the bottom, a pushpin-like positive segregation zone penetrates into the ingot body from top, and a negative segregation ring makes its appearance around the hot-top.

In order to evaluate the accuracy of the current predictions, the predicted concentration C_p at the same positions of concentration measurements C_m are extracted. Then, the concentration scatter points (C_m, C_p) have been collected to evaluate the predictions compared to the measurements (Fig. 5). If the predictions are accurate enough, the scatters should locate at the dash-dotted line $C_p = C_m$ in Fig. 5. However, deviations in the measurements will always exist in predictions due to the model simplifications. Thus, a confidence interval has to be chosen for the accuracy evaluation. Here, the range $C_p \in [0.85C_m, 1.15C_m]$ has been chosen with a relative error $|(C_p - C_m)/C_m|$ of 15% being viewed as credible. Furthermore, the confidence level α is defined as the ratio of the number of credible prediction points N to the number of all the extracted scatters M ($\alpha = N/M$). As for the current concentration predictions, the confidence level α is 0.960 and 0.758 for carbon and sulfur, respectively. Moreover, it can be seen that the unconfident scatters which are out of the confidence intervals ($C_p \notin [0.85C_m, 1.15C_m]$) mostly appear in the positive segregation zones ($C_m > 0.7$ for carbon in Fig. 5a). These scatters are located in the range $C_p \notin (0, 0.85C_m)$, which means that obvious underestimations are made for the predictions of positive segregations which gives the possible instructions on prediction improvement. The neglect of other solute elements which have strong effects on thermo-solutal convection at the late solidification stage may be the reason for the underestimations.

Further quantitative comparisons were made between the predictions and measurements along four selected lines in the ingot. The vertical centerline for the position covering the whole solidification range was chosen along with other three transverse sections A, B and C (Fig. 4c). The heights of section A, section B and section C over the ingot bottom are 600mm, 1800mm and 2800mm, respectively. Section A is located at the bottom for the negative segregation zone due to the sedimentation of solutelean solid grains, section B is in the concerned ingot body zone, and section C is at the hot-top standing for the positive segregation zone formed by soluterich melt at late stages.

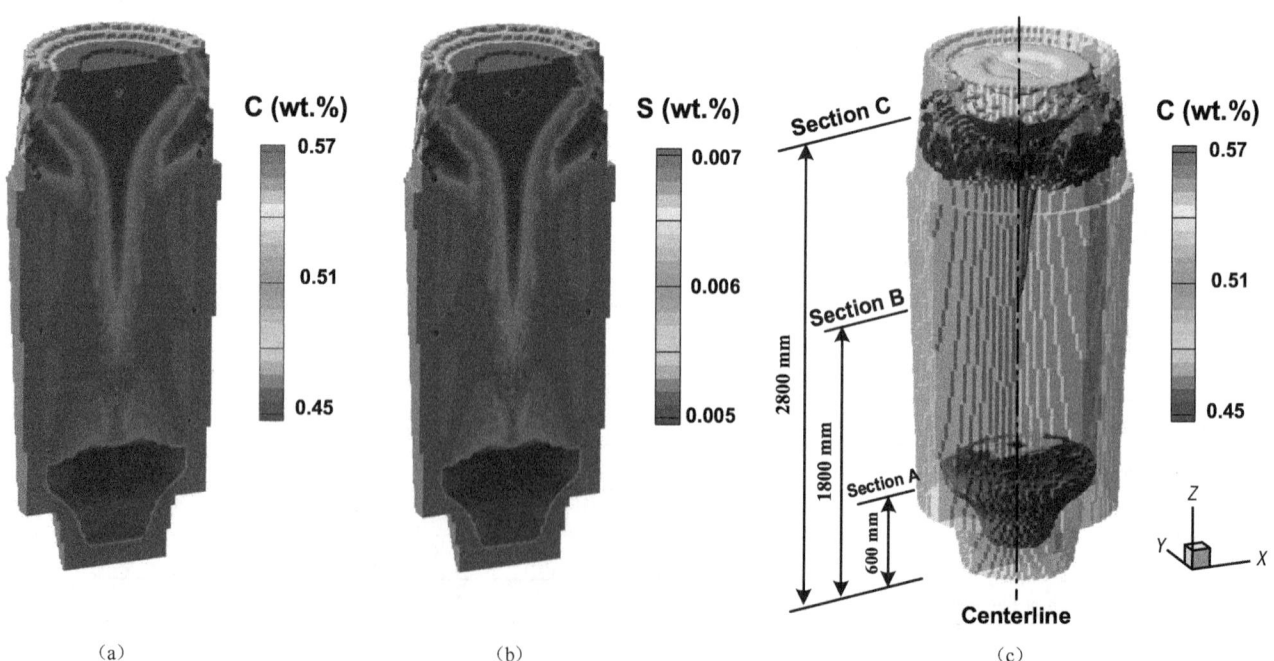

Fig. 4 (a) Predicted carbon concentration, (b) predicted sulfur concentration, and (c) extracted segregation patterns from carbon distribution.

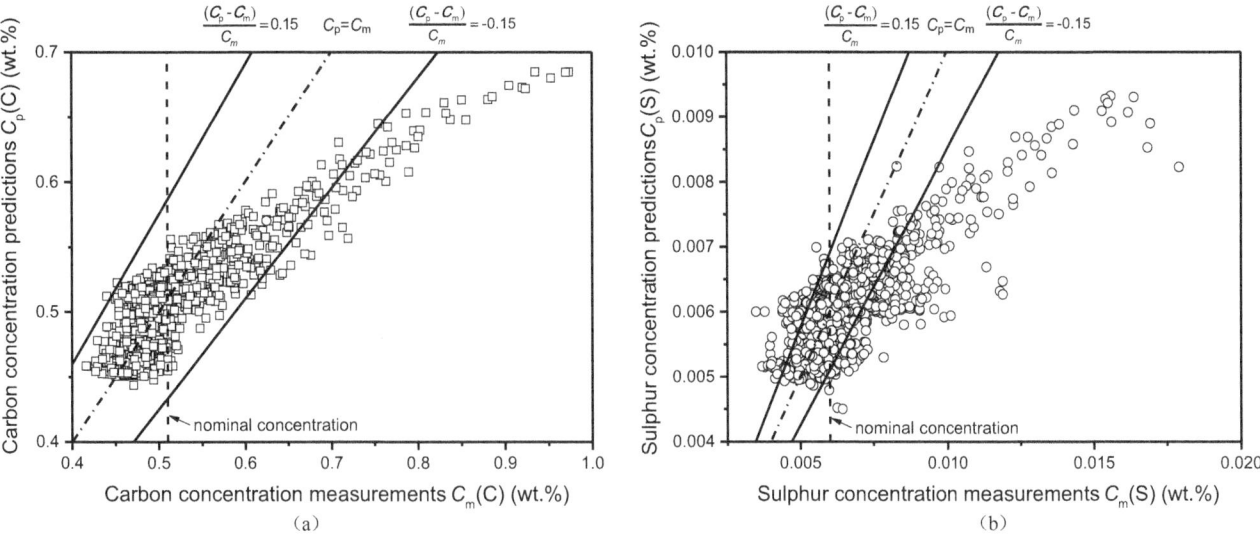

Fig. 5 Accuracy evaluations of concentration predictions to measurements for (a) carbon, (b) sulfur.

The concentration profiles along the selected lines are shown in Fig. 6. In Fig. 6a, the predictions are in generally good agreement with the measurements along the centerline. Obvious underestimations of predictions to measurements can be observed for both carbon and sulfur at the positive segregation zone (the distance to the bottom being higher than 2.5m). The underestimations could be attributed to the neglect of alloying elements as analyzed above. In addition, a sudden decrease of concentrations has been exhibited in the upper centerlines, as shown in Fig. 6a. The sudden decrease corresponds to the isolated negative segregation zones which can also be observed in the rebuilt macrosegregation map of measurements (Fig. 6a). As analyzed by Ge et al.,[20] the thermosolutal convection in the last solidified zone drives the formation of the isolated negative segregations.

Concentration variations for the other three sections are illustrated in Fig. 6b-d. For section A, slight underestimations are observed for the predictions compared with measurements as shown in Fig. 6b. The simplification of solid grain morphology should be responsible for this underestimation as analyzed by Combeau et al.[6] The ideal spherical grains are of greater sedimentation speed due to the larger ratio of volume to surface (thus, the ratio of sedimentation to buoyancy) compared with the probable dendritic solid grains in practice. For section B, relative flat prediction curves follow measurements with fluctuations as shown in Fig. 6-c. As for section C, both the predictions and measurements are in generally decreasing trends as shown in Fig. 6d. However, the concentrations are also underestimated in the predictions compared with the measurements for positive segregations (distance to centerline $x<0.2$m in Fig. 6d) due to the neglect of other solutes.

Above all, current predictions by the multicomponent multiphase model for the 36-ton steel ingot are generally reliable compared with the measurements. Experimental analysis concerning the determination of uncertain parameters for grain nucleation and growth, and numerical developments focused on the extension of other solute elements and dendritic solid grains should be included in future research.

CONCLUSION

A multicomponent multiphase model has been developed to predict the macrosegregation during solidification. The model tackles the interaction between the liquid, the solid and the air. Interfacial solute constraint relationships are derived to close the model. A unidirectional solidification of Al-6.0 wt.%Cu-1.0 wt.%Si is applied as a basic validation. Then, the model is used to predict the macrosegregation of carbon and sulfur in a 36-ton steel ingot.

1. Solidification paths of the ternary Al-Cu-Si alloy system have been calculated through the coupling of phase diagram calculation data and interfacial solute

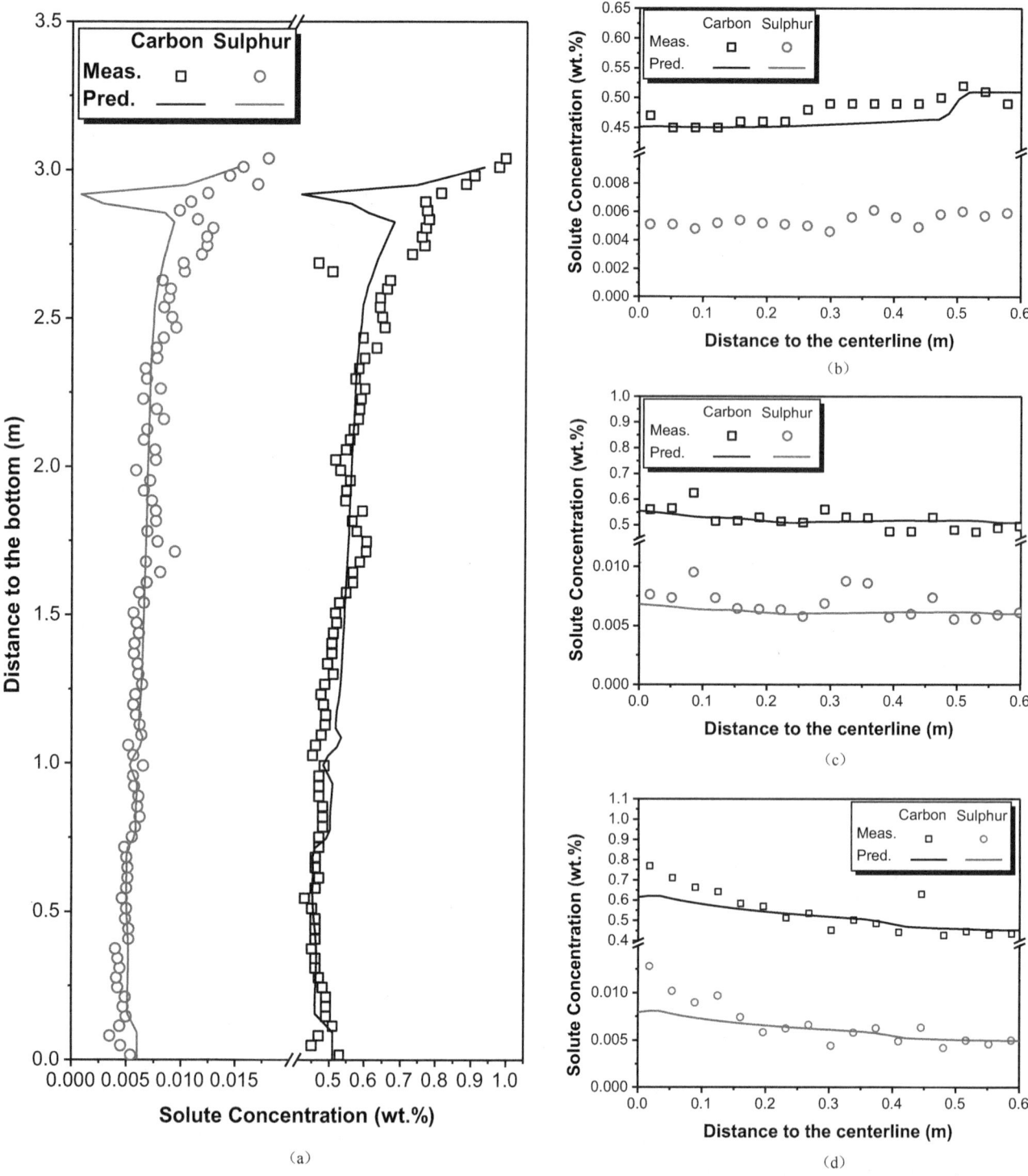

Fig. 6 Concentrations of carbon and sulfur along (a) the centerline, (b) section A, (c) section B, (d) section C in ingot (sections A, B and C as indicated in Fig. 4c).

constraint relationships. The inverse segregations of copper and silicon that are driven by shrinkage have been well captured by the current predictions.

2. Macrosegregation maps of carbon and sulfur have been rebuilt based on 1800 concentration sampling points which have covered the ingot's semi-longitudinal section. Typical macrosegregation patterns, including the bottom-located negative segregation and the pushpin-like positive segregation zone in the upper part, have been reproduced both in the meas-

urements and the predictions.

3. Current predictions, especially for carbon concentration, are in general in good agreement with measurements through the confidence levels analysis and quantitative comparisons along four selected lines in the ingot. Predicted concentrations are extracted at the measurement positions to evaluate the accuracy of the current predictions. The confidence levels with a chosen range of $C_p \in [0.85C_m, 1.15C_m]$ are 0.960 and 0.758 for carbon and sulfur, respectively. Further developments should be carried out for the consideration of dendritic grains and more solute elements.

ACKNOWLEDGEMENTS

This work was financially supported by the National Basic Research Program of China (No. 2011CB012900) and the NSFC-Liaoning Joint Fund (U1508215).

ELECTRONIC SUPPLEMENTARY MATERIAL

The online version of this article (doi: 10.1007/s11837-016-2023-x) contains supplementary material, which is available to authorized users.

REFERENCES

[1] A. Ludwig, M. Wu, and A. Kharicha, *Metall. Mater. Trans. A* 46A, 4854 (2015).

[2] D. Li, X. Q. Chen, P. Fu, X. Ma, H. Liu, Y. Chen, Y. Cao, Y. Luan, and Y. Li, *Nat. Commun.* 5, 5572 (2014).

[3] M. C. Flemings and G. E. Nereo, Trans. *Metall. Soc. AIME* 239, 1449 (1967).

[4] I. Vannier, H. Combeau, and G. Lesoult, *Numiform 92: Numerical Methods in Industrial Forming Processes* (Rotterdam: Balkema, 1992), p. 835.

[5] J. Ni and C. Beckermann, *Metall. Mater. Trans. B* 22B, 349 (1991).

[6] H. Combeau, M. Zaloznik, S. Hans, and P. E. Richy, *Metall. Mater. Trans. B* 40B, 289 (2009).

[7] W. Li, H. Shen, X. Zhang, and B. Liu, *Metall. Mater. Trans. B* 45B, 464 (2014).

[8] J. Li, M. Wu, A. Ludwig, and A. Kharicha, *Int. J. Heat Mass Tran.* 72, 668 (2014).

[9] T. Fujii, D. R. Poirier, and M. C. Flemings, *Metall. Trans. B* 10B, 331 (1979).

[10] M. C. Schneider and C. Beckermann, *Metall. Mater. Trans. A* 26A, 2373 (1995).

[11] J. P. Gu and C. Beckermann, *Metall. Mater. Trans. A* 30A, 1357 (1999).

[12] W. S. Li, H. F. Shen, and B. C. Liu, *Int. J. Miner. Metall. Mater.* 19, 787 (2012).

[13] D. Gidaspow, *Multiphase Flow and Fluidization, Continuum and Kinetic Theory Description* (San Diego: Academic Press Inc, 1994), p. 35.

[14] M. Rappaz and C. A. Gandin, *Acta Metall. Mater.* 41, 345 (1993).

[15] S. Chang and D. M. Stefanescu, *Acta Mater.* 44, 2227 (1996).

[16] S. L. Zhang, D. R. Johnson, and M. J. M. Krane, *Int. J. Cast Metal. Res.* 28, 28 (2015).

[17] I. L. Ferreira, D. J. Moutinho, L. G. Gomes, O. L. Rocha, and A. Garcia, *Philos. Mag. Lett.* 89, 769 (2009).

[18] Thermo-Calc software, version 2006, http://www.thermocalc.com/media/30968/thermo-calc-user-guide.pdf.

[19] Z. Duan, W. Tu, B. Shen, H. Shen, and B. Liu, *Metall. Mater. Trans. A* 47A, 3597 (2016).

[20] H. H. Ge, J. Li, X. J. Han, M. X. Xia, and J. G. Li, *J. Mater. Process. Tech.* 227, 308 (2016).

31. Analysis of internal crack in a six-ton P91 ingot

Jing-an Yang[1], Hou-fa Shen[1], Bai-cheng Liu[1], Ya-dong Xu[2], Yong-ping Hu[2], and Bing-wang Lei[2]

[1] School of Materials Science and Engineering, Tsinghua University, Beijing 100084, China
[2] Special Material Institute, Inner Mongolia North Heavy Industries Group Co, Ltd., Baotou 014033, China

Abstract: P91 is a new kind of heat-resistant and high-tensile steel. It can be extruded after ingot casting and can be widely used for diferent pipes in power plants. However, due to its mushy freezing characteristics, a lack of feeding in the ingot center often generates many defects, such as porosity and crack. A six-ton P91 ingot was cast and sliced, and a representative part of the longitudinal section was inspected in more detail. The morphology of crack-like defects was examined by X-ray high energy industrial CT and reconstructed by 3D software. There are five main portions of defects larger than 200mm^3, four of which are interconnected. These initiated from continuous liquid film, and then were tom apart by excessive tensile stress within the brittle temperature range (BTR). The 3D FEM analysis of thermo-mechanical simulation was carried out to analyze the formation of porosity and interal crack defects. The results of shrinkage porosity and Niyama values revealed that the center of the ingot suffers from inadequate feeding. Several criteria based on thermal and mechanical models were used to evaluate the susceptibility of hot crack formation. The Clyne and Davies' criterion and Katgerman's criterion successfully predicted the high hot crack susceptibility in the ingot center. Six typical locations in the longitudinal section had been chosen for analysis of the stresses and strains evolution during the BTR. Locations in the defects region showed the highest tensile stresses and relative high strain values, while other locations showed either low tensile stresses or low strain values. In conclusion, hot crack develops only when stress and strain exceed a threshold value at the same time during the BTR.

Key words: hot crack; industrial CT; liquid film; thermo-mechanical simulation; steel ingot

CLC numbers: TG142.73   Document code: A   Article ID: 1672-6421 (2016) 03-191-08

Internal crack of an ingot is frequently encountered in casting practice, which directly leads to scrapping the whole product. From many studies [1-7], it appears that hot crack initiates in the brittle temperature range and propagates in the interdendritic liquid film. An extension of the two-phase model, which includes plasticity of the porous network, is reported, considering the void as the crack nucleus, although the pores should not necessarily develop into a crack [8]. The crack may nucleate or develop from other defects and then propagate through a chain of pores. The excessive stress and strain developing during the brittle temperature range are the main reasons for hot crack formation. A coherent dendritic network can sustain and transmit stress. Above the coherency temperature, continuous liquid film still exists as the solid dendrite arms have not yet coalesced. Deformation induced by thermal stress can pull these arms apart quite easily. However, deep in the mushy zone, where the permeability of the mush is very low, and the opening of the non-coherent dendritic network by tensile deformation cannot be compensated by liquid feeding, hot crack forms [9].

So it is essential to investigate the stress and strain evolution in the brittle temperature range when the mush is vulnerable to tensile deformation. Since the 1960s, criteria for hot crack based on thermal considerations and solid mechanics are the primary means to evaluate the hot crack formation. Some criteria are based only on thermal considerations as Clyne and Davies's criterion[10] and Katgerman's criterion[11], while some criteria are based on both thermal and mechanical considerations, such as Guo's criterion[12] and WYSO's criterion[13].

In practice, internal crack was found in P91 ingot, which was extruded to produce heat-resistant pipes for a power station. It is known that P91 steel has a larger freezing range, i.e., 183 K between the liquidus and solidus, and it is estimated that hot crack forms because such an alloy spends a longer time in the vulnerable state in which thin liquid films exist between the dendrites[13]. The mushy zone behavior is very complex, considering feeding, coalescence, deformation, etc. Much effort should be paid to predict hot crack formation. Therefore, a 6-ton P91 ingot was cast and sliced to analyze the formation of internal crack for this study.

1 Experimental procedure

A bottom-poured 6-ton P91 ingot was sliced after solidification to ascertain the internal quality. The ingot body is hexadecagon with a height of 1315mm, bottom diameter 690mm and top diameter 858mm. Composition of P91 grade steel is shown in Table 1.

Table 1 Chemical composition of P91 grade steel (wt.%)

C	Si	Mn	V	Cr	Mo	N	Nb	Fe
0.08	0.2	0.3	0.18	8	0.9	0.03	0.06	Bal.

Figure 1 (a) shows the sliced ingot, which was cut into three parts in height at a distance of 350mm and 940mm from the ingot bottom, respectively. Then the middle part of the ingot was split from the center plane and a longitudinal section of the center plane 90mm was obtained as shown in Fig. 1 (b). After polishing, it was found that the crack-like defects concentrated in the center of the upper part of the longitudinal section. A mapping of internal cracks is schematically illustrated in Fig. 1 (b).

A rectangular block containing crack-like defects with height of 280mm, width of 120mm and thickness of 90mm was sliced again and examined by X-ray high energy industrial CT as shown in Fig. 1 (c). In order to adapt the X-ray penetration ability, the rectangular block (Fig. 1c) was further cut into three long bars with dimension of 28mm × 28mm × 200mm (Fig. 3a). The front view of the first long bar is shown in Fig. 2a. Figures 2b-2i are CT images at the depth gradually penetrating from the front to the back of the bar. It can be imaged that the cracks stretch in the ingot body as bending sheets. In order to gain an overall view, defects in the three long bars were reconstructed according to the obtained CT images (Fig. 3b), where the color indicator represents defect volume. Superficially, the defects are fragmentary but actually, they are more continuous than expected. The total volume of the defects in three bars are 1864.71mm^3, 498.52mm^3, 682.59mm^3, about 1.39%, 0.37%, 0.5% of the entity, respectively. There are five main portions of defects greater than 200mm^3 in Fig. 3 (b), where the color is remarked with red, pink, and green. The blue marks show the remaining small defects below 50mm^3, which may be micro-cracks or porosities. Through recombining the three CT reconstructions, as shown in Fig. 3 (c), it is found that most defects connect with each other,

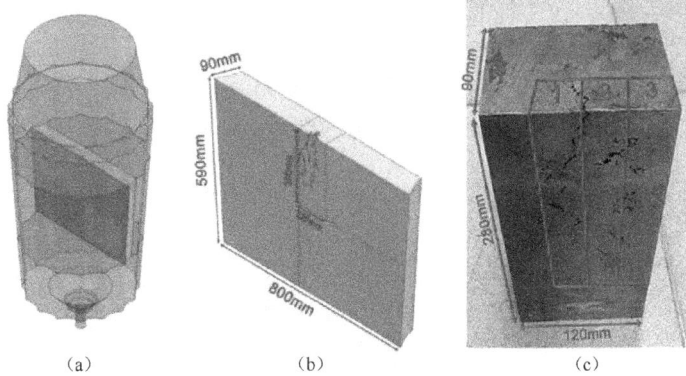

Fig. 1 (a) Schematic of sliced ingot, (b) slice in longitudinal section of ingot, (c) rectangular block cut from the slice

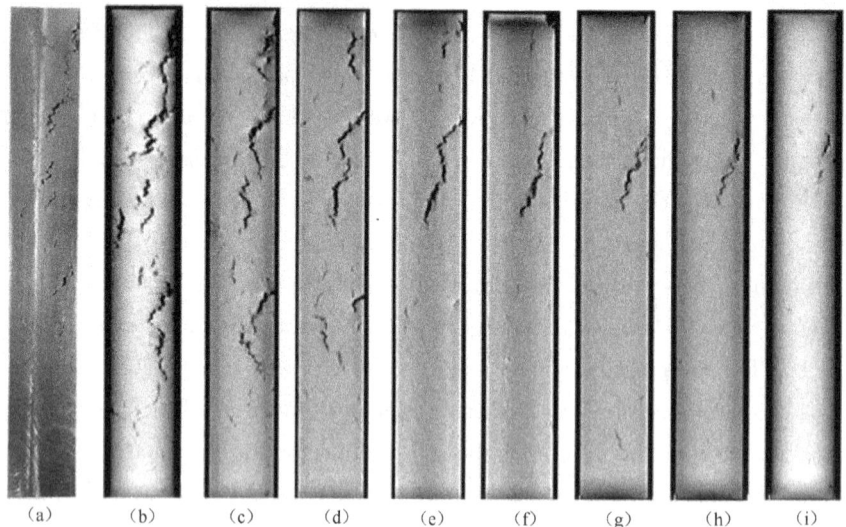

Fig. 2 (a) Front view of first long bar, (b) - (i) CT images at the depth gradually penetrating from the front to the back of bar

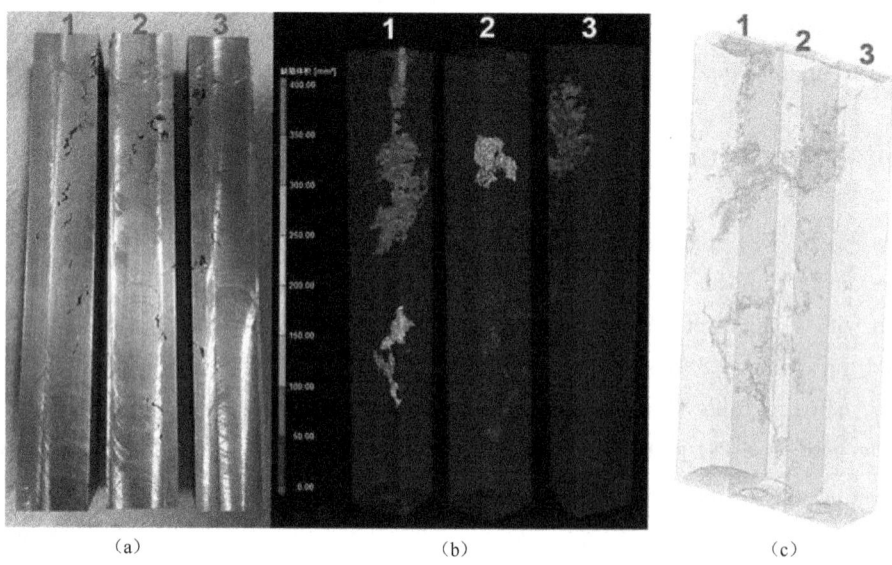

Fig. 3 (a) Three long bars from the rectangular block (Fig. 1c), (b) 3D CT image reconstruction with transparent display, (c) recombination of three CT reconstructions

especially the four main defects greater than 200mm³ on the upper part of the bars. The connected defects derived from continuous liquid films. As the solidification progresses, inadequate feeding and tensile deformation created the opening of the non-coherent dendrite network and induced hot crack formation.

2 Numerical simulation

The 3D FEM analysis of temperature field and stress field was carried out based on ProCAST software. An FEM mesh including the ingot and mold system (Fig. 4a) with 2,638,787 elements was generated for the calculation as shown in Fig. 4 (b). The thermophysical properties, such as thermal conductivity, density, enthalpy, and fraction solid are calculated by CompuTherm thermodynamic database for multi-component Fe-rich alloys of ProCAST. At the same time, the thermomechanical properties, such as Young's Modulus, Poisson's Ratio, yield stress, thermal expansion and plastic modulus are calculated by General Steel database of JMatPro. The stress type of the casting is Elasto-plastic and hardening type is linear isotropic.

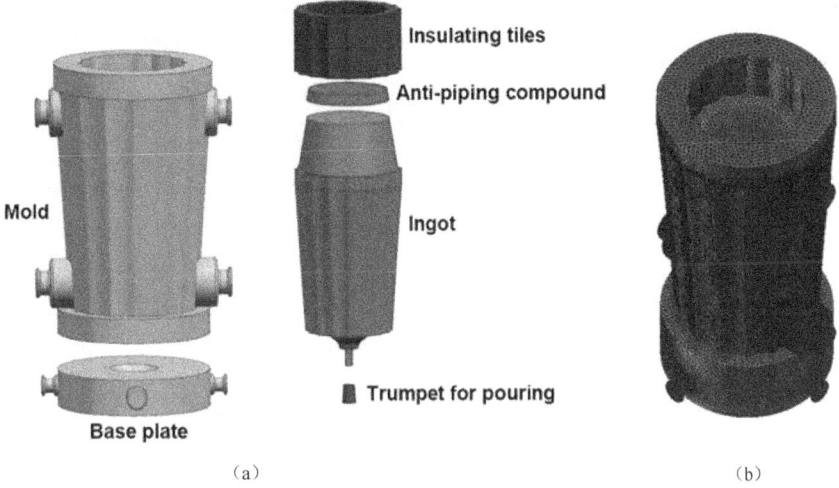

Fig. 4 (a) Geometry characteristic of ingot and mold system, (b) 3D FEM mesh

Shrinkage porosity within the mushy zone including micro-porosity, macro-porosity and pipe-shrinkage formation during solidification was predicted using a dynamic refinement technique[14]. During thermo-mechanical calculation, the gap model assumes that heat conduction through the air gap is progressively replacing the heat transfer coefficient due to the contact. When there is a contact, the heat transfer coefficient is increased as a function of the pressure,

$$h = h_0\left(1 + \frac{P}{A}\right) \quad (1)$$

where h is the adjusted heat transfer coefficient, h_0 is the initial value of the heat transfer coefficient, P is the contact pressure, A is an empirical constant accounting for contact pressure.

Data of model information, temperature field evolution, isochrones of different solid fractions, principal stresses and strains evolution in three directions, and cooling rate information were extracted from the final results of ProCAST and then processed by C++ programming to evaluate the hot crack susceptibility using different criteria, such as Clyne and Davies criterion, Katgerman's criterion, and WYSO's criterion.

Clyne and Davies' criterion[10] considers that in the last stage of solidification, it is difficult for the liquid to move freely so that the strains developed during this stage cannot be accommodated by the mass feeding and liquid feeding. The cracking susceptibility is defined by the ratio of the vulnerable time period where hot tearing may develop, t_V, and time available for the stress-relief process where mass feeding and liquid feeding occur, t_R. The cracking susceptibility cofficient HCS reads:

$$HCS = \frac{t_V}{t_R} = \frac{t_{0.99} - t_{0.9}}{t_{0.9} - t_{0.4}} \quad (2)$$

where $t_{0.99}$ is the time when the volume fraction of solid, f_s, is 0.99, $t_{0.9}$ is the time when f_s is 0.9, and $t_{0.4}$ is the time when f_s is 0.4.

Katgerman's criterion[10] defines the hot tearing index, HCS, as follows:

$$HCS = \frac{t_{0.99} - t_{cr}}{t_{cr} - t_{coh}}. \quad (3)$$

where $t_{0.99}$ is the time when the volume firaction of solid, f_s, is 0.99, t_{coh} is the time when f_s is at the coherency point, and t_{cr} is the time when feeding becomes inadequate.

Guo's criterion[12] is a hot tearing indicator of ProCAST, which is based on the accumulated plastic strain in the last stage of solidification, as follows:

$$e_{ht} = \int_{t_c}^{t} \sqrt{(2/3)\dot{\varepsilon}^P \dot{\varepsilon}^P}\, d\tau \quad t_c \leqslant t \leqslant t_s \quad (4)$$

where t_c represents time at coherency temperature and t_s denotes time at solidus temperature.

WYSO's criterion[3] compares the accumulated strain undergone by the material over the brittle temperature range to a given strain limit. It is expressed as follows:

$$HCC_{WYSO} = \underset{BTR}{Max}\left(\int \hat{\dot{\varepsilon}}(t)\,dt - \hat{\varepsilon}_c\right) \text{ with } \hat{\varepsilon}_c = \frac{\varphi}{(\hat{\dot{\varepsilon}})^{m^*} BTR^{n^*}} \quad (5)$$

where, the three parameters have been deduced by a nonlinear data fitting covering numerous tests performed on different mid-alloyed steel grades: $\varphi = 0.02821$, $m^* = 0.3131$, and $n^* = 0.8638$.

3 Results and discussion

The simulated results of shrinkage porosity in the longitudinal section of the ingot are shown in Fig. 5 (a). The red horizontal lines in Fig. 5 represent the transverse cutting positions of the ingot (Fig. 1a). As can be seen from the figure, pipe-shrinkage forms in the riser of the ingot, and micro-porosity and macro-porosity form mostly along the center line of the ingot, especially in the upper part of the ingot and the bottom of the pipe (i.e, the primary shrinkage cavity). The shrinkage porosities in excess of 2% are composed mainly of macro-porosity, which form a narrow band in the center of the ingot, indicating a lack of melt feeding. The Niyama values under $8(K \cdot S)^{0.5} \cdot cm^{-1}$ in Fig. 5 (b) show a strong possbility of porosity as well.

Hot crack susceptibility was evaluated as shown in Fig. 6. Figures 6 (a) and 6 (b) are hot crack susceptibilities according to Clyne and Davies' criterion and Katgerman's criterion, respectively. They are based only on thermal considerations, mainly taking into account the time spent in a vulnerable state, during which hot crack may develop. They both successfully predicted the high hot crack susceptibility in the ingot center, but additionally showed high susceptibility along the ingot surface, which was not found in the experiment. There are certain limitations when only considering temperature evolution. By thermo-mechanical calculation, treating the ingot body as an Elasto-plastic model, Guo's criterion and WYSO's criterion are tried, but they both show low hot crack susceptibility in the ingot center. The main

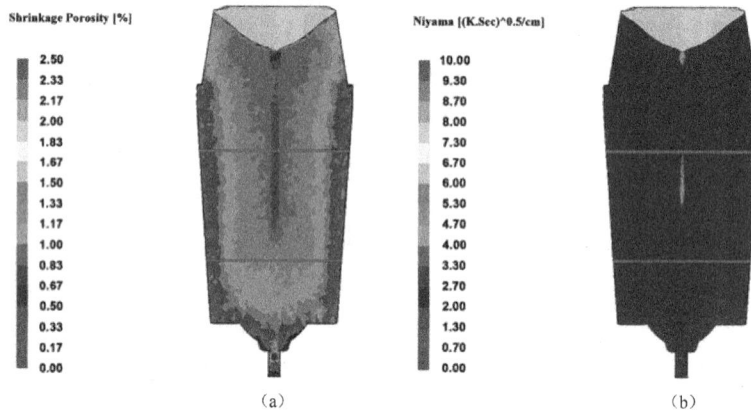

Fig. 5 (a) Shrinkage porosity in the longitudinal section of ingot, (b) Niyama values in the longitudinal section of ingot

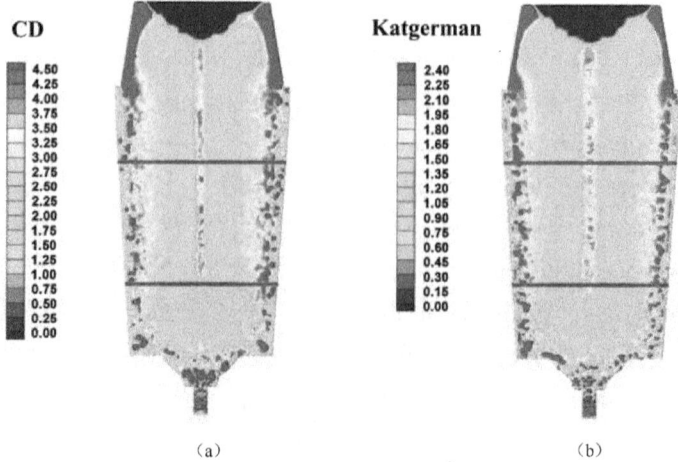

Fig. 6 (a) Hot crack susceptibilities (HCS) according to Clyne and Davies's criterion, (b) HCS according to Katgerman's criterion

reason may be that the two criteria are in essence strain-based criteria and the critical strain is treated as a global constant regardless of porosity formation due to inadequate liquid feeding, mush zone embrittlement due to detrimental elements enrichment, coarse grain due to low undercooling degree, and so on. Additionally, high strain under low stress does not necessarily lead to hot crack formation.

Thermo-mechanical simulation was used to provide a detailed description of the evolution of stresses and strains during the ingot solidification. Six typical locations in the longitudinal section have been chosen for analysis and comparison as shown in Fig. 7 (a). Locations A, B, C, D are in the center line of the ingot and locations E, F are in the radial direction, relative positions of which have been labeled in Fig. 7 (a). Minimum and maximum stress, strain, and time duration within the brittle temperature range at the six locations are listed in Fig. 7 (b). Brittle temperature range is between liquid impenetrable temperature (LIT) and zero ductility temperature (ZDT). The corresponding solid fractions for LIT and ZDT are 0.9 and 0.99, respectively[15]. First, principal stresses and strains are the main indicator for evaluation of stress-strain state. Their detailed evolution with temperature change is shown in Figs. 8 and 9, respectively. In Fig. 8, horizontal axis shows time, left vertical axis shows temperature and right vertical axis shows first principal stress. In Fig. 9, only the right vertical axis changes to first principal strain compared to Fig. 8. The dashed blue horizontal lines in the two figures are used to indicate BTR zone, i.e., temperature between LIT and ZDT when solid fractions are 0.9 and 0.99, respectively.

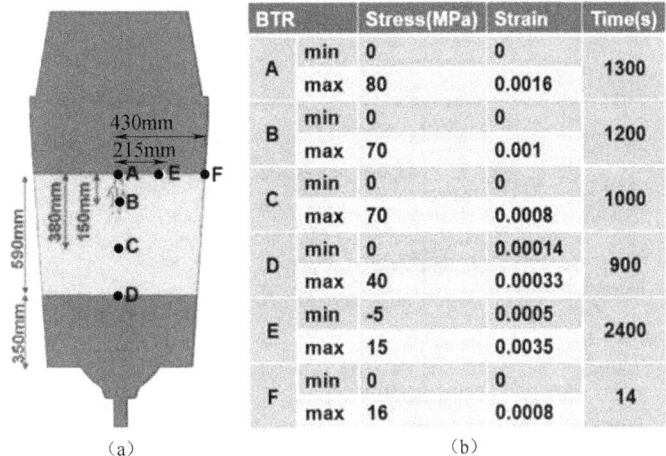

Fig. 7 (a) Six locations of interest in the longitudinal section of ingot, (b) minimum and maximum stress, strain, and time duration of six locations under solidification within BTR

Location A as shown in Fig. 7 (a) is on the top center of the slice of the longitudinal section (Fig. 1b), where the most severe defects were found. 1,300 seconds is spent within the BTR and the maximum stress and strain develop up to 80MPa and 0.0016, respectively. Location B is also located in the defects area, but the degree is much less severe. The time spent within BTR is 1,200 seconds and the maximum stress and strain develop up to 70MPa and 0.001, respectively, which are both less than the corresponding value of location A. Location C is below the defects area, where no defects were found. 1,000 seconds are spent within the BTR and the maximum stress and strain develop up to 70MPa and 0.0008, respectively. Compared to location B, the maximum stress is the same but the maximum strain and time duration within BTR are both less, which makes the area less susceptible to hot crack. Location D is even much lower than the defects range and on the bottom center of the slice. Compared to location C, time duration within BTR is 100 seconds less, and the maximum stress is 40MPa, much less than 70MPa. The strain develops from 0.00014 to 0.00033, much less than 0.0008. For these reasons, it is more likely that the hot crack will not develop.

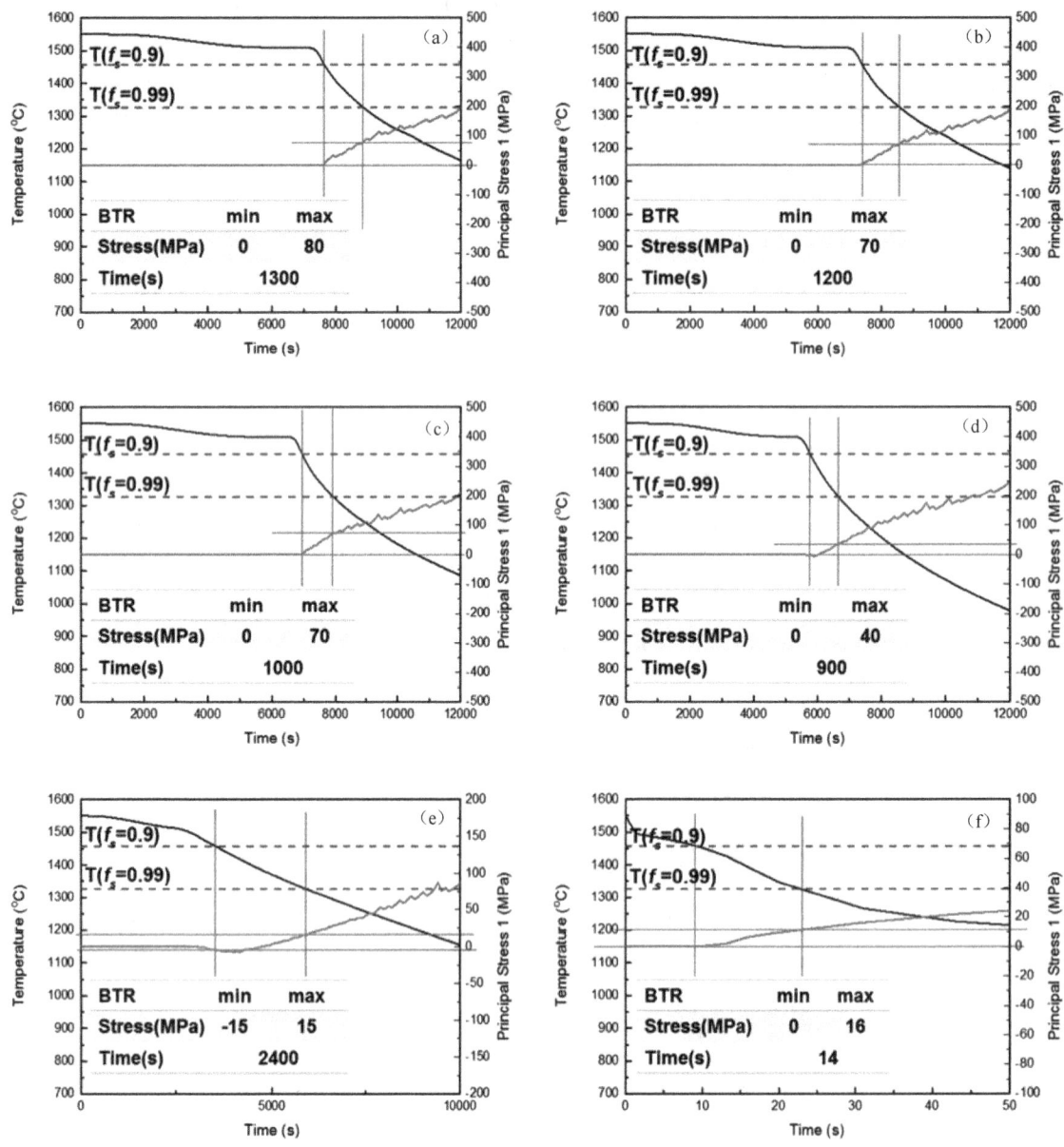

Fig. 8 Temperature and first principal stress evolution in locations A-F as shown in Fig. 7 (a)

Location E is on the top of slice and 215mm from the center (location A), where defects were also not found. Time duration within the BTR is rather long and up to 2,400 seconds, but the stress is in the compress state when temperature begins to fall in the BTR range and then develops to tensile stress and up to 15MPa, which is relatively a very small tensile stress for dendrite network detachment. The strain develops from 0.0005 to 0.0035, which is a relatively high value. But it did not result in hot crack because there is enough time to generate elastic-plastic deformation under a low tensile stress. Meanwhile, this explains the overestimation of hot crack susceptibility by strain-based criteria. Location F is near the ingot surface, where is free from defects. Due to the chilling effect of the ingot mold, its time duration within the BTR is only 14 seconds and the maximum stress and strain develop up to 16MPa and 0.0008, respectively, which are both relatively low values for hot crack formation. Because of the shortness of time duration within the BTR, the criteria based only on thermal considerations, such as Clyne and Davies' criterion and Katgerman's criterion, are not so precise in predicting hot crack in the ingot chill zone.

Equivalent strain and stress in the longitudinal section within the BTR are shown in Fig. 10. Although the equivalent strain of the defects zone is relatively small,

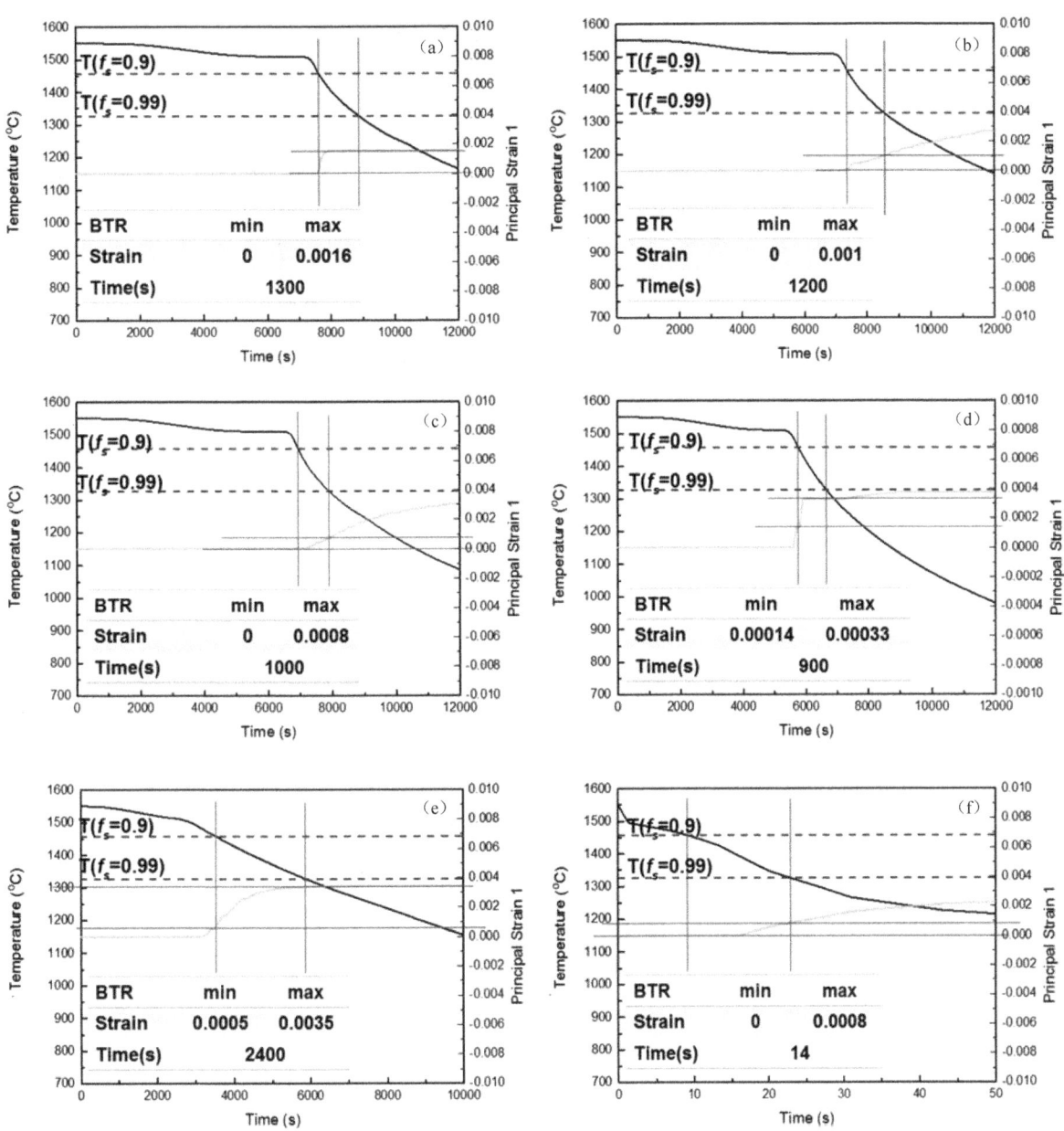

Fig. 9 Temperature and principal strain in locations A-F as shown in Fig. 7 (a)

there are many factors leading to hot crack, such as inadequate feeding (Fig. 5), detrimental elements enrichment, excessive stress (Fig. 10b), and so on. Figure 11 shows the main simulation results compared with the experiment, where Fig. 11 (a) schematically ilustrates the experiment results of the crack-like defects. Figures 11 (b) and 11 (c) reveal that the centerline of the ingot suffers inadequate feeding by shrinkage porosity and Niyama values respectively; Figure 11 (d) indicates that the defects region is under excessive tensile stress within the BTR; Figures 11 (e) and 11 (f) suggest that the centerline of the ingot has the highest hot crack susceptibility. Above all, these factors cause the opening of the non-coherent dendrite network and incur pores nucleation, growth and interaction for crack formation.

4 Conclusion

The internal defects of a 6-ton P91 ingot were characterized by X-ray high energy industrial CT and 3D CT image reconstruction. It was found that the defects are distributed in the upper center part of the ingot and mainly composed of hot cracks, which derive from con-

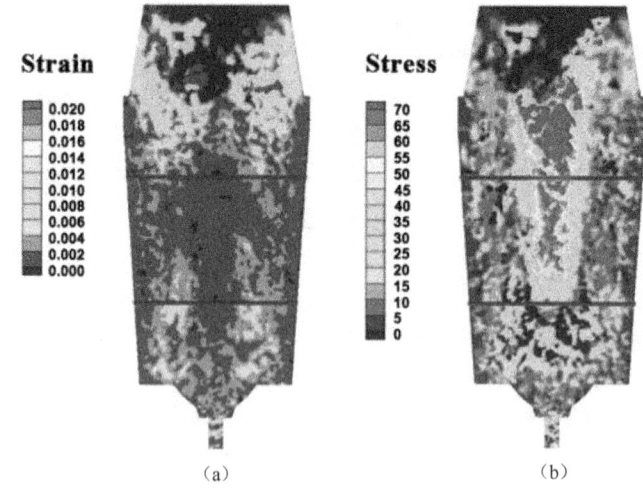

Fig. 10 (a) equivalent strain development in the longitudinal section within BTR, (b) equivalent stress development in the longitudinal section within BTR

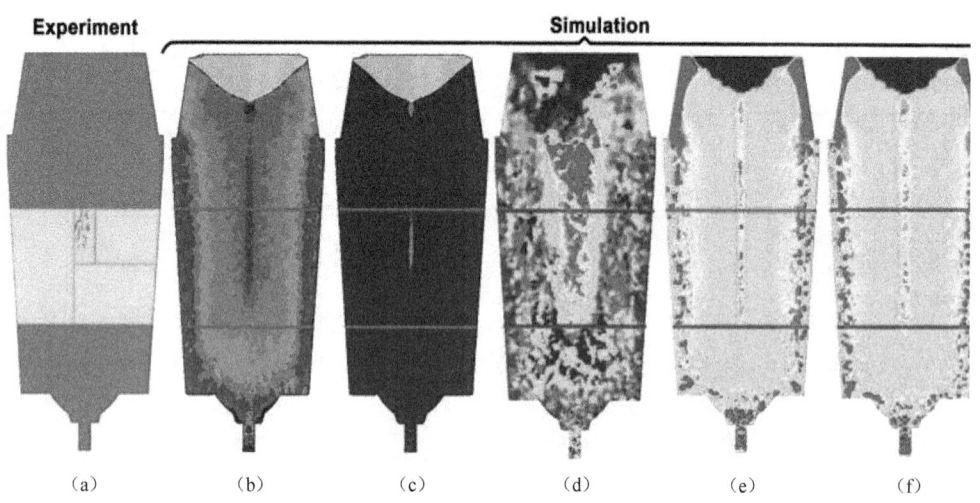

Fig. 11 (a) schematic diagram of crack-like defects in experiment, (b) shrinkage porosity in the longitudinal section of ingot, (c) Niyama values, (d) equivalent stress development within BTR, (e) HCS according to Clyne and Davies's criterion, (f) HCS according to Katgerman's criterion

tinuous liquid flm and develop under tensile stress when the mush is vulnerable, i. e. , within the brittle temperature range (BTR). Thermo-mechanical calculation by 3D FEM analysis based on ProCAST software was carried out and relative data were extracted and then processed by C++ programming to evaluate the hot crack susceptibility. Four criteria were used, two based only on thermal considerations and the others based both on thermal and mechanical considerations. The first two, Clyne and Davies's criterion and Katgerman's criterion, both successfully predicted the high hot crack susceptibility in the ingot center, but were not precise in the ingot chill zone. The latter two, Guo's criterion and WYSO's criterion both strain-based criteria, indicated low hot crack susceptibility in the ingot center.

The stresses and strains evolution and equivalent stress and strain development in the longitudinal section of ingots show that the stress exceeds the limits of noncoherent dendrite network, and then the strain develops over a critical value to initiate hot cracks. The critical value for strain should be an adaptive value considering the diversity of different parts of the ingot, such as porosity formation due to inadequate liquid feeding, mush zone embrittlement due to detrimental elements enrichment, coarse grain due to low undercooling degree, and so on. Therefore, more efforts should be made on numerical simulation to predict hot crack formation, considering the above mentioned factors and other relevant mechanisms.

References

[1] Chojecki A, Telejko I, and Bogacz T. Influence of chemical composition on the hot tearing formation of cast steel. Theoretical and Applied Fracture Mechanics, 1997, 27 (2): 99-105.

[2] Rappaz M, Drezet J M, Gremaud M. A new hot-tearing criterion. Metallurgical and Materials Transactions A, 1999, 30 (2): 449-455.

[3] Won Y M, Yeo T, Seol D J, et al. A new criterion for internal crack formation in continuously cast steels. Metallurgical and Materials Transactions B, 2000, 31 (4): 779-794.

[4] Drezet J M and Rappaz M. Prediction of hot tears in DC-cast aluminum billets. Light Metals: Proceedings of Sessions, TMS Annual Meeting (Warrendale, Pennsylvania), New Orleans, LA, United states, 2001, 887-893.

[5] Olivier C, Yvan C, and Michel B. Hot tearing in steels during solidification: Experimental Characterization and Thermomechanical Modeling. Journal of Engineering Materials and Technology, 2008, 130 (2): 21018.

[6] Bellet M, Cerri O, Bobadilla M, Chastel Y. Modeling hot tearing during solidification of steels: assessment and improvement of macroscopic criteria through the analysis of two experimental tests. Metallurgical and Materials Transactions A, 2009, 40 (11): 2705-2717.

[7] Ridolfi M R. Hot tearing modeling: a microstructural approach applied to steel solidification. Metallurgical and Materials Transactions B, 2014, 45 (4): 1425-1438.

[8] M'Hamdi M and Mo A. Microporosity and other mushy zone phenomena associated with hot tearing. Light Metals: Proceedings of Sessions, TMS Annual Meeting (Warrendale, Pennsylvania), Seattle, WA, United states, 2002, 709-716.

[9] Hatami N, Babaei R, Dadashzadeh M, et al. Modeling of hot tearing formation during solidification. Journal of Materials Processing Technology, 2008, 205 (1-3): 506-513.

[10] Suyitno S T, Kool W H, and Katgerman L. Hot tearing criteria evaluation for direct-chill casting of an Al-4.5pctCu alloy. Metallurgical and Materials Transactions A, 2005, 36 (6): 1537-1546.

[11] Katgerman L. Mathematical model for hot cracking of aluminum alloys during D. C. casting. Journal of Metals, 1982, 34 (2): 46-49.

[12] Guo J and Zhu J Z. Prediction of hot tearing during alloy solidification. Proceedings of the 5th Decennial International Conference on Solidification Processing, 2007: 549-553.

[13] Eskin D G and Katgerman L. A Quest for a New Hot Tearing Criterion. Metallurgical and Materials Transactions A, 2007, 38 (7): 1511-1519.

[14] Pequet C, Gremaud M, Rappaz M. Modeling of microporosity, macroporosity, and pipe-shrinkage formation during the solidification of alloys using a mushy-zone refinement method: Applications to aluminum alloys. Metallurgical and Materials Transactions A: Physical Metallurgy and Materials Science, 2002, 33 (7): 2095-2106.

[15] Won Y M, Kim K, Yeo T, et al. Effect of cooling rate on ZST, LIT and ZDT of carbon steels near melting point. ISIJ International, 1998, 38 (10): 1093-1099.

第 2 篇

学术会议报告

国际会议

1. Experience on Modeling of Casting and Solidification Processes
（铸造及凝固过程建模研究经验）

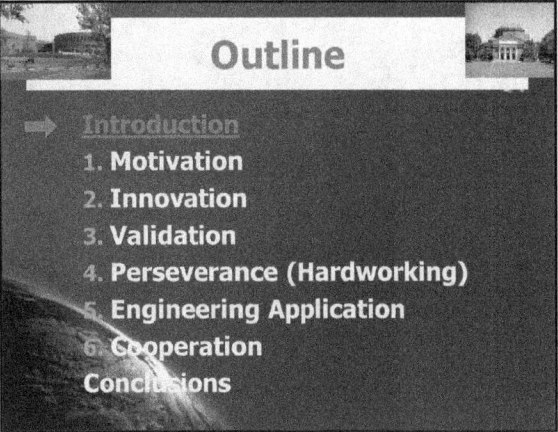
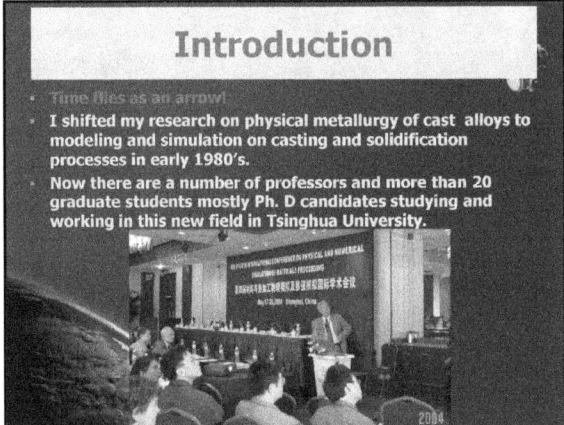

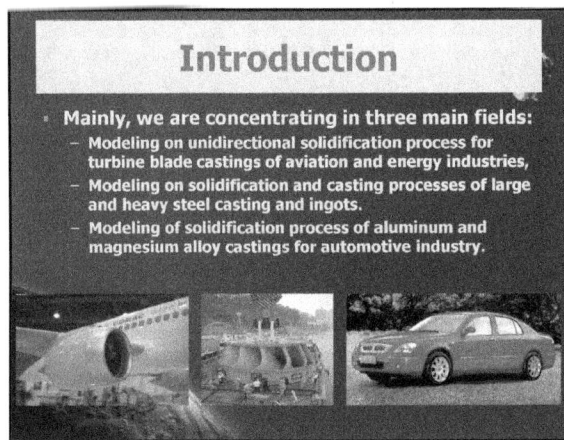
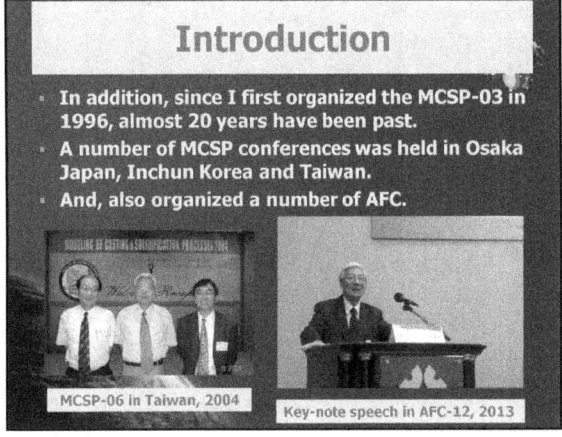

○ 本文为2014年第9届MCSP会议的大会主旨报告，会议地点为日本大阪。

Introduction

- What are the lessons we have learned in these almost 30 years?
- What are my experiences which I would like to share with my colleagues, especially to our young scientists and students?
- In short, my experiences could be summarized in six words. Namely,
  - Motivation
  - Innovation
  - Validation
  - Perseverance
  - Industrial application
  - Cooperation

1. Motivation

China manufacturing industry is now the largest manufacturing industry in the world, but not strong comparing with developed countries.

CMI faces three main issues as follows:
1. Weak in innovation ability.
   - 2013: China: R&D/GDP=2.0%, while that of developed countries are more than 2.5%.
   - 2011: China manufacturing valued added rate is about 21.5%, while developed countries are more than 35%.
2. Weak also in design and manufacturing technology, especially lack of core and enabling technology, such as high value-added manufacturing technology.
3. Serious pollution and waste resource.

1. Motivation

Case One:
- All the aviation turbines (LEAP-X1C) for the new C919 passenger airplane will be imported from abroad.
- Core technologies for heavy duty turbines of energy industry also are relied on abroad.

1. Motivation

Case Two:
- The largest steel casting for forging press in the world was produced in China.
  Liquid steel: 830 tons, steel casting: 520 tons.

By courtesy of China CITIC Heavy Industries Co. Ltd

1. Motivation

Quality Issue - Macrosegregation: 560t steel ingot, vacuum melted and poured for rotor forging of nuclear power station.

By courtesy of China Second Heavy Machinery Manufacturing Group

1. Motivation

An Action Program for a strong manufacturing industry so called "China Manufacturing – 2025" was proposed by CAE in 2014.

- Therefore, facing those main issues of the manufacturing industries, the main motivation of my research group is to improve the casting quality, to optimize the processing parameters. And finally to shorten the R & D time and to reduce the R & D cost, by using Modeling and Simulation Technology.
- Of course, modeling and simulation are also the frontier of materials science and engineering. (so called ICME)

2. Innovation

- I always advice my graduate students especially Ph.D candidates that the doctorate theses could not only be fulfilled by using commercial software with some examples.
- Instead, new ideas, new method and new codes should be innovated or proposed.
- Which means, innovation will be the core part of the doctorate theses.

2. Innovation

Case one: Model for directional solidification process of turbine blade casting:

- Metal pouring and solidification process take place within the directional solidification furnace under vacuum.
- The furnace consists of a heating zone at the top, a cooling zone at the bottom and a baffle in the middle.
- The casting will be solidified when the chill is withdrawn into the cooling zone at a certain rate.

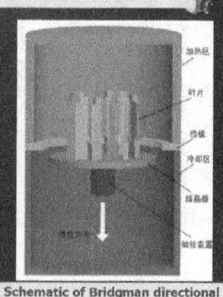

Schematic of Bridgman directional solidification process

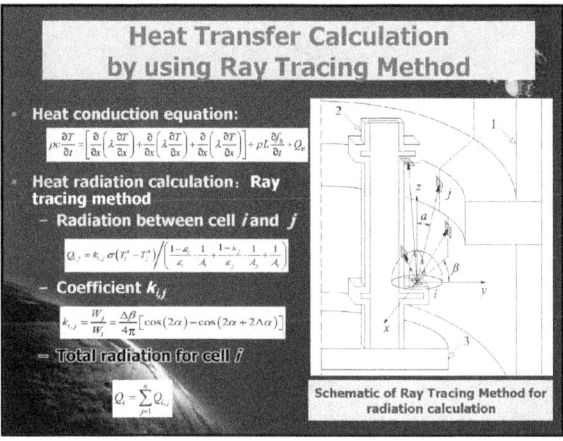
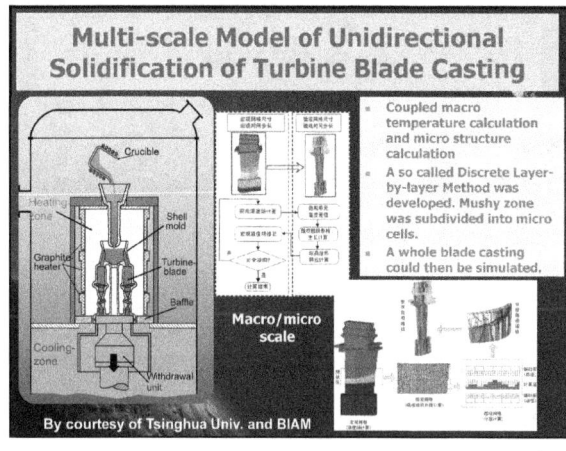
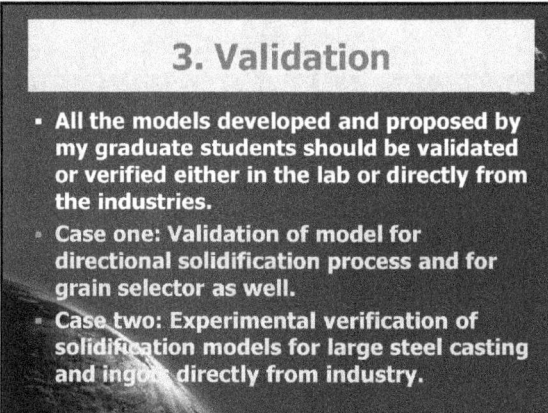
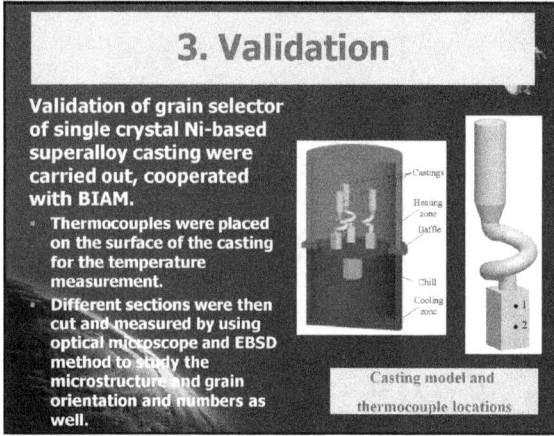
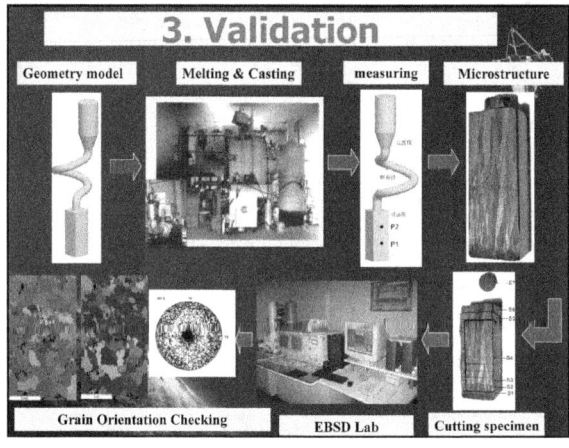
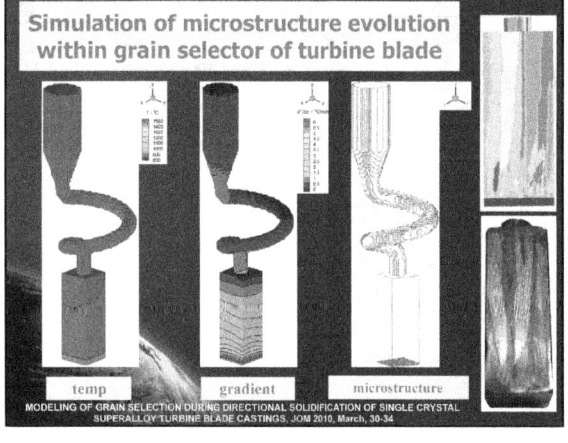
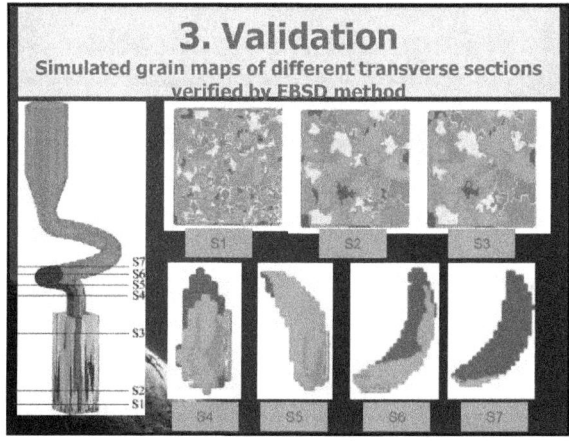
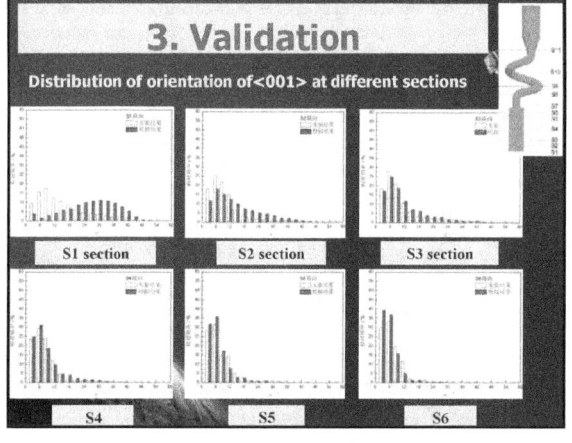

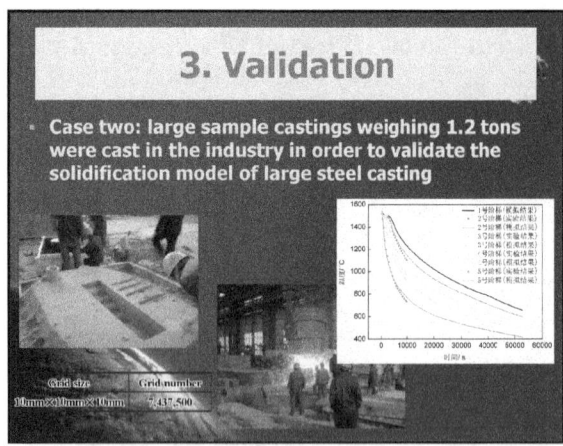
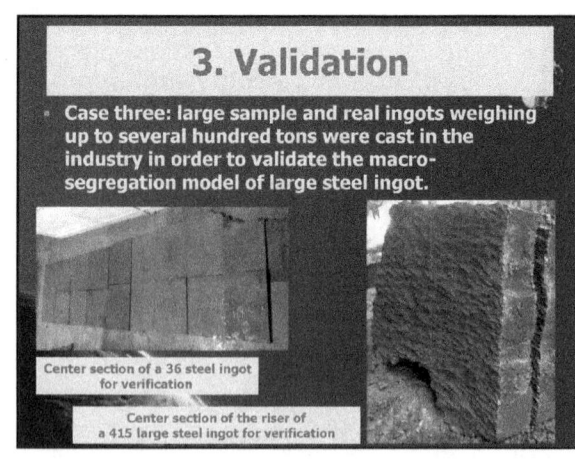
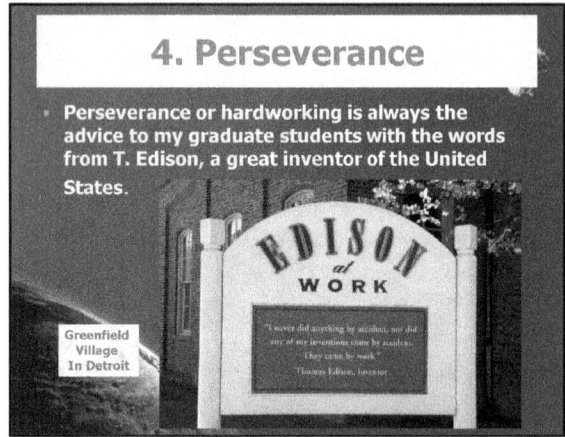
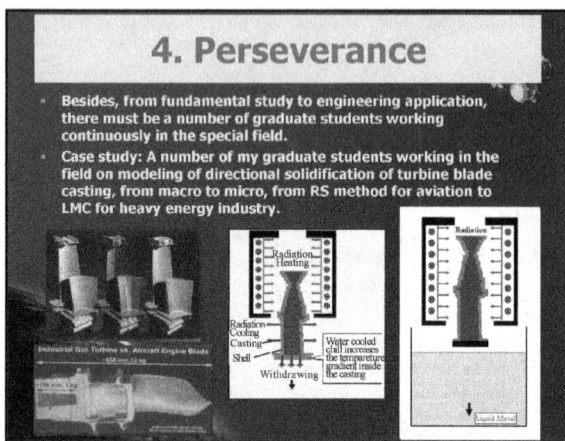
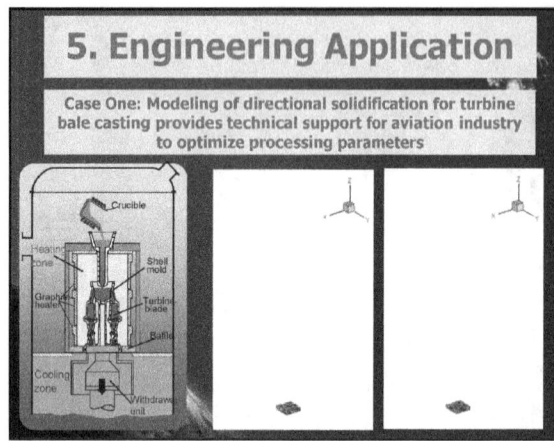
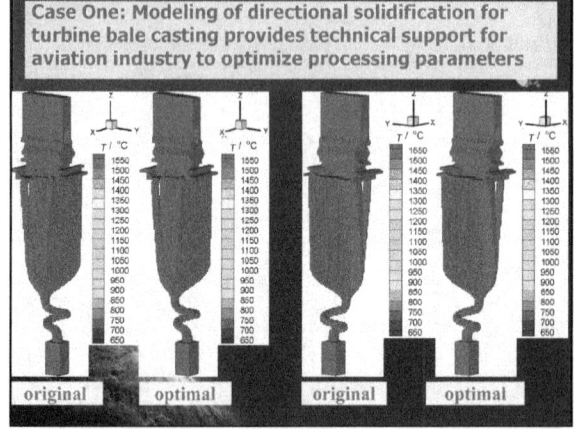
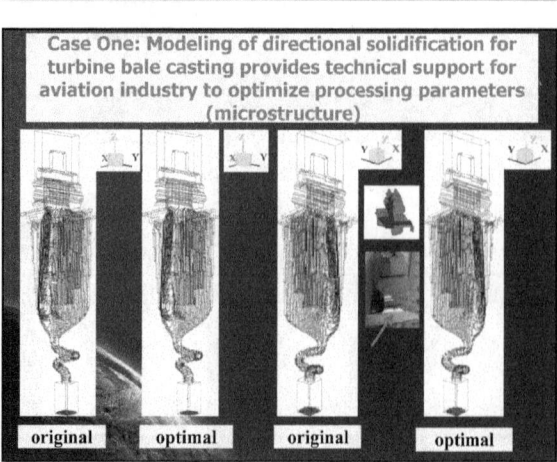
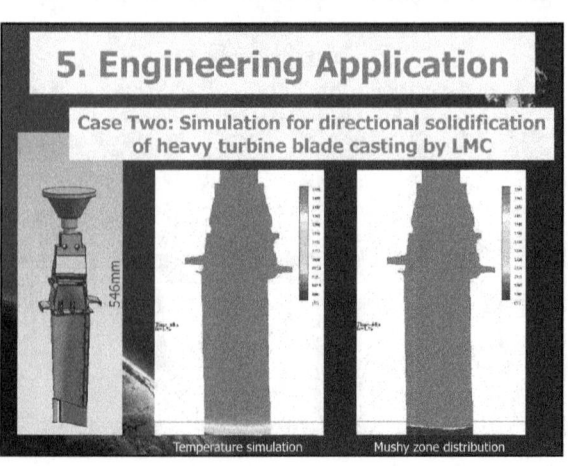

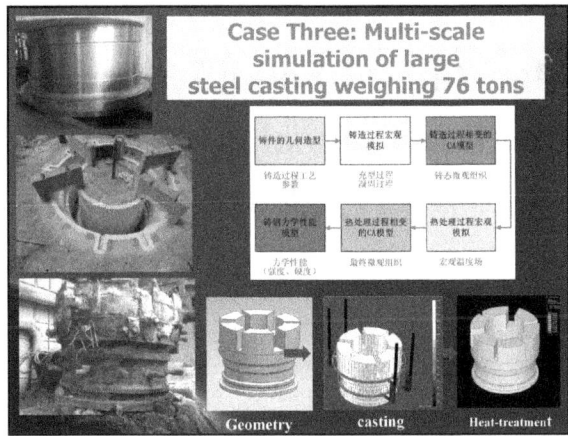

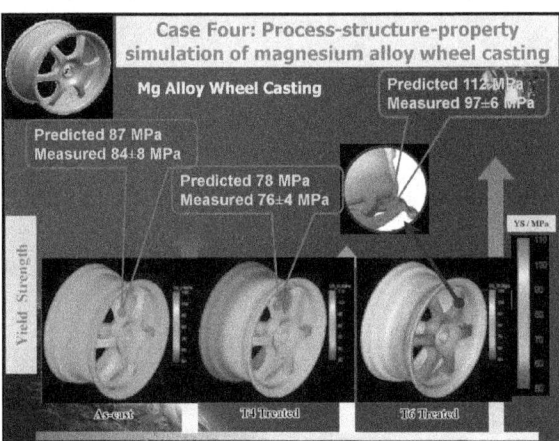

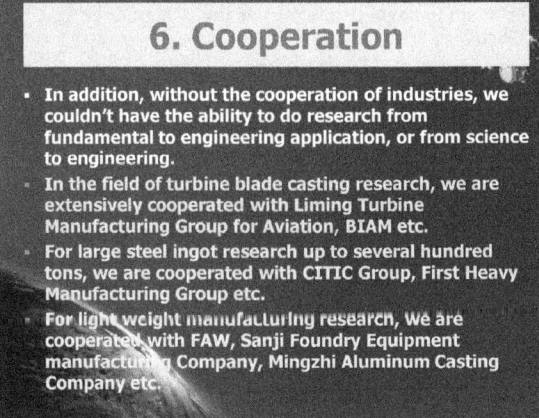

2. Progress on Multi-scale Modeling of Solidification Process of Advanced Casting Technology
（先进铸造技术凝固过程的多尺度建模研究进展）[一]

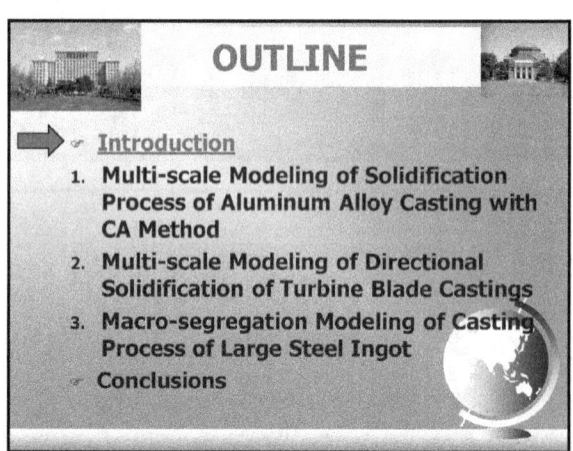

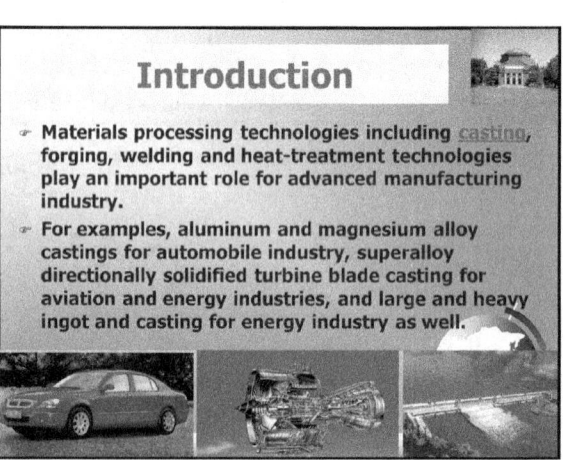
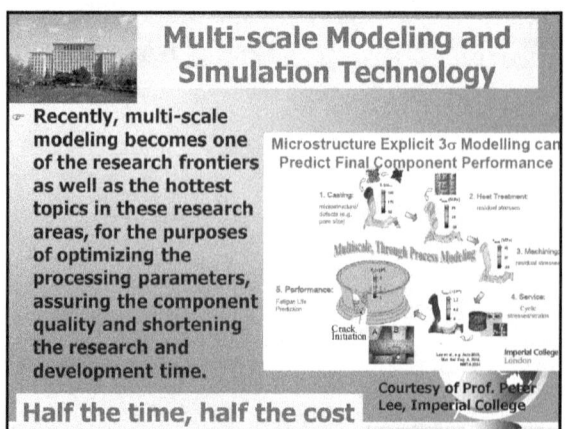
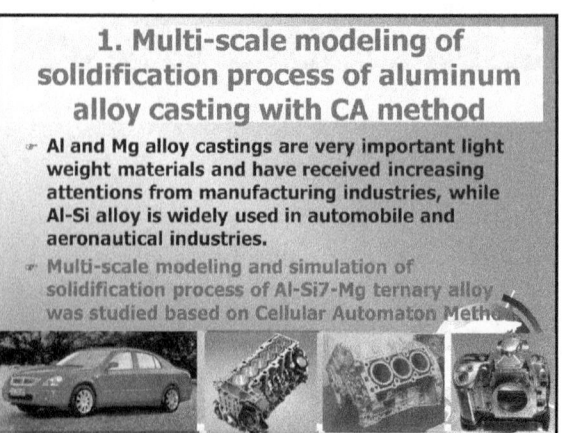

[一] 本文为"International Conference on Casting & Solidification Simulation for Foundry—2015"会议的大会主旨报告，会议地点为韩国。

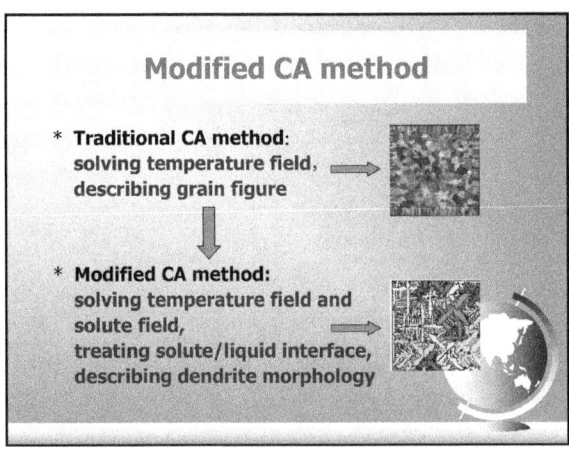
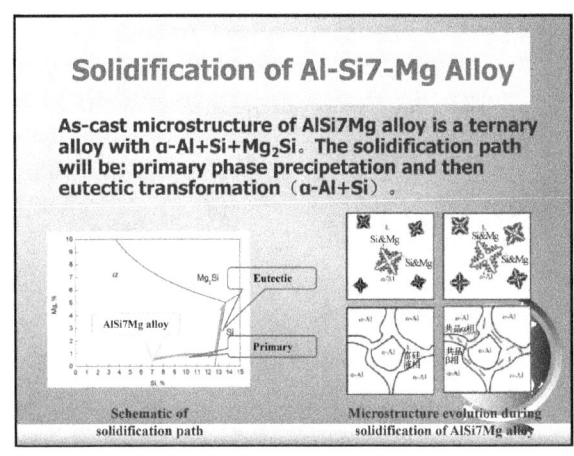
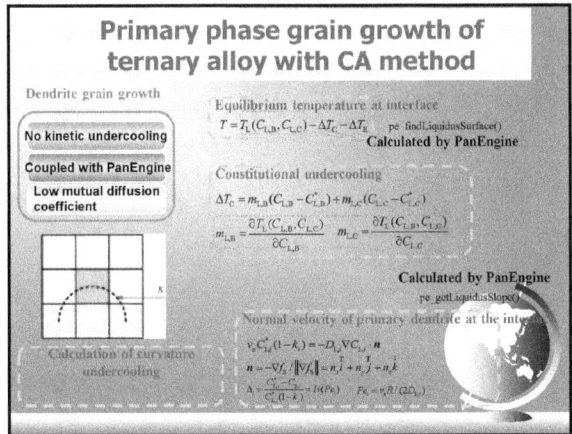
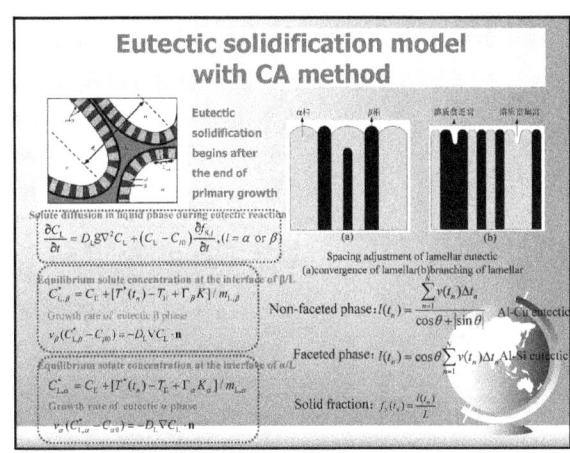
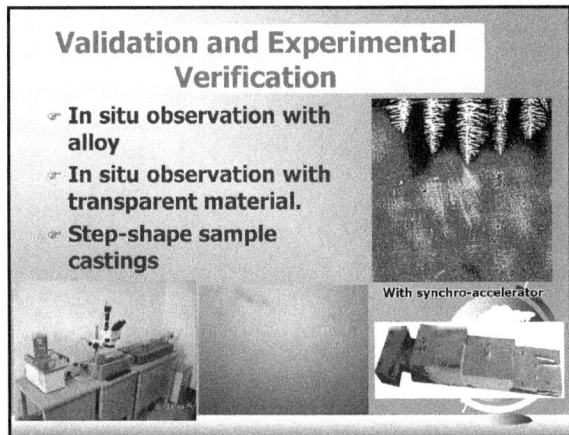
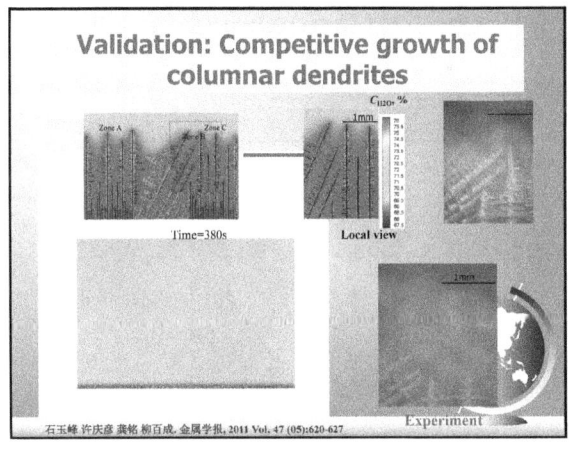
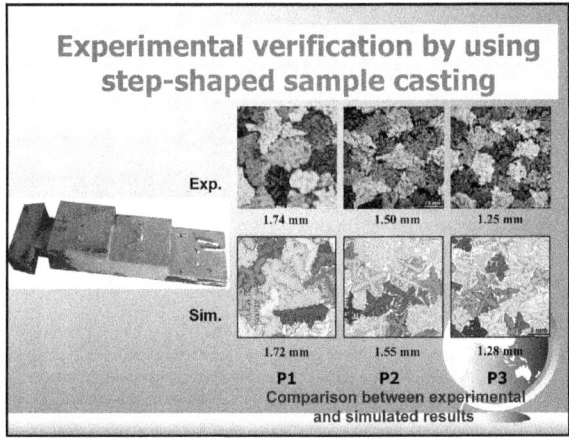
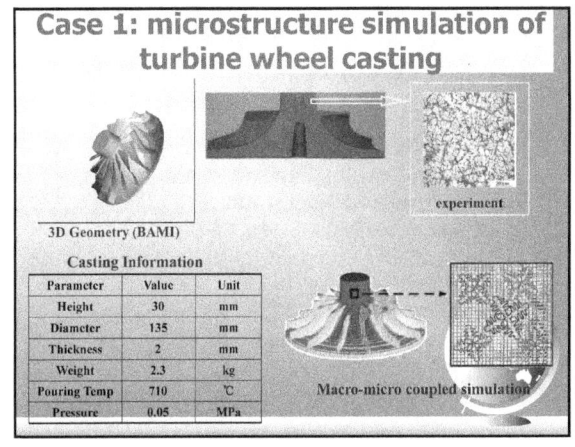

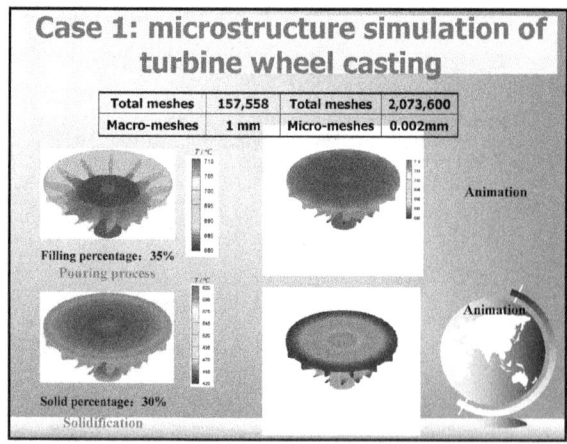
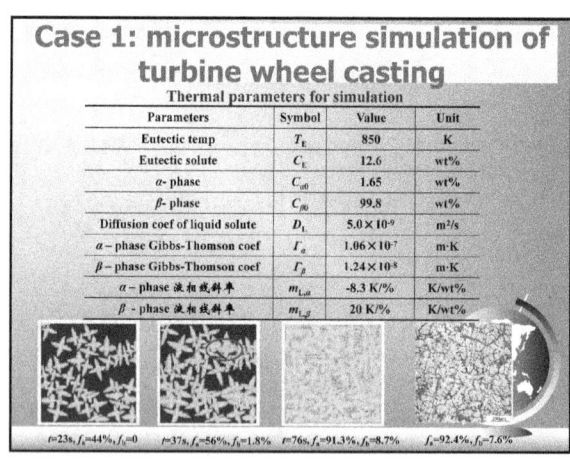
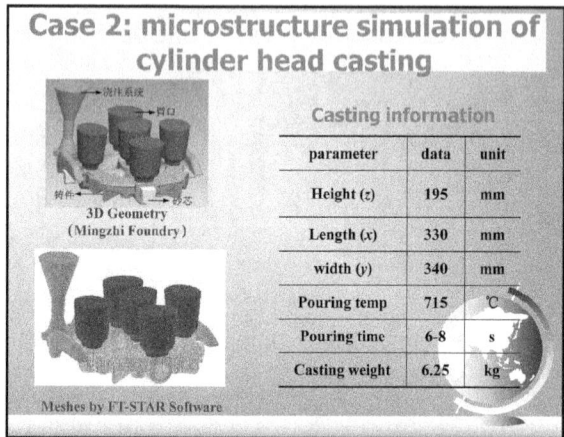
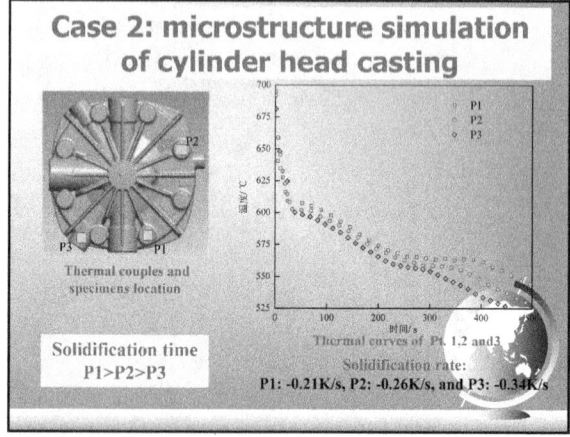
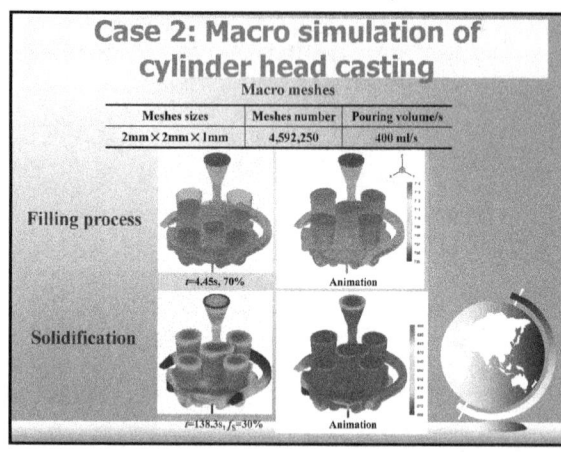
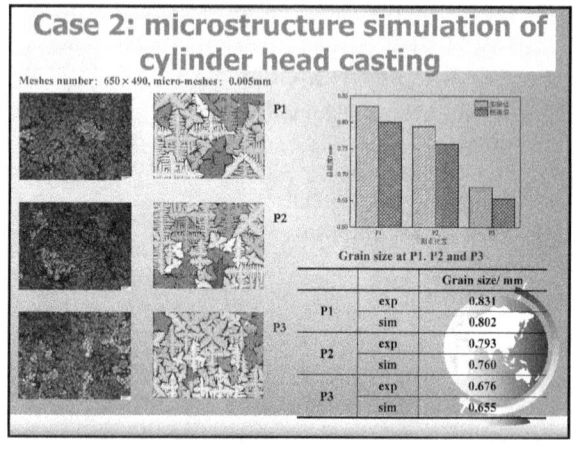
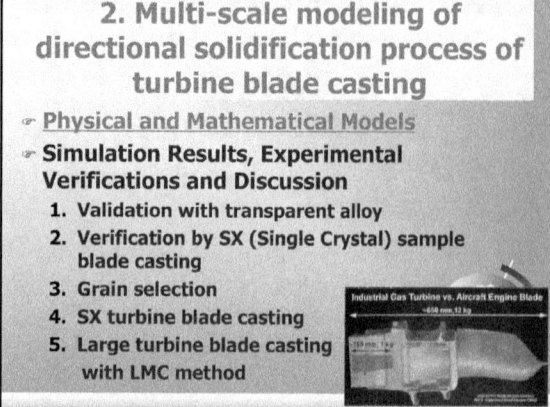
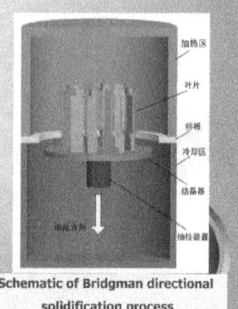

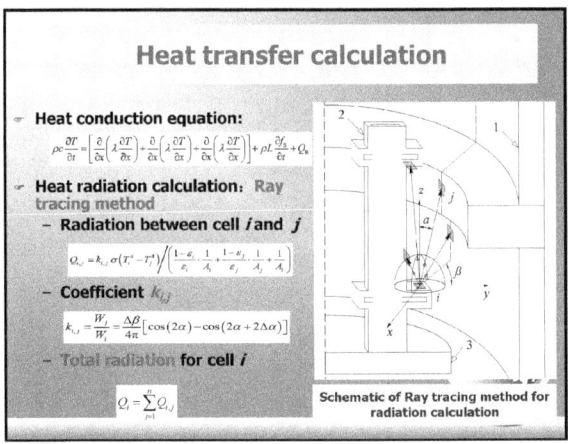
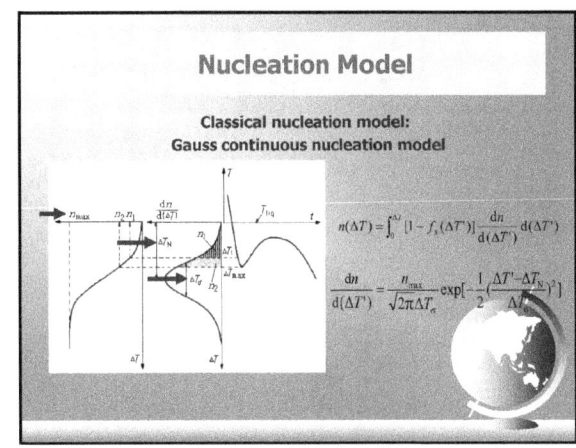
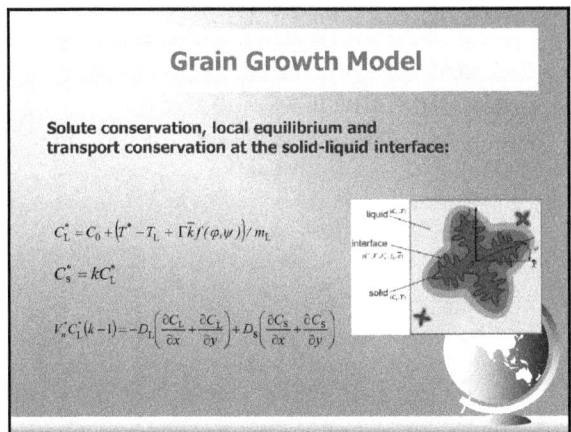
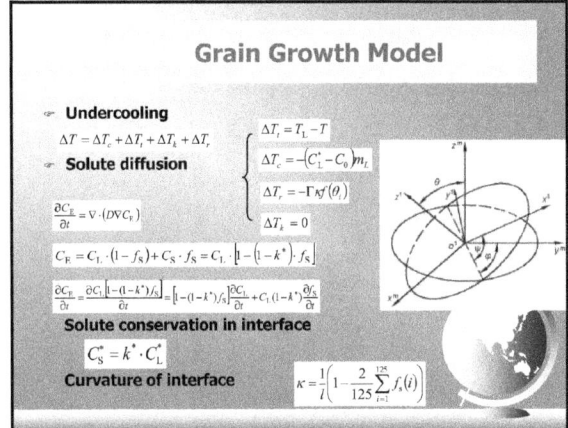
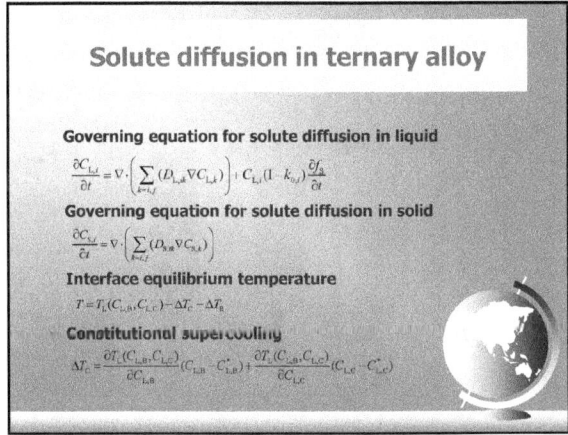
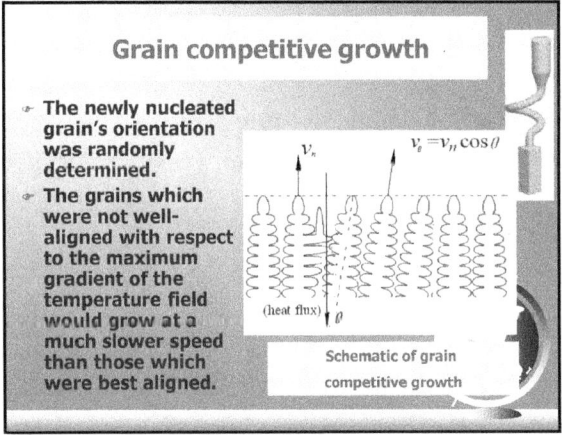
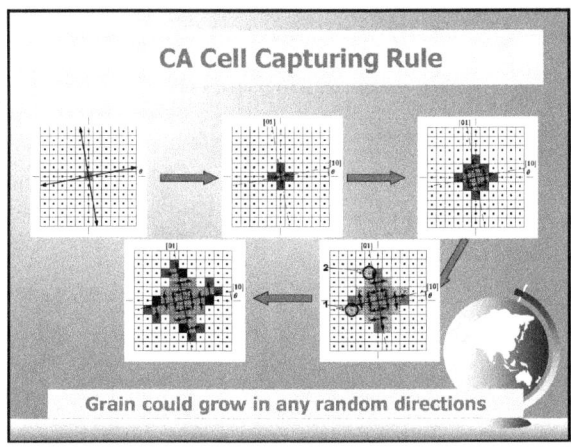
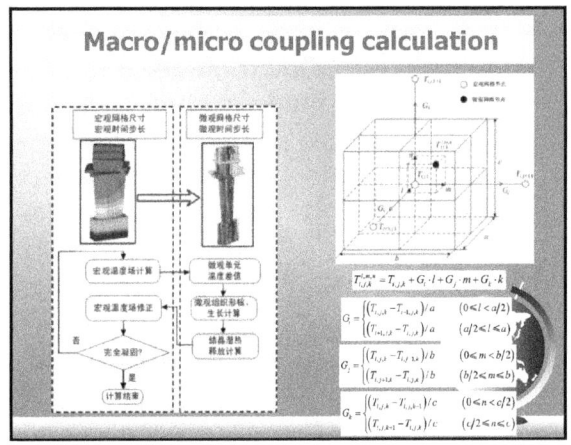

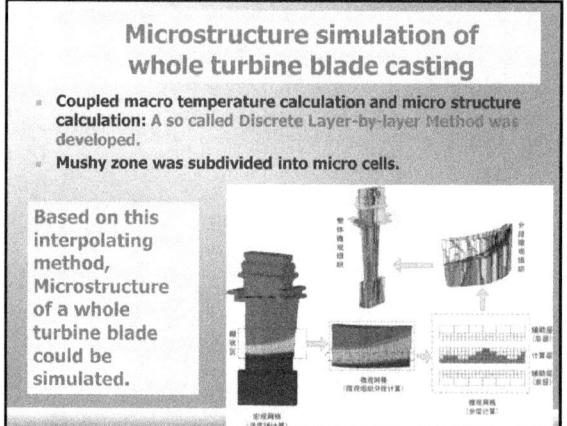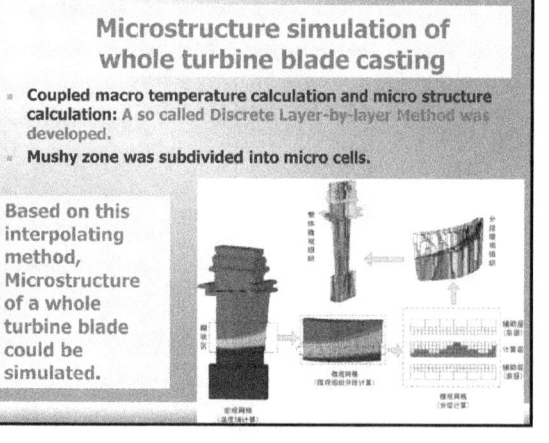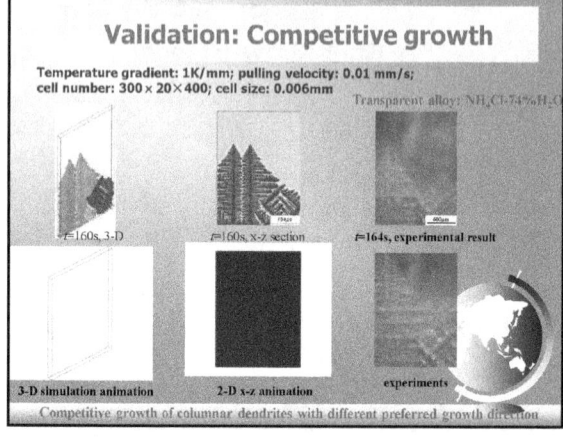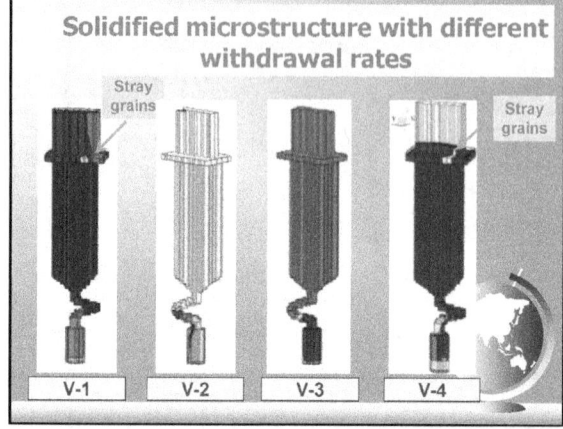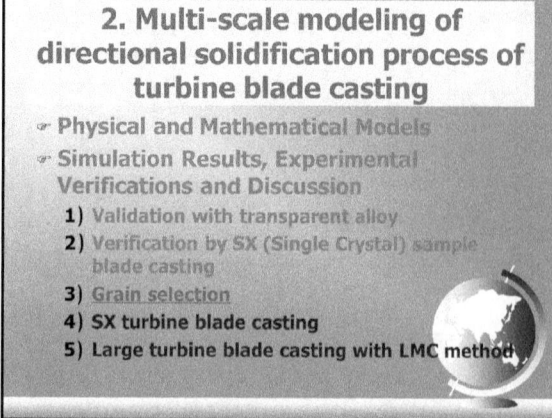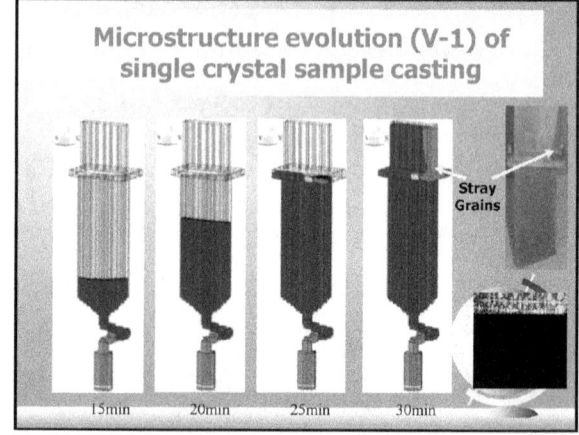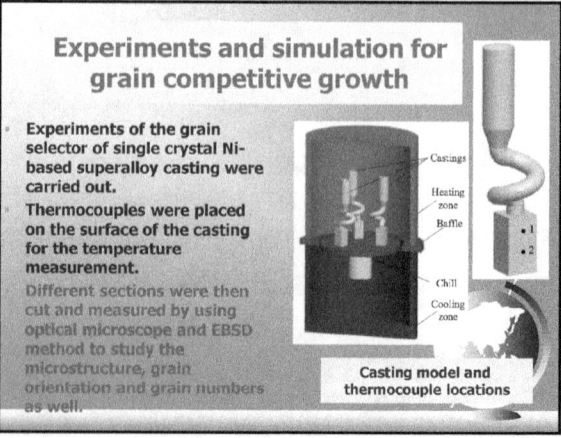

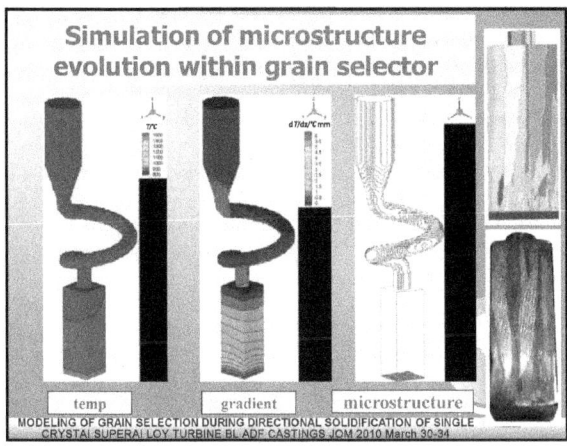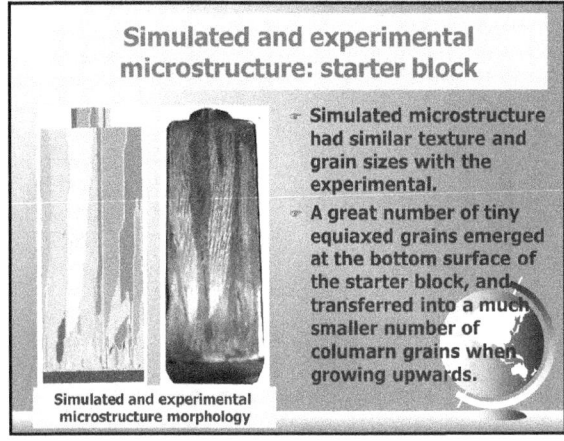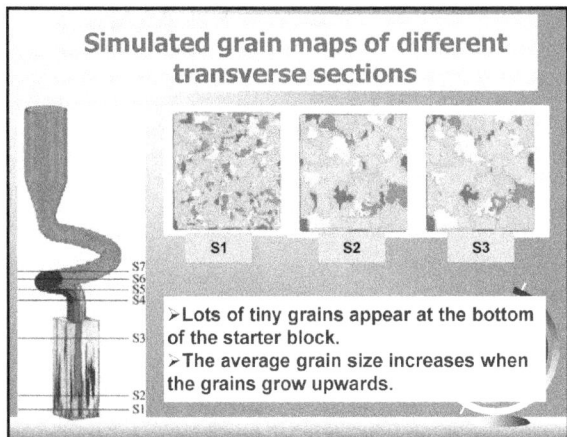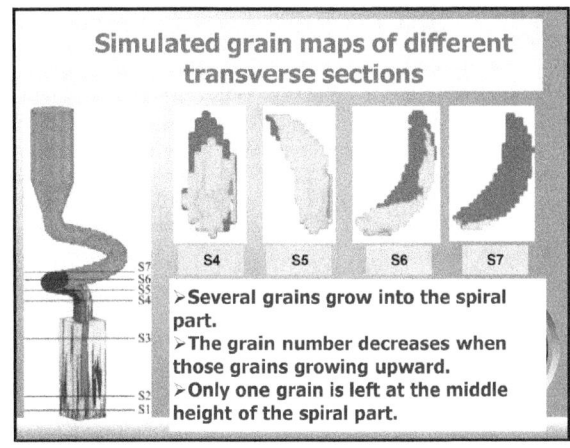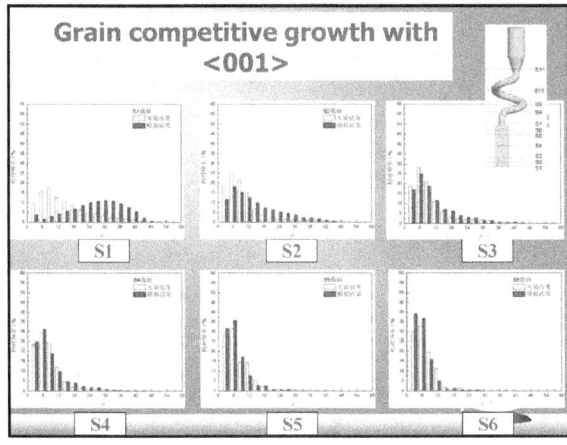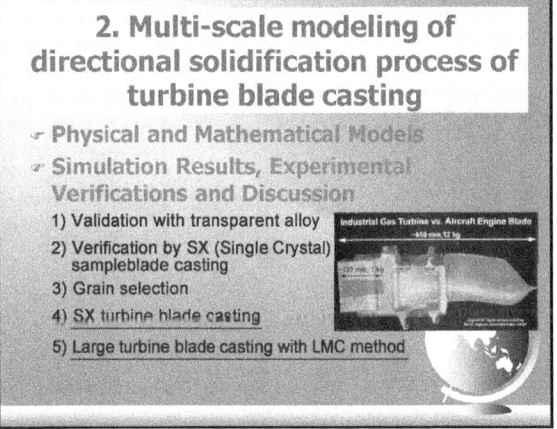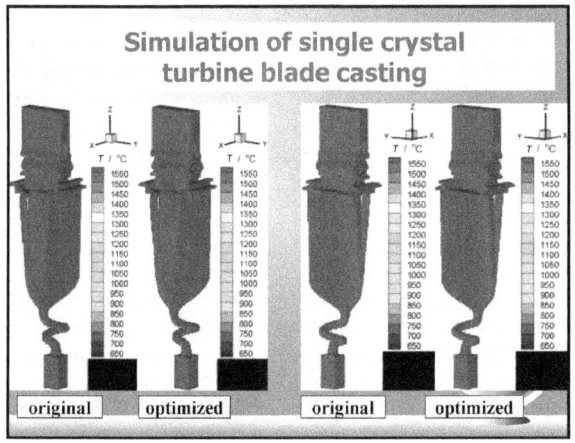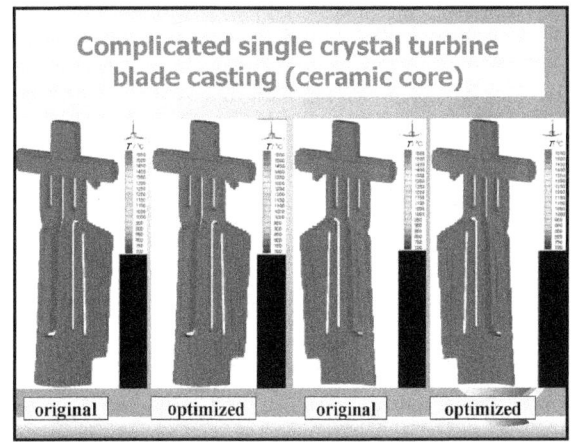

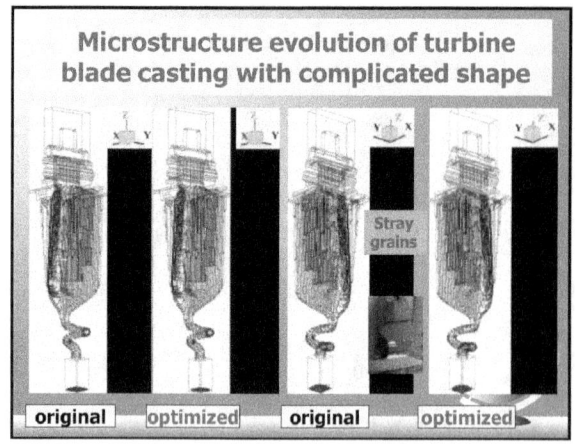
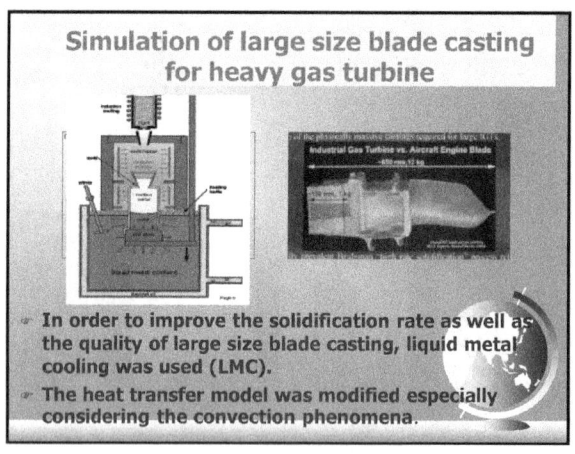
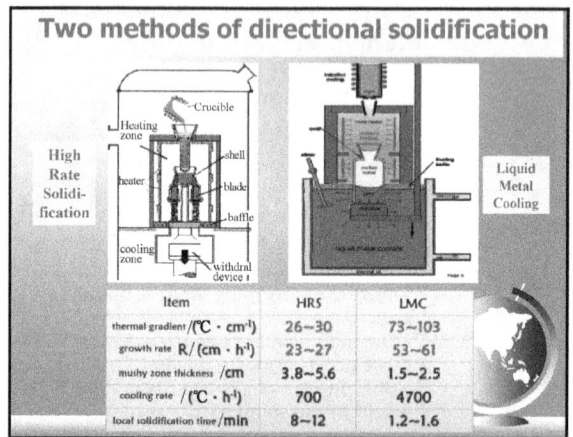
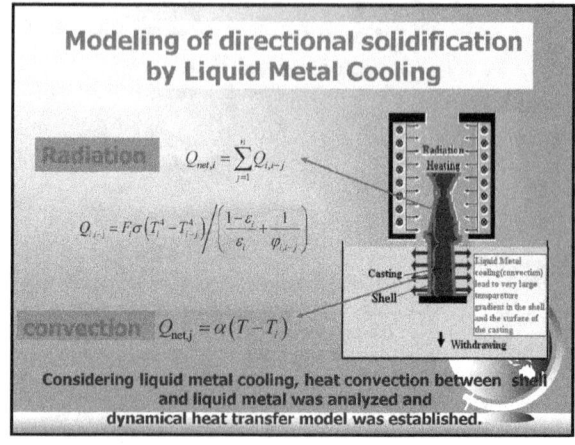
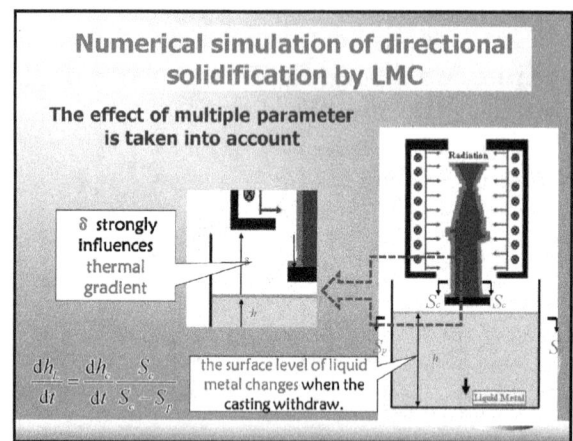
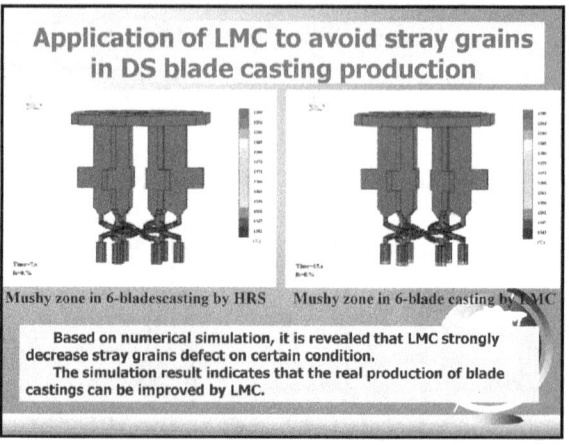
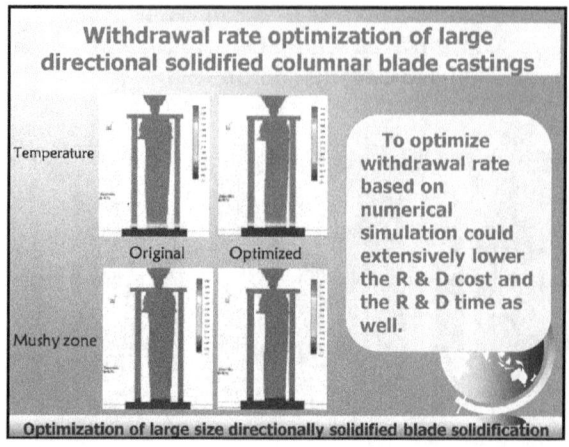

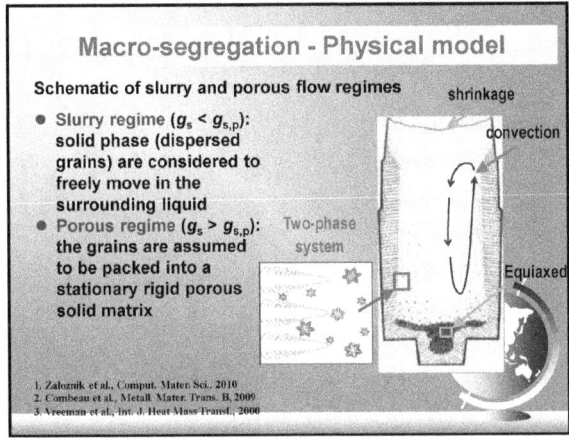
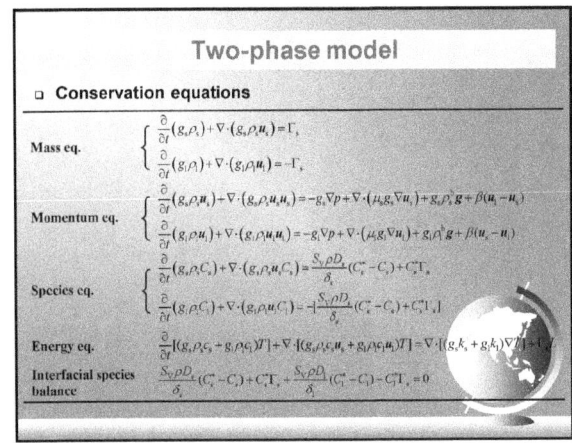
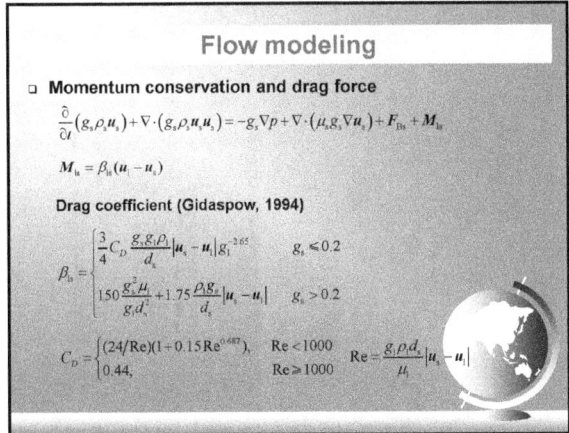
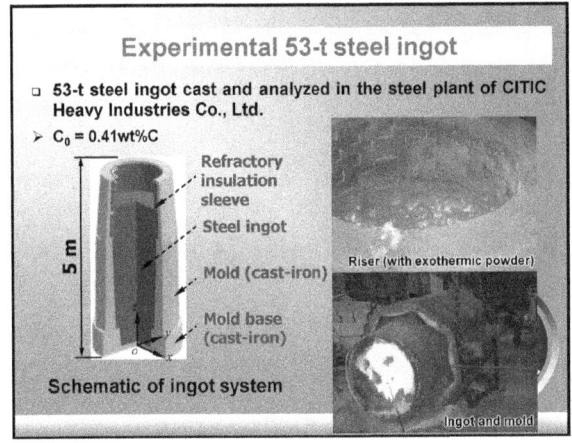
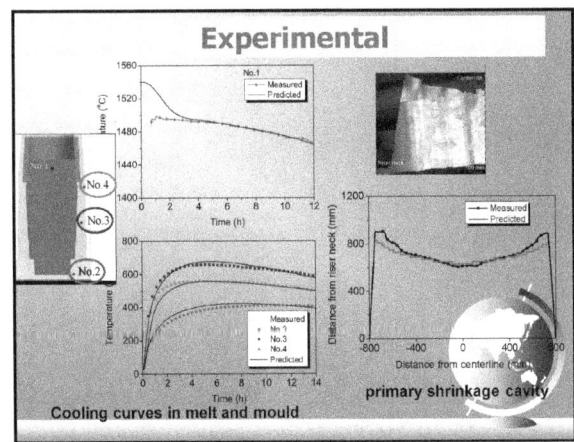
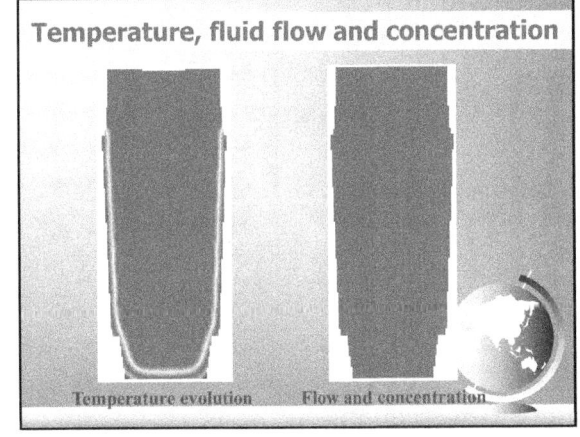
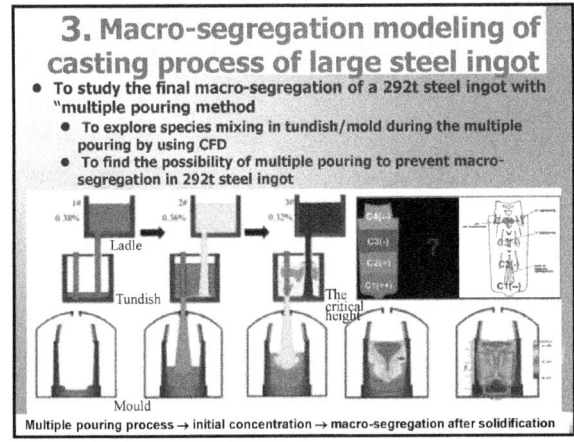
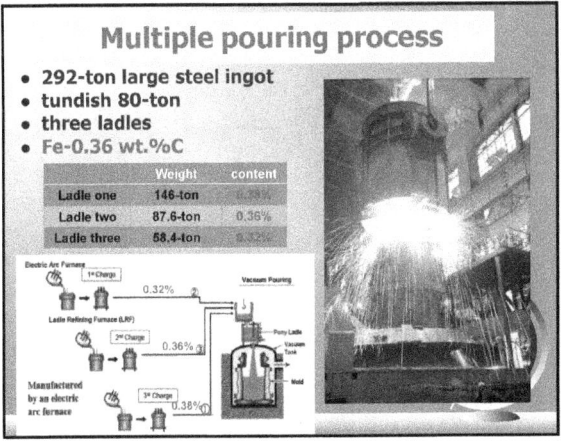

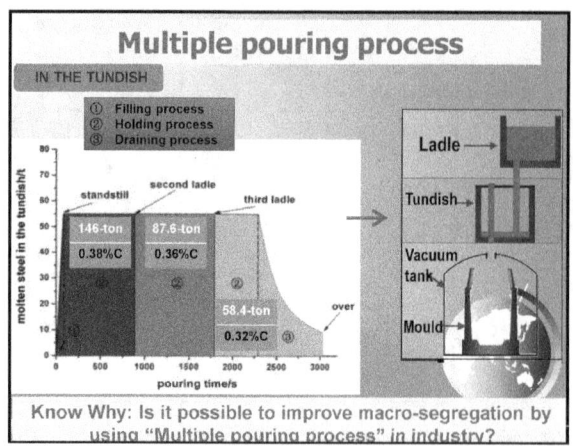
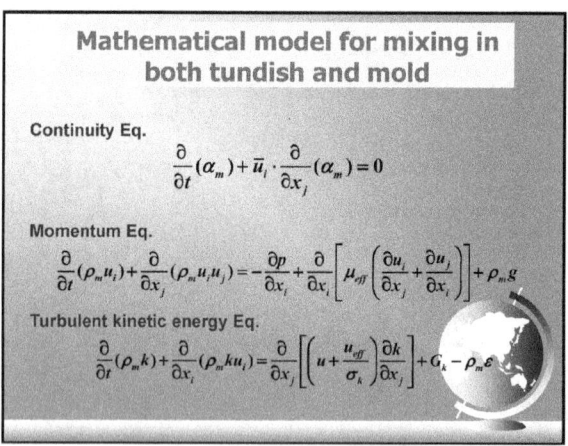
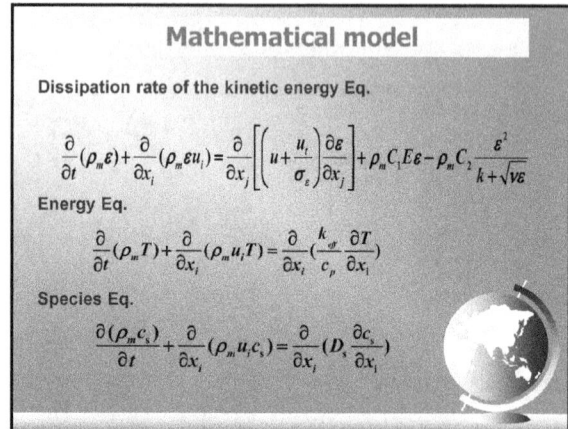
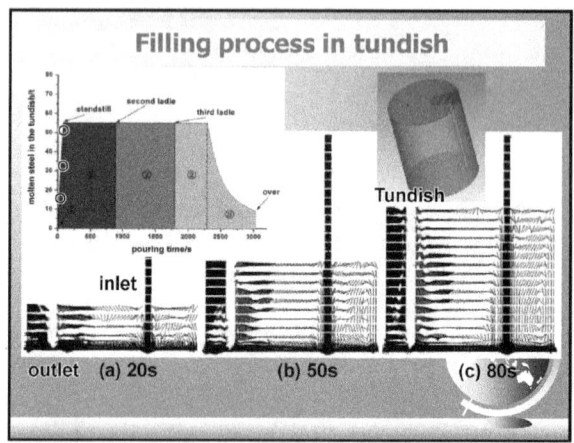
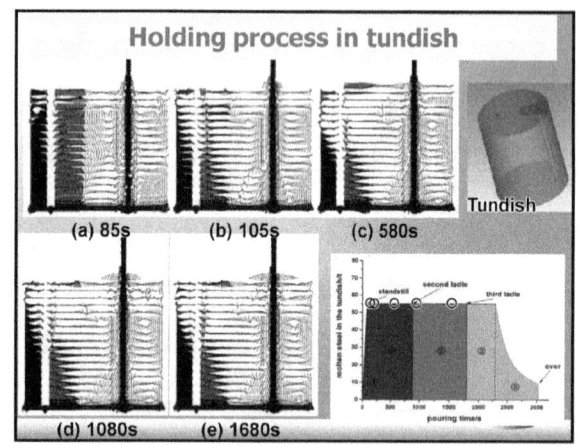
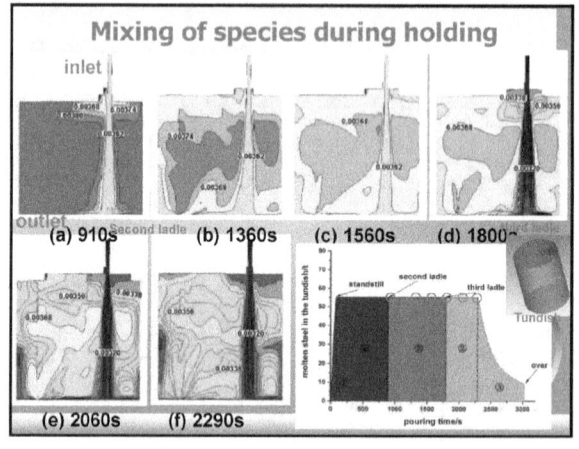
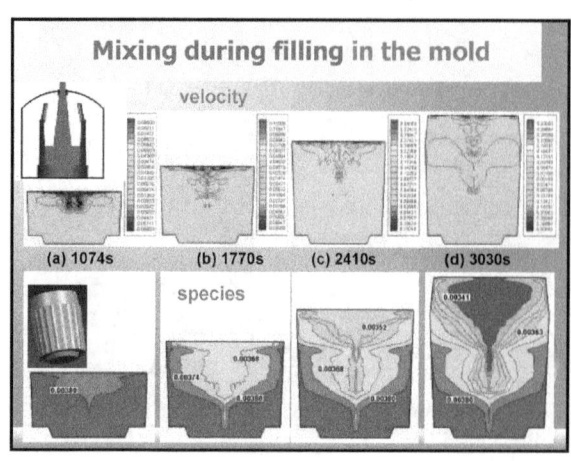
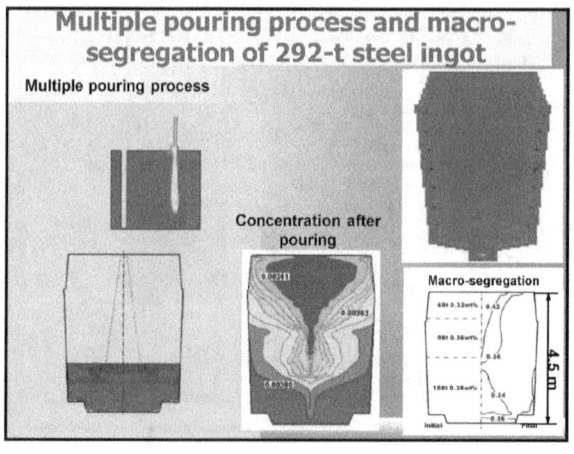

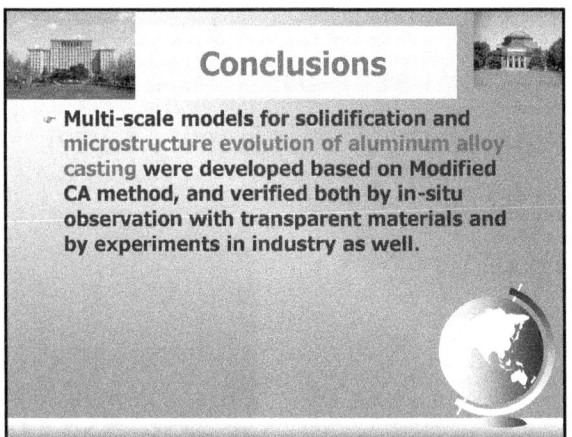

3. Numerical Simulation of Macrosegregation in Large Steel Ingot with Multicomponent and Multiphase Model （基于多成分和多相模型对大型钢锭中宏观偏析进行数值模拟研究）

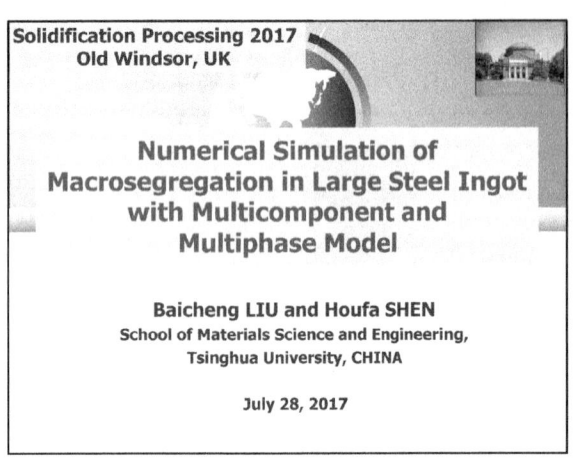
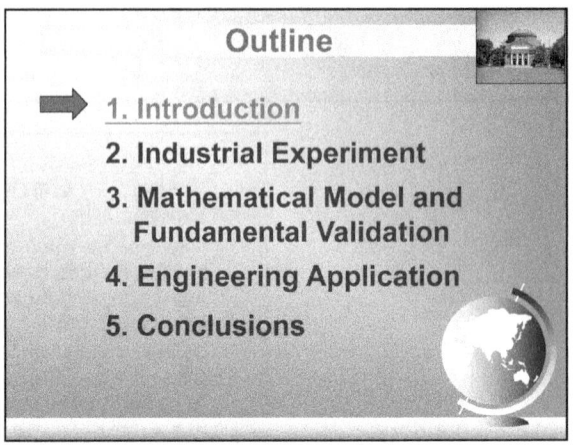
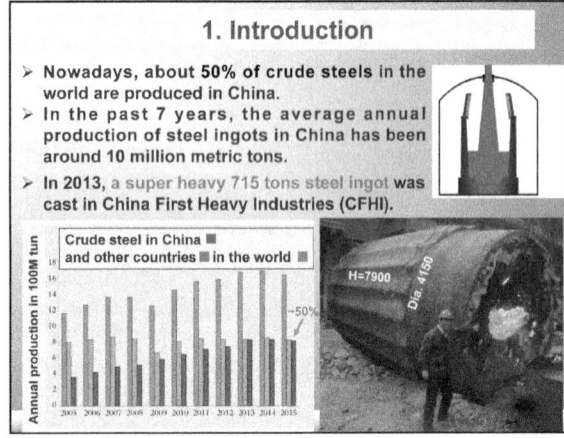
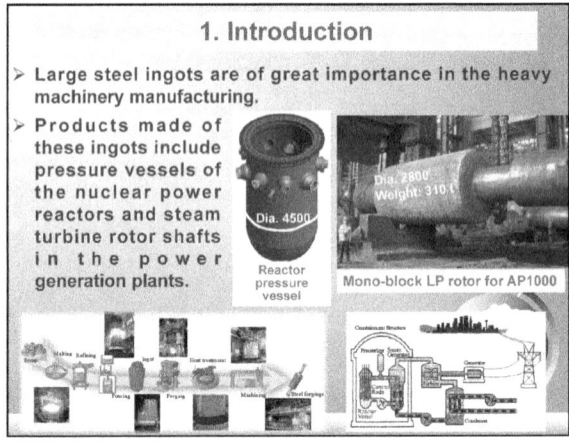
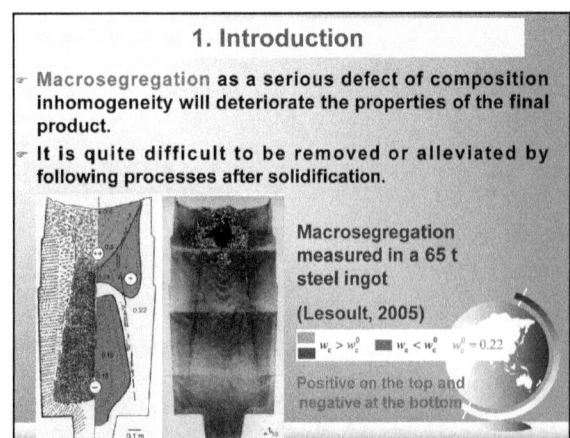
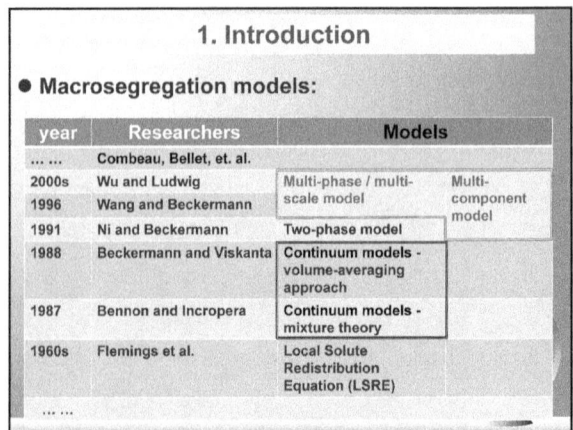

本文为2017年第7届国际凝固过程会议（Solidification Processing 2017）的大会主旨报告，会议地点为英国温莎。

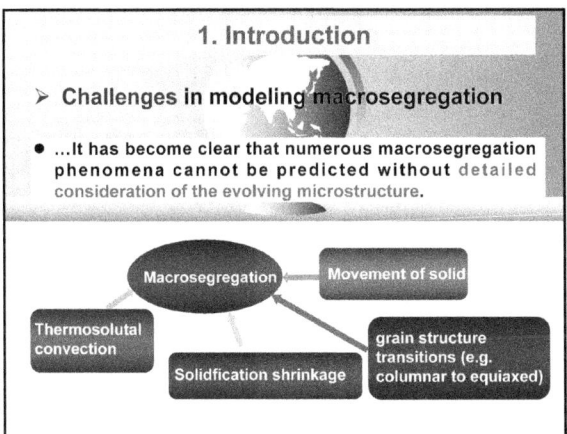
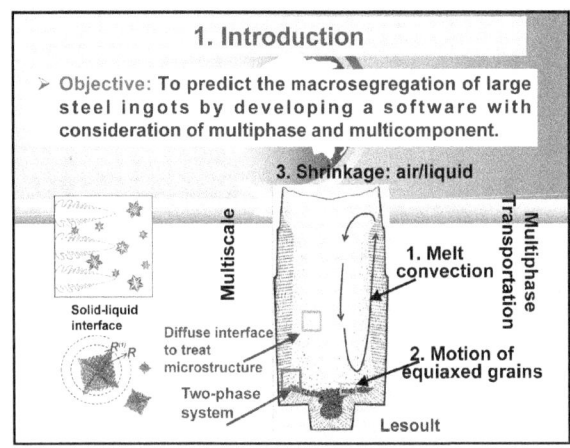
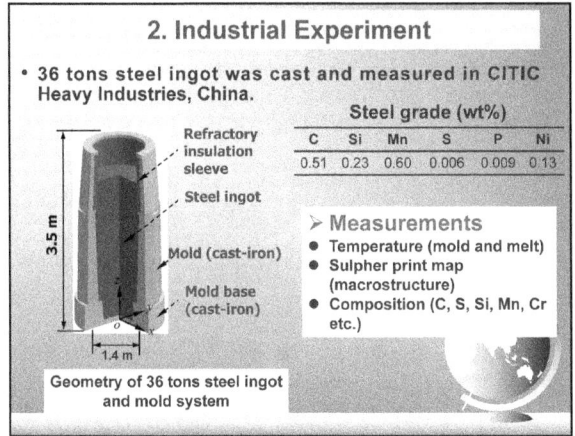
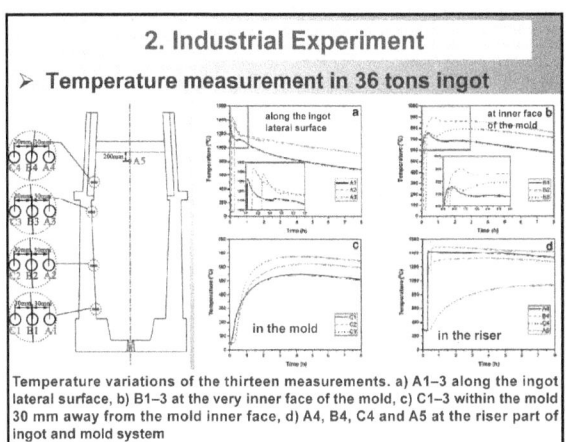
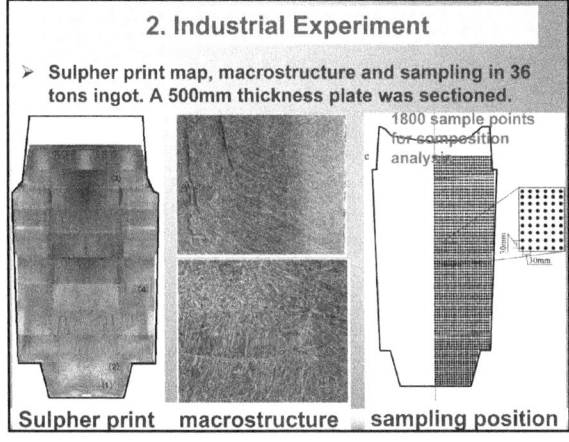
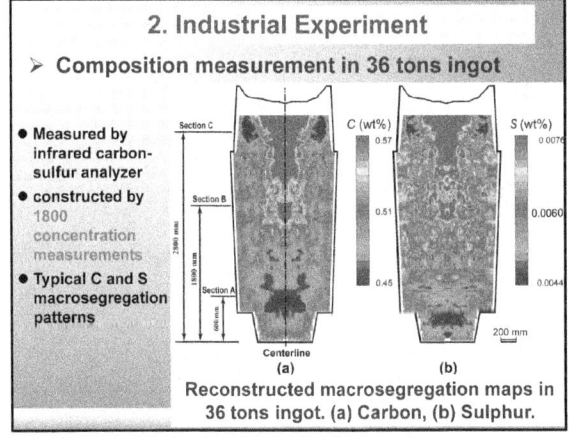
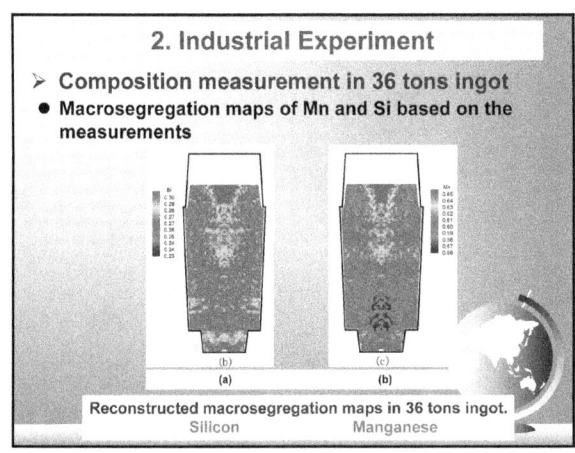
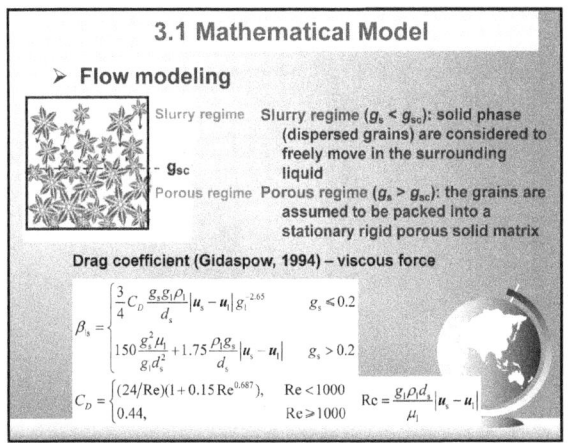

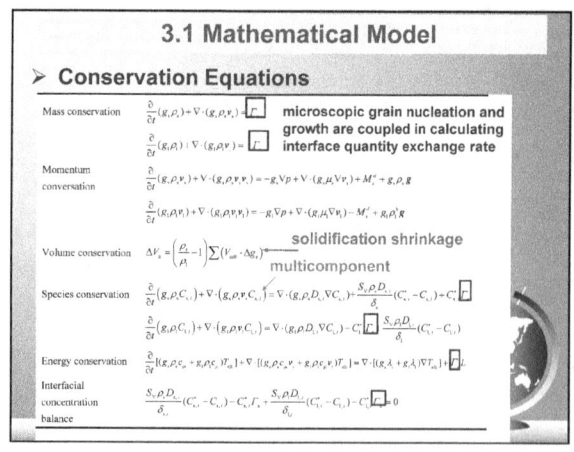
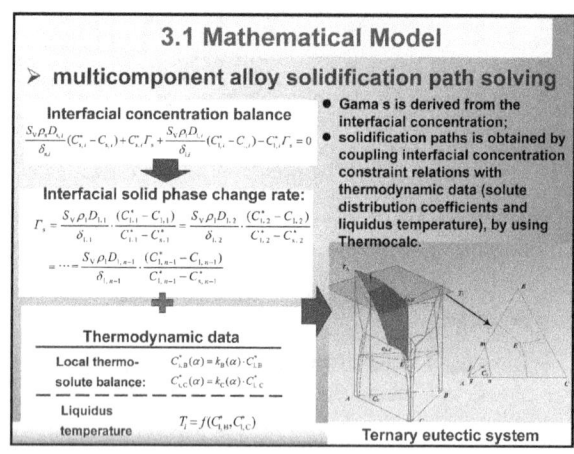
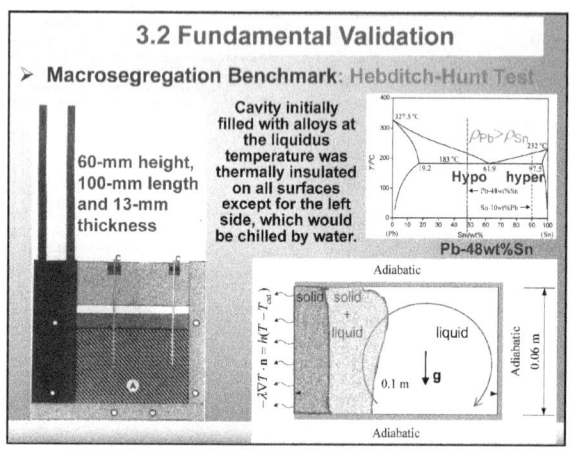
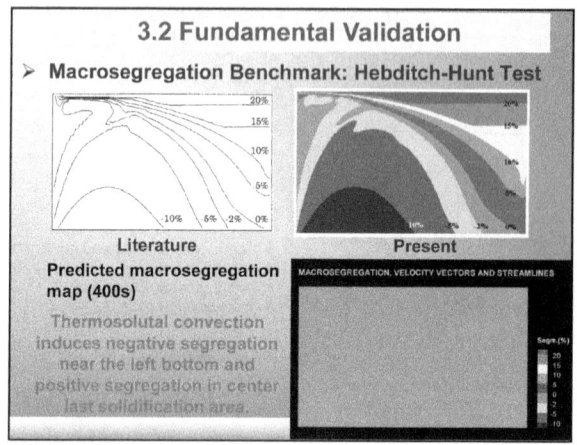
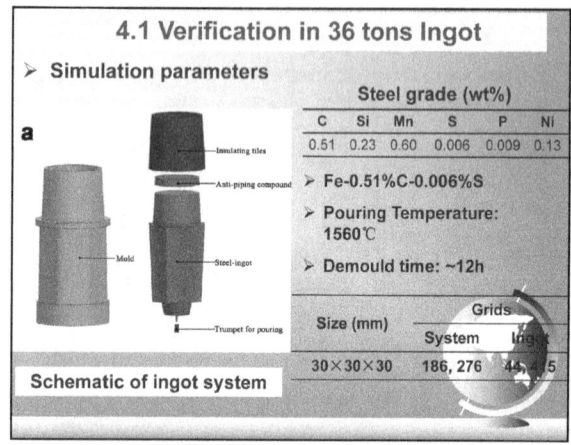
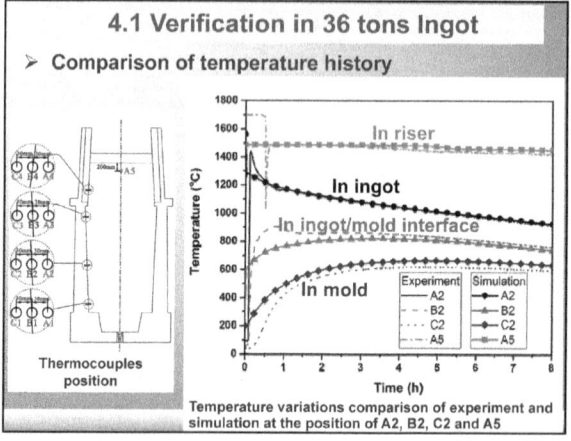
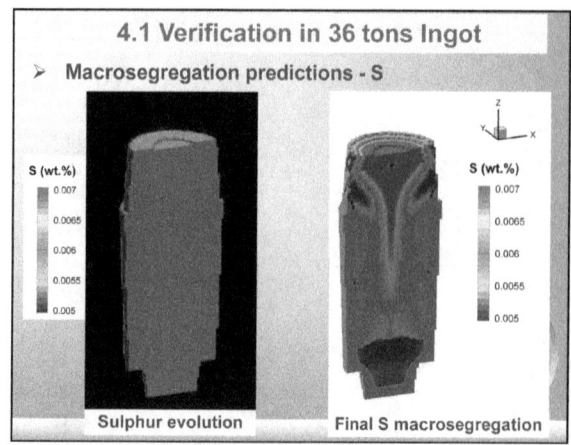
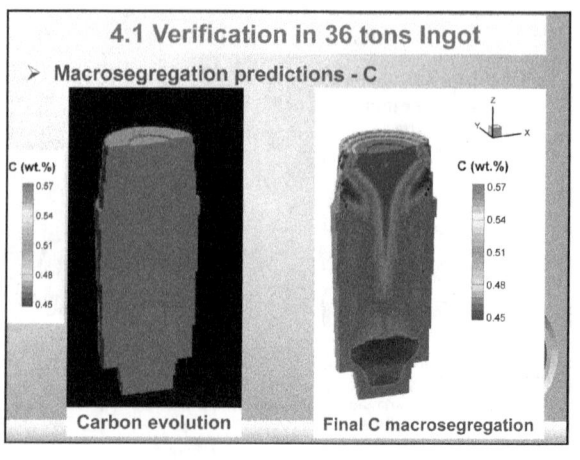

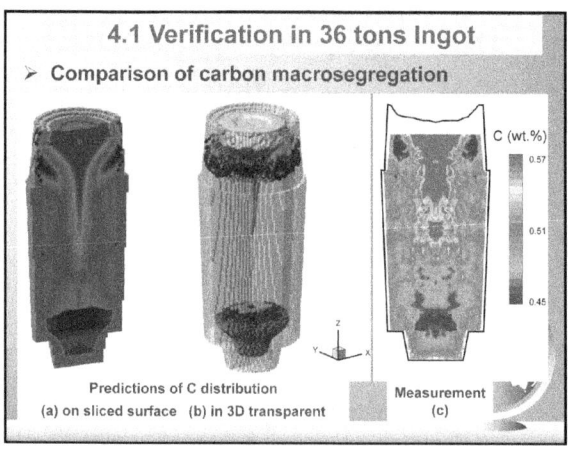
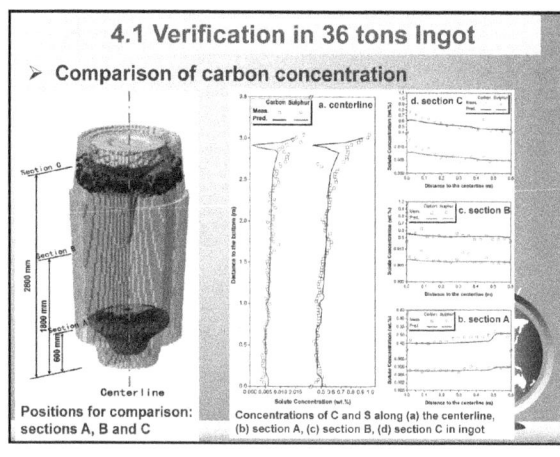
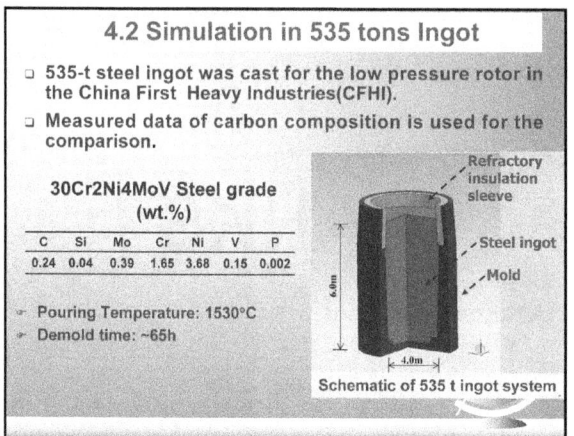
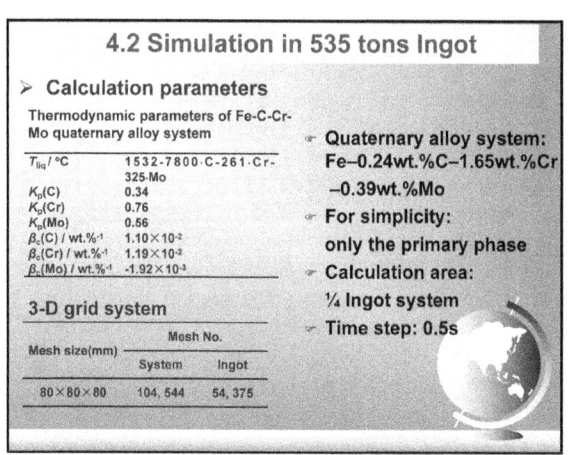
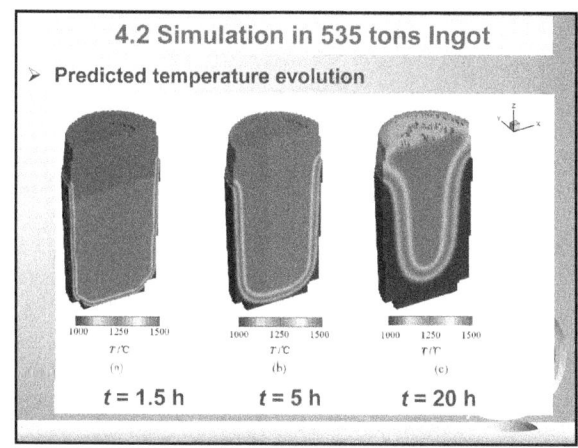
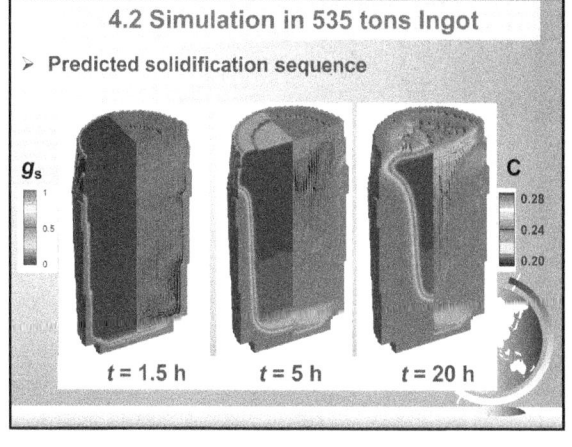
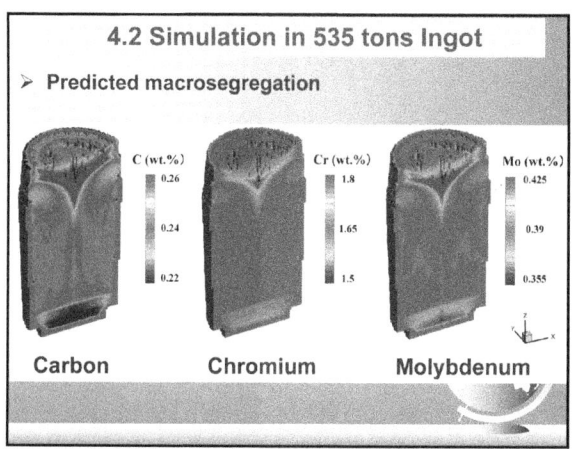
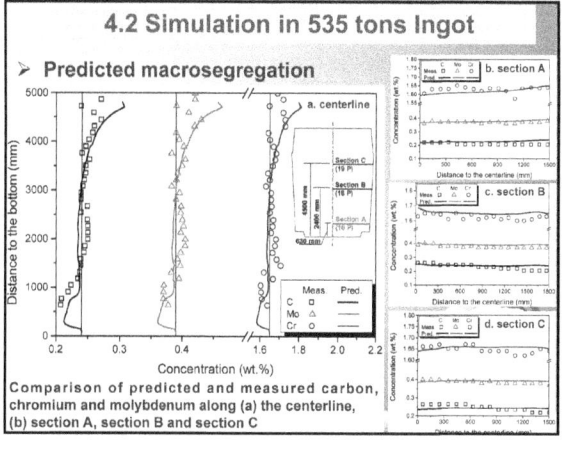

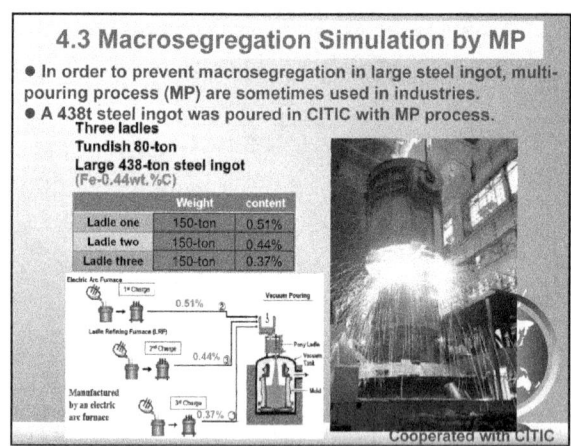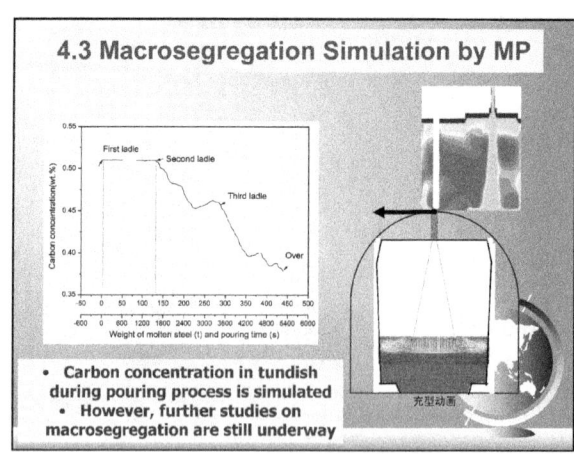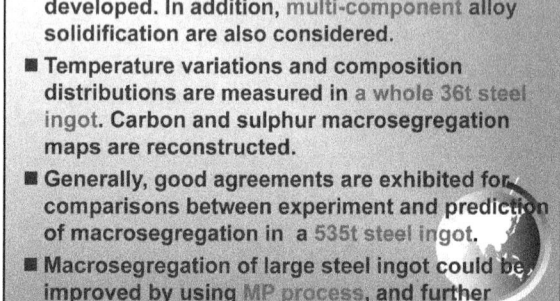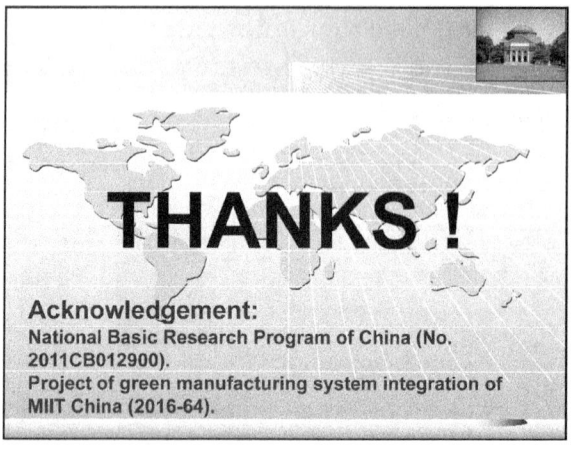

4. Multiscale Modeling and Simulation of Directional Solidification Process of Ni-based Superalloy Turbine Blade Casting
(镍基高温合金涡轮叶片铸件定向凝固过程的多尺度建模与仿真研究)

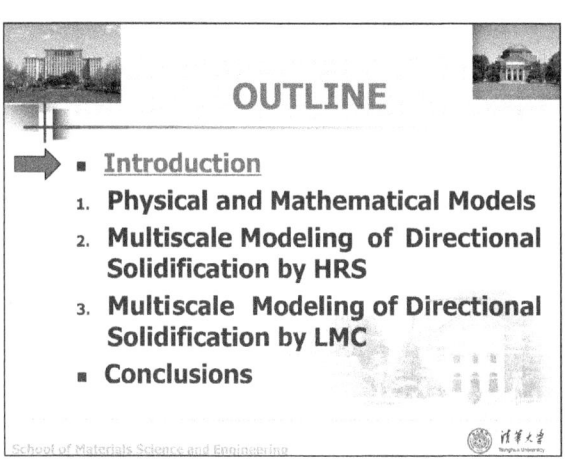

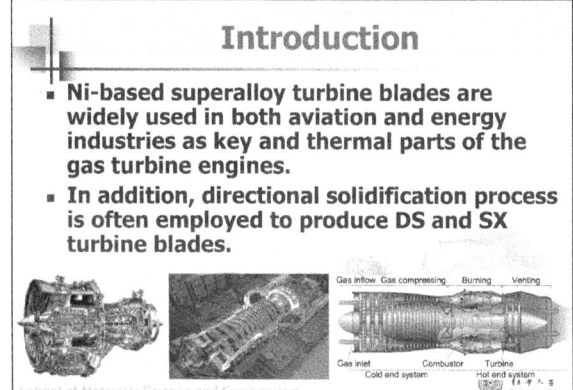

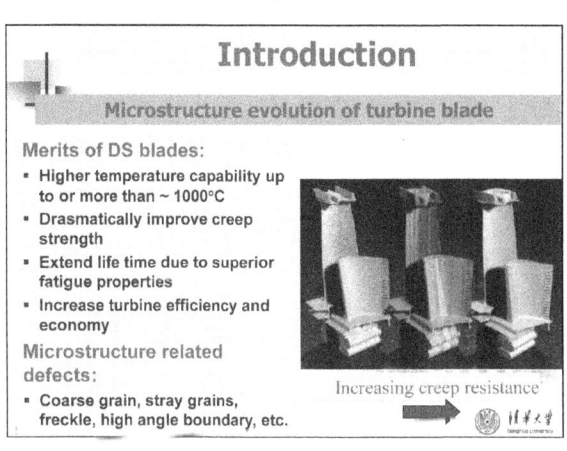

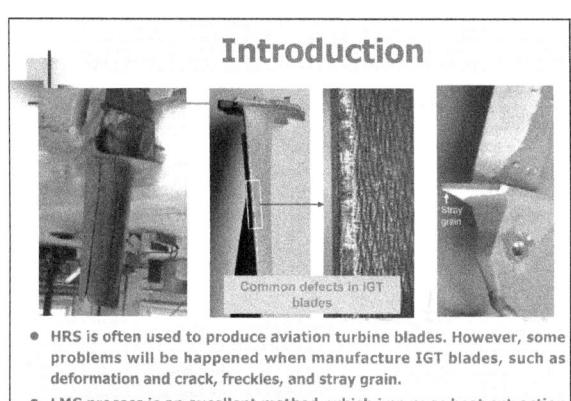

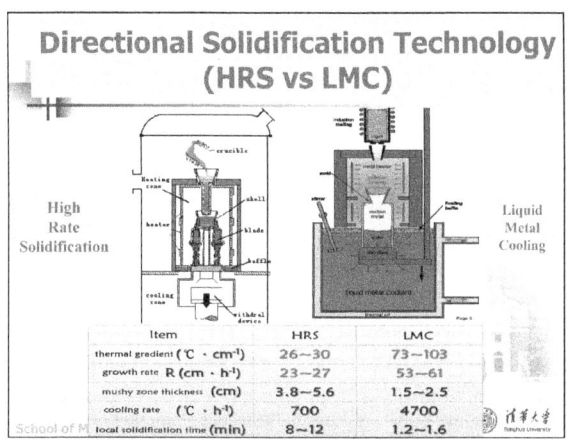

⊖ 本文为2018年"5th UK-China Steel Research Form"会议的大会主旨报告,会议地点为英国伯明翰。

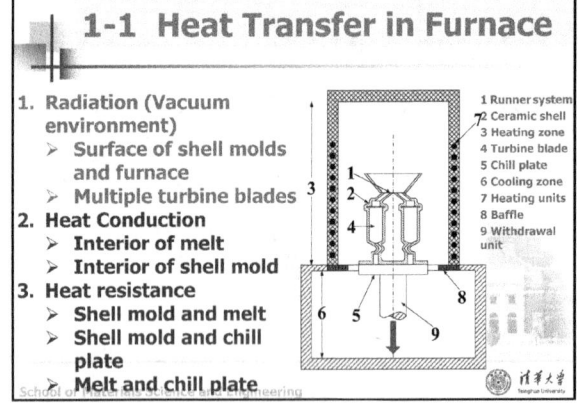
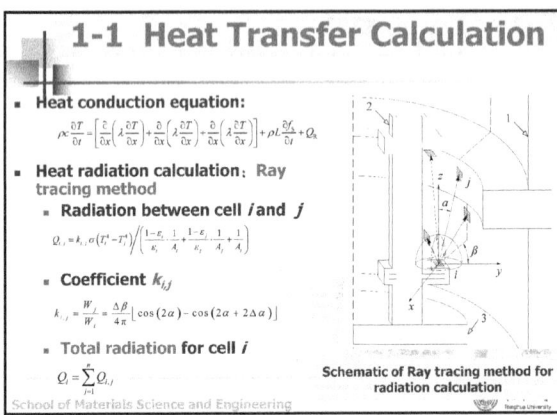
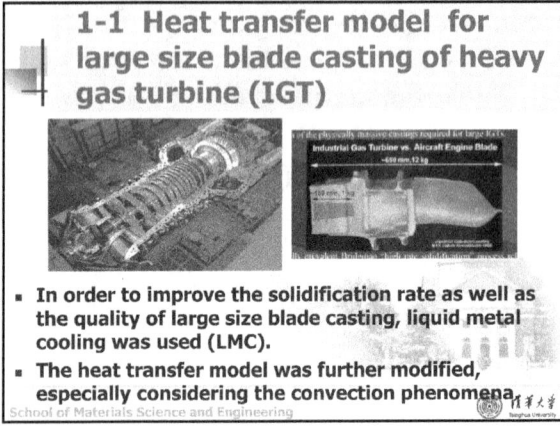
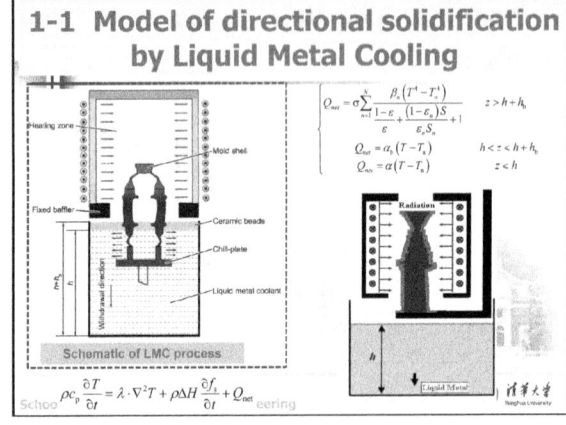
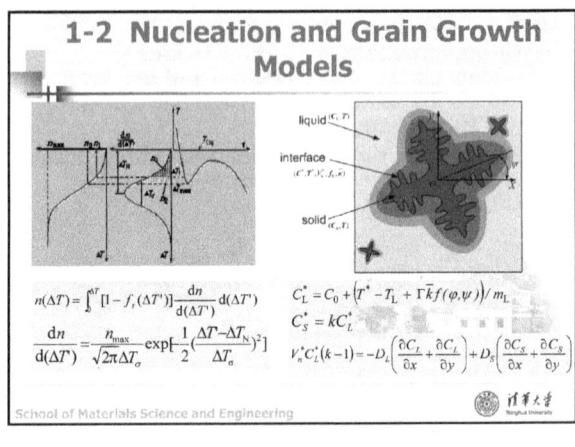
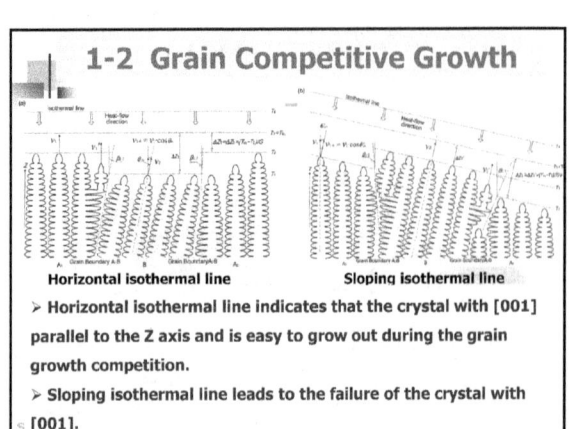
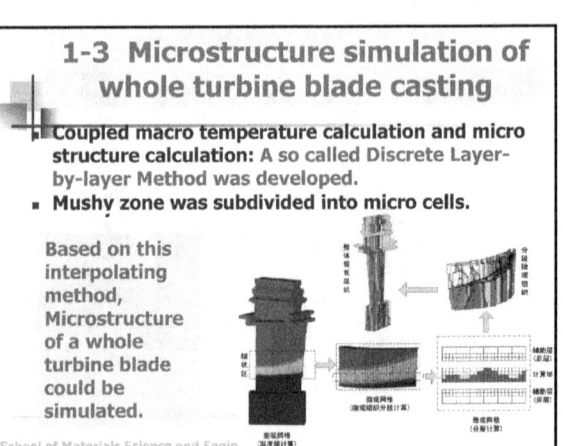

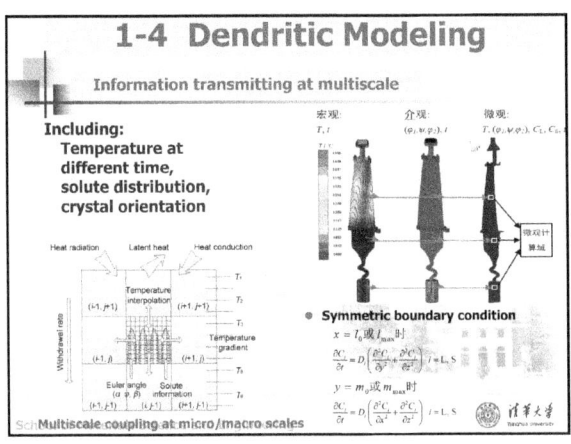
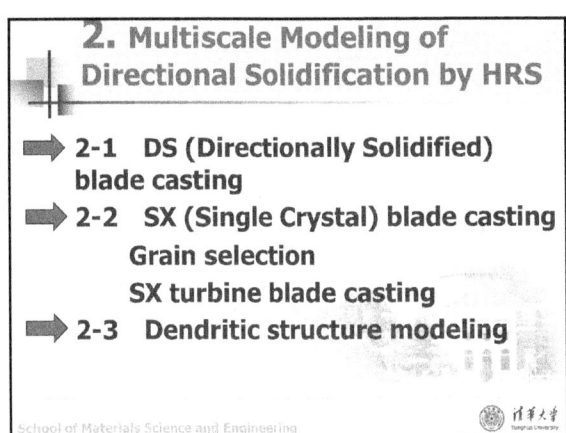
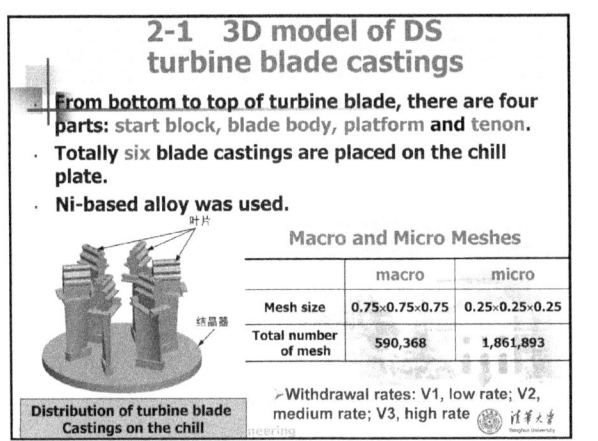
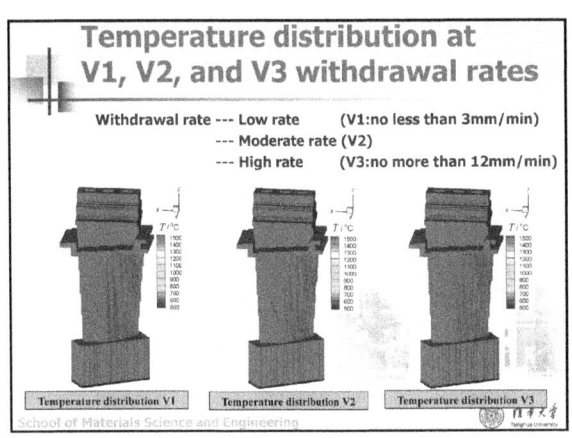
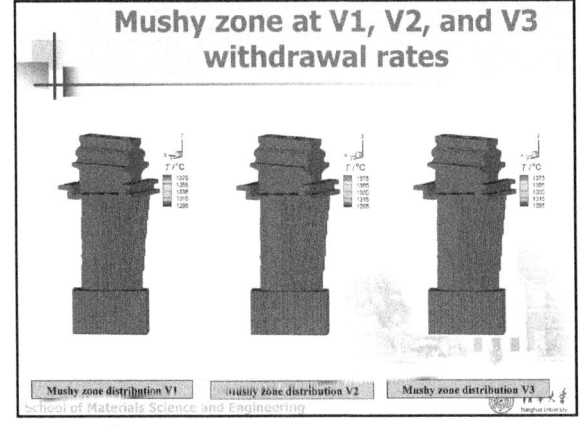
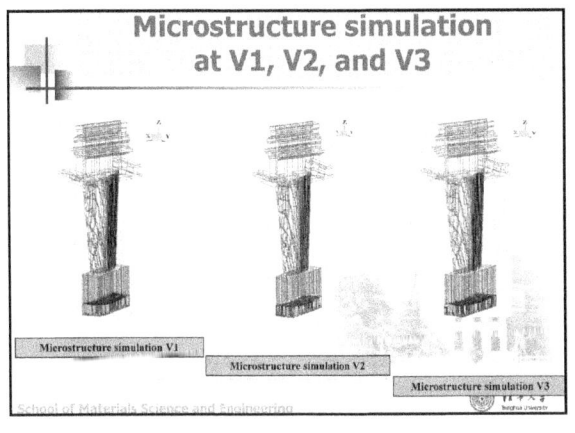
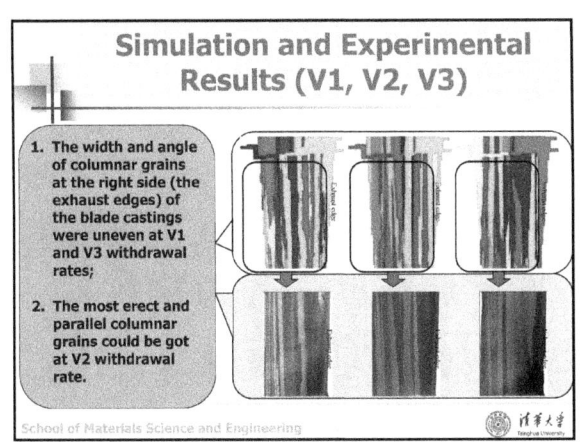
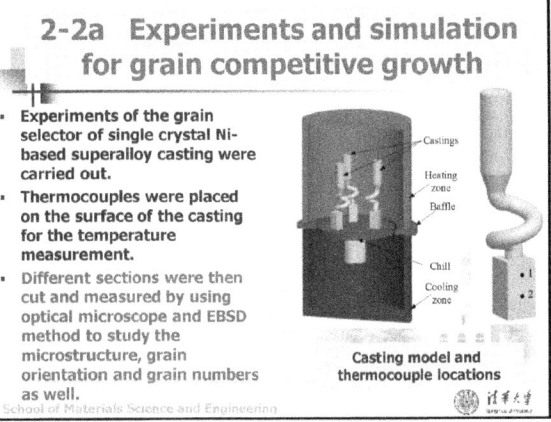

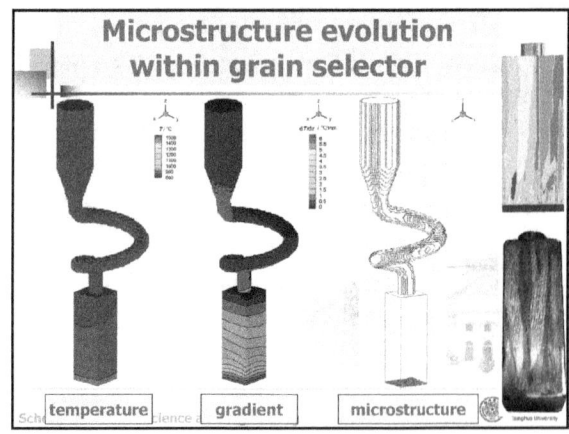
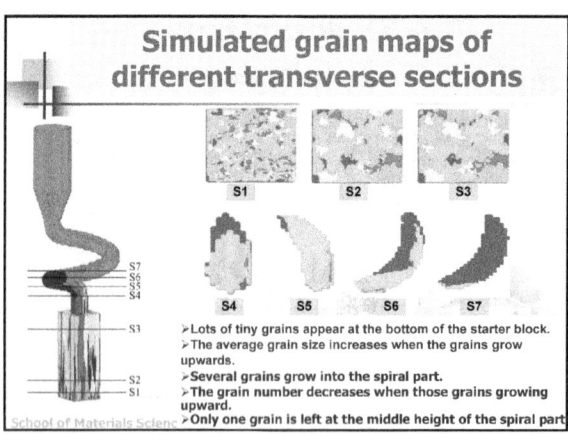
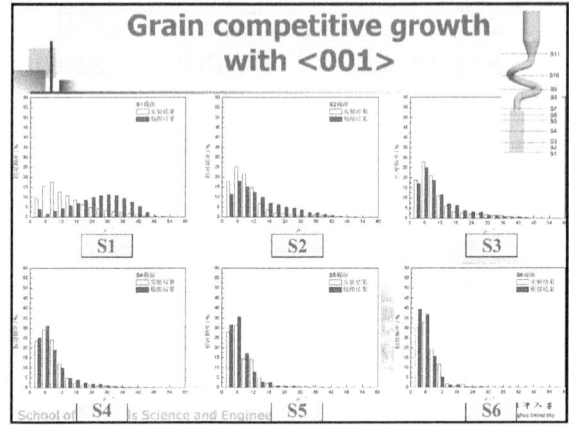
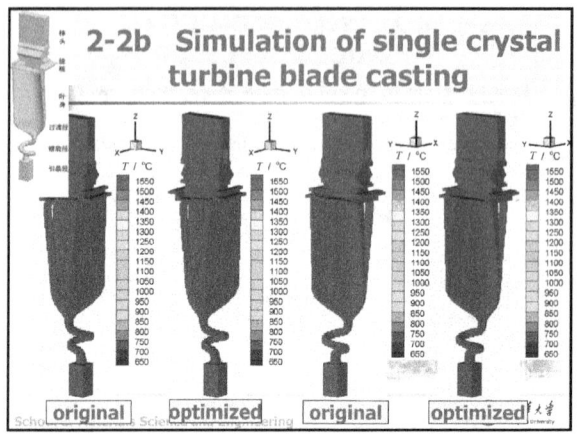
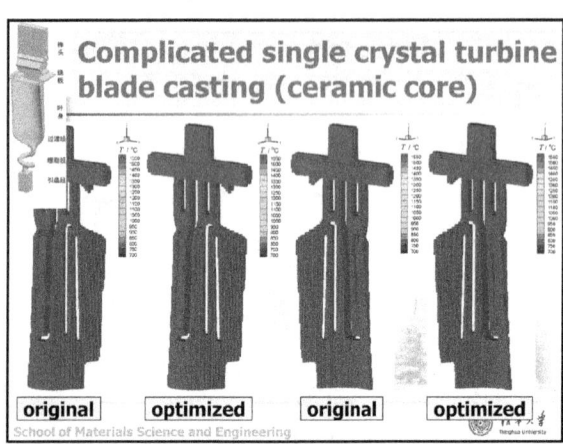
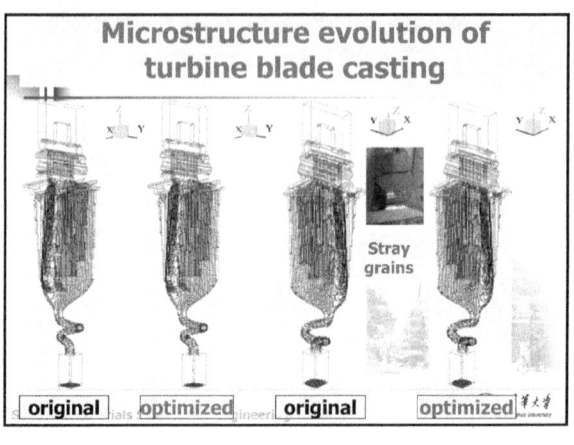
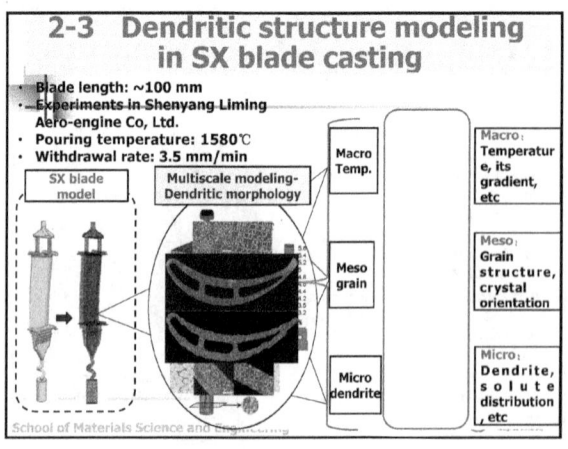
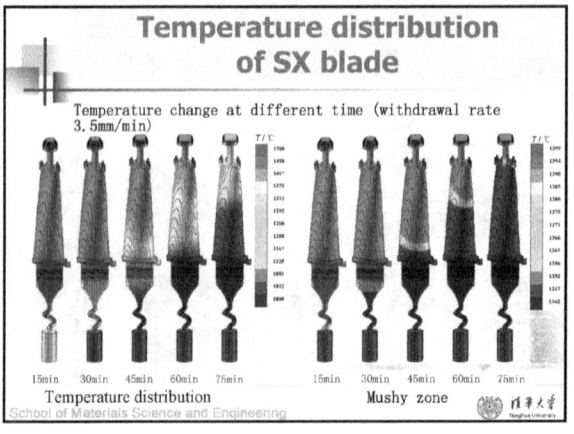

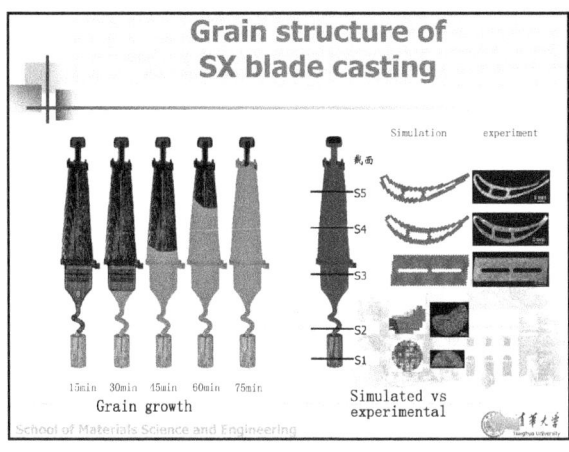
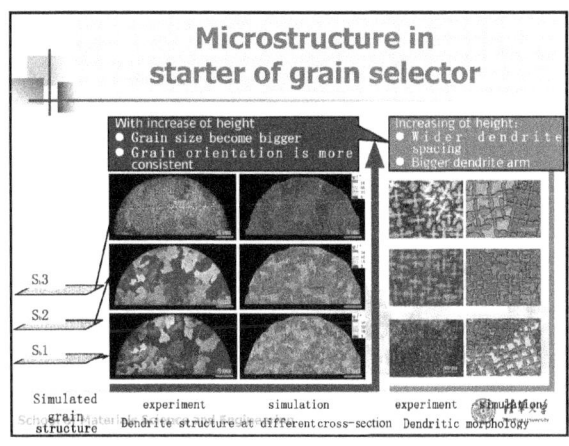
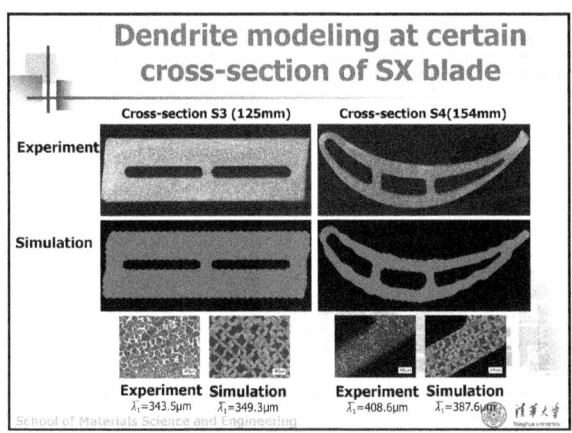
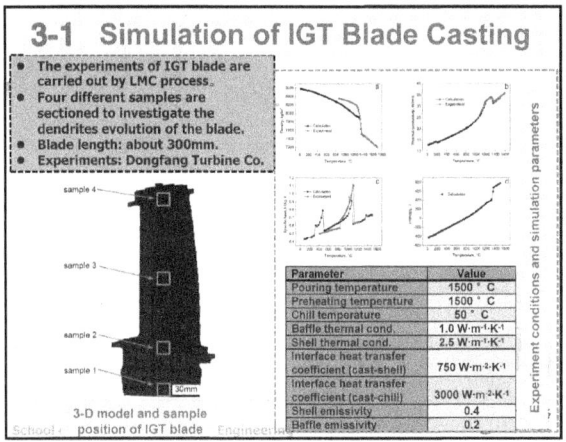
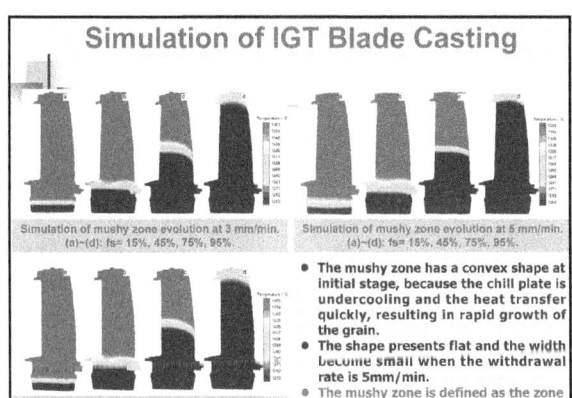
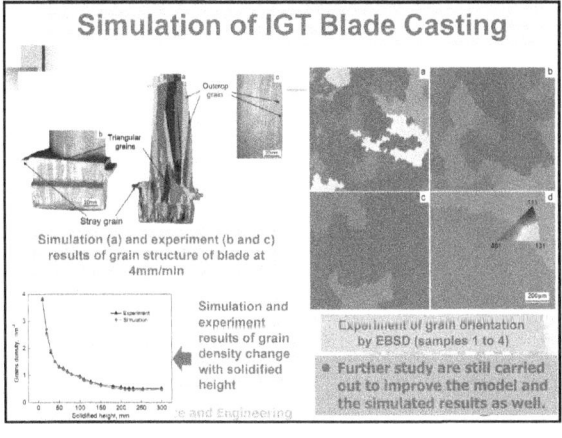
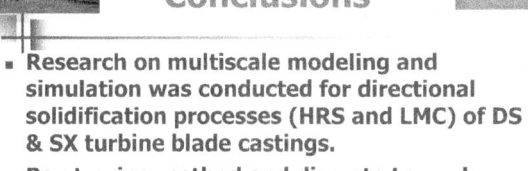
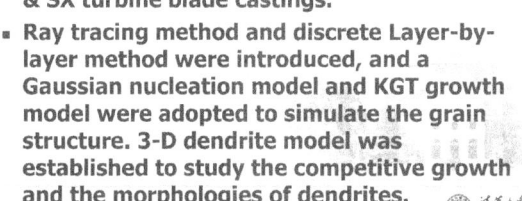
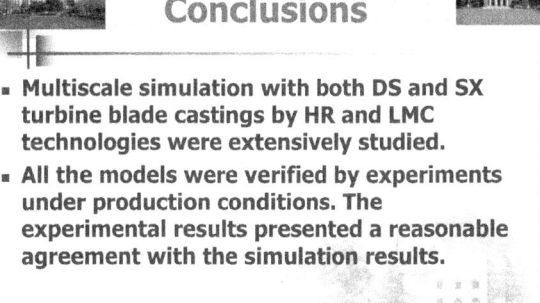

国内会议

5. 建模与仿真在装备制造中的作用与前景[一]

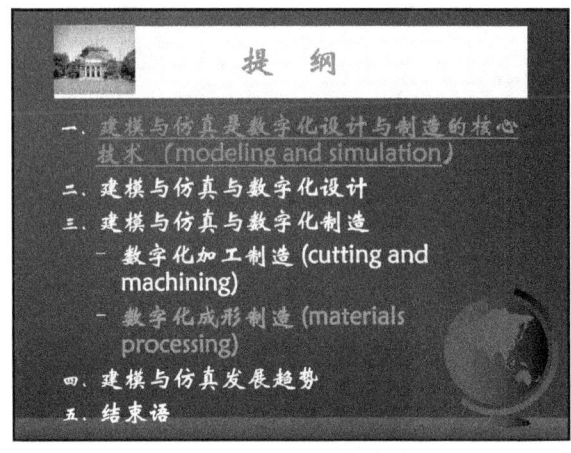

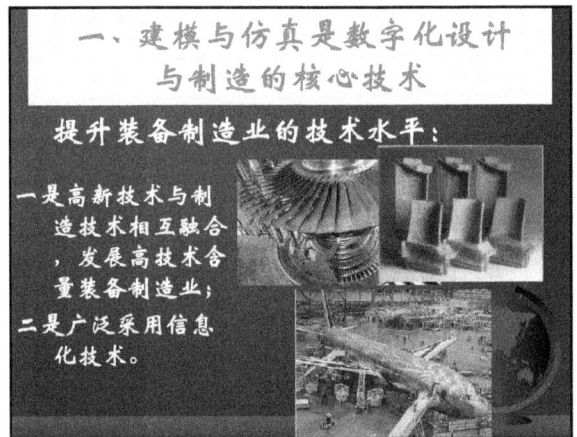

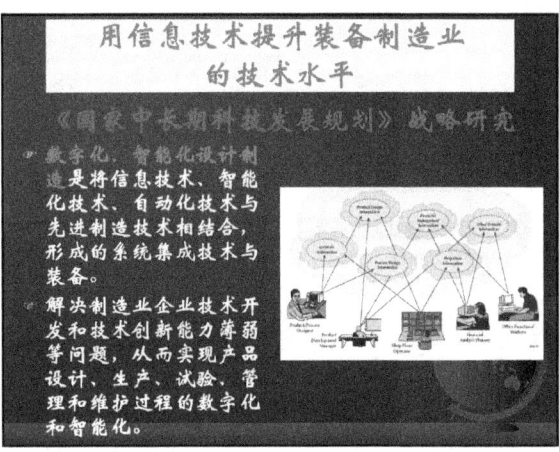

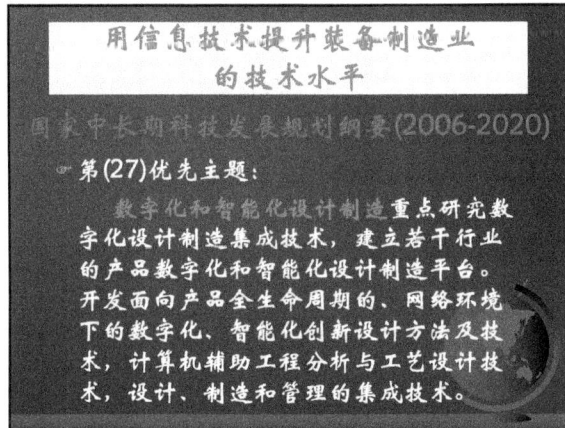

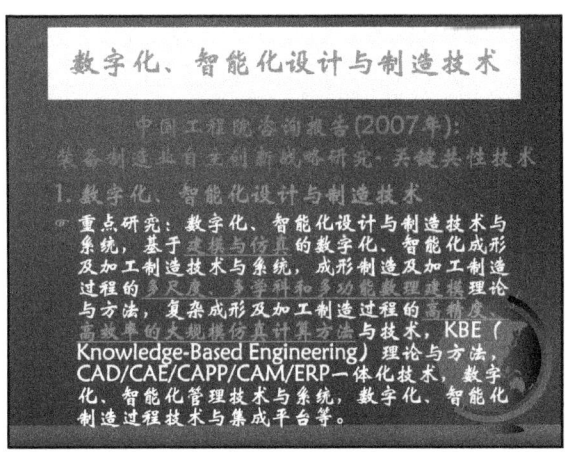

[一] 本文为2007年中国一航北京航空工程研究所建所50周年院士报告会的邀请报告，会议地点为中国北京。

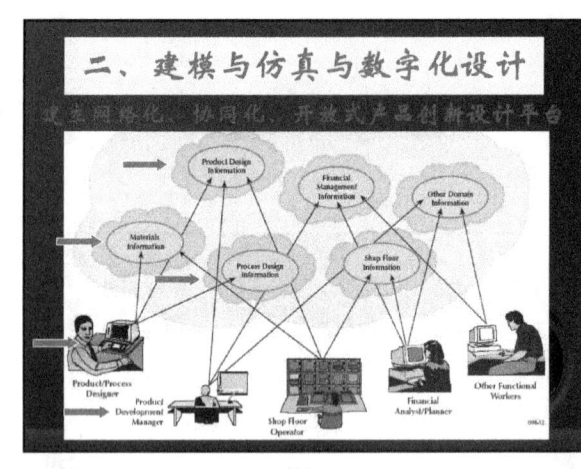
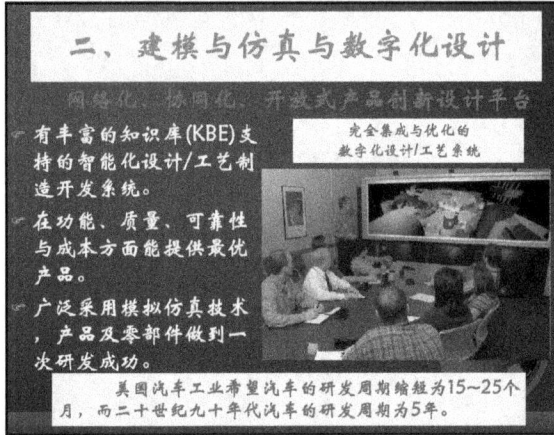
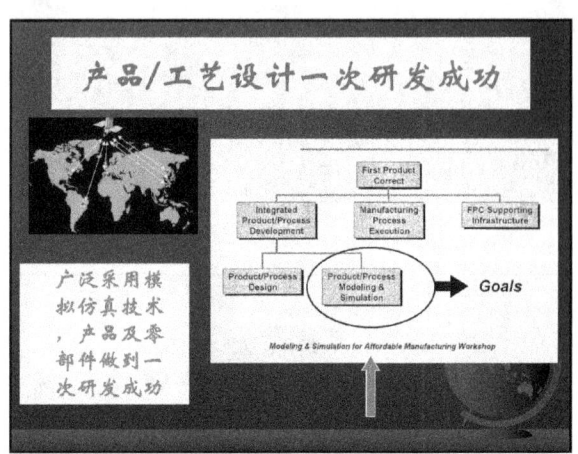
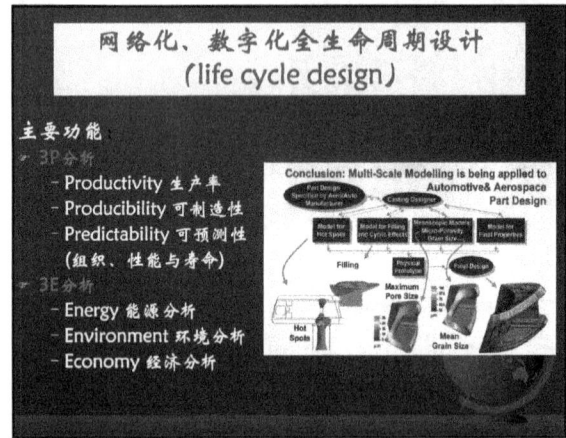

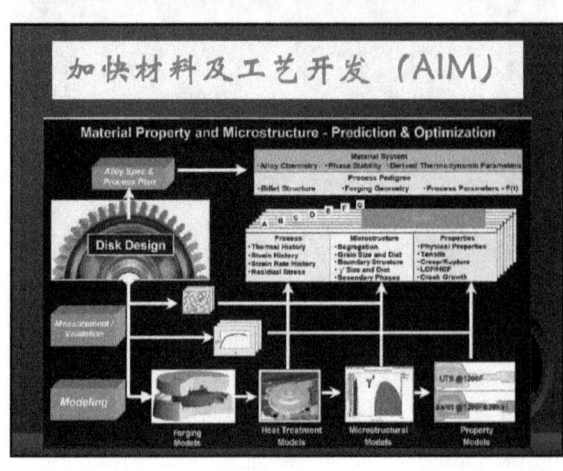
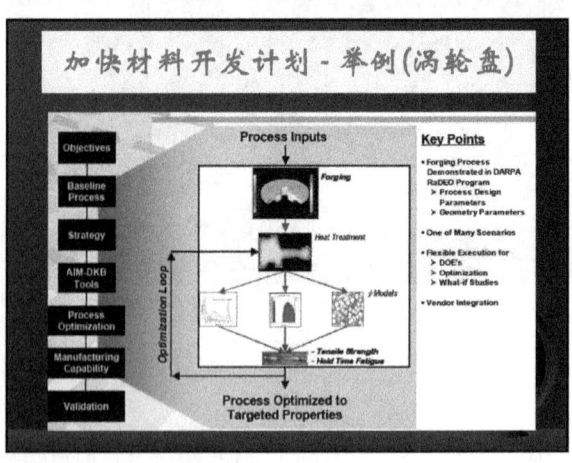

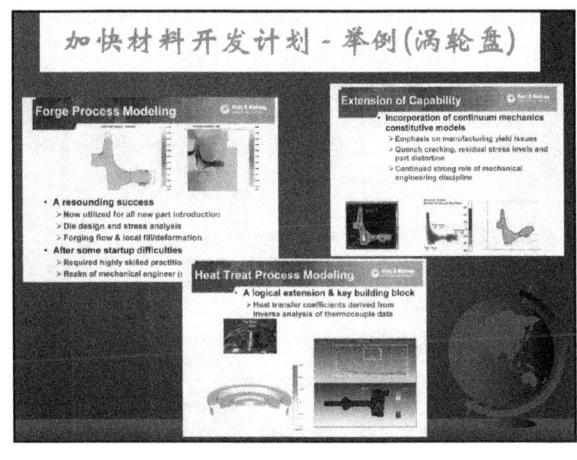

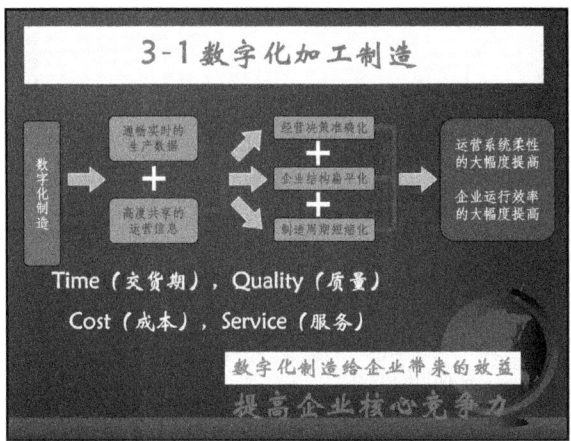
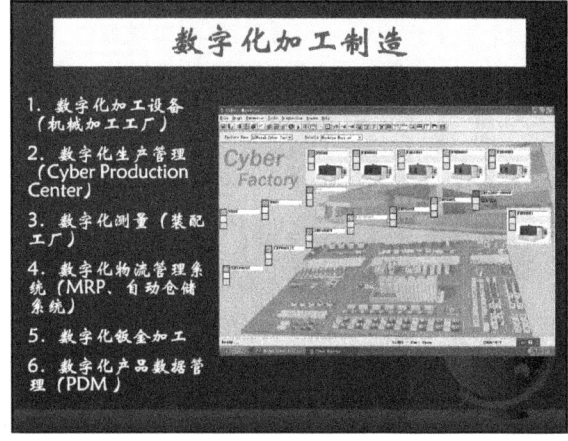
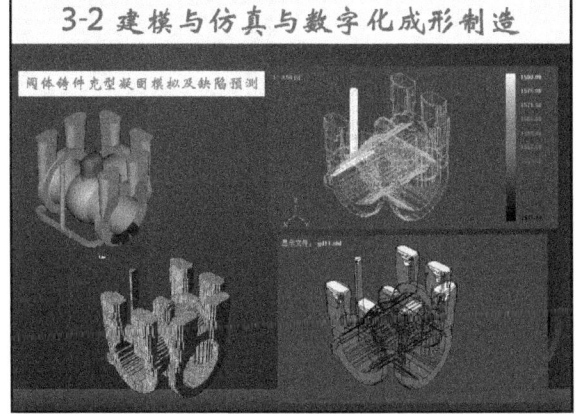
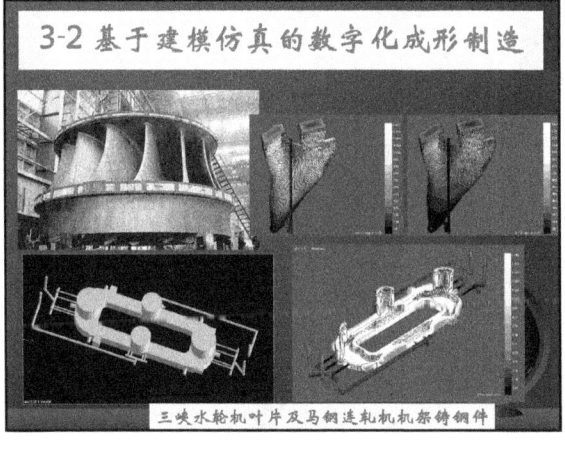
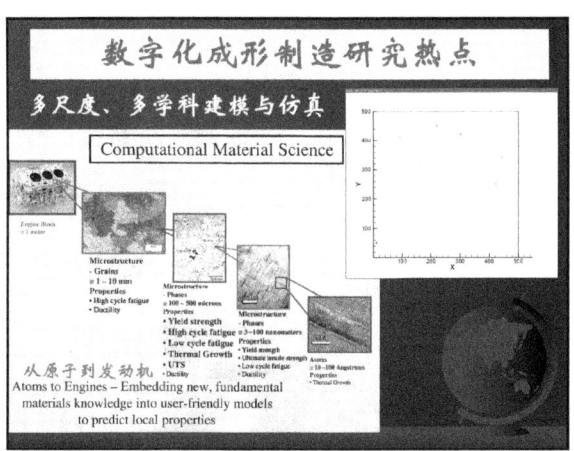
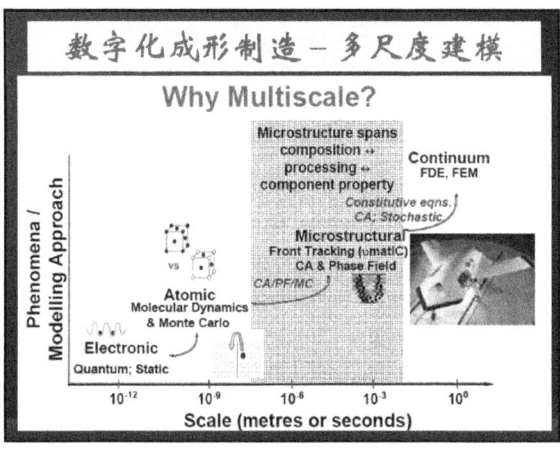

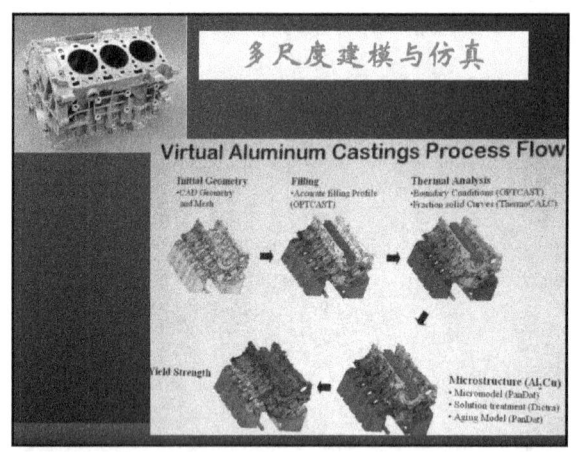
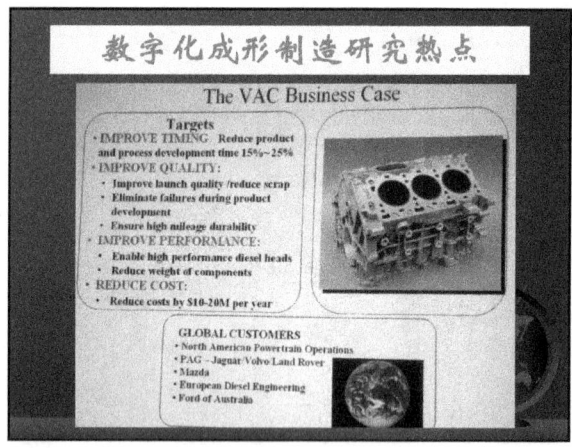
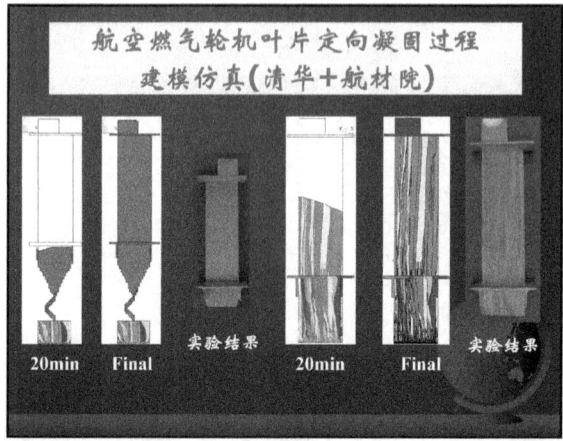
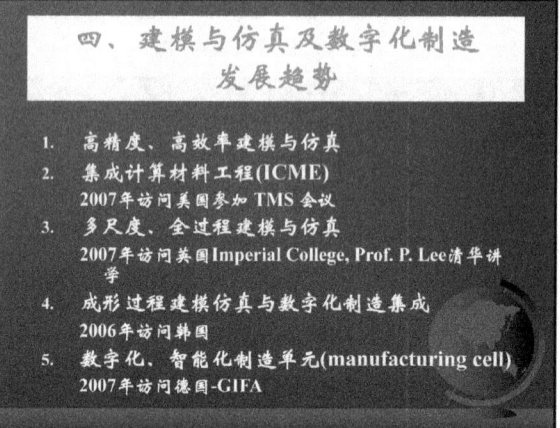
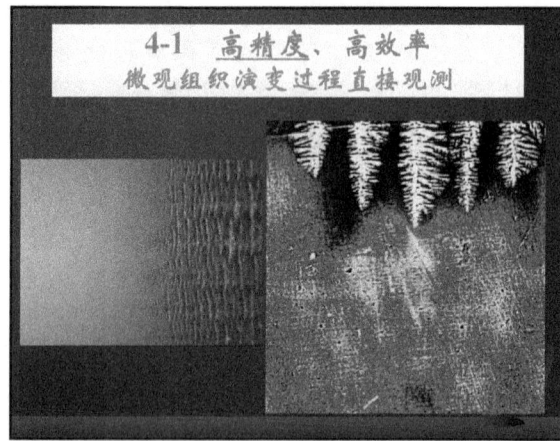

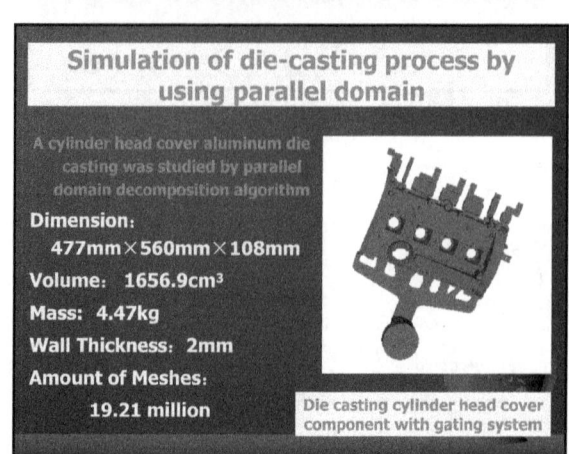
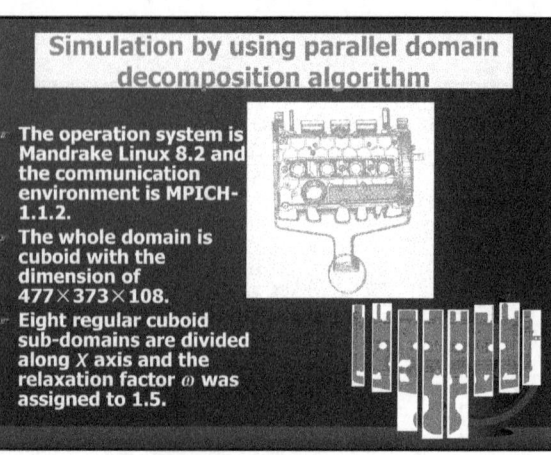

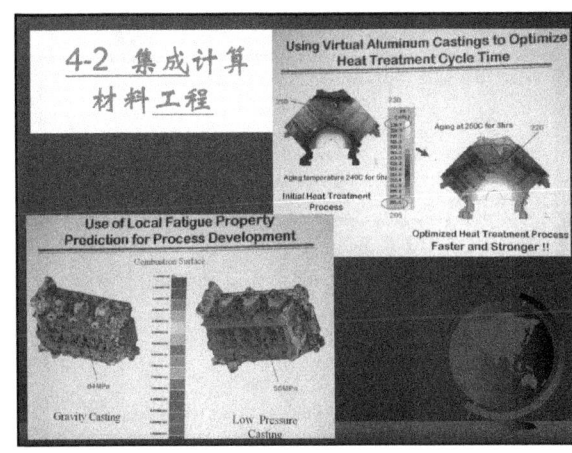
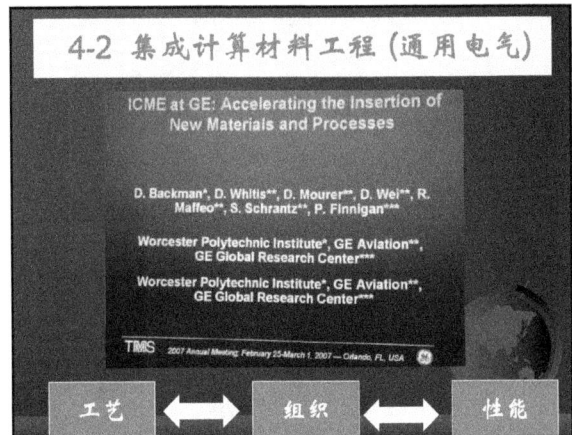
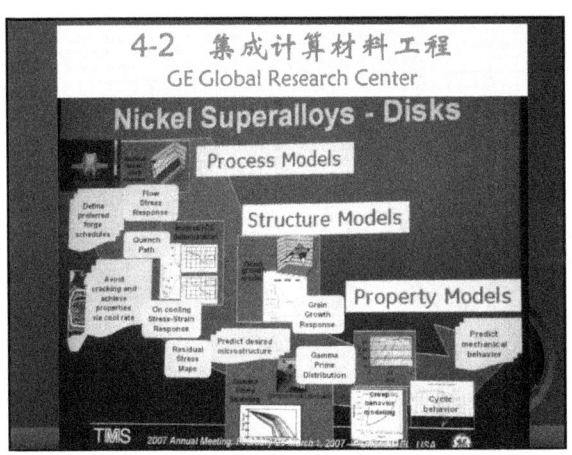
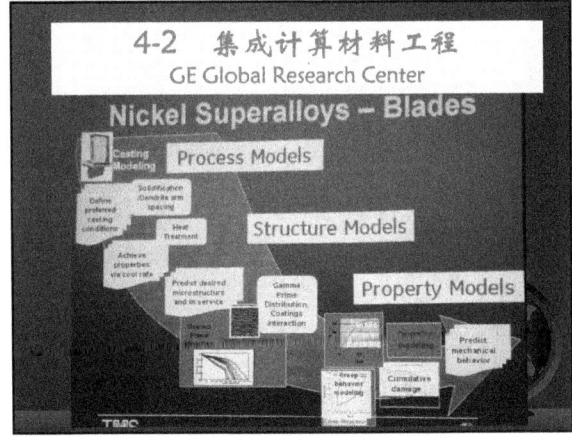
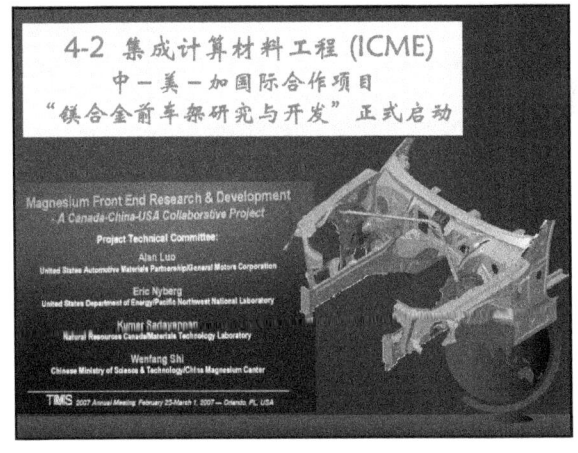

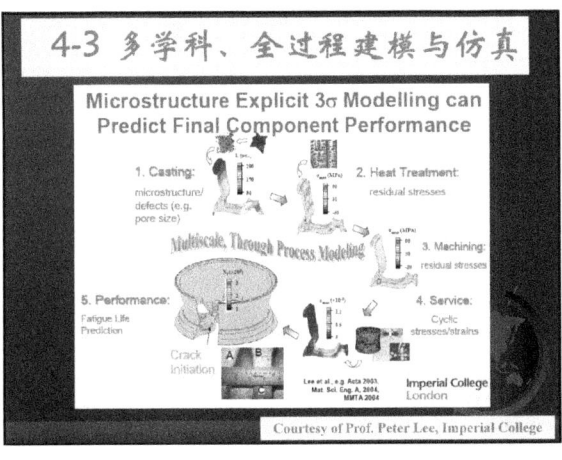

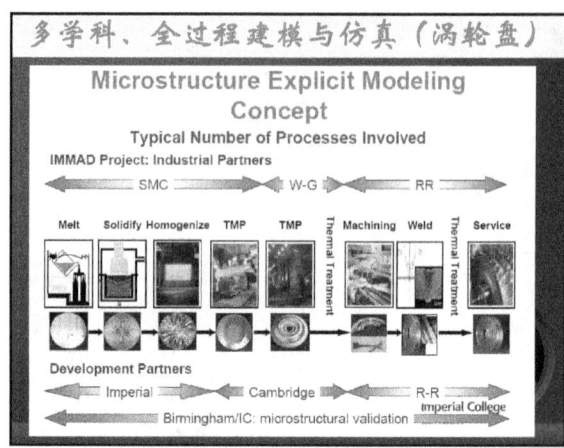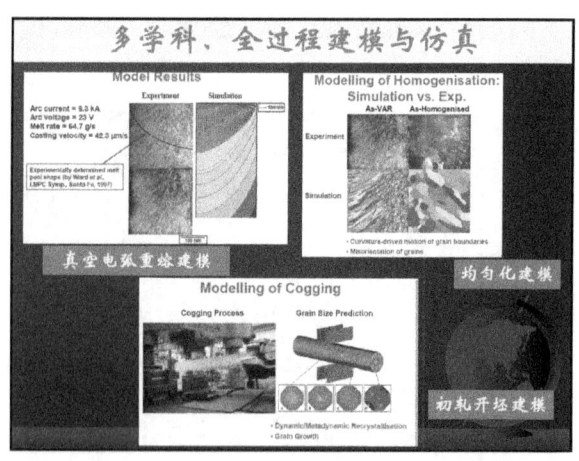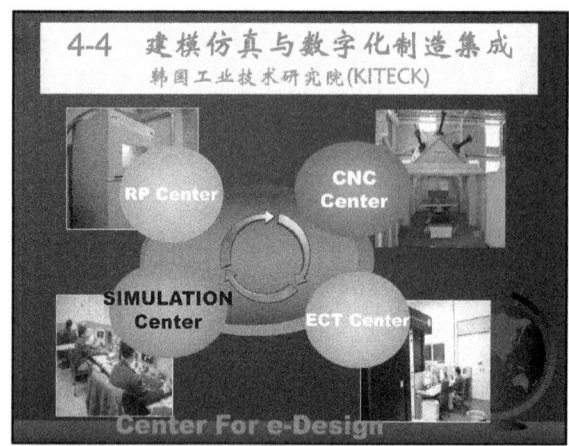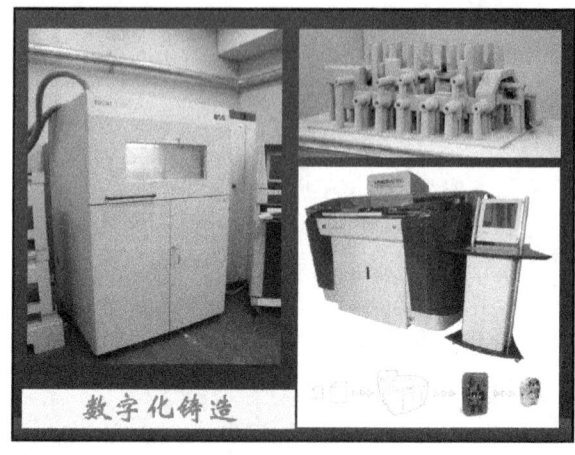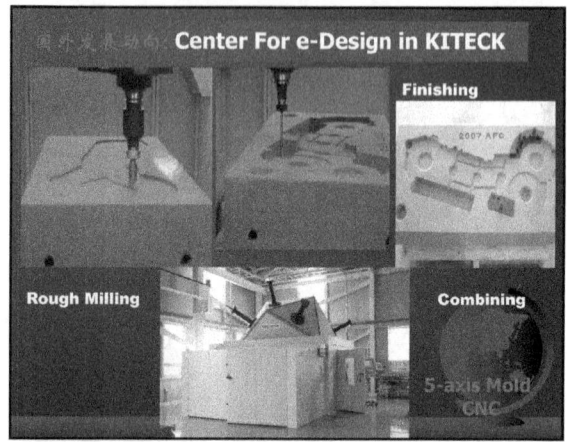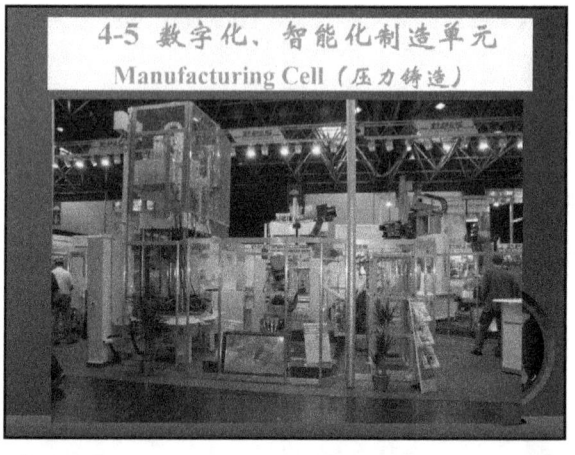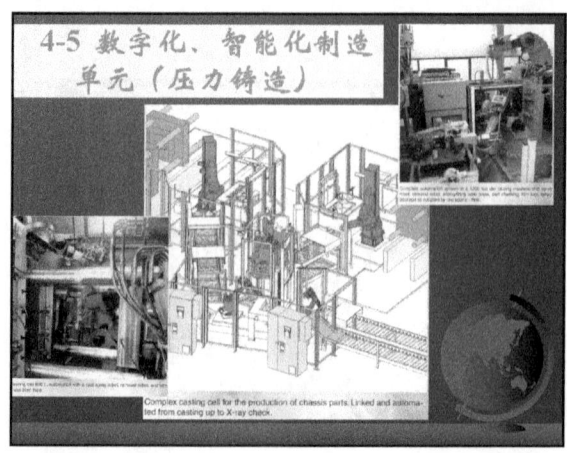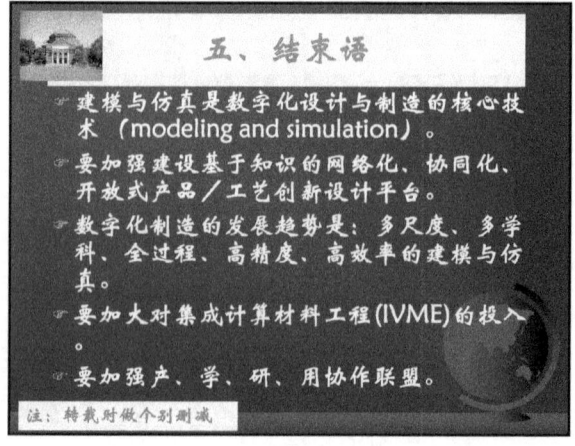

6. 高温合金定向凝固叶片铸件凝固过程建模与仿真进展

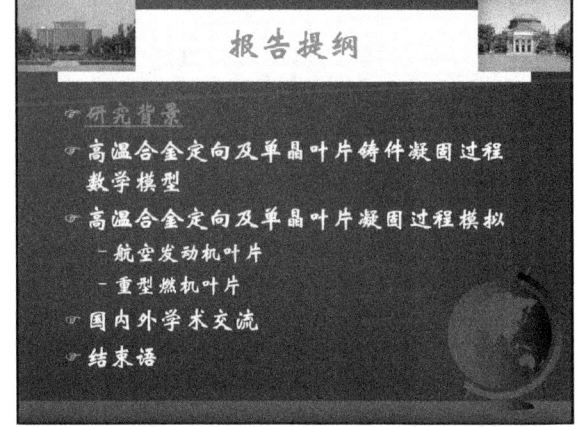
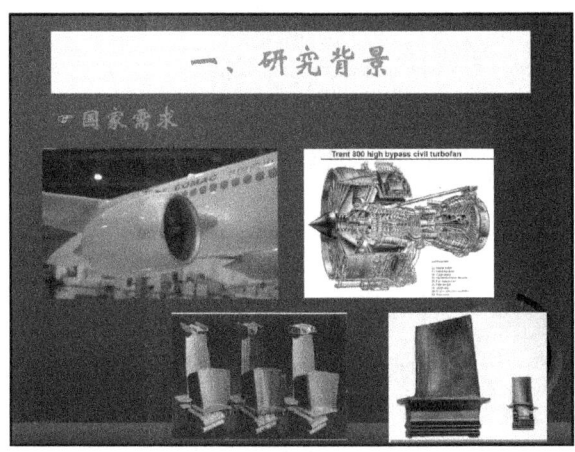
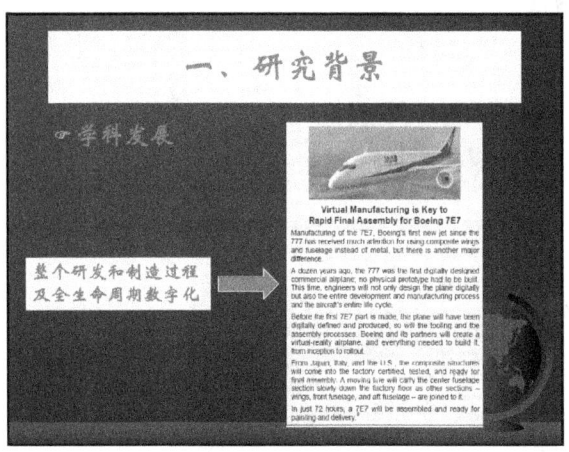
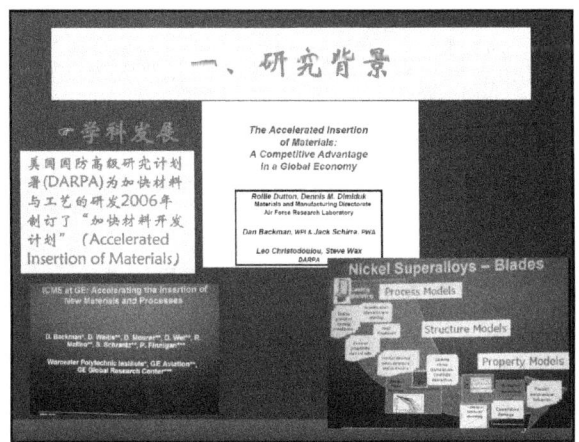
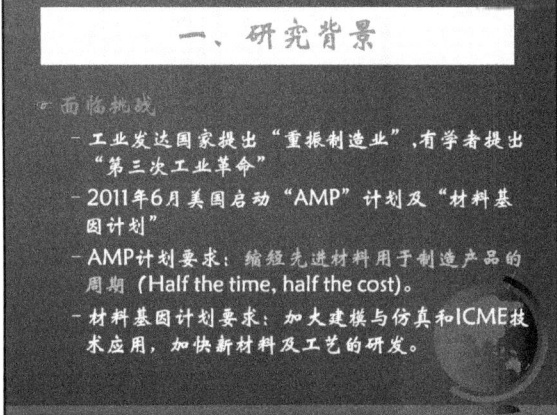

○ 本文为2012年上海燃气轮机高层论坛的邀请报告，会议地点为中国上海。

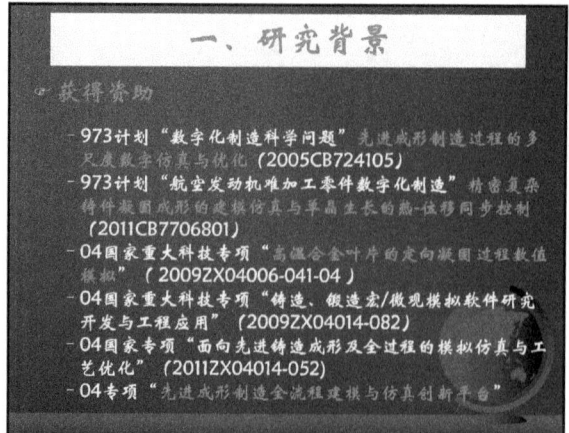
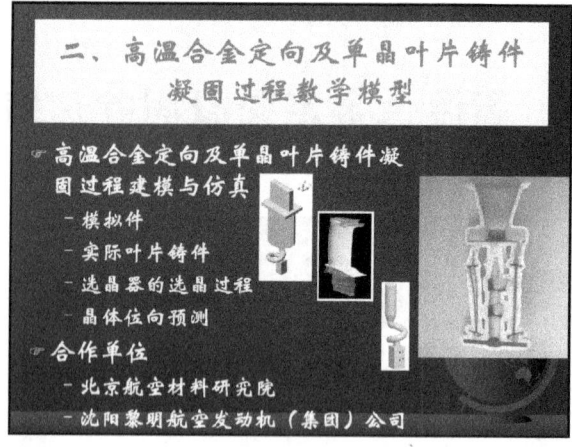
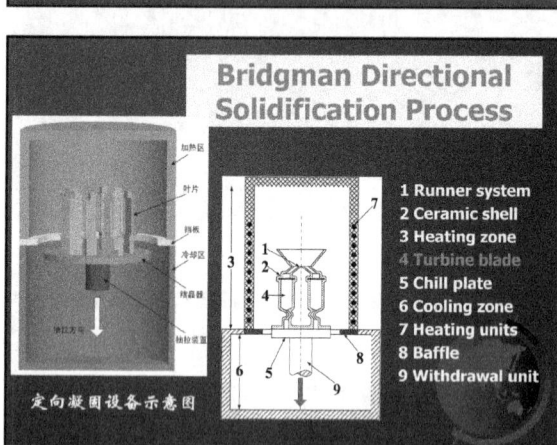
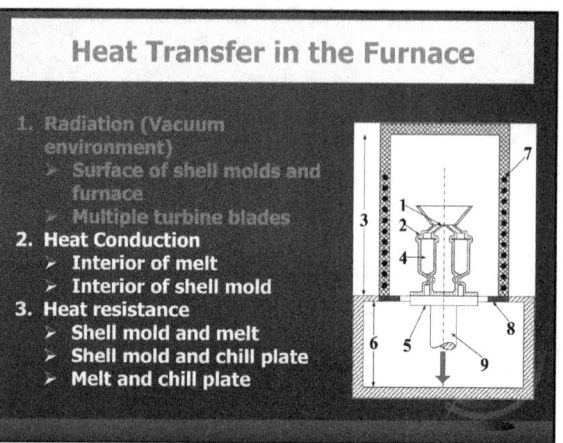
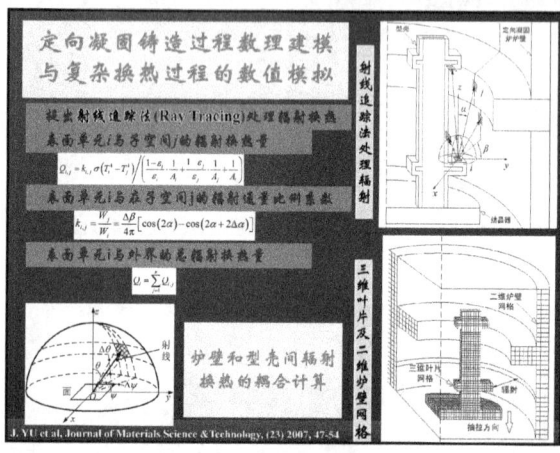
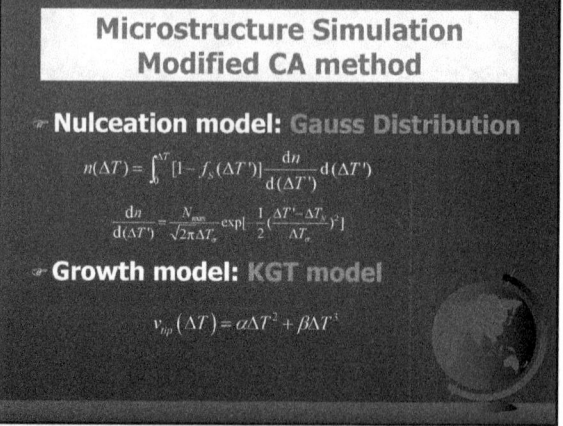
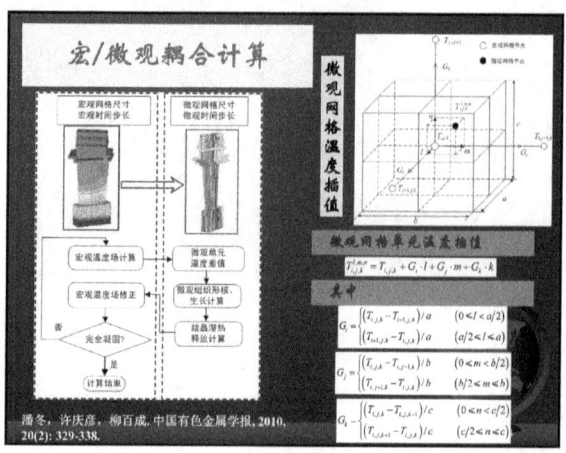
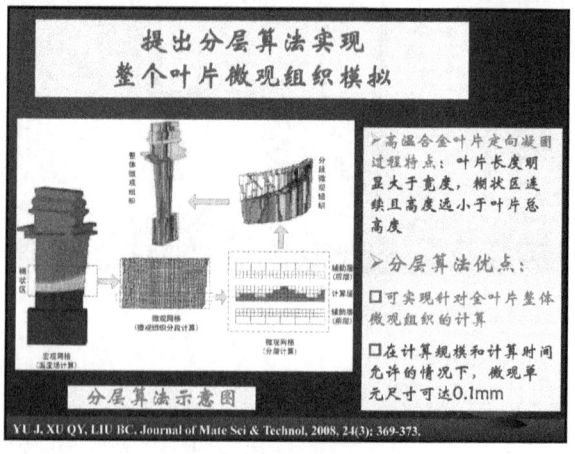

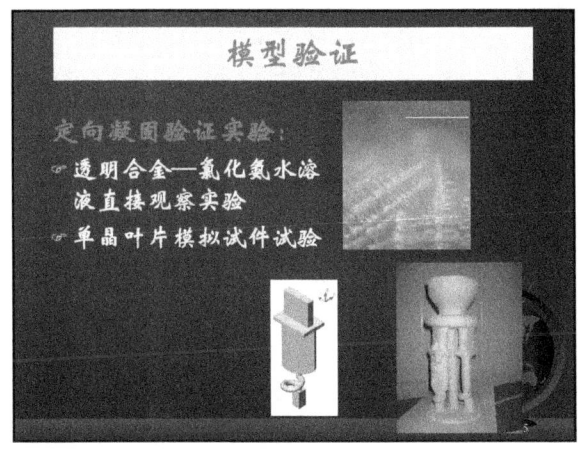

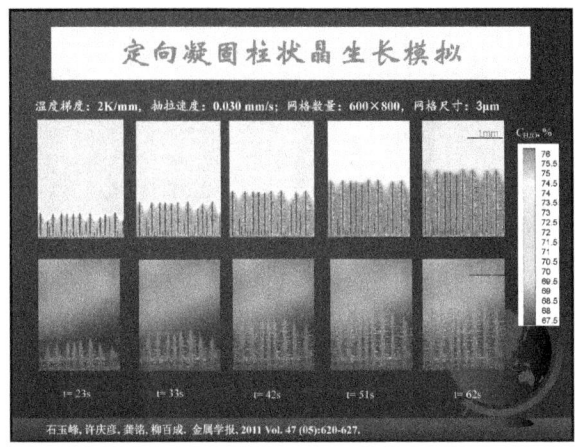
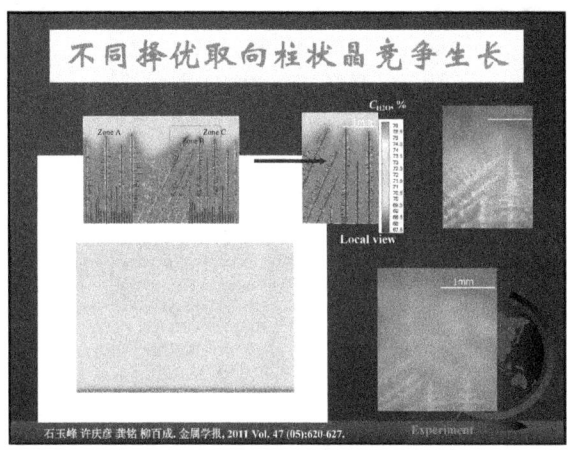
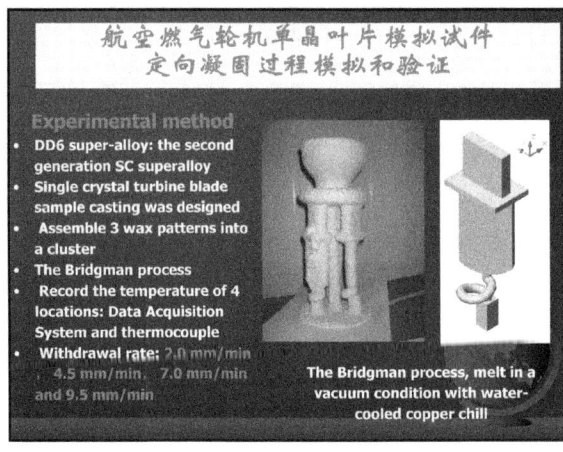
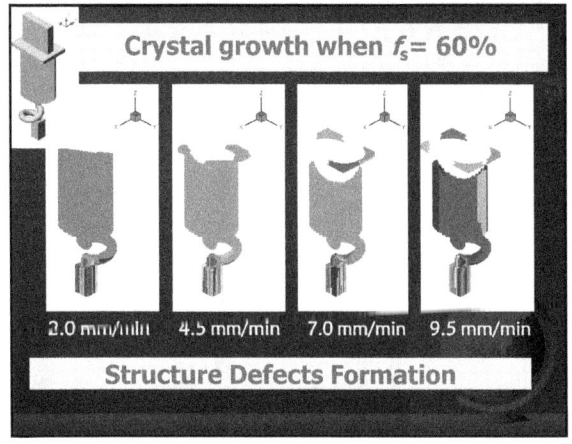
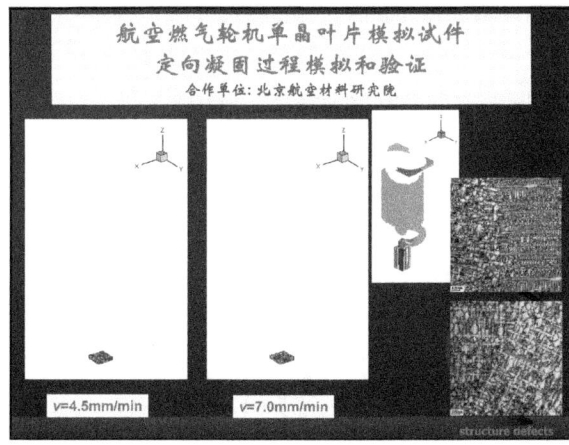
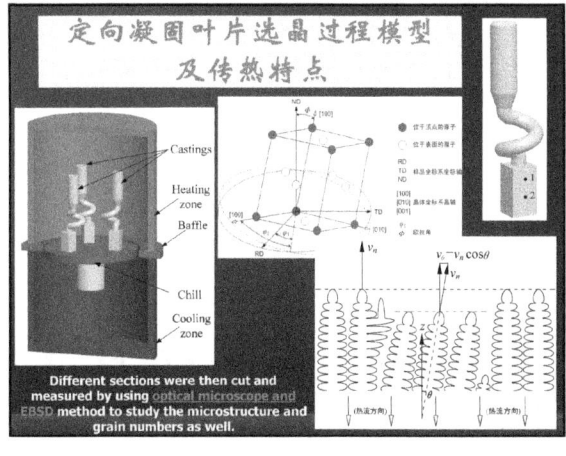

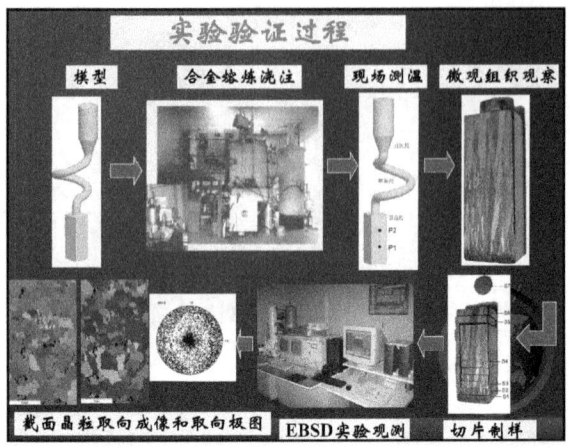
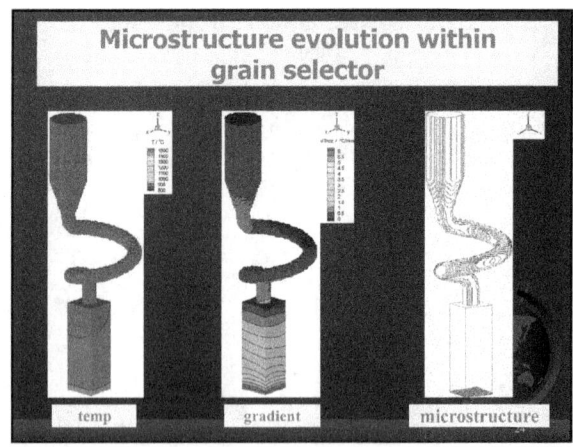
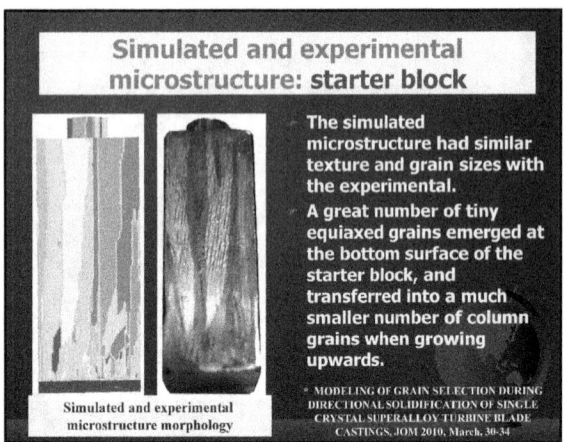
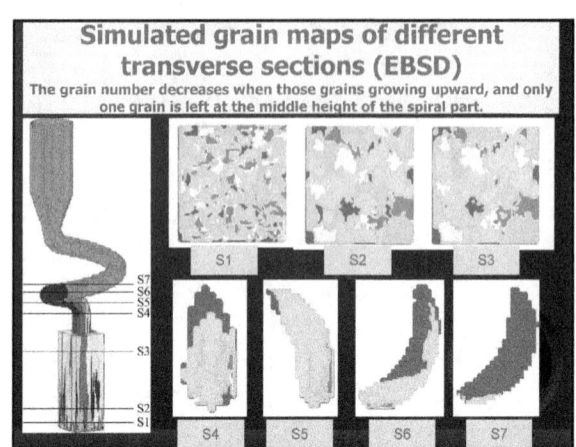
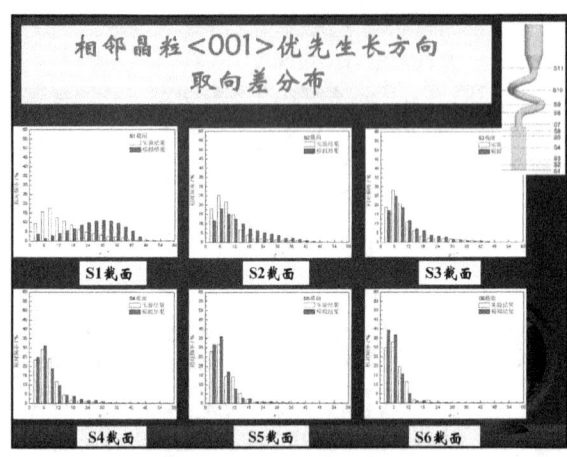
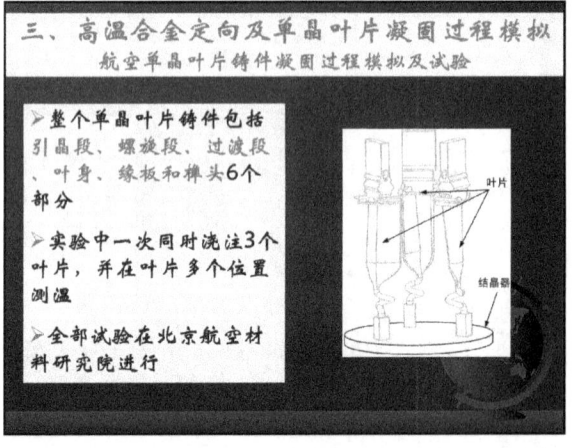
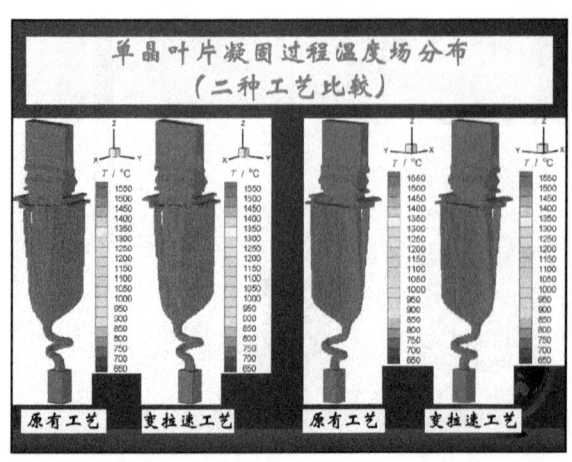
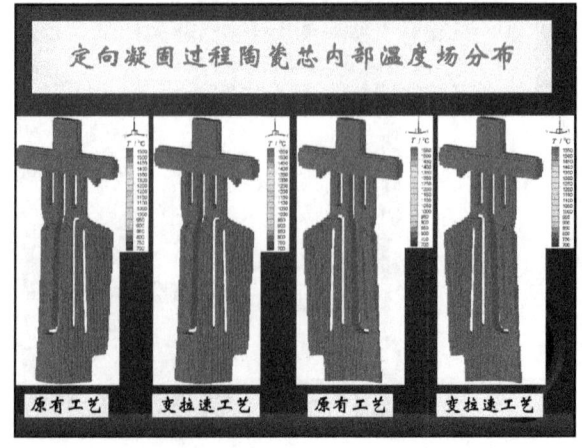

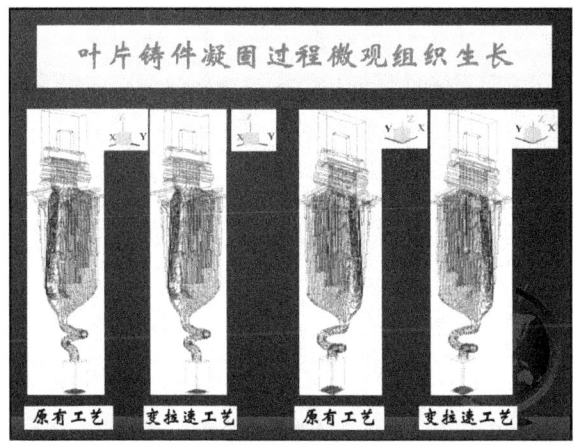
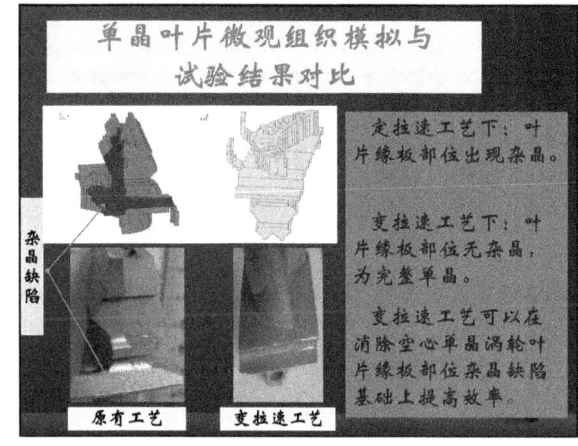
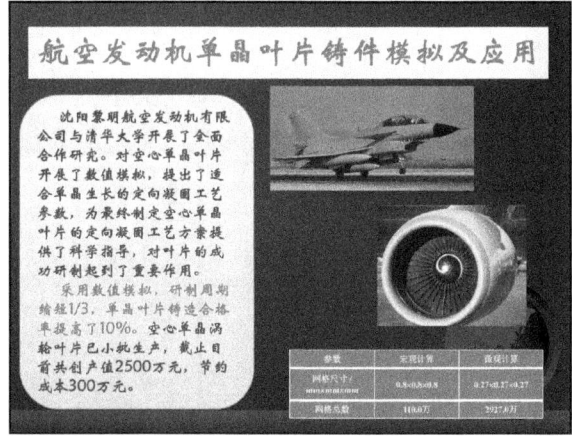
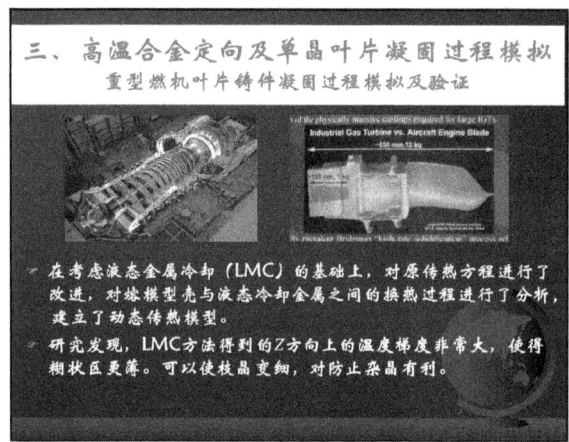
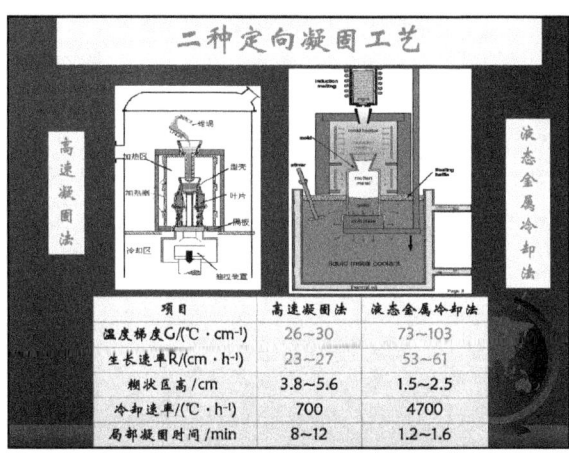
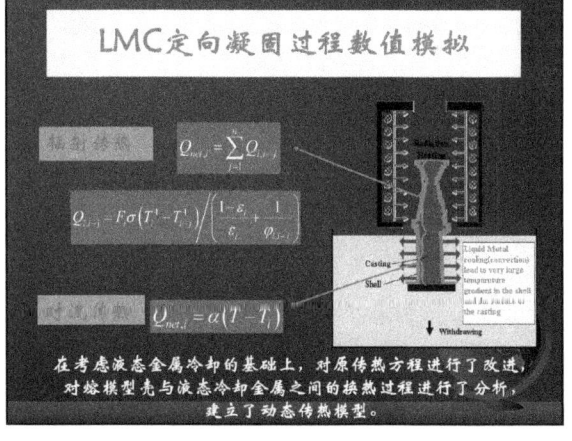
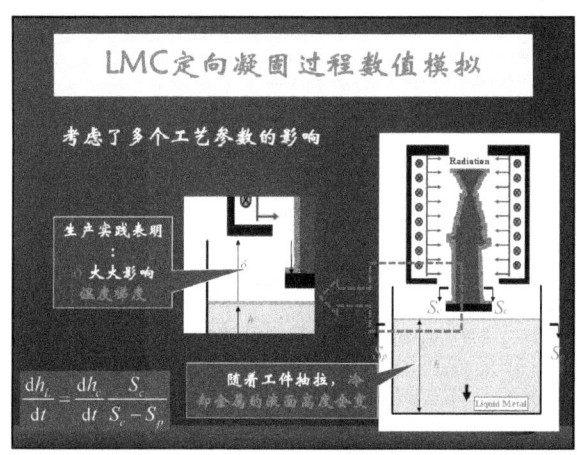
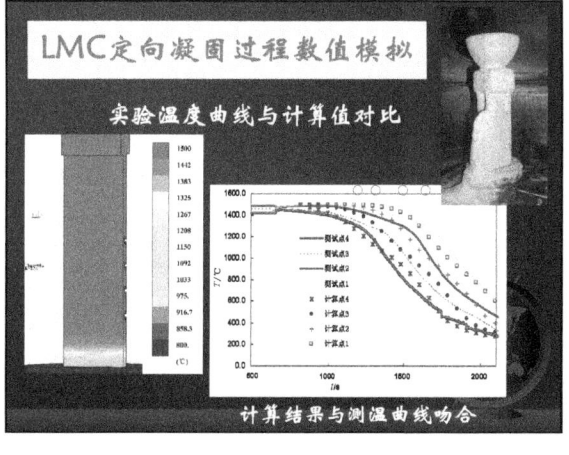

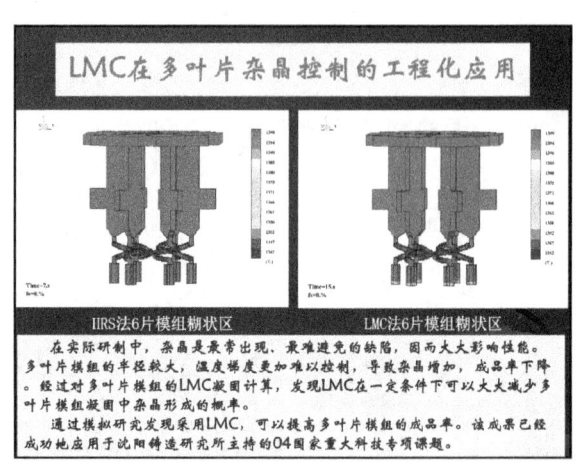
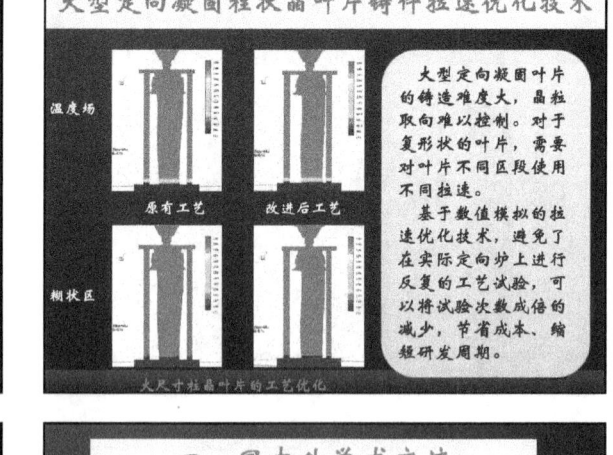
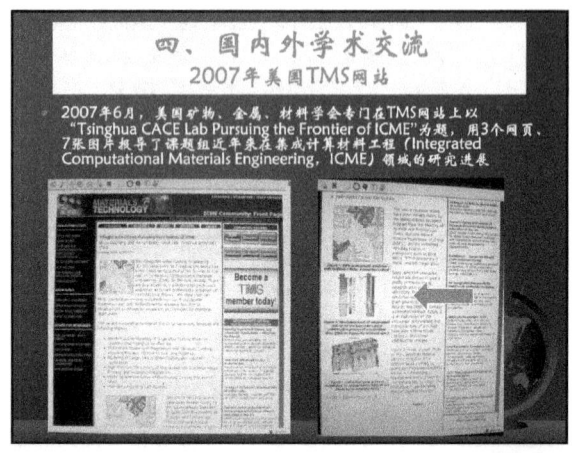

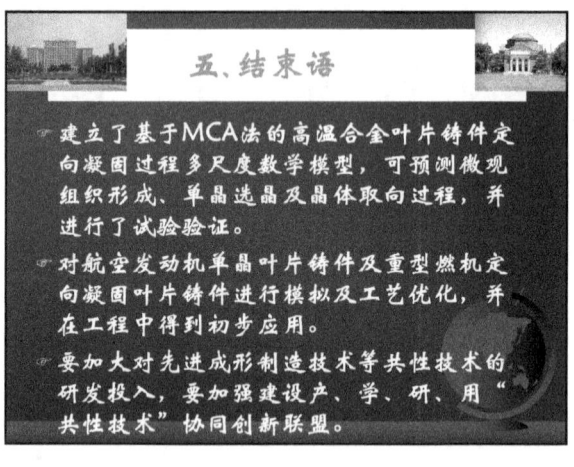

第 3 篇

制造业发展及制造强国战略研究论文

1. 发展资源节约环境友好的先进制造技术

提纲

制造业是建设创新型国家的重要支柱工业，我国已是制造大国，但远不是制造强国。制造业面临巨大挑战：一是缺乏核心和关键技术、基础设计和制造技术薄弱；二是资源浪费、污染严重；三是工业发达国家提出"再工业化"的发展战略。

先进制造技术是制造业及战略性新兴产业的基础技术，要十分重视发展资源节约、环境友好的先进制造技术。先进制造技术发展趋势：一是制造技术与高技术集成融合；二是数字化智能化制造技术；三是极端工作条件下的制造技术；四是清洁及可持续发展制造技术。

一、制造业面临严峻挑战

制造业特别是装备制造业是建设创新型国家的重要支柱工业，关系到国家繁荣和国防安全。我国已是制造大国，但远不是制造强国。在全球创新能力指标（Global Innovation Index）及全球竞争力指标中，我国处在 20~30 名左右。最近在中国社科院的有关研究报告中，我国排在第 15 名。

例如，2012 年全国研发投入与 GDP 之比为 1.97%，而工业发达国家均大于 2.5%。2010 年我国企业的研发投入与销售收入之比仅 0.93%，而国外在 3%~5%，甚至更高。

我国制造业面临三大挑战：

一是关键核心及基础技术缺乏。

我国设计和制造等基础技术十分薄弱，低端产品过剩而高端产品则尚未形成。例如，航空发动机是飞机的心脏，是制约我国大飞机研制的瓶颈。与第一批正在研制的大飞机 C919 配套的发动机，还得采用国外的先进技术（LEAP-X1C 发动机）。我国已是铸锻件生产大国，但火电、水电及核电装备的大型及关键铸锻件仍依赖进口，受制于人。

二是资源浪费、污染严重。

三是工业发达国家提出"再工业化"的发展战略。

工业发达国家的"再工业化"发展战略使我国制造业的科技发展和自主创新形势更为严峻。

2011 年 6 月，美国启动"先进制造伙伴计划（Advanced Manufacturing Partnership，AMP）"，将投入 5~10 亿美元。同时启动了"材料基因计划"。AMP 计划的目的是："在哪里发明，在哪里制造"。具体内容包含：1）在关键的国防工业建立自己的制造能力；2）缩短先进材料用于制造产品的周期；3）确立美国在下一代机器人领域的领先地位；4）增加节能的制造技术；5）研发能显著缩短产品的设计、制造和测试时间的新技术。明确提出"缩短研发周期一半、降低研发费用一半（Half the time，half the cost）"的目标。

2012 年 3 月，美国总统宣布建议建立"国家制造创新网络（National Network for Manufacturing Innovation）"。7 月 17 日，美国总统科技顾问委员会提出新报告："要确保在先进制造领域的竞争优势"，描绘了重振美国制造业和在全球处于领导地位的创新战略及路线图。

总之，先进制造技术是制造业及战略性新兴产业的基础技术，对发展经济和国家安全至关重要。制造技术已成为发展我国制造业的薄弱环节，所以要十分重视发展先进制造技术。

中国工程院十分重视我国制造业和先进制造技术的发展。在 2007 年的"装备制造业自主创新战略研究报告"及 2010 年的"中国制造业可持续发展战略研究报告"中都强调要加快发展先进制造技术。近年来，中国工程院多次举行有关先进制造技术的国际及国内高层论坛。2013 年初正式启动"制造强国战略研究"咨询项目。

先进制造技术的发展趋势可归纳为：

一是制造技术与高技术集成融合；

二是数字化智能化制造技术与信息技术；

三是极端工作条件下的制造技术；

四是清洁及可持续发展制造技术。

○ 本文刊登于《先进制造业》，2013 年 6 月刊。

二、制造技术与高技术集成融合

以航空发动机为例，发动机的叶片工作温度高达1700℃，已超过材料的熔点。要采用的镍基高温合金，陶瓷复合材料表面镀层，复杂冷却气道设计及真空熔炼、定向凝固单晶叶片制备等多项高新技术的集成（图1及图2）。而重型燃机的工作叶片长达600mm，定向凝固制备技术难度更大（图3及图4），需要进一步采用液态金属冷却技术（Liquid Metal Cooling）。

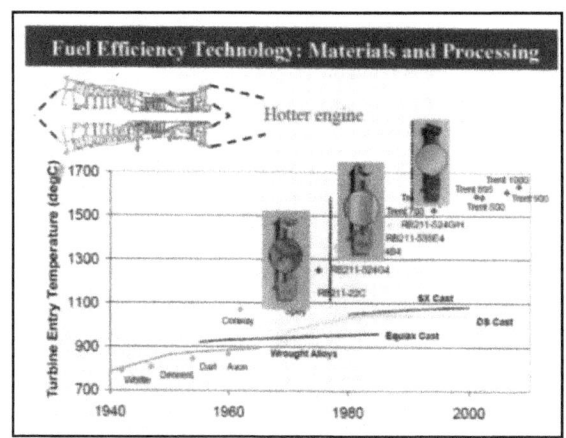

图1　航空发动机叶片发展历程
引自：英国董洪标教授讲学

图2　等轴、定向及单晶三代航空叶片

图3　重型燃机和航空发动机叶片比较

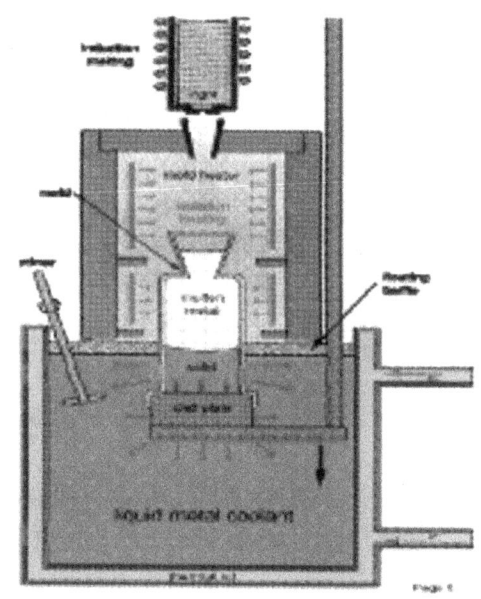

图4　LMC技术制备重型燃机叶片

三、数字化智能化制造技术

数字化制造应是广义的含义，包含数字化设计与数字化制造。其中数字化制造则包含加工制造和成形制造，既涉及装备的数字化，也涉及工艺过程的数字化。最近，国内外十分关注的增材或增量制造（Additive manufacturing），也是数字化制造的重要内容，而3D打印技术只是增材制造技术的一种方法。

智能化制造是信息技术与制造技术的更深度的融合，是数字化技术与人工智能技术的进一步集成。

美国最近公布的波音787的数字化设计内容，包含设计的数字化、研发和制造过程的数字化以及全生命周期的数字化，堪称是数字化设计的典范（图5）。美国国防先进研究计划署（DARPA）提出的加快材料研发计划（Accelerated Insertion of Materials）计划，其核心内容也是要"缩短研发周期一半、降低研发费用一半"（图6）。

图5　波音787数字化与虚拟制造范例

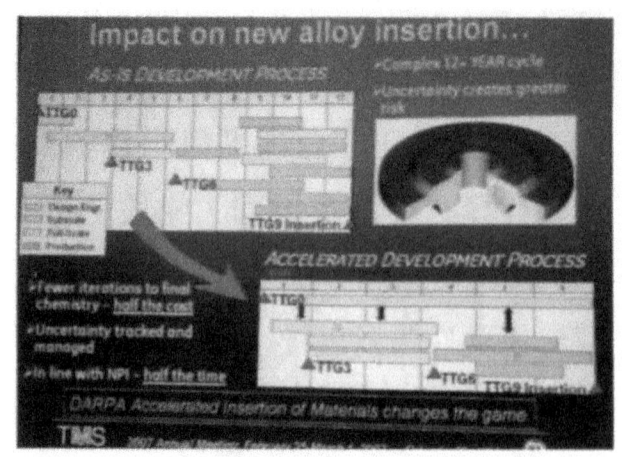

图 6 美国 DARPA 的加快材料研发计划
引自：2007 年美国 TMS 年会

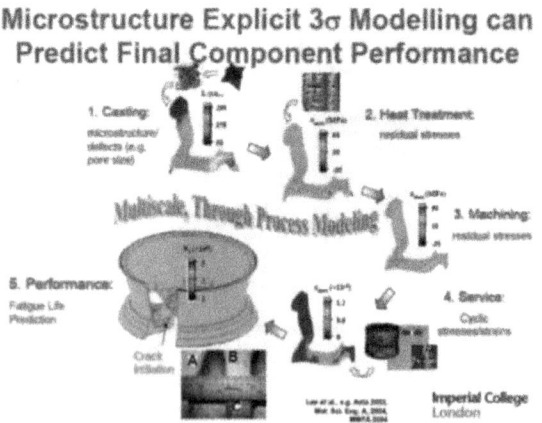

图 8 汽车轮毂铸件多尺度、全流程建模
引自：帝国理工学院 Peter Lee 教授

制造过程的数字化要建立在知识或科学的基础上（Science-based），要广泛采用建模与仿真技术，也可称之为基于科学或知识的数字化制造。最近美国学者提出集成计算材料工程（Integrated Computational Materials Engineering）的新思路（图 7），建立从工艺建模到组织建模再到性能建模。英国帝国理工学院 Peter Lee 教授则提出"多尺度、全流程建模与仿真"的新思维（图 8），从铸造、热处理到加工等全过程的建模与仿真。

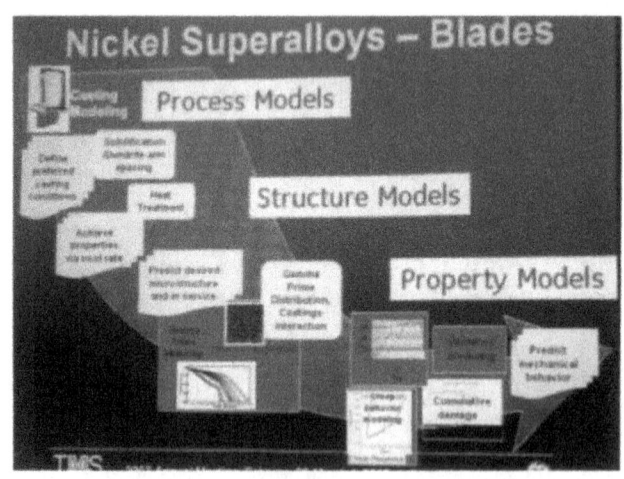

图 7 航空叶片铸件的工艺-组织-性能建模
引自：2007 年美国 TMS 年会

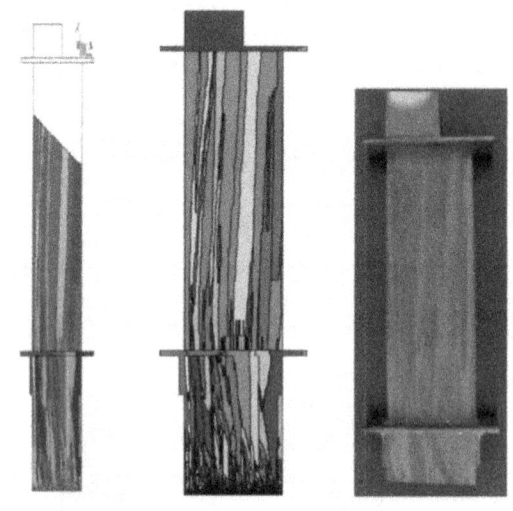

图 9 定向凝固叶片模拟和试验比较

我国在成形制造过程建模与仿真领域已取得突破性进展。例如，清华大学与日本 IHI 公司合作，建立了高温合金叶片定向凝固和单晶叶片的数理建模和仿真技术研究（图 9 及图 10）。清华大学在单晶叶片选晶器和晶体生长位相的建模与仿真也取得了进展（图 11）。

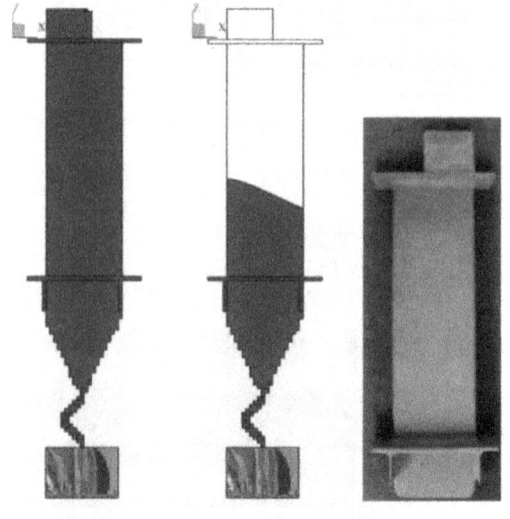

图 10 单晶叶片模拟和试验比较
引自：清华大学与日本 IHI 合作科研项目

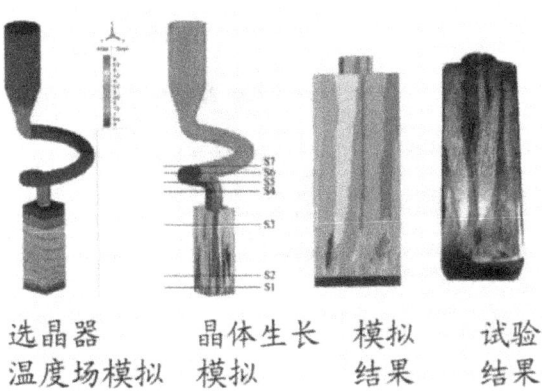

图 11 航空高温合金单晶叶片
螺旋选晶器模拟与试验

四、极端工作条件下的制造技术

极端条件下的先进制造技术,包括特大型装备制造技术、微纳制造技术等在极端工作环境下的各种制造技术。

以特大型铸锻件制造技术为例:中信重工集团已浇铸成功世界最大铸件,18500t 压力机横梁铸钢件,铸件重 520t,钢液重 830t(图 12);中国二重集团公司采用真空冶炼浇铸,成功地铸成核电转子用的 560t 钢锭。

图 12 中信重工集团浇铸成功 520t 铸钢件

特大型钢锭的主要关键点是控制宏观偏析,针对 500~600t 级钢锭的宏观偏析,中信重工集团和清华大学合作开展了系统的试验及建模与仿真研究,图 13 是重 53t 试验钢锭的宏观偏析模拟结果并与实际浇铸的试验钢锭进行了比较。目前,正在开展多包合浇 292t 特大型钢锭的建模与仿真研究。

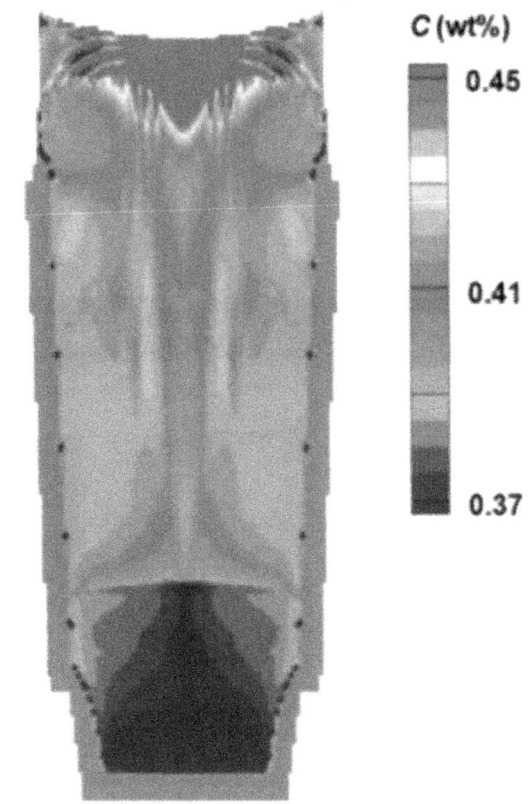

图 13 钢锭宏观偏析模拟(锭重 53t)

五、清洁及可持续发展制造技术

要发展资源节约、环境友好的先进制造技术。要实施减量化、再利用、再循环的 3R(Reduce,Reuse,Recycle)原则。贯彻减量化原则,在提高产品质量的前提下,可以减少生产费用、降低废品率及提高生产率,节省资源和能源,以及保护环境。欧洲的汽车制造商正在进行"超轻型汽车"工程,力争减轻车重 30%。

轻量化、精密或超精密化、绿色化制造技术是贯彻减量化原则的主要先进制造技术。以节能汽车为例,降低 10% 汽车重量,可提高热效率 7% 及降低污染 10%。表 1 列出不同轻量化材料的减重效果。图 14 和图 15 则是汽车采用铝合金零件和镁合金零件的减重效果。

表 1 轻量化材料减重比例

轻量化材料	替代材料	减轻重量(%)
高强度钢	碳钢	10
铝合金	钢、铸铁	40~60
镁合金	钢、铸铁	60~75
镁合金	铝合金	25~35
复合材料	钢	25~35

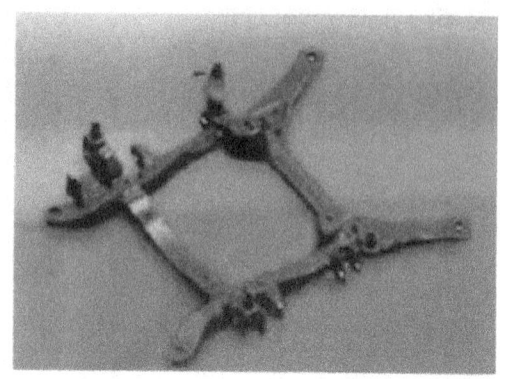

钢支架（共27个零件、重27kg）

铝合金支架（共6个零件、重16kg）

图14　铝合金发动机支架替代碳钢支架
（美国通用汽车公司提供）

钢(1.2kg)多个件组成　　铝合金(0.9kg)　　镁合金(0.6kg)比铝合金轻30%

图15　钢、铝及镁合金汽车方向盘
（通用汽车公司提供，90%的GM车已采用镁合金）

（图18）。

图16　压铸铝合金汽车缸体

图17　半固态铸造铝合金柴油机缸体

图18　3200t压铸机镁合金汽车仪表盘压铸车间和
镁合金再利用（回收）车间（美国Meridian压铸厂提供）

　　国内外广泛采用压力铸造、精密铸造、精密塑性加工、搅拌摩擦焊等精密化成形制造技术，或国外称之为"净成形制造（Net shape processing technology）"。例如，广泛采用大型压铸机或精确砂型可控压力铸造汽车发动机铝合金气缸体铸件（图16）。近年来，开展高真空压力铸造、半固态铸造等净成形新技术（图17）。又例如，镁合金被誉为绿色材料，因为可以再利用、再循环，达到可持续发展的目的

六、结束语

制造业特别是装备制造业对国家的繁荣与安全至关重要。先进制造技术是制造业和战略性新兴产业的基础技术，要十分重视发展资源节约、环境友好的先进制造技术。要发展高技术含量制造技术、数字化智能化制造技术，极端条件下制造技术及清洁与可持续发展制造技术。要加大研发投入，加强企业与高校院所的协同创新联盟。

2. 《中国制造2025》——建设制造强国之路

编者按：近年来，在中国工程院领导下，柳百成院士致力于振兴我国制造业及推广先进制造技术等战略研究，曾担任中国工程院"制造强国战略研究"课题组副组长，而《中国制造2025》的编制正是源于这一重大课题的研究。近日，柳百成院士为本刊撰写专稿，阐释了《中国制造2025》出台的背景、指导思想和主要内容，介绍了中国制造业现状和所面临的新挑战，以及美国的国家制造创新网络的进展，同时也提出了建设制造强国的几点启示等，敬请读者关注。

一、《中国制造2025》出台背景

无论是工业发达国家还是发展中国家都一致认识到，制造业是一个国家的基础和支柱工业，对国家的经济建设、繁荣富强和国家安全至关重要。但是中国制造业可以用四个字来概括："大而不强"。

2013年初，中国工程院专门启动"制造强国战略研究"项目，周济院长亲自担任组长。2014年初，中国工程院向国务院呈报在中国实施《中国制造2025》的建议。马凯副总理十分赞同中国工程院的建议，并委托工信部牵头制订具体实施计划。

2015年3月，李克强总理在全国人民代表大会的政府工作报告中，正式提出要实施《中国制造2025》。5月，国务院正式颁布《中国制造2025》文件。制造业涉及多个部门，为此专门成立了国家制造强国建设领导小组，马凯副总理亲自担任组长。接着，又成立了由一批专家组成的"国家制造强国建设战略咨询委员会"。

《中国制造2025》这个纲领性文件发布以后，引起了国内制造界的热烈反响，也引起了国外的高度关注。欧盟、美国、英国等国家或地区组织有关人士先后访问中国工程院，深切关注《中国制造2025》的内涵和发展动向。

二、中国制造业现状

《中国制造2025》既是面向未来发展，又实事求是地分析了我国制造业的现状。

中国制造"大而不强"。根据世界银行2011年的统计，我国的制造业增加值是23 300亿美元，是世界第一制造大国。美国是18 530亿美元，排第二位。2011年，我国的制造业增加值占全世界的制造业增加值的20%左右，美国占16%左右，第三是日本，第四是德国，德国大概占8%左右。最近公布的2013年的数据，我国制造业增加值占世界的制造业增加值已经超过了20%。我国确实是名副其实的世界制造业大国。

新中国成立以来，特别是改革开放30年以来，我国制造业取得了举世瞩目的成就，而且有相当一部分装备已经达到了国际先进水平，这是大家公认的。但是，中国制造是"大而不强"，可以归纳为三大问题。

1. 创新能力不足

根据世界银行等权威机构公布的数据，我国的全球创新能力指标（GII）和全球竞争能力指标（GCI）大概处在世界的25~30位。根据我国社会科学文献出版社公布的《世界创新竞争力发展报告（2001~2012）》，2010年我国的创新竞争力排名在全世界的第15位。反映创新能力的另一个重要指标，就是研发投入R&D和GDP的比值。最近几年，我国R&D/GDP大大增加了，2014年是2.0%，这已经很了不起了。但是，从世界范围来看，工业发达国家一般均大于2.5%，我们和世界工业发达国家来比，仍有差距。我国企业的研发投入和销售收入之比，与世界著名企业相比则差距更大。

2. 核心技术薄弱，共性技术缺位

我国自主研制的C919是单通道窄体客机，座位是160~180座，但是发动机全部从国外引进，主要材料也大部分依靠进口。正在研制的重型燃气轮

本文刊登于《表面工程与再制造》，2016，16（1）：1-6.

机的关键材料和关键零部件,如高温合金定向及单晶工作叶片仍依赖进口。近年来,我国加大对数控机床的研发投入,但是 80% 的高端数控机床至今仍依赖进口。2013 年,我国已是机器人消费大国,但 80% 的机器人是进口的。

3. 资源浪费,污染严重

2010 年,我国的 GDP 占全世界 GDP 的 7.5%。但是,我国的能耗却占了全世界的 19.6%。2010 年,我国制造业增加值占我国 GDP 的 32.6%,但能耗却占整个国家的 58.0%。就是说,我们制造出相同的产品用了比工业发达国家多 1 倍的能耗。

目前我国 56% 的原油、50% 的铁矿仍然依赖进口。水质和空气污染严重,已成为全国人民十分关心的问题。

三、中国制造业面临新挑战

我国虽然取得举世瞩目的成就,但也面临着新的挑战。

1. 新科技和新工业革命的挑战

当今世界科技发展迅速,迎来了新的工业革命,如大数据、云计算、生物制药、新材料、新能源、增材制造、智能制造等。新的科技和工业革命,对中国的制造业提出了新的挑战。前两年美国《华盛顿邮报》发表一篇文章,很傲慢地说"现在轮到中国制造业担心的时候了,因为美国在人工智能、机器人等方面占有优势"。当然,新的科技和工业革命对我们既是挑战,也是新的机遇。

2. 工业发达国家"再工业化"的挑战

2011 年,美国政府正式启动了"先进制造伙伴计划(AMP)",提出了"在哪里发明,在哪里制造"的口号,要确保先进制造业在世界的领先地位,要重新夺回制造业的世界市场。

德国结合自己的国情,提出了以智能制造为核心的"工业 4.0"计划,以确保德国的世界制造强国地位。

2013 年,英国发布了《未来的制造》报告。同时,为加快促进成果转化,建立了先进制造、成形技术等 7 个"高价值制造(HVM)推进研发中心"。

2015 年 10 月,在韩国国家工程院成立 20 周年会议上,韩国代表提出发展制造业的战略目标就是要发展智能制造,并和物联网集成。

他山之石,可以攻玉。我们也可以学习借鉴工业发达国家"再工业化"的经验和教训。

四、美国制造创新网络[1-3]

2014 年,中国工程院专门组团访问了欧洲,特别是德国。回来以后,对于德国"工业 4.0"做了较详细的介绍。2015 年 5 月,中国工程院再次组团,到美国考察了"先进制造伙伴计划",特别是考察了美国的国家制造创新网络的进展。下面就美国考察结果做概要介绍。

1. 国家制造创新网络(NNMI)

美国建立的"国家制造创新网络",是由一批"制造创新研究院"组成。第一批将建设 15 个制造创新研究院,计划要建立 45 个"制造创新研究院"。为什么要建立"制造创新研究院"呢?美国用技术成熟度来评估研究成果转化的进程。基础研究为 1~3 级,小批量研制为 4~6 级,成果产业化和批量生产为 7~9 级。当前的主要问题是:从实验室到原型小批量研制(4~6 级)缺位。

美国认为中间环节存在一个鸿沟,并用了一个夸张的词汇"死亡谷(valley of death)"来描述。美国认为科技成果从高校院所研究出来申报了很多专利、发表了很多文章后,就掉到了"死亡谷"而消失,最后没有能够产业化。为此,在"先进制造伙伴计划"下,专门建议要建立一批"制造创新研究院",并组成"国家制造创新网络"。在此基础上,2014 年 12 月,美国国会专门通过了"振兴美国制造业与创新(RAMI)"法案。

2. 国家"制造创新研究院"

建设"制造创新研究院"的目的就是要解决"死亡谷"问题,使得科技成果能够产业化。

"制造创新研究院"有四项主要目标:一是提高美国制造业竞争能力,二是将创新技术进行成果转化,三是加快高级劳动力的培训,四是促使研究院运行模式能保持稳定及可持续发展。

"制造创新研究院"的宗旨很明确,凡是一个企业能做的,它绝不支持。这里有两个词,一个是"竞争前技术"或者叫共性技术。另一个是"竞争技术"。美国政府可以支持竞争前技术研发,绝不支持竞争技术研发。"制造创新研究院"主要从事的跨行业的共性技术、竞争前技术研发。

"制造创新研究院"的宗旨是研究成果（竞争前、共性技术）可以共享。我国建立了很多国家级工程实验室等，但研究成果不能共享，没有起到这个作用。我国缺乏共性技术的研究，实际上过去的大院大所改制后，造成了现在的共性技术研发缺位。

美国"制造创新研究院"的特点是组成产学研协同联盟。我们现在也有很多产学研联盟，但是很多联盟貌合神离，只是为了向国家要钱。美国"制造创新研究院"由产（包含大中小企业）、学（包含大学、社区学院）、研（包含国家级研究院所）、政组成非营利的创新联盟。"制造创新研究院"设立具体办事机构，有的"制造创新研究院"还建有示范基地或实验室。"制造创新研究院"的研究开发项目经费，原则上国家按1:1方式给予资助。每个"制造创新研究院"可以获得政府约7000万美元的资助。

美国已建成7个、正在建设2个"制造创新研究院"，其中涉及智能制造和基础工艺的有：增材制造、轻量化材料、数字化制造与设计、先进复合材料及智慧制造（Smart Manufacturing）等5所"制造创新研究院"。

3. 集成计算材料工程（ICME）进展

美国在宣布"先进制造伙伴计划"的同时，宣布了"基因组计划（MGI）"。在"基因组计划"中，特别强调集成计算材料工程。集成计算材料工程就是要把计算工具中的材料信息与工程产品性能分析及制造工艺仿真集成在一起。最终目的是缩短研发周期，降低研发费用；用了一个响亮口号"一半时间，一半费用（half the time, half the cost）"。

例如，美国通用电气公司把航空发动机高温叶片的工艺模拟、组织模拟、性能模拟集成起来，经过反复的工艺模拟和优化，大大提高了产品的质量。福特汽车公司提出了多尺度建模与仿真的口号，称之为"从原子到汽车"，把材料设计、工艺建模、性能预测集成起来。

实际上，这就是我国多年来倡导的制造技术与信息化的深度融合，实施数字化、智能化制造。

五、《中国制造2025》的指导思想和主要内容

工信部苗圩部长对《中国制造2025》曾做过多次解读，高度概括、相当精辟。大体上可以简要概括为"一个目标、三步走战略，五条指导思想，五大工程及十大重点领域"。

1. 一个总目标及三步走战略

《中国制造2025》的总目标就是要由大变强，建设成制造强国。

为建设制造强国又提出了三步走的战略：第一步，到2025年，经过10年努力，能够进入到世界制造业强国行列。第二步，到2035年，希望能够进入世界制造强国阵营较高水平，大体上可以接近或者达到德国或日本的水平。第三步到2045年，或者到新中国成立100周年，也就是2049年，希望我国能够进入到世界强国的前列。

这个纲领文件发布以后，很多省、市和地区积极响应，都在制定地方或区域的2025规划。他们忘掉了"三步走战略"，而是希望到2025年就能全部实现制造智能化等战略任务。因此，要再次强调，我国的建设制造强国的宏伟目标是要经过30年的努力奋斗才能达到。

2. 五项指导思想

文件首先提出"创新驱动、质量为先、绿色发展、结构优化、人才为本"五项指导思想。文件将"质量为先"作为重要的指导思想。应该指出，现在很多产品不合格、质量不过关，主要问题还是出在材料和基础工艺上，甚至是热处理、材料成形、加工精度等基础工艺。因此，中国工程院于2014年，专门启动了"工程强基战略研究"咨询项目。

3. 五大工程及十大重点领域

为具体实施《中国制造2025》，工信部正在积极制定五大工程实施方案，即：制造业创新中心建设工程、智能制造工程、工业强基工程、绿色制造工程及高端装备制造工程。其中高端装备聚焦在新一代信息通信技术产业，高档数控机床和机器人，航空航天装备，海洋工程装备及高技术船舶，先进轨道交通装备，节能与新能源汽车，电力装备，新材料，生物医药及高性能医疗器械，农业机械装备十大重点领域。

六、建设制造强国的几点启示

1. 进一步完善国家技术创新体系

创新驱动，首先企业要转变观念，加大研发投

入，成为技术创新主体。据统计，我国企业研发投入占销售收入的比值不到1%，而工业发达国家一般在3%~5%左右。企业是技术创新主体，主要是指：市场及科技需求的主体，研发投入的主体（主要指竞争技术），科技成果产业化的主体。

其次，我国技术成果转化率仅10%左右。一个重要原因是技术创新体系不完善，在技术研究成果到企业产业化间存在缺位（美国称之为鸿沟）。特别是大院大所改制后，造成"共性技术"研究缺位。这一缺位问题亟待解决，已到了刻不容缓的时刻。

因此，《中国制造2025》的第一个建设工程，就是要建立一批制造业国家创新中心。建设国家创新中心的关键，一是要成果共享；二是要开展竞争前、关键共性技术研究与开发，要为跨行业或全行业服务；三是要集中国内产学研优势单位组成创新联盟，不能遍地开花，低水平重复设置。

2. 加强先进基础工艺研究

现在，很多专家都认为我国很多企业还处在工业2.0阶段，不可能弯道超车，直接进入智能化制造。因此，先进基础工艺一定要补课，不要看不起铸锻焊及热处理等基础工艺。例如，航空发动机的关键零部件，一个是涡轮盘（是锻件或粉末成形件），一个是航空单晶叶片（是铸件）。我们考察美国的"制造创新研究院"、高校或企业的研究与创新中心，都十分重视铸造、塑性加工、焊接、热处理等先进基础工艺的研究。同时又十分重视先进基础工艺及基础材料与信息化（数字化）的深度融合和集成，特别是集成计算材料工程（ICME）的研究。

要加强竞争前、基础共性技术研究，单靠企业不行，需要政府主导、产学研用联合，共同组成协同创新联盟，建设竞争前、关键共性基础技术研发平台。例如，美国政府设立的"轻量化材料制造创新研究院"，研究项目的立项，要根据需求征得企业同意，而该研究院的主要牵头单位则是由一所研究院所和两所大学主持。技术总负责人由具有丰富工程经验的教授担任。

因此，建议在《中国制造2025》"工业强基工程"中，要大力加强基础材料、先进基础工艺研究，并与信息化深度融合，加强"集成计算材料工程（ICME）"的研究。互联网、云计算和大数据等信息技术正深刻改变着制造业的创新发展模式。加强先进基础工艺研究，也要和互联网、云计算和大数据的发展相互融合。

3. 加快培养各层次的工程技术人才

人才建设是建设制造强国的根本。要十分重视各个层次（从领军人才到高级技工）的工程技术人员的培养，特别是第一线的高级技能人员的培养。我国现在特别缺少高水平技工。

我们需要各方面的人才。美国也强调要加强能适应新技术、具有知识和技能的劳动力的教育和培训，并且将劳动力教育和培训作为国家"制造创新研究院"的重要任务之一。

4. 加强高等工科学校学生实践环节及创新能力培养

近年来，我国高等工科学校的教学实践环节有所削弱，有"工科培养理科化"的倾向。其中有很多原因，如企业也不欢迎学生去实习，以及经费问题等。因此，要引起有关部门的注意，要大力加强工科院校实验室建设，加强实践环节培养和训练，通过实践环节等训练，着实提高学生的创新能力。

七、结束语

制造业是国民经济的主体，是立国之本、兴国之器、强国之基。对国家的经济发展、繁荣富强、国家安全至关重要。《中国制造2025》是建设制造强国的纲领性文件，将鼓舞和动员制造领域企业界和学术界等各方面力量，为建设制造强国而努力奋斗。建设制造强国要以创新驱动为指导思想，以强化基础为技术支撑，以智能制造为突破口。

参考文献

[1] 美国国家制造创新网络及先进制造技术考察报告，内部材料，中国工程院赴美考察代表团，2015年7月．

[2] National Network for Manufacturing Innovation Program-Annual Report, Executive Office of the President, USA, Feb. 2016.

[3] National Network for Manufacturing Innovation Program-Strategy Plan, Executive Office of the President, USA, Feb. 2016.

3. 数字化设计与制造是智能制造关键共性技术

作者简介：柳百成教授，1955年毕业于清华大学，获优秀毕业生金质奖章。1978—1981年他以访问学者身份赴美国威斯康星大学及麻省理工学院进修2年。1999年当选为中国工程院院士。2002年获第4届"光华工程科技奖"，2012年获中国机械工程学会第一届"铸造工业杰出贡献奖"。现任清华大学材料学院及机械工程学院教授。他的主要研究领域：多尺度铸造及凝固过程建模与仿真，铸造合金物理冶金学及发展先进制造技术和振兴制造业战略研究。

一、数字化设计与制造是智能制造的关键共性技术

国务院颁布的《中国制造2025》，是建设制造强国的纲领性文件。文件吸取了美国、德国等国的所长，又结合了中国的特点，聚焦在五大工程，即：创新体系建设、智能制造、工业强基、绿色制造及高端装备创新五大工程。并且，把智能制造工程作为主攻方向。

应该指出，智能制造是先进制造技术与信息化技术深度融合的发展趋势和方向，但切忌一哄而起，企图一蹴而成。当今也有不少认识误区，以为用了"机器人"或"增材制造"就是智能制造，以为联上了"互联网"就是智能制造等。我的理解，智能制造应包涵智能产品、智能装备、智能制造过程（智能车间及工厂）及智能制造生产模式。其中智能制造过程是重要组成部分，而基于模型的数字化设计与制造则是智能制造的关键共性技术。美国新成立的智能制造创新研究院则聚焦在：智能传感器、数据分析（建模与仿真及人工智能）及智能控制。

例如，美国波音777大飞机的研发一直被公认是数字化设计的典范，它缩短了研发周期40%，更好、更快、更符合要求制造出创新产品。从波音777又发展到波音787，这是国际上最先进的大飞机。大家都知道，波音787的主要特点是复合材料用量超过50%。但是，波音787还有第二个特点，就是大量广泛采用了数字化设计与制造，可以用4D来表示。从数字化设计、数字化制造、数字化研发到数字化全生命周期，进一步发展了数字化的设计与制造。

二、美、英等国数字化设计与制造发展概况

美国很早就提出"产品设计与制造一体化"提出一个愿景："一次产品开发成功（First Product Correct Model）"。一次研发成功的关键是在产品设计时，考虑产品制造，同时并行进行建模与仿真。现在有了信息化、数字化技术就有可能大大缩短研发周期，降低研发成本，就有可能使产品一次研发成功。

早在2006年，美国国防先进计划研究署（简称DARPA），提出了加快材料的研发周期计划。因为一个新材料研发成功到应用，如大飞机的起落架，需要12年时间。因此，提出要加快研发，就是用信息化技术，把研发周期缩短一半，研发成本缩短一半。例如，GE公司研发航空发动机的关键零部件单晶叶片及涡轮盘，采用了数字化建模与仿真技术，又称之为集成计算材料工程（ICME），做到工艺模型、组织模型，最后到性能模型的集成。英国罗-罗公司是欧洲的航空发动机制造公司，早就提出：全流程建模与仿真技术。罗-罗公司和帝国理工学院、剑桥大学等院校合作，前期的工作主要由院校进行，通过全流程建模与仿真，大大缩短了研发的周期。

近年来，美国政府启动了国家制造创新网络。它是由一批制造创新研究院组成，第一批计划建15所，总计划要建45所。今年9月12日，美国政府又将"国家制造创新网络"用了一个更为明确、让大众通俗易懂的名称，称之为"制造业-美国（Manufacturing USA）"。

到2016年，美国已经建立了9所制造创新研究

---

① 本文刊登于《先进制造业》，2016年9月刊。

院,其中 3 所与智能制造直接有关。今年 9 月,美国宣布正在建立第 10 所"工业机器人"创新研究院。美国制造创新研究院具有四大特点:一是非盈利为目的,为大中小企业服务,二是从事竞争前共性技术研发,三是成果可以共享,四是组成产学研的协同创新联盟。

美国成立的第 3 所数字化制造与设计制造创新研究院,研究任务就是要将设计—研发原型—生产过程—测试过程,一直到销售全过程联系起来,全部数据在每个阶段能够流畅运行。其目的是做到产品在最好的时间、最好的地方做得更好、更快,而且又非常便宜和更具有竞争力。这个研究院虽然称为数字化制造与设计创新研究院,但它宣称:如果真正实施了整个流程、全面的数字化数据交换和处理,也就是一般人所说的智能制造。

今年 6 月在洛杉矶刚刚建立的第 9 所智能制造创新研究院,由 200 多个企业、大学、研究院所组成创新联盟,总部设在洛杉矶,成立了 5 个分中心,遍布美国全国三十几个州。创新研究院的重点聚焦先进传感器、数据分析与控制及共性技术平台。其目的就是要从根本上降低研发成本,提高美国先进制造业的效率及全球竞争力。

下面举几个最新应用实例。2005 年,美国研发波音 767 时,要做 77 次风动实验。现在研发波音 787 时只要 11 次实验。美国通用电气公司研究开发航空发动机的喷嘴,用 10000 个处理器组成的高性能计算机,模拟和优化了发动机的喷嘴设计,大大提高了发动机的效率,降低了成本,降低了油耗等。接着,通用电气又直接用增材制造技术,生产高温合金喷嘴。它采用直接金属激光熔化技术,将喷嘴寿命提高了 5 倍。因为它的批量并不是很大,通用电气已经将增材制造直接用作生产,而不仅仅是原型研发。

我国刚刚成立了航空发动机集团公司,新华社专门做了报道,提到一个新的航空发动机研发要几十年的时间。如何能够做好、加快?可以直接采用数字化、网络化、智能化设计与制造技术。

三、我国在数字化设计与制造研究进展

我国政府及工信部一再强调,工业化要和信息化深度融合,来促进和推动制造业的发展。我国在很多行业也已取得进展,已有较好基础。早在 2000 年,长江三峡水轮机叶片,原来完全依靠进口,中国二重集团采用了我国自主研发的软件,叶片一次试制成功。新华社专门做了报道,认为打破了这个叶片被国外垄断的制造技术。2002 年,马鞍山钢铁公司引进了德国的全套连轧设备,由于经费有限,主要设备要由国内自己制造。他们联合清华大学,对 218t 的轧钢机机架铸钢件工艺,采用数字化模拟和优化技术,铸钢件一次研发成功。接着,在 10 个月内成功生产了 18 件机架铸钢件,为企业节省经费超过 1 亿元。

2013 年,为了配合智能制造,中国工程院启动了网络化数字化设计—制造—服务一体化战略咨询项目。我国在航空及汽车领域,已取得初步成效。航空工业研制飞机,从设计到首飞比传统周期缩短了一半。汽车工业网络化数字化设计与制造研发也取得了进展。中国一汽集团的"数字化发动机",

从数字化设计、数字化加工和生产、数字化检测、到销售,实现了全过程数字化。东风汽车集团也提出建立商用车全过程数字化研发平台,从商品规划、设计、实验、生产到整个流程进行建模与仿真。

四、结束语

实施《中国制造2025》,智能制造是主攻方向。数字化设计与制造则是智能制造过程的关键共性技术,而基于科学或知识的建模与仿真是数字化设计与制造的基础。美国等工业发达国家十分重视发展智能制造,美国建立的国家智能制造创新研究院,其目的是要为大中小企业提供智能制造共性技术服务和平台。我国在基于网络化的数字设计与制造领域已经具有较好的技术基础。但是,要充分认识到全面实施智能制造,仍然是任重而道远。

4. 创新·强基·智能——建设制造强国

柳百成[1,2,3]

1. 清华大学机械工程学院，北京，100084
2. 清华大学材料学院，北京，100084
3. 先进成形制造教育部重点实验室，北京，100084

摘　要：世界工业发达国家美、德、英等国"重振制造业"的发展战略均将智能制造作为发展趋势。我国制造业总体而言，大而不强。我国已是世界制造第一大国，但创新能力弱、缺乏关键核心及共性技术。我国《制造强国发展战略》聚焦"五大工程"，其中将智能制造作为主攻方向，而"五大工程"是相互联系和相互支持的。数字化设计与制造是智能制造关键共性技术，而建模与仿真是数字化设计与制造的科学基础。要全面实施智能制造，建成制造强国，任重而道远。

关键词：创新；工业强基；智能制造；制造业

中图分类号：F424

DOI：10.3969/j.issn.1004-132X.2020.01.002

Innovation · Fundamentals · Intelligence—for Strong Manufacturing Industry

LIU Baicheng[1,2,3]

1. School of Mechanical Engineering, Tsinghua University, Beijing, 100084
2. School of Materials Science and Engineering, Tsinghua University, Beijing, 100084
3. Key Laboratory for Advanced Materials Processing Technology, Ministry of Education, Beijing, 100084

Abstract: National strategies to re-vitalizing manufacturing industry from United States, United Kingdom and Germany were studied, and intelligent manufacturing would be their main trend. China manufacturing industry was big but not strong. China manufacturing values added were in the first position of the world, the weakness in innovation ability and lack of key competitive technologies were pointed. Therefore, China national strategy for strong manufacturing industry focusesd on "five important projects", and intelligent manufacturing would be the first priority. In addition, digital design and manufacturing was the critical and fundamental technology for intelligent manufacturing, while modeling and simulation would be the scientific base. It should be stressed that China are on the way to build strong manufacturing industry as well as intelligent manufacturing.

Key words: innovation; robust industrial foundation; intelligent manufacturing; manufacturing industry

0　引言

制造业是国之重器，是国民经济的物质基础。近年来，在中国工程院的领导下，笔者参与了《制造强国战略研究》《工业强基战略研究》等多个项目的研究工作，参与了工业与信息化部领导下的制造强国建设战略咨询研究。2015年及2017年，笔者还专门访问美国，考察了美国制造业创新研究院。现就创新驱动、强化基础、智能制造、建设制造强国等议题发表个人的见解。

本文刊登于《中国机械工程》，2020，31(1)：13-18。

1 世界工业发达国家制造业发展战略

近年来,世界各国,特别是工业发达国家,都在大力重振制造业,纷纷出台新的制造业发展战略。

2013年,英国提出《未来制造业》(《The Future of Manufacturing》)发展战略。2017年,英国一份咨询报告中更提出了"让制造更智能(Made Smarter)"的愿景。

2013年,德国出台"工业4.0"战略,聚焦智能制造及互联网 2019年,进一步提出《德国工业2035》规划,聚焦若干先进制造领域。应该指出,在德国,"工业4.0"也是处于发展过程之中。2014年,德国西门子总裁在韩国庆祝韩国国家工程院建院20周年的大会上作主旨报告,他的报告主题的副标题是"走在工业4.0的路上(On the Way to Industry 4.0)"。

早在2011年,美国政府提出"先进制造伙伴计划"(Advanced Manufacturing Partnership)战略,提出"在哪里发明,在哪里制造"的口号,要重新夺回制造业的世界市场。美国总统科技顾问委员会的多份报告都认为,美国制造业的主要问题是:在原创性成果到产业化间存在鸿沟,或称之为"死亡谷(valley of death)"[1-6](见图1)。如按技术成熟度来衡量,他们再三强调要重点解决4~7级关键共性技术,或称之为竞争前技术(precompetitive technology)。为此,美国于2013年组建了国家制造创新网络(National Network for Manufacturing Innovation, NNMI),其目标是建设一批制造创新研究院,在原创性成果与产业化间架设桥梁。该计划于2016年更名为"制造业美国"(Manufacturing USA),目前已有14所制造创新研究院并组建成了网络[4-6],网络中各成员可充分利用联盟单位的已有研发基础及条件,如图2所示。值得注意的是:这些制造创新研究院均由产学研机构组成创新联盟来统一管理运行,而联盟成员的66%是企业,企业中66%又是中小企业。

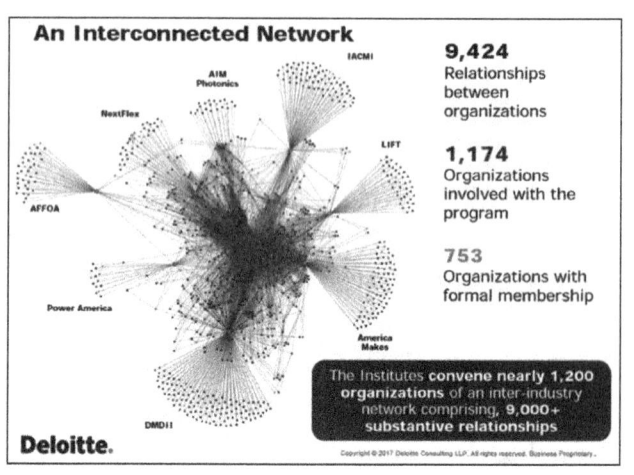

图2 由一批制造创新研究院组建成的美国国家制造创新网络

Fig. 2 National Network for Manufacturing Innovation by a number of manufacturing innovation institutes

美国14所制造创新研究院中,增材制造、数字化制造与设计、清洁能源智能制造及先进机器人4所研究院聚焦智能制造领域,其余研究院则聚焦生物、电子、材料工艺及能源等领域,这些研究院已初步取得成效。在2017年美国国家科学院召开的会议上,洛克希德-马丁公司认为,制造创新研究院为公司提供了竞争前技术,很有价值,他们已参加了多所创新研究院产学研联盟[3]。2019年,美国进一步提出"美国领导先进制造业战略(Strategy for American Leadership in Advanced Manufacturing)"[7]。

总之,他山之石、可以攻玉,国外工业发达国家重振制造业的经验和教训值得我们借鉴。

2 我国制造业现状

我国已是世界制造大国,我国制造业的现状可以归纳为"大而不强"。图3所示是2013年美国公布的数据,可以看出,我国制造业增加值已位居世界第一,美、日、德则分居第2、3、4位[3]。

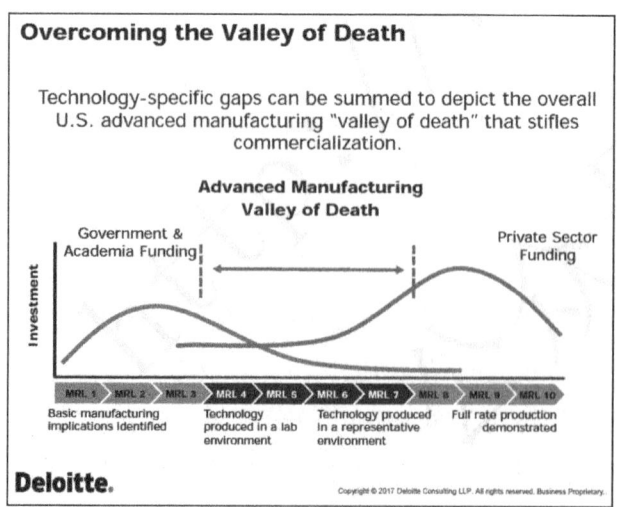

图1 制造业研发与产业化间的"死亡谷"

Fig. 1 "Valley of death" between invention and commercialization

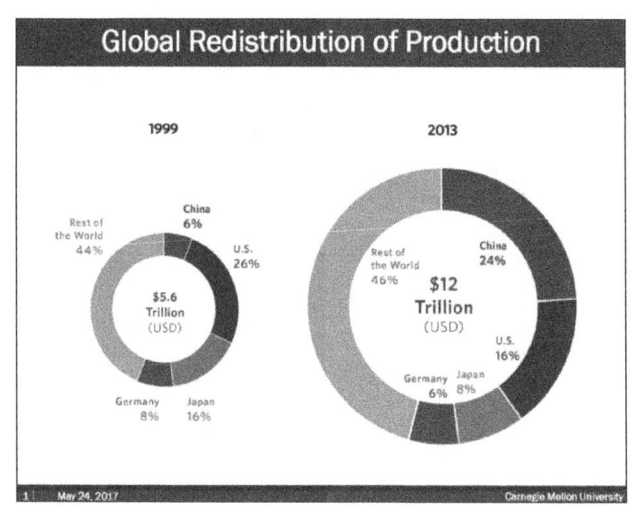

图 3 1999 年及 2013 年世界制造业增加值
分布及比较图

Fig. 3 Distribution of world manufacturing value added in 1999 and 2013

但是,我国制造业的主要问题是:创新能力弱,缺乏关键核心及共性技术。根据国际权威机构发布的全球创新能力指数(global innovation index)及全球竞争力指数(global competitiveness index),我国排位仍处在 15~20 之间。2014 年,中国工程院向马凯副总理汇报"制造强国发展战略"时,马凯副总理提出,是不是制造强国,要有几个重要标志,如航空发动机能不能实现自主研发等。应该指出,我国民用航空发动机及重型燃气轮机与国外相比,仍有相当大的差距。又例如,我国正在大力推广工业机器人,已是世界机器人消费第一大国,但是多数仍依赖进口。2019 年,笔者随中国工程院赴广州考察时了解到,广东已有上百家制造机器人的企业,但是广州汽车制造公司的流水线上,几乎全部是进口的高端工业机器人。因此,我国制造业要从中、低端走向中、高端,仍有很长的路要走,切忌急躁情绪,以为指日可待。

3 我国制造强国发展战略及五大工程

中国工程院十分重视我国制造业的发展。在 2004 年"国家中长期科技发展规划战略研究"报告及 2008 年"装备制造业自主创新战略研究"报告[8]中,都将"数字化、智能化设计制造及基础装备"作为制造业科技发展的重大专项之一。

2013 年,中国工程院正式启动"制造强国战略研究(一期)"咨询项目,有 100 余位院士和专家积极参加。2014 年初,中国工程院正式向国务院汇报,并提出实施"制造强国"发展战略计划。在此基础_上由工业和信息化部牵头,会同有关部委,正式起草《中国制造 2025》战略文件(以下简称《发展战略》)[9]。该文件于 2015 年 5 月由国务院正式颁布,同时分别成立制造强国建设领导小组及由 40 多位专家组成的制造强国建设战略咨询委员会。中国工程院主持的"制造强国战略研究"二期及三期项目仍在进行之中。

《发展战略》提出了三步走的战略目标:到 2025 年,我国制造业进入世界制造强国行列;到 2035 年,我国制造业整体达到世界制造强国阵营中等水平;2045 年或建国 100 周年,制造业科技水平处于国际前列,接近或达到美国水平。

为实施《发展战略》,要聚焦推进"五大工程",即:创新体系建设工程、工业强基工程、智能制造工程、绿色制造工程及高端装备创新工程。

需要强调的是:我们既要重视将智能制造作为主攻方向,又要关注到"五大工程"是相互联系、相互支持的(图 4)。没有传感器等基础元器件,没有基础材料和先进工业,何来智能制造。

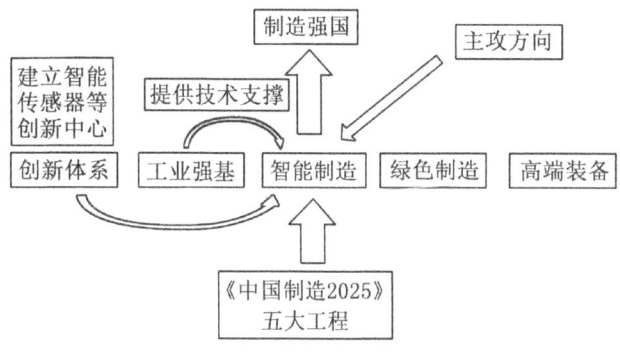

图 4 相互联系、相互支持的"五大工程"

Fig. 4 Five important projects interconnected and integrated

总之,《发展战略》的颁布,极大地调动了企业界、学术界等工程科技人员的积极性,将举全国之力,为建设制造强国而努力奋斗。

4 建设制造业创新体系[9]

我国长期以来关键共性技术(即竞争前技术)缺位的现实严重影响了科研成果的转化[8]。为此,《发展战略》将建设一批国家制造业创新研究中心作为十分重要的战略任务。制造业创新研究中心的目标：一是研发工作，并为大/中/小企业提供关键共性技术（技术成熟度：4~7 级）；二是要培训相关技术的工程技术人员及高级技工；三是要在政府的支持下，逐步实现自主经营，进而具备可持续发展能力。

目前，我国制造业创新研究中心的运行模式主要采用"公司+联盟"方式。要求国内相关领域的主要产（包含大/中/小企业）、学、研单位整合起来，组成协同创新联盟，并形成网络。创新中心要充分利用已有的资源和装备，而不是另起炉灶，从零开始。当然，我国制造业创新研究中心的运行模式仍在探索和积累经验阶段，有待进一步完善。

据不完全统计，到 2019 年 6 月，我国已建成或通过建设方案论证的已有 13 所国家制造业创新研究中心，它们是：动力电池、增材制造、印刷与显示、机器人、信息光电子、轻量化材料与装备、数字化设计与制造、智能传感器、集成电路、先进功能纤维、先进轨道交通装备、智能网联汽车、农机装备等[10,11]。其中有 4 所研究中心聚焦智能制造领域，为智能制造提供创新平台。目前，这些制造业创新研究中心主要集中于我国东部工业发达地区。

5 加强工业基础[9,12]

长期以来，我们受"重产品、重型号，轻基础轻工艺"及"重硬轻软"等思想的影响，存在急于求成、"立竿见影"等急躁情绪，结果是投入虽大但碎片化问题突出，效果适得其反。应该指出，当年我国"大院、大所改制"的做法进一步造成了产业关键共性技术研发缺位[8]。

近年来，工业与信息化部领导多次强调"基础不牢、地动山摇"。加强工业基础建设的重要性日益受到重视，大家一致认为要下大功夫、持之以恒，才能真正打好工业基础。因此，总结以往经验教训，《发展战略》专门将"工业强基工程"作为"五大工程"之一。"工业强基工程"聚焦于"4 基"：基础元器件、基础材料、基础先进工艺及相应的基础标准。最近，各界人士建议应再增加"1 基"，即基础工业软件。

加强工业基础研究，需要政府支持，产、学、研、用四方组成协同创新联盟。加强工业基础，一方面要补短板，解决一批当前国家急需的关键共性技术；另一方面，更要有长远规划，扎扎实实地建设一批工业基础创新平台，解决"大院、大所改制"后长期以来存在的"共性技术"缺位问题。例如，在"创新体系建设工程"中，要建设一批如传感器、轻量化材料、数字化设计与制造等创新平台。

6 数字化是智能制造关键共性技术[13]

智能制造是基于新一代信息通信技术与先进制造技术深度融合，贯穿于设计、生产、管理、服务等制造活动的各个环节，具有自感知、自学习、自决策、自执行、自适应等功能的新型制造模式。智能制造可包括智能生产制造、智能产品、智能装备及智能服务等方面[14]。

现聚焦智能生产制造及智能工厂作进一步论述。应该指出，感知、决策、控制、建模仿真及相关支撑工业软件是智能制造过程及智能工厂的关键共性技术。美国数字化制造与设计创新研究院及智能制造创新研究院也都将感知、控制、高性能计算建模与仿真及软件平台作为关键共性技术。

智能制造不等同于"机器人换人"，也不等同于"黑暗工厂"。总之，智能制造不是自动化，而是应具有自感知、自决策、自控制等功能。其中数字化是关键技术基础，而建模与仿真则是其科学基础。

早在 2006 年，美国国防先进研究计划署（DARPA）就提出"加快材料研发计划（Accelerated Insertion of Materials）"，要求材料工艺研发周期缩短一半，研发经费减少一半（half the cost, half the time），以满足产品研发的需要，而其核心内容就是建模与仿真。美国研发波音 787 飞机时，采用了"4-D"技术，即数字化设计、数字化制造、数字化研发及数字化全生命周期。同样，英国 Rolls-Royes 公司研发航空发动机关键零部件时也采用"全流程建模与仿真技术"（图 5）。2018 年，中国工程院组团访问德国西门子研发机构时，他们提出"数字孪生（digital twin）"是智能工厂（含产品、制造、服务）的心脏（图 6），而建模与仿真则是其核心技术。

据报道，美国 2005 年研发波音 767 飞机时，大飞机需要进行 77 次风洞试验，研发波音 787 飞机时，采用建模与仿真技术，仅需进行 11 次风洞试验，大大缩短了研发周期，并降低了研发成本 2014 年，美国通用电气公司采用高性能计算机模拟和优化航空发动机喷嘴设计，大大提高了发动机的效率，降低油耗，减少污染。

应该指出，我国在数字化设计与制造方面，特

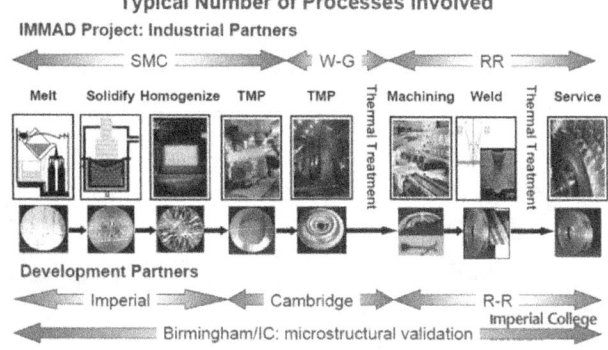

图 5 Rolls-Royce 公司全流程建模技术
Fig. 5 Through process modeling technology by Rolls-Royce

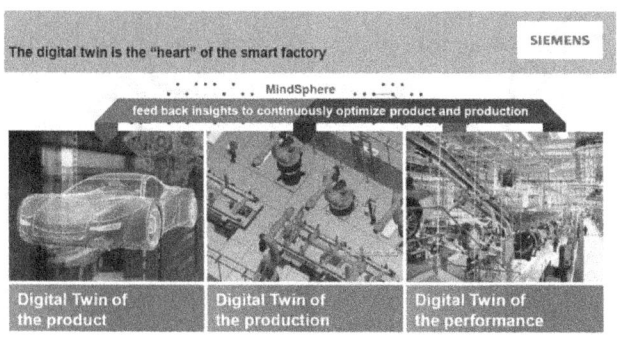

图 6 德国西门子公司产品-制造-服务"三维数字孪生"方案
Fig. 6 "3D digital twin" including product-manufacturing-service by Siemens

别是建模与仿真技术方面已取得重要进展,为发展智能制造提供了重要技术支撑。早在2002年,我国"三峡工程"水轮机叶轮不锈钢叶片铸件在中国第二重型机械集团公司首次浇注成功,打破了水轮机叶轮大型铸件受制于人的局面[15]。该铸件研发过程中采用了清华大学自主研发的"铸造之星"模拟软件,新华社专门对此成果进行了报道,并指出:该铸件的研发成功"打破了国外公司垄断该种叶片关键制造技术的格局"。

近年来,我国航空工业及汽车工业在数字化设计工程应用方面取得了较大进展,华中科技大学在数字化装备,浙江大学在高端数控装备数字化设计,上海交通大学、清华大学、西北工业大学等高校在材料成形制造领域的建模与仿真技术均取得显著进展。例如,清华大学联合中国航空发动机材料研究院、黎明航空发动机集团公司,采用产、学、研联合研发方式,完成了"航空发动机单晶叶片模拟仿真及工程应用"项目,该项目于2019年获北京市科技进步一等奖。

7 结束语

我国已是世界制造第一大国,取得了一批举世瞩目的成果。但是,总体而言,我国制造业"大而不强",创新能力弱,缺乏关键核心及共性技术。我国制定的制造强国发展战略提出了三步走的发展目标,争取在新中国成立100周年进入世界制造强国前列。为实施《发展战略》,需聚焦"五大工程"。"五大工程"相互联系、相互支持;智能制造是主攻方向,要通过建设一批制造业创新研究中心和大力推进工业强基工程,为智能制造工程提供有力的创新平台和技术支撑;数字化设计与制造是智能制造关键共性技术,而建模与仿真是数字化设计与制造的科学基础。我国在数字化设计与制造领域已经具有较好的技术基础。

我们要充分认识到:全面实施智能制造,建成制造强国,任重而道远。

参考文献

[1] President's Council of Advisors on Science and Technology (U.S.). Report to the President on Ensuring the American Leadership on Advance Manufacturing [R]. Washington D C: Executive Office of the President, President's Council of Advisors on Science and Technology, 2011.

[2] President's Council of Advisors on Science and Technology (U.S.). Report to the President on Capturing the Domestic Competitive Advantages in Advance Manufacturing [R]. Washington D C: Executive Office of the President, President's Council of Advisors on Science and Technology, 2012.

[3] Securing Advanced Manufacturing in the United States: the Role of Manufacturing USA [C] // Proceedings of a Workshop, National Academy of Science-Engineering-Medicine, 2017.

[4] GAYLE Frank. Manufacturing USA Program [R]. 北京:中国工程院, 2018.
GAYLE Frank. Manufacturing USA Program [R]. Beijing: Chinese Academy of Engineering, 2018.

[5] 柳百成. 赴美国考察"国家制造创新网络"及"先进制造技术"报告 [R] 北京：中国工程院, 2015.
LIU Baicheng. Report on "National Manufacturing Innovation Network" and "Advanced Manufacturing Technology" in the United States [R]. Bejing: Chinese Academy of Engineering, 2015.

[6] 中国电子信息产业发展研究院. 美国制造创新研究院解读 [M]. 北京：电子工业出版社, 2018.
China Center for Information Industry Development. Interpretation for American Institute of Manufacturing Innovation [M]. Beiing: Publishing House of Electronics Industry, 2018.

[7] Subcomittee on Advanced Manufacturing Committee on Technology of the National Science & Technology Council. Strategy for American Leadership in Advanced Manufacturing, National Science and Technology Counil [R]. Washington D C: Executive Office of the President, President's Council of Advisors on Science and Technology, 2018.

[8] 装备制造业自主创新战略研究咨询研究项目组. 装备制造业自主创新战略研究 [M]. 北京：高等教育出版社, 2007.
Consulting Research Group of Research on Independent Innovation Strategy of Equipment Manufacturing Industry. Research on Independent Innovation Strategy of Equipment Manufacturing Industry [M]. Bejing: Higher Education Press, 2007.

[9] 王鹏. 兴国之器——中国制造2025 [M]. 北京：机械工业出版社, 2016.
WANG Peng. The Instrument of Rejuvenating the Nation—Made in China 2025 [M]. Beiing: China Machine Press, 2016.

[10] 工业和信息化部科技司. 国家智能网联汽车创新中心、国家农机装备创新中心建设方案专家论证会 [EB/OL]. (2019-05-23). http://www.mit.edu.cn/newweb/nl 146285/n1146352/n3054 355/n3057497/n3057504/c6969411/content.html.
Department of Science and Technology, Ministry of Industry and Information Technology. Experr Discussion Meeting on the Construction Scheme of National Itelligent Network Automobile Innovation Center and National Agricultural Machinery Equipment Innovation Center [EB/OL]. (2019-05-23). http://www.miit.gov.cn/newweb/n1146285/n1146352/n3054355/n3057497/n3057504/c6969411/content.html.

[11] 工业和信息化部科技司. 国家先进功能纤维创新中. 心建设方案论证会 [EB/OL]. (2019-06-13). http://www.miit.gov.cn/n1146290/n1146402/n7039597/c7093492/content.html.
Department of Science and Technology, Ministry of Industry and Information T echnology. Discussion Meeting on the Construction Scheme of National Advanced Functional Fiber Innovation Center [EB/OL]. (2019-06-13). http://www.miit.gov.cn/n1146290/nl1 146402/n7039597/c7093492/content.html.

[12] 柳百成. 提升工业基础创新能力 [C] // 2016国家制造强国战略咨询专家论坛. 北京, 2016.
LIU Baicheng. Improve the Ability of Industrial Basic Innovation [C] // 2016 National Manufacturing Power Strategy Consulting Expert Forum. Beijing, 2016.

[13] 柳百成. 数字化设计与制造——智能制造关键共性技术 [C] //2018世界制造业大会智能制造发展论坛. 合肥, 2018.
LIU Baicheng. Digital Design and Manufacturing—the Key Fundamental Technology of Intelligent Manufacturing [C] //2018 World Manufacturing Conference Intelligent Manufacturing Development Forum. Hefei, 2018.

[14] 工业与信息化部装备司. 《智能制造发展规划（2016—2020年）》 [EB/OL]. (2016-12-08). http://www.miit.gov.cn/n1146295/n1652858/n1652930/n3757018/c5406111/content.html.
Department of Equipment, Ministry of Industry and Information Technology. 《Inteligent Manufacturing Development Plan (2016—2020)》 [EB/OL]. (2016-12-08). http://www.mit.gov.cn/n1146295/n1652858/n1652930/n3757018/c5406111/content.html.

[15] 柳百成.加强产学研结合,提高大型铸件自主创新能力 [C]// 2007中国机械工程学会年会——产学研结合典型案例报告会文集.北京：

中国机械工程学会,2007:1-5.
LIU Baicheng. Strengthen the Combination of Production, Teaching and Research, Improve the Independent Innovation Ability of Large Castings [C]//2007 Annual Meeting of Chinese Mechanical Engineering Society—Collection of Reports for Typical Cases of Combination of Production, Learning and Research. Beijing: Chinese Mechanical Engineering Society, 2007: 1-5.

作者简介：柳百成，男，1933年生，中国工程院院士，清华大学机械工程学院/材料学院教授，国家制造强国建设战略咨询委员会委员，《中国机械工程》第三、第四届编委会主任。研究方向为用信息技术提升传统铸造行业技术水平及提高铸造合金性能。发表论文300余篇。E-mail：liubc@tsinghua.edu.cn。

第4篇

战略研究会议报告

国际会议

1. Trend of Advanced Manufacturing Technology (先进制造技术发展趋势)[一]

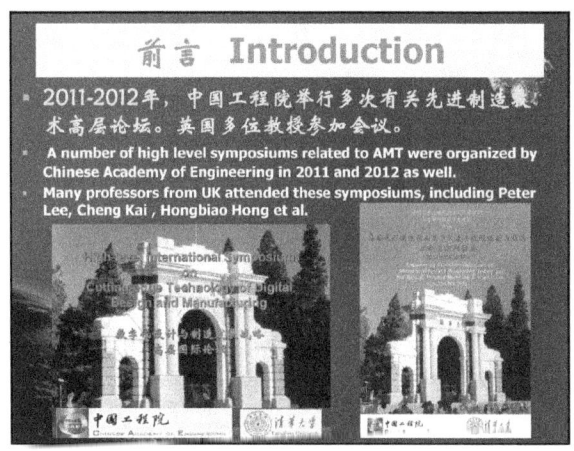

[一] 本文为2012年中-英战略性新兴产业和新兴技术研讨会的邀请报告,会议地点为中国北京。

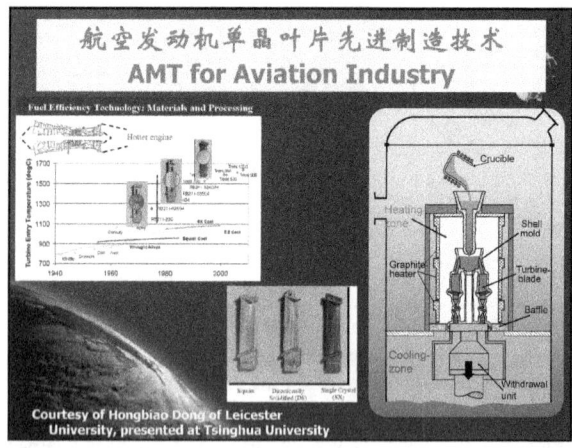
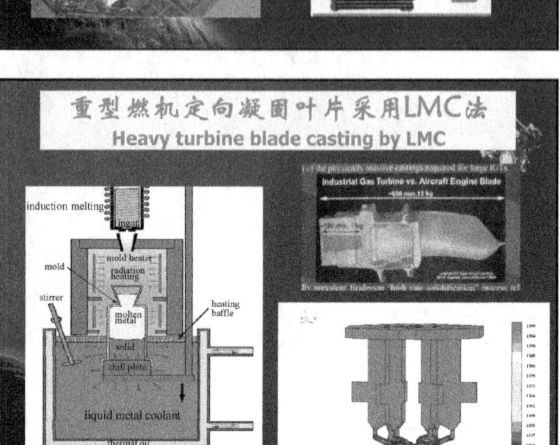

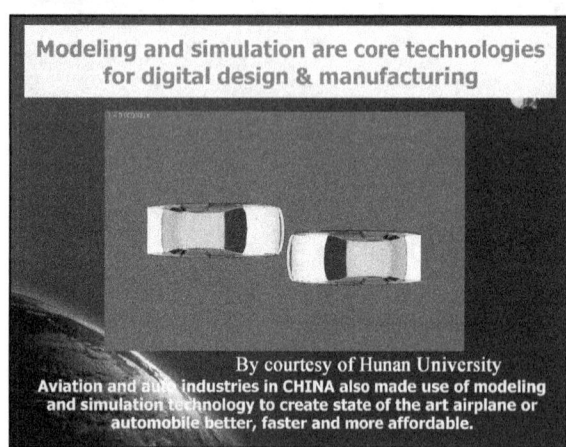

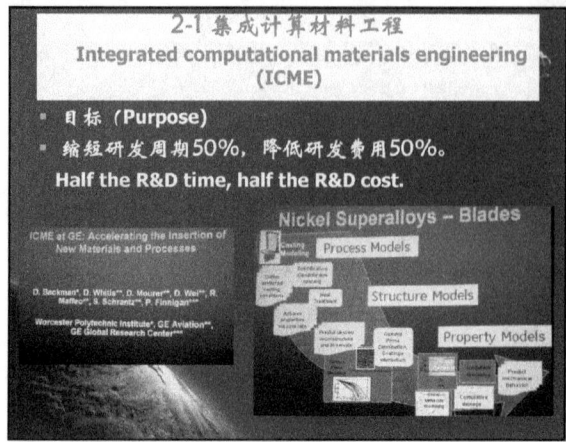
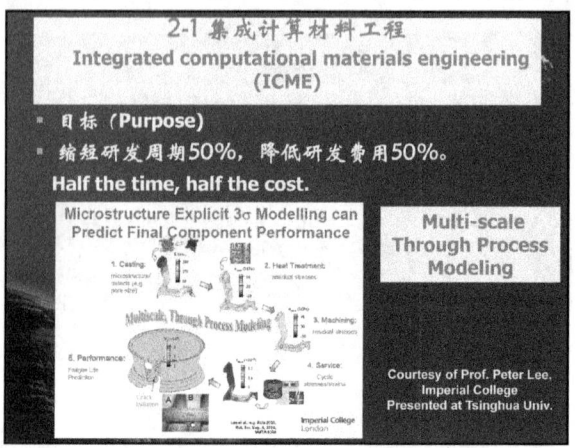

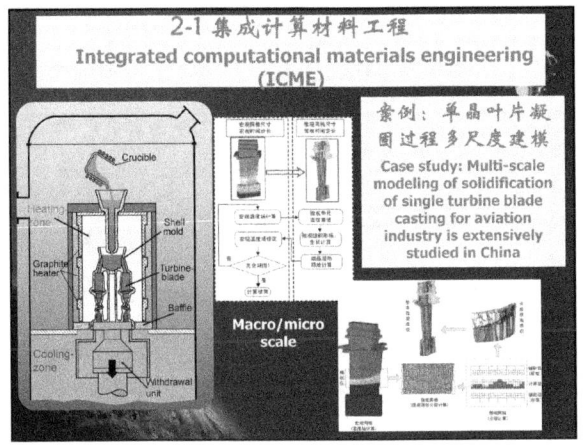
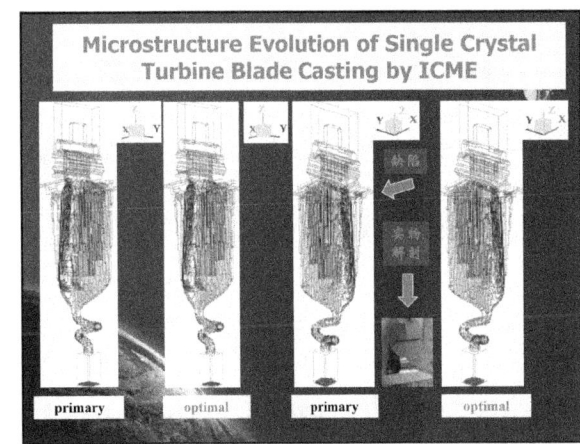
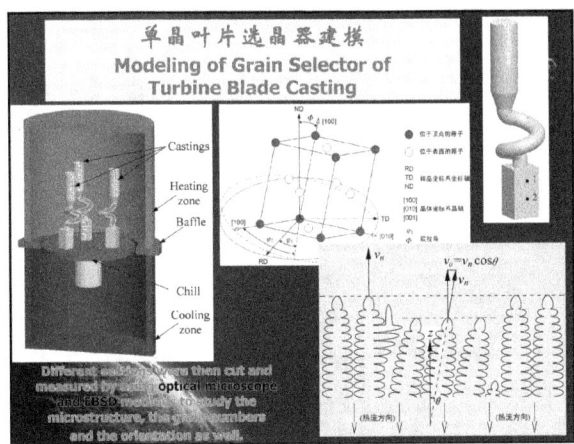
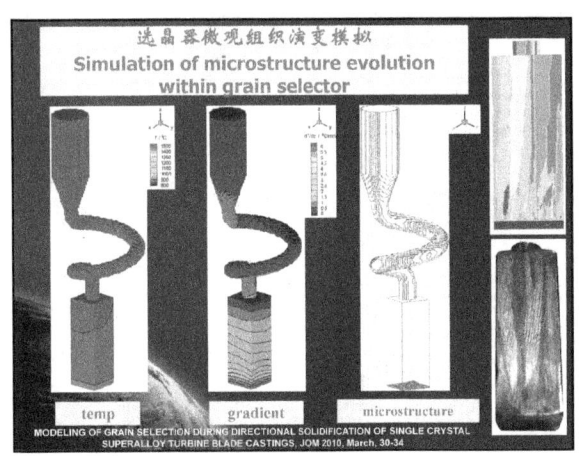
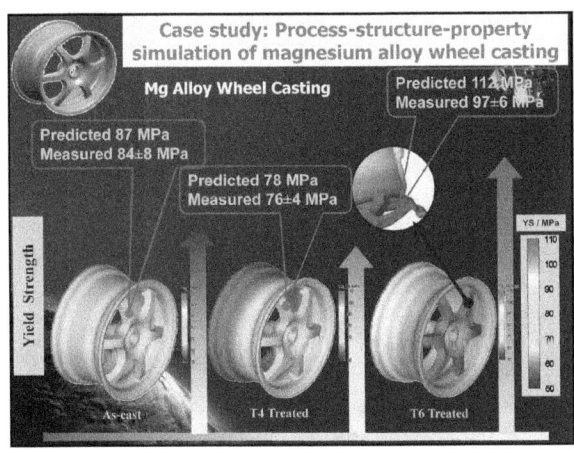
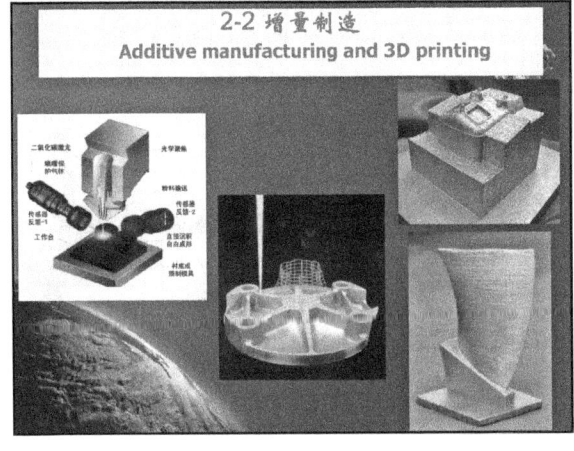
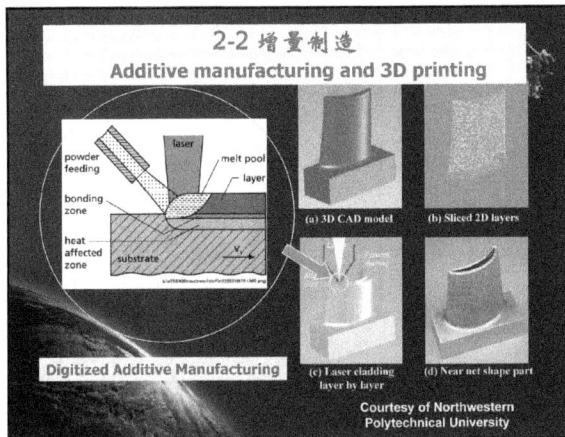

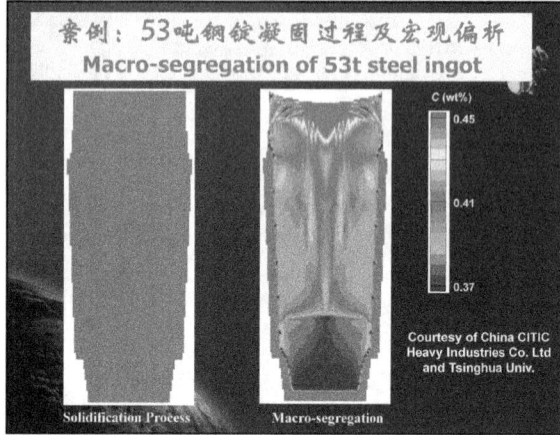
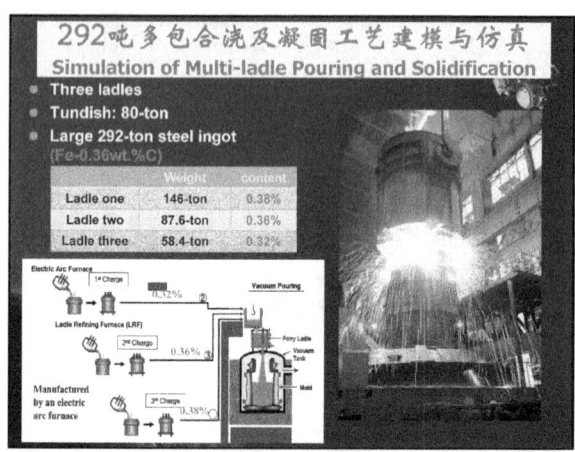
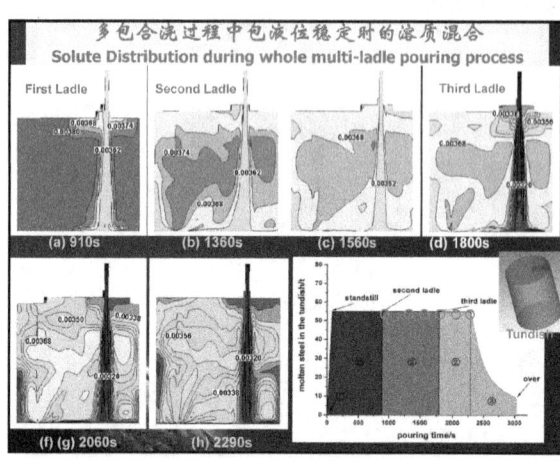
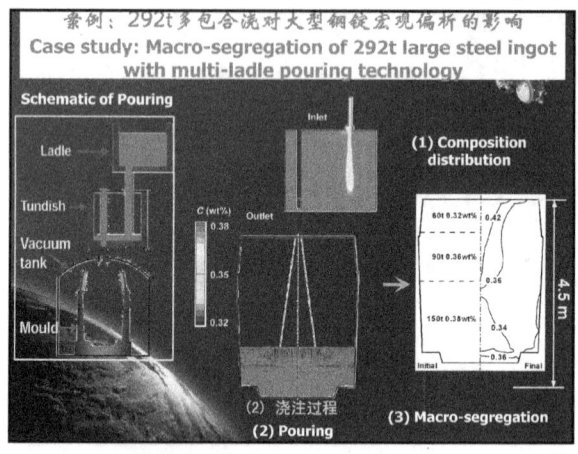

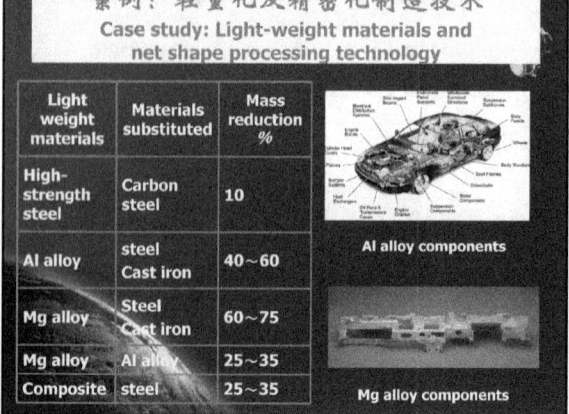

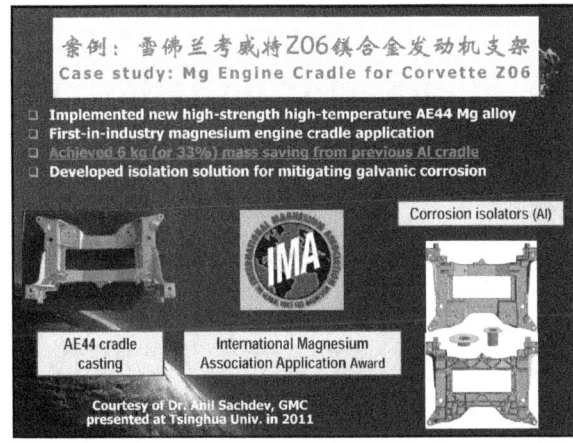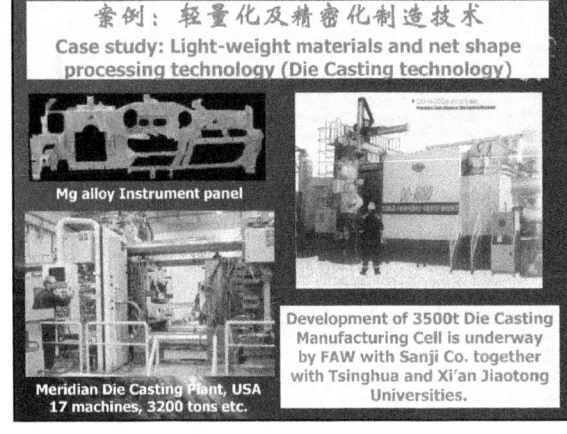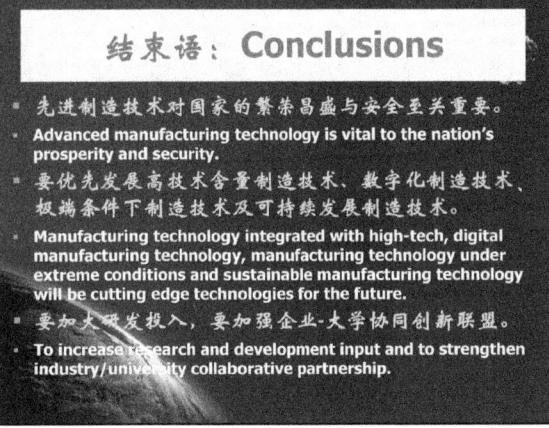

2. Status and Forecast of China Manufacturing Industry
(中国制造业的现状及展望)

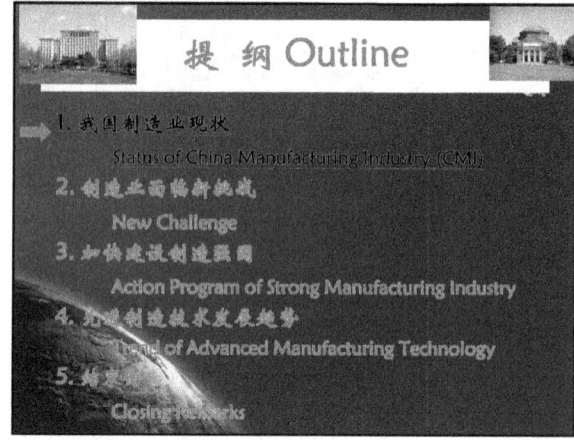

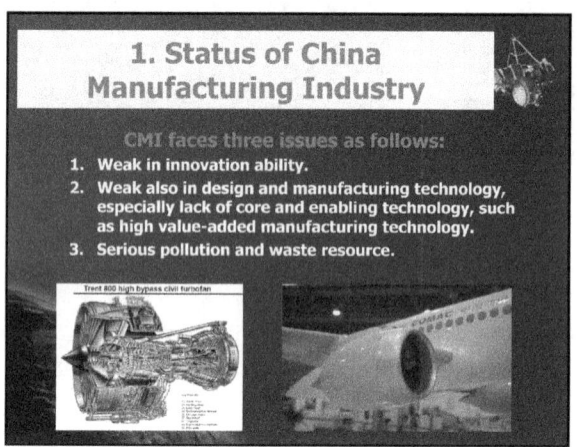

---

① 本文为2014年"SATEC Forum on New Industrial Revolution and Intelligent Manufacturing"会议的主旨报告,会议地点为中国北京。

1. Status of China Manufacturing Industry
(3) serious pollution and waste resource

- 2010: GDP of China is about 7.5% of that of the whole world, while the energy consumption is about 19.6% of the whole world.
- 2010: The ratio of manufacturing value added with the whole GDP of China is about 32.6%, while the energy consumption with GDP is about 58.0%.
- 56.5% of crude oil and more than 50% of iron ore are imported.
- And also, serious pollution as well.

2. Facing New Challenge

- China manufacturing industry faces new science and technology changes and new industry revolution.
- Such as cloud computation, big data, digital and intelligent manufacturing technology, new materials and new energy resources, bio-technology, etc.
- However, It is not only just a great challenge, but also a great opportunity instead.

2. Facing New Challenge
New strategy in United States and UK

- In June 2011, "Advanced Manufacturing Partnership" was announced by President Obama.
- A number of innovation institutes were and will be established, including "Digital Manufacturing and Design", "Light Weight Materials Manufacturing", etc.
- An Integrated Design-Manufacturing-Service Strategy was established by Rolls Royce, so called Total Care Plan. The strategy is from "sold turbine" to "rent turbine" to "rent turbine service"

3. Action Program of a Strong Manufacturing Industry

- CAE pays great attention to re-vitalizing China manufacturing industry in recent years.
- A number of strategy studies were carried out, such as "Strategy Study of Science and Engineering Issues of China Manufacturing Industry" in 2004, "Innovation Strategy Study of China Equipment Manufacturing Industry in 2007", etc.
- "Strategy Study of A Strong Manufacturing Industry" and "Strategy Study of Strengthening 4 basic technologies for manufacturing industry" are extensively studied recently.

3. Action Program of a Strong Manufacturing Industry

An Action Program for a strong manufacturing industry so called "China Manufacturing – 2025" was proposed by CAE in 2014.

5 symbols of a strong manufacturing industry
1. A number of world-known enterprises.
2. High innovation and competitiveness ability.
3. Structural reformation by mastering high tech technology and core technology as well.
4. Quality assurance and efficiency improvement.
5. Potential ability of sustainable development.

3. Action Program of Strong Manufacturing Industry

4 Guiding Principles for The Action Program

- 创新驱动 Innovation Driven
- 质量为先 Quality Assurance
- 绿色发展 Sustainable Development
- 结构优化 Structure Optimization

3. Action Program of Strong Manufacturing Industry
8 action plans for China Manufacturing 2025

1. 推行数字化网络化智能化制造
   1. Developing network based digital and intelligent manufacturing technology
2. 提高创新设计能力
   2. Strengthening innovative design ability
3. 完善技术创新体系
   3. Improving technology innovation system with enterprises, university and research institutes.
4. 强化制造基础
   4. Enhancing manufacturing fundamentals, including components, materials and technologies as well.

3. Action Program of Strong Manufacturing Industry
8 action plans for Action Program

5. 提升产品质量
   5. Strengthening products quality
6. 推行绿色制造
   6. Developing clean and sustainable technologies
7. 培养具有全球竞争力的优势产业和企业群体
   7. Cultivating world-known enterprises with high global competitiveness ability
8. 发展现代制造服务业
   8. Developing modern manufacturing service system

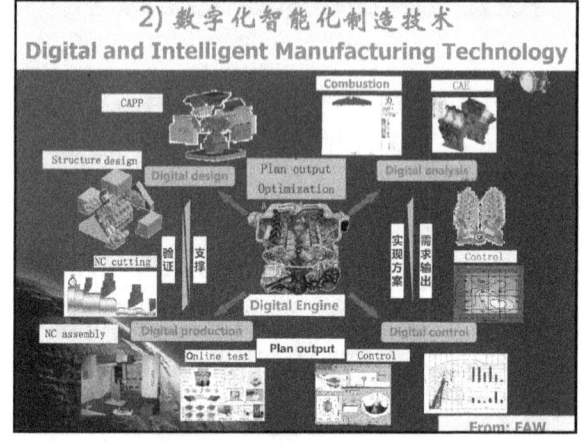

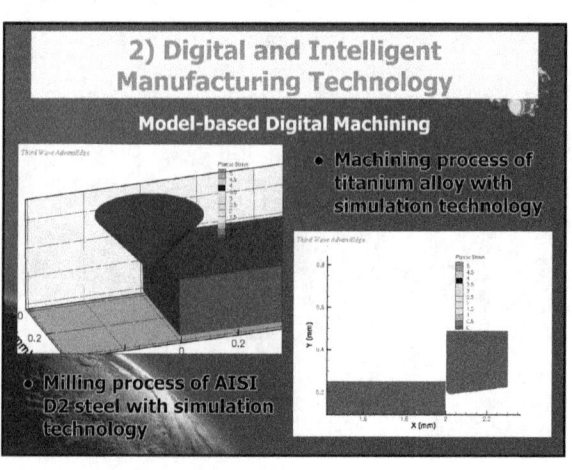

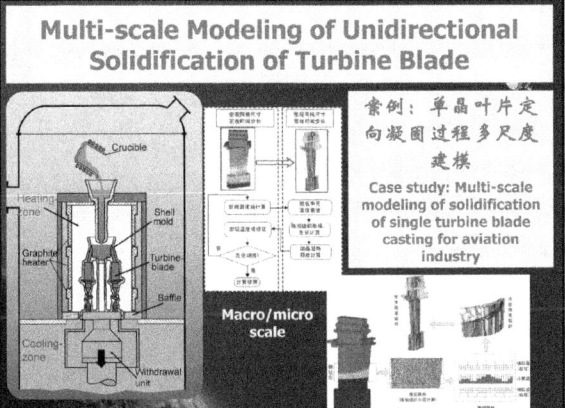
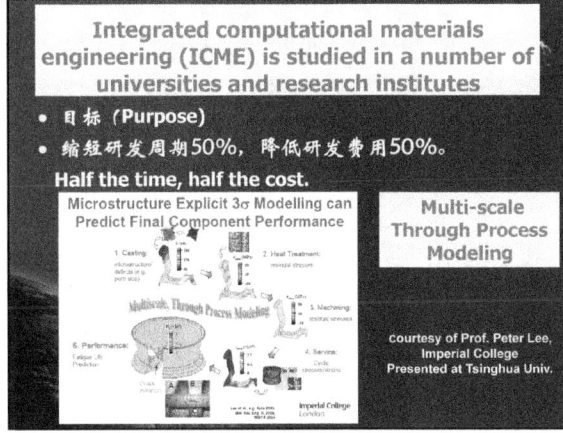
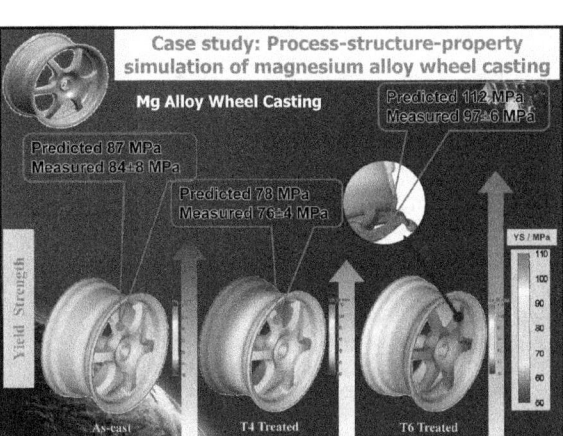
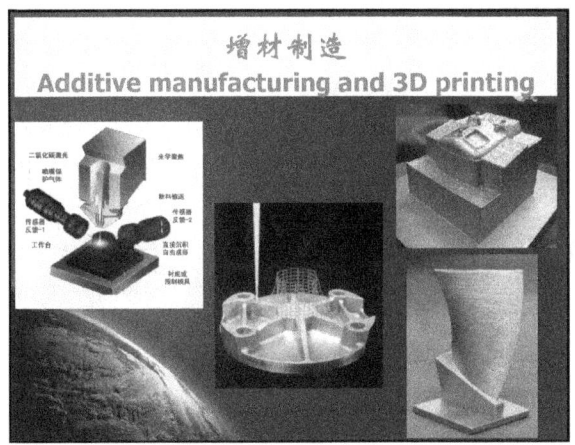

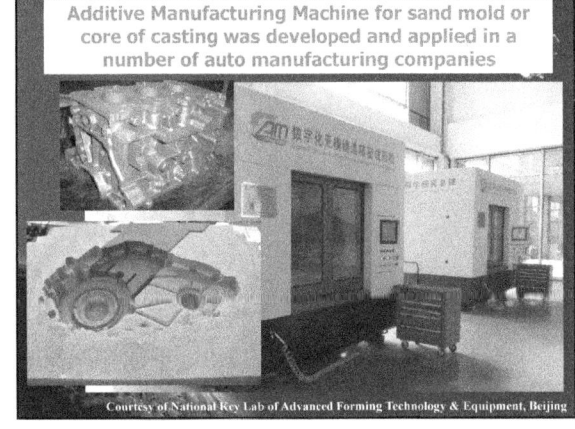

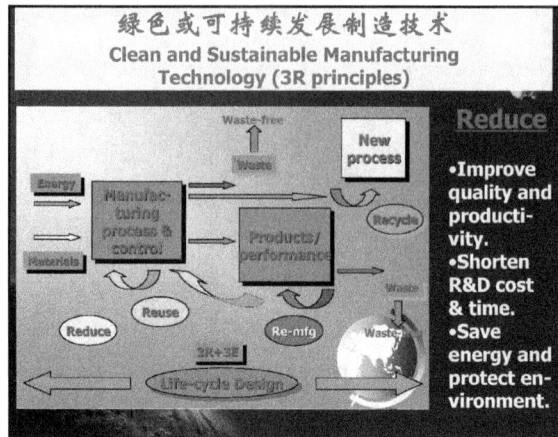

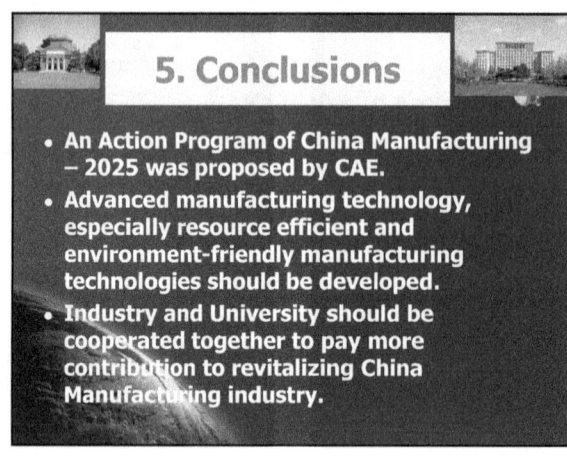

3. CHINA MANUFACTURING 2025
——An Action Program for Strong Manufacturing Industry
(《中国制造2025》——建设制造强国行动纲领)

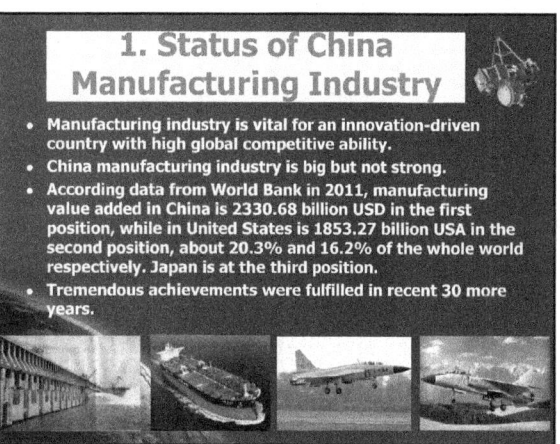

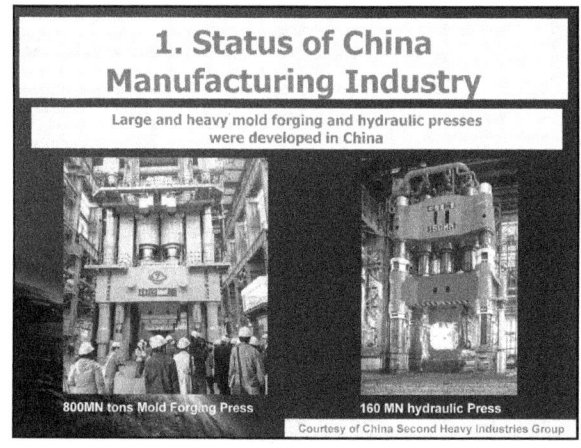

本文为2015年"20th Anniversary International Conference of NAEK"会议的主旨报告,会议地点为韩国。

1. Status of China Manufacturing Industry

However, CMI faces three main issues:

1. Weakness in innovation ability.
2. Lack of core and key manufacturing technology.
3. Serious pollution and waste resource.

1. Status of China Manufacturing Industry
(1) Innovation Ability

- According to Global Innovation Index and Global Competitiveness Index: China is at about 20-30th position, while the data published from the China Academy of Social Sciences is at 15th position.
- 2013: China: R&D/GDP=2.0%, while that of developed countries are more than 2.5%
- 2011: China manufacturing valued added rate is about 21.5%, while developed countries are more than 35%.
- For example, 80% chips and control systems for high level numerical control machine tools are imported from abroad.

1. Status of China Manufacturing Industry
(2) Design and Manufacturing Technology

- All the aviation turbines (LEAP-X1C) for the new C919 passenger airplane will be imported from abroad.
- Core technologies for heavy duty turbines of energy industry also rely on abroad.

1. Status of China Manufacturing Industry
(3) serious pollution and waste resource

- 2010: GDP of China is about 7.5% of that of the whole world, while the energy consumption is about 19.6% of the whole world.
- 2010: The ratio of manufacturing value added with the whole GDP of China is about 32.6%, while the energy consumption with GDP is about 58.0%.
- 56.5% of crude oil and more than 50% of iron ore are imported.
- And also, serious pollution as well.

2. Facing New Challenge

- China manufacturing industry faces new science & technology development and new industry revolution as well.
- Such as cloud computation, big data, digital and intelligent or smart manufacturing technology, new materials and new energy resources, bio-technology, etc.
- However, it is not only a great challenge, but also a great opportunity instead.

2. Facing New Challenge
"Re-industrialization Strategy" from abroad

- In June 2011, "Advanced Manufacturing Partnership" was announced by President Obama in United States.
- "Invents it here, and manufactures it here".
- A national network for manufacturing innovation is established (NNMI). Under NNMI, 15 manufacturing innovation institutes were and will be established, including "Digital Manufacturing and Design", "Smart Manufacturing", "Lightweight Materials Manufacturing", etc.

 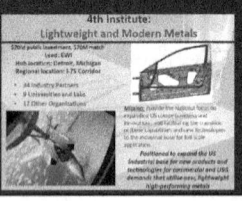

2. Facing New Challenge
"Re-industrialization Strategy" from abroad

- The Future of Manufacturing, as a new vision for UK manufacturing, was established by UK recently.
- A number of high value manufacturing catapult centers were established in UK to strengthen the innovation ability.
- An Integrated Design-Manufacturing-Service Strategy was established by Rolls Royce in UK, so called Total Care Plan.
- "Industry 4.0" was established in Germany to revitalizing manufacturing industry by intelligent manufacturing.

 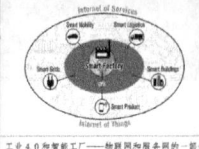

工业4.0智能工厂——物联网和服务网的一部分

3. China Manufacturing 2025

Based on CAE's strategy study, an action program for strong manufacturing industry so called "China Manufacturing 2025" drafted by MIIT was officially announced by State Council in May of 2015.

"China Manufacturing 2025" could be Summarized as:
- 5 guiding principles
- 1+3 strategic targets
- 9 missions
- 5 projects including 10 sectors

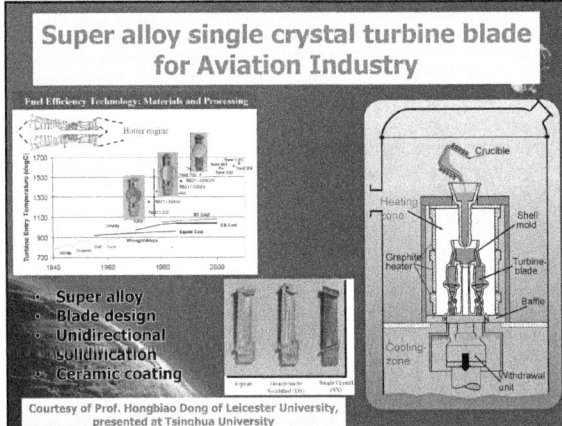

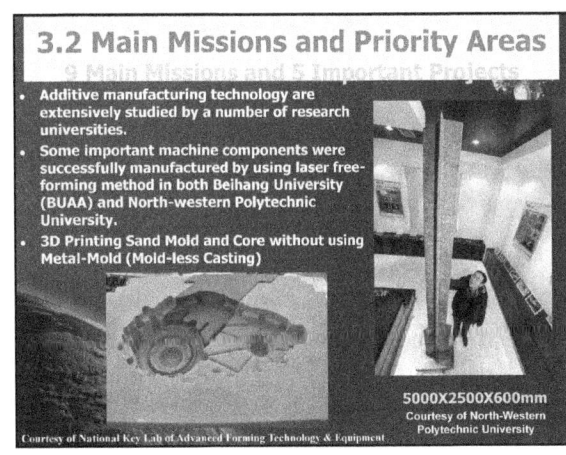

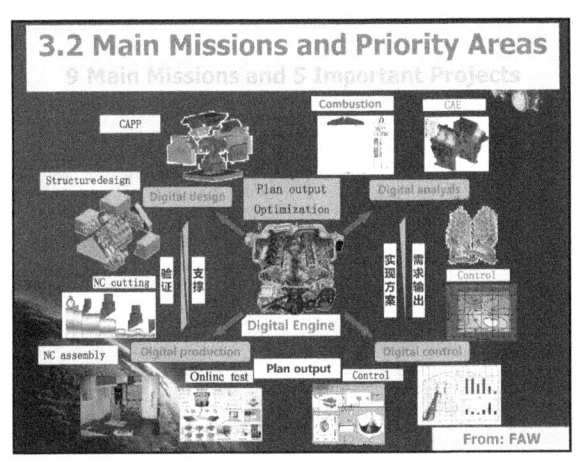

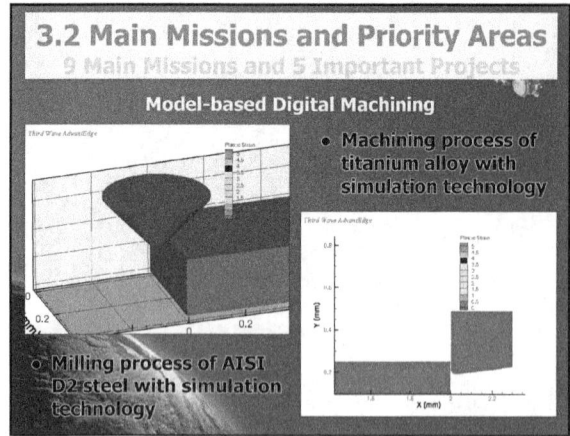
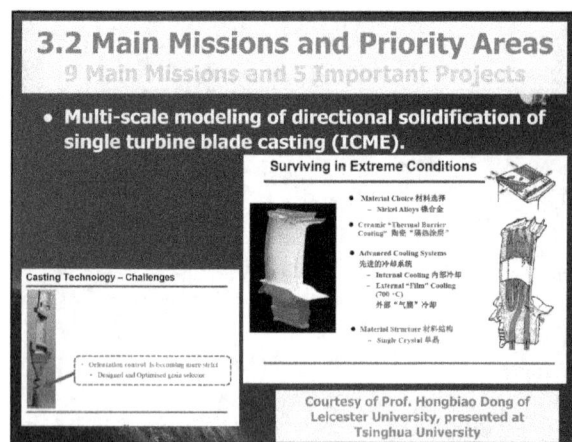
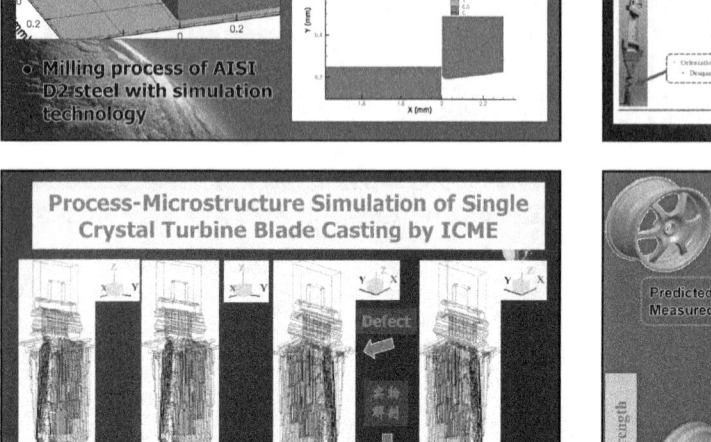
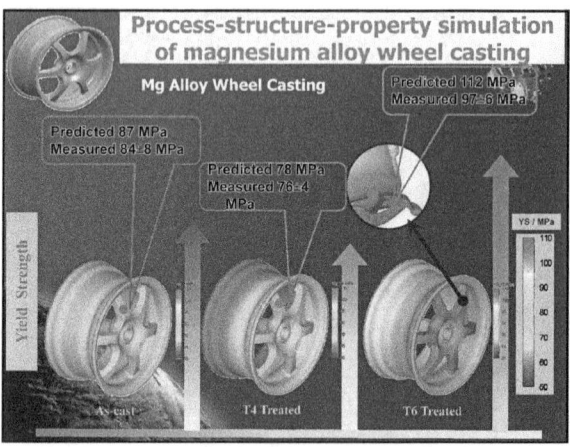
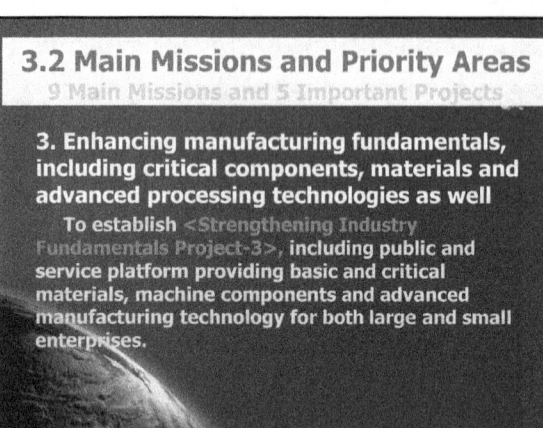
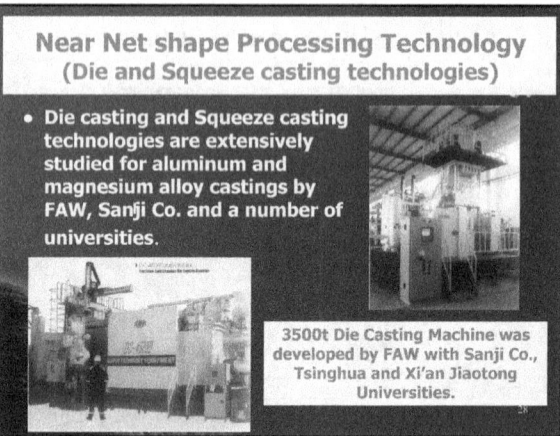

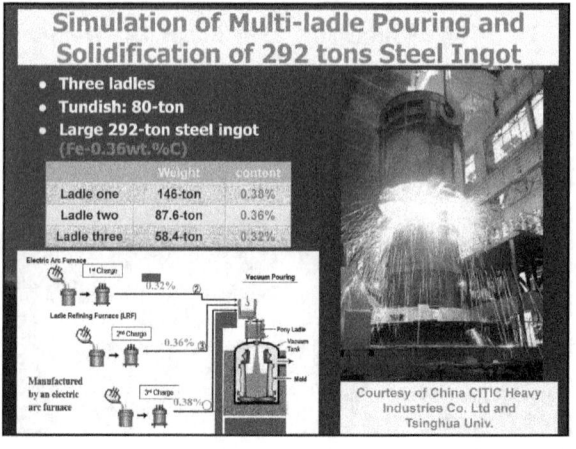

3.2 Main Missions and Priority Areas
9 Main Missions and 5 Important Projects

4. Improving products quality with well-known brands

5. Developing clean and sustainable manufacturing technologies
To establish <Green manufacturing Project-4>. Based on reuse, reduce and recycle principles, developing net shape processing technology, lightweight materials processing technology, precision and ultra-precision machining technologies etc.

3.2 Main Missions and Priority Areas
9 Main Missions and 5 Important Projects

6. Developing and breaking through major and priority areas
To establish <Innovation Project of High Level Manufacturing Equipment-5>, including 10 main sectors, such as: next generation information industry, high level NC machine and industry robotics, sea and ocean engineering project, energy-efficient and new energy automobiles, equipment for aviation and industry, advance transportation equipment for railroad, energy equipment, new materials, bio-medicine and medical equipment, and agricultural equipment.

3.2 Main Missions and Priority Areas
9 Main Missions and 5 Important Projects

High level numerical control machine tools

- High level numerical control machine tools and machining centers are researched and developed by Shenyang Machine Tool Co, Dalian Machine Tool Group, and Beijing Machine Tool Research Institute, etc.
- These machine tool companies are cooperated with a number of universities, including Huazhong University of Technology, Xian Jiaotong University, etc.

3.2 Main Missions and Priority Areas
9 Main Missions and 5 Important Projects

7. Deeply reforming manufacturing structure
To upgrade manufacturing enterprises from low to medium or high level, from low value added to high value added.

8. Developing modern manufacturing service system

9. Enhancing international cooperation under global economy era
To strengthen international cooperation as well as scientific & technological exchanges.

3.2 Main Missions and Priority Areas

- Therefore, a number of policies and measures are also established, for the purposes of:
- To fulfill all the main missions and priority areas,
- To reach the final target of the action program,
- And, to finally transform China manufacturing industry not only big but also strong.

4. Conclusions

- Manufacturing industry is vital to national economy, national security and people's prosperity.
- China manufacturing industry is big but not strong.
- Manufacturing industry faces three main issues, and also faces many new challenges.
- An Action Program of "China Manufacturing 2025" was officially announced by State Council in May 2015.
- "China Manufacturing 2025" could be summarized as 3-step target, 5 guiding principles, and 5 important projects.

4. Developing Intelligent Manufacturing
——For a Strong Manufacturing Industry
（发展智能制造——建设制造强国）

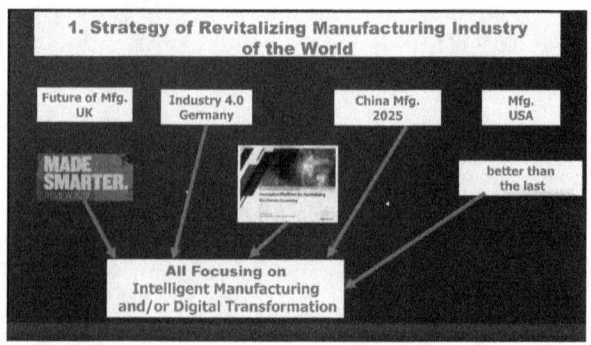

---

① 本文为"2018 Beijing International Forum on Innovation & Development of Advanced Manufacturing Technology"会议的主旨报告，会议地点为中国北京。

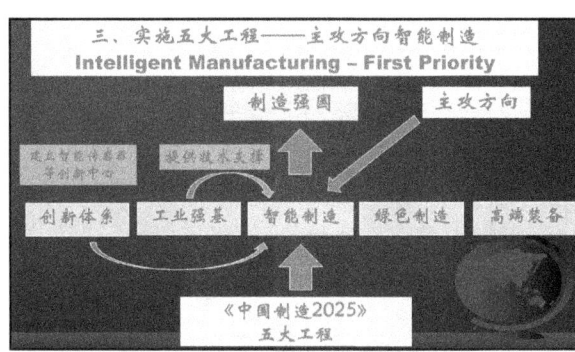

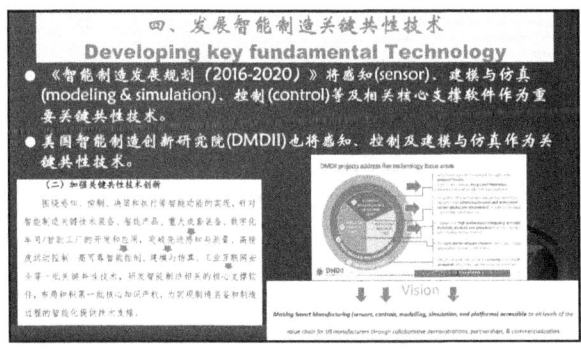
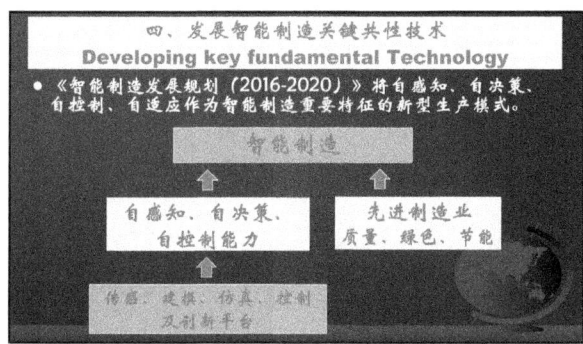
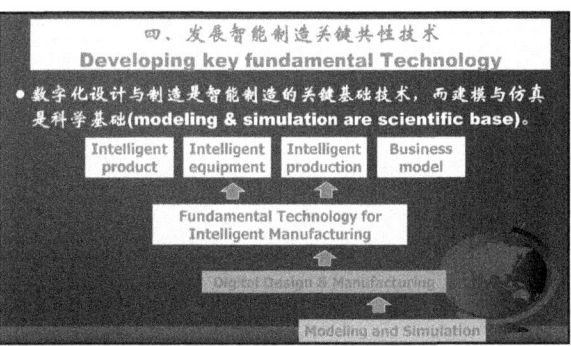

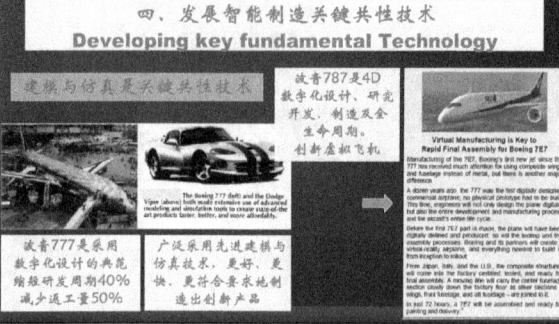
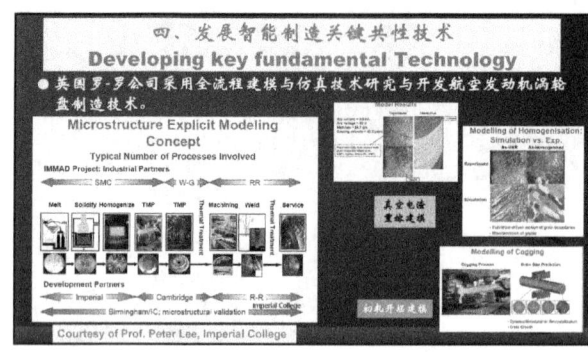
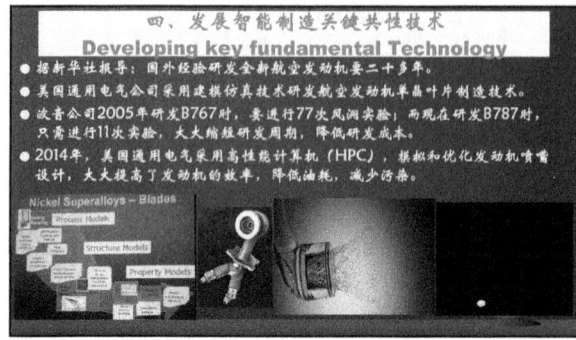
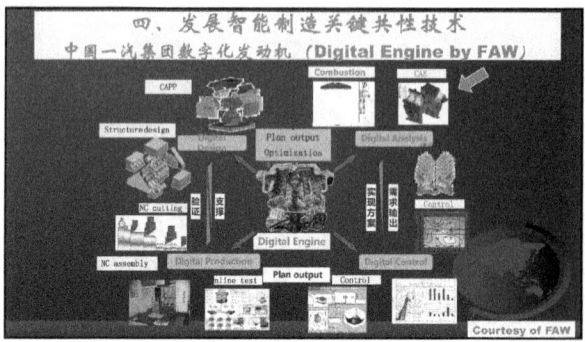
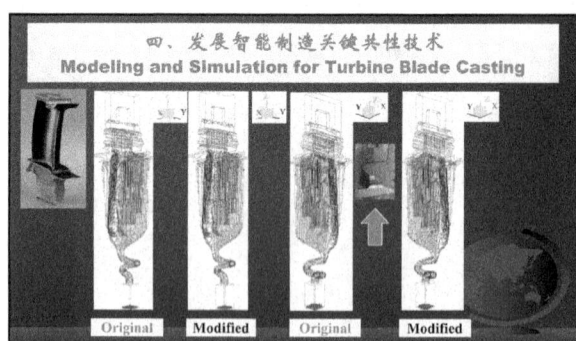
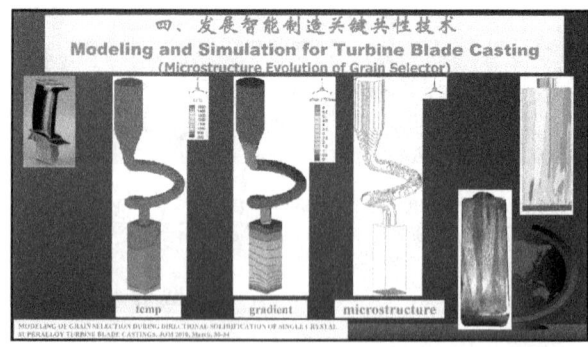

5. Modeling and Simulation——Key Technology for Digital Transformation of Manufacturing Industry
（建模与仿真——制造业数字化转型关键技术）[一]

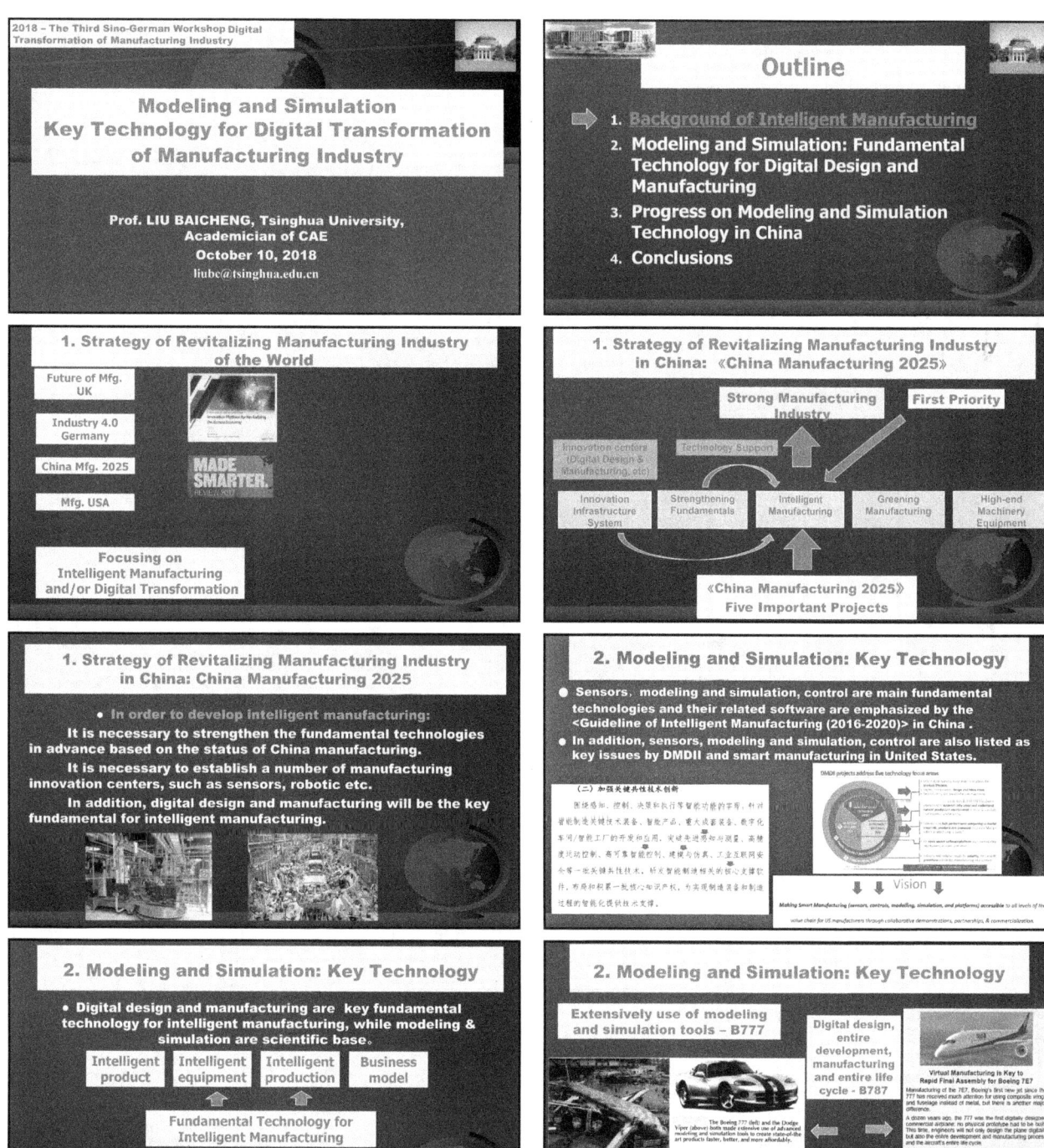

[一] 本文为2018年"The Third Sino-German Workshop: Digital Transformation of Manufacturing Industry"会议的主旨报告，会议地点为德国。

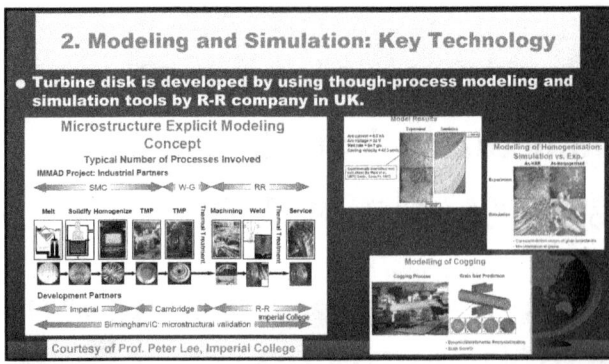
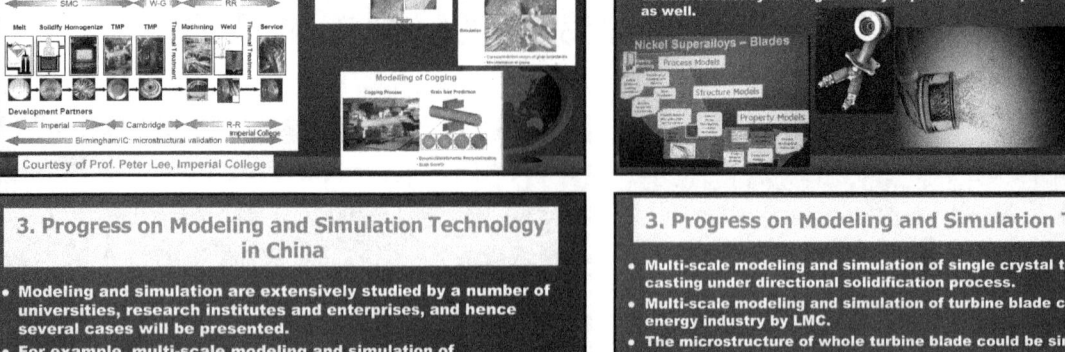
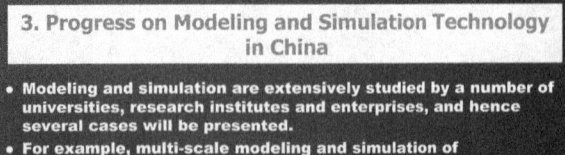

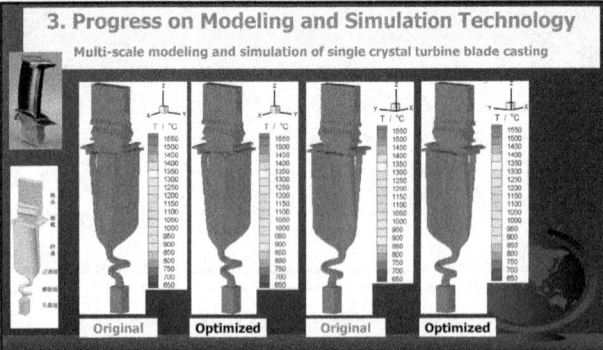
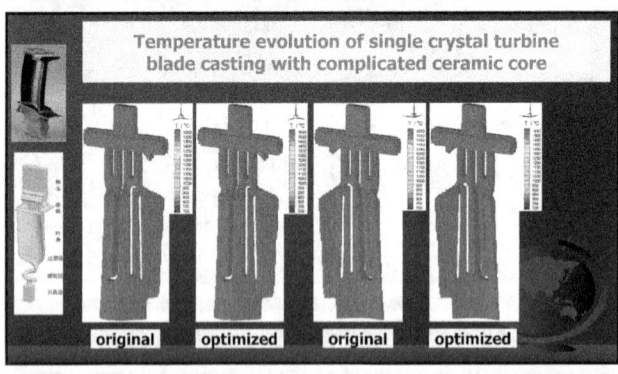
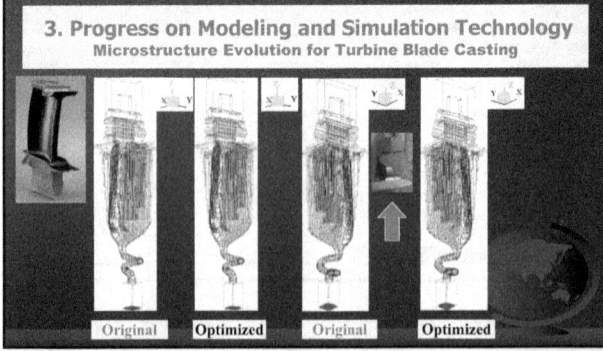
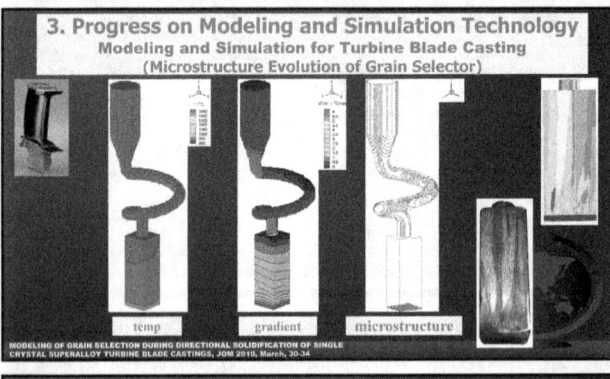
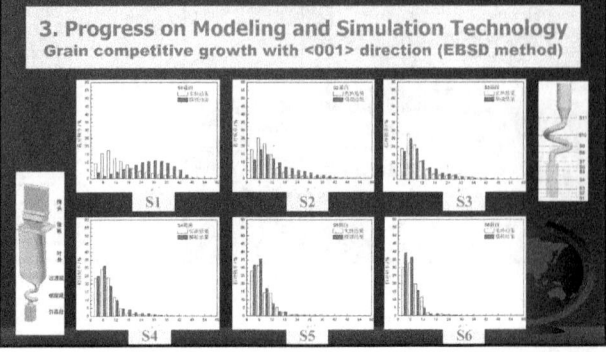
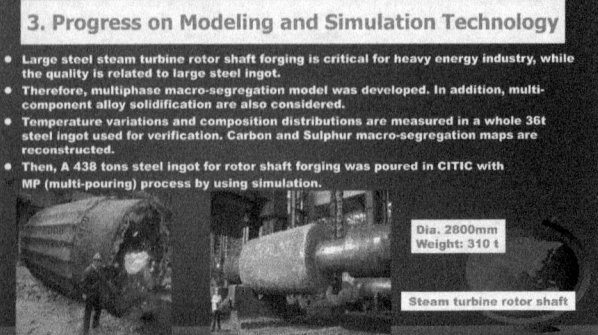

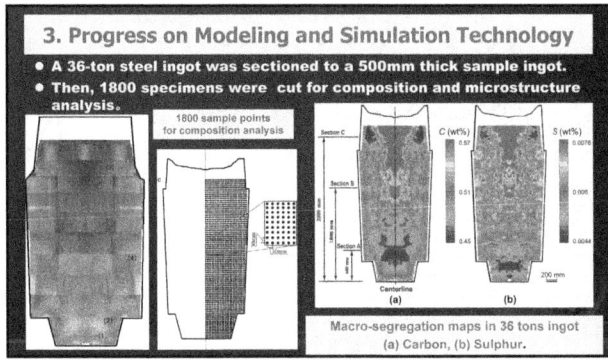
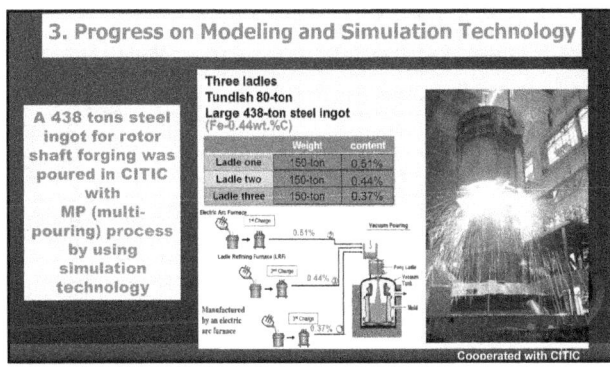
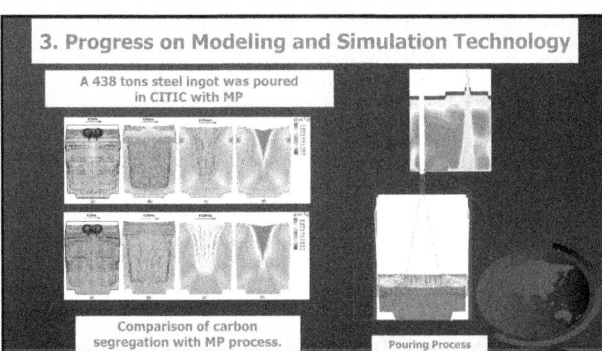
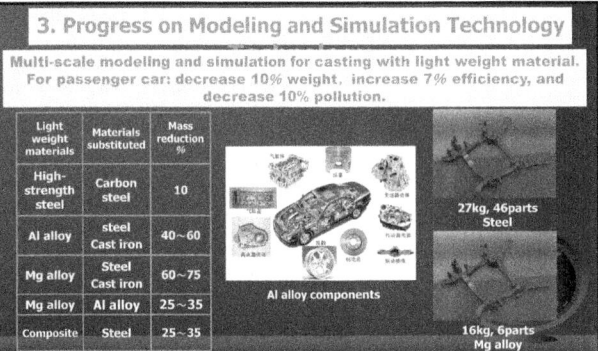
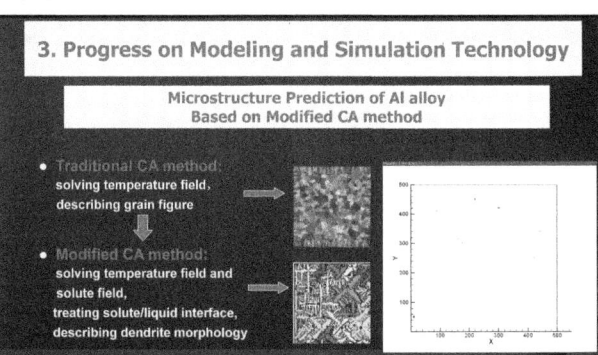
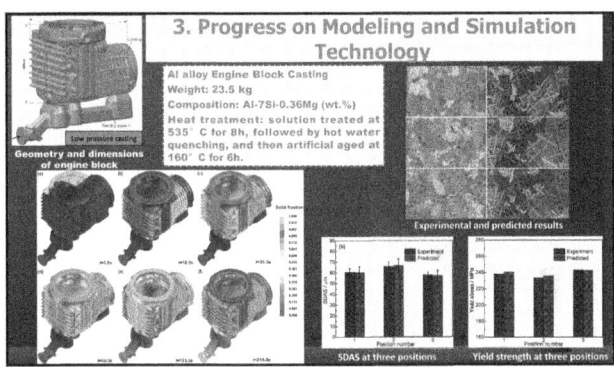
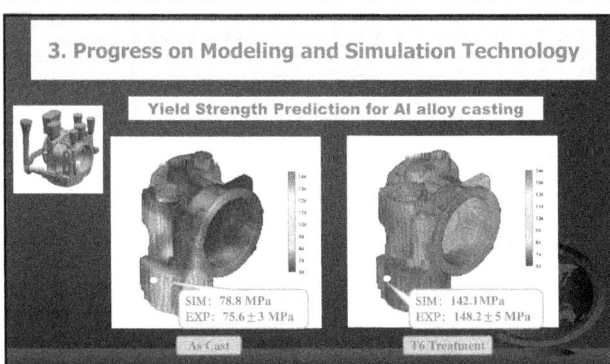
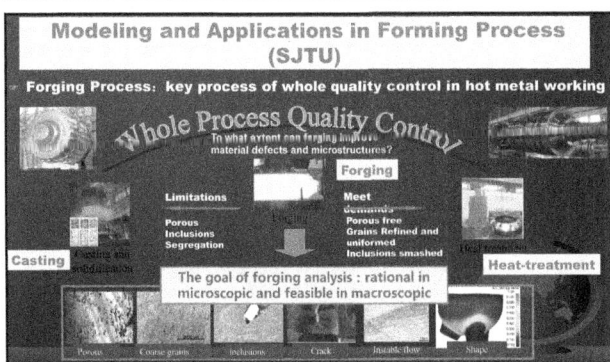
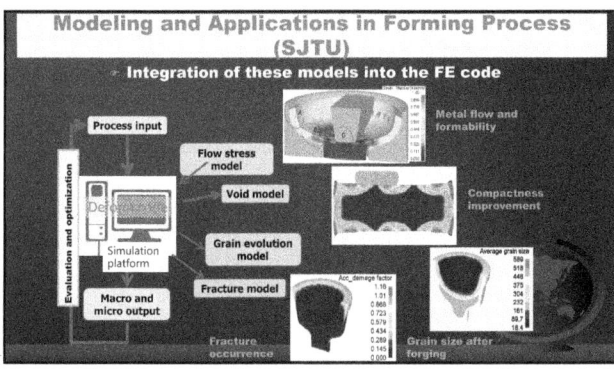
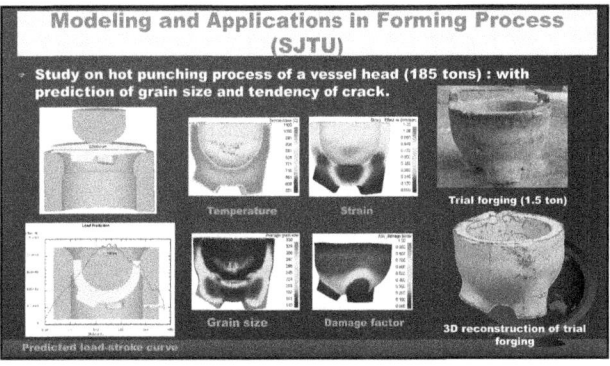

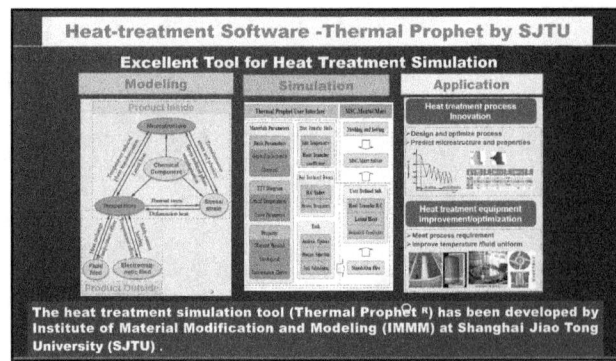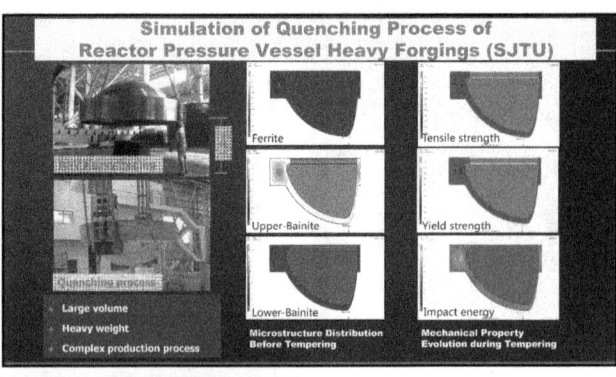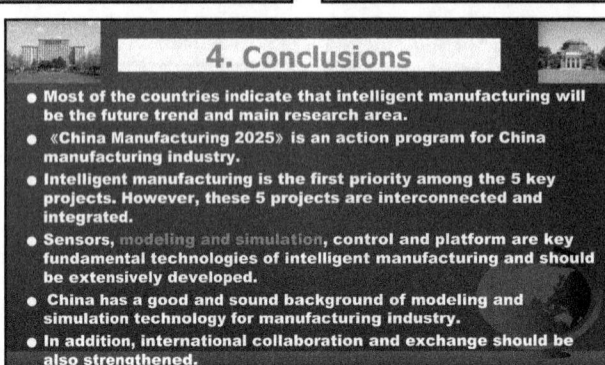

国内会议

6. 我国制造业科技发展战略

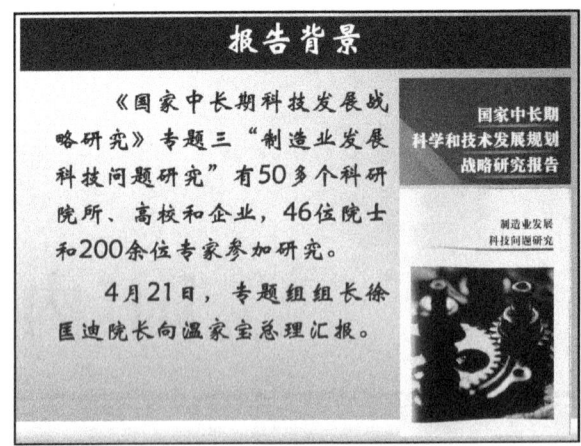
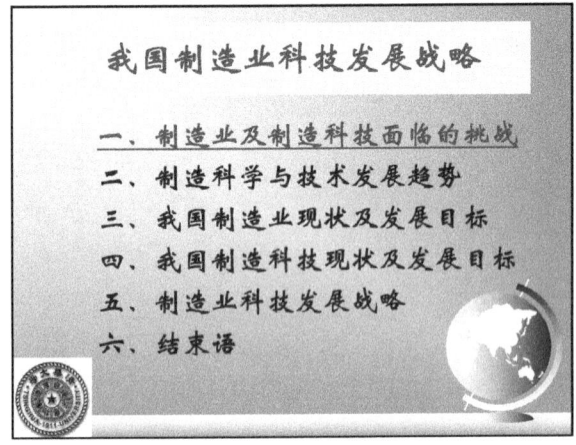

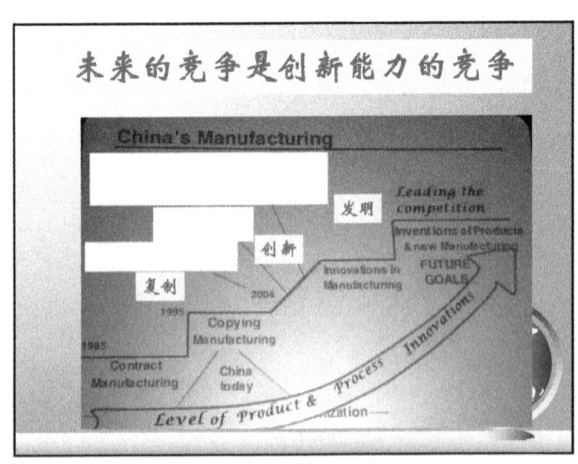
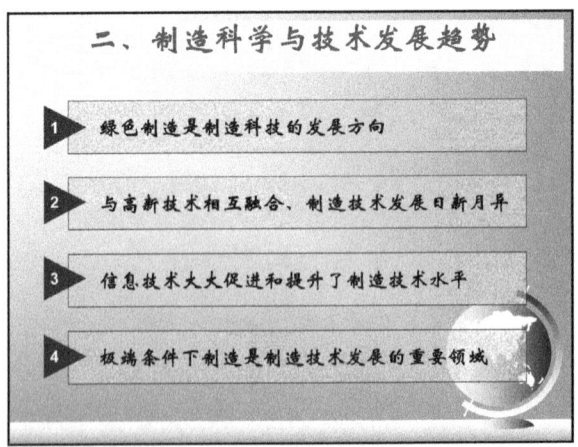

○ 本文为 2005 年振兴辽宁装备制造业高层论坛及浙江省先进制造技术与交流大会的大会主题报告。

趋势一：绿色制造是制造科技的发展方向

- 全世界每年产生废弃物约250万亿吨，预计由于人口的急剧增加，每年产生的废弃物将增加到1000万亿吨。
- 面对日趋严峻的资源和环境约束，世界各国都在制定可持续发展规划。
- 德国制定了《产品回收法规》，日本等国提出了减少、再利用及再循环（Reduce, Reuse, Recycle）的战略，美国提出了"再制造"及"无废弃物制造"（Waste-Free Process）的新理念。
- 欧盟将颁布"汽车材料回收"法规，从2005年起，要求新生产的汽车材料的85%能再利用。

早期工业化时期
工业发达国家江河污染严重

趋势二：与高新技术相互融合、制造技术日新月异

- 科学技术特别是生物、纳米、新能源和新材料等高技术的迅猛发展，对制造科技带来了深刻的变化。
- 制造业是高技术的重要载体；高技术又为制造业前瞻性发展提供了技术支撑。

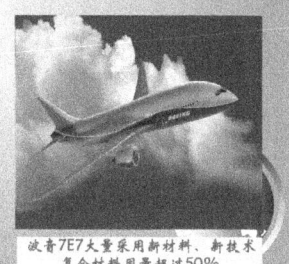
波音7E7大量采用新材料、新技术
复合材料用量超过50%

趋势三：信息技术促进和提升制造技术水平

- 信息技术与制造技术相融合，将进一步给设计与制造技术带来深刻的、甚至是革命性的变化。
- 更好、更快、更省、更可靠地制造出创新产品。

波音777是数字化设计与制造的典范
研发周期缩短40%，工程返工减少50%
数字化设计与制造＝CAD+CAE

趋势三：信息技术促进和提升制造技术水平

- 信息技术与制造技术相融合，将进一步给设计与制造技术带来深刻的、甚至是革命性的变化。
- 更好、更快、更省、更可靠地制造出创新产品。

汽车采用数字化设计与制造（模拟仿真）技术
更好、更快、更可靠地制造出创新产品

趋势四：极端制造是制造技术发展的重要领域

- 制造空天飞行器、超常规动力装备、超大型冶金和石油化工装备等极大尺寸和极强功能的重大装备；制造微纳电子器件、微型光机电系统等极小尺度和极高精度的产品。

长江三峡水轮机转轮重430吨　　微型直升机

三、我国制造业现状及发展目标

中国制造业已发展成为国民经济的重要组成部分，工业增加值占GDP的35.75%。

- 工业增加值占全部工业的78.68%;
- 上交税金约占全部工业的90%;
- 从业人员占全部工业的90.7%。

中国制造业工业增加值居世界第四位，约为美国的1/4、日本的1/2，与德国接近（2001年数据）。

制造业 35.75%
其它 64.25%
2002年
制造业占GDP比重

3.1 我国与发达国家的差距

(1) 资源消耗大，污染严重

- 中国的GDP占世界的4%左右，但消耗世界钢的25%、煤的30%、水泥的50%。
- GDP产出的能耗：日本为1，德国为1.5，美国为2.67，中国为11.5。
- 制造业产品耗能和产值能耗约占全国一次能耗的63%，单位产品能耗平均高出国际先进水平20～30%；单位产值产生的污染远远高出发达国家，全国SO$_2$排放量的67.6%是由大电站和工业锅炉产生的。

3.1 我国与发达国家的差距

(2) 产品以低端为主，附加价值不高

增加值率仅为26.23%，比美国、日本及德国分别低22.99、22.12及11.69个百分点。出口的主要是劳动密集型和技术含量低的产品。

3.1 我国与发达国家的差距

(3) 产业结构不合理

作为先进生产力代表、国家核心竞争力关键的装备制造业工业增加值占制造业的比重比工业发达国家约低10个百分点。

2001年,全国进口装备制造业产品1100亿美元,占全国外贸进口总额48%。集成电路芯片制造装备的95%,轿车制造装备、数控机床、纺织机械及胶印设备的70%依赖进口。

3.2 2020年制造业的发展目标

力争进入世界制造强国行列,成为世界制造中心之一。

- 总体规模进入世界前列,据预测:2020年制造业工业增加值占GDP比重为37.66%。
- 工业增加值占世界总量比重提高到10%以上,制成品出口占世界比重提高到10%以上。
- 锤炼一批技术创新能力强、具有国际竞争力的大型企业集团。
- 形成若干国际知名、各具特色的制造业集中地。

四、我国制造科技现状及发展目标

我国制造科技取得巨大进步

- 为人民生活提供了丰富的轻工和纺织产品及家用电器;
- 为国民经济和国防建设提供了一批重要设备;
- 有100多种重要产品产量已在国际上占据首位。

4.1 制造科技与工业发达国家仍存在阶段性差距

一是技术创新能力不强。

75美元的MP3,国外拿走45美元。

二是制造技术基础薄弱。

三是技术创新体系尚未形成。

差距之一:技术创新能力不强

第一类,以自主创新为主,包括航天技术、轨道交通设备、炼油技术等。但产品技术水平与国外仍有较大差距。

中华之星 时速200公里/小时

差距之一:技术创新能力不强

第二类,在引进技术消化吸收的基础上,创新能力有明显提高。如通信设备、家用电器、发电设备、船舶、军用飞机、载重汽车及钢铁制造、炼油技术等。但产品技术水平与国外仍有较大差距。

30万吨超大型油轮

差距之一:技术创新能力不强

第三类,引进技术处于消化吸收过程,尚未掌握系统设计与核心技术。如轿车、大型乙烯成套设备、计算机系统软件等。

差距之一:技术创新能力不强

第四类,某些重要产品主要依赖购买国外产品,国内基本未开发。如大型飞机、半导体和集成电路专用设备、光纤制造设备、大型科学仪器及大型医疗设备等。

 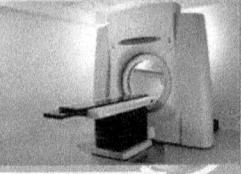

大型科学仪器及大型医疗设备

差距之二：制造技术基础薄弱

- 设计技术、可靠性技术、制造技术及工艺流程、基础材料、基础机械零部件和电子元器件、基础制造装备、仪器仪表及标准体系等发展滞后，制约了制造业的发展。

长江三峡水轮机制造技术
水轮机叶轮
（叶片及下环）

差距之二：制造技术基础薄弱

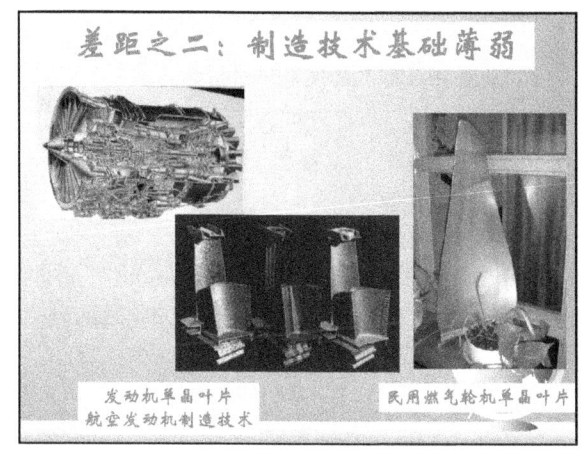

发动机单晶叶片
航空发动机制造技术

民用燃气轮机单晶叶片

差距之三：技术创新体系尚未形成

- 绝大多数企业技术开发能力薄弱，尚未成为技术创新的主体。
- 2001年我国大中型企业有研发机构的仅占25%，有研发活动的仅占30%；
- 50%中央国营企业R&D投入小于业务收入的0.5%，而国际上为5%。
- 缺乏一支精干、相对稳定的力量从事产业共性技术的研究与开发。
- 科技中介服务体系尚不健全，没有充分发挥作用。

国外企业-大学研究中心

4.2 制造科技发展目标

- 2020年发展目标：制造科技的总体水平进入国际先进行列。

五个标志：

一：自主创新能力大大增强。

二：制造科技总体水平进入国际先进行列。

三：重大装备由国内制造和成套的比例大幅度提高。

四：高技术产业产值占制造业产值比重大幅度提高。

五：形成以企业为主体的技术创新体系。

4.3 制造科技发展重点领域

2020年发展目标：制造科技的总体水平进入国际先进行列。

制造科技发展的三个重点领域：

1. 重大成套装备和高技术装备及技术
2. 新一代绿色制造流程工艺与装备
3. 制造业信息化（设计、制造与装备）

1-重大成套装备和高技术装备及技术

- 要特别重视发展战略性的重大成套装备、高技术装备和高技术产业所需装备，掌握核心技术，提高可靠性，大幅度增强自主创新能力和成套能力。
- 如：百万千瓦核电机组、大型水电机组、清洁高效火电机组、精密高效数控装备等。

2-新一代绿色制造流程与装备

以绿色化和信息化为核心，研究开发具有高技术含量产品制造、能源转换和大宗社会废弃物资源化三项功能的新一代制造流程及相关装备。

中国宝钢

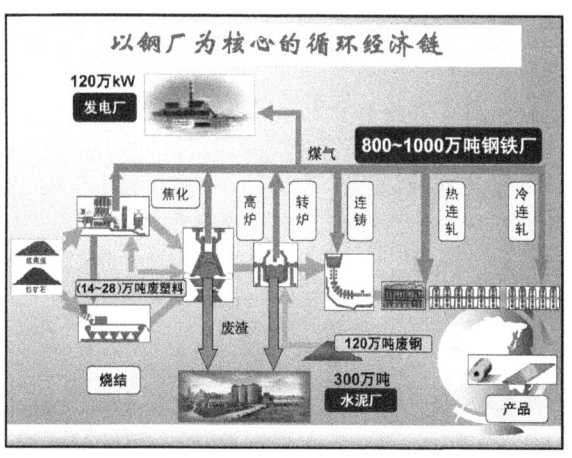

以钢厂为核心的循环经济链

3 - 制造业信息化
— 数字化、信息化设计、制造与基础装备

- 将以信息技术为代表的高新技术融入制造企业的产品设计与制造过程,以及制造业的产品和基础装备,实施制造业信息化工程。

正在研制中的新支线飞机ARJ21
来源:中国航空工业第一集团公司

3 - 制造业信息化
— 数字化、信息化设计、制造与基础装备

- 以高精度、智能化数控机床为代表的数字化基础装备是保障国防和尖端工业的战略性装备。
- 发展发电设备、航空、航天高精度大型专用制造装备。
- 汽车制造所需成套、高效、高精度、高可靠制造系统。
- 发展电子通信设备制造所需高精、高速及微米/纳米制造技术与设备。

五、科技发展战略与对策

(1) 开放式自主创新战略

- 要把制造科技进步的基点从主要依赖引进国外技术逐步转移到增强自主创新能力上。
- 在积极引进国外先进技术的同时,加大研究开发和对引进技术消化吸收的投入,大幅度提高设计方法和制造技术的自主创新能力。
- 集成创新与关键技术的突破相结合,仍将是今后制造业的主要自主创新形式。
- 我国企业重引进,轻消化吸收及创新。据有关统计,引进同等的技术设备,我国用于消化吸收再创新的费用只及日韩的0.7%。(国内100:7;韩国100:1000)

五、科技发展战略与对策

(1) 开放式自主创新战略

- 加快企业成为技术创新主体的进程。企业必须成为研发经费投入的主体、技术开发和技术创新的主体。大型企业均应建立和完善企业技术中心,加大研究开发经费投入。鼓励企业与高校、科研单位合办工程研究中心和产学研联合技术中心。鼓励中小企业采取联合出资,共同委托的方式进行合作研究开发。国家应明确制订有关支持和激励的政策。
- 50%中央国营企业R&D投入小于业务收入的0.5%,而国际上为5%。

五、科技发展战略与对策

(1) 开放式自主创新战略

- 要重组产业共性技术研究体系及建立产业共性技术研究开发平台。
- 当前,我国广大中小型企业无力自主开发,绝大多数企业无力支持共性、基础性及竞争前技术的研究。国家应建立共性技术平台,支持并形成一支高水平、精干的研究队伍,重点承担产业原创性技术、共性技术及战略性关键技术的研究开发,要建设若干个先进制造技术国家实验室和国家工程技术研究中心。

五、科技发展战略与对策

(2) 资源节约、环境友好的可持续发展战略

- 制造业是大量消耗资源的产业,同时对环境质量造成很大影响。要走科技含量高、经济效益好、资源消耗低、环境污染少、人力资源优势得到充分发挥的新型工业化道路。
- 发展节约资源型和环境友好型产业、产品及技术。如:节能型轿车等。
- 优化资源利用和减少环境污染,减缓资源消耗总量和污染排放。如:短流程工艺,清洁工艺等。

五、科技发展战略与对策

(3) 重点突破装备制造业、提高装备设计与制造及系统集成与成套能力战略

- 装备设计能力、制造能力和集成创新能力是构成制造强国的最核心能力。
- 要发展重大成套装备、高技术装备和高技术产业所需装备,推进重大装备的国产化;
- 要将提高单机和系统可靠性作为关键;要大力发展为装备提供零部件、元器件和基础材料等产业,实现专业化和大规模生产;
- 要加强成套技术的开发,培育一批具有国际竞争力的集系统设计、成套、工程总承包和服务为一体的工程公司,实现制造商与用户、制造工艺流程与制造装备的紧密结合。

五、科技发展战略与对策

(4) 用高新技术促进与提升制造技术水平战略

- 推进以信息技术为代表的高新技术全面渗透和融入制造业。用信息技术改造、提升传统制造业和老工业基地,大力推进制造业信息化,是以信息化带动工业化的主要内容。
- 制造业信息化的重点是:数字化、信息化设计与制造及数字化、信息化基础装备。

网络化、协同化、开放式产品数字化设计方法与技术

- 有丰富的基于科学与经验的知识库支持的智能化设计与制造开发系统。
- 在功能、质量、可靠性与成本方面能提供最优产品。
- 广泛采用模拟仿真技术，产品及零部件做到一次研发成功。

完全集成与优化的设计与制造系统

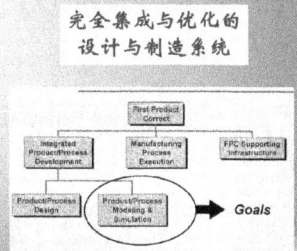

产品一次成功模型

网络化、协同化、开放式产品数字化设计方法与技术

主要功能：
- 3P分析
  - Productivity 生产率分析
  - Producibility 可制造性
  - Predictability 可预测性（组织、性能与寿命）
- 3E分析
  - Energy 能源分析
  - Environment 环境分析
  - Economy 经济分析

美国汽车工业希望汽车的研发周期缩短为15~25个月，而20世纪90年代汽车的研发周期为5年。

基于模拟仿真的数字化、智能化制造

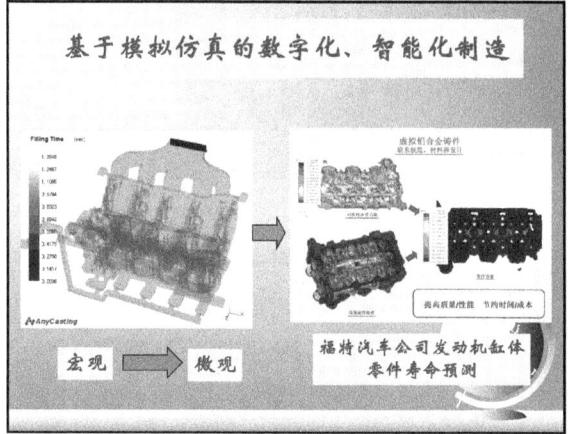

宏观 → 微观

福特汽车公司发动机缸体零件寿命预测

五、科技发展战略与对策

（5）培养创新意识人才和高级技能人才战略

要成为制造强国：
- 需要大批高水平的科技人才。
- 需要大批熟悉国际国内市场、具有现代管理知识和能力的企业家。
- 需要大批能熟练掌握先进技术、工艺和技能的高级技能人才。
- 全国192家中央级企业专业技术人员中，具有硕士以上学历人员也只占总数的2.1%，高级技师仅占工人队伍的0.16%。

六、结束语

制造业是国民经济的物质基础、国家安全的主要保障、国家竞争力的重要体现。

必须依靠科技进步，开拓出一条资源消耗少、环境污染轻、技术含量高的制造业发展道路，从制造大国走向制造强国。

7. 提高装备制造业自主创新能力[一]

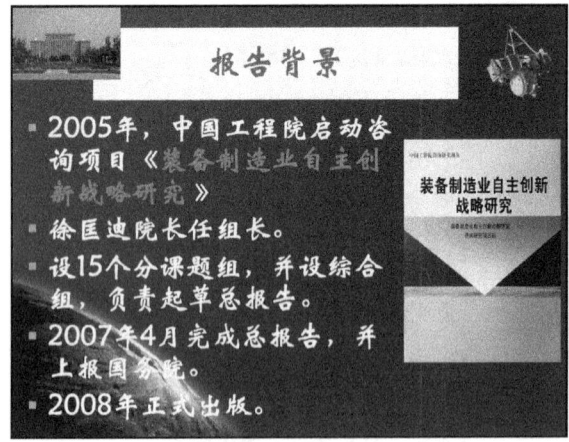
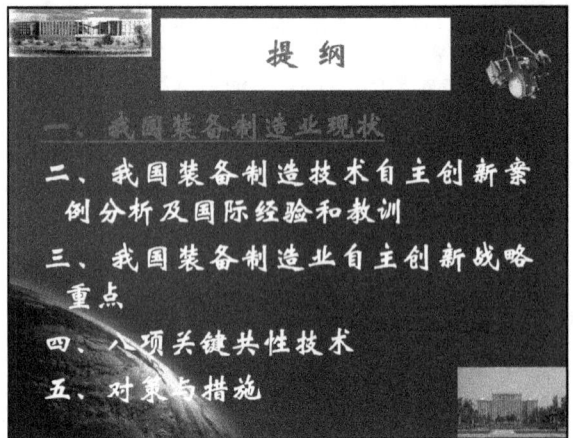

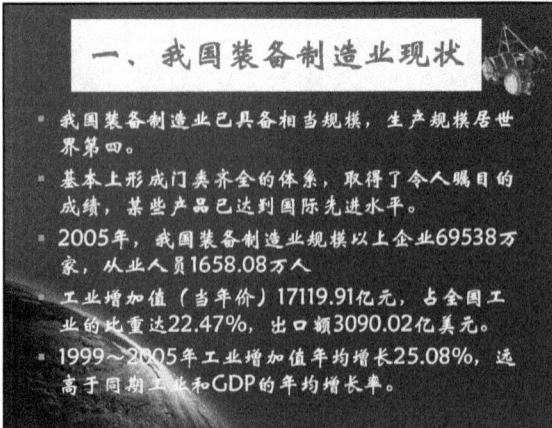

[一] 本文为2008年广东科技报告会及上海"产品现代设计与技术创新"论坛的大会主题报告。

一、我国装备制造业现状

- 突出的问题是自主创新能力不强
- 一是产品以中、低端为主,附加价值不高,某些关键核心技术没有掌握。
- 二是产业制造基础薄弱;
- 三是系统集成和工程成套能力差。

一、我国装备制造业现状

- 一是产品以中、低端为主,附加价值不高
- 全行业增加值率仅为25.44%,而工业发达国家在37%-48%之间。
- 中低档产品和一般加工制造能力大量富余,但国民经济发展所急需的重大成套装备和基础性装备过度依赖进口。
- 2005年,全国进口装备产品3187.05亿美元,占全国外贸进口总额的48.28%。
- 以机床为例:我国已是机床生产大国,经济规模居世界第三位,但高档数控机床仍依赖进口,是世界上最大的机床进口国。

2006年机床数控系统国内生产与进口百分数

2006年机床进出口金额:
进口:72.4亿美元;
出口:11.9亿美元

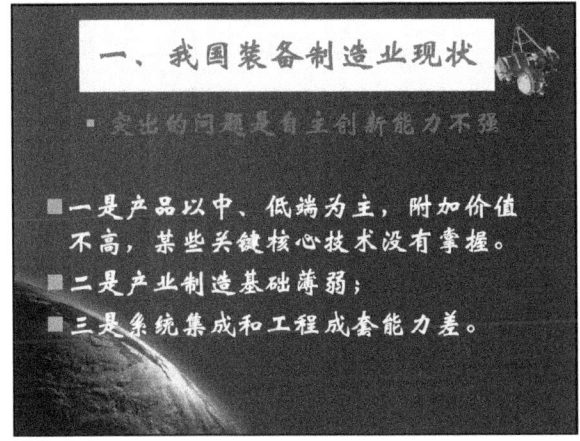

一、我国装备制造业现状

- 二是产业制造基础薄弱-1

我国重要装备制造企业的装备水平已接近或达到国际先进水平,但制造基础仍是十分薄弱。

我国已是铸锻件生产大国,但火电、水电及核电装备的大型及关键铸锻件仍依赖进口,受制于人。

长江三峡水轮机叶轮 重400余吨

一、我国装备制造业现状

- 二是产业制造基础薄弱-2

我国重要装备制造企业的装备水平已接近或达到国际先进水平,但制造基础仍是十分薄弱。

设计与制造技术、基础技术、基础材料、基础元器件、基础装备制造工艺、自动化仪表、标准体系、知识产权等发展滞后。

航空发动机及重型燃机叶片

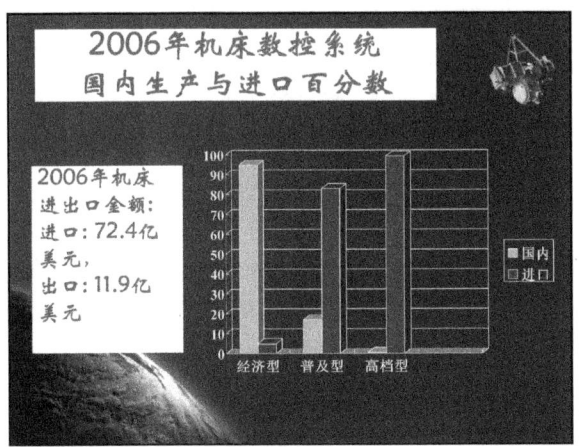

一、我国装备制造业现状

- 三是缺乏核心制造技术及系统集成能力差

装备的控制部分、集成技术等主要依靠国外。缺乏一批具有较强实力、能承担系统设计、工艺和设备成套及工程总承包任务的工程公司。

存在较为严重的制造部门与用户脱节;学、研与生产脱节;装备制造与工艺脱节等。

如:大马力低速柴油机成套制造技术,及大马力曲轴核心制造技术

一、我国装备制造业现状

装备制造业自主创新能力不强主要原因

1. 宏观调控不力,缺乏有效的协调与管理
2. 以企业为技术创新主体的体制没有建立
3. 研发经费投入不足
4. 工程科技人才培养体系不够健全

一、我国装备制造业现状

装备制造业自主创新能力不强主要原因

1. 宏观调控不力,缺乏有效的协调与管理

缺乏完整、系统、有效的政策体系,难以形成激发企业自主创新功能的政策环境和市场环境;

政府对引进技术缺乏有效的管理与协调,没有形成一个集中对外、统一引进、联合消化吸收的格局,一些地方和企业(特别是用户)为了追求局部利益,片面重视技术引进而忽视了消化吸收,重复引进现象严重,造成了大量的资金浪费;

条块分割、有限研发投入、分散使用、各行其是。

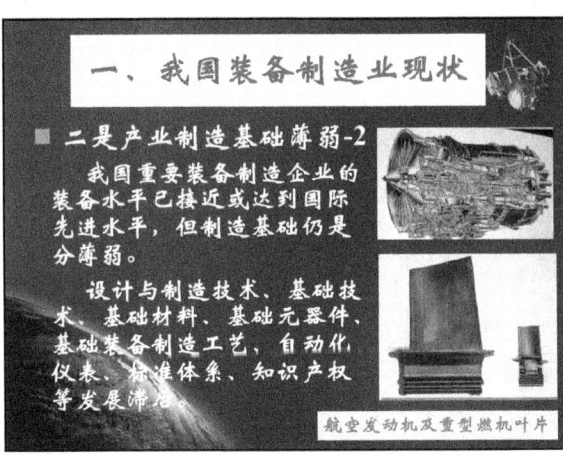

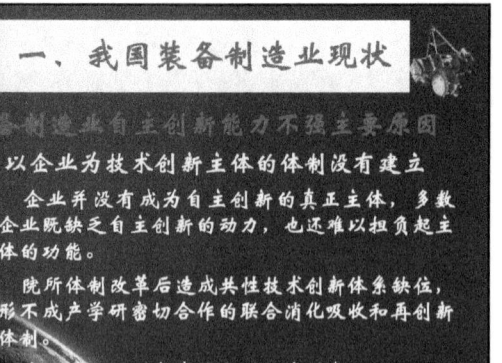
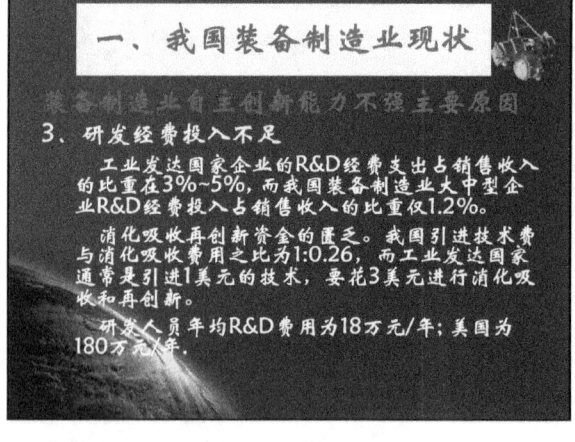
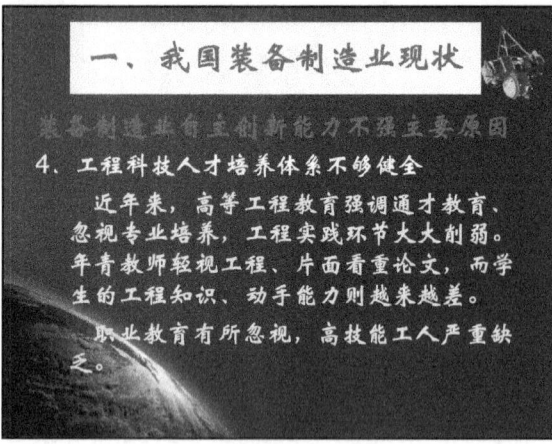
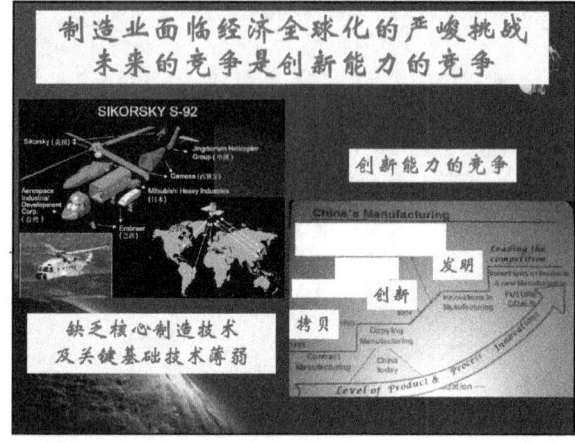
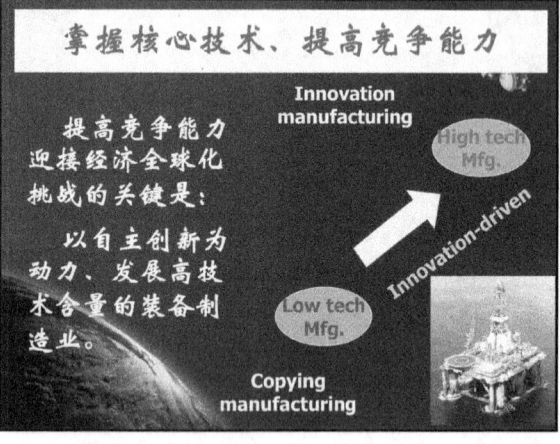

二、装备制造技术自主创新案例分析

1. 国家引导，联合引进，联合消化吸收的模式
- 我国电力装备制造业30/60万千瓦大电机组经验值得重视。
- 目前30万千瓦、60万千瓦大电机组的国产化率已分别达到95%和90%，形成了批量生产能力，国产机组已成为电力建设的主力机组，我国80%的发电机组是国产机组。

二、装备制造技术自主创新案例分析

2. 打捆招标，联合设计，合作制造的模式
- 我国电力装备制造业三峡70MW水电机组的经验值得重视。
- 由于我国大型水轮发电机组设计制造能力明显提高，三峡工程右岸电站的12台70万千瓦水轮发电机组及其辅助设备订单被东电和哈电各夺得4台，使中国大型水轮发电机组的技术水平提高到世界先进水平。

二、装备制造技术自主创新案例分析

3. 以我为主，系统集成，带动成套设备的模式
- 鞍山钢铁集团公司先后在43项重大工程建设、改造过程中，实现自主创新，并取得重大成果。
- 1700中薄板坯连铸连轧（APS）生产线是我国首套自行设计、制造拥有自主知识产权的新型短流程热轧带钢生产线。
- 完成了1780大型宽带钢冷轧生产线，表明我国掌握了冷轧成套装备制造和工艺生产控制两大核心技术。

二、装备制造技术自主创新案例分析

4. 敢为人先，自主创新，跨越发展的模式
- 上海振华港机集团公司依靠不断自主创新，2006年产值达到20亿美元以上。产品主要从集装箱机械扩大到散货装卸机械、大型桥梁用钢梁、海上大型起重机（300吨，正在研制具有世界最高吨位700吨技术及装备）、起重机专用配件等。它们的产品已占领国际市场73%，国内市场90%以上，创造了多项世界领先技术。

二、装备制造技术自主创新案例分析

从企业自主创新成功的案例来分析，主要的经验是：
- 立足自主创新，以我为主、集成与成套，引进部分关键技术、消化吸收再创新，形成自主知识产权的核心技术。

要能做到以上这点：
- 一是企业的领导班子要有创业的奉献精神，要有自主创新的思维，要有高瞻远瞩的战略眼光，要对市场需求和发展有清晰思路，要懂得科学技术知识。
- 二是要有一支具有奉献精神与科技创新的团队。

三、装备制造业自主创新战略及重点

（一）战略（40字）

市场牵引、政府调控；
企业主体、科技先行；
产学研用、紧密联合；
消化吸收、掌握核心；
强化基础、集成创新。

总之，要依托重点工程，突破共性技术，掌握核心技术，促进自主创新，提高研发设计、加工制造和系统集成的整体水平。

三、装备制造业自主创新战略及重点

（一）战略

1. 市场牵引、政府调控

市场需求是推动装备制造业发展和自主创新能力提高的根本动力。

提高重大装备自主创新能力事关国家经济和国防安全，是国家目标，必须充分发挥政府的调控作用，制订重大科技和产业化计划并进行引导，调动各方面力量，集中使用有效的社会资源，力求取得突破。

三、装备制造业自主创新战略及重点

（一）战略

2. 企业主体、科技先行

企业是技术创新的主体，也是提高装备制造业自主创新能力的需求主体、投资主体和实施主体。要加速主体的培育，使之尽快到位是最紧迫的任务。

企业自主创新能力的提高，归根到底要依靠科技。要充分认识"科学技术是第一生产力"的重要意义和巨大作用。

三、装备制造业自主创新战略及重点

（一）战略

3. 产学研用、紧密联合

重大装备技术难度大，涉及多个科技领域，单靠一个企业自身的力量是远远不够的，应该在政府的引导、推动下，实现用户与制造商、产学研、制造企业之间的紧密联合，或进一步结成联盟。在引进技术的企业与消化吸收的企业或科研机构间搭建桥梁。共同对引进技术进行消化吸收和再创新。共同对重大装备的重大共性技术、关键技术进行攻关，实现双赢或多赢。

三、装备制造业自主创新战略及重点

（一）战略

4. 消化吸收、掌握核心

在今后相当长的时期，充分利用开放的国际环境，引进国外先进技术，进行消化吸收和再创新，仍将是提高我国重大装备自主创新能力的重要途径。

但必须摒弃长期存在的重引进、轻消化吸收的顽症，以我为主，加大消化吸收和再创新的力度，掌握核心技术和关键技术，尽快实现由引进模式转变为自主创新模式。

三、装备制造业自主创新战略及重点

（一）战略

5. 强化基础、集成创新

- 装备制造业自主创新能力的提高，必须建立在扎实的产业共性技术、基础技术之上。产业共性基础技术和基础零部件产业的发展滞后已严重制约了装备制造业的自主创新，亟待予以加强。

系统成套能力薄弱是我国装备制造业存在的一个突出问题，而集成创新被证明是一种成本低、周期短、风险少、见效快，往往能取得重大突破的一条创新途径。

对装备制造业而言，高度重视集成创新，提高系统成套能力和工程总承包能力，尤其具有重要意义。

三、装备制造业自主创新战略及重点

（二）目标

- 突破一批重大成套装备的核心技术；
- 创造一批具有自主知识产权的核心技术与产品；
- 建成以企业为主体、产学研结合的技术创新体系；
- 锤炼一批有国际竞争力的大型企业集团或成套工程公司。
- 造就一支高水平的和适用性创新人才队伍。

三、装备制造业自主创新战略及重点

（三）16项重点任务

以基础制造装备、发电设备、新一代钢铁和石化流程工业生产装备、现代交通运输设备四个领域为重点。

同时，也要重视和提高影响国计民生及人民健康的农业装备、医疗设备、纺织机械装备及轻工专用设备的自主创新能力。总共16项重点领域。

三、装备制造业自主创新的战略重点

1) 超精密及重型高档数控机床技术。
2) 600MW~1000MW级超临界及超超临界火电机组设计与制造技术。
3) 百万千瓦等级压水堆核电设备设计与制造技术。
4) 1000KV交流和±800KV直流输变电技术。
5) 新一代钢铁流程工业成套技术与装备。
6) 百万吨乙烯及配套装备。
7) 海洋深水石油开发大型工程设施。
8) 液化天然气（LNG）。
9) 300km/h高速列车设计与制造技术。
10) 新一代节能型轿车及新能源汽车。
11) 研究支线客机以及与支线客机配套的涡扇发动机。（大型干线飞机已列重大专项）
12) 大规模集成电路专用制造设备。
13) 煤矿综采设备及全断面掘进机。
14) 农业装备。
15) 医疗设备。
16) 纺织机械及纸浆造纸设备。

四、突破八项关键共性技术

要形成上述16项重大装备的自主创新能力和系统集成能力，必须集中力量突破以下8项关键共性技术。

→ 1、数字化、智能化设计与制造技术；
2、现代复杂机电产品创新设计及系统集成技术。
3、大型复杂机电系统安全性与可靠性技术及关键基础件制造技术；
4、新型工程材料应用技术；

四、突破八项关键共性技术

要形成上述16项重大装备的自主创新能力和系统集成能力，必须集中力量突破以下8项关键共性技术。

→ 5、重大工程中大型铸、锻、焊结构件及关键零件制造技术；
→ 6、精密成形及超精密加工制造技术。
→ 7、自动化仪表及自动检测控制技术；
→ 8、绿色制造技术。

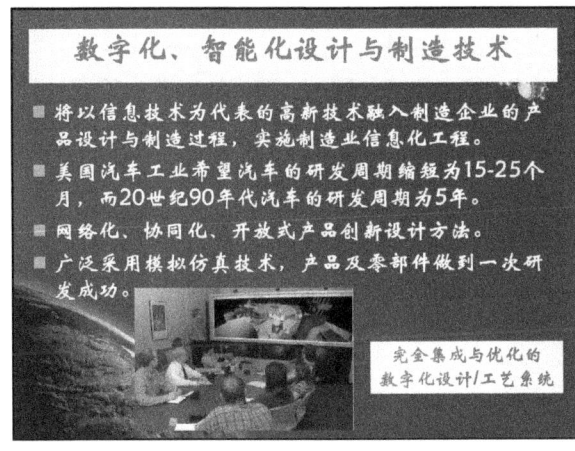

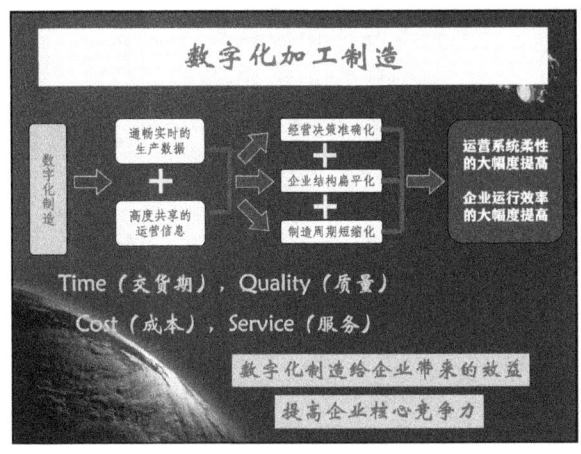
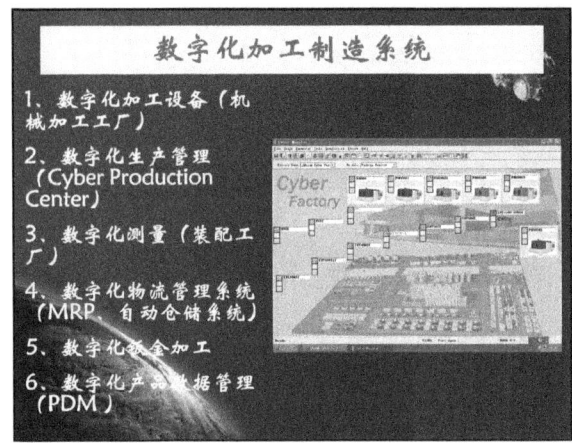
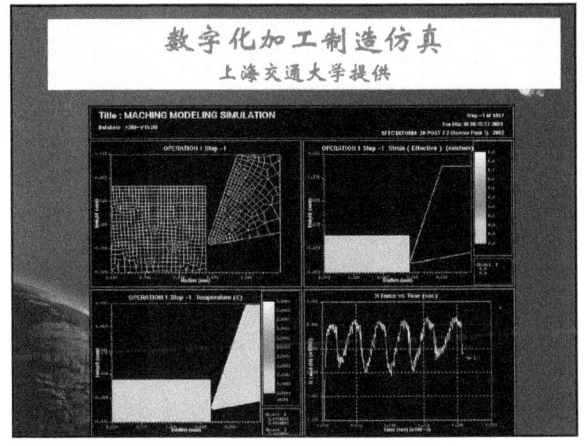
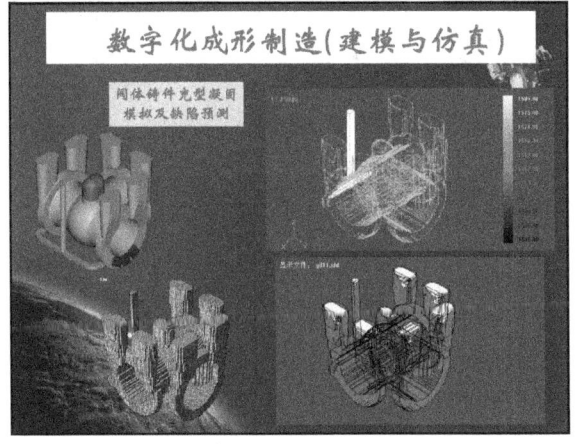
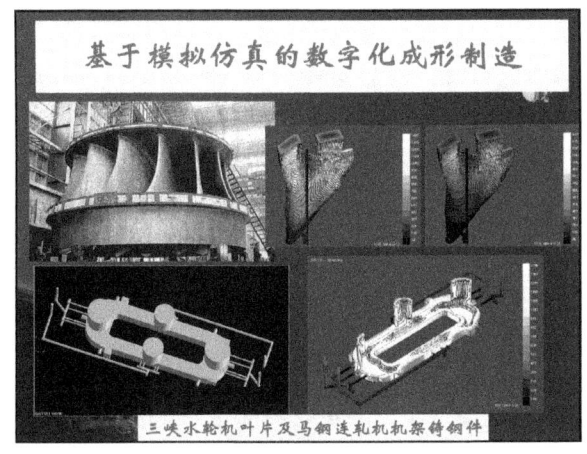
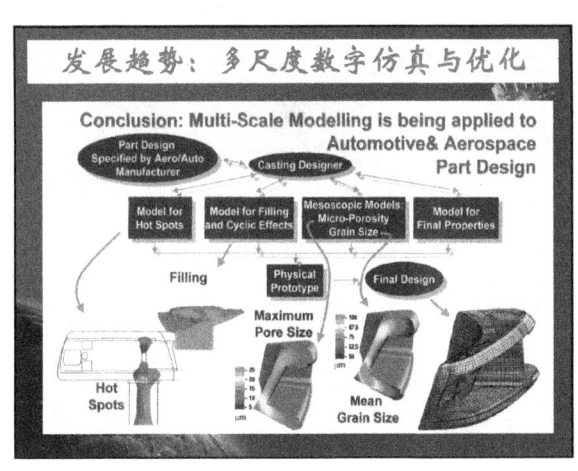

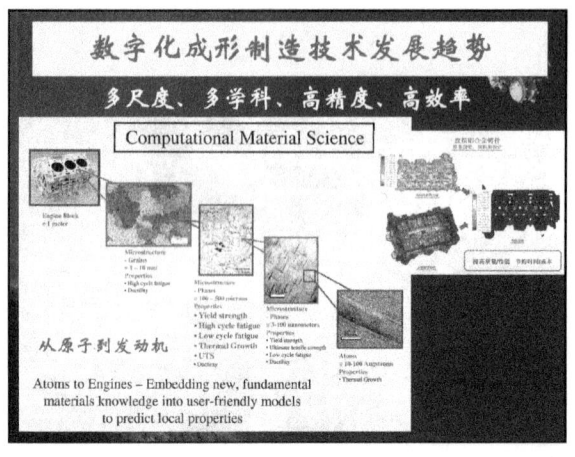
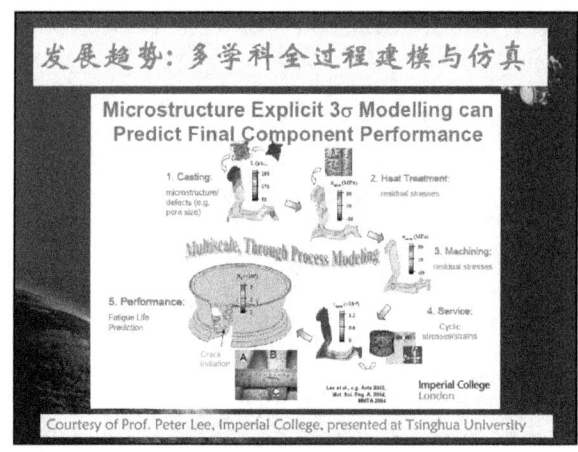

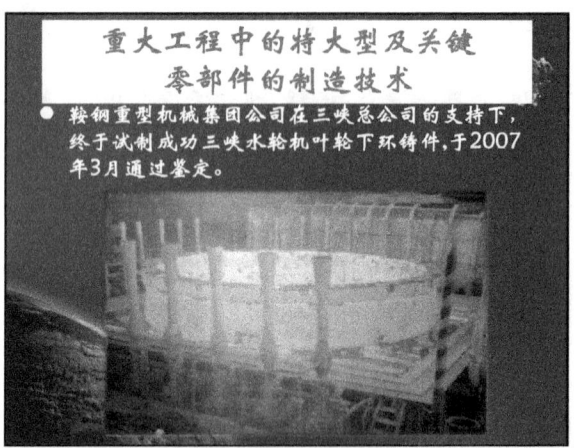

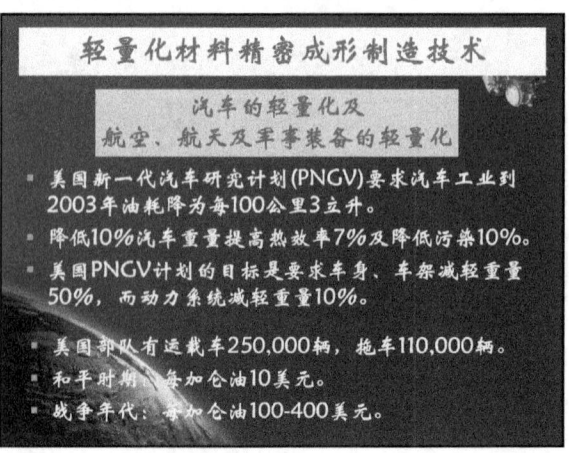

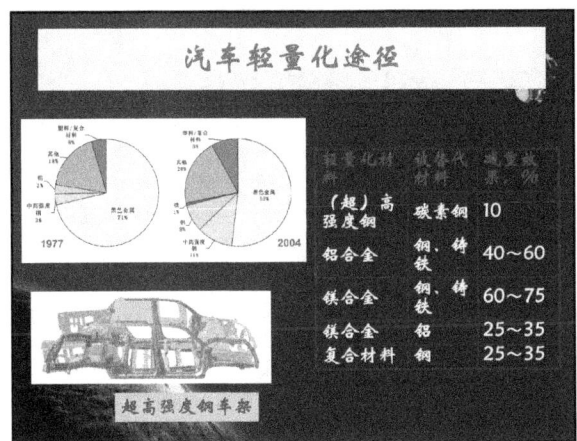

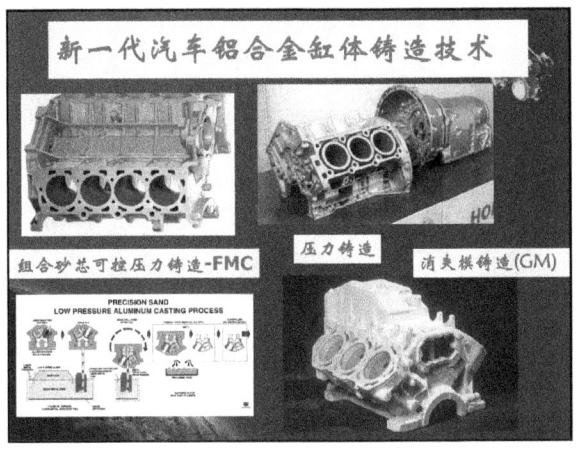
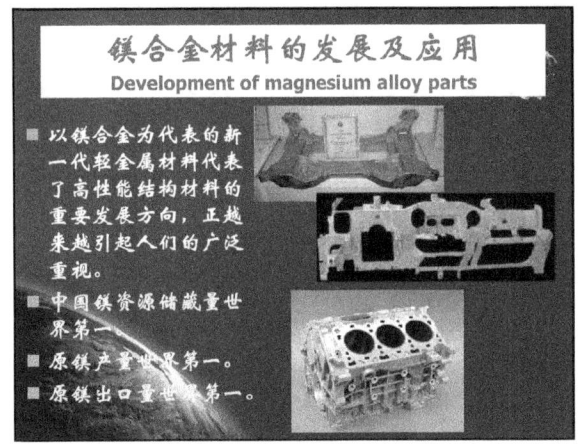
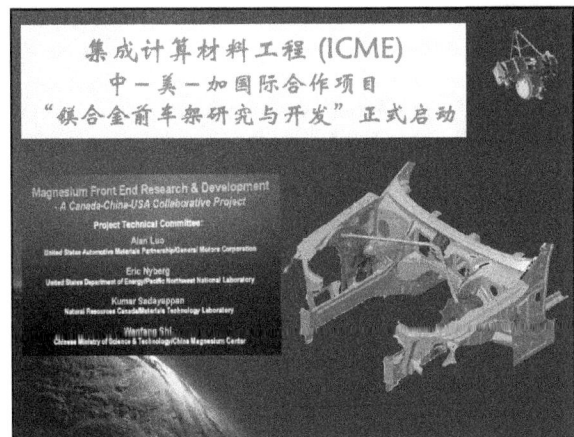
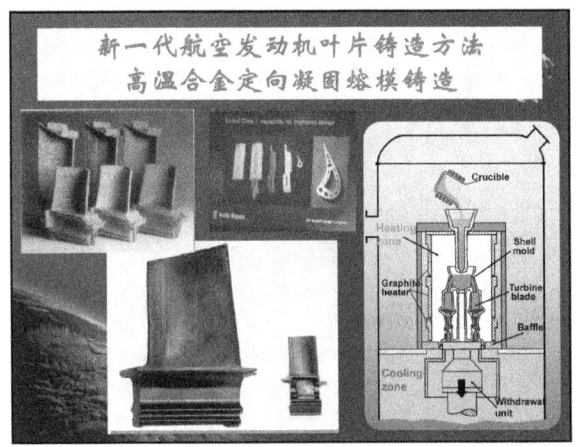
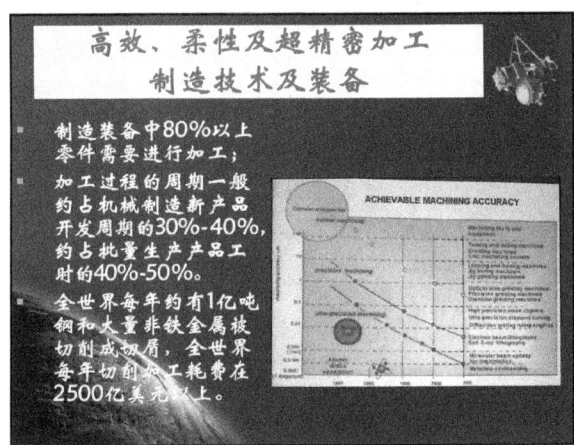
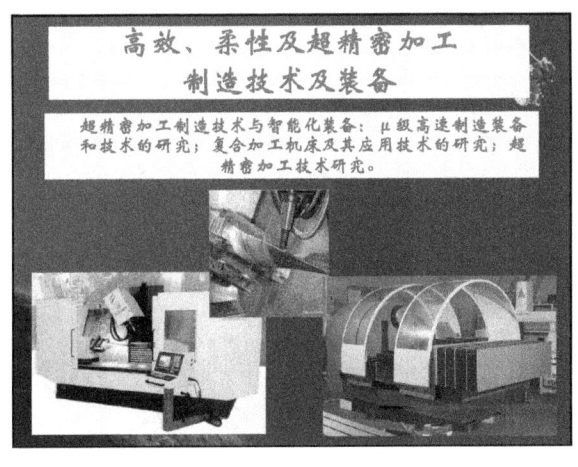

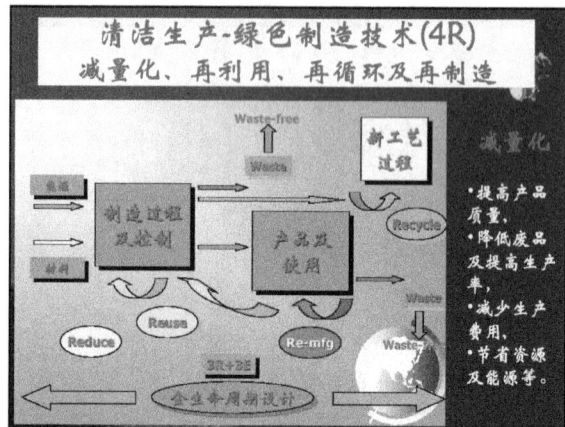

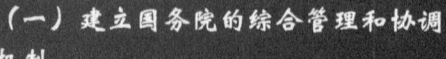

五、对策与措施

（五）重视创新型工程科技人才的培养，弘扬自主创新的民族自强精神

装备制造业的自主创新需要大量的具有坚实理论基础、工程实践、企业实践经验的交叉复合型人才。

高等院校应成为科技创新的源泉，肩负起培养创新型人才的历史使命。高等工程教育要进行改革，要改革高等工科院校的评价体系，改变片面重视论文，忽视工程实践的倾向。

企业也要承担起培养工程科技的责任。

结束语

一、装备制造业是为国民经济和国防建设提供技术装备的基础产业，是国家实力和国际竞争力的主要象征，是国民经济的脊梁，具有极其重要的战略和现实意义。

二、装备制造业的突出的问题是自主创新能力不强。

三、提高装备制造业自主创新能力的战略是：市场牵引、政府调控；企业主体、科技先行；产学研用、紧密联合；消化吸收、掌握核心；强化基础、集成创新。

四、提高装备制造业自主创新能力要以基础制造装备、发电设备、新一代钢铁和石化流程工业装备、现代交通运输设备为重点领域。

五、提高装备制造业自主创新能力要突破8项关键共性技术。

六、提高装备制造业自主创新能力的对策与措施是：建议建立国务院综合管理和协调机制；建立举国协同的科技创新体系；制定重点领域装备自主创新路线图；规范外资并购政策；重视创新型工程科技人才培养。

8. 创新驱动 强化基础——建设制造强国

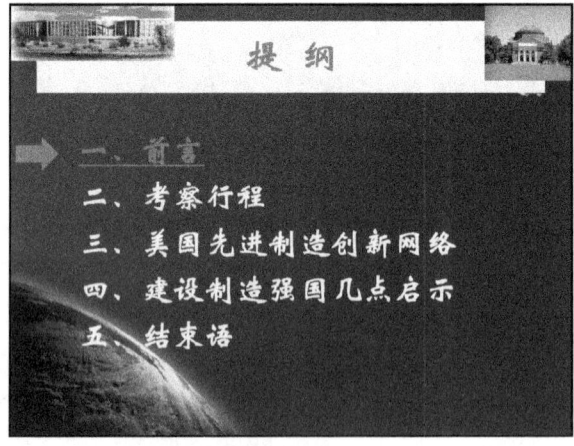
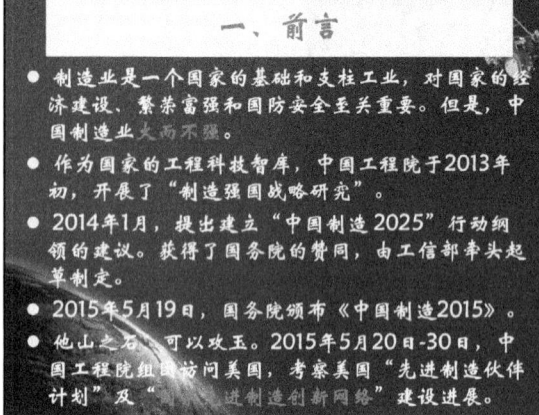

○ 本文为2015年中国制造2025国际论坛的大会主题报告,会议地点为中国深圳。

三、美国先进制造创新网络

3.1 美国总统科技顾问委员会（PCAST）和"美国先进制造（业）伙伴计划(AMP)"
3.2 美国"先进制造伙伴计划"指导委员会
3.3 国家制造创新网络（NNMI）
3.4 制造创新研究院(IMI)

3.1 美国总统科技顾问委员会及AMP

- 2011-2014年，美国总统办公室和总统科技顾问委员会（PCAST）连续向总统提交了《2011-确保美国在先进制造业的领导地位》、《2012-紧握在先进制造业的国内竞争优势》、《2014-加快发展美国先进制造业》等重要报告。
- 2011年6月，美国宣布启动"先进制造（业）伙伴关系"（Advanced Manufacturing Partnership - AMP）计划，呼吁政府、高校及企业之间应加强合作，以强化美国制造业领先地位。同时，设立美国先进制造国家计划办公室（AMNPO）。
- 美国总统科技顾问委员会对推动振兴美国制造业，建立"国家制造业创新网络（NNMI）"发挥了重要战略咨询作用。

3.2 "先进制造伙伴计划"指导委员会

- 由大学校长和专家，及工业界巨头组成的AMP指导委员会在具体实施过程中，发挥了不可替代的作用。第一及第二届均由Dow化工集团CEO和MIT校长分别担任委员会双主席。

指导委员会提出16项具体建议，凝练了3项重要举措：

一是要设立跨部门的AMNPO，
二是要建立制造创新网络（NNMI），以解决基础研究与产业化之间的鸿沟，
三是发挥社区学院（Community College）的作用，特别是（劳动力）技术工人的培训等。

3.3 国家制造创新网络

- 建立制造业创新网络（NNMI）的目的是填补制造技术基础研究和商业化生产之间的空缺，被称之为"Missing Middle"。

制造创新过程可分为：基础研究（basic manufacturing research）、概念验证（proof of concept）、实验室试制（production in laboratory）、原型制造能力（capacity to produce prototype）、生产条件能力（capability in production environment）、生产率示范（demonstration of production rates）等6个阶段。

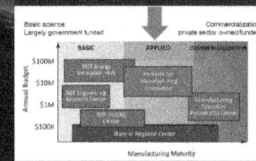
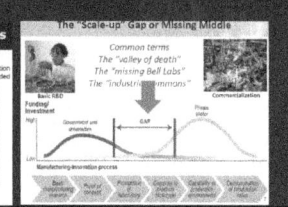

3.4 国家制造创新研究院

- 制造创新研究院由产（包含中小企业）、学（包含社区学院）、研（包含国家研究院所）、政，组成非营利的创新联盟。研究院设立具体办事机构，有的研究院还建有示范基地或实验室。
- 制造创新研究院的主要任务及作用是：1）开展竞争前共性技术研究及示范，2）供应链的技术集成，3）支持中小企业，4）各个层次劳动力的技能教育与培训等。

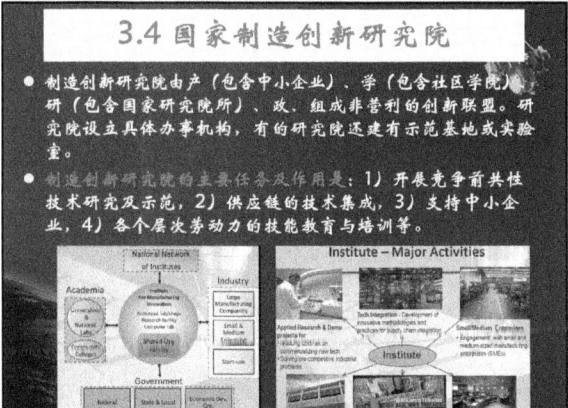

3.4 国家制造创新研究院

- 案例1：国家增材制造创新研究院（National Additive Manufacturing Innovation Institute - NAMII）是在全国建立的15个制造创新研究院中的第一个，目前已由超过85家公司、13个研究型大学、9个社区学院以及18个非营利机构组成。
- 所有成员的共同目标就是要把增材制造技术转变成美国主流的制造技术。
- 美国在增材制造中关键材料方面的研发起步较早并且投入了很大的精力，整个产业链正在逐渐成形。
- 应该指出，虽然我们在增材制造领域也是起步早，但是由于各种原因限制，目前仍没有清晰的产业化架构。各地仍在进行"跑马圈地"运动，这对于产业发展非常不利。

3.4 国家制造创新研究院

案例2：数字化制造与设计创新研究院
主要任务特点

1. 聚焦技术的使命（Focus）
2. 明确的工业价值命题（proposition）
   每个研究院为工业界参加者提供资助和创造价值
3. 产、学、政伙伴关系（Partnership）
   每个研究院由工业、学术界及政府组成联盟
4. 解决关键挑战与技术（Challenges）
   通过技术路线图，只有靠协同联盟才能解决的工业界的优先及关键的技术
5. 平衡的计划（Portfolio）
   通过技术路线图，每个研究院有一个平衡的研究计划（当前与战略投资），由技术顾问委员会驱动。

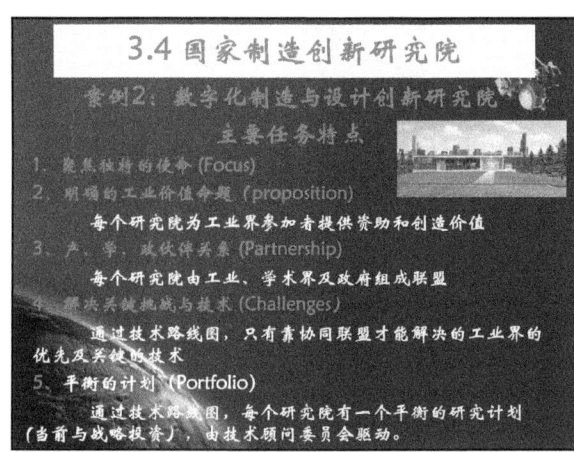

3.4 国家制造创新研究院

- 案例3：轻量化材料制造创新研究院：由34个企业、7所大学及17个其他单位组成联盟，是美国成立的第四个制造创新研究院。由EDI、OSU及UM三单位主持，UM材料科学与工程系Alan Taub教授是技术总负责人。
- 我们访问了轻量化材料制造创新研究院。他们主要集中在高强度钢、铝合金、镁合金及钛合金等金属材料领域。
- LIFT的任务：开展竞争前共性技术的应用研究。

4.1 进一步完善技术创新体系

- 要实施创新驱动,首先企业要转变观念,加大研发投入,成为技术创新主体。
- 根据统计,我国企业研发与销售收入的比值不到1%,而工业发达国家一般在3%~5%左右。
- 企业是技术创新主体,主要是指:市场及科技需求的主体,研发及投入的主体(竞争技术,而不是竞争前技术),科技成果产业化的主体。
- 其次,我国技术成果转化率仅10%左右。技术成果转化率低的原因是多方面的。其中重要的原因是技术创新体系不完善,在技术研究成果到企业产业化间有缺位(美国称之为鸿沟)。
- 特别是大院大所改制后,造成"共性技术"研究缺位。这一缺位现象要抓紧解决,已到了刻不容缓的时刻。

4.1 进一步完善技术创新体系

- 他山之石,可以攻玉。美国的建立"国家制造创新研究院"的做法,解决"死亡谷"的做法,值得借鉴。

The "Scale-up" Gap or Missing Middle

Common terms
The "valley of death"
The "missing Bell Labs"
The "industrial commons"

4.1 进一步完善技术创新体系

- 建议在《中国制造2025》"制造业创新中心建设工程"中,参照德国及美国的经验,在整合原有各类工程实验室或工程研究中心的同时,试点建立一批(10-15个):
  一、非营利的,
  二、从事竞争前、关键共性技术研究,
  三、开放和成果可共享,
  四、人才培训
  的制造创新研究院或中心
  由具有优势企业、高校、院所组成协同联盟。
- 例如,可以试点建立增材制造、数字化设计与制造、轻量化材料等国家制造创新研究中心等。

4.2 加强先进基础工艺研究

- 我们考察的无论是制造创新研究院,或是三所大学,或是福特汽车公司研究与创新中心,都十分重视铸造、塑性加工、焊接、热处理等先进基础工艺的研究。
- 同时又十分重视先进基础工艺及基础材料与信息化(数字化)的深度结合和集成,特别是集成计算材料工程(ICME)的研究。
- 建议在《中国制造2025》"工业强基工程"中要大力加强基础材料、先进基础工艺研究,并与信息化的深度融合,加强"集成计算材料工程(ICME)"的研究。

4.2 加强先进基础工艺研究

- 应该认识到,要加强应用基础共性技术研究,单靠企业不行,需要政府主导、产学研用联合,共同组成协同创新联盟,建设竞争前关键共性基础技术研发平台。
- 例如,我们考察了美国政府设立的"轻量化材料制造创新研究院"。研究院的经费约80%,用来支持竞争前关键共性技术研究。研究项目的立项要根据需求,征得企业同意,而研究院的主要牵头单位则由一所研究院所和二所大学主持。技术总负责人是有丰富工程经验的教授担任。正在建设的"先进复合材料制造创新研究院",由田纳西大学负责。

4.3 加快培养各层次的工程技术人才

- 人才建设是建设制造强国的根本。要十分重视各个层次(从领军人才到高级技工)的工程技术人员的培养,特别是第一线的高级技能人员的培养。
- 美国在实施AMP中,多次强调要加强适应新技术、具有知识和技能的劳动力的教育和培养,特别在"制造创新研究院"的组成中,强调要有社区学院(College)参加,在任务中强调要具有"劳动力教育和培训"功能。这一做法,值得借鉴。

五、结束语

- 制造业是一个国家的基础和支柱工业,对国家的经济建设、繁荣富强和国防安全至关重要。但是,中国制造业大而不强。
- 《中国制造2025》是建设制造强国的纲领性文件。将鼓舞和动员制造业企业、学术界等各方面力量,为建设制造强国而努力奋斗。
- 美国实施"先进制造伙伴"计划,及建设一批制造创新研究院组成"国家制造创新网络"的做法值得借鉴。
- 建设制造强国要以"创新驱动"为指导思想,"强化基础"为根本,"智能制造"为突破口。

9. 加强先进基础工艺创新能力[一]

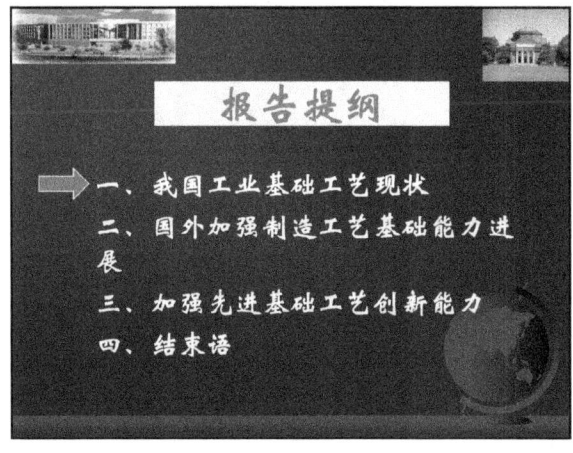
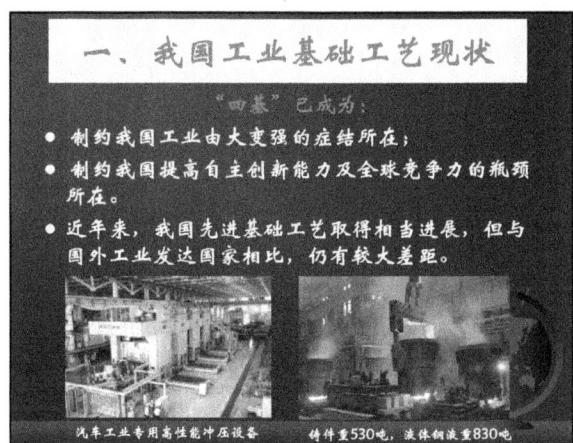

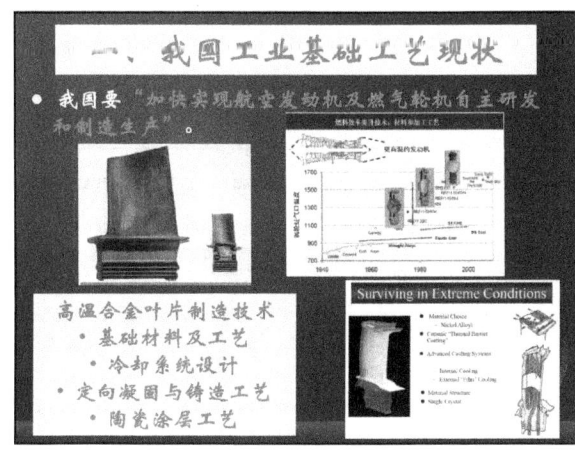
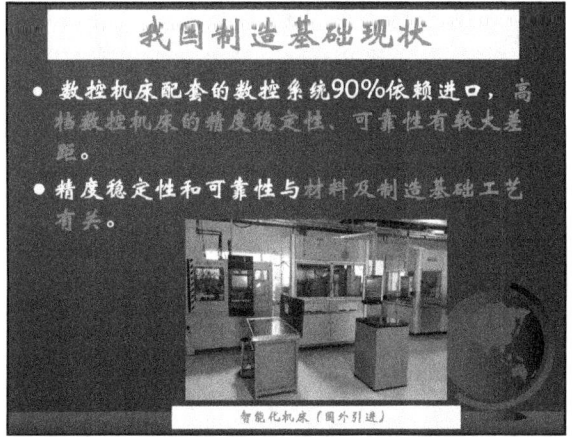

[一] 本文为2016年中国工业强基战略推进论坛的大会邀请报告，会议地点为北京。

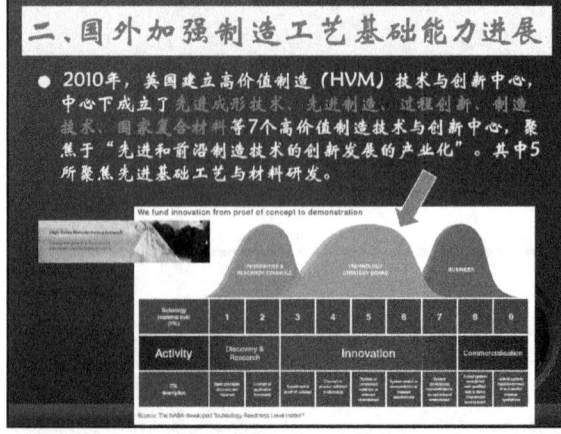
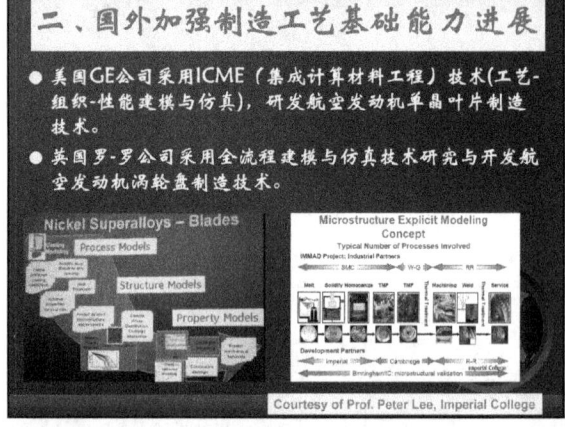
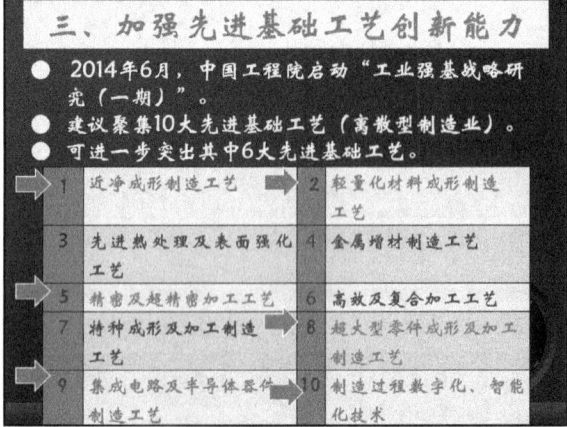
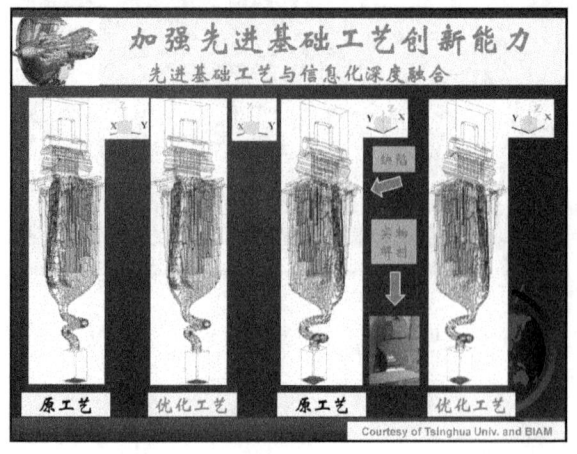
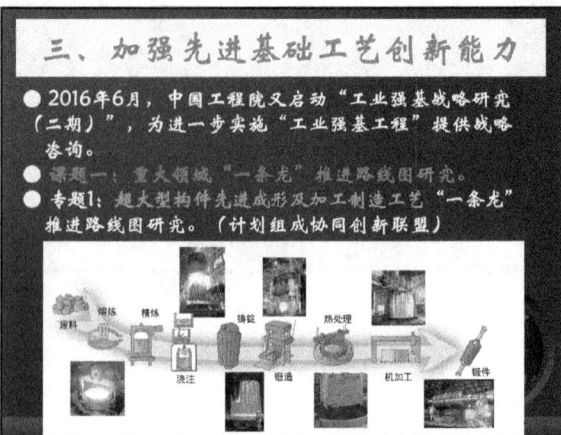

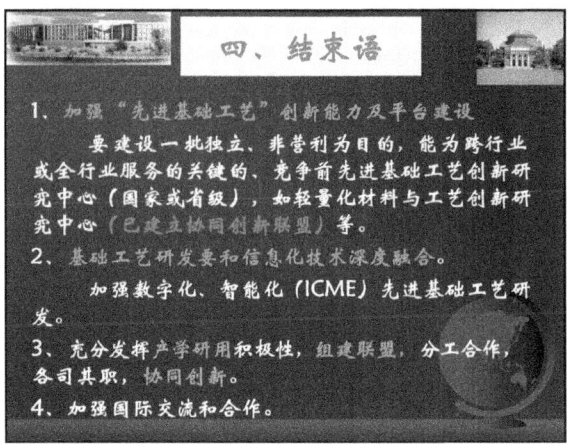

第 5 篇

留学情结与学术人生

1. "中国留学生的四十年"之柳百成：新留学潮开启的见证者

【编者按：适逢中国改革开放40周年，美国格律文化传媒集团全媒体平台携手上海东方网，联合全球多家机构、留学组织和华文媒体，跨越十余个国家和地区，隆重推出"中国留学生的四十年"大型专题报道，记录40年留学潮中40位中国留学生的命运与故事、奋斗与荣光。以海外学人的心路，见证中国崛起；以中国留学生的视角，回望改革开放。今日刊发第十八期，柳百成：新留学潮开启的见证者】

"中国人民是伟大的人民，美国人民也是伟大的人民。我们不仅为学习美国先进的科学技术而来，也是为促进中美两国人民的友谊而来。"

1978年12月27日，纽约机场，镁光灯和照明灯将整个大厅照亮，面对眼前大批西方记者，来自北京协和医院的吴葆桢大夫代表52位改革开放后第一批来自中国的赴美访问学者大声读出了在飞机上已起草好的声明，最后几句正是出自柳百成之手。

他们不卑不亢的友好姿态赢得了现场阵阵掌声，40年后，这幅画面让已到耄耋之年的柳百成激动不已。他深知这批访问学者身上承担着特殊的使命——为中美建交、邓小平访美烘托气氛。

柳百成座右铭

与中美关系正常化同步启动的是中国的改革开放。但当时柳百成并未意识到其深远的意义，他当时一心想的是"报效祖国，我别无二话"。两年后，他没有辜负自己，学成归国，率先应用信息技术改变了"傻大黑粗"的传统铸造行业的面貌。

如约归来的还有其余的51位学者，无人缺席。他们在各个领域的杰出贡献为中国改革开放再添薪火。

柳百成2014年参加中美留学35年会议

从战火中来 一心投入铸造行业

硝烟弥漫，路有冻死骨。这是柳百成的童年记忆，他出生于上海，经历过1937年的八·一三事变以及沦为沦陷区难民的悲痛，很小就意识到"国家兴亡，匹夫有责"，练毛笔字时一遍又一遍用正楷字写文天祥的《正气歌》。

正是基于这样的爱国情操，1951年报考大学时，柳百成坚定地选择了清华大学机械工程系。北京在他心里是革命圣地，而清华大学则充满了新中国成立后的新气象。

当时中国机械工程产业刚刚起步，基础较差。而美国已于1952年研制出世界上第一台数控机床。

在清华大学的院系大调整中，原本没有分专业的机械系多了一个铸造专业，学校领导找到了柳百成，只说了一句"国家需要这个专业，需要人。"没有丝毫犹豫，柳百成便投入到了这片未知的领域

⊖ 本文转载自侨报网，2018年9月13日相关文章。

里，一干便是66年。

柳百成1954年——清华大学图书馆

柳百成1955年——清华大学图书馆

他心里很清楚，当时铸造业的代名词是"傻大黑粗"，劳动环境极差，自然愿意做的人也少，但他完全服从学校的安排。理由在当下年轻人看来有些不可思议，"国家需要就是我的志愿。"

在此期间，他与留学苏联的宝贵机会擦肩而过，看着要好的朋友求学远去的背影，想到自己资产阶级的出身，原本自以为有希望入选的柳百成感到很受挫。后来，他留校任教时，再次错失留学机会。两次失望的经历，让柳百成有些心灰意冷。

局面在1978年有了转机。

"改革开放"之初，邓小平就对中国和世界的科研水平差距忧心忡忡。1978年6月23日，邓小平在听取教育部关于清华大学的工作汇报时，做出了扩大派遣留学生的指示："我赞成留学生的数量增大，主要搞自然科学""要成千成万地派，不是只派十个八个""要千方百计加快步伐，路子要越走越宽"。

在邓小平的大力倡导下，中国出国留学的大门在封闭多年后终于打开。通过派遣留学生，中国教育对外合作与交流开启了新的征程，扩大派遣留学生成为中国对外开放的前奏。

1978年12月26日，中国向美国派出的首批52名留学人员启程出发，其中，清华大学教师9名，柳百成名列其中。

当时柳百成已45岁，本不对留学之事抱希望，但当系主任告诉他这一消息时，他意识到这一次没人再在政治背景上设门槛，命运掌握在了自己手里。

柳百成回忆，选拔考试唯一的科目是英文，这是他的强项。在"文革"期间，即使外面一片混乱，学校科研教学全部停顿，他被迫下放到铸工车间承担繁重劳动，但仍坚持每晚到图书馆里，如痴如醉地阅读美国铸造学会的会刊，光英文笔记就做了一尺多厚。

"原本是为了了解国际上铸造业的知识，谁知道误打误撞让我通过了英文考试，顺利出国，"柳百成笑着说，然后很认真地补充了一句，"我始终相信，知识就是力量。"

见证中美建交历史时刻

52位访问学者的出发时间原本定于1979年1月，但为了让他们赶在中美建交前抵达，他们赴美日程提前了一段时间。

出发前那天上午，时任国务院副总理的方毅在人民大会堂接见了留学生全体成员。当晚，北京大学校长周培源和美国驻华联络处主任伍德科克也到首都机场送行。作为总领队的柳百成对此记忆犹新，他感慨道："如此高的规格，让大家感到此行意义非同寻常。"

当时中美尚未建交，从北京到纽约，需要在巴黎转机。在巴黎机场，前来迎接的中国驻法大使馆人员告诉柳百成，他们得到消息说，在纽约机场已经聚集了大批的美国记者，正等着他们的到来。这是一次临时安排的采访，柳百成等人毫无准备，也无时间向国家请示报批。

"要见！"只思索片刻后，柳百成这样说，"按照外交礼节我们是可以回绝采访的，但我心想，改

柳百成——1979年中国驻美大使馆挂牌时留念照片

柳百成——1979年在华盛顿与清华大学第一批访问学者合影

柳百成——美国留学期间照片

革开放中国的知识分子,为什么怕美国的记者呢?"

这群刚刚迈出国门的知识分子想出了一个颇具外交色彩的办法,起草了一份声明。宣读声明的是当时飞机上英文最好的协和医院大夫吴葆桢。

抵达纽约机场出境后,大家才发现等待他们的不止有记者,也有很多华人自发地来机场欢迎他们。

随后,邓小平应卡特总统夫妇邀请,携夫人卓琳对美国进行了为期8天的正式访问。对于中国领导人的到访,整个美国都表现得极为热情。柳百成一行再次有幸成为这一历史的见证者,他们被随机分为两组,一组前往美国安德鲁斯空军基地迎接邓小平一行抵达,另一组则参加隔天在白宫举行的正式欢迎仪式。

柳百成——1979年在华盛顿生活工作照

柳百成收到的是前往白宫的请柬,他至今还保存着。在卡特夫人为卓琳女士举行的招待会上,全体留学生受到了卓琳的接见。

"我记得她说了三句话,好好学习,学成回国,报效祖国,我觉得最后一句话激励了我们,而且我们第一批52个人,最后全部回国。"

没有任何地方比家更可爱

柳百成与第一批赴美学者抵达纽约机场 1978年12月

1979年1月1日,中美正式建交。访美学者们陪同首任驻美大使柴泽民参加了中国驻美国大使馆的开馆升旗仪式,当鲜艳的五星红旗伴随着慷慨激昂的国歌,迎着新年第一缕晨光,第一次在美国国土上冉冉升起时,柳百成心潮澎湃。

"我是80后,"今年85岁的柳百成总是这样笑着向别人介绍自己。在他身上丝毫看不到清华大学教授或者中国工程院院士的"架子",也看不到任何岁月的痕迹,说话逻辑清晰,酷爱摄影,已出版了三本影集。

按照清华老校长蒋南翔"为祖国健康工作五十

年"的号召，柳百成算是"超期服役"了。

柳百成——1979年美国乔治城大学报纸刊登中国访问学者照片

在外界看来，他早已功成名就，是唯一先后获得"中国铸造杰出贡献奖"和"中国铸造终身成就奖"的获奖者，这两个奖项原本可以为他的学术人生画上一个圆满的"句号"，但现在却变成了"逗号"。"老骥伏枥，志在千里，我讲得再通俗一点，小车不倒，只管推，我还在尽自己的力量。"

对于年轻人，柳百成说自己有20字、五句话的忠告："爱国奉献、敢于创新、顽强拼搏、健康体魄、全面发展。"其中"敢于创新"与他赴美访问的经历息息相关。

从1978年底到1981年，在美国的700多个日夜，给柳百成留下了很深的印象。他至今还记得刚到华盛顿时已是深夜，坐在开往使馆招待所的车上，访美学者们都在惊叹，车水马龙，何等繁华。

而当时，柳百成的家里只有两个小房间，用的还是一个11吋的黑白电视。美国人早已用上了相机和苹果计算机，而当时清华大学机械系1700人，无人拥有计算机。

一位美国的年轻人去往中国访问，正好去了柳百成的家里，"把我的家说的一无是处，脏，还在生炉子。"这句话深深刺激到了当时刚被美国物质丰富所震撼到的柳百成，但他告诉自己，"有差距不要紧，我们找准方向，迎头赶上。"

和其他访美学者不同，柳百成只身一人先后去往威斯康星大学、麻省理工学院进修，同时利用一切可能的机会参加各种学术会议，参观通用汽车公司、福特汽车公司等大型企业。

在威斯康星大学时，他住在一个美国人的家里，始终秉持一个原则"留学生不要抱团"，即使刚开始语言沟通并不顺畅。选择该校的另一个原因是"这里的铸造工程学科在当时是最强的。"

柳百成——1980年在MIT与导师合影

柳百成——1980年在MIT照片

柳百成——1979年在威斯康星大学实验室

柳百成——留学期间学习工作照

他是学校里第一个来自中国大陆的学生,美国正好处于"中国热"期间,大家好奇的眼光都围着他打转。

从那天起,柳百成就给自己定下"来者不拒"的见客原则。"长达三个月的时间里,每个周末,我几乎都不用自己做饭,有不同的人邀请你去吃饭,去聊天。"

他还开始学习当时看起来和铸造业并没有什么关联的计算机语言,有远见地预料到"计算机有一天也许会改变人类的一切"。上课时周围都是二十多岁的年轻本科生,他反而更努力,晚上在计算机中心编制程序直到清晨。

在归国后,柳百成开辟了一个新领域——信息化技术,与传统制造业、铸造业融合在了一起,长江三峡工程所用的水轮机转轮便有他所带领的团队的功劳。他还将美国课堂上"名师上讲堂"的教学理念带回了清华,重新拿起教鞭,至今为国家培养了五十多名博士和大批本科生。

柳百成——2009年在清华办公室

"你要不要留在美国?"在美国,曾有一名中学生这样向他发问。但他没有做过多的回答,只用了一首歌的最后一句来回答:"Home, home, sweet sweet home, there is no place like home(家,家,可爱的家,没有任何地方比家更可爱)。"

2. 改革开放四十年之亲历者记
柳百成：留学岁月照亮我的人生

1978年6月23日，历史将永远铭记这非比寻常的日子。这一天，刚刚第三次复出不久、并主动要求主抓教育和科技工作的邓小平做出关于扩大派遣留学生的重要指示，中国改革开放新的历史时期的留学工作热潮由此掀起。

此时，"文化大革命"刚结束不久，整个国家百废待兴。当时的清华大学领导班子遵照邓小平关于拨乱反正的指示，对学校各项工作进行了清理，提出整顿计划，写出书面报告。

邓小平对这个报告非常重视。1978年6月23日下午，邓小平在听取时任清华大学校长兼党委书记刘达的工作汇报，同方毅、蒋南翔、刘西尧等人谈话时，对留学工作作出重要指示："我赞成留学生的数量增大，主要搞自然科学。要成千成万地派，不是只派十个八个……这是五年内快见成效、提高我国科教水平的重要方法之一。现在我们迈的步子太小，要千方百计加快步伐，路子要越走越宽，我们一方面要努力提高自己的大学水平，一方面派人出去学习，这样可以有一个比较，看看我们自己的大学究竟办得如何。"

在邓小平的大力倡导下，中国出国留学的大门在封闭多年后终于打开。通过派遣留学生，中国教育对外合作与交流开启了新的征程，扩大派遣留学生成为中国对外开放的前奏。

1978年12月26日，中国向美国派出的首批52名留学人员启程出发。同机飞往美国的52人中，除了后来成为中国科学院院士的姜伯驹、张恭庆是以访问教授身份去的，其余50人都是正式称为"访问学者"的留学生，其中清华教师9名。现任清华大学材料学院及机械工程学院教授的柳百成院士便是其中一位。

40年光阴荏苒，如今已85岁的柳百成回顾那段往事，当年抵达纽约机场时的情景仍历历在目——灯火通明的机场大厅，耀眼的镁光灯，52名同样着装的中国留学者昂首挺胸。

"中国人民是伟大的人民，美国人民也是伟大的人民，我们不仅是为学习美国的科学技术而来，也是为促进中美两国人民的友谊而来。"

面对现场数十名西方记者，他们掷地有声、蓄势待发。

而在他们身后，中国宏伟的改革开放蓝图已徐徐展开。作为"首航"的留学生之一，彼时的柳百成难以想象，40年间，中国出国留学的浪花一浪接一浪涛声不竭，当年的涓涓细流如今已汇聚成为壮阔的时代大潮……

亲历者说：

为中美两国友谊而来

1978年，我45岁，是清华大学机械工程系的一名教师。8月份左右，学校里传来一个消息：中国要派留学生赴美学习。新中国成立前我的父亲是上海的资本家，那个年代算作出身不好，之前有两次赴苏联留学进修的机会都未能成行，最初听到这个消息时我没抱多大希望。

当时机械工程系分得了一个名额参加清华大学的选拔，系主任亲自面试，我得了第一名。接着学校、教育部也组织了统一考试，我连闯三关后最终入选。

这次选拔看重业务素质，特别是英语水平，这在当时确实难住了不少人。因为1952年后，学校的外语教学都改成了俄语，学英语的人屈指可数。我能够入选，也是与自己的经历有关。"文革"期间，我在清华大学校办工厂铸造车间干活，白天扛砂子、搬生铁，晚上坚持看英文资料。那时清华图书馆有美国铸造学会出版的会刊，大概存了30多期，我都读过，英文笔记本做了有一尺厚。加之我生在上海，小学和中学上的都是教会学校，英文功底还算扎实。可以说是"养兵千日、用在一朝"。

1978年12月26日，我们一行52人启程飞赴美国，我被任命为总领队。飞机万里西行，满座的中

○ 本文转载自《新清华》2129期第6-7版，2018。

国学者难抑心中兴奋,当时大家对美国就像对月球一样陌生。

美国时间 1978 年 12 月 27 日下午,我们终于抵达纽约国际机场。一出关便看到成群的美国记者,报纸、电视台的记者都来了,镁光灯、照明灯照得机场大厅通亮。来自北京协和医院的吴葆祯大夫,代表大家用英语宣读了我们在飞机上早已起草好的声明。声明最后几句是我执笔的:"中国人民是伟大的人民,美国人民也是伟大的人民。我们不仅为学习美国先进的科学技术而来,也是为促进中美两国人民的友谊而来。"实践证明,我们的声明掷地有声,经受起历史的考验。

其间,有个感人场面我至今难忘。同伴中有位北京大学的老师,他的哥哥在美国多年,"文革"期间,兄弟二人一直处于失联状态。哥哥多方打听得知了弟弟将到美国留学,便立即赶往机场,两人相见后紧紧相拥、热泪盈眶。那一刻,我真切地感受到,中断多年的中美间联系又恢复了。

迎接邓小平夫妇访问美国

首批赴美访问学者团队原定是 1979 年初才出发,后来选择 1978 年 12 月 26 日,是因为我们要赶在中美正式建交(1979 年元旦)及邓小平访问美国前到达,为中美建交及邓小平访美烘托气氛。

到达美国后,我们有幸参加了中国驻美国大使馆开馆和五星红旗升旗仪式,还参与了欢迎邓小平访问美国等许多活动,留下了极为珍贵的记忆。

邓小平夫妇是 1979 年 1 月 28 日下午乘专机抵达的华盛顿安德鲁斯空军基地。第二天上午,卡特总统及夫人在白宫南草坪,举行典礼欢迎小平夫妇。我们 52 人被分成两批,一批去安德鲁斯空军基地迎接,一批去白宫参加欢迎典礼,我很幸运去了白宫。

欢迎仪式上,邓小平夫妇先在卡特总统夫妇的陪同下,登上铺有红地毯的讲台。随后乐队奏两国国歌,礼炮齐鸣。接着,两国领导人又检阅了六军仪仗队。整个欢迎仪式非常隆重。

接着,在卡特夫人为卓琳女士举行的招待会上,我们全体留学生受到了卓琳的接见,她代表小平语重心长地讲了话,勉励我们:"努力学习,学成回国,报效祖国"。我想这是转达了小平同志的嘱咐,我们在座每个人都铭记于心。

把学到的先进知识带回祖国

在美国我去了威斯康星大学学习。这所大学是查了很多有关美国科技研究资料后自己选的,因为我的研究领域铸造工程学,在威斯康星大学处在学科前列。在那里,我见到了一批清华、甚至国内都没有的先进材料、分析测试仪器,学习并利用这些仪器大大提高了所从事的铸造工程学的基础科研水平。我接连发表了几篇有分量的学术论文,其中一篇获得了美国铸造学会杰出贡献论文奖。

为了更多地了解中美间的文化差异,留美期间,我决定要多走、多看。当时的威斯康星大学只有我一个人从中国大陆来,无论是中国香港和中国台湾来的留学生,或是大学里的华裔教授,很多人都想了解中国大陆。每逢周末,总有人打电话约我聊天,我就定了一个原则:"来者不拒",因为我也可以利用这样的机会,告诉世界一个真实的中国。

其中有件事情特别触动我。那时刚到麦迪逊,我住在一个普通美国人家里。刚进门,就看到房东太太七八岁的儿子正在玩苹果计算机,我感到十分惊讶,因为出国前自己从未见过计算机,但在美国,连儿童都能自如操作。我敏锐地感觉到,或许有一天计算机会改变人类的生活。如果能把信息化技术和传统工业进行融合,是否会有新的发现和突破,进一步推进中国制造业的科技进步?

于是,我下决心跟着学校的本科生一起学习计算机高级语言。每天晚上,就进计算机中心,学习编程、解难题。我下定决心把学到的所有先进科学技术都带回祖国去。这也是我想对如今出国学习的清华学子们说的——走出国门,要勇于开拓新视野,接受新事物,提出新思维,要为推进祖国的科技事业而拼搏。

没有任何地方能比家更让我眷恋

留学期间,有件事我印象很深。那是一次在麦迪逊的一个中学作访问演讲,率真的美国中学生问我:"你觉得美国怎么样?想不想留下来?"

我毫不犹豫地唱起了儿时谙熟于心的世界名曲《Home, Sweet Home》的最后两句:"Home, home, sweet, sweet home。There is no place like home."(家,可爱的家,世间没有任何地方能比家更让我眷恋!)。

话音刚落，顿时全场掌声如雷，美国学生也佩服中国人热爱祖国的高尚情操，那个场景我永远不会忘记。

这确实是我的真实心声。记得上小学时，临摹文天祥的《正气歌》，其中有一名句："人生自古谁无死，留取丹心照汗青"。高中时，读范仲淹的"先天下之忧而忧，后天下之乐而乐"，深有感慨。我把这两句话当成自己的座右铭，指导我的一生。多年来，我的心中始终有一个强有力的声音——爱国奉献、报效祖国。在我看来，一个人的能力有大有小，但一定要为国家和人民做出力所能及的贡献，一定要把爱国奉献牢记在心，这是一个中国人一生应有的追求。

1981年初，我如期回国。回国时，根本没想过哪一年能再出国。但最近在整理学术人生资料时发现，目前为止，我已出国100多次，到美国也有30多次了。当年清华去的9人中，如今已有3人当选为中国科学院院士或工程院院士。我也在促进信息化技术与先进制造业深度融合上做出了自己的贡献，使"爱国奉献、报效祖国"的夙愿得以实现。改革开放确实为知识分子带来了春天，使知识分子有了充分发挥聪明才智的平台。

3. 西风千里话转折　水木数载铸人生

——柳百成院士的学术人生

柳百成院士，1955年毕业于清华大学机械工程系，于1978至1981年以访问学者的身份在美国威斯康星大学和麻省理工学院进修，成为改革开放第一批国家公派留美学者。1999年当选为中国工程院院士，并于2002年获"光华工程科技奖"，是我国著名的铸造工艺与装备专家。

主持人： 今天我们非常荣幸邀请到了中国工程院院士，我校机械工程系教授柳百成院士，大家欢迎！

柳百成： 同学们，我今天非常高兴来参加学术人生讲座。我觉得学生是高校的主体，教师应该为学生服务。所以，我认为参加今天的讲座是我应该做的事情。

今年是新中国成立60周年，也是我一生中很光荣、很荣幸的一年。今年我参加了三个有重要意义的喜事。今年的元宵节在人民大会堂，党中央举行了招待知识界人士的元宵晚会，我荣幸地参加了这个晚会。胡锦涛总书记、党和国家领导人都参加了这个会议。今年8月份，党中央国务院又邀请了一批创新、创业、创优的人才在北戴河休假，我被教育部推荐作为教育界的代表参加了这个活动。10月1日，我应邀在天安门观礼台观看了60周年国庆阅兵、游行及晚会的全过程。

柳百成： 今年北戴河的休假又有它的特殊意义，因为是新中国成立60周年。所以，这次它挑选了60位各界代表人物，其中有两弹一星的专家孙家栋院士，有得到国家最高奖励的清华校友金怡濂院士，也有航天英雄翟志刚等。中央组织部部长李源潮同志亲自到北戴河看望大家，而且举行了座谈。

这是我们国家比较重要的事件，人民日报、新华网、光明日报等多个媒体连续报道了这件事情。大家可能会问，为什么柳百成能参加这个活动呢？为什么会作为教育系统的代表呢？因为我是30年前，改革开放后第一批被国家选拔赴美的访问学者。第一批赴美访问学者一共是52个人，清华一共派去了9个人，其中有三个都当选为院士，有李衍达院士、张楚汉院士和我。在第一批派遣的52个人中间，有5个领队，我被选作清华的领队。这5个领队中间我又很荣幸地担任了总领队。

我出生在上海的一个普通家庭，新中国成立以后我的家庭成分被定为民族资产阶级，实际上是个小资本家。我父母文化程度不高，但是他们很看重对子女的教育，所以把我和我弟弟送到上海当时比较好的教会学校。当时教会学校里大多都是家庭经济条件比较好的学生，包括荣毅仁的家族子弟都在我所上的中西女中第二附属小学上学。我上的中学是天主教教会办的圣芳济中学。

在这两个学校，我受到比较严格的教育，如每星期二校长都要来报告考试成绩，稍微有一点偷懒就罚抄写。特别是在外语方面奠定了很坚实的基础——我小学所学的英文课本是美国原版的，书本都要包起来，学完后再还回去。我在中学的时候受到更加严格的英文训练，英语课程包括有 Reading（阅读）、Grammar（文法）、Dictation（默写）、Composition（作文）等；除了这些课程以外，我的代数（Algebra）、几何（Geometry）、地理（Geography）、物理（Physics）都是英文教学。物理课非常严格，全部要背英文的 Definition（定义）。这也就是 1978 年，经过选拔，我能够在清华连过三关通过出国英语考试的原因。

在北戴河的座谈会上，我在会上发言："现在的海归回来，国家给一百万元生活费补贴，我回来的时候，只拿79元的工资。现在，国家经济条件改善了，海归的待遇提高了。但是，我们每个人都要扪心自问：我们为国家做出了什么，我们为人民奉献了什么？"

我们赴美做访问学者之初，中美还没建交、没通航，我们是转道巴黎过去的。我们52个人上飞机的时候，教育部给了我致美国联络处公函、附52人的名单，我现在还保留着。教育部只给了我50美元，是我们全队的零用钱。我们到了巴黎，由中国

㊀ 本文转载自2011年清华大学出版社"学术人生"讲座的采访文章。

驻法国的大使馆代表接待我们。在巴黎上飞机的时候，使馆人员告诉我们："在纽约机场有大批电视台记者要采访，你们见还是不见？"

我们国家与世隔绝了十多年，在"文革"时期，中国人很少见外国记者的。当时我作为总领队，觉得我们是伟大的中国人民，受了党、国家和人民的多年教育。所以，当即表态：见！但是，也有一些顾虑，一些言谈如被西方记者稍加渲染、歪曲，可能会很被动、很尴尬。所以在飞机上我们五个领队起草了一个声明，这个声明的最后几句话是我写的："中国人民是伟大的人民，美国人民也是伟大的人民，我们不远万里来到美国，不仅是为了学习先进的科学技术，也是为了促进中美两国人民的伟大友谊。"30年过去了，我现在回想当时的情景仍然历历在目。而我们作为泱泱中国人民的代表，我们无愧于国家的派遣，无愧于人民对我们的寄托！

我回顾自己的经历，中小学受到严格的教育固然重要，但清华对我最重要的教诲就是要思想、学习、身体几方面全面发展。蒋南翔老校长再三强调，要我们走"又红又专"的道路，要思想进步，要热爱祖国，要为人民服务，同时要踏踏实实学好本领。蒋南翔校长带头在运动场锻炼，要我们为人民健康服务工作50年。我很高兴，我已经"超期服役"，而且我还愿在有生之年培养更多的学生。希望是属于你们的。

留取丹心照汗青

主持人： 非常感谢柳院士刚才跟我们分享了一段这么宝贵的人生经历。我们首先来看一张图片：大家看到的这张黑白图片应该是柳院士在1954年拍摄的。

柳百成： 这张照片大概拍摄于1954年，我1955年毕业，这应该是我大学三年级或四年级拍的，背后是图书馆。图书馆上面曾经有我的名字，因为我1955年获得金质奖章。当时本科毕业有两个头衔，一个叫奖状，一个叫金质奖章。当然，1955年国家经济不是那么好，不像现在奥运会金牌，我们的金质奖章实际上是铜的，但重要的是它的意义。怎么得的金质奖章？三年各科成绩全五分。

我进大一的时候，在班里成绩是中等。我从小喜欢看书，我记得《三国演义》里有那么一句话，"小时了了，大时未必了了"。学习要靠自己的勤奋。我第一年在年级里成绩是中等，我的学号我还记得，1951年进校的，是51543。当时在每个系，

1954年于清华图书馆前

学号越低排名越前。但是经过我几年的努力，我最后毕业时是三年全五分，拿了金质奖章。

主持人： 您在清华度过了非常宝贵的一段时光，您能不能谈一谈您最大的收获是什么？

柳百成： 最大的收获是，清华使我的思想更加成熟了，我的政治立场更加坚定了。是什么精神支柱使我这样的勤奋学习？小学的时候我练毛笔字。我临的帖是文天祥的《正气歌》，里面有两句名言"人生自古谁无死，留取丹心照汗青"，这两句话成为我一生的座右铭。新中国成立后我进入清华。在新中国朝气蓬勃的环境下，我首先明白了做人的道理，政治上更加成熟，思想更加进步。清华当时的名教授直接上讲台授课。近年来，清华有很大的变化，学生进了某个系，名教授四年只见到两次：第一次开学典礼，第二次毕业典礼。在美国我看到所有的教授，包括诺贝尔奖获得者，都要去上大课，清华在当年也同样如此。当时给我们上《力学》的杜庆华院士，现在过世了，他是力学方面的权威。当时学《机械零件》，授课的是郑林庆教授，现在可能也过90岁了，他也是国内的权威。所以，我在清华不仅政治思想上更加成熟，同时又在名师的熏陶下，加上我刻苦学习，打了一个良好的基础。

养兵千日、用在一时

主持人： 您当时作为访问团的领队，是怀着怎样的一种心情踏上美国这片土地的？

柳百成： 1978年"改革开放"，小平同志说要大量、

大批地派遣。一来我觉得我们国家有希望了，开始重视科学技术、知识和知识分子。但是二来我又觉得自己希望渺茫，顾虑到"文革"的极"左"思潮中的"家庭出身论""成分论"的影响。我 1951 年进清华，1952 年派大批留学生到苏联学习。开始我榜上有名，后来不了了之。1955 年毕业后留校，1956 年又有派大批青年教师到苏联、东欧去学习的机会，也把我抽调出来做出国培训的准备，后来又不了了之。所以，我就背了一个思想包袱，这辈子出国渺茫了。

但是，我感谢小平同志的英明决策。"改革开放"以后，小平同志表示，要重在表现。表现是个人的，家庭是历史的，你生在哪个家庭你不能做主，但是自己的道路由自己选择。当时派遣的时候，清华把指标分派到各个系。关于这个指标学校有说明，假如被推荐的人考试不合格，指标就被取消。所以，机械系对于人选的推荐非常慎重。

当时，在德才兼备的条件下，考什么？不是考政治，政治不好考，最后决定考英文。一考英文，我就如鱼得水了。第一关，系主任主考，我通过了。第二关，在主楼后厅考，大约二百人，我通过了，而且成绩名列前茅。紧接着是教育部考试，考试模仿托福，有听力，我依然通过了。我连过三关，而且在清华成绩名列前茅。所以，清华选我做领队，这是一方面的原因。

"文革"的时候，很多教师灰心丧气了。有人说"书越念越蠢"，有人说"书越念越反动"。当时学校的老教授很多都成了"反动学术权威"了，很多老师把书烧了、卖了，从此与书本告别。我有一点书呆子气，我一直相信英国哲学家的名言——"知识就是力量"。所以，在"文革"期间，我白天在学校里的铸造车间从事繁重的体力劳动，晚上则仍然艰苦地看书学习。晚上，我把图书馆中我这个学科领域最有名的外文书刊《Transactions of American Foundrymen's Society》（《美国铸造学会会刊》），从 20 世纪 50 年代开始，一本一本都读完了。在"文革"期间没有互联网，我的读书笔记大约做了有一尺厚。所以，我说"养兵千日，用在一时"。我之所以能够被选为第一批访问学者，一方面在于清华长期的培养，一方面还要有一个坚定的信念。

主持人： 柳老师是以访问学者的身份在美国威斯康星大学以及麻省理工学院进修，那么最初接触到美国大学的科研工作，您的最大感触是什么？

柳百成： 也有电视新闻记者采访我，说你到美国最大的震撼是什么？我谈三点。

第一，到了纽约后转机到华盛顿，晚上七八点钟时汽车开在高速公路上，一路上灯火辉煌、车水马龙，我不禁感叹道——我们跟国外的差距太大了。到了现在，汽车也进入到中国家庭了。大家想象三十年前，北京王府井七点钟就没什么人了。所以，看到了美国现代化的社会，确实是个震撼和冲击。

我的第二个震撼就是美国计算机的高速发展。我到了威斯康星大学，我按照小平同志的指示，尽量要接近美国家庭。所以我住在一个美国家庭里，我看到主人的小儿子（小学三年级）正在玩苹果电脑。当时我在国内，没有见过个人电脑，机械系也没有一台个人电脑。我对新鲜事物有比较敏锐的洞察力，从那时起我在威斯康星大学就开始学习计算机高级语言。我意识到计算机不仅会改变科学技术的进程，还会改变人类社会的进程。

第三个震撼，我到威斯康星大学进入实验室，看到一批现代的材料测试仪器，如扫描电镜、俄歇谱仪、透射电镜、电子探针等。清华、北大是国内一流大学，很多仪器清华当时都没有。清华第一台扫描电镜是 1976 年引进的。我在机械系从事材料方面的研究，过去是用传统的光学显微镜，可放大到一千倍，而扫描电子显微镜就到了几十万倍。所以，我在国外跟大学生一起听课，向他们请教，一起用计算机编程。同时，我又掌握了扫描电镜、电子探针等一批先进测试仪器的使用技术。这两个方面对于我回国以后的成就起了决定性的作用。

1979 年在威斯康星大学电子探针实验室

上图就是当时的电子探针实验室，电子探针在当时是很先进的仪器。为了保持它的电流及数据的稳定，这个设备一工作就要连续数小时保持运行状态，早上七八点钟进实验室，连续工作到下午三四点钟才能结束。扫描电镜实验往往晚上八点钟进去，清晨三四点钟才能结束。

美国大学有值得我们学习的地方。第一，我刚才讲了美国名师上讲堂；第二，实验室24小时开放。电子探针实验室我交了五美元的押金，就把实验室钥匙给我了，回国前再还给它，这五美元仍然还给我。我回国以后开始感觉很不适应，国内学校实验室的开放程度与工作效率要低很多。

主持人： 您在留学期间，在生活上有没有遇到什么困难？

柳百成： 刚到美国我们闹了很多笑话，这个笑话也反映了刚刚改革开放的发展中国家和发达国家的差距，举几个例子。

第一个例子，出国，我们家里都没有西装，当时只有一个地方能做西装——王府井百货大楼后面的出国人员服务部。西装只有几种颜色，大衣两种颜色，又厚又重。因此，到了美国就闹了笑话。首先，美国电视台新闻报道，说中国来了52个人，衣服穿得差不多，没有个性。最大的笑话出在我们欢迎小平夫妇访美的活动，卡特夫人专门为卓琳夫人举行一个招待会，我们全体有幸参加。到招待会时给了我们52个人一个房间放衣帽。但是招待会一结束，大家各自的大衣找不到了。我比较细心，在我大衣后面写了"柳百成"，没有搞错。很多学者回去以后还没有闹清楚到底穿的是自己的还是别人的。这是第一个笑话。

第二个笑话就是黑白胶片。我们52个人到美国去没有一个人有相机。于是我们清华的9个人聚了一下，凑钱买胶卷。彩色胶卷不能买，太贵。于是决定买黑白胶卷。到了美国问中国大使馆借相机照相，冲印时发现价钱比彩色的还贵。原来，在美国彩色已经是自动化、流水线印相了，而黑白的倒变成艺术照相了。

第三个笑话是吃鸡。我们到了美国，大使馆不知道一个中国留学人员要花多少钱。刚去美国给我们定的标准叫实报实销。所以，我们到美国就出好大的洋相，到哪儿买东西都要receipt（收据），包括吃个冰激凌也要receipt，搞得我们很被动。刚到美国的时候，正好中美建交，产生了中国热。有一天，哥伦比亚电视台来采访我。采访记者问我："柳百成先生，我注意到了，你们中国人来了以后，都喜欢吃鸡，为什么？"鸡最便宜啊！但是我不好这样讲。我说："中国人就是喜欢吃鸡。"

但是，我觉得我到美国总体来讲比较适应，为什么呢？第一，我出生在上海；第二，我又在两个教会学校读过书。所以，对于西方文化我还是有点了解。吃西餐也行，自己做中餐也行，各方面我都还比较适应。

见证中美建交

主持人： 在美国留学的时候，您见证了中美两国的建交仪式，能不能给我们大家分享一下当时这个激动人心的场面？

柳百成： 好的。我记得我们第一批的访问学者与第二批、第三批有所不同。我们这一批经历了三件事："见证中美建交""欢迎小平访美"，然后"努力学习进取"。我们在语言学院稍事集训以后就放假了，原本让我们1979年走，并不是1978年走。临时我们接到紧急电话通知。为什么？中美建交公报已经发表，1月1号联络处要改为大使馆，1月下旬小平同志要访美，要求我们提前到美国，营造气氛。所以，我们在12月26号（美国的圣诞节假日）出发了。

我们在1979年1月1号，目睹我们中华人民共和国驻美大使馆挂牌，照了相，同时高唱《中华人民共和国国歌》，看着我们的国旗冉冉升起。30年前的这些情景至今仍然历历在目，难以忘怀。紧接着，更高兴的事情就是欢迎小平同志。我们参加了欢迎小平同志的全部活动。举个例子，小平同志到美国，飞机降在美国安德鲁斯空军基地，我们52个人分成两拨，一拨去空军基地，而我是另一拨参加了白宫举行的欢迎小平夫妇仪式。

在白宫玫瑰园草坪，我们亲眼看到卡特夫妇欢迎小平夫妇，小平同志检阅了美国六军仪仗队，海、陆、空、海岸警卫队、海军陆战队等。紧接着，卡特夫人为卓琳夫人举行招待会，卡特夫人陪同卓琳女士与我们全体见了面。卓琳女士代表小平同志给我们讲了话，归纳起来就是三句话，"**努力学习，学成回国，报效祖国**"。所以，我们这52个人以这12个字作为我们的信念，贯穿始终。

接着小平同志还要到西雅图等地访问，所以大使馆在小平同志离开华盛顿的时候举行了招待会。在这个招待会上我们52个人忙得不可开交。怎么忙法？大使馆人手不够，我们有的洗盘子，有的在衣帽间挂衣服。所以，不要看我们都是四五十岁的知识分子，在国内还有点地位，但我们为中美建交甘做这些服务性的工作。我很是荣幸，作为五个幸运代表之一参加了招待会，因而结识了一批美中友好人士，至今我们仍保持着联系。这个招待会完了以后，小平同志临时决定跟大家照相，跟大使馆人员和访问学者分批照相，很可惜我的照片没留下来。

离开华盛顿前夕，卡特夫妇为小平夫妇举行了盛大文艺晚会。有美国著名的乡村音乐歌唱家 John Denver 唱歌，还有美国 NBA 也表演了几个篮球动作。

所以，我们感到非常荣幸，不仅仅因为我们见证了中美建交，还因为我们很荣幸的和小平同志访美融合在一起，见到了小平，见到了卓琳，而且卓琳代表小平跟我们讲了三句语重心长的话。

主持人：您曾经在接受人民日报的专访中提到1978年的这次赴美留学是您的一个人生转折。您能不能给我们大家诠释一下这样一个转折，或者说在留美期间带给您的这样一份财富？

柳百成：留美以前的学习经历为我出国留学打了个扎实的基础，但是我的学术生涯，我的科学研究成果是回国后才开辟了新的篇章。我现在发表了三百多篇文章，而出国的时候只写了六篇文章。这六篇文章还是瞒着写的。那时候不敢写文章，写文章叫"走白专道路"等。

我的主要成果归纳起来：第一，我的专业是铸造工艺和装备，我通过到美国学了材料领域四大先进仪器，大大提高了我的研究工作的理论水平。这方面我发表的文章现在已经成为研究这个领域的经典引用论文，其中有一篇被美国的铸造学会评为最佳论文。我在美国两年发表了四篇文章，我离开威斯康星大学向研究生院院长告别的时候，他说你工作效率很高，对我做了很高的评价。

第二，我回国以后，开辟了新的研究领域，用计算机信息技术来提升传统产业的科技水平，通俗来讲就是把信息化融合到传统产业。这个方面我在国内研究的比较早，现在我们团队的研究成果在国内处于领先地位，在国际上也占有一席之地。这个和我在国外第一眼看到小学生用计算机有很大关系，回国以后，这个正好符合我们国家提出的结构调整战略。

第三，我也想过，在美国的时间是有限的，我觉得要打下一个为今后发展的基础。所以，我在美国两年，除了在威斯康星大学呆了一年半，我主动要求换学校，最后我到了MIT，结识了MIT材料系的系主任。他一直和我有来往，帮我拓宽了研究思路。

我利用这两年时间，去了通用汽车公司、福特汽车公司和卡特彼勒公司的技术中心。我到福特汽车公司还有一个小插曲，国外的公司和研究中心都是在小城镇，我坐公交汽车后还要走一段公路。在

1979年访问通用汽车公司

公路上，美国的交警开了车停了下来：你干什么？我说我要到福特去访问。美国人很友好，让我上了交警车，他开车送我去。

同时，我还访问了密歇根大学、凯斯西方储备大学及哥伦比亚大学。我利用一切机会广交朋友，现在我的国际交往十分频繁。我当时选择在威斯康星大学，清华几个老师说柳老师，你一个人到威斯康星，不如到伯克利。我们好几个人，大家做个伴。我查了一下，当时我那个专业在威斯康星大学的学术水平最高，当时该校的很多研究生现在都是国际上这个领域的权威。我们在国际会议上经常碰面、聚会，开玩笑叫 Wisconsin Group（威斯康星学派）。

去年我提出建议，我说我们三十年了，大家聚一聚如何？今年，我们隆重地组织了一个小型国际会议，以我们的导师洛伯尔教授为名，称作"Carl Loper Symposium"。今年五月我重访威斯康星大学，做了学术报告，正好是30周年。洛伯尔教授对我特别表示了称赞，他觉得他培养的中国学者在本国做出这样的成绩，感到非常的光荣。

There Is No Place Like Home

主持人：柳老师在美国参加了很多的座谈会，其中不得不讲的一场座谈会就是在美国一个中学的一场座谈会。那个时候，柳老师还唱了一首歌，这首歌就是《Home, Sweet Home》，柳老师，不知道现在您还记不记得这首歌？

柳百成：我先讲一下这件事情的由来。我们当时第一批出国，国内也有很多人担心我们是否一去不返。我在华盛顿的时候，一个在美国定居的中学同学坐飞机来看我。一见面他就问："柳百成，你在'文革'期间怎么样，你想不想留下来"。我一口回绝了，我说我是国家派来的，我一定要回去报效祖国。

这个同学和我非常好,也为我的信念感动。那两年他在各方面关心我,我们生活费很少,冬天他给我寄了厚衣服,还专门陪我到芝加哥看场棒球,重温我们中学时代打垒球的情景。

当时在美国是中国热,到处请我做报告,到了一个中学,报告完后就提问、互动。美国学生提的问题富有美国人的特点,第一个问,中国学生毕业后工作好找吗?大家知道美国现在金融危机,失业率很高,美国学生关心的问题就是毕业以后是否好找工作。最后,有人直率地问我,你对美国的印象怎么样?我说美国有很好的科学技术,我学习很有收获。他马上就追问:"你愿不愿意留在美国?"我毫不犹豫地用一首世界名歌,我小学三年级就学会了这首歌,叫《Home, Sweet Home》的最后两句:"Home, Sweet Home, There is no place like home"。全场响起了雷鸣般的鼓掌声,觉得中国人有志气。美国虽然科学发达,生活水平高,但中国人要回去建设自己的祖国。

这个歌我今天又查了一下,最后两句我可以唱一下:"Home, Home, Sweet, Sweet Home. There is no place like home, there is no place like home!"

主持人: 柳老师回国到现在已经有三十年了,这张照片也是柳老师去年照的,您在这期间也曾经出国访问交流学习达到50多次。那么出国这么多次,对于国外您觉得最大的变化是什么?

柳百成: 中国突飞猛进,一片欣欣向荣,而工业发达国家基本上处在停滞的阶段。但是我要告诉我们的年轻人两点:既要看到我们祖国的伟大,也要看到我们的不足。

我举个例子,大家最近有没有注意,世界经济论坛(World Economic Forum)公布了世界竞争力排名,我国的国际竞争力排29位,第一名是美国,德国、法国、英国、日本都在前十名。另外,这几年我国生态环境有很大的恶化。假如你在国外待一两个月,一回来,在飞机上往下看是一片黄,国外则是一片绿,环境的问题非常突出。这几年北京好一点了,前几年,开玩笑地说,北京小孩儿不知道星星,晚上看不见星星,空气都被污染了。你到国外,包括伦敦,过去说伦敦污染,叫雾伦敦,现在伦敦一片蓝天。所以,国外绿色环境、环境保护、低碳经济值得我们学习,还不能不承认国外现在生活水平还是要高过我们,我们还有漫长的路要走。这个漫长的路有的我已经赶不上了,主要靠你们年轻人。

奉献、创新、拼搏

主持人: 您回国之后,一直潜心科研与教学,您能不能举个简单的例子向我们讲讲您在科研中遇到的最大困难是什么?

柳百成: 科研中遇到的最大困难不是能不能发表文章,而是你的研究成果能不能经受生产考验。我们的科学研究成果,实践是检验真理的标准。我一再告诉我的学生,你搞的研究尽量要和国民经济结合,和国家目标结合,要能够指导生产。举个例子,我们开发的三维铸造模拟软件,工厂用我们的软件计算,算完的结果马上要通过生产校核,校核后一对比跟我们预测的一样,这对我们是最大的欣慰。我们的研究成果确实能指导生产,而不是发表一篇文章,放两张彩图。所以,我觉得我做那么多研究,最困难、最紧张的就是我们在工厂里做实验来验证我们的成果。

主持人: 所谓实践是检验真理的唯一标准,您在刚才的谈话中也谈到您从出国、回国,在科研中一直不断追求创新,特别是把计算机技术融入传统铸造行业中,在国内也处在领先水平。我们在座的学生,一定都非常想问您,我们需要具备什么样的条件和素质来实现创新呢?

柳百成: 我1999年当选中国工程院院士,2002年获得了光华工程科技奖。当选院士的时候,我也回顾了一下,我这几十年有哪些可以总结的。我总结了三条,希望和大家共勉。

第一条,要有远大的理想,要有爱国主义的情操,要有奉献精神,这是我从小学到大学,我一直坚持的精神支柱。大家不要觉得我一帆风顺,大学获得优秀金质奖章,"改革开放"后第一批公派出国,又当了院士。我没给大家讲我的酸甜苦辣。我在学校里挨过很多批评,甚至批判。我在1959年受到很严厉的"批判",闭门思过写检讨三个多月,但是我相信祖国、相信人民、相信党,我坚信我的道路是正确的。

我觉得一个人不可能一帆风顺,但是遇到挫折的时候要有勇气。所以,第一要有坚定的人生观。这人生观不是空洞的,不是学学马列主义的书本知识,而是要踏踏实实、勤勤恳恳。我一直觉得我不是天才,我主张笨鸟先飞。就是说,我们生在伟大的中华人民共和国,我本事不大,但是我尽我所能为国家做点贡献。每个人的能力不一样,贡献不一样，但是我们要有这么一点精神，为祖国增砖添瓦。

第二条，要有敏锐的创新思维。大家知道计算机系李三立院士。1951年，李三立院士跟我一起从上海坐火车到北京进清华。前几年，我的博士生从事计算机模拟分析，计算的网格达到几千万，微机难以胜任。算个题要两个多月，马上要毕业了，他十分着急。正好我在路上碰到李三立院士，他说他们搞了一个并行计算，效率提高很多，但是这项技术找不到人来用。我说正好我们有个大规模的题没地方能算。我马上让学生过去，跟他们的学生协作配合，这是我们国内最早采用并行计算技术解决铸造过程的大规模运算问题。这就是学科交叉。

第三条，科学的道路没有捷径，靠顽强的拼搏、实干的精神，特别是工科学生，要靠长期的勤奋努力，不要企图一天想个巧招就能拿到国家发明一等奖。

主持人： 柳老师在这么多年的教育工作中已经培养了四十多位博士生。其中有很多学生都已经在我们清华机械工程系当教授了，可谓是桃李满天下。我们非常想知道，您对于学生的培养有一些什么样的理念？

柳百成： 首先，我觉得是"严师出高徒"。我有个博士生他的科研工作做得相当不错，但缺乏归纳整理，他最后把他的实验结果整理了八张大表，但没有把里面的规律找出来。我不仅给他指出了方向，而且跟他一起花了一个星期的时间反复琢磨，最后，找出了规律，提炼出两张相平衡图。第二，还要身教重于言教。除了出去开会，我平时都在实验室，与同学一起讨论分析。我有几个博士生到最后毕业还有三个月的时候，开始跟我有点小矛盾。为什么？他觉得论文量已够了，柳老师故意卡他们。经过我再三帮助，既提高理论水平，答辩时又获得较高评价。这些学生毕业十年后回来，对我特别表示感谢。他说你最后这段对我们的教育和提高，让我们受益匪浅，终生难忘。前几年，利用出差机会，我还专门去研究生家做家访，结识他们的家长。

全面发展、热爱生活

主持人： 生活中柳老师也拥有着非常多的兴趣爱好，现在拿在我手上的这本，就是柳院士出的一本摄影习作集，这个摄影集都是柳老师走遍世界各地拍摄的精美照片，其中好像还有一个图章有一段故事，柳老师给我们说一下吧。

2009年在秦皇岛休假

柳百成： 我刚才讲的这三点大家千万不要理解成读书人只顾念书，读死书。我觉得学生兴趣要广泛，要全面发展。在小学、中学我喜欢体育锻炼，我在中学打垒球、踢足球、打篮球。到大学，足、篮、排我都喜欢。我在三年以前，冬天还去滑冰。我有比较广泛的兴趣。过去家庭情况困难，买不起照相机，只能借相机拍照，现在有条件了。我从第一次出国到现在，已超过了50次。我利用这些机会，再加上现在又有数码单反相机满足我的摄影爱好。我这个摄影习作集已经出到第三册了。除此以外，我每年还精选13张照片，自己做台历，赠送至亲好友，最近还学会了做DVD。我希望大家不一定是摄影，音乐等也好。比如我的弟弟柳百新，在音乐方面有很深的造诣，贝多芬、莫扎特的乐章他能给你讲一整套故事。所以，我觉得不要认为现在的大师只会有限元，只是从图书馆到办公室。广泛的兴趣和人文修养与我们的科学研究各方面也是相互融合的。我也很赞成李政道教授所讲的"人文和理工的融合"。所以，我觉得大家前进在科学道路的时候，要健康生活、有所爱好、全面发展，这对我们的工作不仅不会有影响，而是有促进的。

互动

清华园里柳氏兄弟

提问： 柳教授，您刚才说您家里有两位院士，现在能介绍一下吗？

柳百成： 我介绍一下我的弟弟，柳百新。介绍柳百新，大家只要记住三个字，"二、四、六"。这照片是我们在人大会堂参加两院院士大会时照的。怎么叫"二、四、六"呢？第一，柳百新跟我是亲兄弟，"二"，比我小两岁。"四"，中学毕业跟我差四年。我大学毕业是1955年，他1955年进校，我在大操场欢迎他。人家说差两岁，怎么会四年？他小学时身体不如我，因病停学过两年。所以，他中学毕业跟我就差四年。"六"什么意思呢？我在清华是四年制，柳百新进清华是六年制，他一毕业跟我差六年了。但是他的基础比我打得好，应该说我们都在清华，一级学科是同一个学科，材料科学与工程，他是搞材料物理，偏重基础理论。所以，学校里总拿他的文章，SCI收录影响因子，宣传他的成就。而我是做材料加工工程研究。我们家庭不是很富裕的家庭，我的父母文化也不高，但家里舍得花钱，做教育投资。所以，这一点我们很感谢父母，在小学、中学为我们打下了一个比较好的基础。

提问：您和您的弟弟柳百新院士在各自的专业中各有建树，非常的成功。您跟您的弟弟在二十岁、三十岁的时候是怎么交流的，都交流什么？您作为哥哥，当时有没有对弟弟说一些什么话？

柳百成与弟弟柳百新

柳百成：我跟我弟弟是亲兄弟，从小一起生活，一起上学，我们两个的关系亲密无间。他考清华也是受我的影响，我在清华经常给他写信，宣传清华的学风、清华的名师等，所以他考清华是受我的影响。他考的也是机械系，进了清华以后，学校建工程物理系，把他调到工程物理系，后来从工程物理系转到材料系。所以，进清华、选专业是受了我的影响。我们碰到一些重大事件，总是互相交换意见。

另外，我是1999年当选，他是2001年当选。我们当选院士时的年龄都是66岁。

提问：柳院士，您说科研最大的挑战就是你的成果在实践中接受检验，我们在企业和在清华的成长有什么不同？或者说不管在哪里的成长，我们在这个平台最应该获取的是什么东西？

柳百成：我要说明一点，我所讲的还是以工科院系为背景，我指的是工程。工程的博士生，工程的科学研究难点在什么地方？难点是既要面向国家目标，满足国家需要，同时也要能够提炼，有理论成果，出高水平博士论文。我刚才讲的不是说为生产而生产，我们现在选择的课题都是国家重大科学技术关键，如大飞机航空发动机里面的关键零部件的制造与仿真技术。这个零部件制造与仿真技术的解决要在大飞机上获得应用，大飞机上不用，你光写文章，人家认可吗？

所以，第一，国家需求的问题不是一般的问题，是高技术含量、重大关键核心技术的问题。第二，也不能仅仅停留在把这个任务完成。我在1985年专门到美国考察高等工程教育。美国大学的教授跟我讲得很简单，什么叫硕士？什么叫博士？硕士要回答How，博士则要回答Why。硕士回答怎么做出来，博士回答为什么，为什么就是机制和理论。所以，我刚才讲的这个成果必须是重大关键核心技术，不是小打小闹。最近我的博士生从事长江三峡工程重达数百吨的特大型不锈钢铸件的建模与仿真。这铸件过去90%进口，现在国产化了。我们国家航空发动机的高温合金叶片制造技术与国外还有很大差距，我就带领大批研究生从事该项研究。理论和实践重在结合，发表文章是研究成果的最后表现。现在有些人把发表文章作为研究的目的，文章一发表、课题就收摊，是不对的。

提问：柳院士，刚才您也说您有广泛的兴趣爱好，对于我们学生来说自身也有一些兴趣，您平常在做学术和兴趣方面，时间上怎么协调？

柳百成：这个问题难以直接回答，各人情况不一样，我也难以给你安排一个时间表。但是我们在做学生的时候，每天下午五点到六点必须去锻炼，我不知道现在有没有做到。过去蒋南翔校长每天在大操场跑步，大学生五点到六点人人在操场上。1956年，我已经留校了，当时兴起跳伞运动，我报名参加，也跳了六次。前几年，七十多岁了，我还去荷花池滑冰。

最近几年，我鼓励我的学生组织一些集体活动，如郊游等，可以相互沟通。不要光是一天到晚有限元啊，给他们开展一些丰富的活动和培养爱好。我在美国还学到了一点，美国的老师跟学生比较平等，平等到我们难以想象。美国的学生叫老师的夫人可以直接叫名字,我的教授叫 Carl Loper,我都叫 Professor Loper,他的夫人是 Mrs. Loper。我是中国人改不了口,人家学生直接叫她名字 Jane。在美国,每年圣诞节导师都把学生请到家里,二三十人聚在一起,又唱又跳。我刚回国的开始几年,我只有六七个学生,我都请他们到我家里做客,每年两次。现在不行了,我的团队有三十余人,就得去全聚德。马上就要国庆中秋聚会,大家聊聊天,有些女同学再唱个歌。虽然要严师出高徒,但是跟同学是平等的,不能一天到晚板着脸训人。

提问:在铸造行业,中国已经是世界上生产铸件的大国,但是我看到我们的技术主要给国企用,我们有很多的民营企业可能还在手工翻砂、劳动条件极差。我们很多的产品,即便是铸造用的设备都是从日本、德国进口。您是怎么来看待这个问题?

柳百成:这个问题说来话长,我从远的先讲一下。刚才我讲了我的一些成就,1999 年我当选中国工程院院士以后,我的研究工作又有了一个新的台阶。我在中国工程院领导下参与了国家装备制造业的宏观战略研究。最近几年又参加若干大的咨询项目,如装备制造业自主创新战略研究。现在,回答你的问题。

我们国家的铸件年产量约 3000 万 t,占全世界 35% 左右,遥遥领先其他国家。我们现在铸件年产量等于老二加老三加老四可能还要加上几个国家,与我国钢的年产量情况一样。但是我刚才讲了,长江三峡水轮机的转轮铸件 90% 进口,从哪儿进口?韩国铸造行业年产量只有几百万吨铸件,我们还从韩国进口高端铸件,我们还从克罗地亚等一些国家进口。这个问题告诉我们要调整我们的科学研究方向,长期以来对这些制造技术和工艺不重视,这几年正有所转变。最近,我们国家列了 16 个重大科技专项,其中有一个重大专项,题目是"高档数控机床与基础制造装备",其中列了四大铸造设备,如 3500 t 大型压铸机等。所以,我们国家的铸造等工艺技术和国外有较大的差距,其中一个原因是:长期重视不够、投入不足。现在我们国家重视了,加大了投入,相信很快就会扭转这个局面。

提问:刚才您说到在您弟弟的一些人生的重大抉择或者转折的时候,您对他提出了很多建议,而且起到了很大的作用。在您人生当中一些重大的抉择或者转折的时候,是谁给您一些建议,让您有更大的一些改变,是您的家人还是朋友,还是您自己?谢谢。

柳百成:这个问题很简单,两个因素。第一,我自己的坚定信念。第二,我夫人的支持。今天在这儿有很多女同学,我的成就有 50% 或者还多一点,51%,是我夫人的支持。我在 1959 年最困难的时候,闭门思过写检讨三个多月,在大礼堂旁边的阶梯教室,全系三百余人全都奉命来批判我。上到教授、下到大一学生,批判柳百成上到什么纲:有组织、有目的、有纲领地向党进攻。天似乎要塌了下来!我很坚定我的信念,我夫人在旁边也一直支持,毫不动摇。

主持人:您的家庭,您的亲人在您最困难的时候给予您这么大的一份支持,我们也应该珍惜这样的一份亲情,同时也要在这里送一份祝福给您的夫人。

柳百成:所以我制作的这个摄影集上专门放了一张她的照片。刚才问我兴趣爱好,我兴趣爱好很广泛。我父亲会雕刻,我们小时候父亲就教我们画画、雕刻。所以,我从小就刻图章,这个图章现在我仍然还保留着,伴随了我快六十多年了。小时候我还喜欢做模型,现在我和我的小外孙常常一起做模型,做美国的隐形飞机、航空母舰等。

提问:您提到过清华以前的一些大师,经常在课堂直接和同学面对面,包括对本科生的教育。现在为什么很多大师或者是称不上大师的人每天都在外面奔波,在校园里经常看不到人,您对这个问题是怎么看的?

柳百成:别的大师、别的教授,我不敢妄加评论,但是我自己以身作则。我觉得作为一个教师,高等学校的教师,不管你多忙,不管你地位多高,你是大师,你是院士,都要和学生见面,都要讲课,我自己就是这样做的。我回国以后,就用英文开设一门课。我觉得中国的学生外语水平在三十年以前太差,我在美国很有感触,在美国,中国台湾、中国香港、中国大陆去的谁的英文最好?中国香港的最好。为什么?整个是英文环境。第二,中国台湾的学生也比中国大陆的好,整个大学教材是英文的。我们这几年已经变化了。过去二十年以前,我们的大学生、研究生上英文课的时候是英文,英文课以外全部是中文,这是一个致命的问题。所以,回来我就用英文开课。到目前我先后开设了三门课程,给本科生开《材料加工工程概论》,给研究生开两门课。另外,我很反对很多学校一个教授同时带几十个博士生,我认为是误人子弟。我赞成清华的规定,清华规定教授同时带博士生最多不能超过十个。

我觉得教师的神圣职责就是培养人。当然也要搞研究,研究除了为国家做贡献,也是通过研究使得我们的教学水平大大提高。讲授的内容不是书本上的东西，而是有自己亲身经历的东西。所以，有些教师自己办个小公司，搞额外创收等，我不是很赞成。

主持人：非常感谢柳老师。我们校研究生会特别准备了一份礼物，让我们首先掌声有请武晓峰老师上台为柳老师赠予这样一份特别的礼物！

（赠奖环节）

主持人：请柳老师能够在最后给我们所有的同学留一句话，同时也是作为您的一份希望和寄语。

柳百成：我去过美国很多次，我去了美国的Greenfield Village，在底特律，它陈列了美国著名作家、科学家、发明家的生平。其中有爱迪生，大家知道爱迪生是美国早期最伟大的发明家，他有一句名言，我翻译过来了，他说："我做的所有的工作都不是靠偶然或意外，我的工作和发明是靠长期的积累。"我用这句话作为最后赠送给同学。

"学术人生"讲座结束时与部分研究生合影

主持人：今晚真是非常衷心地感谢柳老师能够在百忙之中来到学术人生的访谈，柳老师在今天晚上给我们分享了这么宝贵的人生经历，一定会成为我们每个人在人生中最难忘的一次回忆和一笔财富。在这里，我要代表所有的同学送一份最诚挚的祝福给柳老师，祝您身体健康，工作顺利！同时也祝愿所有的清华学子能够以不懈的努力，共同创造美好的明天！

4. 怀念南翔同志　学习南翔同志

柳百成

一、发扬"又红又专、全面发展"的教育理念

我认为，在新形势下，仍要坚持和发扬南翔同志提出的建设一支"又红又专教师队伍"的教学理念。尽管现在经济发展是以市场经济为主导等，这个指导思想还要继续坚持。回顾我走过的人生道路，正是体现着南翔同志的教育思想。

1951年我考进清华，1955年毕业，并获得了优秀毕业生金质奖章，图书馆里还刻有我的名字。我在清华四年的最重要收获就是在浓厚的政治思想氛围中，培养我们的年轻人的"爱国奉献"精神。1952年在大操场举办的"五四"篝火晚会上，我们高唱革命歌曲，朗诵革命诗词的情景仍然记忆犹新。到毕业的时候，就凝聚成一个口号"到祖国最需要的地方去"。大学四年的教育让我从一个不太懂事的青年学生，成长为一个有比较坚定的革命信仰，随时把自己的知识奉献给祖国的年青教师。

2013年正好也是我80周岁。回顾我的一生，总结为20个字5句话，就是"**爱国奉献、创新思维、顽强拼搏、健康体魄、热爱生活**"。这5句话正好是南翔同志"又红又专、全面发展"的教育理念在我身上的具体体现。我觉得最重要的就是第一条"爱国奉献"。2009年新中国成立60周年时，我参加了中组部组织专家在北戴河的休养活动。当时，召开了座谈会，我也发了言。我说："改革开放"之初我赴美国进修，1981年初回国时我的工资是79元钱。现在国家强大了，经济形势也好了，高薪引进人才，应该不应该？我说应该。但是千万不要忘记第一条仍然是要求我们所有的人才，不管是"海归"还是"土鳖"，都要有"爱国奉献"精神，都要为祖国富强、人民幸福贡献我们所学的科学文化知识。

爱国奉献，为祖国人民服务，当然要有真才实学。我在清华名师的言传身教和"行胜于言"校风的熏陶下，培养了既努力学习、顽强拼搏，又敢于探索、勇于创新的思想和作风。1979年，我刚到美国，看到我的房东太太的10岁小儿子在摆弄一台苹果电脑时，我敏锐地意识到计算机技术将会深刻地改变人类社会的一切。回国后，我开辟了"先进铸造及凝固过程多尺度建模与仿真研究"新领域，经过近30年的顽强拼搏，为我国制造业的技术进步做出了贡献，也为我国在国际铸造学术界占有一席之地。

虽然南翔同志去世多年了，但是我们学校仍一直坚持走"又红又专"的道路，我是深有体会的。1978年刚刚"改革开放"，教育部第一批派遣的赴美访问学者共52人。其中清华派出了9位，党员比例高，政治觉悟也较高，我是清华出国人员的小组长。到了教育部集中时，我被任命为总领队。回国以后，我们9个人中先后有3位当选为院士，是第一批赴美访问学者中比例最高的。

我还可以举一个例子，1978年我们国家经济情况相当困难，国家派我们出去进修，而美国是花花世界。有一次在一个美国中学生座谈会上，当场就有中学生问我："要不要留在美国？"我毫不犹豫，唱了一首美国家喻户晓的世界名曲《Home Sweet Home》的最后一句，"Home! Sweet home, there is no place like home"。全体中学生都热烈鼓掌，他们觉得中国人有骨气，他们也佩服中国人的爱国情操。所以，我归纳的这5句话，第一条"爱国奉献"，是我在清华学到的最宝贵的精华，后面4条都是在这个指导思想的统领之下的延伸。

时至今日，南翔同志的教育思想和理念，应该说是一脉相承，贯彻继承下来了。现在每年博士生入学时，我都要去讲课，我特别强调学生要有"爱国奉献"的精神。同时我再三告诫他们，绝对不要想不劳而获、一夜成名，一定要顽强拼搏、持之以恒，才能有所创新、有所突破。这几年除了学校的

○ 本文转载自2014年出版的《深切的怀念　永恒的记忆：纪念蒋南翔同志诞辰100周年》一书，转载时做个别删改。

学术讲座以外，北京科技大学、华中科技大学、西安交通大学、西北工业大学等很多高校都请我去讲"学术人生"。我总是语重心长地要把我们坚持的"又红又专、全面发展"教育理念和"爱国奉献"思想传授给我们的年青人。

二、学习南翔同志"坚贞不屈、刚直不阿"的崇高品德

在我的学生时期，南翔同志是我们的校长。"文革"时期，我在校办工厂劳动，并当上了铸工车间政治指导员。当时，南翔同志也被安排来车间劳动，我居然"领导"南翔同志。因而我和南翔同志有了近距离地多次接触，更进一步了解到南翔同志的很多优秀品质。

我尽力多方保护南翔同志。当时，南翔同志年事已高、身体不好，我给他安排了最轻微的劳动。我说："你身体不好，劳动半天，下午不必来了，学习资料、思考问题就可以了。"我多次和南翔同志交谈，他身处逆境，仍然坚持真理，他给我讲了几件事使我深受感动。第一，他对"文革"完全不理解。他说："为什么现在我对教育工作有不同意见，就成了走资派？"第二，当时《红旗》杂志发表了很多批判高等教育的文章，要批判旧清华、砸烂旧清华。他对《红旗》杂志等的这些文章写了密密麻麻的批注。他给我举了例子，他说："在一亩地里又种大米、又种小麦、又种杂粮高粱，能长得好吗？他们把高考取消了，有的人只有小学文化，都送到清华来，能培养出国家需要的科技人才吗？"通过这些近距离地接触，我进一步认识到南翔同志"坚持真理、刚直不阿"的崇高革命品质。

过不多久，突然迟群①又要整治南翔同志。迟群一个电话把我叫到工字厅，他先问我蒋南翔表现怎么样，我说表现不错。他问蒋南翔劳动不劳动，我说劳动、全天劳动。他又问蒋南翔有没有什么错误言论或不满情绪？我说没有，南翔在车间里劳动，跟工人师傅相处得都很好。这样，我的"谎言"使得迟群要整治南翔同志的阴谋没能得逞。我和南翔同志从此也结成了忘年之交。

"文革"结束，南翔同志恢复工作后，他专门约请我，和我畅谈了一个晚上。更令人难忘的是1979年，南翔同志当了教育部长，率团访问美国威斯康星大学。正巧我也在威斯康星大学做访问学者，南翔同志十分热情和亲切地见到了我。他不顾疲劳，专门约请我去他下榻的饭店畅谈，他希望能了解到美国高等教育的第一手真实情况，并认真地听取我对访问进修、学习生活及教学改革的意见等。

总之，我们纪念南翔同志、怀念南翔同志，就是要坚持发扬南翔同志"又红又专、全面发展"的教育理念，更要坚持学习南翔同志"坚持真理，坚贞不屈，说真话、不随风"的崇高品德。

---

① 迟群，"文革"期间担任清华大学党委书记，革命委员会主任，1976年10月被免职务，1983年被判有罪入狱。

5. 顽强拼搏、报效祖国[一]

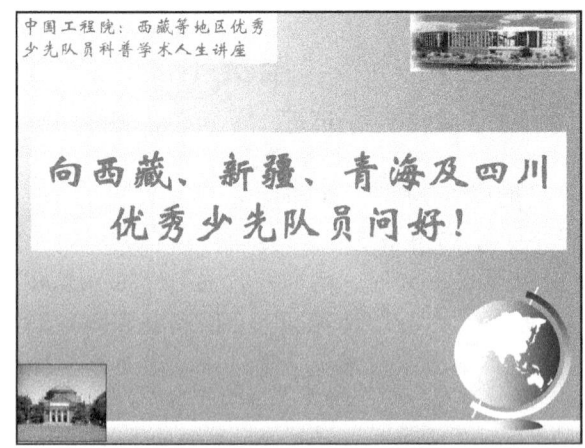
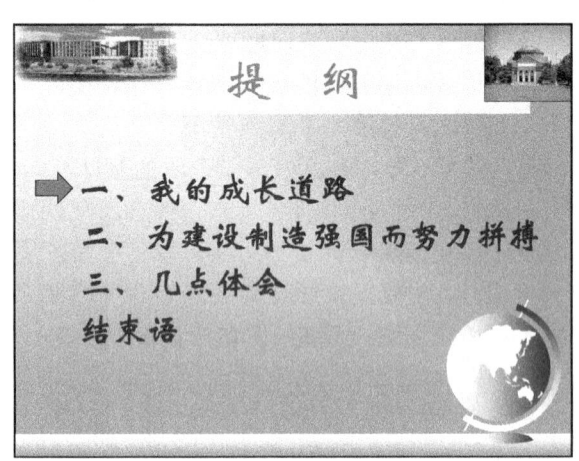

[一] 本文为 2016 年中国工程院为西藏等地区优秀少先队员科普学术人生讲座中的报告。

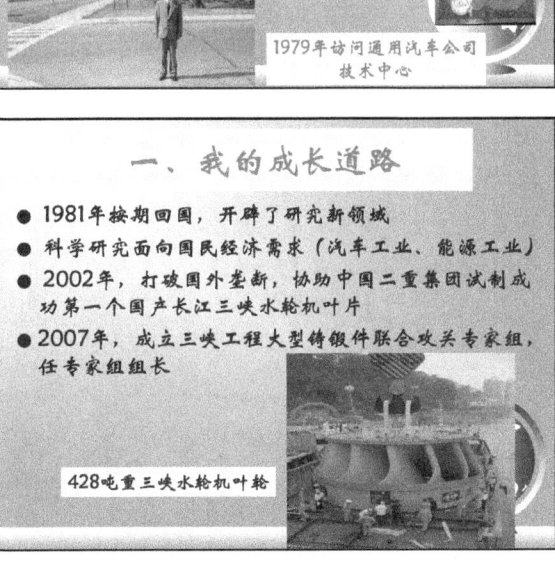
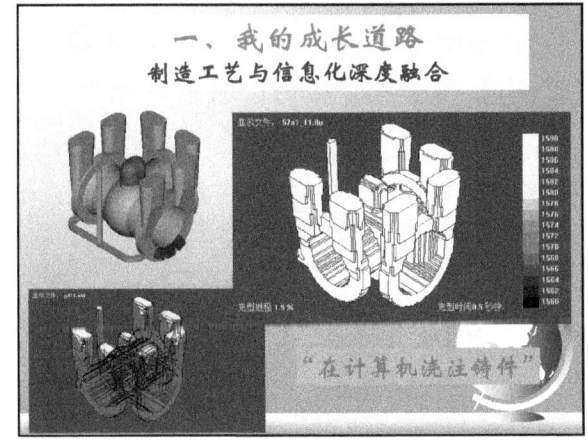

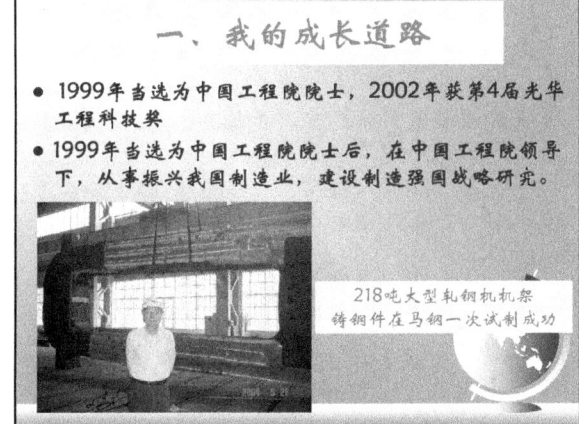

一、我的成长道路

- 2008年12月，在人民大会堂留学生工作30周年会议上，作"顽强拼搏、报效祖国"邀请报告
- 2014年，在人民大会堂"中-美留学35年"会议上，作邀请报告

二、为建设制造强国而努力拼搏

- 2003年，在徐匡迪院长领导下，参加《国家中长期科学与技术发展规划战略研究》专题三"制造业发展科技问题研究"
- 2004年4月21日，陪同徐匡迪院长，向国务院领导汇报"研究报告"

二、为建设制造强国而努力拼搏

- 我国已是世界制造大国，位居第一
- 美国、日本、德国分居第二、三及四
- 我国取得举世瞩目的成就

二、为建设制造强国而努力拼搏

- 我国已是世界制造大国，位居第一
- 美国、日本、德国分居第二、三及四
- 我国取得举世瞩目的成就

二、为建设制造强国而努力拼搏

- 但是，总体上我国制造业大而不强

工业机器人
中国：23/万工人
德国：273/万工人

二、为建设制造强国而努力拼搏

- 2013年，中国工程院开展"制造强国战略研究"
- 2014年1月，提出建立"中国制造2025"行动纲领的建议，并获得国务院的赞同
- 2015年5月，国务院正式颁布《中国制造2015》
- 2015年5月，柳百成院士组团访问美国，考察美国"先进制造伙伴计划"进展

二、为建设制造强国而努力拼搏

《中国制造2025》
制造强国的一个总目标
制造业由大变强，建成制造强国

三步走计划
- 到2025年：进入世界强国行列
- 到2035年：进入世界强国阵营中等水平
- 到2045年（或建国100周年）：进入世界强国前列

二、为建设制造强国而努力拼搏

- 为建设制造强国，中国工程院开展广泛国际合作交流，柳百成院士积极参加，并做邀请报告
- 2015年11月，在武汉召开中-韩-日国际学术会议
- 2015年12月，美国机械工程师协会访问中国工程院，进行学术交流
- 2016年5月，在中国工程院召开中-德-美国际学术会议

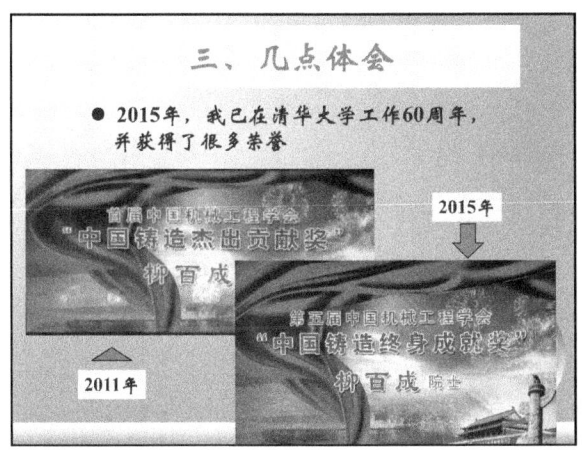

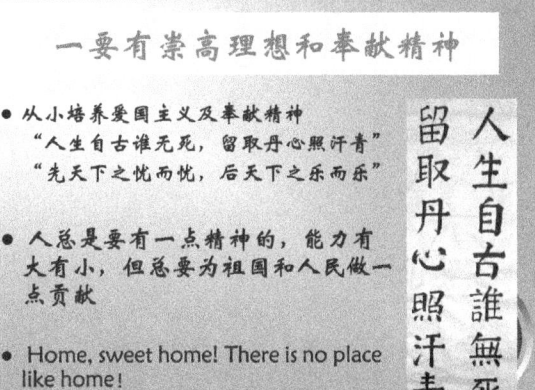

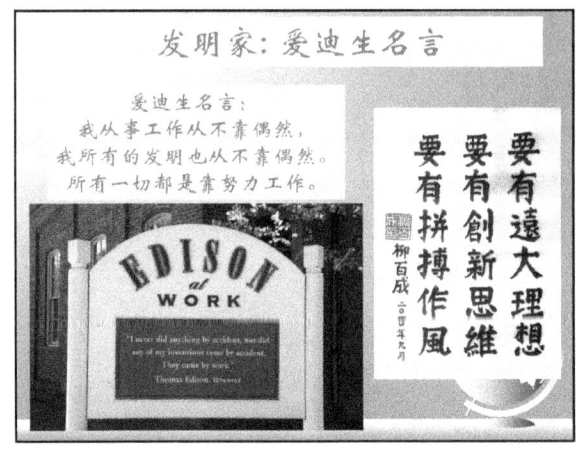

第 6 篇

祝贺与回忆

1. "中国铸造杰出贡献奖"颁奖词

"中国铸造杰出贡献奖"——柳百成院士（2011年）：

您用高瞻远瞩的慧眼，瞄准国际铸造学科的前沿和高端，以信息技术，来推进我国铸造技术进步和理论研究跨越性地发展；

您用"成果必须转化为生产力"的先进理念，在著书育人和推动我国装备制造业的战略理论研究与实践活动中做出了突出贡献！

您，不愧为我国铸造界著名的学者与实践家。

中国机械工程学会
二〇一二年十月

2. "中国铸造终身成就奖"颁奖词

致"中国铸造终身成就奖"获奖者 柳百成院士（2015年）：

您是一位领军人，潜心铸造六十余载，奋战在科研和教育的最前沿，硕果累累、桃李芳菲！

您以独到的创新思维，将传统铸造技术与当代科技相结合，实现着铸造技术理论的跨越式发展！

您用卓越的贡献助推着中国铸造产业迈向高端！

您是一缕阳光，温暖着铸造强国之路上的前行者！

您是一座灯塔，引领着我们在铸造的海洋中扬帆远航！

中国机械工程学会
二〇一五年十月

3. 桃李缘
——贺导师柳百成院士清华任教 60 周年

周昭喜[一]

恩师授业近六年，

奕奕风采映眼帘。

水木耕耘一甲子，

孜孜提振制造圈。

教学科研攻前沿，

桃李天下尽高端。

老骥伏枥志千里，

人生楷模美名传。

2016 年 12 月

[一] 作者简介：周昭喜，1982 年 2 月至 1987 年 12 月在清华大学学习，在柳百成先生指导下攻读硕士、博士，为柳先生培养的第一位博士生。现任上海某投资管理公司总经理。

4. 跟着先生学知识学做人

哈尔滨工业大学材料科学与工程学院　郭景杰

我是一九八六年九月从哈尔滨工业大学考入清华大学，师从柳百成先生攻读博士学位。在一九八六年九月至一九八九年十月这三年期间，柳先生开放式的思维、不断创新的意识和能力、渊博的知识、严谨求实的作风、精益求精的治学态度、平易近人的性格和对学生无微不至地关怀等都给我留下了深刻的印象和永久的记忆，对我日后的工作产生了重大影响。

在撰写博士论文期间，我记忆最深的几件事是柳先生主持和组织的组内学术讨论会、修改论文和一年一度的组内聚会及柳先生的家访。

柳先生主持和组织的组内学术讨论会一般每个月进行一次，组内老师和学生都积极参加。通常由一名或两名研究生做报告，有时老师也做报告。内容非常广泛，如出国访问报告、国内会议报告、课题进展报告、资料调研报告和突发奇想报告等。在柳先生的主持和倡导下，在报告中和报告后老师和学生都可以随时提问和提出不同看法，有时关于一个基本概念、一个实验方法、一条实验曲线分析、一个新的思想、一个数学模型和物理模型等讨论和争论得十分激烈。在组内，无论老师还是学生都有自由表达自己学术观点的平等权利，大家都非常愿意参与讨论。柳先生这种学术民主的大师风范使我们大家都受益匪浅，对我的日后工作起到了重要的指导作用。通过多年的实践，我深深地感到这种组内学术研讨会对学生有许多好处：1. 可以激发学生的想象力和创造力，去积极地思考一些问题，进行开拓性的研究工作。2. 开阔眼界，增长知识，拓宽思路。通常学生刚刚开始进行研究工作时，看的资料仅限于自己的研究方向，知识面较窄，经常参加学术讨论会，可以听到不同方向的研究情况和各种不同的研究方法。3. 提高学生的表达能力和讲演能力。做报告要做认真地准备，从内容的确定、语言的组织，到表达的方式都需要认真思考。4. 提高学生的竞争意识和能力。大家轮流做报告，如果别人无论从研究深度，还是从表达能力都很好，而自己表现却很差，这是一件很难堪的事情。5. 密切了师生关系。

先生修改论文是非常严谨的。大到文章的主题、内容和层次，小到标点符号和文字，都改得十分认真，有时一篇文章要改两三次。每修改一次文字水平就上一个台阶。记得有一次我写了一篇关于球铁激光表面改性过程中组织演化规律的文章，我将显微组织和化学成分及激光扫描速度之间的关系总结成一个表，柳先生审查后，建议我改成一个显微组织随工艺参数变化图。这样既清晰明了，又实用。果然，文章发表后引起国外研究者的重视，被多次引用。后来，作为项目的部分内容，获得了教育部自然科学一等奖。

那时候柳先生主持和组织的一年一度组内聚会都在柳先生家里进行。柳先生和曾老师会准备丰盛的食品和饮品，大家围着桌子坐一圈，一边吃一边聊。大家来自全国各地，各自介绍自己家乡的风土人情、饮食文化等，气氛非常热烈。有时，大家也问先生一些与研究无关的问题，或与先生开玩笑，使我感到就像生活在一个温暖的大家庭中一样。

柳先生的家访是在1988年的夏天。那时，哈尔滨非常热，我正在哈尔滨家里休暑假。柳先生给我打电话，告诉我他要到我家里看看。虽然柳先生在哈尔滨的日程排得满满的，但还是挤出时间来家访，使我和我的家人非常感动。柳先生到我家后，问长问短，不但关心我个人情况，而且关心我家的生活情况，询问有什么困难需要帮助解决，使我爱人深受感动。柳先生反复对我爱人说你的先生人真好，不但学术水平高，而且为人又这么好，你真有福气！

总之，在清华大学跟先生学习的三年中，不但从先生身上学到了科学知识和组织课题组的工作方法，而且学会了做人的道理，这对我的一生都将产生重要影响。

毕业后，我回到哈尔滨工业大学工作。虽然远隔千里，但是每年都能通过学术会议和各种其他会议见到先生几面，亲耳聆听先生所做的富有很强前瞻性、引导性和战略性的大会特邀报告以及先生作为973项目专家组负责人对项目所做的点评和建议等。对先生的认识越来越深入，从先生身上学到的东西也越来越多。另外，经常阅读先生指导博士生撰写的博士学位论文，也受益匪浅。虽然已经毕业参加工作，但是，向先生学习的脚步一刻也未停止。

对我影响最深和最大的是先生 2005 年在中国铸造活动周上作的《提高铸造技术水平促进国民经济发展》大会特邀报告。这一报告对我国铸造行业发展现状、世界铸造技术发展趋势、铸造与国民经济的关系以及 2020 年我国铸造发展的目标和重点等全局性战略性问题进行了系统深入地分析，以独到的眼光，提出了许多创新性的建议。同时，又对具体研究领域指出了明确的、详尽的发展方向，例如，不但对我国铸造行业存在的 5 大问题和世界铸造技术发展的 4 大趋势进行了分析，而且对铸造过程模拟仿真这一具体方向的未来发展目标给出了明确的回答，即全过程、多尺度、多功能、多学科、高精度和高效率的模拟方法。这份报告我特意向先生要了 PPT，可以毫不夸张地说：我看了多少遍，已经记不清楚了。2007 年和 2008 年中国铸造学会让我代表学会在日本第 150 次铸造会议和在印度的世界铸造大会上先后作了《中国铸造产业现状及未来发展》的报告。这一报告主要内容就是参考先生的报告，可谓受益良多。令我印象深刻的另一件事是先生作为我们多家单位承担的国防 973 项目专家组负责人，每年对项目进行检查、把关和指导。记得第一次会议是在西北工业大学召开的，项目和各个课题汇报完之后，先生对项目和课题做出了精准的点评，对项目存在的问题和未来工作提出了明确的建议。会后有的教授跟我说这老先生太聪明了，真有水平，句句切中要害。我很自豪地说那是我的博士导师。

先生经常让我评审先生指导的博士学位论文，我先后阅读了十几本，这对我来说是十分难得的学习机会。每篇论文我都要仔细阅读两遍以上，体会和分析先生指导博士学位论文的方式方法，作为我自己指导博士的方式方法。通过对先生指导的论文的认真分析和总结，同时比较我审阅的其他近 200 本博士学位论文，发现先生指导博士学位论文有几个特点：1. 首先是培养学生对所研究课题的兴趣，使学生对论文研究有热情，当作自己的事业来进行，这样才能全身心地投入，才能发挥自己的主观能动性，而不是当成一项任务来完成。2. 先生非常注重集成创新性。这一点从一篇论文很难看出，但是，仔细阅读多篇论文后，会发觉先生指导博士学位论文不是急功近利，打一枪换一个地方，以多出论文为目的。而是有着很好的顶层设计，既注重每篇论文的创新性，又注重各篇论文创新的集成性。3. 先生对博士学位论文的科学性给予了很高的重视。学术论文是某一学术课题在实验性、理论性或观测性上具有新的科学研究成果或创新见解和知识的科学记录，或是某种已知原理应用于实际中取得新进展的科学总结。因此，没有科学性就不称其为论文，只能是研究报告。在先生指导的博士学位论文中，不但揭示了大量的规律，而且阐明了这些规律形成的机制，并建立相应的物理模型和数学模型来描述这些规律。4. 先生也非常重视一篇博士论文的系统性。纵观通篇博士论文，会发现整个论文结构非常严谨，系统性特别强。每一章都有自己的明显特征，章与章之间又联系非常紧密，是一个存在内在联系的有机整体。5. 实用性也是先生一直强调的。我看到的论文几乎都是针对铸造生产实践中提炼出的重要科学问题开展研究工作，反过来又对铸造生产实践进行理论指导，对我国关键铸件的生产起到了巨大的助推作用。

另外，我作为颁奖嘉宾，亲身经历了先生荣获中国机械工程学会"中国铸造杰出贡献奖"及"中国铸造终身成就奖"两个奖项的颁奖过程。先生是第一位先后荣获这两个奖项的学者。中国机械工程学会的颁奖词代表了我们的心声，对先生的贡献做出了很高的评价："您是一位领军人，潜心铸造六十余载，奋战在科研与教育的最前沿，硕果累累，桃李芳菲！您以独到的创新思维，将传统铸造技术与当代科技相结合，实现着铸造技术理论的跨越式发展！您用卓越的贡献助推着中国铸造产业迈向高端！您是一缕阳光，温暖着铸造强国之路上的前行者。您是一座灯塔，引领着我们在铸造的海洋中扬帆远航。"每当我读起颁奖词，就感到十分自豪和对先生无比的崇敬。

最后，祝柳先生身体健康，万事如意！

5. 久违的回忆

郝守卫

恰逢感恩节之际，柳先生的弟子们张罗着征集纪念文章庆祝先生在清华任教六十周年及八十三岁高寿。师恩如海！多年对柳老师及夫人曾晓萱老师的感恩及思念之情一直在心中。这次无论如何一定要用文字表达出来。

我是1984年成为柳先生的硕士研究生，1986年转直博，1989年获博士学位，留校任教到1992年初出国。可以说在柳老师的指导下学习工作了八年，基本是我二十多岁时的整个成长过程。其间学了几门曾老师的课，受益匪浅，尤其是世界科技史，让我记忆犹新！可能当时属于年少时期，所以我在柳老师和曾老师面前没有感觉到任何拘束。经常借与柳老师学术讨论之机去吃曾老师做的点心、冰淇淋。在我心目中，曾老师绝对是师母中的典范。在回忆柳老师的师恩之际，对曾老师的感恩也是一定要表达的。

三十年过去了，我也到了当年柳先生带我时的年纪了。我从柳先生那学到的最重要的是什么？我觉得可以总结为以下几点：站得高，看得远。勇于突破自我。理论用于实际。认认真真做学问。下面我就用具体的事例来点评。

首先是站得高，看得远。1984年，刚师从柳先生，我以为我的课题一定是球墨铸铁。柳先生是世界球墨铸铁的权威，做出过重大的发现。当时周昭喜师兄的项目也有很多突破。没想到的是，柳先生给我定的是数值模拟凝固过程。第一次讨论课题，柳先生就给了一堆英文的资料，让我学习和总结。并要求找到突破口，争取一年在美国铸造年会杂志上发表论文。1984年，国内的计算机能力是非常有限的。刚开始用的是286机，Fortran 77编程序。微软公司的Windows操作系统还没问世，只能用MS-DOS操作系统。由于计算机能力，我们只能从二维模拟开始。就这样柳先生带着我成长为清华铸造数值模拟的第一人。1986年，柳先生让我直读博士，1987年，我到了日本东北大学在新山英辅教授处做了一年的联合培养博士生。同新山先生及安斋浩一教授结下了终身友情。现在回过头来想，柳先生真是站得高，看得远。在柳先生的指导下，加上后来其他人的努力，特别是荆涛、熊守美等师弟的努力，清华的数值模拟一直是走在世界前列的。

柳先生第二个让我佩服的是他勇于突破自我。我现在也五十多岁了，越来越感觉到突破自我是多么的不容易。当年柳先生不满足于在铸铁方面的成就，带领我们不仅做数值模拟，而且也进入铸铝及大型铸钢件的领域。用数值模拟大型铸铝及大型铸钢件的项目后来都取得了成功。先后获得教育部及北京市的科技奖。20世纪80年代正是国外汽车业大举应用铝铸件的关键时期，汽车铝发动机体也被大量应用。可以说在国内我们是走在前列的。从我个人的经历，我也是受益于柳先生的这种勇于突破自我的精神。在日本、新加坡学术界工作了几年后来到了美国，2000年时跳出学术界，正式进入工业界，也彻底地离开了铸造业。在克莱斯勒汽车公司管理供应商的质量。2008年又跨入锂电池业为新能源汽车做电池。2012年初到苹果公司负责锂电池的生产工艺及质量管理。每次的转变，都能激发我的好奇心及求知欲。每次都能让我看得更清楚到底自己想要做什么。

第三点要谈的是柳先生对理论用于实际的重视。在20世纪80年代，数值模拟的最大挑战是要算得准，能处理复杂的三维形体，还要能形象地显示三维计算结果。当时有许多理论研究及基础研究足够写博士论文的，但很幸运的是柳先生和新山先生都是非常重视实际应用的。所以我在课题里有大量的实例，包括一些国家科研项目。为了攻克三维复杂铸件形体输入，我们还在计算机系孙家广教授的支持下，应用孙教授的三维CAD，开发出了三维铸件形体输入及网格自动生成软件。同时也成功地开发了三维立体模拟结果显示软件。它可以形象地显示整个凝固过程并预测缺陷大小及位置。这为计算机在铸造界的实际应用扫清了一大障碍。在当时这是非常不易的。后来清华大学和日本东北大学都有了自己的商用软件，为计算机在铸造界的应用都做出了贡献。我很幸运能成为最早期的参与者之一。

最后，也是我从柳先生那学到的最宝贵的财富，就是柳先生认认真真做学问的执着。我印象深刻的是，当我和柳先生讨论论文时，每一个数据的来源，每一篇引用的出处及原著者的发现过程必须是清清楚楚。宁可少写不可乱写。柳先生还经常指出一些原著中的英文语法错误，让我佩服得五体投地。不是认真做学问的人，英文是不可能达到柳先生的境界的。这个认真劲我还一直保持到今天。我所在部门的人都知道，每一个报告、每一封邮件，必须是实事求是，有根有据。我的供应商也经常说，给我们写报告可以把他们给逼疯了。我对自己和下属的要求是，所有的报告十年、二十年之后还能站得住脚，经得起考验。我想这也是我从柳先生及清华的教育中最深、最长久的受益。

在这里祝柳先生及曾老师健康长寿，万事如意！

2016 年 12 月

6. 科学严谨治学、厚德载物育人
——写在柳百成先生从教 60 周年之际

程 军

光阴似箭，日月如梭。时间过得真快，不知不觉中，柳先生已从教 60 年了，迈入了耄耋之年。是啊，想想自己也早就鬓生白发，接近退休年龄的人了。1985 年我有幸师从先生攻读硕士、博士研究生学位，期间 5 年多时间，在先生的言传身教下顺利完成了学业，打下了扎实的学术功底，拓宽了科研和人生视野。之后不论在科研工作还是管理岗位，近 30 年来，工作时间越长，越觉得先生的桃李春风、谆谆教诲让我受益匪浅。

先生是一位严师。在先生身上，我学到了严谨治学的工作态度。师从过先生的弟子们、许多与先生共过事的人都讲，先生对工作非常严谨，对自己，不论是学术研究还是教学工作，每个数据、每项实验、每一堂课，总是一丝不苟，总是尊重事物的本来面目，探寻着事物的客观规律。严谨来自于认真，先生不仅严于律己，而且要求每位学生都要讲认真，这种讲认真是一种负责，是一种期待，更是催人上进的无形力量，进而一个又一个高徒脱颖而出，一批又一批高水平的科研成果接踵而至。先生这种科学严谨的治学精神，也在潜移默化中长久影响着包括我在内的众多弟子。在高校教学科研以及后来的管理岗位中，我始终把精益求精、严谨认真作为座右铭，尊重事实、注意细节，每一次工作完成中的不足哪怕是小的欠缺，都会不时勾忆起先生当年孜孜教诲、身体力行的场景。

先生是一位明师。在先生身上，我学到了善抓重点的科学方法。先生从教 60 年来，科研成果颇丰，始终保持着创新、领先的学术地位，既是他始终保持着对学术研究和教学工作浓厚兴趣和热情的结果，更与他掌握的科学研究方法密不可分。不论多么复杂的研究工作，到了先生这里，他都能化繁为简、抓住重点，很快取得突破。每一个研究选题，他都能见微知著，很快判断出是否处于学术前沿，并提出从哪里着手开展研究；每一道技术难题，他都能抽丝剥茧，用强大的逻辑分析方法拨云见雾，找到攻克的途径。在我后来的工作中，特别是从事管理工作中，更加真切体会到这种"大道至简"的工作方法之妙。管理工作往往纷繁复杂、千头万绪，作为管理者必须懂得"弹钢琴"，清楚哪些是自己要亲自抓的和关注的，哪些是要更多发挥大家的积极性的，做到善抓重点。正是如此，我才能在别人看来角色转换难度很大的科研管理、战略规划以及党务工作等岗位调整中，很快适应岗位要求，并做出一定的成绩。

先生是一位良师。在先生身上，学到了厚德载物的人格魅力。"自强不息、厚德载物"是清华大学的校训。先生淡泊名利、潜心学术，把学术研究作为毕生价值追求，60 年来在科研上投入了主要的精力，不懈践行着科学精神、工匠精神，在科学技术研究中取得了一个又一个成就，成了先进制造技术研究领域的大师级人物，同时为社会培养和输送了一大批栋梁之材。先生宽以待人、平易近人，从不求全责备，注重为学生创造宽松的科研环境；老师识人之异、用人之长，善于发现学生的优点长处并加以鼓励，让学生在如沐春风中成长成才。这种人格魅力，让人不由得肃然起敬，为我们的人生态度、人际交往方式中留下了深深的印记。几十年来，尽管我的岗位多次调整，但都保持着一颗本心，坚信厚德载物，干一行爱一行、爱一行精一行，注重团结周围的同事、员工，集众之力、用人之长，才能出色履行好岗位职责。

古人云：师者，所以传道授业解惑也。先生就是这样一位长于传道、精于授业、善于解惑的严师、明师、良师。他不仅教给了我们当时这些初出茅庐的年轻人以知识、方法，为我们插上了科学的翅膀、注入了思想的力量，把我们培养成为国家现代化建设的有用之材，还在于他教给我们做人做事、治学治业的道理，为学生们的学术探索、职业生涯乃至人生发展树立了思齐看齐、可信可学的标杆，让我们在风吹雨打、披荆斩棘的路上始终充溢着满满的正能量。

到今年，先生已经在学术和教学岗位上整整耕耘了一个甲子，但这些年一直保持着乐观的心态、学术的青春，每次见面都能感受到他的精神矍铄、思维敏捷，每次见面都能让我们有新的受教，如同 30 年前师从时一般。这种"活到老、学到老、研究到老"，对科学、对事业追求无止境的精神值得我们后来者学习和发扬，也必将激励着我们不断前行。

2016 年 12 月 16 日

7. 教书育人，勇攀科技高峰

北京航空材料研究院　李嘉荣

1990年秋，我到清华大学机械工程系师从柳百成先生攻读博士学位研究生。从那时至今已27年了，现在柳百成先生已到耄耋之年，谨以此文纪念。

敢于挑战，勇于创新，善于创新，准确把握科技发展方向

入学后不久，我便开始进行博士论文课题的选题工作。开始，柳先生给我指出了两个研究方向：一个方向是铸造合金研究；另一个方向是铸造凝固过程数值模拟研究。由于上述两个研究方向差别较大，在当时的情况下我难于判断和选择研究方向，博士论文课题选题工作艰难而痛苦。1991年，柳先生的研究方向发生了重大转变：在此之前，柳先生以铸造合金为主要研究方向；在此之后，柳先生以铸造凝固过程数值模拟为主要研究方向。博士论文选题期间，我查阅了国内外大量文献，同期柳先生采用言谈和环境熏陶的方式使我全面和深入了解上述研究方向的情况。铸造合金研究是柳先生已取得很大成就的研究领域，该研究方向基础强、难度小、风险低，易于取得成绩；而铸造凝固过程数值模拟研究是柳先生刚开始从事的研究方向，基础弱、难度大、风险高，难于取得成绩。在柳先生的启发和指导下，我下定决心选择了铸造凝固过程数值模拟的研究课题，并发挥了我在工厂工作期间积累的实践经验，将数值计算与试验研究密切结合，圆满地完成了博士论文的课题工作。

20世纪90年代以来，柳先生高瞻远瞩，辛勤耕耘，克服条件以及技术等方面的困难，带领研究团队解决了多项技术难题，突破了多项关键技术，在铸造凝固过程数值模拟研究方向取得显著成就，培养了大批人才，为国家做出了很大贡献。从铸造合金研究发展到铸造凝固过程数值模拟研究，显示出了柳先生敢于挑战、勇于创新的胆略和魄力；在铸造凝固过程数值模拟研究方向取得公认的成就，体现了柳先生善于创新的高超的科研能力和水平。

我从清华大学毕业后到了新的工作岗位，从事新型单晶高温合金的研究，研究方向发生了很大变化，科研工作中经常困难重重，柳先生敢于挑战、善于创新的思想和工作方法对我影响很大，使我带领团队勤奋努力、不断创新、自主发展的单晶高温合金在我国航空发动机上获得广泛应用。

重视高新技术与传统产业结合，强调科研成果实际应用，促进传统产业升级换代

铸造在我国是一个具有悠久历史的传统产业。20世纪末，随着以计算机为代表的高新技术的迅猛发展，铸造等传统产业受到了很大的冲击，产业发展缓慢，效益下降，从业人员减少，高校招生困难。在这种情况下，柳先生在国内较早地提出了用高新技术改造传统产业，从而促进传统产业发展的思想。30多年来，柳先生不辞辛苦，奔波于祖国大地，宣传用高新技术改造传统产业，推广铸造凝固过程数值模拟技术，为以铸造为代表的传统产业的升级换代做出了重要贡献。近年来，柳先生参加了《中国制造2025》国家规划的编制，继续为我国制造业由大变强献计献策。

长期以来，柳先生集中主要精力，从事铸造凝固过程数值模拟的研究。这个研究方向就是高新技术改造传统产业的一个具体体现，柳先生注重科研成果的实际应用，强调必须把促进经济发展作为工程科学技术发展的首要任务。在从事基础研究的同时，他要求研究生将研究成果编制出具有重要应用价值的工程软件，并将这种软件应用到工厂的实际生产中。不要小看这一要求，工程技术科研成果能否获得良好实际应用是科研成果的一个试金石，该要求给研究工作提出了更高的目标，并由此带来很大的工作量，这既检验了研究成果，促进了研究成果的实际应用，又强化锻炼了研究生，明显提高了科研水平。

柳先生注重科研成果实际应用的另一个例子是重视试验工作。在研究生的具体工作中，他反复强

调试验工作的重要性。他说，如果没有试验数据和试验验证，数值模拟就成为无源之水。由于柳先生正确处理数值计算研究与物理试验研究两者之间的关系，将计算机技术与铸造专业密切结合，才使得他领导的研究团队取得今天这样的成就。

热爱祖国，勤奋工作

柳先生是"文革"后1978年国家教委第一批选派到美国进修的高级科研教学人员。2000年以前，与美国相比，我国的科技与经济水平差距很大，上述进修的高级科研教学人员中有一部分人定居国外。柳先生有过数次在国外工作的机会，但他都放弃了。他经常教育研究生："人总是要干点事情的，中国人要干点自己的事情还得在中国。"朴素的语言折射出深刻的哲理和他的爱国之心。柳先生的言传身教影响着他的学生，目前柳先生指导的许多研究生在国内工作，为祖国的建设和富强而努力工作着。

初识柳先生给我的主要印象是：步履快捷、目光睿智、言语简洁、做事干练。追根究底，这些特点都与柳先生工作节奏快有关，都源自于他的勤奋。柳先生认真努力，工作勤奋。我在读期间，他每年都在忙，忙讲学、忙讲课、忙论证、忙答辩、忙与研究生讨论、忙听研究生汇报、忙修改研究生论文……2001年，柳先生不慎右脚骨折。我去看望柳先生时，他正在克服身体上的困难，认真修改研究生的论文。在三九天寒冷的早晨，在三伏天酷热的下午，柳先生经常是第一个到实验室的人。2016年，柳先生接受北京航空材料研究院主办的先进航空材料技术发展论坛组委会的邀请，在柳先生夫人曾晓萱教授的陪同下，忍着左胳膊桡骨骨折的病痛，带着夹板做了精彩的学术报告。柳先生是一个不断进取、奋进不息的人，他勤奋工作的动力源自于他对祖国的热爱、对科学的追求、对真理的探询。

实事求是，治学严谨，教书育人

柳先生实事求是，治学严谨。记得20世纪90年代初，柳先生无论是给本科生、硕士生，还是给博士生上课，尽管很熟悉讲课内容，但他都一丝不苟，认真备课。柳先生课堂教学的特点是条理清晰，深入浅出，语言简洁，理论联系实际，感染力强。由于柳先生备课认真、学识渊博，他的课深受学生的欢迎。在指导研究生的过程中，他坚持高标准、严要求，严把论文关。有的研究生的论文要修改多遍，甚至他要求研究生补充试验或计算工作。柳先生常说，我现在对你们要求严，是对你们负责、是对国家负责，这对你们的未来有好处。我步入中年后，越来越深刻地理解柳先生的话语与思想。

在申报课题和课题论证时，柳先生不讲过头话，不写达不到的指标。在科研成果申报和评价时，柳先生实事求是，其公平合理得到广泛认可。

很多人直接或间接地了解柳先生实事求是、学风严谨的一面，但知道柳先生宽以待人一面的人并不多。铸造凝固过程数值模拟研究的重要结果表现在编制的计算机软件上，在柳先生的研究团队中，为了加强交流、提高研究水平，研究生经常相互交流使用软件，所以柳先生的研究生经常使用多个自主研制的软件。某研究生经柳先生推荐到国外某大学去攻读学位，他不妥当地使用了柳先生研究团队的其他科研成果。柳先生知道这件事后，严肃批评教育了这个研究生，但未向该研究生就读的国外学校正式提出这件事，保证了这个研究生继续在国外攻读学位。柳先生对这件事情的处理深刻反映了他治学严谨、宽以待人的思想品德。

柳先生对学生的严格要求，是出于他实事求是的科学态度和对学生的无私关爱；他对学生的真心挚爱，又表现为柳先生对学生的严格要求和宽厚仁慈。无论学生在读期间，还是毕业以后，柳先生指导学生、鼓励学生、帮助学生、批评学生、爱护学生，他的言行感染并影响他的学生的一生。我有幸成为柳先生的研究生，从他身上学到了很多宝贵的东西，并对我产生重要影响。

柳先生勇攀科技高峰，教书育人，桃李满天下。

柳先生已到耄耋之年，但仍壮心不已，敬祝他健康长寿！

2017年2月18日

8. 贺柳老师执教六十年

康进武

执教一甲子，桃李满天下。
忆昔年少时，负笈清华园。
佳绩又金奖，毕业即教师。
未逃十年乱，学术不停辍。
阴霾一朝尽，开放追赶忙。
首批兼领队，中年涉重洋。
白宫玫瑰园，见证伟人访。
威星暴雪寒，验室仪器暖。
铁中有乌金，奥秘趣无穷。
家乡苦也甜，雁去无留意。
感怀新科技，引入计算机。
铸造虽千年，凝固不得见。
仿真展神奇，模拟觅玄机。
辛勤数十载，荣登院士堂。
足迹五大洲，环球有一席。
声名播海内，魅力中国人。
授业三尺台，解惑恍然开。
指导在实践，讨论着前沿。
弟子不胜数，自是多才俊。
中间多教师，再传广又广。
老骥志千里，白发不畏霜。
心系国制造，振臂呼强基。
日日奔走忙，犹胜壮年郎。

2016 年 12 月 26 日

9. 李文胜博士回忆[一]

1. 对柳老师印象最深的是什么？

柳老师严谨求实、注重方法，对科技前沿和宏观方向的把握很准确，注重与工程实际相结合做学术研究，厉行节约，关心学生，指导有方，心系学科、院系、学校发展，将很大的精力投入到促进我国制造业发展的事业中。注重国际交流与合作，把握了国际前沿，在国际上有一定的话语权和影响力。

2. 他在讲课、指导您的工作、学习，特别是博士阶段，您有哪些收获，对当时的博士论文有什么帮助？对您以后的工作、学习、为人有何影响？

博士阶段受柳老师的帮助很大。柳老师亲自确定了我的博士课题方向"大型钢锭宏观偏析数值模拟"，强调与工程实际相结合，帮助落实好博士课题试验的工厂。记得我撰写的第一篇英文论文，柳老师从英语写作、研究结果的表达等方面将我写的初稿通篇改了一遍，之后就放手让我去改。博士论文的撰写工作中，柳老师专门组织了博士论文工作的讨论，包括研究的整理和提高、技术路线的梳理、关键内容的表述，给出了高水平、高屋建瓴的指导。

科学求实，利用先进的模型和方法，密切结合工程实际，解决重大工程问题，是导师指导我做博士课题的启示。坚持不懈，刻苦钻研，追求卓越，不断创新，尊重客观实际，不盲从，柳老师坚守、践行并提倡的这些精神和理念，深刻影响着我的学习、工作和为人。

3. 他的教育理念、培养方式、科研学风和同学的关系等方面，您有何评价？

柳老师多次跟我们提到：钱要用在刀刃上；做研究只有踏踏实实，没有一夜成名。教育学生时，一"严"一"松"，一方面在宏观方向和研究思路上严格把关，一方面在具体做研究的过程中给学生充分的自主权。柳老师强调课题组学术研究的传承和积累，强调在传承基础上的创新与超越。柳老师注重学生定期学术交流和工作汇报。鼓励学生之间相互讨论，启发研究思路，有问题多请教、多讨论。鼓励学生参加重要的国际会议和学术交流。鼓励学生多下工厂，研究过程注重试验，注重研究的实际工程应用。

柳老师与国内外学术同行交流密切。聘请国际上知名学者来课题组做讲座、短期授课，这些前沿讲座使我们课题组的同学受益匪浅。由于国内主要高校和研究机构的一些研究者也常来参加，这样在一定程度上也促进了国内学科的整体发展。柳老师对学术始终抱着交流、开放的态度，目标是解决前沿研究和实际工程问题。

4. 他对工作、对生活，有何特色？他有哪些特长？

柳老师工作上孜孜不倦，保持学习，耄耋之年还坚持去实验室工作，柳老师八十岁还骑自行车上班，柳老师骑自行车矫健、匆匆的身影深深印在我的脑海中，这是老清华人、老科学家朴实而又卓越的印记。柳老师生活简朴，柳老师常年穿着一件灰黄色带深色线条的夹克的模样，我是不会忘记的。柳老师的英文很好，从小接受英文教育，早年坚持阅读英文学术期刊，后来又赴美访学，柳老师在专业领域始终瞄准国际学术前沿，与国际知名学者开展深入学术交流，与英文好也是密不可分的。

后记

"人生天地之间，若白驹之过隙，忽然而已。"一晃之间，认识柳老师已经是十多年前了。那是2005年9月，去清华参加面试。在英文面试环节，我对一个英文单词procedure（程序）发音不准确，柳老师在提问时要我重说这个单词。柳老师一丝不苟、严谨的治学态度，从这时就给我留下了深刻的印象。

入学以后，柳老师就给我确定了博士课题方向："大型钢锭宏观偏析数值模拟"，我很早就进入了课题。在博士阶段的前期，柳老师还给我安排了大型

[一] 作者系柳院士2006级入学、2012届毕业的博士生。目前工作单位：广东电网有限责任公司电力科学研究院。

铸件铸造工艺优化的相关研究项目，使我得到锻炼和提高，特别是铸造过程模拟仿真、试验研究的能力，多次赴工厂开展试验和应用。

博士课题是通过数值模拟的方法研究大型钢锭宏观偏析，是一个国际上的难题。柳老师请来了奥地利 Ludwig 教授课题组的老师，介绍国际上宏观偏析的最新研究成果，特别是先进的数学模型，对我的研究启发很大，我也与该课题组建立了学术上的联系。

柳老师支持我赴韩国参加第二届中韩先进制造技术学术会议并作口头报告。会上，国际知名的铸造模拟软件公司 AnyCasting 展示了他们在宏观偏析模拟仿真与试验研究方面的最新进展。这些研究从未发表在公开的学术刊物，对我来说很珍贵。会议开拓了我的研究思路，特别在钢锭试验方面取得很好的借鉴。

柳老师强调理论研究的试验验证，注重工程应用，解决工程实际问题。柳老师联系中信重工机械股份有限公司，落实了工厂试验。我有很长一段时间是在车间摸爬滚打，多次开展大型钢锭凝固过程测温、钢锭解剖、成分分析等现场试验，获得了大量的试验数据和宝贵的一手资料。博士课题研究建立了较先进的宏观偏析两相模型，实现了准确求解，在工厂解剖了 53t 大型钢锭，对模型进行了验证，取得了国际上比较领先的结果。

我曾有几年时间担任柳老师科研秘书，协助柳老师处理一些日常事务，还要接触一些人。柳老师办事的风格、待人的态度，真是"高山仰止，景行行止"，让我心里一直向往。柳老师崇高、正直、无私，总是想着学科发展、我国制造业发展。"君子之交淡如水"，柳老师赢得同行的广泛尊敬。柳老师的爱国、奉献，通过言传身教，潜移默化影响着我们。

柳老师关心学生，不仅仅是在课题研究上给予高水平的指导，在生活、思想上都很关心。有一件事令我感激、感动，终生难忘。2011 年，我家人患重病做手术，柳老师给我批准了假期，让我全心去照顾家人，柳老师时刻关心治疗进展，经济上给予了极大的帮助。记得那时柳老师也刚刚做了一个手术，却将自己的营养品给我家人服用。后来我家人对这份营养品记忆特别深刻，因为术后吃不下东西、心态也低落，柳老师给的营养品无论是物质上还是精神上都促进了术后恢复。此后，柳老师经常问起我家人的康复情况，并给予关心鼓励。我们一家对柳老师的帮助十分感激。

2012 年我博士毕业赴广州工作。柳老师的弟子之前在广州的就只有华南理工大学的一位教授。柳老师要我们师兄弟常联系，也跟我分享前些年赴广州出差的经历。毕业后回学校，柳老师一家还专门请我喝粤式早茶。从今年开始，单位安排我往电力机器人方向攻关，对我来说是一个全新的方向，柳老师一方面叮嘱我要保持清醒的头脑，客观理性认识机器人技术的发展和应用；一方面给我提供了一些重要资料和信息，帮助我了解机器人技术。柳老师始终关心学生的发展，其他师兄弟的情况，柳老师也同样关心。

柳老师耄耋之年，老骥伏枥，壮心不已。柳老师给我的总是正能量、积极的力量。感谢恩师！祝福柳老师健康长寿！柳老师孜孜以求的"中国制造梦"一定能够实现！

2016 年 12 月 24 日于广州

附录　赴国外及中国港澳台地区参加重要学术交流活动表（1978—2019）

附录 赴国外及中国港澳台地区参加重要学术交流活动表（1978—2019）

1978—2019年共出访国外及中国港澳台地区100余次，访问36个国家及地区，其中美国27次，日本11次，德国10次，英国9次。连续多次代表中国参加世界铸造会议（WFC），作大会邀请报告，多次参加凝固过程国际会议（SP）、模拟仿真国际会议（MCWSP）、亚洲铸造会议（AFC）及美国材料年会（TMS）等，作主旨或邀请报告。

No.	日程	国家或地区	学术及考察任务
01	1978-12-26—1981-01-02	美国	第一批访问学者，在 University of Wisconsin 及 MIT 学习2年期间： 参加国际扫描电镜会议，作邀请报告，参加美国铸造学会年会 考察通用汽车公司、福特汽车公司及卡特彼勒公司及它们的技术中心
02	1984-03-25—1984-04-12	法国、瑞士	代表中国参加国际标准会议，考察大型球墨铸铁技术
03	1985-09-14—1985-12-15	美国	清华机械工程系组团考察美国教育，访问 MIT, Case Western Reserve Univ., Univ. of Michigan, Univ. of Wisconsin, UC-Berkley 期间： 参加铸钢国际会议，作邀请报告 访问 Michigan-Tech Univ.，作邀请报告
04	1986-09-04—1986-09-12	捷克	代表中国参加第53届世界铸造会议（WFC）
05	1988-03-25—1988-04-05	美国	参加马鞍山市代表团考察美国球墨铸铁管技术
06	1988-06-30—1988-07-17	保加利亚、德国	参加国际铸造模拟会议，作邀请报告 访问德国亚琛工业大学
07	1989-05-08—1989-06-06	德国、波兰、捷克	赴德国，代表中国参加第56届世界铸造会议（WFC） 访问波兰，捷克布尔诺大学
08	1989-08-28—1989-09-15	日本	访问东北大学、名古屋大学、九州大学 东京，参加第4届铸铁国际会议（Cast Iron）
09	1990-09-18—1990-10-08	日本	大阪，代表中国参加第57届世界铸造会议（WFC），访问早稻田大学，作邀请报告
10	1991-05-30—1991-06-22	印度	首钢组团考察高炉技术 访问孟买，应邀印度铸造学会作学术报告
11	1991-08-28—1991-09-26	立陶宛、苏联、波兰	赴波兰克拉科夫，代表中国参加第58届世界铸造会议（WFC） 访问立陶宛 Kaunas 大学，莫斯科高等工业学校、列宁格勒工学院等
12	1992-09-16—1992-10-10	巴西、美国	赴巴西，代表中国参加第59届世界铸造会议（WFC） 访问美国 MIT、UM-Rolla、UW 等
13	1992-10-13—1992-10-30	日本	带领石油制造企业组团考察日本铸造技术 仙台，参加第1届亚洲铸造会议（AFC-1），作报告
14	1993-09-25—1993-10-17	荷兰、德国、英国	赴荷兰，代表中国参加第60届世界铸造会议（WFC） 访问德国及英国 Manchester Univ.、Liverpool Univ.，作学术报告
15	1993-12-15—1993-12-21	中国香港	参加第2届"制造技术"会议
16	1994-09-26—1994-10-08	法国	南锡，参加第5届铸铁国际会议（Cast Iron）
17	1994-10-23—1994-11-03	日本	福冈九州大学，第2届亚洲铸造会议（AFC-2），作报告，访问大阪大学、广岛大学、早稻田大学
18	1994-05-23—1994-05-31	中国香港	访问香港理工大学
19	1995年11月	韩国	参加第3届亚洲铸造会议（AFC-3），宣读论文 访问韩国汉城大学、延世大学
20	1996-04-11—1996-05-16	美国	费城，参加第62届世界铸造会议（WFC），作邀请报告 访问宾夕法尼亚州立大学，作报告 访问福特汽车公司 访问加拿大福特汽车公司铝合金铸造厂
21	1997-01-06—1997-01-17	美国	西雅图，国家自然科学基金会组团参加美国 NSF 会议
22	1997-04-15—1997-05-06	美国	访问福特汽车公司技术中心，讨论科技合作
23	1997-06-05—1997-06-19	英国	谢菲尔德，参加第4届凝固国际会议（SP-4）作报告，访问 Manchester Univ.

(续)

No.	日程	国家或地区	学术及考察任务
24	1998-03-14—1998-04-04	美国	机械工业部组团、任副团长，考察材料成形加工模拟仿真技术
25	1998-06-07—1998-06-14	美国	圣迭戈，参加第8届国际凝固、铸造、焊接模拟会议，宣读论文
26	1998-09-29—1998-10-12	美国	伯明翰，参加第6届铸铁国际会议（Cast Iron）作报告
27	1999-09-05—1999-09-16	韩国	汉城，参加第4届环太平洋国际会议（Pacific-Rim），作主题报告
28	2000-02-19	新加坡	访问新加坡理工学院
29	2000-08-19—2000-08-30	德国	亚琛大学，参加第9届国际模拟会议，作报告
30	2000-12-13—2000-12-20	韩国	访问韩国工业技术研究院，作报告
31	2001-02-05—2001-02-18	美国	新奥尔良，参加美国2001年TMS会议，作报告
32	2001-05-25—2001-06-02	罗马尼亚	参加国际凝固与铸造会议，作报告
33	2001-08-14—2001-08-21	墨西哥、乌拉圭、巴西	中国工程院组团访问南美 赴巴西作"中国机械工程教育与科技发展"报告
34	2002-02-20—2002-02-27	日本	名古屋，参加第5届环太平洋国际凝固与铸造国际会议（MCSP），作报告
35	2002-08-04—2002-08-14	中国台湾	台南，成功大学讲学，访问台湾大学
36	2002-09-02—2002-09-11	西班牙	巴塞罗那，参加第7届铸铁国际会议（Cast Iron）作主旨报告
37	2002-10-22—2002-10-27	韩国	庆州，参加第65届世界铸造会议（WFC），作报告
38	2002-11-15—2002-11-26	美国	新奥尔良，美国2002机械工程国际会议，作报告 访问WPI及MIT
39	2002-12-02—2002-12-06	韩国	仁川，第2届中-韩先进制造技术会议
40	2003-09-15—2003-09-21	澳大利亚	布里斯班，轻量化材料技术会议，作报告
41	2003-09-27—2003-10-09	美国	访问WPI，Univ. of Michigan，Purdue Univ.，作学术报告
42	2003-12-06—2003-12-12	中国香港	第7届"制造技术"会议，作大会报告"中国制造科学与技术新进展"
43	2004-03-01—2004-03-07	新加坡	精密制造工程会议，作报告
44	2004-06-27—2004-07-02	日本	访问东洋公司，商讨科研合作 访问东京早稻田大学，作报告
45	2004-08-07—2004-08-12	中国台湾	高雄，第6届环太平洋国际会议，作报告
46	2004-08-13—2004-08-23	英国	伯明翰，第10届中-英学者材料会议，作报告 访问剑桥大学、帝国理工学院
47	2004-09-04—2004-09-11	匈牙利	第4届凝固与重力会议，作报告
48	2004-11-14—2004-11-21	印度	班加罗尔，国际凝固科学与工艺会议
49	2005-02-12—2005-02-21	美国	旧金山，TMS会议，作报告
50	2005-08-13—2005-08-25	美国	访问福特公司及通用公司技术中心，卡特彼勒公司等
51	2005-10-31—2005-11-02	韩国	全州，参加中-韩先进制造技术会议
52	2006-02-26—2006-03-02	日本	横滨，访问IHI，参加中-日科技合作会议
53	2006-05-24—2006-06-05	法国	尼斯，第12届国际MCWASP会议，作报告
54	2006-07-13—2006-07-26	美国	访问密苏里大学-罗拉分校、圣路易、夏威夷等地
55	2006年09月	韩国	济州岛，参加国际材联-亚洲国际会议，作大会特邀报告
56	2007-02-24—2007-03-05	美国	奥兰多，参加2007年TMS会议，作报告 参加中-美-加三国镁合金科技合作会议
57	2007-05-08—2007-05-15	韩国	首尔，参加第7届亚洲铸造会议（AFC），作报告
58	2007-06-13—2007-06-20	德国	杜塞尔多夫，参加世界铸造博览会（GIFA） 访问亚琛工业大学

（续）

(续)

No.	日程	国家或地区	学术及考察任务
59	2007-07-21—2007-08-02	英国	谢菲尔德，第5届国际凝固过程会议（SP）报告 访问帝国理工学院，作报告
60	2007年08月	中国澳门	访问澳门大学
61	2007-09-16—2007-09-25	美国	底特律，参加材料科学与技术会议 访问通用汽车公司技术中心
62	2007-10-05—2007-10-20	德国	法兰克福，参加世界书展
63	2007-11-05—2007-11-10	韩国	济州岛，第6届PRICM会议，作报告
64	2008-02-20—2008-02-25	日本	横滨，访问IHI公司，讨论合作事宜
65	2008-05-21—2008-05-25	日本	名古屋，参加第10届亚洲铸造会议（AFC），作报告
66	2008-06-13—2008-06-23	奥地利	格拉茨，参加国际先进凝固过程会议，作报告
67	2008-07-17—2008-07-24	英国	牛津，Oxford Univ.，参加12届中-英学者材料会议，作报告，访问帝国理工学院
68	2009-05-09—2009-06-01	加拿大、美国	参加中-美-加ICME会议，作报告 美国麦迪逊，C. Loper国际铸铁会议，作报告
69	2009-08-23—2009-09-04	德国、瑞士、法国	柏林，参加2009-Thermec会议，作报告
70	2009-11-02—2009-11-07	韩国	晋州，参加中-韩先进制造技术会议
71	2010-02-14—2010-02-28	美国	西雅图，参加2010年TMS会议，作报告
72	2010-04-12—2010-04-16	韩国	仁川，参加第8届（MCSP）会议，作报告
73	2010年06月	挪威	奥斯陆，参加中国工程院与挪威工程院会议，作报告
74	2010-07-27—2010-08-09	澳大利亚	凯恩斯，参加第7届（PRICM）会议，作报告
75	2010-10-23	美国	安娜堡，参加"中-美-加镁合金ICME"科技合作会议
76	2010-11-08—2010-11-19	埃及	卢克索，参加第9届国际铸铁会议（Cast Iron） 访问开罗
77	2011-01-16—2011-01-24	美国	华盛顿，参加中-美两国"清洁能源"会议 密歇根，参加分主题会议，作报告
78	2011-02-26—2011-03-09	美国	圣迭戈，2011年TMS会议，作报告
79	2011-05-21—2011-06-07	美国	加州长滩，参加Aeromat-2011会议，作报告
80	2011-08-23—2011-09-20	加拿大、美国	参加中国工程院访问加拿大、美国工程院活动 不慎脑部受伤，在波士顿外科手术
81	2012-06-16—2012-06-29	奥地利	参加第12届MCWASP国际会议，作报告
82	2012-09-22—2012-10-05	澳大利亚	Wollongong，参加国际材料及工艺技术会议 访问悉尼
83	2013-05-18—2013-05-28	芬兰、瑞典、丹麦	芬兰、瑞典参加国际会议，作报告 访问丹麦
84	2013-07-07—2013-07-11	美国	盐湖城，参加第2届世界集成计算材料工程会议，（ICME）任国际委员会委员
85	2013-09-09—2013-09-14	英国	莱斯特，国际相场会议，作大会主旨报告《Progress in Multi-scale Modeling and Simulation of Solidification and Casting Processes》
86	2013-12-08—2013-12-11	中国台湾	台北，参加第12届亚洲铸造会议（AFC），作大会主旨报告《Multi-scale Modeling of Solidification Process of Advanced Casting Technology》
87	2014-07-21—2014-07-31	西班牙、法国	西班牙，参加第11届世界计算力学会议，作报告《Three-dimensional Dendritic Morphology and Branching Mechanism in Directionally Solidified Mg-Zn Alloy》
88	2014-11-23—2014-12-03	日本	大阪，参加第9届"MCSP"会议。作大会主旨报告《Experiences on Modeling of Casting and Solidification Processes》

(续)

No.	日程	国家或地区	学术及考察任务
89	2015-01-29—2015-02-04	韩国	International Conference on Casting & Solidification Simulation for Foundry，作大会主旨报告《Progress on Multi-scale Modeling of Solidification Process of Advanced Casting Technology》
90	2015-05-19—2015-06-05	美国	中国工程院组团 7 人，赴美考察"国家制造网络"及创新研究院，访问 AMNPO、Ohio State Univ.、Univ. of Michigan、Ford Research and Innovation Center 等，作报告《China Manufacturing 2025-An action Program for a Strong Manufacturing Industry》 赴 Colorado Spring，参加第 3 届世界 ICME 会议，作报告《Modeling and Simulation of Directional Solidification of Ni-Based Super-alloy Turbine Blades Casting by Liquid Metal Cooling》
91	2015-10-13—2015-10-15	韩国	受中国工程院委托，赴韩国，出席韩国国家工程院（NAEK）建院 20 周年庆祝活动暨国际学术会议，作大会主旨报告《China Manufacturing 2025-An Action Program for Strong Manufacturing Industry》
92	2016-04-25—2016-04-29	韩国	参加中国工程院组团，参加"中-韩企业创新论坛" 考察韩国创新企业
93	2016-11-22—2016-11-25	德国	慕尼黑，中国工程院组团，参加中-德工程院会议，主题："制造业数字化转型"
94	2016-12-11—2016-12-14	日本	横滨，参加华为主办"国际结构技术"会议，作主旨报告
95	2017-05-21—2017-05-31	美国	密歇根，参加第 4 届世界 ICME 会议，华盛顿参加"美国制造业任务"研讨会，访问福特技术中心
96	2017-07-07—2017-07-12	法国	波尔多，参加国际会议。作邀请报告《Multi-scale modeling of the microstructure and tensile property evolution in Al-7Si-Mg cast aluminum alloys》
97	2017-07-23—2017-08-04	英国	温莎，第 7 届国际凝固过程会议（SP），作主旨报告《Numerical Simulation of Macrosegregation in Large Steel Ingot with Multicomponent and Multiphase Model》 访问 Leicester Univ.，作邀请报告
98	2018 年 07 月	英国	伯明翰，参加"中-英钢铁研究"会议，作主旨报告《Multiscale Modeling and Simulation of Directional Solidification Process of Ni-based Superalloy Turbine Blade Casting》
99	2018 年 10 月	德国	中国工程院组团参加中-德工程院会议，主题"制造业数字化转型"，作大会报告《Modeling and Simulation：Key Technology for Digital Transformation of Manufacturing Industry》
100	2018 年 11 月	阿联酋	迪拜，参加世界经济论坛未来制造分会会议
101	2019 年 10 月	德国	慕尼黑，参加世界经济论坛先进制造分会会议